Neuropsychology

The Neural Bases
of Mental Function

Marie T. Banich
University of Illinois at Urbana-Champaign

Houghton Mifflin Company   Boston   New York

To Mom for the push, to Wend for the pull, and to Mary for the shove that got this book finished.

Thanks for enduring my absences.

Sponsoring Editor: David C. Lee
Senior Associate Editor: Jane Knetzger
Senior Project Editor: Charline Lake
Senior Production/Design Coordinator: Jennifer Waddell
Manufacturing Manager: Florence Cadran
Marketing Manager: Pamela J. Laskey

Cover design: Harold Burch, Harold Burch Design, New York City
Cover image: *Mona Lisa*, Leonardo da Vinci, 1452–1519, Florentine, Musée du Louvre, Paris—Superstock; brain, MRI/Axial, © Howard Sochurek—The Stock Market

Printed in the U.S.A.

Library of Congress Catalog Card Number: 96-76859

ISBN: 0-395-66699-6

8 9 -DC- 05 04 03 02

Brief Contents

Contents

Preface

This book was written in response to the frustration I suffered every year for the past 10 years when it came time to choose a text for the introductory course in neuropsychology geared toward advanced undergraduate and beginning graduate students. I was looking for a text that surveyed the neural basis of a large variety of mental functions in a systematic fashion; that included research from animal, human experimental, and human clinical perspectives; and that provided a balance in presenting knowledge both about the brain and about cognition. When I continually failed to find one, I decided that the only way to remedy this situation was to write this book. Although the book is best suited for a course in human neuropsychology, the breadth and nature of the material that is covered also make it appropriate either for a course in cognitive neuroscience, which emphasizes insights garnered from neuropsychological research on how the brain meets the computational requirements of different mental processes (see, for example, chapter 5, Object Recognition), or for a clinical neuropsychology course, which emphasizes not only the phenomenology of specific neuropsychological syndromes, but also their implications for the neural bases of mental function (see, for example, chapters 7, Attention, and 9, Memory).

To introduce human neuropsychology to the student in a comprehensible manner, one must invariably decide on the approach to take—either to emphasize particular regions of brain tissue (and then discuss the functions that they perform) or to emphasize mental functions (and then discuss how they are instantiated in neural tissue). I have taken the latter approach, organizing the book with regard to specific cognitive functions. However, I have taken great care to write the book so that the student also gains an appreciation of the neural organization of the brain, starting in the early chapters by introducing basic concepts about the brain's behavioral topography (e.g., posterior regions are important for sensory functions and anterior regions for motoric ones), and building upon this knowledge in subsequent chapters (e.g., introducing the ventral and then the dorsal visual-processing streams).

The book also emphasizes the notion of converging operations—that is, the idea that we can only truly understand the neural basis of mental function by examining it from different perspectives, using different techniques and different populations of individuals in our investigations. Thus, for each mental function examined, knowledge gained from studies using behavioral, electrophysiological, and brain imaging techniques is discussed, as well as studies examining processing in animals, neurologically intact individuals, and patients with brain damage.

TEXT ORGANIZATION

A striking difference between this book and other neuropsychology texts is that it is organized to systematically survey the neural bases of a wide variety of mental functions, whereas other books cover functions selectively. To this end, I divided the book into three main parts. The first part, comprising the first three chapters, provides students with a basic foundation for the exploration of neuropsychology. The introductory chapter provides information about the basic parts of the nervous system. This chapter is probably unnecessary for students who already completed a course in physiological psychology, but it will be of use to students who have not. The second chapter acquaints students with the many techniques available to both clinicians and scientists in their quest to understand the neural bases of mental function. This chapter discusses not only the tried and true methods, such as examining the behavior of patients with localized lesions, but also the newest brain imaging techniques, such as functional magnetic resonance imaging. Chapter 3 provides an overview of lateralization of function because hemispheric differences are prominent for many of the functions discussed in the subsequent chapters. This chapter is notable in that it covers many current issues in this field, including the nature of interhemispheric integration and interaction.

The second part of the book, chapters 4 through 12, provides a survey of the neural bases of mental function, with each chapter devoted to a distinct cognitive function. The chapter topics discussed are, in order, motor processes, object recognition, spatial processing, attention, language, memory, executive function and goal-oriented behavior, emotion, and artistry.

These chapters have been carefully sequenced so that information learned in earlier chapters is built upon in later ones. Notably, the processes most linked to motoric and sensory functions are presented earlier, and those that depend on more integrative aspects of brain function, such as memory, are presented later. For example, the chapter on object recognition directly precedes that on spatial processing, so that the student is introduced to the ventral and dorsal visual-processing streams in consecutive chapters. The chapter on spatial processing precedes that on attention because the most prominent neuropsychological disorder of attention, hemineglect, has a large spatial component. The chapter on memory is preceded by the language and object recognition chapters so that the distinction between generalized memory disorders and the "memory" problems that are specific to certain domains (e.g., anomia in language or agnosia with regard to objects) is clear. And artistry concludes this section of the book because this chapter emphasizes many previously discussed issues in a synthetic way—for example, by demonstrating the spatial and emotional contributions to the visual arts and the auditory and "reading" abilities required for music.

Each chapter in this part introduces the basic neural circuitry that underlies the mental process under examination, as well as prominent neuropsychological theories of that function. When a particular syndrome adds markedly to our understanding of a given function, such as hemineglect in the case of attention or amnesia in the case of memory, the chapter is organized so that the phenomenology of the disorder is followed by a discussion of its implications for understanding brain-behavior relationships.

The final part of the book, comprising the last two chapters, looks at broad-based issues in neuropsychology. To disabuse students of the idea that the brain is a static organism, chapter 13 examines neural plasticity from a life-span perspective. This chapter examines not only developmental changes in the brain, but also those that occur with aging. In addition, it discusses recovery of function in children and in adults, and the neural bases of developmental disabilities. Chapter 14 examines syndromes that are characterized by generalized cognitive disorders (rather than the specific disorders discussed in chapter 4 through 12), including closed head injury, dementia, demyelinating diseases, disorders due to substance abuse or exposure to toxins, and epilepsy.

PEDAGOGICAL FEATURES

This book has many features designed to make the material accessible and engaging to students without sacrificing accuracy or oversimplifying the material. Each chapter begins with an opening case history to pique the students' interest and preview issues that are discussed later in the chapter. For example, the opening case history in chapter 4 discusses how Muhammad Ali's boxing career led him to have a Parkinsonian disorder, and the opening case history in chapter 14 discusses the mental decline of my maternal grandmother due to dementia. The text is written in a conversational tone rather than in a technical style, to grab the students' interest and retain it. So that difficult conceptual issues can be presented in a tractable manner, analogies are used extensively. Each chapter has a special-interest box designed to provide students with a better feel for either a particular issue in neuropsychological research or one of the implications of neuropsychology for everyday life. For example, in chapter 5, Object Recognition, the box discusses visual imagery; that in chapter 8, Language, examines the brain organization of bilinguals; and that in chapter 12, Artistry, examines the use of melodic intonation therapy in the rehabilitation of patients with aphasia. To keep students oriented to neuropsychological terminology, I have introduced key terms in boldface and provided a glossary at the back of the book. Chapter summaries are also included so that students can either review the material that they learned or preview what is to be discussed, and chapter outlines provide the reader with a clear conceptual structure of the material to be discussed. All in all, these features have been designed to make this book heavily user-friendly.

ACKNOWLEDGMENTS

This book has benefited greatly from the generous help of a number of colleagues who aided in the review process. I was genuinely touched by the amount of time and effort that these individuals took to improve the book. Their enthusiasm for the project bolstered me when the process seemed to be dragging on forever. They kept me on my toes, and although I may not have taken all of their advice, I thought about each and every one of their suggestions. I am most appreciative of their input.

Mark Beeman, Rush Medical College; Robert Bohlander, Wilkes University; Robert Bornstein, Ohio State University; Joan C. Borod, Queen's College of CUNY; Brian Butterworth, University College London; James V. Corwin, Northern Illinois University; Verne C. Cox, University of Texas, Arlington; Suzanne Craft, University of Washington; Martha J. Farah, University of Pennsylvania; Deborah Fein, University of Connecticut; Susan M. Garnsey, University of Illinois; Siegfried Gauggel, Phillips University; Jordan Grafman, National Institute of Neurological Disorders and Stroke; Gary Greenberg, Wichita State University; Daniel Kimble, University of Oregon; Karen E. Luh, University of Wisconsin; James V. Lupo, Creighton University; Loraine K. Obler, CUNY Graduate School; Shelley Parlow, Carleton University; Michael Peters, University of Guelph; Graham Ratcliff, Harmarville Rehabilitation Center; Patricia Reuter-Lorenz, University of Michigan; John D. Salamone, University of Connecticut; Sid Segalowitz, Brock University; Matthew L. Shapiro, McGill University; Myra O. Smith, Colgate University; Christopher Sullivan, Butler University; James Tanaka, Oberlin College; Eli Vakil, Bar-Ilan University; Janet M. Vargo, Hennepin County Medical Center and University of Minnesota; and Daniel B. Willingham, University of Virginia.

I also need to thank my graduate students, Alessandra Passarotti, Joel Shenker, and Daniel Weissman, for their input at various stages of this project; to thank Mary Greenpool for being the "naive" reader of the book; and to thank Linda May for secretarial assistance. I was also fortunate to have Doug Bernstein share with me his insights and wisdom regarding the textbook publishing process, which spared me many headaches. Furthermore, I am most grateful to both Neal J. Cohen and Wendy Heller for their willingness to contribute to this project and for the superlative job each has done on his or her respective chapter: Neal for chapter 9, Memory, and Wendy for chapter 11, Emotion. In addition, the help from the staff at Houghton Mifflin has far exceeded my expectations. In particular, I am greatly indebted to Jane Knetzger for her extremely thought-provoking and useful suggestions, expert editorial advice, enthusiasm for this project, and cheerleading when I was dragging behind schedule.

Finally, I would like to acknowledge the way in which the three people to whom this book is dedicated have played a substantial role in its coming to fruition. Mary Greenpool lived equally with me and this book for 3½ years.

Although this project precluded me from being anything resembling a normal human being, she nonetheless provided me with an encouraging and loving shove when I despaired at the enormity of the task. Wendy Heller provided the pull for this project because our conversations about neuropsychology, which began 17 years ago when we first met in graduate school and have continued ever since, have only drawn me deeper into study of the field. Finally, my mother provided the push for this book. Through the example of her life, I became passionate about the process of learning and acquired dogged persistence—traits critical to completing this text. But most important, the dinnertime conversations of my childhood, in which my mother spoke about her day's work, provided me with informal lessons about teaching that two and a half decades later pervade every sentence of this book.

MARIE T. BANICH

*I*ntroduction to the *N*ervous System

In this book, we explore how the neurological organization of the brain influences the way people think, feel, and act, an area of inquiry known as **human neuropsychology.** Since the mid-1970s, not only has our knowledge in the realm of neuropsychology grown rapidly, but the number of individuals who specialize in this area of psychology also has increased. Experimental neuropsychologists work as scientists attempting to understand the neural bases of cognition by doing scientific studies with individuals who have sustained brain damage and with individuals who are neurologically intact. In their studies, these researchers use a variety of techniques to divide complicated mental functions into meaningful categories and to isolate the contribution of specific brain regions to each of these functions. Although clinical neuropsychologists work with individuals who have sustained brain damage through either trauma or disease, they also work in hospitals and clinics to diagnose the cognitive deficits resulting from brain trauma, to plan programs of rehabilitation, to evaluate the degree to which an individual is regaining function, and to determine how environmental factors (e.g., family structure, educational background) may moderate or exacerbate the effects of brain dysfunction. In this book, we provide an overview of the current state of knowledge in neuropsychology as derived from findings in both the laboratory and the clinic.

The endeavor of understanding the relationship between the brain and the mind may be undertaken from two distinct vantage points, one that emphasizes the neurology of the brain and one that emphasizes the psychology of the mind. The neurologically oriented approach emphasizes the brain's anatomy; therefore, the major objective of this approach is to understand the function of specific circumscribed regions of brain tissue. For instance, a researcher might want to investigate a particular brain structure, such as the hippocampus, to determine its anatomical characteristics, its pattern of connectivity to other brain regions, and its role in mental functioning. Information derived from this approach can be extremely useful to medical personnel, such as neurosurgeons, who want to know which functions are likely to be lost or impaired if a certain region of brain tissue is excised. In contrast, the psychologically oriented approach emphasizes the brain's mental capabilities, so the major objective of this approach is to understand how different aspects of cognition, such as language, memory, and attention, are supported by the neurological organization of the brain. For example, psychologists may want to know whether the brain structures that support our ability to read are the same as, or distinct from, those that support our ability to write. Neuropsychologists can address this question by determining whether the type of brain damage that compromises the process of reading always compromises the process of writing as well. In fact, both reading and writing are not always affected after brain damage, a finding that tells us that although they are similar functions, they are controlled by separate brain regions.

In this book we lean more toward the psychologically oriented approach than the neurologically oriented one. This bias can be seen most clearly by taking a quick glance at the table of contents, which includes chapter titles such as "Language," "Memory," and "Attention," indicating that our discussion of the relationship between the brain and the mind emphasizes cognitive functions. If this book were written from a more neurologically oriented approach, the chapters would have been organized by brain regions and been titled "The Basal Ganglia," "The Cerebellum," and "The Frontal Lobes." Although we take a more psychologically oriented approach, a working knowledge and understanding of the neurological organization of the brain is indispensable, for only with that knowledge can we intelligently discuss the relationship between psychological functions and the specific regions of brain tissue that support those functions.

By the nature of the field, neuropsychology is at the intersection of a variety of fields, including neurology, biological psychology, and cognitive psychology. To study such a cross-disciplinary subject, we must be willing not only to examine questions from different perspectives, but also willing to work to integrate information provided from these alternative perspectives. You may find that some of the concepts raised in the book are ones with which you are already familiar through previous course work in either cognitive or biological psychology. However, the perspectives on such concepts provided in this book are likely to be different because throughout the book we integrate, interrelate, and synthesize material from both a biological perspective and a cognitive perspective. Although we cannot go into the detail that separate courses in each area would entail, we can obtain a large-scale, integrative picture of the topic under study. For example, when discussing face recognition in chapter 5, we learn not only which salient features enable people to recognize the face of someone they haven't seen for 30 years, but also which regions of the brain support such feats and why.

Now is a particularly exciting time to study neuropsychology because the vast advances in our knowledge in neurology, medical science, and cognitive psychology provide the opportunity to synthesize findings in ways that were impossible just a few years ago. Research in cognitive psychology has tremendously increased the sophistication of models of mental functioning so that we can take a complicated function such as language and divide it into specific subcomponents and subprocesses. At the same time, incredible advances in medical technology now allow us to examine the neuroanatomy and physiological functioning of the brain in ways unimagined even as recently as the 1980s. We discuss these advances in methods in more detail in chapter 2.

Before we begin to attempt to link cognitive functions to the brain, however, we need some background knowledge, which is the focus of this chapter. First, we must have a common base of knowledge about the anatomy and physiology of the brain, especially the cells that form the building blocks of the nervous system. Then we must have a common and somewhat specific vocabulary so that we can discuss the locations and characteristics of brain regions. Finally, we need to know the major

regions of the brain and a brief idea of each region's major functions.

NEURONS: BUILDING BLOCKS OF THE NERVOUS SYSTEM

Our nervous systems are comprised of two main classes of cells: **neurons** and **glia.** Neurons are the cells in the nervous system that carry information from one place to another by means of a combination of electrical and chemical signals. Glia, which outnumber neurons by at least 10 to 1, are support cells. In this section, we first briefly discuss the functions of glia, then delve into a discussion of the structure and function of neurons. We present only an overview of how neurons work, highlighting the aspects of neuronal function that are important to remember for discussions in later chapters. More detailed explanations of how an electrical signal is generated by a neuron and the nature of chemical processes that aid in communication between neurons can be found in almost any physiological psychology or neuroscience text.

Although glia are not the main carriers of information, they are critical to the functioning of the nervous system. Their tasks include influencing the communication between neurons by modifying the chemical milieu between them, aiding with reorganization after brain damage by removing dead neurons, and serving some of the nutritive needs of neurons. Glia are critical to maintaining the **blood-brain barrier,** which is the mechanism by which many harmful substances, such as toxins, are prevented from reaching the brain. Developmentally, glia guide neurons as they migrate from the site of creation to their final position within the brain. Compared with our knowledge about neurons, our knowledge about glia is scant, but has increased tremendously in recent years (see Hawrylak & Greenough, in preparation, for a review of recent findings).

Neurons have three main parts: a **dendritic tree** (composed of individual dendrites), a **cell body,** and an **axon.** The dendritic tree is the part of the neuron that receives input from other cells. The cell

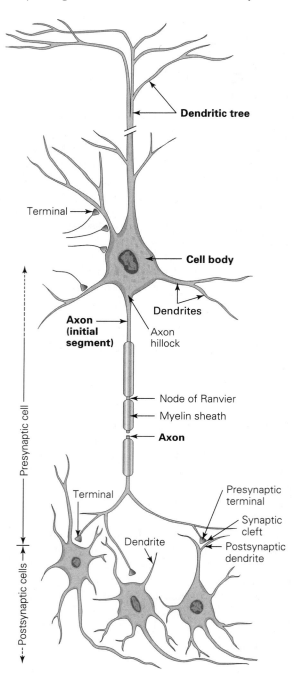

body is the part of the cell containing the nucleus and other cellular apparatus responsible not only for the manufacture of proteins and enzymes that sustain cell functioning, but also for the production of **neurotransmitters,** the chemical substances neurons use to communicate with one another. The axon is the appendage of the cell across which a large electrical signal is propagated. It can vary in length; in some cases it is very short, extending a distance not much farther than the length of the dendrites and cell body, and in other cases the axon is very long, traversing inches (as in the case of an axon that extends from one half of the brain to the other). The points at which neurons make connections are known as **synapses** (Figure 1.1).

Neurons transfer information by means of a combination of electrical and chemical processes. Typically, the electrical charge within a neuron is 70 mV less than the electrical charge outside the neuron, a difference known as the **resting potential.** This resting potential of −70 mV is maintained by a mechanism known as the *sodium-potassium pump,* which essentially works incessantly to pump out positive charged particles (ions) and make the inside

Figure 1.1 The basic parts of a neuron.
The dendritic tree, made up of individual dendrites, is the main region that receives information from other cells. The cell body contains the nucleus and the machinery necessary to support basic cell functions. The axon hillock is the location at which a large electrical signal is generated. The axon is the long shaft of the cell across which this large electrical signal is propagated. Many axons are covered with a myelin sheath, which has intermittent gaps, known as nodes of Ranvier. The myelin speeds conduction of the electrical signal down the axon. The branches at the end of the axon contain bulbous-shaped terminals (or boutons), which have vesicles filled with neurotransmitters. These neurotransmitters, which can be either inhibitory or excitatory, are released into the space between adjacent neurons, which is known as the synaptic cleft. The neuron on the terminal side of the cleft is known as presynaptic and the neurons on the opposite side are referred to as postsynaptic. Some synaptic connections are made onto postsynaptic dendrites, whereas others are made directly onto the postsynaptic cell body. An axon can have many branches, synapsing with as many as 1,000 other neurons. (*Note.* Adapted from Kandel et al., 1991, p. 19.)

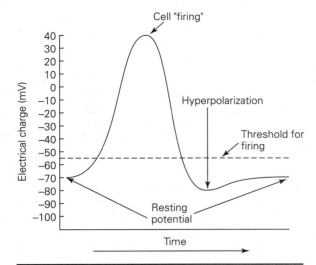

Figure 1.2 The firing of an action potential.
The cell is initially at the resting potential of −70 mV relative to the outside of the cell. Once the threshold is passed, the cell fires and the polarity reverses to +40 mV. After the cell fires, it hyperpolarizes for a short period, meaning that its voltage becomes more negative than −70 mV. After this phase, the cell returns to the resting potential.

of the cell negative relative to the outside. After the cell receives enough stimulation to reduce the difference in the electrical charge between the inside and the outside of the cell to about −55 mV, a threshold is passed and the cell "fires." When a cell fires, the electrical charge of the neuron reverses from −55 mV to a peak of +40 mV and then retreats toward the base-line resting potential. After the cell fires, a brief *hyperpolarization* occurs whereby the differential in charge becomes greater than −70 mV (usually to −90 mV), and is followed by a return to base line (Figure 1.2). This reversal in the differential between the electrical charge inside and outside the neuron is known as an **action potential.** This potential is generated at a point in the cell body known as the **axon hillock** and is carried down the axon. We do not discuss here the exact chemical properties that cause this firing, other than to say that it has two main properties of importance. First, it is self-propagating, which means that once it is set in motion nothing else must be done,

much as knocking down one domino causes all the others in a line to fall as well. Second, its strength does not dissipate with the distance that it travels, meaning that it remains +40 mV for its entire trip down the axon, unlike sound, for example, which loses energy the farther it travels. This potential is carried to the terminal bouton of the axon, which contains **synaptic vesicles,** which are little balloons filled with neurotransmitters. The electrical potential causes the synaptic vesicles that are fused to the outside walls of the neuron to burst open, pouring their contents into the area between neurons, known as the *synaptic cleft.* At this point, the signal that was previously propagated down the axon electrically is transformed into a chemical message.

Once out of the vesicles, the neurotransmitters diffuse across the cleft and bind with receptors on the dendritic trees of the adjacent neurons. In this context, *binding* is the ability of a neurotransmitter to fit into a particular region of the postsynaptic membrane that is characterized by a specific configuration, much the way a key fits into a lock. These particularly figured regions of the postsynaptic membrane are known as **receptor sites.** Once bound, the neurotransmitters cause the difference between the electrical charge inside and outside the neuron to change within a small local area. These changes can make the electrical charge of the cell either more positive than the resting potential, in which case they are known as **excitatory postsynaptic potentials (EPSPs),** or more negative than the resting potential, in which case they are known as **inhibitory postsynaptic potentials (IPSPs).** At this point, the chemical signal is transformed back into an electrical signal. These postsynaptic potentials are much lower in magnitude than the potential that occurs when an axon fires. If excitatory, the postsynaptic potentials make the cell's electrical charge more positive—that is, reduce the difference in electrical charge between the inside and the outside of the cell. This reduction brings the differential closer to the value of −55 mV at which the cell will fire. If inhibitory, the postsynaptic potentials make the inside of the cell more negative than the outside and move the cell away from the threshold at which it will fire.

Postsynaptic potentials differ from action potentials in three important ways. First, they are graded: The farther they travel from their source, the more they dissipate. Unlike the action potential, which remains constant for the entire course of its journey, postsynaptic potentials weaken as they travel across time and space. Second, as mentioned, postsynaptic potentials are much smaller in magnitude than an action potential, usually in the range of 0.2 to 0.4 mV. Third, whereas action potentials are always excitatory in that they make the cell fire, postsynaptic potentials can be either excitatory or inhibitory.

Because of its small value, one postsynaptic potential is highly unlikely to cause a cell to fire. Rather, the combined effect of these potentials influences the firing of the neuron. These graded postsynaptic potentials exert their influence by summating, both across time and across space. Hence two EPSPs that occur close together in time have a greater influence than if a gap in time separates them. Likewise, if two IPSPs occur at the same part of the dendritic tree, they are likely to have a larger influence than if they occur in spatially disparate regions of the dendrite. The complexity of this summation process can be appreciated if you consider that the average neuron has hundreds to thousands of other neurons synapsing upon it. Thus, whether a single cell fires depends not on a single voice from a neighboring neuron, but rather on the chorus of EPSPs and IPSPs produced by its neighbors and whether those voices occur close together in time and space.

The cacophony of postsynaptic potentials is summated at the axon hillock (see Figure 1.1). If the summed value of EPSPs and IPSPs manages to change the differential in charge from inside the cell to outside from −70 mV to around −55 mV, the cell will fire. If this value is not surpassed, the cell will not fire. Because the postsynaptic potentials are graded and lose their potency as they travel from their source to the axon hillock, potentials generated close to the axon hillock have a larger influence on whether or not the cell fires. Consequently, if we go back to our chorus analogy, the cells that synapse closer to the axon hillock have a louder voice in the chorus than those that do not.

We discuss the cellular basis of the nervous system because it is important to our understanding of certain syndromes discussed in later chapters. In some of these syndromes, the problem has been linked to a specific neurotransmitter. For example, Parkinson's disease, which is a motor disorder, is linked to a lack of dopamine, one of many chemical compounds that can act as a neurotransmitter. Other diseases, such as Alzheimer's disease, are characterized by changes in the morphology of neurons, in particular the appearance of tangles in the cellular matrix. These tangles may interfere with the transport of neurotransmitters from the cell body, where they are produced, down the axons, to the terminal, where they are packaged into synaptic vesicles. In other diseases, such as epilepsy, the cell's electrical activity is disrupted. In this case, an abnormal lowering of a cell's firing threshold causes it to misfire (Morselli & Lloyd, 1985).

Although we have discussed the mechanics of how information is propagated from one neuron to another, we have not discussed the mechanism that allows most of our thoughts and actions to appear to occur instantaneously. The speed at which neurons propagate electrical signals down their axons varies, in large part according to the degree to which the axon is insulated by a fatty sheath called **myelin.** The larger the myelin sheath, the greater the speed with which the electrical signal is propagated down the axon. The axons of some neurons have no myelin sheath. Unmyelinated neurons typically are small and do not carry information over long distances, generally synapsing on neighboring neurons. In contrast, neurons whose axons project to distant places in the nervous system are typically myelinated because myelination decreases the time needed to transport information from one neuron to the next. To demonstrate the increase in speed afforded by myelin, let's consider a specific type of neuron in the brain known as a *pyramidal cell,* which, among other things, is involved in controlling muscle movement. The axon of a pyramidal cell that controls movement of the right leg must extend from the brain to the bottom reaches of the spinal cord, a distance of more than 3 ft, or approximately 1 m. Unmyelinated fibers convey information at the rate of only about 0.5 mm/ms. If the pyramidal neuron were unmyelinated, it would take approximately 2,000 ms (i.e., 2 s) to convey information from the brain to the base of the spinal cord (2,000 ms × 0.5 mm/ms = 1 m). Such a time delay would not enable people to move or react very quickly. The myelination of pyramidal neurons allows information to be relayed at about 50 mm/ms, reducing the time between the generation of the signal in the brain to its arrival at the spinal cord more than 100 fold to about 200 ms.

The myelin sheath is not produced by the neuron but rather by a particular class of glia. In the brain, these are known as **oligodendrocytes.** A portion of the oligodendrocyte wraps itself around the axon much in the same way that a carpet is wrapped around a cardboard tube; such wrapping creates a discrete section of myelin. The more turns around the neuron, the greater the insulation and hence the greater the conduction speed. Gaps between myelinated sections of an axon are known as *nodes of Ranvier.* Because the electrical signal must jump across these nodes, they serve to keep the electrical signal constant in size, rather than degrading, as it travels down the axon (Figure 1.3).

Because myelin is fatty, it is white. Areas of the brain through which myelinated fibers run are known as the *white matter* of the brain. Concentrations of cell bodies, which are unmyelinated, constitute the *gray matter.* When a group of cells sends their axons to the same place, the group of axons is known as a **fiber tract,** and because these axons usually traverse long distances, they tend to be myelinated. For example, the *corpus callosum,* which is the main fiber tract connecting the two halves, or hemispheres, of the brain, is composed mainly of myelinated fibers, which allow a speedy transfer of information from a neuron in one hemisphere to a distant neuron in the other hemisphere.

Later in this book, we discuss the myelination of neurons in two contexts: with regard to development and with regard to certain diseases. As discussed in chapter 13, myelination of the brain follows a development course in which sensory and motor regions myelinate early in life, but the connections between more distant regions involved in

higher cortical processing do not become fully myelinated until as late as the teenage years or early 20s (Yakovlev & Lecours, 1967). The result is that regions of the brain become functionally more connected with age. Some of the disease states we discuss later, such as multiple sclerosis (see chapter 14), cause the myelin that is surrounding neurons to be thinned in a patchy or haphazard manner. This process leads to a significant disruption in neural processing affecting both motor function and cognitive function (e.g., Peyser & Poser, 1986).

Now that we have a basic understanding of the brain's cellular structure, we examine the major subdivisions of the central nervous system.

NEUROANATOMICAL TERMS AND BRAIN "GEOGRAPHY"

Anytime you begin a long journey, you need a road map to guide your path and you need some understanding of common directional terms such as *north, south, east,* and *west.* So, to begin our trip around the "geography" of the central nervous system, we must identify the major neural regions and introduce terms that can help to orient us on our journey. Distinguishing between regions of the central nervous system, and in particular the brain, serves a function similar to that of drawing boundary lines on a map. Such lines on a map may tell us not only about differences in geography between regions, but also about differences in the behavior, attitudes, and customs of people on either side of boundary. Likewise, boundaries between brain regions are often drawn to demarcate differences in structure and function of the brain tissue on either side of the boundary. Sometimes we find that boundaries between brain regions are based on large and obvious anatomical landmarks, like major geographical features on a map such as rivers or mountains. In other cases, the physical distinction between regions is not as obvious from the neuroanatomical terrain.

We must first learn the anatomical equivalents of north, south, east, and west. Unlike most geographical maps, which have only two dimensions, the brain has three. Thus, we need terms not only for the brain's left, right, top, and bottom, but for its

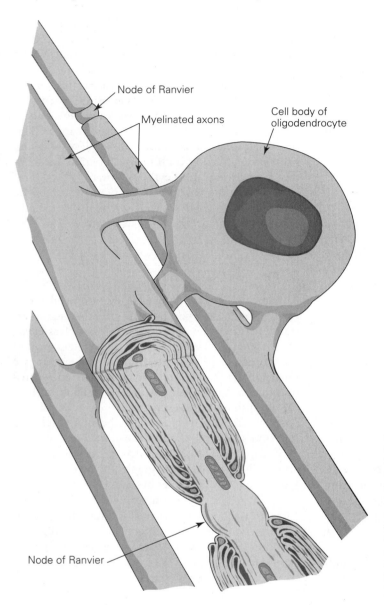

Node of Ranvier

Myelinated axons

Cell body of
oligodendrocyte

Node of Ranvier

**Figure 1.3 The structure of the myelin
sheath around an axon.**
Oligodendrocytes in the brain form a short
section of the myelin sheath on each of a
number of adjacent neurons by wrapping a
paddlelike process around each axon. A
gap between sections of myelin is known
as a node of Ranvier and helps the electrical signal to be propagated at a constant
strength along the axon. (*Note.* Adapted
from Carlson, 1994, p. 27; Kahle et al.,
p. 31.)

back and front as well. The front of the brain is referred to as **anterior** and the back as **posterior.** Because the head of an animal is situated in front of its tail, sometimes regions toward the front are referred to as **rostral** (toward the head), whereas regions toward the rear are referred to as **caudal** (toward the tail). The top of the brain is referred to as **superior,** and the bottom is referred to as **inferior.** With regard to the human brain, **dorsal** and **ventral** have meanings similar to superior and inferior, respectively. However, with regard to other portions of the central nervous system, such as the spinal cord, dorsal and ventral are better understood in reference to a four-legged animal or a fish. In these cases, dorsal means toward an animal's back, whereas ventral means toward an animal's stomach. If you have aquatic interests, you can remember that dorsal means top because the dorsal fin of a shark sticks out of the water. Finally, areas in the middle of the brain are referred to as **medial,** whereas areas that are far from the brain's midline are **lateral.**

Throughout this text, the brain is portrayed from one of three planes. When the brain is sliced to separate the front from the back, the view, or slice, is **coronal.** If we view the brain so that the top is separated from the bottom, the view is **horizontal.** Finally, if the left side of the brain is separated from the right side, the view is **sagittal.** A sagittal slice down the middle of the brain is known as a *midsagittal,* or *medial,* section, whereas a section taken more toward one side is known as a *lateral* section (Figure 1.4).

Knowledge of these terms can help us understand the location of specific brain structures. So, for example, when we are first introduced to the anatomical structure called the *lateral ventricles* (a ventricle is a space within the nervous system that is filled with fluid), we can deduce that they must be positioned away from the midline of the brain (i.e., laterally). Indeed, if you examine the picture of the ventricular system presented in Figure 1.5, you can see that the lateral ventricles are positioned toward the outside of the brain. As another example, consider how we might go about locating **nuclei,** which are distinct groups of neurons whose cell bodies are all situated in the same region, in a brain structure called the *thalamus.* As discussed later in this chapter, the thalamus helps to regulate and organize information from the outer reaches of the nervous system as it ascends toward the cortex and also modifies information descending from the cortex. If we need to find the anterior ventral nucleus of the thalamus, we now know from our discussion of anatomical terms that it should be located at the front and bottom part of the thalamus. You can give yourself a quick test of how well you learned

these anatomical terms by trying to locate the dorsal medial nucleus, the ventral lateral nucleus, and the lateral posterior nucleus of the thalamus in Figure 1.6.

Other terms we need to know include **contralateral** and **ipsilateral.** *Contralateral* means on the opposite side from, and *ipsilateral* means on the same side as. So, for example, the left half of your brain is contralateral to your right hand, whereas it is ipsilateral to your left hand. To make these definitions more concrete, remember the familiar adage that the right side of your brain controls the motor movements of the limbs on the left side of your body, and vice versa. Put in the terms we just learned, motor control occurs contralaterally. Anything that occurs or is situated to only one side of the brain (or space) is known as **unilateral,** whereas that which holds for both is known as **bilateral.** Other terms often used to describe brain regions and their relation to body parts are **proximal,** which means near, and **distal,** which means far. For example, distal muscles are in your far extremities such as your hands. Now that we know the spatial terms of directionality in the nervous system, we turn our attention in more detail to the major subdivisions of the nervous system.

MAJOR SUBDIVISIONS OF THE CENTRAL NERVOUS SYSTEM

We now start our journey across the different territories or regions of the **central nervous system.** The central nervous system encompasses the brain and the spinal cord, whereas the **peripheral nervous system** involves all neural tissue beyond the central nervous system, such as neurons that receive sensory information or synapse on muscle, and those that relay information to or from the spinal cord or the brain. Because of its fragility and because nerve cells do not regenerate, the entire central nervous system is encased in bone. The spinal cord is enclosed within the spinal column and the brain within the skull. Although these bony structures protect the central nervous system, at times they can cause damage. For example, if the spinal column presses against the spinal cord, it can pinch a nerve and cause pain. Likewise, as discussed in chapter

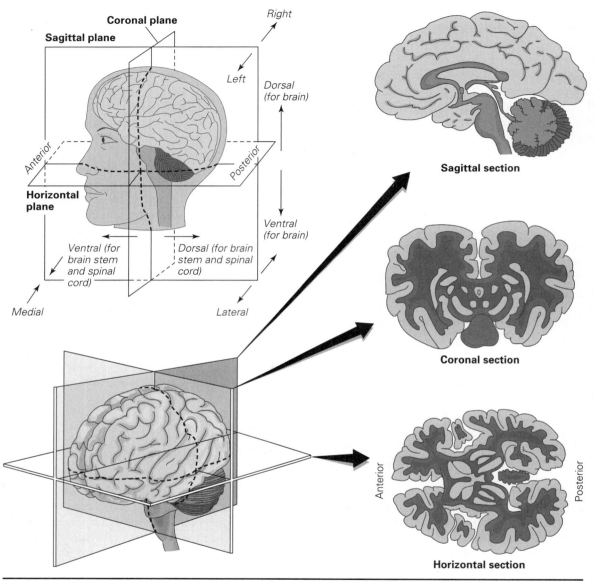

Figure 1.4   The main planes in which the brain is viewed.
A sagittal section divides left from right, a coronal section divides front from back, and a horizontal section divides top from bottom. (*Note.* Adapted from Rosenzweig & Leiman, 1989, p. 29.)

14, the brain can be damaged from compression against the skull.

Between the neurons and their bony encasements is **cerebrospinal fluid (CSF),** which is similar in composition to blood plasma. It both physically cushions the neurons and is the medium through which nutrients can diffuse into the neurons. Essentially, the brain floats in CSF, which makes it more buoyant and prevents it from being knocked around every time we move. CSF also

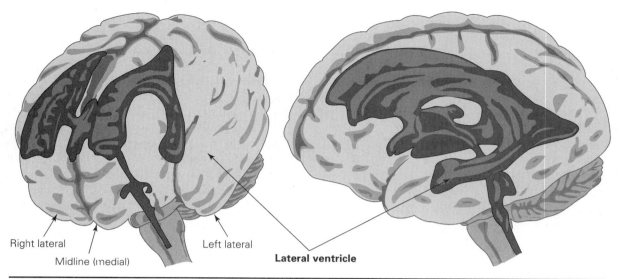

Figure 1.5 An important laterally located structure in the brain.
The ventricular system of the brain is a system of canals filled with cerebrospinal fluid, which is similar in composition to blood plasma. The two large lateral ventricles are located toward the exterior surface of the brain and away from the midline. (*Note.* Adapted from Rosenzweig & Leiman, 1989, p. 30.)

serves metabolic needs because nutrients can diffuse across it to reach neurons. Typically, cells outside the nervous system receive nutrients from the blood. However, under normal conditions, nutrients and many other compounds carried in the blood, such as drugs, bacteria, and cells of the immune system, never directly enter the nervous system because of the blood-brain barrier, which is produced by a tight packing of glial cells between blood vessels and neurons. Rather, nutrients from the blood reach nerve cells through CSF.

Because the molecules of the immune system, such as antibodies and phagocytes (cells, such as white blood cells, that engulf foreign bodies), have difficulty crossing the blood-brain barrier, the immune system is prevented in large part from protecting the central nervous system against infection. Thus, the central nervous system relies heavily on the blood-brain barrier to deflect bacteria and other infectious agents and to block the entry of toxins. Although the blood-brain barrier works well, when an infection does reach the brain it can be difficult to arrest because standard treatments used for infections in other regions of the body are unlikely to

be effective. A neurologist will often draw a sample of CSF from a region near the spinal cord (commonly known as a *spinal tap*) to determine if the brain is being affected by an infectious or a toxic agent. For example, an unusually high bacteria count in the fluid may indicate infection.

In the following sections, we examine the seven main subdivisions of the central nervous system depicted in Figure 1.7: (1) the spinal cord, (2) the medulla, (3) the cerebellum, (4) the pons, (5) the midbrain, (6) the hypothalamus and thalamus (diencephalon), and (7) the cerebral cortex. In addition, we discuss two major subcortical systems, the basal ganglia and the limbic system.

Spinal Cord

The **spinal cord** is the portion of the nervous system whereby most (but not all) sensory neurons synapse on their way to the brain, and whereby motor commands from the brain are sent to the muscles. The *spinal column,* the bony structure housing the spinal cord, is composed of many sections, or vertebrae. At each vertebra, sensory information enters the

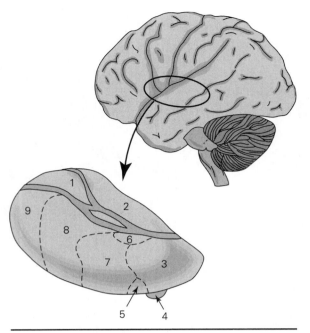

Figure 1.6 The different nuclei of the thalamus.
(1) Anterior nucleus, (2) dorsal medial nucleus, (3) pulvi-nar, (4) medial geniculate nucleus, (5) lateral geniculate nucleus, (6) ventral lateral posterior nucleus, (7) lateral posterior nucleus, (8) ventral lateral nucleus, and (9) ventral anterior nucleus. (*Note.* Adapted from Kolb & Whishaw, 1990, p. 26.)

cord and motor information leaves it. If the spinal cord were cut in cross section, two clumps of nerve cells, one located ventrally and another located dorsally, as shown in Figure 1.8, would be prominent. Cells in the dorsal section of the spinal cord (remember, dorsal is located toward the back) receive sensory information, whereas those in the ventral region (remember, ventral is located toward the stomach) are responsible for conveying motor commands to the muscle as well as for receiving input from the brain and from other regions of the spinal cord.

Damage to the spinal cord leaves an individual without sensation or motor control for all body areas that are connected to the brain by spinal segments distal to the point of injury. The damage prevents impulses from the periphery from being carried up the spinal cord past the point of injury

to the brain, and precludes information from the brain from being relayed down past the point of injury to the muscles. How much of the body is paralyzed and how much sensation is lost depends on where in the spinal cord the damage occurs. The vertebrae at which information from each part of the body enters the spinal cord are shown in Figure 1.9. Compression of the spinal column that causes a vertebra to be broken or crushed may result in a damaged or severed spinal cord. For example, when damage to the spinal cord occurs at the level of the fifth cervical vertebra (C-5; see Figure 1.9A), the person is often left quadriplegic, without control of muscles or sensation from either the arms or the legs (see Figure 1.9B). If, however, the damage is sustained at a lower level, perhaps waist level (e.g., at vertebra T-12, the twelfth thoracic vertebra), the person is often paraplegic, with loss of sensory information and motor control for just the bottom half of the body.

Medulla

The **medulla** is the section of the brain directly superior to the spinal cord. For our purposes, we should know a few main things about the medulla. First, it is the region of the brain that contains many (but not all) of the cell bodies of the 12 **cranial nerves.** Whereas the spinal cord is the point of synapse for sensory and motor nerves of the body, some cranial nerves are responsible for receipt of sensory information and motor control of the head. Other cranial nerves are responsible for the neural control of internal organs. A list of the 12 cranial nerves and their functions, and a diagram of the region of the brain where their nuclei are located are presented in Figure 1.10. Second, at the medulla, most of the motor fibers cross from one side of the body to the other, with the result that the left side of the brain controls the right side of the body and the right side of the brain controls the left side of the body. Third, the medulla controls many vital functions and reflexes, such as respiration and heart rate. Because the medulla serves these functions, damage to it can be fatal. One common accompaniment of either diffuse or specific brain damage is swelling of the entire brain. When this swelling puts enough

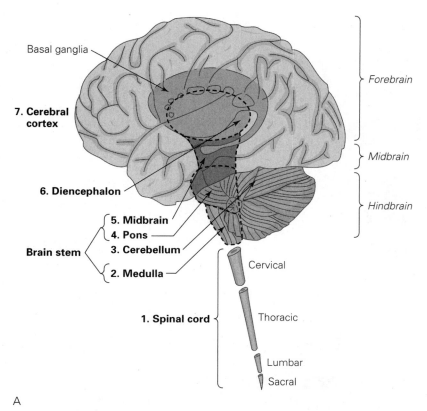

A

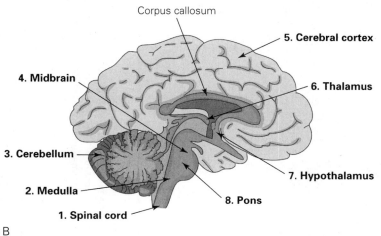

B

Figure 1.7 Major subdivisions of the brain.
(A) Left hemisphere, midsagittal view of the major subdivisions: the spinal
cord, medulla, cerebellum, pons, midbrain, diencephalon (thalamus and hypothalamus), and cerebral cortex. The medulla, pons, and midbrain are often referred to as the *brain stem*. Sometimes the brain is conceived of as having
three broad sections: the hindbrain (medulla, pons, and cerebellum), the midbrain, and the forebrain (diencephalon and cerebral cortex). (B) Left hemisphere, lateral view. (*Note.* Adapted from Kandel et al., 1991, p. 8; Kolb &
Whishaw, 1990, p. 13.)

13

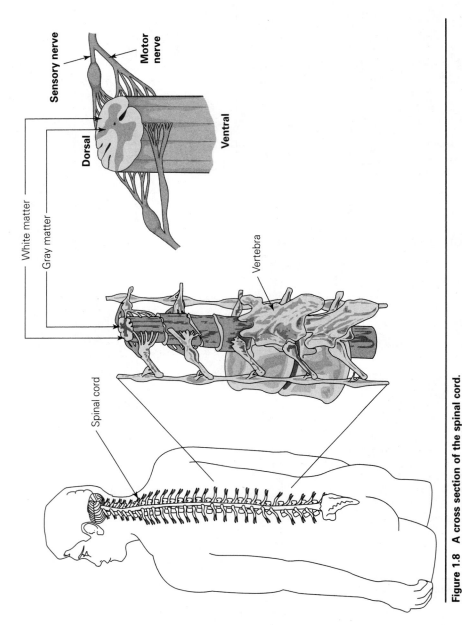

Figure 1.8 A cross section of the spinal cord.
Sensory information enters the spinal cord through the dorsal region, and nerves exit through the ventral region to control muscle movements. The gray matter consists largely of cell bodies. The surrounding white matter is composed of axons, some of which carry information down from the brain and higher levels of the spinal cord, and others of which carry information from lower levels upward. (*Note.* Adapted from Kalat, 1992, p. 101; Rosenzweig & Leiman, 1989, p. 68.)

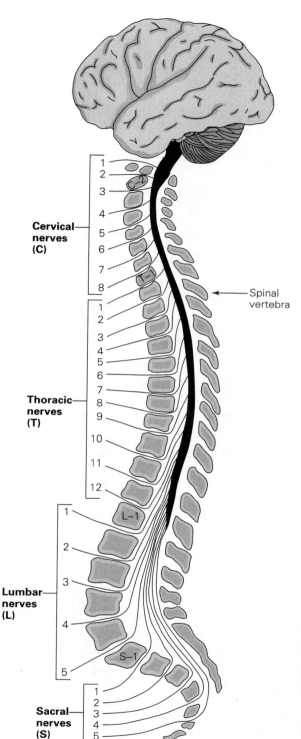

Cervical nerves (C)

1
2
3
4
5
6
7
8

Thoracic nerves (T)

1
2
3
4
5
6
7
8
9
10
11
12

Lumbar nerves (L)

1
2
3
4
5

Sacral nerves (S)

1
2
3
4
5

T–1

L–1

S–1

← Spinal vertebra

A

Figure 1.9 Spinal nerves and areas that they control.
(A) The four segments of the spinal cord: cervical (C), thoracic (T), lumbar (L), and sacral (S). There are 8 cervical spinal nerves, 12 thoracic nerves, 5 lumbar nerves, and 5 sacral nerves. A spinal nerve exits at each vertebra of the spinal column. (B) A map indicating the vertebra through which sensory information enters the spinal cord for each region of the body. Determining the locations of sensory loss after trauma to the spinal cord by using such maps helps medical personnel determine the level of the spinal cord at which damage occurred. (*Note.* Adapted from Kandel et al., 1991, p. 716.)

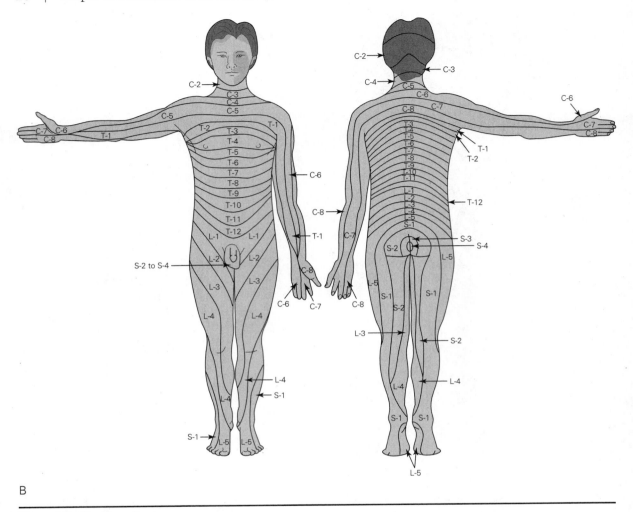

B

Figure 1.9 (Continued)

pressure on the medulla to interfere with its functions, death can result. Fourth, the medulla is the home to part of a set of the neurons known as the **reticular activating system.** These neurons receive input from the cranial nerves and project diffusely to many other regions of the brain, including the hypothalamus, thalamus, and cortex. The reticular activating system is important for overall arousal and attention, as well as for regulation of sleep-wake cycles. We discuss this system in more detail in chapter 7.

Cerebellum

The **cerebellum,** located posterior to the medulla (see Figure 1.7) is a region of the brain that is important for the regulation of muscle tone and guidance of motor activity. In large part, it is the region of the brain that allows a pianist to play a piece of music seamlessly or a pitcher to throw a ball fluidly. Damage to the cerebellum does not result in paralysis, but instead interferes with the precision of movement and disrupts equilibrium.

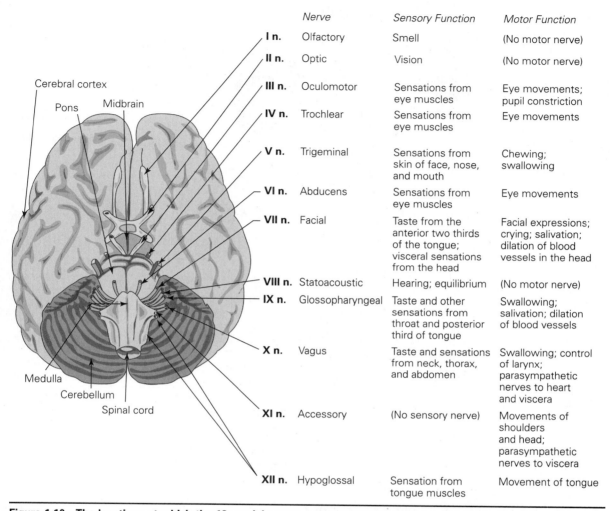

	Nerve	Sensory Function	Motor Function
I n.	Olfactory	Smell	(No motor nerve)
II n.	Optic	Vision	(No motor nerve)
III n.	Oculomotor	Sensations from eye muscles	Eye movements; pupil constriction
IV n.	Trochlear	Sensations from eye muscles	Eye movements
V n.	Trigeminal	Sensations from skin of face, nose, and mouth	Chewing; swallowing
VI n.	Abducens	Sensations from eye muscles	Eye movements
VII n.	Facial	Taste from the anterior two thirds of the tongue; visceral sensations from the head	Facial expressions; crying; salivation; dilation of blood vessels in the head
VIII n.	Statoacoustic	Hearing; equilibrium	(No motor nerve)
IX n.	Glossopharyngeal	Taste and other sensations from throat and posterior third of tongue	Swallowing; salivation; dilation of blood vessels
X n.	Vagus	Taste and sensations from neck, thorax, and abdomen	Swallowing; control of larynx; parasympathetic nerves to heart and viscera
XI n.	Accessory	(No sensory nerve)	Movements of shoulders and head; parasympathetic nerves to viscera
XII n.	Hypoglossal	Sensation from tongue muscles	Movement of tongue

Figure 1.10 The locations at which the 12 cranial nerves enter (sensory) or exit (motor) the brain, and each nerve's functions.
A ventral (*bottom*) surface view of the brain is shown on the left. The majority of cranial nerves enter at the medulla and the pons. The cranial nerves and their sensory and motor functions are shown in the table on the right. (*Note.* Adapted from Groves & Rebec, 1988, p. 103; Kalat, 1992, p. 110.)

The classic test that neurologists use to detect cerebellar damage is one in which the doctor asks a person to alternate between touching his or her own nose, and then the doctor's. Although a person with cerebellar damage can follow this command, the path taken by the hand from one nose to the other will be imprecise and jagged. Damage to the cerebellum also contributes to the lack of balance and motor control. A common manifestation of temporary disruption to the cerebellum is seen in the *punch-drunk syndrome,* in which an individual temporarily loses balance and coordination after sustaining a hard blow to the head.

Traditionally, a specific region of the cerebellum, the *lateral cerebellum,* was thought of as a brain structure mainly involved in motor control and the learning of motor skills (e.g., the skill of precisely serving a tennis ball). However, more recent evidence suggests that this region may be linked to certain aspects of cognitive processing, allowing for fluidity and precision in mental processes as well (Akshoomoff & Courchesne, 1992).

Pons

The **pons,** which lies directly superior to the medulla and anterior to the cerebellum (see Figure 1.7), has a multiplicity of functions. Because of its anatomical location, it acts as the main connective bridge from the rest of the brain to the cerebellum. It is the point of synapse of some of the cranial nerves, and it acts as an important center for the control of certain types of eye movements and for vestibular functions (e.g., balance). Finally, the pons is the site of the *superior olive,* one of the points through which auditory information is relayed from the ear to the brain. At the superior olive, information from both ears converges, and this convergence allows comparison of information received at each ear. Such comparison is thought to be important for localization of sounds in the horizontal dimension (Masterton, 1992).

Midbrain

The **midbrain** lies superior to the pons (see Figure 1.7). Like the pons and medulla, this region of the brain contains the nuclei of the cells that form some of the cranial nerves. The midbrain also contains two important structures on its dorsal side, the **inferior colliculus** and the **superior colliculus,** which play a role in allowing us to orient to stimuli in the auditory and visual modalities, respectively (Figure 1.11).

Like the superior olive, the inferior colliculus is a relay point for auditory information as it travels from the ear to the brain and appears to be involved in sound localization. However, it also contributes to reflexive movements of the head and eyes in response to sound, which provides us with the rudimentary ability to orient toward salient auditory stimuli.

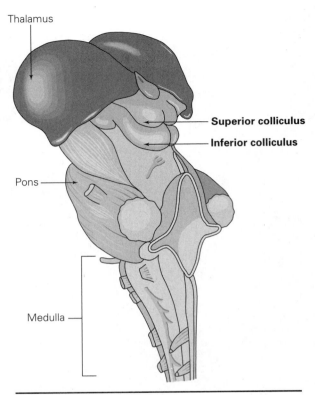

Figure 1.11 The brain stem, including the medulla, the pons, and the midbrain.
Note the position of the inferior and superior colliculi on the dorsal surface of the midbrain. Above the midbrain lies the thalamus, an important portion of the diencephalon. (*Note.* Adapted from Kalat, 1992, p. 109.)

The superior colliculus is the visual system's equivalent of the inferior colliculus, allowing us to perceive and orient toward large moving objects in the periphery. So, if a car comes speeding toward you from the far left, the superior colliculus signals your brain that something is approaching. The superior colliculus also aids, along with other brain regions to be discussed later, in guiding your eyes toward that large object so that it falls in the center of your vision, a process known as *foveation.* The midbrain visual system, however, cannot make fine discriminations of visual objects (e.g., recognize the object as a car), thus only after the object is in central vision can it be identified by other brain regions that are specialized for object recognition. The role of the superior colliculus in orienting toward certain types of visual information and guiding the eyes toward objects of interest makes it a structure that we revisit in chapter 7.

Hypothalamus

The general role of the **hypothalamus** (see Figure 1.7B) is to control behaviors that help the body maintain an equilibrium or satisfy its needs. When organisms have a particular need, they generally emit a behavior designed to bring the body back to a stable state (this stable state is known as *homeostasis*). For example, when hungry or thirsty, a person will engage in behaviors that lead to food or drink, or if cold, the person will search for a sweater or a blanket. The hypothalamus provides the signals telling the brain that these sorts of behaviors are called for.

Let's now examine the role of the hypothalamus in each of a variety of functions in more detail. One of the main functions of the hypothalamus is to aid in feeding and drinking behavior. For example, research with animals has demonstrated that damage to the ventromedial region of the hypothalamus leads an animal to eat more than is required to maintain a normal body weight; such behavior eventually causes obesity. Likewise, *lesions* (wounds, damage, or injuries) to dorsal and lateral regions of the hypothalamus can interfere with water intake. Another main function of the hypothalamus is to aid in regulation of body temperature. Some neurons in both anterior and posterior sections of the hypothalamus detect changes in the temperature of the skin or blood and hence act similar to a thermostat.

The hypothalamus also has an intimate relationship with the hormonal system, which is the system whereby chemical messengers are carried throughout the body, by means of the bloodstream, to exert their influence on target organs far from their point of production. The hypothalamus either secretes hormones itself or produces other factors that regulate activity of additional brain regions that secrete hormones. This linkage of the hypothalamus to the hormonal system helps explain its role in sexual behavior, daily (diurnal) rhythms, and fight-or-flight reactions. Certain regions of the hypothalamus, such as the sexually dimorphic nucleus vary in size between males and females, a difference seen in many mammalian species, including humans. Other regions of the hypothalamus, such as the suprachiasmatic nucleus, play a role in diurnal rhythms. This region of the hypothalamus, which receives input from the retina, controls fluctuations in the release of hormones during the day. Finally, lateral areas of the hypothalamus are important for activating certain bodily responses such as the fight-or-flight reactions that animals have in threatening situations.

Thalamus

Along with the hypothalamus, the **thalamus** (see Figures 1.7B and 1.11) is part of the **diencephalon.** It is a large relay center for almost all sensory information coming into the cortex and almost all motor information leaving it. A **relay center** is a brain region in which the neurons from one area of the brain synapse onto neurons that then go on to synapse somewhere else in the brain. Often, the pattern of connections between neurons at relay centers serves to reorganize information before it is sent elsewhere in the nervous system. For example, in the visual system, information from the retina comes, via the optic tract, to synapse onto the *lateral geniculate nucleus* of the thalamus. The pattern of connections is such that one layer of the lateral geniculate, the *magnocellular layer,* tends to receive input from cells that are extremely sensitive to low levels of light and quite insensitive to color, whereas the *parvocellular layer* receives information from cells that are color sensitive and need higher levels of light to function. Thus, at this relay point, information is reorganized on its way to the brain so that information about color and light intensity are segregated (Zeki & Shipp, 1988).

To give you a better sense of how certain brain regions, including the thalamus, act as relay centers, consider the analogy to the distribution of eggs laid by a group of chickens, each of which has a particular roost. In this case, eggs, rather than information, are being relayed from one point to another. Initially, each hen lays a set of eggs in her nest. These eggs are then sent down the conveyor belt toward the processing plant in a systematic order so that eggs laid by hens with roosts next to each other end up on the belt next to each other. However, as the eggs reach the plant, they are sorted into two piles on the basis of size, so that all the small eggs are packaged together and all the large ones are packaged together. Such a system preserves basic information about life in the hen house (because eggs from hens with adjacent roosts get packaged next to each other), but nonetheless also sorts the information in a novel way (because the eggs are now segregated with regard to size). Likewise, if we go back to the visual system, when information leaves the retina it does so with regard to where in the retina a cell is located but without regard to a cell's sensitivity to color or the degree of illumination. However, the partitioning of information between the magnocellular and parvocellular layers ensures that the information leaving the thalamus is segregated on the basis of sensitivity to light intensity and color, at the same time preserving information about where in the retina those cells originated.

The connections of the thalamus are extremely complicated, and understanding all of them could be a course unto itself. For our purposes, we should know that the pattern of connections both coming into and leaving the thalamus are very specific. For example, one particular region of the thalamus receives information from just one sensory system and projects to only one particular region of the cortex.

Major Subcortical Systems

Two important neural systems reside mainly within regions of the midbrain and diencephalon: the basal ganglia, which is important for motor control, and the limbic system, which is important for emotions. Because many or all the structures in these systems are located in regions below the cerebral cortex, they are referred to as *subcortical* systems.

The **basal ganglia** consist of the *caudate nucleus,* the *putamen,* and the *globus pallidus,* all of which are structures located near the thalamus (Figure 1.12).

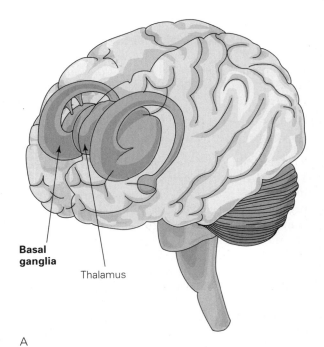

Basal ganglia

Thalamus

A

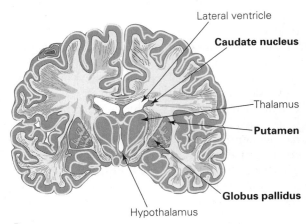

Lateral ventricle

Caudate nucleus

Thalamus

Putamen

Globus pallidus

Hypothalamus

B

Figure 1.12   The location of the basal ganglia in relation to other cortical and subcortical structures.
(A) Left hemisphere, lateral perspective.
(B) Coronal view. (*Note.* Adapted from Carlson, 1994, p. 93; B, Adapted from Kandel et al., 1991, p. 648.)

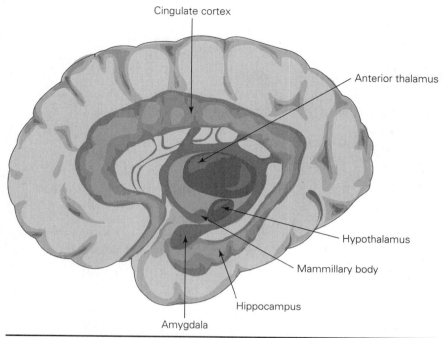

Cingulate cortex

Anterior thalamus

Hypothalamus

Mammillary body

Hippocampus

Amygdala

Figure 1.13 The structures that comprise the limbic system.
Left hemisphere, medial view of the limbic system, which comprises the amygdala, the hypothalamus, the cingulate cortex, the anterior thalamus, the mammillary body, the hippocampus, and the hypothalamus. (*Note.* Adapted from Kalat, 1992, p. 112; Kandel et al., 1991, p. 736.)

Degeneration or destruction of these areas leads to difficulty in motor control, generally characterized by involuntary movements. Damage to the globus pallidus leads to involuntary twisting and turning of the limbs, whereas damage to the caudate nucleus and putamen causes involuntary movements, such as tremors, while the person is at rest, and the introduction of extra movements into a standard progression of voluntary movement, such as walking. We discuss the role of these structures in motor behavior in much more detail in chapter 4.

The **limbic system** is a series of subcortical structures that were initially believed to be a circuit for integrating emotional information between various parts of the nervous system, although we now know that these structures play a much more complicated role in a variety of functions. As initially conceived, these structures were mainly thought to allow for

the processing of emotional information by linking information from the sensory world and an individual's internal state with information from the cortex. For example, if a small animal sees a larger one, it must integrate (a) information from its hypothalamus about fear, (b) information from its visual cortex identifying the large animal, and (c) information from the brain regions involved in memory that reminds the small animal whether previous encounters with this type of large animal were dangerous.

The structures comprising the limbic system include the *amygdala*, the *hypothalamus*, the *cingulate cortex*, the *anterior thalamus*, the *mammillary body*, and the *hippocampus* (Figure 1.13). We discuss the roles of these structures in more detail in later chapters. For example, the amygdala has been implicated in the control of rage and is thought to play a prominent role in emotional functioning, as dis-

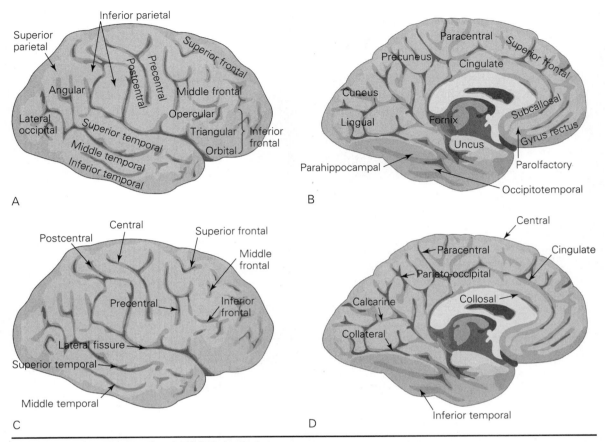

Figure 1.14 The major gyri and sulci of the brain.
(A) The major gyri of the right hemisphere, lateral surface of the brain. (B) The major gyri as viewed from the longitudinal fissure. (C) The major sulci on the right hemisphere, lateral surface of the brain. (D) The major sulci as viewed from the longitudinal fissure. (*Note.* Adapted from Kolb & Whishaw, 1990, p. 16.)

cussed in chapter 11. The hippocampus plays an important role in memory, specifically the formation of new long-term memories, as described in chapter 9, and the cingulate cortex has been implicated in motor control and in the selection of actions, as discussed in more detail in chapters 4 and 12.

Cerebral Cortex

The cerebral cortex is the region that most often comes to mind when we think of the brain (see Figure 1.7). The cortex plays a primary role in the majority of functions that we discuss in the remainder of this text—such as language, memory, attention, and artistry. The cortex is divided into two physically separated halves, each called a **cerebral hemisphere.** Although at first glance these two hemispheres look similar, we find in chapter 3 that they differ both in function and in anatomy. Each convolution, or bump, of the brain is called a **gyrus** (plural: gyri) and basically is a giant sheath of neurons wrapped around the other brain structures just discussed. These convolutions serve to pack more brain tissue into a smaller space, much as rolling your clothes allows you to get more of them into your suitcase. Each valley between the bumps is called a **sulcus** (plural: sulci), and if it is deep it is known as a **fissure.** Every brain has the same basic gyral pattern, just as every face has the same basic pattern (i.e., eyes above the nose, mouth below the nose). However, subtle individual variations exist in the gyral pattern, just as facial configuration varies (e.g., some people have wide-set eyes, whereas in others the eyes are close together). The major gyri and sulci of the brain and their names are shown in Figure 1.14.

Three major fissures serve as prominent landmarks in the brain because they provide a means for conceptualizing distinctions in function between major brain regions. The first of these is the **central fissure,** sometimes called the *Rolandic fissure,* which separates each hemisphere of the brain in an anterior-posterior dimension. In general, areas of the brain in front of the central fissure are more involved in motor processing, whereas those behind are more involved in sensory processing. The second major fissure is the **Sylvian (lateral) fissure,** which sepa-

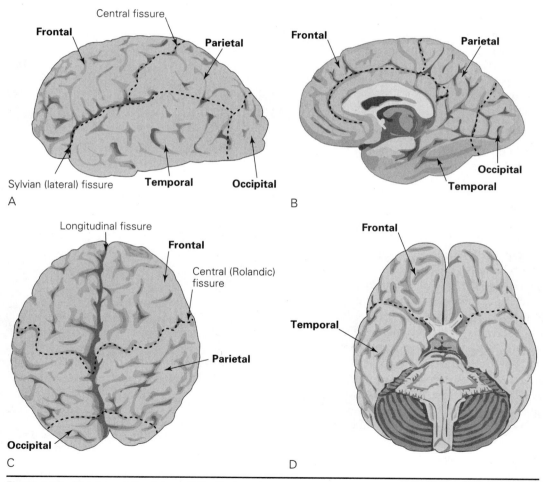

Figure 1.15   The four major lobes of the brain.
(A) Left hemisphere, lateral, (B) right hemisphere, midsagittal, (C) dorsal, and (D) ventral perspectives of the brain, showing the frontal, temporal, parietal, and occipital lobes. (*Note.* Adapted from Kolb & Whishaw, 1990, p. 17.)

rates each hemisphere of the brain in the dorsal-ventral dimension. This division is important because the area of the brain below the Sylvian fissure is the temporal lobe, which plays an important role in memory, emotion, and auditory processing. The third major fissure is the **longitudinal fissure,** which separates the right cerebral hemisphere from the left. This division is important because each hemisphere has a unique specialization with regard to both cognitive and emotional functioning.

These three major fissures also divide each hemisphere into four major regions, or lobes. The area in front of the central fissure is known as the **frontal lobe.** The area below the Sylvian fissure is the **temporal lobe.** The region directly behind the central fissure but above the Sylvian fissure is the **parietal lobe,** and the remaining region of the brain behind the parieto-occipital sulcus the **occipital lobe.** These three fissures, as well as the four major lobes of the brain, are depicted in Figure 1.15.

A CLOSER LOOK AT THE CEREBRAL CORTEX

Because the cortex plays a prominent role in many functions that we think of as uniquely human, we must examine it in more detail. We begin by briefly discussing the anatomical characteristics of the cortex and a system of how cortical regions can be distinguished on the basis of the pattern of cellular organization, often referred to as *cytoarchitectonics.* Then, we switch to examining regions of the cortex according to the functions that each serves. We discuss not only the areas of the brain that are important for receiving sensory information from the outside world, but also the areas that are important for controlling the motor output of the body. Finally, we examine an overview of the functions of the remaining areas of the cortex, most of which are devoted to cognitive and emotional function.

Cytoarchitectonic Divisions

Although all regions of cortex have five or six layers, or *laminae,* of cells, the relative thickness of each layer as well as the size and the shape of cells within

those layers, varies between brain regions. Neuroanatomists have identified the areas of the cortex in which the laminar organization and nature of cells within those layers are similar and have created what is known as a **Brodmann map** (named after its creator), which is shown in Figure 1.16. It is useful to bear in mind that these boundaries on the Brod-

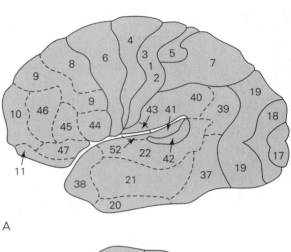

A

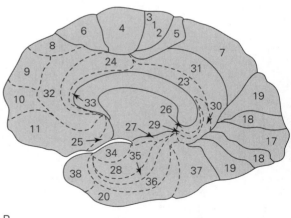

B

Figure 1.16 Brodmann map of the cortex.
The Brodmann map is based on cytoarchitectonic differences between brain regions. Borders between areas that have distinct cytoarchitectonic characteristics are depicted by solid lines, whereas less distinct borders are depicted by dashed lines. (A) Left hemisphere, lateral view. (B) Right hemisphere, midsagittal view. (*Note.* Adapted from Kolb & Whishaw, 1990, p. 21.)

mann map are not always absolute. Sometimes, they reflect smoother transitions; therefore, the borders may be considered "fuzzy."

Although the distinctions between regions in the Brodmann map are made entirely on the basis of anatomy, with no regard to function, in some cases regions with distinct cytoarchitectonic characteristics also have distinct functions. In other cases, the correlation between neuroanatomy and function is less clear. One of the main reasons to be familiar with the Brodmann map is because some scientists find this system convenient to use when attempting to refer to particular regions of brain tissue. For example, later in the text we discuss brain imaging techniques that are designed to determine which regions of the brain are physiologically active during performance of a specific task. To convey the location of these regions to the reader, scientists often refer to the activated brain region by means of the number assigned to that region on the Brodmann map. For example, *Broca's area,* a region of the left hemisphere that is important to speech output, is often referred to in Brodmann's terminology as areas 44 and 45. Alternatively, this same region could be called the *frontal opercular region* (see Figure 1.14A).

Primary Sensory and Motor Cortices

The first region in the cortex to receive information about a particular sensory modality (e.g., visual information) is known as **primary sensory cortex.** **Primary motor cortex** is the region of the cortex that is the final exit point for neurons controlling the fine motor control of the body's muscles. The locations of the primary sensory areas and primary motor cortex are presented in Figure 1.17.

The organization of primary sensory regions is dictated by the physical attribute of the world to which our sensory receptors are sensitive. Let's use *audition* (the sense or power of hearing) to illustrate this point. In some alternative universe, we might have evolved so that the sensory receptors in the cochlea of the ear, known as *hair cells,* were organized to allow certain receptors to respond only to loud sounds and others only to soft sounds. However, in our world this is not the case. Rather, the hair cells in the cochlea of the ear are differentially sensitive to sounds of different frequencies (i.e., low tones vs. high tones), which we perceive as tones of different pitch. Thus, frequency is the attribute of auditory information that is coded by the nervous system. Later in this chapter, we see that the sensitiv-

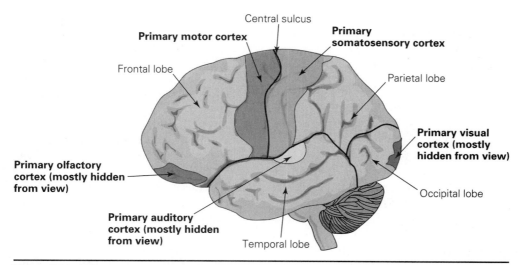

Figure 1.17   Primary sensory and motor cortices.
All the primary sensory areas are posterior to the central sulcus, whereas primary motor cortex is anterior. (*Note.* Adapted from Carlson, 1994, p. 89.)

ity of the sensory receptors to frequency is reflected in the organization of primary auditory cortex because some regions are active when high tones are heard and other regions are active when low tones are heard.

The organization of primary sensory and motor areas share some general characteristics of organization that are worth noting now, before we discuss the specifics of each system. First, all these brain areas are organized so that specific attributes of the physical world are "mapped" onto brain tissue. For example, motor control of a specific region of the body is controlled by a specific region of primary motor cortex. Thus, movement of the index finger is controlled by one specific region of the motor cortex rather than a multiplicity of areas. Second, these maps are distorted relative to the physical world. Rather, they appear to reflect the density of receptors (or effectors) within a system. For example, we have a much higher density of receptors at the fovea, the focal point of our vision, than for more lateral locations. Likewise, much more of primary visual cortex is devoted to processing visual information from the central part of the visual world as compared with the periphery. Third, the mapping of the world onto brain tissue occurs in an upside down and backward manner for vision, touch, and motor control. For example, information from the upper right-hand portion of the body or world is processed by primary sensory or motor cortex in the ventral portion of the left hemisphere.

Motor Cortex

Primary motor cortex resides directly in front of the central fissure in a long, narrow band sometimes called the *motor strip*. It begins deep within the longitudinal fissure and continues down until the Sylvian fissure. Look at Figure 1.18, which depicts the body regions that are controlled by each portion of the motor strip. This map is often referred to as the *homunculus*, meaning "little man." As you look at Figure 1.18, note that a couple of features bear out the generalizations we just discussed. First, notice that the mapping of the body onto the brain is inverted both with regard to top and bottom and with regard to left and right. The inversion left-

right occurs because the left motor strip controls the right side of the body and the right motor strip controls the left side of the body. The inversion top-bottom occurs because the area of the motor strip controlling the toes and feet are at the top end of the motor strip, actually within the longitudinal fissure, and the control of the face is most ventral on the lateral surface of the brain. Second, notice that the mapping is distorted because the size of the area of brain tissue devoted to control of a particular body part is disproportionate to the size of that body part. Notice which regions of the body have large amounts of cortex devoted to their control, despite their relatively small size: the face, the larynx, the vocal cords, and the hands. As you may surmise, the distortion of the map depends, in large part, on the degree to which we have fine motor control of a body part. The body parts for which we have a large degree of fine motor control, such as the face and the hand, have a disproportionately larger area of brain tissue devoted to their control than do areas of the body for which we have little fine motor control, such as the thigh. The functional significance of this distortion can be understood when we consider the extremely precise fine motor control needed to express emotion, speak, and manipulate objects, actions that are performed by the face, the vocal apparatus, and the hands, respectively. Hence, large sections of the motor cortex are devoted to control of these body regions. In comparison, we have little fine motor control of the back muscles, so only a small region of the motor strip is devoted to their control, even though the back is one of the larger regions of the body.

What are the effects of damage to the motor strip? Because the neurons in the motor cortex control the amount of force to be applied by muscles, damage to primary motor cortex leads to muscle weakness on the contralateral side of the body. For example, damage to dorsal regions of the motor strip results in weakness of the bottom part of the body (recall the upside-down orientation of the homunculus), whereas damage to ventral regions of the motor strip often leads to weakness in face and arm muscles. As discussed in chapter 4, the body has multiple systems for muscle control. Hence, damage to the motor cortex does not cause total paralysis because

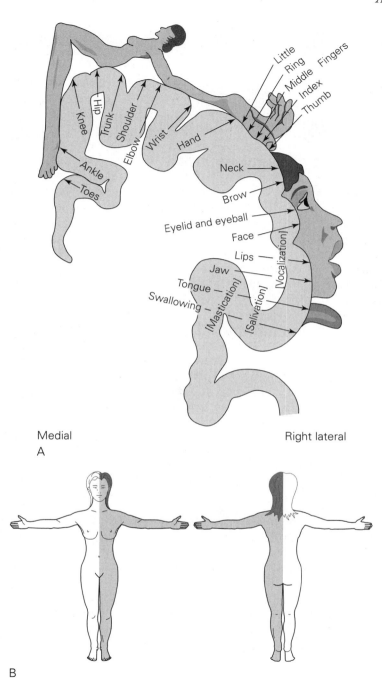

Little
Ring
Middle Fingers
Index
Thumb
Hip
Knee
Trunk
Shoulder
Elbow
Wrist
Hand
Neck
Brow
Eyelid and eyeball
Face
Lips
Jaw
Tongue
Swallowing
Ankle
Toes
[Vocalization]
[Mastication]
[Salivation]

Medial
A

Right lateral

B

Figure 1.18 The motor homunculus in the right hemisphere.
(A) The regions of the body for which we have precise motor control, such as the hand and vocal musculature, have a large region of motor cortex devoted to their control. In contrast, large body parts for which we have relatively poor fine motor control, such as the trunk, have a relatively small region of the cortex devoted to their control. (B) The motor cortex in the right hemisphere controls movement on the left side of the body as depicted by the shaded regions on the body. (*Note.* Adapted from Kandel et al., 1991, p. 372; Posner & Raichle, 1994, p. 14.)

Discovery of the "Homunculus"

Our knowledge about the organization of the motor cortex is derived in large part from the search for a therapeutic intervention for a particular disease—epilepsy. Although scientists knew from the late 1800s that the left motor strip controlled the right side of the body and vice versa, the precise nature of the homunculus was revealed only in the course of attempting to obtain a better understanding of epilepsy (Novelly, 1992). Observations by neurologists of a particular type of epileptic seizures known as *Jacksonian seizures* (named after the famous neurologist John Hughlings Jackson) revealed that the body was mapped onto the brain in an orderly fashion. In an **epileptic seizure,** neurons in the brain fire in an abnormal manner typified by great bursts, or volleys, of firing, often called *spikes*. In Jacksonian seizures, the tremors follow an orderly pattern, starting in one body part, such as the leg, and moving systematically, next to the trunks then to the arms and face. Such a pattern indicates that the seizure begins in one part of the motor strip and proceeds along it in an orderly fashion.

The creation of therapeutic interventions to reduce and control epilepsy earlier in this century dramatically revealed the degree of distortion of the brain map of the motor area. Working at the Montreal Neurological Institute, Dr. Wilder Penfield pioneered the use of surgical interventions to excise regions of brain tissue that cause epileptic activity (Penfield & Rasmussen, 1950). Even today, when seizures cannot be controlled by drugs and originate from a specific brain region, often referred to as an *epileptic focus,* physicians sometimes remove brain tissue at the focus. The rationale for this intervention is that continued seizure activity will recruit otherwise healthy neurons and cause them to become more prone to seizure activity. Although the neurosurgeon wants to remove the region of brain tissue that is misfiring, he or she must ensure that both the incisions required to reach the focus and the removal of the misfiring tissue do not have devastating effects. Therefore, during surgery, the neurosurgeon needs the ability to map out precisely which regions of the brain control which functions. This is especially true for the motor strip because excision of portions of it can leave a person with severe muscle weakness on the contralateral side of the body.

Let's move into the operating room to see how the mapping is performed. The patient is lying on the operating table, covered with green surgical sheets that are used to form a tent of sort, with one open side around the patient's head. The patient's face protrudes

the other motor systems can compensate for the damage. However, the ability to move muscles independently of one another, and the required fine motor control is lost, such as is needed to grasp something between the thumb and forefinger. When massive destruction to the motor strip occurs along with damage to the basal ganglia (as often occurs after stroke), paralysis on the contralateral side of the body is observed and results in a deficit known as **hemiplegia.**

Somatosensory Cortex

The *primary somatosensory cortex* is the portion of the cortex that receives information about tactile stimulation, **proprioception** (the perception of the position of body parts and their movements), and pressure and pain sensations from internal organs and muscles. It is located directly posterior to the central fissure.

The skin contains various nerve endings, or receptors, that are sensitive to different aspects of tactile information, such as pain, pressure, vibration, and temperature. This information travels to the cortex along two main routes. Crude tactile information, along with information about pain and temperature, is sent to the cortex by neurons that synapse at *dorsal regions of the spinal cord,* from which the information is carried to the thalamus and then to the cortex. Information about fine touch and

from under one side of the tent, whereas the surgeon is situated on the other side at the opening of the tent. Procedure in this operating room is different from what you might expect: Instead of an unconscious patient on the operating table, this patient is alert and talking! Because the brain has no pain receptors, only local anesthetics are used as the surgeon removes a piece of skull to expose the brain underneath. After the brain is exposed, the surgeon places an electrode on the brain, and a sheet with a number on the brain, adjacent to the electrode. Let's assume that the surgeon starts by placing the electrode directly in front of the central fissure at the most dorsal portion of the brain. Although the patient is lying perfectly still, as soon as the surgeon runs some current through the electrode, the patient's leg begins to twitch involuntarily! As soon as the current is turned off, the twitching stops. The neurosurgeon then announces "Leg movement at position 4" and moves the electrode more ventrally, leaving the marker in place. He or she now places another marker number on the brain and stimulates at the next spot. Now, the patient's thigh begins to twitch. The neurosurgeon continues in this fashion until the whole motor strip is identified.

The need for such mapping is important if you consider, as we already discussed, that each individual's brain is as distinct as each person's face. Although neurosurgeons know that the motor strip lies in front of the central fissure, they don't know exactly where. Consider by analogy the organization of the face. Just as we know that the eyes are always located above the nose, so the neurosurgeon knows that the motor strip is in front of the central fissure. However, this landmark alone is not enough, just as knowing where a person's nose is located does not tell you exactly where his or her eyes are situated. Likewise, precise mapping is needed to determine the extent and range of the motor strip. In addition to mapping the motor area, a neurosurgeon will also map the primary somatosensory cortex during surgery for epilepsy. In this case, the active cooperation of the patient is even more critical. Only if the patient is conscious can he or she convey to the surgeon where the sensations, such as a tingle, a tickle, or an itch, are being felt as different regions of the somatosensory strip are stimulated. This mapping technique, originally designed to aid the neurosurgeon in therapeutic interventions for epilepsy, provided extremely useful information about the organization of the primary motor and somatosensory areas.

proprioception enters the spinal column but does not synapse until the medulla, from which point it is carried to the thalamus and subsequently onto the cortex.

Like the motor homunculus, the map of the body onto primary somatosensory cortex is inverted left-right and top-bottom. The distortion of body parts in the somatosensory map is proportional to the density of touch receptors. In general, areas that have a high density of tactile receptors have large areas of the somatosensory strip devoted to receiving information from them, and areas of the body that have relatively few tactile receptors have relatively small regions of brain tissue devoted to receiving information from them. The mapping of the

body's sense of touch onto the somatosensory cortex is illustrated in Figure 1.19.

If you compare this map with that of the motor strip in Figure 1.18, you can see that the map of somatosensory cortex looks similar, but it is not identical to that of the motor homunculus. The differences clearly arise because what is being mapped in the somatosensory strip is sensitivity of touch, not precision of motor control. Yet, striking similarities are apparent. These similarities should not be surprising because the parts of our body for which we have fine motor control, such as our hands, are the same areas for which we need a fine sense of touch. Agile manipulation of an object requires not only that we be able to move the hands

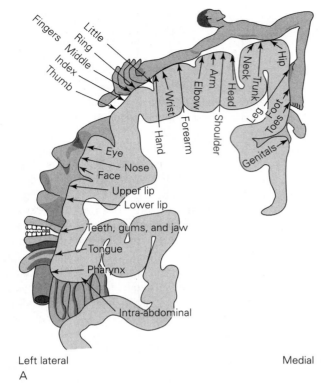

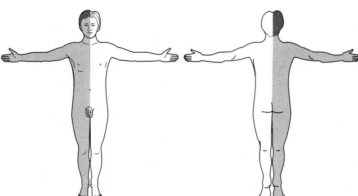

Figure 1.19 The somatosensory homunculus in the left hemisphere.
(A) Like the motor homunculus, the somatosensory homunculus is distorted with regions of high tactile sensitivity occupying large regions of cortex. Although the distortion is similar to that of the motor homunculus, it is not identical. (B) Sensory information from the right side of the body is sent to the primary somatosensory cortex of the left hemisphere. (*Note.* Adapted from Kandel et al., 1991, p. 372; Posner & Raichle, 1994, p. 14.)

and fingers, but also that our sense of touch is equally fine so that we have tactile feedback on which to base our movements. If this relationship is not intuitively obvious, consider, for instance, how difficult deftly manipulating something like your car keys is in the winter when you are wearing a pair of gloves and your sense of touch is reduced.

What are the consequences of damage to the somatosensory strip? Rather than obliterating all sense of touch, such damage compromises fine discriminations of touch on the side of the body contralateral to the damaged primary somatosensory cortex. So, for example, if you put a piece of cloth in the hand of a individual who sustained damage to the somatosensory strip, the person would know that something was placed there but would have difficulty determining whether the cloth was velvet or burlap. Furthermore, if touched multiple times in quick succession, the person likely would have trouble determining the number of times that she or he was touched. Finally, if an individual was touched in two places near each other (e.g., two places on the back of the palm about 5 mm apart), he or she would have difficulty knowing that the touch had occurred in two separate places. This type of discrimination is known as *two-point discrimination,* and our sensitivity to it varies depending on the body part. The distance required to perceive two points as distinct is smallest for the hands and fingers (with the largest number of receptors) and largest for the shoulders, thighs, and calves (with the smallest number of receptors).

One interesting aspect of the somatosensory map of the body is that it appears to provide a means for understanding some phenomena associated with phantom limb pain, a symptom common after the loss of a limb. With phantom limb pain, the limb is usually in a particular position and may also be perceived to move. In addition to pain, other sensations, such as itchiness, may be perceived. However, reorganization of the primary somatosensory region after limb loss can lead to some atypical feelings. For example, in the case of an individual who lost a hand, touch on his face leads him to report that he feels the phantom hand. Although at first such a claim may seem odd, it isn't if you think about the organization of the somatosensory strip. By referring to Figure 1.19, you can see that the primary somatosensory region that receives tactile information from the hand is adjacent to the area that receives information from the face. In this individual, the reorganization of the somatosensory strip probably led neurons in regions previously devoted exclusively to receiving tactile information from the hand to interact with neurons that receive informa-

tion from the face (Ramachandran, Rogers-Ramachandran, & Steward, 1992).

Visual Cortex

The *primary visual cortex* is the first region of the cortex that processes visual information. The information it receives first impinges on the nervous system in the retina by two types of visual sensory receptors: the *rods,* which are very sensitive to small degrees of light but are insensitive to color, and the *cones,* which are extremely sensitive to color but require a high degree of illumination to function. The light energy detected by these cells is transformed into a neural signal and relayed to the *ganglion cells,* which reside in the retina. The axons of the ganglion cells form the **optic nerve,** which is the conduit whereby information is carried from the eye to the brain. Ganglion cells synapse on the **lateral geniculate nucleus** of the thalamus, and cells in this brain structure project to primary visual cortex (Figure 1.20).

Although this is the basic outline of the major relay points from the eye to the brain, we must examine the visual system in a bit more detail for a number of reasons. First, doing so enables us to better understand the nature of the mapping of the visual world onto primary visual cortex. Second, a thorough understanding of the wiring of the visual system is important to understanding how researchers can examine differences in processing between the two halves, or hemispheres, of the brain (we learn more about these differences in chapter 3). Third, an understanding of visual processing is important because vision is one of the keenest senses that humans have, and fourth, our understanding of the neurology of the visual system probably surpasses that of any other sensory system.

To understand the organization of the visual system, take a look at Figure 1.21, and fix your eyes on the dot in the center of the arrow. When you look straight ahead like this, information to the right of fixation, known as the **right visual field,** which in this case contains the arrowhead, projects to the left half of the retinas of both your eyes. Information to the left of fixation, known as the **left visual field,**

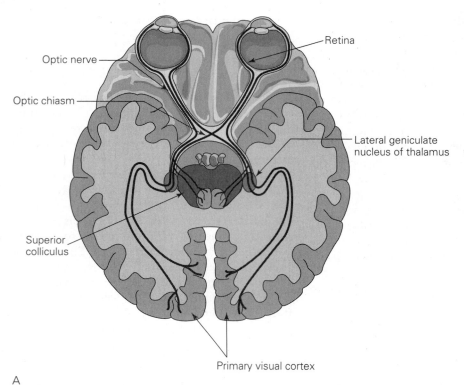

Retina

Optic nerve

Optic chiasm

Lateral geniculate
nucleus of thalamus

Superior
colliculus

Primary visual cortex

A

Thalamus

Calcarine
fissure

**Optic
chiasm**

**Primary
visual
cortex**

**Optic
nerve**

**Optic
tract**

Superior colliculus

B

**Figure 1.20 The pathway
from the visual receptors in
the retina to the brain.**
(A) Horizontal view. The
brain receives visual information through two routes.
One goes from the retina
by means of the lateral geniculate nucleus to visual
cortex. The other goes from
the retina to the superior
colliculus in the midbrain.
Information from the inside
retina of each eye crosses
over to the other side of the
brain at the optic chiasm.
(B) Right hemisphere, midsagittal view. The group of
axons carrying information
from the retina to the brain
is called the *optic nerve* before it reaches the optic chiasm, but the *optic tract* afterward. (*Note.* Adapted
from Kalat, 1992, p. 235;
Kandel et al., 1991, p. 423.)

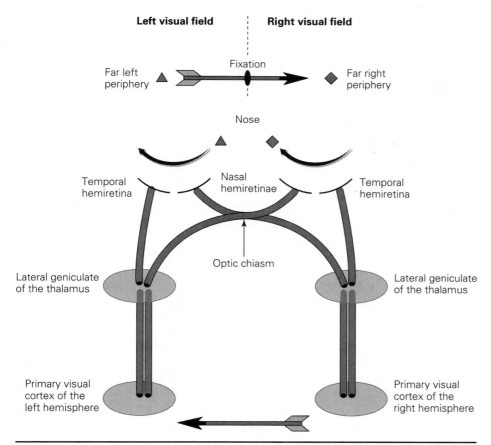

Figure 1.21 The mapping of the visual world onto the retina and visual cortex.
Except for information in the far periphery, all visual information projects to both eyes. Because information from the nasal hemiretinas cross over at the optic chiasm, the arrowhead projects only to the left hemisphere, whereas the arrow tail projects only to the right hemisphere.

in this case the arrow tail, projects to the right half of the retinas of both your eyes. Except for information in the far periphery of the visual world, all visual information reaches both eyes. The far peripheral portion of the left side of the visual world is detected only by the left eye (in part because the nose precludes the right eye's perception of that part of the visual world); likewise, the far right side is detected only by the right eye. Ultimately, information from the right visual field is directed solely to the primary visual cortex of the left hemisphere, and information

from the left visual field projects only to the primary visual cortex of the right hemisphere.

The routing of information from each retina through the optic nerve to the lateral geniculate is tricky. Information from the inside half of each retina, known as the *nasal hemiretina* (because this half of the retina is near your nose), crosses the midline of the body at the **optic chiasm** and projects to the contralateral lateral geniculate. In contrast, information from the outside, or *temporal, hemiretina* projects to the ipsilateral lateral geniculate. This aspect of the visual system's wiring is important because at the lateral geniculate, for the first time, information from one side of space is confined to one half of the brain, and information from the other side of space is confined to the other side of the brain. From the lateral geniculate, information then projects back to the ipsilateral visual cortex.

In Figure 1.21, notice that information about the arrowhead that has landed on the nasal hemiretina of the right eye crosses the midline of the body at the optic chiasm on its way to the lateral geniculate nucleus of the thalamus in the left hemisphere. There, it is joined by information about the arrowhead that has landed on the temporal hemiretina of the left eye. Likewise, information about the arrow tail that has landed on the nasal hemiretina of the left eye crosses midline to project to the right lateral geniculate, which is also receiving information from the temporal hemiretina of the right eye. From here, information travels ipsilaterally to the visual cortex. Thus, if you trace the path of information separately for the arrow's head and the arrow's tail, you can see that information from the right visual field projects to the left hemisphere and information from the left visual field projects to the right hemisphere.

Because of the organization of the visual system, determining whether a difficulty in vision arises from a problem in the eye or a problem in the brain is relatively easy. If the source of the problem is in the eye, the world looks different when viewed by one eye alone than when viewed by the other eye alone. For example, if part of the retina of the left eye is damaged, the visual problem is present when only the left eye is open, not when only the right eye is open. In contrast, if the problem resides in the brain, the problem is identical no matter which eye is open because *all* information from a specific region of the visual world converges on the same region of the lateral geniculate or primary visual cortex, regardless of whether it was initially received by the right eye or the left. (This is why the crossover of information at the optic chiasm is so important—it allows information from a specific region of space detected by *each* eye to converge on the same region of brain tissue.)

Not only is the mapping of the visual world onto the brain reversed left-right, but as we have seen with other modalities, it is inverted top-bottom as well. Thus, information above the fixation point projects to ventral portions of the visual cortex, and information below the fixation point projects to dorsal portions of the visual cortex. Furthermore, as with the other senses already discussed, the map by which the physical world is transformed onto brain tissue is distorted. Once again, this distortion is related to the density of receptors. The greatest concentration of light receptors is in the *fovea,* or central region of vision. From there, the density of receptors decreases dramatically. Hence, a much larger area of the occipital cortex is devoted to processing information from the central part of vision than is devoted to processing more peripheral regions.

Destruction of visual cortex results in an inability to perceive light-dark contrast. If the entire occipital cortex of only one hemisphere is damaged, no visual information can be detected in the contralateral visual field. This condition is known as a **homonymous hemianopsia.** Sometimes just the dorsal or ventral portion of occipital cortex is damaged, in which case just one quadrant of the visual world is lost; this disorder is known as **quadranopsia.** In other cases, only small portions of the visual cortex are damaged; the result is particular regions in the visual field, known as **scotomas,** in which light-dark contrast cannot be detected.

To determine how well you understand the organization of the visual system, take a look at Figure 1.22. Each picture shows a view of the visual world as it appears to a person with damage in a particular portion of the visual system. Try to determine the location of the lesion in the visual system for each situation shown.

Auditory Cortex

The human auditory system is sensitive to sound, which is essentially pressure waves in the air. The physical energy in sound waves causes vibration of the eardrum and the bones in the ear. These vibrations are transformed into pressure waves in a liquid

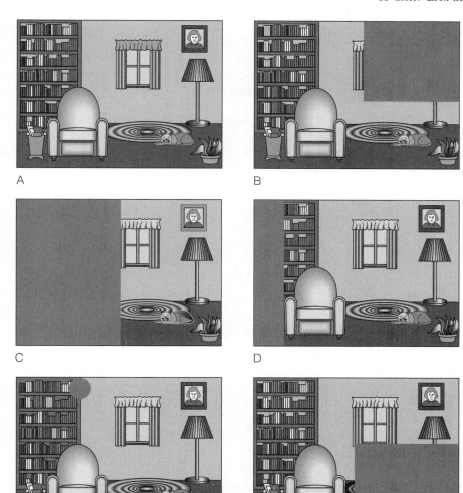

Figure 1.22 Visual field disorders.
(A) The visual world as it appears to an individual with an intact visual system. Where would the damage be located to create the views in (B), (C), (D), (E), and (F), and what disorders would result? *Answers:* (B) Ventral regions of the left occipital lobe, quadranopsia; (C) all regions of right occipital lobe, homonymous hemianopsia; (D) damage to the left eye, damage to the left eye; (E) damage to a small portion of the ventral region of the right occipital lobe, scotoma; (F) damage to the dorsal region of the left occipital lobe, quadranopsia.

in the cochlea, which contains hair cells that transduce pressure waves into a neural signal. Hair cells are aligned so that those nearest the bones in the ear are more sensitive to high-frequency sounds and those farther away are more sensitive to low-frequency sounds. These hair cells synapse on spiral ganglion cells, the axons of which form the **auditory nerve,** which is the main conduit of auditory information to the central nervous system, where it synapses on the *cochlear nucleus* in the medulla.

Unlike other sensory systems in which information from one side of the body projects solely to the contralateral hemisphere, the organization of the auditory system is such that there are both ipsilateral and contralateral projections from the ear to the brain. Hence auditory information received at the right ear projects to the left and right hemispheres. The point at which two copies of information are created is the cochlear nucleus in the medulla. There, some nerve fibers cross the midline and synapse on the contralateral superior olive, whereas others remain ipsilateral and synapse on the ipsilateral superior olive. From the superior olive, information is sent to the *inferior colliculus,* then to the **medial geniculate of the thalamus** (the thalamic relay station of auditory information), and finally onto primary auditory cortex. In addition, some information projects directly from the cochlear nucleus to the inferior colliculus. The primary auditory cortex of the human brain is located in the superior portion of the posterior temporal lobe in an area called **Heschl's gyrus.** The pathway whereby information is carried from the ear to the primary auditory area is depicted in Figure 1.23.

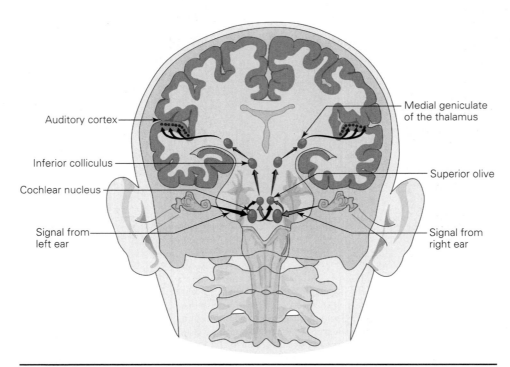

Medial geniculate of the thalamus

Auditory cortex

Inferior colliculus

Cochlear nucleus

Superior olive

Signal from left ear

Signal from right ear

Figure 1.23 The auditory pathway from the cochlea to the cortex.
After the cochlear nucleus receives input from the ipsilateral ear, all other connections are both ipsilateral and contralateral. (*Note.* Adapted from Kalat, 1992, p. 201.)

Like other primary sensory areas, the primary auditory cortex has a specific organization, described as **tonotopic,** meaning that it is organized with regard to the frequency of a tone. In the auditory cortex, information from cells that all respond maximally to the same frequency converge on the same region of cortex. The mapping of auditory cortex is such that the lowest tones are processed caudally and laterally and tones of increasing frequency are processed as one moves rostrally and medially through the cortex (Figure 1.24).

Unilateral damage to primary auditory cortex does not impair the ability to perceive all sound because of the redundancy provided by both crossed and uncrossed connections in the auditory system. If primary auditory cortex in the right hemisphere is damaged, primary auditory cortex in the left hemisphere can still process sound from both ears because it receives ipsilateral and contralateral connections. So, what types of deficits are observed after damage is sustained by auditory cortex in one hemisphere? First, the softest intensity that can be perceived—that is, the *sound threshold*—becomes higher contralateral to the damaged hemisphere. In addition, the ability to perceive the location of a sound becomes poorer for the contralateral side of space. If you previously had a course in physiological psychology or perception, this finding should not be surprising. You may remember that the mechanisms used to determine the location of the sound involve a comparison of the difference in the intensity and time at which auditory information arrives at each ear. Quite simply, if a sound is located closer to your right ear than to your left, the sound will be louder at the right ear (and will arrive there sooner). Because unilateral damage to primary auditory cortex disrupts the ability to judge the loudness of sounds, you can see why individuals with such damage have difficulty localizing the source of a sound.

Olfactory Cortex

Our sense of smell comes from receptors in the nasal mucosa that send information about odors to the **olfactory bulb.** Each of the two bulbs (one in each hemisphere) is a thin strand of neural tissue located directly below the frontal lobe (Figure 1.25). From the olfactory bulb, information is projected in one of two directions. One pathway, which probably mediates our emotional responses to smell, travels to various parts of the limbic system. Another projection is to the medial dorsal thalamus, which then projects to the cortex, specifically, the orbitofrontal lobe, which can hence be considered *primary olfactory cortex.* Olfaction is unique in the human because it is the only sensory system in which information is received ipsilaterally. Hence, information received in the right nostril is sent to the right olfactory bulb, and information received in the left nostril is sent to the left olfactory bulb. The actual means whereby smell is mapped onto the nervous system is unknown, but damage to primary olfactory cortex appears to impair odor discrimination in humans.

At this point, we have discussed how sensory information is first received by the cortex. After processing by primary sensory regions, this information is relayed to *secondary sensory cortex,* which, like primary sensory regions, processes information from only one sensory modality. However, secondary sensory cortex has a more specialized organization. For example, more than 30 regions of secondary visual cortex have been identified, each of which varies in its sensitivity to important visual attributes, such as color, orientation, and motion. However, primary and secondary sensory cortices account for only a small proportion of the overall mass of the cortex. Next, we overview the type of processing performed by the remainder of the cortex.

Association Areas

An area of the brain where information from multiple sensory modalities is processed is known as an **association area.** As we shall see, these regions of the brain support the abilities that we tend to think of as distinctly human, such as language, compassion, and foresight. Because it is mainly involved in processing visual information, the occipital lobe does not serve as large an associative function as the other three major lobes of the brain: the frontal, the parietal, and the temporal. We now turn to a

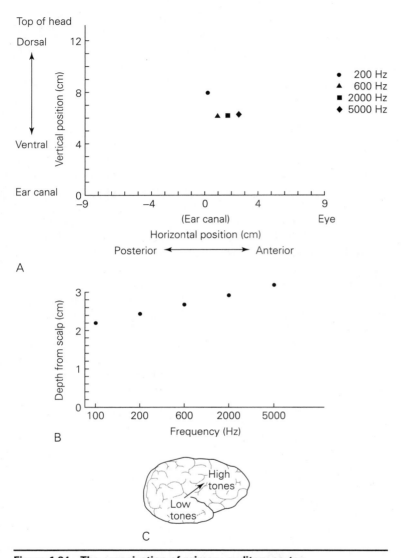

Figure 1.24 The organization of primary auditory cortex.
(A) The tonotopic map of the primary auditory cortex of the right hemi-sphere emphasizing its vertical and horizontal dimensions. This map de-picts areas that are most sensitive to sounds ranging from low, 200 Hz, to high, 5000 Hz. It is organized so that low tones are represented more caudally and high tones more rostrally. (B) A map of the primary audi-tory cortex of the right hemisphere emphasizing depth from the scalp. Low-frequency tones are processed closer to the scalp, whereas high-fre-quency tones are processed more deeply within the cortex. (C) Right hemisphere, lateral view of the oblique angle at which the tonotopic map in primary auditory cortex is aligned. (*Note.* A & B, Adapted from Ro-mani et al., 1982.)

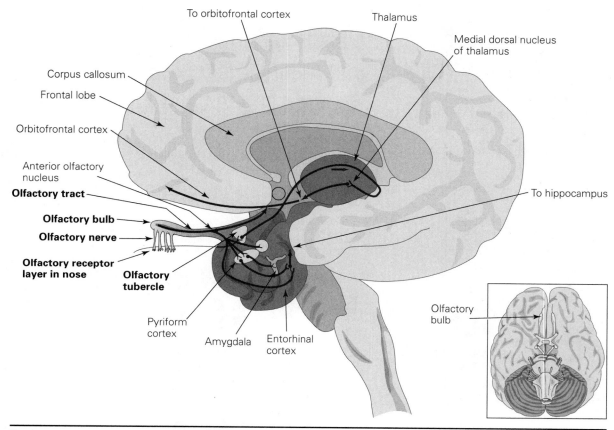

Figure 1.25 The path of olfactory information in the cortex.
The connections from the olfactory bulb to the cortex from a right hemisphere, midsagittal view. Olfactory information can reach the cortex, specifically orbitofrontal cortex, via two main projections: one via the medial dorsal nucleus of the thalamus and the other via structures in the limbic system. (Inset) The position of the olfactory bulb from a ventral vantage point. (*Note.* Adapted from Groves & Rebec, 1988, p. 103; Kandel et al., 1991, p. 517.)

brief overview of the multiplicity of functions by each of these three lobes.

Frontal Lobe

In discussing the frontal lobes, researchers and clinicians generally describe it as having three distinct regions: the *primary motor region* (previously discussed), the *premotor region*, and the *prefrontal region*. Prefrontal regions are often further divided into dorsolateral, orbital, and medial regions (Figure 1.26). The distinction among these regions is

based on major cytoarchitectonic subdivisions (see Figure 1.16). Although controversy exists as to whether damage to these different regions leads to distinct behavioral syndromes (e.g., Levin, Goldstein, Williams, & Eisenberg, 1991), we introduce these subdivisions of frontal cortex because we refer to them in later chapters, such as when we discuss the role of specific frontal regions in different memory processes (chapter 9).

Frontal regions are often thought of as the source of some of the most uniquely human abilities. A good generalization about the role of frontal re-

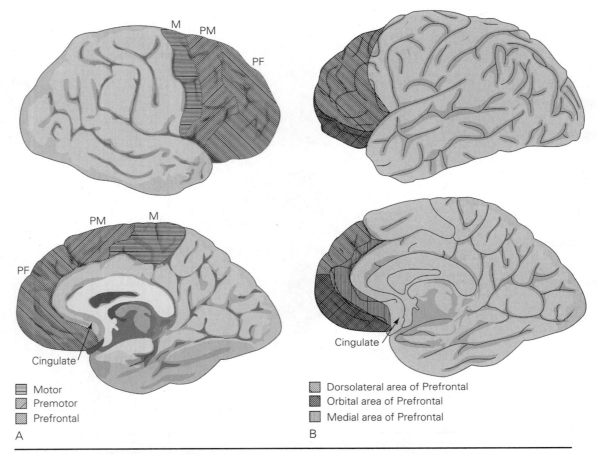

Figure 1.26 Divisions of the frontal lobe.
(A) The three major divisions of the frontal lobe: primary motor (M), premotor (PM), and prefrontal (PF) regions. (Top) Right hemisphere, lateral view. (Bottom) Right hemisphere, midsaggital view. (B) The prefrontal regions are further divided into dorsolateral, orbital, and medial areas. (Top) Left hemisphere, lateral view. (Bottom) Right hemisphere, midsaggital view. (*Note.* A, Adapted from Damasio, 1991b, p. 103; B, Adapted from McCarthy & Warrington, 1990, p. 357.)

gions is that they are associated with the planning and guidance of behavior. Just as the head of a corporation oversees its day-to-day operations and plans long-term goals for it, the frontal lobes are considered the "executive" of the brain. Not only are the frontal regions important for organizing behavior coherently, but research also suggests that they may allow us to extrapolate forward in time,

enabling us to realize the future consequences of our current behavior.

The abilities that are destroyed by frontal lobe damage are not easily categorized under a simple rubric, but the loss of these abilities can nonetheless be profound. For example, individuals with frontal lobe dysfunction may exhibit little decrement in performance when given standardized IQ tests that assess fact knowledge and academic skills, such as knowing the definitions of words, knowing how to solve arithmetic problems, knowing how to put together jigsaw puzzles, and so forth. Although these abilities may be minimally affected after frontal lobe damage, impairments in functioning may nonetheless be severe. Disruptions may occur in any or all of the following areas: the ability to organize and sequence behavior; the ability to modulate behavior, especially its initiation or its cessation; the ability to generate an appropriate emotional response; and the ability to use strategies and tags for retrieving memories.

People with frontal lobe damage generally have difficulty knowing how to organize behavior to reach a goal. Although they may know the component or steps in a process, they are unable to put them together in a coherent manner to reach a goal. For example, in making an omelet, a patient with frontal damage might beat the eggs, place them in the skillet, turn up the heat, and then add the butter. As this example illustrates, the individual knows that making an omelet requires eggs, grease, and heat, but the component cannot be organized in a systematic way to reach the desired endpoint.

Another problem observed in individuals with frontal lobe damage is an increase in what has been called *psychological inertia,* the force that must be overcome to either initiate a process or stop one. Individuals with frontal lobe damage have an inability to overcome the inertia required to initiate a new behavior or the inertia required to cease the task in which they are engaged. This handicap may take many forms. For example, persons with frontal lobe damage may not bathe and change clothes each day on their own volition, but they will do so if directed to by another individual. Or, an individual may sit on a couch for hours without initiating any behavior. Initiating some behavior seems to take a monumental effort that the person just cannot muster. Conversely, once involved in a behavior, an individual with frontal lobe damage may find it impossible to stop acting in a particular manner. Such patients are likely to **perseverate:** They perform a behavior repeatedly. Because of this tendency, some researchers speculate that obsessive-

compulsive disorders, which are characterized by individuals who engage in the same stereotyped motor behavior to ward off some danger (e.g., constantly washing one's hands to prevent infection by germs), may result from dysfunction of the frontal lobe, specifically the orbitomedial areas, as well as from dysfunction from some subcortical regions to which the frontal lobe connects (e.g., Malloy, 1987).

Developmentally, the frontal lobes are relatively immature in young children; thus, these youngsters often exhibit perseverative tendencies. You may have had the experience of hiding a child's favorite toy behind one of many pillows. The young child will reach out and move the pillow behind which he or she believes the toy to be, but then sees that the toy is not there. Rather than moving another pillow, the child again moves the same pillow, which still does not conceal the toy. The child is likely to repeat this behavior not once or twice, but many times. Although the child appears to forget where the toy is hidden, research suggests that very young babies, only 2 to 2.5 months old, can remember the location of an object even when it is hidden behind another one (e.g., Baillargeon, 1994). The problem is not so much one of memory, but rather the child seems to be locked into a perseverative behavioral loop in which the only way to look for the toy is to reach out and move that one particular pillow. This sort of behavioral loop is exactly the type of perseverative behavior that may be exhibited after frontal lobe damage. However, the young child engages in perseverative behavior not because frontal lobes are damaged but because they are relatively immature (A. Diamond, 1990).

Not only do individuals with frontal lobe damage have difficulty in starting and stopping behavior, but they have more general difficulties in modulating behavior. For example, patients with frontal lobe damage are often socially uninhibited and socially inappropriate. They may make unwanted sexual advances to medical personnel, may tell jokes at inappropriate times, may be insensitive to the social context in which they find themselves (such as a man dressed in a business suit, who after obtaining his boarding pass for an overbooked flight, skips past the remaining long line of haggard customers yelling, "It's Friday, be happy!"), and so forth. This inability to modulate behavior leads to the paradoxical effect that at times individuals with frontal lobe damage are insensitive to their social surroundings, whereas at other times they are unduly swayed by them. For example, by talking about depressing topics, physicians and other medical personnel may find an individual with frontal lobe damage moved to tears but can reverse the effect and put him or her in an ecstatic mood within minutes by talking about the person's favorite possessions or activities.

From what we just learned, you should not be surprised that frontal regions of the brain have been implicated in emotional functioning. Although we discuss the role of the frontal lobes in emotion in more detail in chapter 11, let's briefly consider some important points. Commonly, the family and other loved ones of an individual who has sustained frontal lobe damage will comment that the individual doesn't really seem like him- or herself anymore. A formerly quiet and peaceful person may be described as argumentative and prone to outbursts, a previously conscientious and hardworking person may be characterized as irresponsible and lazy, and a previously kind and considerate person may now be found to be selfish and uncaring. In sum, people often say that the individual with frontal lobe damage has undergone a change in personality. One of the most famous early cases in which such changes were documented was that of Phineas Gage, a railroad worker. While clearing a way for the railroad in 1848, an explosion blew a steel rod through his skull, damaging sections of his frontal cortex. Family and friends complained that Phineas just "wasn't Phineas anymore," and that although his body was the same, the man they knew seemed to have vanished.

More recent research suggests not only that frontal lobe functioning influences personality, a characteristic considered to be constant over time, but that such functioning can also influence a person's internal emotional state, or mood, which can vary over time from happy to sad, from calm to frustrated, from peaceful to agitated. Investigators suggest that certain aspects of mood are related to the

difference in activation between the right and left frontal regions. In particular, relatively higher activation of the left frontal region as compared with that of the right is associated with positive mood. In contrast, relatively higher activation of the right frontal region as compared with that of the left is generally associated with negative or dysphoric mood (e.g., Davidson, 1992). For example, after damage to left frontal regions, activation of such regions is clearly lower than that of right frontal regions—an imbalance associated with depressed mood. In fact, in one study, approximately 60% of individuals with damage to left frontal regions due to stroke fit psychiatric definitions of either major or minor depression (Starkstein & Robinson, 1988). You may be thinking, "Well, of course. Anyone who sustains brain damage could have a good reason to be depressed!" However, the probability of depression is much higher after left rather than right frontal damage. Furthermore, the extent of the depression does not depend on the severity of the person's cognitive deficits, but is related to the location of the lesion within the left frontal lobe. We discuss these research findings in more detail in chapter 11.

Frontal regions of the brain are also involved in what are known as **metamemory** functions, which can be thought of as the abilities that allow for the strategic use, deployment, and retrieval of memories. These functions clearly are related to memory, but they don't involve actually remembering a particular item, individual, or fact. In general, the difficulties in metamemory observed after frontal lobe damage are problems with the temporal sequencing or tagging of memories. For example, individuals with frontal damage are unable to determine which of two items in a sequence occurred more recently (B. Milner, Corsi, & Leonard, 1991), even though they can clearly distinguish between items that appeared in a sequence and those that did not (B. Milner & Petrides, 1984). Moreover, if you show individuals with frontal lobe damage a series of items, in which some items randomly appear on multiple occasions (e.g., three times, five times, seven times), these persons have difficulty in estimating how often an item occurred, although they have no difficulty in discerning whether an item was previously viewed (Smith & Milner, 1988).

The frontal lobe, especially dorsolateral frontal regions, are also considered important for keeping memory information on-line to be used in giving a response. Evidence for this function of frontal regions comes from various sources, including work with monkeys (e.g., Goldman-Rakic, 1990), young infants (A. Diamond, 1990), and adults. Suggesting that frontal areas are indeed undeveloped in young children are findings that children exhibit deficits in working memory that are similar to those observed in monkeys with damage to dorsolateral regions of the frontal lobe. Such findings are discussed in more detail in chapter 10.

As this short review illustrates, the frontal regions of the brain are involved in a vast array of behaviors. Rather than being important for specific domains of cognitive activity such as language, spatial processing, or object recognition, frontal regions provide us with executive capabilities that are used across a vast number of domains and allow for flexible and novel behavior.

Parietal Lobe

The parietal lobe of the cortex plays a role in (a) integrating information from various sensory modalities, (b) integrating information from the sensory world with information stored in memory, and (c) integrating information about an individual's internal state with information from the external sensory world. Because this integrative function can occur in various ways, the deficits observed after parietal lobe damage are often diverse and difficult to conceptualize as all falling under the same rubric. However, if you keep in mind that the parietal lobe is critical for associating different forms of information, the array of functions performed by the parietal lobe will not seem all that disjointed.

One way to begin to conceptualize the role of parietal cortex is to consider the results of experiments done with macaque monkeys, because such results nicely illustrate some of the ideas discussed next. In these studies, an electrode is placed into the brain of an animal to record a single cell's activity. The investigator determines what type of stimulus will make the cell, which is in contact with the electrode, fire. This procedure is performed for a multiplicity of different cells all over the area of interest, until the researcher can deduce the critical characteristics required to make cells in that region fire. To understand the role of the parietal lobe, we need to consider what we would observe if we recorded from other brain regions as well. Let's suppose that a banana is in a monkey's field of view. If we recorded from a cell in *inferior temporal cortex* (discussed in the next section), we might find a cell that would fire consistently whenever the banana was within the monkey's field of view but would not fire when other visual forms, such as other monkeys, people, or objects, were within view. (This pattern would occur because regions of inferior temporal cortex are specifically involved in distinguishing between distinct visual forms.) If we recorded from a cell in the parietal lobe, however, we would find that it too would fire whenever the banana came into view but if and only if the banana was within the monkey's reach. Alternatively, another cell in the parietal lobe might not fire at the sight of the banana alone, but would fire only if the animal was also hungry. Thus, in both cases, the cell would fire in response to some *conjunction* of attributes: the visual stimulus of the banana *and* its position in space, or the visual stimulus of the banana *and* the animal's internal state (e.g., Lynch, 1980). For this reason, we can say that processing by the parietal lobe is *multimodal* in nature.

In humans, the role of the parietal lobe in multimodal integration is seen in many syndromes that occur after damage to this region, including agnosia, alexia, agraphia, and apraxia, all of which we discuss in turn. **Agnosia** is a modality-specific deficit in recognizing objects that occurs in the absence of major deficits in basic sensory processing. What we mean by *modality-specific* is that the person cannot recognize an object in one sensory modality but can recognize it in other modalities. For example, if an individual has a *visual agnosia,* he or she will be unable to identify an item as a rose merely by looking at it. However, if the person is pricked by a thorn or smells the flower, she or he will instantly recognize it. An important point about agnosia is that the deficit can be attributed neither to the inability to perform basic sensory processing nor to a memory deficit. Persons with visual agnosia are not blind. They can distinguish light from dark, and they can discriminate basic shapes (e.g., square from rectangle) (Warrington & James, 1988). So, for example, when looking at a rose, a person with visual agnosia can see that an object is there, describe its color, and maybe even crudely describe its shape, but cannot use this information to gather a visual impression of a rose. Furthermore, memory for an item is intact. So, for example, if asked what kinds of flowers compose the garland that is placed around the neck of the horse that wins the Kentucky Derby or which popular flower associated with romance has thorns, the person with visual agnosia could easily answer "rose."

Agnosias can occur in all modalities. In *auditory agnosia,* an individual knows that a sound has occurred but doesn't know its significance. For example, a person with auditory agnosia cannot identify a particular sound as a car horn even though he or she knows that some sound just occurred. Likewise, in *tactile agnosia,* objects cannot be recognized by touch. What is common to all these agnosias is that basic sensory processing in the affected modality is intact, as are memory processes. Agnosia is discussed in more detail in chapter 5. For now, we should note that parietal damage is most often associated with tactile and visual agnosia rather than auditory agnosia. Auditory agnosia is more often associated with damage to the temporal lobe, which, you may surmise from our discussion of primary auditory regions, plays an important role in the processing of auditory information.

Two other deficits common after parietal lobe injury are **alexia** and **agraphia,** which are, respectively, the inability to read and the inability to write as a result of brain damage. We discuss both these syndromes in more detail in chapter 8. The reason that alexia and agraphia are caused by parietal lobe damage makes sense if you consider how we come to read and write. Two strategies or routes can be used when you are reading and writing. The first route requires two steps: The first step is making a linkage between each letter and a sound, and the second step requires making a linkage between the sound pattern and information stored in memory. The alternative route bypasses sound entirely because a pattern of letters (e.g., d-o-g) is directly linked with meaning (e.g., a favorite household pet). For both routes, a person must take a visual form and associate it with meaning, which, like other functions for which the parietal lobe is important, requires different types of information to be linked.

Still another deficit observed after damage to parietal regions is **apraxia,** which is the inability to perform skilled motor movement in an abstract manner. Although we already discussed how almost all aspects of motor processing occur in frontal regions, the motor movements affected in apraxia are the exception. In the case of apraxia, basic motor control is intact; the individual is not paralyzed. Yet, these people have trouble linking motor movement to a representation. Individuals with apraxia can usually make certain voluntary movements without difficulty but cannot pantomime them. For example, an individual with apraxia might be able to put a spoonful of sugar into his or her coffee cup, but when asked to pantomime the same gesture, might use one finger to represent the spoon, rather than positioning the hand as appropriate for stirring sugar into coffee. Apparently, individuals with apraxia lack the capacity to program the motor sequences that allow for the representation of an act, but these persons have the capacity to perform the act itself. Apraxia is discussed more thoroughly in chapter 4.

Other abilities affected by parietal lobe damage include disturbances in spatial processing. Damage to parietal regions disrupts the ability to localize points in space, to know the angle of lines, and to understand spatial relations between items. Hence, parietal regions of the brain appear to contain the map of space that we use for navigation, for placing our limbs in the correct position for the manipulation of objects, and for knowing what part of space to explore. The importance of parietal regions in creating a map of space is seen most prominently in the syndrome called **hemineglect,** or **hemi-inat-**

tention. In this syndrome, individuals ignore information on one side of space, usually the left, and act as if that side of the world does not exist. It is as if one half of the world has been erased from their spatial map of the world. Details about spatial processing and hemineglect are given in chapters 3, 5, and 7.

As you can probably tell from this brief review, damage to the parietal regions can cause a heterogeneous array of syndromes. In general, however, they all are syndromes in which sensory information cannot be integrated across modalities and/or with internal representations or memories.

Temporal Lobe

Temporal regions of the brain are associated with four main functions: memory, visual item recognition, emotion, and auditory processing. Classically, the temporal lobes have been associated with memory function, as documented most clearly in the famous case of H.M., who in early adulthood underwent bilateral removal of anterior portions of the temporal lobe for the relief of intractable epilepsy. Although the surgery was successful in reducing his seizures, he was left with the inability to learn almost all types of new information, even though most of his memories from the years before the operation were intact. This case was pivotal in demonstrating that specific regions within the temporal lobe, more notably the hippocampus, are critical for the formation of new long-term memories. Additional research by Milner and colleagues demonstrated that the memory deficit tends to be greater for verbal material after removal of only the left temporal lobe (e.g., Frisk & Milner, 1990) and greater for spatial information after removal of only the right temporal lobe (Smith & Milner, 1981).

In addition to being important for the formation of new long-term memories, temporal regions of the brain play important roles in visual processing, contributing to visual item recognition. Single-cell recordings in the inferior temporal lobes of monkeys have revealed that these cells respond only to highly specific visual stimuli. Unlike cells in primary visual cortex, which respond to bars of light oriented at

particular angles and moving in particular directions, the cells of the inferior temporal lobe respond to very specific shapes, such as a hand, a brush, or a face (Gross, Rocha-Miranda, & Bender, 1972). In fact, some of the cells may respond only to faces of particular people or certain features on a face (e.g., eyes) (Perrett, Mistlin, & Chitty, 1987). This specificity of visual processing in temporal regions appears to be a characteristic of the mammalian nervous system. For example, certain cells in temporal cortex of sheep respond only to horned sheep, not unhorned sheep, whereas other cells respond only to sheepdogs, but not wolves or dogs with pointy ears (because they resemble wolves) (Kendrick & Baldwin, 1987). In people, damage to temporal regions can lead to deficits such as the inability to recognize a given face as belonging to a specific individual (A. R. Damasio, Damasio, & Van Hoesen, 1982). Thus, at least for visual items, temporal regions appear to be important for item identification. The role of the temporal lobe in item recognition is discussed in more detail in chapter 5.

This specialization of temporal regions for visual item processing seems to reflect a segregation of the processing of visual information in the mammalian brain into two streams or systems, one of which is important for processing the shape of items and another of which is important for processing the location of items. On the basis of neuroanatomical, neurophysiologic, and behavioral work with animals, Mishkin (Ungerleider & Mishkin, 1982) suggested that visual information leaving primary occipital areas bifurcates into two pathways, one of which courses dorsally to the parietal lobe and the other ventrally to the temporal lobe. The parietal visual processing system is considered the "where" system, which is responsible for localizing objects in space with little regard for the item's identity. In contrast, the temporal visual processing system is the "what" system, which is responsible for determining what an item is regardless of its location. One way to think about these two systems if you are a sports fan is to consider the contrast between a zone defense and a person-to-person defense. The parietal region of the brain treats items much the way a defender in a zone defense does. The job of these parietal regions is to process the location of items in space regardless of who they are. Thus, for parietal regions, localization of objects, not their identities is important. In contrast, the temporal region of the brain treats items much the way a defender in a person-to-person defense does. These regions are sensitive to a specific person or object regardless of its location in space, much as a defender will stick to his or her person regardless of where on the court or field that person may wander.

Temporal regions of the brain have also been implicated in the processing of emotional information. Some structures in the temporal lobe are portions of the limbic system, which, as we learned earlier in the chapter, can act to integrate information from the sensory world with internal urges (e.g., urges for food, sex, and so forth). Moreover, disruptions of temporal lobe functioning can have emotional consequences. For example, some investigators have suggested that temporal regions may be dysfunctional in a certain proportion of persons with schizophrenia, most notably those suffering from delusions (Schroder et al., 1995).

Finally, because auditory processing areas are located in the temporal lobe, damage to this region of the brain can have consequences for the processing of auditory material. For example, damage in the temporal lobe can lead to auditory agnosia or to difficulties in the appreciation of certain aspects of music, such as melody. We discuss these issues in more detail in chapter 12.

SUMMARY

The building blocks of the nervous system are neurons and glia. Neurons are the cells that carry information by means of electrical and chemical signals, whereas glia are the support cells that serve as a conduit for nutrients and help after damage to the nervous system. Neurons carry information by means of an action potential, which is an electrical signal propagated down the length of an axon. When this signal reaches the terminal of the cell, it induces vesicles to release neurotransmitters into the synapse, or space, between neurons. These chemicals cross the synaptic cleft where they join with receptors of the next neuron and cause a small graded electrical potential known as either an excitatory postsynaptic potential (EPSP) or an inhibitory postsynaptic potential (IPSP). These postsynaptic potentials summate both spatially and temporally, and if they exceed a certain threshold, they cause the neuron to fire. Some neurons are myelinated, meaning they are covered by a fatty sheath that speeds conduction of the electrical signal and generally connect distant regions of the nervous system. Neurons making connections between local regions tend to be unmyelinated.

When discussing the location of various structures in the nervous system, clinicians and researchers use different terms. An area toward the front is known as anterior or rostral, whereas a region toward the back is known as posterior or caudal. Toward the top of the body is known as superior or dorsal, and toward the bottom is known as inferior or ventral. Structures situated near the midline are described as medial, whereas those further toward the periphery are known are lateral.

The central nervous system has many important subdivisions. The spinal cord, housed within the spinal column, is the portion of the nervous system whereby sensory information comes into the nervous system through its dorsal section, and control of the musculature occurs by neurons leaving its ventral section. The medulla is important for controlling such life-sustaining functions as the beating of the heart and breathing and for overall alertness and arousal. The cerebellum is a region of the brain that is important for skilled motor movement and possibly fluidity of cognitive functions. The pons is a region in which information from many of the cranial nerves enters the nervous system. The midbrain contains two important structures involved in orienting toward sensory stimuli, the inferior colliculus, which processes auditory information, and the superior colliculus, which processes visual information. The hypothalamus is the region important for motivational behavior, such as seeking food, a sexual partner, and so forth. The thalamus is a major relay center in the brain whereby information from the sensory world is reorganized on its way to the cortex and information from the cortex is reorganized on its way to the periphery. Two major systems involve subcortical structures; these systems are the basal ganglia, which are important for the control of movement, and the limbic system, traditionally thought to be important for emotion, but now known also to be involved in other functions, such as memory.

Only a small portion of the cerebral cortex is involved in basic sensory and motor processes; the remainder is association cortex. The primary somatosensory and motor cortices are located behind and in front of the central fissure, respectively. Primary visual cortex is located in the occipital lobe, and primary auditory cortex is located in the superior and posterior region of the temporal lobe. All primary cortices contain a map of the external world. Except for audition and olfaction, information about the physical world is mapped onto the cortex upside down and left-right reversed. Furthermore, the map is distorted such that the regions of space or the body to which we have the most sensitivity are disporportionately represented in primary sensory or motor cortex.

The three main association areas of the brain are the frontal, parietal, and temporal lobes. The frontal lobe is considered the executive control center of the brain and is important for many mental functions including planning and goal-directed behavior, psychological inertia, emotional processing, and metamemory functions. The parietal region is a multimodal association area. Damage to it can result in agnosia, alexia, agraphia, apraxia, spatial-processing deficits, or hemineglect. The temporal lobe has been implicated in memory, visual object recognition, emotional functioning, and auditory processing, including the processing of music.

Chapter

2

*M*ethods in *N*europsychology

In this chapter, we discuss the different methods that can be used to understand how the brain influences the way we think, feel, and act. Because neuropsychology is an interdisciplinary field of research, it requires integration of information about the brain and information about behavior. The question under investigation has a major influence on which aspects of information about the brain and behavior are examined and at what level of analysis an issue is investigated.

In terms of the brain, we may want to obtain information at the neuroanatomical, neurochemical, or neurophysiological level. At a neuroanatomical level, we may need information about the integrity of brain structures, their connections to other brain regions, and their relationship to particular behavioral patterns. For example, knowing that people have specific difficulties in recognizing faces after sustaining trauma to the right temporal lobe may allow us to infer a connection between that cognitive process and that brain structure. We may also require information about the brain at the neurochemical level. For example, we may want to know how the dysregulation of the neurotransmitter dopamine contributes to the symptoms observed in schizophrenia. Finally, at the neurophysiological level, we may want to observe which brain regions are electrically or metabolically active during performance of a specific task. For example, we may want to know the degree to which the right hemisphere is electrically responsive during a musical judgment task.

We can also observe behavior at different levels. On one hand, we may want to observe the integrity of sensory processing in an individual (e.g., determine whether a person can distinguish high tones from low tones). On the other hand, we may need to examine more central aspects of mental processes, such as the integrity of the memory system. In still other cases, we may want to decompose specific mental abilities, such as determining whether a memory deficit occurs only when a person is learning new information or whether the deficit extends to retrieving previously learned information as well.

To investigate each of these issues requires particular tools: Research methods are neuropsychologists' tools. We refer to the research methods and ideas introduced in this chapter throughout the book as we explore the neurological underpinnings of mental activity. During all our discussions, understanding the strengths and limitations of different research methods is important because the adage "You need the right tool for the job" is as apt in neuropsychology as in carpentry. If you ever tried to use a knife or a dime when you needed a screwdriver, you know that having the correct tool can mean the difference between success and failure or between ease and hardship. In neuropsychology,

the proper tool may be a particular clinical population, a specific brain imaging technique, or a certain experimental method.

Neuropsychologists must consider how the information they gather in any investigation is molded by the choice of a particular population and a particular method. Each choice directs the researcher toward observing some aspects of processing and not others. Consider, as an analogy, that the form of transportation you choose to take from one city to another influences what you see along the way. If you take an airplane from Chicago to New York City or from Toronto to Montreal, you can "see" the overall topography of land and observe the flat open plains as they blend smoothly into the forested hills of the East. However, you cannot clearly "see" the architectural differences between the farms of the central region and the row houses of the eastern cities. If, however, you make the trip by car, the overall change in topography as you drive east is less apparent, but your ability to see smaller details such as differences in houses is much better.

Because the choices researchers make in investigations influence their observations, we must also remember throughout our discussion that in science, as in other areas of life, no single method solves all our problems or answers all our questions. Rather, each method or population provides only a vantage point from which to seek the answer to a question. Thus, given the limitations imposed by a single method of neuropsychological research, you may wonder how scientists can be certain of the conclusions that they draw about brain-behavior relationships. Are these scientists as foolhardy as the inhabitants of the Emerald City in the Wizard of Oz, who thought the city looked emerald because they were wearing green eyeglasses?

As we discuss in more detail later in the chapter, the answer to the previous question is "no" because neuropsychologists invoke a strategy akin to changing your eyeglasses often. In general, information is gathered on the same question by using a variety of methods with a variety of populations. This technique of examining whether all the answers obtained from a set of interrelated experiments converge on the same conclusion is known as the

method of converging operations. When researchers have examined a question from multiple perspectives and all answers point to the same verdict, the researchers can be relatively confident that they understand a basic aspect of the relationship between the brain and behavior. Because the method of converging operations requires information from multiple subject populations and multiple investigatory techniques, the body of work cannot usually be performed by a single scientist; instead, it is generally performed by individuals across the scientific community.

Let's consider an example of converging operations by examining three representative findings, from different methods, regarding the role of the parietal lobe in attending to particular regions of space. Let's also consider the potential pitfalls of each method. First, research with monkeys indicates that the response of neurons in the posterior parietal cortex is modified when the animals must pay attention to particular regions of space (e.g., Lynch, Mountcastle, Talbot, & Yin, 1977). However, interpolating from animals may not always be justified because their repertoire of behavior and the organization of their brains are distinct from those of humans. Second, brain imaging in neurologically intact individuals reveals an increase in the metabolic activity of the parietal region when a person directs attention to a specific portion of visual space (Corbetta, Miezin, Shulman, & Petersen, 1993). Yet, some brain imaging techniques provide an "average" of activity across a number of individuals with such poor resolution that conclusions with regard to specific anatomical locations are difficult to make. Third, after a person sustains a unilateral parietal lobe lesion, he or she often ignores the contralateral portion of visual space (e.g., Vallar & Perani, 1986). However, findings from patients with brain damage are always subject to variability among individuals both in the extent of the neurological damage and in the diversity of the individuals' experiences both pre- and postdamage. Hence, although the evidence from any one of these studies alone is not convincing, evidence from all three methods of inquiry converge on the same conclusion, namely that the parietal region plays an important role in directing our

attention to a given region of space. When such convergence occurs, researchers can have much more faith that the answer arrived upon is accurate and that the inherent biases of each method are not so great as to obscure their usefulness.

We now turn our discussion to the specific subject populations and the specific methods used in examining the relationship between the brain and behavior. In this endeavor, we need three critical ingredients. First, we need a population of individuals on which to test our hypothesis about the relationship between the brain and behavior. The group of participants chosen will vary depending on the question asked. Second, we need to be able to gather information about the brain of each individual. Depending on the question, we may want information about brain structure, brain function, or both. Third, we need a way to measure behavior. In some cases, we may want to use specific measures of behavior, and in other cases, large test batteries. In the remainder of the chapter, we survey the options available for each of these three critical ingredients and outline the advantages and disadvantages conferred by each choice.

POPULATIONS OF RESEARCH PARTICIPANTS

In this section of the chapter, we examine the specific advantages and disadvantages of using three major populations—individuals with delineated brain damage, neurologically intact individuals, and nonhuman animals—to investigate neuropsychological issues.

Patients With Delineated Brain Damage

Examining patients who sustained brain damage to understand mental functioning has a long and venerable history, stretching back some 2,000 years. In the time of the Romans, Galen, a physician who ministered to the wounds of the gladiators, noticed that contestants sustaining injury to the arm, leg, or torso retained their powers of thought, whereas those who sustained injury to the head or the brain did not. From these observations, he inferred that the brain was linked to the mind, becoming one of the first scientists to use individuals with brain damage to understand brain-behavior relationships. Although today we take for granted that the brain supports our mental capabilities, Galen's inference was revolutionary for his time. Until that point, the mind had been associated with other regions of the body, such as the gut. For example, when an Egyptian Pharaoh was buried with all the necessities for the afterlife, his embalmed viscera were included because ancient Egyptians believed that the viscera would preserve his mind for the world to come. However, because the Pharaoh's brain was discarded, we can only wonder how well he functioned if he went on to the hereafter!

Galen deduced the role of the brain in thought by examining the consequences of brain damage. This approach was a precursor of the logic we use today to determine which regions of the brain are important for a given mental function. If damage to a particular region of the brain results in an inability to perform a specific function, scientists usually assume that the function was supported by that particular brain region, an approach known as the **lesion method.** During the history of neuropsychological investigation, this method has proved very powerful in expanding our knowledge about the neurological bases of thought and emotion. One noteworthy aspect of this method is that it led us to conceptualize the brain as being composed of different modules, each supporting a different mental function. Although researchers have different ideas about exactly what constitutes a module (e.g., Fodor, 1985), for our purposes it can be considered a portion of a processing system that is dedicated to a single function not performed elsewhere within that system (e.g., reading, verbal short-term memory, or face recognition). Furthermore, we now realize that these modules are located in specific regions of brain tissue, a concept called **localization of function.**

The brain was not always believed to work in the manner just described. In the early 20th century, scientists debated whether functions were localized or whether the brain worked by **mass action,** meaning that all pieces of brain contributed to all func-tions. One of the most notable supporters of the mass action viewpoint was the psychologist Karl Lashley, who did much of his work in this area in the 1920s and 1930s (K. S. Lashley, 1929). He argued that the nature of cognitive deficits observed after brain damage did not hinge on which region of the brain was destroyed but on the extent of the damage: The larger the amount of tissue destroyed, the greater the decrements in performance. In contrast, the researchers supporting localization of function argued that the site of brain damage, not just the overall amount of destruction, predicted the nature and degree of the deficit observed.

Today, the debate has been resolved more firmly on the side of localization of function than on that of mass action, in part as a result of improved techniques for measuring lesions (or in the case of animals, creating lesions), and because more sophisticated methods of measuring behavior have evolved. With these improvements, researchers realized that not all lesions have the same effect on behavior and concluded that behavioral differences must occur because of differences in brain structure.

Despite the apparent localization of function that makes us think of the brain as being composed of modules, we must not forget that the brain is comprised of about 50 billion *interconnected* neurons. Therefore, even complex cognitive functions for which a modular description seems apt rely on a number of interconnected brain regions or systems. The smooth and integrated functioning of these areas provides for many of our unique cognitive abilities. Consider by analogy a car. Although it is made of specific parts or systems such as an engine, a drive train, wheels, and a suspension, all these parts are useless for travel unless they are interconnected in a specific manner so that the power from the engine can be transferred to the drive train to move the wheels.

Throughout this book, we see that the modular description of functioning is more useful for certain cognitive abilities than for others. For example, the components of language—the comprehension of spoken language, the production of spoken language, reading, and writing—seem to be performed by different brain regions and hence are well modularized. In contrast, components of other cognitive functions, such as certain aspects of memory, are much more diffusely organized across many brain regions. Thus, we must remember that the brain relies both on localization of function and on diffuse processing to carry out cognitive function in a seamless fashion.

Uses of the Lesion Method

The basic strength of the lesion method is that a specific region of brain tissue can be directly linked to a specific aspect of mental processing. The ability to make such a linkage is critically important to understanding many aspects of human cognition because nonhuman animal models, which have historically provided much information on the relationship between the brain and behavior, are often insufficient due to limitations in the cognitive repertoire of nonhuman animals.

Unlike animal models, in which scientists carefully create lesions in a certain region of the brain and then observe the effect on behavior, the lesion method in humans requires investigators to rely on cases of brain damage that result from unfortunate circumstances, such as war, accident, injury, or disease. Hence, the neuropsychologist has no control over the location, extent, and cause of the lesion in any given patient. A researcher interested in the role of a particular brain structure in cognition must work with medical personnel to comb hospital records until the appropriate patient or set of patients is found who can be asked to participate in a research project. The success of this method depends critically on the cooperation, courage, and goodwill of these patients, who despite struggling with the ill effects of brain damage agree to participate in studies. Although testing starkly reveals the abilities that these patients have lost, they participate in the hope that the knowledge gained will help other individuals who find themselves in the same unfortunate circumstance in the future.

When using the lesion method, a researcher can take one of two conceptual approaches, which differ in emphasis. One approach emphasizes knowledge about neural substrates, the other knowledge about cognitive function. The approach that a researcher takes has a large influence on the population that is recruited for the study. Throughout the book, we find many examples of these two conceptual approaches of the lesion method, so we discuss them next in more detail.

If the question to be asked is "What functions are supported by a particular piece of brain tissue?" the researcher assembles a group of individuals in whom the site, cause, and extent of damage are as comparable as possible. An example of this approach is the research of Brenda Milner and colleagues at the Montreal Neurological Institute, who examined the role of the temporal lobe in memory. Their population consisted of patients with epilepsy who underwent removal of areas of the temporal region (the brain region that is the center of epileptic activity). For this procedure, the neurosurgeon excises a particular region of brain tissue and documents the extent of tissue removal at the time of the operation; therefore, a relatively uniform population can be obtained. Using this approach, Milner and colleagues found that removal of a particular structure within the temporal lobe, the hippocampus, leads to difficulties in forming new long-term memories (e.g., B. Milner, 1978).

Studies of this type usually include not only a group of patients who have brain damage or have undergone removal of the brain structure under investigation, but also one or more groups of patients with damage elsewhere in the brain. This practice allows researchers to determine whether the behavioral disruption is linked specifically to the brain structure under investigation and not others. Returning to the previous example, we must consider that the ability to form new long-term memories may have been disrupted by damage to many brain regions; the hippocampus may be just one. To rule out this possibility, Milner and colleagues typically included one or more groups of individuals with damage to a different brain region, such as the frontal lobes. Because individuals with damage to these other regions did not exhibit problems in forming new long-term memories, the researchers concluded that the hippocampus specifically supports the formation of new long-term memories.

Because such an approach allows us to identify a particular brain region as critically important to a specific component of cognition, it can provide invaluable information to physicians, clinical neuropsychologists, and other medically related professionals. For example, neurosurgeons must know which cognitive functions are likely to be disrupted if a particular region of brain tissue is excised. Likewise, knowing the site of brain damage allows neuropsychologists to predict which intellectual abilities are likely to be compromised, to tailor their evaluation of cognitive deficits, and to plan for appropriate rehabilitation.

The other conceptual approach to the lesion method emphasizes cognitive function. When taking this approach, researchers are likely to select a group of individuals that exhibit the same behavioral symptoms; the selection is made with little regard for the location of the brain damage. For example, in chapter 7 we learn about a syndrome called *hemineglect,* which, as we discussed in chapter 1, causes individuals to ignore information on one side of space. Although most common after damage to parietal regions of the right hemisphere, hemineglect can occur after damage to many other regions of the brain, including the basal ganglia, the frontal lobes, and the thalamus. Hence, researchers may assemble a group of individuals who have hemineglect, regardless of the location of the lesion that caused it, so that they can ask questions about the nature of hemineglect. For example, researchers might design a study to determine whether the neglect can be minimized if fewer rather than more objects are located in the environment. Having a clearer understanding of the nature of a behavioral deficit aids our understanding of the subcomponents of cognition and can be useful in designing effective methods of rehabilitation.

This approach can also be useful in aiding our understanding of the neural basis of a given cognitive or emotional function. By carefully examining the neurological records of the assembled group of patients (all of whom exhibit the same behavioral deficit), researchers can determine the locus of damage in each patient. The pattern of findings among patients can help to identify the specific neural structure or the set of neural structures that is likely to participate in that given function.

Not only can the logic of the lesion method allow us to infer which regions of the brain are important for different cognitive functions, but observing the patterns of cognitive disability among individuals with lesions in different locations can provide important insights into the architecture of the mind. A particularly powerful method, the method of **double dissociation,** allows researchers to determine when two cognitive functions are independent (e.g., Shallice, 1988; Teuber, 1955). A double dissociation occurs when lesions have converse effects on two distinct cognitive functions: One brain lesion causes a disruption in Cognitive Function A but not Cognitive Function B, whereas a different lesion causes a disruption in Cognitive Function B but not Cognitive Function A. We infer that the functions are independent because the viability of one cognitive function does not depend on the viability of the other.

To make the concept of a double dissociation more concrete, let's consider a classic example, the dissociation between Broca's aphasia and Wernicke's aphasia, both of which are disruptions in language processing (which we discuss in more detail in chapter 8). Without any background knowledge, we might think that all aspects of auditory language processing rely on the same region of the brain. If this were the case, we would predict that if a person lost the ability to understand auditory language, he or she would also lose the ability to speak. However, Broca's aphasia and Wernicke's aphasia illustrate that the ability to produce and the ability to comprehend spoken language are distinct. In Broca's aphasia, comprehension of auditory language is intact for the most part. However, individuals with this syndrome have great difficulty with speech production. In Wernicke's aphasia, the converse is observed. The individual cannot understand what is said to her or him but nonetheless fluently produces grammatically correct sentences (although as we learn in chapter 8, these sentences are usually nonsensical). Hence, disruptions in speech output are independent of whether a disruption in speech comprehension occurs, and vice versa.

Without a double dissociation, we could not infer that speech comprehension and speech output are separable cognitive functions. For example, if we were to observe only individuals with Broca's aphasia (and never those with Wernicke's aphasia), we might assume that a single auditory language system existed and that damage to any part of the system would preclude speech output because it was the final stage of processing. This model would be analogous to a situation in which damage to any part of an assembly line would make getting products off the line impossible. However, Wernicke's aphasia demonstrates that auditory language processing in the brain is not like a single assembly line because even though speech comprehension is disrupted, speech output occurs fluently.

The importance of the lesion method in expanding our knowledge in neuropsychology cannot be underestimated. It has led to classic conceptualizations about the neural underpinnings of language, memory, and perception, to mention just a few areas (see H. Damasio & Damasio, 1989, for further discussion). Throughout this book, we often discuss evidence provided by the lesion method, yet for all its power, the lesion method, like any other method, has its limitations. We now turn to a discussion of these limitations.

Difficulties With the Lesion Method

The lesion method imposes two major limitations on researchers. First, variability in characteristics of the participant population and variability in the location and the extent of the lesion can make straightforward inferences difficult. This variability is especially prominent when compared with that which occurs in animal experimentation. Second, although the lesion method has an obvious intuitive appeal and appears to allow straightforward inferences about the relationship between the brain and behavior, in some cases this logic can lead us to inaccurate conclusions. We discuss both the major sets of problems in turn.

Compared with lesion experiments done with nonhuman animals, research performed with people who sustained brain damage is "messy" because the sample is much less homogeneous in a number of dimensions. In animal experiments, the population usually consists of littermates (which are genetically similar) raised in the same environment, given the same lesion at the same age, provided with the same experiences before and after the lesion, and are assessed behaviorally at the same age. Furthermore, the lesion given to each animal is designed to be as identical as stereotactic surgery allows. Thus, genetic and environmental characteristics of the sample are as comparable as possible.

In contrast, populations of individuals who sustained brain damage are quite different. Individuals typically vary widely in age, socioeconomic status, and educational background. Prior to brain damage, these individuals may have had diverse life experiences. Afterward, their life experiences likely vary too, depending on the type of rehabilitation they receive, their attitudes toward therapy and recovery, and their social support network. Compared with research on animals or even the standard psychology experiments typically performed on college sophomores, the individuals with brain damage who participate in studies examining the neural underpinnings of human cognition are a heterogeneous group.

Furthermore, lesions sustained by humans are much less specific, both in extent and origin, than those created in animal experiments. Although a researcher can assemble a group of patients in whom the lesion is more or less in the same location (e.g., the dorsolateral regions of the frontal lobe, the posterior parietal lobe), he or she has no control over the size and severity of the lesion, thus variability increases across the population being investigated. In animals, we can induce lesions in different brain regions in a uniform manner (e.g., apply electrical current to destroy brain tissue). In humans, the cause of damage can vary from a bullet wound to a stroke to an infectious disease to surgical removal of a region due to epilepsy or tumor. These different sources yield very different types of damage. For example, damage due to stroke causes more diffuse effects and has a higher probability of involving subcortical regions than damage inflicted by a bullet or another missile does. Often researchers attempt to assemble groups of individuals with similar causes of brain damage, yet in some cases doing so may be impossible. For example, a researcher would have difficulty comparing the effects of occipital and temporal lobe damage if restricted to using individuals with herpes simplex because this virus often destroys temporal regions of the brain but not occipital regions.

The diversity of characteristics among people who sustain brain damage and the heterogeneity of the situations in which the damage is sustained may impede our ability to isolate the specific neural structures that influence a given behavior. For example, the severity of a cognitive deficit associated with damage to a particular brain region may be influenced by an individual's life experiences. Even if we compare groups of individuals who have similar demographic characteristics, such as age, educational background, and gender, the participants will still differ on myriad other individual characteristics. Likewise, if the size and extent of the lesion varies among individuals, identifying the exact brain region critical to a given function may be very difficult. In situations such as these, the effects of the damage may be masked by the variability in these factors. However, when a relationship is uncovered, it is more likely to be robust because it was discerned despite variations in populations and differences in the nature of the damage.

The second major limitation of the lesion method is that it does not allow us to observe directly the function that the damaged portion of the brain performs. Rather, all we can do is observe how the rest of the brain performs *without* that particular area and from these observations infer the previous role of the damaged brain region. Although such inferences are usually sound, they may have certain limitations and liabilities. First, we can determine only the regions of the brain *critical* to a given cognitive function, but we cannot identify the entire set of brain regions that may participate in that function. Second, behavioral impairment may result after damage to a region not because that region is critical to the task, but because that region *connects* other brain regions that must interact for correct performance of the function. Finally, a brain

region's contribution to a particular cognitive function may be masked if the task can be performed in more than one way. In such cases, the individual is competent at performing the task, although the strategy used is different than that used before damage.

To appreciate the lesion method's limitations in identifying all brain regions that are critical to performing a task, think about putting on a play. If the person playing the main character is ill (and there is no understudy), the show cannot go on; therefore, we can identify that person as critical for the performance of the play. But if one of the stagehands or prop masters becomes ill, the show still goes on, even though clearly the individual contributes to the production. The show can continue because the chores of the remaining crew are likely to be shuffled to compensate for the absence of this individual. Similarly, if brain damage destroys a region that participates in but is not critical for the performance of a function, behavior can appear to be more or less intact because other brain regions can act to support that function.

The lesion method is also limited in that it doesn't allow us to discern whether damage to a particular region of the brain alters performance because that region is critical to task performance or because it contains axons, known as *fibers of passage,* that connect two or more brain regions critical for the function. In effect, when damage occurs, information carried by these fibers cannot be transmitted from one brain region to another; the result is a behavioral deficit called a **disconnection syndrome.** To understand this concept more clearly, consider a case during severe weather in which food from the farms is not reaching the city. Perhaps the food is not reaching the city because the farms were destroyed and are no longer producing food. Such a situation would be similar to the case in which a brain lesion damages a portion of the brain critical for performance of a task. Alternatively, perhaps the farms are intact but the highway between the farms and the city was ruined and the food could not be transported. This situation would be similar to what occurs in a disconnection syndrome. Throughout the book, we find many examples of disconnection syndromes, including *split-brain syndrome* (discussed in chapter 3) and *conduction aphasia* (discussed in chapter 8). We can sometimes identify disconnection syndromes by referring to brain anatomy. If the region of the brain that leads to cognitive deficits contains few cell bodies and many nerve tracts, we might consider a disconnection syndrome as an explanation for the deficit.

A final potential limitation of the lesion method is that it may cause us to underestimate the role of a specific brain region in a given cognitive function. After brain damage, a person may compensate for the damage by using a different strategy to perform the task, one that relies on intact areas. Suppose that after damage to Region A of the brain, a person navigates around her or his world without much difficulty, behavior that makes us assume that the functioning of Region A is unrelated to the cognitive skill of navigation. Yet, in actuality, Region A *is* important for navigation, playing a role in constructing the geographical relationship between objects or places (e.g., that Montreal is north-northwest of Boston). Little difficulty occurs because Region B of the brain provides the ability to navigate point to point by means of landmarks, not by compass directions. Now, instead of heading north-northwest from Boston to go to Montreal, the person sequentially travels from point to point (e.g., "I take Interstate 90 out of Boston until I reach Interstate 87, at which point I take a right; I take this road until I reach the border, after which I take Route 15 until I reach Montreal"). The ability to uncover the distinct roles of Regions A and B in navigation is possible only if we carefully break down general cognitive skills into their components and test each component individually, which sometimes can be difficult.

Single-Case Versus Group Studies

Our discussion of the lesion method would be incomplete without a review of the debate about single-case versus group studies of individuals with brain damage, because much has been written on this issue in recent years. In **single-case studies,** a single individual with brain damage is studied intensively with regard to a variety of neuropsychological tests. In contrast, in **group studies,** individuals with brain damage who have similar characteristics (e.g., lesions in similar areas) are studied as a group. Some researchers argue that group studies may obscure patterns of behavior or cause misleading interpretations of data. They argue that a group of patients may be so heterogeneous in their patterns of performance that the group average does not typify the majority of individuals and may be a composite that is rarely, if ever, found in any individual (e.g., Caramazza & Badecker, 1989). Suppose, for example, as illustrated in Table 2.1, that researchers test a group of nine individuals with localized brain damage and a group of nine neurologically intact controls on three tasks. If you look at the average percentage correct for each group at the bottom of the table, you can see that on each of the three tasks the percentage is lower for the individuals with brain damage than for the controls. However, if you look at the pattern for the individuals you should be able to identify three subgroups of patients with brain damage: one group that does poorly on Task 1 (Individuals 1–3), one that does poorly on Task 2 (Individuals 4–6), and a third that does poorly on task 3 (Individuals 7–9). Although on average the individuals with brain damage do worse than the controls on all three tasks, no single individual with brain damage performs more poorly than the controls on all three tasks!

Because of the difficulties that arise when we generalize from group studies, some researchers endorse the single-case study, in which the performance of a single patient with brain damage is examined in extensive detail. However, the single-case study approach has its difficulties too (for instances of problems with single-case studies, see Zurif, Gardner, Brownell, 1989). One problem is that we may never know whether the pattern observed for a single individual is representative of people in general. For example, we know that left-handers, who compose about 10% of the population, have a neural organization for cognitive function that is distinct from that of right-handers. If handedness, genetics, or some special environmental influence causes an individual's brain organization to be atypical, the

Table 2.1   Hypothetical Example of Potential Distortion of Performance Patterns When Group Averages Are Used

The average score for the nine individuals with brain damage does not adequately reflect the performance of any given individual. Although the average for individuals with brain damage is lower than that of neurologically intact individuals for all three tasks, all individuals with brain damage score as well as neurologically intact individuals for two of three tasks.

Individual with brain damage	Performance as measured by percentage correct		
	Task 1	Task 2	Task 3
1	20	75	70
2	25	70	80
3	30	80	75
4	75	25	75
5	80	30	70
6	70	20	80
7	75	80	25
8	70	75	30
9	80	70	20
Average of nine individuals with brain damage	58.3	58.3	58.3
Average of nine neurologically intact individuals	78	80	83

pattern of disability after damage may also be atypical. This issue is especially a problem when the syndrome and its causative lesion are so rare as to have ever been observed in only one or two individuals. In such cases, our power of interpretation is restricted.

If both group and single-case studies have limitations, what are researchers to do? One approach, known as the **multiple-case study approach,** is to validate research findings on a series of patients, each of whom is also treated as a single-case study. In this approach, data for each individual within each group are provided, so that researchers can determine the variability across individuals and the degree to which the overall group average typifies the behavior of individuals within the group (Figure 2.1).

Multiple single-case studies have other advantages as well. A series of multiple single-case studies in which the individuals all have damage in the same general region may help clinicians to determine the

cognitive profile of a "typical" patient with damage to that region. In addition, such studies can be used to examine whether a relationship exists between a cognitive deficit and some other factor of interest, such as the amount of tissue destroyed. For example, in a previous example in this chapter, Milner and colleagues found that the hippocampus is involved in the formation of new long-term memories. They reasoned that additional confirmation for this relationship could be provided by demonstrating that the degree of hippocampal damage is proportional to the degree of memory loss. However, a single-case study can reveal only whether the hippocampus is related to memory, not whether the degree of hippocampal damage predicts the severity of the memory problem. Thus, Milner and colleagues turned to a group study approach, examining a group of patients with varying amounts of hippocampal damage and assessing the extent of memory impairment that these patients exhibited. As predicted, Milner and colleagues found that the greater

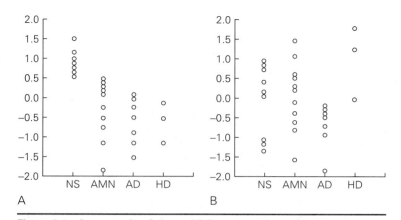

Figure 2.1 An example of the multiple-case study approach.
To determine the extent of differences between patients with brain damage (AMN, patients with amnesia; AD, patients with Alzheimer's disease;
HD, patients with Huntington's disease) and neurologically intact subjects (NS), the researcher treats each member of the group as a single-
case study as well. (A) For a measure of recognition memory, every patient is performing at a level worse than that of the neurologically intact
controls (0 indicates average performance, positive values represent
above-average performance, and negative values below-average performance). (B) In contrast, for a measure of memory "priming" (i.e., facilitation of processing of material due to prior exposure), much more variability exists across the groups; the result is an overlap between the
performance of the neurologically intact participants and that of the different patient populations. Whereas individuals with brain damage can
clearly be characterized as having poorer recognition memory than controls, the same is not true for memory priming. (*Note.* Adapted from Jernigan & Ostergaard, 1993, p. 19.)

the hippocampal damage, the greater the memory
loss (e.g., Pigott & Milner, 1993). This additional
support for their claim could be obtained only by
examining a group of individuals.

Neurologically Intact Individuals

Studying neurologically intact individuals can also
aid our understanding of the linkage between brain
function and structure. First and foremost, these
persons provide the important control group that
allows us to determine the degree to which the
performance of individuals with brain damage is
compromised. Clearly, a problem is much more severe if, after brain damage, an individual performs
worse than 98% of the individuals in a neurologically

intact reference group than if he or she performs
worse than 40% of those individuals. The larger
the control group assembled for any given test, the
more certainty researchers can have in such comparisons.

Well-designed neuropsychological studies must
include careful consideration of the characteristic of
the individuals composing the neurologically intact
control group. These individuals must be matched,
on a case-by-case basis, as carefully as possible
against the individuals with brain damage for demographic variables such as age, gender, and educational history. In this manner, the study homes in
on the degree to which the brain damage, and not
other factors, affects performance on a particular
task. Consider, for example, a hypothetical study in

which the researchers do not match for educational history and most patients have a college education, but the neurologically intact group completed only high school. When tested, the two groups perform equivalently, so the researchers conclude that the brain damage was inconsequential. Yet, because the group with brain damage had more schooling, if they had been tested prior to injury, they would have *outperformed* the control group. Thus, relative to their preinjury state, the individuals with brain damage did experience a deficit, but it was masked by the poor choice of a control group.

When choosing a control group, we may also want to select individuals who are experiencing stresses similar to those of individuals recently brain damaged. Individuals with brain damage are often inpatients in a hospital, and hospitalization can be stressful. Patients lose control over the simplest aspects of their lives, such as their privacy and their eating schedule. They have anxiety about the outcome of their hospitalization and often worry about their finances as well. Because individuals under stress often perform poorly on cognitive tasks, a well-designed study should demonstrate that any cognitive deficit can be attributed to the brain damage and not to the stresses associated with hospitalization, illness, or misfortune. For this reason, neurologically intact subjects gathered from a hospital population are often good control subjects because they are under similar stresses but do not have brain damage. One example of such a population is individuals who, like the individuals with brain damage, are in a rehabilitation unit but are there because of physical injury to a limb rather than injury to the brain.

Neurologically intact individuals may aid our understanding of brain-behavior relations in other ways besides acting as a control group. They can aid researchers' understanding of how individual variations in the neuroanatomical structure of the brain are related to cognition. For example, in most right-handers, the *planum temporale*, a region of the brain at the junction of the temporal, parietal, and occipital lobes, is much larger in the left hemisphere than in the right (e.g., Geschwind & Levitsky, 1968). In contrast, this asymmetry is not ob-

served as often in left-handers and usually is less striking when it is observed (e.g., Steinmetz, Volkmann, Jancke, & Freund, 1991). Because right-handers, but not left-handers, almost always have left-hemisphere specialization for language, these neuroanatomically asymmetrical areas, such as the planum temporale, may be the neurological substrate for certain aspects of language processing (e.g., Ratcliff, Dila, Taylor, & Milner, 1980; Strauss et al., 1985). Finally, neurologically intact subjects are important as research participants because, along with brain imaging techniques (discussed later in this chapter), they can provide evidence on how brain structures work together under normal conditions, insights that cannot be obtained from individuals with brain damage.

Nonhuman Animals

Until this point, we have considered only the populations of humans that aid our understanding of the neural underpinnings of cognition; however, many of the insights we gain about the neural organization of cognition are derived from studies performed with animals, most notably monkeys. Although the brains of monkeys and humans are distinct, they appear to share some basic organizational principles, some of which are exhibited in all mammalian brains. Because monkeys can be trained to perform sophisticated cognitive tasks, many mental functions can be investigated with these animals, such as object recognition (e.g., Gross, Rocha-Miranda, & Bender, 1972), attention (Moran & Desimone, 1985), and memory (Miskin, 1982). In numerous instances throughout the text, we discuss research of this nature.

For many of the reasons we just mentioned, such as better control over environmental conditions, the size and nature of lesions, and previous life experiences, research with animals can be more straightforward than that with people. In addition, certain techniques that we discuss later in the chapter, such as single-cell recordings, can be done with groups of animals, but only with very particular groups of people. However, as with research involving human participants, researchers must adhere to careful guidelines concerning the ethical treatment of their subjects. They are responsible for designing and following protocols that ensure the animals are subjected to the minimal amount of pain possible and are not unduly traumatized by the procedures.

Now that we discussed the different populations of individuals that are used to examine brain-behavior relationships, we turn our attention to the different methods available for both research and clinical work that inform us about brain anatomy, brain function, and behavior.

TECHNIQUES FOR ANALYZING BRAIN ANATOMY

Linking specific regions of neural tissue to specific cognitive functions requires that researchers and clinicians be able to determine *where* damage was

sustained in the brain. Our ability to make such linkages has been undergoing a revolution since the mid-1970s because of the advent of different brain imaging techniques. These techniques opened a new world to researchers because they allow the location of damage to be pinpointed much more exactly in individuals who are still alive. Prior to this revolution, researchers had to wait for postmortem examination of brain to localize damage that occurred years or decades prior, or they had to guess the location of brain damage from scant medical records. To appreciate the advances provided by these new brain imaging methods, look at Figure 2.2, which depicts the older methods. All they provide is information about what part of the skull is missing as a result of the entry of a bullet or another missile. Such records clearly give us no idea of how extensive or how deep the damage is, and they provide only a gross measure of the location of the damage.

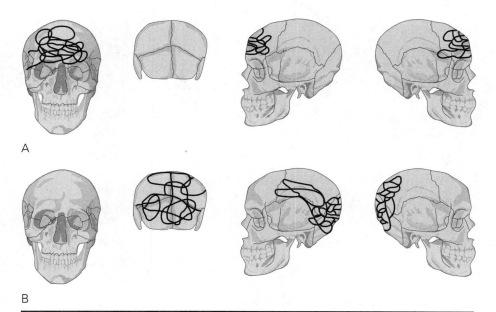

A

B

Figure 2.2 Composite diagrams of skull x-rays showing the entrance (and sometimes the exit) points of missiles that caused damage in two groups of 20 men.
X-rays were used in the days before brain imaging techniques to infer the extent and location of brain damage. Localization was not precise and allowed only gross differentiation such as that shown between (A) individuals with anterior lesions and (B) those with posterior lesions.

The intricacies of some of the new brain imaging techniques can take a career to master and in one case led its inventors to receive a Nobel Prize. The goal of this section of the chapter is to present a practical overview of how these techniques work, the basic principles behind them, and, most important, the type of information they provide. We start with the first of modern brain imaging techniques, computerized axial tomography.

Computerized Axial Tomography

CAT, **computerized axial tomography** (sometimes called CT), uses x-rays to provide information on the density of brain structures. Cerebrospinal fluid (CSF) is less dense than brain tissue, which is less dense than blood, which is less dense than bone. In a CAT scan, dense tissue such as bone appears white, whereas material with the least density, such as CSF, appears black. Typically, CAT scans provide a series of slices of the brain (usually between 9 and 12), stacked one above the other. In CAT scans, regions of the brain that were damaged long ago appear darker than the surrounding tissue because they are filled with less dense CSF. In contrast, areas in which a hemorrhage recently occurred are indicated by lighter areas, because blood is denser than brain tissue.

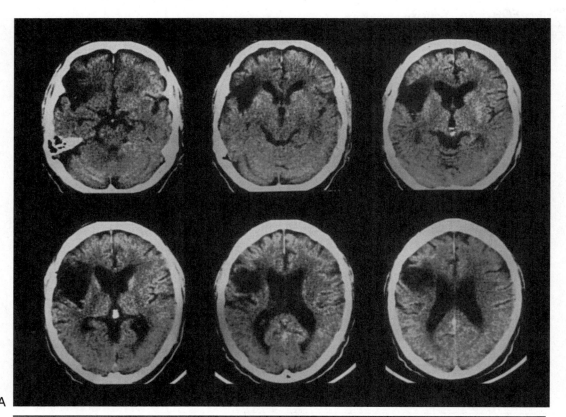

A

Figure 2.3 Slices of a computerized axial tomography (CAT) scan showing regions of low density.
(A) Note the dark regions in the frontal opercular region and underlying white matter of the left hemisphere. As a result of a stroke, tissue was lost in these areas, which now appear dark because they are filled with cerebrospinal fluid. (B) Affected brain regions, with the Brodmann's areas labeled. The slices depicted are at the same angles as Slices 3 to 8 in Figures 2.5A and 2.5B. (*Note.* A, From *Lesion Analysis in Neuropsychology* by Hanna Damasio and Antonio R. Damasio. Copyright © 1989 by Oxford University Press, Inc. Used by permission of Oxford University Press, Inc. B, Adapted from Damasio & Damasio, 1989, pp. 56, 57.)

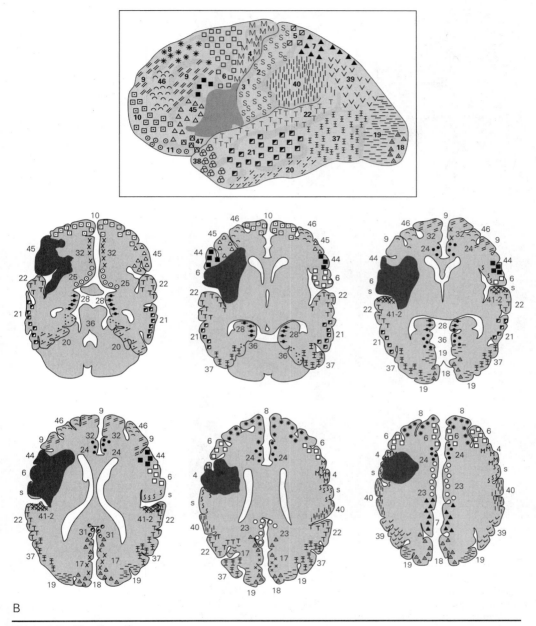

B

Figure 2.3   (Continued)

When you look at a CAT scan (Figures 2.3 and 2.4), the slices appear to cut through the middle of the brain in a manner similar to that of a horizontal slice. However, this is not the case because the slices provided by CAT, and all the subsequent brain im-aging techniques we discuss, are typically *oblique slices* through the brain. Oblique slices are obtained because when an individual's head is positioned in the machine, a line is usually drawn from the eyes to the *meatus*, the point where the skull meets your

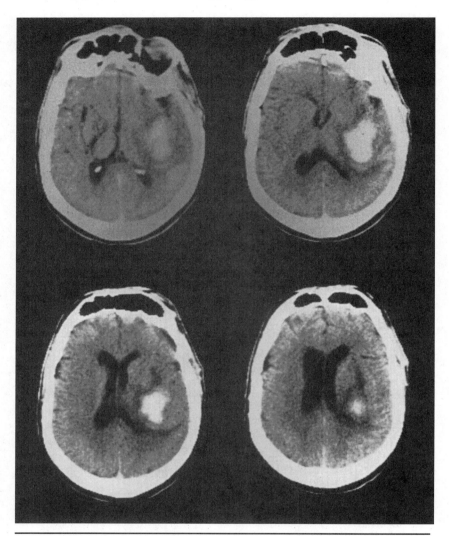

Figure 2.4 Slices of a computerized axial tomography (CAT) scan showing regions of high density.
In this case, a collection of blood, known as a *hematoma,* appears as an area of increased brightness in the right temporal lobe. The presence of the hematoma causes a displacement of the lateral ventricle on that side of the brain. (*Note.* From *Lesion Analysis in Neuropsychology* by Hanna Damasio and Antonio R. Damasio. Copyright © 1989 by Oxford University Press, Inc. Used by permission of Oxford University Press, Inc.)

neck in the middle of your head (if you place your hand about two thirds of the way down the middle of the back of your head, you can feel an area of depression; this is the meatus). This line is known as the *orbitomeatal line,* which typically is at an oblique angle varying between 10 and 30 degrees.

To learn how to orient with regard to the position of the brain imaging slices, look at Figure 2.5. Depending on the depth of the slice, all lobes or just some of them will be depicted. For example, the first top slice provides only information about regions of the frontal and parietal lobes. Notice that the top four slices (numbered 8 to 11 in Figure 2.5) do not cut through the temporal lobes. As you go lower in the stack of slices, they course through regions of all four lobes: the frontal, temporal, parietal, and occipital lobes. The lowest slices provide information about only the frontal and temporal lobes.

CAT scans and all other brain imaging techniques are immensely useful because they provide pictures of the brain that allow researchers and clinicians to determine where damage has occurred in the brain and to correlate that damage with certain behavioral problems. This ability to immediately associate behavior and brain anatomy has proved extremely useful in neuropsychology in recent years.

Magnetic Resonance Imaging

Although CAT scanning was a breakthrough, in many ways it has been superseded by **magnetic resonance imaging (MRI).** This technique relies on the use of magnetic fields to distort the behavior of atoms, and the information gained on how long the atoms take to recover from this distortion can then be used to create an image of the anatomy of the brain. The description of how this technique works is somewhat more complicated than that for a CAT, so we examine it in a bit more detail.

MRI relies on three magnetic fields. The first is the **static field,** a constant magnetic field, whose strength is referred to when we describe the magnet. Clinical machines generally vary in strength between 0.5 and 1.5 tesla (for a reference point, the magnetic field of the earth is 0.0001 T). This static magnetic field causes all the magnetically sensitive particles to align themselves within the magnetic field in the same direction. Such uniformity is important because only if the particles are all acting in the same manner can we interpret the effects of the perturbation of the static field, which is provided by the second magnetic field, the **pulse sequence,** emanating from a radio antenna placed around the patient. This pulse sequence varies depending on the particular substance to be imaged (e.g., water or fat) and is applied at a set frequency (*resonant frequency*)

specific to that substance. It affects only one particular substance, much the way that a particular frequency of sound makes only one but not all tuning forks vibrate. The time for the atoms to revert to their original state, the *relaxation time,* is recorded through a **receiver coil.** The intensity of the signal received by the receiver coil indicates the concentration of the particular substance in the brain but by itself cannot provide information on the location in the brain from which the signal is coming. This information is provided by the third magnetic field, the **gradient field,** which varies in intensity over the area being imaged. It provides a way to identify particular locations within the static field, thus enabling identification of the location from which signals are emanating. The combination of spatial information from the gradient field and the signal intensity received after a series of radio-frequency pulses allows a three-dimensional image of the brain to be reconstructed (for a more advanced but readable discussion of this method and some of its applications, see Andreasen, 1989).

Typically, MRIs are tuned to substances such as water and fat. Water is the molecule that composes much of our body, and the resulting image reveals a picture of tissue density. These images can be used to detect brain atrophy and increases in CSF much as CAT scans do. When MRIs are tuned to fat, they are often used to detect demyelinating diseases, such as multiple sclerosis, in which myelin, the fatty sheath surrounding the neurons that speeds the transmission of nerve impulses, is selectively pockmarked.

MRI has two main advantages over CAT. First, MRIs do not require x-rays and hence do not involve transmitting high-energy radition through the body. Second, the clarity of the picture—that is, the spatial resolution of the image—is superior in MRIs. If you look at Figure 2.6A, which is a coronal section of the brain provided at autopsy, you can see how well a similar slice provided by MRI in Figure 2.6B, compares with what is revealed on anatomical dissection.

Yet, not everyone can be subjected to a MRI scan. Because magnetic fields interfere with electrical fields, individuals with pacemakers (which gener-

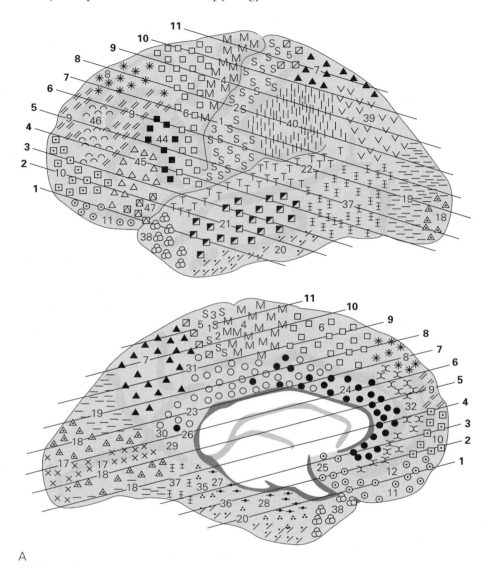

A

Figure 2.5   Typical oblique slices through the brain often provided by brain imaging techniques.

(A) The location of the slices as seen from a left hemisphere, lateral view (top) and a left hemisphere, midsagittal view (bottom). The numbers on the brain represent the different Brodmann's areas (which are also differentiated in the diagrams by different symbols). (B) The slices corresponding to the locations depicted in (A). Note the correspondence between the figures. For example, look at Slice 7 in this figure and notice that the Brodmann's areas labeled around the lateral surface of the brain from front to back (i.e., 8, 6, M, S, 40, 22, 37, 19, and 18) are all transected by Slice 7 in the lateral view in (A). Also note that the areas labeled medially at Slice 7 in this figure (i.e., 8, 24, 23, and 18) are all transected by Slice 7 in the midsagittal view in (A). (*Note.* Adapted from Damasio & Damasio, 1989, pp. 190, 191.)

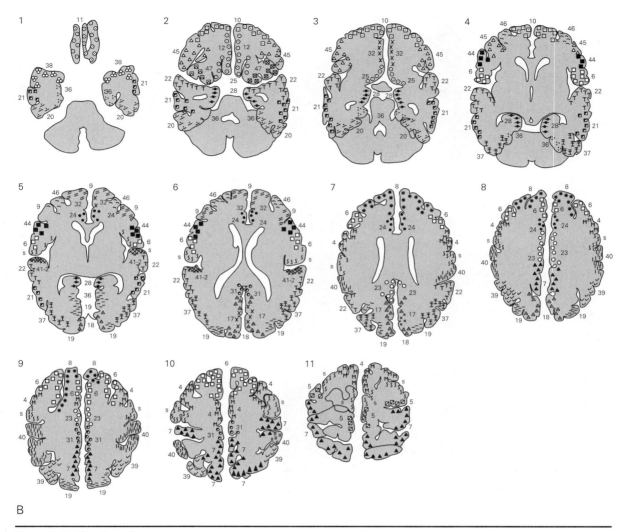

B

Figure 2.5 (Continued)

ate electrical signals to the heart) cannot undergo MRI. Also, any individual with metal in her or his body that is not connected to hard tissue (e.g., a clip on an artery or a metal shaving in the eye from welding) cannot have an MRI taken because the attraction of the metal to the magnet could cause it to move or dislodge. (Metal embedded in hard tissue [such as the fillings in teeth] is not a problem). Other than these exceptions, MRI is becoming the anatomical imaging technique of choice because of

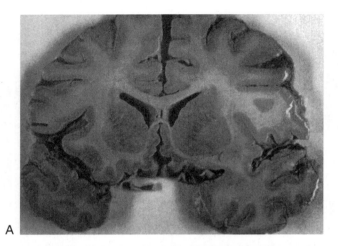

A

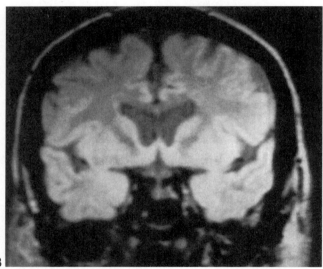

B

Figure 2.6   A comparison of the clarity obtained in anatomical dissection and magnetic resonance imaging (MRI).
(A) A coronal section through the brain as seen on anatomical dissection. The temporal lobes, Sylvian fissure, putamen, globus pallidus, lateral ventricles, and frontal lobes can be seen. (B) The same coronal slice as imaged by MRI. Note how precisely the MRI reveals anatomical detail. (*Note.* Reprinted with permission from "Introduction and Overview," by E. D. Bigler, R. A. Yeo, and F. Turkheimer, in *Neuropsychological Function and Brain Imaging* (p. 10), edited by E. D. Bigler, R. A. Yeo, and E. Turkheimer, 1989, New York, Plenum Press.)

its superior imaging capabilities and the lack of high-energy radiation.

TECHNIQUES FOR ANALYZING PHYSIOLOGICAL FUNCTION

The brain imaging techniques we just discussed provide a picture of the anatomical structure of the brain. However, they cannot tell us about brain function. Analogous to these anatomical brain imaging techniques are devices that measure the thickness of metal on a car's body (which is a good way of spotting areas on a used car that may have previously been rusted and painted over). These devices provide information about the structural integrity of the car, much the way anatomical brain imaging techniques provide information about the structural integrity of the brain. However, this information does not tell how well the car runs. A similar limitation befalls anatomical brain imaging techniques.

For many reasons, neuropsychologists often want to know how well the brain is functioning. But, just as is the case with cars, many different ways to measure function are available. To determine how well a car is functioning, we might examine how much fuel the car is using. In the analogous case with the brain, we may want to know how much of the brain's fuel, such as oxygen or glucose, is being used by different areas. In other situations involving the car, we might want to examine the chemical composition of certain systems, such as the amount of antifreeze in the cooling system. In the brain, we might want to measure the concentration of a specific neurotransmitter, such as dopamine. In still other cases involving the car, we might want to know about the integrity of the electrical system. In the case of the brain, we might measure whether aberrant electrical signals are being generated, or we might want to record the sum of the brain's electrical activity.

Notice that we have been talking about the mechanics of how the car functions, not its overall behavior. We have not discussed ways to measure overall performance: how a car handles in sharp turns, how quickly it brakes, how it climbs steep, narrow roads. Similarly, in this section of the chapter we discuss methods for measuring the mechanics of brain function, rather than its overall performance, which is covered in a later section.

Brain Imaging Methods

Not only has there been a revolution in the ability to image the brain anatomically, but there has also been a revolution in the ability to measure the functioning of the brain. In this section of the chapter, we discuss the methods that discern which areas of the brain are metabolically active by measuring the compounds used by different brain regions. The two main techniques are **positron emission tomography (PET),** which uses a radioactive agent to determine the brain's metabolic activity, and **functional magnetic resonance imaging (fMRI),** which uses a variation of MRI techniques distinct from those just discussed.

Although these functional brain imaging techniques are often used with individuals with known or suspected brain damage, these techniques can be used with neurologically intact individuals to great advantage. Functional brain imaging techniques with neurologically intact individuals allow researchers to observe the degree to which a brain region is activated by a task, so that its contribution to task performance under normal circumstances can be directly observed. This contrasts with the lesion method, in which inferences about a brain region's contribution to a task are made as a result of dysfunction. These functional brain imaging methods also allow researchers to observe the entire network of brain structures that participate in performing a particular cognitive function because such methods detect all brain regions that are active.

Positron Emission Tomography

Positron emission tomography (PET) allows researchers to determine the amount of a particular compound being used by specific brain regions. Like CAT, PET relies on the use of radiation to obtain a picture of brain function, although in this case the radiation is emitted by a substance introduced into the body rather than by radiation passing through the body. Like MRI, this technique is somewhat complicated, so we examine it in more detail next.

In PET, molecules altered to have a radioactive atom are introduced into the blood supply and carried to the brain. One commonly used molecule is 2-deoxy-D-glucose, a physiologically inert sugar similar to the one that supplies the brain with energy, which is altered by the introduction of a radioactive fluorine atom (^{18}F) into 2-deoxy-2-fluoro-D-glucose. Radioactive molecules are unstable but reach a more stable, nonradioactive state by releasing a charged particle. PET uses a particular class of radioactive molecules, which become stable by emitting a positively charged electron called a *positron*. When a positron is emitted, it collides with an electron, which has a negative charge of the same value, and they annihilate each other. This annihilation produces energy in the form of two photons of light that travel from the site of annihilation exactly 180 degrees opposite each other. A person having a PET scan sits with his or her head in a ring of photocells that are designed to detect the coincident arrival of two photons of light from exactly opposite directions. (Because light travels at 186,000 mi/s, the arrival of the two photons is, for all intents and purposes, simultaneous.) Areas of the brain that are very metabolically active emit that many photons of light. By extrapolating back from the detectors to the point from which the photons emanated, the region or regions of the brain that are most active can be determined. The time required to obtain a picture is linked to how quickly a given isotope goes from a radioactive state to a nonradioactive state (known as its *half-life*), because a certain number of photons must be detected to create an image (Figure 2.7).

A related technique, *SPECT (single photon emission tomography),* uses a much scaled-down version of the same technique as PET. In this case, however, a small set of sensors rather than a ring of sensors is used, which reduces the spatial resolution of the obtained brain image. In addition, because the isotope used with these techniques usually takes longer to decay than the isotopes used with PET, the picture of the brain activity is less precise because it

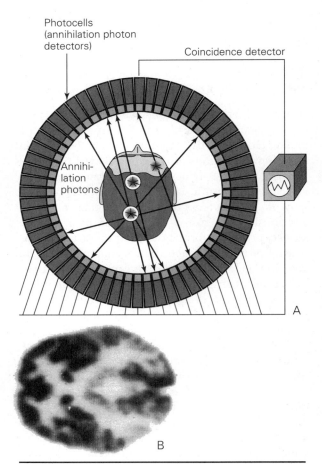

Figure 2.7 An explanation of positron emission tomography (PET).
(A) When a positron is annihilated by an electron, two photons of light traveling in opposite directions are emitted simultaneously. The coincidence of arrival of two photons 180 degrees apart is detected by photocells. Brain regions that are very active give off many photons, whereas those that are less active give off fewer. By extrapolating backward, the source of the photons can be determined. (B) A sample PET scan. Typically, the level of activity in different regions is color-coded, not depicted in gray scale as shown here. (*Note.* A, Adapted from Posner & Raichle, 1994, pp. 19, 63. B, From "Images of the Brain in Action," by M. E. Raichle, in *The Oxford Companion to the Mind* (p. 348), edited by Richard L. Gregory, 1987, Oxford University Press.)

is averaged over a much longer time interval than with PET.

PET's main advantage is that it allows researchers to examine the use of a variety of molecules over many regions of the brain, provided that a radioactive (positron-emitting) version of the molecule can be created. (If you are a neuropsychologist, such study usually calls for having a clever biochemist as your collaborator.) Suppose we are interested in looking for regional increases in cerebral blood flow because we know that local changes in blood flow are associated with increases in neural activity (e.g., Sandman, O'Halloran, & Isenhart, 1984). To do so, we can inject subjects with radioactive water that contains the positron-emitting ^{15}O, which accumulates in the brain in direct proportion to the local blood flow (for a readable account of how this technique was fruitfully applied to the study of cognitive functions, see Posner & Raichle, 1994). In contrast, if we are interested in the distribution of a neurotransmitter, such as dopamine, we can introduce a radioactively tagged substance that binds to receptor sites (e.g., Wong et al., 1986).

Despite this major advantage, PET has some drawbacks. First, like CAT, it involves radiation; therefore, an individual can undergo only about four or five scans a year. Second, the time periods required to obtain a picture of brain activity (which is determined by an isotope's half-life) are much longer than those typically used to measure mental activities in the brain. For example, 2-deoxy-2-fluoro-D-glucose will yield a picture of brain activity averaged over about an hour. This time lapse is a problem when you consider all the activity that may have occurred in the subject's mind in that amount of time—besides the task she or he was instructed to do. All of the subject's thoughts (not just those related to the experiment) cause brain activity that is conglomerated into one picture. Even the half-lives of isotopes, such as ^{15}O, which provide an image of brain activity averaged over a minute and a half, are long considering that most people can make a cognitive decision, such as whether a letter string is a word or not, in 700 ms or less. An additional drawback of these isotopes with a shorter half-lives is that they must be continually infused if the person is to be engaged in the task for any length of time (i.e., more than a minute and a half). This continual creation of the radioactive isotope requires a machine, called a *cyclotron*, which is expensive and often available only at major medical centers.

A third disadvantage of PET is that it often cannot provide enough information from a single person to provide a reliable picture of brain activity. Rather, scans often portray the areas of the brain that are active during a specific task or activity averaged across many people. Hence, although PET can be used to determine, on average, whether different functions (e.g., speech output and speech comprehension) rely on different brain regions, it may not be as accurate at determining localization of function for a given individual. The process of averaging across individuals requires that each individual's PET scan be "normalized" by superimposing an anatomical scan (usually an MRI) to a brain atlas that shows an "average" brain. Because the position of the subject's head in the PET and MRI images is likely to vary, the images may be difficult to superimpose, although techniques that align the images can partially correct for the problem. Furthermore, brains are as unique as faces, which can make averaging difficult. Think about the variation in morphology of your friends' faces: Some are wide whereas others are thin, some have eyes spaced far apart whereas others have eyes quite close, and some have prominent ridges at the eyebrows whereas others do not. If you imagine how your face would be modified to match that of the "average" person's face, you can get a sense of the potential distortion imposed by this averaging process. Thus, PET sometimes cannot provide a precise demarcation between the brain regions that are active and those that are inactive during performance of a given task.

Although many difficulties are associated with PET, it is still a good technique for identifying the multiplicity of brain structures involved in a cognitive function, and, at present, is uniquely suited for examining the brain's processing of certain substances such as neurotransmitters and acid-base balance (M. E. Raichle, 1994). If the researcher need not precisely locate active brain regions during short time periods, the advantages of PET can more than outweigh its disadvantages.

Functional Magnetic Resonance Imaging

Although we previously discussed MRI as a means of obtaining images of brain anatomy, recently a

Participating in a Functional Magnetic Resonance Imaging Study

What is it like to participate in MRI studies of brain function? I was involved in one such study, both as a researcher and as a participant, so I can provide a short description of some of this work from both perspectives. The fMRI studies described here are the result of a collaborative effort of a large number of neuropsychologists and chemists at the University of Illinois and the University of Chicago (e.g., N. J. Cohen et al., 1993). The psychologists in the group, including myself, Neal Cohen, and Art Kramer, all participated as initial subjects so that we could determine what difficulties might arise in experiments that are run in the atypical environment of a magnet and to know exactly what participants would experience.

Our study was simple; it was designed to determine whether we could detect changes in blood oxygenation over the occipital lobe while a person stared at a checkerboard of red and green squares that reversed color seven times a second. However, I could not just go and sit in the magnet to be tested. First, I had to carefully look over a checklist to make sure that I did not have characteristics that would preclude a scan. Such characteristics included having ever had a metal clip placed on any blood vessel during surgery, having a pacemaker, and even having "permanent" eyeliner!

Next, I had to check that my clothes contained no metal. Although this task might seem easy, remember that most pants have zippers and that undergarments, especially those for women, usually have metal clasps.

Once outfitted correctly in a pair of surgical scrubs and a long-sleeve T-shirt, I had to be custom-fitted with a mask that would help keep my head in place during the experiment. Next, because MRIs are loud, I needed earplugs to lessen the noise. At this point, I was positioned on my back on a table outside the magnet, which is a rather large cylinder, about 8 ft tall by 8 ft wide, with a small hole (known as the *bore*) in the middle, in which the person is placed. The customized face mask was put over my face and was affixed to the table assembly so that my head would stay still. The receiver coil of the magnet, which is like an enlarged baseball catcher's mask, was then put around my head. Finally, two angled mirrors positioned directly above my eyes were adjusted so that I could view a screen, positioned near my feet, onto which the visual stimuli would be projected. Then I was moved into the machine headfirst, which placed my head in the middle of the magnet so that the best image could be obtained.

The experience of being moved into the magnet was disconcerting. The bore of the magnet is a small

variation of this method was devised that allows examination of certain aspects of brain function. This method is known as *functional* magnetic resonance imaging (fMRI) to distinguish it from MRI used to obtain neuroanatomical images of the brain. Because changes in neuronal activity are accompanied by local changes in cerebral blood flow and blood oxygenation (e.g., Fox, Raichle, Mintun, & Dence, 1988), these local changes can be used to infer the activity levels of different brain regions. fMRI methods examine brain metabolism by using a contrast agent with magnetic properties, such as gadolinium, to measure blood flow (e.g., Belliveau et al., 1991). When a contrast agent is used, the areas with the most activity have the highest concentration of the magnetic agent. Like PET, though, this approach requires the introduction of a foreign substance into the body.

A much less invasive fMRI method is to assess the oxygenation of blood, which takes advantage of a change in the magnetic properties of blood. It should not surprise you that blood has magnetic properties if you consider that a lack of iron in the blood causes anemia, which is the reason that many people, especially women, are encouraged to ensure that their diet contains enough iron. Oxygen-rich blood carried from the heart by the arteries is *diamagnetic*, meaning it has magnetic properties. As this blood passes through the capillary beds, oxygen is extracted and the blood loses its magnetic proper-

semicircular opening that leaves little room for even the smallest arm movements and places your nose just inches from the top of the magnet. If you are a spelunker (that is, a cave explorer), you'd probably feel comfortable, but for people who have claustrophobia, the experience would be nerve-racking. I must admit that the first time I was rolled into the magnet my heart started to race and I felt uncomfortable. But I chattered to my colleagues and forced myself to think about being safely and snugly tucked into bed rather than trapped in a magnet. Because of such thinking, I subsequently found the magnet a comfortable place to relax.

Once the screen was positioned at my feet for optimal viewing, the studies began. MRIs work because they set up a homogeneous static magnetic field around an object. Because a body and a head in the magnet disrupt that field, the machine had to be "shimmed," or adjusted, to take into account the peculiarities of my individual head and body, and to optimize the signal that the machine would receive. During this time, the machine made low, deep "a-clump, a-clump, a-clump" noises, like the sound of a large steel horse slowly loping around a racetrack. After the shimming, an anatomical scan of my brain was taken. The first time I participated in this procedure, my colleagues

thoughtfully let me know through an intercom system between the control room and the magnet that the structural scan revealed that I did indeed have a brain!

Because we were interested in visual processing, the machine was programmed to take a "slice" of my brain's activity that would pass through the calcarine fissure (see Figure 1.14), which is where the primary visual areas of the brain are located. During each pair of scans, I first had to close my eyes, a task designed to provide a base line of the activity level in my occipital cortex when it receives no visual input. Then, a checkerboard was flashed to measure the response of my occipital cortex to visual stimulation. The noise made by the machine became different, more tinny and staccato than previously. To round out the day, a high-resolution anatomical scan of my brain with 128 slices was obtained to allow a computerized three-dimensional rendering of my entire brain to be constructed. One and a half hours after we started, my colleagues told me through the intercom that we were done, came into the magnet room, and wheeled me out of the magnet. Although being in the magnet was relaxing, I was glad to get out, stretch my legs, and hear more familiar noises.

ties (a *paramagnetic* state). When a particular area of the brain is active, the local increase in oxygen-rich blood is greater than the amount of oxygen that can be extracted by the brain tissue. Thus, the relative proportion of oxygenated blood to deoxygenated blood changes in that local region. The difference between the magnetic properties of the oxygen-rich blood in the vein and the deoxygenated blood in the surrounding brain tissue can be detected as an increased signal with certain MRI techniques (e.g., Kwong et al., 1992).

For a number of reasons, fMRI provides particularly exciting prospects for making brain-behavior inferences. First, scans can be obtained with standard clinical MRI machines that are located in many

hospitals in different countries. Second, certain varieties of the technique are noninvasive. Third, fMRI can be used with many populations (except individuals with cardiac problems or metal in their bodies). Fourth, scientists can obtain an anatomical MRI and an fMRI in immediate succession and can overlay them with great precision. Fifth, multiple scans can be run on a single subject, unlike the limitations imposed by PET. Finally, the precision of scans obtained from fMRI enables us to examine brain-behavior relationships for individuals rather than only for groups (as is often the case with PET).

Because many of these new fMRI techniques are still in the developmental stage, both their advantages and their limitations will be revealed in more detail in the coming years. At present, fMRI techniques allow us to obtain information only about blood flow and, by inference, oxygen consumption, whereas PET scans can image the distribution of many metabolically active substances. Because MRI can be tuned to specific atoms, the potential to scan for other substances exists, but MRI has not been used to date, for example, to detect the concentration of neurotransmitters in the human brain. Whether the concentration of such substances is high enough to be detected with these methods remains to be seen.

Electrical Recording Methods

The methods we discussed so far examine the metabolic activity of the brain. In other cases, however, we may want to record the electrical activity of the brain that results from neuronal firing. In animals, we can place electrodes directly into cells and determine which stimuli make a cell fire. In humans, we record the summed electrical activity of many neurons. Compared with the brain imaging techniques we just discussed, electrical measures in humans currently do a poor job of identifying where activity is occurring in the brain. Yet, the electrical methods provide an accurate measure of brain activity on a millisecond-by-millisecond basis, much more rapidly than even with the fastest fMRI methods.

Single-Cell Recordings

Many of the studies performed with animals that we discuss in this book examine the electrical responses of cells in particular regions of the brain. In these studies, an electrode is placed into the brain region of interest and the experimenter records the electrical output of the cell or cells that are contacted by the exposed electrode tip. After establishing a base-line firing rate for a given cell, researchers attempt to discover the properties of a stimulus that will make a cell fire maximally above that base line. Depending on the location of the cells being moni-

tored, researchers may want to address various issues. They may want to determine whether the cells are sensitive to input in only one sensory modality or are multimodal in sensitivity, whether they respond to information from only specific places in the sensory world or from broad regions of space, and whether a cell's response is modified depending on whether or not the animal's attention is directed at the stimulus.

Studies involving single-cell recording techniques in animals have been enormously helpful in providing information about the organization of many brain regions. For example, such studies have demonstrated that cells in primary visual areas are responsive to basic orientation of bars of light whereas cells in higher order visual regions are responsive to much more elaborate forms (e.g., Desimone, Albright, Gross, & Bruce, 1984), that frontal regions are important for keeping information available in memory during a delay period (e.g., Funahashi, Bruce, & Goldman-Rakic, 1991), and that parietal areas are important for directing arm movements into particular regions of space (Georgopolous, Schwartz, & Kettner, 1986). Because studies such as these provide a basis for conceptualizing how particular regions of the human brain may be organized for certain cognitive functions, we discuss them throughout the text where appropriate.

In humans, opportunities for such studies are limited. However, there are cases during surgery for the removal of epileptic tissue in which electrodes are either placed on the surface of the brain during surgery or implanted into the brain for about a week before surgery to better isolate the source of seizure activity. Although implanted electrodes may be more invasive than surface electrodes, they allow for a more thorough mapping of the brain. Because the seizure activity can be more precisely located and because the organization of mental functions can be more thoroughly mapped, useful tissue is less likely to be removed. In these cases, we can record from groups of cells during these procedures and attempt to determine the stimulus properties that make cells fire (e.g., Allison et al., 1994). In addition, small amounts of current can be passed through the electrodes and the effect on behavior can be observed. For example, some researchers have mapped the regions of the left hemisphere that lead to an arrest in speech when stimulated (G. A. Ojemann, 1983).

Electroencephalography

Electroencephalography (EEG) is a method of recording the brain's electrical activity. Clinically, it is often used to detect aberrant activity such as that which accompanies epilepsy and sleep disorders. Experimentally, it is used to detect certain psychological states, such as drowsiness and alertness, because these states are associated with particular patterns of electrical activity.

In EEG, the electrical signals produced by the brain are typically recorded by metal electrodes positioned on the scalp (Figure 2.8), and then amplified. Each electrode (sometimes called a *lead*) acts as its own recording site or channel. An electrode is also attached to an electrically inactive site, such as the mastoid bone (located behind the ear), which acts as a ground that provides a base line for comparing the activity at each electrode. An electrode simply placed on the skin is an inappropriate ground because it covers muscles, whose contractions are induced by electrical signals. To avoid mistaking muscle movement for brain activity, researchers usually place an electrode near the eyes so that EEG signals from the time periods when eye movements occur can be discarded from further analysis.

The **electrical potential** recorded at an electrode on the scalp is the summed or superimposed signal of electrical activity of fields of neuronal dendrites. The waveform recorded at the scalp has a particular voltage (which is a measure of its size) and a particular frequency, meaning that it oscillates at a specific rate (Hertz; cycles per second). The frequency and form of the EEG signal varies according to whether a person is wakeful or asleep, drowsy or alert. When a person is awake, the EEG shows a mixture of many frequencies, but those that are relatively fast (>15 Hz), known as *beta activity,* tend to predominate. In contrast, when a person is relaxed with his or her eyes closed, slower frequencies, or *alpha activity*, at 9 to 12 Hz, are much more common.

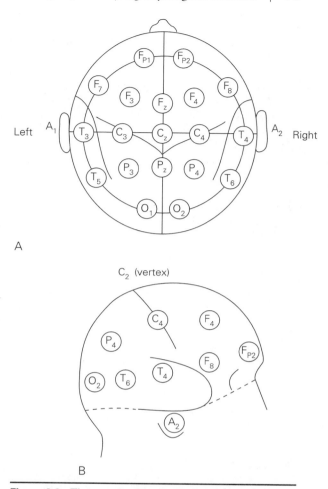

Figure 2.8   The standard placement of electrodes during electroencephalography (EEG) recording. Electrodes over the left hemisphere are labeled with odd numbers, those over the right hemisphere are labeled with even numbers, and those on the midline are labeled with a *z*. The uppercase letter is an abbreviation for the location of the electrode: A, auricle; C, central; F, frontal; Fp, frontal pole; O, occipital; P, parietal; and T, temporal. (*Note.* Adapted from Kandel et al., 1991, p. 779.)

During sleep, very slow frequencies of *delta activity*, at 1 to 4 Hz, predominate.

As we noted earlier, EEG is useful for the detection of certain clinical disorders. Because each stage of sleep and wakefulness has a characteristic EEG pattern, EEG can be used to diagnose such prob-

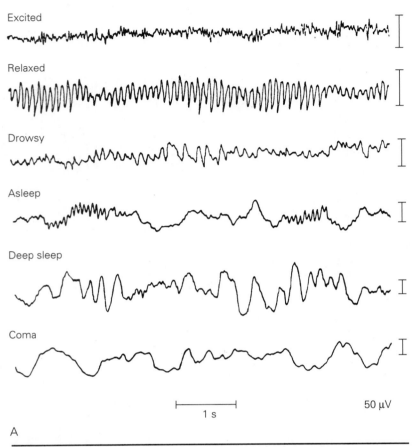

Excited

Relaxed

Drowsy

Asleep

Deep sleep

Coma

1 s

50 μV

A

Figure 2.9 Examples of electroencephalography (EEG) recordings.
(A) Characteristic EEG activity during various mental states. Note the cyclicity of activity that can be observed, for example, when an individual is in a relaxed state. (*Note.* A, From *Epilepsy and the Functional Anatomy of the Human Brain*, by W. Penfield and H. H. Jasper, 1954, Boston, Little, Brown. Reprinted by permission of Lippincott-Raven Publishers.)

lems. In addition, epilepsy, which can be conceptualized as an electrical storm in the brain, can be detected by EEG. Neurons normally fire in a synchronous manner, leading to the alpha, beta, and delta waveforms we just discussed. In epilepsy, however, rather than firing in a synchronous rhythm at random times, neurons fire in large quantities at once (a burst, or "spike"). The result is an increase in the amplitude of firing that can be observed on the EEG record. After an individual is treated with

anticonvulsants, the EEG can be performed again to ensure that the spiking activity decreased. Figure 2.9 provides some examples of different types of brain waves seen in neurologically intact individuals as well as those that occur in clinical conditions.

EEG can also be used to examine experimental questions. Because alpha waves indicate that a person is relaxed and resting, the absence or suppression of alpha activity is often used as an indicator

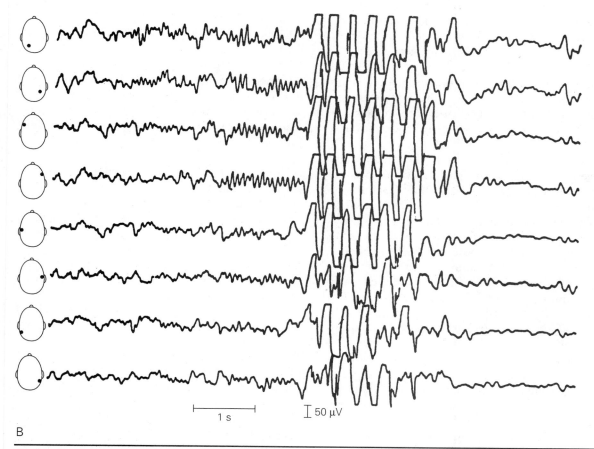

B

Figure 2.9 (Continued) (B) An example of "spiking" activity, which is a discrete increase in the voltage of the EEG, that accompanies epilepsy. In this case, the seizure occurred over many regions of the brain simultaneously, as can be seen by the occurrence of high-voltage activity over all electrodes. The position of the electrode for each line of recording is indicated by a dot on the diagram of the head on the left. The square shape of the wave during seizure activity is an artifact owing to limitations of the recording apparatus, which could not adequately record the intensity of the voltage associated with this seizure. More typical waveforms during seizure activity can be seen in the third recording from the bottom, in which square waves are less prominent. (*Note.* B, From *A Primer of Electroencephalography*, by G. D. Vander Ark and L. G. Kemp, 1970. Copyright 1970 by Hoffmann-La Roche. Reprinted by permission of Hoffmann-La Roche.)

of the degree of activation of the brain. The degree of **alpha suppression,** as it is known, is examined to determine how active the brain is under different conditions. For example, in the chapter on emotion (chapter 11), we discuss evidence that when individuals are depressed, they exhibit greater alpha suppression over right frontal areas than over left frontal areas. This finding indicates that depression is accompanied by greater activation of right frontal regions than of left frontal regions.

Event-Related Potentials

Event-related potentials (ERPs) are recordings of the brain's activity that are linked to the occurrence of an event (e.g., the presentation of a stimulus). Whereas EEG recordings provide a continuous measure of brain activity, ERPs, are recorded only in reference to a specific event. The common alignment and firing of dendritic fields in the brain after this event causes a *dipole,* which is a small region of electrical current with relatively positive end and a relatively negative end (hence *di*pole, or *two*-pole, system). Electrodes at the scalp can detect this dipole. Because the potential is recorded at the scalp, it does not provide information about where in the brain the electrical activity is emanating from (a focus of current research is to create methods that will allow more precise localization of the dipole).

With time from the onset of the stimulus, the active groups of neurons, and hence the locations of the dipoles, change. Thus, the waveform recorded on the scalp changes as well. The waveform can be divided into **components,** which are characteristic portions of the wave that have been linked to certain psychological processes, such as attention and memory. ERP components are usually given names that have two parts: a letter and then a subscript number (e.g., P_3). The letter is always a *P* or an *N* and denotes whether the deflection of the electrical signal is positive or negative. The number represents, on average, how many hundreds of milliseconds after stimulus presentation the component appears.

Components are often divided into two categories: exogenous and endogenous. **Exogenous components** are linked to the physical characteristics of a stimulus and usually occur early in the waveform. (Because they are evoked by an external stimulus, they are sometimes referred to as *evoked potentials.*) In contrast, **endogenous components** appear to be independent of stimulus characteristics and driven by internal cognitive states. They typically occur later in the waveform. An example of a typical waveform with the different components is presented in Figure 2.10.

Next, let's discuss the major classes of important components, starting with those that occur earliest in time: the early sensory components, the early negative components, the P_3, and the N_4. The very early components, occurring within 100 ms of stimulus onset, are linked to sensory processing. This property makes them useful in assessing the integrity of nerve fiber pathways from the sensory receptors to the brain. For example, the synapse points from the cochlea of the ear to the cortex are the cochlear nuclei (and superior olive) at the level of the me-

dulla, the inferior colliculus, the medial geniculate nucleus of the thalamus, and then Heschl's gyrus, the primary auditory region of the brain (see Figure 1.23). Information takes time to reach each of these relay points, and when it does, a characteristic component of the waveform is produced. Because of this relationship between the transmission of information along the neural pathway and the ERP, disruptions at a specific relay point in the flow of information from the sensory receptors to the cortex can often be detected as an abnormality in a specific early component of the ERP.

Components that appear approximately 100 ms poststimulus are no longer driven only by sensory information but can also be modulated by attention. The effect of attention can be demonstrated by asking individuals to pay attention to information presented in one place but not another, such as paying attention to information presented to the right ear but not the left. The stimulus presented in each ear does not vary between conditions, only attention does. Typically, researchers find that the size of the P_1 component, a positive deflection observed between 80 and 140 ms postpresentation, and that of the N_1, a negative deflection observed about 100 ms postpresentation for auditory stimuli and between 160 and 200 ms postpresentation for visual stimuli, are increased when a stimulus appears in an attended location as compared with an unattended location (Mangun & Hillyard, 1990).

A negative deflection at about 200 ms postpresentation, known as the *mismatch negativity,* occurs when an individual is presented with an item that is physically deviant from that of the prevailing context. For example, if someone is listening to a series of tones, most of which are low in pitch, an N_2 is elicited by a high-pitched tone. Unlike the N_1, this effect occurs regardless of whether the individual is attending to the location in which the deviant stimulus appears (e.g., Naatanen, Gaillard, & Mantysalo, 1978).

One of the most studied components is the P_3, which is a positive deflection found approximately 300 ms poststimulus. Although researchers disagree on exactly what the P_3 measures, it appears to be related to attention and the updating of memory, in that the current model of the environment is modified by incoming information (Donchin & Coles, 1988). The P₃ occurs in numerous situations; however, the classic situation in which it is usually observed is in an experimental procedure called the *oddball paradigm*. In this paradigm, an individual hears a series of tones at consecutive intervals, most of which are at one pitch (e.g., a "beep") and a minority of which are at another pitch (e.g., a "boop"). A P₃ is elicited when the individual must respond to the oddball, the boop, but not the regular items, the beeps. The P₃ appears to be elicited by conditions in which the individual must pay at-

tention to an item, the oddball, and when the oddball is distinct from the information currently held in memory (which necessitates the updating of memory). The P₃ is distinct from the mismatch negativity, which occurs when a physical deviance is detected, because a P₃ can be elicited by the lack of sensory stimulation, such as silence. If, for example, a person hears a series of tones punctuated periodically by silence when a tone should occur, a P₃ is elicited to the silence because memory must now be updated.

Another late component that has been linked to

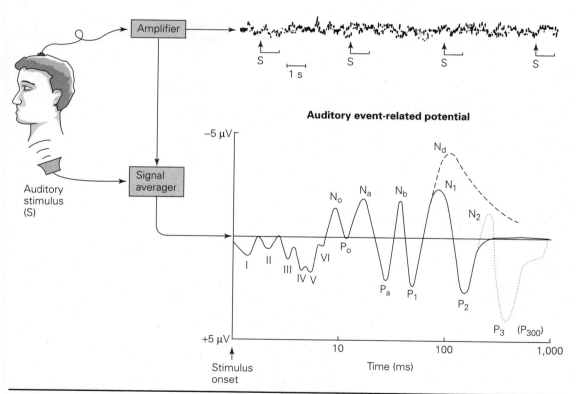

Figure 2.10 The method of recording event-related potentials (ERPs).
The ongoing electroencephalography (EEG) (top) is recorded on the scalp through an amplifier. Every time a stimulus occurs (denoted by an *S* in the ongoing EEG), the electrical signal is recorded for a discrete period (e.g., 1 s). Signals from all such time periods are then averaged because ERPs are too small to be detected in the ongoing EEG. The resulting ERP waveform to an auditory stimulus is shown below, with time plotted logarithmically to allow differentiation of early responses from the brain stem (Waves I–VI), early components (<100 ms) that indicate the response of the brain to sensory characteristics of the stimulus (N$_o$, P$_o$, N$_a$, P$_a$, N$_b$), and later (endogenous) components (>100 ms) that tend to be linked more to cognitive processes (N$_d$, N$_2$, P$_3$). (*Note.* Adapted from Hillyard & Kutas, 1983, p. 35.)

psychological processing is the N_4. This negative-going component appears approximately 400 ms poststimulus presentation and occurs when individuals detect semantic anomalies. So, for example, if your ERP were being recorded at this moment, an N_4 would probably be observed as you read the last word of the following sentence: "Running out the door, Patty grabbed her jacket, her baseball glove, her cap, a softball, and a skyscraper." In contrast, the N_4 would be absent if the same sentence ended with the word *bat*. The amplitude of the N_4 increases with deviance of a word relative to the prior context of the sentence. For example, your N_4 to the following sentence, "Running out the door, Patty grabbed her jacket, her baseball glove, her cap, a softball, and a lamp," would be smaller than your N_4 to the first sentence because *lamp* is less deviant a word than *skyscraper* (i.e., Patty could actually grab a lamp, but not a skyscraper). However, an N_4 would still be elicited by the second sentence because you would expect Patty to grab another piece of softball equipment, not a piece of furniture (e.g., Kutas & Hillyard, 1980).

A review of the components and the psychological processes with which they are associated is presented in Table 2.2. (A more detailed review of ERPs and their relations to psychological processes is presented in Rugg & Coles, 1995.)

In this section, we discussed various techniques for assessing brain function. Because we need the proper tool for the job, the relative advantages and disadvantages of each method must be considered when we choose a method for each question to be investigated. A summary of the information provided by each method, as well as its strengths and weaknesses, is presented in Table 2.3.

Table 2.2 Basic Components and Psychological Processes Associated with Event-Related Potential (ERP) Components

ERP component	Time period (ms)[a]	Eliciting conditions	Associated mental processes
Sensory components	0–100	After the receipt of sensory information	Transmission of sensory information from the periphery to the cortex
N_1–P_2 (N_d)	100–300	When subjects are paying attention to the portion of the stimulus stream in which the material was presented	Selective attention
Mismatch negativity (N_2)	200–300	When a stimulus is physically deviant from other recent stimuli; it is not much affected by whether the individual is paying attention to the portion of the stimulus stream in which the deviant item is presented	Detection of physical deviance
P_3	300–800	When individuals must pay attention to the rarest of two events, even if that rare event is the absence of sensory stimulation (e.g., silence)	Memory of context updating
N_4	400–600	When items deviate in meaning from what is expected	Detection of semantic deviance

[a]Indicates time postpresentation.

Table 2.3 Comparison of Different Methods of Investigating the Brain

Method	Information provided	Advantages	Disadvantages
CAT (computerized axial tomography)	*Anatomical image* of brain density	1. Can be used with almost all individuals	1. Involves the use of radiation 2. Does not provide a picture with high spatial resolution
MRI (magnetic resonance imaging)	*Anatomical image* of the distribution of a certain substance, such as water or fat	1. Provides an anatomically precise image 2. Can be used to detect different substances	1. Cannot be used with individuals who have metal in their bodies or pacemakers 2. Can induce claustrophobia in some individuals
PET (positron emission tomography)	*Functional image* of brain physiology for various substances, including glucose, oxygen, and neurotransmitters	1. Can be used to assess many aspects of physiological function	1. Involves the use of ionizing radiation 2. Provides images that are averaged over times longer than thought processes require 3. Often necessitates the averaging of data among subjects 4. Does not provide high spatial resolution
fMRI (functional MRI)	*Functional image* of blood flow or oxygenation	1. Provides good spatial resolution in relatively short periods 2. Can be performed repeatedly on the same individual 3. Does not require the averaging of data across individuals	1. Cannot be used with individuals who have metal in their bodies or pacemakers 2. Is a relatively new technique, so all its limitations may not yet be apparent
Single-cell recordings	*Electrical signal* that provides information about the firing rate of a cell	1. Provides information on the type of stimulus a cell responds to	1. Cannot be used with humans except under very specific circumstances
EEG (electroencephalography)	*Electrical signal* that provides information about the frequency of averaged electrical activity	1. Provides information on the general state of the person (e.g., alert, drowsy) 2. Provides a millisecond-by-millisecond record of activity	1. Cannot be used to identify the region in the brain producing the activity
ERPs (event-related potentials)	*Electrical signal* that provides a record of the averaged electrical activity that is time-locked to an event	1. Provides information that has been linked to specific psychological processes such as memory and attention 2. Provides a millisecond-by-millisecond record of activity	1. Cannot be used to identify the region in the brain producing the activity

TECHNIQUES FOR ANALYZING BEHAVIOR

Careful and thoughtful behavioral testing is one of the most powerful tools we have for analyzing how the brain constrains and influences the way we think. Just as we need precise tools to measure brain anatomy and brain physiology, we also need precise tools to examine behavior.

The Role of Cognitive Theories

Although we might assume that the deficits a person has sustained due to brain damage can be ascertained simply by observing behavior, this is not the case. Think for a moment about the task of seeing a picture of an animal, such as a zebra, and providing its name. If we find that a patient cannot supply the name "zebra," how are we to determine the exact cause of this problem? Clinical and experimental neuropsychologists must determine, from among an array of possibilities, exactly why the naming problem exists. Perhaps the visual attributes of the stimulus can't be processed because occipital regions were damaged and the person is blind. Or maybe basic visual processing is intact, but the patterns of light and dark cannot be interpreted as the black-and-white stripes of a zebra. Alternatively, maybe the physical form can be perceived (which we know because the patient correctly chooses a horse and not an elephant as looking similar to the zebra) and the patient's memory for zebras is intact (which we know because when asked which African animal is similar to a horse and has stripes, the patient correctly points to the word *zebra*), but that form can't be identified as a zebra. Or, perhaps, the verbal label cannot be specifically accessed (that is, if you said "zebra," the patient could point to a picture of one, but if shown a picture of a zebra, he or she couldn't name it). Finally, the patient may have sustained some damage to the vocal musculature that does not allow production of the sound sequence of *zebra*, even though she or he knows that the picture is that of a zebra.

As this example demonstrates, what appears on the surface to be a simple problem may actually stem from numerous complex sources. Often the job of both clinical and experimental neuropsychol-

ogists is to carefully tease apart the possibilities and pinpoint the probable locus of the deficit. The degree to which we know how to parcel a cognitive ability into subcomponents relies not only on logic and common sense, but also to a large degree on having sound theories of cognitive functioning. For example psycholinguists often describe language as being composed of three parts: phonology, syntax, and semantics. *Phonology* refers to the rules governing the sounds of language, *syntax* its grammar, and *semantics* its meaning. As we discuss in chapter 8, individuals with brain damage may have deficits in one of these domains but not in the others.

Why is it so important to be aware of cognitive theories? Let's suppose that a naive neuropsychologist doesn't know or consider psycholinguistic theories of language and encounters an individual who cannot correctly repeat a sentence spoken to her. The neuropsychologist might conclude, erroneously, that the patient doesn't "understand" the sentence. However, if the neuropsychologist knew from theories of language that the ability to use grammar correctly can be separable from knowing what words mean, the neuropsychologist not only would test the patient's ability to repeat the sentence, but also would test her comprehension—for example, by asking her to point to a picture that depicted what she just heard. The results might show that although the individual cannot repeat the sentence, she can point to the picture depicting the sentence. This result would suggest a different conclusion from the initial one, namely that the patient *can* understand the meanings of words. The neuropsychologist would discover that the problem does not lie in comprehension and could go on to systematically test whether the individual has difficulties in producing the correct grammar or syntax.

Throughout this book, we discuss different theories of mental function. They help to guide investigations into the relationship between the brain and behavior by providing a means of conceptualizing overarching cognitive functions such as "language" or "spatial ability" as actually consisting of a set of more specific cognitive capacities. These theoretical frameworks for understanding cognitive functions can help delineate the many possible causes of a behavior and allow behavior exhibited in either the clinic or the laboratory to be decomposed into its parts.

We must also remember that not only do psychological theories inform neuropsychological investigations, but neuropsychological investigations can inform cognitive theories, especially differentiating those that are plausible and those that are not. For example, as discussed in chapter 8, data from neuropsychological studies support the conceptualization of syntax and semantics as distinct aspects of language because brain damage can disrupt one of these abilities while leaving the other intact.

Clinical Assessment of Behavior

In the final section of this chapter, we discuss some of the methods commonly used in clinical settings for assessing the effects of brain damage on cognitive and emotional processing. We begin by discussing the test-battery approach, which is designed to assess a variety of cognitive abilities with the intention of obtaining a profile of an individual's strengths and weaknesses. Usually contained within the test battery is at least one test designed to measure overall intelligence. We discuss several standard tests designed to measure overall intelligence in the second part of this section of the chapter. In some cases, more specific tests, such as those measuring memory, attention, spatial ability, and abstract reasoning, are used to elucidate a more fine-grained profile of an individual's strengths and weaknesses. Myriad tests can be used for assessing specific functions, far too many to be discussed here. If you are interested in knowing more about these specific tests as well as other aspects of clinical assessment of neuropsychological dysfunction, the definitive reference is Lezak (1995).

A **neuropsychological assessment,** which is performed by a clinical neuropsychologist, is used to evaluate the degree to which damage to the central nervous system may have compromised a person's cognitive, behavioral, and emotional functioning. The goals and uses of this assessment are numerous. First, the assessment provides a profile of cognitive capacity exhibited by a subject. It can demonstrate both the strengths and the weaknesses of an individual, identifying the domains likely to cause difficulty

and highlighting the retained skills that can be used to offset potential problem areas. Second, the assessment provides a base line from which to evaluate the person's progress during rehabilitation. As time passes from the insult, neuropsychologists often want to know whether the person is making additional gains in performance or whether a particular therapeutic regimen is helpful. Third, the assessment yields information that can be used to provide a prognosis for the individual. The individual, as well as his or her family and loved ones, must be given not only insight into the level at which the individual is currently functioning, but also reasonable expectations about the likely level of functioning in the future. If expectations are too high, the patient and family may become frustrated, and if expectations are too low, the person may not recover to her or his full potential (Lezak, 1983).

Batteries and Customized Approaches

Because brain damage can affect a range of cognitive abilities, one approach is to administer a **neuropsychological test battery** that can be used to assess a range of functions. Probably the most widely used neuropsychological test battery is the *Halstead-Reitan battery,* which consists of a number of tests that generally require about 6 to 8 hours to administer. The abilities examined in this battery range from simple tests of sensory function to complex tests of reasoning, from tests of verbal function to tests of spatial function, and from tests of immediate recognition to tests of memory. In addition, the battery is used to assess functioning in different sensory modalities. A complete Halstead-Reitan battery for adults include the tests described briefly in Table 2.4 (Boll, 1981).

Besides the Halstead-Reitan, other test batteries, such as the Luria-Nebraska, can be administered in about half the time of the Halstead-Reitan. The tasks on the Luria-Nebraska are divided into 12 content scales: motor functions, rhythm and pitch, tactile and kinesthetic functions, visual functions, receptive language, expressive language, reading, arithmetic, writing, memory, intermediate memory, and intelligence. This battery is a formalized set of tests that reflects the philosophy of Alexander Luria,

Table 2.4 Components of the Halstead-Reitan Neuropsychological Test Battery

Test	What it measures	How the ability is measured
MMPI-2 (Minnesota Multiphasic Personality Inventory—Second Edition)	Psychiatric symptomatology, such as depression and schizophrenia	The individual answers a large number of yes-no questions to provide a profile relative to individuals who have been diagnosed with specific psychiatric disorders.
Categories Test	Abstract reasoning	The individual views four items on the screen and pushes one of four buttons; different sets of items require different responses (e.g., push the button corresponding to the atypical item, push the button corresponding to the Roman numeral on the screen). The only feedback provided is a bell for correct answers and a buzzer for incorrect responses.
Rhythm Test	Auditory perception and timing	The individual decides whether two patterns of sounds are similar.
Speech Sounds Perception Test	Verbal abilities Attentional abilities	In each trial, the individual chooses a previously heard sound from among a number of choices. The sounds are nonsense syllables that begin and end with different consonants.
Finger Tapping Test	Motor function	The tapping rate of each index finger is determined.
Grip Strength Test	Motor function	The strength with which a dynamometer can be squeezed by each hand is assessed.
Trail Making Test	Visual search Attention	*Part A:* The individual's ability to draw a line connecting consecutively numbered circles is assessed. *Part B:* The individual's ability to connect, in an alternating manner, numbered and lettered circles (e.g., A1B2C3) is examined.
Aphasia Screening Test	Language	The individual's ability to use and perceive language, to pantomime simple actions, and to reproduce simple geometric forms is assessed.
Tactile Perception Test	Tactile ability	The individual is tested as to whether he or she can identify objects by touch (each hand separately), can identify letters traced on the fingertips (with the eyes closed), and can perceive being touched on different fingers of both hands.
Tactile Performance Test	Tactile memory Spatial localization	Without any visual input (blindfolded or eyes closed), the individual must place a set of felt shapes into a single board from which they were cut out. Afterward, with eyes open and the board obscured from view, the individual must draw each shape at its correct location on the board.
Sensory-Perceptual Exam	Sensory loss Hemineglect	The individual's perception of simple information in the visual, tactile, and auditory modalities is examined. To determine whether neglect is present, the investigator presents stimuli to just one side of the body or to both sides simultaneously.
WAIS-R (Wechsler Adult Intelligence Scale—Revised)	General intellectual abilities	Eleven subtests are used to assess various intellectual functions of the individual (see Table 2.5).

who believed the brain to be composed of three functional and interrelated systems: a brain-stem system that is important for overall tone and arousal, an anterior system that is important for the planning and output of behavior, and a posterior system that is important for the reception of information and its processing (Golden, 1981).

These batteries were designed to determine whether or not an individual suffered brain damage, and they are effective at discriminating patients with brain damage from neurologically intact individuals (e.g., C. J. Golden, Hammeke, & Purisch, 1978; Vega & Parsons, 1967). However, these batteries may not be as effective at discriminating between individuals with brain damage and persons with psychiatric disorders (e.g., Adams, 1980).

In addition to providing data about the absolute level of performance, test batteries can provide data on the qualitative nature of performance—that is, the strategies an individual uses to perform a task. Such information can be important in gaining a more precise understanding of the cognitive deficit.

An alternative strategy to the test-battery approach is **customized neuropsychological assessment.** In such assessment, a small set of standard tests is used (e.g., WAIS-R [Wechsler Adult Intelligence Scale—Revised], Boston Diagnostic Aphasia Exam), then more specific tests are selected to test particular hypotheses about the nature of the individual's deficits. Conceptually, the examiner uses information from the initial set of tests to generate hypotheses about the set of particular abilities that were compromised by the brain damage. Each hypothesis is evaluated with a specific neuropsychological test, and, depending on the individual's performance, the hypothesis is either pursued further with another test or abandoned (e.g., Lezak, 1983). If it is abandoned, a new hypothesis is generated and the cycle is repeated until the behavioral deficit is well characterized. In such a situation, not only the level of performance, but also the manner in which an individual performs tasks can provide important clues to the nature of the underlying deficit. Compared with a standardized battery, the individualized approach requires a more skillful examiner. Such expertise on the part of a neuropsychologist may be critical to elucidating the nature of the disorder, especially in atypical or unusual cases.

Measures of Overall Intelligence

Probably the set of tests most widely used to assess intellectual abilities is the Wechsler family of intelligence tests: the WPPSI-R (Wechsler Preschool and Primary Scale of Intelligence—Revised [Wechsler, 1989]), for children aged 3 years 7 months to 7 years 3 months; the WISC-III (Wechsler Intelligence Scale for Children—Third Edition [Wechsler, 1991]), for children aged 6 years to 16 years 11 months; the WAIS-R (Wechsler Adult Intelligence Scale—Revised [Wechsler, 1981]); and the WAIS-NI (Wechsler Adult Intelligence Scale as a Neuropsychological Instrument [E. Kaplan, Fein, Morris, & Delis, 1991]). All these tests provide an overall, or full-scale, estimate of IQ (FSIQ) as well as two major subscale scores, a verbal IQ (VIQ) and a performance IQ (PIQ), which in general break down into verbal tests and nonverbal tests, respectively. Because our discussion centers mainly on adults, rather than on children, the subscales and tests that compose the WAIS-R and WAIS-NI are presented in Table 2.5. The WISC-III and WPPSI-R contain many of the same subscales with some minor modifications and substitutions.

For many of the subscales in the Verbal portion of the test (e.g., Vocabulary and Similarities), responses are not timed but are scored according to the completeness and complexity of the answer. For example, if asked to define *commerce,* a person who answers "money" will receive 1 point, whereas a person who answers "a system of exchanging goods and currency" will receive 2 points. Likewise, if a carrot and celery are described as alike because they are both long and thin, 1 point will be given, whereas if the reply is that they are both vegetables, 2 points will be given. In contrast, on the Performance subtests, an individual must either respond within a set time to receive points, such as on Picture Completion, or receive fewer points the longer he or she takes to reach an answer (until no points are awarded after a certain time limit), such as on Object Assembly.

The WAIS-R is useful because it provides a profile of abilities, not just a single score. So, for example, poor scores on Block Design, Object Assembly, and Picture Completion along with relatively normal

Table 2.5 Wechsler Adult Intelligence Scale—Revised (WAIS-R) Subscales

Subscale	What it measures	How the ability is measured
Verbal subtests		
Vocabulary	Vocabulary	The individual defines words such as *commerce*.
Information	Factual knowledge	The individual answers questions such as "If you were to go from New York to Los Angeles, in which direction would you be traveling?"
Similarities	Abstract thinking	The individual answers questions such as "How are celery and a carrot alike?"
Comprehension	Social knowledge	The individual answers questions such as "If you were at a beach without a lifeguard and someone in the water was having trouble, what would you do?"
Digit Span	Verbal short-term memory Freedom from distractibility	The individual hears a string of digits ranging in length from three to eight and must repeat the string to the experimenter. In half the trials, the string must be repeated in the same order as presented (e.g., hear: "2-5-3" and respond: "2-5-3"), and in the other half in the opposite order (e.g., hear: "2-5-3" and respond: "3-5-2").
Arithmetic	Arithmetic abilities Freedom from distractibility	The individual solves math problems, such as the following, in his or her head without aid of pen and paper: "If it takes 18 days for 12 workers to manufacture one automobile, how many workers would you need to manufacture an automobile in 6 days?"
Performance subtests[a]		
Picture Completion	Visual processing	The individual views a series of pictures and within the allotted time must identify in each picture the critical portion that is missing (e.g., a car viewed from the back is missing taillights).
Picture Arrangement	Visual processing Sequencing	The individual views a series of frames, much like those in a comic strip, and must put them in order so that they make a coherent story.
Block Design	Visuomotor ability Spatial processing	The individual is given cubes that are red on two sides and white on two sides and two that are half red and half white (the color divide goes along the diagonal). The cubes must be arranged so that their tops match a picture.
Object Assembly	Visuomotor ability Spatial processing	The individual must perform a task similar to completing a jigsaw puzzle, except the pieces are large and have few distinctive shapes or markings.
Digit Symbol	Visuomotor ability Freedom from distractibility	The individual sees a series of symbols, each of which is associated with a number. The template is in front of the person. A series of numbers with blank boxes is given below and the corresponding symbol must be written in.

Note. The examples in this table are similar to but not actual items from the test.
[a]All these tests are timed.

performance on other tests might suggest problems in visuospatial processing. Such results are only suggestive because a specific hypothesis should be assessed more thoroughly with specialized tests designed to evaluate that particular mental function more completely.

Another useful aspect of the WAIS-R is that the test is well-normed, based on a large sample of individuals who were chosen to match the demographics of the U.S. population with regard to gender, region of the country in which they reside, and type of environment (i.e., rural or urban). In addition, the WAIS-R provides different norms for different age ranges, which is an important feature. As a person ages, the ability to perform tasks quickly is compromised (e.g., Salthouse, 1985). Therefore, because superior scores on the Performance subscales are obtained not only by performing the task correctly but also by performing it quickly, different norms are necessary for younger and older individuals to account for the slowing that accompanies aging.

Finally, the WAIS-NI, a recently released version of the WAIS-R, was designed specifically for use in neuropsychological assessment (E. Kaplan, Fein, Morris, & Delis, 1991). In this version of the test, certain items were changed to take into consideration the way in which difficulties in motor output might unduly decrease an individual's test score. Let's consider an obvious but nontrivial example. On the Information subtest, the individual must answer specific "fact" questions, such as "If you were to go from New York to Los Angeles, in which direction would you be traveling?" An individual with Broca's aphasia, a condition that makes speech output difficult but leaves language comprehension intact, might have difficulty saying "west" and thus would not receive credit for that question even if she or he knew the answer. To preclude such a situation, researchers designed the WAIS-NI so that Information questions can be given in a multiple-choice format. As a further aid, the written question and the four possible answers are shown to the patient while the examiner reads the question and the four answers aloud.

The WAIS-NI is also designed to be scored to provide the examiner with information on the strategies and approaches that a patient uses in solving problems. For example, the manner in which the individual attempts to arrange the blocks on the Block Design test can be informative. In the standard form of the test, the individual is scored only on the basis of whether he or she completes a particular design in the allotted time. However, there are numerous ways in which someone can fail to receive credit on items in this subtest. For example, some individuals receive no credit on this subtest because they perform the test too slowly or because they misorient just one of the blocks. Performance of this nature would indicate that, for the most part, visuospatial faculties are not compromised, except maybe with regard to how quickly they can be translated to motor output. However, other individuals are unable to manipulate the blocks to form the correct overall shape (e.g., a square). Such performance is suggestive of a problem in visuomotor or visuoperceptual processing.

The administration of the WAIS usually takes at least 2 hours, if not longer. If an individual is easily fatigued or if less time is available, another means of assessing general intellectual ability may be preferred. In some cases, this may involve obtaining an estimate of overall IQ by using just a subset of the WAIS-R tests, such as Similarities, Comprehension, Block Design, and Object Assembly. These subtests are used because the first two correlate well with the basic ability measured by the Verbal subscale, whereas the latter two correlate with that measured by the Performance subscale (Crawford, 1992).

Measures of Premorbid Functioning

The test batteries and tests of general intellectual abilities discussed so far can tell us how well a person is functioning. When brain injury has profound consequences, these consequences are reflected in deviant scores on such tests. Yet in other situations, the deficits may be more subtle or difficult to assess. Consider the case of a midlevel manager for a small business, who after a car accident performs about average on the WAIS-R. How can a neuropsychologist differentiate between the possibility that this person initially had average intelligence and the possibility that brain damage compromised his functioning? To make such a distinction, neuropsychologists must obtain an **estimate of premorbid functioning**—that is, a reasonable guess of how well the person was performing before the injury. Sometimes a person's educational and occupational history can serve as such a standard, but in other cases it may be inadequate. The Vocabulary subtest of the WAIS-R has been used to estimate premorbid IQ because the abilities it measures seem relatively resistant to brain damage, even that which affects many different arenas of intellectual functioning, such as Alzheimer's disease. Another test used to estimate premorbid functioning is the National Adult Reading Test (H. E. Nelson, 1982), which is an oral reading test consisting of 50 words, most of which are short and irregular, meaning they don't follow normal rules of pronunciation (e.g., *ache*). Because the words cannot be sounded out, the ability to read them indicates some previous familiarity with them and hence provides an estimate of premorbid abilities (Crawford, 1992). When estimates of premorbid intelligence are much higher than present test scores, the results suggest that the brain damage adversely affected the individual's intellectual abilities.

SUMMARY

The relationship between the functional architecture of the mind and the functional architecture of the brain can be investigated by using a variety of subject populations and techniques. Depending on the question that researchers want answered, they may focus on the neuroanatomy or neurophysiology of the brain or the way in which the brain controls behavior. Various techniques are often used in combination because converging evidence from different techniques is a powerful tool in uncovering fundamental aspects of brain-behavior relationships.

Historically, the lesion method has been one of the most prominent means of understanding brain-behavior relationships. This method is based on the inference that if damage to a particular brain region impairs the ability to perform a specific cognitive task, that brain region must be critically involved in performing the task. Additional insights into the architecture of the mind can be obtained by observing patterns of cognitive disability among individuals with lesions in different locations. When two distinct lesions have converse effects on two cognitive functions, a pattern known as a double dissociation, we can infer that these two mental operations are performed independently of each other.

Although the lesion method is powerful, it has some drawbacks. First, it does not identify all brain regions that participate in a function, but rather identifies only the areas critical for task performance. Second, an individual with brain damage may use new, clever strategies to cope with dysfunction. Such strategies may mask the role that the damaged region played in task performance. Third, the diversity of characteristics among people who sustain brain damage and the heterogeneity with which the damage is sustained may impede our ability to isolate the specific neural structures that influence a given behavior. These sources of diversity have led to a debate concerning whether single-case studies or group studies of individuals with brain damage should be used. The main argument against group studies is that the "average" performance of the group may be an amalgam, and not like that of any individual patient in the group. The argument against single-case studies is that any one person may have an atypical brain organization; therefore, the pattern observed may not generalize to the population at large. To avoid the pitfalls inherent in both these approaches, many investigators use the multiple-case study method, in which both individual and group data are examined.

Neurologically intact individuals are also helpful in investigating brain-behavior relationships. First, and most important, their performance provides a base line for comparison with the cognitive performance of individuals who sustain brain trauma. Such a comparison is most effective when the two populations are matched for demographic characteristics, such as age, gender, and socioeconomic status. Second, these individuals provide information on the basic neuroanatomical organization of the brain. Third, along with brain imaging techniques, neurologically intact individuals provide evidence on how brain structures work together normally, insights that cannot be obtained from individuals with brain damage.

Research with animals also aids in our understanding of brain-behavior relationsips in humans. Because human brains share certain characteristics with other mammalian and primate nervous systems, research in nonhuman species, especially monkeys, provides useful information. In addition, certain techniques, such as single-cell recording, that are either not feasible in humans or applicable only under highly unusual circumstances, can be performed with animals.

Two main methods are available for obtaining information about the anatomical structure of the brain: computerized axial tomography (CAT) and magnetic resonance imaging (MRI). CAT uses x-rays to provide information on the density of tissue, which can differentiate bone, blood, brain tissue, and cerebrospinal fluid (CSF). The spatial resolution of this method has been surpassed by MRI, in which magnetic fields are used to provide a picture of the distribution of specific atoms in the brain. For example, when tuned to water, MRI reveals a picture of tissue density, but when tuned to fat, it provides a picture of myelinated regions of the brain.

Various methods can provide information about the physiological functioning of the brain. Images of the brain's metabolic functioning are provided by positron emission tomography (PET) and functional MRI (fMRI), whereas information about the brain's electrical activity is provided by electroencephalography (EEG) and event-related potentials (ERPs). PET uses a radioactively tagged molecule to provide a measure of physiological function. For example, radioactively tagged oxygen, ^{15}O, is used to determine how much oxygen the brain consumes during performance of certain tasks. The advantage of PET is that brain activity can be measured for any substance that appears in a relatively high enough concentration, as long as a radioactive version of the molecule can be constructed. fMRI works either by introducing a compound with magnetic properties, such as gadolinium, into the blood system or by examining differences in the magnetic properties of blood as it changes from an oxygenated state to a deoxygenated state. One main advantage of this latter type of fMRI is that it does not require the introduction of a radioactive tag and provides better spatial and temporal resolution than that of PET.

Most recording of electrical brain activity in humans is done through a series of electrodes placed on the scalp. These electrodes detect synchronous firing in the dendrites of populations of neurons. EEG is used to examine the frequency of the electrical signal; is useful for distinguishing states of alertness, drowsiness, and sleepiness; and can be used for detecting electrical spiking that occurs in epilepsy. ERPs are electrical potentials that are recorded in response to an event and are time-locked to that event. They typically have a characteristic form, composed of specific components that occur at particular times after stimulus presentation and have a characteristic polarity (either negative or positive). Early potentials are related to sensory characteristics of the stimulus and are often used to investigate the integrity of pathways through which sensory information reaches the cortex. Late potentials have been linked to cognitive functions such as attention, memory, and the detection of semantic anomalies.

In addition to information on brain anatomy and physiology, detailed information is required for understanding behavior. Almost all cognitive skills are complicated, having many components. To link the brain to behavior requires that each of these component processes be identified and evaluated separately. The identification of component processes is aided by having a theory or a hypothesis about how a cognitive task is accomplished. In a clinical setting, test batteries are often used to survey a large number of cognitive abilities in a variety of modalities. One of the most widely used batteries is the Halstead-Reitan battery. These test batteries usually include some measure of general intellectual ability. The most widely used tests of general intellectual ability are the Wechsler family of tests, including the WAIS-R, the WAIS-NI, the WISC-III, and the WPPSI-R, which allow for the assessment of intellectual abilities in individuals ranging from young children to older adults. In some cases, more specific tests, such as those measuring memory, attention, spatial ability, and abstract reasoning, are used to elucidate a more fine-grained profile of an individual's strengths and weaknesses. When deficits are subtle, other tests are used to obtain an estimate of the level at which an individual was functioning prior to injury, so that the degree to which brain damage has compromised functioning can be determined.

*H*emispheric *S*pecialization

Close to the edge, a little off center,

More than a dreamer, a real believer,

Visual but I take heart,

I've been born right brained in a left brain world, it's true!

—Carrie Newcomer, folksinger, 1991[1]

As the lyrics to the song on the opening page of this chapter attest, it is common knowledge that the cerebral hemispheres are specialized for different aspects of cognitive and emotional functioning. We should not be surprised that the brain's functions differ left and right, because as we learned in chapter 1, they also differ in the anterior-posterior and dorsal-ventral dimensions. The difference between the hemispheres in their processing is often referred to as **hemispheric specialization,** or **lateralization of function.**

BASICS OF HEMISPHERIC SPECIALIZATION

Although at first glance the hemispheres of the brain look like mirror images, this impression is deceiving in some important ways. In actuality, the hemispheres are distinct with regard to neuroanatomy, neurochemistry, and, most important, function. Many asymmetries in the neuroanatomy of the cerebral hemispheres have been noted. The right frontal lobe tends to extend farther forward toward the skull and is wider than the left frontal lobe, whereas the left occipital lobe extends farther back toward the skull and is wider than the right occipital lobe (e.g., Galaburda, LeMay, Kemper, & Geschwind, 1978) (Figure 3.1A). In most individuals, the Sylvian fissure extends farther in the horizontal dimension in the left hemisphere but takes more of an upward turn in the right hemisphere (Hochberg & LeMay, 1975; Rubens, Mahowald, & Hutton, 1976) (Figure 3.1B). This asymmetry has a long evolutionary history, having been observed in a Neanderthal fossil 60,000 years old (LeMay, 1976) and in australopithecine fossils dating back as far as 3.5 million years (Holloway, 1980). In addition, the region of the brain at the end of the Sylvian fissure in the temporal lobe, known as the **planum temporale** (i.e., temporal plane), usually is larger on the left than on the right, in fact, sometimes as much as 10 times larger (Geschwind & Levitsky, 1968) (Figure 3.1C).

[1] By Carrie Newcomer from ''Right Brain Born (in a Left Brained World)'' on *Visions and Dreams* (Philo Records, 1995). Reprinted with permission.

91

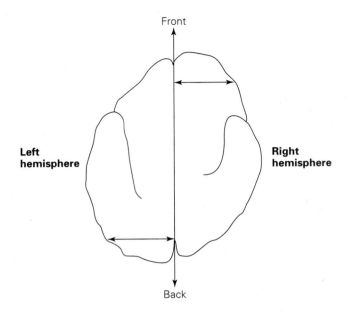

A

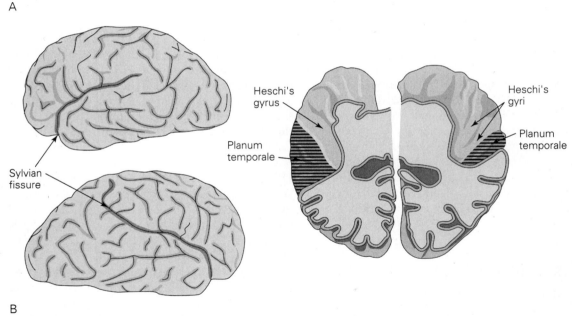

B

Figure 3.1 · Some anatomical asymmetries of the human brain.
(A) The right frontal region typically extends farther forward and is wider than the left frontal region, whereas for the occipital region the opposite is true: This region of the left hemisphere extends farther back and is wider. (B) The Sylvian fissure extends farther horizontally in the left hemisphere (top), whereas in the right hemisphere (bottom), it takes more of an upward turn. (C) The planum temporale, which can be clearly seen after the cortical tissue above the Sylvian fissure, as is shown by the solid line in (B), is removed, is typically larger on the left than on the right. (*Note.* A, Adapted from Hellige, 1993a, p. 116; B & C, Adapted from Kolb & Whishaw, 1990, p. 349.)

These anatomical asymmetries are of interest because they may account for some hemispheric differences in functioning. For example, the planum temporale of the left hemisphere is an area that has been implicated since the late 1800s as being important in language comprehension, and asymmetry of this region, as measured by magnetic resonance imaging (MRI), is related to lateralization for language (Foundas et al., 1994). Another region of the brain that differs between the hemispheres is the frontal opercular area (see Figure 1.14A). A portion of this region in the left hemisphere, Broca's area, is believed to be important for speech output (Falzi, Perrone, & Vignolo, 1982) and exhibits greater branching of dendrites than in the homologous region of the right hemisphere (Scheibel, 1984). Because animals raised in complex (rather than simpler) environments also exhibit greater dendritic branching (Greenough, 1975), the more elaborated dendrites of cells in this region of the left hemisphere may indicate that they have a larger or more specialized processing capacity. Another brain region, Brodmann's area 39 (see Figure 1.16A), which is approximately akin to the angular gyrus (see Figure 1.14A), is larger on the left than on the right side of the brain, a finding consistent with the specialization of this region in the left hemisphere for reading. In contrast, a more dorsal parietal area, which is hypothesized to be important for spatial processing, is larger on the right than on the left (Eidelberg & Galaburda, 1984).

Neurochemical differences between the hemispheres also abound, mainly expressed as asymmetries in neurotransmitter concentrations. For example, larger concentrations of norepinephrine can be found in certain regions of the right thalamus than in the left (Oke, Keller, Mefford, & Adams, 1978). A different brain region, the globus pallidus (which, as we learned in chapter 1, is a portion of the basal ganglia), has not only greater concentrations of dopamine in the left than in the right (Glick, Ross, & Hough, 1982), but also more terminals for the reception of dopamine in the left than in the right (Wagner et al., 1983). Because dopamine and norepinephrine have different effects on behavior, these findings have led to the hypothesis that mental processes more dependent on dopamine, such as those that require a readiness for action, are lateralized to the left hemisphere. In contrast, processes more dependent on norepinephrine, such as those that aid a person in orienting toward new or novel stimuli, are lateralized to the right hemisphere (D. Tucker & Williamson, 1984).

Most dramatic, however, are the differences in function between the hemispheres, a distinction that was first observed in the late 1800s. We now turn back the pages of time to explore how the distinct specialization of each hemisphere was uncovered.

Historical Perspective

The idea that the hemispheres had different functions first caught the attention of the scientific community in the 1860s, when Paul Broca, a French neurologist and anthropologist, provided evidence from numerous case studies that the left hemisphere, but not the right, was critical in language processing. (A similar observation in the 1830s by a French country doctor, Marc Dax, went virtually unnoticed, being neither as systematically pursued nor presented to as wide a scientific audience as was Broca's.) The imagination of the scientific community may have been captured by Broca's findings, in part, because a hot topic of scientific inquiry in the late 19th century was the relationship between brain anatomy and mental function. Broca's discovery was sparked by a patient he met on his rounds who had an unusual syndrome. The man could utter only the syllable "tan," yet he could understand language because he could follow simple verbal commands. His problem was specific to speech output in that he did not exhibit paralysis of the vocal musculature or the vocal tract. When the man died relatively soon thereafter, Broca autopsied his brain and noticed that a specific region of the left hemisphere was damaged. Broca then proceeded to accumulate a small series of brains from individuals who had the same type of language problem. He noticed that in each case the damage was restricted to the same brain region, but more important, it was always located in the left hemisphere. Furthermore, individuals with damage to the analogous area of the right hemisphere displayed no difficulties in language.

The importance of the left hemisphere for language processing was confirmed by other neurologists such as Karl Wernicke, who observed individuals with the converse syndrome of that discovered by Broca. Wernicke noticed that damage to yet another region of the left hemisphere caused individuals to lose almost all ability to comprehend language, although they retained their ability to speak fluently (even though what they said made little or no sense). Like Broca, he found that this syndrome occurred only after left-hemisphere damage.

By the end of the 1860s, the English neurologist John Hughlings Jackson had introduced the idea of **cerebral dominance** (although he had not named it as such), which is the idea that one hemisphere dominates or leads mental function. Because at the time language was considered to be the quintessential mental act (following the logic that language equals thought), the left hemisphere was viewed as the dominant hemisphere. As a result, even today you may find a research article in which the right hemisphere is referred to as the "nondominant hemisphere." Although in the late 1800s, Jackson had documented the deficits that occur after right-hemisphere damage, these findings were generally overlooked and ignored. The prevailing thought was that the right hemisphere was important only for receiving sensory information from the left side of space and for controlling motor movement of the left half of the body. In this view, the right hemisphere was like a spare tire, available in case the left hemisphere sustained damage, but having few functions of its own (see Springer & Deutsch, 1993, for a discussion of the history of these ideas).

Building on a groundwork laid in the 1930s, research in the late 1950s and early 1960s dramatically changed scientists' conceptions of the functioning of the hemispheres, revealing each to have its own specialization. Research performed by Brenda Milner and colleagues at the Montreal Neurological Institute demonstrated that the surgical removal of temporal regions of the right hemisphere for the relief of epilepsy did have consequences,

such as disrupting memory for unfamiliar faces and other stimuli that could not be easily named (e.g., B. Milner, 1968). Other evidence for the role of the right hemisphere in specific tasks was provided by research performed by Henri Hécaen and colleagues in France (e.g., Hécaen, 1962) and by Arthur Benton and colleagues at the University of Iowa (e.g., A. L. Benton, 1969). Probably the most dramatic demonstration of differences in function between the hemispheres, however, came from the research of Roger Sperry and associates at the California Institute of Technology, who tested the competency of each hemisphere in a unique set of patients (e.g., Sperry, 1974). The findings from this research were so definitive and compelling that they were cited as part of the reason that Sperry was awarded the Nobel Prize for Physiology and Medicine in 1981. We turn next to this body of research.

Studies of Patients With the Split-Brain Syndrome

Sperry came to demonstrate the distinct specializations of each cerebral hemisphere because he had been attempting to elucidate the function of the **corpus callosum,** the massive neural tract of more than 250 million nerve fibers that connects the hemispheres. By studying this structure in cats and monkeys, he had found it to be critical in the transfer of information between the hemispheres of the brain. Around the same time, the neurosurgeons Joseph Bogen and Philip Vogel were severing the corpus callosum in a small group of people for a different reason—to control intractable epileptic seizures. These seizures did not diminish with anticonvulsant medication and were so frequent and severe as to make any semblance of a normal life impossible, and in some cases, they had life-threatening consequences. The surgical procedure performed by Bogen and Vogel became known as the **split-brain procedure** because it severed the primary route by which the left and right cerebral hemispheres interact, thereby splitting the brain in half. This procedure is also sometimes referred to as *commissurotomy* because it severs the corpus callosum, one of the brain's *commissures* (a name for brain structures that connect the hemispheres). Figure 3.2 illustrates the nature of the split-brain procedure.

Because severing the callosum precludes the hemispheres from communicating with each other at the cortical level, the procedure provides an excellent means of testing the processing capabilities of each hemisphere individually. Through specific techniques to be discussed shortly, the competency of each hemisphere to perform a large variety of tasks could be established. In a person with an intact callosum, the hemispheres can coordinate their processing, shuttling information back and forth with great rapidity (in ≤20 ms) over millions of nerve fibers. However, with the callosum severed, infor-

mation initially directed to one hemisphere cannot be sent to the other; essentially, the information is trapped within a hemisphere. By taking advantage of the neuroanatomical structure of the human nervous system, Sperry and colleagues could direct information to only one hemisphere and then assess its competence to process that information.

Basic Findings

Because the observations of Broca and subsequent neurologists suggested that the left hemisphere was dominant for speech output, one of Sperry and colleagues' first goals was to determine lateralization of speech output in the patients with split-brain syndrome. To do so, these researchers asked the

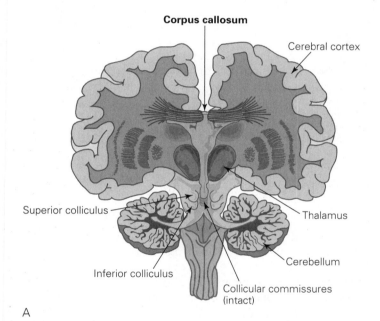

A

Figure 3.2   The split-brain procedure.
(A) In this procedure, the hemispheres of the brain are separated, mainly by cutting the corpus callosum. With this pathway severed, information from one cerebral hemisphere cannot be transferred to the other. (B) The surgery does not affect the crossover of sensory and motor information from one side of the body to the opposite side of the brain because these crossovers occur before information reaches the cerebral cortex. (*Note.* B, Adapted from Sperry, 1964.)

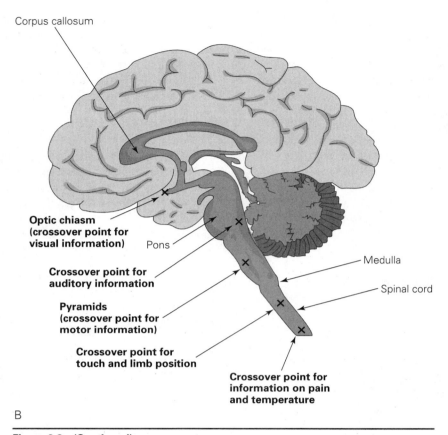

Corpus callosum

**Optic chiasm
(crossover point for
visual information)**

Pons

**Crossover point for
auditory information**

**Pyramids
(crossover point for
motor information)**

**Crossover point for
touch and limb position**

**Crossover point for
information on pain
and temperature**

Medulla

Spinal cord

B

Figure 3.2   (Continued)

patients to feel objects with just one hand, either the left or the right. The objects were hidden from view so that the only source of information about them was from the tactile domain. With this procedure, objects felt by a given hand are perceived exclusively by the contralateral hemisphere. Thus, objects felt by the right hand of a patient with split-brain syndrome would be perceived only by the left hemisphere and those felt by the left hand would be perceived only by the right hemisphere.

The patients were able to name the objects placed in the right hand but not those placed in the left hand. At this point, the researchers were faced with two possible explanations for their results. One was

that the right hemisphere was indeed a stupid spare tire with little knowledge of the world, unable to identify even simple objects. The other was that, as Broca suggested 100 years earlier, only the left hemisphere can control speech output. Hence, when asked about the object in the left hand, the right hemisphere would be unable to reply because it is incapable of speaking, and the left hemisphere would respond appropriately by saying that it didn't know what the object was because it hadn't perceived it (remember, the object was felt only by the left hand).

To distinguish between these possibilities, the researchers changed the task so that the patient had to demonstrate the correct use of familiar objects, such as pencils, cigarettes, and drinking glasses. If the right hemisphere does know about the world but is merely mute, it should be able to demonstrate correctly the use of objects placed in the left hand, which it controls. In contrast, if the right hemisphere is only a spare tire, it should be dumbfounded when asked how to use the object. The researchers found that objects placed in the left hand could be used correctly, an indication that the right hemisphere does have knowledge about the world (Gazzaniga, Bogen, & Sperry, 1962).

Although the right hemisphere has been revealed to be much more than a spare tire, its linguistic capacity is somewhat limited. The right hemisphere can read most concrete words (that is, words that represent real objects in the world) and can make simple grammatical comparisons (e.g., differentiate between "The boy went to the store" vs. "The boy did not go to the store") (e.g., E. Zaidel, 1990). Yet it does not seem to possess many language abilities. Not only can't the right hemisphere control speech output, but it also cannot process more complicated grammatical constructions, such as long, nonredundant sentences in which word order is important (e.g., "The dog that the cat chased ran under the table behind the garage that had been condemned by the sheriff last week") (E. Zaidel, 1978). It also seems to be unable to break down words into their constituent sounds, a task known as *phonologic processing,* which is required to determine whether two words rhyme (e.g., Levy & C. Trevarthen, 1977). The exact degree of right-hemisphere competence for language remains an issue of some debate (see, for example, the contrasting viewpoints of Gazzaniga, 1983a,b, vs. Levy, 1983, and E. Zaidel, 1983b).

Because the right hemisphere's language was revealed to be relatively poor in the patients with the split-brain syndrome, researchers began to focus their attention on what the right hemisphere *could* do. As they performed more experiments, they found that they could describe the tasks at which the right hemisphere excelled as spatial or nonverbal in nature. For example, when given the Block De-

sign subtest of the Wechsler Adult Intelligence Scale—Revised (WAIS-R) (see page 85, chapter 2), in which blocks must be arranged to form a pattern, the right hand performed in a hapless and disorganized manner. In contrast, the left hand performed the task rapidly and accurately. In addition, the left hand could depict three-dimensional structures in a two-dimensional plane, such as is required when a cube must be drawn on a piece of paper, but the right hand could not (Gazzaniga, 1970). On the basis of such findings, some researchers suggested that the right hemisphere was specialized for manipulative or motor aspects of spatial processing (Gazzaniga & LeDoux, 1978).

However, other studies revealed that the right hemisphere exhibited a superiority on spatial tasks even when no manual manipulation was required. In a series of studies, patients with the split-brain syndrome were asked to view chimeric figures (i.e., figures composed of two different objects) (Figure 3.3). Although these figures seem strange to us, the hemispheres of patients with the split-brain syndrome do not have a similar perception. The hemispheres of such patients are unaware that they are viewing different things because each hemisphere receives only one half-item, whose identity cannot be communicated to the other hemisphere.

To preclude the need for manual manipulation, the researchers tested each hemisphere's competence by having the contralateral hand point to the object that was just viewed. When the left hand (controlled by the right hemisphere) had to choose the face it had just viewed, it pointed to the face in the left visual field (LVF) (which was information received by the right hemisphere) and did so with a high degree of accuracy. In contrast, when the left hemisphere was required to respond (either through pointing or a vocal response), performance was much poorer. This pattern was found not only for real-world objects, such as faces, but also for abstract forms (Levy, Trevarthen, & Sperry, 1972). Therefore, the results of research with patients with the split-brain syndrome demonstrated the complementarity of the hemispheres for different aspects of mental functioning. The left is superior at pro-

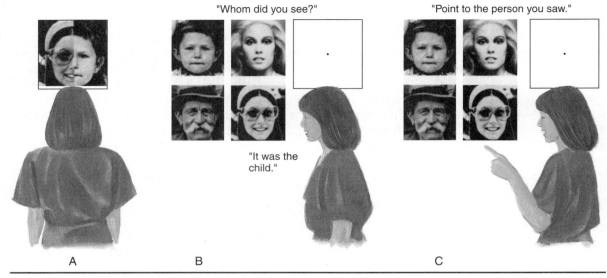

"Whom did you see?"

"Point to the person you saw."

"It was the child."

A   B   C

Figure 3.3 Examining the competency of each hemisphere in a patient with split-brain syndrome.
(A) An example of a chimeric stimulus, composed of two half-faces, used with patients with split-brain syndrome.
(B) When asked to indicate verbally which face was seen (a task under control of the left hemisphere), the patient
names the child, whose picture was located in the right visual field. In such cases, accuracy is not high. (C) When
asked to use the left hand to point to the face that was seen (a task under control of the right hemisphere), the patient points to the picture that was in the left visual field. Under these conditions, accuracy is higher, a finding that indicates a right-hemisphere superiority for face-recognition processing. (*Note.* From Levy, Trevarthan, & Sperry,
1972.)

cessing verbal material, but the right has expertise
in the spatial domain.

Caveats in Interpretation

Although studies of patients with the split-brain
syndrome provide fascinating, compelling, and dramatic data, we must keep certain caveats in mind
when interpreting these results. One potential problem is that the brains of these patients may not
be typical. To sever the corpus callosum, which is
located deep within the longitudinal fissure (see
Figure 3.2), the surgeon must *retract* (pull back)
the hemispheres, which provides the opportunity
for damage to regions other than the callosum. Furthermore, the brain organization of these patients
may be unusual as a result of their long-standing
history of epileptic seizures. A second problem is
that investigations with these patients have typically
used a limited population of individuals, and sig-

nificant variations in performance can occur among
these individuals. The population of patients who
have been extensively tested is small (only about
five to seven) because most individuals who undergo
split-brain surgery have IQs so low as to preclude
them from participating in research studies. Usually,
no more than two or three individuals are included
in a single study (see page 57, chapter 2, for a
discussion on the potential problems in studies with
so few patients). Further compounding this problem, results from these patients can sometimes be
difficult to interpret because different patients may
exhibit different patterns of performance. For example, the patients vary not only in the degree to which
their hemispheres truly act independently of each
other (Sergent, 1990), but also in the competency
of the right hemisphere for language (Sidtis et al.,
1981). Hence, we may need to be careful not to
overgeneralize when drawing conclusions from the
results of studies of patients with the split-brain syndrome.

Despite the issues just raised, some striking and consistent results observed with these patients have clearly demonstrated hemispheric specialization of function. Furthermore, long before the advent of imaging techniques, these patients provided a means of examining hemispheric differences in a relatively intact, but isolated, hemisphere. In contrast, observing patients whose damage is restricted to a single hemisphere, a popular approach for determining hemispheric asymmetries, has the same difficulties as any other study involving the lesion method (see page 55, chapter 2): It cannot reveal how an intact hemisphere functions, but rather allows us to observe only how the rest of the brain functions when portions of one hemisphere are damaged. Hence, because studies of patients with split-brain syndrome provide information on the functioning of a reasonably intact hemisphere, they are a powerful tool in our attempts to understand asymmetry of function in the human brain.

Research With Individuals With Lateralized Lesions

While dramatic demonstrations of lateralization of function were being provided by split-brain research, studies with other neurological patients were also revealing the distinct capabilities of the hemispheres. Although scientists knew for some time that left-hemisphere lesions compromise language functioning, especially speech output, other methods provided converging evidence. One such method is the **Wada technique,** which is used to determine the hemisphere responsible for speech output in patients about to undergo tissue removal to control epileptic seizures. Although the left hemisphere is almost always dominant (except in left-handers), the surgeon wants to know unequivocally which hemisphere is dominant for speech before beginning surgery. In this technique, a barbiturate is injected into one of the carotid arteries (which lead from the heart to the brain). Because the blood supply to the brain is unilateral, the barbiturate anesthetizes only one hemisphere. The onset of the barbiturate's effect can be readily detected because, shortly after injection, it causes paralysis on the con-

tralateral side of the body. At this point, the neuropsychologist determines whether the individual can speak. If the person is mute, the anesthetized hemisphere is inferred to be responsible for speech output. This determination must be made quickly, in about 5 min, because after that point the barbiturate reaches the other side of the brain and the individual becomes groggy. Typically, the procedure is repeated some time later, except then the opposite hemisphere is anesthetized to determine its contribution, if any, to speech output. Research with this method has revealed that the left hemisphere is dominant for speech in 95% of right-handers, a finding consistent with that observed in patients who sustain unilateral brain damage (Rasmussen & Milner, 1977b).

In addition to confirming the role of the left hemisphere in language functions, studies also demonstrated that right-hemisphere lesions have different consequences than those of left-hemisphere lesions. Whereas left-hemisphere lesions disrupt language-related processing, right-hemisphere lesions disrupt many spatial and visuospatial abilities. For example, individuals with right-hemisphere damage are poor at making judgments about line orientation (A. L. Benton, Hannay, & Varney, 1975), have difficulty recognizing objects that are not in a standard or canonical form (Warrington & Taylor, 1973), and are poor at distinguishing between faces that were previously viewed and those that were not (Yin, 1970). In addition, patients with right-hemisphere damage have difficulty with distinguishing different pitches of sound or tones of voice (E. D. Ross, 1981) and cannot interpret the emotional expression of faces (Bowers, Bauer, Coslett, & Heilman, 1985). This body of research revealed the right hemisphere to have cognitive abilities equally sophisticated to those of the left hemisphere, albeit in nonverbal, nonlinguistic domains.

Research With Neurologically Intact Individuals

Because for most sensory modalities the organization of the human nervous system is such that information from one sensory half-world is directed initially to the primary sensory regions of the opposite hemisphere, examination of hemispheric differences in neurologically intact individuals is relatively easy. The large body of evidence in this regard provides a third converging approach that illustrates the specialization of the hemispheres for different cognitive and emotional processes. Before discussing this evidence further, though, we first turn to a discussion of the methods used to investigate lateralization of function.

Methods

Lateralization of function is mainly investigated in the visual, auditory, and tactile modalities. Measuring hemispheric differences in the visual modality takes advantage of the arrangement of the neural pathways from the eye to the brain (see Figure 1.21). Most critical is the fact that information in the right visual field (RVF) is directed to the left half of both eyes but eventually projects exclusively to the primary visual cortex of the left hemisphere. Conversely, information presented in the LVF is directed to the right half of both eyes but then eventually projects exclusively to the primary visual cortex of the right hemisphere. Because information is presented separately in each visual field, this technique is often referred to as the **divided visual field technique.**

In divided visual field studies, two methods of presentation can be used: bilateral and unilateral. In **bilateral presentation,** two items are presented, one in each visual field. In **unilateral presentation,** a single item is presented entirely within one visual field. Regardless of the type of presentation, we infer how well each hemisphere can process information by comparing performance for items presented in the RVF with performance for items presented in the LVF. Performance is generally measured by either the speed or the accuracy of responding. For example, if the recall of information is, on average, superior when presented in the RVF than when presented in the LVF, the left hemisphere is assumed to be specialized for processing that type of information. In contrast, an advantage for information presented in the LVF is considered indicative of right-hemisphere specialization. Note that what

we actually observe is an asymmetry in the perception of information depending on which part of the sensory system we stimulate. Hence, these differences in performance are often referred to as **perceptual asymmetries.** Because different parts of the sensory system project to different hemispheres, the perceptual asymmetries are then interpreted as reflecting hemispheric differences.

One constraint imposed by the divided visual field technique is that information must be presented for 200 ms (one fifth of a second) or less because this is the amount of time required to move the eyes from one position to another. Only if the eyes are maintaining fixation on a single point will the region of space that constitutes the RVF and the LVF stay static. If an individual's eyes move to a new fixation point, different information will fall into each visual field and hence different information will be projected to each hemisphere than that which was intended by the researcher. By having a person fixate on a central point and precluding eye movements, the investigator can ensure that information presented in the RVF will project initially to the left hemisphere and that information presented in the LVF will project initially to the right hemisphere. To ensure that the information presented is initially received by only one hemisphere, the researcher usually positions stimuli somewhat lateral (at least 1 or 2 degrees) from midline so that they fall exclusively within one visual field even if the individual is slightly off fixation. (The divided visual field technique is also sometimes referred to as *tachistoscopic presentation* from the days before personal computers, when a machine called a *tachistoscope* and timers were used to control precisely the temporal duration of displays.)

Similar logic can be applied to investigate hemispheric differences in the somatosensory modality. In **dichaptic presentation,** a person is asked first to feel two items simultaneously, one in each hand, and then to identify these items in some manner (e.g., Witelson, 1974). Often, the items are behind a screen or the person is blindfolded so that information can be obtained only from the somatosensory modality and not other modalities (e.g., through vision). Because tactile information from the left side of the body projects to the primary somatosensory region of the right hemisphere, an advantage in processing information presented to the left hand is generally interpreted as a right-hemisphere superiority for the task. Likewise, an advantage in processing information presented to the right hand is generally interpreted as a left-hemisphere superiority for the task.

Examining hemispheric differences in the auditory modality is a bit more complicated. As you should remember from chapter 1, information from each ear connects both to the primary auditory cortex of the contralateral hemisphere and to the primary auditory cortex of the ipsilateral hemisphere. If each ear connects to both hemispheres, how are we to interpret differences in the ability to report information from each ear? Under special conditions known as **dichotic presentation** the situation becomes simplified. In dichotic presentation, *different* information is presented simultaneously to each ear so that each hemisphere receives two competing pieces of information, one from the ipsilateral ear and one from the contralateral ear. Because of this competition, information traveling to a hemisphere from the ipsilateral ear is suppressed relative to information from the contralateral ear (B. Milner, Taylor, & Sperry, 1968). Thus, information from the right ear is processed almost entirely by the left hemisphere and information from the left ear is processed almost entirely by the right hemisphere (Figure 3.4). In dichotic studies, individuals are typically asked to report what they heard in one ear or what they heard in both ears. In other situations, they are asked to monitor for a specific target item and to press a button as soon as they hear it.

Research Findings

Empirical studies examining perceptual asymmetries have served as fertile ground for revealing differences in the processing capabilities of the hemispheres. Because these studies are relatively simple to undertake and can be performed on a variety of neurologically intact individuals, thousands of such studies have been performed. As a gross generalization, when information of a verbal nature must be processed, performance is superior when it is directed initially to primary sensory regions of the left hemisphere. In contrast, when certain kinds of nonverbal information must be processed, an advantage in processing occurs when information is directed initially to primary sensory regions of the right hemisphere. For example, in the visual modality, a RVF (or left-hemisphere) advantage is usually observed for words (e.g., S. C. Levine & Banich, 1982) and a LVF (or right-hemisphere) advantage for faces (S. C. Levine, Banich, & Koch-Weser, 1988). In the tactile modality, a right-hand advantage is found for identifying letters drawn in the palm (e.g., O'Boyle, Van Wyhe-Lawler, & Miller, 1987) and for identifying dichaptically presented letters made of sandpaper (Gibson & Bryden, 1983). In contrast, when individuals must feel two complex shapes simultaneously and match them to a visual array (e.g., Witelson, 1974) or otherwise identify them (e.g., Gibson & Bryden, 1983), a left-hand advantage is found. In the auditory modality, the report of or response to words (e.g., Kimura, 1967) and other speech sounds (e.g., Studdert-Kennedy & Shankweiler, 1970) is more accurate or faster when the words or sounds are presented to the right ear than when they are presented to the left ear. In contrast, the report of or reactions to nonverbal material, such as animal noises, sounds in the environment (e.g., doors opening, train whistles), and musical tones, are better processed when the material is presented to the left ear (e.g., H. W. Gordon, 1980).

The advantage in performance generally observed under divided visual field, dichaptic, or dichotic conditions is on the order of a 10% difference in accuracy and usually between a 20- and a 100-ms difference in speed of response. Although these differences may seem small, they are actually impressive if you consider that they occur even though the hemispheres are connected by the 250 million nerve fibers of the corpus callosum. How do such differences in the accuracy and speed of processing by each hemisphere arise in the face of such a vast network of interconnections between the hemispheres? No single account is agreed upon, but researchers have a number of ideas about how percep-

Spoken response: "Cat"

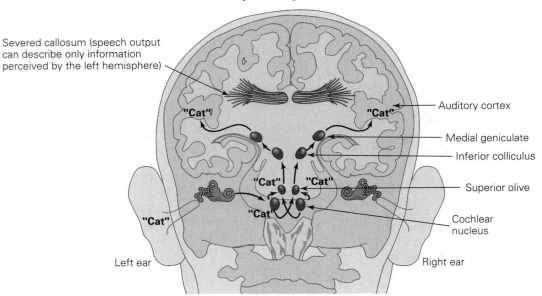

Severed callosum (speech output can describe only information perceived by the left hemisphere)

Auditory cortex

Medial geniculate

Inferior colliculus

Superior olive

Cochlear nucleus

Left ear

Right ear

A

Spoken response: "Dog"

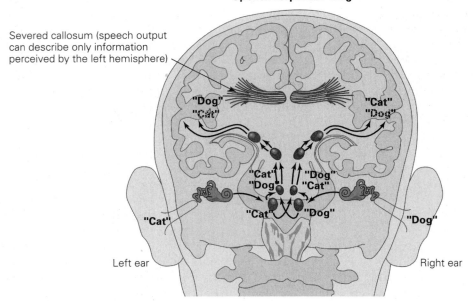

Severed callosum (speech output can describe only information perceived by the left hemisphere)

Left ear

Right ear

B

tual asymmetries are generated in neurologically intact individuals. One idea, referred to as the **direct access theory,** involves the assumption that when a hemisphere receives sensory information, it processes it. When information is received by the hemisphere less suited to a task, performance is poorer than if it is received by the hemisphere better suited to the task. Another idea, the **callosal relay model,** is based on the assumption that when information is received by the hemisphere less suited for a given task, the information is transferred to the opposite hemisphere. This callosal transfer is believed to degrade the information and lead to poorer performance than if the information is received by the hemisphere more suited to the task (see E. Zaidel, 1983a, for a discussion of these issues).

A different type of model, known as the **activating-orienting model,** suggests that an attentional set or bias can contribute to perceptual asymmetries (Kinsbourne, 1975). According to this theory, engaging in a particular type of process (e.g., word recognition) causes greater activation in the hemisphere best suited to the task (e.g., the left hemisphere). This increased activity is thought to result in an attentional bias to the side of space contralateral to the more active hemisphere (i.e., the right side), making perceptual information on that side of space more salient and allowing it to be processed in a superior manner. Evidence for this model comes from studies in which larger visual field advantages are observed on tasks when they have just been preceded by a task that activates the same hemisphere rather than the opposite hemisphere (e.g., a larger LVF advantage is observed on a face task when preceded by a face task than when preceded by a word task) (Klein, Moscovitch, & Vigna, 1976).

CHARACTERIZATION OF HEMISPHERE DIFFERENCES

Until this point, we implied that the hemispheres are specialized for processing different types of material: verbal versus nonverbal. Yet the situation isn't quite so simple. In fact, a fair amount of debate has been generated regarding how to best characterize the differences in processing between the cerebral hemispheres. Some researchers posit that the hemispheres differ in their ability to process basic sensory features of information. These researchers assume that such basic asymmetries in sensory processing underlie hemispheric differences for more complicated cognitive tasks. Another group of theorists suggests that the hemispheres differ not so much in *what* type of information they process, but rather in *how* they process information. These theorists suggest that the hemispheres have different modes of processing (e.g., holistic vs. piecemeal) and that certain material or tasks are better handled by one mode than the other. We now examine these two classes of theories regarding hemispheric specialization.

Differences in Sensitivity to Particular Sensory Features

One group of theorists argues that the differences in hemispheric specialization arise early in processing, soon after receipt of sensory information, because the hemispheres differ in their ability to process basic sensory attributes of stimuli. One influential theory of this sort, the **spatial frequency hypothesis,** proposes that the hemispheres differ in their ability to process a particular attribute of visual in-

←

Figure 3.4 Ipsilateral suppression in the dichotic listening technique.
(A) Under conditions of monaural stimulation (a stimulus presented to one ear), the left hemisphere of a patient with split-brain syndrome can name, with a high degree of accuracy, the word that was presented monaurally in the left ear. This ability must rely on the use of ipsilateral auditory fibers from the left ear to the left hemisphere because only the left hemisphere can produce speech output and information received by the right hemisphere cannot be transferred to the left. (B) Under conditions of dichotic stimulation, the patient with split-brain syndrome cannot report both words. Only the word presented to the right ear, which projects contralaterally to the left hemisphere, can be reported with a high degree of accuracy. The word presented in the left ear is not reported because of the suppression of information carried through ipsilateral fibers. (*Note.* Adapted from Kalat, 1992, p. 201.)

A

Figure 3.5 Information of varying spatial frequency.
(A) Examples of three pieces of information with different spatial frequencies. The frequency increases from top to bottom. (B) A plot of the spatial frequency of each of the three stimuli in (A). Spatial frequency describes how
quickly visual information switches from black to white. Note that the spatial
frequency of the middle row is twice that of the top row and half that of the
bottom row. The right hemisphere is posited to be superior at processing information of relatively lower spatial frequency, whereas the left hemisphere
is believed to be superior at processing information of relatively higher spatial frequency. (*Note.* A, Adapted from Hellige, 1993, p. 80.)

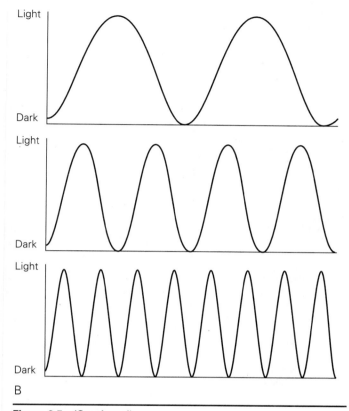

Figure 3.5 (Continued)

formation, known as *spatial frequency* (e.g., Sergent, 1983). Visual information has a low spatial frequency if, over a given expanse of space, it oscillates slowly from black to white. In contrast, it has a high spatial frequency if information switches quickly from black to white. To obtain a better appreciation of visual information of high spatial frequency versus that of low spatial frequency, look at Figure 3.5. Visual information of low spatial frequency generally provides the broad outline of form without much detail. You can get a poor approximation of what low spatial frequency information is by squinting your eyes and looking at this page. Notice that you can perceive broad general forms but not details. Visual information of high spatial frequency provides the details.

Sergent's theory hypothesizes that the right hemisphere is more adept at processing low spatial frequency, whereas the left hemisphere is specialized for processing high spatial frequency. This distinction is somewhat akin to an earlier suggestion that in general the right hemisphere is specialized for coarse coding of information, whereas the left is specialized for fine coding of information (Semmes, 1968). To understand how differences in the processing of visual information of varying spatial frequencies might cause differences on more cognitively complicated tasks, let's consider the example of a face-processing task in which an individual decides whether two faces are identical. If the faces were to differ by only one feature, a left-hemisphere advantage would be observed because detailed high spatial frequency information is required to differentiate between two similar faces. In contrast, if the faces were substantially different, a right-hemisphere advantage would emerge because low spatial

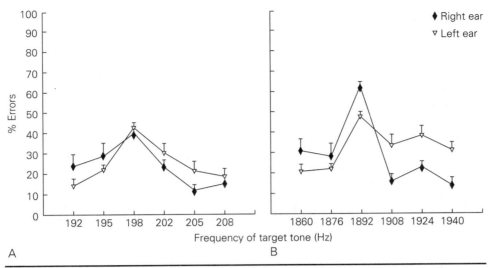

Figure 3.6 Hemispheric differences for the processing of different auditory frequencies.
The percentage of errors in the tone-judgment task for the set of low-tone targets (left) and
the set of high-tone targets (right). For relatively lower tones within both sets (192–198 Hz,
and 1860–1892 Hz), fewer errors are made on left-ear trials (open inverted triangles) than on
right-ear trials (solid diamonds). In contrast, for the relatively higher tones within each set
(202–208 Hz, and 1908–1940 Hz), right-ear performance is superior. This pattern of performance indicates that the right hemisphere is specialized for processing information of relatively lower (rather than absolutely lower) frequency and the left for processing information of
relatively higher frequency. (*Note.* Adapted from Ivry & Lebby, 1993, p. 42.)

frequency information is best suited to determine
whether the overall forms of the faces are identical
(e.g., Sergent, 1985).

Results of investigations of the spatial frequency
hypothesis have been equivocal; some, but certainly
not all, studies have yielded results consistent with
its predictions (see Christman, 1989, for a review).
The discrepancies among some of these studies may
have occurred because more recent research suggests that hemispheric differences are driven by the
relative, rather than the *absolute,* spatial frequency
of visual information. What is important, then, is
not whether the spatial frequency of information is
high or low on an absolute scale, but rather what the
relative spatial frequency of information is within a
given context (Kitterle, Hellige, & Christman,
1992).

A recent study illustrates this phenomenon and
demonstrates how these effects generalize to the

auditory modality as well (Ivry & Lebby, 1993). In
this study, each participant decided whether a target
tone was "higher" or "lower" than the average of
all the tones within a set. In one set of trials, all the
target items were of low frequency (e.g., 192–208
Hz) (Figure 3.6A). In another set of trials, all the
target items were of high frequency (e.g., 1860–
1940 Hz) (Figure 3.6B). If absolute frequency of
information dictates hemispheric differences, a left-
ear advantage (indicative of right-hemisphere superiority for the task) should be observed for detection
of all target items (192–208 Hz) in the Low-Tone
Set, and a right-ear advantage (indicative of left-
hemisphere superiority) should be observed for all
items (1860–1940 Hz) in the High-Tone Set. In
contrast, if *relative* frequency is important, a different pattern should be observed: A left-ear advantage
(indicative of right-hemisphere superiority) should
be observed for low tones within *each* set (i.e., 192–

198 Hz, and 1860–1892 Hz), and a right-ear advantage should be found for the high tones within *each* set (i.e., 202–208 Hz, and 1908–1940 Hz). As we can see in Figure 3.6, the results are dictated by relative frequency rather than by absolute frequency. Within both the Low-Tone Set (Figure 3.6A) and the High-Tone Set (Figure 3.6B), a left-ear advantage is observed for lower frequencies and a right-ear advantage for the higher frequencies. Thus, the differences between the hemispheres in the processing of basic perceptual information are greatly influenced by the context in which this information appears.

Not all researchers agree that the hemispheres differ in their processing of basic sensory attributes, such as the spatial frequency of visual information or the frequency of auditory information. Instead, some investigators argue that hemispheric differences in processing emerge only after basic sensory information has been transformed into a more abstract code (e.g., a visual letter is no longer coded by its form, but rather by how it sounds), a process that occurs within the first few hundred milliseconds postpresentation (e.g., Moscovitch, 1979; Moscovitch & Radzins, 1987). Thus, at present, a debate remains, which is beyond the scope of this chapter, as to how soon after initial receipt of sensory information the processing in the cerebral hemispheres diverges.

Differences in Modes of Processing

In other approaches to hemispheric differences, researchers are less concerned with where hemispheric asymmetries emerge in the time course of processing but are more interested in providing a heuristic for understanding hemispheric differences at any stage of processing. Whereas earlier models suggested that the hemispheres differed in *what* kinds of information they each processed (e.g., spatial vs. verbal), more recent research suggests that the hemispheres differ in *how* they process information. Although many dichotomies have been suggested to describe the differences between the hemispheres, they are well summed up by saying that the left hemisphere processes information in a piece-meal and analytic fashion with a special emphasis on temporal relationships, whereas the right hemisphere processes information in a gestalt and holistic fashion with a special emphasis on the spatial relationships.

The concept that the hemispheres are specialized for different modes of processing implies that both hemispheres can simultaneously contribute to performance. If only the left hemisphere processed verbal material and only the right processed nonverbal material, we would be left with a situation in which the right hemisphere would "take a nap" while we read and the left hemisphere would "snooze" while we tried to recognize a friend's face. Going around the world in such a half-brained manner doesn't seem, on the face of it, a good strategy. However, if each hemisphere can bring its own mode of processing to bear on any given task, having specialized hemispheres affords us two ways of examining the world at once. Even if one hemisphere is better than the other when tested head-to-head (no pun intended!), two modes of processing provide extra information than that which could be obtained from one perspective alone.

One of the first studies to illustrate clearly that the hemispheres differ in processing styles was performed with patients with the split-brain syndrome by Levy and C. W. Trevarthen (1976). In their study, they presented the patients with chimeric figures, such as those in Figure 3.7, under two conditions. In one condition, the patients were told to point to the item that "looks like" the one just seen. In the other, they were told to point to the item that "goes with" what was just seen. What was critically important in this study was that the stimuli were *identical* in the two conditions. All that varied was the nature of the decision, which, as it turns out, had profound effects on the patients' behavior. If they were told to point to the item that "looks like" what they just saw, they made a match on the basis of what had been presented in the LVF (viewed by the right hemisphere). However, given the same picture, but told to choose the item that "goes with" what they just saw, they made a match on the basis of what had been presented in the RVF (viewed by the left hemisphere). This experiment

Chimeric stimuli

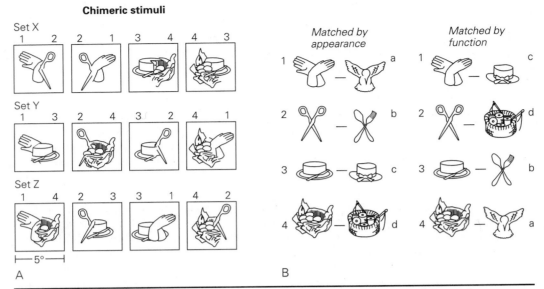

A

B

Figure 3.7 A demonstration of hemispheric specialization for different modes of processing.
When patients with split-brain syndrome viewed these chimeric stimuli, they responded differently depending on whether they were instructed to match by appearance or by function. For example, look at the left-most stimulus in Set X. When instructed to match by appearance, the patient selected the dove (a) because it looks like the gloves (1) (which was viewed by the right hemisphere). However, when given the same stimulus but instructed to match by function, the patient chose the sewing basket (d) because it is similar in function to the scissors (2) (which were viewed by the left hemisphere). (*Note.* Adapted from Levy & Trevarthen, 1976.)

demonstrated that both hemispheres were capable of processing the information provided, so their differences were not adequately explained as a distinction between *what* types of information each could process. Rather, the findings were more consistent with the idea that the hemispheres differ in terms of *how* they process information because the hemisphere that controlled the response varied depending on the task instructions.

Research with neurologically intact individuals has also demonstrated that the hemisphere most adept at processing can vary depending on the demands of the task, even when the stimulus remains the same. For example, remember that the right hemisphere is generally superior at deciding whether two faces represent the same person. However, if the faces differ by just one feature, such as the eyes, a left-hemisphere advantage is observed (Sergent, 1982a). We can interpret these results within theories of hemispheric specialization that

emphasize differences in modes of processing by positing that a right-hemisphere advantage emerges for differentiating two distinct faces because this task can best be performed by a gestalt, or holistic, comparison between the faces. But when the faces differ by just one feature, the task can best be performed by paying attention to the details, a mode of processing at which the left hemisphere excels.

These differences in modes of processing between the hemispheres can also be observed by comparing the performance of patients with unilateral damage to the left hemisphere with that of patients with unilateral damage to the right hemisphere. For example, look at the figures in Figure 3.8, which are often referred to as *hierarchically organized figures*. After sustaining right-hemisphere lesions, individuals have difficulty paying attention to the global form of the item (i.e., an *M* or a triangle) but have no difficulty paying attention to the local pieces or parts (i.e., the *Z*s or the rectangles). Conversely,

Target stimulus | Patients with right-hemisphere damage | Patients with left-hemisphere damage

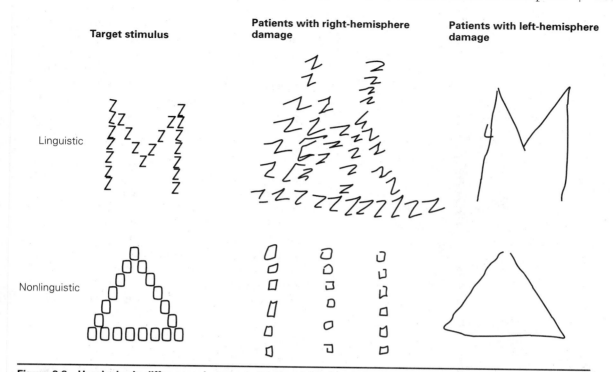

Linguistic

Nonlinguistic

Figure 3.8 Hemispheric differences between global and local processing.
Patients who sustain damage to the right hemisphere can correctly draw the local, or component, parts of the objects, as illustrated by the correct drawing of the *Z*s and the rectangles. However, the overall global form is incorrect; it is neither an *M* (in the case of the linguistic stimulus) nor a triangle (in the case of the nonlinguistic stimulus). In contrast, patients who sustain damage to the left hemisphere can correctly draw the global form of the items but not the local, or component, parts. (*Note.* Reprinted from *Neuropsychologia*, vol. 24, D. Delis, L. Robertson, and R. Efron, "Hemispheric Specialization of Memory for Visual Hierarchical Stimuli," pp. 205–214, Copyright 1986, with permission from Elsevier Science Ltd., The Boulevard, Langford Lane, Kidlington OX5 1GB, UK.)

after left-hemisphere damage, patients have difficulty paying attention to the parts (i.e., the *Z*s and the rectangles) but no difficulty with the global form (i.e., the *M* and the triangle) (for a review of this research, see Robertson & Lamb, 1991). Notice that a similar pattern is obtained regardless of the *type* of stimulus, either linguistic or nonlinguistic. As we can see, the hemispheres take complementary roles in processing. In this case, metaphorically, the right hemisphere pays attention to the forest, while the left hemisphere pays attention to the trees.

Although we presented theories of hemispheric specialization with regard to differences in sensory processing as distinct from the theories of differences in modes of processing, some overlap exists.

For example, if the right hemisphere is biased to extract information of relatively lower spatial frequency, this bias may cause the right hemisphere to process information in a more coarse and global manner (as shown in Figure 3.8). Similarly, if the left hemisphere is superior at processing information of relatively higher spatial frequency, this bias may cause the left hemisphere to process information in a more detailed and local manner.

INTEGRATION OF INFORMATION BETWEEN THE HEMISPHERES

Although our hemispheres are clearly specialized for different processes, our actions and everyday experiences reflect the unified processing of a single

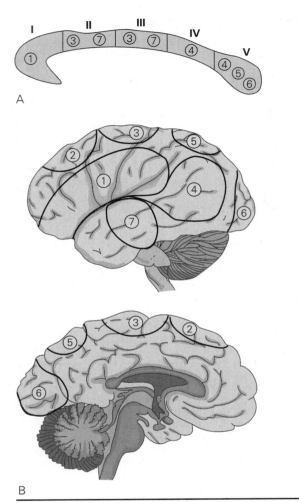

Figure 3.9 Different brain regions connected by different sections of the corpus callosum.
(A) Diagram of the corpus callosum. The numbers shown in each section indicate the brain regions depicted in (B)—(top, left hemisphere, lateral view; bottom, left hemisphere, midsaggital view), which are connected through that section of the callosum. The connections occur in a topographic manner: Anterior sections (I) of the callosum connect anterior sections of the brain (Region 1, which is frontal), middle sections of the callosum (II and III) connect brain regions that are more central (Regions 3 and 7), and posterior sections of the callosum (IV and V) connect posterior sections of the brain (Regions 4, 5, and 6). Some brain regions, such as the frontal region labeled 2, have few, if any, callosal connections. (*Note.* Adapted from deLacoste et al., 1985.)

brain, rather than the output of two distinct minds. This fact raises a major conceptual question. If the left hemisphere is processing information in a fundamentally verbal, analytic, and temporally based manner while the right is processing information in a nonverbal, holistic, and spatially based manner, how do they manage to communicate with each other and coordinate processing to yield a seamless response?

This question has just recently begun to receive more attention from researchers. In this section of the book, we examine this issue from three vantage points. First, we examine the properties of the main conduit through which the hemispheres communicate, the corpus callosum. Second, we examine the functions served by interaction between the hemispheres. Third, we discuss the variety of mechanisms or strategies that are invoked when the hemispheres have the opportunity to coordinate processing.

Nature of Information Carried Over the Corpus Callosum

Although other subcortical commissures allow information to traverse from one side of the brain to the other, the corpus callosum is the main nerve-fiber tract whereby information is transferred between the cerebral hemispheres. Studies indicate that the callosum is a multifaceted structure with a specific anatomical and functional organization. Structurally, anterior sections of the callosum connect anterior sections of the brain, and posterior sections of the callosum connect posterior sections of the brain (Figure 3.9). Because of this organization, different types of information are transferred across different parts of the callosum depending on the brain regions connected by that section of the callosum. For example, information about motor signals is transferred in the middle of the callosum (known as the *body*), whereas visual information is transferred in the back of the callosum (a region known as the *splenium*).

Researchers can determine the nature of information transferred by the callosum by asking patients with the split-brain syndrome to compare items directed to different hemispheres. Because the callo-

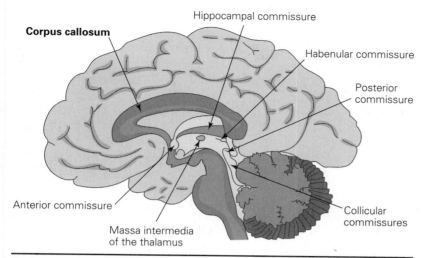

Figure 3.10 **The position of the corpus callosum compared with the locations of other brain commissures.**
Information that allows an item to be uniquely identified can be transferred between the hemispheres only by the corpus callosum. Some evidence exists that other commissures can support the transfer of information coded in a dichotomous manner (e.g., old/young) or information about basic emotional tenor (e.g., positive/negative). (*Note.* Adapted from Sperry, 1964.)

sum is severed in these patients, we can infer that if the patients *are* incapable of comparing two items, each of which is sent to a different hemisphere, such integration must rely on the callosum. If, however, the patients can make such a comparison, that comparison must rely on commissures other than the callosum (Figure 3.10). Studies based on such logic have revealed that detailed information required to uniquely identify an item can be transferred between the hemispheres only by the callosum, whereas some evidence exists that more general information can be transferred through subcortical commissures. For example, researchers have reported that patients with the split-brain syndrome cannot determine whether two faces, each directed to a different hemisphere, are the same person (e.g., Madonna). However, the subcortical commissures may be able to transfer dichotomous information, such as whether the face is of a younger adult or an older one, or is a female and not a male (Sergent, 1990).

The subcortical commissures also appear to be able to transfer information about general emotional tone. For example, in one study, faces were shown only to the right hemisphere, and the left hemisphere had to attempt to signal its response to that face with a "thumbs-up" or "thumbs-down" sign made by the right hand. The left hemisphere could respond appropriately, giving the thumbs-down sign to pictures of people like Hitler and the thumbs-up sign to pictures of family members (Sperry, Zaidel, & Zaidel, 1979).

The conclusion from all these studies is that the corpus callosum is the major conduit for transfer of higher order information between the hemispheres. Interhemispheric transfer of only basic and rudimentary information occurs through other brain commissures.

Functions of Interhemispheric Interaction

Part of the corpus callosum's function in interhemispheric interaction is to act much like an office mes-

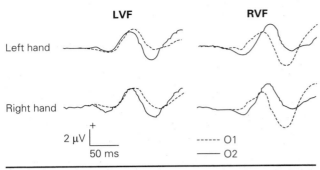

Figure 3.11 The rapid transfer of sensory information from one hemisphere to the other.
Shown here are evoked responses to visual checkerboards presented either in the left visual field (LVF) or the right visual field (RVF). These responses were recorded at sites O_1 (occipital lobe, left hemisphere) and O_2 (occipital lobe, right hemisphere) (see Figure 2.8), when individuals were asked to respond to the presentation of the stimulus with either the left hand or the right hand. For LVF stimuli, the response occurred earlier over the right hemisphere (site O_2, solid line) and then later over the left hemisphere (site O_1, dotted line) after the signal was transferred across the callosum. In contrast, for RVF stimuli, the response occurred earlier over the left hemisphere. The hand used to give the response did not influence the event-related potential (ERP) patterns because the electrodes were located over occipital regions and hence were detecting responses to visual information (as opposed to motor responses). (*Note.* Adapted from Saron & Davidson, 1989, p. 1120.)

senger service, providing photocopies of each hemisphere's experience for the other and sending information that allows the hemispheres to coordinate processing. We first discuss this function of the callosum and then explore its additional roles.

The callosum keeps the hemispheres aware of each other's doings by allowing for immediate transfer of information received by one hemisphere to the other. One way this fast transfer can be demonstrated is by examining event-related potentials (ERPs) to sensory stimuli. A response recorded over the hemisphere contralateral to presentation of a stimulus is followed only a few milliseconds later by a response over the other hemisphere (e.g., Saron & Davidson, 1989) (Figure 3.11). The difference in time between the peak of the ERP recorded over the hemisphere that received the information and the opposite hemisphere is often considered an estimate of callosal transfer time, which ranges from 5 to 20 ms in the average adult.

As we mentioned earlier when discussing the source of perceptual asymmetries, sometimes information acquired by means of callosal transfer may be somewhat "degraded" compared with the original, much as a photocopy is degraded compared with the original. Such degradation is most often observed in memory studies in which participants view an inspection series of items, some of which appear in the RVF and some of which appear in the LVF. After a short delay (e.g., 5 min), the participant views a series of test items and decides, on each trial, whether the item was viewed in the inspection series. Some items in the test series are shown to the same hemisphere as in the inspection series (e.g.,

RVF/RVF), whereas others are shown to the hemisphere opposite that in the inspection series (e.g., RVF/LVF). In general, performance is superior when the item is initially and subsequently presented in the same visual field (not requiring interhemispheric interaction) than when the item is initially viewed by one hemisphere and subsequently seen by another (e.g., Banich & Shenker, 1994a). The inferior performance on these latter trials suggests that information received through callosal transfer can be poorer in quality than that received directly.

More recent evidence indicates that interaction between the hemispheres does not act merely as a message transfer service. It may, in fact, enhance the overall processing capacity of the brain under high-demand conditions, such as when the processing is relatively complex and much information must be simultaneously processed within a short period. This phenomenon was demonstrated in a series of studies in which two types of trials were compared: those on which critical items were directed to opposite hemispheres and had to be uniquely identified and compared (across-hemisphere trials), and those on which the critical items were directed initially to just one hemisphere (within-hemisphere trials). The across-hemisphere trials required the hemispheres to interact in order to perform the task, whereas the within-hemisphere trials did not (Figure 3.12). When the task was relatively easy, such as making a simple decision about whether two items looked physically identical (e.g., 2 and 2), processing was faster on within-hemisphere trials. Yet when the same type of stimuli were used but the task was more complicated, such as determining whether the sum of two numbers equaled ten or more (e.g., 2 and 8), an across-hemisphere advantage was observed. These more demanding tasks required not only that a physical form be recognized, but that additional processing be performed, such as adding one value to another (e.g., Banich & Belger, 1990; Belger & Banich, 1992).

How might dividing processing across the hemispheres and forcing them to communicate aid performance when tasks are difficult? Because each hemisphere can analyze information somewhat separately, dividing processing across the hemispheres may allow different portions of the task to be performed in parallel. The cost of such a division of labor, however, is that information must be "put back together" at some point. For difficult tasks, the advantages afforded by parallel processing probably outweigh the costs associated with having to recombine information. In contrast, when a task is easy, the costs of coordinating processing across the hemispheres do not outweigh any advantages derived from dividing processing. Consider, as a simple analogy, that you have an easy task to do. Asking a friend to help you may take longer than if you just do it yourself because explaining the task and coordinating your work with that of your friend would take too long. But, as the task gets harder, the time and effort required for such coordination is small compared with having an extra helping hand. Thus, in demanding situations interhemispheric processing appears to be advantageous to task performance and actually increases the brain's processing capacity (see Banich, 1995a,b, for a more detailed discussion of these issues).

Varieties of Interhemispheric Interaction

Research since 1990 suggests that the hemispheres do not have a single way of interacting with each other but can do so in a variety of ways. Next, we briefly outline the varieties of interhemispheric interaction that have been observed. What is not known at present is which factors determine when a particular variety of interaction is observed instead of another type of interaction.

To investigate how the hemispheres work together, researchers often compare performance under three conditions: when information is sent initially to only the right hemisphere (as on LVF trials), when it is sent initially to just the left hemisphere (as on RVF trials), and when both hemispheres receive the same information simultaneously (bilateral visual field [BVF] trials). Peformance on BVF trials can then be compared with that on the unilateral

Physical identity task

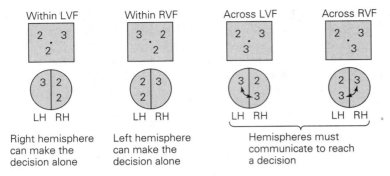

Ordinal task

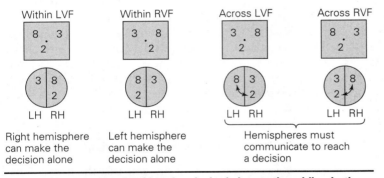

Figure 3.12 An example of interhemispheric interaction aiding in the performance of more demanding tasks.
In the physical identity task, which is easier, individuals must simply decide whether the bottom item looks identical to either of the top two items, whereas in the more demanding ordinal task, individuals must not only identify the digits but also add them. Two types of trials are compared: those in which the critical items are directed initially to only one hemisphere and the correct decision can be reached without interhemispheric interaction (within–left visual field [LVF] and within–right visual field [RVF] trials), and those in which each hemisphere receives one of the critical digits and both hemispheres must communicate for the task to be performed correctly (across-RVF and across-LVF trials). Performance is better on within-hemisphere trials for the easier task, but requiring the hemispheres to interact, as is mandatory in across-hemisphere trials, leads to better performance on the more demanding task.

(RVF and LVF) trials. A task is chosen in which the pattern of performance, such as that exhibited when the person is making errors, differs between the hemispheres (e.g., on LVF trials, individuals are more likely to misreport the last letter of a consonant-vowel-consonant [CVC] string rather than the first, whereas on RVF trials, the difference between first- and last-letter errors is not that large). In this manner, the pattern of performance on BVF trials can be compared to determine whether it is more like that exhibited on RVF/left-hemisphere trials or that exhibited on LVF/right-hemisphere trials.

Studies using such an approach have yielded a variety of results. In some cases, the hemispheres appear to interact by means of **metacontrol:** One of them dominates performance. For example, on the CVC task just described, the error pattern on BVF trials mimics that on LVF trials but not RVF trials (Hellige, Taylor, & Eng, 1989). This result may seem surprising because we may think that the hemisphere superior at the task, the left, would dominate performance on BVF trials. However, some investigators contend that this counterintuitive result may reflect processing at the level of the "lowest common denominator" (Hellige, 1993b). Consider, as an analogy, that an English speaker with a poor knowledge of French is trying to communicate with a French speaker who knows no English. Their better course of action may be to communicate in fractured French than in perfect English because at least they have some French in common. In other cases, researchers have observed an "averaging" of performance on BVF trials relative to LVF and RVF trials. In these situations, performance on BVF trials mimics that of neither hemisphere but seems to represent a midpoint, average, or compromise between the two. For example, sometimes the error pattern on BVF trials in the CVC task is midpoint between the patterns observed on RVF trials and LVF trials (Luh & Levy, 1995). In still other cases, one hemisphere dominates one aspect of processing while the other hemisphere dominates a different aspect of processing (Banich, Nicholas, & Karol, submitted).

One of the most surprising findings to result from this sort of research is that in certain cases

the interaction between the hemispheres can have unique properties that cannot be predicted by what each hemisphere alone is doing. Because this finding is somewhat counterintuitive, we present the relevant evidence next: Two studies were performed in which individuals viewed a target word, such as *key,* and then had to decide if either of two words appearing 1 s later rhymed with the target. Sometimes both words were presented in the LVF, sometimes both were presented in the RVF, and sometimes the words were divided so that one word appeared in each visual field (BVF trials). In one experiment, the two words were presented in the identical case (uppercase or lowercase) and typeface (or font) (e.g., *BEE* and *BEE*). In a second experiment, the words were presented in different cases and fonts (e.g., *BEE* and **bee**), so that they would look dissimilar (the reasons for this manipulation and some others in the experiment aren't germane to the present discussion, so they are not discussed here).

The important finding in these two studies was that although the patterns of performance on RVF and LVF trials were identical in the two experiments, meaning that font and case affected neither hemisphere, case and font were important on BVF trials, so the result was a different pattern of responses in the two experiments (Banich & Karol, 1992). Hence, the physical form of the words was important when the hemispheres were conversing with each other, but not when each hemisphere was processing information by itself. These findings indicate that we would be overgeneralizing to think of the processing of the whole brain as simply the sum of the processing by the left hemisphere and the processing by the right. A phenomenon similar to that found in this study is also observed in other areas of psychology, such as social behavior, in which people do not exhibit certain behaviors as individuals, yet exhibit the behaviors when in a group.

As we already mentioned, at present the specific factors governing which pattern of interaction will be observed are unclear. What is clear, however, is that the means by which the hemispheres can interact with each other are multifaceted and flexible, a finding suggesting that interaction between the hemispheres is dynamic.

DEVELOPMENTAL ASPECTS OF HEMISPHERIC SPECIALIZATION

Now that we examined the manner in which the hemispheres are specialized and how they interact, we need to consider whether such patterns are observed from an early age or whether they change as a child develops. In his influential book, *Biological Foundations of Language,* Lenneberg (1967) hypothesized that the hemispheres of the brain were equipotential at birth and that lateralization increased until puberty, after which it remained constant. He based this hypothesis, in part, on evidence that younger children who sustained left-hemisphere damage have less severe deficits than older children and adults with similar lesions do. He posited that the recovery in younger children occurred because the right hemisphere, which he assumed was not yet fully specialized, took over the language processing.

However, subsequent investigations suggest that the basic specializations of the hemispheres are in place at birth and that the degree of specialization is not modified much with development, except in cases of profound environmental influence, such as occurs with traumatic injury to the brain. The evidence for the lack of an increase of lateralization of function comes from four major areas, each of which is briefly discussed next (one of the best early discussions of these issues is contained in Segalowitz & Gruber, 1977).

The first piece of evidence that a child's brain is lateralized at birth comes from neuroanatomy. As we discussed earlier in the chapter, neuroanatomical asymmetries exist in certain regions of the human brain; the most noteworthy is the asymmetry of the planum temporale. Because these neuroanatomical asymmetries have been related to asymmetries in function (e.g., Ratcliff, Dila, Taylor, & Milner, 1980), we would expect that if lateralization did develop with age, these neuroanatomical asymmetries should become more pronounced with age. However, this is not the case. The gyral patterns of the human brain are present sometime between the 10th and 31st gestational weeks, and the asymmetry in the planum temporale can be observed at this time (Wada, Clarke, & Hamm, 1975) and at birth (Witelson & Pallie, 1973). Thus, neuroanatomically, an infant's brain is already lateralized.

The second piece of evidence comes from studies examining the size of perceptual asymmetries in children. If asymmetry developed with age, the size of the left-hemisphere advantage for verbal material and the right-hemisphere advantage for spatial information would be smaller in younger children than in older children. Because many of the methods used to assess lateralization of function require a certain level of cognitive capacity (e.g., the ability to read), a comparison across studies with different-aged children focused on those of school age and older. A vast review of these studies by Witelson in 1977 revealed that the size of perceptual asymmetries does not increase with age, a finding suggesting that specialization of the brain does not increase between kindergarten and puberty.

The third piece of evidence that asymmetry does not increase with age comes from measurements of asymmetries in infants. Because standard techniques for assessing lateralization of function could not be used owing to the limited cognitive repertoire of infants, clever techniques had to be utilized. Some researchers recorded the electrical brain activity of young infants while they were exposed to verbal materials, such as nonsense syllables (e.g., "pa" or "ba"), or to nonverbal materials, such as musical chords. In children as young as 1 week old, brain activation over the left hemisphere was greater for the verbal material and over the right hemisphere was greater for nonverbal material (Best, Hoffman, & Glanville, 1982; D. L. Molfese, Freeman, & Palermo, 1975). In other cases, rather than recording brain waves, investigators determined whether the hemispheres are specialized at birth by relying on normal behaviors in the repertoire of babies, such as sucking on a pacifier. When young babies are interested in something, they suck at a fast rate, whereas when they get used to, or habituate to, a stimulus, their sucking rate decreases. Researchers found that when verbal material was played, the sucking rate was more affected by changes in sound in the right ear than in the left. In contrast, when nonverbal material was presented, the sucking rate was more affected by changes in the left ear (Bertoncini et al., 1989; Entus, 1977). Hence, the results of these studies suggest that the hemispheres of young children are as specialized as they are in older children.

The fourth piece of evidence comes from studies of young children who were born with one extremely small and malformed hemisphere. Because this malformed hemisphere often becomes a focus for epileptic activity, the prognosis for these children is better if the hemisphere is removed at birth, a procedure known as **hemispherectomy.** If the hemispheres are equipotent at birth, the performance of children with just a left hemisphere should be identical to those with just a right hemisphere, even years after the hemispherectomy. Otherwise, if the hemispheres are specialized at birth, performance should differ depending on which hemisphere was excised. Because the performance of children with only a left hemisphere differs from that of those with only a right hemisphere, the hemispheres are probably not equipotent at birth. On language tasks, most notably those in the domain of syntax, children who have only a left hemisphere outperform children with only a right hemisphere (Dennis & Kohn, 1975; Dennis & Whitaker, 1976). Likewise, children with only a left hemisphere do not acquire spatial skills to the degree of children with only a right hemisphere (Kohn & Dennis, 1974).

We should mention that these children do acquire some skills typically performed by the removed hemisphere, albeit not at a very high level. Children who have only a right hemisphere generally acquire the ability to speak and to comprehend language, although not to the degree of children with only a left hemisphere. Likewise, children with only a left hemisphere can acquire some spatial skills. Thus, we can conclude that each hemisphere is specialized for a particular type of processing and from birth provides the best neural substrate for its expression. However, under extreme circumstances, such as the removal of one hemisphere early in development,

the opposite hemisphere is sufficiently *plastic* (capable of being shaped or formed) to take over those functions to at least a moderate degree, a plasticity lacking in adults (we discuss plasticity in more detail in chapter 13).

As the preceding sections of the chapter should have made clear, distinctions in processing that occur between the two hemispheres of the human brain are one of the fundamental aspects of the neurological organization of the brain. Throughout this book, we find that certain syndromes or cognitive dysfunctions are associated with damage to one hemisphere but not the other. We also observe hemispheric differences in processing for almost all the intellectual functions that we discuss in this book, including language, attention, emotion, and memory. We next turn our attention to the ways in which this basic pattern of brain organization may vary among individuals.

INDIVIDUAL DIFFERENCES IN BRAIN ORGANIZATION

Although we described the pattern of lateralization of function that is observed for most individuals, this brain organization is not observed in *all* individuals. Rather, some variability in brain organization appears to be linked to specific individual characteristics. In this section of the chapter, we discuss two of these factors: handedness and gender.

Handedness

Scientists have known for some time that the brain organization for left-handed individuals is distinct from that for right-handed individuals. Historically, left-handers have been believed to be different in a non-too-flattering way. For example, the Latin word for *left* is *sinister,* whereas the French word is *gauche.* In certain cultures such as India, the left hand is never used to eat a meal (nor is it extended to someone for a handshake) because it is the hand reserved for bathroom functions. Even in the early to mid-20th century, individuals who wrote with their left hand were considered evil, stubborn, and

Is Being Left-Handed a Health Hazard?

In 1991, two researchers made the provocative claim that left-handers are likely to have a shorter life span than that of right-handers (Coren & Halpern, 1991). By examining a 1979 yearbook providing information on professional baseball players, these investigators found that, on average, right-handers lived an extra 8 months longer than left-handers. By examining death records in one community, the researchers found that the older the age of the deceased, the less likely the person was to be left-handed, so of the individuals who had died at an advanced age, few, if any were left-handers. Where had all the left-handers gone? As best the researchers could tell, the left-handers must have died at an earlier age, so none had reached an advanced age.

The researchers proposed that left-handers might have an elevated death rate, in part, because they are forced to live in a right-handed world, where everything from telephones to scissors are not made for them.

Support for this conjecture came from findings that left-handers were 1.89 times more likely than right-handers to report injuries that required medical attention. However, the researchers also claimed that left-handedness may be a marker for a stressful birth and/ or is associated with a variety of maladies, including developmental disabilities, reduced immunological competence, and neural abnormalities, all of which could decrease life span.

As you can imagine, these findings sparked some interest, not only among left-handers, who were concerned for personal reasons, but also among the research community in general. As with any new and intriguing finding, this result generated a large debate and a number of subsequent studies. Some researchers suggested that alternative explanations existed for the data (e.g., Harris, 1993a). For example, the decreasing percentage of left-handers in the death records might reflect a decrease in the base-line rate of left-

defiant, and subsequently they were often forced to write with the "right" hand. Left-handers often were subjected to such indignities because they compose a minority of the population, approximately 10%.

Although left-handers have been unfairly labeled with negative stereotypes, these people do appear to be different from right-handers, at least with regard to their brains. For right-handers, verbal processing is almost always lateralized to the left hemisphere and visuospatial processing is lateralized to the right, but this is not the case for left-handers. Rather, their brain organization is heterogeneous, some being the same as that of right-handers (verbal, left hemisphere; visuospatial, right hemisphere), some the opposite (verbal, right hemisphere; visuospatial, left hemisphere), and some different (verbal and spatial processing performed by both hemispheres). For example, whereas in 95% of right-handers, speech output is controlled by the left

hemisphere and in 5% by the right, in 70% of left-handers speech is controlled by the left hemisphere, in 15% by the right, and in 15% by either hemisphere (Rasmussen & Milner, 1977b). Thus, when we average across all these types of left-handers, as a group they appear to be less lateralized than right-handers (e.g., Bryden, 1965), although a given left-hander may not be less lateralized than a given right-hander.

Because on average left-handers are less lateralized than right-handers, the consequences of brain injury for a given function may not be as dire for left-handers. For example, after damage to the left hemisphere, left-handers may exhibit less severe language deficits than right-handers do, because language output may be controlled by one hemisphere and language comprehension by the other (e.g., Naeser & Borod, 1986). Yet, such apparent sparing of function is illusory. Although right-handers often exhibit little to no visuospatial deficit after left-hemisphere damage, the deficit observed in left-handers

handedness with age in the population as a whole. The individuals who went to school in the mid-1900s were likely to be under much less pressure to switch to being right-handed than those who attended school in the early 1900s. Thus, the decreased rate of left-handedness among the very elderly might not indicate that they had all died, but rather that they never existed because they had all been forced to become right-handers! Although the original researchers do not believe such an explanation, or other possible rationales (e.g., Halpern & Coren, 1993), the debate over the interpretation of the original data continues (Harris, 1993b).

Other researchers also performed studies to follow up on the original findings. A reanalysis of the 1979 data on baseball players (Fudin, Renninger, Lembessis, & Hirshon, 1993) and an updated analysis of 5,441 players in a 1993 baseball yearbook (Hicks et al., 1994) indicated no difference in age of death for left- and right-

handers (see Coren & Halpern, 1993, and Lembessis & Rudin, 1994, for a debate about these data). The results from still other studies are divided. Some studies did not indicate an elevated accident rate among left-handers (e.g., Merckelbach, Muris, & Kop, 1994). Other studies indicated that individuals who are neither strongly right-handed nor strongly left-handed have elevated accident rates (e.g., Hicks et al., 1993), that college-age individuals who are not right-handed (either mixed or left-handed) have higher accident rates (Daniel & Yeo, 1994), and that left-handed females are more likely to suffer traumatic brain injury, especially in automobile accidents (MacNiven, 1994). At present, the issue as to whether being left-handed is a health hazard remains unresolved. However, left-handers may still want to search out that pair of left-handed scissors because even if doing so doesn't reduce their accident rate, it might make their lives a bit easier.

usually is more severe (J. C. Borod, Carper, Naeser, & Goodglass, 1985).

These differences in lateralized functions between right- and left-handers may derive in part from differences in brain morphology between the groups. Anatomical asymmetries that are observed in the planum temporale, for example, are not as consistent or as large in groups of left-handers (e.g., Hochberg & LeMay, 1975). Furthermore, some researchers have suggested that physiological aspects of functioning may differ between left- and right-handers as well. One theory that has received much attention is that of Geschwind and Galaburda (1985a–c), which posits that the expression of patterns of lateralization (and left-handedness) are related to sex hormones, the immune system, and profiles of cognitive abilities. One of their specific suggestions is that left-handedness is associated with autoimmune disorders, in which the body incorrectly identifies its own tissue as foreign. How-

ever, evidence for this broad theory is sparse (see McManus & Bryden, 1991, for a thoughtful critique of the model; *Brain and Cognition, 26*(2), 1994, for a variety of commentaries on the theory; and Bryden, McManus, & Bulman-Fleming, 1995, for a response to those commentaries).

At this point, although we know that the brains of left-handers differ from those of right-handers, the reasons for such variation and the ability to predict the pattern of brain organization for any given left-hander are beyond our grasp. In addition, although various genetic models have been proposed, the most noteworthy of which is that by Annett (1985), the causes and many consequences of left-handedness still remain a mystery.

Gender

One of the more heated debates about individual variations in brain organization revolves around differences between the genders. Not only is the question of whether gender is linked to neurological organization of interest, but another area of investigation is the importance of the extent and degree of gender differences in predicting cognitive function. Much evidence in other species indicates that hormones influence brain organization and behavior for reproductive functioning (e.g., Breedlove, 1992). However, the degree to which these hormonal differences in other species influence nonreproductive aspects of behavior is less certain (e.g., van Haaren, van Hest, & Heinsbroek, 1990), although anatomical differences between the sexes have been noted in areas of the brain that are not associated with reproduction (for a review of these differences, see J. Juraska, 1991). Furthermore, in humans the degree to which hormones rather than patterns of learning and cultural influences contribute to mental function is difficult to determine. (For a critique of the overgeneralizations from animals to humans and an appraisal of some of the conclusions drawn about gender differences in lateralization of function, see Bleier, 1984, especially chapter 4.)

For many years, researchers have debated whether lateralization of function is less pronounced in females than in males. If so, females would be more akin to left-handers and males more akin to right-handers. Although some researchers report such a pattern, others find no differences between men and women, and some even find women to be more lateralized (see McGlone, 1980, for the diverse spectrum of viewpoints on this issue). Two recent reviews of hundreds of tachistoscopic (Hiscock et al., 1995) and dichotic listening studies (Hiscock et al., 1994) revealed that depending on the criterion used as support for gender differences, between 5 and 15% of these studies yield results consistent with the idea that females are less lateralized than men. These authors concluded that although statistically the average degree of lateralization found for a group of men may differ from that found for a group of women, gender differences account for little of the variability (1–2%) in patterns of lateralization of function among individuals.

Even if gender differences are observed, we must remember that they may result from other factors

besides differences in neural organization. This consideration applies to both anatomical and behavioral studies. We discuss the results of some sample studies in both the anatomical and behavioral domains to illustrate the factors that we must consider when interpreting gender differences.

One anatomical structure for which gender differences have been reported is the corpus callosum. A relatively consistent finding involves both sex and handedness: Portions of the callosum are larger in non-right-handed men than in right-handed men, but the same is not true of women (e.g., Habib et al., 1991; Witelson & Goldsmith, 1991). This finding has been attributed to the effects of sex hormones (Witelson & Nowakowski, 1991). Furthermore, gender differences have been observed in the shape of the posterior section of the corpus callosum—the splenium—which is more bulbous in women than in men (e.g., L. S. Allen, Richey, Chai, & Gorski, 1991). However, the functional implications of this finding, if any, are unclear. (Originally, the callosum was reported to be larger in women than in men [deLacoste-Utamsing & Holloway, 1982], but this finding has not been replicated in numerous studies [e.g., Byne, Bleier, & Houston, 1988].)

One potential problem in interpreting any observed gender differences in anatomy is that they could be due to other factors that co-vary with gender, such as size. For example, a woman generally has a smaller brain than that of a man. Perhaps people with smaller brains have a more bulbously shaped splenium. Hence, a difference between men and women might be attributed to gender when it actually reflects differences between people with larger and smaller brains (regardless of gender). Consequently, investigating alternative explanations for gender differences and attempting to rule them out is extremely important. For example, a researcher may want to compose a sample in which male and female individuals are matched for approximate overall brain size and then determine whether gender is related to the shape of the splenium.

Similar issues must be considered when we interpret the results of behavioral studies. For example, recent functional brain imaging studies indicated differences between the genders in regional brain activation not only when the participants are at rest (R. C. Gur et al., 1995), but also during processing of linguistic information (Shaywitz et al., 1995). We must consider whether men and women may exhibit distinct patterns of brain activation on these tasks not because they have differentially organized brains, but because they use different strategies to perform a task (similar consideration should be given to gender differences in perceptual asymmetries). The use of different strategies by men and women may arise as a result of differential schooling, socialization, and other environmental factors. To demonstrate definitively that the genders have distinct brain organizations, researchers will have to show that distinct brain regions are activated in the genders even when both groups are using identical strategies to perform a task.

Because interpreting differences between the genders can be difficult, researchers have turned to other approaches to examine whether gender and hormonal influences on lateralized functioning exist. One approach is to examine differences in cognitive function during the menstrual cycle, as the level of female hormones varies. For example, estrogen and progesterone are at high levels directly after ovulation and at low levels during menstruation. By testing women at different points in the menstrual cycle, researchers can determine whether fluctuations in the ability to perform lateralized tasks are related to hormonal levels. In this manner, researchers need not compare women with men, but can just compare the performance of a given woman at two points in time. The way she has been influenced by culture will be constant, so researchers can sidestep the cultural issue. These types of studies have yielded some evidence that when female hormones are high, such as just after ovulation, women tend to perform better on certain fine motor tasks that are more likely to be lateralized to the left hemisphere and poorer on spatial tasks, such as the mental rotation of objects, that are more likely to be lateralized to the right hemisphere. Women exhibit the opposite pattern when female hormones are low, such as during menstruation (e.g., Kimura & Hampson, 1994). However, the differences in ability are small and are found for only a limited set of tasks. Put practically, the differences are not large enough that a woman would want to use the phase of her menstrual cycle to determine the best date to take an entrance examination for graduate or professional school.

As we now know, the debate regarding gender differences in brain organization, and specifically lateralization, has not been satisfactorily resolved. In fact, public imagination on the issue is often fueled by sensational stories in the popular press. The bodies of men and women clearly differ in a number of anatomical features and physiological functions, and we would probably not be surprised to find that such differences apply to the brain as well. However, what is critically important is how differences in brain lateralization are interpreted, with regard to both their nature and their magnitude. When differences are observed, they tend to be relatively small, and the variation among individuals within a gender are much greater than any variation between men and women.

In this chapter, we reviewed many, but not all, of the differences between the hemispheres in their anatomy and function. For example, we did not discuss findings that asymmetries are observed in other species, or theories about the evolution of asymmetry. For a more extensive discussion of these topics and others related to cerebral asymmetry, you may want to investigate two very readable yet scholarly books on the topic, one by Springer and Deutsch (1993) and another by Hellige (1993a).

SUMMARY

One of the fundamental aspects of human brain organization is a differentiation in anatomy and function between the cerebral hemispheres. Although at first glance the hemispheres look like mirror images, they are not. For instance, asymmetries can be found in the neuroanatomy of the brain. Most notably, the planum temporale, an area implicated in language comprehension, is typically larger in the left hemisphere than in the right. Asymmetries also exist in neurotransmitter distribution and reception; the left hemisphere is more influenced by dopamine and the right by norepinephrine.

The most dramatic differences between the hemispheres, however, are observed in behavior. In the 1860s, Paul Broca reported that damage to a region of the left, but not the right, frontal lobe disrupted the ability to produce fluent speech (although language comprehension remained intact). The importance of the left hemisphere for language was later corroborated by Karl Wernicke, who observed that damage to a different region of the left hemisphere produced the opposite syndrome: disrupted language comprehension with intact production. These findings led to the idea of cerebral dominance, which is the notion that one hemisphere dominates or leads mental function.

In the 1960s, the differences in the processing capacities of the hemispheres were revealed dramatically in studies of patients with the split-brain syndrome. These individuals underwent severance of the massive nerve-fiber connection between the hemispheres—the corpus callosum—for the relief of intractable epilepsy; this procedure allowed the competencies of each hemisphere to be assessed in isolation of each other. Studies with these patients confirmed the superiority of the left hemisphere for language processing, especially in the domain of speech output and phonology. The right hemisphere was shown to be superior at visuospatial tasks, such as the arrangement of blocks, the transformation of spatial patterns, and the recognition of faces. Corroborative evidence for hemispheric specialization has been provided by studies of patients with unilateral brain damage. As known since the time of Broca, left-hemisphere lesions disrupt language processing. Right-hemisphere lesions disrupt a variety of abilities, including face recognition, judgment of line orientation, recognition of objects, and tonal processing of auditory material.

Hemispheric specialization can also be demonstrated in neurologically intact individuals by directing sensory information so that it is received initially by a single hemisphere. In the visual modality, lateral specialization is demonstrated by the divided visual field technique, in which subjects fixate on a central point so that information in the right visual

field (RVF) is received initially by the left hemisphere and information in the left visual field (LVF) is received initially by the right hemisphere. In the tactile modality, the dichaptic technique is used. In this technique, a person is asked to feel two items simultaneously, one in each hand, and then to identify them in some manner. In the auditory modality, lateralization is tested by means of dichotic presentation, in which two items are presented simultaneously, one in each ear. In all cases, a superiority in processing information for one visual field, hand, or ear is believed to represent specialization of the contralateral hemisphere for the task.

Many studies performed with the use of such techniques have shown an advantage for processing verbal material when it is presented in the RVF, in the right hand, or to the right ear. In contrast, nonverbal material is better processed when presented in the LVF, in the left hand, or to the left ear. These perceptual asymmetries may occur for various reasons. First, information directed to the nonspecialized hemisphere may not be processed as effectively as information directed to the specialized hemisphere. Second, the nonspecialized hemisphere may transfer the information it receives to the specialized hemisphere, and that information may degrade during the transfer across the corpus callosum. Third, the task demands may induce the specialized hemisphere to be more active, causing more attention to be paid to information in the contralateral sensory fields.

Two major classes of theories have been formulated about the nature of hemispheric specialization. One class suggests that the hemispheres process sensory information in fundamentally different ways. For example, researchers have proposed that the right hemisphere is superior at processing information of relatively lower spatial or auditory frequency, whereas the left hemisphere is superior at processing information of relatively higher spatial frequency. Asymmetries in higher order cognitive processes are believed to result from these sensory asymmetries. Another class of theories suggests that each hemisphere applies a different strategy to analyzing information, which leads to differences in performance. These theories suggest that the left hemisphere is most adept at analyzing information in a piecemeal, detailed, and time-locked manner, whereas the right hemisphere is most adept at analyzing information in a holistic, gestalt, and space-based manner.

Although the hemispheres have different functions, they act together in a seamless fashion because they can coordinate processing through the corpus callosum. The callosum is critical for transferring information that can be uniquely characterized (e.g., a picture of Madonna's face), as compared with that categorized dichotomously (e.g., a female face rather than a male face). This latter type of information, as well as that of general emotional tenor, can be transferred through subcortical commissures. Interaction between the hemispheres also increases the brain's processing capacity. Under demanding conditions, dividing processing between the hemispheres leads to better performance than if a hemisphere must perform the task alone. Furthermore, the hemispheres have multiple ways of coordinating processing. In some cases one hemisphere dominates performance, sometimes both hemispheres equally contribute, and in other cases the hemispheres interact in ways that neither would by itself, much the way that groups of people act in ways they never would as individuals.

Four pieces of evidence suggest that hemispheric asymmetry is present at birth and does not increase with age. First, anatomical asymmetries, which predict asymmetries in function, can be observed in utero and at birth. Second, the degree of asymmetry observed on divided visual field and dichotic tasks remains constant among children of different ages. Third, behavioral asymmetries can be observed in infants. Fourth, children who have only a left hemisphere do not acquire spatial skills to the degree of those with only a right hemisphere, whereas children with only a right hemisphere do not acquire verbal skills to the degree of those with only a left hemisphere.

Patterns of lateralization may be influenced by individual traits, such as handedness and possibly gender. On average, left-handers have less of a division of labor between the two halves of the brain than right-handers do. This functional difference appears to have a genetic and neuroanatomical basis because the brains of left-handers are more likely to lack the neuroanatomical asymmetries observed in right-handers. At present, much debate exists as to whether the gender of the individual influences lateralization of function. A common suggestion is that women are less lateralized than men, but this finding is not obtained consistently. Furthermore, determining whether differences between the genders are due to biological or social factors is difficult. One way to avoid this issue is to study variations in the performance of women as their hormonal status changes during the menstrual cycle. Such studies provide some evidence that hormones can influence how well each hemisphere can process different tasks.

*M*otor *C*ontrol

The life story of Muhammad Ali, one of the 20th century's most famous boxers, interweaves not only boxing and politics, but also the neural basis of motor control. Ali, who was known as Cassius Clay before his conversion to Islam, rose to prominence as an Olympic boxer. He eventually turned pro and became a world champion. Ali said that his boxing strategy was to "float like a butterfly, sting like a bee," meaning that his fancy footwork allowed him to flutter around the ring to evade his opponents' punches, after which he would move in for a knockout. At the height of his career, Ali was drafted to serve in Vietnam, but he refused induction because of his religious beliefs. He was convicted of draft evasion, stripped of his crown, and did not box for the next 3 years.

During his exile from the ring, Ali's ability to "float" deteriorated substantially. When he was allowed to resume his boxing career (shortly before the Supreme Court overturned his conviction), he adopted a different fighting style that capitalized on the strength he had gained during his time out of the ring. This new style, however, would have deleterious effects later in his life. Ali would let an opponent get him against the ropes in the early rounds, either blocking or absorbing an onslaught of punches that would have felled most men. This technique became known as the "rope-a-dope" style, because a boxer was traditionally considered a fool if he allowed himself to get caught against the ropes by an opponent. However, Ali would patiently wait for the later rounds when his opponent was exhausted, frustrated, and getting sloppy. Then, he would move in for the knockout blow.

After his retirement from boxing, Ali became a popular speaker on the lecture circuit. In time, however, people began to notice that he was slurring his words and stumbling. When signing autographs, he was slow and his writing was poor. To many observers, Ali appeared to be drunk, but heavy drinking was not his style. Medical examinations revealed that Ali had sustained neurological damage and that he was most likely displaying signs of Parkinsonism. In Parkinsonism, motor control is disrupted so that previously simple motor acts become extremely difficult. The three basic attributes of Parkinsonism are slowness of movement, rigidity of movement, and tremors (which are usually observed when a person is at rest). Generally, Parkinsonism is observed in older people as a progressive neurological disorder. But Ali, although well past the years when most boxers are in the ring, was only middle-aged. Why was he exhibiting these symptoms?

As best as his neurologists could surmise, years of boxing had taken their toll on Ali. Although he had never been knocked out, the barrage of punches Ali absorbed with his rope-a-dope style had the cumulative effect of damaging regions of his brain important for motor control. As we discuss later in this chapter, Parkinsonian symptoms, which are caused by damage to specific (dopaminergic) neurons in a specific brain region (the substantia nigra), appear only after more than one-half of the neurons are destroyed. As cells die, the remainder try to do all the work, but at some point the number of damaged cells is too great and motor control deteriorates. Thus, although Ali sustained the damage during his long and illustrious boxing career, only afterward did the effects of this damage become apparent (Hauser, 1991).

Muhammed Ali's Parkinsonism was caused by destruction to just one of the many brain regions that permit the great diversity of motor skills that humans display. Before we discuss these various brain regions, let us first consider several of the many types of motor movements that humans can exhibit. In some motor acts, such as when hitting a tennis serve, you must coordinate movement of the gross and postural muscles in a smooth and seamless fashion. When learning to serve, you break down the process into a series of steps: Start to toss the ball, dip your legs, bring the racquet behind your back, push up on your legs, extend the racquet skyward, rotate your torso, and hit the ball. Consider how different such a step-by-step process is from the smooth, well-learned tennis serve of professionals like Martina Navratilova and Andre Agassi. Rather than seeming like a concatenation of separate movements, the swing of a tennis pro or even a good amateur player appears to be one smooth, continuous motion. As we learn later in this chapter, such smooth, rapid movements are aided by the cerebellum.

Other actions require that fine motor movements be precisely timed. When you touch-type (that is, when you type with five fingers instead of pecking with two), little gross muscle movement occurs because the position of your hand remains relatively static. Typing speed is increased by reducing the time between individual keystrokes. One way to do so is to adjust the typing of a given key on the basis of the keystrokes that precede and follow it. Our ability to make such adjustments implies that we create an overall motor program of the series of movements that we want to produce, then invoke this program when a series of finger strokes is executed. As we learn later, these motor programs are probably produced by a specific brain region known as the *supplementary motor area*. This area transmits information about the motor program to the primary motor area, which then activates the specific muscles required to institute the program.

In other motor acts, performance is linked to specific external cues, such as when you press on the gas pedal upon seeing a green light and step on the brake upon seeing a red light. When movements require us to break well-learned associations (e.g., pressing the gas pedal for a *red* light and stepping on the brake for a *green* one), when they are novel, or when they are less well rehearsed, the anterior cingulate region (a part of the limbic system, see chapter 1, page 21) is called into action.

Motor acts often involve multiple brain regions because they require many types of motor control to occur simultaneously (e.g., control over both the fine and gross muscles). However, as this brief introduction should illustrate, specific brain regions may play a more prominent role in certain motor acts than in others. We begin this chapter by reviewing the major brain regions involved in motor control and by pointing out the important contribution each makes. Afterward, we examine clinical syndromes in which motor processing is disrupted. These syndromes fall into two major categories: those resulting from damage to subcortical regions of the brain and those resulting from damage to the cortex. The subcortical syndromes that we discuss—Parkinson's disease, Huntington's disease, Tourette's syndrome, and tardive dyskinesia—all involve a disruption in the form of movements. These syndromes may lead to slowness or imprecision in movement, or to movement that should not occur (e.g., tremors, such as the head bobbing, or head-nodding, exhibited by Katharine Hepburn in her older years). In contrast, the cortical syndromes impair the conceptualizing, planning, and sequencing that underlie learned movements. In these cases, individuals have difficulty playing the piano or knowing how to program muscles to make the sign of the Christian cross.

BRAIN STRUCTURES INVOLVED IN MOTOR CONTROL

As we mentioned, a multiplicity of brain regions are involved in motor control. In this section, we review the five main brain structures involved in such control: the motor tracts, cerebellum, basal ganglia, motor cortices, and parietal lobes.

Motor Tracts

Before discussing the role of different brain regions in motor control, we must first discuss the basic underlying mechanism that makes muscles move. Muscles can be either in a contracted state or in an uncontracted state. Muscle contraction is caused by an impulse from a neuron at the **neuromuscular junction,** which is a place at which a neuron synapses on a muscle (Figure 4.1). Hence, for muscles to move, information must be relayed from the nervous system to the muscles. Without such control, paralysis occurs.

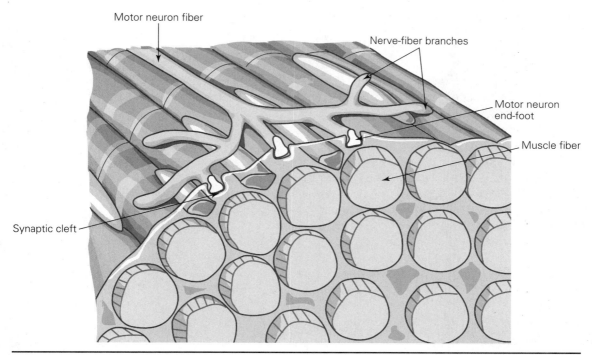

Motor neuron fiber

Nerve-fiber branches

Motor neuron end-foot

Muscle fiber

Synaptic cleft

Figure 4.1 The neuromuscular junction.
At this junction, a motor neuron fiber makes extensive contact with muscle fibers. When an action potential reaches the motor neuron end-foot, acetylcholine is released into the synaptic cleft, which generates an action potential in the muscle fiber. This action potential causes contraction. (*Note.* Adapted from Beatty, 1995, p. 253.)

The brain has not one, but four basic routes whereby information is transferred from the brain to the muscles: the corticospinal, corticobulbar, ventromedial, and rubrospinal pathways. Each of these routes innervates different types of target muscles (e.g., finger muscles vs. leg muscles) and hence is involved in different aspects of motor control (e.g., fine motor control vs. posture). These pathways are the mechanisms whereby motor movements planned in the brain are sent to target muscles to be executed. To better conceptualize the role that these pathways play in motor control, we might consider them akin to the infantry in the army: They carry out the orders but do not make them. Instead, the subcortical and cortical regions that we discuss later are the key regions for determining the form,

sequencing, and planning of these movements. The subcortical regions can be thought of as lieutenants who make sure that their platoons are moving along in proper form, whereas the cortical regions are more like generals who plan the actions of vast numbers of platoons. The lieutenants and generals do not cause the actual movement. Rather, the movement occurs because of the action of the infantry.

The first of the four pathways, the **corticospinal pathway,** links the cortex to the spinal cord, just as its name suggests. The cell bodies for these tracts are located mainly in the motor cortex. Two corticospinal tracts are of most importance. One, the **lateral corticospinal tract,** is responsible for the control of distal (i.e., far) limb muscles, such as those that innervate the arms, hands, fingers, lower leg,

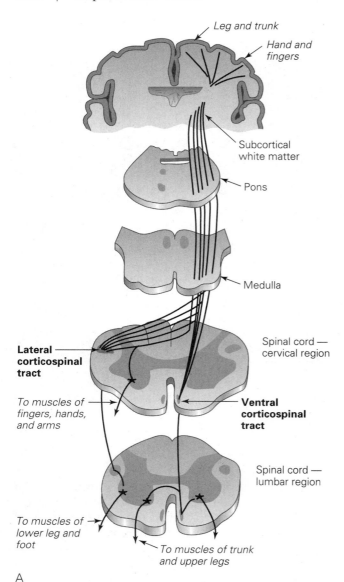

Leg and trunk

Hand and fingers

Subcortical white matter

Pons

Medulla

Lateral corticospinal tract

Spinal cord — cervical region

To muscles of fingers, hands, and arms

Ventral corticospinal tract

Spinal cord — lumbar region

To muscles of lower leg and foot

To muscles of trunk and upper legs

A

Figure 4.2 The four major motor pathways.
(A) The lateral and ventral corticospinal tracts of the corticospinal pathway. The lateral corticospinal tract, which controls fine motor movement of the distal extremities, crosses the midline at the level of the medulla so that motor control by this fiber tract is exclusively contralateral. In contrast, fibers of the ventral corticospinal tract, which are important for posture and locomotion, synapse both ipsilaterally and controlaterally. (B) The corticobulbar pathway, which is important for motor control of the face and tongue. In contrast to the corticospinal pathway, this pathway crosses the midline at the level of the pons. (C) The ventromedial pathway. This pathway is important for controlling movement of the trunk and proximal limbs; contributes to posture; coordinates head, trunk, and eye movements; and controls muscles involved in autonomic functions. (D) The rubrospinal pathway, which is important for independent movement of the forearms and hands from that of the trunk. Although this tract originates mainly in the red nucleus of the midbrain, it projects to primary motor cortex as well as to the cerebellum. (*Note.* Adapted from Carlson, 1986, pp. 304, 306.)

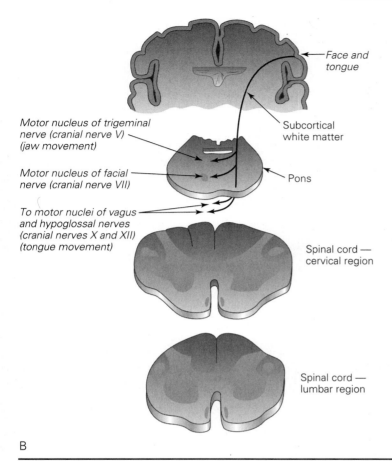

B

Figure 4.2   (Continued)

and foot. Damage to the lateral corticospinal tract has profound effects on the ability to reach and grasp objects and to manipulate them. After damage to this tract, a person would have difficulty grabbing and manipulating a key or twirling a pencil with his or her toes (as some talented individuals can do). Because this motor tract crosses the midline entirely in the medulla (as discussed in chapter 1, page 12), damage to it results in deficits in motor movement on the opposite side of the body. The other major tract within the corticospinal pathway, the **ventral corticospinal tract,** is important for controlling muscles of the trunk and upper legs, and it plays a more prominent role in the ability to walk and run

(i.e., to locomote) and to maintain posture. This tract projects both ipsilaterally and contralaterally (Figure 4.2A).

The second major motor pathway is the **corticobulbar pathway,** which also has most of its cell bodies located in the motor cortex. However, instead of synapsing in the spinal cord, these cells synapse in the pons on the fifth, seventh, tenth, and twelfth cranial nerves (Figure 4.2B). As we learned in chapter 1, these cranial nerves are important for innervation of the face and tongue. Some portions of the corticobulbar pathway have only contralateral projections, whereas other portions have both ipsilateral and contralateral connections. In particular,

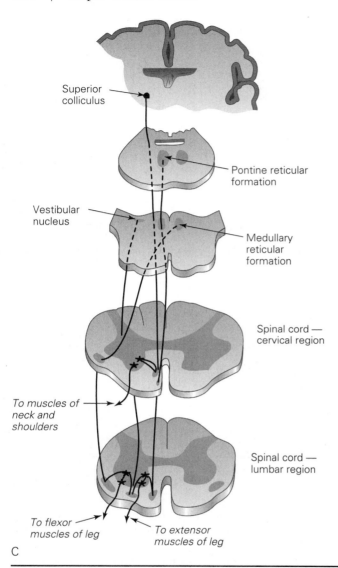

Superior colliculus

Pontine reticular formation

Vestibular nucleus

Medullary reticular formation

Spinal cord — cervical region

To muscles of neck and shoulders

Spinal cord — lumbar region

To flexor muscles of leg

To extensor muscles of leg

C

Figure 4.2   (Continued)

the regions of the motor cortex that control movements of the upper part of the face project both ipsilaterally and contralaterally. Therefore, the forehead area is usually unaffected by a unilateral lesion. As a result, people with unilateral lesions can still furrow their brows in frustration or raise their eyebrows in surprise, and they can wink each eye separately. In contrast, the regions controlling movement of the lower part of the face project only contralaterally. Because one side of the mouth cannot move, whereas the other is motile (i.e., can move), after damage to these regions, the result is often asymmetrical mouth movements. For example, drooping of one side of the face is common

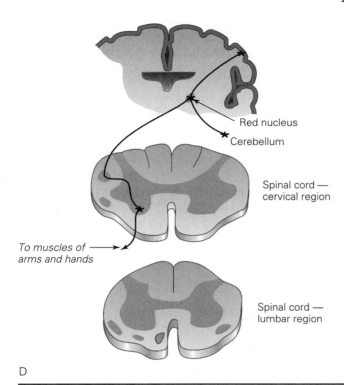

Red nucleus

Cerebellum

Spinal cord —
cervical region

*To muscles of
arms and hands*

Spinal cord —
lumbar region

D

Figure 4.2 (Continued)

after a stroke. Therefore, when the face region of the motor strip is damaged unilaterally, the lower half of the face on the contralateral side is deprived of any motor control, whereas the upper half of the face can still receive innervation from the undamaged ipsilateral hemisphere.

The two other major pathways, the ventromedial pathway and the rubrospinal pathway, do not originate in the cortex but mainly have their cell bodies in the brain stem. Both terminate in the spinal cord and have indirect linkages to primary motor cortex. The **ventromedial pathway** has a variety of functions. Primarily, it controls movements of the trunk and proximal (i.e., near) limb muscles. Along with the ventral corticospinal tract, it also contributes to posture. Hence, posture is severely compromised when both the ventromedial and corticospinal pathways are damaged. A division of the ventromedial

pathway is important for coordinating eye movements with those of the head and trunk. The cell bodies of these tracts originate, not surprisingly, in the superior colliculus, which, as we learned in chapter 1 (and discuss further in chapter 7), is important in eye movements. Other tracts in the ventromedial pathway control muscles involved in autonomic (involuntary) functions, such as sneezing, breathing, and muscle tone, along with other motor functions, such as walking. The cell bodies for these tracts reside in the nuclei of the brain stem (such as the vestibular nucleus and the medullary reticular formation) and in the pontine reticular formation (Figure 4.2C).

The last major pathway, the **rubrospinal pathway,** originates mainly in the cell bodies of the red nucleus located in the midbrain. This nucleus receives input from both the motor cortex and the

Table 4.1   The Four Major Motor Pathways and Their Characteristics

Pathway	Origin	Termination	Target muscles	Purpose
Corticospinal	Motor cortex: 1. Finger, hand, arm, lower leg, and foot regions 2. Trunk and upper leg regions	Spinal cord	1. Fingers, hands, arms, lower legs, and feet 2. Trunk and upper legs	1. Grasping and manipulating objects 2. Locomotion and posture
Corticobulbar	Motor cortex: Face region	Pons: Nuclei of cranial nerves V, VII, X, and XII	Face and tongue	Face and tongue movements
Ventromedial	Superior colliculus, nuclei in the medulla and pons	Spinal cord	Trunk, neck, and legs	1. Posture 2. Coordination of eye movements with those of trunk and head 3. Autonomic functions (e.g., respiration) 4. Walking
Rubrospinal	Red nucleus of the midbrain	Spinal cord	Hands (not fingers), feet, forearms, and lower legs	Allows independent movements of forearms and hands from that of the trunk

Note. Adapted from *Physiology of Behavior* (3rd ed., p. 308), by N. Carlson, 1986, Boston: Allyn & Bacon.

cerebellum, to which it also projects, forming a loop (Figure 4.2D). Loops in the nervous system usually provide an opportunity for modulation of control, and the role of the rubrospinal pathway can be well characterized as that of modulating motor movement. Damage to this pathway disrupts the ability to control movements of the forearms and hands, independent of the trunk. When this system is damaged in animals, limb movements are clumsy and usually cannot be produced without associated movements of the trunk (e.g., an animal cannot raise just an arm and have the rest of the body remain static) (Lawrence & Kuypers, 1968). In humans, however, the red nucleus is very small and the fibers of this tract are unmyelinated, facts suggesting that it may not play as prominent a role as in other species (Carpenter, 1976).

The basic characteristics of the major motor pathways, including their points of origination and termination, and their purposes, are summarized in Table 4.1.

Cerebellum

The **cerebellum,** looking much like a small cauliflower attached to the back of the brain, often does not receive much attention because it lies outside the cortex. Nonetheless, it plays an extremely important role in motor control, especially in the modulation of motor movements and in the learning of motor skills. The anatomy of the cerebellum is such that it contains two hemispheres and three divisions within each hemisphere. From the midline, the three divisions are the vermis, the intermediate zone, and the lateral zone. Embedded within the cerebellum are three nuclei, which are known as deep cerebellar nuclei: the **fastigial nucleus,** the **interpositus nucleus,** and the **dentate nucleus.** Each region of the cerebellum projects to a different deep cerebellar nucleus: The vermis projects to the fastigial nucleus, the intermediate zone projects to the interpositus nucleus, and the lateral zone projects to the dentate nucleus. The structure of the cerebellum is shown in Figure 4.3.

Before we examine the inputs and outputs of each of these major zones of the cerebellum and examine how damage to each of them affects motoric processing, a few general principles about the

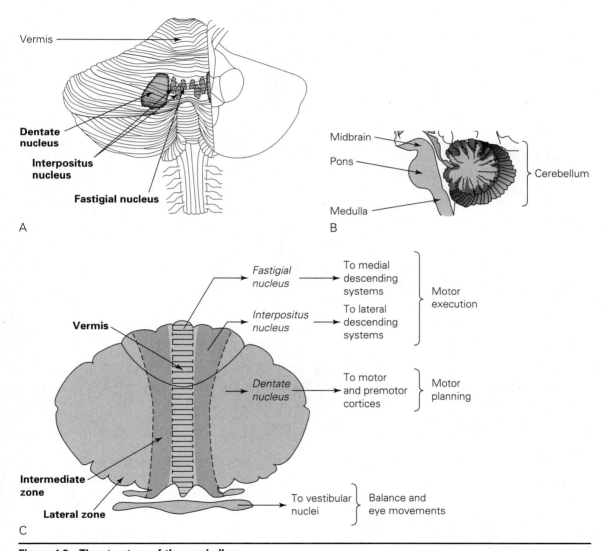

Figure 4.3 The structure of the cerebellum.
(A) Dorsal view showing the location of the deep cerebellar nuclei. (B) Midsagittal view of the cerebellum. (C) Main functional divisions of the cerebellum with their outputs. (*Note.* A, Adapted from Kandel et al., 1995, p. 538; B & C, Adapted from Kandel et al., 1991, pp. 629, 633.)

cerebellum are worth noting. First, in our discussion of cerebellar organization, you should notice that the projection of information through the cerebellum often forms loops that connect with other brain regions important for motor functioning. In this way, the cerebellum is perfectly positioned to have a modulatory effect on motor processing, and it may act as a mechanism to determine whether the ongoing movement is matching the intended movement. Second, unlike motor cortex, which acts on contralateral muscles, the cerebellum modulates *ipsilateral* muscles. Finally, areas of the cerebellum near the midline are responsible for functions associated with the body's center, including posture and control of speech. In contrast, more lateral areas of the cerebellum control the lateralized structures, including the limbs and the eyes.

We now examine the three main divisions of the cerebellum. The **vermis,** located on the midline of the cerebellum, receives somatosensory and kinesthetic information from the spinal cord. It projects to the fastigial nucleus, which in turn influences some of the ventromedial pathway tracts, which, as we discussed earlier in the chapter, are important for posture. Given the type of information that is fed into the vermis (i.e., somatosensory and kinesthetic) and the pathways to which it projects, we should not be surprised to learn that damaging the vermis leads to difficulty with postural adjustments and with movement such as walking. If you deactivate the fastigial nucleus unilaterally in a monkey, the animal tends to fall to the side of space ipsilateral to the deactivated cerebellar hemisphere (because of the ipsilateral cerebellar control). Other movements, such as those made with the arms and fingers, are unaffected because, as we learned earlier, these are controlled by the corticospinal pathways, to which the fastigial nucleus has no connections.

The **intermediate zone of the cerebellum** receives information from the red nucleus (which receives projections in part from motor cortex) and somatosensory information from the spinal cord. This zone projects to the interpositus nucleus, which in turn projects to the red nucleus, creating a loop. Damage to the intermediate zone of the cerebellar cortex results in rigidity and difficulty in moving the limbs. In monkeys, deactivation of the interpositus nucleus causes tremors, which are observed most often when the animal reaches for something, such as a piece of food. Similar problems have been observed in humans with localized cerebellar atrophy and are most often characterized as an inability to make smooth movements to a target location. An affected person makes such movements in a staggered manner, especially as he or she zeroes in on the target. This behavior is sometimes referred to as an **action tremor (intention tremor)** because it occurs during the performance of an act. This type of tremor is distinct from that seen with disorders of the basal ganglia, in which the tremor is much more likely to occur at rest. As mentioned in chapter 1, neurologists often screen for cerebellar damage by having an individual touch his or her nose and then the neurologist's nose. An individual with damage to the lateral zone of the cerebellum can perform this task, but the path the hand takes from one nose to the other is often staggered, jerky, and zigzag.

The **lateral zone of the cerebellum** receives input from both motor and association cortices through the pons. This zone projects to the dentate nucleus, which in turn projects back to the the primary motor cortex through the red nucleus and the ventrolateral thalamus. Damage to the lateral zone affects four types of movements. One type is rapid and smooth **ballistic movement,** which is a movement that occurs so quickly that it leaves little or no time for the movement to be modified by feedback. In a ballistic movement, the precise time at which the movement of individual muscles start and stop is preprogrammed. The swing of a batter trying to hit a ball moving at 90 mph (144 km/hour) is a good example of a ballistic movement. Although the adage says to "Keep your eye on the ball," the ball moves so rapidly that the batter has no time to adjust the swing as the ball nears the plate, but rather must preprogram movements on the basis of the initial flight path of the ball soon after it leaves the pitcher's hand. (Often pitchers throw sliders or knuckle balls, which, because they make the ball take an irregular curved path rather than a straight trajectory, taxes the batter's ability to produce the correct ballistic movement that will cause good contact with the ball.) The typical problem with ballistic movements after lateral cerebellar damage is an overshooting of the target. This overshooting occurs because individuals cannot calculate when each muscle group must be turned on and then off to land at the target. These patients tend to put the brakes on a movement only when they see that their arm or finger is almost at the target, which is too late (e.g., C. Marsden et al., 1977).

The second set of difficulties experienced by individuals with damage to the lateral cerebellar cortex involve the coordination of multijoint movements. Because multijoint coordination breaks down, movements are best accomplished by moving one joint at a time in a serial manner, a strategy known as **decomposition of movement.** For example, rather than lifting a glass by moving the entire arm, an individual with damage to the lateral cerebellar cortex is taught in rehabilitation to place an elbow on a table, to lean forward, and to bring the glass to his or her mouth. With the elbow stationary, the number of joints that must be moved is decreased, which increases the likelihood of a successful movement (Thach, 1992). In the monkey, inactivation of the dentate nucleus (which receives projections from the lateral cerebellar regions) results in both overshooting and lack of coordination of compound finger movements.

Third, damage to the lateral zone of the cerebellum can hamper the learning of new movements. Let's consider the case of throwing a dart at a target. The ability to coordinate eye fixation on a target with arm movement is an acquired skill (which explains the difference in accuracy between the throw of a major league baseball player and that of an amateur in a hometown league). An individual with cerebellar damage who had decent eye-hand coordination prior to injury can throw a dart with relative accuracy. However, if this task is changed a bit so that new learning must occur, deficits are exhibited. For example, if a person is wearing prism eyeglasses that displace the view of the world 15 degrees to one side, hitting the target will require a recalibration of the relationship between the position of the gaze and the arm movement. Neurologically intact individuals can gradually make this adjustment if given

enough practice. When the prisms are removed, the throws are once again off target, but these individuals learn to recalibrate the relationship between the gaze and the throw back to its original value (Figure 4.4A). In contrast, patients with cerebellar damage who are wearing prisms never learn to adapt their movement to hit the target, even after much practice. Because they never learn the new gaze-throw relationship, they, unlike the neurologically intact individuals, can hit the target as soon as the spectacles are removed (Figure 4.4B) (see Thach, Goodkin, & Keating, 1992, for a description of this research, as well as a general research review of the role of the cerebellum in the coordination of movement).

Finally, the lateral zone of the cerebellum seems to be important in the timing of not only motor movements, but cognitive functions as well. Lesions in this region compromise the ability to perform simple but precisely timed tapping movements. In addition, they impair the ability to make judgments about time, such as whether one tone lasts longer than another. Thus, this region of the brain seems to act as a central timing mechanism, or clock (Ivry & Keele, 1989). This function may overlap with the cerebellum's role in making mental and motor processes fluid (e.g., J. Fiez, Petersen, Cheney, & Raichle, 1992; also refer to chapter 1, page 16).

As we just learned, the cerebellum has a multiplicity of roles with regard to motor control: It is important for posture, smooth movements, coordinated multilimb movements, ballistic movements, and motor learning. In part, these different roles are the province of different regions of the cerebellum. Damage to the cerebellum does not eradicate motor movements so much as it degrades motor capabilities. A summary of the different parts of the cerebellum and their roles in motor control is presented in Table 4.2.

Basal Ganglia

The **basal ganglia** are a complex collection of subcortical nuclei consisting of the **caudate nucleus** and **putamen** (known collectively as the *striatum*) and the **globus pallidus** (or *pallidum*). The caudate

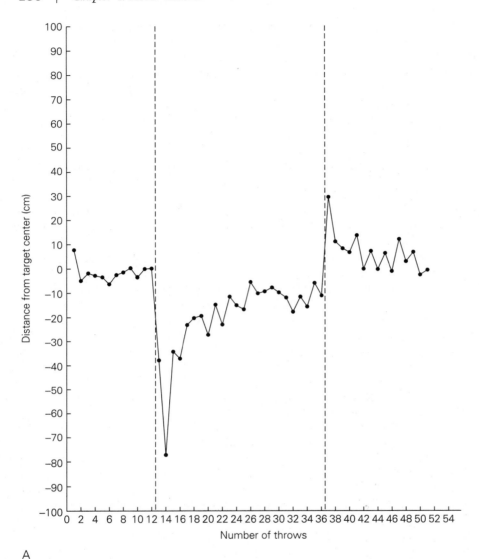

A

Figure 4.4 The role of the cerebellum in motor learning.
Shown here are plots of dart-throwing accuracy for a series of throws by two individuals. The first dashed line indicates when the individual puts on the prism spectacles, and the second dashed line indicates when they are taken off. (A) Plot for a neurologically intact individual. After putting on the prisms, the person's throw is far off target, but with practice, the individual's aim improves. After the eyeglasses are removed, the throw is off again but quickly becomes recalibrated. (B) Plot for an individual with cerebellar damage. The introduction of the eyeglasses leads to inaccurate throws, which are not adjusted with practice. Because no learning has taken place, the individual's accuracy returns to the preprism base line almost immediately after the eyeglasses are removed. (*Note.* Adapted from Thach et al., 1992, pp. 429, 431.)

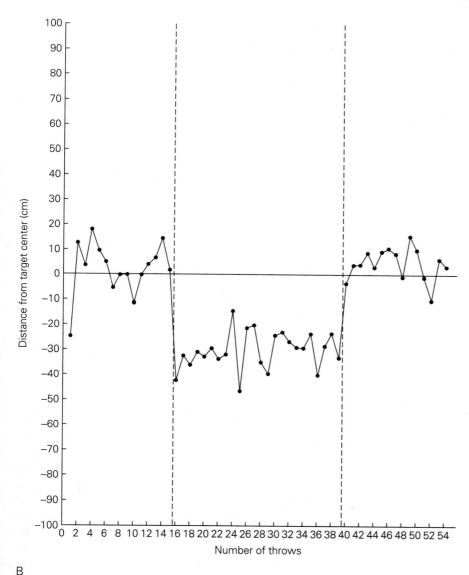

B

Figure 4.4 (Continued)

and putamen receive all the input to the basal ganglia, input that comes from practically all the different regions of the cerebral cortex, as well as the substantia nigra (discussed later in this paragraph) and the thalamus. The globus pallidus is the main output pathway from the basal ganglia and connects with the thalamus. Through the thalamus, the basal ganglia are connected to both motor and nonmotor regions, including, in the latter case, the dorsolateral prefrontal cortex, lateral orbitofrontal cortex, and anterior cingulate cortex. Thus, the basal ganglia help to form a loop of sorts, up from the globus

Table 4.2 The Different Parts of the Cerebellum and Their Roles in Motor Control

Cerebellar region	Inputs	Associated nucleus	Output from associated nucleus	Function
Vermis	Somatosensory and kinesthetic information from the spinal cord	Fastigial	Ventromedial pathway	Modulation of posture and walking
Intermediate zone	Red nucleus (with projections in part from motor cortex) and somatosensory information from the spinal cord	Interpositus	Red nucleus	Smooth, unrigid limb movements
Lateral zone	Motor and association cortices through the pons	Dentate	Primary motor cortex through the red nucleus and ventrolateral thalamus	1. Ballistic movements 2. Coordination of multijoint movements 3. Learning of new motor skills 4. Timing of motor and cognitive processes

pallidus to the thalamus and cortex, which then connects back down into the striatum. Output from the basal ganglia also influences eye movements through the superior colliculus. Two other nuclei, the **substantia nigra** and the subthalamic nucleus, are also associated with the basal ganglia. The substantia nigra projects to the basal ganglia through the **nigrostriatal bundle,** whereas the subthalamine nucleus has input into one part of the globus pallidus and receives connections from another (Alexander, DeLong, & Strick, 1986). The basal ganglia, thus, are at the crossroads of the neural circuits involved in motor control (Figure 4.5) (for a description of the multiple anatomical connections of the basal ganglia, see Alexander & Crutcher, 1990).

Unlike the cerebellum, which plays a role in the rapid ballistic movements, the basal ganglia are more important for the accomplishment of movements that may take some time to initiate or stop. The basal ganglia have been suggested to have multiple roles in motor control: "setting" the motor system with regard to posture, preparing the nervous system to accomplish a voluntary motor act, acting as an autopilot for well-learned behaviors, controlling the timing and switching between motor acts, and, because both motor and nonmotor information feed into the basal ganglia, playing a role in motor planning and learning, especially when motor acts have motivational significance (i.e., lead to a reward) or involve more cognitive components (e.g., motor learning). (See Graybiel, Aosaki, Flaherty, & Kimura, 1994, for a description of how the modular neural organization of the basal ganglia makes them particularly well-suited for learning).

To best understand the role of the basal ganglia in movement and movement disorders, look at Figure 4.6. The caudate and putamen, which receive all the input to the basal ganglia, connect to the main output region of the basal ganglia, the internal section of the globus pallidus, by two routes. One route, the direct route, directly connects these two regions in an inhibitory fashion. The other is an indirect route in which the caudate and putamen

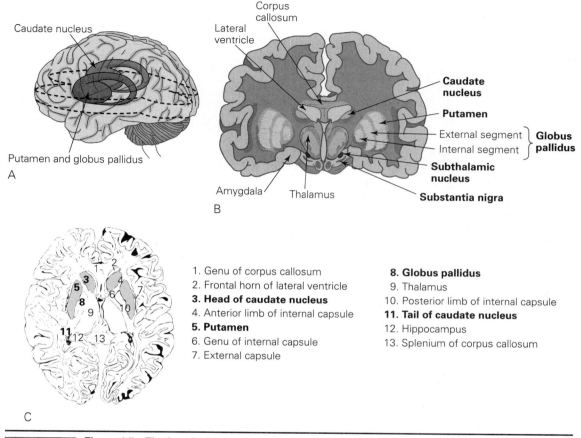

Figure 4.5 The basal ganglia in relation to other brain structures.

1. Genu of corpus callosum
2. Frontal horn of lateral ventricle
3. **Head of caudate nucleus**
4. Anterior limb of internal capsule
5. **Putamen**
6. Genu of internal capsule
7. External capsule

8. **Globus pallidus**
9. Thalamus
10. Posterior limb of internal capsule
11. **Tail of caudate nucleus**
12. Hippocampus
13. Splenium of corpus callosum

Figure 4.5   The basal ganglia in relation to other brain structures.
(A) The basal ganglia in relation to the neocortex. (B) Coronal and (C) horizontal sections indicating the location of the basal ganglia. (*Note.* A & C, Adapted from Rosenzweig & Leiman, 1989, p. 64; B, Adapted from Kandel et al., 1991, p. 648.)

connect to the external section of the globus pallidus in an inhibitory fashion, which in turn connects to the subthalamic nucleus in an inhibitory fashion, which then connects to the internal section of the globus pallidus in an excitatory fashion. The internal section of the the globus pallidus then has inhibitory connections to motor nuclei of the thalamus. The motor nuclei of thalamus serve to excite the cortex. Activity in the direct route causes inhibition of the internal sections of the globus pallidus, so that it can no longer inhibit the thalamus from exciting the cortex. Thus, activity in this route allows for

sustaining or facilitating ongoing action (because inhibition of the thalamus is decreased). In contrast, activity in the indirect pathway causes the subthalamic nuclei to activate the internal section of the globus pallidus, which suppresses thalamic activity. This pathway is thought to be important for suppressing unwanted movement.

Damage to the basal ganglia produces various motor disorders, depending on which regions of the ganglia are affected. Parkinson's disease is characterized by **akinesia** (the lack of spontaneous movement), **bradykinesia** (slowness of move-

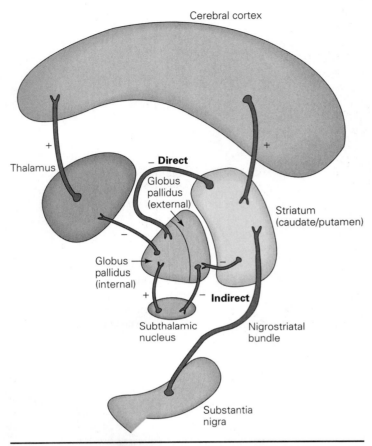

Cerebral cortex

Thalamus

− **Direct**

Globus
pallidus
(external)

Striatum
(caudate/putamen)

Globus
pallidus
(internal)

Subthalamic
nucleus

Indirect

Nigrostriatal
bundle

Substantia
nigra

Figure 4.6   The connections between different sections of the basal ganglia.
Inhibitory connections (indicated by a minus sign) and excitatory connections (indicated by a plus sign). Two routes exist between the caudate and putamen (which receive all the input to the basal ganglia) and the internal section of the globus pallidus (the main output region of the basal ganglia). One route is a direct route (inhibitory) between these two regions. The other is an indirect route from the caudate and putamen to the external section of the globus pallidus (inhibitory), to the subthalamic nucleus (inhibitory), then finally to the internal section of the globus pallidus (excitatory). The globus pallidus has inhibitory connections to motor nuclei of the thalamus. The motor nuclei of the thalamus serve to excite the cortex. (*Note.* Adapted from Graybiel, 1990, p. 246; Mink & Thach, 1993, p. 952.)

ment), and **tremors** (rhythmic, oscillating movements). In Parkinson's disease, the major problem is that the section of the putamen from which the direct pathway arises is not receiving the excitatory effects of a specific neurotransmitter, *dopamine*. This dopamine deficiency is caused by the death of cell bodies in the substantia nigra, which project to the basal ganglia through the nigrostriatal bundle.

The death of cells in the substantia nigra (meaning "black substance") can be seen easily on autopsies of patients with Parkinson's disease because this region does not stain the usual dark color that is seen in neurologically intact individuals. Because there is no input to the direct pathway, the indirect pathway becomes overactive (see Figure 4.6), which causes much activity in the internal portion of the globus pallidus, which in turn inhibits the thalamus and results in decreased motor activity (Albin, Young, & Penney, 1989).

If the striatum of the basal ganglia itself is damaged, however, as in Huntington's disease, a different set of motor problems is observed. In this disorder, **hyperkinesias,** which are involuntary undesired movements, are common. One type of hyperkinesia is **chorea** (derived from the Greek *khoros,* meaning "dance"), which is uncontrollable, jerky movements such as twitching and abrupt jerking of the body. Another type is **athetosis,** which is involuntary writhing contractions and twisting of the body into abnormal postures. In Huntington's disease, neurons in the striatum that use the neurotransmitters *gamma-aminobutyric acid (GABA)* and *acetylcholine,* both of which are inhibitory, are most affected. Acetylcholine appears to be the transmitter used by interneurons that connect with one another within the striatum, whereas GABA is the neurotransmitter used by cells that connect from the striatum to the globus pallidus (C. D. Marsden, 1986). In Huntington's disease, the indirect pathway from the striatum to the internal section of the globus pallidus is underactive due to destruction of particular regions of the caudate and putamen from which these fibers arise (see Figure 4.6). In this case, the output from the globus pallidus is decreased, which lessens inhibition on the thalamus and leads to more motor activity (Albin, Young, & Penney, 1989).

The role of the basal ganglia in the initiation and termination of movements, particularly those oriented toward a goal or in response to a stimulus can be well illustrated by some of the symptoms of Parkinson's disease and Huntington's disease. For example, a person with Parkinson's disease may take a long time to begin to walk across a floor, but once

started, the individual may continue like a runaway train. Also in Parkinson's disease, a person may be unable to initiate the leg movement required to kick a stationary ball, but if the ball is rolled toward him or her, the ball will act as a trigger, and the person will respond with a kick. Conversely, researchers have suggested that chorea observed in Huntington's disease may result from an inability to suppress a response to sensory stimuli (see Albin, Young, & Penney, 1989, for a discussion of basal ganglia anatomy and how damage to them leads to motor disorders). Later in this chapter, we discuss the motoric aspects of Parkinson's disease and Huntington's disease in more detail.

Motor Cortices

Several regions of the brain are involved in creating the motor plans that underlie coordinated, skilled movements. After first reviewing the concept of a motor plan, we examine three of the areas involved in creating motor plans: the supplementary motor area, the anterior cingulate cortex, and the frontal eye fields.

Concept of a Motor Plan

As we learned earlier in this chapter and in chapter 1, the primary motor cortex relays information to the spinal cord (and in the case of facial muscles, to the pons) to enable muscle control on the contralateral side of the body. When the motor cortex is damaged, the force with which muscles are exerted cannot be controlled, and the result is weakness and imprecise fine motor movements. Yet, skilled movement requires more than being able to move the muscles: It also requires coordination and timing of muscle movements. For example, the physical ability to move our muscles is clearly insufficient if we want to give a speech or play the piano. Such complicated motor tasks require a plan of action. Areas of the cortex that are distinct from yet project to primary motor cortex are believed to be important for the creation of such plans.

A plan of action, or **motor program** as it is often called, is believed to be an abstract representation of an intended movement. It must contain not only general information about the goal that a series of movements is intended to achieve, but also specific information about the neuromuscular control that will allow the goal to be reached (see Keele, 1968). Suppose that the goal of the plan is to type the sentence, "The lazy white cat just languished in the sun as the bunny bolted across the yard." In this case, the motor program should contain information about which fingers will move, the order in which they will move, the direction in which they will move, the timing between movements, and so forth.

Evidence that the human brain creates an overall plan of a series of complicated motor movements comes primarily from studies examining motor control in the oral and manual domains. One phenomenon suggestive of motor planning is **coarticulation,** in which we see differences in how the vocal muscles produce different sounds (most notably vowels), depending on what precedes them. For example, the sound /u/ requires the lips to be rounded (unless you are a ventriloquist!). Consonants, however, can be produced acceptably with or without lip rounding. Thus, if a series of consonants precedes a vowel requiring lip rounding, the consonants will be produced with rounded lips. Look at yourself in the mirror as you say "construe." Notice that your lips are rounded as you begin to say "str" of the second syllable. Now look in the mirror at the shape of your lips as you say "constrict." You should have noticed that when you said the "str" of this word, your lips were not rounded because the vowel *i* did not require it. Examples such as these indicate that some preplanning of speech must have occurred. However, is the *entire* utterance planned in advance? Perhaps motor commands are generated in a chainlike manner allowing movements to be planned only a couple of steps ahead rather than requiring the entire sequence to be planned before an action begins (see Wright, 1990, for a further description of some of these phenomena).

Researchers have found evidence that humans can indeed plan an entire motor sequence before initiating action. In their experiments, the researchers told their participants to produce a fluent stream of words, but only after a signal let them know to do so. The utterances were well practiced so that the subjects could produce them fluently. The critical variable in the study was the time an individual took to begin to say the utterance after the signal appeared. The researchers reasoned that if the motor plan were being continually created "on-line," the number of words in an utterance would not influence how long a person would take to start the utterance. The person would plan speech "on the fly," keeping a step or two ahead of what he or she was actually saying. Such a strategy would be invoked in an equivalent manner regardless of whether the individual was saying an utterance that consisted of three words or one that consisted of seven. However, if a motor plan of the entire utterance was created before the person began to speak, the time to initiate speech would be related to the length of the utterance. Because short utterances would require little time to plan, an individual would begin to speak more quickly with these than if she or he was asked to say a longer utterance, which would require more time to plan. The logic behind these experiments is shown in Figure 4.7. The results of these experiments indicated that the latency to begin speaking increased linearly with the number of words in the utterance, indicating that each word increased the latency to begin speaking by a set amount. Hence, the brain generates an entire plan of action before movement commences, rather than just creating the plan as actions are being performed (e.g., Sternberg, Monsell, Knoll, & Wright, 1978).

As mentioned previously, the regions of the brain that are involved in creating these motor plans lie outside the primary motor cortex. Most are located in the frontal cortex or are associated with frontal cortex. They include the supplementary motor area, the anterior cingulate cortex, and the frontal eye fields. Parietal regions are also involved in skilled motor action, linking motoric movements to extrapersonal space and to their meaning, as in gesture. In the following sections, we turn our attention to these frontal areas, which are depicted in Figure

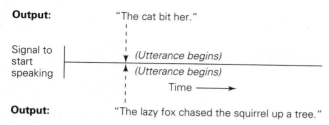

Planning: The cat bit her.

Output: "The cat bit her."

Signal to start speaking — (Utterance begins) / (Utterance begins) — Time ⟶

Output: "The lazy fox chased the squirrel up a tree."

Planning: The lazy fox chased the squirrel up a tree.

A

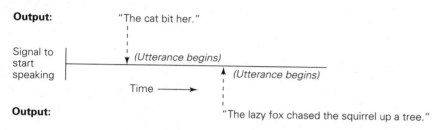

Planning: The cat bit her.

Output: "The cat bit her."

Signal to start speaking — (Utterance begins) / (Utterance begins) — Time ⟶

Output: "The lazy fox chased the squirrel up a tree."

Planning: The lazy fox chased the squirrel up a tree.

B

Figure 4.7 Testing for the existence of a motor program.
(A) If the brain just plans a step or two ahead, the time required to initiate an utterance should not be affected by the length of the utterance—in this case, four versus nine words. (B) In contrast, if the brain must plan the entire utterance before initiating speech, the longer the utterance, the longer the delay before its initiation.

4.8, and to the way in which they influence motor planning. Afterward, we discuss the role of the parietal region.

Supplementary Motor Area

One of the main regions of the brain that plays a role in planning, preparing and initiating movements is the **supplementary motor area (SMA).** The SMA is located on the medial surface of each hemisphere (in the longitudinal fissure) anterior to the region of the primary motor cortex that controls movement of the foot and dorsal to the cingulate sulcus (see Figure 4.8). The SMA connects to the primary motor area in a topographic fashion and is often called the *premotor* area, a name that aptly describes its position in front of the motor area and also its role in sending commands to the motor area, making it prior in the chain of command. Unlike motor cortex, which has totally contralateral outputs, each SMA projects to both the ipsilateral and the contralateral motor cortex, as well as to the contralateral SMA. This neuronal wiring allows one SMA to influence motor control on both sides of the body.

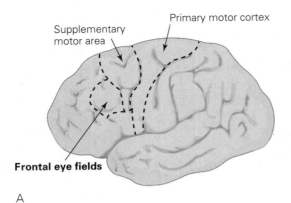

A

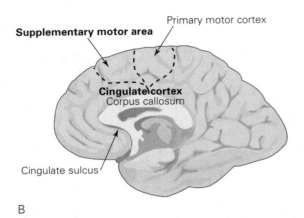

B

Figure 4.8   The major regions of the cortex involved in motor control.
(A) Left hemisphere, lateral view. (B) Right hemisphere, midsagittal view. (*Note.* Adapted from Kolb & Whishaw, 1990, p. 464.)

Unlike unilateral damage to the primary motor areas, which produces difficulties in exerting force, damage to the SMA in nonhuman primates mainly produces difficulty in bimanual coordination. These animals are unable to execute different movements of the fingers on each hand because the hands no longer work independently but rather tend to make the same movement at the same time. These deficits are abolished when the corpus callosum is sectioned, a finding that suggests that connections between the SMAs in each hemisphere are also important

for coordinating hand movements (Brinkman, 1984).

The SMA's role in motor planning has been demonstrated in studies with both animals and humans. In monkeys trained to plan a simple response to a stimulus, the firing of SMA neurons (as examined using single-cell recording techniques) was found to change systematically when the movement was being planned. By comparing the time at which the firing rate of a cell in the SMA changed with the time when electrical activity began in the limbs associated with the movement (remember, neuronal firing is necessary for a muscle to move), researchers determined that the firing rate in the SMA changed *before* electrical activity was recorded at the limb (Tanji, Taniguchi, & Saga, 1980). Thus, these data indicate that the SMA is involved in planning movement prior to initiation of an action.

Research with humans provides a similar picture regarding the role of the SMA in the planning of complex movement. First, functional brain imaging studies indicate that this area becomes active during tasks that require complicated motor sequencing. For example, an increase in SMA activity is observed when an individual must guide a finger by touch (not vision) to a specific place within a grid of rectangular rods, or when he or she must repetitively touch the limb of one hand to the fingertips in a 16-sequence set of movements (Roland, Larsen, Lassen, & Skinhøj, 1980). As suggested in animal studies, activity in the SMA is linked to planning of both hands because even in tasks in which only one hand was moving, an increase in blood flow occurred *bilaterally* (i.e., over both SMAs). In contrast, changes in blood flow over the primary motor cortex occurred only contralateral to the hand that was moving. The SMA is specifically involved in *complex* movements. No increase in SMA activity occurs during a simple repetitive task, such as pressing a spring between the thumb and index fingers one time a second, even though blood flow increases substantially (30%) over the contralateral primary motor area.

Second, the SMA is active even when participants are asked to imagine, but not actually perform, a complex finger-sequencing task. Although blood flow to the SMA increases about 20% under these conditions, blood flow does not increase over primary motor cortex; this finding indicates that the individuals were not performing the motor task but merely managing it (Roland, Larsen, Lassen, & Skinhøj, 1980). Such evidence suggests that the SMA plays an important role in planning complex movements. Because of the topographic relationship between the SMA and the motor cortex, scientists think that commands are programmed in the SMA, which feeds them to the primary motor cortex, which in turn directly controls the muscles that perform the movement (see Goldberg, 1985, for a review of much research in animals and humans on the SMA and its role in motor planning).

Anterior Cingulate Cortex

The **anterior cingulate cortex** has also been implicated in the control of motor movements, especially when they are novel or require much cognitive control. It is located below the cingulate sulcus but above the corpus callosum (see Figure 4.8B). Unlike most other areas of cortex, it has five cell layers rather than six, and from an evolutionary viewpoint, is one of the more primitive parts of the brain.

The anterior cingulate cortex appears to be involved not only in motor movements but in their planning as well. Whereas lesions of the cingulate cortex interfere with motor function, extra activity in this region, such as that generated during epileptic seizures, causes motor activity. Moreover, stimulation of the anterior cingulate gyrus in monkeys leads to vocalization as well as to movements of the body, some of which can be complex (e.g., sucking). Evidence that the region is involved in the preparation for movement comes from single-cell recordings. Activity is observed in the anterior cingulate cortex before the beginning of hand movements, regardless of whether they are initiated internally by the animal (i.e., in self-paced tasks) or occur in response to a sensory signal from the environment (Vogt, Finch, & Olson, 1992).

A group of researchers at McGill University suggest that the anterior cingulate cortex plays a role in modulating and funneling motor commands in humans, especially when the movements to be produced are novel or unrehearsed and hence influenced by cognitive factors (Paus, Petrides, Evans, & Meyer, 1993). To test their hypothesis, these investigators recorded regional brain activity with positron emission tomography (PET) while individuals performed motor tasks that required manual, oral, or ocular movements. For each manner of movement (oral, manual, or ocular), the researchers administered two types of tasks: one that was well practiced and one that was not. For example, in the well-practiced oral task, after hearing "A," subjects responded "B," or after hearing "L," they responded "M." In the novel task, the stimuli were the same, but the task demands were different. In this task, when individuals heard "A," they responded "M," and when they heard "B," they responded "L."

The study revealed two important findings. First, these investigators found that the anterior cingulate cortex had a specific topography. Tasks requiring manual movements activated the most caudal region of the anterior cingulate cortex, those requiring oculomotor movements the most rostral, and those requiring speech the area between. Hence, like the organization of primary and supplementary motor areas, the organization of the anterior cingulate region is topographic. Second, the researchers found that this region was most active when a novel response was required but was not very active when the response had been ingrained over the course of a lifetime (such as saying "B" in response to "A") or over hundreds of trials preceding the PET scan. These findings suggest that the anterior cingulate cortex plays a role in linking motor and cognitive behavior, especially when that linkage is novel or newly learned.

Frontal Eye Fields

Another region in the frontal lobes that play a role in voluntary movement is the **frontal eye fields**, which are located anterior to the SMA and dorsal to Broca's area (see Figure 4.8A). As their name suggests, the frontal eye fields control voluntary eye movements. These movements are distinct from reflexive eye movements, which occur when something such as a loud noise or a large bright moving object pulls a person's attention to a particular point in space. Such reflexive eye movements are under the control of the superior colliculus (which we discuss in chapter 7). In contrast, voluntary eye movements are programmed by the individual, such as when searching a crowd for a friend's face.

The neural system controlling voluntary eye movements (involving the frontal eye fields), and that controlling reflexive eye movements (involving the superior colliculus), can work independently. For example, eye movements that occur when the frontal eye fields are stimulated in the monkey are not affected by removal of the superior colliculus (Schiller, True, & Conway, 1980). Yet, both of these systems synapse on brain-stem centers that direct the actual eye movements by means of the third, fourth, and sixth cranial nerves. Thus, the neural control of both voluntary and involuntary eye movements appears to occur through a final common output pathway, even though they can work separately.

If each of these two systems can control the eye-movement centers in the brain stem, why doesn't massive conflict occur? The conflict seems to be avoided because the frontal eye fields have precedence: They strongly influence the superior colliculus. In humans, damage to the frontal eye fields makes suppressing automatic eye movements that occur when an attention-grabbing stimulus appears in the periphery difficult because the frontal eye fields can't inhibit the response (Paus et al., 1991). In monkeys, cells in the frontal eye fields excite the cells in the superior colliculus that are important for moving the eyes in the same direction, while inhibiting the cells important for movements in other directions (Schlag-Rey, Schlag & Dassonville, 1992).

In humans, the frontal eye fields are also important for **conjugate lateral eye movements,** which are rapid eye movements in a sideways direction. The right frontal eye field controls movements in a leftward direction, and the left frontal eye field controls movement in a rightward direction. Because of this directional specificity, some researchers attempted to use conjugate lateral eye movements to index hemispheric activation (with leftward movements indicating right-hemisphere activation and rightward movements indicating left-hemisphere activation). In these studies, individuals are asked questions designed to engage one hemisphere more than the other, such as "Think of your mother's face" (presumably a right-hemisphere question) or "Think of the definition of the word *commence*" (presumably a left-hemisphere question). As the participants begin to think about the correct answer, their gaze usually deviates to one side, and its direction of movement is recorded by an experimenter. Although some studies revealed that leftward deviations were more common after tasks requiring greater right-hemisphere processing and rightward deviations were more common after tasks requiring left-hemisphere processing, these findings have not been robust. For instance, some investigators have suggested that certain methods used in some studies to measure the direction of eye movements might be problematic (e.g, the participant could have been distracted by having an experimenter watching his or her eye movements) (see Ehrlichman & Weinberger, 1978, for a review of some of these studies).

Although examining hemispheric involvement by using conjugate lateral eye movements fell into disfavor, some newer methods have provided evidence that eye movements might be used to index not only hemispheric differences, but other cognitive processes as well. In these studies, eye movements are monitored less intrusively by an infrared beam bounced off the eyes and recorded by a computer. This method has revealed differences in eye movements depending on the stimulus examined. For example, in one study, more leftward eye movements were made to faces than to vases, a finding consistent with a special role for the right hemisphere in processing faces above and beyond other complex visuospatial stimuli (Mertens, Siegmund, & Gruesser, 1993) (Figure 4.9). Later in this book, in chapter 9, we revisit the issue of using

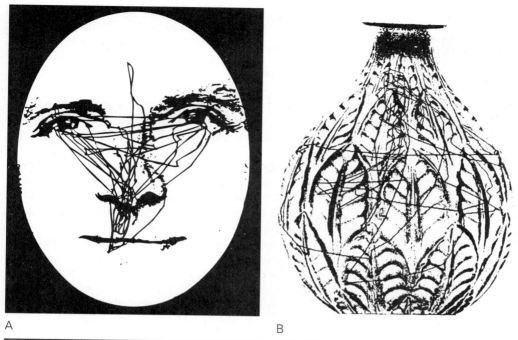

A B

Figure 4.9 The use of eye movements to investigate hemispheric differences.
Patterns of eye position during a 20-s inspection period for (A) a face and (B) a vase. Note that with regard to the face, much more time is spent looking at the left side of the figure, especially the mouth, whereas for the vase more time is spent on the right (this is most noticeable at the top of the figure). (*Note.* Reprinted from *Neuropsychologia*, vol. 31, I. Mertens, H. Siegmund, and O. J. Gruesser, "Gaze Motor Asymmetries in the Perception of Faces During a Memory Task," p. 991, Copyright 1993, with permission from Elsevier Science, Ltd., The Boulevard, Langford Lane, Kidlington OX5 1GB, UK.)

eye movements to make inferences about cognitive processing.

Parietal Lobes

The role of the parietal lobe in motor programming is twofold: First, it is involved in the control of movements in space; second, it contributes to the ability to produce complex, well-learned motor acts. These two aspects of motor control appear to rely on different regions of the parietal lobe, the former on the superior regions and the latter on the inferior regions. These regions are depicted in Figure 4.10.

As demonstrated in both monkeys and humans, the superior parietal lobe is involved in spatial aspects of motor function. It appears to integrate sensory information with motor movements so that the

limbs can be guided correctly during motor acts. Parietal regions are sensitive to *proprioceptive information*, a type of sensory information about the position of body parts relative to one another and to points in space. In addition, parietal regions receive feedback from motor and premotor areas. Motor feedback and proprioceptive information may be integrated in this lobe to ensure that movements are being executed according to plan and to allow for correction if they are not (e.g., Mountcastle et al., 1975). Damage to the superior parietal region in humans causes individuals to lose the ability to guide their limbs in a well-controlled manner and is often accompanied by a tendency to misreach (D. N. Levine, Kaufman, & Mohr, 1978).

Damage to more inferior regions of the parietal

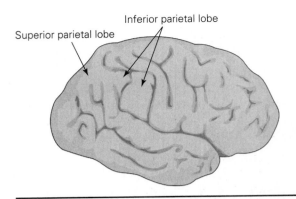

Figure 4.10 **Superior and inferior regions of the parietal lobe involved in motor programming.** The superior regions are important in controlling movements in space, whereas the inferior regions are important in the ability to produce complex, well-learned motor acts. (*Note.* Adapted from Kolb & Whishaw, 1990, p. 16.)

lobe can affect the ability to perform complex, well-learned motor acts. Like damage to some other brain regions, damage to inferior parietal regions may cause apraxia. Apraxia is a syndrome in which an individual is unable to perform certain complex, learned motor tasks when asked to do so (Lezak, 1983) despite intact motor innervation of the muscles, an intact ability to coordinate sensorimotor actions spontaneously, and an ability to comprehend what is being asked. As stated by Bogen (1979, cited in Lezak 1983, p. 31), "The hallmark of apraxia is the appearance of well-executed but incorrect movements." Apraxia is discussed in more detail later in this chapter.

The neural control of these aspects of motor function are well lateralized because damage to the *left* inferior parietal lobe almost always causes apraxia. Researchers have hypothesized that the left parietal lobe links different types of information, such as visuokinesthetic information and internal conceptual representations, to motor programs. Considered this way, the performance of complex, learned acts fall well within the domain we characterized in chapter 1 as the purview of the parietal lobe, namely, that of a multimodal association area.

For example, the inferior parietal lobe might link the visual and kinesthetic information of a match and a matchbook cover with the motor act that involves lighting the match against the matchbook cover. Such linkages do not require a physical object, because the parietal lobe may also link motor acts to internal representations, such as occurs during pantomime or gesture (e.g., waving good-bye) (K. M. Heilman & Rothi, 1985).

At this point, we have reviewed the major regions of the brain that are involved in motor movement and have briefly outlined some of the motor disorders that occur after damage to these brain regions. We now turn our attention to the neurological basis of some of the more common motor disorders. In our discussion, we divide motor disorders into those that occur because of damage or disruption to subcortical areas and those that occur after cortical damage. As was discussed at the outset of this chapter, we can broadly characterize subcortical motor disorders as affecting the form and timing of movements, whereas cortical motor disorders affect the conceptual clarity of motor acts, either by disrupting the sequencing of complex motor acts or by disrupting the ability to have a motor act represent a concept.

SUBCORTICAL MOTOR DISORDERS

In this section of the chapter, we discuss the motor disorders that are characterized mainly by damage to subcortical regions: Parkinson's disease, Huntington's disease, Tourette's syndrome, and tardive dyskinesia. Two of these, Parkinson's disease and Huntington's disease, are characterized not only by motor disorders, but also by cognitive and emotional disruptions. We discuss the motor components of these diseases next but save our discussion of the cognitive and emotional aspects for chapter 14.

Parkinson's Disease

As we learned earler, **Parkinson's disease** results from damage to the cells of the substantia nigra, which stops producing the neurotransmitter dopamine. This damage may result from a variety of causes, including encephalitis, toxins, and trauma. The behavioral effects of the disease are not evident, however, until 60% of nerve cells and 80% of dopamine are lost. The delay in symptom onset occurs because the brain tries valiantly to compensate for the loss of dopamine in a number of ways, such as by having the remaining dopaminergic neurons increase their synthesis of dopamine or by decreasing the inactivation or clearance of dopamine once it crosses the synaptic cleft (Zigmond et al., 1990). At some point, however, often later in life, when a person reaches age 60 or 70 years, these compensatory mechanisms fail. At this point, cell loss, which is a normal part of the aging process, reduces the population of cells in the substantia nigra below a critical point, and behavioral effects are observed.

The movement disorder of Parkinson's disease has four major symptoms: **tremors, cogwheel rigidity, akinesia,** and **disturbances of posture.** These symptoms are generally observed on both sides of the body (Bannister, 1992). However, in some cases, the dopamine depletion occurs in just one half of the brain, so symptoms are evident only on the contralateral side of the body; this condition is known as *hemi-Parkinsonism*. Let us now examine each of the symptoms in more detail.

As we mentioned earlier, tremors are repetitive rhythmic motions. Parkinsonian tremors generally affect the arms and hands. These tremors are rarely seen during deliberate and purposeful movements but are most obvious when the person is at rest (e.g., just sitting in a chair listening to a conversation). Hand tremors are often described as looking like "pill-rolling" because they resemble movements of an individual who is rolling a pill between the thumb and forefinger.

The rigidity observed in Parkinson's disease occurs because increased muscle tone in the extensor and flexor muscles makes the person appear stiff. In fact, the mechanical nature of the movements is referred to as **cogwheel rigidity.** If you try to move a limb of someone with Parkinson's disease, the movement is resisted. Yet, if you push hard enough, the limb can be moved, but only so far until once again the movement is resisted. When sufficient force is applied, the limb can be moved again. Thus, rather than moving smoothly, the limb moves in specific, rigid steps, much as a cogwheel does.

Another symptom of Parkinson's disease is **akinesia,** a poverty, or bradykinesia, a slowness of movement. Some Parkinson's patients sit motionless, just like live mannequins in a store window. Even facial movements can diminish to such a degree that these individuals are said to have a *Parkinsonian mask.* As we saw in the case of Muhammad Ali, this lack of movement can disrupt communication. Speech is affected because individuals have trouble producing sounds, and writing is affected because the production of letters is slow and labored.

Parkinsonian symptoms also include difficulty in posture and locomotion. Unlike tremors, which mainly affect the arms and hands, these difficulties affect muscle groups throughout the body. The posture of a person with Parkinson's disease suffers because he or she has difficulty counteracting the force of gravity. For example, the person's head may droop or the person may bend so far forward as to end up on his or her knees. The posture required for sitting or standing may be impossible to maintain without support. The ability to make postural adjustments may also be impaired. For example, individuals with Parkinson's disease may fall when bumped because they cannot right themselves quickly after losing balance. Movements that require postural transitions are also difficult, such as standing up from a seated position. Walking is compromised not only because it requires continual postural adjustments, but also because it requires a series of movements (and akinesia renders this difficult). When patients with Parkinson's disease walk, they tend to shuffle, much as normal individuals do when walking on ice or in other situations in which maintaining balance is difficult.

Although Parkinson's disease has been described as having four major symptoms, all these symptoms are not typically observed in any one person. Some patients have a rigid-bradykinetic-predominant form (remember that bradykinesia is slowness of movement), whereas others have a more tremor-predominant form. These two varieties of the disease differ not only with regard to behavior, but also in their biochemical bases, in the degree of intellectual impairment observed, and in the clinical course of the disease. The clinical course may decline more sharply and the intellectual impairment may be more severe in patients with the rigid-bradykinetic-predominant form than in those with the tremor-predominant form (Huber, Christy, & Paulson, 1991). Likewise, akinesia is associated with depletion of dopamine and **homovanillic acid (HVA),** a by-product of dopamine synthesis, in one part of the nigrostriatal system (the caudate nucleus), whereas tremor is associated with HVA depletion in another region (the globus pallidus) (Bernheimer et al., 1973).

As already noted, the causes of Parkinson's disease seem to vary. In some cases, the disease runs in families. In other cases, it may be related to carbon monoxide, toxins, syphilis, or tumors. Still other cases may be viral in origin. In the 1910s and 1920s, individuals with *encephalitis lethargica* (also known as *von Economó's encephalitis*) caught the flu and either soon thereafter or as long as 20 years later exhibited Parkinsonian symptoms. (If you want to know more about the story of these individuals and their subsequent treatment, read the book *Awakenings* by Oliver Sacks, or rent the movie of the same name starring Robin Williams and Robert DeNiro.) Finally, Parkinson's disease can be caused by drugs that individuals voluntarily ingest. For example, in the mid-1980s, young adults in their 20s and 30s began appearing in hospital rooms exhibiting symptoms of the disease, especially those related to lack of movement. Because such symptoms are highly unusual in this age group, doctors looked for a commonality between the patients and discovered that all were drug users. As a result, the afflicted individuals were called "the frozen addicts." Some detective work revealed that these cases of Parkinson's disease could be linked to a synthetic heroin that was contaminated with a compound, MPTP (1-methyl-4-phenyl-1,2,3,6-tetrahydropyridine), which, when converted by the body into MPP$^+$ (methylphenylpyridinium), is toxic to dopaminergic cells.

Although Parkinson's disease cannot be cured,

it can be treated. Two types of drugs are typically administered to affected persons: agents that increase the level of dopamine and those that inhibit cholinergic receptors. Because the nigrostriatal pathways are damaged, dopaminergic pathways are underactive. To augment the level of dopamine, physicians give these patients a metabolic precursor of dopamine, L-**dopa,** because dopamine itself cannot cross the blood-brain barrier. This precursor, however, can reach the brain when taken orally. Damage to the nigrostriatal pathways also disrupts the usual balance between dopaminergic and cholinergic systems so that the cholinergic systems are relatively overactive. Thus, anticholinergic drugs are also given, which are particularly helpful in reducing tremors (Bannister, 1992). Unfortunately, these drugs have numerous side effects. They may alter a person's mood, leading to euphoria or depression. Sometimes, they interfere with the ability to pay attention. In other cases, people's thought patterns and their sexual behavior may be altered. In extreme cases, the individual may even experience hallucinations and delusions. These effects tend to go away when the person stops taking the drug or when the dosage is reduced (Cummings, 1991). Furthermore, the drugs tend to be effective at first but may be of little use after a number of years.

Some experimental therapies for Parkinson's disease are being explored, but they are far from becoming standard treatment. One that has received much attention is the grafting of tissue rich in dopamine-producing cells to the substantia nigra of an affected person. The strategy is for cells from the graft to produce dopamine and thus offset the loss of dopamine-producing cells in this region. Tissue for the grafts generally comes from either the medulla of the affected person's adrenal gland or from a fetal brain. The possibility of such a treatment was first demonstrated in monkeys, in whom the substantia nigra had been destroyed in a matter of days (as compared with years as is typical for Parkinson's) by the neurotoxin MPTP. Afterward, a graft was introduced into the animal and the amount of recovery was measured. Multiple implants of tissue from the substantia nigra of fetal monkeys into two Parkinsonian monkeys were found to improve behavior (fewer tremors, less motor freezing, and fewer eating problems). In addition, biochemical analyses suggested that more dopamine was being produced because higher levels of HVA (which is created when dopamine is broken down) were found and tyrosine hydroxylase (TH), which is the enzyme that converts tyrosine to L-dopa, was present. Whether such methods can be converted into successful therapy for humans remains to be seen (see Kimble, 1990, for a review of these studies). The surgery requires probing deeply into the human brain, which is likely to damage tissues, especially those of the frontal lobes. Whether the benefits of this treatment are large enough to offset the risks is still unclear (Bannister, 1992).

Huntington's Disease

Huntington's disease, an inherited neurologic disease caused by degeneration of the striatum, produces abnormal movements, cognitive deficits (eventually dementia), and psychiatric symptoms. As with our discussion of Parkinson's disease, in our discussion of Huntington's disease we concentrate here on the motor aspects and leave a description of the intellectual and cognitive deficits for chapter 14. Although Huntington's disease is rare (1.6 cases per million), when the Huntington's gene is inherited, it always expresses itself. This gene acts much like a time bomb that remains dormant until sometime between the ages of 30 and 45 years, when the symptoms begin. Afterward, the disease involves a slow decline for 10 to 15 years and eventually leads to death.

The main motor symptom of Huntington's disease is chorea, a variety of jerky movements that appear to be well coordinated but are performed involuntarily and ceaselessly in an irregular manner. Although individuals with Huntington's disease initially seem to be fidgeting, the movements eventually increase until they are almost incessant. They never involve just one muscle but affect whole limbs or parts of a limb. Eventually, all movement becomes uncontrollable and the chorea affects most of the body, including the head, face, trunk, and limbs. In the later stages, not only is the person

unable to communicate through speaking or writing, but other basic movements required for independent living, such as walking or swallowing, are also lost (Bannister, 1992).

Although chorea is considered the classic motor sign in Huntington's disease, individuals with this condition have additional motor difficulties, specifically in the realm of akinesia and bradykinesia. These difficulties in the execution and initiation of movements can be observed in experimental paradigms, such as one in which visual information presented in advance could be used as a cue to aid in a sequential button-pressing procedure. Although neurologically intact individuals can use such advance information to initiate and execute movements, individuals with Huntington's disease cannot. These difficulties may be a marker for the disease because they may even precede the onset of chorea, which is generally considered the definitive motor symptom. Furthermore, difficulty in using cue information and initiating movement in the absence of other symptoms has been found in a subset of individuals who are at risk for Huntington's disease (because one of their parents had the disease). Researchers speculate that this group might exhibit the disease later in life (Bradshaw et al., 1992).

The speed and initiation of eye movements are also affected in Huntington's disease. For example, in a task requiring individuals to visually track a target that moved predictably between positions, patients with the disease could not direct their eyes to the correct location at the correct time. As we discussed earlier in the chapter, such voluntary eye movements are under the control of frontal brain regions. Voluntary eye movements may be affected in Huntington's disease because the basal ganglia, which are damaged, project to the frontal eye fields. However, movements to an unexpected stimulus that appears in the periphery, which are likely under the control of the superior colliculus, are unaffected. Huntington's disease spares the superior colliculus, which probably explains why more reflexive eye movements remain intact (Tian, Zee, Lasker, & Folstein, 1991).

The severity of motor slowing in Huntington's disease is predicted by the degree of degeneration of

The Wexler Family's Role in Finding the Genetic Basis of Huntington's Disease

Although a tragic and harrowing illness, Huntington's disease has an interesting history, and the discovery of its cause is a testimony to the efforts of personally involved and determined scientists. Even before the first medical description of Huntington's disease, investigators knew that choreas inherited in families were associated with a progressive dementia. For example, Vessie (cited in Kolb & Whishaw, 1990) claims that the disease was introduced to the United States by immigrants from England who were attempting to escape persecution as witches (a perception probably reinforced by their movement disorders).

Because the disease is most common among White persons of European descent and is rare in other racial groups, the introduction of the gene to a particular region of the world can usually be traced to one or two immigrants from Europe. For example, individuals with Huntington's disease in mainland China and Hong Kong generally have family origins from the coastal provinces of China, which suggests that the Huntington's gene was introduced into the Chinese gene pool by European travelers (Leung et al., 1992).

One family touched by Huntington's disease has played a prominent role in the discovery of its cause. Nancy Wexler, whose mother died of the disease, worked with molecular biologists to find the responsible gene. Research funds were provided in part by the Hereditary Disease Foundation, which her father helped to found. Tracking down the gene required a population not only with a high incidence of the disease, but also isolated enough so that the genetic status of most of the individuals within the population could be determined (a prerequisite for obtaining a highly complete genealogy). So, Nancy Wexler and other scientists packed their bags and headed for the small towns near Lake Maracaibo in Venezuela because the local population has one of the highest concentrations of people with Huntington's disease in the world. The scientists carefully charted the genealogies of these people and then painstakingly took blood and skin samples so that the chromosomes of these individuals could be examined.

Then, it was back to the laboratory. The scientists examined the chromosomes for a marker, a characteristic telltale portion of the chromosome that would be easily identifiable. This marker, although not the gene for Huntington's disease itself, would be positioned so close to the Huntington's gene that it would be inherited along with it. Although skeptics believed that finding such a marker would take 50 to 75 years, the 12th marker tested, which was located on the short arm of chromosome 4, was the correct one (Gusella et al., 1983). Nancy Wexler said, "It was as though, without the map of the United States, we had looked for a

---

a particular portion of the basal ganglia, the caudate nucleus (see Figure 4.5). Using magnetic resonance imaging (MRI) techniques, researchers measured the degree of caudate atrophy in a group of patients with Huntington's disease and found that it correlated not only with eye-movement abnormalities, disruptions on tests requiring writing speed, and tests of complex psychomotor processing, but also with the severity of cognitive impairment (Starkstein et al., 1988). However, no correlation was found between the caudate degeneration and the severity of chorea, a finding indicating that the atrophy was linked specifically to motor slowing and not to all the motor manifestations of Huntington's disease.

Tourette's Syndrome

Tourette's syndrome is a relatively rare disorder that manifests itself as a variety of vocal and motor **tics,** which are repetitive involuntary movements of a compulsive nature. Unlike the other motor disorders discussed so far, all of which affect individ-

killer by chance in Red Lodge, Montana, and found the neighborhood where he was living" (Murray, 1994, pp. 30–31).

The discovery of the gene, however, raised a number of gut-wrenching dilemmas. Once the gene was known, a genetic test for the disease was created. Imagine for a moment that one of your parents died of Huntington's disease, meaning that the chances that you have the disease are 50/50 and that you have a 50/50 chance of passing it on to your offspring. Would you REALLY want to be tested to learn whether you have the gene? Would you make different decisions about your life, about marriage, children, and a career, if you definitely knew your fate, be it good or bad, than if all you knew was that you had a 50/50 chance of having the disease? What would you do if you found out that you had the Huntington's gene? Because the test would tell you only that you have the gene but not the age at which you will be affected or the speed of your demise, how would you handle the uncertainty?

Because of the ethical and psychological dilemmas raised by the test, Nancy Wexler, trained as a clinical psychologist, has become a specialist in counseling individuals who are deciding whether to learn their status. She says that people often claim that if they knew their fate, they would live their lives differently, spending more time with their families or traveling. She points

out to these people that they might not want to wait until they are diagnosed with a fatal disease to give themselves license to pursue their desires. Studies with individuals at risk for Huntington's disease suggest that they often want to be tested because of decisions about having children and planning for the future. The effect of counseling remains unclear. For example, a group study in Wales found that many applicants were ill prepared for what they learned (A. Tyler et al., 1992), whereas other studies have suggested that the knowledge provided by the test increases the psychological well-being of individuals (e.g., Wiggins et al., 1992).

How has Nancy Wexler decided to deal with her own genetic legacy? When she was in her 20s and her mother was first diagnosed with Huntington's disease, Nancy decided not to have children. She will not say publicly whether she has been tested for the gene, believing that the issue is very personal and not wanting to influence others in their choice. She has stated, however, that she took many years to reach her decision. In October 1993, she received the Albert Lasker Public Service Award, one of the most distinguished awards in medicine, for "her groundbreaking work . . . toward finding a cure for Huntington's disease and for increasing awareness of all genetic disease" (Murray, 1994, p. 28).

uals in their middle to late adult years, Tourette's syndrome is seen in childhood, usually before the age of 11 years. In the least severe form of the syndrome, the tics typically involve the face and head, although the limbs, and even the entire body, may be affected. Complex movements, such as touching, hitting, and jumping can also occur. In these patients, the jumping and movements are akin to those seen in pogo dancing or the head banging of punk rockers (Lees, 1990). The next level of severity includes cries and vocalizations. The most

severe level is characterized by the articulation of words; *echolalia,* the repeating of what has just been said; and obscene speech (*coprolalia*). Because of the unusual behavior of these children, they are often misdiagnosed as having psychiatric disorders, and in extreme cases they may be considered to be possessed by evil external forces that need to be exorcised.

Tourette's syndrome appears to run in families and has been linked to a gene on chromosome 18 (Bannister, 1992). Studies of family genealogies suggest that it may be a sex-linked trait that, when present, expresses itself to a high degree in males and to a much lesser degree in females. Tourette's syndrome is also associated with obsessive-compulsive disorder. Half the children with the syndrome exhibit obsessive-compulsive behaviors, whereas approximately a quarter manifest a full-blown obsessive-compulsive syndrome. Like compulsive behaviors, in which an urge becomes stronger and stronger until relieved by the production of an act, people with Tourette's syndrome claim that the more they try to suppress a tic, the greater their compulsion to produce it; this compulsion is relieved only after the tic occurs (G. S. Golden, 1990).

The association with obsessive-compulsive disorders, as well as the effects of pharmacological agents on Tourette's syndrome, suggests that it involves dysfunction of the basal ganglia. A number of other motor syndromes that involve basal ganglia dysfunction are also associated with obsessive-compulsive disorders (Rapoport, 1990), including von Economo's encephalitis and Sydenham's chorea (a motor disorder characterized by sudden, aimless, and irregular movements of the extremities that usually occur after rheumatic fever). The dysfunction in Tourette's syndrome appears to be specifically related to the dopaminergic system, of which the basal ganglia are a major part. Drugs that block dopamine receptors ameliorate the disorder, whereas drugs that increase dopamine turnover aggravate the symptoms. Moreover, levels of HVA, a metabolite of dopamine, are lower than normal in children with Tourette's syndrome. In fact, the level of HVA predicts behavior: Children with lower levels of HVA perform more poorly in school and have more motor restlessness. These findings are believed to indicate that dopamine receptors are hypersensitive and that negative feedback is sent to the presynaptic dopaminergic neurons so that they reduce their production of dopamine. Treatment for Tourette's syndrome usually involves antidopaminergic agents, such as haloperidol, which have been found to reduce vocal tics in a majority (85%) of patients. However, haloperidol has side effects that include lethargy, increased appetite and weight gain, depressed mood, and in some cases, social phobias and avoid-

ance of school; other drugs tend to have equally disruptive effects. Hence, the advantages and disadvantages provided by drug therapy must be carefully considered case by case (G. S. Golden, 1990).

In general, Tourette's syndrome does not have major deleterious effects on cognitive functioning. Most children with the syndrome have normal IQs, although 35% also have difficulties in certain realms of learning, most often those related to visuomotor and visuographic skills. At present, scientists know neither the degree to which these difficulties are part of the core constellation of symptoms associated with the syndrome, nor how much these problems can be attributed to associated factors, such as the side effects of medication taken to relieve the disorder, social stigmatization, or difficulties in concentration because of frequent tics. Fortunately, the symptoms of this syndrome may ameliorate somewhat by adulthood, with the severity of childhood tics having little predictive value for later functioning (Goetz et al. 1992).

Tardive Dyskinesia

Tardive dyskinesia is a movement disorder that has been estimated to occur in 20 to 40% of individuals who are long-term users of antipsychotic drugs that act to block dopamine, such as some patients with schizophrenia (e.g., Morgenstern, Glazer, Niedzwiecki, & Nourjah, 1987). As we learned earlier when discussing Parkinson's disease, decreased dopaminergic output causes slowness, lack of motor movements, and/or tremors. However, people with tardive dyskinesia do not tend to show Parkinsonian symptoms. Rather, they often exhibit increased motor movements that usually affect the face, especially the mouth and lips, and sometimes the trunk and limbs. Some of these motor movements include chorea, tics, **akathisia** (compulsive, hyperactive, and fidgety movements of the legs), and **dystonia** (painful, continual muscle spasms). How then are we to explain these abnormal motor movements? Just as in Tourette's syndrome, these motor movements are speculated to result from a supersensitivity to dopamine because the symptoms are similar to those that occur when L-dopa is given.

Researchers have proposed that dopamine receptors in the striatum become supersensitive as a result, in part, of the inactivation of dopaminergic neurons in the substantia nigra (Breggin, 1993). The abnormal movements can be lessened in some patients by anticholinergic agents and/or by the blockage or depletion of dopamine, but unfortunately the symptoms ameliorate in only less than one-half of all individuals treated (Bannister, 1992). Somewhat paradoxically, and by a mechanism that is not clearly understood, a significant number of individuals may have overlapping tardive dyskinesias and Parkinsonian symptoms.

The motor-related problems induced by antipsychotic medications are extremely troublesome for several reasons. First, determining which individuals will exhibit tardive dyskinesia is nearly impossible because the symptoms appear only after a person has been taking such drugs for at least 3 months. Research indicates that older individuals and females are more at risk for the disorder, and the risk may also be increased for patients with mood disorders and those who have sustained brain injury (Wirshing & Cummings, 1990). Second, once the symptoms appear, they are irreversible because lowering the dosage of medication does little to improve them. Consequently, the patient and the person prescribing the medication often find themselves in a Catch-22: Starting the patient on a low dosage of antipsychotic drugs might help reduce the possibility of motor symptoms, but too low a dosage will not suppress the psychotic behavior.

CORTICAL MOTOR DISORDERS

As we have learned, most of the subcortical motor disorders manifest as a slowness of movement or as an increase in movements. As we turn our attention to cortical motor disorders, we see that they have a different effect, tending to disrupt the ability to pursue specific plans of motor action or to relate motor action to meaning. We first examine one specific cortical disorder of motor control, alien limb syndrome, and then a family of such disorders, the apraxias.

Alien Limb Syndrome

One of the more unusual disorders of motor function is **alien limb syndrome.** Patients afflicted with this disorder feel as if one of their limbs is alien, either because it seems to move on its own, feels as though it doesn't belong to its owner, or seems to have its own personality. Patients with this disorder commonly complain that their limbs do not obey them or that they make involuntary and complex movements. The most typical types of movements displayed by the alien limb are groping and grasping. As described in one case study, "The left hand would tenaciously grope for and grasp any nearby object, pick and pull at her clothes, and even grasp her throat during sleep" (Banks, et al., 1989, p. 456). In almost all cases, only one limb is affected, and it is located contralateral to the site of the lesion, which is typically caused by a stroke.

Another common symptom among patients with this disorder is competition between the hands or difficulty in bimanual control. For example, one person noted that, while driving, one hand tried to turn the car to the left, while the other tried to turn it to the right. In other cases, each hand would try to hold a glass from a different side, or the hands would fight over which one would pick up the telephone. Not only do the difficulties in bimanual coordination result in power struggles, but they may also manifest as mirror movements, in which one hand mimics the motions of the other (Doody & Jankovic, 1992).

Any limb can be affected in this syndrome, altough the distal parts of a limb (e.g., the hand and forearm) are usually involved. Of all body parts, the hand is most commonly affected, and if the syndrome first manifests there, it may evolve to include other limbs. Although the individual retains the ability to move the affected limb voluntarily, control of such movement is clumsy. The affected limb seems as if it can be controlled only from proximal regions (e.g., the shoulder), which allow only gross motor control, rather than from distal regions (e.g., the hand), which provide fine motor control. Under extreme conditions, the limb can take on a personality. In one case study, a patient thought her left arm was named Joseph and was a baby.

When her limb acted in strange ways, she would make up a story to explain the alien limb's behavior in the context of her belief about the limb's personality. For example, when this arm acted on other parts of her body (like pinching her nipples), she interpreted this action as baby Joseph's biting her while nursing.

At present, no consensus exists about exactly which neural structures must be damaged for alien limb syndrome to occur. However, the syndrome is usually observed after an *infarction* (i.e., blockage of a blood vessel) in the territory of the anterior cerebral artery, which supplies blood to the medial frontal cortex, the anterior two thirds of the corpus callosum, and the anterior cingulate cortex; thus, these structures are implicated as likely candidates (Gasquoine, 1993). The damaged areas of frontal cortex tend to include the SMA, which may help to explain some of the symptoms observed in alien limb syndrome. As you may remember from our discussion of the SMA earlier in the chapter (see page 144), in monkeys damage to this region and the callosum affects bimanual control (Brinkman, 1984).

Although no cure exists for alien limb syndrome, several methods can be used to alleviate it. One approach is to keep the limb "busy" performing a repetitive motor activity or holding an object. Another approach is to use muscle relaxation or the application of warm water or a shower spray to calm the limb. Still another approach is to attempt to increase control over the limb by concentrating on it or by directing it with verbal commands.

Apraxia

Apraxia is an inability to perform *skilled,* purposeful movement, an inability that cannot be accounted for by disruptions in more basic motor processes, such as muscle weakness, abnormal posture or tone, or movement disorders (such as tremors or chorea). This disorder is almost invariably observed after damage to the left hemisphere, although as we discuss later, the exact region of the left hemisphere that is damaged varies depending on the type of apraxia exhibited.

Two main pieces of evidence suggest that apraxia is a higher order motor deficit rather than a deficit associated with more low-level aspects of motor control. First, apraxia exhibits itself bilaterally. If the deficit were at a low level and concerned the control of specific muscles, it would be expected to be observed only for the limbs contralateral to the site of damage. Second, low-level motor processes are intact in some patients with apraxia because they can spontaneously perform skilled motor movements. They encounter difficulty only when the movement must be performed purposefully, as when imitating someone or responding to a verbal command (Poeck, 1986).

Dichotomous Classifications of Apraxia

Because apraxia can take many forms, currently there is an ongoing debate as to how to classify the different varieties of apraxia. A number of classification schemes dichotomously categorize the disorder. For example, some classification schemes focus on the part of the body affected (e.g., a limb vs. the face). Others categorize apraxias depending on whether simple or multisequence movements are affected, whereas still others distinguish between apraxias exhibited when objects are used and apraxias that are seen when objects are not used. We next briefly highlight and review these distinctions.

As mentioned, one method of classifying apraxia is to refer to the part of the body that is affected. If facial movements are disordered, the condition is known as oral (buccofacial) apraxia; if limb movements are affected, it is known as limb apraxia. **Oral (buccofacial) apraxia** is associated with difficulties in performing voluntary movements with the muscles of the tongue, lips, cheek, and larynx. As is usually the case in apraxia, automatic movements are preserved. However, tasks such as sticking out your tongue, clearing your throat, blowing a kiss, and yawning are impaired. These difficulties may also extend to oral movements used to manipulate or act upon objects, such blowing out a match or sucking on a straw.

Limb apraxia disrupts the ability to use the limbs to manipulate items such as screwdrivers, scissors,

Correct pantomime   **Apraxic behavior**

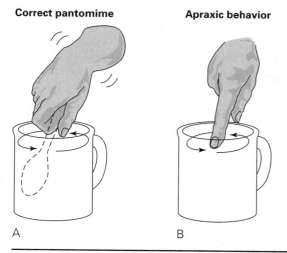

A   B

Figure 4.11   An example of apraxic behavior.
When attempting to pantomime, an individual with
apraxia often uses a limb to represent an object.

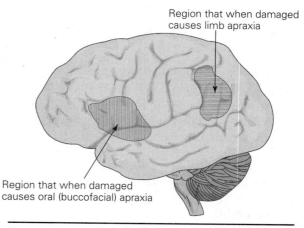

Region that when damaged
causes limb apraxia

Region that when damaged
causes oral (buccofacial) apraxia

**Figure 4.12   The locations of lesions associated with
oral (buccofacial) and limb apraxia.**
A lesion in the frontotemporal region produces oral
apraxia, whereas limb apraxia is often caused by a left
parietal or parietotemporal lesion.

and hammers (e.g., DeRenzi & Lucchelli, 1988). It can also disrupt the ability to perform more complex series of movements, such as opening a can of soup or opening a door with a key (e.g., Poeck & Lehmkuhl, 1980). In addition, limb apraxia affects the ability to use motor movements in a symbolic way, as occurs in gestures, such as waving good-bye or saluting, and in pantomime (e.g., K. M. Heilman & Rothi, 1985). One common error individuals with this type of apraxia exhibit is to use a body part to represent the object that they would be manipulating in their pantomime. For example, if asked to imitate putting a spoonful of sugar into a cup of coffee and then stirring it, an individual with limb apraxia is likely to do the following: Rather than putting her hand in the typical posture of grasping a spoon, the person will extend the index finger below the others, as if to represent the spoon, and will move it around in a circular manner (rather than rotating the wrist as would occur in a correct pantomime) (Figure 4.11). The person with limb apraxia may also have difficulty copying and imitating meaningless motor movements or unfamiliar hand or arm positions (e.g., Kimura, 1977; Kolb & Milner, 1981). A frontotemporal lesion usually pro-

duces oral apraxia. More specifically, the lesion includes the frontal and central opercula, a small area of the superior temporal gyrus adjacent to these two frontal regions, and the anterior part of the insula, which is the region tucked into the Sylvian fissure (see Figure 4.11) (Tognola & Vignolo, 1980). In contrast, limbapraxia is generally associated with damage to left parietal or parietotemporal regions (Figure 4.12) (e.g., DeRenzi, Motti, & Nichelli, 1980; Hécaen & Rondot, 1985).

Another, and classic, way of distinguishing between types of apraxia was introduced in 1905 by Liepmann, who differentiated between ideational and ideomotor apraxia. He suggested that **ideational apraxia** involves disruptions in the ability to form an "idea" of the movement. According to Liepmann, this disorder would impair a person's ability to carry out a complex motor act because the person could not determine which actions would be necessary and in what order they should occur. For example, a person might not be able to light a candle because he or she might not be able to sequence the necessary events (e.g., tear a match out of a matchbook, close the matchbook cover, strike the match against the cover, bring the match to the candle's wick). Despite this inability to organize complex motor movements correctly, single simple motor movements would be undisturbed. Returning to the candle-lighting example, the person would be able to strike a match against a matchbook or bring the match to the candle's wick if each was performed as a single, isolated act. In contrast, Liepmann conceptualized **ideomotor apraxia** as a disconnection between the idea of movement and its execution. He believed that in this case, single simple actions, mainly gestures, would be impaired because the commands for action could not reach the motor center. These problems would be most pronounced for motor actions that were the least concrete (e.g., gestures, meaningless movements) or that had to be imitated, although the production of most everyday motor actions would be relatively undisturbed. Unlike individuals with ideational apraxia, these individuals would be able to sequence complex movements, although the constituent acts would be disrupted. Unfortunately, the degree to which Liepmann's types represent two separate syndromes is unclear. For example, Zangwill (1960) suggested that ideational apraxia might just be a more severe version of ideomotor apraxia, because it was difficult to find many case studies in which an individual with ideational apraxia did not also have ideomotor apraxia. Further complicating matters, other theorists use the terms *ideational apraxia* and *ideomotor apraxia* differently than Liepmann did (presumably because they do not find his distinctions useful for categorizing deficits), but also without agreement among themselves (see Mozaz, 1992, for an overview of how these different terms have been used and how one might distinguish between them).

One camp of researchers that defines ideational apraxia differently from Liepmann argues that the distinction between ideomotor apraxia and ideational apraxia does not rest on whether a person can sequence complex motor acts, but on whether the apraxia involves the use of objects (DeRenzi, Pieczuro, & Vignolo, 1968). For these researchers, the cardinal symptom of ideomotor apraxia is an inability to imitate gestures that are conceptual in nature and that do not act upon an object. (These are sometimes called *intransitive gestures,* because, like intransitive verbs, they do not have an object upon which they act.) Under this conceptualization, ideomotor apraxia manifests as an inability to produce motor actions that are meaningful gestures, such as making the sign of the cross, saluting, or thumbing your nose. In contrast, ideational apraxia is defined by an inability to use an actual object, such as a hammer, a toothbrush, or a pair of scissors. These syndromes have been conceptualized as distinct because researchers find only a loose association between ideational apraxia, as defined by the inability to use objects, and ideomotor apraxia, which they define as the inability to gesture (e.g., salute). What DeRenzi and colleagues classify as ideational apraxia is most closely associated with aphasias caused by occipitoparietal lesions of the left hemisphere that disrupt language comprehension (see chapter 8 for a more complete discussion of aphasias). Because of this association, these investigators argue that individuals with ideational apraxia may have disrupted "concept formation." Considered from this vantage point, ideational apraxia does not seem to have as much to do with motor programming as with conceptual processing.

As should be clear from the foregoing discussion, researchers have not formed a clear consensus on how to divide the apraxias into meaningful subtypes. Because of the difficulties in distinguishing between types of apraxias on theoretical grounds, some researchers instead categorize them on descriptive grounds. Thus, rather than talking about ideational versus ideomotor apraxia (which may mean different things to different people), some researchers use descriptive terms such as "apraxias of symbolic actions" or "apraxias of object utilization" (e.g., Dee, Benton, & Van Allen, 1970).

Nature of the Underlying Deficit in Apraxia

Not only do researchers disagree on how to classify apraxia, but they also disagree over what deficit underlies apraxic behavior. As we just discussed, Liepmann thought that either the "idea" of a movement was disrupted (in what he called ideational apraxia) or the linkage of that idea to motor control was disrupted (in what he called ideomotor apraxia). Other researchers, however, consider what Liepmann called ideomotor apraxia to be a basic deficit in using action patterns or "visuokinesthetic motor" memories, which are stored in the left parietal cortex. Under this conceptualization, these memories of action patterns contain not only information about the selection and production of specific gestural actions, but also linkages to information about the visual and kinesthetic feedback that will occur during the performance of the motor act. Such action patterns are fed forward for execution by premotor and motor areas (K. M. Heilman & Rothi, 1985). Although actions can be performed in everyday life, they cannot be performed to verbal commands or in imitation of someone else, because the action patterns, which are stored in the angular and supramarginal gyri, cannot be accessed. Because access to the stored action pattern is gone, the person is unable both to perform gestures correctly and to discriminate between them (e.g., know the difference between the gesture for brushing your teeth and that for flipping a coin). In line with Liepmann's idea of a disconnection syndrome, these researchers suggest that apraxia may also result by a different means, namely, by a disruption in the linkage between the stored program and motor control. In this case, the person can discriminate between correctly and incorrectly performed gestures made by others (because the stored program is intact) but cannot produce correct gestures (because the stored program cannot reach motor areas) (K. M. Heilman, Rothi, & Valenstein, 1982).

Other researchers have suggested that in some forms of apraxia, the person can access the motor programs and send them to frontal motor areas for execution, but that once received by frontal areas, difficulty occurs in reading the program or in keeping the memory of the correct program "on-line" to perform the task (Schwartz, Mayer, Fitzpatrick-DeSalme, & Montgomery, 1993). This disorder manifests as errors in motor behavior characterized by the blending of two motor tasks. For example, a man wanting to shave might raise the razor to his face but then move it to his hair and make a combing gesture. The lesion causing this syndrome is usually

bilateral and in orbital frontal regions. The [f]
lobes are considered important for working me[m]
ory, the memory that allows us to keep things available for use in pursuit of particular tasks and goals
(this idea is discussed in more detail in chapters 9
and 10). Thus, this type of apraxia may result because a frontal lesion disrupts working memory for
motor programs.

Still other researchers suggest that apraxia arises from a disrupted sense of "the conceptual organization of actions" (Lehmkuhl & Poeck, 1981), which can be considered a variation on Liepmann's ideational apraxia. This conceptualization is based on findings that individuals with apraxia have difficulty arranging pictures about motor actions in a coherent sequence. For example, these patients cannot assemble a scrambled set of the following pictures in proper order: (a) a telephone and a telephone book, (b) a person looking up a number in the telephone book, (c) the person picking up the receiver with the right hand while pointing to the number in the book with the left hand, (d) the person holding the receiver in the left hand while looking at the open telephone book and dialing the number, and (e) the person talking on the phone with the telephone book closed. This deficit is not one of sequencing in general but specifically relates to motor acts because other sequencing tasks, such as the picture arrangement task in the Wechsler Adult Intelligence Scale—Revised (WAIS-R), and sequencing of everyday events, like shopping, can be performed without difficulty.

Another theory of apraxia emphasizes not the sequential nature of action but the role of posterior sections of the left hemisphere for making transitions in postural adjustments from one movement to another (e.g., Kimura, 1977). For example, in one test, individuals with apraxia were asked to sequence three relatively gross motor movements across three objects positioned on a box: pushing on a button (located at the top), pulling on a handle, and then pressing down on a bar (located on the bottom). They found this task extremely difficult, often perseverating by producing the motor movement they had correctly performed at the previous position on the box. In contrast, when these persons

of repetitively turning a screw, ch greater fine motor control does, they had fewer problems 0). Thus, their difficulty could the degree of fine motor control Rather, the push-pull-press sequence of the box task required continual postural adjustments, whereas the repetitive turning of the screw did not. Similar effects were also found in the oral domain. Patients with posterior left-hemisphere lesions had difficulty under conditions in which different oral movements, rather than a single one, had to be produced. For example, they had more difficulty saying "badaga" rather than "bababa," or, in sequence, opening the mouth, pursing lips, and then clicking teeth, rather than just blowing.

Unlike the distinction we made earlier between limb apraxia and buccofacial apraxia, Kimura conceptualizes the left hemisphere's control over manual and oral movements as falling under the rubric of a single system, called **praxis,** which is thought to control all aspects of movement. This conceptualization is based in part on findings that difficulties in oral and manual movement often co-occur. Furthermore, rather than viewing linguistic movements (e.g., speech sounds) as being controlled by a separate system from that for other oral movements (e.g., blowing out a match), Kimura is a vocal proponent (no pun intended!) of the idea that apraxia and aphasia, a specific deficit in language processing, are both manifestations of a deficit in this same unitary system for motor control (e.g., Kimura, 1982). In fact, aphasia and apraxia co-occur with high frequency (e.g., Kertesz, Ferro, & Shewan, 1984). Moreover, Kimura and Watson (1989) found a high correlation in performance between tasks requiring speech production and nonspeech oral movements (e.g., blowing). For patients with posterior left-hemisphere damage, the ability to copy visually presented single oral movements was predictive of the ability to reproduce single speech sounds (e.g., a vowel, a consonant). In addition, the ability to copy single oral movements was predictive of how well these patients could rapidly articulate a single syllable (e.g., "bababa"). These correlations did not prove, but rather suggested, that

single oral movements and motor programming of speech often rely on the same neural mechanism. However, in at least some cases, a double dissociation occurs between apraxia and aphasia, which suggests that motor control for language and nonlanguage systems can be distinct. Nonetheless, in many cases, these two syndromes co-occur, a finding that indicates at least a fair degree of overlap between the systems (e.g., Papagno, della Sala, & Basso, 1993).

Other Varieties of Apraxia

Other syndromes referred to as apraxia because the person has difficulty performing complex motor acts should not be considered true apraxias because they arise from difficulty in the spatial domain rather than the motor domain. Two examples of such syndromes are constructional apraxia and dressing apraxia. In **constructional apraxia,** items cannot be correctly manipulated with regard to their spatial relations. For example, wooden blocks cannot be manipulated to copy an arrangement created by someone else. In **dressing apraxia,** the affected individual has difficulty manipulating and orienting both clothes and his or her limbs so that clothes can be put on correctly (e.g., opening a jacket so that the arm can be inserted, and properly putting an arm out and bending it at the elbow to put on the jacket). These syndromes are generally observed after right-hemisphere lesions and are often associated with spatial-processing difficulties and hemineglect. As such, many neuropsychologists do not consider these apraxias per se, but rather motor manifestations of visuoconstructive disorders.

Other apraxias result from a disconnection syndrome rather than from difficulties in motor programming. We already discussed the idea that in certain cases of apraxia, visuokinesthetic programs may not reach motor areas because of a disconnection between parietal and frontal areas. Another type of apraxia that results from a disconnection syndrome is **callosal apraxia.** Unlike other apraxias that affect motor control bilaterally, this apraxia selectively disrupts the ability to perform movements or manipulate objects with the left hand in response to verbal commands. This type of apraxia is associ-

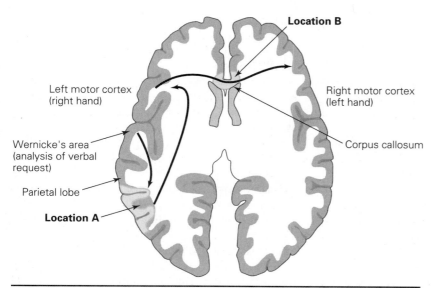

Location B

Left motor cortex
(right hand)

Right motor cortex
(left hand)

Wernicke's area
(analysis of verbal
request)

Corpus callosum

Parietal lobe

Location A

Figure 4.13   Anatomical mechanisms of unilateral and bilateral apraxia.
Wernicke's area analyzes a verbal request and transmits this information to the left parietal region (Location A), where the correct movements are selected. If this region is damaged, bilateral apraxia results. In contrast, in unilateral apraxia of the left hand, the left parietal region is intact, so information about the correct movements is sent forward to the left motor cortex, where the motor commands are executed. Hence, the right hand is not apraxic. However, because of a lesion of the corpus callosum (Location B), the information cannot be relayed to the right hemisphere and apraxia of the left hand results. (*Note.* Adapted from Kolb & Whishaw, 1990, p. 309.)

ated with damage to the corpus callosum and has been suggested to occur because of a disconnection between the left hemisphere, which is specialized for skilled motor sequencing, and the right hemisphere, which controls motor functioning of the left hand (e.g., Rubens, Geschwind, Mahowald, & Mastri, 1977). According to this account, when a person is verbally instructed to perform a skilled motor act, the left hemisphere interprets the command and relays it to left parietal regions so that the appropriate motor program can be assembled. Once formed, the motor command is forwarded to the premotor and motor cortices of the left hemisphere. These areas receive an intact program, so there is no apraxia of the right hand. However, because of

the callosal disconnection, the motor programs are trapped in the left hemisphere and have no way of reaching the right hemisphere, which controls the left hand. Because motoric information cannot reach the right hemisphere, the left hand is apraxic. Figure 4.13 diagrams the essential anatomical relations of this syndrome.

SUMMARY

Motor control can take various forms, from the basic movement of muscle groups to skilled motor actions. These different types of motor control rely on different regions of the brain. The four basic pathways whereby information is transmitted from the brain to muscles are the corticospinal, corticobulbar, ventromedial, and rubrospinal pathways. The corticospinal pathway controls the distal muscles, fine motor movements, and basic postural adjustments, whereas the corticobulbar pathway controls the face and the tongue. The ventromedial pathway controls autonomic motor functions, posture, and coordination of eye and trunk movements, whereas the rubrospinal pathway controls separate movement of the trunk and limbs, although its importance in humans is debatable.

The cerebellum plays diverse roles in motor control. It is important for gross posture, the smooth coordination of movements, ballistic movements (i.e., rapid movements that must be planned with little chance for feedback), the learning of skilled motor movements, and timing of movements (and possibly cognitive functions as well). Two main subcortical areas involved in motor control are the caudate nucleus and the putamen, which along with the globus pallidus make up the basal ganglia. Damage to these structures can cause not only a slowing or cessation of motor movements, but also involuntary motor movements. Two syndromes characterized by prominent motor disorders, Parkinson's disease and Huntington's disease, are associated with dysfunction of the basal ganglia.

The cortical regions involved in motor control include the primary motor cortex, the supplementary motor area (SMA), the frontal eye fields, and the anterior cingulate cortex. Primary motor cortex is responsible for the control of muscles, and damage to this region of the brain results in the inability to effectively exert force with the muscles on the contralateral side of the body. Prefrontal areas involved in motor control include the SMA and the frontal eye fields. The SMA becomes activated as someone begins to plan a motor action, even before the act is initiated. This region of the brain is thought to relay motor programs to primary motor areas so that they can be executed. The frontal eye fields program voluntary eye movements. Both the SMA and the frontal eye fields are associated with the anterior cingulate cortex, which plays an im-

portant role in the selection of motor responses, especially when they are novel or atypical.

The parietal lobe is also involved in various aspects of motor control. First, it links movements with a representation of the space in which those movements occur. Second, it links information about motor programs with visuokinesthetic information about the motor acts. Finally, it links a motor act with its conceptual significance (e.g., knowing that touching the forehead, chest, left shoulder, and right shoulder in rapid succession with the hand is a symbol for the sign of the cross and has religious significance).

Two of the most prominent motor disorders with a subcortical basis are Parkinson's disease and Huntington's disease. Parkinson's disease is characterized by a slowing or halting of motor behavior, rigidity of movement, and tremors that usually occur when the individual is at rest. This disorder appears to result from damage to dopaminergic neurons whose cell bodies reside in the substantia nigra and that project to the basal ganglia. Huntington's disease is associated with a specific loss of cells in the caudate and putamen. The major motoric sign of this disease is chorea, a variety of jerky movements that appear to be well coordinated but are in fact involuntary. Recent research has suggested that Huntington's disease may also involve a decrease in the ability to control voluntary motor behavior, which manifests as difficulty in initiating and planning movements. A third, rare motor disorder that is subcortical in origin but manifests in childhood is Tourette's syndrome. In this syndrome, the child has tics and twitching of the face, the limbs, and other regions of the body. In more severe cases, vocalizations, such as cries, grunts, and curses, are also produced. Finally, a motor disorder associated with antipsychotic medications that reduce the amount of dopamine in the brain, known as tardive dyskinesia, is also associated with subcortical dysfunction. This disorder typically manifests as an excess of motor symptoms similar to those exhibited by individuals with Huntington's disease, but in some cases, decreases in motor behavior may also occur. One of the most worrisome aspects of this disorder is that it afflicts a substantial proportion of individuals on antipsychotic medication, and, once manifest, is irreversible, even if the medication is stopped.

Disorders of movement resulting from cortical damage interfere with the conceptualization, coordination, and creation of skilled motor movement. Damage to the SMA disrupts coordinated bimanual activity and in some cases leads to alien limb syndrome, in which an individual's appendage seems to move of its own free will in ways that are destructive or unhelpful. In apraxia, which typically results from left inferior parietal lesions or left frontal lesions, the person cannot perform skilled motor acts. Apraxia can take many forms, affecting either facial and oral movements or limb movements. The types of functions that can be compromised include the ability to perform skilled movements (e.g., blowing out a match or stirring a spoonful of sugar into a cup of coffee), the ability to use motor actions in a symbolic manner (e.g., gesturing), the ability to perform complex motor acts (e.g., folding a letter, placing it in an envelope, and sealing the envelope), and the ability to use objects to perform a complex motor act (e.g., using a hammer to drive a nail into a piece of wood). The taxonomy for describing apraxic disorders varies considerably, and numerous theories have been formulated about the mechanisms of apraxia, but currently researchers have not arrived at a consensus.

Chapter 5

*O*bject *R*ecognition

One crisp autumn night, Betty yearns for a midnight snack when she remembers that some deliciously spiced tart apple pie is sitting in her refrigerator. She thinks, That would be wonderful right now with a hot cup of tea! Although for most people getting the pie out of the refrigerator and making a cup of tea would be simple, for Betty it will be a difficult task.

She walks into the kitchen and identifies the refrigerator by its large size and black color. But now she knows that she must find the pie, and that doing so will not be easy. As she peers inside the refrigerator, she sees a large round object but deduces from its red color that it must be the leftover pizza pie, not the apple pie. Searching a bit more, she sees a tan round-shaped object and reaches for it. But alas, as soon as she feels how flexible it is, she realizes it's the package of tortillas, not the desired pie. Searching some more, she spies another tan round-shaped object. This one feels stiff, like a pie pan, and is covered with plastic wrap. She pulls it out, takes off the plastic wrap, and sniffs. Ah, it is the pie she has been searching for! She carefully places it on the breakfast table.

Now for the cup of tea. Because she knows that the stove is to the left of the refrigerator, her usual strategy is to leave the teakettle sitting on the stove so that she can easily find it. Unfortunately, it's not there. Ah, she sighs, why didn't I just put the teakettle back where it belongs? Now she begins to feel all the objects on the counter next to the stove. Hmm, that one feels tall and thin and a little greasy—must be the bottle of olive oil. That one feels cylindrical and as if it's made of paper—must be either the large container of salt or the carton of oatmeal. Soon after, she feels the distinctive curved arm of the teakettle and its wide round body. Next to it, she feels the box of tea bags. That was fortunate, she thinks, or I would have spent the next 5 minutes searching for the tea bags. She carefully places the box of tea bags on the stove; the box is now easily identifiable because its bright green color stands out against the white stove.

She then turns around to the sink, which she knows is located directly across from the stove, and fills the teakettle with water. Waiting for the water to boil, she puts her hand in the silverware drawer, feels for the tines of a fork, and takes one out. Soon, the teakettle whistles. She makes her cup of tea, walks over to the breakfast table, and gets ready to eat her piece of pie. That was a bit of a trial and tribulation, she thinks, but after the first bite of pie and sip of tea, she knows that all her work was worthwhile.

At this point, you are probably wondering what strange disorder this woman has. As you think about this story, a number of possibilities may come to mind. Maybe she has a visual problem and is blind. This seems unlikely. She recognized the pizza pie (if only by its distinctive round shape and red color) and incorrectly grabbed an item that looked similar to the apple pie, a package of tortillas, rather than something quite different in shape and size, like a milk carton. Another possibility is that she has a memory problem and can't remember where things are located or the specific attributes of an item. This possibility seems somewhat unlikely too. She remembered the locations of the stove and the sink. Furthermore, her memory for specific items must be intact because she recognized the apple pie as soon as she smelled it and the kettle as soon as she felt it.

The neurologic syndrome that this woman has emanates neither from a problem in basic aspects of visual perception nor from a memory problem. Rather, her disorder is visual agnosia, a syndrome that deprives an individual of the ability to link perceptual information in a particular sensory modality (in this case, vision) to meaning. The goal of this chapter is to examine the neural mechanisms that allow people to recognize objects in the visual modality as well as in other modalities. Our discussion, however, concentrates on visual object recognition because this process has undergone much study and because vision is a very salient human sense.

To set the stage for appreciating distinctions between types of deficits in visual object recognition, we begin the chapter by discussing the neural hardware, in both humans and other mammals, that allows us to recognize objects visually. This hardware is known as the *"what" visual system,* or **ventral visual system,** which we were introduced to in chapter 1 (see page 45). Then, we discuss clinical syndromes in which specific aspects of visual object recognition are lost. To aid in our understanding of these disorders, we briefly review some of the cognitive mechanisms that have been proposed to account for our ability to recognize visual objects. Afterward, we discuss the recognition of faces because they appear to be a special category of visual items that are analyzed by highly specific neural tissue. Then we discuss disorders of object recognition that are limited to specific categories of objects, such as fruits and vegetables or human-made objects, and discuss what these types of disorders imply about the neural mechanisms of object recognition and how they may provide insights into the organization of memory systems. To conclude the chapter, we briefly discuss object-recognition difficulties that occur in modalities besides vision.

THE "WHAT" VENTRAL VISUAL SYSTEM FOR IDENTIFICATION

A clear understanding of deficits in visual object recognition requires us to consider how the brain processes visual information after it leaves primary visual cortex. As we discussed in chapter 1, information departing from primary visual cortex is funneled into two distinct processing streams, one that courses ventrally toward anterior temporal regions and one that courses dorsally toward parietal regions. As we learned in chapter 1, the ventral visual system is important for item identification. We now examine this system in more detail. The ventral visual-processing stream consists of the areas of the occipital, occipitotemporal, and temporal regions

that are solely devoted to processing visual stimuli and are unresponsive to information from other modalities as well as multimodal information. Much of our knowledge about the basic processing characteristics of the ventral visual system comes from research with other species, such as monkeys, in which techniques not typically used with humans, such as single-cell recordings, are employed.

The mammalian brain is confronted with a number of difficult problems to solve when attempting to recognize a visual object. One major problem is that information from the three-dimensional (3-D) world is projected onto the retinas, which are just two-dimensional (2-D) planes. Hence, the brain must *reconstruct* and put the third dimension back into the pictures solely on the basis of 2-D information. Another major hurdle is that items must be recognized no matter where they fall on the retina and no matter how much of the retina they fall upon. For example, a cup in your hand projects onto a much larger area of your retina than a cup on a table across the room. Yet, in both cases, you must recognize the object as a cup. In addition, objects must be recognized regardless of the orientation in which we view them. Your brain needs to recognize that a cat walking directly toward you, facing forward, is the same object as when viewed sideways skittering across the floor in pursuit of a mouse. Recognition must occur even though the visual information you receive in each case is distinct. In sum, although the same object can project upon the retina in various ways, the brain must nonetheless interpret the object as being the same, regardless of variations in retinal size, retinal position, and orientation (see Plaut & Farah, 1990, for a discussion of these issues from both neuroscientific and computational viewpoints).

By examining the response characteristics of cells in the ventral visual system with single-cell recording techniques, researchers can uncover many of the mechanisms that the brain uses to solve these problems. If information is recorded from various electrode sites in the ventral visual-processing stream, which is depicted in Figure 5.1, three important trends emerge regarding the types of stimuli that make the cells fire. The first trend is that relatively simple stimuli make the cells fire in posterior

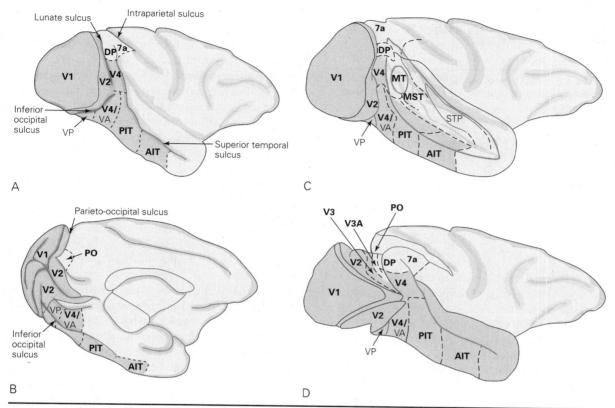

Figure 5.1 The ventral processing stream of the brain in the macaque.
(A) Right hemisphere, lateral view. (B) Left hemisphere, midsagittal view. (C) View showing the areas buried within the superior temporal sulcus. (D) View showing the areas buried within the lunate, intraparietal, parieto-occipital, and inferior occipital sulci. The ventral processing stream (shown here shaded in gray) goes from V1, V2, V3, VP, and V4 to the posterior and anterior inferotemporal areas (PIT and AIT, respectively). DP, dorsal prelunate; VA, ventral anterior; VP, ventral posterior; PO, parieto-occipital; MT, middle temporal; MST, medial superior temporal; STP, superior temporal polysensory. (*Note.* Adapted from Maunsell & Newsome, 1987, pp. 365, 367.)

regions, but for anterior regions the stimuli must be more complex and specific. So, whereas the areas just beyond primary visual cortex, such as V2, are likely to respond to one or more simple stimulus qualities (e.g., color, texture, length, width, orientation, direction of motion, spatial frequency), the cells in inferotemporal (PIT and AIT) regions fire only in response to much more complex visual stimuli.

In fact, cells in the inferotemporal cortex of monkeys can be tuned to specific forms, such as hands (Gross, Bender, & Rocha-Miranda, 1969) or faces (Gross, Rocha-Miranda, & Bender, 1972). The dis-

covery that these cells are so selective in their response occurred serendipitously. The researchers were having difficulty determining what type of stimulus would make a cell in the inferotemporal region fire, and in frustration one of them moved a hand across the monkey's visual field. To their amazement, they found that the cell fired more strongly than it had to any other object! They then tested other complex visual stimuli and found that in all cases the cell fired only in response to highly specific forms (Figure 5.2). Because the stimuli that makes a cell fire is highly specific, the brain is able to distinguish among many complex visual forms.

Figure 5.2 Examples of stimuli used to test the responsiveness of cells in the inferotemporal region of the macaque.
These stimuli are arranged from left to right in order of the degree to which they elicited a response, from 1 (no response) to 2 and 3 (little response) to 6 (maximal response). Note that the forms that make the cell fire are complicated and specific. (*Note.* Reprinted with permission from "Visual Properties of Neurons in Inferotemporal Cortex of the Macaque," by C. G. Gross, C. E. Rocha-Miranda, and D. B. Bender, 1972, *Journal of Neurophysiology, 35,* p. 104.)

To recognize objects, however, the brain must be able not only to distinguish among different complex visual stimuli, but also must recognize an object regardless of variations in the conditions under which it is viewed, such as lighting and orientation. In fact, the response of cells in inferotemporal cortex is unaffected by changes in retinal position, retinal size, and orientation (e.g., Desimone, Albright, Gross, & Bruce, 1984), a neural mechanism that allows us to recognize an object from various perspectives.

The second trend observed is that the receptive fields of cells are larger for anterior regions than for posterior regions. The **receptive field** of a cell is the area of visual space to which the cell is sensitive. If a stimulus to which a cell is tuned falls within the receptive field, the cell fires. However, if the same stimulus falls outside the receptive field, the cell does not fire. You can consider the receptive field of a cell to be similar to a window or a field of view. The view of the world through a window is limited, so if something is happening beyond the view provided by the window, you do not respond to it because you cannot see it. Remember that each section of primary visual cortex is responsible for receiving information from only a precise region in space. For a cell in primary visual cortex, the receptive field is small and could be considered analogous to a peephole or a porthole on a ship. How-

ever, the farther the cell is positioned along the ventral visual-processing stream in an anterior direction, the larger the area of space to which it responds. For example, cells in area V4, a region beyond primary visual cortex and near anterior temporal areas, have receptive fields that are between 16 and 36 times larger than the receptive fields of cells found in primary visual cortex. The most anterior region of the ventral visual-processing stream, the inferotemporal area, has cells with large receptive fields that can encompass as much as 130 degrees of the 180-degree field of view in front of the head. In addition, the receptive fields of these cells *always* include the foveal, or central, region of processing (e.g., Desimone & Gross, 1979). In contrast to the peepholes of the primary visual cortex, which are distributed all over space, the receptive fields of the inferotemporal area can be considered analogous to a large picture window or glass wall that runs the length of one side of a house and always provides a view of what is directly in front. Figure 5.3 provides a comparison of the relative sizes of the receptive fields for cells in posterior and anterior regions of the ventral visual system.

A large receptive field that encompasses almost all of the visual field is useful for object recognition because it allows an object to be identified regardless of where it is located in space and regardless of its size (e.g., Gross & Mishkin, 1977). Consider that when you look out a peephole, you see just a small portion of an object, which often doesn't allow you to determine what you are viewing. Such is the problem with the small receptive field sizes of the more posterior regions of the ventral processing stream. However, as your field of view increases, so does your ability to detect whole objects because the interrelations among its parts can be appreciated. Thus, having a large receptive field allows the cell to respond to objects on the basis of their global shape, rather than just the size or location of local contours (the features that cells in more posterior regions of the ventral visual-processing stream respond to). Having a receptive field that always includes the central region of visual space also aids object recognition. The region of the retina that receives information about the central area of visual

A

B

Figure 5.3 The receptive-field size for cells in primary visual cortex compared with that for cells in the inferotemporal region.
The receptive field is the region of space to which the cell is sensitive. If the optimal stimulus for an object falls outside its receptive field, the cell does not respond. In these pictures, the receptive field of a cell is indicated by a dashed circle. Areas within the receptive field are denoted in black, whereas those outside the receptive field are denoted in gray. (A) In primary visual cortex, the size of a cell's receptive field is small. (B) In contrast, the receptive field of a cell in the inferotemporal region is much larger, usually encompassing a wide expanse of visual space that always includes the midline.

space, the fovea, has the greatest density of sensory receptors and hence the best acuity, providing for the highest possible resolution when attempting to recognize an object.

The final important attribute of cells in the ventral processing stream is that they are often sensitive to color (e.g., Zeki, 1980). Color is a visual attribute that aids in object recognition because it allows us to separate an object from the background in which it is embedded. This process is often referred to as **figure-ground separation.** For example, consider an average street scene including parked cars, trees, buildings, and parking meters. Color may aid in quick identification of a car if it is yellow or aqua, a color distinct from the red brick building, the gray parking meter, the tan sidewalk, and the green trees that surround the car.

We have now described the basic attributes of visual information that are important to cells in the ventral system and allow for object recognition. Next we discuss neuropsychological deficits in object recognition caused by brain injury and examine the degree to which the ability to perceive these basic attributes is disrupted.

VISUAL AGNOSIA

As mentioned previously, **visual agnosia** is an inability to recognize a visual object, an inability that is not attributable either to a basic deficit in processing of visual information or to a pervasive memory disorder. Furthermore, the deficit is modality specific because the item can be recognized through other sensory channels. For example, a woman with visual agnosia might be able to describe an object as a fuzzy brown, white, and black ovoid balanced on four short, stocky cylinders with a triangular-shaped appendage at one end and a very thin, very pointy, and constantly in motion appendage at the other end. This description would illustrate that her rudimentary visual abilities are intact. Furthermore, if this fuzzy ovoid nuzzled up to her to be petted so that she could feel its stout body, its round wet nose, and its whiplike tail, she would probably have little trouble identifying it as a dog, and possibly even as a beagle. And, if she heard the plaintive "booooaaaaahhhhhh, woooaaaaaahhh, woooooaaa hhh" that the fuzzy ovoid makes, she would instantly recognize it as the distinctive bark of a beagle. Thus, although the woman cannot recognize the beagle in the visual modality, she can do so by the sense of touch or sound. Hence, her disorder is **modality specific,** meaning that it manifests in one modality or sense but not others.

The word *agnosia* is Greek, meaning "without knowledge." One of the most famous figures in psychology, a man who is not traditionally known for his contributions to neuropsychology—Sigmund Freud—first used this word to describe the neuropsychological disorder. He chose to call this syndrome agnosia because he argued that it was not the result of disruptions in sensory processes but rather reflected an inability to gain access to previous knowledge or information about a sensory experience.

Traditionally, visual agnosias have been divided into two types: apperceptive and associative. This distinction dates to the 1890s and has been attributed to Lissauer. He suggested that **apperceptive agnosia** is a fundamental difficulty in forming a *percept* (a mental impression of something perceived by the senses). Although visual information is processed in a rudimentary way (e.g., distinctions between light and dark can be made), it cannot be bound together so that a meaningful whole can be perceived. In contrast, in **associative agnosia** basic visual information can be integrated to form a meaningful perceptual whole, yet that particular perceptual whole cannot be linked to stored knowledge. If we consider this distinction differently, persons with apperceptive agnosia in some sense have trouble "seeing" objects, whereas persons with associative agnosia can "see" objects, but they don't know what they are looking at. We now discuss these two main types of agnosia in more detail.

Apperceptive Agnosia

In apperceptive agnosia, rudimentary visual processing is intact at least to the degree that basic perceptual discriminations involving brightness, color, and simple form can be made. However, the ability to coalesce this basic visual information into a percept, an entity, or a whole is lost. The term *apperceptive agnosia* has been applied to a diverse population of individuals who vary in the degree to which they can identify objects, from having no ability whatsoever to having a severely disrupted ability. As you might expect, the loci of their lesions and the causes of their damage also vary somewhat.

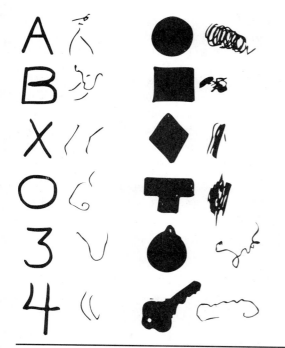

Figure 5.4 An example of the inability of a person with apperceptive agnosia to copy even the most basic of forms.
The objects that the patient was asked to copy are on the left of each column, and the patient's attempts to do so are on the right. (*Note.* Reprinted with permission from "Visual Form Agnosia," by D. F. Benson and J. P. Greenberg, 1969, *Archives of Neurology, 20,* pp. 82–89. Copyright 1969, American Medical Association.)

Persons with apperceptive agnosia who have little or no ability to discriminate between objects also have no ability to copy or match simple shapes and seem to perceive only extremely small or local aspects of contour (Figure 5.4). Generally individuals with such a severely compromised ability to recognize objects have diffuse damage to the occipital lobe and surrounding regions, such as damage that occurs with carbon monoxide poisoning (Farah, 1990). As an example of how severe these deficits can be, one patient was unable to distinguish between Os and Xs (Benson & Greenberg, 1969). As best as could be discerned, the patient had sustained significant damage to the ventral processing stream that precluded the recognition of letters based on their form. However, slowly moving the paper on which the letters appeared or drawing the letters slowly sometimes enabled the patient to recognize them. In such cases, recognition was probably occurring through the intact dorsal visual system, which is specialized for processing the spatial relationships among visual information, including direction of motion. In some cases, the structure of an object can be discerned from motion information because points moving in the same direction with the same velocity generally belong to the same object. Thus, although the patient could not recognize form per se (because his ventral system was damaged), he was able to infer form from motion cues, which he could readily perceive because his dorsal visual system was intact.

Other individuals with apperceptive agnosia, whose brain damage typically involves posterior regions of the right hemisphere, have somewhat better visual abilities. These persons can distinguish two simple visual forms from each other, such as discriminating between an oval from a circle and a square from a rectangle. Furthermore, they can successfully find a fragmented letter, such as an *X*, in a mottled background. From these findings, researchers have argued that these individuals can at least coalesce *contour* information into a meaningful gestalt (Warrington, 1982). Yet these patients exhibit difficulties when the contour information is degraded and must be interpolated (Figure 5.5A) or when an object's contour must be disembedded from among other contours (Figure 5.5B).

A deficiency in deriving contours under degraded conditions, however, does not explain all the difficulties of these individuals because their object recognition also suffers when the object looks atypical as a result of transformations of either position or lighting. In everyday life, we generally view most objects from a particular vantage point. For example, we usually view a pail from the side rather than from above (Figure 5.6A). Yet, when we encounter an "unusual view" of an object, such as that of the pail from above, we still recognize it as a pail (Figure 5.6B). However, individuals with apperceptive agnosia cannot recognize an item in an atypical position, even though they can do so when the same

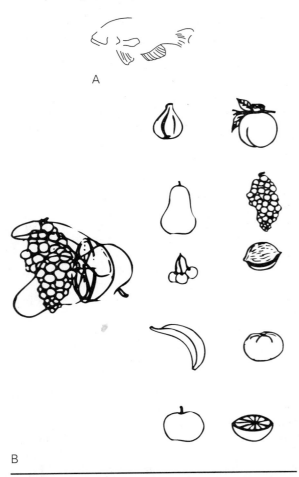

B

Figure 5.5 Examples of how contour information influences recognition in persons with apperceptive agnosia.
(A) Patients with apperceptive agnosia have difficulty recognizing this object as a fish because they cannot interpolate the missing contours. (B) Because the contours of each item in the drawing on the left are difficult to disentangle, patients with apperceptive agnosia cannot distinguish the different items (right), such as the pear and the banana. (*Note.* A, From "Visual Apperceptive Agnosia: A Clinicoanatomical Study of Three Cases," by E. K. Warrington and M. James, 1988, *Cortex, 24,* p. 23. B, From "Neuropsychological Studies of Object Recognition," by E. K. Warrington, 1982, *Philosophical Transactions of the Royal Society of London, B298,* fig. 2, p. 16. Reprinted with permission from The Royal Society.)

item is viewed in a prototypic, or usual, position (Warrington & Taylor, 1973). They may also have difficulty recognizing objects when a lighting source causes atypical, or unusual, shadows to fall across an object. For example, these individuals have more difficulty recognizing a keyboard when the light source is from the side, illuminating only half the keys and causing shadows, than when the light source is from above.

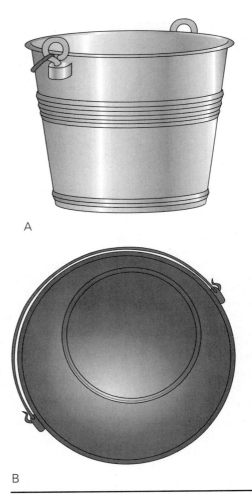

Figure 5.6 A common item viewed from a typical and nontypical perspective.
(A) In this case, a pail is in the position from which we typically view it. (B) The same object but in an atypical, or nonprototypic, view. Persons with apperceptive agnosia have difficulty recognizing the item in its atypical orientation. (*Note.* Adapted from Marr & Nishihara, 1978, p. 19.)

What underlying problem might account for all these deficits? One suggestion is that these individuals cannot perform basic **perceptual categorization,** which is the ability to categorize an object as being the same item despite variations in the information received by the sensory system (in this case, the image that falls on the retina). As mentioned earlier in the chapter, we must recognize objects under a variety of conditions that cause different types of retinal images: when the item is in different positions, when it appears under different types of light, when it is different colors (e.g., an apple whether it is red, green, or yellow), and when it is viewed from different distances.

The evidence presented so far indicates only that persons with apperceptive agnosia cannot identify items, but it does not directly address whether they can perceptually classify objects. To make the idea of perceptual classification clear, consider an example from the auditory modality. Imagine that you heard two different cat meows. If asked what those sounds meant, you might not be able to link a gurgling sound to the meaning of "I'm happy," or a high-pitched mew to "I'm hungry," much the way persons with apperceptive agnosia can't determine the meaning of visually presented objects. Nonetheless, you could perceptually classify the meows, determining that two high-pitched mews sounded similar and that both of these were different from a gurgle.

To determine whether persons with apperceptive agnosia can perceptually categorize items, researchers showed them pairs of photographs. Some pairs consisted of one item in a typical view (e.g., a picture of a cat sitting on its back legs and facing the camera) and the same item in a nontypical view (e.g., the same cat viewed from above with its face turned away). Other pairs consisted of an unusual view of an object (e.g., a closed umbrella) and a different object that has similar visual characteristics (e.g., a cane). The task was simply to decide whether the items were the same or different—that is, whether they represented the same type of object. It did not require the individual to link the visual pattern to meaning, as is required when the item must be identified (e.g., determine that a particular visual object is a chair). Even so, the individuals with apperceptive agnosia performed poorly (Warrington & Taylor, 1978).

To summarize, although persons with apperceptive agnosia can process crude visual information, such as item contour, the ability to derive more complex visual information is lost. The result is that object recognition is impaired across a variety of situations in which information is degraded or objects are presented atypically. Researchers have suggested that the underlying deficit is an inability to determine perceptual equivalence of items across viewpoints, especially when they are present in a nonstandard or noncanonical form. This basic deficit plays a prominent role in theories of visual object recognition discussed later in this chapter.

Associative Agnosia

In associative agnosia, individuals retain the ability to perform the perceptual grouping that persons with apperceptive agnosia find difficult. When given an object to copy, patients with associative agnosia can do so relatively easily. For example, if given a picture of an anchor to copy, the patient can do a credible job, even though the same task would be impossible for a person with severe apperceptive agnosia. However, if required to draw the same picture from memory, the patient with associative agnosia would be unable to do so (Figure 5.7). This difficulty does not arise from a general problem in memory because when asked, for example, what an anchor is, an individual with associative agnosia can provide a reasonable definition, such as "a brake for ships" (Ratcliff & Newcombe, 1982). In some cases, persons with associative agnosia are able to extract enough information from a visually presented item to determine its superordinate category (e.g., mammal, insect, or bird) but cannot correctly determine other attributes (e.g., whether it is tame or dangerous) (Warrington, 1975).

Because individuals with this disorder can copy objects and can detect identical items from a set of similarly shaped objects, researchers originally presumed that these persons' perceptual processing was intact. The difficulty in recognizing objects was attributed to an inability to link particular perceptual patterns to information retained in memory. However, more recent evidence suggests that the perceptual abilities of these people, although better than those of patients with apperceptive agnosia, are not

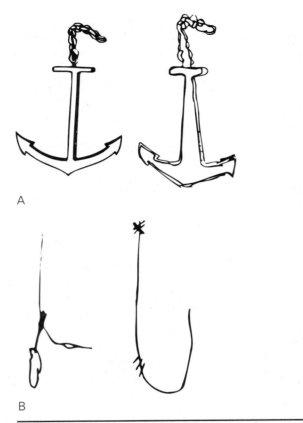

A

B

Figure 5.7   Drawing abilities of a person with associative agnosia.
(A) The patient's copy (right) of the model (left). Compared with the copying ability of a person with apperceptive agnosia (see Figure 5.4), this patient's ability to copy is much better. Yet, despite the patient's ability to copy the figure and assert that an anchor is "a brake for ships," he could identify neither the model nor his copy as an anchor. (B) The patient's attempts to respond to the request to draw an anchor. He was unable to retrieve the correct visual form from memory. (*Note.* Reprinted with permission from "Object Recognition: Some Deductions From the Clinical Evidence," by G. Ratcliff and F. Newcombe, in *Normality and Pathology in Cognitive Functions* (p. 162), edited by A. W. Ellis, 1982, London: Academic Press.)

truly normal. In associative agnosia, the affected individual appears to perform the matching and copying task by using a point-by-point or part-by-part comparison that enables him or her to decide whether two items look similar, but this method may not provide the person with a percept of the entire form. When copying objects, these patients often do so in a "slavish" manner, or "line by line," while taking much time and making long pauses for cross comparing the original and the copy. This strategy is different from that of neurologically intact individuals, who tend to draw the broad features first and then fill in the details. In some matching tasks, persons with associative agnosia consider slight variations between the two copies to be important when these variations have no bearing on the object. For example, an individual with associative agnosia might decide that two visual items are not identical because the photocopier produced an extra dot on one picture but not on the other (Farah, 1990). This mistake suggests that persons with associative agnosia do not have a percept of the entire form, because if they did they would realize that the dot is superfluous rather than integral to the object.

Differences Between Apperceptive Agnosia and Associative Agnosia

What then are the main differences in perceptual processing between persons with apperceptive agnosia and those with associative agnosia? Individuals with associative agnosia can perceive much more detailed information than persons with apperceptive agnosia can, as evidenced by their ability to match items and to copy drawings with a fair degree of accuracy. In addition, patients with associative agnosia apparently can extract some information about general shape because when they misidentify an item, they generally assume it to be an object that looks similar in shape (e.g., misidentifying a pig for a sheep). In contrast, individuals with apperceptive agnosia have a poor ability to extract shape information and must rely on other cues, such as color and texture, to segregate figure from ground. Common to both syndromes, however, is the loss of the ability to link visual information to meaning.

Given the differences in processing abilities between persons with apperceptive agnosia and associative agnosia, we would expect the site of brain damage to differ between these two populations, and indeed this is the case. As you may remember from earlier in the chapter, persons with appercep-

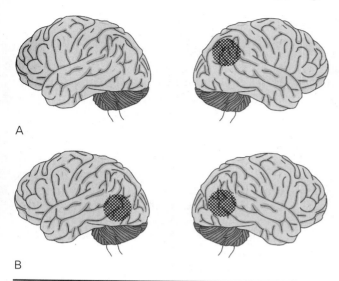

A

B

Figure 5.8   The regions of the brain typically damaged in apperceptive and associative agnosia.
(A) In apperceptive agnosia, damage is usually restricted to posterior sections of the right hemisphere. (B) In associative agnosia, the damage tends to be bilateral at the occipito-temporal border. Relative to the lesion in apperceptive agnosia, the typical lesion in associative agnosia is more ventral.

tive agnosia who have only the most rudimentary visual functions usually have diffuse damage to the occipital lobe and surrounding areas. Those who have better visual functions but who are unable to perform perceptual classifications generally have posterior right-hemisphere damage. Those patients who can recognize objects in their prototypical position but not in unusual views also have damage to the posterior region of the right hemisphere; the damage varies among occipital, parietal, and temporoparietal regions across different case reports (e.g., Warrington & James, 1988). In individuals with associative agnosia, the lesion site varies but typically involves the occipitotemporal regions of both hemispheres. When damage is restricted to one hemisphere, the lesion tends to be in the region of the occipital lobe bordering on the posterior temporal lobe (Farah, 1990). A diagram summarizing the location of damage that is typically seen in each of these syndromes is provided in Figure 5.8.

Now that we have some idea of the different ways in which visual object recognition can be disrupted, it is time to turn our attention to models of visual-information processing that might help explain some of the difficulties we observe in these clinical syndromes.

NEUROPSYCHOLOGICAL PERSPECTIVES ON THEORIES OF VISUAL COGNITION

We have just seen how the recognition of visual objects may be disrupted by brain damage. To better understand how these deficits may arise, we next examine two major theoretical frameworks that propose specific cognitive mechanisms that allow visual items to be recognized. At present, neither can satisfactorily explain all the phenomena observed in patients with agnosia, so investigations in this area are the source of much interest and debate. The first framework, provided by David Marr, arises from computer science and examines which computational problems must be solved to recognize an object over its different instantiations. The second framework proposes that a visual item's overall form is analyzed simultaneously and in parallel with its parts, but that one neural system, the left hemisphere, analyzes the parts while another neural system, the right hemisphere, analyzes the whole. This framework, based in part on work done by gestalt psychologists in the early 20th century, has been championed both by Robertson and by Sergent.

A Computational Perspective

David Marr was a computer scientist interested in how computers could be made to recognize visual objects (Marr, 1982). His approach was to devise a **computational theory,** which is a theory that outlines the computations that must be performed by a system to solve a problem, regardless of whether the system is composed of neurons or microchips (Marr & Nishihara, 1978). As we mentioned earlier, visual object recognition requires elaborate computations and inferences not only because the brain must reconstruct a 3-D world from the 2-D information that falls on our retinas, but also because it must do so simply on the basis of light intensity and wavelength (color).

Marr theorized that the brain constructs a series of representations of the world by making inferences derived from basic retinal information; these representations eventually allow an object to be recognized. He proposed three main types of representations: the primal sketch, the 2½-D representation, and the 3-D representation. Marr viewed the **primal sketch** as a "rough draft" of information in the visual world that is easily derived from the basic information that reaches the retina. He proposed two types of primal sketches, a raw one and a full one. Although the retina receives information about light intensity at different places in space, the primal sketch specifically computes the *changes* in light intensity across the visual array, providing information on light-dark contrasts and their geometric relations. Adjoining areas with similar levels of contrast

are represented in the primal sketch by lines or edges, which are used to help define the edges of objects. The full primal sketch is a slightly more sophisticated representation in which local elements of shape are grouped by gestalt-like principles that govern how parts are grouped to be perceived as whole forms. For example, one gestalt principle is that of proximity. This principle states that elements located close to one another are perceived as belonging to a common object. Hence, if we view a row of dots that have little space between them, we perceive it as a line.

The **2½-D representation** is a more elaborate representation of the visual world that provides information about the relative depth of surfaces (e.g., whether something is in front or behind). Depth information is squeezed out of the primal sketch by various means. First, the difference in the retinal images received by each eye, known as **binocular disparity,** provides information about the relative depth of surfaces and can be used to infer whether two surfaces belong to distinct objects. Second, some depth information can be inferred from motion, because points moving in the same direction and at the same velocity tend to be associated with the same surface. For example, the fact that the speed and direction of all the points on a moving car are the same helps us to distinguish it as a separate object not only from a woman walking down the street (because she is moving more slowly than the car), but also from the houses and trees (which are not moving unless a *very* strong wind is blowing). Third, color, as already mentioned, allows for the separation of foreground from background, providing information on relative depth and thus aids in the identification of objects. Texture helps in a similar way because points of similar texture usually all reside on the same item and objects nearer to the viewer generally have a finer grain than those farther away. Occlusion also provides relative depth information and helps to parse figure from ground because what is in front occludes the view of that which is in back. Although these many mechanisms provide information on relative depth, a full 3-D construct of the item is not yet available. Front and back or nearer and farther are identified, but the volumetric properties of an object—that is, how far back one surface is from another—is not yet specified.

At the final level, a **3-D representation** of the object is constructed, which is a **volumetric representation** of the object that is **orientation invariant,** meaning that the relationships among different parts of an object can be specified regardless of the angle from which it is viewed. A volumetric representation describes the actual 3-D overall shape of the object as well as other features. The main aspects of the object specified are its center of mass, its overall size (mean diameter or volume), and the principle axis of elongation or principle axis of symmetry. (In humans, for example, the principle axes of elongation and symmetry are identical because in both cases it is the axis that runs from our head to our toes.) Also specified are the proportion and locations of parts relative to the principle axes. The 3-D model allows the person to have a conceptualization of a rigid construction of the object that is orientation invariant. As such, the representation of the object is now considered an **object-centered representation** rather than a **viewer-centered representation.**

To better understand the difference between object-centered and viewer-centered representations, we need to consider the coordinate system whereby information is coded in the primal sketch and the 2½-D representation as compared with that of the 3-D representation. In the primal sketch and the 2½-D representation, the visual world is specifically referenced to the coordinates of information falling on the retina. Hence, the representation is considered viewer centered because if the position of the viewer changes, the relative positions among the parts of an item change and so does the representation. For example, when a mug is viewed sideways, the distance in the retinal image between the handle and the main cylindrical body is far, but if the cup is turned so that the handle faces you, this same distance in the retinal image is substantially decreased. Thus, although a mug is being viewed in both cases, the representations are different because the viewer's position relative to the mug is different. In contrast, the 3-D model is considered object centered because once the major and minor axes of the object have been identified and the volumetric

properties of the object have been ascertained, the object and its parts are always referenced with regard to the same coordinate system. If we consider the mug example, in the 3-D representation the distance between the handle and the main body of the mug remains invariant regardless of the angle from which the item is viewed because parts of the object are specified with regard to its principle axis of elongation or principle axis of symmetry. Such an orientation invariant representation is critical if an object is to be recognized from any angle and any direction.

Marr's theory is useful because it provides a theoretical framework from which deficits in different persons with apperceptive agnosia can be understood. Researchers have suggested that the person with apperceptive agnosia who cannot even distinguish letters unless they are moving may be able to create only a raw primal sketch but not a full one (Farah, 1990). Thus, although the person can distinguish local aspects of color, brightness, depth, and contour, she or he cannot group these fundamental visual features to have an appreciation of form (unless, as mentioned earlier, it can be inferred from motion). In contrast, an individual with apperceptive agnosia who can perform perceptual grouping but has trouble recognizing items in atypical configurations may lack the ability to build a 3-D model of an object. If an object is seen from a prototypical viewpoint, the person recognizes it because the ability to build a viewer-centered representation is intact. However, if the person must recognize the object from an unusual vantage point, which requires an object-centered representation, he or she will fail (Marr, 1982).

The hypothesis that certain persons with apperceptive agnosia cannot build a 3-D model of an object has been investigated empirically and has received partial support. In one study, the researchers placed a standard object (Figure 5.9A) in two different types of nonprototypic orientations (G. W. Humphreys & Riddoch, 1984). In some cases, objects were positioned so that a salient feature of an object was minimized (e.g., photographing a pepper shaker turned on its side so that the top with the holes was not so salient), a manipulation that should have little effect on object recognition according to

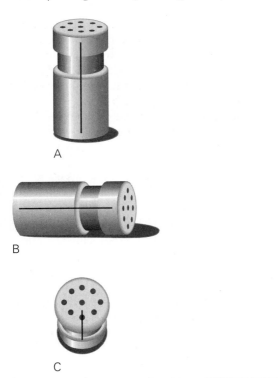

A

B

C

Figure 5.9 Stimuli used to determine the importance of the major axis of symmetry in deriving a three-dimensional (3-D) model of an object.
(A) An example of an object, a pepper shaker, in its prototypical view. (B) The same object in a nonprototypical view in which its major axis of symmetry is still apparent but its distinguishing feature, the holes on top, is not salient. (C) The same object from a different nonprototypical perspective in which its distinguishing feature is obvious but its major axis of symmetry has been foreshortened. According to Marr's theory, this axis foreshortening should create great difficulties in object recognition, whereas minimizing its salient features should not. (*Note.* From "Routes to Object Constancy: Implications from Neurological Impairments of Object Constancy," by G. W. Humphreys and M. J. Riddoch, 1984, *Quarterly Journal of Experimental Psychology*, 36A(3), pp. 401, 402. Copyright © 1984. Reprinted by permission of Experimental Psychology Society.)

Marr's theory (Figure 5.9B). In other cases, objects were positioned so that the major axis was foreshortened (e.g., photographing the pepper shaker almost directly from the top so that the length of its longest axis [i.e., from its base to top] was foreshortened

relative to the prototypical view) (Figure 5.9C). This manipulation should, according to Marr's theory, make object recognition difficult because deriving the major axes is critical for creating a 3-D model. Of the five patients tested, four with right-hemisphere lesions had significantly more difficulty recognizing the object in its foreshortened condition than when its salient feature was minimized, as was predicted by Marr's theory. However, one patient who was presumed to have a small bilateral occipitoparietal lesion identified the object when its salient feature was minimized rather than when its major axis was foreshortened. This latter result suggests that another route to recognizing objects may exist—namely, by identifying salient features.

To further pursue the idea that certain persons with apperceptive agnosia have trouble recognizing objects because they have difficulty identifying the major axes of an object and deriving a 3-D representation, Warrington and James (1986) examined the ability of individuals with posterior right-hemisphere damage to identify 3-D shadow images of common objects. These shadow images, which are devoid of texture cues and color information, basically provide only contour information. In one condition, the vertical axis of the object was perpendicular to its base for all images and the object was rotated from a head-on view (in which the horizontal axis could not be seen) to a sideways view (Figure 5.10A). In another condition, the same object was placed with the base toward the viewer (which precluded the person from receiving information about the major vertical axis) and was rotated toward an upright position in which the vertical axis was obvious (Figure 5.10B). Warrington and James hypothesized that if the individuals with brain damage had difficulty ascertaining the major axes of symmetry, they would exhibit more difficulty, relative to neurologically intact individuals, when the major axes of symmetry were foreshortened. Surprisingly, however, they did not, which suggested that the patients were not particularly impaired at determining the major axes of symmetry. Because the results of the studies of G. W. Humphreys and Riddoch, and Warrington and James are inconsistent, whether these patients actu-

Figure 5.10 Examples of shadow images (devoid of features) used to examine the degree to which individuals can recognize an object rotated with regard to one of its major axes.
(A) An example of lateral rotation in which the major vertical axis is unaffected but the horizontal axis undergoes varying degrees of foreshortening. On the far left, the horizontal axis is completely foreshortened, whereas on the far right it is not foreshortened at all. (B) An example of rotation around an item's base in which the horizontal axis is unaffected but the vertical axis undergoes varying degrees of foreshortening. On the far left, the vertical axis is completely foreshortened, whereas on the far right it is not foreshortened at all. (*Note.* From "Visual Object Recognition in Patients With Right-Hemisphere Lesions: Axes or Features?" by E. K. Warrington and M. James, 1986, *Perception, 15,* pp. 355–366, fig. 2. Reprinted with permission from Pion Limited, London.)

ally have difficulty in extracting the major axis of symmetry remains unclear. Nonetheless, most studies suggest that these patients lack the ability to recognize objects from a variety of perspectives, a finding consistent with the idea that such patients are unable to compute an object-centered 3-D representation.

Marr's computational theory is useful in understanding agnosia because he makes two important distinctions: between a raw and a full primal sketch and between viewer-centered and object-centered representations. Persons with apperceptive agnosia who have little or no ability to recognize objects and have difficulty in grouping local features seem to be unable to create a full primal sketch. In contrast, individuals with apperceptive agnosia who have difficulty recognizing objects in nonprototypic views appear to have an inability to create an object-centered representation. Hence they lose their ability to determine the perceptual equivalence of an object across variations in position and lighting.

Global Versus Local Processing

Marr's theory described how an object is recognized from basic local features, by building from the small parts, the lines and edges of the primal sketch, to create a 3-D representation of an object. Yet evidence also exists that under some conditions the overall form of an item can be recognized more quickly than its local features. This observation led to the idea of **global precedence,** advanced by the gestalt psychologists in the early 20th century, who contended that the overall shape or relation among parts may be analyzed before the parts themselves. Today, evidence of two distinct neural mechanisms for recognizing objects exists, one of which is important for analyzing the parts of objects, known as **local processing,** and the other of which is important for analyzing the wholes, which is known as **global processing.**

Much research examining the separation of global and local processing has made use of a task invented by David Navon (1977) involving *hierarchical stimuli*. We were already introduced to these stimuli briefly in chapter 3 (see Figure 3.8, page 109). As a reminder, items (e.g., Zs) that are small (e.g., 0.25 in., or 0.64 cm) are arranged in a particular spatial array so that they form a large item (e.g., an *M* that is 2 in. or 3 cm square). On each trial, a hierarchical letter is shown. The individual is generally instructed to respond only to the information at one level (e.g., the global level) and to ignore the information at the other level (e.g., the local level). The participants in the study generally have to discriminate items; for example, they must press one button if a *Z* is present at the specified level and another button if an *M* is present. (In some forms of the experiment, a *Z* or an *M* is always present. In other forms, other letters may be present, such as a *V* or an *X*, and in this case the subject presses neither button.) On some trials, the small letter and the large letter are the same (e.g., a large *Z* composed of little *Z*s), which is known as the *congruent condition.* On other trials, the small letters lead to one response and the large letters to another (e.g., a large *M* composed of little *Z*s), which is called the *incongruent condition.* Not surprisingly, there is interference in the incongruent condition; that is, the person takes longer to respond than in the congruent condition. However, this interference is much greater when the person must respond to the local information (e.g., respond to the little *Z*s) than when the response is to the global information (e.g., respond to the global *M*). This finding has been suggested to indicate global precedence; that is, the global information is processed first. As such, global information interferes with the ability to extract local information, but the reverse is less likely to occur because global information has already been extracted before local information is analyzed.

Recent research both with patients with brain damage and with neurologically intact individuals suggests that the ability to perceive global aspects of an object may rely on a different neural substrate than that required to identify its parts. More specifically, right-hemisphere mechanisms seem to support the global analysis of form, whereas left-hemisphere mechanisms seem to support the local analysis of form. Whereas large lesions of the left hemisphere disrupt the ability to perceive local, but not global, aspects of an item, right-hemisphere lesions have the converse effect, disrupting the ability to perceive overall, but not local, aspects of form (Delis, Robertson, & Efron, 1986). The lesions most likely to cause such effects are those in the temporal region (as opposed to more dorsal parietal lesions), which is consistent with the idea that temporal regions, a part of the ventral visual-processing system, are specialized for object recognition (Robertson, Lamb, & Knight, 1988). Such effects do not depend on using verbal stimuli because damage to the right temporal lobe disrupts the appreciation of global form even when geometric shapes, rather than letters, are used to create such hierarchical stimuli (Doyon & Milner, 1991).

These impairments after brain damage in recognizing form at a given level (e.g., impairments in recognizing global form after right-hemisphere damage) have been shown to be independent of the ability to allocate *attention* to that level. As we learn in chapter 7, attention is the ability to tune in certain portions of a stimulus and tune out others. Because patients are told to pay attention and respond to targets only at one level but not the other (e.g., the local level but not the global level), the task also has an attentional component. Hence, researchers wanted to demonstrate that after temporal damage the deficits in recognizing form could not be explained by difficulties in allocating attention. To do so, they asked patients with brain damage to perform the hierarchical stimulus task under three conditions that varied in their attentional demands: a no-bias condition, in which the target letter appeared at the global or local level with equal probability; a global-bias condition, in which the target appeared more often at the global level; and a local-bias condition, in which the target appeared more often at the local level. If attentional mechanisms are intact, the ability to perceive form at a given level (e.g., global), even if poor, should vary across these three attentional conditions. The performance of patients with temporal lobe lesions did differ across the three conditions, an indication that their difficulties in perceiving form at a given level could not be explained by a difficulty in allocating attention. In contrast, patients with left parietal lesions reacted equivalently across all three conditions, which indicated that they had difficulty with attentional control (this finding is consistent with the results of research discussed in chapter 7 that implicate the parietal lobe as important in the control of attention).

Confirmatory evidence for a distinction in the neural control of local and global processing comes from studies with neurologically intact individuals. For example, when given Navon-like tasks, these individuals exhibit a left visual field (LVF) advantage for detecting the letter at the global level and a right visual field (RVF) advantage for detecting it at the local level (e.g., M. Martin, 1979). Although not all researchers have found this pattern, the general pattern emerging from the half dozen or more studies on this issue is that the right hemisphere plays a greater role in global processing and the left in local processing (Van Kleeck, 1989).

A related theory by Sergent (1982b) suggests that the hemispheres play different roles in visual processing and that these differences have implications for object recognition. As we discussed in chapter 3, Sergent's theory proposes a right-hemisphere superiority for processing visual information of low spatial frequency and a left-hemisphere superiority for processing visual information of high spatial frequency. This model seems to hold if the hemispheric difference is reconceptualized slightly with regard to *relative* rather than absolute spatial frequency (e.g., a right-hemisphere superiority for the *lower* spatial frequencies within a display) (e.g., Christman, Kitterle, & Hellige, 1991). Remember that spatial frequency refers to how often transitions from dark to light occur within a given region of space (see page 105, chapter 3). In this chapter, we want to examine how these differences in visual processing between the hemispheres could affect object-recognition capabilities.

Sergent suggests that data contained in the low spatial frequency provide information about the coarse outline, or general form, of an item. This information is exactly the kind that would allow processing of the global features of an item. In contrast, high spatial frequency data provide information about details, which would allow the local features of an item to be ascertained (Sergent, 1982b). For example, if a person were attempting to recognize a house, the right hemisphere would ascertain information about global form (e.g., whether the house is an A-frame or a bungalow), and the left hemisphere would analyze local features (whether the house is composed of bricks or shingles, whether the windows have panes or not) (see Sergent, 1985, for a discussion of this issue as it specifically relates to face recognition).

Sergent's theory that the hemispheres differ in the processing of spatial frequency is consistent with that of Robertson and colleagues, who argue that the hemispheres differ in their ability to analyze global and local information. In fact, when low spatial frequency is filtered out of a stimulus, global information loses some of its effectiveness, no longer causing interference with local information (i.e., global precedence is lost) (Hughes, Fendrich, & Reuter-Lorenz, 1990). However, these two perspectives are not identical. Sergent believes that hemispheric differences in object recognition arise at a fundamental and low level of visual processing, namely in the analysis of spatial frequency. In contrast, Robertson and colleagues' theory is more specifically concerned with object recognition and with the distinction between an object's parts and its wholes.

Nonetheless, both theories contend that the hemispheres work in parallel to process different visual aspects of an object and posit that a complete description of an object requires information from both hemispheres. These common conceptualizations may help us to understand some of the deficits observed in agnosia. For example, they may explain why some persons with apperceptive agnosia retain the ability to process local aspects of color, brightness, depth, and contour but cannot group these fundamental visual features to have an appreciation of form. In such a case, right-hemisphere object-recognition mechanisms, which are independent of those of the left, have sustained more damage. The result is a loss of the ability to analyze information regarding low spatial frequency information and global form even as the analysis of high spatial frequency information and local detail is spared, at least to some degree.

FACE-RECOGNITION DIFFICULTIES AS A SPECIAL TYPE OF VISUAL AGNOSIA

So far, we discussed agnosia as a deficit in which the person loses the ability to recognize or identify all information within a specific modality. However, at least one type of visual agnosia is specific to a particular class of visual items, namely faces. This disorder is known as **prosopagnosia,** and it is a selective inability to recognize or differentiate among faces, although other objects in the visual modality can be correctly identified. Individuals with prosopagnosia can recognize a face as a face, which suggests that high-level visual processing is intact. In fact, they may even be able to determine the sex or relative age (old or young) of a person's face and the emotion that it is expressing (e.g., Tranel, Damasio, & Damasio, 1988). Yet, the ability to recognize a particular face as belonging to a specific person is lost. The impairment can be so severe that the patient with prosopagnosia may not be able to recognize her or his spouse, children, or own face (in the mirror). Like other individuals with agnosia, those with prosopagnosia do not have a general memory deficit. They can remember information about specific individuals and can recognize these people through other modalities (e.g., by tone of voice), even when the individual's face cannot be recognized. Commonly, persons with prosopagnosia attempt to compensate for their deficit by relying on distinctive visual nonfacial information, such as a person's hairstyle or a distinctive piece of clothing, or by relying on information in a nonvisual modality, such as tone of voice or gait (A. R. Damasio, Damasio, & Van Hoesen, 1982).

Researchers have been interested in face recognition not only because the syndrome of prosopagnosia suggests that faces may be a special type of visual object, but for a number of other reasons as well. As already mentioned, face recognition seems to be the task for which the right hemisphere is highly skilled, much as the left hemisphere is skilled for processing language. Thus, researchers are interested in understanding face recognition to gain better insight into the types of processes at which the right hemisphere is most adept. Another reason for the interest in faces is that findings from studies of patients with prosopagnosia seemingly indicate that the ability to identify an item as belonging to a specific category (e.g., determining that the visual pattern is a face) is distinct from the ability to remember the particulars about members within that category (e.g., determining that the face you are viewing is John's and not Tim's). As we discuss later, these findings have implications for how perceptual information is linked to memory. Still another reason for an interest in faces is that face recognition is an ecologically important task. The ability to distinguish among people's faces is critical for many aspects of social interaction and communication. Moreover, these abilities have probably been honed over evolutionary time. Whereas humans as a species have known how to read and write for only the last 5,000 years (therefore the brain probably did not evolve to specifically perform such tasks), the ability to distinguish family from friend and friend from foe on the basis of facial features has been of great importance for the survival of humans for a much longer period. In fact, the evolution of a neural substrate for face-recognition abilities appears to encompass a period far longer than that in which humans have been on the earth, because specific

neural machinery for distinguishing among the faces of animals has been found in other mammalian species. To provide a broader perspective, we now briefly review some of what has been learned about the neural substrates of face-recognition abilities in other species.

Face Recognition in Other Species

Many mammals appear to have a specific brain region that is important for recognizing faces, especially those of their own species. As we discussed in chapter 1, single-cell recording in the temporal regions of sheep indicate that certain cells respond selectively to horned sheep, others to unhorned sheep, some to dogs that look like sheepdogs, and others to dogs that look like wolves (e.g., Kendrick & Baldwin, 1987). These findings provide evidence that the mammalian brain has the ability to divide a larger category of visual forms (e.g., sheep) into subcategories (e.g., horned sheep vs. unhorned sheep). Notice, however, that this evidence does not imply that, on the basis of visual cues, the sheep brain is capable of distinguishing different individual sheep from one another.

Single-cell recordings in monkeys provide additional evidence for a specific neural substrate underlying face recognition. As mentioned earlier in the chapter, cells in the inferotemporal cortex can be tuned to highly specific visual information. In some cases, the cells in this region are tuned to fire specifically in response to faces, regardless of whether the faces belong to monkeys or persons. Indicating their specificity to faces, these cells do not fire in response to other round objects, such as alarm clocks, or to other emotionally important stimuli, such as snakes. Even more specialized cells in the inferotemporal cortex fire in response to specific aspects of faces or only in response to faces that have particular characteristics. For example, just as global and local aspects of an item are processed by distinct neural systems in humans, there is also a specificity of cell responses, some firing only in response to a global facial configuration and others to certain facial features. Some cells in the inferotemporal cortex fire only when a specific facial feature, such as the eyes, is present, either when embedded within the whole face or when presented by itself. The critical feature varies from cell to cell. Some cells fire only when the mouth is present and others fire only when the eyes are present. In contrast, another class of cells are particularly sensitive to the configuration of features that form a face (e.g., two eyes positioned laterally above a nose on midline that in turn is positioned directly above a mouth). These cells fire in response to the components of monkeys' faces only if the components are correctly positioned but not if their positions are scrambled. Other cells have still different types of specificity. Some fire only in response to faces in particular orientations (e.g., those facing directly forward; those turned 45 degrees from front view). Others fire only in response to faces with a particular emotion. Hence, cells within inferotemporal cortex can be finely tuned for specific aspects of face processing.

As we discussed earlier in the chapter, recognizing an object requires that its equivalency be appreciated across variations in retinal size and orientation. Cells in the inferotemporal region of monkeys have this characteristic, being responsive to faces under a variety of illuminations and configurations (such as variations in facial orientation and viewing distance). A small number of cells are even more finely tuned, firing only in response to a specific person's face (usually that of an experimenter), regardless of orientation, size, color, or emotional expression on the face. Furthermore, these cells do not fire in response to other individuals (Perrett, Mistlin, & Chitty, 1987, provide a good review of these results). Taken together, these findings provide evidence that cells in inferotemporal cortex are highly sensitive to faces and to facial features, and, in some cases, are selectively responsive to individual faces.

Because these cells respond to specific aspects of faces and in some cases to specific people's faces, we might be tempted to think that these cells are *the* place in the brain where recognition of a particular face occurs. In fact, at one time a predominant theory posited the existence of "the grandmother cell" (see H. B. Barlow, 1985, for an account of

this viewpoint). According to the **grandmother cell theory,** a small set of cells would fire only in response to a highly specific visual object, such as your grandmother, and no other objects. Hence, these cells alone would be the brain mechanism responsible for recognizing your grandmother. They would recognize a specific object because they received information from other cells that analyzed parts of that specific object and conjoined them (e.g., received information from cells that recognized your grandmother's nose, her hair, her eyes, her chin line, etc., to perceive her face). However, current understanding of brain organization reveals that a cell exhibiting a highly specific firing pattern isn't likely to be *the* place in the brain that recognizes your grandmother so much as it is part of a diffuse cortical network that *participates in recognizing* your grandmother. The reason that scientists think this scenario is more likely is that although some cells show high specificity in their response for shape, most cells in inferotemporal cortex are simultaneously selective for a particular aspect of color, a particular aspect of shape, and a particular aspect of visual texture. Furthermore, these cells usually tend to give a small response to a variety of somewhat dissimilar stimuli. Hence, the brain more likely codes a particular visual object as a highly specific pattern of activation across a population of neurons rather than having a small pool of neurons dedicated to responding to that object and no other (see Gross, 1992, for a good historical and theoretical description of this work and its relevance to face recognition).

Researchers have also moved away from the idea of a grandmother cell because they realize that although a cell can appear to be specific in its response (e.g., it responds only to a researcher's face), determining with certainty exactly which specific stimulus makes the cell fire is practically impossible. Consider the following rather contrived example, which nonetheless makes this point. Assume, for example, that an experimenter finds a cell that fires in response to the face of his grandmother but not that of his grandfather. He might conclude that this cell is highly specific for recognizing his grandmother. However, unbeknownst to the researcher, the same cell fires in response to potato chips (which the researcher doesn't know because he can't test all possible objects and potato chips didn't seem like a likely candidate). The common denominator between the face of his grandmother and the potato chips that makes the cell fire is that they share a particular oval shape, a characteristic not shared by his grandfather's face, which is round. As this theoretical example illustrates, ascertaining the specific visual configuration that makes a cell fire may be difficult in principle. Recent empirical evidence illustrating this difficulty comes from recordings of a subpopulation of cells that traditionally were considered "face" cells because they respond vigorously to faces. However, researchers found that a subpopulation of these cells also fire in response to views of the body, even when the face is occluded. These findings suggest that these cells might be more aptly described as "body" cells rather than "face" cells (e.g., Wachsmuth, Oram, & Perrett, 1994).

Overall, what implications do these findings in monkeys have for face-recognition abilities in people? They suggest that the brains of monkeys (and most likely people) have specific regions that are especially adept at performing the computations that are important for recognizing faces. Furthermore, these same brain structures can in certain cases individuate among faces of different people. If these regions are damaged, disruptions of face recognition can occur. We now turn our attention to such disruptions seen after neurological insult in humans.

Face Recognition in Humans

As we mentioned in chapter 3, much evidence exists from studies of patients with the split-brain syndrome, from divided visual field studies of neurologically intact individuals, and from individuals with right-hemisphere damage that the right hemisphere of the human brain is particularly adept at recognizing faces. In fact, Yin (1970) suggested that posterior sections of the right hemisphere are specifically organized for recognizing faces above and beyond other types of complex visual stimuli. To investigate this hypothesis, he compared the ability of individuals with right-hemisphere damage to recognize faces with their ability to identify other visually complex stimuli that are also generally viewed in only one orientation, such as houses. In these studies, individuals viewed an inspection series of items (either faces or houses). Afterward, they were given a test series of items that contained, on each trial, a pair of items, one of which had appeared in the inspection series and one of which had not. The individuals were asked to pick the face viewed previously.

The participants were required to perform this task twice, once when the items in both the inspection and test series were in their regular upright orientation and once when they were presented in an inverted orientation. The rationale behind this manipulation is that the items are identical in visual complexity, regardless of orientation. However, when the items are inverted, configurational information is lost (e.g., the nose is no longer below the eyes, the chin is not at the bottom of the face). Yin theorized that this configurational information was especially important for recognizing faces. To appreciate the role that configurational information plays in face recognition, let's consider the picture in Figure 5.11, which is a demonstration created by Thompson (1980). In the inverted orientation, the woman does not look very odd, although on closer inspection you may notice that in the right-hand picture her eyes and mouth seem a bit strange (because they are actually upside down). Now, turn your book upside down and view the woman in an upright position. In the picture on the left, her face should now look bizarre and somewhat ghoulish. Because we have a configuration for recognizing upright faces but not one for recognizing inverted faces, her face looks much more distorted when viewed upright than when viewed inverted.

Yin found that neurologically intact individuals exhibited an **inversion effect,** which is a greater difficulty in remembering inverted stimuli than upright stimuli. Of most importance, however, the inversion effect was significantly larger for faces than for houses, which suggests that configural properties play a more important role in recognizing faces than in recognizing houses. In contrast, patients

 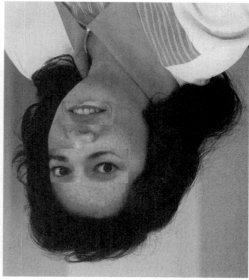

Figure 5.11 An example of the importance of configural information for recognizing faces. Examine the two faces and notice how from this vantage point they look similar. Now turn your book upside down so that the two faces are right-side up. You should immediately see a difference. This exercise, called the Thompson illusion, demonstrates the degree to which configural strategies are important for the processing of faces in the upright orientation and how they are minimized when the faces are inverted. (*Note.* After "Margaret Thatcher: A New Illusion," by P. Thompson, 1980, *Perception*, 9, pp. 483–484.)

with right-hemisphere damage showed a reduced inversion effect for faces. Although these patients did as well as neurologically intact subjects at recognizing inverted faces, they were selectively poor at recognizing upright faces. These findings led Yin to suggest that the posterior section of the right hemisphere was specialized specifically for face recognition and for the configural processing that such recognition required. This suggestion is consistent with a vast literature of face-recognition studies of neurologically intact subjects. Typically, a LVF advantage is found for face recognition (e.g., Geffen, Bradshaw, & Wallace, 1971), but this effect diminishes when faces are presented in an inverted orientation (e.g., Leehey, Carey, Diamond, & Cahn, 1978).

Other researchers have attempted to build upon Yin's findings, with the idea of both determining more specifically which regions of the brain are critical for face processing and determining whether these regions are specialized for processing faces

above and beyond other visually complex mono-oriented stimuli. At present, data from various converging methods, such as electrophysiologic methods, brain imaging studies, and analysis of lesion location in patients with prosopagnosia, confirm that only certain regions of the posterior sector of the right hemisphere are involved in face processing.

Recordings of electrical potentials from electrodes placed on the surface of the brains of patients about to undergo surgery for the relief of epilepsy are one source of information about the neural substrates of face processing. A particular brain wave with a negative amplitude at about 200 ms post-stimulus presentation (i.e., an N_{200}) occurs when individuals are asked to view faces but not other categories of stimuli, such as cars, butterflies, scrambled faces, and scrambled cars (Allison et al., 1994). The location of the source of this potential varies from patient to patient but generally is recorded bilaterally from fusiform and inferotemoral regions (Figure 5.12A). In any given patient, however, the

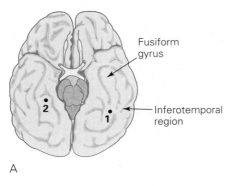

A

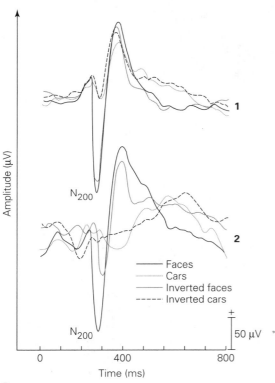

B

Figure 5.12   Examples of N$_{200}$ responses to faces and cars recorded from the cortex of one individual about to undergo surgery for the control of epilepsy.
(A) The sites (labeled 1 and 2) in the fusiform gyrus at which the potentials were recorded. (B) The potentials recorded over the left hemisphere (top) and over the right hemisphere (bottom). Note that the N$_{200}$ response is larger to faces than to cars. Also notice that the larger response over the right hemisphere to upright faces than to inverted faces (bottom) does not occur for the left hemisphere (top). (*Note.* Adapted from Allison et al., 1994, p. 548.)

size of the region providing such a response is small, perhaps only 1- to 2-cm wide, a finding suggesting a fair amount of anatomical variability with regard to the exact location of face-specific regions. Hemispheric differences have also been found in these recordings, with the right hemisphere, but not the left, exhibiting different responses to upright faces than to inverted faces (Figure 5.12B).

The findings from electrophysiological studies mesh well with those of functional imaging studies of face processing, with regard both to the location of the brain region important for face processing and to its specificity of response to faces but not other complex visual stimuli. In a recent positron emission tomography (PET) study, a group of researchers sought to distinguish among the regions of the brain that are important for object recognition in general, those important for making overall categorizations about faces (e.g., deciding whether a face is male or female), and those important for specifically identifying a face as belonging to a particular individual. These investigators' results yielded a number of interesting conclusions. First, large regions of the ventral areas of the occipital and temporal lobes were found to be involved during face-processing tasks, a finding suggesting that face processing is supported by a network of brain regions. Second, ventral regions of extrastriate cortex in the right hemisphere were involved in the face-gender categorization task but not the object-recognition task, which suggests that these regions are particularly sensitive to the visual features of facial stimuli. Third, when specific faces had to be identified, more anterior regions of both hemispheres, such as the medial fusiform gyrus and the anterior temporal lobes, including the temporal pole, were involved. For the left hemisphere, activity in all but the most anterior region of the temporal lobe occurred in both face- and object-recognition tasks, which suggests that these regions of the left hemisphere are not specifically specialized for face recognition. However, the pattern for the right hemisphere was different. The researchers found that the fusiform gyrus and the parahippocampal gyrus were active only during the face-identification task but not during the gender-identification task; therefore, these two regions of the right hemisphere

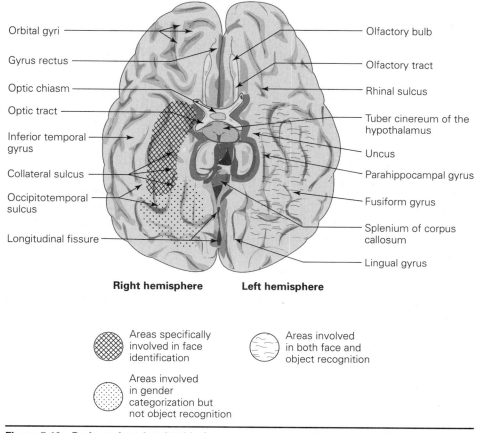

Orbital gyri

Gyrus rectus

Optic chiasm

Optic tract

Inferior temporal gyrus

Collateral sulcus

Occipitotemporal sulcus

Longitudinal fissure

Olfactory bulb

Olfactory tract

Rhinal sulcus

Tuber cinereum of the hypothalamus

Uncus

Parahippocampal gyrus

Fusiform gyrus

Splenium of corpus callosum

Lingual gyrus

Right hemisphere   **Left hemisphere**

Areas specifically involved in face identification

Areas involved in both face and object recognition

Areas involved in gender categorization but not object recognition

Figure 5.13   Brain regions involved in face recognition, gender categorization, and object recognition.
Large areas of ventral brain regions are involved in face processing and object recognition. In the right hemisphere, more posterior areas are important for processing the general aspects of facial form (whether the facial form is that of a woman or a man) as is required in a gender-categorization task, whereas more anterior areas are important for linking facial information to a specific person. In contrast, in the left hemisphere, the homologous brain regions are not specifically involved in face recognition because they are responsive to objects as well.

may be specifically specialized for the operations required to determine facial identity (Figure 5.13) (Sergent, Ohta, & MacDonald, 1992).

These findings are also consistent with lesion locations observed in patients with prosopagnosia. Some researchers had suggested that prosopagnosia occurred only after bilateral lesions (which was proposed as one reason that prosopagnosia is so rare) (e.g., A. R. Damasio, Damasio, & Van Hoesen, 1982). However, a more recent review of lesion locations in case studies of prosopagnosia indicates that some patients had lesions restricted to the right hemisphere. Because sometimes diffuse or microscopic damage may not manifest itself on neuroanatomical scans, PET scans have been used to provide converging evidence that the left hemisphere is functioning normally in cases of prosopagnosia. In a small sample of patients whose magnetic resonance imaging (MRI) scans showed a lesion confined to the right hemisphere, reduced metabolism was found only for right hemisphere regions; this finding confirmed that the left hemisphere was functioning normally and implicated the right hemisphere as critical for face processing (see DeRenzi et al., 1994, for some of the empirical data and for a review of this literature). Furthermore, case studies of patients with prosopagnosia suggest that different portions of the occipitotemporal area of the right hemisphere play different roles in different aspects of face processing, a finding consistent with those of PET studies. Case reports of two patients with prosopagnosia who had difficulty performing basic perceptual face tasks (such as determining whether two identical photographs of the same face represented the same individual) but who didn't have such difficulties with other objects, such as cars, were found to have damage in occipital regions and posterior parts of the medial temporal cortex. In contrast, two patients who were relatively unimpaired at matching pictures of faces but were unable to determine the identity of a given face, had damage in more anterior regions—in the right fusiform gyrus or the parahippocampal gyrus (Sergent & Signoret, 1992b).

The conclusion that can be drawn from these studies is that many ventromedial areas of the right hemisphere are involved in face processing. In general, posterior regions seem to be important for the perceptual processes that must be performed to create a configural representation of a face and to extract the invariants of the face that make it unique. In contrast, more anterior regions are involved in linking a particular facial representation to the pertinent biographical information about that person. Furthermore, these regions appear to be specific to faces and are neural structures not invoked in the recognition of other complex objects (see Sergent & Signoret, 1992a, for a very readable account of the research that supports such a viewpoint).

Role of Experience or Expertise in Face-Processing Capacities

Although the evidence we just reviewed clearly indicates that the right hemisphere is specialized for determining facial identity, we haven't directly addressed the degree to which these right-hemisphere mechanisms are specific to faces. For example, we haven't considered whether the right hemisphere might be specialized for individuating among members of any general class of complex visual objects, of which faces is only one (for an example of this position, see DeRenzi & Spinnler, 1966). In the studies we just discussed, participants had to determine whether a given face belonged to a certain person, but similar demands were not required for other complex objects, such as requiring them to differentiate their own cat from the neighbor's cat.

To address this question, researchers considered the different pieces of evidence suggesting that the role of the right hemisphere in face processing was special; one such piece of evidence was the inversion effect (remember, Yin found that the inversion effect was greater for faces than for other mono-oriented stimuli). One group of researchers hypothesized that the inversion effect might be observed for any class of objects with which a person has had vast experience. According to these investigators, experience would allow a configurational strategy to be developed for that particular class of objects, and this strategy would be disrupted by inversion. By their reasoning, the inversion effect is observed for faces because faces clearly are a class of objects with which we have much experience. The researchers further reasoned that if the right hemisphere is specialized for individuating members of any class of objects with which we are extremely familiar, rather than faces specifically, the inversion effect for that class of objects should be as large as that observed for faces (R. Diamond & Carey, 1986).

The trouble these researchers faced in attempting to prove their hypothesis was finding such a set of objects. What other type of object besides faces requires extensive expertise in carefully individuating among members of a category over a long period? To solve this problem, these investigators devised a plan to compare how well college students and judges of show dogs could individuate among pictures of different dogs in a paradigm similar to that used by Yin. As expected, the researchers found that college students exhibited a much larger inversion effect for faces than for show dogs. The results for the show-dog judges didn't clearly support their hypothesis because although the show-dog judges exhibited a larger inversion effect for the dogs than the college students did (consistent with their hypothesis), the effect was still smaller than for faces (inconsistent with their hypothesis). In the meantime, the researchers had learned that a show-dog judge does not judge all kinds of dogs but instead specializes in judging a particular class of dogs (toy dogs, retrievers, terriers). Hence, some of the items on the test had been beyond the expertise of the show-dog judges. To remedy this problem, the researchers chose a group of show-dog judges expert at judging sporting dogs. They then tested how well these judges could recognize, in both upright and inverted orientations, members for two breeds of sporting dogs with which they were highly familiar, Irish setters and cocker spaniels. This time, the show-dog judges had as large an inversion effect for show dogs as for faces, and the researchers concluded that expertise plays an important role in the inversion effect.

You should not be surprised to learn that experience influences the way we process not only faces, but also other stimuli. This point is well illustrated by the following study. The ability to remember a particular chest x-ray that is abnormal and indicative of disease (e.g., congestive heart failure, pneumonia, collapsed lung) increases with expertise from someone with no medical training through medical residents, junior radiologists, and senior radiologists. However, if these same groups of individuals must remember x-rays that don't indicate disease, greater expertise is associated with *poorer* performance, although memory for other items, such as faces, is identical across the four groups (Figure 5.14) (Myles-Worsley, Johnston, & Simons, 1988).

Why are the highly trained radiologists significantly worse at remembering normal x-rays? One likely explanation is that they have devised a system of encoding information about x-rays that emphasizes certain markers associated with disease. When given x-rays that are distinguished by other attributes unrelated to disease (e.g., thickness of the ribs), the radiologists do not pay attention to them, which makes remembering these x-rays more difficult. Thus, this study illustrates how expertise can

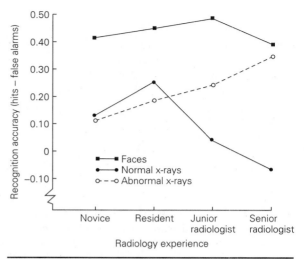

Figure 5.14 An example of how experience can influence the way in which visual information is processed. Shown here is the accuracy of identifying faces and x-rays for four groups of individuals who vary in their expertise in reading x-rays: novices, medical residents, junior radiologists, and senior radiologists. All four groups are equally skilled at remembering faces (scores depicted by black squares). Also, as might be expected, the greater the expertise with reading x-rays, the better the memory for abnormal x-rays (scores depicted by white circles). However, greater expertise with reading x-rays is associated with *poorer* memory for normal x-rays (scores depicted by black circles). These results suggest that expertise can hone the ability to observe certain visual characteristics, which has the effect of reducing the ability to observe other visual characteristics. (*Note.* Adapted from Myles-Worsley et al., 1988, p. 556.)

affect the way in which information is encoded and retrieved from memory.

Expertise also affects the ability to recognize faces. With experience, faces, like other classes of objects, can be well processed by using a configurational strategy that likely relies more on right- than left-hemisphere processing. Evidence that experience aids in the configurational processing of faces comes from both cross-cultural and developmental studies. For example, the inversion effect has been found to be greater for same-race faces, with which a person has had much experience, than for different-race faces. For instance, Chinese individuals exhibit a greater inversion effect for Chinese faces than for European faces, whereas European individuals exhibit the opposite pattern (Rhodes, Tan, Brake, & Taylor, 1989). These results may occur because we have more experience with the configurational nature of the faces of individuals of our own race than with that of other races. When asked to differentiate among faces, we can do so more easily if they fit into a configuration with which we are familiar.

Developmental studies suggest that such a configurational strategy is not fully developed until about 12 years of age. Before that age, children tend to rely on salient features and can be fooled—by clothing, hairstyle, eyeglasses, or expression—into thinking that two individuals are the same person (Carey & Diamond, 1977). Also suggesting that the right hemisphere is important for this configurational processing of faces is the finding that young children do not show the typical right-hemisphere advantage for faces until 12 years of age, after which a LVF asymmetry emerges. However, experience can speed up this process because a LVF advantage can be found in younger children, but only for faces with which they are highly familiar, such as their third-grade classmates. In contrast, no visual field asymmetry is observed for faces of other third-graders in either their own school or that of a neighboring town. The longer experience with their classmates probably allows these children to devise a configurational strategy for this particular set of faces, a strategy that relies on the right hemisphere (S. C. Levine, 1984).

Given that expertise affects the recognition of faces and other objects, we now need to consider other evidence that the right hemisphere might play a special role in processing faces, such as whether the right hemisphere is more involved in individuating among faces than among members of other well-known mono-oriented objects. In certain clinical case reports of patients with prosopagnosia, researchers have informally asserted that the ability to distinguish among members of other categories is also affected. For example, in one case report, a farmer who became prosopagnosic could no longer

distinguish among the cows in his herd (B. Bornstein, Sroka, & Munitz, 1969), and in another case, a bird watcher could no longer individuate among birds of a given species (B. Bornstein, 1963). Yet in other case studies, these abilities dissociate: The ability to distinguish among faces was found to be disrupted, although the ability to differentiate among cows (Bruyer et al., 1983) or to differentiate personal objects from other objects (e.g., DeRenzi, 1986) was intact.

Two case studies are of particular interest because they probably best address the issue of expertise. In one case, the individual with prosopagnosia was a car expert, possessing a set of miniature cars that numbered more than 5,000 at one point. To test his ability to distinguish among cars, researchers showed him 210 pictures of cars and asked him to identify each car's make, model, and year of production (within 2 years). He identified all three aspects correctly for 172 of the pictures, and of the remaining 38, he correctly identified the company in 31 cases and the model in 22 cases (Case R.M., Sergent & Signoret, 1992b). In another case, a patient was able to learn the individual faces of a flock of sheep he acquired after becoming prosopagnosic, even though his inability to distinguish among human faces remained disrupted (McNeil & Warrington, 1993). Thus, at present, the ability to distinguish among individual faces appears to be distinct from the ability to distinguish among members of other well-known classes of objects.

The evidence we discussed suggests that the right hemisphere is indeed specialized for the types of visuospatial analyses, such as configurational processing, that are likely to be tuned by experience and honed with time. The high degree of right-hemisphere involvement in face recognition most likely occurs because our vast experience with faces allows for the extraction of common configural aspects of faces (see S. C. Levine, Banich, & Koch-Weser, 1988, for an elaboration of this argument). At present, however, we do not know which specific regions of the posterior section of the right hemisphere support a general mechanism of extracting configural invariants across a set of stimuli. Evidence also suggests that the neural processing of faces is special, to the degree that the neural mechanism that allows us to differentiate among individual faces is distinct from that which allows us to distinguish among individuals of other classes of mono-oriented objects, such as cars or sheep faces.

Although we emphasized the importance of the right hemisphere for face processing, we must not lose sight of the fact that the left hemisphere also seems to be involved to some degree. For example, PET studies indicate that regions of the left hemisphere are also active during face recognition (as they are during recognition of other objects) (Sergent, Ohta, & MacDonald, 1992). The left hemisphere may contribute to face recognition by allowing for the processing of specific features, such as the nose or mouth. For example, a RVF advantage is found for face processing when decisions must be made about the identity of faces that either are identical or differ by just one feature (e.g., the nose differs) (e.g., Hilliger & Koenig, 1991). Thus, as with many other processes that we discuss in this book, both hemispheres are involved, although they contribute in different manners.

Implicit Recognition of Faces

One intriguing aspect of face processing that has been revealed by studying individuals with prosopagnosia is that in some cases they can recognize faces even though they do not have conscious access to that information. Traditionally, agnosia has been conceptualized as a disruption in the ability to link perceptual patterns to information in memory. However, evidence for a degree of preserved face processing, at least in some patients with prosopagnosia, suggests that the connection between perceptual information about a face and its meaning is not always totally destroyed. Covert processing of faces has been demonstrated in two major ways: through measurements of electrodermal skin conductance and through behavioral priming studies.

Although individuals with prosopagnosia cannot verbally distinguish between familiar and unfamiliar faces at more than a chance level, electrodermal skin conductance is greater to previously known faces than to unknown faces (Tranel & Damasio, 1988).

The electrodermal skin conductance response (which is basically a lowering in the impedance to electrical current due to sweat and is the same method as used in a lie-detection test) is related to activity of the autonomic nervous system, although its exact source is unknown. As a reminder, the autonomic nervous system is the part of the nervous system responsible for control of smooth muscles (such as those that cause goose bumps and the hair on your arms to stand up), the heart, and glands (including sweat glands).

Other evidence for covert recognition of faces in patients with prosopagnosia is the existence of interference effects that should not occur if the individual truly has no access to information about facial identity. In one study, a patient was taught (to the limited degree possible) to face-name pairs for a set of faces. Some of the faces in the set were faces he had previously known but now could not identify and claimed not to know. However, he had more difficulty learning to associate these faces with incorrect names than with correct names. Thus, at some level, information about the face had to be accessed or no interference should have occurred when he was learning a new name for an already-known face (Bruyer et al., 1983). In another study, a patient had to read a person's name or after reading the name had to classify the person by occupation (e.g., a musician or a politician). A prior study with neurologically intact individuals had demonstrated that such tasks take longer if the name is situated next to the face of someone in a different occupation rather than next to the face of the correct person or someone in the same occupation. If the patient is not retrieving any information about faces, the face should have no effect on how quickly the name is read or how quickly the person's occupation is classified. Yet, the patient demonstrated covert recognition of the faces because, like neurologically intact adults, he took longer to read an individual's name when it was situated next to the face of someone in a different occupation (De Haan, Young, & Newcombe, 1987). This interference effect occurred even though the individual with prosopagnosia did not recognize the faces, being able neither to name them nor to sort them according to occupa-

Figure 5.15 **Examples of stimuli used to demonstrate covert recognition in a patient with prosopagnosia.**
In studies such as these, the patient was asked to read the name inside the bubble. Then, three types of trials were given: in some the name of the individual (such as Dianne Feinstein, an American politician) was paired with (A) her own face (Reuters/Corbis-Bettmann), (B) in others with the face of another American politician (in this case, Patricia Schroeder) (UPI/Corbis-Bettmann), and (C) in still others with the face of a nonpolitician (in this case, Barbara Walters) (Reuters/Bettmann). Although the individual with prosopagnosia could not recognize any of the faces, he was still slower to read the name when it was paired with an individual from a different profession, as in (C), than when it was paired with either (A) or (B).

tion. Examples similar to the type of stimuli used in this study are shown in Figure 5.15.

The results of all these studies suggest that a subset of patients with prosopagnosia can retain some information about faces in memory, although it is not available in a way that allows explicit naming or categorizing of faces. These cases of prosopagnosia do not fit well with a model that presumes a total disconnection in the linkage between a face's perceptual features and its associated biographical information in memory. Rather, the amount of information that can be encoded from a face by these individuals may be scant, or the threshold for recognizing a face may be increased so that gaining access to information is impossible under ordinary conditions but can nonetheless influence performance under specific conditions. We revisit the issue of implicit memory in more detail in chapter 9.

CATEGORY-SPECIFIC DEFICITS IN OBJECT RECOGNITION

So far we discussed agnosia as a deficit in which the person loses the ability to recognize or identify information within a specific modality. However, in other cases a person has trouble identifying a certain category of objects even though the ability to recognize other categories of items in that same modality is undisturbed. This disorder is knowns as a **category-specific deficit.** For example, a person may have difficulty identifying fruits and vegetables but not have difficulty identifying human-made objects (Warrington & Shallice, 1984). These deficits are perplexing because they are difficult to understand within the framework in which we previously considered agnosias.

When discussing agnosias, we emphasized that they do not arise from a fundamental disruption in basic sensory processing. Rather, apperceptive agnosia has been conceptualized as an inability to use basic sensory attributes to form a percept. Associative agnosia has been conceptualized as a difficulty in linking meaning to a particular visual pattern (e.g., the visual form of a chair), which itself can be categorized perceptually (e.g., matched to an identical chair). How then are we to understand

these category-specific deficits? Clearly, neither of these problems arises here. First, the ability to form percepts must be intact because objects outside specific categories can be recognized. For example, although apples and oranges cannot be recognized, cars and trains can, which indicates that an overall ability to form a visual percept is intact. Second, in limited cases, the percept can be linked to meaning because items in the nonaffected category can be recognized.

Most evidence suggests that such deficits are not agnosic deficits. Rather, they arise either from difficulties within the semantic memory system (i.e., the system for meaning) or from difficulty in being able to name certain items, which is known as *selective anomia*. For example, Warrington and Shallice (1984) found patients who could neither recognize a particular class of objects when they were presented visually, nor provide an adequate definition of those items when told the names of the objects (remember that individuals with agnosia *can* provide definitions for items they can't identify). Such findings suggest that these individuals have lost access to memory for the affected class of items. In other cases, individuals cannot name certain categories of items, such as fruits and vegetables, but their deficit is limited to naming and therefore appears to be a problem in word retrieval rather than in semantic memory (e.g., J. Hart, Berndt, & Caramazza, 1985).

How could such category-specific deficits in memory arise? One possible explanation is that gaining access to information in memory about certain items, such as fruits and vegetables, is more difficult than doing so for others, such as human-made objects. However, this possibility is unlikely because other patients exhibit the converse syndrome; they have more difficulty recognizing human-made objects than fruits and vegetables (Warrington & McCarthy, 1987). If the problem were merely one of difficulty in gaining access to certain portions of memory, we would not expect to find the categories that are the most difficult for some individuals to be the easiest for others. Another argument against the idea that gaining access to certain categories of items is more difficult is the finding that access may

Visual Imagery: Seeing Objects With the Mind's Eye

Have you ever imagined yourself on a tropical island in the Caribbean? Can you see the long white sandy beach? The blending of the water's colors from pale green to jade to aquamarine to royal blue? The palm trees with their fronds waving in the breeze? And, to complete the picture, your latest romantic interest looking perfectly enticing in an ever-so-alluring bathing suit? If so, then even though our discussion of objects has centered on recognizing objects in the real world, you realize that we also have the ability to examine and manipulate objects in our mind's eye by mental imagery.

The nature of mental imagery has been the subject of a long-running debate whose resolution was based, in part, on neuropsychological data. Stephen Kosslyn, a researcher at Harvard University, had proposed that mental imagery was much like visual processing, except in the mind's eye. Some support for this position came from studies in which he found that the time needed to "see" particular parts of an image was proportional to the distance that we would expect the mind's eye to have to move to get to that part. For example, participants were told to imagine an item (e.g., an airplane) and to focus on one end (e.g., the propeller). Then they were given the name of a particular feature to look for ("the tail") and instructed to press a button when they could see it. Kosslyn (1973) found that individuals took longer to press the button if the feature was located at the other end of the imagined

item (e.g., the tail) than if it appeared in the middle (e.g., the wing).

In contrast, Zenon Pylyshyn (1973, 1981) argued that we don't actually draw mental images. Rather, he suggested, the results of Kosslyn's experiment could just as easily be explained by *propositional knowledge*. Propositional knowledge describes entities (e.g., a propeller, a wing), their relations (next to, behind), their properties (long, silver), and their logical relations (if). He argued that a person takes less time to decide about the wing than the tail because the individual must remember only that the wing is behind the propeller, which is fewer propositions than remembering that the tail is behind the wing, which is behind the propeller.

The arguments for and against each theory oscillated for more than another 10 years, until Kosslyn and Martha Farah turned to neuropsychological evidence, which played a large role in settling the matter (for a more detailed but readable account of this debate, see Kosslyn, 1990). These researchers reasoned that if imagery does rely on producing a picture in the mind's eye, it should require some of the same neuronal machinery required by vision (e.g., Farah, 1988). Alternatively, if imagery tasks can be performed simply by resorting to propositional knowledge about objects in the world, then the memory and/or semantic-processing areas of the brain should be active, but visually related areas should not. Studies of regional brain activation and patients with brain damage both suggest

be hampered only for specific attributes of the affected category. For example, in one case report, researchers described a patient who could retrieve nonvisual aspects of information about living things (e.g., "Are roses given on Valentine's day?") and nonliving things (e.g., "Was the wheelbarrow invented before 1920?") equally well but who had more difficulty gaining access to information about the visual form of living things (e.g., "Are the hind legs of a kangaroo larger than the front legs?") than

that of nonliving things (e.g., "Is a canoe widest in the center?"). If gaining access to information from memory about living things were harder than doing so for nonliving things, the same pattern would be expected to hold regardless of the type of information that was being retrieved from memory (i.e., the type of question asked) (Farah, Hammond, Mehta, & Ratcliff, 1989).

An alternative explanation is that memory is organized so that the "living things" section is distinct

that visual areas play a major role in imagery. For example, Kosslyn and colleagues (1993) reasoned that if imagery relies on the visual cortex, some relationship should exist between the size of the imagined object and the area of visual cortex that is activated. This finding would be expected because, as we discussed in chapter 1, visual space is mapped onto visual cortex in a retinotopic manner. Consistent with their hypothesis, these investigators found that when a person was imaging small letters in the center of the mind's eye, activation was greatest in posterior regions of the medial occipital lobes, which is the region that processes information from the fovea. In contrast, when a person was imaging larger letters, activation occurred over a larger area of visual cortex that included more anterior regions, which is where more peripheral regions of visual space are processed (short, readable accounts of this and related work on occipital activation during imagery can be found in Kosslyn & Ochsner, 1994, and in Moscovitch, Behrmann, & Winocur, 1994).

Additional evidence that imagery relies on visual cortex comes from an unusual case study in which an individual had elective surgery to remove the occipital lobe of one hemisphere because it was the source of intractable epileptic seizures (Farah, Soso, & Dasheiff, 1992). The researchers calculated the visual angle of the patient's mental image before and after the surgery (see the original article for details on how this was done). The researchers reasoned that if imagery relies on the visual cortex, after surgery the visual angle of

images in the horizontal dimension should be half what it was previously, because the visual cortex of one hemisphere is responsible for processing information from one half of visual space. In contrast, the visual angle of images should be unchanged in the vertical dimension because the remaining intact occipital cortex could process information from both the upper and lower halves of space. These investigators found, as expected, a reduction by approximately half for the visual angle of images in the horizontal dimension, but no change for the visual angle of images in the vertical dimension.

Like many of the other mental abilities we discussed, mental imagery does not rely on only one hemisphere; both are involved (e.g., Kosslyn, 1987). The generation of multipart high-resolution images that require a person to compute the relationships between image parts (e.g., Do a German shepherd's ears protrude above its head?) has been found to rely on the left hemisphere (e.g., Farah, 1984; Farah, Gazzaniga, Holtzman, & Kosslyn, 1985). In contrast, the right hemisphere is better at doing computations that require a coarse overall assessment of the image (e.g., Is a pig taller than it is wide?) (e.g., Kosslyn, Holtzman, Farah, & Gazzaniga, 1985). Thus, since the mid-1980s, not only has the neural machinery required for imagery been shown to overlap with that of vision, but also each hemisphere has been shown to have a distinct role in imagery.

from the "nonliving things" section. In this case, the argument would be that in category-specific deficits, one section of memory can be retrieved whereas another cannot. The problem with this account is that some individuals can *generally* distinguish one semantic category from another (e.g., living vs. nonliving items) but exhibit important exceptions to the rule. For example, one patient can't recognize fish, flowers, or fruit, all of which are living. Yet he recognizes body parts perfectly

well, which are also living. Likewise, although nonliving items such as clothing, kitchen utensils, and vehicles can be identified, musical instruments cannot. Such findings cast doubt on the idea that the deficit in these patients is restricted to a specific topical area (e.g., living items, nonliving items) (Warrington & Shallice, 1984).

A more likely explanation for the deficits is that when a person is accessing memory, information from different modalities may have a differential weight or influence. For example, when recognizing human-made objects, we generally differentiate them according to function. Chalk, crayons, and pencils are all used for drawing and writing, but they are distinguished from one another by the surfaces on which they are used (blackboard, construction paper, and writing paper, respectively). Nothing inherent in the sensory attributes of the items might point to this distinction in function. However, this is not the case for living things. For example, the best way to distinguish a leopard from a lioness and a tiger is by sensory attributes in the visual modality (the leopard has spots, the lioness is all one tawny color, and the tiger has stripes). According to this explanation, a more severe deficit might arise in recognizing animals than in identifying writing utensils because the information in memory relies more heavily on the visual attributes of the item (see Warrington & Shallice, 1984, for the original articulation of this idea).

Yet even this explanation is lacking. We still need to be able to explain why some patients have trouble recognizing fruits and vegetables but can recognize other items such as flowers, all of which are probably differentiated on the basis of visual attributes, and why other patients can recognize certain objects such as keys and pens but not airplanes and helicopters, even though they all are probably differentiated on the basis of function. One possible explanation is that particular channels of information within a sensory modality may be more affected by a brain lesion than other channels are. In our discussion of visual processing, we noted that different visual attributes, such as color, shape, motion and location, are processed in different regions of the brain (see page 167). Thus, the nature of brain damage may be such as to affect the processing of certain visual attributes more than others. Depending on the area damaged, identification of certain items is more likely to be affected than that of others. For example, consider the case of round fruits such as oranges, peaches, and apples. For these items, color is the visual attribute that most helps us to differentiate among them. In contrast, differentiating among flowers is much less likely to rely on color. For example, the various colors of violets can overlap with those of irises and hyacinths. The distinguish-

ing feature among these flowers is their shape. Thus, depending on where the damage is, one patient may have a greater disruption in gaining access to information about one channel (e.g., color) than another (e.g., shape), which is a possible explanation for the seemingly strange dissociations observed in patients with category-specific deficits (Warrington & McCarthy, 1987).

These dissociations raise issues about how the memory system is organized. One group of theorists argues that a centrally organized semantic system exists for all categories of items. They posit that category-specific deficits arise because certain types of information (e.g, visual features) may be more important attributes of certain items than others (e.g., Caramazza, Hillis, Rapp, & Romani, 1990). Other theorists suggest that knowledge is organized in parallel subsystems, one organized for sensory information and one for functional information. From this perspective, these category-specific deficits can be explained by a disconnection between peripheral information from a sensory modality and the functional-associative portion of memory (e.g., Farah & McClelland, 1991). Yet another possibility is that modality-specific meaning systems exist (e.g., Warrington & McCarthy, 1994). This suggestion has been based in part on a case report of a patient who has a category-specific disorder that appears to be limited to a single modality, the visual one. The deficit was shown to be category specific because he could name line drawings depicting animals and flowers but was poor at doing so for objects. The difficulty was shown to be modality specific because he could easily and quickly define items whose pictures he could not recognize. Furthermore, when given the name of an object, he could pantomime its use flawlessly (an indication that he did not have difficulties in word retrieval and that he had intact memory for objects), but he was poor at pantomime when shown the object visually. Thus, he appeared to have a specific difficulty in retrieving information about objects through the visual modality. This individual's brain damage was located in the right parietal lobe and the inferior left occipitotemporal region; therefore, at least some disruption in the ventral processing stream was likely. At present, no one knows exactly which of these theories provides the best explanation of the available data. These category-specific deficits do, however, suggest that sensory information from different modalities may allow for differential access to a memory system and/or that memory itself is organized in some way with regard to sensory attributes.

AGNOSIAS IN OTHER MODALITIES

Much of our attention in this chapter has been directed to agnosias in the visual modality. However, we must remember that agnosias can occur in other modalities as well. In this section of the chapter, we discuss the characteristics of auditory and somatosensory (tactile) agnosias.

Auditory Agnosia

Auditory agnosia, like other agnosias, is characterized by unimpaired processing of basic sensory information but an inability to link that sensory information to meaning, despite the fact that memory, as assessed through other modalities, appears to be normal. The integrity of basic auditory processing is generally assessed through **pure tone audiometry.** In this method, an individual is tested on the ability to perceive a tone that consists of only one frequency (e.g., 1000 Hz). In the test, a large number of trials are given so that the ability to process these pure tones is assessed over the range of frequencies that can be detected by humans (e.g., ~125–8000 Hz). Individuals with auditory agnosia do well on tests of pure tone audiometry. They can perceive when a sound occurs and at thresholds generally equivalent to that of the average person without agnosia.

In real life, however, sounds are typically made up of a complex pattern of tones that are overlaid much the way that chords in music are the result of combining different single notes. When persons with auditory agnosia hear a complex sound, they cannot classify it. Auditory agnosia usually manifests in one of three ways. In **verbal auditory agnosia** (also known as **pure word deafness**), words cannot be understood, but the ability to attach meaning to nonverbal sounds is intact. In **nonverbal auditory agnosia,** the ability to attach meaning to words is

intact, but the ability to do so for nonverbal sounds is disrupted. In **mixed auditory agnosia,** the ability to attach meaning to both verbal and nonverbal sounds is affected.

In verbal auditory agnosia, or pure word deafness, the individual can read, write, and speak normally, an indication that this condition is not a disorder of linguistic processing. However, patients with this type of auditory agnosia complain that although they know that a noise has occurred, speech sounds like "an undifferentiated continuous humming noise without any rhythm" or "like foreigners speaking in the distance." Likewise, in nonverbal auditory agnosia, which is rarer than verbal auditory agnosia, the individual knows that a sound has occurred but cannot categorize it as either a car horn, a dog bark, or a lawn mower. This difficulty can be quite a problem in real life. For example, if a car's driver is honking a horn as a warning for people to move out of the way, an individual with auditory agnosia would hear a noise but might not hurry across the street because the sound was "unintelligible, sort of like how I remember crickets chirping or static on a telephone line." In contrast, persons with mixed auditory agnosia can recognize neither verbal nor nonverbal sounds, although they can determine whether two sounds are identical or different and whether one sound is louder than the other. That is, their ability to *hear* the sounds is intact and they are not deaf.

Just as we discussed for visual agnosias, the degree to which higher order perceptual problems can account for such disturbances is an issue debated by researchers and clinicians. Some authorities claim that one form of pure word deafness involves the compromise of some important basic aspects of auditory perception (e.g., Auerbach et al., 1982). This type of verbal auditory agnosia is associated with damage to the bilateral temporal lobe and because such damage interferes with the ability to process basic acoustic parameters, it has been suggested that higher order auditory processing cannot occur (e.g., M. L. Albert & Bear, 1974). For example, compared with neurologically intact individuals, patients with pure word deafness require a much longer separation in time between two tones to perceive them as distinct. As we learn in more detail in chapter 8, fine temporal discrimination is an important aspect of language processing. Similar difficulties have been reported for patients with mixed auditory agnosia. For example, one particular patient required 250 ms to perceive sounds as separate, whereas neurologically intact subjects could do so with only a 15-ms interval. Indicating that the problem was limited to the auditory modality, times to perceive two flashes of light as separate were normal (H. A. Buchtel & Stewart, 1989). In addition to difficulties in sequencing sounds, individuals with auditory agnosia may have difficulty determining the duration of tones. In contrast, the ability to judge the pitch (frequency) of a sound and its intensity are much less affected (Mendez & Geehan, 1988). Thus, at least some persons with auditory agnosia appear to have what might be considered an apperceptive disorder because they cannot integrate component sounds into a whole, much the way patients with visual agnosia can't integrate local features of light and dark into a meaningful gestalt.

Why processing of the same types of acoustic parameters should be affected in individuals with pure word deafness and nonverbal auditory agnosia is unclear. In part, the distinction between verbal auditory agnosia and nonverbal auditory agnosia may arise depending on the degree to which the perception of specific acoustic parameters is impaired. For example, speech and nonverbal sounds tend to occur at different frequencies, and speech is also noteworthy for the transient nature of some of its acoustic cues. Our understanding of the conditions that produce pure word deafness as compared with those that produce nonverbal auditory agnosia is likely to improve when the specific acoustic parameters compromised in each of these disorders become better characterized.

A disruption in processing different acoustic parameters may also account for two proposed varieties of pure word deafness (e.g., Auerbach et al., 1982), one that involves a disruption in relatively basic auditory processing and another that involves a more specific disruption of processing of the constituent sounds of language (this type of pure word deafness is associated with left temporal lobe lesions). The type of word deafness based on more basic auditory cues (as well as mixed auditory agnosia) causes difficulty for cues that are related to the location in the vocal tract where a sound is produced (for example, the *p* in *pot* is produced at the lips, whereas the *g* in *got* is produced toward the back of the mouth) (e.g., Miceli, 1982). These sounds may be difficult to differentiate because they rely on quick temporal transitions in the frequency of the acoustic signal (S. E. Blumstein, Tarter, Nigro, & Statlender, 1984). In contrast, in the other form of word deafness, cues that relate to the temporal offset between particular sounds are more likely to be compromised (e.g., voicing contrasts such as the difference between "b" and "p," which relate to when the vocal tract begins to vibrate relative to the burst of air produced at the lips). (We discuss some of these contrasts in more detail in chapter 8, see page 288.)

In sum, the evidence suggests that auditory agnosia disrupts the ability to coalesce sounds into a percept that allows meaning to be obtained. The particular acoustic parameters that cannot be integrated may vary among verbal, nonverbal, and mixed auditory agnosias, but in all cases, the processing of temporal parameters seems to be more affected than the processing of the parameters involved in pitch or intensity.

Somatosensory Agnosia

Somatosensory agnosia, or **tactile agnosia** (sometimes referred to as *astereognosia*), is a condition in which a person is unable to recognize an item by its touch but can recognize the object in other modalities. As with other agnosias, two types have been proposed, one in which the affected person has an inability to use tactile information to create a percept, and another in which the percept is more or less intact but cannot be linked to meaning. This latter agnosia is sometimes called **tactile asymbolia** because the tactile information cannot be linked to its symbolic meaning (e.g., a small metal object that is big at the top and thin at the bottom with a jagged edge and is about 1 in., or 2.5 cm, long cannot be linked to the concept of a key). Although these two distinct types of tactile agnosia have been proposed, researchers disagree as to whether tactile asymbolia actually exists.

As with the other agnosias we discussed, the degree to which sensory impairments preclude object recognition is also a debated issue for the tactile modality. Some researchers have argued that deficits in recognizing objects in the tactile modality occur only in the presence of sensory deficits, such as difficulty in two-point discrimination and pressure sensitivity. For example, in one study, most individuals (83%) who exhibited unilateral difficulties in recognizing objects through the tactile modality had severe sensory loss for the affected hand and damage to the hand area of the contralateral postcentral gyrus (Corkin, Milner, & Rasmussen, 1970). Although these sensory deficits often lead to poor object recognition, they do not always do so because many different cues can be used to recognize an object tactilely, such as its shape, texture, weight, temperature, and so forth. If the ability to process some of these cues remains intact, some object recognition may still be possible.

At least some authors (e.g., Semmes, 1965) have argued the opposite, namely that tactile recognition of objects can be disrupted even when no sensory deficit exists. These researchers found that individuals were impaired in the ability to identify an item's shape, although they could tell whether the item was smooth or scratchy, hard or soft, large or small. Although their intact perceptual-processing abilities would suggest an agnosia, the deficit did not appear to be modality specific because these individuals also had trouble identifying the same items visually. Hence, these individuals appeared to have difficulties in visuospatial processing that exhibited itself in multiple modalities.

A recent and detailed case study (Reed & Caselli, 1994) of a woman with unilateral tactile agnosia provides evidence that tactile agnosia can occur when basic and intermediate sensory functions are intact; therefore, her difficulties could clearly be attributed to forming a percept of the item or to linking that percept to information in memory. She exhibited normal thresholds for detecting touch, vibration, and proprioception, and she had normal

two-point discrimination (i.e., the distance required so that two touches are perceived as occurring in separate locations rather than the same location was normal), so basic sensory function appeared to be intact for the affected hand. She also performed well with the affected hand on tests of more elaborate somatosensory functions, such as distinguishing objects of different weights and different textures, and identifying simple shapes. Moreover, her difficulties did not appear to be caused by an impaired ability to acquire sensory data because the types of motor behaviors she exhibited when exploring objects was similar for both the affected hand and the unaffected hand. Nonetheless, when given complex objects that she could identify visually and tactilely with the unaffected hand, she was deficient in doing so with the affected hand. For example, she misidentified a pine cone as a brush, a ribbon as a rubber band, and a snail shell as a bottle cap. This individual had a lesion in the left inferior parietal area (Brodmann's area 40 and, to a lesser degree, Brodmann's area 39—the ventromedial area of the somatosensory association cortices), as has been observed in other case reports of tactile agnosia (Figure 5.16) (e.g., Caselli, 1993).

The evidence reviewed in this section of the chapter illustrates that agnosia can occur in modalities besides the visual one. However, the distinctions between apperceptive and associative disorders do

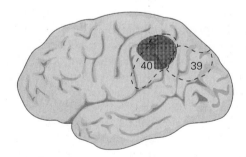

Figure 5.16 The location of the lesion that typically causes tactile agnosia.
Damage to the left inferior parietal area (Brodmann's area 40 and, to a lesser degree, Brodmann's area 39—the ventromedial area of the somatosensory association cortices) typically causes tactile agnosia. (*Note.* Adapted from Reed & Caselli, 1994.)

not seem to be as clear-cut in the auditory and tactile modalities as those observed in the visual modality.

SUMMARY

Research with animals has suggested that the visual-processing stream that courses ventrally from the occipital regions toward the pole of the temporal lobe plays a major role in our ability to recognize objects. Lesions of the anterior temporal region create difficulties in recognizing objects, and single-cell recordings from this region reveal that the cells fire only in response to very specific visual forms. In addition, the receptive fields of cells in inferior temporal cortex, the last purely visual-processing area in the ventral stream, are large and always include the center of the visual field. The large receptive field size may allow an object to be recognized regardless of location, and sensitivity to the center of the visual field may allow objects to be recognized at the region of highest acuity.

Agnosia is the inability to recognize an object in a particular sensory modality even though basic perceptual processing in that modality is intact and the individual does not have a generalized memory disorder. Although agnosia can appear in all modalities, it has been studied most commonly in the visual modality. Traditionally, a distinction has been made between two types of agnosia: apperceptive agnosia and associative agnosia. In general, apperceptive agnosia is viewed as an inability to combine fragmentary sensory information into a unitary percept. In some cases of apperceptive agnosia, diffuse bilateral damage near and extending into occipital regions causes disruption in all but the most basic of visual processes. In cases associated with damage to posterior regions of the right hemisphere, basic visual processing is less disturbed, but the ability to classify visual objects perceptually is lost. Persons with associative agnosia traditionally have been considered to have intact perceptual processes but an inability to link that information to meaning. However, more recent research suggests that these individuals also have some perceptual difficulties, albeit not to as severe a degree as that exhibited by individuals with apperceptive agnosia. These difficulties preclude the patients from deriving meaning from visual information and are associated with bilateral damage near the occipitotemporal border.

Various theories examine how information is recognized in the visual modality. One of these theories, proposed by David Marr, examines the computational steps required to identify an object. One major difficulty in recognizing visual objects is that the brain must reconstruct a three-dimensional (3-D) model of the object from the two-dimensional (2-D) information received on the retina. Marr suggests that this process has three steps. The first step is to construct a primal sketch in which basic distinctions between light and dark information are made. The second step is the construction of a 2½-D sketch in which information about relative depth is derived from texture, occlusion, and other visual cues. Both representations are considered viewer centered because the information about the relationships among an object's parts is linked to the specific perspective from which the viewer is seeing the object. Finally, a 3-D representation is derived in which the major axes of the item are identified and the volumetric relationships among different parts of the object are known. This representation is considered object centered because the representation of the relationships among an object's parts is with reference to the object itself, which allows it to be recognized from many different vantage points. Researchers have suggested that patients with apperceptive agnosia cannot perform perceptual classification of objects because they lack the ability to create a 3-D representation of an object.

Evidence also exists that both global and local aspects of visual objects can be processed simultaneously and by different neural systems. On the basis of studies of individuals with brain damage and neurologically intact subjects, the right hemisphere appears to be specialized for processing global aspects of a visual object, whereas the left hemisphere appears to be specialized for processing local aspects of a visual object. These findings are consistent with other research suggesting that the right hemisphere is superior at processing information of a relatively lower spatial frequency, which is used to identify coarse outline and global features of an item, whereas the left hemisphere is superior at processing information of a relatively higher spatial frequency, which is used to identify detailed information in a visual figure.

The ability to recognize faces seems to have a strong evolutionary history because specialized cells for recognizing faces are found in the temporal lobes of other species, such as sheep and monkeys. Data from individuals with brain damage, neurologically intact subjects, patients with the split-brain syndrome, and brain imaging studies all suggest that the right hemisphere may play a predominant role in the visual processing of faces. However, some debate has been generated as to whether or not face processing is supported by a general-purpose mechanism in the right hemisphere that is honed by experience and is used for any class of objects that share a common configuration. At present, the evidence suggests that the regions of the right hemisphere that are specialized for face processing are distinct from those that process other objects. Furthermore, the ability to distinguish among individual faces appears to be a separate capacity than that required to distinguish among individual members of other categories, such as individual cars or individual sheep in a herd.

Another piece of evidence supporting the role of the right hemisphere in face recognition is the existence of prosopagnosia, a condition that occurs after right-hemisphere damage and disrupts an individual's ability to recognize previously familiar faces even though other visual objects can be recognized. Prosopagnosia traditionally has been considered to be a disconnection of facial information from meaning; however, evidence exists that some persons with this disorder can implicitly recognize faces. Even when these individuals cannot name the face they are viewing or sort faces into categories (e.g., by occupation), their responses to familiar and unfamiliar faces differ when measured by other means. For example, they have different electrodermal skin responses to familiar and unfamiliar faces and exhibit interference in learning or processing names when the names are paired with incorrect or inappropriate faces.

Some category-specific disorders affect the ability to recognize items within certain categories (e.g., fruits and vegetables), whereas items within other categories (e.g., items manufactured by humans) are recognized without difficulty. These disorders generally either are not modality specific or are specific to the naming of items. Some theorists explain category-specific disorders by suggesting that the memory system is unitary and that the degree to which we gain access to information in memory varies from item to item, so that differentiating some items relies more on attributes in one modality than in the others (e.g., we rely more on visual attributes to differentiate animals than to differentiate tools). Other authorities claim that we have two types of memory stores: a sensorally based store and a conceptually based store. Still other investigators posit that we may have separate memory systems for different modalities.

Agnosias can also occur in modalities besides vision. Auditory agnosia can take one of three forms. In verbal auditory agnosia, or word deafness, the ability to recognize auditory words is disrupted but the ability to recognize musical and nonverbal sounds is retained. In nonverbal auditory agnosia, the recognition of nonverbal sounds is disrupted but the ability to understand words is spared. In mixed auditory agnosia, the recognition of both words and sounds is disrupted. All three types of auditory agnosia are associated with an inability to process certain acoustic features. In somatosensory, or tactile, agnosia, the individual cannot recognize items by touch. Often these deficits are accompanied by severe deficits in tactile sensory processing or occur concomitantly with disruptions in spatial processing in other modalities, which suggests that they may not represent true tactile agnosia. However, in at least a few case studies of individuals with true tactile agnosia, spatial abilities as well as basic and intermediate tactile perception are intact.

Spatial
Processing

A fun-loving middle-age woman, C.J. had spent her entire adult life as an outdoor enthusiast. Recently, she had suffered a mild stroke that damaged a small portion of the posterior section of her right hemisphere. She had hated the confinement of the hospital during her month-long stay and had eagerly awaited her chance to spend some time outdoors again. Because her basic visual-processing abilities were intact (an indication that the lesion had spared primary and secondary visual areas), she didn't anticipate having any problems doing the things she loved—hiking, skiing, and backpacking.

A few weekends after being released from the rehabilitation unit, C.J., along with her friend Sarah, decided to take a day hike up to a mountain pass. As they started up the trail, it was a beautiful, crisp autumn day with great views of the valleys below them. They hiked for about an hour, passing a number of turnoffs until they entered a more forested area, where the trail became less well defined and had many switch backs. The hiking was difficult, but C.J. was feeling like her old self again. Soon afterward, they came to a fork in the trail. They knew from the map that their cutoff should be nearby, but they weren't sure exactly where, so C.J. decided to pull out the map and compass. Once she had them out, though, she had difficulty determining how to align the map with reference to the compass. Having had a strong sense of direction previously, C.J. was surprised to find herself confused as to which way was north, east, south, or west. At that point,

Sarah called out, saying that she had found a trail marker indicating that they wanted the rightward fork. C.J. was relieved to realize that despite her trouble with the map and compass, she had no trouble correctly distinguishing the rightward fork of the trail from the leftward fork.

They reached the top of the pass after a couple of hours and were rewarded with a spectacular view of mountains all around them. As was their usual routine, they pulled out their map and tried to identify the surrounding peaks. Even though both the compass and the position of the sun could be used for orienting their direction, C.J. once again found herself confused. She was unable to translate what was on the map with the fantastic vista in front of her. Although she and Sarah would usually disagree about the position of at least one mountain (after which a lively discussion would ensure), this time C.J. just listened carefully, startled at her own confusion.

C.J. was subdued on the hike down. Usually fit, she was a bit out of shape from her hospital stay, and as with any trauma, her body had not yet fully recovered. Sarah asked C.J. whether she was feeling OK, and although C.J. said that she was just tired, her mind was elsewhere. She was wondering whether her stroke might have had some unexpected consequences that would interfere with one of her favorite pastimes.

The story about C.J. helps to illustrate that spatial processing is not a simple cognitive function but consists of many different abilities. Some of C.J.'s spatial abilities, such as understanding the relationship between the map and the surrounding terrain, and knowing geographical points of reference (north, south, east, and west), were compromised. Other abilities, however, such as determining left and right, were unaffected. In this chapter, we examine the many ways in which spatial relations among items can be computed and the brain systems that underlie these computations.

To understand spatial relations, we start by examining basic spatial processes, including localizing points in space, perceiving depth, comprehending the orientation of lines, understanding the geometric relations among parts of objects and whole objects, perceiving motion, and rotating items mentally. These basic spatial skills underlie more complex spatial operations, which we examine next, such as being able to construct items in either two or three dimensions and understanding how to read a map and follow a route. All these types of spatial operations require you to compute the relations between two points in space with regard to each other but not in relation to your body. Such abilities rely on the right hemisphere, in particular, the parietal lobe. We then examine the ability to understand how your body relates to the external spatial world and the ability to comprehend the spatial relationships among parts of your body. For these spatial processes, parietal regions may participate as well.

After discussing these spatial skills, we examine their interplay with two other mental processes, memory and attention. We learn that the neural structures supporting the retention of long-term spatial representations rely on right temporal and hippocampal regions and are independent of the spatial operations performed by the right parietal region. We also examine how particular disturbances in attentional processing can have profound effects on the ability to process spatial information.

In many places throughout this chapter, we learn about the importance of the right hemisphere for spatial processing. In fact, the right hemisphere's role in spatial processing is so large that people often refer to this hemisphere as the "spatial" hemisphere. However, as is the case with almost all the mental processes discussed so far, we find that both hemispheres contribute to processing, albeit in different ways. Therefore, our final discussion is a review of not only the ways in which the left hemisphere contributes to spatial operations, but also of one theoretical framework used to distinguish the contributions of each hemisphere to spatial processing.

THE "WHERE" DORSAL VISUAL SYSTEM FOR SPATIAL PROCESSING

As we learned in chapter 5, research with macaques has provided many clues as to how the brain is organized for processing visual information. In chapter 5, we examined this research to gain insights into the functioning of the ventral visual-processing stream. In this chapter, we examine similar research to learn about the contributions of the dorsal visual stream. This visual stream, which supports spatial processing, projects from primary visual areas to parietal regions (Figure 6.1).

Just as the properties of cells in the ventral visual system make them well suited for the task of object recognition, properties of cells in the inferior parietal area (area 7) of the monkey made them well suited to process spatial information. These cells are sensitive to different attributes than those that stimulate cells in temporal regions. Unlike cells in the ventral processing stream, cells in parietal areas are not sensitive to form or color, so they are not particularly well tuned to the visual properties from which shape can be derived. Furthermore, the cells in area 7 are not sensitive to items positioned in central vision, where acuity is the highest, which is additional evidence that these cells are not involved in object recognition.

The attributes of visual information to which cells in area 7 are most responsive appear to make these cells geared for processing spatial relations. First, their receptive field generally encompasses almost all of the contralateral visual space as well as a substantial portion of ipsilateral space so that information can be provided about the locations of items and their movements over a large expanse of space. Second, within these large receptive fields, the cells seem to fire in response to a specific direction, either inward toward the center of the visual field or outward toward the periphery. Such sensitivity provides a means for objects to be tracked as they move across space. Third, the velocity of movement that is optimal for making these cells fire is about that at which objects would appear to be moving if the animal were not stationary but were either walking or running (Motter & Mountcastle, 1981). Sensitivity to this range of speeds provides a way to analyze space and update the positions of items as the animal is locomoting. Fourth, cells in this area appear to be responsive to a combination of the retinal location of the visual stimulus and the position of the animal's eyes and/or head (e.g., Andersen & Mountcastle, 1983), which allows for the creation of a stable spatial map of the world. Consider that although a particular region of space falls on a specific region of the retina, the mapping of a spatial location to a retinal location changes as soon as the animal turns its head or moves. If the animal needs

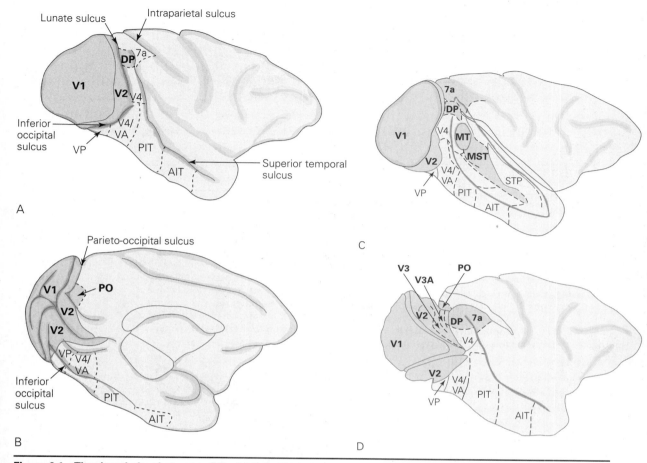

Figure 6.1 The dorsal visual stream of the brain in the macaque.
(A) Right hemisphere, lateral view. (B) Left hemisphere, midsagittal view. (C) View showing the areas buried within the superior temporal sulcus. (D) View showing the areas buried within the lunate, intraparietal, parieto-occipital and inferior occipital sulci. The dorsal processing stream, shown in gray, includes areas V1, V2, V3, and V3A; the middle temporal (MT) area; the medial superior temporal (MST) area; the dorsal prelunate and parietal-occipital areas; and area 7a of the parietal lobe. DP, dorsal prelunate; VA, ventral anterior; VP, ventral posterior; PIT, posterior inferotemporal; AIT, anterior inferotemporal; PO, parieto-occipital; STP, superior temporal polysensory. (*Note.* Adapted from Maunsell & Newsome, 1987, pp. 365, 367.)

to respond to that portion of space (e.g., needs to reach for an object located there), it must be able to reference the position in a spatial map of the world that is constant regardless of head or retinal position. Cells in inferior parietal regions are equipped to provide just such a map because they are sensitive not only to particular retinotopic areas of space, but to head position as well (Motter & Mountcastle, 1981). This constant framework can be considered the spatial equivalent of the constancy

provided by inferior temporal neurons, which respond to a particular object regardless of variations in lighting, size, and orientation.

Lesion studies with monkeys provide converging evidence for the role of the parietal region in spatial processing. Monkeys with parietal lobe lesions are impaired on tasks that require the animal to compute spatial relations among items. In one such task, monkeys are shown two food wells that have identical covers. A small tower, which acts as a landmark,

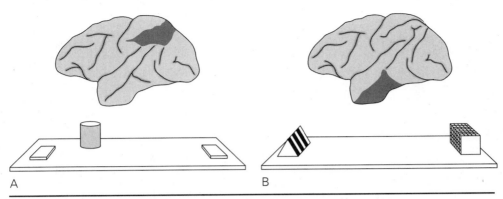

Figure 6.2   Tasks sensitive to dorsal vs. ventral stream damage in monkeys.
(A) In the landmark-discrimination task, the monkey sees two identical food-well covers and a landmark. A reward is hidden under the food-well cover closer to the landmark. The position of the landmark varies randomly from trial to trial, sometimes closer to the left food well and sometimes closer to the right well. When bilateral damage to the posterior parietal region, shown in black, is sustained, monkeys cannot perform this task. (B) In the object-discrimination task, the monkey sees two distinct food-well covers, one with which it has been familiarized prior to the trial. A reward is hidden under the food-well cover that was not previously viewed. This task is known as a *nonmatch-to-sample paradigm* because the animal must choose the well covered by the object that was not viewed previously. When bilateral damage to inferior temporal areas, shown in black, is sustained, the monkey cannot perform this task. (*Note.* Adapted from Mishkin et al., 1983, p. 415.)

is situated closer to one of the covers than to the other. The position of the landmark changes from trial to trial; sometimes it is closer to the right food well and sometimes it is closer to the left food well. However, it is always positioned nearer the well containing the food. Thus, to learn the task, the animal must be able to encode relative position to know that the reward is hidden under the well nearer the landmark (Figure 6.2A) (e.g., Pohl, 1973).

Furthermore, an object-based variation of the same task demonstrates that damage to parietal regions does not interfere with object discrimination. In this version of the task, the monkey is famliarized with an object placed in a central location (e.g., an elongated striped pyramid). This object is then placed over one food well, whereas another object (e.g., a checkered three-dimensional rectangle) is placed over the other food well. In each trial, the reward is hidden under the object with which the animal was *not* familiarized (i.e., the novel object), in this case the checkered three-dimensional rectangle. This procedure is known as a *nonmatch-to-sample paradigm*. As you might expect on the basis of

what we learned in chapter 5, animals with temporal lobe lesions find this task difficult even though they can perform the spatial-location task with ease (Figure 6.2B) (Mishkin, Ungerleider, & Macko, 1983). This dissociation between the performance of animals with temporal lesions and the performance of those with parietal lesions provides additional evidence for a functional distinction between the dorsal and ventral visual-processing streams (see Andersen, 1988, for a review of the anatomical, physiological, and behavioral research implicating parietal regions in spatial processing).

Before we end our discussion of the role of parietal regions in spatial processing, one point should be mentioned: At least some researchers suggest that the distinction between the ventral and dorsal systems is not so much a distinction between "what" and "where" as it is a distinction between "what" and "how" (e.g., Goodale & Milner, 1992). From this perspective, the role of the dorsal system is to know *how* motor acts must be performed to manipulate an object—for example, how the hands and fingers must be positioned to grasp an object. Support for this idea comes from a double dissociation observed in human patients. A case study of one patient with bilateral parietal damage revealed that she could recognize line-drawings of common objects but couldn't adjust the gap between her index finger and thumb to grasp items, such as a block, even though she could correctly move her hand to the region in space where the item was located (Jakobson, Archibald, Carey, & Goodale, 1991). In contrast, patients with damage to ventral extrastriate regions could not recognize the size, shape, and orientation of visual objects, yet they could accurately guide both the hand and fingers to these same objects (e.g., A. D. Milner et al., 1991).

The emphasis by Milner and colleagues on the role of parietal regions in motor manipulations is consistent with the results of single-cell recordings in monkeys. These results indicate that some neurons in the inferior parietal lobe are active when the animal is involved with motor acts to particular locations, such as reaching, fixating on an object, or tracking an item with the eyes. Because these cells exhibit both sensory- and movement-related activity, some researchers have suggested that these areas of the brain are important for integrating external information about space with the commands for motor actions in extrapersonal space (e.g., Lynch, Mountcastle, Talbot, & Yin, 1977; Mountcastle et al., 1975). Furthermore, some cells in parietal regions have been found to be sensitive to the visual qualities of an object that influence how the hand and fingers should be positioned if the object is to be grasped (Taira et al., 1990). Thus, regardless of the exact perspective taken, much evidence from research with monkeys and humans supports the idea that the parietal lobes play an important role in spatial processing in primates. Let us now turn to evidence for the neurological basis of spatial processing in humans.

DISRUPTIONS IN BASIC SPATIAL PROCESSES IN HUMANS

As suggested by the results of studies with animals, posterior parietal areas in humans are important for computing the location of an object in space and for integrating information about location with bodily movements so that a person can direct his or her movements, either limbs or eyes, to a particular location. In humans, damage to these areas of the brain causes spatial deficits that can take numerous forms. For example, let's consider some difficulties that can be encountered in the copying or drawing of objects. Individuals may have difficulty (a) because they switch, elongate, or truncate the main axes on an item to be copied; (b) because they cannot correctly represent the relationships among parts of an item; (c) because they give an item an incorrect form; (d) because they make lines intersect that should not; or (e) because they rotate lines or object parts.

Spatial difficulties may also affect other mental skills. For instance, an individual may be unable to perform arithmetic because he or she cannot keep columns straight, or a person may have an inability to use maps for navigation (e.g., McFie, Piercy, & Zangwill, 1950).

Because many of these spatial abilities appear to rely on a confluence of spatial skills, researchers have attempted to extract the basic component abilities that contribute to these more complicated spatial skills and have attempted to identify the neural hardware required for each basic skill. Thus, we now examine six fundamental spatial skills: localizing points in space, perceiving depth, judging line orientation, understanding geometric relations, perceiving motion, and rotating items mentally, and the neural substrates necessary for these skills.

Localization of Points in Space

Probably the most basic aspect of spatial processing is the ability to find a point in space. Difficulties in this arena were first noted in individuals with brain damage by Holmes in 1918. Holmes reported on patients who could recognize objects, like a fork, placed directly in front of them, but who would act as if blind, groping and misreaching for the item, when it was placed somewhere else, such as on a table set for dinner. All three dimensions of space were affected because patients would reach too near or too far, too much to the left or too much to the right, or too high or too low. These individuals were at just as much of a loss at determining relative position (e.g., determining which of two objects was farther left) as they were at determining absolute position (i.e., determining the precise point in space at which an object was located). As you might imagine, such deficits greatly disrupted these patients' lives.

The syndrome that Holmes observed could not be called a specific deficit in spatial localization, however, because his patients exhibited various other disruptions in spatial processing as well. Nonetheless, these findings hinted that the parietal region might play a role in spatial localization because Holmes's patients typically had bilateral parietal lesions. Since the time of Holmes, more evidence has accrued for the role of the parietal lobe of humans in spatial localization. Unilateral damage to superior regions of the parietal lobe can cause an inability to accurately reach for items on the contralateral side of space, regardless of the arm used, while leaving accuracy of localization for ipsilateral targets intact (e.g., Cole, Schutta, Warrington, 1962; Ratcliff & Davies-Jones, 1972).

In the patients discussed so far, difficulty in spatial localization was demonstrated by an inability to direct movement toward a particular position in space. We can also attempt to determine which neural mechanisms are important for *perceiving* the location of a point in space. This issue can be investigated in the laboratory in diverse ways—for example, by asking individuals to decide whether two dots, presented successively, appear in the same location, or by displaying a dot on the screen briefly and then asking the individual to locate its position among an array of dots. Although some variation occurs in findings across studies (e.g., Hannay, Varney, & Benton, 1976; Warrington & James, 1988; Warrington & Rabin, 1970), deficits are most likely to be observed on such tasks when individuals have damage to posterior regions of the right hemisphere. Converging evidence for the role of the right hemisphere in this function comes from divided visual field studies with neurologically intact individuals. In these types of studies, a left visual field (LVF) advantage has been found regardless of whether the point must be localized with a Euclidean coordinate system (Figure 6.3A) or a polar one (Figure 6.3B) (Kimura, 1969). Subsequent research, however, has suggested that the size of the LVF advantage is usually small and not always consistent (Bryden, 1976).

Although the ability to localize the information in space has been examined mainly in the visual modality, a similar role for parietal regions in auditory localization has been noted. Lesions in parietal regions disrupt the ability to localize sounds (e.g., Pinek, Duhamel, Cave, & Brouchon, 1989; Ruff, Hersh, & Pribram, 1981). You may remember from chapter 1 that sound localization can also be disrupted by damage to primary auditory areas of the temporal lobe, but this disruption occurs for a different reason. Whereas parietal lobe damage interferes with sound localization because it disrupts a spatial map of the world, damage to primary auditory cortex disrupts sensitivity to interaural differences in intensity and timing that are used for localizing sounds in space.

Although the results of studies of patients with brain damage differ as to whether left or right parietal lobe damage is more likely to disrupt spatial localization, research with neurologically intact individuals suggests that at least for nonverbal noise the right hemisphere is better at localizing sound. This conclusion is based on findings that monaural localization of a sound was better with the left ear than with the right (R. A. Butler, 1994) and for positions on the left side of space than for those on the right (K. A. Burke, Letsos, & Butler, 1994). Information received by the left ear or from the left side of space is assumed to be preferentially processed by the contralateral hemisphere because patients who undergo hemispherectomy have deficits in sound localization on the contralateral side of space (e.g., Poirier et al., 1994).

Depth Perception

Most of the research that we just discussed with regard to localizing points in space has involved localization in a two-dimensional plane. However, space has three dimensions. Thus, another basic spatial ability is the ability to perceive the third di-

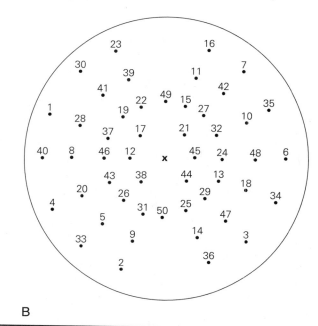

Figure 6.3 Two choice arrays used in divided visual field studies to assess the ability of each hemisphere to local-ize points in space.
A single dot is shown on a trial and the individual must point to the corresponding location on the choice array. (A) A choice array arranged in Euclidean coordinates (rows and columns). (B) A choice array arranged in polar coordi-nates. (*Note.* Adapted from Kimura, 1969, pp. 447, 452.)

mension of depth. Depth perception, also known as **stereopsis,** is the specific ability that helps us to localize items in the near-far plane. Because each eye is in a slightly different position with regard to what we are viewing, there is a difference in the visual images that fall on corresponding points of each retina when both eyes are focusing on the same position in space. This offset is known as **binocular disparity** and is one of the important visual cues that provides us with a sense of relative depth (i.e., knowing which locations are closer to and which are farther from the viewer).

In general, depth perception is divided into two types: local and global. Local stereopsis, or *ster-eoacuity,* is the ability to use local detailed features of objects in a point-by-point manner to determine its relative position. For example, differences be-tween information reaching each eye about particu-lar local cues, such as the front leg of a chair and the right-hand corner of a table, can be compared

to determine whether the chair or the table is nearer the viewer. This type of depth perception can be disrupted by either right- or left-hemisphere lesions (e.g., Danta, Hilton, & O'Boyle, 1978).

In contrast, global depth perception requires that the disparity between information reaching each eye be computed over the whole visual scene. This abil-ity cannot be tested with ordinary stimuli but must be examined with specially constructed stimuli known as *random-dot stereograms* (Julesz, 1964). These stereograms are two large squares that consist of a patchwork of many smaller squares, each of which is randomly determined to be either dark or light. The patchwork pattern in the two large squares is identical except that the pattern in one is shifted a couple of small squares relative to the other. The result is that when viewed binocularly, one of the two large squares appears to be in front of the other. Because no discrete object can be seen in these stereograms, depth cannot be computed on the basis of local cues. Rather, to perceive depth, an individual must calculate disparity across the entire display. This type of stereopsis, *global stereopsis,* is disrupted by right-hemisphere damage (e.g., A. L. Benton & Hécaen, 1970; Carmon & Bechtoldt, 1969).

Orientation of Lines

In our discussion of localization of places in space, we have assumed, so far, that we are interested in finding a particular point in space. Yet, often in our visual world we must be able to calculate the location and orientation of a string of points, which together constitute a line. The ability to judge the orientation or angles of lines is another basic visuospatial ability that appears to rely on the right hemisphere. Disruption of this basic ability can have troublesome effects in everyday life. As a simplistic example, think of how difficult reading a clock face would be if you couldn't determine the angle at which the arms were pointing.

One task commonly used both in the laboratory and in the clinic to assess the ability to discern line orientation requires individuals to differentiate among a set of 11 lines, all of which radiate at different angles from the same point. The individual views a display with 2 lines and must identify them from the set of 11 (Figure 6.4). Right-hemisphere damage compromises the ability to perform either a visual or a tactile version of this task (e.g., A. L. Benton, Hannay, & Varney, 1975). Because deficits in the two modalities are correlated (Meerwaldt & Van Harskamp, 1982), the deficit is truly spatial and not modality specific. Converging evidence for the role of the right hemisphere in line orientation comes from studies of neurologically intact individuals who exhibit a LVF advantage on this task (e.g., Atkinson & Egeth, 1973; Umilta et al., 1974). However, the LVF advantage appears to be limited to the orientations that cannot be easily verbalized, because for vertical or horizontal lines, a right visual field (RVF) advantage is observed (Umilta et al., 1974).

The finding of a LVF advantage for judging certain orientations but not others raises the important

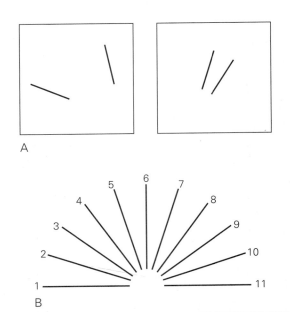

Figure 6.4 One test commonly used in assessing the ability to judge the orientation of lines.
(A) Two sample trials from the test. In each trial, the two lines must be matched to the lines in the choice card shown in (B). (*Note.* From *Contributions to Neuropsychological Assessment: A Clinical Manual*, by A. L. Benton, K. D. Hamsher, N. R. Varney, and O. Spreen, 1983, New York: Oxford University Press.)

point, which we revisit frequently in this chapter, that alternative modes of processing can be used to perform the same spatial task. For example, as we just discussed, a RVF advantage may occur for line orientation if certain angles can be described verbally (e.g., horizontal, vertical); otherwise, a LVF advantage occurs. As another example, consider the Euclidean dot-localization tasks described earlier. Although on each trial only a single dot is seen, the array of dot positions from which an individual must choose follows a regular pattern (e.g., the dots are placed in rows and columns). After some experience with the task, a subject could estimate a dot's location with a verbally mediated strategy ("That dot seemed like it was located in the second row, third column"). When such a verbal analytic strategy is used, the role of the right hemisphere in spatial processing is minimized. We discuss this issue in more detail at the end of this chapter, but for now we should consider that inconsistent findings with regard to hemispheric differences in spatial tasks may reflect, in part, differences in strategies that individuals use to perform a task.

Geometric Relations

As we think about processing the components of our spatial world, we can progress from our ability to perceive points and lines to the ability to perceive the spatial relationships among parts of basic forms, which we refer to under the umbrella term *geometric relations*. As with the abilities discussed so far, these, for the most part, depend more on the right hemisphere than on the left.

One ability that falls under the rubric of geometric relations is the ability to determine whether different forms have similar spatial properties. For example, a LVF advantage is observed for judgments of curvature (Longden, Ellis, & Iversen, 1976) and for deciding whether an arc has the same curvature as a circle (Hatta, 1977). These findings are consistent with studies in which the left-hand (right-hemisphere) performance of patients with the split-brain syndrome is superior to that of the right when they are asked to tactilely feel arcs and match them to circles. Left-hand performance is also superior to that of the right when the pattern inherent in an array of raised dots must be detected and when a solid object must be felt and matched to an "exploded" visual depiction of the same object in which the pieces of the object retain the same relationship to one another but are no longer connected (Nebes, 1978).

Another way to examine the neural substrates of geometric spatial processing is to investigate the capacity of each hemisphere to process different types of mathematically defined geometric relations. Such an approach was taken with patients with the split-brain syndrome by examining the capacity of each hemisphere to understand four major classes of geometric relationships: Euclidean, affine, projective, and topological. Euclidean geometry is the type we learned in school; it provides mathematical equations for the properties of simple forms that

can be easily verbalized (e.g., the area of a triangle = width × ½ height). Topology is the branch of geometry that relates to curved spaces and forms. As we move from Euclidean to affine to projective and then to topological geometry, the characteristics or constraints that define similarity among forms become fewer and fewer. Although the right hemisphere was equally good at all four types of geometry, the left was as good as the right only for Euclidean geometry, and its performance systematically decreased across the spectrum (Franco & Sperry, 1977).

Yet another way in which the ability to process geometric relations among item parts can be examined is to investigate the ability to remember complex figures that do not represent anything in life. Because the complex figure has never been seen in the individual's lifetime, the person must process its spatial relations to encode the item in memory. This process is somewhat different than that required to recognize common objects, because in those cases the individual can refer to a template stored in memory (e.g., a template for the shape of birds). Studies with neurologically intact individuals generally revealed a LVF advantage when the person must determine whether a given complex figure was previously viewed (e.g., Fontenot, 1973; Umilta, Bagnara, & Simion, 1978), although some studies do not yield this result (Hannay, Rogers & Durant, 1976). The degree to which a verbal label can be assigned to a particular nonsense shape may account for some of the variations in findings. For example, the size of the LVF advantage for remembering nonsense designs has been found to be greater for items that are judged difficult to label verbally than for items that can more easily be given a verbal label (Figure 6.5) (J. I. Shenker, M. T. Banich, & S. Klipstein, unpublished observations, 1993).

Motion

So far, we have considered a spatial world in which the relations among points in space or geometric relations are static. However, often in the spatial world these relations can change with time; that is, they may involve motion. Thus, motion is another

Figure 6.5 Some examples of complex nonsense shapes.
These stimuli vary in how easily people can provide a verbal description of them. Although individuals had difficulty providing a verbal label for the stimuli shown in (A), these persons were more likely to provide a label for those shown in (B), which, from left to right, might be described as a pile of rocks, a nose with eyeglasses, a leaf, and interlocking horseshoes. A left visual field (LVF) advantage in recognition is more likely to be observed when verbal labels cannot be easily applied to the figures, as for the items shown in (A).

basic process underlying competence in spatial processing that we need to consider.

Research with monkeys has shown that a particular region of the brain—the superior temporal gyrus, an area at the border of parietal, temporal, and occipital regions—contains cells that are especially sensitive to motion (e.g., Dubner & Zeki, 1971; Komatsu & Wurtz, 1988) and are active when an animal is visually tracking a moving object (e.g., Sakata, Shibutani, & Kawano, 1983). In humans, brain imaging studies suggest that the area sensitive to motion is a bit more dorsal, in the inferior parietal lobe. Activity in parietal regions is observed in positron emission tomography (PET) studies of humans in which stimuli similar to those presented to monkeys are used (e.g., Zeki et al., 1991), and in studies in which a target must be tracked with the eyes across space (Colby & Zeffiro, 1990). Furthermore, when an individual must selectively attend to the speed of a moving object, medial regions of the left inferior parietal lobe become active (Corbetta et al., 1991).

The findings in one case study suggest that the analysis of motion in humans has a separate neural substrate than that which supports spatial skills. Although the woman in this study lost her ability to perceive motion in all three dimensions, her other basic visual and spatial functions, including visual acuity, binocular vision, color discrimination, discrimination of visual objects and words, and localization of items in space, were all intact (Zihl, Von Cramon, & Mai, 1983). Furthermore, her difficulty in perceiving motion could not be accounted for by difficulties in integrating visual information across time (which in turn might selectively impair the ability to detect movement), because the researchers found that her thresholds for flicker fusion were normal. **Flicker fusion** is when the time delay between the presentation of two successive flashes of light is brief enough that a person perceives them as a steady stream of light.

As you might imagine, this woman's difficulty in perceiving motion created much difficulty in her life. When she would pour liquid, such as tea or coffee, the flowing stream would appear to her as a glacier or a snapshot, much the way flowing liquids look in magazine ads. Because she could not see the rising level of fluid in a container, she could not determine when to stop pouring liquids. Even more troublesome was her difficulty in judging the speed of cars (which she had no trouble recognizing); this impairment made crossing streets extremely dangerous. In describing her dilemma, she said, "When I'm looking at the car, first it seems far away. But then, when I want to cross the road, suddenly the car is very near" (Zihl, Von Cramon, & Mai, 1983,

p. 315). Eventually, she learned to rely on auditory cues, such as the loudness of a car, to estimate how close or far away it was.

In this patient, damage was localized to a broad range of parietal regions in the right hemisphere and a more restricted range in the left hemisphere, as well as the middle and superior temporal gyri bilaterally (Figure 6.6) (Hess, Baker, & Zihl, 1989).

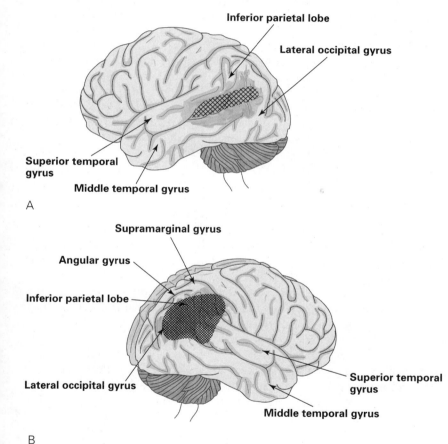

Figure 6.6 Localization of damage in a case study of an individual who had difficulty perceiving motion but not other aspects of visual or spatial processing.
(A) The damage to the left hemisphere involved the inferior parietal gyrus, the lateral occipital gyrus, and the superior and middle temporal gyri. (B) The damage to the right hemisphere involved the supramarginal gyrus, the angular gyrus, the inferior parietal gyrus, the lateral occipital gyrus, and the superior and middle temporal gyri. Both lesions are located in the same area as the macaque's dorsal processing stream shown in Figure 6.1. (*Note.* Adapted from Zihl et al., 1983.)

Neuroimaging and neuropsychological data suggested that primary visual cortex as well as the remainder of the parietal region was intact. According to a subsequent case report, an individual who had difficulty perceiving motion (but in this case in only two, not all three, dimensions) had also sustained damage in a similar location, namely bilaterally in posterior temporoparietal areas. However, this individual's spatial deficits were not restricted to the perception of motion but included other difficulties, such as localizing objects in space. These additional findings suggest that the patient's damage affected not only neurological structures important for perceiving motion, but also other portions of the "where" visual system (Vaina, et al., 1990). Hence, results from these case studies and PET studies suggest that inferior parietal and temporoparietal regions are important for the analysis of motion and that this basic spatial ability can be distinct from other aspects of spatial processing.

Rotation

To finish our review of basic spatial skills, we examine rotation, which might be considered a special class of movement detection. Rather than detecting movement from one location in space to another, we must be able to comprehend the movement of an object around an axis to perceive rotation. Just as single-cell recordings in monkeys reveal that some cells are sensitive to the detection of motion, cells in the superior temporal regions (e.g., Saito et al., 1986) and the inferior parietal region (e.g., Sakata, Shibutani, Kawano, & Harrington, 1985) are sensitive to rotation, especially in a rotary manner (e.g., clockwise or counterclockwise). Other cells respond to rotations in depth (e.g., front to back).

In humans, the ability to rotate objects mentally has been studied extensively by Shepard and colleagues (for a review, see for example, R. Shepard, 1988), who have found that the greater the degree of mental rotation required to align two three-dimensional objects (Figure 6.7A), the greater the time required to decide whether they are identical. For example, if two items are positioned 180 degrees apart, a person will take longer to decide

whether they are identical than if they are only 60 degrees apart in rotation (Figure 6.7B).

However, the neural basis of such abilities remains controversial and seems to be affected by a variety of factors. One group of studies suggests that mental-rotation abilities rely on the right hemisphere. Increased blood flow to the right hemisphere was found during a rotation task similar to that depicted in Figure 6.7A (G. Deutsch, Bourbon, Papanicolaou, & Eisenberg, 1988), and when simplified versions of the same stimuli were used, rotational abilities were more disrupted by right parietal lobe damage than by left parietal lobe damage (e.g., Ditunno & Mann, 1990). The right parietal lobe has also been implicated for another rotational task in which a man with outstretched hands holds a black orb in one hand. The individual's task is to determine whether the orb is held in the man's right hand or the left hand. When the man is positioned upside down, reaching the correct answer requires mental rotation. Under these conditions, patients with posterior right-hemisphere damage have difficulty performing the task (Ratcliff, 1979).

The results from divided visual field studies of rotational abilities are more equivocal; some studies yield a RVF advantage (e.g., Corballis & Sergent, 1989), others a LVF advantage (e.g., Ditunno & Mann, 1990), and some no difference (e.g., Simion et al., 1980). Two factors, the nature of the stimuli and the direction of the rotation, may influence the type of visual field advantage that is observed. The results of some studies indicate that verbal stimuli may be more likely to yield a RVF advantage, whereas spatial stimuli may be more likely to yield a LVF advantage (e.g., Corballis & McLaren, 1984). Furthermore, at least two studies have yielded findings suggesting that hemispheric superiorities in rotation may differ depending on the direction of rotation required. In particular, the right hemisphere seems to be superior for clockwise rotation and the left hemisphere for counterclockwise rotation; therefore, each hemisphere appears to be specialized for rotation inward toward the center (Burton, Wagner, Lim, & Levy, 1992; Corballis & Sergent, 1989). Although no clear explanation exists for this effect, perhaps it provides a conceptual-

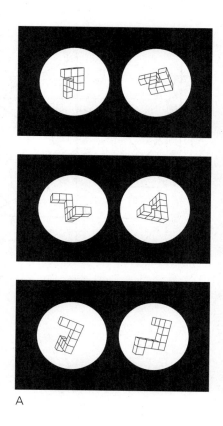

A

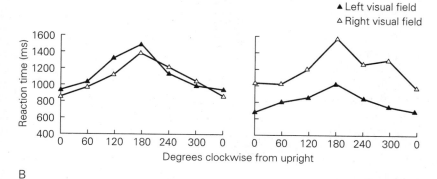

B

Figure 6.7   A classic paradigm for examining mental rotation.
(A) The type of three-dimensional stimulus often used to assess the ability to
rotate objects in three dimensions. Whereas the top two pairs can be rotated to
match each other—the first by an 80-degree rotation in the sideways plane and
the second by an 80-degree rotation in depth—the final pair cannot because
the forms are mirror images. (B) Typical performance on such rotational tasks
for a group of neurologically intact individuals (left) and for a patient with split-
brain syndrome, L.B. (right). For both L.B. and the neurologically intact individuals, the more rotation required, the longer the reaction time. However, whereas
L.B. showed a strong left visual field (right-hemisphere) superiority for the task,
the neurologically intact control subjects did not. (*Note.* A, From *Mental Images
and Their Transformations* (p. 35), by R. N. Shepard and L. A. Cooper, 1986,
Cambridge, MA: MIT Press. Copyright © 1986 The MIT Press. B, Adapted from
Corballis & Sergent, 1989, p. 20.)

ization of space that allows mirror-image motor movements to be performed.

Now that we reviewed the neural bases of basic spatial processes, we turn our attention to more complex spatial skills.

CONSTRUCTIONAL ABILITIES

In our discussion so far, we emphasized the ability to *perceive* spatial relations but did not yet discuss the ability to motorically produce or manipulate items so that they have a particular spatial relationship. These latter abilities are often referred to as **constructional praxis.** In everyday life, such basic abilities can be critical for the performance of more complex tasks. For example, the ability to manipulate items into particular spatial arrangements is critical for many daily activities, from putting groceries into the refrigerator to manipulating a key so that it fits correctly into a lock.

In the laboratory and the clinic, constructional skills are examined with tasks that are relatively simpler than the real-life instances just discussed. Some examples are copying a complicated nonsense drawing, building a block world, and manipulating and arranging colored cubes to match a particular pattern. One example of such a test is the Rey-Osterrieth Complex Figure, which is often used to assess spatial-constructional skills and perceptual skills (Figure 6.8A). For the most part, such abilities are disrupted by damage to the right hemisphere (e.g., A. L. Benton, 1967). The role of the right hemisphere in such tasks can be seen by looking at the copies of the Rey-Osterrieth figure drawn by three individuals who had strokes that damaged the temporoparietal region of the right hemisphere (Figure 6.8B).

Although right-hemisphere damage is usually associated with deficits in spatial-constructional skills, sometimes hemispheric differences are not observed (e.g., Black & Strub, 1976). This inconsistency in the hemispheric locus of damage across studies probably occurs for one of two reasons. First, although all these tasks measure constructional abilities, they are likely to involve other subskills as well

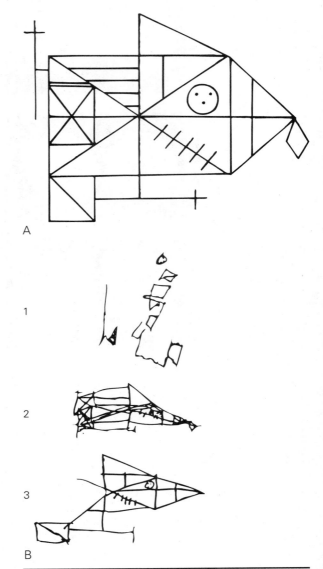

A

B

Figure 6.8   The testing of visuospatial drawing abilities.
(A) The Rey-Osterrieth Complex Figure. (B) Examples of attempts to copy this figure by three individuals with damage to posterior sections of the right hemisphere. (*Note.* A, From *Neuropsychological Assessment* (2nd ed., p. 396), by M. D. Lezak, 1983, Oxford, England: Oxford University Press. B, Adapted with permisssion from "The Role of the Right Cerebral Hemisphere in Evaluating Configurations," by L. I. Benowitz, S. Finkelstein, D. N. Levine, and K. Moya, in *Brain Circuits and Functions of the Mind* (p. 327), edited by C. Trevarthen, 1990, Cambridge, England: Cambridge University Press.)

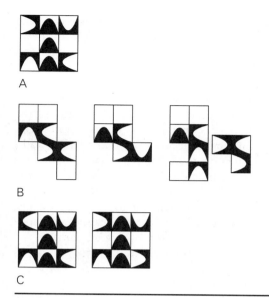

A

B

C

**Figure 6.9 Constructional skills as measured by a
Block Design subtest.**
(A) An example design that individuals must copy.
(B) Three steps in an attempt to copy the design by an
individual with right-hemisphere damage. The patient
does not even recognize the basic square pattern of the
design. (C) The first and second attempts to copy the
same figure by an individual with left-hemisphere damage. The overall configuration is correct, but the details
are incorrect. In the first attempt, the block in the upper
left-hand corner is rotated 180 degrees from the correct
position, whereas in the second attempt, the block in
the lower right-hand corner is rotated 180 degrees.

(e.g., fine motor control plays a larger role in copying than in manipulating large blocks). Thus, the
location and extent of the brain region that causes
an inability to perform any of these tasks probably
depends on additional regions besides the one critical for the constructional component of the task.
Second, many of these tasks can most likely be performed by using a variety of strategies and varying
degrees of verbal mediation. For example, Figure
6.9 shows a Block Design subtest that requires an
individual to arrange blocks with colored sides (either solid white or with a black and white design)
so that the top of the blocks matches a template

pattern (Figure 6.9A). One way to perform such a
task is to analyze the spatial relationships in a given
template (i.e., perceive the overall form and recurring spatial patterns) and manipulate the blocks to
match the template. Another approach is to use a
verbal strategy to perform the task, such as saying,
"I need a solid white block and must place that to
the left of a block that has the black design at the
bottom with the white part on top." Sometimes
such differences in strategy can be detected by
qualitative differences in how individuals perform the test. For example, after right-hemisphere
damage, a distinctly different type of error is seen,
involving the overall arrangement of the blocks
(Figure 6.9B), than that observed after left-hemisphere damage, which is much more likely to involve a specific piece of the pattern (Figure
6.9C).

DISTURBANCES OF ROUTE-FINDING AND TOPOGRAPHICAL SKILLS

In our lives we are often called upon not just to
perceive spatial relationships but to understand their
ramifications so that we can skillfully negotiate or
navigate a route from one point to another. This
navigation often is not simple because although we
may know the direction of travel between the beginning and endpoint of our journey, we can rarely
travel a straight line between the two. Whether traveling from one building on campus to another or
driving from home to the grocery store, our route
probably takes us around other buildings, trees,
people, and cars. What is common in all these cases,
however, is that we must follow a route to reach
our destination.

The ability to follow a route appears to require
different neural substrates depending on the framework in which the spatial relations between points
are embedded. In this section of the chapter, we
discuss how the ability to perceive spatial relations
in extrapersonal space dissociates from the ability
to do so in a personal framework. The former ability
requires you to perceive the relationship between
two points in space, whereas the latter requires you
to perceive the relationship between your body and

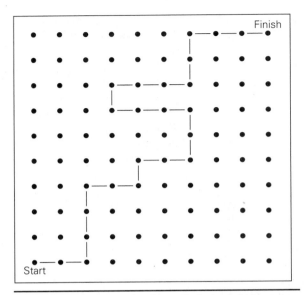

Figure 6.10   An example of a path that might have to be learned through the stylus maze.
The maze is an array of identical metal bolt heads, depicted here by black circles. Although the path is shown in this diagram, it is not presented to the individual. Rather, each time the person touches an incorrect bolt head, a loud click occurs. Thus, the individual must discover the correct direction of movement at each choice point and remember information about previously discovered portions of the maze. (*Note.* Adapted from Milner, B. 1962b, 257–272.)

a point in space (e.g., My body is to the left of the table). In this section, we also learn that the ability to comprehend spatial relations on a large scale, such as that required for reading a national map, may dissociate from route-finding abilities either in a town or in a neighborhood. Moreover, these abilities may be separable from finding the way around your house or hospital corridors, which in turn may be separable from knowing whether you turn left or right at the next landmark, which in turn may be separable from knowing your left hand from your right. Thus, the evidence suggests that we use multiple spatial frameworks in understanding relationships between points. We compute some relationships between points in space that are within our range of view, we compute others between

points that are outside our range of view (and can be symbolized on maps), and in some cases we compute relationships between points in space and our bodies.

Often damage to right posterior areas disrupts these route-finding abilities because, as we learned earlier, this region of the brain is important for the construction of a spatial map of the world. Yet, because different types of route finding place additional burdens on an individual, other brain regions may play a prominent role as well. For example, the route-finding abilities that have memory demands can also be affected by damage to temporal regions, whereas those that have a strong planning component may be more affected by frontal damage.

One task often used in the labortory to assess route finding is the stylus maze task, in which the individual must maneuver a stylus through an orderly array of bolt heads to reach a goal (Figure 6.10). All the bolt heads are identical, but the person learns the maze because when she or he moves in the wrong direction, a counter clicks loudly to indicate a mistake. The ability to perform this task is compromised by damage to the right hemisphere (Newcombe & Russell, 1969) and more specifically by damage to posterior and parietal regions (Newcombe, 1969). Because this task involves learning a spatial sequence of movements, individuals with damage to the right hippocampal region and those with right frontal damage have also been reported to show deficits. The former group seems to have difficulty remembering the series of turns that must be taken, whereas the latter group may have more difficulty with the sequential nature of the task (first right, then left, then left again, etc.) (B. Milner, 1965).

Another type of route-finding ability requires an individual to maneuver him- or herself through a maze (rather than moving an object through a maze as in the stylus maze task) (Ratcliff & Newcombe, 1973). In one such task, the locomotor maze, a series of nine dots are placed on the floor of a large room, in a grid (Semmes, Weinstein, Ghent, & Teuber, 1955). The individual is given a map, which designates a route from start to finish that the person is to walk as quickly and accurately as possible. For orientation, one wall of the room is designated "north," and the person must always hold the map so that north is at the top and south is at the bottom. (In other words, the person is not allowed to rotate the map when changing directions as some people do when driving!) Damage to the parietal region has been found to be associated with poor performance on this task; some researchers claim that task performance is compromised by right-hemisphere damage (Semmes, Weinstein, Ghent, & Teuber, 1963) and others suggest that deficits are not observed unless bilateral posterior lesions exist (Ratcliff & Newcombe, 1973). As we discussed with regard to other spatial tasks, this discrepancy may arise because alternative strategies are available for performing the task: one that relies more on mental rotation and the right hemisphere and another that is verbally mediated (turn left, turn right) and depends more on the left hemisphere. Perhaps deficits are most easily observed after bilateral damage because the ability to invoke both strategies is compromised in such a case.

Although the ability to perform this maze and that required to complete the stylus maze can be impaired simultaneously, some patients show a dissociation: Either they are impaired at performing the stylus maze but not the locomotor maze, or vice versa (Ratcliff & Newcombe, 1973). Various reasons have been postulated to explain why the ability to perform the locomotor maze task may dissociate from the ability to perform the stylus maze task. First, the stylus maze task is much smaller in scale. The individual can view the entire map in a bird's-eye fashion while maneuvering through it. This is not the case with the locomotor maze. Second, in the stylus maze task, a person's orientation with regard to the maze remains constant, whereas in the locomotor maze task, even though the map direction stays static, the individual's orientation relative to the map constantly changes. Another difference is that in the stylus maze task the individual must remember the route, whereas in the locomotor maze task the route is given.

Yet another way to test route-findings abilities with the Money (1976) Standardized Road-Map Task, in which a person is shown a path through a fictional town and at each choice point must determine whether the direction turned to follow the route is right or left. Rather than being affected by parietal lobe damage, this task is compromised by frontal lesions (e.g., Butters, Soeldner, & Fedio, 1972), possibly because movements must be planned in a sequential, orderly manner. This task seems to assess a different aspect of route finding than the locomotor maze does. In the road-map test, a person must determine her or his own position in space (e.g., turning right, turning left) at different points in the route; that is, the individual must determine his or her personal spatial orientation. In contrast, in the locomotor maze the person's orientation is irrelevant. Rather, the important factor is the relationship between two points in space relative to each other.

In some cases, we are required to understand topographic spatial relations over much larger distances than those just discussed, such as when geographical knowledge and orientation are involved. These types of geographical knowledge can be assessed by such diverse means as asking the direction of travel from one major city to another within a person's homeland or requiring major cities of a familiar country to be located on a map. Such abilities do not appear to depend on one specific brain region and can be disrupted by both right- and left-hemisphere brain damage (e.g., A. L. Benton, Levin, & Van Allen, 1974). As with route-finding abilities, different strategies may be available to perform geographical tasks. A right-hemisphere strategy would be based on topographical relations, whereas a left-hemisphere strategy would rely on verbal and analytic mediation. For example, a verbal strategy that would allow Nova Scotia to be located reasonably well on a map of Canada might involve knowing that Nova Scotia is located on the southern portion of Canada's Atlantic Coast, reasoning that the Atlantic Ocean is off Canada's east coast, knowing that east is on the right-hand portion of maps, and knowing that north is on the upper part of maps. As another example, an individual might deduce that the direction of travel from New York to Los Angeles is west by knowing that New York is three time zones ahead of L.A.

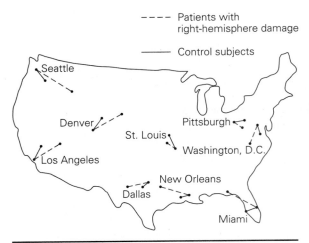

Figure 6.11 Difficulties in the mental representation of geographic space after brain damage.
The locations of nine major U.S. cities and the locations of the same cities based on mileage estimates between each possible pair of cities (e.g., Denver and Seattle, Denver and Los Angeles, Denver and Dallas, etc.) provided by individuals with right-hemisphere damage and by neurologically intact control subjects. The displacement of the cities from their actual locations is greater for individuals with right-hemisphere damage (dotted lines) than for the control subjects (solid lines). (*Note.* Adapted from Morrow et al., 1985, pp. 269, 270.)

Brain damage may affect the ability to construct a mental representation of geographical space even when basic map-reading skills are intact. For example, in one study, neurologically intact individuals and individuals with right-hemisphere lesions, with no map in front of them, were asked to estimate the distance between each of 36 pairs of cities (this represented all possible pairings of nine major cities in the United States). From their responses, a map could be produced showing where the nine cities would have to be located given their estimates. As you can see in Figure 6.11, the estimates of patients with brain damage were farther from the actual locations of the cities than the estimates of neurologically intact individuals. These difficulties could not be attributed to a lack of knowledge about the nine cities' locations or from general difficulty in estimating distance. When given an outline map of the

U.S. cities, the patients with brain damage accurately located the cities, and when asked to estimate the distance between geometric forms arranged in a similar configuration to that of the nine major cities, they did no worse than neurologically intact individuals did.

Thus, the deficit appears to be specifically in their ability to use an internal representation about the geographical relations between cities to guide their estimate of distance. Whether such deficits are limited to patients with right-hemisphere lesions is unclear from this study because a left-hemisphere control group was not tested (L. Morrow, Ratcliff, & Johnston, 1985).

In this section, we reviewed the varieties of disruptions in route-finding and topographic skills that can occur as a result of brain damage. We also illustrated that these disruptions should not be considered to represent the same underlying function because many functional dissociations can occur between the abilities to perform these different topographical tasks. These findings suggest that we use multiple frames of reference to understand our spatial world.

DISTURBANCES OF BODY SCHEMA

In this section of the chapter, we explore the inability to comprehend the spatial relations among parts of your body, deficits that are generally conceptualized as disturbances of **body schema.** This ability to understand the topography of the body appears to dissociate from the ability to recognize the other topographies that we just discussed.

Probably the best documented disturbance of body schema that arises after brain damage is the inability to tell right from left. Traditionally, right-left confusion has been most often associated with damage to the left parietal region (e.g., McFie & Zangwill, 1960). However, although the concepts of left and right are first learned with regard to your own body, they are later applied to other individuals and objects (Belmont & Birch, 1963), in which case a spatial transformation or rotation is necessary (e.g., such as when discerning which hand the woman across the net is using to hold her tennis racquet). Whereas individuals with left-hemisphere damage often have difficulty making simple left-right distinctions on their own body, especially when they also have aphasic disorders, individuals with right-hemisphere damage cannot easily determine right and left when those terms are applied to another person who is facing them (A. L. Benton, 1985), presumably because of the required spatial transformation.

Right-left disturbances have been linked to other types of disturbances in body schema, especially **finger agnosia,** which is a bilateral inability to recognize or localize your own fingers. Because the syndrome occurs bilaterally, it is not likely to represent a specific sensory deficit. In the 1920s and 1930s, Gerstmann proposed that the association of finger agnosia and right-left disturbances along with *dysgraphia* (an inability to write) and *dyscalculia* (the inability to perform arithmetic) represented a specific syndrome—**Gerstmann syndrome**—that was indicative of damage to the left parietal cortex (Gerstmann, 1957). Although case reports of a pure Gerstmann syndrome (without any accompanying deficits such as aphasia) have been cited after damage to the left angular gyrus (e.g., Mazzoni et al., 1990), these four symptoms co-occur no more frequently than other signs of parietal damage (A. L. Benton, 1961). Hence, they do not appear to form a unique syndrome that is diagnostic of left parietal damage. In fact, finger agnosia seems to be associated with many types of damage, including diffuse damage and lesions in the posterior parietal, frontal, and temporal areas (A. L. Benton, 1985). When caused by a more circumscribed lesion, finger agnosia is usually associated with a left-hemisphere lesion that leads to an aphasic disorder in which a lack of language comprehension is the most prominent sign (e.g., Gainotti, Cianchetti, & Tiacci, 1972; Kinsbourne & Warrington, 1962).

Other disturbances of body image can also be produced by brain insult. Individuals with hemiplegia may exhibit **anosognosia,** in which a unilateral disturbance of body schema exists because they deny, with both verbal and nonverbal behaviors, that the affected limb is paralyzed. For example, when questioned about the hemiplegic limb, they

say it is not paralyzed. When asked to move it, they make the facial expressions that would accompany raising a limb and then look to where the limb would be if raised, although, of course, the limb has not moved. This syndrome is usually observed after a stroke associated with the right middle cerebral artery (although sometimes it can be caused by a lesion of a subcortical structure, the internal capsule) and usually dissipates by 1 to 2 weeks after the stroke. Some authorities have suggested that the syndrome results because somesthetic information from the hemiplegic limb is not being properly processed (Cumming, 1988).

In some other cases of neurological disease, most notably in cases of epilepsy, individuals have the sensation that parts of their body are either too big, known as **macrosomatagnosia,** or too small, known as **microsomatagnosia.** For example, in one case described by Williams (cited in Trimble, 1988), an 11-year-old boy had an epileptic disturbance centered in the left temporal lobe. During seizure activity, his hands would "seem too big, they were unnatural, he could not understand why they were there." Seizure activity may also make the relation of the person's body to the outside world feel distorted. Microsomatagnosia and macrosomatagnosia are observed not only in cases of epilepsy, but also in cases of other brain disorders including migraine, drug-induced psychoses, and schizophrenia. Because both epilepsy and schizophrenia have been associated with temporal lobe dysfunction (e.g., Trimble & Rogers, 1987), the temporal lobe may play a role in how we create a mental map of our bodies.

Body schema can also be disrupted by hemineglect, a syndrome in which an individual does not pay attention to the side of space contralateral to a lesion. Typically, this syndrome is produced by damage to the right parietal lobe, but it can occur after left parietal lesions as well. In some cases, body schema is affected because an individual with hemineglect does not use or pay attention to the limbs on the unattended side of space. In some dramatic cases, the individual even denies that the limb belongs to him or her (e.g., K. M. Heilman, Watson, & Valenstein, 1985). We discuss the relationship of this syndrome to spatial processing in more detail later in this chapter when we discuss attentional disturbances in spatial processing.

SPATIAL MEMORY

So far in this chapter, we centered our attention mainly on the ability to *perceive* spatial relations, which appears to depend on right parietal regions, rather than on the ability to *store* these relations in memory. Like the perception of spatial relations, memory for spatial relations relies on the right hemisphere. However, for spatial abilities that require long-term storage of information, the right temporal lobe and especially the hippocampus play a prominent role.

Short-Term Spatial Memory

Short-term memory, or **working memory,** is the memory that we use to hold information for a brief amount of time or that we hold "on-line" as we perform a task. Storage in this type of memory is generally considered to be limited to about seven

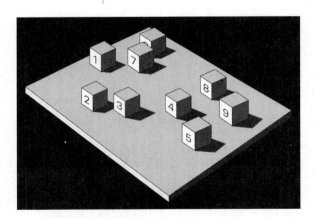

Figure 6.12　The Corsi Block Tapping Test as seen by the experimenter.
The individual being tested sees only an array of nine identical blocks. The experimenter taps a series of blocks (e.g., 4-1-3-9-2). Depending on the condition (forward or backward), the individual taps the blocks either in the identical order or in the reverse order. (*Note.* Adapted from DeRenzi et al., 1977, p. 426.)

items, and the information dissipates quickly if not rehearsed. We were introduced to the idea of verbal short-term memory in chapter 2 when we discussed the Digit Span subtest, in which a person hears a series of digits and then must recite them in order (similar to when you are trying to remember someone's telephone number). Short-term spatial memory can be assessed by a nonverbal equivalent of the Digit Span subtest known as the Corsi Block Tapping Test (B. Milner, 1971). In this task, the individual sees a series of identical blocks that are spatially dispersed across a board. The sides of the blocks facing the subject have no identifying marks, whereas those facing the experimenter are numbered to aid in test administration. The experimenter taps the blocks in a specific order and the subject is required to immediately tap the blocks in the same sequence (Figure 6.12). In another version, similar to backwards verbal Digit Span, the experimenter taps the blocks in a specific order and the individual must touch the blocks in the reverse order. Patients with damage to the posterior sections of either the right or left hemisphere have difficulty with this task (e.g., DeRenzi & Nichelli, 1975), exhibiting spans of only about three items rather than the five or six exhibited by neurologically intact individuals.

Other tests of visual short-term memory place more demands on an individual to keep information on-line simultaneously, without the sequential component inherent in the block tapping test. In situations such as these, the right frontal area appears to play a prominent role in short-term visual memory. For example, in one study, individuals were given a series of patterns to remember briefly (for either 2 or 10 s) (Pigott & Milner, 1994). Each pattern was composed of small squares, which were randomly arranged so that half were white and half were black. After initially viewing the pattern, participants were shown it again, except this time one white box was missing, and the individual had to indicate where in the pattern the white box should be. The first pattern in the series consisted of only two boxes, a single white one and a single black one. After each correct response, a more complicated pattern with two additional boxes was shown until the partici-

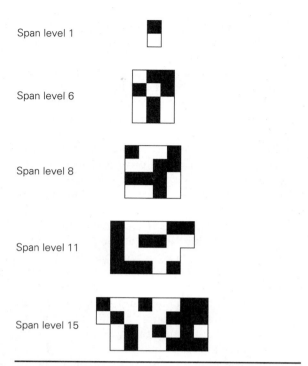

Span level 1

Span level 6

Span level 8

Span level 11

Span level 15

Figure 6.13 The visual span test of Pigott and Milner (1994).
Each individual was shown a simple pattern such as the one at Span Level 1 and was instructed to remember it. Then, after a short delay, the person was shown the same pattern except one of the small white boxes was missing. The individual was told to indicate the location where the white box should appear. After each correct response, the person was shown a more complicated pattern with two additional boxes and the process was repeated until he or she made two errors. Whereas neurologically intact individuals could remember patterns at Span Level 11 (consisting of 22 small squares), individuals with right frontal damage could remember patterns only up to Span Level 8 (consisting of 16 small squares). (*Note.* Reprinted from *Neuropsychologia*, vol. 32, S. Pigott and B. Milner, ''Capacity of Visual Short-Term Memory After Unilateral Frontal or Anterior Temporal-Lobe Resection,'' p. 975, Copyright 1994, with permission from Elsevier Science Ltd., The Boulevard, Langford Lane, Kidlington OX5 1GB, UK.)

pant made two incorrect responses (Figure 6.13). Individuals with right frontal damage could remember patterns composed of only about 16 squares (Span Level 8 in Figure 6.13), whereas neurologically intact individuals and individuals with right temporal lobe damage could remember patterns composed of about 22 squares (Span Level 11 in Figure 6.13).

Converging evidence from brain imaging studies also implicates right frontal regions as important for spatial working memory. For example, in one PET study, activation during a working memory condition was compared with that during a perception condition in which no memory load was imposed. In the perception condition, individuals saw a pattern of three dots for 200 ms, then viewed the dots along with a circle for 1,500 ms. Their task was to decide whether the circle surrounded any of the dots. The working memory condition was similar in that individuals saw the pattern of three dots for 200 ms, except then the screen went blank for 3 s. Afterward, only a circle appeared on the screen (no dots were present), and the individual had to decide whether one of the dots in the original display would have been surrounded by the circle. Thus, in this condition, subjects had to keep the dot positions on-line in working memory until the circle appeared. The difference in activation between the working memory condition and the perception condition occurred most prominently over the right frontal region, an indication that this area is important for spatial working memory (Jonides et al., 1993).

Long-Term Spatial Memory

Right-hemisphere damage affects a variety of long-term spatial memory abilities, including the ability to remember spatial patterns of movements, the locations of objects, and nonverbal spatial patterns such as nonsense designs. For the most part, these long-term spatial memory deficits are observed after damage to temporal regions rather than frontal regions, which, as we just learned, are more important for spatial working memory.

Difficulties in the ability to remember a spatial span of sequential movements is impaired by right-hemisphere damage if that spatial sequence must be retained for an extended period or exceeds an individual's working memory capacity. For example, temporal lobe damage does not interfere with the ability to retain a spatial span on the Corsi Block Tapping Test if the individual mimics the pattern immediately. However, when the delay before recall is extended to 8 or 16 s, or the number of items to be learned exceeds the individual's short-term span by more than two items, individuals with right-hemisphere damage exhibit a deficit (DeRenzi, Faglioni, & Previdi, 1977).

Difficulties in remembering the spatial locations of objects, but not their identities, are observed after removal of right temporal regions, especially when the removal includes large sections of the hippocampus (e.g., Smith & Milner, 1981, 1984). One group of individuals who underwent such removal had their memories tested by viewing 16 small objects positioned on a board in an essentially random manner. Immediately after viewing the board, the patients were given a piece of paper and asked to place the objects in the same locations in which they had just appeared. These individuals were retested 24 hours later. Compared with neurologically intact control subjects, individuals with right temporal lobe resection that included the hippocampus had more difficulty remembering item locations both immediately after viewing the board and 24 hours later.

Individuals with right temporal lobe damage may have difficulty remembering item locations even when the items are in a more naturalistic visual scene (as compared with the essentially random nature of the displays Smith and Milner used). In one test, individuals were shown a series of complex scenes (e.g., a beach scene) that contained multiple objects (e.g., a person, a sandcastle, a pail and shovel, a beach towel, a motorboat, a sailboat, a sea gull). After a 15-min delay, each person's memory for the scene was assessed. Individuals with right temporal lobe removal that impinged on the hippocampus were unable to detect changes in a scene when the locations of two objects were switched. In addition, the researchers found that damage to the right temporal lobe disrupted the ability to remember other aspects of the spatial composition of complex scenes. For example, the patients could not detect when an object's position within the scene had been

moved laterally or when an object had been removed from the scene. The size of these latter two deficits was not related to the degree of hippocampal removal but was associated with right temporal lobe damage in general (Pigott & Milner, 1993).

Right temporal lobe damage also disrupts the ability to remember complex spatial patterns, such as nonverbal nonsense designs (see Figure 6.5). As we discussed earlier in this chapter, this task places special demands on spatial processing because the nonsense designs cannot be remembered with reference to spatial schemata already stored in memory such as those that can be invoked for common objects (e.g., a house tends to be a rectangular form with a slanted triangular roof above the rectangle). Deficits resulting from right temporal lobe damage include not only difficulty in remembering items in a series of nonsense figures when there is a delay between initial presentation and the memory test, but also difficulty in recognizing the entire pattern of a large nonsense figure that was initially viewed piece by piece and then built into a whole (Jones-Gotman, 1986a). This latter task seems to be affected more by right hippocampal damage than by general damage to the right temporal lobe. In addition, right hippocampal damage interferes with the ability to learn a list of abstract designs (Jones-Gotman, 1986b). Thus, all these findings implicate right temporal regions in long-term spatial memory.

Topographical Memory

A result of brain trauma, **topographical disorientation** is a specific loss of spatial memory in which an individual may not be able to learn his or her way around a new environment or may not be able to remember routes through familiar places. The disorder is specific to remembering routes around the environment, sparing the ability to recognize buildings and landmarks, and leaving short-term and long-term spatial memory undisturbed. Furthermore, these topographical abilities are distinct from route-finding abilities because some individuals with topographical disorientation have intact geographical knowledge, as indicated by the ability to localize major cities on blank maps of their native countries, and can learn the stylus maze within normal limits (e.g., Habib & Sirigu, 1987).

In some cases of topographical disorientation, the difficulty arises only in environments encountered since the brain trauma. These individuals may have great difficulty negotiating the corridors of the ward in the hospital but have few difficulties negotiating around their own house. Likewise, they may be able to traverse familiar paths through their hometown but have difficulty navigating new routes through the same town. In other cases, the ability to negotiate in both old and new environments is lost (e.g., Habib & Sirigu, 1987). The underlying problem that these individuals have is unclear. One suggestion is that they have a deficit in which they cannot link the sensory information about the relations of points in the environment with information in memory (much the way a person with agnosia cannot link sensory information about objects with information in memory) (e.g., Landis, Cummings, Benson, & Palmer, 1986). Another suggestion is that these individuals have a highly specific amnesia in which a personal route through space cannot be remembered (e.g., Habib & Sirigu, 1987). The location of the lesion that typically causes such a syndrome—the medial temporal region of the right hemisphere, including almost all of the lingual and parahippocampal gyri that border the occipital lobe—is consistent with either an impairment to memory itself or the linkage of information to memory.

ATTENTIONAL DISTURBANCES IN SPATIAL PROCESSING

So far we discussed syndromes in which the inability to process spatial material occurred because of difficulties either in constructing a spatial map of the world or in comprehending the spatial relationships among parts of items or locations in space. However, in a variety of syndromes, spatial processing is disrupted not so much because the relationships among items cannot be comprehended, but because of difficulties in directing attention to a particular spatial location. In everyday life, we often direct our attention to a particular sector of space, such as

when we go to the airport to pick up a friend and direct our attention to the area around a specific gate while ignoring the activity and people at other locations. When attention cannot be allocated to certain regions of space, the ability to process spatial relations in that region suffers. The two main syndromes in which attentional problems interfere with spatial processing are Balint's syndrome and hemineglect.

Balint's Syndrome

Balint's syndrome is similar to what Holmes (1918) observed in his patients, because individuals with this syndrome have trouble localizing items in space, groping for objects as if blind. **Balint's syndrome** has three major aspects: **optic ataxia,** which is the inability to point to a target under visual guidance; **ocular apraxia,** which is the inability to voluntarily shift gaze toward a new visual stimulus; and **simultanagnosia,** which is the inability to perceive different pieces of information in the visual field simultaneously because the person cannot direct attention to more than one small location in the visual world at a time (A. R. Damasio, 1985). The last component defines this syndrome as a disruption of spatial attention rather than a disruption of spatial processing.

Individuals with Balint's syndrome often appear as if they are blind for all but the most limited area in the visual world. For example, if a doctor holds a pencil at arm's length in front of the face of a person with Balint's syndrome, the pencil is recognized but not the doctor's face or any other object in the room. These individuals do not have cortical blindness because they can view objects anywhere in their visual field, but only one at a time. A case of Balint's syndrome observed by Godwin-Austen (1965) and discussed in Farah (1990) illustrates this phenomenon well. The individual was asked to describe a drawing similar to that shown in Figure 6.14. She described the pieces one after the other, first mentioning the helmet, then the handlebars, then the telegram, and finally the car. Only after quite a bit of time did she infer that the girl was waving to flag down the car, but she never really

Figure 6.14 A picture used to reveal simultanagnosia, an inability to direct attention to more than one part of the visual world at a time.
When asked to describe this picture, an individual with this syndrome could describe the handlebars, the telegram, the car, and the helmet but could not perceive why the girl was trying to flag down the car. (*Note.* Adapted from Farah, 1990, p. 18.)

understood why because she never noticed that the front tire was disconnected from the bicycle. She could never "see" the whole picture but could comprehend only parts at a time. Subjectively, individuals with this syndrome report that one object in the world comes into focus while all the others fade. Furthermore, such patients have little control over what is in focus and when that focus switches.

The incidence of Balint's syndrome is relatively low because the causative lesion is rare. The syndrome is typically observed after a **watershed lesion,** which is caused by lack of oxygen to brain regions especially susceptible to oxygen deprivation because they fall between the main "watershed" areas of the arterial blood supply. The lesion that causes Balint's syndrome falls in a watershed region

between the supply of the posterior and middle cerebral arteries and often occurs after a sudden and severe drop in systemic blood pressure. In almost all cases of Balint's syndrome, a bilateral lesion can be found in the dorsal occipitoparietal region (A. R. Damasio, 1985). Because of the dorsal location of the lesion and the individual's inability to pay attention to more than one location in space simultaneously, Balint's syndrome is sometimes known as **dorsal simultanagnosia** (Farah, 1990).

Hemineglect

As we discuss in more detail in chapter 7, damage to parietal regions is associated with hemineglect. Because hemineglect is observed more often after right-hemisphere damage than after left-hemisphere damage, the neglect is typically observed for information on the left side of space. What is important about hemineglect for the purposes of the present discussion is that it provides additional evidence that we have multiple frames of reference by which we map the spatial world.

Studies of patients with hemineglect have revealed that what constitutes a "side" of space can be influenced by different spatial frameworks. For example, we can map the world not only by a spatial framework with regard to the body, but also by a spatial framework with regard to the head. When a person is standing and looking straight ahead, these spatial frameworks coincide, but when he or she turns or tilts the head, or lies on one side, these spatial frameworks dissociate. The region of space neglected by patients with hemineglect is influenced not only by what is to the left of body midline, but also by what is to the left of the midline of the head (e.g., Ladavas, 1987).

Studies of patients with hemineglect also provide evidence that the spatial framework for extrapersonal space can dissociate from the framework for personal space. In one case, an individual exhibited no neglect for the extrapersonal world; he was attentive to all aspects of his surroundings and used objects to perform activities on both sides of space (e.g., serving tea or dealing cards). Yet, he exhibited neglect for personal space because when objects such as razors and combs had to be used on his own body, he ignored the left side of his body. So severe was this neglect that in one instance he woke up his wife in the middle of the night and asked her for help in finding his left arm (Guariglia & Antonucci, 1992).

In summary, both Balint's syndrome and hemineglect reveal that when attention cannot be directed to particular regions of space, the ability to comprehend spatial relations in that region is disrupted as well.

ROLE OF THE LEFT HEMISPHERE IN SPATIAL PROCESSING

For most of this chapter, we emphasized the predominant role of the right hemisphere in visuospatial processing. However, we did discuss a number of cases in which deficits in spatial processing appeared after left-hemisphere damage as well. These deficits may arise because certain spatial tasks can be performed by using different strategies, some of which may rely on the left hemisphere. One way to uncover the strategies that the left hemisphere uses is to examine the compensatory mechanisms invoked by individuals with right-hemisphere damage when they must perform visuospatial tasks. One case study that provides some interesting insights into left-hemisphere modes of spatial processing is that of a young woman who wanted to become an architect even though she had sustained right-hemisphere damage (Clarke, Assal, & DeTribolet, 1993). This case is notable because the researchers assessed many of the visuospatial functions that we discuss in this chapter.

For many of the tasks, the woman used a piecemeal strategy in which spatial relations were computed on a point-by-point basis rather than in a holistic manner. For example, when copying the Rey-Osterrieth figure (see Figure 6.8A), she did not perceive its overall rectangular form (which probably jumps out at you). Rather, her strategy was to copy the figure, small piece by small piece. Although she did manage to include all the basic elements of the figure, she misplaced half of them relative to

one another and added extraneous details. Not surprisingly, she was also poor at drawing the item from memory after a delay, an indication of a problem in spatial memory as well. Her piecemeal strategy was also evident in the house plans that she drew for her architecture classes. If she had to change the scale of the plan, she would misplace the subparts in relation to one another, although she could meticulously reproportion all the subparts to the correct size. The only spatial relations she could correctly depict were left and right and front and back, which probably rely on left-hemisphere processing (as we discuss further later in this chapter). Moreover, she used a feature-by-feature approach when trying to recognize pictures of European towns or villages in her native Switzerland. She managed to recognize many towns by some distinctive feature, such as a castle or a riverside. However, such a strategy led her to mistake towns with similar features for one another because she could not take into account the spatial composition of those features (e.g., a castle with a central tower that sits high above a lake vs. a castle with a side tower situated at lakeside).

In addition to the visuospatial skills just discussed, this woman's geographical and route-finding abilities were impaired. She had difficulty locating cities on a map. Although she could generally localize them to the correct region, she misplaced them with regard to landmarks, such as lakes and rivers. These deficits could not be accounted for by a lack of knowledge about the cities because she could verbally name the countries in which foreign cities were located and the regions in which Swiss cities were found. Because her sense of the direction from point to point was impaired, sometimes off by more than 45 degress, her method of remembering a route through an unknown town was to use a verbal point-by-point strategy. In all cases, her compensatory strategies seemed to be verbally mediated, detailed, and linear, in which the relations among different locations in space were processed in a point-to-point manner.

Case studies, such as these, help us to understand the way in which the left hemisphere may go about performing visuospatial tasks. Although we gener-

Although successful piloting requires a multiplicity of skills, including the ability to divide attention and the ability to prioritize tasks, spatial abilities are undoubtedly critical to aviation. Unlike earthbound mortals in cars, pilots must navigate in two, not three, dimensions and under conditions in which their major landmarks, the earth and the horizon, may sometimes be obscured from view. As we learned in this chapter, neuropsychological evidence suggests that certain types of spatial processes are distinct from one another and may rely on distinct neural subsystems. These dissociations among spatial processes and their neural substrates may have implications for the design of aircraft and for the type of spatial skills required for competent piloting. We now look at how two issues examined by neuropsychologists—the dissociation between different frames of reference and the distinction between categorical and coordinate processes—may be applied to aviation.

As we discussed, neuropsychological evidence suggests that processing information with regard to a personal frame of reference is distinct from processing it with regard to positions in extrapersonal space. To the degree that these systems are separate, they may involve fundamentally distinct cognitive operations that are not easily compatible. In fact, the displays that pilots use tend to provide either a personal frame of reference or an extrapersonal frame of reference, but not both. One system, known as track-up alignment, provides a view of the world that is aligned perfectly with the world outside the cockpit window: What is straight ahead of the window is straight ahead on the map. As the plane turns, the alignment of the display turns with it so that the pilot has an egocentric, or personal, frame of reference (Box Figure 6.1A). The other system, known as north-up alignment, provides a map of the world that remains static; north is always straight ahead regardless of the direction in which the plane is moving. This map provides an earth-based, or extrapersonal, frame of reference (Box Figure 6.1B). The advantage of the track-up map is the direct mapping between locations on the display and locations outside the cockpit window. However, its disadvantage is that it hinders

a pilot's ability to build a static mental map of the world because the display constantly changes. In contrast, the north-up map, which provides an earth-centered frame of reference, aids in composing a cognitive map, but it requires the pilot to mentally rotate either the display or the view outside the cockpit so that both are aligned, an operation that takes time (Aretz, 1991; Aretz & Wickens, 1992).

Psychologists interested in cockpit design attempt to invent new displays that will maximize the benefits of each system while reducing their costs (e.g., Aretz, 1991) or to determine which type of map is most advantageous under specific conditions. For example, aircraft, such as helicopters, which are to be flown close to the ground, may be best guided by track-up maps so that the map is continuously aligned with terrain, whereas aircraft flow at higher altitudes may be best flown by using north-up maps (e.g., Harwood & Wickens, 1991).

As we also learned, neuropsychological evidence suggests that processing spatial relations in a categorical manner is distinct from processing them in a metric manner. Research with pilots indicates that these individuals are superior to nonpilots in their ability to process metric spatial relations, such as judgments about the distance between spatial locations, but they are no better at processing coordinate spatial relations, such as knowing whether one location is above or below another. Pilots have also been found to be superior at mental rotation, a skill required to use a north-up display effectively. As we discussed earlier in the chapter, these two types of spatial abilities, metric spatial processing and mental rotation, appear to place particular demands on right-hemisphere processing (see Dror, Kosslyn, & Waag, 1993, for a discussion of the spatial skills at which pilots excel and their neural bases). Thus, some test batteries designed to screen aviators for neuropsychological dysfunction due to disease or substance abuse are heavily weighted toward testing the spatial processes that rely on the right hemisphere (e.g., Banich, Stokes, & Elledge, 1989; Stokes, Banich, & Elledge, 1991).

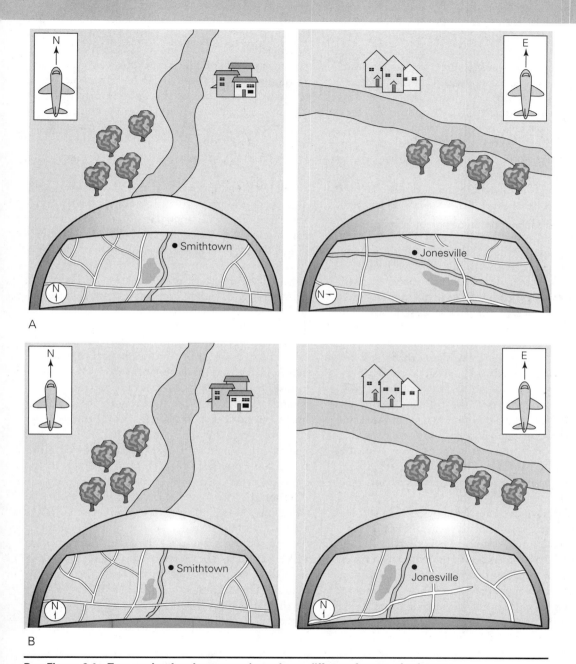

A

B

Box Figure 6.1 Two navigational systems that rely on different frames of reference.
(A) An example of track-up alignment: What is outside the cockpit window corresponds directly with the map. (B) An example of north-up alignment: The map always provides a constant view of the space; therefore, the pilot must mentally rotate it to align it with the view outside the cockpit window.

ally think about the right hemisphere's large role in visuospatial processing, the left hemisphere appears not only to participate in different aspects of spatial processing, but also to excel at certain spatial tasks. Some researchers have suggested that the left hemisphere may be involved in visuospatial processing under certain conditions: when distracting or extraneous information is included in the spatial array, when complex spatial processing is required to perform a task (as opposed to just a single basic process such as detecting the orientation of a line), and when Euclidean geometric principles must be used (Mehta & Newcombe, 1991). Such a conceptualization meshes well with the finding that for many basic aspects of spatial function, such as the perception of motion, depth, and so forth, the right hemisphere is superior. It also meshes well with findings that the left hemisphere of the patient with the split-brain syndrome is most involved in performing Euclidean geometry. Yet such a description does not provide an overall rubric for conceptualizing the role that each hemisphere plays in spatial processing.

One overarching theory suggests that the hemispheres are specialized for mutually exclusive ways of computing spatial relationships (Kosslyn, 1987). According to this theory, the right hemisphere is specialized for computing **metric (coordinate) spatial relations,** or the distance between two locations. In contrast, the left hemisphere is hypothesized to be especially skillful at determining **categorical spatial relations,** or one position in relation to another (e.g., above vs. below, top vs. bottom, front vs. back, left vs. right). These types of relations are considered categorical because a position must fall into a single category (e.g., you can't be below and above something at the same time).

One important feature of this model is that metric and categorical spatial relations are considered independent of each other because describing relations between two points from a metric perspective provides no information about their relationship from a categorical perspective, and vice versa. For example, if we describe the relationship between two points metrically, by saying that Point A is 3 feet from Point B, we are given no information

about their categorical relationship. We do not know whether Point A lies to the left of Point B or whether it lies above Point B. These processes are viewed as relying on mutually exclusive ways of computing spatial relations that can be carried out better by two distinct subsystems, in this case different hemispheres, than if they had to be computed by the same system (see Kosslyn, Chabris, Marsolek, & Koenig, 1992, for a computer simulation of the computational advantages of two distinct subsystems).

Evidence to support the distinction between categorical and metric processing comes from studies both of patients with brain damage and of neurologically intact individuals. As we discussed, individuals with left-hemisphere damage often have difficulty discerning right from left, a task that involves categorical descriptions of spatial relations. In contrast, individuals with right-hemisphere damage have difficulty localizing items in space, which implies that they are unable to compute the distance of an item from some reference point within a spatial framework. In neurologically intact subjects, divided visual field techniques have been used to assess responses to the same set of stimuli, but under two separate conditions, one that requires a judgment about categorical spatial relations and one that requires a judgment about metric spatial relations. For example, in one study, subjects viewed a dot and a blob on the screen (Figure 6.15A). In the categorical task, the subjects merely had to decide whether the dot was on or off the blob. In the metric task, they had to decide whether the dot was within a certain distance of the blob. Typically, a RVF advantage is found for the categorical task, and a LVF advantage for the metric task (e.g., Kosslyn et al., 1989). However, this is not always the case. For example, sometimes no visual field advantage is seen for the categorical task (e.g., Hellige & Michimata, 1989; the stimuli for this study are shown in Figure 6.15B), sometimes the LVF advantage for metric processing dissipates as the number of trials increases (e.g., Rybash & Hoyer, 1992), and sometimes different visual asymmetries are not found for categorical and metric tasks (e.g., Sergent, 1991).

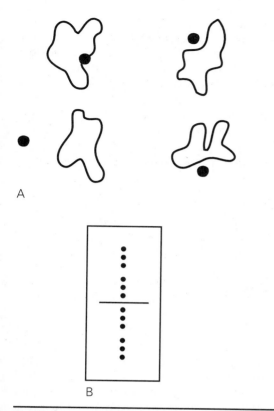

A

B

Figure 6.15   Examples of stimuli used in divided visual field studies to investigate the difference between categorical and metric spatial relations.
(A) Each of these four stimuli were shown individually. In the categorical task, an individual was asked to decide whether the dot was on or off the blob. In the metric task, the person was asked to decide whether the dot was near or far from the blob. Typically, a right visual field (RVF) advantage is seen for the categorical task and a left visual field (LVF) advantage for the metric task. (B) In this task, the bar and one dot were shown in each trial. The figure depicts the 12 possible locations of dots. In the categorical task, subjects decided whether the dot was above or below the bar. In the metric task, they decided whether the line was near (within 0.79 in., or 2 cm) or far away (farther than 0.79 in., or 2 cm) from the dot. Only a trend toward a RVF advantage was seen for the categorical task, whereas, as expected, a LVF advantage was observed for the metric task. (*Note.* A, From "Seeing and Imagining in the Cerebral Hemispheres: A Computational Approach," by S. M. Kosslyn, 1987, *Psychological Review, 94,* p. 164. Copyright © 1987 by the American Psychological Association. Reprinted with permission. B, From *Memory and Cognition, 17,* 1989, p. 772, reprinted by permission of Psychonomic Society, Inc.)

These discrepancies across studies led Sergent to suggest that the distinction between the hemispheres with regard to how they compute spatial relations may not be as clear-cut as originally proposed (see Sergent, 1991, for a conceptual and empirical criticism of the original theory). However, the discrepancies may also result because individuals become highly familiarized with a small set of stimuli and change their strategy during the course of testing. When task conditions are manipulated to minimize these types of changes in strategy, a RVF advantage is found for categorical judgments and a LVF advantage is found for metric judgments (e.g., Banich & Federmeier, 1995), which suggests that computing each of these types of spatial relations does rely on a different neural substrate.

Before we leave our discussion of categorical and metric spatial relations, one fact worth mentioning is that knowledge about categorical spatial relations may be particularly important for object recognition. As we discussed in chapter 5, objects must be recognized across various orientations and positions. Generally, the categorical relations among the parts of an item are invariant regardless of how and where the object is positioned in space. For example, we need to recognize a cat as the same object regardless of whether it is sitting curled up on the windowsill or scampering across the floor after a mouse. In both cases, the cat's ears are *above* its whiskers. These invariants in categorical relations may aid in the ability to recognize an object across a variety of transformations (Kosslyn, 1987).

SUMMARY

Spatial processing is not a single cognitive function but encompasses a large variety of abilities, most of which rely on the right hemisphere. The perception of spatial relations depends heavily on the parietal lobe, which is part of the dorsal, or "where," visual system (as distinct from the ventral, or "what," visual system discussed in chapter 5). Evidence for parietal involvement in processing spatial locations comes from single-cell recordings and lesion studies of monkeys. Cells in the parietal region have attributes that make them well suited for processing spatial relations because they are sensitive to information over a wide expanse of the visual field (especially the regions that fall outside the fovea), are sensitive to a combination of eye and head positions, and are sensitive to motion in the range of speeds at which animals locomote. All these attributes are useful for constructing a map of external space that can serve as a constant reference regardless of the animal's position or movements. Furthermore, these cells tend to be insensitive to the attributes that are important for item recognition, such as color and shape. Thus, animals with lesions to the parietal area retain the ability to recognize objects but cannot make decisions about the relative positions of items in space.

In humans, the right parietal lobe plays a role in many basic aspects of spatial processing, such as localizing points in space, determining the depths of objects, recognizing the orientation of lines, comprehending geometric relations, detecting and processing motion, and rotating objects mentally, although in some cases, depending on the strategy used, the left hemisphere may contribute to these abilities as well. Not only does right-hemisphere brain damage disrupt the ability to perceive basic spatial relations, but it also disturbs the ability to construct representations of the spatial world.

A different set of spatial skills is used when we navigate around the world. These route-finding abilities appear to be distinct from the more basic spatial processes just mentioned. Disruptions in route-finding abilities take many forms. In some cases, individuals cannot perform simple maze tasks in which a pen or a finger must be moved along a route. In other cases, the individual may be unable to use a map to follow a route around a room. In still other cases, the ability to follow a route through a city may be lost or the ability to comprehend the relation between two landmarks may be compromised. Part of the reason that these different abilities may dissociate is because some involve computing relations in personal space whereas others involve determining relations in extrapersonal space. The ability to understand the relationship between two points in space seems to be different than under-

standing the relationship of your body to a point in space. Furthermore, the ability to follow a route appears to be distinct from the ability to remember geographical locations on a map. Although route-finding and topographical skills are usually compromised by right-hemisphere damage, they are sometimes affected by left-hemisphere damage, especially in cases when verbal strategies can be used to perform the function.

The ability to understand the relations among points in space is also distinct from the ability to understand the relations of your body parts. Individuals may lose the ability to distinguish their left from their right and to differentiate among their fingers. Unlike most of the other spatial problems we discussed, these disturbances are caused by left-hemisphere lesions. Sometimes brain malfunctioning can distort body schema so that body parts seem especially large or small. These types of problems are often associated with epilepsy.

Whereas the perception of spatial relations often relies on parietal regions, other brain areas are important for spatial memory. Short-term, or working, spatial memory is the system used to store spatial information for relatively brief periods. Many brain areas appear to contribute to this skill when it is assessed by a task such as the Corsi Block Tapping Test, in which a sequence of locations must be remembered. However, when spatial information must be held on-line simultaneously, right frontal regions play a prominent role. Long-term spatial memory involves remembering spatial information during the course of minutes, hours, or days. Right temporal regions are important for retaining such long-term spatial information. Damage to these regions leads to difficulties in remembering where items were located in space, the form of complex nonverbal figures, and the spatial composition of complex scenes.

Spatial processing can also be disrupted by attentional disorders. In Balint's syndrome, the individual has difficulty processing spatial relations because attention can be directed to only a single position in space. Individuals with this disorder cannot comprehend the relation between two items because they cannot pay attention to two points in space at the same time. Hemineglect, which is an inattention to one side of space, also disrupts spatial processing because information in certain spatial locations is ignored. Studies of patients with hemineglect provide converging evidence that we map our spatial world according to multiple spatial frameworks (e.g., a head-centered framework, a body-centered framework.

Although the right hemisphere is usually thought of as the "spatial" hemisphere, the left hemisphere can also contribute to certain aspects of spatial processing. When the left hemisphere processes spatial relations, it tends to use a verbal point-to-point strategy. To account for such findings, researchers have proposed that each hemisphere has a distinct way of computing spatial relations. According to this view, the left hemisphere is specialized for determining categorical spatial relations, in which the relationship of two points is described according to categories of locations (above vs. below, to the left vs. to the right). In contrast, the right hemisphere is specialized for computing metric (coordinate) spatial relations, or the distance between two points. Evidence to support such a distinction comes both from patients who sustained unilateral brain damage and from divided visual field studies of neurologically intact individuals. Categorical spatial relations may aid in item recognition because any two given parts of an item generally retain the same categorical relation relative to each other (e.g., the head is generally above the neck) regardless of transformations in object position.

*A*ttention

As he did every morning after waking, Bill went into the bathroom to begin his morning ritual. After squeezing toothpaste onto his toothbrush, he looked into the mirror and began to brush his teeth. Although he brushed the teeth on the right side of his mouth quite vigorously, for the most part he ignored those on the left side. Then he stepped into the shower and began rubbing a bar of soap to produce a frothy lather. He started to generously distribute the suds all over his body, but once he finished lathering his right arm, he didn't bother to do so for the left side of his body. Back in front of the mirror he shaved all the stubble from the right side of his face impeccably but did a spotty job on the left side.

After getting dressed, Bill went to his favorite local diner for breakfast. He ordered the daily special of two eggs, toast, bacon, and hash browns; the last two items were his favorites. When his order arrived, the waitress placed the plate in front of him with the fried eggs and the toast toward the right, and the bacon and hash browns to the left. He took one bite each of bacon and of hash browns, and then turned to the eggs and toast. Strangely, once he started eating the eggs and toast, he never took another bite of hash browns

or bacon. While Bill was sipping his coffee, a busboy, walking to the kitchen off to Bill's left, dropped a stack of dirty dishes, creating a commotion. Bill, like everyone else in the diner, watched the rattled busboy clean up the mess. Afterward, Bill resumed eating his breakfast and now heartily consumed the hash browns and bacon he had previously ignored.

When Bill asked for the check, the waitress placed it on the left side of the table. After a few minutes, he waved the waitress over and complained, saying, "I asked for my tab 5 minutes ago. What is taking so long?"

She looked at him quizzically, pointed to the bill on the table, and replied, "But sir, it's right here. I put it there a while ago."

"It's not such a great idea to hide the bill from the customer," he replied. With that, Bill rose to leave, and the waitress, still bemused by the whole encounter, watched him bump into the left-hand part of the door frame as he walked out into the street. As she turned to clean the table, she saw that Bill had left a generous tip. Shrugging, she said softly to herself, "I guess the customer is always right."

The seemingly bizarre behavior that the gentleman in this story displayed can be attributed to a syndrome known as **hemineglect**, or **hemi-inattention.** Despite having intact sensory and motor functioning, individuals with hemineglect ignore, or do not pay attention, to one side of space. Not surprisingly, this disorder is typically observed after a parietal lobe lesion. As we discussed in chapter 6, the parietal lobe plays an important role in spatial processes, including creating a mental map of space, locating points in space, guiding movement in space, and attending to particular points in space. Hemineglect can be considered a space-based phenomenon because the neglect of information occurs with reference to a spatial frame (i.e., information in the half

of space located contralateral to the lesion is ignored) and because all types of information, regardless of modality, are ignored on the neglected side of space.

Because attention is a multifaceted process that has been conceptualized in different ways, we begin the chapter by briefly outlining some cognitive theories of attention. These conceptual frameworks help us to understand some specific neuropsychological disorders of attention that are discussed later in the chapter. Next, we identify and discuss the multiplicity of brain structures that play a role in attention. Unlike some of the other abilities discussed so far that seem to be under control of a relatively circumscribed area of the brain, attention is controlled by a large and diverse network of brain structures. We conclude by devoting a considerable amount of time to discussing hemineglect, a syndrome that has received much attention (no pun intended) not only because the pattern of deficits is so bizarre and intriguing, but also because this particular syndrome provides much insight into the nature of the neural organization for attention.

THEORIES OF ATTENTION

Attention is a concept often invoked by psychologists, but one that does not have a standard, universally accepted definition. Nonetheless, most psychologists agree that the brain has some inherent limitations to the amount of information that it can process. For example, people cannot pay attention to or do 12 things simultaneously. These limitations mean that to function effectively, we must have a way of filtering or selecting particular information, whether it be from the vast array of incoming sensory information that impinges upon our brain every moment of the day or from the many possible responses that can be given in any particular situation. This selective process that occurs in response to the limited processing capacity of the brain is known as **attention.** In discussing attention, cognitive psychologists often divide it into four general categories: alertness and arousal, sustained attention (vigilance), selective attention, and resources (capacity) (see D. L. LaBerge, 1990, for a short review of the different varieties of attention and some of the major theoretical debates). We briefly discuss each of these four categories next.

Basic Categories of Attention

Alertness and arousal are the fundamental aspects of attention that enable a person to extract information from the environment or to select a particular response. Our alertness and arousal are low when we are tired or sleepy, which is why we often have difficulty paying attention to information in our sensory world and choosing our actions at these times. In some extreme cases, such as coma, alertness and arousal are so disrupted that the person is almost totally unresponsive to the outside world and has no control over his or her responses.

Another general category of attention is **vigilance,** which is also known as *sustained attention.* Vigilance is the ability to maintain alertness continuously. In common parlance, we often say that someone has a "short attention span" when he or she cannot maintain attention for long periods. Vigilance is important when a task must be performed nonstop and alternately "tuning in" and "tuning out" would be deleterious. Your ability to sustain attention is taxed every day in class as you try to listen to every word of a lecture for an entire class period.

A third general category of attention is **selective attention.** Because we are bombarded with vast amounts of information and have myriad ways of choosing to respond to this information, attention often involves selection of both the material to be received and the response to be given. For example, as you read this page and try to understand what is written on it, you cannot simultaneously listen to a song on the radio and monitor the movements of people around you. Selective attention is the cognitive mechanism that allows you to select—from all the possibilities before you—the words on the page and the task of comprehension as the most salient aspects of processing that need to be accomplished at this time.

A fourth way in which attention has been conceptualized is as the **resource** or effort that must be devoted during information processing. Such resources are required because our capacity to process information is inherently limited. Originally, these resources were assumed to be undifferentiated; that is, they were assumed to be the same. Thus, when either multiple tasks or a multifaceted task had to be performed, these resources would be doled out for different component processes, much like pieces of a pie, until none were left (e.g., Kahneman, 1973). However a more recent **multiple-resource theory** suggests that a limited set of distinct resource pools may exist, each of which can be applied to only certain types of processes. From this perspective, the system has a larger processing capacity when tasks draw from different resource pools than from the same one (e.g., C. D. Wickens, 1980). Later in this chapter, we discuss how neuropsychological data support the notion of multiple resources.

Issues in Selective Attention

Now that we know the different ways in which attention has been conceptualized, we turn to two prominent issues with regard to how selective attention occurs—issues on which neuropsychological data can shed some light. The first issue that we discuss is *when* this selection process occurs; does it occur relatively early or relatively late after the receipt of sensory information? The second issue that we discuss is *how* the selection process occurs; does it occur with regard to particular locations in space or with regard to particular objects? Although the different possibilities have traditionally been expressed as dichotomies (early vs. late selection and space-based vs. object-based attention), experts now know that attention can operate in a variety of ways that need not be mutually exclusive.

Early and Late Selection

Because attention is conceptualized as a filter, researchers have long debated whether this filtering of material occurs at a relatively early stage of processing or a relatively late stage. Hence, we next discuss the two distinct viewpoints and the neuropsychological evidence that addresses this issue. One viewpoint is that selection occurs early in the stream of processing, soon after the receipt of sensory information and before an item is identified (e.g., A. Treisman & Gelade, 1980). This position is known as the **early selection viewpoint.** According to the other viewpoint, the **late selection viewpoint,** selection occurs later in processing, only after information is identified and categorized (e.g., J. A. Deutsch & Deutsch, 1963). For example, a person who adopts the early selection viewpoint assumes that a long vertical bar with a shorter horizontal bar can be identified as the letter *T* only after attention is directed to the point in space where the

two bars are located. In contrast, a person advocating the late selection viewpoint assumes, for instance, that only after the visual patterns of the letters *A, C, R,* and *T* are identified as distinct letters and their meaning is derived can the letter *T* be selected for further processing so that a decision or response can be reached. Although these two viewpoints were once thought to be mutually exclusive, researchers now think that attention may act at different points in processing. Let's examine some of the evidence for both late and early selection.

Evidence for late selection was provided by studies demonstrating that information to which an individual was not paying attention could nonetheless be categorized. In one such study, individuals were given a dichotic listening task in which a continuous stream of information was provided to each ear. (This use of dichotic listening is somewhat different than that typically used in studies of lateralization of function; in such studies, information is provided in discrete pairs rather than continuously.) The individual was asked to attend to the information being presented to one ear and to repeat it verbally. Nonetheless, some information from the unattended ear, such as the subject's name, could be reported (e.g., Moray, 1959). Such findings suggest that items can be categorized (e.g., "that was my name") even when they have not been attended.

However, evidence also exists that selection can occur relatively early in processing. This evidence comes from research examining how quickly a particular target item can be found in a multi-item visual display with many nontargets. The logic of these experiments is that if attention is required to filter out distracting information, the larger the number of nontargets and hence the more filtering that must occur, the longer the person should take to find the target. Indeed, when a target item, such as a red *X*, must be identified on the bais of a conjunction of basic visual attributes (e.g., both shape and color) from among the nontargets, such as red *O*s (which share the same color as the target) and green *X*s (which share the same shape as the target), the time required to find the target increases with the number of nontargets. Researchers have proposed that this result occurs because attention can be directed to only one point at a time. Hence, the more items in the display, the more points that must be sampled before the target is located. The important concept for the purposes of the present discussion is that directing attention to a point in space *precedes* the identification of information, which means that selection must occur early in processing, before identification. Because the attribute of "red" appears at many points in the display, as does the attribute of *X*, the only way to identify an item is to first direct attention to a given location, subsequently combine the basic attributes (e.g., color and shape) of the information located there, and then identify the item (e.g., "It is a red *X*"). This combining of basic visual attributes that occurs by directing attention to a given spatial location is a prerequisite to item identification (A. Treisman & Gelade, 1980). Additional support for the idea that attention must occur before an item can be correctly identified comes from studies in which people report viewing illusory conjunctions of item attributes when they are not paying attention to the locations at which these items appear. For example, if a display contains a red *X* and a green *O* at unattended locations, an individual may report having seen a red *O*, incorrectly combining one item's color with another item's shape (A. M. Treisman & Schmidt, 1982).

One notable exception to the pattern described for the multi-item task is that when a target, such as a red *X*, can be differentiated from all the nontarget stimuli on the basis of a simple visual attribute, the time required to find the target does *not* vary with the number of nontarget items. For instance, if all the nontargets are green *X*s or curved *O*s, people say that the red *X* "pops out" at them regardless of how many nontargets surround it. In such situations, processing is said to be "preattentive," which means that attention needn't be implemented to find the target. Because the target can be identified on the basis of a simple visual attribute and both of its visual attributes do not need to be combined, attention is not required.

Researchers wanting to know more precisely when attentional selection occurs have used event-related potentials (ERPs) because they provide a millisecond-by-millisecond record of the brain's averaged electrical activity. Researchers using such techniques traditionally determine the effect of attention by comparing two conditions. In one, the person is instructed to direct attention to the place at which the stimulus is being presented, whereas in the other, the identical stimulus is presented but the individual is paying attention to information at a different location. In this design, ERPs are being recorded to identical stimuli; the only difference in the conditions is whether the person is attending to the place at which the signal is presented. Hence, if any difference in response is observed between these conditions, it can be attributed to attention. Researchers obtain an estimate of when attention begins to exert its influence by discerning the point in time when the amplitude of the ERP to the attended stimulus begins to differ from that of the unattended stimulus.

In a classic example of this type of experiment, individuals are instructed to listen and count the number of target tones that occur. Target tones are of long duration, whereas most tones are nontargets and are of short duration. As mentioned previously, researchers record the ERPs for two conditions. In one condition, targets are presented to the attended ear (e.g., the left ear). In the other condition, the identical target stimuli are presented to the same ear (i.e., the left), but the individual is instructed to pay attention to stimuli presented to the other ear (i.e., the right ear). Both conditions are then repeated for the opposite ears (e.g., the attended ear becomes the right ear and the unattended ear becomes the left ear). In each case, the ERP in the attended condition begins to become more negative in amplitude than that in the nonattended condition approximately 80 ms after stimulus presentation, and this difference may continue for some time (Hillyard, Hink, Schwent, & Picton, 1973). This increased negative shift for the attended stimulus is often called the N_d *(negative difference) component* and is shown in Figure 7.1.

Because the onset of the N_d occurs as soon as 80 ms after stimulus presentation, attention can exert itself relatively early in the stream of processing. Still, 80 ms is more than enough time for the infor-

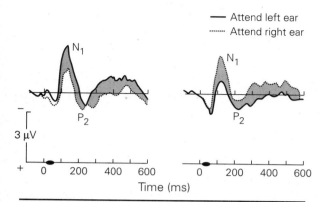

Figure 7.1 **Modulation of early event-related potential (ERP) components by attention.**
The response to the stimulus is enhanced when it is presented in the attended location as compared with when it is not. (Left) For example, the amplitude of the N_1 is greater to a left-ear tone when the individual is attending to the left ear (solid line) than when the same tone is heard but the individual is attending to the right ear (dotted line). (Right) Likewise, the response to a right-ear tone is greater when the right ear is attended (dotted line) than when the left is (solid line). The difference between these two waveforms (shaded area) is the N_d component. This effect begins relatively soon after stimulus presentation, within the first 100 ms. (*Note.* Adapted from Andreassi, 1989, p. 124.)

mation to have traveled from the sensory receptors to the primary sensory cortex of the brain, so these modulatory effects are probably occurring within the central nervous system rather than at the peripheral sensory receptors (e.g., the cochlea).

Although we used auditory stimuli in this example, a similar negative electrical shift can be observed for visual (Van Voorhis & Hillyard, 1977) and somatosensory (Desmedt & Robertson, 1977) information. These findings suggest that the early negativity in the ERP reflects a general attentional process that is not modality specific.

Later ERP components can also be affected by attentional requirements. For example, the P_{300} (which occurs at least 300 ms postpresentation) is found only when an individual is paying attention and monitoring the sensory world for a target. The typical P_{300} paradigm forces study participants to pay attention by having them count the number of

times a target occurs or by requiring a specifc response to target stimuli (see Hoffman, 1990, for a review of this issue). Moreover, the amplitude of the P_{300} is modified by the amount of attention paid to a task (e.g., C. Wickens, Kramer, Vanasse, & Donchin, 1983). The results from ERP studies examining the N_1 and P_{300} indicate that attention can moderate the brain's response not only soon after a stimulus is received, but for a while thereafter as well.

Space-Based and Object-Based Selection

Another topic that psychologists have discussed extensively is whether attention modulates processing mainly with regard to particular points in space or whether it can also modulate processing with regard to specific objects. As we just discussed, some models suggest that attention is directed to a particular point in space and that the information at this location is processed more fully. For example, we discussed how directing attention to a particular point in space is thought to allow for the identification of items and how attending to a specific location can moderate the N_1 response. This is known as a **space-based viewpoint of attention.** In contrast, according to the **object-based viewpoint of attention,** attention is directed toward particular objects. To make the distinction between space-based and object-based attention more concrete, let's assume that you have arranged to pick up your friend outside a train station. Suppose that you have agreed beforehand that she will be standing at the northeast corner of the plaza in front of the station. When you arrive and begin to look for your friend, you can direct your attention in a space-based manner by processing information from only a specific location (i.e., the northeast corner of the plaza), while ignoring information at other locations. In contrast, you may direct your attention in an object-based manner if you know that your friend will be wearing her long oversized wool coat. As you look for your friend, you can selectively pay attention only to particular objects, long oversized wool coats, while ignoring other objects such as ski jackets, short coats, and parkas.

One classic experimental paradigm for demonstrating space-based attention abilities was designed by Posner (1980). In this paradigm an individual is shown a display that contains a central cross and two peripheral boxes. Throughout the trial, the person must fixate his or her eyes on the central cross. Next, one of the two peripheral boxes brightens, and shortly afterward, a target to which the person must respond, an asterisk, appears inside the box. In approximately 80% of the trials, known as *valid trials*, the cue correctly identifies the location at which the target will subsequently appear. For the remaining 20% of the trials, known as *invalid trials*, the target appears in the box opposite where the cue appeared. Thus, paying attention to the cue should aid the participant in performing the task. The essentials of this paradigm are shown in Figure 7.2.

Posner and colleagues reasoned that if attention works in a space-based manner, responses to valid cues should be faster than those to invalid cues. These researchers argued that once the cue appears, your attention (but not your eyes, which remain fixed on the cross) should move to the cued location because the cue predicts the location of the target with a high degree of accuracy. When a target appears in the same location (valid trials), you can respond quickly because your attention is already directed to that position in space. In contrast, if the target appears in the other location (invalid trials), your responses will be slower because your attention must be moved from the cued location to the target's position.

As we discuss in more detail later in this chapter, hemineglect provides powerful evidence for space-based allocation of attention. In this syndrome, individuals are unable to direct their attention to a particular region of space, namely the region contralateral to the damaged hemisphere. We also discuss how Posner's paradigm has been used to demonstrate deficits in space-based attention in such patients.

Recent research suggests that attention may be directed not only to certain locations, but also to certain objects. One experimental paradigm that demonstrates object-based attention is the negative

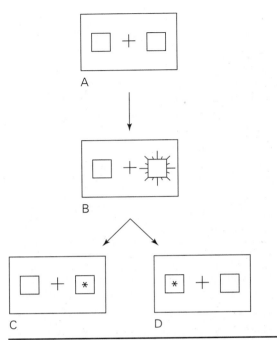

Figure 7.2 Posner's spatial attention paradigm.
(A) The individual is told to fixate on a central location (the cross) for the duration of the trial. (B) At some point a cue occurs, which is the brightening of a peripheral box. This cue predicts with a high degree of accuracy the location of the subsequent target. The target, to which the individual must respond, an asterisk, appears after a variable interval. Two types of trials are given: those in which the cue correctly predicts the location of the subsequent target, *valid trials* (C), and those in which the cue incorrectly predicts the location of the subsequent target, *invalid trials* (D). Responses to invalid trials take longer because the individual must move attention from the cued location to the location of the target.

priming paradigm (e.g., Neill, 1977; Tipper, 1985). In every trial in this paradigm, a person sees two overlapping figures, one that is red and one that is green. The individual must respond to the red item while ignoring the green one. The logic of the experiment is that if attention can be directed to one object, responses should be hindered when attention must be redirected to a previously unattended object, just as performance is impeded when attention must be redirected to a previously unattended location. In these experiments, two types of trials are compared: those in which the target was the unattended object in the previous trial (which requires a redirecting of attention) and those in which the target did not appear in the previous trial (which does not require a redirecting of attention). Slower responses are found to targets that were unattended in the prior trial, indicating a cost of redirecting attention to a previously ignored object. The results cannot be explained by space-based attention because all items appear in the same spatial location. The essentials of this paradigm are shown in Figure 7.3.

Later in this chapter, we discuss how studies of

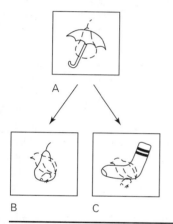

Figure 7.3 An example of the negative priming paradigm that demonstrates object-based attention.
In each trial, two items are superimposed but are distinguishable. (A) For example, one item might be presented in red (denoted by dark black lines) and the other in green (denoted by dotted lines). The individual must respond to the red item. The critical contrast occurs in the subsequent trial. (B) In some trials, such as this one, the item to which the individual must now respond is the item that was ignored in the prior trial (in this case, the pear). (C) In other cases, such as this one, the item to which the individual must respond was absent in the prior trial. Responses are slower in the former condition (B) than in the latter (C) because in (B) attention must be engaged to an item that was previously ignored, whereas in (C) no such redirection of attention is required because the item was not previously viewed.

individuals with hemineglect and other patients with neurological damage provide evidence that attention can be object based in certain situations. Whereas the patients described thus far ignore information in one half of space, these patients ignore one half of objects regardless of where the objects are located in space.

Issues in Resource-Based Models of Attention

Neuropsychological evidence suggests that distinct neural substrates may exist for some of the separate resources posited by multiple-resource theory. As we mentioned at the beginning of the chapter, Kahneman (1973) first suggested that attentional abilities could be partitioned like a pie (in this case a pizza pie) and that pieces of the pie, which were identical, would be gobbled up whenever a task required effort until no pieces were left. Elaborating upon this idea, multiple-resource theory suggested that a distinction may exist among resources (e.g., C. D. Wickens, 1980) much the way different pieces of a pizza pie can have different toppings (e.g., mushrooms vs. pepperoni vs. anchovies). Certain tasks would tap specific resources, whereas other tasks would tap different resources, much the way certain individuals eat just mushroom pizza, others eat only pepperoni pizza, and still others eat just anchovy pizza.

Some of the models that postulate multiple resources can be mapped, at least in part, to different neural substrates. C. D. Wickens (1980) has identified three dichotomous pools of resources: early vs. late processing, auditory vs. visual processing, and verbal vs. spatial processing. We already discussed the idea that sometimes attention can exert its influence early in processing (e.g., about 80 ms post-presentation), whereas other times it exerts its influence later (e.g., about 300 ms postpresentation). These two types of modulation appear to rely on different brain regions, because although attentional modulation early in processing is observed mainly over secondary sensory areas, that occurring later is observed more often over parietal and temporoparietal regions. Likewise, auditory and visual processing each rely on different regions of the brain. This distinction provides a framework for understanding why two visual streams of information are more likely to interfere with each other, whereas an auditory stream of information and a visual one yield much less interference. If the processing capacities of different brain regions are thought of as somewhat distinct pools of resources, then when all processing requires the same region, it will deplete resources to a greater degree than if the processing is spread across regions.

Researchers have also suggested that verbal and spatial processing may rely on different brain regions, namely the left and right hemispheres, respectively. To investigate this proposition, these researchers have used a **dual-task method,** in which the amount of interference that occurs when two tasks are performed simultaneously is determined relative to when each task is performed in isolation. If the two tasks compete for resources, interference should occur when both tasks are performed simultaneously. If they do not compete for resources, little decrement should be observed. Likewise, if each hemisphere has a distinct pool of resources, more interference should occur between two tasks that rely on the same hemisphere than between two tasks relying on opposite hemispheres (e.g., Friedman & Polson, 1981; Hellige & Cox, 1976; Polson & Friedman, 1988). To illustrate this idea and the way it is investigated by use of a dual-task method, we next discuss one experiment of this nature in depth.

To investigate whether the hemispheres have separate resources, we need to choose tasks for which we can reasonably estimate which hemisphere's resources will be required. One such task is the pronunciation of visually presented consonant-vowel-consonant (CVC) sequences (e.g., GEK). Although both hemispheres can recognize the letters that compose the CVC, only the left hemisphere can determine the correct sound that goes with each letter (phoneme-to-grapheme correspondence) so that the syllable can be pronounced (Rayman & Zaidel, 1991). Typically, these CVCs are presented by means of the divided visual field technique, in which information is directed initially to either the right hemisphere (left visual field [LVF] presenta-

tion) or the left hemisphere (right visual field [RVF] presentation). Subjects must also perform another task concurrently with the lateralized CVC task, such as keeping 4 CVCVCs (e.g., GOMIS) in memory that must be reported later. As with the CVC, making the letter-sound correspondence relies exclusively on left-hemisphere processes, hence this task should also tax the resources of the left more than those of the right.

If the hemispheres are separate modules, performance should be worse when the CVCs are presented in the RVF than when they are presented in the LVF. In all trials, the left hemisphere must remember the CVCVCs because only it can make the phoneme-to-grapheme correspondences. Hence, in RVF trials, the left hemisphere should have a large additional burden because it must also process the lateralized CVC. In contrast, in LVF trials, the right hemisphere should be able to ameliorate the load on the left hemisphere because it can identify the letters, even if the later stages of processing (e.g., phoneme-to-grapheme correspondences) must be performed by the left hemisphere. Researchers have found that relative to single-task conditions, a greater decrement in performance does occur when the memory task is combined with RVF trials than when it is paired with LVF trials, an indication that the hemispheres are, in part, separate pools of resources (Friedman, Polson, Dafoe, & Gaskill, 1982).

Studies such as these indicate that the hemispheres do have some distinct resources. However, these studies should not be overinterpreted to mean that the hemispheres are totally separate processors. After all, our hemispheres act as a unified system. Furthermore, research with patients with split-brain syndrome indicates that the hemispheres share some resources. If the hemispheres had totally separate resources, the performance of a task by one hemisphere of a patient with split-brain syndrome would be completely unaffected by the difficulty of a task being performed simultaneously by the other hemisphere. However, experiments indicate that the hemispheres of patients with split-brain syndrome share resources through subcortical commissures (see page 111, chapter 3) because one hemisphere's task performance is better when the opposite hemisphere is performing an easier task rather than a harder task (Holtzman & Gazzaniga, 1982).

Now that we have seen how neuropsychological data provide important insights into particular conceptualizations of attention, we turn to a discussion of the network of brain structures that is critical for the neural control of attention.

ATTENTIONAL CONTROL BY A CORTICAL NETWORK

Attention relies on complex interaction among many neural areas (e.g., D. L. LaBerge, 1990; Mesulam, 1981; Posner & Petersen, 1990). The six main brain areas that are conceptualized as forming the neural network controlling attention are depicted in Figure 7.4. These areas are distributed throughout the central nervous system and are the reticular activating system, whose cell bodies are located in the brain stem; the superior colliculus, which is located in the midbrain; the thalamus; and the anterior cingulate, the posterior parietal lobe,

and the frontal lobe, all of which are in the cortex. The nature of attentional control exerted by these areas varies from the basic, as in the case of the reticular activating system, to the much more sophisticated, as in the case of parietal and frontal regions.

Parts of the Network

Although attention is controlled by a network of brain structures and their functions interact and overlap, each brain region we discuss plays a more prominent role in certain attentional functions than in others. We next outline the prominent role of each structure in the attentional network.

Reticular Activating System

At the most basic level, the ability to pay attention requires the nervous system to be receptive to stimulation. The brain system responsible for alerting and arousal aspects of attention is the **reticular activating system (RAS).** Not surprisingly, this system is also responsible for controlling sleep-wake cycles.

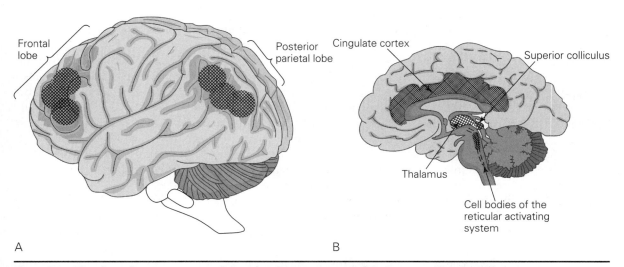

Figure 7.4 The six major components of the neural system responsible for controlling attention.
These six components are the reticular activating system, the superior colliculus, the pulvinar of the thalamus, the cingulate cortex, the posterior parietal lobe, and the frontal lobe. (A) Left hemisphere lateral view. (B) Midsagittal view of the right hemisphere.

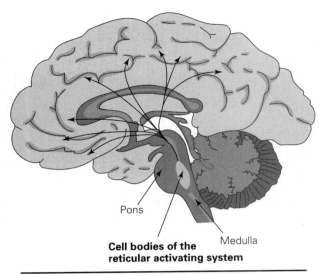

Pons

Medulla

**Cell bodies of the
reticular activating system**

Figure 7.5 The reticular activating system.
This system is the portion of the attentional network responsible for overall attention and arousal. The cell
bodies of the reticular activating system are located in
the medulla and the pons, but they project diffusely to
many areas of the cortex (arrows). Coma results from bilateral damage to this system.

The cell bodies of the RAS are located in the brain
stem and have diffuse connections to most regions
of the cortex (Figure 7.5). These diffuse connections are thought to enable the system to modulate
the alertness and wakefulness of the entire brain and
to keep the brain tonically aroused. To the degree
that this system keeps the brain in a constant attentive state, it is likely to contribute to sustained attention.

The RAS is so critical to alertness that damage
or disruption of it results in coma. Individuals in a
state of **coma** are seemingly unresponsive to most
external stimuli, lying with their eyes closed. In severe cases, they may not even exhibit defensive
movements to noxious or painful stimuli, although
in less severe cases they will do so. Coma occurs
either after bilateral lesions to the RAS or because
of diffuse problems that interfere with RAS functioning. In some instances, the causative factor affects the brain but not the body, as in the case of

meningitis, a tumor, hemorrhage, head trauma, or
seizures. In other instances, the causative factor affects other regions of the body as well, as in the
case of a metabolic disorder, an abnormal gas in the
blood (e.g., carbon monoxide), lack of a certain
vitamin (e.g., thiamine), or the presence of a toxin
(e.g., alcohol or heavy metals) (Weiner & Goetz,
1989).

Individuals who go into a coma may come out
of it with time, for example, after a metabolic disturbance is corrected or as time passes from an acute
brain trauma. Before returning to a regular state of
consciousness, an individual usually progresses to a
state of **stupor,** in which the individual can be
aroused when shaken vigorously or called by name
but cannot speak rationally and falls back into unconsciousness quickly. Generally, the longer that
someone is in a coma, the worse the long-term
prognosis. Sometimes the person never regains consciousness and enters a **chronic vegetative state,**
in which some RAS elements are intact, so self-
maintenance of certain basic bodily functions is possible (Plum & Posner, 1980). Patients in a chronic
vegetative state often regain some sort of sleep-wake
cycle, have control of autonomic and respiratory
functions, respond with primitive reflexes, and may
even follow people with their eyes. However, they
have no additional awareness of the outside world
or their internal needs, are unable to voluntarily
control movement, and have no ability to communicate. If their physical condition can be maintained
at an optimal level (e.g., nutrition by a feeding tube,
elimination by bladder management, peripheral cir-
culation by changes in body positioning, etc.), they
may survive for years (Gunderson, 1990).

In addition to tonic arousal, the RAS is important
for alerting the brain that it should get ready to
receive information or make a response. In fact, the
brain's electrical activity changes when it is in such
a preparatory state. Soon after an individual receives
a warning signal indicating that he or she will soon
receive a stimulus to which a response must be
made, a long, slow-going negative shift called the
contingent negative variation (CNV) starts to appear. This potential is thought to reflect higher levels of arousal as the brain, now in an expectant state,

anticipates the occurrence of a stimulus. The CNV can be decreased by depressant drugs (e.g., Tecce, Cole, Mayer, & Lewis, 1977) and enhanced by stimulants (e.g., Tecce & Cole, 1974), which suggests that it measures some general aspect of the brain's arousal and alerting capacity. Investigators have hypothesized that the CNV reflects activity of the RAS, which then activates the rest of the cortex, including prefrontal and posterior regions (e.g., Donchin, 1984).

Superior Colliculus

Paying attention requires more than simply being alert and awake; we must also have a means of directing our attention. If we are to flexibly allocate attention, we must be able to move it from one position or object to another. The midbrain structure that has been implicated in this process, at least for visual stimuli, is the **superior colliculus** (Figure 7.6).

The superior colliculus aids in shifting attention to new locations or objects by controlling eye movements responsible for bringing peripheral stimuli quickly into foveal vision. Although our focus of attention need not be the same place as our eyes, the position of our eyes often follows our focus of attention. The process of bringing a peripheral item or location into central vision is accomplished by a **saccade,** an eye movement in which the eyes, rather than moving smoothly across space, jump from one position to the next with no processing of the intervening visual information. Saccades come in two varieties: express saccades and regular saccades. *Express saccades,* which are fast and require about 120 ms, tend to be reflexive and are triggered by the appearance of a novel visual stimulus in the periphery. In contrast, *regular saccades* are under voluntary control and take longer, about 200 to 300 ms (Schiller, Sandell, & Maunsell, 1987). Research with monkeys indicates that the superior colliculus plays a special role in express saccades because when this structure is damaged, such saccades are extinguished. In contrast, damage to the superior colliculus does not influence regular saccades, which are instead disrupted by damage to the frontal eye fields, a region of the frontal lobe implicated in the control of eye movements (see page 145, chapter 4) (Guitton, Buchtel, & Douglas, 1985). From an anatomical perspective, the superior colliculus is well situated for controlling reflexive eye movements because regions of the superior colliculus that receive sensory and motor information are tightly coupled to the oculomotor regions of the brain stem that are the final common pathway for control of eye movements (R. H. Wurtz & Goldberg, 1972).

The role of the superior colliculus in attention in humans has been aided by the study of individuals with supranuclear palsy, which is characterized by degeneration of parts of the basal ganglia as well as specific degeneration of the superior colliculus. Insights into the contribution of the superior colliculus in attentional control can be gained both by observing the behavior of these patients in their daily interactions and through experimental manipulations. In everyday life, these individuals often behave as if blind. As noted by some researchers, "They often fail to turn towards those who approach them, to maintain eye contact during conversation, or to look at their plates when eating, even though they may still be able to do so on command" (R. D. Rafal et al., 1988, p. 268). In the laboratory, researchers have demonstrated that these patients have a specific problem in being able to move their attention from one point in space to another. We revisit these difficulties later in the chapter when we discuss a specific neural model of visual attention (i.e., Posner, Inhoff, Friedrich, & Cohen, 1987). Before we leave our discussion of the superior colliculus, it is important to note that the inferior colliculus is believed to play a similar role in attention for information in the auditory modality.

Pulvinar of the Thalamus

Now that we identified the brain structures that keep us alert and awake and allow our attention to be attracted reflexively, we need to discuss the **pulvinar,** a nucleus of the thalamus that plays an important role in selective attention (Figure 7.7). Experts have suggested that this brain region helps to filter specific information for further processing

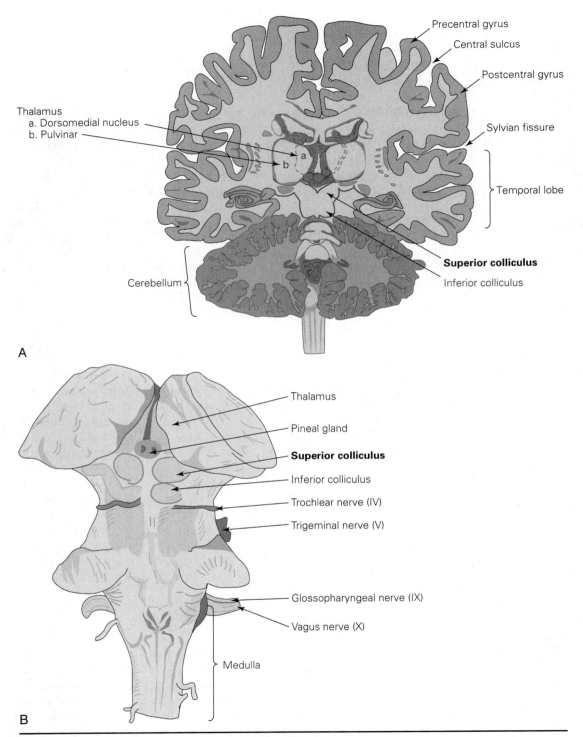

A

B

Figure 7.6   The superior colliculus.
This structure, located in the midbrain, is responsible for moving attention to particular points in space. (A) Coronal view. (B) View from above with the overlying cortex removed.

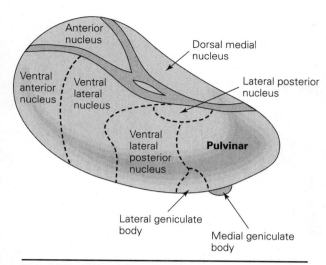

Figure 7.7 The pulvinar of the thalamus.
This brain structure is responsible for filtering incoming sensory information and for engaging attention at particular points in space. (*Note*. Adapted from Kolb & Whishaw, 1990, p. 26.)

from among the barrage that constantly impinges upon our sensory systems. In chapter 1, we mentioned that the thalamus can be considered to reside at a crossroads in the brain because information from almost all sensory receptors is relayed to the brain through the thalamus. As such, the thalamus would seem a logical candidate to play a role in attention because if a place exists in the brain where sensory information is to be gated or modulated, the thalamus is well positioned to do so.

Evidence that the thalamus plays a role in attention is provided by positron emission tomography (PET) studies in humans (e.g., D. LaBerge & Buchsbaum, 1990). In one experiment, individuals viewed displays confined to one visual field, so that the information was received exclusively by the contralateral thalamus (remember that past the optic chiasm all information in one visual field projects contralaterally; see page 33 in chapter 1). The participant's task was to decide whether the visual display contained an *O*. The critical contrast was between two conditions in which the *O* appeared. In one, the *O* was surrounded by eight other letters, which meant that attention was required to detect

the *O* because it had to be filtered out from the extraneous letters around it. In the other condition, no filtering of information (and hence little control of attention) was required to detect the *O* because it appeared alone. Activity was greater in the pulvinar contralateral to the *O* when the *O* was surrounded by other letters than when it was not, a finding consistent with the idea that the pulvinar plays a role in selective attention.

These results, however, are not sufficient to *prove* a gating role for the thalamus. The thalamus could be more active when the *O* is surrounded by other letters just because this display is more visually complex than when the *O* appears alone. One way to differentiate these possibilities is to compare activity in primary visual areas during both conditions as well. If the extra activity in the pulvinar when the *O* is surrounded by other letters is due to greater visual complexity, a similar difference in activity between the two conditions should be observed over primary visual areas as well. However, the increase in activity for the surrounded *O* as compared with the lone *O* was observed only for the pulvinar, not for primary visual cortex. This finding suggests that the filtering aspect of the task, rather than its visual complexity, was activating the pulvinar.

The study of individuals with damage to the thalamus also provides evidence that this structure plays a role in attentional functioning. Earlier in the chapter, we discussed the idea that directing attention to a particular region in space allows information at this location to be processed more effectively. Patients who have sustained damage to the thalamus have difficulty engaging their attention to particular places in space (R. Rafal & Posner, 1987). Thus, they cannot attend to one location and use that as a means to filter out information at other locations. We also revisit this issue later in the chapter in conjunction with our discussion of a model of visual selective attention (i.e., Posner, Inhoff, Friedrich, & Cohen, 1987).

Cingulate Cortex

Thus far, we discussed how the brain becomes alert and aroused, how it orients toward previously non-

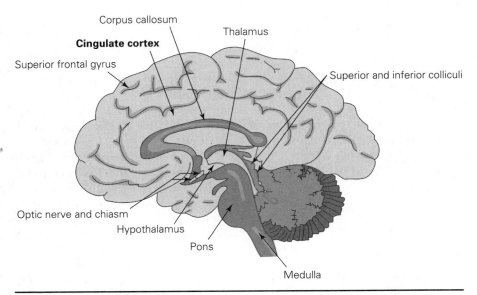

Figure 7.8 The cingulate cortex.
This structure is important for imparting emotional significance to information that has captured attention and is involved when attention must be used to override automatic motor responses.

attended information, and how it filters the vast amounts of information received by our nervous system. Once the brain has accomplished all these processes, another useful process would be for the attentional network to integrate such information with emotion and to help select a response. The region of the brain that is responsible for doing so is the **cingulate cortex,** which can be thought of as an interface between subcortical and cortical regions (Figure 7.8).

Think for a moment about what needs to happen *after* your superior colliculus causes eye movements to a large fast-moving object in your periphery. For instance, imagine standing in the middle of the street outside your favorite campus coffee shop, when suddenly your attention is drawn to a fast-moving object in your periphery. As you begin to foveate on the object, you recognize it as a car. Now you must process the emotional significance of that object and initiate an action. At this point, the cingulate cortex comes into play. It imparts the emotional information appropriate to this situation

(e.g., Oh my God, I'm about to get run over!!!!!!!) and aids in the motor response of getting the [expletive deleted] out of the middle of the street. (Good thing that you had that extra cup of Mocha Java!)

Although little research on humans directly implicates the cingulate cortex with imparting emotional significance during attentional processing, monkeys with unilateral lesions of the cingulate cortex demonstrate hemineglect (Watson, Heilman, Cauthen, & King, 1973). Anatomically, this structure is considered well positioned to link emotional and sensory information because it connects subcortical regions important for modulating the internal state of the animal (with regard to such things as hunger, thirst, fear, and so forth) with cortical areas that are important for processing sensory information from the outside world.

The role of the anterior part of the cingulate cortex may be particularly important in the selection of appropriate responses. You may remember that in chapter 4 we discussed a PET study in which the anterior cingulate cortex was found to be particularly active when a new or novel response had to be emitted (e.g., responding "L" to "A" and "M" to "B" rather than responding "B" to "A" and "M" to "L") (Paus, Petrides, Evans, & Meyer, 1993). This task requires attentional control over response selection because the person must effortfully inhibit a typical automatic response to produce the correct response. Another case in which a fair amount of control must be exerted to inhibit an automatic, but incorrect, response involves the use of the conflicting condition of the Stroop task. In this condition, a person must name the color of ink in which a word is printed (e.g., "blue") when the word itself spells a conflicting color name (e.g., red). Because reading is so automatic, the individual usually wants to say the name of the word (e.g., "red") and must use attention to suppress this response and produce the correct one (e.g., "blue"). Under such conditions, increased activity, as measured by PET, occurs in the anterior cingulate cortex (Pardo, Pardo, Janer, & Raichle, 1990).

Cingulate activity during PET scans is also observed when a response must be selected from an array of possibilities or when the selection of an appropriate response is somewhat complicated. For example, cingulate activity is observed when a person is given a noun (e.g., *wood*) and must choose one word, from a large set of possible words, that would go with it (e.g., *hammer*) (Petersen et al., 1988). Greater cingulate activity is also found when the determination of a response is complicated because it relies on multiple attributes of a stimulus rather than a single one. For example, greater cingulate activity is observed when people must decide whether two complex displays, presented in quick succession, differ with regard to any one of three attributes—color, speed, or shape—than when they are told exactly which one attribute (e.g., color) they should use to make their decision (Corbetta et al., 1991).

Parietal Lobe

The parietal lobe is important for spatial aspects of attention and the allocation of attentional resources to a particular stimulus or task (Figure 7.9). Evi-

dence for a role of the posterior parietal lobe in visual selective attention comes from single-cell recordings in monkeys. The firing rate of cells in this region is enhanced anytime attention is directed to a visual object. Furthermore, this increase cannot be attributed to motor actions toward a stimulus because it is independent of eye or arm movements to the stimulus (e.g., R. H. Wurtz & Goldberg, 1989).

We know that the parietal region makes an important contribution to spatial aspects of attentional functioning in humans because lesions in this area of the brain are most likely to cause hemineglect (Vallar & Perani, 1986). Intuitively, the idea that damage to the parietal lobe would lead to such a syndrome makes sense because, as we learned in chapter 6, parietal regions are specialized for processing spatial relations.

Parietal regions have also been implicated in the allocation of attentional resources to a particular task or stimulus because the amplitude of the P_{300}, which occurs only when an individual must attend to specific information (e.g., an oddball "boop" in a series of "beeps"), is typically largest over parietal regions. Although investigators have extensively discussed exactly what the P_{300} measures (e.g., Donchin & Coles, 1988) and associated commentaries, one hypothesis is that the amplitude of the P_{300} measures the degree of attentional resources that an individual voluntarily allocates to a particular stimulus or task. For example, in dual-task situations, subjects may give the same amount of attention to both tasks (50% to Task A, 50% to Task B) or may divide their attention unequally (e.g., 80% to Task A, 20% to Task B or 20% to Task A, 80% to Task B). The greater the amount of attention that a subject voluntarily allocates to a given task in a dual-task situation, the greater the P_{300} to that task. So, for example, when an individual concentrates on Task A with 80% of her or his effort and on Task B with only 20%, a larger P_{300} is elicited from Task A than from Task B (A. F. Kramer, Wickens, & Donchin, 1985).

Although, as we discussed in chapter 2, a large response recorded by an electrode positioned at a particular region of the scalp does not necessarily

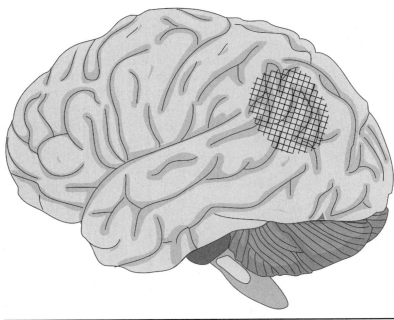

Figure 7.9 The parietal lobe.
This structure, especially the posterior portion, may play a role in attention. It provides a spatial map of the world so that attention can be directed to particular regions of space and may also contribute to the allocation of attentional resources.

imply that the electrical activity is being generated in the cortex directly below, converging evidence suggests that the parietal lobe plays an important role in the generation of the P_{300}. When patients have a lesion at the temporoparietal junction, no P_{300} is observed, whereas it can be observed in patients with lesions in other locations, such as in the frontal lobe (R. T. Knight, Scabini, Woods, & Clayworth, 1989).

Frontal Lobe

Frontal regions appear to be important for the selection of particular motor responses and for recruiting attentional resources in service of a goal or a plan (Figure 7.10). In monkeys, unilateral damage to the dorsolateral frontal area causes a hemispatial hypokinesia in which the animals fail to move the limbs contralateral to the lesion (Watson, Miller, &

Heilman, 1978). So, for example, after right-hemisphere damage, little movement of the left limbs occurs. Such a deficit appears to be the motor equivalent of the sensory neglect observed after parietal lobe damage. In humans, frontal damage can cause a directional hypokinesia in which extra time is required to initiate movements in the direction contralateral to the lesion (e.g., leftward movements in individuals with right-hemisphere lesions) (K. M. Heilman et al., 1985). Neglect can also be observed after frontal lesions (e.g., A. R. Damasio, Damasio, & Chui, 1980) and tends to exhibit itself more as an inability to make motor movements toward the neglected side of space, rather than a neglect of sensory information, as is typically observed after parietal lobe damage (e.g., Bisiach et al., 1990).

Another frontal function related to motor aspects of attention is the voluntary control of eye move-

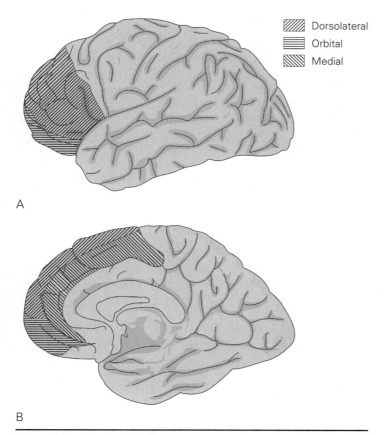

Dorsolateral
Orbital
Medial

A

B

Figure 7.10 The frontal lobe.
Frontal regions play numerous roles in attention. They are important
for selecting particular motor programs, for inhibiting reflexive eye
movements, and for responding to particularly novel information. (A)
Lateral view of the left hemisphere. (B) Midsagittal view of the right
hemisphere. (*Note.* Adapted from McCarthy & Warrington, 1990, p.
357.)

ments and the inhibition of reflexive eye movements. As we discussed earlier in the chapter, the
direction of attention to a particular region is usually
accompanied by the movement of gaze to the same
location. You may remember from chapter 4 that
portions of the frontal region, the frontal eye fields,
are important for volitionally directing the eyes to
a particular point in space and that the orbital and
medial regions, but not the dorsolateral regions,
of the frontal lobe are important for inhibiting or
overriding the reflexive eye movements that are controlled by the superior colliculus (Paus et al., 1991).
The need for such an inhibitory control mechanism
becomes obvious if you consider how difficult maintaining your attention on a location would be without it. Every time a novel object occurred in the
periphery, your gaze would be directed toward it.
For example, your attention would be drawn away
from the road in front of you every time a car on
the other side of the median passed you!

Not only do frontal regions contribute to the
motoric aspects of attentional processing, but they

also appear to be important when a novel stimulus captures attention. As mentioned earlier, an oddball stimulus that must be attended causes a P_{300} that is maximal over parietal regions (this P_{300} is sometimes referred to as the P_{3b}). A similar component known as the P_{3a}, occurs 20 to 50 ms earlier and is maximal at frontocentral leads when a novel or an unexpected stimulus captures attention. For example, the P_{3b} is elicited if an individual must count or attend to the rare boops interspersed within a series of frequent beeps. If a totally unexpected or novel item, such as a dog bark, is inserted into the series of beeps and boops, a P_{3a} is elicited (R. T. Knight, 1991). We can be relatively certain that frontal regions of the brain contribute to the generation of this potential because the P_{3a} decreases in amplitude after lesions to prefrontal cortex are sustained. However, frontal regions are not the sole source of the P_{3a} because its amplitude is also reduced after damage to temporoparietal regions (Yamaguchi & Knight, 1991).

Models of Attentional Control by a Cortical Network

As we emphasized from the beginning of the chapter, attention is a function that relies on multiple brain regions, not just one. Therefore, we need a model that will help to integrate the role of the specific brain regions just discussed. To provide a flavor for how attention might be coordinated among brain regions, in this section, we briefly discuss two classes of models of attention, one that examines how attention in general might be controlled by disparate brain regions and one that proposes a brain network for a specific aspect of attention, that required when information is selected in the visual modality.

A General Model of Attentional Control

One prominent model of attention, proposed by Mesulam (1981), views directed attention as being controlled by a diffuse cortical network that is simultaneously specialized and redundant. In this model, each region in the network has some specialization

because the role it plays is not exactly like that of any other, yet this specialization is not absolute because lesions to different areas of the network can have similar effects. Thus, this model takes neither a strict localizationist approach nor one of mass action (see page 52 in chapter 2 regarding debates about these two positions).

According to this model, each of four major brain regions plays a prominent, but not necessarily exclusive, role in controlling a certain aspect of attention. The main role of the RAS is to maintain vigilance and arousal; the main role of the cingulate cortex is to impart motivational significance to information; the main role of the posterior parietal region is to provide a sensory map of the world; and the main role of frontal regions is to provide the motor programs for moving our attentional focus around the world by exploring, scanning, reaching, and fixating.

Because this model views attention as being supported by an interconnected neural network, it has three important implications regarding the relationship between the brain and behavior. First, it implies that even though a lesion is confined to a single brain region, the lesion will affect not only attentional behaviors, but other behaviors as well. For example, although frontal regions are part of the attentional network, they also are involved in executive functions. Second, the same complex function can be impaired as a result of a variety of lesions in different locations. For example, as we discuss in more detail shortly, hemineglect has been reported after lesions to many different regions of the brain. Third, the most severe disruption of a complex function will be observed after damage to more than one region that is involved in the network. For example, neglect would be expected to be more severe if damage occurred to both frontal and parietal regions rather than just parietal regions.

More than 10 years after Mesulam originally formulated his model, PET studies provided strong support for his idea that attention is controlled by the coactivation of a network of brain regions and that the composition of the network varies depending on the nature of attentional control. These studies were those discussed earlier in the chapter in which participants decided whether two successive displays with multiple perceptual attributes were different. In the selective-attention condition, individuals were told to base their decision on one of the attributes (e.g., color) and to ignore the others (e.g., speed and shape). In contrast, in the divided-attention condition, individuals had to divide their attention across all three attributes—color, speed, and shape—to determine whether the displays differed with regard to any of these attributes (Corbetta et al., 1991).

Under both conditions, a large set of neuronal structures was activated, and for both, activity in visual areas increased. However, each attentional condition (i.e., divided vs. selective) also activated a unique set of brain structures. In the divided-attention condition, but not the selective-attention condition, activity was noted over the anterior cingulate cortex and the right prefrontal cortex. In contrast, in the selective-attention condition but not the divided-attention condition, activity increased over a set of structures including the caudate, the globus pallidus, the insular cortex (i.e., the cortex around the Sylvian fissure), the lateral orbitofrontal cortex, and the premotor cortex. Furthermore, the brain regions activated in the selective-attention condition varied depending on the visual attribute to which the participant was paying attention. When the person was attending to shape (but not color or speed), greater activation was found in areas that are part of the ventral processing stream, including the fusiform and parahippocampal gyri, the superior temporal sulcus, and areas bordering the juncture of the parietal, occipital, and temporal lobes. When the person was attending to speed, activation was greatest in an area that is part of the dorsal processing stream, the inferior parietal lobe. When the person was attending to color, ventral visual regions that are sensitive to color, such as those of the occipitotemporal junction and the dorsolateral occipital cortex, were most active.

We can conclude from this study that attention can modulate activity in a range of brain structures. Furthermore, exactly which brain areas are affected depends on the task demands. When selective attention must be paid to a particular attribute (e.g., color), activity in the secondary sensory regions most sensitive to that perceptual attribute are enhanced. Furthermore, the nature of attentional control, either divided or selective, also influences which brain regions become active. Different types of attentional control appear to activate unique networks of brain structures.

Specific Model for Visual Selective Attention

A different type of model has been proposed for the control of visual selective attention. In this model, each neural structure has a unique function, providing the machinery for only one component of the total number of operations involved in the attentional selection of a particular visual location (e.g., Posner, Inhoff, Friedrich, & Cohen, 1987). The model task used to explore the nature of visual selective attention was also discussed earlier in this chapter (see Figure 7.2). As a brief reminder, in this task an individual fixates on a central point in a display that also contains two laterally displaced boxes. In every trial, one of the two boxes brightens, which acts as a cue for the subsequent target, an asterisk that appears within one of the boxes. The cue provides important information because in most trials the cue indicates the location at which the target will subsequently appear (valid trials). In the remainder of the trials, the cue appears in the box opposite where the target will subsequently appear (invalid trials).

On the basis of work with neurologically intact individuals, Posner theorized that changing attention from one spatial location to another relies on three component operations. First, the individual must *disengage* attention from the spot at which it is currently engaged. Second, the individual must *move* attention to a new location, and third, the individual must *engage* attention at the new location. This three-step model can account for faster reaction times to valid trials than to invalid trials in the following manner. On valid trials, attention is engaged at the location of the cue so that when the target appears in the same location, no disengagement, movement, or reengagement of attention is required. In contrast, on invalid trials, attention must be disengaged from the location of the cue, moved to the opposite visual field, and then engaged to the location of the target, all of which take time.

Posner further hypothesized that there is a unique brain region responsible for each of the three component operations: the *disengage* operation is performed by parietal areas, the *move* operation is performed by the superior colliculus, and the *engage* operation is performed by the thalamus. Support for such a contention has been provided by studies of patients with circumscribed lesions who are asked to perform the visual-attention task just described. Patients with parietal lobe damage show a different pattern of deficits than that of patients with damage to the superior colliculus, who in turn exhibit a different pattern than that of patients with thalamic damage.

Individuals with unilateral parietal lobe damage are exceedingly slow to respond when they are given a cue in the nonneglected field and must disengage from that cue to respond to a target in the neglected field. These difficulties can be shown to be specifically related to the disengage function and not to engaging attention to the target in the neglected field. Attention can be engaged, even to a target in the neglected field, as demonstrated by the essentially normal responses of these patients when both the cue and the target appear in the neglected field. Thus, Posner argues that poor performance on the invalid trails indicates a deficit in being able to disengage attention from a location in the nonneglected field (Posner, Walker, Friedrich, & Rafal, 1984).

The attribution of difficulty to a disengage operation in the nonneglected field (rather than an engage operation in the neglected field) is consistent with clinical observations in cases of hemineglect. In hemineglect, the lack of a response to the item contralateral to the lesioned hemisphere is most often observed when items are present on both sides of the midline. In contrast, neglect is not as likely to occur when a single item appears in the neglected field, presumably because there is no information in the nonneglected field from which attention must be disengaged. An interesting demonstration of this phenomenon was provided by a study in which pa-

tients with unilateral neglect performed two versions of a cancellation task often used to assess hemineglect (Mark, Kooistra, & Heilman, 1988). In this task, a person must "cancel" lines that are randomly distributed across the page. In one version, individuals canceled the targets on a dry-erase board by writing over them in a darker color ink. In this way, the lines remained even after they were canceled. In the second version, individuals were given an eraser and canceled the lines by erasing them. The neglect for left-side stimuli was less severe in the second condition than in the first. Because cancellation of the lines by erasure decreased the number of items in right hemispace, attention needed to be disengaged from fewer items and hence the neglect was less severe.

Patients with collicular damage from supranuclear palsy have a different pattern of attentional disruption, exhibiting deficits in the *move* function. One peculiarity of this disease is that it affects vertical movements of gaze more than horizontal movements. Hence, if the colliculus is important for moving attention (with which gaze is often coupled), we could expect greater deficits for vertical shifts of attention than for horizontal shifts. Indeed, these patients exhibit little facilitation from a valid cue (which predicts the location of the subsequent target) when attention must be moved in the vertical dimension, but they show relatively normal facilitation for horizontal movements. Remember that when a cue in presented, individuals must move their attention from the fixation cross to the cued location. If attention has already been moved to the cued location by the time the target appears, responses should be facilitated. However, if the movement of attention is slow, it will not reach the position of the cue before the target appears there. For horizontal shifts of attention, a 50-ms interval between the cue and the target was enough time to speed responses. In contrast, for vertical movements, a delay of approximately 350 ms between cue and target was required before the cue provided any facilitation of responses, an indication that the individuals with supranuclear palsy were slow in moving their attention vertically (R. D. Rafal et al., 1988).

Patients with thalamic damage exhibit a third pattern of attentional disruption; they have difficulty with the *engage* operation. Anytime a target appears contralateral to the lesioned hemisphere, regardless of whether the cue is valid or invalid, their response to the target is delayed. Such findings suggest that these patients have difficulty engaging attention in the field contralateral to the lesion. The deficit appears to be attributable specifically to thalamic damage because it occurs even in the absence of visual problems, such as blind spots and neglect, which might make detection of items in the contralateral field difficult (R. Rafal & Posner, 1987).

This system that we just discussed, which controls the allocation of spatial attention, is often referred to as the *posterior attentional network*. Posner also hypothesized the existence of another attentional network, the *anterior attentional network,* which consists of the anterior cingulate and midline frontal regions. He postulated that this network is important for "locking onto" or selecting a target, especially with regard to its meaning (e.g., Posner, 1992). The anterior attentional network becomes active when, for example, an individual must monitor a list of words for targets that have specific meanings (e.g., animal names). As the number of targets in the list increases, so does activation of the anterior cingulate cortex (Posner, Petersen, Fox, & Raichle, 1988). Furthermore, the anterior and posterior networks are conceptualized to be mainly independent but somewhat overlapping systems. For example, listening to a story, which would rely on the anterior system, slows the ability to simultaneously shift attention to a cued visual location, which would rely on the posterior system (e.g., Posner, Sandson, Dhawan, & Shulman, 1989).

Comparison of the Two Models

You may have noticed that Mesulam's and Posner's models conceptualize the relationship between attention and the underlying neural tissue that supports it somewhat differently. In Posner's model, the brain structures controlling attention do not have overlapping functions. Instead, each operation (engage, disengage, move) is thought to be con-

trolled by a different area of the brain (the thalamus, the parietal regions, and the superior colliculus, respectively). This network can be considered a cortical network for two reasons. First, selective visual attention requires all these operations to occur, and second, the operations occur in physically distinct regions of the brain. However, in Mesulam's model, functions are not localized as specifically and the control of attention is more diffusely organized. Each model informs us about brain-behavior relationships and provides a heuristic as to the way attention may be implemented in human neural tissue, albeit from different perspectives.

HEMINEGLECT: CLINICAL FEATURES

Now that we discussed the different brain regions that contribute to attentional control and the ways in which they may interact, we turn our attention to one of the most prominent syndromes in which attentional dysfunction occurs: hemineglect. In this section of the chapter, we describe the clinical features of neglect and save for the next section a discussion of how the implications of this syndrome affect our understanding of the neuropsychology of attention.

Description of Hemineglect

As mentioned previously, hemineglect, sometimes referred to as hemi-inattention, is a syndrome in which an individual ignores or does not pay attention to the side of space contralateral to the lesion. The side of space ignored is usually defined with reference to body midline, but as we discuss later, may occur with regard to other spatial reference frames as well (e.g., information to the left of the head's midline when the head is not a body midline). This inattention is seen regardless of the modality in which information is presented. Depending on the severity of hemineglect, individuals may not eat food on the left side of the plate, draw the left side of objects, read the left side of words, use the left side of the body, and, as we discussed in chapter 6, in severe cases they may even deny that the left side of the body belongs to them.

Two case studies illustrate the severity of neglect of the body and its sometimes bizarre consequences. In one case study, a patient with hemineglect pushed a call button for assistance and with great agitation told the nurse that he thought one of the staff had played an extremely cruel and inappropriate joke on him by placing a severed leg in his bed. However, when he attempted to throw the offensive leg out of bed, he managed only to hurl himself onto the floor because he was attempting to throw his own leg out of bed (Sacks, 1985).

Sometimes patients with hemineglect not only deny ownership of a limb, but even claim that the limb belongs to someone else. Despite this strange belief, the rest of the patient's reasoning is normal. This syndrome, although rare, has been recognized since the late 1800s and is called **somatoparaphrenia.** Rode and colleagues (1992) described one patient with this condition, a 69-year-old woman who had sustained a right-hemisphere stroke in the territory of the middle cerebral artery 6 months earlier:

> She repeatedly affirmed that her left upper limb was not hers but the examiner's. When the examiner brought the patient's left arm in her good visual field and asked whose it was she answered: "It's not mine. I found it in the bathroom, when I fell [during her stroke she fell in the bathroom]. It's not mine because it's too heavy; it should be yours. It can move and do everything; when I feel it too heavy, I put it on my stomach. It doesn't hurt me, it's kind." When asked where her own arm was, she answered: "Behind the door." (p. 204)

Neglect is usually observed when damage occurs to the supramarginal gyrus of the parietal region and extends to include subcortical areas (e.g., Vallar & Perani, 1986). The cause is typically vascular damage (K. M. Heilman, Watson, & Valenstein, 1985). Because neglect is observed more commonly and is more severe after right- than left-hemisphere lesions (e.g., M. L. Albert, 1973; Ogden, 1985), left neglect is more common than right neglect. Although more often observed after damage to the right parietal lobe, neglect can also be observed after damage to frontal regions (e.g., K. M. Heilman & Valenstein, 1972), the basal ganglia (e.g., A. R. Damasio,

Damasio, & Chui, 1980), and the thalamus (e.g., Watson, Valenstein, & Heilman, 1981). The degree of neglect is usually severe at first; all items on the neglected side of space are ignored. However, within weeks to months, this profound neglect usually dissipates so that some information on the neglected side is processed, although the neglect rarely, if ever, disappears completely (K. M. Heilman, Watson, & Valenstein, 1985). The residual deficit is usually most prominent when there is competing information on both sides of space. To test for residual deficits, neurologists and neuropsychologists often use the **double simultaneous stimulation technique,** in which the patient is confronted with two similar items simultaneously, one on each side of space, and is asked how many items have been presented (i.e., one or two). Testing is done separately in the visual, auditory, and tactile modalities. Typically, under double simultaneous stimulation, the patient will say that he or she sees, hears, or feels only a single item, ignoring the item on the neglected side. However, if the same item is presented singly on the neglected side of space, the patient will respond correctly.

Hemineglect Is an Attentional Syndrome

So far we presented the neglect syndrome as a deficit in attentional processing, but we did not discuss the evidence to support such an assertion. In this section, we examine two lines of evidence for this viewpoint. First, we discuss findings that demonstrate that neglect cannot be attributed to deficits in sensory processing. Then, we discuss evidence revealing that neglect can be moderated by attentional factors.

No Sensory Explanation for Neglect

To evaluate the possibility that neglect could merely result from deficits in sensory processing, let us reconsider the story that appeared at the beginning of the chapter. One of the first explanations for the gentleman's strange behavior that may have popped into your mind was that he had sustained right-hemisphere damage that precluded him from receiving sensory information from the left side of space and interfered with motor control on the left side of his body. However, is this explanation plausible? Probably not, when you consider that the gentleman could perform motor acts competently, as evidenced by his ability to shave, shower, dress, and eat. Despite such competence, motor acts appeared to be directed mainly to the right side of his body. Furthermore, when his attention was drawn to the neglected side (by a loud noise), his performance improved. Thus, the motor acts themselves were probably not disrupted. Rather, the mechanisms for directing these acts to the left side of body appeared to be impaired.

Is it possible that a sensory deficit in the visual modality could explain his behavior? You might hypothesize that he had dense hemianopsia of the LVF because, as we learned in chapter 1, that would preclude him from receiving all visual information situated to the left of fixation. Although such a prominent deficit in visual processing would account for an inability to process information to the left of fixation, it cannot account for a lack of processing to the left of body midline. In cases of hemianopsia, patients can process visual information from the left side of space by simply moving their gaze so that the center of fixation falls at a point to the far left side of space.

For a fuller appreciation of this point, look at Figure 7.11A. Assume that you have left hemianopsia and are sitting at the center of the table. Previously, you lit a candle and placed it on the left side of the table. Now you want to make sure that it is not dripping wax. If your gaze is fixed straight ahead, you will be unable to see the candle and all information to the left of body midline. However, if you simply turn your head so that your eyes are now fixated on the left edge of the table, as shown in Figure 7.11B, you will still be unable to see all information to the left of fixation, but you will be able to see the candle because it now falls entirely within your RVF. Thus, even though the candle remains to the left of body midline, it can be perceived simply because the point of visual fixation has changed.

Hence, even if the gentleman discussed at the beginning of the chapter had hemianopsia, turning

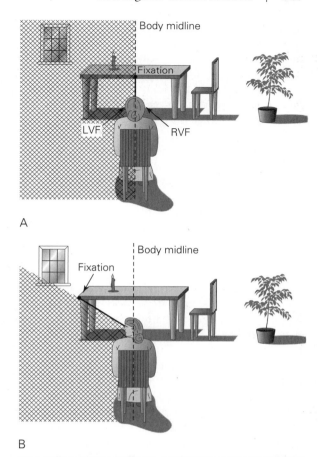

Figure 7.11 The influence of head position on the information that falls in each visual field.
(A) When someone is looking straight ahead, information to the left of body midline falls in the left visual field (LVF) and information to the right of body midline falls in the right visual field (RVF). If the individual has hemianopsia for the LVF (gray crosshatching), the candle in this picture will not be visible. (B) However, the individual can view the candle by simply turning her head so that the candle now falls within the good visual field, the RVF. Although patients with hemineglect who simultaneously have visual field defects could use such a strategy, they do not because they ignore the left side of space.

his head or diverting his gaze to the left side of space would have enabled him to see things positioned there. One of the reasons it is important to demonstrate that visual deficits cannot account for hemineglect is that the lesion that causes hemineglect often extends into the occipital lobe, leading to cuts or scotomas (i.e., blind spots) in the visual field. Hence, there may be regions of space for which the patient with hemineglect is functionally blind. Nonetheless, even when such visual cuts are present, they cannot fully explain the hemineglect.

Our analysis of the gentleman's deficits so far should make you skeptical that hemineglect can be explained by sensory loss in the visual modality. However, individuals with hemineglect might be relatively insensitive to *all* sensory material that is received by the damaged hemisphere. This hypothesis might be plausible because posterior regions of the brain are important for sensory processing and hemineglect is observed after damage to posterior parietal regions. However, we now entertain this hypothesis just long enough to disprove it!

If this hypothesis were true, we should observe that the severity of neglect varies with the degree to which information in a given modality is exclusively processed by a single hemisphere. For the purposes of this discussion, let us assume that the person is ignoring information on the left as the result of a right-hemisphere lesion. Because visual and somatosensory information from the left is received exclusively by the right hemisphere, the hypothesis would predict that little visual and somatosensory information would be processed from the left, whereas processing of that same type of material from the right would be normal. Inattention to material on the left would be less severe in the auditory modality because some information from the left ear projects ipsilaterally to the intact left hemisphere. Concomitantly, some neglect of auditory information on the right might be found because the right hemisphere would be unable to proficiently process information from the right ear that is received through ipsilateral pathways. Finally, because the left nostril projects to the left hemisphere and the right nostril to the right hemisphere, no neglect should be observed for smells on the left,

but neglect should be evident for smells on the right. In sum, if the neglect resulted from an inability of the right hemisphere to process sensory information, it should be exhibited by an extreme insensitivity to visual information in the LVF and tactile information from the left side of the body, less extreme neglect for auditory information on the left side of space, and no neglect for olfactory information on the left side of space. However, such variations in the degree of neglect across modalities are not observed in cases of hemineglect. Instead, information from the contralateral side of space is generally ignored, regardless of whether it is presented in the visual, tactile, auditory, or olfactory modality. Thus, the evidence we reviewed illustrates that neglect does not appear to have a sensory basis.

Moderation of Neglect by Attentional Factors

Now that we know that hemineglect is not the result of sensory malfunction or damage, we examine some research that suggests it is specifically a disruption in attentional processing. Let's return to the scenario at the beginning of this chapter. One odd aspect of the gentleman's behavior was that information on the left side of space that was seemingly ignored on some occasions was not ignored on others. So, although he initially ignored his hash browns and bacon, he eventually ate them, but only after his *attention* had been drawn leftward by the ruckus produced by crashing dishes. Furthermore, even though his attention was drawn leftward by an auditory event, all information on that side of space, regardless of the modality through which it was perceived (e.g., visual, auditory), was processed.

As this scenario suggests, neglect can be moderated by attentional factors. According to anecdotal reports, particularly salient or emotional information in the neglected half of space will not be ignored, such as a long needle in the hands of a nurse. Even in experimental situations, neglect can be diminished by the manipulation of attention. For example, a classic sign of hemineglect is the inability to bisect a line correctly. Patients with hemineglect most often place the halfway point about one quarter of the way from the line's right end and three

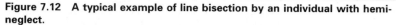

Figure 7.12   A typical example of line bisection by an individual with hemi-neglect.
Because the person with hemineglect ignores the left half of space, the line is bisected far to the right, as if it extended only from its midpoint to its right endpoint. (*Note.* Adapted from Heilman et al., 1985, p. 246.)

quarters of the way from the left end (e.g., Reuter-Lorenz & Posner, 1990). They act as if the line extends only from the middle to the right and has no left side (Figure 7.12). However, line bisection can be improved (although it is still not totally accurate) if attention is first drawn to the left side of space by a preceding task. Typically, this directing of attention is accomplished by placing a salient marker at the left edge of the line that must be identified, such as a digit or letter that must be named (e.g., Riddoch & Humphreys, 1983).

Furthermore, if information on the neglected side of space is critical for the understanding or comprehension of material, it tends to receive attention. For example, if a patient with hemineglect for the left side of space fixates on the center of the word *antiballistic,* which is centered on a page, he or she is much more likely to read the word as *ballistic,* even though the letters to the right of midline are only *llistic.* Thus, patients with hemineglect attend to information from the left side of space to the degree that it is needed so that they can devise a reasonable interpretation of sensory information.

Finally, motivational factors can also mitigate the degree to which attention is allocated to the left. For example, Mesulam (1985) discussed the performance of a patient with hemineglect on two occasions in which the motivation for finding *A*s in a letter-cancellation task varied. On one occasion, the patient was simply told to cross out all the *A*s. On the other occasion, he was told that he would receive a penny for every *A* correctly detected. When he was provided with a motivation to pay attention to the left side of space, neglect was reduced. We might speculate that the cingulate cortex played a role in

increasing the emotional or motivational value of detecting an *A.*

We have just seen that neglect can be decreased by manipulations that draw attention to the left. These manipulations include external factors such as the presence of particularly salient items or emotionally charged information. Attention to the left can also be increased by internal factors, such as a pressing motivation to process the left side of space or the need to do so in order to make sense of the world.

Lack of a Conceptual Representation for One Half of Space

The most striking aspect of hemineglect is that individuals seem to have no awareness that they are ignoring one side of space. Often when first learning about hemineglect, students comment, "I just don't understand. If an individual is ignoring the left side of space, why don't you just tell him that it is important to pay attention to the left?" Because individuals with hemineglect do not realize that they are ignoring one side of space, telling them to orient in that direction is of little use. For them, that region of space does not exist.

As an analogy, consider how you usually conceptualize the area behind your head. Generally your attention is focused on the world in front of you and you give little thought to the region behind you. Even if you were instructed to pay attention to that part of space, you would most likely begin by looking over your shoulder every few seconds, but you would soon stop doing so. However, the behavior might be extended for a longer period if you were paid a dime every time you reported on an event that occurred behind your head. Or, you might pay attention to the world behind you if some extremely significant information were coming from that region, such as the sound of quickly approaching footsteps when you were walking down a dark street alone. The patient with hemineglect treats one side of the world the way you normally treat the world behind your head.

Researchers have tried to uncover why this profound neglect occurs. One possible explanation is that the pull of sensory stimuli on the nonneglected side of space is so salient as to prevent these patients from attending to the information on the neglected side. We reviewed evidence that such an explanation may in part be true because patients with parietal lesions often have difficulty disengaging attention from the nonneglected field. But another explanation may exist; patients with neglect may ignore one side of space because they lack the conception that the neglected side of space even exists! One way to investigate this latter hypothesis is to examine the performance of patients with neglect when no sensory stimuli are present. If these persons merely have problems being distracted by sensory information in the nonneglected field, their neglect should not be obvious when sensory stimuli are absent. On the other hand, if these patients lack a representation of one side of space, the neglect should be present whether or not the individual is receiving sensory information.

Researchers have demonstrated that sensory stimuli are not required to produce behavior typical of neglect. For example, patients with neglect and neurologically intact individuals were placed in a totally darkened room with no sensory stimuli, and their eye-movement patterns were compared. Whereas the neurologically intact individuals moved their eyes to positions all over the darkened room, those with neglect moved their eyes only to positions in the nonneglected field, as if they didn't perceive that the other half of space existed (Hornak, 1992). Although this study demonstrates that sensory stimuli are not required to observe neglect, it doesn't directly address whether patients with neglect do not perceive the existence of one side of space.

The lack of a conception of one side of space in patients with hemineglect was demonstrated in a particularly ingenious study by Bisiach and Luzzatti (1978). They worked with two Milanese individuals who had hemineglect for the left side of space. While the patients were in their hospital room, Bisiach and Luzzatti asked them to imagine an extremely popular plaza in Milan that contains a variety of buildings, including a famous and ornate cathedral. Because this plaza is a major Milanese landmark, the two individuals had visited it many times and could be expected to have an excellent mental representation of the area.

Bisiach and Luzzatti first asked the individuals to imagine that they were standing at the end of the plaza opposite the imposing cathedral and then to describe what they saw. The landmarks that the patients mentioned are designated on the map of the square shown in Figure 7.13A. Notice that the patients could aptly describe the major landmarks on the right but not those on the left. Why not? Perhaps in their mind's eye, they were exhibiting neglect of information on the left. Alternatively, maybe they just couldn't remember which buildings were situated in that part of the plaza.

To distinguish between these two possibilities, the researchers next asked the patients to imagine that they were at the opposite end of the plaza—standing on the steps of the cathedral with their backs toward it. If the patients had restricted memory for the plaza, they should name the structures as before, which at this point were positioned to their left. On the other hand, if their conception of *left* was disrupted, they should describe all the features of the plaza that they previously failed to mention. As you can see in Figure 7.13B, the patients described a whole new set of landmarks—those that were previously to the left but were now to the right.

We can draw a number of conclusions from this study. First, clearly the subjects' memory for the entire plaza was fine. If we combine their first and second imaginings of the plaza, all aspects of it were described, so any deficit in their performance cannot be attributed to a memory problem. Second, the patients were missing the conception of one side of

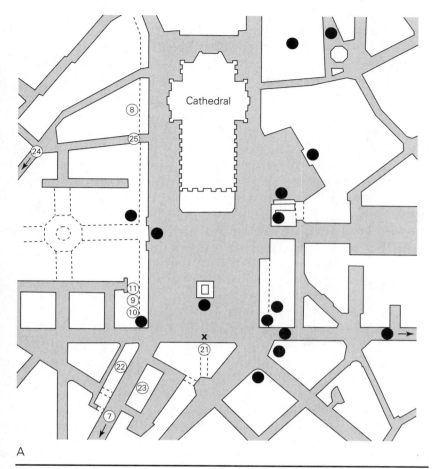

Figure 7.13 Maps indicating which structures were reported by patients with hemineglect when they imagined standing in the Piazza del Duomo in Milan, Italy.
The position in the plaza where the individual imagined him- or herself to be standing is marked with an *X*. The landmarks that the patients described are designated by filled circles. (A) The landmarks mentioned by patients when they imagined themselves facing the cathedral. These landmarks are situated mainly on the right. (B) The landmarks mentioned when the patients imagined themselves standing on the steps of the cathedral and facing away from it. Once again, mainly the landmarks on the right are mentioned. These individuals' memory for the square is intact because they mention most of the square's major landmarks across the two imagined positions. (*Note.* Adapted from Bisiach & Luzzatti, 1978, p. 130.)

space, in this case the left, because from either mental vantage point, they failed to report information on the left. Third, the attentional disruptions of hemineglect need not be driven by external stimuli.

In this case, the patients were in their hospital rooms, not the plaza, imagining the square. These findings imply that patients with hemineglect fail to represent one side of space or fail to pay attention

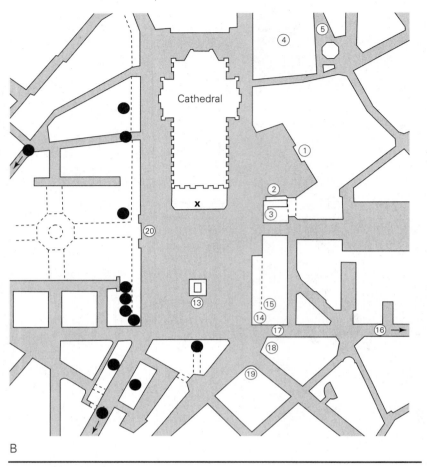

B

Figure 7.13 **(Continued)**

to one side of their mental representations of the world.

Treatment of Hemineglect

As we mentioned earlier, although hemineglect may dissipate with time, it rarely if ever disappears. Hemineglect can be vexing because of the degree to which it can interfere with everyday life. For patients with hemineglect, simple actions like crossing the street or driving a car can be extremely dangerous and in some cases impossible. Therefore, finding

an effective means of reducing neglect is of great clinical interest.

One of the more intriguing recent findings is that a technique known as **caloric stimulation** can lead to remission of a variety of the symptoms in patients with hemineglect. In caloric stimulation, 20 ml of water that is at least 7 °C warmer or colder than body temperature is poured into the ear canal during the course of 15 s. Because the water induces convection currents in the semicircular canals of the vestibular system, a person's balance is destabilized. The introduction of cold water makes the eyes begin to move in the opposite direction from the side of stimulation, whereas the introduction of warm water makes them move in the same direction (a mnemonic that medical students use to remember this is *COWS*—cold opposite, warm same). Unfortunately, this technique also makes the person experience vertigo and nausea (Gunderson, 1990).

Although caloric stimulation has side effects that prevent its regular use to reduce neglect, it has been found to ameliorate not only neglect in the sensory and motor realms, but also neglect of mental representations (Cappa, Sterzi, Vallar, & Bisiach, 1987; Rubens, 1985; Vallar et al., 1990). Furthermore, caloric stimulation applied soon after the lesion (Bisiach, Rusconi, & Vallar, 1991) or as much as 6 months later (Rode et al., 1992) seems to reduce the anosognosia associated with neglect. In at least one case, the reduction in anosognosia was long-lasting, but determining whether such a remission would have occurred spontaneously without caloric stimulation is impossible.

At present, the mechanism by which caloric stimulation reduces neglect is not understood. One possible link is that unilateral vestibular stimulation increases brain activation (as measured by regional blood flow) in the temporoparietal region of the brain (Freiberg et al., 1985); thus, caloric stimulation may modify parietal functioning, which in turn reduces neglect. Although caloric stimulation cannot be used as an everyday therapy, it may allow the mechanisms of neglect to be better understood so that an effective method of reducing it may be devised.

HEMINEGLECT: IMPLICATIONS FOR UNDERSTANDING BRAIN-BEHAVIOR RELATIONSHIPS

Now that we discussed the way in which hemineglect manifests as a clinical syndrome, we turn our attention to a number of issues regarding brain-behavior relationships that can be illuminated by hemineglect. We explore the degree to which hemineglect reveals the multiple frameworks that we use to understand our spatial world, how it provides additional evidence for object-based attention, how

it reveals a special role for the right hemisphere in attention, and how it provides insights into the degree to which the nervous system processes unattended stimuli.

Multiple Spatial Frames of Reference

In chapter 6, we discussed evidence that the maps we build of our spatial world can be constructed with reference to multiple spatial frameworks. For example, the ability to negotiate through space with regard to an egocentric framework can be distinct from the ability to do so with regard to an extrapersonal framework. In this section, we discuss how hemineglect also provides evidence for distinct spatial frameworks, especially with regard to left and right.

Frames of Reference With Regard to Left and Right

So far in our discussion of hemineglect, we used body midline as the frame of reference from which to determine left and right. However, left and right can be determined with regard to a number of other reference points, including the retina, the head, and gravity. In fact, in chapter 6 we discussed evidence from research with monkeys that suggests that we need to be able to integrate the spatial reference frame of the head with that of the body. Often, we experience a world in which spatial frames are all aligned. For example, what is to the left of our head is also to the left of our body, which in turn is to the left side of space as determined by gravitational coordinates. However, these frames of reference can be dissociated, for example by turning the head to one side so that head and body coordinates dissociate or by leaning to one side so that egocentric (head and body) coordinates are disentangled from gravitational (environment-centered) coordinates.

Neglect provides a powerful way to determine whether these frames of reference can dissociate. If they can, the degree of neglect should depend not only on the location of a region of space with regard to one frame of reference (e.g., the head), but also on the location with regard to another frame of reference (e.g., the body). For example, neglect should be demonstrated not only for items to the left of the head's midline, but also for those to the left of body midline.

To make this hypothesis more concrete, let's consider a specific example in which researchers investigated whether neglect for information to the left side of the body and neglect for information to the left side of the environment can dissociate (Calvanio, Petrone, & Levine, 1987). Normally, as shown in Figure 7.14A, body-centered and environment-centered coordinates are the same. If you look at the four quadrants of space, not only are Quadrants 1 and 3 to the left of body midline, but they are also to the left of the environment as defined by gravity. Likewise, Quadrants 2 and 4 are to the right of body midline and to the right of the environment as defined by gravity. To dissociate these frames of reference, the researchers asked individuals to recline on one side. When a person reclines so that the head is to the right, although the environment-centered left and right remain the same, Quadrants 3 and 4 are to the right and Quadrants 1 and 2 are to the left of body midline, as shown in Figure 7.14B. When a person reclines so that the head is to the left, environment-centered coordinates once again remain the same, but Quadrants 3 and 4 are now to the left of body midline, whereas Quadrants 1 and 2 are to the right, as shown in Figure 7.14C. Thus, if left is determined with reference to the middle of the body, then when the body is reclining with the head to the left, neglect should be observed for Quadrants 3 and 4, and when the body is reclining with the head to the right, for Quadrants 1 and 2. In contrast, if all that matters is environment-centered coordinates, neglect should be seen for Quadrants 1 and 3 across all three conditions (head centered, head turned right, head turned left).

The degree of neglect was found to be influenced by *both* environment-centered and body-centered coordinates, which suggests that these frames of reference are separable. The neglect is most severe for the quadrant that is left with regard to the body *and* left with regard to gravity (e.g., Quadrant 1 when the head is turned right and Quadrant 3 when the head is turned left), whereas it is least severe for

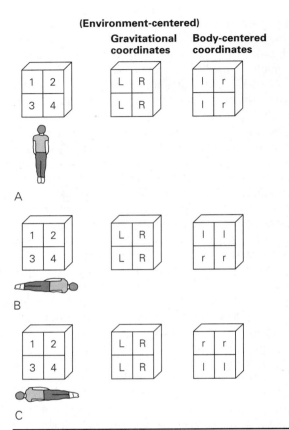

Figure 7.14 Examples of how body-centered and gravitational (environment-centered) frames of reference can dissociate.
(A) When a person is looking straight ahead, information that is to the left of the body is also to the left as defined by gravity. (B) When the person reclines with the head to the right, the frames dissociate so that information to the left of gravitational midline, Quadrants 1 and 3, is distinct from that to the left of the body, Quadrants 1 and 2. (C) When the person reclines with the head to the left, information to the left of gravitational midline, Quadrants 1 and 3, is distinct from that to the left of the body, Quadrants 3 and 4. Both gravitational and body-centered frames of reference influence what patients with hemineglect ignore.

the quadrant to the right of both body midline and the gravitational midline. Across other studies of patients with neglect, dissociations among retinotopic, head-centered, body-centered, and gravity-centered coordinates have also been demonstrated (e.g., Bisiach, Capitani, & Porta, 1985; Ladavas, 1987).

Frames of Reference in Other Dimensions

To this point, we discussed neglect only with regard to the horizontal plane (i.e., left and right). However, our three-dimensional world has two other planes—the top-bottom (vertical) plane and the near-far plane. If these three dimensions are dissociable in our mapping of space, we might expect to find specific cases of neglect for each of these dimensions in space as well.

In fact, evidence from case studies indicates that neglect can occur with regard to the vertical plane, which has been dubbed **altitudinal neglect** (for top vs. bottom) (Rapcsak, Cimino, & Heilman, 1988). In one case, the individual could detect a single stimulus in all four quadrants of her visual field. However, when shown two objects, one above the horizontal meridian and one below (which makes this situation similar to the double simultaneous stimulation example discussed earlier in the chapter), she always ignored the one below. She was also given a rod-bisection test in which her ability to find the midpoint of vertically oriented sticks of wood was assessed under three conditions: when she inspected the rod just visually, just tactilely (with the eyes closed), or visually and tactilely. In all three cases, she estimated the midpoint significantly above the true midpoint of the rod. These findings suggest that her difficulties arose in paying attention to the bottom portion of space rather than from a problem in a specific sensory domain (e.g., visual, tactile). This individual's lesion was a watershed lesion in dorsal parietal regions (as is typical with such a lesion, she also had Balint's syndrome).

An individual with the opposite problem, neglect of the upper part of space, was also reported. This patient had a bilateral temporo-occipital lesion, which is more inferior than the lesion that typically causes Balint's syndrome. Behaviorally, he bisected vertical lines below their midpoint and ignored the upper portions of visual stimuli (Shelton, Bowers, & Heilman, 1990). This patient exhibited another interesting neglect phenomenon. He seemed to have a neglect for far portions of space because he consistently bisected radial lines too close to his body.

Because this patient ignored both the upper part of space and the far part of space, the researchers wondered whether Rapcsak's patient who had neglected the lower part of space might also show a neglect of near space. Upon retesting, she was found to have a significant tendency to bisect radial lines too far away from her body, an indication of neglect of near space (Mennemeier, Wertman, & Heilman, 1992). Hence, in both these patients, representation of space in the vertical dimension was linked to representation of space in the near-far dimension. One patient neglected both the upper half and far region of space, while the other patient neglected both the lower and near part of space. Although this conjecture is speculative, these two reference frames may be coupled because information at the top of our visual world is usually far away (e.g., the horizon), whereas information near to us is usually lower in our visual world. More exploration of this issue is warranted, however, because the available evidence is based on just a few case studies. In contrast, no pairing of neglect between positions in a left-right frame and neglect between positions in either a top-bottom or a near-far frame of spatial reference has been observed.

Object-Based Attention

So far, we considered neglect with regard to a spatial framework. However, at the beginning of the chapter we discussed how attention could be directed either to certain regions of space or to certain objects. Additional evidence for object-based attention could be garnered if neglect could be found for certain portions of objects (rather than certain regions of space). To make this distinction clearer, consider the following. An individual with spatially based neglect for the left half of space will fail to read all words on the left half of the page. In contrast, a person with object-based neglect will be unable to read the left *half* of words, regardless of where they occur on the page.

Recently, a number of case studies of object-based neglect have been reported both for nonverbal and verbal material (e.g., Behrmann & Moscovitch, 1994; Driver, Baylis, Goodrich, & Rafal,

1994). For example, in the nonverbal realm, Young, DeHaan, Newcombe, and Hay (1990) reported on a patient who exhibited a specific neglect for the left half of faces, but not for the left half of other objects such as cars. Although the individual could recognize people from a full view of the face or just the right half of the face, he made many errors in identification when shown just the left half. The researchers demonstrated in a number of ways that the neglect was not spatially based. First, they showed that the patient exhibited no neglect for the left half of space on a standard item-cancellation test. Second, they demonstrated that neglect for the left half of the face occurred regardless of the face's position in space. To do so, they used chimeric faces (recall that a chimeric face is two different half-faces merged at midline). These investigators found that the patient's behavior (such as deciding the emotional tone of a face) was dictated solely by the right half of the face and not by the left. The neglect of the left side of the face was observed even for the rightward of two faces presented side by side, an indication that the patient's deficit was with processing material on the left half of the face, not on the left half of the display. A subsequent patient tested with similar tasks also exhibited a pattern of left-sided neglect, except in her case it occurred not only for faces, but for other common objects as well (Young, Hellawell, & Welch, 1992).

Evidence for object-based neglect in the verbal domain comes from two case studies of patients, who, regardless of a word's length and position in space, ignored one side of the word. The neglect did not exhibit itself with retention to body or head midline, but rather with regard to where letters were located in the overall frame of the word. For example, one patient who had sustained left-hemisphere damage made errors when reading the right half of words, regardless of the length of the word. For example, if given a six-letter word such as *fabric*, she would read the first three letters correctly but not the others and pronounce the word as "fable." For longer words, she would read more letters correctly, but once again only the beginning letters and not the ending letters. For example, when asked to read *banister*, she said "banish," and when asked

to read *familiar*, she said "family" (Caramazza & Hillis, 1990). Another patient, who sustained a right parieto-occipital lesion, made reading errors on the left half of words regardless of word length. The farther a letter was from the right end of the word, the more likely it was to be misread (Hillis & Caramazza, 1991).

These case studies are important because they demonstrate that attention can be object based rather than spatially based. In all cases, neglect was exhibited for a particular portion of the object regardless of the object's position in space. We should not be surprised that attention might work in both an object-based manner and a space-based manner if we consider that, as discussed in chapters 5 and 6, the regions of the brain that process spatial information and those that process objects are different. To the degree that these two functions are performed by distinct brain regions, we might imagine that attentional control in each of these domains might be separate as well.

Role of the Right Hemisphere in Attention

One of the most striking aspects of the hemineglect syndrome is that it is extremely prominent and severe after right-hemisphere damage but much less so after left-hemisphere damage. To account for this finding, researchers have proposed that the hemineglect exhibited after right-hemisphere damage reflects the effects of two distinct factors: an attentional bias of each hemisphere for information on the opposite side of space and a larger role of the right hemisphere in overall attention and arousal. We next discuss the evidence for each of these two factors and then examine how they might combine to cause the observed effects in hemineglect.

Various pieces of evidence suggest that each hemisphere exhibits an attentional bias for information located in the contralateral space. Some evidence is provided by ERP studies of attention. When a study participant is instructed to attend to information in one visual field, the ERP recorded over the contralateral hemisphere is larger than that over the ipsilateral hemisphere. For example, if a person is asked to attend to information in the LVF, an enhanced ERP will be recorded over the occipital lead over the right hemisphere (e.g., Mangun & Hillyard, 1988). Other evidence is provided by divided visual field studies. When task demands activate one hemisphere, an attentional bias to the contralateral side of space appears to enhance the processing of material in that location (Kinsbourne, 1974). For example, the size of visual asymmetries is influenced by the hemisphere that was most likely engaged in performance of an immediately preceding task. RVF asymmetries on verbal tasks are larger if immediately prior to performance of the lateralized task, an individual's left hemisphere was activated by performing a verbal task (rather than a nonverbal task, which would have activated the right hemisphere). Likewise, LVF asymmetries are

larger if immediately prior to performance of the lateralized task, a nonverbal rather than a verbal task was performed (e.g., Klein, Moscovitch, & Vigna, 1976).

In fact, these attentional biases for one side of space can be observed even for tasks in which subjects are not presented material by divided visual field techniques but are presented items in free vision and allowed to scan as much of visual space as they like. In each trial of one study, subjects were presented with two chimeric faces that were identical except that they were mirror images. The chimera in each pair was composed of a smiling half-face and a neutral half-face. People were asked to judge which of the two faces looked happier (Figure 7.15). Because these pictures are mirror images, the participants had no reason, on the basis of percep-

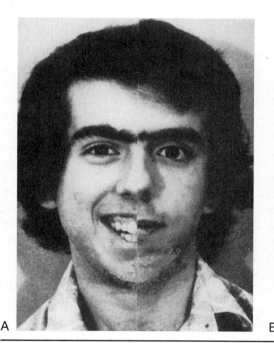 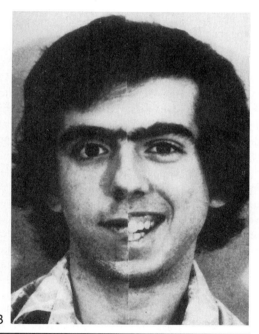

A   B

Figure 7.15 Examples of chimeric faces that demonstrate attentional biases to one side of space. Although these faces are identical except that they are mirror images, most right-handed individuals perceive the face in (A), which has the smile on the left, as happier than the face in (B), which has the smile on the right. Experts think that the left half-face is perceived as more expressive because the right hemisphere is more adept at processing emotional and facial information, which causes an attentional bias toward the left side of space. Hence, information located on the left is perceived as more salient. (*Note.* Reprinted with permission from "Asymmetry of Perception in Free Viewing of Chimeric Faces," by J. Levy, W. Heller, M. T. Banich, and L. A. Burton, 1983, *Brain and Cognition, 2*, p. 406.)

tual factors, to perceive one as happier than the other. Nonetheless, on average, right-handers chose the chimera with the smiling left half-face as looking happier 66% of the time, and the chimera with the smiling right half-face only 34% of the time. The researchers suggested that the task demands of processing emotional information in faces, for which the right hemisphere is specialized, made it more activated, which in turn led to an attentional bias to the left side of space. Thus, when a right-hander was asked which face seemed happier, the chimera with the smiling half-face on the left side of space seemed more salient and hence was judged as happier (Levy, Heller, Banich, & Burton, 1983b).

Similar attentional biases can be obtained for verbal material as well. In a verbal counterpart to the chimeric face task, more than 200 words were aligned at different angles all over a standard page on each of 10 pages. The individual was given 60 s to call out all occurrences of words that rhymed with *een*. Consistent with left-hemisphere specialization for verbal processing, individuals detected more target words when they appeared to the right of midline than when they appeared to the left (Levy & Kueck, 1986).

PET studies also indicate that each hemisphere is important for localizing attention to the contralateral visual field. In one task, attention had to be shifted among various locations, all of which were restricted to one visual field. For RVF locations, activation was greatest over left superior parietal and left superior frontal cortex, whereas for LVF locations, activation was greatest over right superior parietal and right superior frontal cortex (Corbetta, Miezin, Shulman, & Petersen, 1993). On the basis of evidence of this nature and others (e.g., Reuter-Lorenz, Kinsbourne, & Moscovitch, 1990), each hemisphere appears to have an attentional bias for the contralateral side of space.

The evidence for a large right-hemisphere role in alerting and arousal comes from various sources. For example, after right-hemisphere damage, patients exhibit slow responses to simple stimuli. Although brain damage slows the responses of almost all individuals, damage to the right hemisphere, and

more specifically the right posterior regions, causes the greatest decrement in performance (Coslett, Bowers, & Heilman, 1987). Heart-rate responses to warning signals are also disrupted by right-hemisphere damage (Yokoyama et al., 1987), and passive vigilance tasks are performed more poorly by the isolated right hemisphere than the isolated left hemisphere of patients with the split-brain syndrome (e.g., Dimond & Beaumont, 1973). Moreover, PET studies indicate that the right hemisphere is important in sustaining overall attention, for example in vigilance tasks (e.g., R. M. Cohen et al., 1988).

These two factors, a hemispheric attentional bias for the contralateral hemispace and a greater right-hemisphere involvement in attention and arousal, both appear to contribute to the pattern of neglect. The contribution of each factor was shown in a study in which two item-detection tasks were given to three groups of individuals: patients with right-hemisphere damage, patients with left-hemisphere damage, and neurologically intact individuals (Weintraub & Mesulam, 1987). In one task, individuals were asked to circle as many target items as they could find within a visual display, and in the other they were to search and find a plastic bead as quickly as possible while blindfolded. The results for the visual condition (which were essentially the same as those for the tactile condition) are presented in Table 7.1. As expected, the neurologically intact individuals missed practically no targets on either side of space. The results for patients with brain damage yielded two important findings. First, regardless of whether individuals had right- or left-hemisphere damage, they missed more targets on the side of space contralateral, rather than ipsilateral, to the lesion. These results provide additional evidence that each hemisphere is primarily responsible for attention to information in the contralateral hemispace. Second, as you can see in Table 7.1, the overall performance of patients with right-hemisphere damage was worse than the performance of patients with left-hemisphere damage; that is, they missed more items overall on both the left *and* right sides of space. In fact, patients with right-hemisphere damage missed more items in their *non-*

Table 7.1 Number of Items Missed in the Visual Search Task Used by Weintraub and Mesulam (1987)

Patients with unilateral lesions miss more items on the side of space contralateral to the lesion than on the ipsilateral side. Overall, the patients with right-hemisphere damage miss many more targets than those with left-hemisphere damage do.

Group	Average no. of items missed	
	Left side	Right side
Patients with left-hemisphere lesions	1.25	2.38
Patients with right-hemisphere lesions	17.13	8.00
Neurologically intact control subjects	0.56	0.30

neglected hemispace (i.e., right hemispace) than patients with left-hemisphere damage missed in their *neglected* hemispace (i.e., right hemispace). This piece of evidence, along with the others cited previously, suggests that the right hemisphere may exert more influence over overall attention and arousal than the left does.

Processing of Unattended Stimuli

Thus far we presented attention as a mechanism whereby the brain can choose what it wants to process from the vast array of information available. But what is the fate of unattended stimuli? Do they fall into a black hole of mental consciousness, leaving not even a trace of their existence, or are they processed but to a much lesser degree than attended stimuli? In chapter 5, we discussed the fact that patients with prosopagnosia appear to be able to extract some information about faces that they cannot recognize. Such findings provide evidence that information may be processed to some degree even if it doesn't reach consciousness. Next, we examine evidence that although patients with hemineglect appear to ignore all information on the unattended side of space, under certain conditions this information can nonetheless influence their behavior.

In one of the first reports to suggest that patients with hemineglect might process information in their unattended half of space, a patient with left-sided hemineglect was shown drawings of two houses that were identical, except on one flames were coming

out of the left side (J. C. Marshall & Halligan, 1988). Although the patient claimed to detect no difference between the houses, when asked which house she would prefer to live in, she picked the one without flames. Asked to explain her decision, she was unable to. This case report suggested that even though the patient was not consciously aware of information on the left side of space, she was processing some information from this portion of space.

Although subsequent studies failed to replicate this particular finding (e.g., Bisiach & Rusconi, 1990), other researchers have found evidence that information in the neglected field can be processed. Most of this evidence comes from priming studies in which information on the left cannot be explicitly recognized but still influences performance. For example, in one study researchers determined the speed with which patients with right-hemisphere damage, who exhibited a neglect of the contralateral space, could categorize a picture in the RVF (their nonneglected field) as an animal or fruit. The important factor in this study was that 400 ms earlier a picture from either the same category or a different category was presented in the neglected field (i.e., the LVF). Responses to information in the RVF were faster when a related rather than an unrelated item was presented in the neglected field. This finding suggests that information in the neglected field was being processed to some degree and could prime responses in the nonneglected field (Berti & Rizzolatti, 1992). A similar priming phenomenon

Neurological Bases of Consciousness

How are we aware of who we are and the world around us? What makes us conscious, willful beings? The question of consciousness has intrigued philosophers for centuries, and now increasingly is intriguing neuroscientists as well. In Descartes's view, the answer boiled down to "I think, therefore I am." If we believe a basic premise of neuropsychology that the brain is important for mental function, we might give Descartes's theory a modern twist by saying, "I have a brain, therefore I am."

Recently, neuroscientists and philosophers have been examining the question of how consciousness arises. Does a special place exist in the brain from which consciousness emanates? In Descartes's view, the likely source of consciousness was the pineal gland (a structure that hangs from the floor of the brain) because it was the one structure associated with the brain that did not appear to have two halves. Some investigators say that a central executive area in the brain guides our actions and thoughts, whereas others believe that consciousness emerges from the complex interactions of neurons, which at present cannot be well described (see Dennett & Kinsbourne, 1992, and associated commentaries for an overview of different viewpoints).

What is clear, however, is that changes in brain function can alter what we often conceive of as consciousness. As we discussed earlier in the chapter,

damage to the reticular activating system (RAS) can alter responsiveness to sensory information and impair the ability to perform willful acts on a basic level. In epilepsy, an alteration of consciousness, or an aura, often precedes a seizure. These auras are usually characterized by distortions of sensory experience, such as having a feeling of smelling an especially intense aroma or a feeling that the size of certain body parts is either too large or too small. Such distortions often extend to a sense of time and place as well. In some cases, individuals even experience visual hallucinations. At least some investigators have speculated that certain "visions" seen by particular religious figures of the Middle Ages may have been the result of a neurological disorder (Sacks, 1985). (For a particularly interesting self-report of such visual hallucinations as a result of viral encephalitis, see Mize, 1980.)

Brain injury can often cause a seeming lack of awareness or knowledge about certain aspects of the world (see Prigatano & Schacter, 1991, for a multifaceted discussion of this issue). In fact, when individuals have brain damage, their lack of awareness about the nature of their dysfunction can be one of the most vexing aspects of neuropsychological rehabilitation. Without some self-awareness of the problems to be overcome, a patient is unlikely to engage in behaviors, whether they are restructuring the physical environment or devising compensatory strategies, that will mitigate the

was found in another study, in which a letter string was presented in central fixation. In this case, a presentation of a picture in the LVF related to the letter string speeded performance equally for neurologically intact individuals and patients with left-sided neglect, another indication that patients with neglect are processing information in the neglected field to some degree. To demonstrate that such priming should not occur if information from the LVF cannot be processed, researchers gave the task to an individual with LVF hemianopsia. Her responses, as expected, were not speeded by the presentation of a related picture in the LVF (McGlinchey-Berroth et al., 1993). Hence, the available evidence suggests that patients may be processing information in the neglected field to some degree, but not in a way that allows them conscious access to the information.

SUMMARY

Attention is the cognitive ability that allows us to deal with the inherent processing limitations of the human brain. It permits us to select specific informa-

effects of brain damage (see chapter 13 for a more detailed discussion of compensatory strategies). For example, a patient whose brain damage left her hemiplegic was spending 1 hour a day in a rehabilitation hospital learning to use a set of handrails to negotiate in and out of the bathtub. Yet when asked what renovations she was planning for her bathroom at home to accommodate her disability, she replied, "None."

In specific syndromes, such as hemineglect and amnesia, the lack of consciousness occurs with regard to particular aspects of space and time but not others. As we just discussed, hemineglect causes an inattention to one side of space. Individuals with this disorder apparently have no conscious awareness that an entire half of the world exists. This unawareness occurs at the same time that consciousness for the non-neglected side of space seems perfectly normal. In cases of amnesia (which we discuss in more detail in chapter 9), the distortion occurs for particular portions of time. The individual has intact consciousness for the here and now and for the region of time prior to the brain injury, but not for the portions of the past that occurred after the insult. As stated by H.M., one of the most famous patients with amnesia, "You see, at this moment everything looks clear to me, but what happened just before? That's what worries me. It's like waking from a dream; I just don't remember" (B. Milner, 1966, p. 115). (See Newcombe, 1985, for a review

of alterations in consciousness as a result of brain damage and the way that they may be similar to experiences that we may have in our everyday lives, such as waking from sleep or sensory deprivation.)

Recently, much interest has centered on findings that information that seemingly appears to evade consciousness can nonetheless influence an individual's actions. As we discussed previously, information in the neglected field that is ignored and cannot be identified will, under certain conditions, prime behavior. Furthermore, as we discussed with regard to face recognition and as we discuss in more detail in chapter 9, information that cannot be recognized or recalled may influence a behavioral or physiological response (e.g., learning an inappropriate name for a face may be difficult, or the galvanic skin response to previously known faces may differ from that for faces never seen before). These laboratory findings, which indicate that the nervous system is processing information even though it doesn't appear to be doing so, have caused a heightened awareness among clinicians about different levels of consciousness. For example, such findings have been used, in part, to justify coma stimulation therapy, in which patients in coma are given specific types of stimulation even though they appear unresponsive (for a sample description of such therapy, see Freeman, 1991).

tion for further processing from the vast array of information that bombards our sensory receptors and to select specific responses from the large set of possible options. In discussing attention, cognitive psychologists often divide it into four general categories: alertness and arousal, sustained attention (vigilance), selective attention, and resources (capacity).

Data from neuropsychological studies have been important in aiding our understanding of two issues with regard to selective attention: (a) the time course of selection and (b) how the selection process

occurs, with regard to particular locations in space or with regard to particular objects. Scientists debate whether information is selected for further processing relatively soon after receipt of sensory information or whether that process occurs later in time, only after information has been processed to the level of meaning. Because event-related potentials (ERPs) indicate that differences in the electrophysiological response to attended stimuli as compared with the response to unattended stimuli can be detected as soon as 80 ms postpresentation, these ERPs provide evidence that attention can occur very early in processing, although it may continue for some time thereafter. Research with patients with hemineglect indicates that information can be selected for further processing choosing a specific region of space from which information will be processed more fully or by selecting a specific item for additional processing.

Neuropsychological data also provide evidence that attention can be conceptualized as a pool of multiple resources from which certain resources can be used to perform a task. According to this theory, tasks can be performed better when they draw from separate resources rather than from the same one. Evidence suggests that different brain regions, such as each of the cerebral hemispheres, may act as separate pools of attentional resources.

Attention appears to be controlled by a network of neural structures in the brain. The six major brain regions that are conceptualized as part of this network are the reticular activating system (RAS), the superior colliculus, the pulvinar of the thalamus, the cingulate cortex, the posterior parietal regions, and the frontal lobes. The RAS, which resides in the brain stem, plays a role in regulation of alertness and arousal. The superior colliculus, located in the midbrain, plays an important role in automatically orienting attention to particular locations in space. The pulvinar of the thalamus has been suggested as a gating mechanism for selecting or filtering incoming information. The cingulate cortex aids in selecting motor responses and in providing an emotional or a motivational tenor to attentionally salient information. The posterior parietal lobe provides a spatial frame of reference for attentional processing. Finally, frontal regions are important not only for motor planning and movement as they relate to attentional demands, but also for the detection of novel stimuli.

Different theorists surmise how brain regions work together as a network to support attentional processing. According to one conception, each brain region has a somewhat specialized role in attention but one that overlaps at least to some degree with other brain regions. This type of a system would explain why certain disorders of attention can be caused by brain lesions to disparate areas and

why the severity of attentional disorders increases with the number of components in the network that are damaged. Other theorists posit that attentional control occurs through a series of operations, each of which is performed by a unique brain region. One such model has been proposed for visual selective attention. In this model, attention must be disengaged from a location, an operation performed by parietal areas; moved to a new location, an operation performed by the superior colliculus; and then engaged at a new location, an operation performed by the thalamus.

One of the most prominent manifestations of a disorder of attentional processing is the syndrome of hemineglect, in which an individual ignores information on the side of space contralateral to the lesion. At times the neglect can be so severe that an individual denies that parts on one half of the body belong to him or her. Hemineglect can be shown to be an attentional syndrome because it cannot be explained by sensory deficits and its severity can be modulated by attentional factors. Attention can be drawn to the neglected side by external factors such as particular salient items or emotionally charged information, or by internal factors, such as motivation to process that side of space or the need to do so to make sense of sensory information. Furthermore, neglect can be shown to result from the lack of attention to, or conceptualization of, one side of space. Clinically, neglect is often most severe immediately after injury but dissipates with time. However, it usually never disappears and can often be demonstrated when similar stimuli are presented simultaneously on either side of the midline. In such cases, responses to stimuli on the neglected side are usually extinguished. Because hemineglect is such a vexing problem, clinicians want to find an effective treatment. Caloric stimulation therapy, in which either hot or cold water is introduced into the ear canal, has been shown to reduce neglect temporarily. However, its side effects (e.g., nausea) make it unsuitable as a regular treatment. Nonetheless, this therapy may aid in revealing the mechanisms for reducing neglect and hence may help researchers to create an effective treatment.

Hemineglect also provides insight into four issues regarding brain-behavior relationships. First, because hemineglect of information can occur with regard to either body-centered coordinates or gravitational coordinates, it helps to demonstrate the existence of multiple mental maps of extrapersonal space. Furthermore, neglect of the body can dissociate from neglect of items in the world, further evidence for a dissociation of personal and extrapersonal space. Second, neglect illustrates that attention can be either space based or object based. Support for such a viewpoint comes from case studies of individuals who either ignore information on one side of space (space-based attention) or ignore one side of objects regardless of where they are located in space (object-based attention). Third, neglect suggests that the right hemisphere is more intimately linked to the control of overall attention and arousal. This conjecture is based, in part, on findings that neglect is more severe after right- than left-hemisphere lesions. Fourth, hemineglect reveals that unattended information undergoes at least some processing. Evidence to support this assertion comes from studies in which material that cannot be identified in the neglected field can prime performance on other tasks.

*L*anguage

Dr. Sheila Chorpenning, a neurologist, had just joined the staff of a hospital for U.S. Army veterans. In the large patient recreation room, she noticed two men sitting on a sofa, one middle-aged and one younger. The middle-aged man, Bill Rieger, had been a rising star in high school—academically talented and a top athlete. But then his mother died unexpectedly. Confused by her death, he turned down a scholarship to college and joined the army. During a combat mission in Vietnam, he was hit by shrapnel that damaged his left frontal lobe as well as parts of his parietal lobe. Dr. Chorpenning introduced herself and asked Bill to tell her about his history. He replied:

> My un mother died . . . uh . . . me . . . uh fi'tenn. Uh, oh, I guess six month . . . my mother pass away. An'uh . . . an'en . . . un . . . ah . . . seventeen . . . seventeen . . . go . . . uh High School. An uh . . . Christmas . . . well, uh, I uh . . . Pitt'burgh. (Goodglass, 1976, p. 239)

He told the story with much effort, and the words seemed to explode as they came out of his mouth. His intonation was uneven, which made his speech difficult to follow initially, but with time Dr. Chorpenning found him easier to understand.

The younger man, who was in his late 20s, was named Jim Hurdle. He had had a carotid artery aneurysm (the ballooning then breaking of the carotid artery), which caused brain damage. As Dr. Chorpenning began to converse with him, he attempted to explain that he didn't live at the hospital but had just been brought there by his father to have some dental work performed:

> Ah . . . Monday . . . ah, Dad and Jim Hurdle [referring to himself by his full name] and Dad . . . hospital. Two . . . ah, doctors . . . , and ah . . . thirty minutes . . . and yes . . . ah . . . hospital. And, er Wednesday . . . nine o'clock. And er Thursday, ten o'clock . . . doctors. Two doctors . . . and ah . . . teeth. Yeah, . . . fine. (Goodglass, 1976, p. 238)

Like the first man, Jim spoke in a slow, halting cadence, and his words were produced in a harsh and guttural manner.

Despite their difficulties in speaking, both men seemed to understand most of what Dr. Chorpenning said to them. When she mentioned that the weather was springlike, Bill pointed to the open window through which a warm breeze was blowing. When she discussed what a relief the weather was compared with the cold, hard winter that they had been experiencing, Jim pulled his sweater tightly around himself and imitated a shiver. Before she left, she thanked both men for chatting with her, realizing how frustrated they were with their inability to communicate.

Language is the mental faculty that many people consider most uniquely human and that most distinctly separates us from the other species that inhabit the earth. It is such a wonderful communicative tool that for more than a century scientists have tried to understand how the brain's organization endows us with such a superb faculty. In fact, language difficulties such as those experienced by Bill Rieger and Jim Hurdle first led Paul Broca in the late 1800s to realize that the hemispheres have different functions, an event that heralded the advent of modern-day neuropsychology. Broca found that a lesion to a specific region of the left hemisphere causes a loss of fluent speech even though the person's speech comprehension is relatively spared. This syndrome, known as **Broca's aphasia** (**aphasia** is the loss of a language-processing ability after brain damage), has revealed more than just hemispheric specialization: It has also provided a window to understanding the neurological organization for language.

In this chapter, we discuss a variety of aphasias, including Broca's aphasia, gleaning from each some lessons about the neurological organization for language. We consider the neural underpinnings for spoken and written language and examine the degree to which their neural substrates are similar and the degree to which they are distinct. Although most of our discussion is on the neural organization for Indo-European languages, such as English, we also consider the neural underpinnings for other languages, including those from Asia and a language created for persons who are deaf. We take such an approach because if some aspects of the neurological organization for language are universal, they should reveal themselves despite the different grammatical structures found across languages (e.g., Indo-European vs. Asian languages) and despite differences in the modality in which the information is conveyed (e.g., sound in English vs. hand movement in American Sign Language). We also examine the degree to which the right hemisphere is involved in language processing. Although this hemisphere was initially thought to be relatively uninvolved in language, more recent evidence suggests that it contributes to language comprehension.

NEUROLOGICAL BASES FOR AUDITORY LANGUAGE PROCESSING

To begin our discussion of the neural bases for language, we invoke a classic approach used since the mid-1800s, namely a characterization of patterns of language impairment that accompany specific brain lesions. Afterward, we consider the degree to which evidence from other methods, including some modern ones, converges with the conclusions drawn from the study of individuals with brain damage. In this section, we focus mainly on auditory language, saving our discussion of written language for later in the chapter.

Evidence From Studies of Patients with Brain Damage

At the beginning of this book, we discussed how the relationship between the brain and mental function can be examined from either of two vantage points—one emphasizing the neurological organization of the brain and one emphasizing the psycho-

logical processes performed by the brain. These two vantage points are extremely well illustrated by the differing perspectives on language breakdown after brain trauma. The early advances in this field, made in the late 1800s, came squarely from a neurological or medical, perspective. The early *aphasiologists* (i.e., people who study aphasia) were especially interested in the language problems that arose from damage to specific regions of the cortex. These investigators proposed models in which each region of the cortex had a specific role in language processing: One area was deemed critical for recognizing sound images of words, and another critical for producing speech. As we learn shortly, according to these models the brain processes language much as a factory manufactures products along a conveyor belt. Input is received at one region, then is packaged and sent to another region for output. From this perspective, these models have a "knee bone is connected to the thigh bone" flavor about them.

Since the 1960s, psycholinguists have examined the neurological bases for language from a different perspective. In attempting to understand the results of brain damage on language processing, these researchers have emphasized the organization of language rather than the organization of the brain. This approach has led them to ask very different questions about aphasia. For example, they have used aphasia to help test theories about the fundamental components of language.

In this chapter, we examine language processing from both perspectives, the neurological and the psychological. Because each can provide useful information, these views should be considered complementary rather than mutually exclusive ways to conceptualize the neurological organization for language. After discussing each perspective (according to historical precedent—the neurological viewpoint first and the psychological second), we determine the generalizations about language that can be made regardless of the viewpoint taken.

Neurological Perspective

As we mentioned, the two men discussed in the opening vignette of the chapter, Bill and Jim, had an aphasia similar to that experienced by Broca's patients. If you reread what the two men said, you may be struck by certain characteristics. You may have noticed the paucity of speech output: People with Broca's aphasia have great difficulty producing words. Broca deduced that the deficit he observed in his patients was specifically linguistic in nature because their difficulty with speech output was not accompanied by motoric problems of the vocal musculature, such as paralysis. The patients could utter sounds, albeit not linguistic ones, and were sometimes able to use the mouth and lips to perform orofacial movements, such as blowing out candles. Because the deficit appeared to be limited to the language domain, Broca conceptualized the region of the brain that now bears his name as the area that is critical for programming speech output.

Although difficulty in speech output is a glaring symptom of Broca's aphasia, you may have noticed other characteristics as well. For instance, the sentences do not fit a standard structure but seemed more like a telegram (e.g., "Need help, send money"). This characteristic is often referred to as **telegraphic speech** because the words produced tend to be only content words, such as nouns and verbs. Function words and word endings are missing. Function words, although they convey little information, are nonetheless important for speech comprehension because they provide information about the relations among words. Some good examples of function words are conjunctions (e.g., *but, and*) and prepositions (e.g., *around, behind, about*). Word endings also convey meaning. Although *-ing* and *-s* have little meaning by themselves, when appended to the end of a word, they designate, respectively, an action that is happening at the present time, and more than one item. We return to a discussion of these characteristics in the next section, when we discuss the psychological perspective on this type of aphasia.

Until this point, we have not discussed the specific location of the lesion that causes Broca's aphasia other than to say that it is in the left hemisphere. However, with the knowledge we gained in the previous chapters about general attributes of brain organization, we should be able to make a well-

educated guess as to the general location of the lesion that causes this syndrome. To discern whether the lesion is located anterior or posterior to the central fissure, remember that the most prominent behavioral deficit in Broca's aphasia is a disruption of speech output and that comprehension is relatively intact (later, when we discuss the psychological model, we qualify this statement about comprehension abilities, but for now it provides a fair description). You should have reasoned that the lesion causing Broca's aphasia is anterior to the central fissure because anterior regions are specialized for motor output. Now, decide whether you think the lesion critical for producing Broca's aphasia must include the motor strip. You should have guessed that it does not because Broca's aphasia is not a result of facial or vocal muscle paralysis. Finally, consider whether you think the location of a lesion causing Broca's aphasia should be located ventrally or dorsally in the frontal lobe. This decision is more difficult, but if you remember the organization of the motor strip, you might be inclined to choose ventral because the head and the face are represented at the base of the motor strip. In fact, the lesion that typically causes Broca's aphasia is in the frontal region, just anterior to, but not in, the section of the motor strip that is responsible for control of the face (Figure 8.1). In more recent eras, research has suggested that the lesion necessary to produce Broca's aphasia must include not only cortical tissue, but also underlying subcortical tissue and white matter (e.g., H. Damasio, 1991a).

As we discussed in chapter 3, about 20 years after Broca characterized his aphasia, Karl Wernicke described the converse syndrome—disrupted speech comprehension along with fluent (but nonsensical) speech output—which became known as **Wernicke's aphasia.** *Fluent* is the operative word in describing this syndrome because the output occurs without hesitation, the sounds are well formed, and all parts of speech are present. Yet, what these individuals say makes little sense because their output is much like a jumble of words, often referred to as a *word salad*. In fact, the speech of a person with Wernicke's aphasia can be so disjointed that someone without proper training in a medically relevant

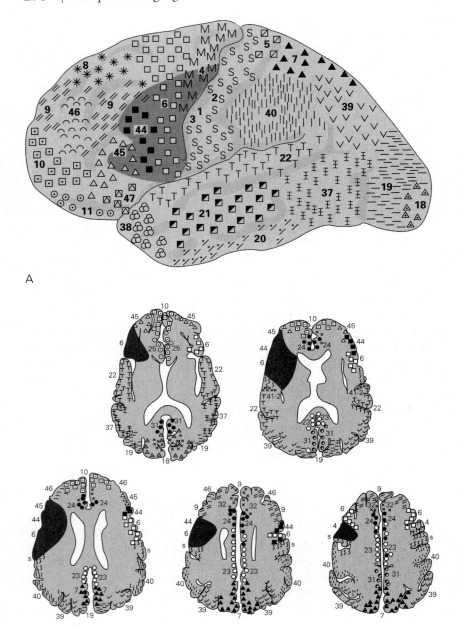

A

B

Figure 8.1 The site of damage that causes Broca's aphasia.
Shown here is the location of the lesion in one patient with Broca's aphasia, as
viewed (A) laterally and (B) in oblique brain slices that go from the lowest region
of the brain that is affected (top row, left-hand slice) to the highest region (bottom row, right-hand slice). The damage in this patient involves not only Broca's
area proper (Brodmann's areas 44 and 45), but also other areas that are often
damaged, such as the motor and premotor areas (areas 4 and 6). (*Note.* Adapted
from Damasio, 1991a, p. 56.)

field might be tempted to refer the individual to a psychiatrist rather than a neurologist.

Following is an example of speech from a 70-year-old man who acquired Wernicke's aphasia after blockage of part of his middle cerebral artery. Unlike the speech of individuals with Broca's aphasia, his speech was produced at a normal rate and rhythm and with an intonational pattern that was, if anything, exaggerated:

> I feel very well. My hearing, writing been doing well, things that I couldn't hear from. In other words, I used to be able to work cigarettes I don't know how. . . . This year the last three years, or perhaps a little more, I didn't know how to do me any able to. (Goodglass, 1976, p. 239)

The output of persons with Wernicke's aphasia is incomprehensible not only because the words are combined in a way that makes no sense, but also because these individuals often make errors in producing specific words, errors known as **paraphasias.** Paraphasias manifest in numerous forms. A **verbal paraphasia** occurs when one word is incorrectly substituted for another. When the substituted word has a meaning similar to that of the intended word, the error is known as a **semantic paraphasia** (e.g., substitution of "barn" for "house"). When a similar sound is substituted for an intended sound, the error is a **phonemic paraphasia** (e.g., "table" becomes "trable" or "fable"). On other occasions, persons with Wernicke's aphasia produce sounds that could be words because they follow the rules by which a language combines its sounds, but in actuality are not words (e.g., "galump," "trebbin"). These sounds are known as **neologisms.**

Despite the fluency of their output, individuals with Wernicke's aphasia generally have much trouble understanding language. Even when given simple commands such as "Point to the blue square" or "Pick up the spoon," they may not be able to discern the meaning of the sentence and hence do not take the appropriate action. Wernicke postulated that individuals with this type of aphasia could not link the "sound images" of language to meaning. Considered in this manner, the breakdown is viewed as an inability to process auditory language

input. This characterization is not entirely adequate as these individuals also often have difficulty reading.

From what we just learned about the behavioral manifestations of Wernicke's aphasia, you should be able to make an educated guess as to the location of the lesion that typically results in this disorder. Given a choice between a location anterior to or posterior to the central fissure, you should have guessed posterior because those regions of the brain are involved in receiving and interpreting sensory information. But where in posterior cortex is the lesion typically located? Consider that Wernicke described the aphasia as an inability to link a sound image to meaning or stored information. Which posterior brain regions might be plausible candidates? First, because we are discussing a sound image, you might consider regions in the superior temporal lobe near Heschl's gyrus, which is the primary auditory area. Because a correspondence must be made between sensory input and meaning, the parietal lobe might be considered a candidate, and because the retrieval of meaning is also important, other regions of the temporal lobe might be considered plausible candidates as well. As you can see in Figure 8.2, the lesion that typically causes Wernicke's aphasia is close to all these areas; it is situated typically at the junction of the temporal lobe with parietal and occipital regions, near Heschl's gyrus.

Not only did Wernicke discover a specific type of aphasia, but he also postulated the existence of other aphasic syndromes, some of which were later documented. Wernicke assumed a basic blueprint for the neurological organization for language in which Broca's area is responsible for speech output and Wernicke's area is responsible for speech comprehension. He went on to suggest that damage severing the connection between these two areas should also result in an aphasic syndrome in which individuals would have difficulty repeating what they just heard. Because the damage would spare both Broca's and Wernicke's areas, the comprehension of language and the production of speech would be intact. Yet information just heard could not be repeated because sound images received by

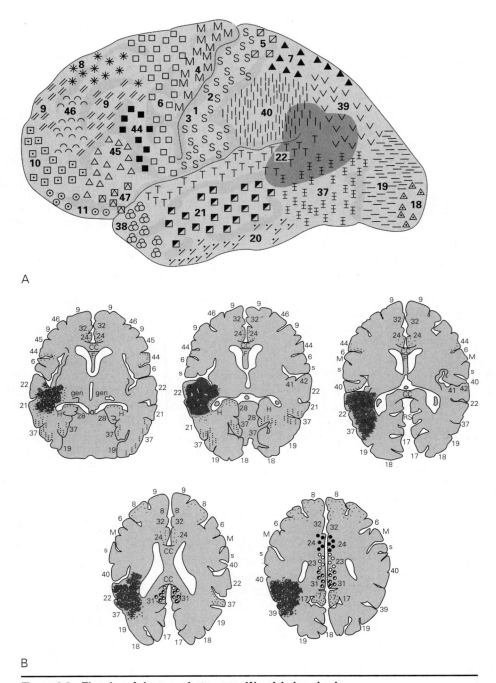

Figure 8.2　The site of damage that causes Wernicke's aphasia.
This diagram shows a composite of the lesions observed in patients with Wernicke's
aphasia, as viewed (A) laterally and (B) in oblique brain slices that go from the lowest region of the brain that is affected (top row, left-hand slice) to the highest region (bottom
row, right-hand slice). In general, not only is Wernicke's area (Brodmann's area 22) affected, but so is primary auditory cortex (areas 41 and 42). The lesion sometimes extends
into regions of the second temporal gyrus (portions of areas 37 and 21) and the angular
gyrus (area 39). (*Note.* A, Adapted from Damasio & Damasio, 1989, p. 184; B, Adapted
from Damasio, 1981, p. 33.)

Wernicke's area could not be conducted forward to Broca's area to be produced. Notice that the underlying assumption of this model is that processing occurs serially, beginning in posterior regions and moving forward with time to anterior regions, much like a product being constructed on an assembly line.

Indeed, a specific inability to repeat, combined with intact comprehension and speech output, is associated with damage between Wernicke's and Broca's areas. Because the difficulties are conceptualized to arise in the conduction of information from Wernicke's area forward to Broca's area, this syndrome is called **conduction aphasia.** When asked to repeat words, individuals with conduction aphasia often make phonemic paraphasias, may substitute or omit words, or may be unable to say anything. You may remember from chapter 2 that syndromes caused by severed connections between intact brain regions are called *disconnection syndromes.* Conduction aphasia meets the criteria for a disconnection syndrome because the behavioral dysfunction does not arise from damage to either the brain region that processes the sound image (Wernicke's area) or the region of the brain that produces the output (Broca's area). Instead, the dysfunction arises from an inability to relay information from one intact area to another intact area—as if a communication cable between the two regions is broken. In fact, a large nerve-fiber tract, known as the *arcuate fasciculus,* connects these two regions, and part of this tract is almost invariably damaged in conduction aphasia. Surrounding tissue usually must also be damaged before the syndrome is observed (Figure 8.3).

Lichtheim and other aphasiologists of the late 1800s elaborated Wernicke's model to include not only a brain region that was responsible for speech output and a brain region that processed sound images, but another region as well, known as the *concept center,* which was thought to be the place in the brain where meanings were stored and from where they originated. This three-part model is shown in Figure 8.4. Although the model itself is flawed, it was used to predict the existence of certain aphasic syndromes that do occur regularly. We next discuss the characteristics of these syndromes that are observed in the clinic. Afterward, we provide one example of why the model is flawed.

Aphasiologists were interested in the implications of a disconnection that could arise between the proposed concept center and the other components of the language-processing system. These researchers reasoned that if the concept center was disconnected from the output center (Broca's area), most of speech output would be disrupted because no route would be available through which ideas could be conveyed to Broca's area for output. However, because Broca's area wasn't damaged, some output should be possible if access to this area could be gained by another means. Because in the model the sound image system is connected to the output center by two routes—not only through the meaning system, but also directly (see Figure 8.4)—the aphasiologists predicted that the intact direct route should enable the person to automatically feed what had just been heard forward for speech output, which would enable repetition of what had just been said. The disruption in transferring information from the concept center to the motor output center, however, would preclude spontaneous speech. A syndrome with this behavioral profile has been observed and is called **transcortical motor aphasia.** Symptomatically, these patients show the same deficits as those shown by patients with Broca's aphasia, except they retain the ability to repeat. In addition, they often seem to have a compulsion to repeat what has just been said, a characteristic known as **echolalia.** The area of brain tissue typically damaged in this syndrome is shown in Figure 8.5.

The aphasiologists also considered the behavioral consequences of a disconnection between the region that processed the sound images of words and the concept center. They reasoned that such a disconnection should preclude an individual from interpreting the meaning of words because the information about sound images could not be relayed to the concept center. Yet, the intact sound image center should allow information received by it to be repeated because the direct connection to the output area would be unaffected (see Figure 8.4). A syndrome with this behavioral profile has also

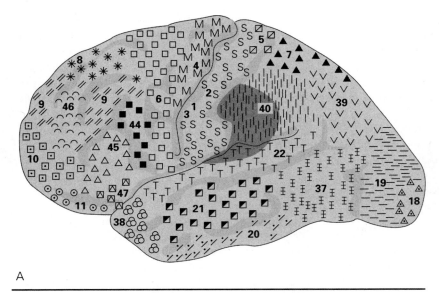

A

Figure 8.3   The site of damage that causes conduction aphasia.
This diagram shows a composite of the lesions observed in six patients with conduction aphasia, as viewed (A) laterally and (B) in oblique brain slices that go from the lowest regions of the brain that are affected (top row) to the highest region (bottom row, right). The lesion generally affects an area in the insula (the region tucked into the Sylvian fissure) that includes Brodmann's areas 22, 41, and 42. More superior regions of the supramarginal gyrus (area 40) are often affected as well. Notice that the damaged area depicted here is located between those shown in Figures 8.1 and 8.2. (*Note.* A, Adapted from Damasio & Damasio, 1989, p. 184; B, Adapted from Damasio, 1981, p. 31.)

been observed and is called **transcortical sensory aphasia.** These patients' symptoms are similar to those of patients with Wernicke's aphasia, except they can repeat and they exhibit echolalia. The damage typically associated with this syndrome is shown in Figure 8.6.

Finally, the aphasiologists speculated that individuals who had extensive damage to multiple parts of the system (e.g., the output center and the sound image center) would be left with neither the ability to comprehend language nor the ability to produce it. Behaviorally, such a syndrome is observed and is known as **global aphasia.** This syndrome is associated with extensive left-hemisphere damage that typically includes not only Wernicke's and Broca's areas, but the area between as well (Figure 8.7).

Although useful, the three-part model of Licht-

heim and other 19th-century aphasiologists does not provide an adequate explanation of the symptomatology in aphasia. For example, the model posits that Broca's aphasia is caused by damage to the language output center. However, as we discuss next, the difficulties experienced by patients with Broca's aphasia are not limited to speech output. Before we analyze the symptoms of aphasia from a psycholinguistic perspective, however, see Table 8.1, which lists the major aphasic syndromes observed in the clinic and their characteristics. Because different nomenclatures are used for these various syndromes, you may also find Broca's aphasia referred to as *nonfluent, agrammatic,* or *anterior aphasia,* whereas Wernicke's aphasia is also sometimes referred to as *fluent,* or *posterior, aphasia.* Figure 8.8 provides a summary schematic of the

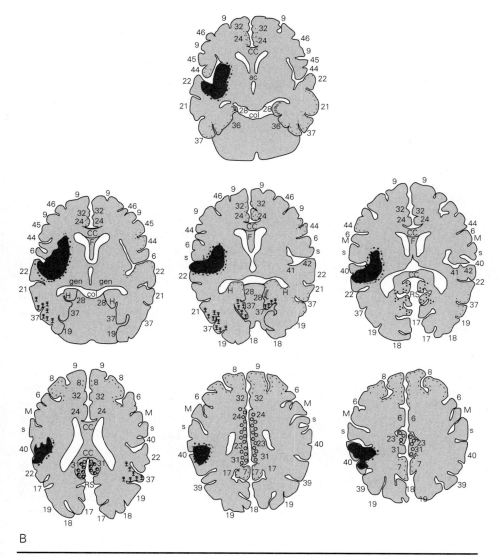

B

Figure 8.3 (Continued)

---

typical lesion locations for each type of aphasia discussed in Table 8.1.

Psychological Perspective

Since the 1960s, interest in aphasia has been renewed because psychologists and psycholinguists have been examining aphasic disorders as a means for understanding the mental structure for language (for a detailed and scholarly discussion of this approach, see Caplan, 1987). By examining the way in which language breaks down in aphasia, these investigators can garner evidence either for or against their theories about the organization of language. To understand how aphasia might inform us about the nature of linguistic processing in the

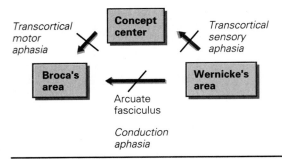

Transcortical motor aphasia

Concept center

Transcortical sensory aphasia

Broca's area

Wernicke's area

Arcuate fasciculus

Conduction aphasia

Figure 8.4 Lichtheim's model of language processing. In Lichtheim's conception, Wernicke's area processes the sound images of words, and this information is then fed forward through a nerve-fiber tract, the arcuate fasciculus, to Broca's area, which is responsible for speech output. Damage to the region between Broca's area and Wernicke's area leads to conduction aphasia. Language disruption can also occur if either the input from Wernicke's area is disconnected from the concept center (which causes transcortical sensory aphasia), or the output from the concept center cannot reach Broca's area (which causes transcortical motor aphasia).

human brain, we must first have some knowledge about the basic components of language as conceptualized by psycholinguists. These individuals consider language to have three main components: phonology, syntax, and semantics. **Phonology** examines the sounds that compose a language and the rules that govern their combination. For example, the difference in sound between a /p/ and a /b/ falls within the domain of phonology (/ / is used to symbolize a linguistic sound, allowing, for example, the sound /b/ to be differentiated from the letter *b*). **Syntax** is the rules of grammar. For example, in English, regular word order is subject, verb, object (SVO), as in the sentence "The dog [subject] chased [verb] the squirrel [object]." **Semantics** is the meaning of language. So, although "The dog chased the squirrel" and "The squirrel was chased by the dog" have different syntactic structures, they are approximately equivalent semantically. In both cases, the big household pet is chasing the smaller nut-eating wild animal. We now discuss phonology, syntax, and semantics in more detail.

Phonology As we just mentioned, phonology refers to the rules governing the sounds of language. Linguists have conceptualized two ways of representing the sounds of speech: phonemically and phonetically. A *phoneme* is considered the smallest unit of sound that can signal meaning. For example, /b/ and /p/ mean nothing by themselves, but they nonetheless cause /bat/ and /pat/ to have different meanings. In contrast, the *phonetic* representation of a speech sound describes how it is produced on particular occasions or in particular contexts. For example, /p/ can be articulated in a number of ways. The /p/ in *pill* is created differently than the /p/ in *spill*. In *pill*, the /p/ is aspirated (produced with a burst of air), whereas the /p/ in *spill* is not aspirated. Different phonetic representations of the same phoneme are known as *allophones*.

To learn more about the neural organization for phonology, researchers have investigated the ways in which both the phonetic and the phonemic representations of sounds are disrupted in aphasia. Persons with Broca's aphasia, and other groups with aphasia whose speech is nonfluent, have difficulty producing the correct allophone of a phoneme (S. Blumstein, 1991), meaning that they cannot produce the correct *phonetic* representation of a speech sound. This finding should not be surprising if you consider that the production of different allophones of the same phoneme requires precise control over the articulatory muscles, with each version varying in subtle but important ways. Because patients with Broca's aphasia produce speech imprecisely, they can often be difficult to understand. In contrast, patients with Wernicke's aphasia (and other fluent aphasias) have little difficulty producing the correct allophone of a given phoneme. Thus, although the phonetic representation of a speech sound is disrupted in Broca's aphasia, it is not disrupted in Wernicke's aphasia.

Even though individuals with Wernicke's aphasia have no difficulty producing the correct phonetic representation of a speech sound, they often have difficulty producing the correct phoneme. This dissociation indicates that the phonemic representa-

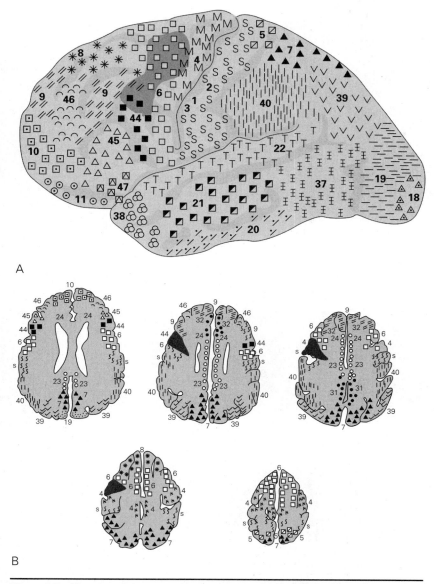

A

B

Figure 8.5   The site of damage in a typical case of transcortical motor aphasia.
Shown here is the damage as viewed (A) laterally and (B) in oblique slices that
go from the lowest region of the brain affected (top row, left) to the highest region (bottom row, right). In general, the lesion is located outside Broca's area
and is either more anterior or more superior. In this particular case, left premotor and motor cortices, just above Broca's area, are affected. (*Note.* Adapted
from Damasio, 1991a, p. 57.)

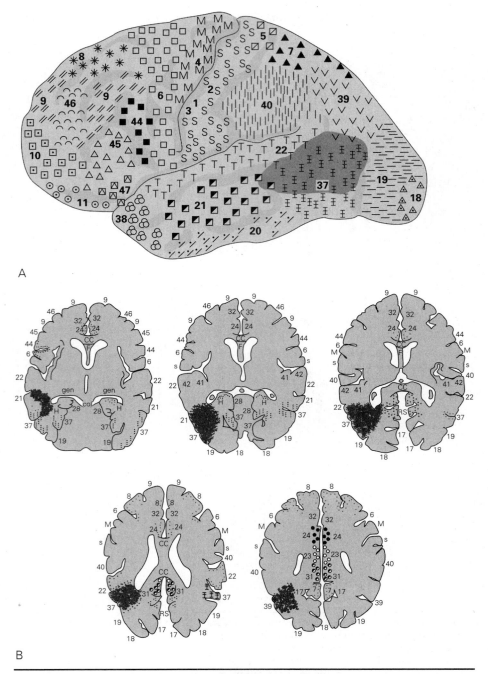

Figure 8.6 The site of damage in transcortical sensory aphasia.
This diagram shows a composite of the lesions observed in six cases of transcortical sensory aphasia, as viewed (A) laterally and (B) in oblique brain slices that go from the lowest region of the brain that is affected (top row, left) to the highest region (bottom row, right). In this type of aphasia, Wernicke's area (area 22) is never completely damaged, but more posterior regions of the temporal lobe (area 37) are always damaged. Sometimes the angular gyrus (area 39) and extrastriate regions (area 19) are also affected. (*Note.* A, Adapted from Damasio & Damasio, 1989, p. 184; B, Adapted from Damasio, 1981, p. 34.)

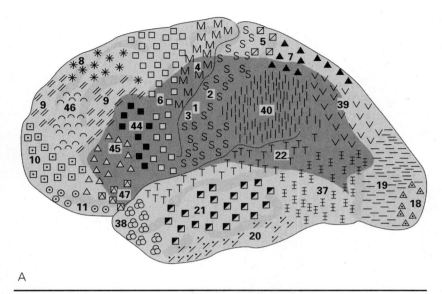

A

Figure 8.7   The site of damage in one case of global aphasia.
Shown here is the damaged area as viewed (A) laterally and (B) in oblique brain
slices that go from the lowest region of the brain that is affected (top row) to the
highest region (bottom row, right). The massive left-hemisphere damage affects
almost all regions implicated in causing the other types of aphasias. (*Note.*
Adapted from Damasio, 1991a, p. 59.)

tion of a speech sound is distinct from its phonetic representation. Thus, whereas a person with Wernicke's aphasia would be highly unlikely to produce an aspirated /p/ for a nonaspirated one, he or she might substitute a /b/ for a /p/. Patients with Broca's aphasia, however, appear to have difficulty producing both the correct phonetic and the correct phonemic representations of a speech sound (see Nespoulous et al., 1984, for a somewhat different perspective, but a similar conclusion that persons with anterior aphasia have difficulty with the execution of word sounds).

Table 8.1   Basic Characteristics of the Major Aphasic Syndromes

Type of aphasia	Spontaneous speech	Paraphasia	Comprehension	Repetition	Naming
Broca's	Nonfluent	Uncommon	Good	Poor	Poor
Wernicke's	Fluent	Common (verbal)	Poor	Poor	Poor
Conduction	Fluent	Common (literal)	Good	Poor	Poor
Transcortical motor	Nonfluent	Uncommon	Good	Good (echolalia)	Poor
Transcortical sensory	Fluent	Common	Poor	Good (echolalia)	Poor
Global	Nonfluent	Variable	Poor	Poor	Poor

Note. Adapted from Benson, 1985, p. 32.

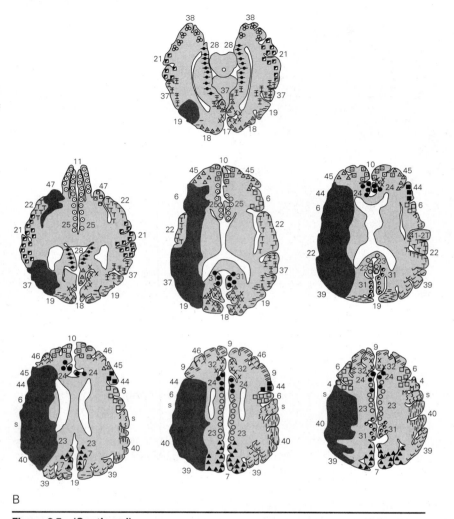

Figure 8.7 (Continued)

The disruption of the phonemic representation of a speech sound in aphasia occurs systematically and can be well explained by considering sounds as being composed of a set of distinctive features. To explain this idea, we need to digress to provide some background information on the production of different speech sounds.

Vowels and consonants are produced differently. Whereas the airflow that produces vowels is unobstructed and continuous, for consonants the air from the lungs runs into some kind of roadblock on its voyage out of the vocal tract. According to linguistic theory, consonants vary in distinctive features, two of which are place of articulation and voicing. **Place of articulation** describes *the location* in the vocal tract where airflow is obstructed. We demonstrate this distinction with *stop consonants*, which are the consonants in which airflow is initially stopped completely. For example, /b/ and /p/ are known as *labial stops* because obstruction occurs

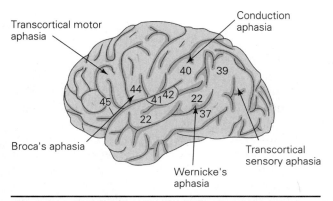

Figure 8.8 A composite diagram indicating the regions associated with the various major types of aphasias.
The numbers in this diagram refer to Brodmann's areas.
(*Note.* Adapted from Damasio, 1991a, p. 47.)

at the lips, /d/ and /t/ are *alveolar stops* because the obstruction occurs from tongue placement at the alveolar ridge behind the front teeth, and /g/ and /k/ are *velar stops* because the air is obstructed at the velar, or soft, palate in the back of the mouth. You can easily determine where the airflow is obstructed if you simply notice where the closure in the vocal tract occurs as you produce these sounds. **Voicing** describes the timing between the release of the air for the stop consonant and the vibration of the vocal cords. When a consonant is voiced, the release of air and the vibration of the vocal cords coincide (/b/, /d/, /g/), whereas in an unvoiced consonant (/p/, /t/, /k/), the vocal cords don't begin to vibrate until after the release. Hence, the only difference between a /b/ and a /p/ is that for a /b/ vocal cord vibration and air release are coincident in time, whereas for a /p/ the air release precedes vocal cord vibration by 40 to 80 ms. As such, incredibly precise timing in the movements of the vocal muscles is necessary to correctly produce a /b/ that is distinct from a /p/. Likewise, precise temporal resolution in the perceptual auditory apparatus is required to perceive the difference between a /b/ and a /p/. The next time you say "bat" or hear it, consider that your vocal apparatus and auditory system distinguish that word from "pat" on the basis of a mere 40 ms.

We can now examine whether the production errors of patients with aphasia are related to a phoneme's distinctive features. For example, /b/ and /p/ differ only in the distinctive feature of voicing, thus they are more similar than /b/ and /t/, which vary with regard to two distinctive features, voicing and place of articulation. Studies have demonstrated that when making phonemic errors, persons with aphasia are much more likely to substitute a sound that differs on the basis of only one distinctive feature rather than two. Phonemic errors of this nature are observed in both fluent and nonfluent aphasias (S. Blumstein, 1991).

We can also examine whether the perception of individuals with aphasia is influenced by distinctive features. Many researchers have found that most persons with aphasia exhibit some problems in discerning these features (e.g., Miceli, Gainotti, Caltagirone, & Masullo, 1980). This is not to imply that all distinctive features have equal saliency, because some may be less resistant to confusion than others. For example, errors based on place of articulation (e.g., /pa/ vs. /ta/) are more common than errors based on voicing (e.g., /pa/ vs. /ba/) (e.g., E. Baker, Blumstein, & Goodglass, 1981). In some cases, individuals with aphasia know that two phonemes sound different (e.g., /ba/ and /da/), but they cannot provide the linguistic value of a sound—for example, identify a sound as a /d/ either by pointing to a card with the letter *D* or by saying "d" (S. E. Blumstein, Cooper, Zurif, & Caramazza, 1977). These individuals appear to be able to distinguish the acoustic differences between the sounds (i.e., distinguish the time offset between vocal cord vibration and airflow release) but have difficulty ascertaining the linguistic value of the sounds that they can discriminate.

Interestingly, the degree of difficulty in linguistically categorizing the acoustic patterns of speech sounds does not predict the level of auditory comprehension (S. E. Blumstein, Baker, & Goodglass, 1977). Some individuals with aphasia who have great difficulty linguistically labeling certain speech sounds may have adequate comprehension. You can probably appreciate this effect if you know what a word means but can't linguistically categorize its constituent sounds well enough to spell it correctly. In addition, persons with aphasia may use information about sentence structure, the legal combination of sounds in words, and the context in which words are presented to overcome their difficulties in linguistic categorization. Conversely, some patients who can linguistically label acoustic patterns may have poor comprehension. Knowing each phoneme in a word does not ensure that you can extract meaning from words and sentences (S. Blumstein, 1991). This effect is similar to knowing all the sounds in a word (and probably also knowing how to spell it) but having no idea of what the word means.

Phonological theory describes not only the sounds of language, as we have just been discussing, but also the rules by which sounds can be combined. So, for example, in English a valid combination of sounds would be "casmeck," whereas an invalid combination would be " *cnamzik." (Linguists denote a word or a sentence that is not legal in a language by preceding it with an asterisk.) As you may remember from our earlier discussion, patients with aphasia, most notably Wernicke's aphasia, often construct novel series of sounds called *neologisms*. These neologisms *could* be words because they follow the rules for combining sounds, but the particular combination used does not compose a

valid word. In this sense, persons with aphasia appear to respect the rules of phonology for the language that they speak.

In summary, phonologic processing can be disrupted in aphasia in two major ways. First, phonetic representations of phonemes are often disrupted in patients with nonfluent aphasias (but remain intact in patients with fluent aphasias). Second, phoneme substitution in production and difficulty in phoneme discrimination are common occurrences in both fluent and nonfluent aphasias and appear to be governed by the similarity of phonemes to each other along the dimensions of distinctive contrasts. Analysis of language breakdown in aphasia suggests that the phonetic and phonemic representations of sounds are distinct because the phonemic representation may be compromised even when the phonetic representation is intact. Despite these difficulties, the rules that govern the combination of specific phonemes are preserved in aphasic speech.

Syntax The second fundamental component of language, syntax, describes the rules governing how words are put together in sentences. For example, in English we generally use a subject-verb-object (SVO) word order, as in the sentence "The cat sat on her lap." This is not true of all languages. In Turkish, for example, the standard word order is subject, object, verb (SOV). Within a language, various syntactic forms or frames are often allowed. For example, SVO word order in English is considered the active voice. In contrast, OVS is considered the passive voice, as in the sentence "The robber [object] was chased [verb] by the police officer [subject]." In addition to order, other indications that this sentence is in the passive voice are the auxiliary verb *was* and the preposition *by*.

When speaking, individuals are sensitive to the syntactic frames available in a language. Studies of slips of the tongue indicate that when words are incorrectly inserted in a sentence, they tend to respect the nature of the information that should be in that slot in the frame (e.g., Garrett, 1975). Consider the following sentence: "The loon was swimming toward the island quickly." In this sentence, the structure is such that a noun (the loon) is taking action indicated by a verb (was swimming) that is followed by a prepositional phrase (toward the island), which indicates the goal of the action, and an adverb (quickly), which specifies how the action is taking place. A person is unlikely to have a slip of the tongue in which she or he says, "The loon was swimming toward the pretty quickly" because the noun in the prepositional phrase would be replaced by an adjective. Rather, a person is much more likely to say, "The loon was swimming toward the table quickly," replacing the intended noun in the prepositional phrase, *island,* with another noun, *table.*

Persons with certain types of aphasia, most notably those with anterior lesions, often have specific difficulties with the syntactic aspects of language processing. If you reread the opening vignette, you should notice that function words and word endings are missing, and that the words produced lack a standard syntactic frame. Historically, researchers assumed that persons with anterior aphasia failed to produce function words and prepositions not because they had difficulty with syntax, but because their difficulty in producing speech biased them to produce words that carried the most meaning, usually nouns and verbs. If this explanation were correct, we would strongly predict that even though syntactic markers should be absent in speech production, they should be used to aid in comprehension. However, if there is a basic underlying disturbance in syntactic processing, it should manifest not only in production, but in comprehension as well.

By examining the comprehension of syntactic structures by individuals with anterior aphasia, investigators revealed that these patients have a deficit in both the production *and* the comprehension of syntax. Because they have difficulty with the grammatical aspect of language, they are sometimes said to have **agrammatic aphasia.** For example, persons with anterior aphasia often have difficulty discerning the difference between active and passive sentences such as "The cat chased the kitten" versus "The cat was chased by the kitten." In the former case, the word structure is in the standard SVO (subject-verb-object) form, whereas in the latter it is in the nonstandard OVS (object-verb-subject) form, as

signaled by the grammatical markers of the auxiliary verb *was* and the preposition *by.* Because of their insensitivity to syntactic markers, these patients assume a SVO word order for both sentences. Hence, when asked to select a picture representing the meaning of each sentence, these individuals select the same picture for both sentences, one of an adult feline chasing an immature feline.

Because languages vary widely in their syntactic structure, many opportunities exist to obtain converging evidence for the role of anterior brain regions in the processing of syntax (see Bates, Wulfeck, & MacWhinney, 1991, and related articles in the same issue of *Brain and Language* for a discussion of the commonalities and peculiarities of aphasia across different languages). For example, in English, we have only one definite article, *the,* and our nouns are not gendered (male, female, neuter). However, in many other languages, one *the* is used for male nouns, another *the* for female nouns, and yet another *the* for neutral nouns. Furthermore, *the* for a noun that is the subject of the sentence may differ from *the* for a noun that is the object. For example, in German, *the* for male nouns that are the subject of the sentence is *der*, whereas when a male noun is the object of a sentence, *the* becomes *den* and an *-n* is added to the end of the noun. Hence, the sentence "Der Junge küsste das Mädchen" means "The boy kissed the girl," whereas "Den Jungen küsste das Mädchen" means "The girl kissed the boy." The *den* and the *-n* at the end of *Junge* indicate that the boy is playing the role of the object. Given these two sentences, persons with anterior aphasia who are fluent in German have difficulty realizing that the boy is being kissed in the second sentence because they assume SVO word order (von Stockert & Bader, 1976).

Despite having problems differentiating between different syntactic constructions, patients with anterior aphasia have little trouble understanding sentences such as "The ice-cream cone was eaten by the boy" because their ability to understand the meaning of words (i.e., semantics) restricts the interpretation of such sentences. When faced with the sentence just mentioned, an individual with anterior aphasia knows that ice-cream cones cannot eat boys and hence is not confused by the OVS word order. In contrast, because cats can chase kittens and kittens can chase cats, who is chasing whom is not constrained. Only when syntax must be relied upon to distinguish meaning do persons with anterior aphasia have difficulty.

In contrast, persons with posterior aphasia appear to have little difficulty processing syntactic aspects of language. As mentioned at the beginning of the chapter, their speech is fluent and contains all the grammatical markers (e.g., verb endings, prepositions, auxilliary verbs) that would normally be found in intact speech production (although what they say is largely devoid of meaning). Thus, their knowledge of syntax appears to be spared.

Semantics The third fundamental component of language, semantics, is concerned with the meaning of words and word combinations. Sentences may have different syntactic structures yet have approximately the same meaning. For example, "The beaver appeared among the reeds on the far side of the lake from where I was standing" has the same basic meaning as "On the side of the lake opposite from where I was positioned, the beaver appeared among the reeds."

The ability to extract meaning from language or to use words to produce meaning is seriously compromised in patients with posterior aphasia. In a severe case, a patient with this disorder may be unable to follow even simple commands such as "Point to the blue circle" and "Point to the big red square," which are included in a quick screening device for aphasia known as the *Token Test* (DeRenzi, 1980). In other cases, simple nouns are understood but comprehension of more complicated linguistic material is difficult. Furthermore, this difficulty in comprehending the meaning of language is pervasive across modalities, extending to both auditory and written language. This finding indicates that the meaning system itself, as compared with some modality-specific access to that system, is disrupted. In contrast, patients with anterior aphasia appear to have intact semantic processing. They can usually follow simple commands with ease, although, as mentioned previously, they

might exhibit minor problems in comprehension when syntax plays a large role in interpreting sentences. For example, if told to "Place the blue circle *on top of* the big red square," patients with anterior aphasia might react by putting the blue circle *next to* the big red square because their problems with syntax would hinder their comprehension of the prepositional phrase that describes the desired relationship between the two items.

Comparison of the Neurological and Psychological Viewpoints

In conceptualizing the difference between anterior and posterior aphasias, we provided evidence for two types of contrasts. On the one hand, we conceptualized anterior areas as important for speech output and posterior areas as important for speech comprehension. On the other hand, we suggested that anterior areas are important for syntactic processing and that posterior areas are involved in semantic processing. Each of these models has some validity, but a melding of the two probably best characterizes the manner in which these brain areas process language. Thus, anterior areas undoubtedly are important for speech output. However, this region of the brain also appears to play a primary role in syntactic processing. Likewise, posterior areas appear to be important for processing speech input. But the function of this area is clearly more all-encompassing because damage to this region disrupts many aspects of semantic processing. Individuals with posterior aphasia don't have difficulty comprehending only auditory language, they have difficulty comprehending *all* language, regardless of modality. Thus, they read and write no better than they can understand speech, and their speech output conveys no more meaning than they appear to extract from spoken language.

Regardless of how the processing difficulties experienced in the two types of aphasias are distinguished (input-output or syntactic-semantic), these syndromes represent a double dissociation in language processing. On a theoretical level, this dissociation tells us that no *unitary* language center or language system exists in the brain. Rather, the system has specific components that can act more or less independently of one another. Coming to such a realization is important both for understanding the neural control of language more completely and for practical reasons. For example, realizing that the input and output of auditory language are governed by different systems allows us to know that therapies geared toward speech production are likely to have little effect on comprehension. Likewise, knowledge that a language's grammar and its meaning are under separate neural control tells us that being tutored in the rules of grammar is unlikely to aid a person with aphasia who is having difficulty producing sentences that make sense. In sum, the human brain appears to have two distinct and separable subsystems that play different roles in language functioning. Although the anterior and posterior systems are intimately linked and interact seamlessly in the normally functioning brain, their separability can be revealed by brain damage.

Until this point, our discussion of the neurological bases for language centered on evidence from individuals with brain lesions. However, as mentioned in chapter 2, converging evidence from different neuropsychological techniques is important if we want to be fairly certain of our findings. We next turn to such evidence.

Converging Evidence From Other Research Methods

In this section of the chapter, we examine the converging evidence that exists for two important generalizations we made about language. First, we study additional evidence that the left hemisphere plays a special role in auditory language processing. Then we analyze further evidence for a distinction between anterior and posterior language systems.

Evidence for the left hemisphere's special role in speech production comes not only from patients with anterior aphasia and those with the split-brain syndrome (as discussed in chapter 3), but also from two methods used during surgery for epilepsy to isolate brain regions involved in language processing. One of these, the Wada technique, was discussed in chapter 3 (see page 99). As a reminder, this procedure involves the injection of sodium amobarbital, a barbiturate, into one of the two carotid arteries. The injection anesthetizes only one of the hemispheres. After the drug takes effect, the test administrator asks the patient to name a series of items, depicted on cards, that he or she was able to name prior to injection. If the anesthetized hemisphere is responsible for speech output, the person is unable to name the items. To ensure that only one hemisphere is capable of speech output, the usual practice is to repeat the procedure, except the barbiturate is now injected into the other carotid artery to anesthetize the opposite hemisphere. The second procedure is necessary because in a relatively small percentage of cases, speech output is controlled by both hemispheres. Table 8.2 presents the percentages of left- and right-handed individuals who have left-hemisphere, right-hemisphere, and bihemispheric control of speech output (Rasmussen & Milner, 1977a). As you can see for right-handers, speech output was rarely controlled by the right hemisphere, and in no case was speech output controlled by both hemispheres. This information is

Table 8.2 Control of Speech Output in a Sample of Left- and Right-Handed Patients as Determined by the Wada Technique

Handedness	No. of cases	Speech representation (%)		
		Left	Bilateral	Right
Right	140	96	0	4
Left	122	70	15	15

Note. Data from Rasmussen & Milner, 1997a, p. 359.

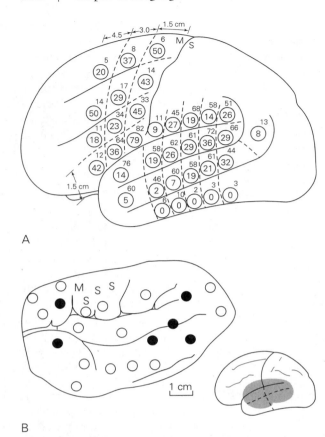

A

B

Figure 8.9 Language localization in the left hemisphere as determined from electrical stimulation studies. (A) Variability among 117 patients for the regions of the left hemisphere that when electrically stimulated disrupt the ability to name objects. The number within each circle denotes the percentage of individuals whose language was disrupted by stimulation at that point, whereas the number above indicates the absolute number of individuals who produced naming errors when stimulated at that point. *M* and *S* mark the locations of the motor and sensory cortices, respectively. Variability can be seen among individuals both for anterior regions (which control the production of the object's name) and for posterior regions (which are involved in gaining access to the object's name). (B) The sites at which electrical stimulation disrupted naming in one female patient. Circles represent the locations tested. Stimulation at the open circles caused no disruption in naming, whereas stimulation at the solid circles did. A relatively well circumscribed anterior language region is located near Broca's area and the motor cortex, whereas the posterior region is more diffuse although still located near those regions that are classically considered Wernicke's area. (*Note.* Adapted from Ojemann et al., 1989, pp. 318, 320.)

consistent with the clinical observation that **crossed aphasia**—that is, aphasia that results from a right-hemisphere lesion in a right-hander—occurs with a frequency of 1% or less (Benson & Geschwind, 1972). However, knowing which hemisphere is responsible for speech output in left-handers is a more difficult proposition. Although left-handers, like right-handers, are most likely to have speech output controlled by the left hemisphere, in a significant proportion of left-handers the *right* hemisphere is specialized for speech output. Furthermore, in still other left-handed individuals, each hemisphere is capable of producing speech, a pattern, rarely if ever, observed in right-handers.

Another means of investigating the localization of auditory language processing in the brain is to stimulate the brain electrically before or during surgery for the removal of epileptic tissue. This stimulation is performed in much the same manner as discussed in chapter 2 to determine the location and extent of the motor and somatosensory regions. This method reveals language to be lateralized to the left hemisphere in nearly all right-handers, a finding consistent with the results of lesion studies. Such stimulation also reveals, however, that the exact locations within the left hemisphere that are responsible for language processing vary considerably among individuals (Figure 8.9A). Furthermore, the specific regions that are critical for language tend to be much smaller than those estimated from lesion studies and tend to have distinct boundaries (G. Ojemann, Ojemann, Lettich, & Berger, 1989). Lesion studies are likely to provide larger estimates because they are usually determined by pooling lesion sites from a variety of patients. Given the degree of variation in the morphology of human brains (e.g., Belliveau et al., 1991), such pooling provides only a ballpark estimate of the area responsible for a specific function. For any given individual, the critical area is only a portion of this ballpark area (Figure 8.9B) (G. A. Ojemann, 1991).

In addition to showing that language is controlled by a network of left-hemisphere regions, studies of electrical stimulation reveal that anterior and posterior regions of the left hemisphere play different roles in language. Stimulation of areas in the left inferior frontal, left parietal, and superior temporal lobes disrupts both sequential orofacial movement used in speech production *and* the identification of speech sounds. Although this finding might seem to suggest that anterior and posterior language areas are undifferentiated, only a small population of neurons (located in the left superior temporal gyrus) have been identified in which the change in activity is the *same* during speech perception and production. Thus, the roles in language played by anterior and posterior regions are likely to differ because the neural activity in each region is different during production than during comprehension. Nonetheless, anterior and posterior language regions of the left hemisphere appear to be linked because they must coordinate functions to process auditory language.

Positron emission tomography (PET) studies not only provide converging evidence that anterior and posterior brain regions play different roles in language, but also highlight the importance of the left hemisphere in linguistic processing. For example, increased activity in the superior temporal regions of the brain, especially those of the left hemisphere, is observed when individuals must distinguish aurally presented words from aurally presented nonwords. The activated area overlaps with that described by Wernicke as processing the sound images of words (e.g., Frith, Friston, Liddle, & Frackowiak, 1991). In contrast, when words must be repeated rather than just heard, activation of the frontal regions, including Broca's area, is found (Petersen et al., 1988).

In addition to confirming findings from other methods, PET studies have expanded our knowledge of the cortical anatomy underlying language processing (see J. A. Fiez & Petersen, 1993, for a succinct review of some of this research). For example, such studies have revealed that well-rehearsed sequences or words are produced by a different cortical pathway than that used when novel words must be generated. In one study, researchers examined the brain regions that are involved in generating a verb in response to a noun (M. Raichle et al., 1994). When subjects were naive to either the task or the particular set of stimuli used, activation occurred over the regions of the left hemisphere that when damaged typically cause Wernicke's aphasia. However, when the subjects were given a familiar and well-practiced set of stimuli, activation was more anterior, in an area typically associated with conduction aphasia (which, as you should remember, disrupts the ability to repeat sequences). Hence, the particular regions of the left hemisphere's neural circuit for language that are used for a given task appear to depend on the facility or automaticity with which the output can be generated.

In this section, we learned that besides lesion studies, various methods—such as electrical stimulation, Wada procedures, and PET studies—all provide evidence of left-hemisphere specialization for auditory language processing and of different roles for posterior and anterior regions of the auditory language system. Next, we turn our attention to how the brain processes visual language.

NEUROLOGICAL BASES FOR VISUAL LANGUAGE PROCESSING

The portions of the neurological system that support processing of written language functions are distinct from those that support auditory language functions, although in right-handers both reside within the left hemisphere. We should not be surprised that the neural machinery for auditory language and that for written language differ in some respects. First, these two types of language processing occur in different modalities and to the degree that they interact with different sensory regions of the brain, they might be presumed to differ in their neural organization. Second, from an evolutionary perspective, although auditory language has existed for some time, written language is a relatively new invention. Third, as we see in the following section, interpretation of written language does not always rely on using spoken language as an intermediary. To the degree that processing visual words is independent of spoken language, these two types of language processing might be expected to have different neurological bases. We now turn to a more detailed discussion of the neurological bases for visual language.

...nce From Studies of Patients with ...ain Damage

As we did when discussing the neurological bases for auditory language processing, we begin this section by examining the information about written language that can be gleaned from studies of patients with brain damage. Then we discuss converging evidence from other methods.

Alexia Versus Agraphia

Just as the production of auditory language is distinct from the perception of auditory language, so too is the production of written language (writing) distinct from the perception of written words (reading). When, as a consequence of brain damage, the ability to read is lost, the ensuing syndrome is known as **alexia.** In contrast, when a person loses the ability to write as a result of brain damage, the deficit is known as **agraphia.** Although typically alexia and agraphia co-occur after damage to the angular gyrus (which is located in the ventral region of the parietal lobe above the Sylvian fissue), in some cases individuals have alexia without agraphia (e.g., Greenblatt, 1973) or in other cases agraphia without alexia (e.g., Hécaen & Kremin, 1976). These dissociations can lead to some strange situations. Although an individual who has alexia without agraphia can write a sentence with little difficulty, the person is unable to read sentences, including those that she or he previously wrote. Thus, even though the brain of a person with this condition knows the motor commands for forming letters and sentences, the ability to decipher the same material is lost. Likewise, individuals who have agraphia without alexia are unable to write sentences but can read without much difficulty.

As you should recognize by now, the syndromes of alexia without agraphia and agraphia without alexia are another example of a double dissociation. In this case, the double dissociation indicates that the neural control systems for reading and writing are separable to some extent and do not critically rely on each other. Hence, we do not have a single module in the brain that is important for written language; instead, we have distinct systems, one for interpreting written language and one for producing it.

Phonological Route Versus Direct Route to Meaning

To better understand how the brain processes written language, we first examine the cognitive processes underlying written language. In the discussion that follows, we use reading as an example, then later describe how these findings generalize to writing.

Reading   Researchers have proposed two distinct routes whereby information in a visual linguistic format can be linked to meaning (e.g., Meyer, Schvaneveldt, & Ruddy, 1974; however, see Seidenberg & McClelland, 1989, who argue for a single route on the basis of a computational model, a variant of which was shown by K. E. Patterson, Seidenberg, & McClelland, 1989, to mimic some aspects of reading impairments resulting from brain damage). The first route is known as the **phonological route to reading** because sound is a mediator in the process of associating print with meaning. You may have been exposed to this route when you learned to read if you were taught that each letter has a different sound. When confronted with a written word for the first time, such as *cat*, you probably visually parsed the word into three letters (*c, a, t*), sounded out each letter (/k/, /a/, /t/), then blended the three sounds to produce a word ("cat"). Once you pronounced the word, you could recognize its meaning because you already associated this sound pattern with the concept that it represents ("a small, furry household pet with claws that is known for its taste for tuna and mice and for an aloof and independent demeanor"). Thus, the auditory sounds were the intermediary allowing you to link print to meaning.

The rules whereby print is associated with sound are known as **grapheme-to-phoneme correspondence rules.** *Graphemes* are the smallest units of written language that are combined to make words. For example, the visual pattern "c" is a grapheme, and this grapheme can take many forms, such as "C," "*c*," "C," and "**C**." Grapheme-to-phoneme correspondence rules let us know how each grapheme should sound (e.g., "c" is usually pronounced /ka/) and how graphemes should be combined. For example, these rules dictate that for most words ending in *vowel-consonant-"e"* (e.g., *lake, mike*), the first vowel is long and the final "e" is silent.

The second route is known as the **direct route to reading** because print is directly associated with meaning, without the use of a phonological intermediary. For a certain proportion of words in the English language, the direct route *must* be used because these words do not follow grapheme-to-phoneme correspondence rules and hence are impossible to sound out correctly. These words are known as **irregular words.** For example, if grapheme-to-phoneme correspondence rules are used to pronounce *colonel*, the result will be the incorrect "koe-loe-nell," rather than "kur-nel." When the direct route is used, an association is made between a particular visual form of a word (e.g., *colonel*) and its meaning (e.g., "a high-ranking military officer whose rank is just below that of a general").

Whether neurologically intact readers use the phonological route or the direct route was, at one time, a source of much debate among cognitive psychologists. According to one viewpoint, the phonological route was mainly used when a person was acquiring the ability to read and whenever a skilled reader encountered a new word (as we usually attempt to sound out unfamiliar words). For known words, skilled readers were assumed to use the direct route because sounding these words out was no longer necessary. Hence, the intermediate step of linking print to sound was mostly abandoned because it was time consuming and unnecessary (e.g., Taft, 1982). According to a second viewpoint, even skilled readers were assumed to rely heavily on a phonological route (e.g., Chastain, 1987).

To try to resolve this issue by using information from patients with brain damage, researchers needed a way to examine the integrity of each route separately. To assess the integrity of the phonological route in individuals with brain damage, these investigators determined whether the patients could read words that they had never seen before and whether they could read nonwords. Reading new words would rely on the phonological route because no prior linkages from the visual form to meaning would exist, thus direct access would be impossible. Similarly, the phonological route would be used in reading nonwords because they have no meaning. (For instance, until now, you probably never saw the nonword *glimay*, but you can read it using your knowledge of grapheme-to-phoneme correspondence rules.) Likewise, these researchers assessed the integrity of the direct route by determining how well the patients could read words that do not follow the grapheme-to-phoneme correspondence rules (i.e., common irregular words), such as *colonel* and *yacht*.

Such neuropsychological research helped to clarify the issue by demonstrating that both routes are available and that each can be used independently of the other. One set of individuals was found to have a disruption in the direct route but not in the phonological route. These individuals are said to have **surface alexia** (this syndrome is sometimes referred to as *surface dyslexia*, although, as we learn in chapter 13, the term *dyslexia* is typically used to describe either dysfunctional reading or an inability to learn to read in childhood, rather than a loss of reading ability after brain damage). This syndrome is so named because the individuals cannot link the surface information—that is, the visual form of a word—directly to meaning. Persons with surface alexia cannot read irregular words correctly. They sound out the words (using the phonological route) and hence misread them. They often confuse *homophones*, words that sound the same but have different meanings, such as *beat* and *beet*. For example, when asked to define the word *pane*, these patients may say "to feel distress," or when asked to define *mown*, they may say "to complain." Their spelling errors also indicate their reliance on the phonological route because their spellings are often phonologically correct but graphemically incorrect (e.g., writing *whisk* as *wisque*, or *mayonnaise* as *mayenaze*) (e.g., Coltheart, 1982; Shallice, Warrington, & McCarthy, 1983). In contrast, when given nonwords or regular words to read, these individuals do well because they can use the intact phonological route. Even though these patients probably read regular words by means of the direct route before damage (e.g., read *cat* by recognizing the visual pattern), they retain the ability to read such words after damage because regular words can just as easily be read by using grapheme-to-phoneme correspondence rules. The lesion that causes surface alexia usually involves temporal structures in the left hemisphere, although the exact location varies (Vanier & Caplan, 1985).

Individuals with the contrasting syndrome, **phonological alexia,** have a disrupted phonological route but an intact direct route. They have relatively little trouble reading previously learned words because regardless of whether the words are regular or irregular, these individuals can extract meaning directly from the visual form. Their disability becomes apparent only when they are asked to read nonwords or words with which they are unfamiliar. In these cases, the direct route does not suffice because either they do not have an association between the visual form and meaning (as is the case with unfamiliar words) or no such association exists (as in the case of nonwords) (e.g., K. Patterson, 1982). The lesion that causes such a deficit has not been well localized but, as might be expected, usually involves posterior regions of the left hemisphere.

If you understand the distinction between phonological and surface alexia, you should be able to predict the performance of each group for the following three tasks. In each task, the individual is shown two pairs of items and must decide which pair contains two items that sound identical. The first task involves regular words (e.g., *sail/sale* vs. *sail/salt*), the second task irregular words (e.g., *berry/bury* vs. *ferry/fury*), and the third task nonwords (e.g., *fex/phects* vs. *fex/phox*). If you were a person with phonological alexia, which pairs would cause you difficulty? Remember that in phonological alexia the grapheme-to-phoneme route is disrupted. Hence, patients with phonological alexia should have relatively little difficulty with real words, regardless of whether they are regular (e.g., *sail/sale*) or irregular (e.g., *berry/bury*). These individuals use the direct route to meaning, which in turn can be used to generate the sound. For example, seeing *sail* allows a person with phonological alexia to gain access to the idea of a piece of cloth on a ship that is used to capture the wind's energy and propel the ship forward. Once meaning is obtained, the individual with phonological alexia can conjure the name of the word, just as seeing a picture of a sail or thinking about a sail allows you to say "sail." In contrast, nonwords (e.g., *fex/phects*) cannot be distinguished because gaining access to the sounds of nonwords relies on grapheme-to-phoneme correspondence rules, which are lost.

What type of performance would you expect from a person with surface alexia? Because the phonologic system is intact, little difficulty with the nonwords (e.g., *fex/phects*) and regular words (e.g. *sail/sale*) would be expected because these pairs can be translated into sound according to grapheme-to-phoneme correspondence rules. In contrast, because the direct route is damaged, correct pronunciation of irregular words (e.g., *berry/bury*) would be difficult because using grapheme-to-phoneme correspondence rules would lead to the wrong pronunciation. For example, *bury* would probably be mispronounced because it does not follow the same grapheme-to-phoneme correspondence rules as words like *fury* and *jury* do.

In a related syndrome, known as **deep alexia,** individuals show many of the deficits exhibited by persons with phonological alexia (such as the inability to read nonwords), so much so that some individuals have suggested that phonological alexia is just a milder form of deep alexia (e.g., Glosser & Friedman, 1990). However, the patients with deep alexia exhibit additional difficulties. First, when reading, individuals with deep alexia often make **semantic paralexias,** which are reading errors in which a word is misread as a word with a related meaning. For example, *forest* may be read as "woods" and *tulip* as "crocus." Second, these individuals have more difficulty reading abstract words (e.g., *sympathy, faith*) than words that represent concrete entities in the physical world (e.g., *refrigerator, basket*). Third, these patients have difficulty reading small function words that serve as grammatical markers. Because of this constellation of symptoms, Coltheart (1980) suggested that the syndrome may represent reliance on the right hemisphere for reading. As demonstrated by the reading performance of the isolated right hemisphere in patients with the split-brain syndrome, this hemisphere is better able to read concrete words than abstract words, has no ability to use grapheme-to-phoneme conversion rules, and cannot distinguish among the meanings of words that are closely associated (E. Zaidel, 1990).

Writing   Just as two routes to reading can be used, studies of patients with unilateral brain damage suggest that two routes can be used to transform thoughts into writing. One route goes from thought directly to writing, whereas the other uses phoneme-to-grapheme correspondence rules as an intermediary. In **phonological agraphia,** individuals can manually or orally spell regular and irregular words to dictation but perform poorly with nonwords (e.g., Shallice, 1981). In **lexical agraphia,** the opposite occurs: A reasonable spelling, both manually and orally, can be produced for virtually any nonword, but spelling of irregular words is poor (e.g., Beauvois & Derouesne, 1981). Hence, just as is the case for reading, writing seems to entail two routes, a direct one and a phonological one. Although you may have anticipated such a distinction on the basis of what we learned about reading, this needn't have been the case because even though reading and writing are similar, the process of writing is not just reading in reverse order. For example, phoneme-to-grapheme rules are not the opposite of grapheme-to-phoneme rules. Consider the following case in point. Although /k/ is the most common sound for the grapheme "k," the most common grapheme for the sound /k/ is "c."

The dissociation between these two routes to writing is supported by findings that the typical lesion in each syndrome differs from that of the other. Damage that causes phonological agraphia, in which the sound-based route is disrupted, tends to be found in the left supramarginal gyrus, an area of the parietal lobe directly above the posterior section of the Sylvian fissure (Roeltgen & Heilman,

1984). This location makes sense if you consider that it is situated near parietal regions implicated in reading and is close to regions that are known to process sound-based aspects of language, such as Wernicke's area. In contrast, the location of the lesion that causes lexical agraphia is more posterior, at the conjunction of the posterior parietal lobe and the parieto-occipital junction (Roeltgen & Heilman, 1984). In this case, the lesion is closer to areas involved in processing visual representations, which is consistent with the loss of an ability to go directly from a word's meaning to its graphemic (i.e., visually based) representation.

Other Components of Visual Language Processing

The syndromes we discussed so far are sometimes called *central* alexias or *central* agraphias because the problem arises in the linkage to or from meaning. In contrast, the peripheral processes required for reading and writing, such as the ability to analyze letters visually or to produce the motor patterns for writing graphemes, are intact. However, in other syndromes, these peripheral processes may be affected in a manner that is specific to reading. An individual unable to recognize many types of visual forms would not be considered to have a specific problem in reading. Yet if these difficulties were limited to processing visual forms of linguistic relevance, such as letters, we would be more inclined to categorize the problem as one that involved reading. When a specific disruption in the reading process occurs outside the linkage of form to meaning, it is sometimes referred to as a *precentral* alexia (when the difficulty arises prior to gaining access to meaning) or as a *peripheral* alexia. These disruptions include the inability to process more than one letter at a time, to read all the letters in a word, or to appreciate the overall form of a group of letters.

Some precentral dyslexias result from a disruption in attentional processes that affects only reading. In a syndrome known as **attentional dyslexia,** the individual can recognize a single letter or a single word in isolation but cannot recognize the same letter or word if it is presented along with items of the same kind (i.e., other letters or other words) (e.g., Shallice & Warrington, 1977). This attentional problem is similar to that observed in Balint's syndrome (also known as *dorsal simultanagnosia*), which we discussed in chapter 6. At present, the lesion critical for causing this syndrome is unknown, but typically individuals have posterior left-hemisphere damage that includes subcortical structures. In **neglect dyslexia,** the individual consistently misreads the beginning or the end of a word, such as misreading *this* as "his" or misreading *discount* as "mount" (e.g., Ellis, Flude, & Young, 1987). This syndrome is similar to hemineglect. Not surprisingly, neglect dyslexia involves damage to the parietal lobe. As we mentioned in chapter 7, neglect of words may occur not only with regard to an external frame of reference, as in neglect dyslexia, but also with regard to a frame of reference inherent to a word. In this case, the neglect is exhibited for a particular portion of a word regardless of its length or orientation (Caramazza & Hillis, 1990). In one case study of a patient with this syndrome (who had sustained a lesion to the parietal lobe of the left hemisphere), the last half of the word was neglected despite variations in orientation. For example, the horizontally presented word *hound* was read as "house," the vertically oriented word *blending* was read as "blemish," and the mirror-image word инишшоэ was read as "comet." Hence, the end of the word was neglected, regardless of where it was positioned in space.

In another syndrome known as **letter-by-letter reading** (sometimes referred to as *spelling dyslexia* or *pure alexia*), individual letters can be identified, but they cannot be integrated to form a word (e.g., K. E. Patterson & Kay, 1982; Warrington & Shallice, 1980). Individuals with this syndrome use oral spelling as a means to reading; they say each letter aloud and then use that information to deduce the word. Thus, a letter-by-letter reader sees the word *cat* and identifies it by saying "*C, a, t,* oh, that must be *cat*!" The lesion that typically causes such a syndrome is located in inferior portions of the occipital lobe bordering on the temporal lobe of the left hemisphere.

In review, studies of patients with neurologic disorders demonstrate that difficulties in visual language can occur either in the linkage to meaning or in other processes specific to visual language skills. We now examine converging evidence about the neurological bases for visual language.

Converging Evidence from Other Research Methods

Studies of individuals with brain damage suggest that the neural substrates of auditory language and those of visual language are distinct, and converging evidence for this assertion comes from imaging studies of brain activation in neurologically intact individuals. Reading pronounceable nonsense words and real words activates a region at the occipitotemporal border in the left hemisphere, whereas a different region of the brain, the temporoparietal area, becomes activated when subjects hear an auditory word or when they decide whether two visually presented words sound similar (Petersen et al., 1988). These findings suggest that the brain regions specific to reading words are distinct from those required for pronouncing words.

Brain imaging studies, electrophysiologic studies, and behavioral studies of neurologically intact individuals also provide insights into how the brain processes visual word form. These studies suggest that the analysis of visual word form is supported by two separate systems, which are located in opposite hemispheres. The right-hemisphere system encodes words in the specific forms or fonts in which they are presented, whereas the left-hemisphere system appears to extract an abstract representation of word form that is common across different instances of a word, such as variations in font or case. Let's explore, in more detail, evidence that the right hemisphere extracts the specifics of the visual form of a word. PET studies reveal that activation over the right hemisphere is great when people are presented with strings of letterlike forms that look similar to distorted letters from the Cyrillic alphabet or with consonant letter strings (e.g., JVJFC) (Petersen, Fox, Snyder, & Raichle, 1990). The right hemisphere appears to process the visual form of linguistic information soon after receipt because event-related potential (ERP) studies reveal a larger positive amplitude (P_{100}) over the right posterior cortex than that over the left about 80 to 120 ms after the presentation of words or nonsense strings (Posner & McCandliss, 1993). Moreover, divided visual field studies indicate that the right hemisphere can better distinguish among different fonts of the same letter than the left hemisphere can (Bryden & Allard, 1976). Finally, priming studies of neurologically intact subjects reveal that if a particular physical shape of a word is presented to the right hemisphere, subsequent processing of that word is facilitated to a greater degree when it appears in the same case (e.g., uppercase) than when it is presented in a different case (e.g., lowercase) (e.g., Marsolek, Kosslyn, & Squire, 1992). The priming effect for words in identical visual form appears to be specific to the lingual gyrus of the right hemisphere but not the left, as ascertained in PET studies (Squire et al., 1992).

In contrast, the left hemisphere appears to be less influenced by the specific visual form of a word. Rather, it has a more abstract or general representation of words. In neurologically intact individuals, the left hemisphere is facilitated by previous exposure to a word to an equal degree when the word appears in a physical form that is identical to the original presentation and when it appears in an altered form (e.g., Marsolek, Kosslyn, & Squire, 1992). Furthermore, left-hemisphere damage is associated with syndromes that appear to indicate a disruption of a word's abstract form. For example, as we discussed earlier, individuals with damage to the left ventral occipital area can read only one letter at a time, which suggests that they cannot integrate the letters into a general word form (e.g., Reuter-Lorenz & Brunn, 1990). We also mentioned a case in which a left parietal lesion resulted in neglect of the end of all words regardless of how they were oriented in space (e.g., horizontally, backward, vertically). Hence, the neglect exhibited by this individual was with regard to a framework of a word's general abstract form (rather than a framework

linked to a specific form, spatial position, or orientation of the word).

The left hemisphere may also have mechanisms that are sensitive to the rules that govern how letters are combined, known as *orthography,* and/or the phonological status of a letter string. This process occurs early as the ERP waveforms in response to real words and pronounceable nonsense words begin to diverge from the waveforms observed for consonant strings 200 ms after exposure (Posner & McCandliss, 1993). PET data indicate that a region at the occipitotemporal border in the left hemisphere becomes activated during the reading of pronounceable nonsense words (e.g., *floop*) and real words but not in response to consonant strings or letterlike forms (Petersen, Fox, Snyder, & Raichle, 1990).

All the evidence we discussed so far suggests that many dissociations exist in the neural machinery supporting language processing. Because most of our evidence has come from studies involving speakers and readers of Indo-European languages, we now turn our attention to other linguistic systems that provide evidence about the neurological bases for language.

PROCESSING OF NON-INDO-EUROPEAN LANGUAGES

Many languages are used around the world, some of which do not rely on the kind of phonological system that is used in English. By investigating the organization of the brain for other types of languages, we can determine the degree to which certain aspects of brain organization for language are universal.

Kana and Kanji

Although as speakers of English we are most familiar with a phonetic alphabet based on phoneme-to-grapheme correspondences, there exist other writing systems. For example, some languages use syllabic writing systems, in which each symbol is linked to a whole syllable rather than to an individual sound. For example, a syllabically based language

ア	イ	ウ	エ	オ	カ	キ	ク	ケ	コ
a	i	u	e	o	ka	ki	ku	ke	ko
サ	シ	ス	セ	ソ	タ	チ	ツ	テ	ト
sa	shi	su	se	so	ta	chi	tsu	te	to
ナ	ニ	ヌ	ネ	ノ	ハ	ヒ	フ	ヘ	ホ
na	ni	nu	ne	no	ha	hi	hu	he	ho
マ	ミ	ム	メ	モ	ヤ	イ	ユ	エ	ヨ
ma	mi	mu	me	mo	ya	i	yu	e	yo
ラ	リ	ル	レ	ロ	ワ	キ	ウ	エ	ヲ
ra	ri	ru	re	ro	wa	i	u	e	o
ガ	ギ	グ	ゲ	ゴ	ザ	ジ	ズ	ゼ	ゾ
ga	gi	gu	ge	go	za	ji	zu	ze	zo
ダ	ヂ	ヅ	デ	ド	バ	ビ	ブ	ベ	ボ
da	ji	zu	de	do	ba	bi	bu	be	bo
パ	ピ	プ	ペ	ポ	ヴ	ン			
pa	pi	pu	pe	po	vu	n			

A

	Meaning	Japanese pronunciation
甘	"sweet"	
感	"be affected"	
刊	"print"	
慣	"be accustomed to"	
観	"view"	
勘	"investigate"	
緩	"slow"	"kan"
管	"tube"	
鐶	"a ring"	
歓	"enjoy"	
巻	"a volume"	
韓	"Korean"	
漢	"Chinese"	

B

Figure 8.10 Some examples of kana and kanji.
(A) Almost all of the 77 symbols in kana represent a consonant-vowel combination. (B) In kanji, the symbol has little relation to how the word is pronounced. Pictured here are various symbols, all of which are pronounced "kan" but each of which has a different meaning. (*Note.* A, Reprinted with permission from *Writing Systems of the World* (p. 94), by A. Nakanishi, 1980, Tokyo: Charles E. Tuttle. B, Adapted with permission from *Writing Systems* (p. 178), by G. Sampson, 1985, Stanford, CA: Stanford University Press.)

might have a symbol for the sound "tor." This symbol would appear as the first of three symbols in a word such as *torrential,* the first of two symbols in *torrid,* and the second of two symbols in *motor.* Although syllabic languages retain a linkage between the sounds of the word and the symbol, the symbol is linked to a specific syllable rather than to a specific phoneme.

In contrast, other languages use a logographic writing system, in which a symbol stands for a concept and the form of the word has no systematic relationship to how it sounds. In such systems, little information in the symbol allows the reader to know how the symbol is pronounced. Sometimes these symbols have iconic properties; that is, they look something like what they mean. Learning to read and write such a language requires an extremely good memory because each word is associated with a different symbol. Typically, thousands of basic logographs are used in such languages.

Our discussion of these different systems should be reminiscent of some distinctions we made earlier with regard to phonological and direct routes to meaning. Syllabic systems are sound based, just as alphabetic systems are, so a phonological route is possible. In contrast, in logographic systems a direct route must be invoked because little or no information in the symbol provides hints to its pronunciation. Some languages, such as Japanese, contain both types of written language systems. One system, known as *kana,* is sound based and syllabic. The other system, known as *kanji,* derived from the Chinese system, is logographic (Paradis, Hagiwara, & Hildebrandt, 1985). Some examples of kana and kanji characters are presented in Figure 8.10. Given that sound-based and meaning-based routes for the same word are distinguishable in languages such as English, you should not be surprised to learn that the ability to read words in kana, a system based on phonology, is distinct from the ability to read words in kanji, a system based on visual form. In fact, these two systems doubly dissociate: In some cases, individuals who lose the ability to read kanji retain the ability to read kana, whereas in other cases, individuals who retain the ability to read kana lose the ability to read kanji (Sasanuma, 1980). This dissociation provides evidence from a language other than English that access to meaning through a sound-based system is independent of access to meaning through a visually based system.

American Sign Language

Other evidence about the neurological organization for language can be derived from examining "spoken" language systems that are not aurally based but are instead completely visual. American Sign Language (ASL), the language used by most deaf individuals in the United States, is one such language. Examination of ASL provides converging evidence for a distinction between anterior and posterior brain systems for language. Recall that previously in this chapter we discussed how the anterior language system plays a major role in syntactic processing. In ASL, certain aspects of syntax are communicated through the position of the hands in space rather than through word order (e.g., SVO vs. OVS) or by the type of hand movement rather than by word endings (e.g., *-ly*). If anterior areas of the left hemisphere are important for all syntactic aspects of language, damage to these regions should disrupt the production of syntactic markers in speakers of ASL, even though these markers are produced by hand movements with a particular spatial relationship rather than by vocal cord movements with a particular temporal relationship. Furthermore, comprehension of syntax should be disrupted even though that information is conveyed in the visual modality.

To evaluate the evidence that ASL provides, we first need a brief introduction to its organization. Each noun in ASL is represented by a particular hand shape that is made in a particular way at a particular location in space with regard to the body. Just as distinctive contrasts exist among phonemes (e.g., voicing), distinctive contrasts can be seen among signs in ASL. One distinctive feature that can be used to distinguish among different words is hand shape itself. Place of articulation is another important feature. The same hand shape placed on the side of the face has a different meaning than if it is placed on the chin. An example of three words

A   B   C

Figure 8.11   The distinctive contrast of place of articulation in American Sign Language (ASL).
The same hand shape has a different meaning depending on where the shape is produced. (A) If produced at eye level, this sign means "summer"; (B) if produced at nose level, it means "ugly"; and (C) if produced at the chin, it means "dry." (*Note.* Adapted from Poizner et al., 1987, p. 4.)

in ASL that differ only in place of articulation is presented in Figure 8.11. Finally, the nature of the hand movement can also distinguish between two words.

Syntactic structure in ASL differs from that of spoken language. For instance, when a sentence is produced in ASL, a noun is placed within a frame, or theater of space, that is directly in front of the speaker's body. For example, a speaker of ASL might make the symbol for the word *dog* with her or his right hand and point with the left hand to a particular location in space—in front of the body and to the left. From then on, that point in space represents the noun that the person just signed, the noun *dog*. When another noun is introduced, a different sign is made and a different point in space is demarcated. For example, the speaker might make the symbol for *cat* with the right hand and point with the left hand to a location on his or her right. This point in space now represents the noun *cat*. If the speaker wants to communicate that the dog bit the cat, she or he makes the symbol for *bit*, moving the hand through space from the "dog" point to the "cat" point. The direction of movement from the "dog" point to the "cat" point indicates that the dog is the subject (and doing the biting), whereas the cat is the object. Thus, the syntactic distinction between subject and object is made spatially, by the direction of hand movement. In contrast, if an individual wants to communicate that

Dog index_a   Cat index_b   _aBite_b

A

Dog index_a   Cat index_b   _bBite_a

B

Figure 8.12 The use of a spatial frame of reference in American Sign Language (ASL) to make a syntactic distinction between subject and object.
(A) In this case, the individual is signing the sentence "The dog bit the cat." First, the speaker makes the sign for the word *dog* and notes a particular spatial location for this noun (left frame). Then, he makes the sign for *cat* and notes a different spatial location to denote this noun (middle frame). He then makes the sign for *bit*, moving his hand from the "dog" position to the "cat" position (right frame). (B) In this case, the individual is signing the sentence "The cat bit the dog." The procedure of signing this sentence is identical to that for the other sentence, except the motion is made from the spatial position denoting *cat* to the one denoting *dog*. (*Note.* Adapted from Poizner et al., 1987, p. 52.)

the cat bit the dog, the direction of hand movement changes; it is initiated at the "cat" position (on the right) and continued until the "dog" position (on the left) is reached. The distinction between these two examples is depicted in Figure 8.12.

The type of hand movement can also provide syntactic information, such as inflections of a verb. In English, we indicate verb inflection by different word endings (e.g., *-ed*, *-ing*). In ASL, inflection is coded by the type of hand movement. For example, if a person wants to say that something occurred repeatedly, the hand movement is different than if the event happened only once, just as in English an ongoing action is indicated by an *-ing* ending. Examples of some of these distinctions are provided in Figure 8.13.

Now that we know the basics about the structure of ASL, we can discuss how it provides converging evidence for a distinction between anterior and posterior brain systems. If anterior portions of the left hemisphere are specialized for syntax and for language output in all languages, a native signer of ASL who has sustained damage to this region of the brain should show deficits in these arenas. More specifically, we would predict that output would be disrupted, as evidenced by both a paucity of signs and a lack of fluency. We would further expect that the production of ASL would be agrammatic, with disruptions of hand movements that serve as syntactic markers. In addition, we would expect that the elaboration of hand movements that act as inflections would be lost. Concomitant with these production difficulties, we would expect that signers of ASL who sustain anterior left-hemisphere damage would also have difficulty interpreting some aspects of syntax. In contrast to these difficulties, the signs produced should be semantically correct, although some errors in "phonological" processing might occur (such as mis-signing a word by producing it at the wrong place of articulation).

Although you might imagine that such predictions would be nearly impossible to test because finding native speakers of ASL who have become aphasic would be difficult, a group of researchers at the University of California at San Diego managed to do so (Poizner, Klima, & Bellugi, 1987). Their case studies reveal that the distinction between anterior and posterior language systems holds for ASL as well.

One of their patients, who sustained a large lesion to her left frontal lobe, exhibited the classic signs of anterior aphasia. Her signing was effortful and composed of short utterances mainly consisting of nouns. Following is a short interchange in which she attempted to relate a story from her childhood. Notice that she had little difficulty comprehending the examiner's questions.

EXAMINER: What else happened?
GAIL D.:   CAR . . . DRIVE . . . BROTHER
           . . . DRIVE . . . I . . . S-T-A-D
           [attempts to gesture "stand up"]

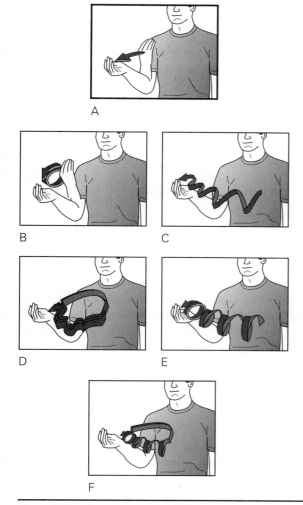

Figure 8.13   Some examples of the way in which variations in hand movement denote verb inflection in American Sign Language (ASL).
(A) The basic sign and hand movement for *give*. (B–F) Variations indicating the duration of the action and to whom it is directed. The various signs mean (B) "give continuously"; (C) "give to each"; (D) "give to each, that action recurring with time"; (E) "give continuously to each in turn"; and (F) "give continuously to each in turn, that action recurring with time." (*Note.* Adapted from Poizner et al., 1987, p. 15.)

EXAMINER: You stood up?
GAIL D.:   YES . . . I . . . DRIVE . . . [attempts to gesture "wave goodbye"]
EXAMINER: Wave goodbye?
GAIL D.:   YES . . . BROTHER . . . DRIVE . . . DUNNO . . . [attempts to gesture "wave goodbye"]
EXAMINER: Your brother was driving?
GAIL D.:   YES . . . BACK . . . DRIVE . . . BROTHER . . . MAN . . . MAMA . . . STAY . . . BROTHER . . . DRIVE

(Poizner, Klima, & Bellugi, 1987, p. 120)

Another signer whose damage included anterior regions but also extended posteriorly exhibited a linguistic profile much more like that of a person with Wernicke's aphasia. Although his comprehension was adequate, it was impaired compared with that before his stroke. His signing in ASL was fluent but did not have much meaning. As with Wernicke's aphasia, these difficulties transcended "spoken" language and affected his writing as well. Following is a translation of a sample of his signing in which he described the layout of his apartment, which had a glass-enclosed patio off the living room:

> And there's one (way down at the end) [unintelligible]. The man walked over to see the (disconnected), an extension of the (earth) room. It's there for the man (can live) a roof and light with shades to (keep pulling down). And there's a glass wall with four different. . . . He hammered. The man (makes hands), makes mobiles, many on the wall. A wonderful (always brillianting) man. (Poizner, Klima, & Bellugi, 1987, p. 98)

These case studies illustrate that the same neurological systems underlie the processing of many different language systems, including those that are visual and mark syntax spatially rather than with word order or word endings. These studies also suggest that anterior regions of the left hemisphere are specialized for syntactic aspects of language and language output, whereas posterior areas are specialized for semantic aspects of language processing.

Brain Organization in Bilinguals

One issue that has intrigued neurolinguists for some time is whether the neural organization for language in bilingual individuals differs from that observed in monolinguals. Investigations of this issue have taken a number of twists and turns, some that suggest differences and some that do not.

One of the most obvious ways to examine the organization for language in bilinguals is to examine a person's functional abilities in both languages after he or she sustains a brain lesion that affects language processing. If the organization for both languages is controlled by the same neural apparatus, we would expect that language loss in one language would parallel language loss in the other. In contrast, if organization for each language is controlled by a different neural apparatus, any linguistic problems exhibited in one language would be independent of (that is, not correlated with) language loss in the other language. Unfortunately, the results in this area are not so clear-cut as to provide a definitive answer because an extremely wide variation in the pattern has been observed. In some individuals, language loss in one language parallels that in the other. In other individuals, no relation appears to exist. Complicating the picture is the fact that the pattern observed directly after injury may differ

from that observed later. Hence, in some cases, language loss may be initially greater in one language than in the other, but the situation may eventually reverse (e.g., Paradis, Goldblum, & Abidi, 1982).

Scientists' attempts to understand the relation between brain structures and language processing in bilinguals are complicated by a number of factors. Whereas almost all individuals start to learn their initial language at birth, often called the *mother tongue,* bilinguals may acquire the second language either simultaneously with or at some point in time after they acquire their first language. Hence, age of acquisition of a second language may be an important variable in how the brain processes that language. The facility a speaker has in each language is another issue to consider, especially if someone has not been raised to speak two languages from birth. Whereas for some individuals the facility in both languages is equal, for others it may be disparate. Furthermore, facility in a language needn't be correlated with its age of acquisition. For example, an individual who spoke the mother tongue until the age of 3 years, then acquired a second language that was the only one spoken for the next 20 years might have poorer abilities in the mother tongue due to limitations in vocabulary and lack of exposure to complicated

ROLE OF THE RIGHT HEMISPHERE IN LANGUAGE PROCESSING

Since Broca first discovered lateralization of function by examining language processing, one major tenet underlying our understanding of the neurological organization for language is that it depends on the left hemisphere. In fact, the left hemisphere's role in language has been considered so important that this hemisphere is often referred to as the *verbal* hemisphere. However, recent evidence suggests that the right hemisphere is not as silent a partner in language processing as is typically assumed. Thus,

we next turn our attention to the right hemisphere's contributions to language processing (for recent research in this area, see Beeman & Chiarello, 1997).

Right-Hemisphere Contributions to Language Processing

As we discussed in this chapter and in chapter 3 (see page 97), studies of patients with the split-brain syndrome revealed that although the right hemisphere can comprehend written and auditory language, its abilities are limited. It has a poor un-

grammatical structures. A third issue to consider is the individual's linguistic environment at the time of damage and the amount of time spent in that linguistic environment. Some individuals use both languages their entire lives, whereas other individuals use just one language at a time, each spoken during a different time of life. As you might imagine, disentangling the contribution that each of these factors may play in the brain organization for language in bilinguals is a daunting task. Thus, you should not be surprised that the language most affected by brain damage varies radically among individuals. In fact, cases arise in which the greatest decrement is *not* for the mother tongue, the language used most frequently by an individual, or even the language used in the environment in which the individual resides (Paradis, 1977).

Despite all this uncertainty, researchers agree on two aspects of the neurological organization for language in bilinguals. First, bilinguals do not appear to have less lateralization of language processing than that of monolinguals. Some researchers had suggested that language lateralization might differ between monolinguals and bilinguals, that the right hemisphere might play a larger role in processing language in bilinguals. Although some studies report evidence consistent with a larger role for the right hemisphere, it is usually restricted to a specific population (e.g., bilingual men who acquired their second language late in life) or to specific tasks. Furthermore, the findings across studies are often contradictory, providing little support for the idea that bilinguals have a more bihemispheric brain organization for language (e.g., Paradis, 1990), although some debate still continues (e.g., Berquier & Ashton, 1992; Paradis, 1992).

The second aspect of neural organization in bilinguals on which experts agree is that the brain regions *within* the left hemisphere that are activated during processing of one language can be somewhat distinct from those activated during processing of the other language, although some overlap may occur. For example, naming an object in one language can be disrupted by electrical stimulation of a different region of the brain than that which disrupts naming in another language (e.g., G. A. Ojemann, 1983). Separation of processing for different languages has been observed during oral language processing (e.g., object naming) as well as during written language processing and for sites in both temporoparietal cortex and frontal cortex.

derstanding of complicated syntax, cannot produce speech or use phoneme-to-grapheme correspondence rules, and has a vocabulary restricted mainly to concrete words as opposed to abstract words. Despite these limitations, some aspects of language processing performed by the right hemisphere help to extract meaning from linguistic material. The right hemisphere's contributions fall into two main areas. First, the right hemisphere is involved in processing certain aspects of **prosody,** which is the intonation pattern, or sound envelope, of an utterance. Second, the right hemisphere plays an important role in narrative and inference. **Narrative** refers to the ability to construct or understand a story line, whereas **inference** refers to the ability to "fill in the blanks" and make assumptions about material that is not explicitly stated (i.e., implied). We now examine these two contributions of the right hemisphere to language processing in more detail.

Prosody

To understand the role of the right hemisphere in prosody, we need to know more about what prosody is and how it can aid in language comprehension. The sound envelope around words can be useful in providing information about the intended meaning of an utterance. For example, in English, when we make a declarative statement, the pitch of our voice usually goes down during the course of the utterance. In contrast, a question is usually said with a raising intonation pattern. Hence, intonation pattern provides a clue as to how a statement should be interpreted.

In some cases, intonation pattern may be the only cue that can differentiate between two ambiguous interpretations of a sentence. Consider the four words "She did it again." Said with a rising intonation, it could be a question, as in the following dialogue:

LYNN: Alice is way into this mountain-biking thing. Yesterday I saw her riding around again, jumping over every curb and obstacle she could find. After breaking her arm, you'd think she'd be a little more cautious. Then I heard last night that she took a bad tumble.

SARA: She did it again?

In this case, Sara is asking whether Alice hurt herself again. On the other hand, if Sara said these same words in a falling tone of voice to be emphatic in a declarative manner (e.g., "She did it again!"), the intonation would indicate that she is asserting what she already knows: Alice has managed to injure herself once more. Prosody can clearly differentiate whether the words are meant as a question or as a declaration.

On the basis of case studies of individuals with right-hemisphere damage, investigators have proposed that the right hemisphere's organization for prosody is homologous to the left hemisphere's organization for linguistic output (E. D. Ross, 1981). Under this conception, the right-hemisphere region that is homologous to Broca's area is important for the *production* of prosody in speech output. Furthermore, the right-hemisphere region homologous to Wernicke's area is considered important for the *comprehension* of prosody. Just as Broca's aphasia and Wernicke's aphasia can be conceptualized as a double dissociation, so can the distinctions between prosodic output and prosodic comprehension.

Evidence that the brain region important for the production of prosody is distinct from that important for the perception of prosody comes from studies of individuals with brain damage and from studies of neurologically intact individuals. The speech output of individuals with damage to frontal areas tends to lack prosody (is **aprosodic**), which can be well characterized as speaking in a monotone. Nonetheless, the same individuals can correctly interpret tone of voice (e.g., warm and friendly, sarcastic, condescending, excited). Conversely, damage in posterior sections of the right hemisphere results in an inability to interpret tone of voice but does not disrupt the ability to produce the correct prosody in speech output. Studies of regional blood flow in neurologically intact individuals reveal that complex discourse containing multiple words (which requires comprehension of prosody) activates posterior regions of the right hemisphere (e.g., Lechevalier et al., 1989), whereas speech production (which requires prosodic output) activates anterior regions of the right hemisphere (e.g., Wallesch, Henriksen, Kornhuber, & Paulson, 1985).

For the most part, the right hemisphere is superior to the left in its ability to perceive prosodic cues. Even though patients with severe aphasia (and hence left-hemisphere damage) can distinguish between questions and statements on the basis of prosodic cues (e.g., K. Heilman, Bowers, Speedie, & Coslett, 1984), evidence from patients with the split-brain syndrome, individuals with epilepsy, individuals undergoing the Wada test, and dichotic listening studies suggests that the right hemisphere is extremely important in the perception of prosody (e.g., Benowitz et al., 1983). A role for the right hemisphere in understanding prosody is not limited to situations in which prosody implies an emotional state (e.g., a brief high-frequency monotone might imply surprise), but can also be found when prosodic information is emotionally neutral (i.e., rising and falling intonation contours) (e.g., Weintraub, Mesulam, & Kramer, 1981; Zatorre, Evans, Meyer, & Gjedde, 1992). The right hemisphere's perception of prosodic cues appears to depend on the tonal aspects of the stimuli because poor tonal memory has been found to correlate with an inability to interpret prosody (e.g., C. Tompkins & Flowers, 1985).

In contrast to the right hemisphere's predominance in interpreting prosodic cues, both hemispheres seem to play a role in the production of prosody, but each makes a different type of contribution. Prosody appears to consist of two classes of cues: those related to pitch or tone and those related to timing. As you may remember from our discussion of hemispheric differences in chapter 3, the left hemisphere tends to excel at temporal aspects of processing, whereas the right is better at tonal processing. These findings suggest that different types of prosodic deficits should be observed after right-hemisphere damage than those occurring after left-hemisphere damage. For example, the aprosodic speech observed after damage to anterior regions of the right hemisphere can be attributed to the individual's speaking all at one pitch (Behrens, 1988), which is not surprising considering that pitch perception depends more on the right hemisphere than on the left (e.g., B. Milner, 1962a). After damage to the left hemisphere, speech is not so much aprosodic as **dysprosodic,** meaning that it has disordered intonation. The dysprosodia seems to result from the ill-timed prosodic cues. For example, neurologically intact individuals tend to elongate the final word rather than the initial word of an utterance. In contrast, persons with Broca's aphasia do the opposite, elongating the first word rather than the last (e.g., Danly & Shapiro, 1982).

Before we end our discussion of prosody, one point is worth mentioning: The production of prosody can be disrupted by damage to other regions of the brain besides the cerebral hemispheres. Prosody can be compromised by damage to the basal ganglia and cerebellum (e.g., Cancelliere & Kertesz, 1990; Kent & Rosenbek, 1982), but such damage simultaneously disrupts various other processes that depend on precise timing of motor control.

Inference and Narrative

Because the meaning of language is not always clear, readers and listeners use certain strategies to aid comprehension. For example, determining the theme of a story can help in interpreting ambiguous information, in making inferences about what has not been explicitly stated, and in anticipating what information will be presented next. To demonstrate this effect, read the following sentence: "Thinking about all the things he could buy if he won the lottery, the man approached the bank." The first part of the sentence biases you to interpret the ambiguous word *bank* to refer to a place where people deposit money rather than the region next to a river. Now read this sentence: "With mosquitoes, gnats, and grasshoppers flying all about, she came across a small black bug that was being used to eavesdrop on her conversation." Because of the way the initial part of the sentence biased you, you probably did a double take to reinterpret the meaning of *bug*. These sentences are examples of how we build upon previous information to make inferences about upcoming words.

Individuals with right-hemisphere damage have difficulty with the types of tasks just discussed: following the thread of a story (e.g., J. A. Kaplan, Brownell, Jacobs, & Gardner, 1990), making inferences about what is being said (e.g., Beeman, 1993), and understanding nonliteral aspects of language such as metaphors (e.g., H. Brownell, 1988). The difficulty appears to occur across spoken and written sentences, and for stories, dialogues, and paragraphs. We now examine these specific difficulties in more detail.

To comprehend language, individuals need some structure superimposed upon discourse. This structure allows them to organize information so that clauses within sentences, or episodes or events within stories, can be linked to one another. Individuals with right-hemisphere damage have difficulty building such structures. They have deficits in the ability to generate orderly presentations of material and to build upon previously presented materials. Some examples of the difficulties exhibited by individuals with right-hemisphere damage include problems in ordering sentences so that they form a story (e.g., Delis, Wapner, Gardner, & Moses, 1983), ordering words so that they form a sentence (Cavalli, DeRenzi, Faglioni, & Vitale, 1981), and determining whether an utterance is relevant to a conversation (that is, determining whether it builds upon previously presented material) (e.g., Rehak, Kaplan, & Gardner, 1992). Individuals with right-hemisphere brain damage also have difficulty extracting the theme of a story (e.g., Moya, Benowitz, Levine, & Finklestein, 1986) or using information about a story's theme to help them in other tasks, such as arranging sentences into coherent paragraphs (e.g., Schneiderman, Murasugi, & Saddy, 1992).

One interesting ramification of this inability to comprehend a coherent theme in stories is that patients with right-hemisphere brain damage have difficulty comprehending jokes. Certain researchers have suggested that jokes are funny because most of a joke forms a coherent story, but then the punch line contains a surprise or twist that nevertheless coheres with the overall story. Given that individuals with right-hemisphere damage have difficulty following the thread of a story, we can easily see why they have difficulty selecting the correct punch line for a joke. They are likely to pick a surprising ending but not one that is compatible with the previously presented material (e.g., H. H. Brownell, Michel, Powelson, & Gardner, 1983).

Some authorities have suggested that individuals with right-hemisphere damage may have difficulty comprehending discourse, in part, because the right hemisphere gains access to the meaning of words in a different manner than the left hemisphere does. Experts have known for some time that when we hear or read a word, it primes our ability to process a network of words that are related in meaning. For example, individuals are quicker to process the word *doctor* if it is preceded by *nurse* rather than by *butter*. *Doctor* can be processed more quickly because the prior presentation of *nurse* activated words with related meaning, *doctor* being one of them. In contrast, reading the word *butter* does not activate *doctor* (but does activate other words such as *bread*), so that the processing of *doctor* is not enhanced. Divided visual field studies have demonstrated that the network of associated words activated is more restricted in the left hemisphere than in the right. For example, whereas the right hemisphere retains activation of both meanings of an ambiguous word (e.g., *bank*) for about 1 s, the left hemisphere retains only the dominant meaning (e.g., "repository for money"), not the subordinate one (e.g., "side of a river") (e.g., Burgess & Simpson, 1988; Chiarello, 1991). Furthermore, weakly related words facilitate the processing of a word presented in the left visual field (LVF) but not a word presented in the right visual field (RVF) (e.g., Rodel, Cook, Regard, & Landis, 1992). These results have been interpreted to suggest that the semantic aspects of words are coded relatively more coarsely in the right hemisphere than in the left hemisphere (e.g., Beeman, 1997). Whereas fine semantic coding by the left hemisphere allows information that occurs near one another in a sentence to be integrated, the coarser and more diffuse semantic processing of the right hemisphere has been suggested to play an important role in integrating information over larger linguistic expanses (Beeman et al., 1994).

Because individuals with right-hemisphere damage often have trouble understanding or maintaining the overall coherence of a story, they also have difficulties making inferences or using discourse to distinguish the meaning of an ambiguous phrase. For example, after hearing "John walked in the water near some glass" and "John grabbed his foot and called the lifeguard for help," most people infer that John cut himself. In contrast, individuals with right-hemisphere brain damage have difficulty doing so (Beeman, 1993).

Individuals with right-hemisphere brain damage also have difficulty with the nonliteral aspects of language such as metaphors and indirect requests. For example, individuals with such damage may be horrified to hear that someone was "Crying her eyes out" because they interpret the sentence literally, so they visualize a gruesome scene. When asked to point to a picture of someone who has a "heavy heart," an individual with right-hemisphere brain damage is likely to point to a picture of a large heart rather than to a picture of someone who looks sad (Winner & Gardner, 1977). When given a sentence such as "Can you open the door?" an individual with this type of brain damage might respond defensively, saying, "Of course I can open the door. Why do you ask? Do you think I'm such a weakling that

I can't even open a door!?" when what was really meant was "Please open the door for me" (e.g., Foldi, 1987).

The deficits in language processing exhibited by individuals with right-hemisphere damage are not so severe as to disrupt their ability to comprehend language and convey meaning. Yet, these deficits do dilute the linguistic experience. The aspects of language that we may find most appealing, such as a wonderful metaphor or an unexpected twist or turn of phrase, go unappreciated or are left unsaid.

Why the Right Hemisphere Isn't Specialized for Language

The differences in the right and left hemispheres' abilities to process language are one of the most basic and fundamental aspects of human brain organization. Because the distinction is so striking, you might wonder, "Why does the left hemisphere have special language capacities?" Three main answers have been proposed to this question: The first suggests that the left hemisphere is specialized for all symbolic and abstract processing (e.g., J. Brown, 1977), the second says that the left hemisphere is specialized for precise temporal control of oral and manual articulators (e.g., Kimura, 1982), and the third says that the left hemisphere is specifically specialized for linguistic processing (e.g., D. Corina, Vaid, & Bellugi, 1992).

From the first perspective, all expression and comprehension of symbols occurs in the left hemisphere. Language is considered just one other symbolic system (e.g., the word *dog* becomes a symbol for a common household pet) and hence is lateralized to the left hemisphere. Such a perspective does not take a flattering view of right-hemisphere capabilities, ignoring many of the ways in which the right hemisphere can perform symbolic associations (e.g., interpreting the symbolic aspects of a map).

From the second perspective, the left hemisphere is specialized for precise motor control and timing regardless of whether language is expressed orally or manually. Hence, language is lateralized to the left hemisphere because it relies on precise timing in the motor control of oral articulators. From this

position, apraxia and problems in speech output arise from the same system, and the system is lateralized to the left hemisphere. In fact, oral and manual movements are often linked. For example, during the oral recounting of a story, gestures related to the story line are much more often made with the right hand than with the left. The interpretation of this finding is that a single left-hemisphere system controls both the oral articulators for speech and the manual articulators for gesture (which must be precisely coordinated with speech). In contrast, self-touching movements that have nothing to do with the story line, such as moving your hair, occur equally often with either hand (e.g., Lavergne & Kimura, 1987).

From the third perspective, the left hemisphere is specifically lateralized for linguistic processing, regardless of whether linguistic information is conveyed in speech, as in conventional English, or in hand symbols, such as in ASL. The argument is that the left hemisphere's contribution to language is above and beyond that which occurs for gesture. Support for this viewpoint is provided by a single case study of a deaf signer who, after sustaining a left-hemisphere lesion, could neither produce nor comprehend ASL but retained the ability to communicate by using gestures in nonlinguistic domains (D. P. Corina et al., 1992). These findings suggest that we do not have one unitary linguistic-gestural system; rather, the control of language and the control of nonlinguistic gesture are distinct.

At present, the debate between the last two positions continues. One camp argues, on the basis of deficit patterns in ASL signers, that the left hemisphere is specialized for language. They say that all symbolic processing is not lost because these individuals can use symbolic gestures to pantomime. Furthermore, these researchers assert that their signers with aphasia do not necessarily have apraxia. Thus, apraxia and aphasia are not linked. The other camp retorts that the tests of apraxia in this special population have not been sensitive enough. Given that speakers of ASL are more sophisticated than most individuals in the use of manual movements, they argue, more stringent tests are required to reveal deficits, and if such tests were given, a co-relation between aphasia and apraxia would be found.

Although this debate remains unresolved, the hemispheres clearly differ in their contributions to language functioning. The left hemisphere has a much more elaborate language system, but the right hemisphere plays an important role as well. Like many other cognitive skills discussed in this book, the complete functioning of language skills relies on an entire brain, not just one hemisphere.

SUMMARY

Language is one of the uniquely human cognitive abilities, and as such its neural organization has received much scrutiny. A breakdown in language functioning after brain insult is known as aphasia. Aphasia is considered from two major conceptual viewpoints, a neurologically based viewpoint and a psychologically based perspective. The neurologically based model suggests that anterior regions of the left hemisphere, more specifically Broca's area, are specialized for speech output. In contrast, posterior regions of the left hemisphere, most notably Wernicke's area, are specialized for speech comprehension. Broca's aphasia is characterized by disrupted output in which speech is slow, halting, and ill formed, although the ability to understand language remains relatively unimpaired. In contrast, in Wernicke's aphasia, language comprehension is lost, although output remains fluent and sentences are well formed. However, the output has little meaning and sounds much like a word salad.

The neurological model elaborated by Lichtheim and others predicted the existence of a number of other types of aphasias. A disruption in the pathway between Broca's and Wernicke's areas produces conduction aphasia, in which language comprehension and production are intact but the ability to repeat is lost. Other major aphasias are transcortical sensory aphasia, which is similar to Wernicke's aphasia, and transcortical motor aphasia, which is similar to Broca's aphasia, except in both cases the ability to repeat is intact. Finally, global aphasia, which is associated with large left-hemisphere lesions, im-

pairs both language comprehension and language production.

In contrast, psychologically based models of aphasia emphasize the specific language processes that are lost. Language is thought to comprise three fundamental components: phonology, syntax, and semantics. Phonology is the rules by which sounds in a language are formed and the rules by which they can be combined. Syntax is the rules of grammar dictating the ways in which words are conjoined to form sentences. Semantics is the aspect of language that specifies meaning of words and sentences. From this perspective, damage to anterior regions of the brain is considered to disrupt syntax while leaving semantics undisturbed. In contrast, damage to posterior regions of the brain is considered to disrupt semantic aspects of language without disturbing syntax. Phonology is disrupted in both anterior and posterior aphasias, although the ability to produce the correct sound for a given phoneme (i.e., phonetics) is more disrupted by anterior damage. Both the input-output and syntactic-semantic views of aphasia suggest that posterior and anterior regions of the brain are specialized for different aspects of linguistic processing and represent independent systems.

Evidence from other methods of neuropsychological investigation supports the idea that the left hemisphere is specialized for speech processing and the concept that anterior and posterior portions of the left hemisphere play different roles in language. The Wada test, in which one hemisphere is anesthetized, provides evidence of left-hemisphere specialization for speech output in all but a fraction of right-handers. Positron emission tomography (PET) studies suggest that anterior and posterior regions of the brain are specialized for different language functions; studies of electrical stimulation of brain regions during surgery for epilepsy corroborate this finding.

The ability to process visual language also depends heavily on the left hemisphere. A disruption in the ability to read after brain insult is known as alexia, whereas the inability to write is known as agraphia. As with auditory language, the input and output of visual language are dissociable: Alexia can occur without agraphia, and agraphia can occur without alexia. Evidence from patients with brain lesions suggests that written language can be linked to meaning through two routes, one that directly links the visual symbols to meaning (the direct route) and one that involves the intermediary of sound (the phonological route). Individuals with phonological alexia have a specific disruption in the phonological route, as evidenced by their inability to use grapheme-to-phoneme correspondence rules to sound out pronounceable nonwords. Nonetheless, they retain the ability to read words that they already know. In contrast, patients with surface alexia have a specific disruption in the direct route, meaning that they cannot read irregular words, such as *colonel*, for which grapheme-to-phoneme correspondence rules lead to incorrect pronunciation.

In addition to disruptions in the ability to link print to meaning, other subprocesses in reading can be disrupted by brain damage, such as the ability to perceive all the letters in a word and the ability to combine the individual letters into an overall word. Specific patterns of disability after brain damage provide evidence that these subprocesses can be dissociated; evidence from event-related potential (ERP) studies, PET studies, and divided visual field studies in neurologically intact individuals confirms these findings.

Our understanding of the neurological underpinnings for language is also enhanced by studying a variety of language systems. For example, the distinction between a direct route and a phonological route to meaning is supported by studies of individuals with brain damage who exhibit dissociations in the processing of kana and kanji, two written language systems in Japanese. Kana is a syllable-based system in which each symbol is related to sound, much like the alphabetic system in English. In contrast, kanji is a logographic system, in which the symbol for each word is unique. After brain damage, the ability to read kanji can be lost while the ability to read kana is preserved, and vice versa. Another language system that has added to our knowledge of the neurological organization for language is American Sign Language (ASL). In this language, information is conveyed by hand symbols, and syntax is marked not only by word order, as in English, but also by the spatial location where a symbol is made and by the type of hand movement. Speakers of ASL who become aphasic after anterior damage have disrupted production of ASL that is noticeably agrammatic. Conversely, those who become aphasic after posterior damage have fluent production but have impaired comprehension of ASL. These findings suggest that anterior and posterior regions of the left hemisphere are specialized for different aspects of language processing regardless of the mode of language production, manual or oral.

Although language deficits are most profound after left-hemisphere damage, the right hemisphere does play a role in language processing. Two areas in which it seems to make a significant contribution are with regard to prosody and with regard to understanding narrative and making inferences. One aspect of prosody is the intonation contour of speech, such as the rising intonation pattern associated with questions and the falling pattern associated with declarative statements. The production of such tonal aspects of prosody is disrupted by damage to anterior regions of the right hemisphere, whereas the perception of prosodic cues is disrupted by damage to posterior regions of the right hemisphere. In addition, the right hemisphere plays a major role in discourse by aiding a person in comprehending a story line and in making inferences based on this story line.

Debates have arisen as to why the left hemisphere and not the right is specialized for language. One point of view is that the left hemisphere is specialized for processing all symbolic systems, of which language is just one. This viewpoint denies the ability of the right hemisphere to make abstractions in a number of nonverbal domains. According to another viewpoint, the left-hemisphere contributes more to language because it is specialized for fine motor control of the vocal and manual muscles. A third viewpoint suggests that the left hemisphere is specialized specifically for language. The first position seems untenable, but the debate over the other two continues.

*M*emory

Contributed by Neal J. Cohen

In response to a seizure disorder that could not be controlled effectively by anticonvulsant medications, a young man underwent an experimental surgical procedure involving the removal of medial temporal lobe structures that (we only now know) are critical to memory. Since the surgery in 1953, he has been unable to keep track of daily events, to learn the names of people with whom he has come into contact since the surgery (such as his physicians and other caregivers), and to learn much about either public or personal events. At present, he does not know his age, the current date, his recent history (such as where he lives and how long he has lived there), or the status of his parents, who died subsequent to his surgery. He has on occasion misidentified a current picture of himself as a picture of his father.

Yet, this man can reason and solve problems, he can recognize objects and perform both voluntary and reflexive motor acts, and he has normal language abilities. His memory for the remote past is intact, including the world knowledge he learned early in life. Also spared is his ability to hold onto information temporarily while he is working with it, but only if he is not interrupted.

He enjoys solving crossword puzzles and watches many television programs. But he can do the same crossword puzzles or watch the same television shows repeatedly without noting the repetition. Understanding television shows is difficult because the commercials interspersed throughout a show cause him to forget the story line. Following the plot of an ongoing show that features an ensemble cast in which many or all of the actors have continuing, interwoven story lines (e.g., a soap opera) is also beyond his capabilities.

This man can hold a perfectly reasonable conversation with you, except his conversation is devoid of current content; he cannot tell you about recent weather conditions, the latest books that he read, the movies that he saw recently, or the people or events currently in the news. If you were to avoid such topics in your conversation with him, his amnesia would be easy to overlook, unless your conversation was interrupted and you left for a short while. Even if the interruption lasted only a few minutes, upon returning you would find not only that he could not remember what you were conversing about minutes earlier, but also that he most likely would not remember having ever met you.

The patient described in the opening vignette of the chapter, who is known by the initials H.M., has been studied extensively since his surgery in 1953, initially by Brenda Milner and her colleagues, and in the last few decades by Suzanne Corkin and her colleagues, mostly at the Massachusetts Institute of Technology (MIT) Clinical Research Center (where this author had the good fortune to spend several years). H.M.'s memory loss, known as **amnesia,** is remarkably profound and pervasive. Since his surgery, H.M.'s impairments have been exhaustively documented to include memory for such materials as words, text, names, faces, spatial layout, routes, geometric shapes, nonsense patterns, tunes, tones, public events, personal episodes, and more (see Scoville & Milner, 1957, and reviews by Corkin, 1984, and B. Milner, Corkin & Teuber, 1968). H.M.'s amnesia apparently affects all aspects of his life and has been said to cause him to forget the events of his daily life "as quickly as they occur" (Scoville & Milner, 1957, p. 15). Although H.M. is undoubtedly the most carefully and intensively studied patient in the annals of neurology or neuropsychology, his memory impairment prevents him from remembering that he is so "famous."

The extraordinary aspect of H.M.'s amnesia is that it is *selective,* affecting only certain facets or kinds of memory. Even from the description of his condition in the opening vignette of the chapter, you can see that although some aspects or kinds of memory are grossly impaired, others remain fully intact. The spared memory includes that which guides reasoning and problem solving, that which is measured in intelligence tests, memory supporting his perceptual and motor competence, memory supporting his language competence, and memory for social etiquette.

An analysis of the selectivity of the amnesia exhibited by H.M. and other patients with amnesia guides much of the rest of our discussion in this chapter. We describe and characterize the spared and impaired memory abilities with the goal of answering the following question: How must memory be organized in the undamaged brain for us to ever see such selective memory loss? As we learn in this chapter, the way in which memory breaks down following brain insult tells us much about the nature and organization of normal memory. Thus, this chapter mirrors the field in its disproportionate coverage of the phenomenology and implications of amnesia. However, we also consider the relationship between particular memory capacities and specific brain systems. Such brain-cognition relationships are derived

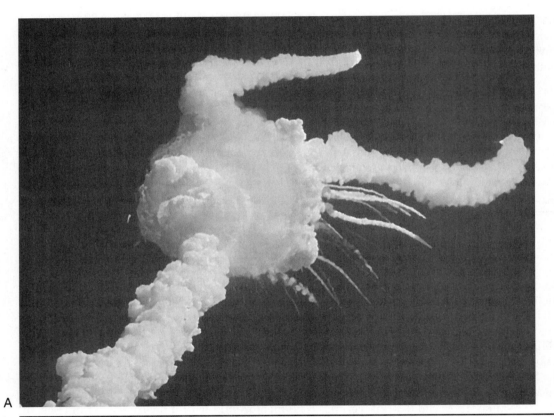

A

Figure 9.1 Two events for which multiple types of memory contribute to what we remember.
(A) News photograph of the U.S. space shuttle *Challenger* exploding in midair in January 1986. (B) News photograph of the Alfred P. Murrah building in Oklahoma City after a terrorist bombing demolished it in April 1995. Our memory of these particular photographs and the associated events is aided by the participation of many types of memory, including memory supporting perceptual knowledge, working memory, memory supporting knowledge of the world, memory for public events and public figures, memory for specific photographs, and memory for autobiographic information. (*Note.* A, Copyright © 1986 Michele McDonald. B, Reproduced with permission from AP/Wide World Photos.)

not only from studies of different neuropsychological patients with memory disorders, but also from neuroimaging studies of people without brain injury and from neuropsychological and electrophysiologic studies of animals.

The most basic message that we attempt to communicate and illustrate throughout this chapter is that memory is not a unitary process. Rather, it must be thought of as a collection of memory systems that operate cooperatively, each system making different functional contributions and supported by different brain systems. Normal memory performance requires many of the brain's various systems, which ordinarily operate together so seamlessly that intuitively appreciating the separate systems and the dis-

tinct contributions of each is difficult. Occasionally, however, circumscribed instances of brain insult can selectively disrupt one or another of these systems so that, through neuropsychological studies, we can infer the contribution of that particular system. By studying different instances of brain insult, we can discover the role of each brain system in memory.

MEMORY AS A COLLECTION OF MEMORY SYSTEMS

One way to illustrate that memory is a collection of distinct systems is to perform the following simple task. Look at the news photographs depicted in Figure 9.1 and try to remember the famous public

B

Figure 9.1 (Continued)

event associated with each. You probably will quickly recognize that the first photograph is of the explosion of the U.S. space shuttle *Challenger* in 1986 and that the second photograph is of the Alfred P. Murrah building in Oklahoma City that was demolished in a 1995 terrorist bombing.

This memory task appears to be simple, so simple that it seems unlikely to reveal much about the nature and organization of memory. However, insight comes from asking why we can recognize famous scenes such as these so easily. The answer is that performance in this task is multiply determined—it reflects the separate contributions of each of the following aspects of memory:

- *Memory supporting perceptual knowledge:* This aspect of memory permits you to identify the various objects in the scenes—the demolished building, the smoke trail, and so forth.
- *Working memory (or short-term memory):* This aspect of memory permits you to maintain the results of your various perceptual analyses online in an active state as you look around each scene; it permits you to temporarily "hold" in your head for a short period the various objects constituting the scene until you can "see" the scene as a whole. However, it does not allow you to retain information for many minutes.
- *Memory supporting knowledge of the world:* You know something about explosions and their consequences.
- *Memory for public events and public figures:* You know about space shuttle flights and the tragic explosion that ended this one; and you know about terrorism and the reaction in the United States to this bombing. You also can probably associate these events with public figures such as Christa McAuliffe and Timothy McVeigh.
- *Memory for specific photographs:* You probably saw these specific photographs many times because they were highly visible at the time of the events and have become the photographs that are shown whenever these events are discussed in the media.

- *Memory for autobiographic information:* If you are old enough, you will likely remember watching news reports in the aftermath of these two disasters.

Each of the aspects of memory just described contributes to your recognition of the scenes. However, following brain insult, each of these can be selectively impaired; that is, for each type or aspect of memory, a group of individuals exists in whom that type of memory is impaired but all other types are intact. By studying the pattern of sparing and loss of memory function in each of these cases, we can determine the separate functional roles that the various systems play in normal memory processing.

AMNESIA: A DESCRIPTION

A large portion of the neuropsychological work on memory involves examination of one particular example of selective memory loss, the type of amnesia that H.M. has. We begin by discussing the various causes of such amnesia. Then we turn to a more detailed description of the pattern of impairment and sparing of memory exhibited in amnesia.

Etiology of Amnesia

The type of amnesia that H.M. has is not limited to him but is characteristic of a variety of patients who sustained damage either to the portions of the brain surgically removed from H.M. or to a closely related brain region. The portion of the brain removed in H.M. is the **medial temporal lobe region** (specifically, the **hippocampal system,** which includes the hippocampus, the amygdala, and adjoining cortex—the entorhinal and parahippocampal gyri). Damage to the closely related **midline diencephalic region** (specifically, the **dorsomedial nucleus** of the thalamus and the **mammillary bodies** of the hypothalamus) can also cause amnesia (see Figure 9.2). Damage to these brain systems can originate in a number of ways; those most frequently observed are listed in Table 9.1. Because the amne-

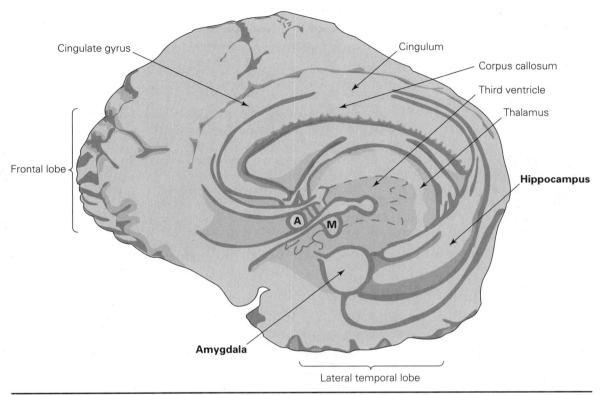

Figure 9.2   The network of neural structures underlying our ability to remember and learn.
Illustrated here are the structures in the medial temporal lobe, specifically the hippocampal system (which includes the hippocampus, the amygdala, and adjoining cortex), and the midline diencephalic structures, specifically the dorsomedial nucleus of the thalamus and the mammillary bodies of the hypothalamus (M), that, when damaged, cause amnesia. For reference, structures outside the system but located nearby (e.g., the corpus callosum, the anterior commissure [A], and the frontal region) are also shown. (*Note.* Adapted from Squire, 1984.)

sias produced by the causes listed in Table 9.1 share a set of fundamental characteristics, we can discuss certain aspects of amnesia in a general way, which we do later in this section. However, first we need to note that the amnesias resulting from these different causes do not form a homogeneous group with respect to the precise details of their behavioral profiles. In fact, these amnesias vary considerably in the severity of memory impairment, in their natural history (that is, the way in which the memory impairment appears or changes with time), and in whether they are accompanied by other cognitive deficits that influence the expression of the memory impairment. These differences are discussed in turn.

Severity of Memory Impairment

The severity of memory impairment varies considerably among patients with amnesia. H.M.'s recall is near-zero and his recognition of information seen since his surgery is near-chance on practically every test of memory he has ever taken in which the amount of material to be remembered exceeded the capacity of his working memory. In contrast, most

Table 9.1 Causes of Amnesia

Cause	Description
Medial temporal lobe damage causing amnesia	
Herpes simplex encephalitis	A virus that tends to affect medial temporal and orbital frontal areas; it can also compromise lateral temporal neocortical areas.
Vascular accident	For example, a blockage of the posterior cerebral artery preventing a normal blood supply.
Hypoxic ischemia	Oxygen deprivation leading to brain damage, especially hippocampal damage.
Closed head injury	For example, head injury from a motor vehicle accident; it tends to cause damage to medial temporal and frontal areas.
Bilateral electroconvulsive therapy (ECT)	A series of ECT treatments for the relief of depressive illness; when administered bilaterally, ECT produces a memory deficit that disappears with time.
Alzheimer's disease	A disease producing damage to medial temporal lobe structures as well as to various cortical areas, apparently as a result of primary damage to nuclei in the basal forebrain that project to those areas. Memory impairment is frequently the earliest sign and the most telling deficit in the early stages, although it is complicated by additional cognitive (and memory) deficits that are part of a progressive dementia.
Midline diencephalic damage causing amnesia	
Korsakoff's disease	The most frequently studied instance of amnesia, resulting from many years of chronic alcohol abuse and a thiamin (vitamin B_1) deficiency that causes hemorrhaging of midline diencephalic structures.
Vascular accident	For example, a stroke affecting the paramedial artery and preventing a normal blood supply to midline thalamic structures.
Third-ventricle tumors	For example, a pituitary tumor; the tumor may press on critical thalamic and hypothalamic structures.

patients with amnesia perform better than this, although they are still profoundly impaired compared with the norm. For example, many patients with amnesia cannot report much information contained in paragraphs or visual figures studied 30 min earlier, but some patients (such as H.M.) are so severely amnesic that they cannot recollect even the fact that paragraphs or visual figures were presented earlier.

Despite the large differences in severity of amnesia among patients, in all cases the amnesia has a profoundly adverse effect on these individuals' lives. A patient who cannot remember the events of daily life from previous days—for example, whether a prescription for anticonvulsant medications has been refilled or whether the broken furnace has been repaired—has a significant problem. This is true whether memory for the events of daily life is "lost" within minutes after the events occur, as

seems to be the case for H.M., or whether such memory can survive for hours but is eventually lost by the next day, as in less severe amnesias. In either case, the patient has lost the sense of continuity and the cumulativeness of events that memory provides us. And, in either case, the person will miss appointments, will fail to get things repaired, and so on. One of the patients we test at the Amnesia Research Laboratory at the Beckman Institute of the University of Illinois is unlike H.M. in that she can drive herself to her appointments, has learned to keep an appointment book, and knows that she has a car. However, she is sufficiently amnesic that she cannot remember which car is hers, so each time she drives she can find her car only by walking through the parking lot and comparing each car with the description of her car that she's written in her notebook. Moreover, like H.M., she cannot remember appointments without external memory aids, and she is no more able than H.M. to remember aspects of her recent past.

Natural History

The natural history of the amnesia also varies considerably among patients with different types of brain insult. Although most of the causes of amnesia listed in Table 9.1 produce chronic, stable impairments, in some instances deficits are more temporary. For example, in most cases of **posttraumatic amnesia** following closed head injury (closed head injury is discussed in more detail in chapter 14), memory is recovered with time, often completely. Likewise, the amnesia associated with bilateral **electroconvulsive therapy (ECT),** which is a series of treatments for the relief of severe depressive illness, disappears during the weeks and months following the end of treatment. ECT is administered bilaterally by passing an electrical current across two electrodes on the surface of the head, one of which is placed over each temporal lobe. By the fifth or sixth treatment, an amnesia has accumulated that persists for as long as several weeks but then dissipates completely within a few months. This amnesia is thought to be caused by the direct effects of passing electrical current across the temporal lobes. These two types of amnesia are discussed further later in this chapter, when we consider retrograde amnesia.

Another related difference among the causes of amnesia has to do with the onset of memory impairment. Whereas the amnesias caused by head injuries or strokes have a sudden onset, the amnesias associated with tumors and, perhaps, **Korsakoff's amnesia,** an amnesia related to chronic alcoholism, have a more gradual, insidious onset. Korsakoff's amnesia is difficult to categorize with respect to its natural history because it involves both the cumulative, debilitative effects of years of alcohol abuse and, experts generally agree, an acute event involving hemorrhaging of midline diencephalic brain structures. This hemorrhaging elicits the acute onset of a full-blown amnesia, often together with gross confusion (Korsakoff's psychosis). In a different category is the slowly progressive dementia associated with Alz-

heimer's disease, a syndrome discussed in more detail in chapter 14.

Accompanying Cognitive Deficits

Perhaps the most obvious difference among the amnesias is the presence or absence of cognitive deficits that are superimposed upon the amnesia. For instance, the amnesia in Alzheimer's disease, although initially much like that seen in other cases of medial temporal lobe damage, gradually worsens and becomes complicated not only by additional memory deficits associated with damage to regions outside the medial temporal lobe, but also by other cognitive deficits (e.g., agnosia, apraxia). Korsakoff's disease is often accompanied by certain deficits in problem solving and other cognitive abilities, typically attributable to frontal lobe pathology. Although the additional deficits seen in Korsakoff's disease and Alzheimer's disease make the analysis of their memory impairments in relation to other instances of amnesia a considerable challenge, these additional deficits prove important in identifying the structures outside the medial temporal lobe and midline diencephalic regions that contribute to memory.

Despite the variations among the amnesias, most researchers agree that all the causes of amnesia noted in Table 9.1 seem to affect the same *domain* of memory: They selectively disrupt the long-term remembering of new facts and events, and, as we see later, the relationship among multiple, perceptually distinct items. We now describe in detail the nature of the aspects of memory that are impaired and those that are spared in amnesia.

Anterograde and Retrograde Components of Amnesia

Amnesia generally has two components: **anterograde amnesia,** which is the impairment of memory for information acquired *after* the onset of amnesia, and **retrograde amnesia,** which is the impairment of memory for information that was acquired normally *prior* to the onset of amnesia. In the time line illustrated in Figure 9.3, the onset of amnesia due to injury is indicated by the vertical line. To the

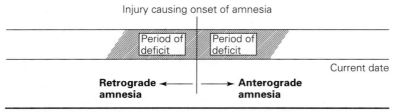

Injury causing onset of amnesia

Period of deficit | Period of deficit

Current date

Retrograde ◄——— ———► Anterograde
amnesia | amnesia

Figure 9.3 Time line illustrating the anterograde and retrograde components of amnesia.
Any memory deficit that extends forward in time from the onset of amnesia and prevents the formation of new, enduring memories is known as *anterograde amnesia.* Any memory deficit that stretches backward in time from the onset of amnesia and prevents retrieval of information acquired prior to the onset of the amnesia is known as *retrograde amnesia.*

right of the vertical line, extending forward in time from the onset of amnesia, is anterograde amnesia; to the left of the vertical line, stretching backward in time from the onset of amnesia, is retrograde amnesia. We next consider each in turn, although we spend more time on anterograde amnesia, which is currently better understood.

Anterograde Amnesia

In this section, we discuss five central features of anterograde amnesia and indicate what each illuminates about the nature and organization of normal memory. First, anterograde amnesia selectively compromises long-term memory abilities while leaving working memory intact. Second, anterograde amnesia is global, affecting memory regardless of modality or material. Third, anterograde amnesia disrupts only a specific domain of long-term remembering, namely that of new facts and events. Fourth, this amnesia spares the acquisition and expression of skilled performance. Fifth, the information that can be acquired in anterograde amnesia is inflexible in that it can be expressed only in limited contexts.

Selective Impairment of Long-Term Memory Anterograde amnesia impairs long-term memory, leaving working memory, which is the ability to hold relatively small amounts of information on-line while it is being processed, intact. Accordingly, pa-

tients with amnesia can perform normally when the delay between material acquisition and the memory test is short, but they cannot maintain the information across longer delays. Formal testing of **digit span,** which provides an index of working memory, and **extended digit span,** which indexes long-term memory, illustrates the dissociation between these systems in amnesia. In the digit span task, the experimenter reads aloud a list of 3 to 9 digits, one at a time. For example, a 4-digit string might be 3-7-8-2. Patients are asked to immediately repeat aloud each string verbatim. H.M. and many other patients with amnesia have digit spans that are basically within the normal range (7 ± 2 digits). When meaningful materials are used instead of digits, we can hold more information in working memory than might be suggested by a digit span of 7. Real-world materials, such as words or passages of text, can be *chunked* into meaningful units. Hence, a moderately sized sentence or the names of as many as 7 people can be held in working memory despite the large number of letters contained in the words or names. Each chunked unit can constitute a single item in working memory.

In the extended digit span task, which requires long-term memory, multiple repetitions of the same digit string are presented with an additional digit added to extend the span. For example, a person with a digit span of 7 would receive multiple trials with an 8-digit string (e.g., 2-7-9-1-3-4-8-6) until she or he could correctly recall it. Then the person would be given multiple trials with a 9-digit string that was identical to the 8-digit string but with one additional digit (e.g., 2-7-9-1-3-4-8-6-5) until that string could be correctly recalled, and so forth. Although neurologically intact subjects can generally recall strings of at least 20 digits when tested in this manner, H.M. could not recall even a single string that was 1 digit larger than his span, despite 25 repetitions of the same string (Drachman & Arbit, 1966).

The fact that working memory is intact permits patients with amnesia to comprehend scenes and events normally and to engage in reasonable discourse. However, because their memory impairment "emerges" over significant delays, they are unable to retain this information. Thus, they cannot learn new facts and data about themselves or about the world. These individuals exhibit little of the cumulativeness across events or learning episodes that marks everyday life for most of us. For example, you can probably comprehend this paragraph and then integrate it with the knowledge acquired from the previous paragraphs in this chapter and the preceding chapters, in this way acquiring the cumulative meaning of the ideas and examples provided in the text. Patients with amnesia, such as H.M., cannot do this, and, indeed, patients with the most severe forms of amnesia often comment on the difficulty that reading presents to them.

As suggested by H.M.'s normal performance on the digit span task and grossly impaired performance on the extended digit span task, working memory has certain time and capacity limitations. The way in which these properties or limitations of working memory determine H.M.'s memory performance is clearly illustrated in the following interaction I had with him:

> One day during a lengthy car drive to MIT's Clinical Research Center to be tested, H.M. proceeded to tell me about some guns that were in his house (actually, he had them only in his youth). He told me that he had two rifles, one with a scope and certain characteristics, and the other with just an open sight. He said that he had magazines from the National Rifle Association (actually, just a memory of his earlier family life), all

about rifles. But, he went on, not only did he have rifles, he also had some handguns. He had a .22, a .32, and a .44. He occasionally took them out to clean them, he said, and had taken them with him on occasion to a shooting range. But, he went on, not only did he have some handguns, he also had rifles. He had two rifles, one with a scope and the other with an open sight. He had magazines from the National Rifle Association, all about rifles, he said. But, not only did he have rifles, he also had some handguns. . . . On and on this went, cycling back and forth between a description of the rifles and a description of the handguns, until finally I derailed the conversation by diverting his attention to a newspaper.

Apparently, the two pieces of H.M.'s story were sufficiently associated in his memory of the remote past (which, remember, is intact) that the telling of each piece reliably evoked the memory of the other. Furthermore, the two pieces were large enough—completely filling his working memory span—that by the time he finished telling one piece, he had forgotten that he just told the other, which caused him to recycle the whole story repeatedly.

Global Nature The anterograde amnesia exhibited by H.M. and various other patients is considered global because it is so pervasive. It has been shown to occur under different modes of memory testing, different modalities of information delivery, and different categories of to-be-remembered information. For example, profound impairment in amnesia extends to each of the following three modes of testing memory:

1. In **free recall,** memory is assessed by using only a general cue about an event or a circumstance. An example is "What public events were depicted in photographs at the outset of this chapter?"
2. In **recognition,** memory is assessed by having an individual make a judgment about a previous occurrence or by having an individual distinguish between items that were previously encountered and those that were not. An example is "Which of the following two public events was depicted in a photograph at the outset of the chapter: a scene from the first manned lunar

landing or the explosion of the space shuttle *Challenger?*"

3. In **cued recall,** memory is assessed with the use of direct cues. An example is "One of the photographs at the outset of the chapter had something to do with an act of terrorism. Can you remember exactly what the photograph depicted?"

These modes of testing are not of equal difficulty and do not have exactly the same sensitivity for detecting amnesia. Although the cued recall and recognition memory of patients with amnesia may be above-chance on some tests and better than their abysmally poor free recall, these patients' performance is nonetheless nearly always impaired compared with that of neurologically intact individuals (e.g., Haist, Shimamura, & Squire, 1992; but see Hirst et al., 1986). Thus, the fact that changing the mode of testing does not abolish the amnesia is important in attempting to understand the nature of the underlying deficit in amnesia, which is discussed subsequently.

Amnesia in patients such as H.M. is modality general as well. For example, H.M.'s impairment has been shown to affect remembering of material presented in the visual, auditory, somesthetic, and even olfactory modalities (see Corkin, 1982, and B. Milner, Corkin, & Teuber, 1968). Indeed, this modality generality helps to distinguish amnesia from other kinds of neuropsychological impairment. Someone who has problems remembering visually presented words or stories but can remember the same materials presented aurally is likely to have a deficit within the visual-processing pathway rather than a global memory disorder associated with damage to medial temporal lobe or midline diencephalic structures.

Finally, the deficit in amnesia is material general, affecting both verbal and nonverbal memory, spatial and nonspatial memory, and so forth. The brain damage that causes global amnesia invariably affects critical medial temporal lobe, midline diencephalic, and/or other related structures *bilaterally*. Unilateral damage to the same structures has been shown to produce **material-specific memory disorders,** selectively impairing memory for either verbal or nonverbal materials depending on whether the damage is to the left or the right hemisphere (e.g., B. Milner, 1971; see page 94, chapter 3).

The modality and material generality of amnesia has been crucial in identifying that the disorder compromises specifically *mnemonic* functions, rather than any perceptual, linguistic, or other cognitive processing functions. Damage to the cortical brain systems critical for processing language, visual objects, or motor sequences causes memory problems that are invariably modality and/or material specific. For example, agnosias affect only the ability to gain access to knowledge in a specific modality. The global nature of the impairment in amnesia is illuminating because it suggests that long-term memory for any kind of material presented in any modality can be compromised.

Although amnesia is material and modality general, it is not *totally* global. It selectively impairs memory for events and facts (verbal and nonverbal, regardless of modality), but not the memory that supports skilled performance. We next discuss evidence suggesting a selective loss of memory for facts and events, then we discuss the sparing of skilled performance.

Profound Impairment of Memory for New Events and Facts Patients with amnesia show profound deficits in remembering specific personal and public events. H.M. is unable to report *any* personal events since the time of his surgery (or for the preceding 11 years) and is impaired in performing a variety of tests of public events that occurred after the onset of amnesia (Corkin, 1984). Similar impairments in tests of memory for public events are seen in other cases of amnesia as well (e.g., N. J. Cohen & Squire, 1981). Patients with amnesia also show markedly impaired performance on all the list-based tasks typically used in the laboratory to test recall or recognition memory. In most such memory tests, subjects are asked to study a list of common words, faces, visual objects, and so forth, and are asked to report (in recall tests) or to judge (in recognition tests) which items—all of which are familiar from previous occurrences—appeared on that particular study list.

Even for memory tests in which lists of novel information are presented (e.g., visual shapes, melodies, nonsense words), the ability of patients with amnesia to recall or recognize the items that had been studied is markedly impaired.

You may note that these examples of impairment seem to involve the learning of relations—relations of the people and actions that constitute an event, or relations of items and their context. More direct tests of memory for relations illustrate the deficit in amnesia particularly clearly, as in studies of paired-associate learning. In **paired-associate learning,** words (or other objects) that have no preexisting association are arbitrarily paired in presentation and then must be remembered as pairs. For example, study participants may be shown or read a set of word pairs, one at a time, such as *obey-inch, crush-dark,* and others. The individuals are then presented, immediately afterward, with one member of each pair (e.g., *obey, crush*) and asked to report the other member of the pair. Patients with amnesia, are profoundly impaired at performing this task. Some patients fail to learn *any* arbitrarily related pairs, even with three consecutive study-then-test attempts with the same items.

The markedly impaired performance of these patients on paired-associate learning in the laboratory is mirrored by a severe impairment in a real-world task that seems closely analogous: learning people's names. When you meet a new person and are told the person's name, you must learn the face-name pairing so that when you next see the person, you may be able to greet him or her by name. This real-world task of face-name paired-associate learning is a challenge for anyone, but it is particularly challenging to patients with amnesia. H.M. still does not know the face-name pairings of any of the people who see and test him each year.

One last example of arbitrary relations among items that we learn in our everyday lives, but that patients with amnesia have extraordinary difficulty acquiring, is new vocabulary—that is, learning the meanings or definitions of words. Except for persons with considerable knowledge of etymology, who can trace the development and transmission of words in the language, most people have no idea

why particular words have the meanings that they do. Thus, most people are forced to acquire new vocabulary as paired-associate learning between words and their definitions. Researchers found H.M.'s vocabulary-learning ability to be severely impaired, even when he was tested in two ways (J. D. Gabrieli, Cohen, & Corkin, 1988). First, H.M. was tested in the 1980s on his knowledge of words such as *Jacuzzi* and *granola*, which had been added to *Webster's Dictionary* after the onset of his amnesia in 1953. H.M.'s performance was impaired when he was required to recall or recognize definitions of these words, and he was unable to decide whether they were real English words. Second, the researchers attempted to teach H.M. new vocabulary in the laboratory, using low-frequency words of the type that appear on graduate record exams (GRE), such as *tyro, cupidity,* and *manumit.* The procedure involved the study and test of definitions (e.g., *cupidity,* "an inordinate desire for wealth"), then the study and test of synonyms (e.g., *cupidity-greed*), and finally the use of words to complete sentence frames (e.g., "The king demanded excessive taxes from the people in order to satisfy his "_____"). The results, shown in Figure 9.4, reveal H.M.'s profound impairment relative to the performance of control individuals. Whereas neurologically intact individuals learned the new vocabulary words readily, producing errorless choices of definitions, synonyms, and sentence-frame completions within about two trials apiece, H.M. showed no measurable learning.

A deficit in learning the relations among objects or events is also clearly seen in work with animal models of amnesia using both rodents and nonhuman primates. More specifically, impairment has been shown in learning and remembering not only spatial locations, but also the relation between items and study context in a variety of procedures. For example, O'Keefe and Nadel (1978) summarized a large body of work showing that rats with damage to the hippocampal system exhibit marked deficits in learning and remembering spatial locations (place learning) across a variety of tasks. One often-used task, the **Morris water maze** (R. G. M. Morris, 1981), depicted in Figure 9.5A, employs an appara-

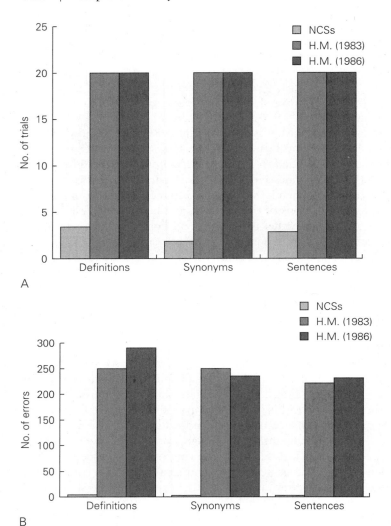

Figure 9.4 An illustration of the profound inability of H.M., a patient who underwent bilateral removal of the temporal lobe, to acquire new information.
In this study (J. D. Gabrieli, Cohen, & Corkin, 1988), H.M. and neurologically intact control subjects (NCSs) were taught the definitions of vocabulary words that they did not previously know. (A) This graph depicts the number of trials required to meet the learning criterion. Note that when tested in both 1983 and 1986, H.M. received the maximum number of trials, 20, whereas the NCSs could learn the definitions, synonyms, and appropriate sentence frames for words in fewer than 5 trials. (B) When tested on their knowledge of the vocabulary words, by selecting either the appropriate definition, the appropriate synonym, or the correct sentence frame, the NCSs retained their knowledge, showing almost no errors, whereas H.M. made more than 200 errors in each case. (*Note.* Adapted from Cohen & Eichenbaum, 1993, p. 255.)

tus consisting of a 2-m-diameter circular tank filled with an opaque fluid (milk or colored water) in which an escape platform sits slightly submerged under the water's surface. This platform is positioned at a constant location relative to various extramaze visual cues (i.e., objects placed around the room, such as light fixtures, doors, and windows).

Animals are placed individually into the tank at various locations around the circumference of the pool on successive trials. During a trial, the animal swims around until it finds the platform and can escape from the water. Across trials, normal animals swim to the platform increasingly rapidly, learning where the platform is located sufficiently well to permit them to navigate directly to it from any starting location (Figure 9.5B). In contrast, damage to the hippocampal system profoundly impairs the ability to learn the location of the escape platform (Figure 9.5C). Placed into the pool at various starting positions, a rat with hippocampal system damage is not able to swim directly to the platform; instead, it must search exhaustively for its location each time, with the result that its escape latency is abnormally long (e.g., Schenk & Morris, 1985; Sutherland, Whishaw, & Kolb, 1983).

In a variant of the **delayed nonmatch-to-sample task** mentioned briefly in chapter 6, animals must remember the identity of recently presented objects (Gaffan, 1974; Mishkin & Delacour, 1975). Each trial of the task consists of a sample phase and a match phase. In the sample phase, the animal is exposed to one of a large set of objects. Following a variable delay interval, the match phase occurs, in which the object from the sample phase is presented together with another from the set of available objects. To receive a reward, the animal must select the object that was not previously presented (the nonmatch object). Thus, the animal must remember across a delay which objects were presented and which were not. Following extensive hippocampal system damage, performance is normal in short-delay conditions (about 10 s) but is markedly impaired after longer delays (e.g., Gaffan, 1977; Mishkin, 1978, 1982; Zola-Morgan & Squire, 1985).

Sparing of the Acquisition and Expression of Skilled Performance Despite the profound im-

pairments shown in amnesia on many memory tasks, certain instances or kinds of new learning remain fully intact even in patients with the most severe forms of amnesia. Furthermore, the patients retain this knowledge even though they cannot remember that they were previously exposed to these tasks.

One main category of preserved learning in amnesia is **skill learning,** which refers to the acquisition, which usually occurs gradually, of new skills such as motor, perceptual, and cognitive skills. We discuss each type of skill learning in turn. The sparing of H.M.'s perceptual-motor skill was shown by using a **mirror tracing task,** which involves tracing the outline of a figure (such as a star) when visual information about the figure and about the individual's hand is conveyed only by means of a mirror (Corkin, 1968; B. Milner, 1962b). Learning is seen as a decrease, across sessions, in the number of times that the pencil falls outside the outline of the figure and as a decrease in the time taken to trace the entire figure. Another perceptual-motor skill, **rotary pursuit,** entails manual tracking of a circularly moving target. Learning is seen as an increase in the amount of time spent on target and a decrease in the number of times that the individual loses contact with the target. Patients with different types of amnesia (i.e., from different causes) have also been shown to exhibit such a preserved learning capacity for motor skills (e.g., Brooks & Baddeley, 1976; Cermak, Lewis, Butters & Goodglass, 1973).

Other researchers (e.g., N. J. Cohen & Squire, 1980) have shown that skill learning in amnesia extends beyond the motor sphere to include perceptual skills—and can be fully intact—in patients with a variety of causes of amnesia. Such sparing was demonstrated with a **mirror-image reading task,** in which word triplets were presented as mirror images, as shown in Figure 9.6A, and the individual was asked to read the words aloud as quickly and accurately as possible. Half of the word triplets were presented multiple times, appearing once in each block of trials and half were presented only once during the experiment. With practice, all participants, neurologically intact control individuals and patients with amnesia alike, learned to read the multiply presented triads with increasing speed and accuracy across blocks (see the graphs to the right in

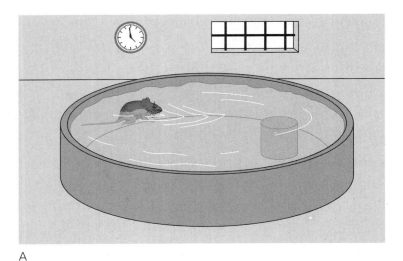

A

Figure 9.5   The Morris water maze task used in animal models of amnesia.
(A) The rats are placed in a circular pool near the perimeter. Sub-merged in the pool is a platform on which the animal can rest, but which is hidden from view because the liquid in the pool is opaque. The position of this platform is constant relative to various objects around the room. (B) The path (black line) from a specific starting point to the escape platform for each of 10 normal rats who had only sham lesions. Normal animals can learn the location of the escape platform, which permits them to swim short, direct paths to the platforms. (C) The paths for 7 animals with hippocampal system damage. Because these animals fail to learn the location of the escape platform, they spend much time swimming around the pool. (*Note.* A, Adapted from Eichenbaum et al., 1990; B & C, Adapted from Eichenbaum, 1994, p. 162.)

Figure 9.6B). Hence, the ability of patients with amnesia to read particular words in a mirror-image orientation increased. These patients also exhibited improvement in reading times for unique word triplets across blocks, which indicated that these individuals had acquired the basic perceptual, pattern-analyzing skills that allow a person to read any mirror-image word (see the graphs to the left in Figure 9.6B). Furthermore, both neurologically intact control individuals and patients with amnesia retained this skill learning during a 3-month interval, a period long enough that none of the patients with amnesia could explicitly recollect their earlier training on this task (see Martone et al., 1984; and Moscovitch, Winocur, & McLachlan, 1986, for similar findings).

Subsequent work has shown that skill learning in amnesia extends further still, to include cognitive skills. One such demonstration involved teaching patients to solve the **Tower of Hanoi puzzle,** a problem in which subjects are confronted with a set of five blocks arranged by size on the left-most of three pegs. These blocks must be restacked onto the right-most peg by moving only one block at a time and never placing a larger block on top of a smaller one (Figure 9.7A). Subjects are asked to solve the problem on multiple occasions, with the ultimate goal of solving it in the shortest number of moves. The optimal solution requires 31 moves, which far exceeds the capacity of working memory and makes this a difficult task. Performance is aided by discovering the recursive structure of the task,

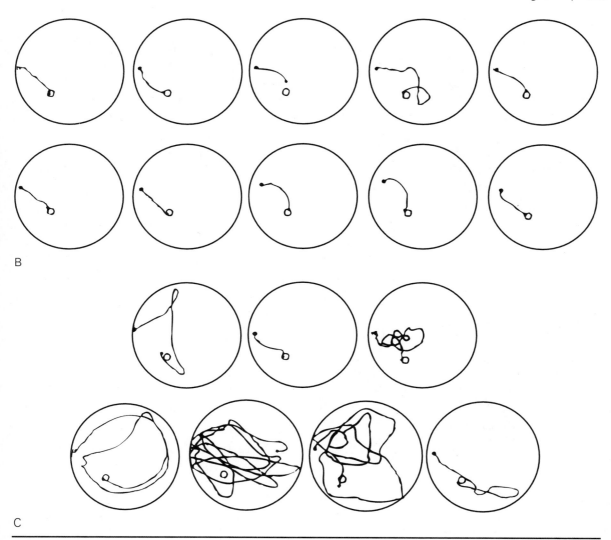

Figure 9.5 (Continued)

namely that solving the five-block puzzle entails first solving a four-block puzzle, which in turn entails first solving a three-block puzzle, and so on. Generally, with successive trials, subjects improve their performance, requiring fewer moves and making fewer detours on their way to gradually approaching the optimal solution. Patients with amnesia, including H.M., can learn to produce the optimal solution (Figure 9.7B) by taking advantage of the recursive-

ness of the task, even though they may be completely unable to describe what they learned to support their increasing skill (N. J. Cohen, Eichenbaum, Deacedo, & Corkin, 1985).

Recent work by Knowlton and Squire has provided other examples of the ability of patients with amnesia to learn the underlying structure of certain cognitive problems. In one of their studies, patients learned the statistical structure of complex sets of

bedraggled grandiose capricious
impotence geometric adjunct
lethargy abrogate brakeman
bedraggled grandiose capricious
paranoia hydrant dinosaur

A

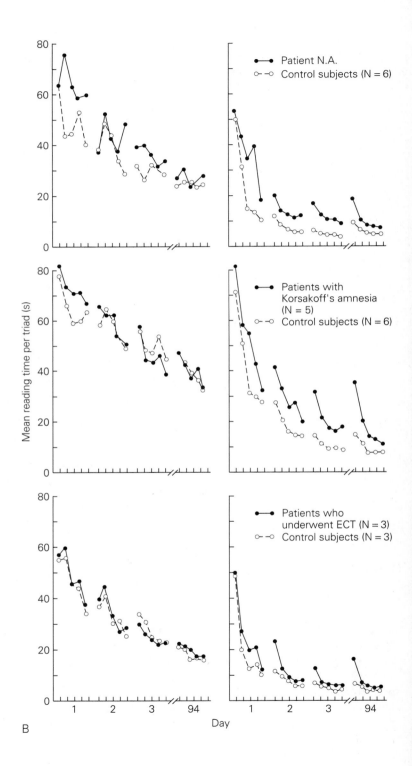

Figure 9.6 An example of a spared perceptual skill in patients with amnesia.
(A) Examples of the mirror-image word triads used in a mirror-image reading task (N. J. Cohen & Squire, 1980). (B) Just like control individuals, patients who have amnesia from different causes—patient N.A., who has midline diencephalic damage (top); patients with Korsakoff's amnesia (middle); and patients who underwent electroconvulsive therapy (ECT) (bottom)—increased the speed with which they could read the triads. This increase occurred not only for repeated triplets (triplets that they saw before; graphs on the right), but also for new (nonrepeated) triads (graphs on the left). The increase in the reading speed for novel triplets indicates that the patients with amnesia were learning the perceptual skill of mirror-image reading. (*Note.* A, Adapted from *Memory, Amnesia, and the Hippocampal System* (pp. 38–39), by N. J. Cohen and H. E. Eichenbaum, 1993, Cambridge, MA: MIT Press. Copyright © 1993 The MIT Press.)

B

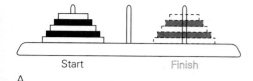

Start   Finish

A

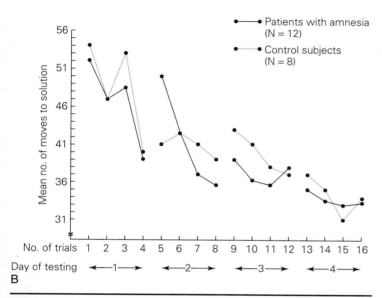

B

Figure 9.7   **The Tower of Hanoi puzzle, which has been used to demonstrate that patients with amnesia can acquire cognitive skills.**
(A) The starting and intended ending configurations of the puzzle.
(B) In this graph, we see that, with practice, patients with amnesia and neurologically intact individuals both can converge on the puzzle's optimal solution in 31 moves. (*Note.* Adapted from Cohen et al., 1985, pp. 57, 63.)

materials. They learned which letter configurations tended to occur across a series of letter strings generated by "artificial grammars" (made-up rules specifying which letters can follow which other letters) and which configuration of symptoms tended to occur in certain made-up diseases (Knowlton, Ramus, & Squire, 1992; Knowlton & Squire, 1994). As with the Tower of Hanoi puzzle, the patients were able to use the information that they acquired about the structure of the problem to categorize stimuli that they had not studied, despite being unable to articulate that knowledge in their verbal reports.

A second main category of preserved learning in amnesia is **repetition priming,** which is an item-specific facilitation of performance based on previous experience. Among the earliest demonstrations of repetition priming in patients with amnesia is the work of Warrington and Weiskrantz (1968, 1970). In one of their studies, patients were presented with a series of visually degraded line drawings, similar to those shown in Figure 9.8, and were asked to name the objects depicted. The patients were first shown the most incomplete drawings (bottom row of Figure 9.8), then somewhat less degraded drawings of the same objects (second row from the bottom in Figure 9.8). This procedure was repeated with sets of increasingly complete drawings of the

Figure 9.8   An example of visually degraded line drawings for which patients with amnesia show repetition priming.

Individuals are shown line drawings of three objects in different stages of completeness, ranging from very degraded (bottom row) to fully complete (top row), and the level of completeness at which an individual can first recognize the figures is determined. When shown the figures again after some delay, neurologically intact individuals recognize the objects at a less complete stage than initially, which indicates that prior exposure to the items influenced their performance. Individuals with amnesia show the same effect, which is indicative of repetition priming. (*Note.* From "Priming Effects in Picture Fragment Completion: Support for the Perceptual Closure Hypothesis," by J. G. Snodgrass and K. Feenan, 1990, *Journal of Experimental Psychology: General, 119,* p. 280. Copyright © 1990 by the American Psychological Association. Reprinted with permission.)

objects until the subject could name all the objects. The number of trials necessary to produce this performance was recorded. Finally, after some delay, the procedure was repeated once more. Both the control individuals and the patients with amnesia benefited from the previous exposure; they were better able to identify the objects in their more degraded versions than they could the first time. B. Milner, Corkin, and Teuber (1968) reported similar results for H.M.

Repetition priming can be seen with verbal materials as well. Perhaps the best known example is the paradigm of **word-stem completion** first used by Graf, Squire, and Mandler (1984), in which individuals are given a list of words to study. The initial three letters of each word in the list is a "stem" for several words in the language. For example, the study list might include *motel* and *cyclone,* whose initial three letters also begin the words *mother* and *cycle,* which are not included on the study list. After a delay, the subjects' retention is tested with the three-letter stems (e.g., *mot* and *cyc*) in two ways, with two outcomes. One way of testing was by cued recall. Tested in this way, patients with amnesia performed poorly compared with control participants. The other way of testing was by word-stem completion, in which subjects were to report "the first word that comes to mind" that completes each stem. As seen in Figure 9.9, patients with amnesia performed normally on this task. Thus, they exhibited priming because they were biased to complete the stems with items from the study list, just as control participants were.

Thus far, we discussed studies in which we inferred, on the basis of increases in response accuracy or decreases in reaction times, that patients with amnesia can be influenced by prior experiences. By using newly developed **eye-movement monitoring techniques,** in which the position of an individual's eyes are monitored as they view a visual stimulus, researchers have recently shown that the nature of processing can be changed by previous experience. The way people move their eyes around visual stimuli (more specifically, the number and kinds of transitions among eye-fixation positions) has been found to distinguish, for any given individual, be-

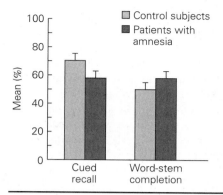

Figure 9.9 Evidence of the dissociation in patients with amnesia between disrupted cued recall and intact word-stem completion.
Patients with amnesia are impaired relative to control individuals on cued recall of words from a previously studied list. However, when asked to complete the word stems with the "first word that comes to mind," these individuals are just as biased as neurologically intact control individuals to report the word that they saw previously on the list. Hence, the prior exposure primes their behavior even though they cannot explicitly recall their experience. (*Note.* Adapted from Graf et al., 1984.)

tween stimuli that were viewed before and those that were not (N. J. Cohen et al., 1995). This effect also holds for patients with amnesia. For example, although one patient with profound amnesia could recognize only 7/48 (15%) of the famous faces for which she was tested, her eye movements demonstrated familiarity with 46/48 (96%) of the same famous faces (Althoff, Maciukenas, & Cohen, 1993). Her previous exposure to these famous faces, in magazines and on television, affected her subsequent perceptual scanning of these faces, even though she could neither explicitly recall the names of the people whose faces she was viewing nor report whether she had seen them before.

These and a host of other examples of skill learning and repetition priming illustrate that, when tested in certain ways, patients with amnesia can be influenced by their prior experiences, despite profound impairment in other aspects of their memory. Their preserved skill learning and priming performances occur despite the following problems:

- *Impaired recollection of the training events:* Patients with amnesia often cannot remember the sessions during which they acquire new skills (such as mirror-image reading, mirror tracing, or solving the Tower of Hanoi puzzle).
- *Impaired recall or recognition of the test materials:* Patients with amnesia show markedly impaired performance on recall or recognition tests for same materials for which they show acquisition of a skill or the influence of previous exposure.
- *Impaired insight into the nature of the newly acquired skills:* Patients with amnesia typically cannot describe what they learned that permits their performance to improve across trials, often being unaware that their performance has even improved.

In summary, amnesia seems to differentiate between the ability to benefit from training experiences, as seen in spared repetition priming and skill learning, and various aspects of memory for or about the training experiences, as seen in impaired recall and recognition.

Sparing of Information Acquired in an Inflexible Manner When normal learning does occur in patients with amnesia, it is fundamentally inflexible in that it can be expressed only in a narrow range of conditions that closely reproduce the conditions of initial learning. Consider the skill-learning and repetition-priming tasks just discussed. In such tasks, performance is assessed on multiple occasions in the same way: Each is a repetition of the original processing circumstances. The intact facilitation of performance that these patients show in priming and skill-learning tasks does not carry over to other tasks or other test contexts, however. As mentioned previously, the patients fail when asked to recall or recognize the materials presented during the earlier learning occasion(s) (the same materials for which they demonstrate priming and skilled performance), and they fail to recollect that earlier learning occasions even occurred. These types of tests present a context different from the original learning context.

Only when the materials are re-presented, and the test conditions replicate the original learning conditions in critical respects, can learning in patients with amnesia be revealed.

The inflexibility of memory acquired by patients with amnesia is particularly evident in Glisky and Schacter's work on teaching a patient with amnesia several computer terms (Glisky & Schacter, 1987; Glisky, Schacter, & Tulving, 1986). These researchers were able to teach computer terms (such as *print*) by using a method that permitted the gradual and incremental learning of what the individual should type into the computer in response to repeatedly presented cues. However, what the patient learned could be used only in the context of this particular computer task with these particular completion cues. When tested outside this context, the patient was impaired. These authors termed the memory that was acquired under such circumstances *hyperspecific.*

One final example of inflexible learning in amnesia comes from an animal study by Eichenbaum, Stewart, and Morris (1990), who used a novel variant of the water maze task. Rather than using the standard method of instruction described previously, in which animals are placed in the maze at different starting locations across trials, a constant starting location was used throughout training. Under these training conditions, rats with hippocampal system damage were able to learn to navigate to the escape platform. However, a subsequent probe test, which assessed the ability of the animals to reach the platform when presented with novel starting positions, revealed that learning in the animals with hippocampal damage was inflexible compared with learning in normal animals. Normal animals readily navigated to the platform from novel starting positions even though their training with regard to the platform's position had been obtained from only one starting position. They were able to use information learned during initial training in a flexible manner, which allowed them to complete the task successfully under conditions distinct from those in the original training situation. In contrast, animals with hippocampal system damage required much longer to find the platform from novel starting positions because these animals, like humans with amnesia, have only an inflexible form of memory.

Retrograde Amnesia

In this section we leave behind the discussion of anterograde amnesia and examine the central features of retrograde amnesia—the impairment of memory for information that was acquired normally prior to the onset of amnesia (see Figure 9.3). We focus on four features of retrograde amnesia that illuminate important issues about the nature and organization of normal memory. First, various instances of retrograde amnesia differ substantially in their temporal extent; some last for decades and others for only several months or years. Second, most instances of retrograde amnesia, regardless of the temporal extent, exhibit a **temporal gradient,** which means that they affect recent memories more so than remote memories. Third, no retrograde amnesia in adulthood permanently affects all long-term memory because much information overlearned early in life is preserved. Fourth, memory supporting skilled performance is spared in retrograde amnesia, just as it is spared in anterograde amnesia.

Variations in Temporal Extent We can distinguish between at least two broad categories of retrograde amnesia: **temporally extensive retrograde amnesia,** which affects decades' worth of memory, and **temporally limited retrograde amnesia,** which affects only years or months. The extent of retrograde amnesia varies with the cause of the amnesia. Patients with Korsakoff's, Alzheimer's, Parkinson's, or Huntington's disease are likely to exhibit an extensive retrograde amnesia. For example, when asked to name the current U.S. President, such patients frequently report Harry Truman or Dwight Eisenhower (whose terms ran from the mid-1940s through the beginning of the 1960s) rather than Bill Clinton. Consider, for example, a pair of studies conducted in the late 1970s and early 1980s, by M. S. Albert, Butters, and Levin (1979) and N. J. Cohen and Squire (1981), that formally document such deficits. In these researchers' famous-faces task,

the examiner asked patients with Korsakoff's disease to identify the photographs of public figures who became prominent during different decades from the 1930s though the 1970s. Even when given cues about the public figures (e.g., the person's profession, the person's initials), the patients exhibited a retrograde amnesia that extended back to the earliest time periods measured by the test (Figure 9.10). Similar results were obtained in formal testing of patients with Alzheimer's disease or Huntington's disease (e.g., Brandt & Butters, 1986; Sagar et al., 1988; B. Wilson, Kaszniak, & Fox, 1981).

Extensive retrograde amnesia is also seen in some, but not all, instances of amnesia associated with encephalitis or anoxia, both on the famous-faces test and on a test of public events in which participants are asked to recall or recognize specific newsworthy events that occurred in various time periods (e.g., the explosion of the space shuttle *Challenger,* the dissolution of the former Soviet Union, the war in Bosnia).

In contrast, other patients, such as those who have undergone bilateral ECT or those with selective damage to the hippocampal region, exhibit a temporally limited retrograde amnesia. One well-studied example involves the amnesia associated with bilateral ECT. Because ECT is a scheduled event, producing an amnesia that emerges gradually during a series of treatments and then dissipates during a period of weeks to months, patients who undergo such treatments can be tested numerous times. In a series of studies, Squire and colleagues (e.g., Squire & Cohen, 1979) showed that after receiving five or six bilateral ECT treatments, patients had a selective retrograde amnesia that was limited to memory for the recent past and left more remote memories intact. For example, patients were prompted to provide all the information that they could recall about television programs that had aired for just one season 1 to 8 years prior to ECT. After ECT, the patients were disproportionately impaired at recalling information about recent shows (Figure 9.11). They often could not remember even the single most salient fact about the shows that aired 1 to 2 years previously (such as that it was a sitcom or a "cop show"), whereas they could remember

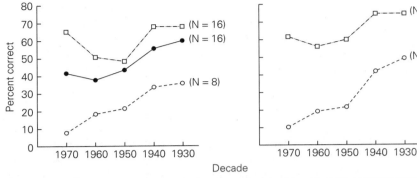

Figure 9.10   Evidence of the extensive retrograde amnesia in patients with Korsakoff's disease.
Alcoholic and nonalcoholic control individuals and patients with Korsakoff's disease were asked to identify photographs of public figures who became prominent during different decades from the 1930s through the 1970s. Across all decades, the performance of patients with Korsakoff's disease was impaired compared with that of the control individuals. (Left) Results of research by N. J. Cohen and Squire (1981). (Right) Results of research by M. S. Albert, Butters, and Levin (1979). (*Note.* Left, Adapted from Squire & Cohen, 1982, p. 289; Right, Adapted from Albert et al., 1979, p. 211.)

much more, even specific episodes, about shows that aired 3 to 5 years prior to ECT.

Temporally limited retrograde amnesia is also associated with other causes of amnesia, such as temporal lobe damage circumscribed to the hippocampus and amygdala (with temporal neocortical areas intact), as occurred in H.M. Formal testing many years after H.M.'s surgery showed his retrograde amnesia to cover 11 years (Corkin, 1984; Sagar, Cohen, Corkin, & Growdon, 1985), a somewhat longer period than what was initially estimated on the basis of clinical observations, but still temporally limited compared with the instances of amnesia discussed earlier in this section. Temporally limited retrograde amnesia can also be found in some cases, but not others, of anoxia and restricted infarctions to the medial thalamus (see Kapur, 1993; Parkin, 1987). However, probably the most frequently encountered instances of temporally limited retrograde amnesia can be seen following closed head

injury. By the time their condition becomes stable, most patients who sustain such injury exhibit a very brief retrograde amnesia. In the classic early study by W. R. Russell and Nathan (1946) of more than 1,000 consecutive cases, greater than 80% of the patients had retrograde amnesia affecting less than a week's worth of memory.

Temporal Gradient   Another important temporal characteristic of retrograde amnesia is that it exhibits a temporal gradient in which recent memories are affected more than remote memories. A temporal gradient such as the one shown in Figure 9.11 is the hallmark of the temporally limited retrograde amnesias. However, even some of the extensive retrograde amnesias are temporally graded, as we can clearly see in Figure 9.10, which depicts the performance of patients with Korsakoff's disease on the famous-faces test. Although the deficit in patients with Korsakoff's amnesia extends across all decades

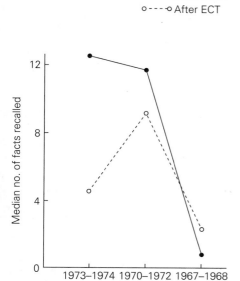

Figure 9.11 **Evidence of temporally limited retrograde amnesia in patients who have undergone electroconvulsive therapy (ECT).**
Before and after a series of ECT treatments, 20 individuals were asked to recall information about former television programs that aired for just one season. Shown here is a graph of the median number of facts recalled. Before ECT (solid line), patients showed a normal forgetting curve; their best recall was for shows from the most recent time period, and their poorest recall was for shows from the most remote time period. After ECT, a selective impairment occurred in the recall of shows from the most recent time period. (*Note.* Adapted from Squire & Cohen, 1979, p. 118.)

tested, the deficit is largest for the most recent time periods and smallest for the most remote periods. This state of affairs results in a peculiar pattern of performance on the famous-faces test when a public figure has been famous for many decades, such as Ronald Reagan. The patients are more likely to correctly identify older photographs of Ronald Reagan, as the 1930s- to 1950s-era actor, than more contemporary photographs of Ronald Reagan, as the 1970s- to 1980s-era politician.

Although the retrograde amnesia associated with closed head injury is eventually temporally limited,

it can start out as a much more extensive amnesia in the immediate aftermath of injury. The resolution of an extensive retrograde amnesia over time into a temporally limited amnesia is known as **shrinking retrograde amnesia.** This type of amnesia clearly reveals the temporal gradient associated with amnesia, as illustrated in Figure 9.12, in which we see three time lines representing the memory status of a patient at three examination times after his closed head injury. In Figure 9.12A, the time line illustrates the patient's status 5 months after injury, when the patient still has a full-blown anterograde amnesia caused by her injury, which is often referred to as *posttraumatic amnesia.* This anterograde amnesia impairs memory for the entire period since the time of the head injury. In addition, the patient has a retrograde amnesia that extends back in time as far as can be measured. In Figure 9.12B, the time line represents the patient's status 3 months later, at which point recovery has begun. On the anterograde side of the time line, we see that the posttraumatic amnesia is beginning to resolve, so some new memories can be formed, although memory for the earlier period posttrauma remains impaired. On the retrograde side of the time line, we see that the extent of retrograde amnesia has begun to shrink, now covering only 1 year of complete amnesia and a few additional years of patchy amnesia. In Figure 9.12C, the time line shows the situation after recovery has run its course. On the anterograde side, new memories are being formed normally, but amnesia remains for the earlier period posttrauma. Amnesia for this period is permanent because the head injury prevents events that occurred soon after that time from being made into robust, retrievable, memories. On the retrograde side, the amnesia has shrunk further, rendering permanently inaccessible only the events that occurred during the 2 weeks prior to the injury. The formerly extensive retrograde amnesia has become temporally limited, and the recovery shows a clear temporal gradient: The most remote memories recovered soonest; less remote memories recovered somewhat later; and the most recent memories are most likely to remain impaired. Even in the latter portion of the 19th century, Theodule Ribot appreciated the disproportionate vulnerability

A Unique Opportunity to Examine the Nature of Temporally Graded Retrograde Amnesia

Perhaps we should not be surprised that, given their decades of alcoholism, patients with Korsakoff's amnesia have a temporally graded retrograde amnesia, showing poorer memory for information from recent years than for information from more remote decades. However, how can scientists determine whether the temporally graded retrograde amnesia of these patients is caused by the cumulative effects of many years of drinking as opposed to the acute effects of hemorrhaging of midline diencephalic structures oc-

curring at the onset of the amnesia? What kind of evidence would permit us to disentangle these two possible sources of the temporal gradient?

In an ideal world, neuropsychologists would find a patient with Korsakoff's amnesia who religiously kept a diary for most of his or her adult life. In this way, the scientists could have a record of the events and facts that the individual considered of consequence at the time and could then use that material to assess the patient's amnesia for recent and remote time periods.

of recent memories, which are least recoverable in a shrinking retrograde amnesia and the only memories affected in temporally limited anterograde amnesias. He observed, in the form of what is now known as **Ribot's Law,** that the most recently acquired memories are most susceptible to disruption by brain damage (Ribot, 1881/1882).

Because retrograde amnesias are temporally graded and have differential effects for events at various periods prior to the injury, laypersons often misinterpret the type of memory deficit experienced by the individuals with amnesia. They tend to consider the inability of patients with amnesia to report what they had for breakfast that day or where they currently live as a deficit in "short-term" memory and assume that these patients' ability to report who they are, where they grew up, and so forth indicates intact "long-term" memory. That is, these people misuse the term *short-term memory* to refer to memory for the events of recent days, months, and years and the term *long-term memory* for memory of more remote events and facts. However, referring to several *years'* worth of events as short-term memory does not capture either the commonsense meaning or the technical definition in psychology of *short-term memory,* which is the memory used during the period when individuals are actively working on information (e.g., the memory used to immediately

repeat 7 digits). As we learned earlier, patients with amnesia can maintain information for such limited periods; that is, they have normal short-term memory. The time period of these memories is seconds and minutes, not years. Accordingly, the terms *recent memory* and *remote memory* are perferable for distinguishing between the long-term memories of different time frames that are lost in retrograde amnesia.

We should note that in some cases the retrograde amnesia is *flat,* or temporally uniform, showing little if any temporal gradient. This pattern is observed when considerable additional damage to neocortical areas has occurred, as in the late stages of Alzheimer's disease (B. Wilson, Kaszniak, & Fox, 1981), in some patients after encephalitis (Cermak & O'Connor, 1983), and in patients with Huntington's disease (see chapter 14, page 530). In such cases, the damage includes areas that, as we learn later in this chapter, are likely to be the sites of long-term memory storage. A loss of stored memories may occur without regard to temporal information; if so, the result is a retrograde amnesia without a temporal gradient.

Sparing of Information Overlearned Early in Life No matter how extensive the retrograde amnesia, unless the patient sustains extensive additional

In fact, as unlikely as it seems, Butters and Cermak (1986) were provided with such an opportunity. They had the unique experience of being able to study a man who, after a long history of drinking, developed Korsakoff's amnesia, shortly after completing his autobiography. In his book, the man, who was a scientist, discussed many events from his long and rich career. In addition, his autobiography included references to many other scientists and to many conceptual issues that were prominent during different periods of his

career. The timing of these two events—the completion of his book followed by the onset of his amnesia—permitted the investigators to test his memory for information from different periods that, just a short time earlier, the patient remembered well enough to include in his book. Tested on information from his book, this patient exhibited a typical temporally graded retrograde amnesia; this finding demonstrated that the temporal gradient can appear full-blown at the acute onset of Korsakoff's disease.

damage to neocortical brain regions, where long-term memories are believed to be stored, he or she can retain information overlearned early in life that, for all people, forms the foundation for perceptual, motor, and linguistic competence. Despite their extensive retrograde amnesias, patients with amnesia associated with Korsakoff's disease, anoxia, or encephalitis have intact knowledge about the world; preserved language, perceptual, and social skills; and spared general intelligence. Only the extensive retrograde amnesias associated with progressive dementias, as in Alzheimer's disease or Huntington's disease, impair this kind of information, and then only later in the progression of the disease (e.g., Weingartner, Grafman, Boutelle, & Martin, 1983).

Sparing of Memory Supporting Skilled Performance Finally, the dissociation seen in anterograde amnesia between impaired remembering on direct tests of memory (e.g., free recall) and spared performance on indirect tests of memory (e.g., priming) is also seen in retrograde amnesia. This dissociation was demonstrated by Squire, Cohen, and Zouzounis (1984), who tested patients receiving bilateral ECT. Prior to the administration of ECT, patients were given a training session to acquire skill in reading mirror-image text. After several ECT treatments were administered, these patients

were given another session of mirror-image reading. The ECT treatments impaired the patients' ability to explicitly remember the earlier training session. Nonetheless, the initial training session had a beneficial effect on their subsequent performance. Hence, skill learning was *not* affected by retrograde amnesia.

Debate About Multiple Forms of Amnesia

The fact that retrograde amnesias differ so radically in their temporal extent suggests the possibility that they reflect different varieties of impairment—different forms of amnesia. Furthermore, because many medial temporal lobe and midline diencephalic regions cause amnesia when damaged, different forms of amnesia may exist depending on exactly which subset of structures is impaired. No matter how anatomically interconnected these brain regions might be, multiple brain structures are unlikely to have identical functional roles, each making exactly the same contribution to memory. Moreover, neuropsychological analysis of the other cognitive domains covered in this textbook shows that brain damage can selectively disrupt different components of a cognitive process. In the study of patients with deficits of language, attention, visual object recognition, and so forth, we learned that

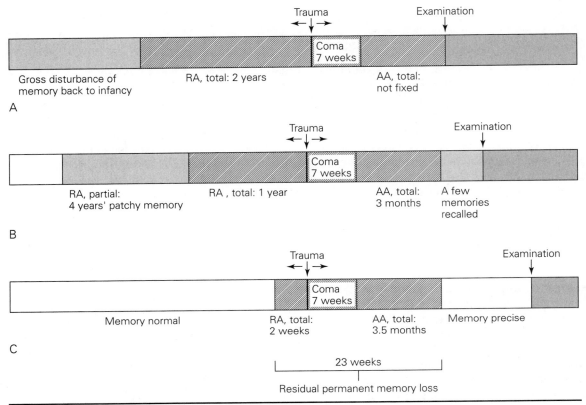

Figure 9.12 An illustration of the phenomenon of shrinking retrograde amnesia.
The memory status of a patient was assessed at three examination times: (A) 5 months, (B) 8 months, and (C) 16 months after closed head injury. The time of the head injury is indicated by the heavy vertical line in each time line. The portion of time for which memory was impaired is depicted by diagonal lines, and times of patchy impairment are represented by lightly shaded areas. The portions of time affected to the right of the heavy vertical line indicate the extent of the anterograde amnesia (AA). The portions of time affected to the left of the heavy vertical line indicate the extent of the retrograde amnesia (RA). Across the three time lines, the retrograde amnesia shrinks from an initially extensive impairment encompassing years to a more limited amnesia affecting only weeks. (*Note.* Adapted from Barbizet, 1970.)

deficits that appear similar on a gross level can, with more precise assessment, be revealed to have different neural bases. Such deficits reflect damage to different component processors. Thus, it seems inevitable that these findings will prove true of memory deficits as well.

Similar claims have been entertained about the nature of anterograde amnesia. F. Lhermitte and Signoret (1976) and Squire (1982) have argued that the anterograde amnesia associated with medial temporal lobe damage differs in important basic ways from the amnesia associated with damage to midline diencephalic structures (e.g., Korsakoff's amnesia). However, Weiskrantz (1985), among others, has disagreed, suggesting that the behavioral data currently available fail to support such a claim. At present, the issue remains unresolved. Whether fundamentally different forms of amnesia exist is, in the end, an empirical question that can be resolved only with the collection and analysis of more data.

WHERE IN TIME AMNESIA EXERTS ITS EFFECT

All, or virtually all, patients with amnesia have a retrograde amnesia as a component of their impairment. The apparently obligatory presence of retrograde amnesia in these patients provides important constraints on our thinking about where in the chain of memory processing, from the initial receipt of information to its eventual retrieval, amnesia exerts its effect. In principle, amnesia might reflect problems either in the initial **encoding of memories,** which is the process whereby information is placed in memory storage so that it can later be retrieved in the **storage, maintenance, or consolidation of memories,** which are the processes operating during the time after learning that allow information to be retained in memory; or in the **retrieval of memories,** which is the process whereby previously stored memories are recalled. If the initial encoding of memories is affected, information is not being fully processed or is not being placed in storage in a form that is sufficiently robust to be easily retrieved later. Alternatively, amnesia could reflect a failure in the storage, maintenance, or consolidation of memories with time, in which case information in memory is decaying abnormally rapidly with time despite having been properly encoded. Finally, amnesia could instead reflect a failure in the retrieval of memories, in which case the information is being stored and maintained in memory in a fully intact manner but is not being retrieved normally.

Let's examine each of these possibilities in turn. An encoding deficit is probably the easiest to rule out because all amnesias include a retrograde component. Because retrograde amnesia is, by definition, an impairment in memories that were previously encoded normally, amnesia cannot simply result from a deficit in encoding.

A disruption in consolidation might be considered because it could account for both anterograde amnesia and temporally graded retrograde amnesia.

Anterograde amnesia would result because memories for events occurring after the onset of amnesia would never receive the benefits of consolidation and therefore would have increased vulnerability to loss with time. In addition, memories acquired recently before the onset of amnesia would not have had the opportunity to benefit fully from consolidation. Thus, they would be more vulnerable to amnesia than more remote—more fully consolidated—memories would be, which would result in a temporally graded form of retrograde amnesia.

Yet consolidation alone may not entirely explain the changes in memory with time. Note that if changes in memory were due solely to consolidation, the extent of the retrograde amnesia would provide some estimate of the time course of consolidation. Because temporally limited retrograde amnesia extends out to a few years, we would conclude that consolidation of memory continues for a few years. However, if we consider the clear temporal gradient that occurs with more extensive retrograde amnesias, we would have to conclude that consolidation extends out to include many decades. Although we could reasonably suppose that memory might continue to change for years after learning, we would have more difficulty envisioning that consolidation would continue to exert its effects and that memory would continue to change for many decades. Furthermore, the great variability in the temporal extent of retrograde amnesias across patients poses a problem for a consolidation viewpoint because it suggests that consolidation continues for decades in some people but for just a few years or less in other people. Hence, attempting to explain both temporally limited retrograde amnesia and graded temporally extensive retrograde amnesia in terms of memory consolidation may not make sense.

Instead, the extensive retrograde amnesias would seem to require an explanation based on either failure to retrieve stored memories or the loss of stored memories, as some researchers, most notably Warrington and Weiskrantz (1970), have argued. Another reason that temporally extensive retrograde amnesia has been conceptualized as a retrieval deficit is that performance of patients with amnesia is often aided by powerful retrieval cues (Warrington &

Weiskrantz, 1970). In certain situations in which patients with amnesia have negligible free recall of some previous event or materials, their recognition memory performance and cued recall performance can be significantly above-chance (although still impaired relative to the performance of neurologically intact individuals). The fact that the existence of these memories can be revealed under the appropriate retrieval conditions indicates that more information was encoded and stored than the negligible free recall performance led us to believe. Furthermore, this fact raises the prospect that the ability to remember might increase as ever more powerful retrieval cues are used. The increase observed when retrieval is aided in this fashion might be used to argue that the problem lies in unaided retrieval processes.

An explanation of amnesia as a retrieval deficit has considerable intuitive appeal. We have each had experience in which a particularly powerful retrieval cue elicited a recall of memories that were believed to be long lost, such as hearing a song or seeing a photograph that triggered rich memories of a specific time in our life or a particular relationship from our past. In addition, we have all heard claims that memories that were apparently forgotten could be elicited during psychotherapy or with the aid of hypnosis. These considerations would seem to suggest that we can easily underestimate, on the basis of performance on any given memory test, the extent of memory that a person has for an event. The right retrieval cues, the proper testing context, or both permit us to get access to rich veins of memory that we might have considered to be long forgotten. In such cases, "forgetting" would seem to be a loss of access to what are demonstrably adequately stored memories. Arguing by extension from normal forgetting to amnesia, and considering the ability of retrieval cues to improve the memory performance of patients with amnesia, we could advance a retrieval deficit theory of amnesia.

However, we must be careful not to overinterpret the findings of strong beneficial effects of powerful retrieval cues. All that we can reasonably conclude from a finding of better memory in response to more powerful retrieval manipulations is that more memory is encoded and stored than was previously appreciated. We cannot infer from such findings that memory was encoded and stored *normally* and that the only deficit is in getting access to it at retrieval time. Perhaps, instead, these memories were encoded, stored, maintained, or consolidated poorly, so that whatever memories were still available at the time of a test were relatively fragmentary and relatively poorly tied to other items, which made them difficult to retrieve. But, as increasingly powerful cues were used, the likelihood of making contact with even fragmentary or degraded memories undoubtedly increased and performance benefited. Accordingly, the finding that more powerful cueing improves memory performance in amnesia does not permit us to distinguish possible deficits at the different stages of memory processing. A retrieval deficit provides no better fit to these data than an encoding or a consolidation deficit would.

Keep in mind that this argument also holds for issues concerning normal forgetting and even when we are talking about the recovery of memories during psychotherapy: Poorly encoded and poorly stored or maintained memories will benefit just as much from cueing procedures used during therapy as will memories that are fully intact but difficult to retrieve. Hypnosis is another matter, however. Most researchers no longer believe that hyponosis acts to reveal memories that are being actively repressed. Rather, most investigators now believe not only that hypnosis serves to lower an individual's criteria for making reports so that she or he can comply with and please the examiner, but also that hypnosis is just as likely to lead to false reports as it is to reveal true memories (see Pettinati, 1988). Indeed, reports by people under hypnosis are so unreliable that these reports are typically banned from court proceedings.

Consequently, despite the intuitive appeal of a retrieval deficit explanation for temporally extensive retrograde amnesia, the jury is still out. Such an explanation could account for the amnesia, but the available evidence does not provide any more support for this explanation than for an explanation based on failure of the storage and maintenance of memories with time. However, the temporally extensive retrograde amnesias clearly differ in important ways from the temporally limited retrograde amnesias, and these differences continue to motivate researchers to consider the possibility that fundamentally different kinds of amnesia exist.

WHAT AMNESIA REVEALS ABOUT THE ORGANIZATION OF MEMORY

Consideration of the central features, and more particularly the specificities, of anterograde and retrograde amnesia illuminates a great deal about the organization of normal memory. As we learned so far, amnesia affects some aspects of memory while leaving others intact. In this section, we consider what these patterns of impairment and sparing tell us about the organization of memory and its neural substrate.

A Distinction Between Long-Term and Working Memory

As we discussed, anterograde amnesia selectively compromises certain aspects of long-term retention while leaving working memory intact. Evidence that these two memory processes doubly dissociate comes from patients who have the opposite impairment—a selective working memory deficit with intact long-term memory. Later in this chapter, we discuss working memory in more detail. At that point, other evidence is provided to distinguish between the brain systems that are active during working memory processing and those that are necessary for long-term memory processes.

The Dynamic Nature of Memory

The existence of temporally limited and temporally graded retrograde amnesia points to the dynamic nature of memory, showing the extent to which memory undergoes change during the time after learning. These two phenomena clear-

ly indicate a difference between recent memory and remote memory in terms of their susceptibility to amnesia. That is, although with time some memories are being forgotten, other memories which survive the passage of time, are apparently increasing their resistance to disruption. Many investigators call this change with time *memory consolidation*. The specific details of the processes underlying memory consolidation are not well understood, but they seem to depend critically on the interaction between the hippocampal system and the neocortical sites of memory storage (e.g., McClelland, McNaughton, & O'Reilly, 1995; Squire, Cohen, & Nadel, 1984).

The Hippocampal System Does Not Store Long-Term Memories

The nature of retrograde amnesia indicates that the hippocampal system and related structures cannot constitute the storage site of all long-term memories. Memory for the remote past remains intact in all patients with temporally limited retrograde amnesia, and even patients with extensive retrograde amnesia still retain information (over)learned early in life. Instead, the neocortex appears to be the site of permanent long-term memory storage. We discuss this issue in more detail later in the chapter.

MULTIPLE MEMORY SYSTEMS

The intact acquisition and expression of skilled performance observed in amnesia across a variety of domains (motor, perceptual, and cognitive) that co-occurs with profound deficits in other aspects of long-term remembering suggests that the medial temporal lobe and midline diencephalic regions make a critical contribution to a particular kind of memory. The question then arises as to how we can best characterize that domain or kind of memory. This issue has been the subject of a large and growing body of work and is a topic of considerable discussion and controversy in the field. A number of theoretical accounts have been offered that distinguish between kinds of memory or memory systems, each of which tends to focus on different aspects of the amnesic syndrome. In the discussion that follows, we primarily consider two of these theoretical accounts—those that have received the most attention in the literature—and end by endorsing one of them on the grounds that it provides the most comprehensive coverage of the data on amnesia and normal memory. However, a number of the theories have much in common, and further work in the field will surely continue to shape these ideas.

Explicit and Implicit Memory

One important aspect of the dissociation between impaired and spared memory abilities in amnesia seems to involve the extent to which the memory test requires *conscious recollection* of the prior learning experiences, requiring that subjects gain conscious access to a representation of a prior learning episode. **Direct (explicit) tests of memory** are those that depend on conscious recollection of the learning event and refer the individual to a particular study episode or learning event, as assessed

- in the query "What did you have for breakfast yesterday?"
- in the instructions for a multiple-choice recognition memory test: "Which of the following items did you see on the previous list?"

To respond appropriately, the subject must refer back to a specific event (breakfast yesterday) or a specific context (the study list).

Indirect (implicit) tests of memory are those that refer individuals to a processing task without requiring conscious recollection of prior learning experience. Changes in performance on the task

are considered a measure of the *influence* of that previous experience (Graf & Schacter, 1985; Richardson-Klaven & Bjork, 1988; Schacter, 1987a). Each of the following instructions is an implicit test of memory:

- "Report the first word that comes to mind that completes the stem *mot___*."
- "Read these words aloud as quickly and accurately as you can."

Participants can respond to these instructions without referring to specific prior experiences. However, to the extent that stem-completion performance is biased in favor of words seen recently and that words encountered previously are read faster, there is evidence of the effects of prior experience.

With these definitions in mind, let's return to considering impaired and spared memory performances in amnesia. Notice that the examples of preserved learning and memory capacities we discussed earlier in the chapter all occurred when the individual's memory was assessed by indirect (implicit) tests of memory. In contrast, patients with amnesia were impaired on direct (explicit) tests of memory. For example, patients showed increased skill in reading mirror-imaged text, but they could not recollect their previous training experiences. They showed priming effects, such as being biased to use words that they recently studied to complete word stems, but they could not explicitly remember those words.

This characterization seems to capture a key aspect of amnesia: a normal ability to acquire and express skilled performance but an absence of the ability to consciously recollect learning experiences. Even while showing normal repetition priming and skill learning, patients with amnesia seem to have no familiarity with the test situation or with the test materials. Because these patients cannot consciously introspect about the contents of their knowledge, they are said to have "memory without awareness" (Jacoby, 1984; Moscovitch, 1994). Rarely, if ever, are neurologically intact individuals so devoid of familiarity when exhibiting memory performance.

Some investigators have focused on this experiential aspect of amnesia, emphasizing the extent to which recollective experience and consciousness are related to the nature of the deficit in amnesia and hence to hippocampal function (e.g., Gray, in press; Moscovitch, 1994). However, this approach has several shortcomings. First, the hippocampal system neither produces conscious awareness nor is critical for it to be produced. Large lesions of the hippocampal region, resulting in profound memory impairments, have no demonstrable effect on consciousness in humans. Furthermore, conscious recollection is still possible after amnesia, not for new memories but for remote memories.

A second problem with this approach is that it provides no ability to explain amnesic deficits observed in animals. As mentioned previously, damage to the hippocampal system in rodents and nonhuman primates also produces an amnesia that exhibits selectivity in the aspects of memory that are impaired. Such animals show impairments in learning and remembering spatial relations among environmental cues, configurations of multiple perceptually independent cues, contextual or conditional relations, and comparisons among temporally discontinuous events—all cases in which information learned in a given context must be expressed in or related to novel contexts. Yet the same animals can show normal learning and remembering of a large variety of conditioning, discrimination, and skill tasks. This dissociation among memory capacities is every bit as compelling as that seen in human amnesia and, in fact, parallels closely the dissociation in human amnesia. A description of impaired versus spared memory abilities in amnesia comprehensive enough to be capable of accommodating the phenomena for both humans and animals seems preferable.

Third, and most fundamental, the extent to which tests require conscious recollection does not seem to be the critical determinant of whether memory performance is impaired or spared. In at least two experiments, patients with amnesia did not perform normally on indirect (implicit) tests of memory when they had to learn relations among arbitrarily associated items. Because these studies provide critical evidence that we will have to look beyond the implicit-explicit memory hypothesis if we are to understand amnesia, we discuss these two studies in some detail next.

Consider first the vocabulary-learning experiment (J. D. Gabrieli, Cohen, & Corkin, 1988) in which patients with amnesia were taught the definitions for uncommon words, such as *tyro* and *cupidity,* the type that might appear on the GREs. In each of the three test phases of this experiment, an implicit test of memory was used. For each vocabulary word, participants indicated from a list of choices the definition that "goes best" with it, the synonym that "goes best" with it, and which sentence frames would "best complete" it. At no time were participants asked to make reference to or to consciously recollect any specific learning experience. They were not asked whether they remembered having seen any of the words, definitions, synonyms, or sentence frames before, nor were they asked to indicate why they made their choices. Yet, H.M.'s performance on this indirect test of memory was profoundly impaired.

The other example we consider involves an experiment using eye-movement monitoring to assess memory for the relations among objects (Whitlow, Althoff, & Cohen, 1995). Stimuli were pairs of real-world scenes consisting of an original scene, an example of which is shown in Figure 9.13A, and a manipulated version in which the relations among objects in the scene were changed, as shown in Figure 9.13B. Participants viewed each of the scenes in their original (unmanipulated) version twice, then viewed half the scenes in their original version and half with some aspect of the scene manipulated but still perceptually reasonable. To the extent that view-

A

B

Figure 9.13 Eye-movement monitoring as a means of assessing implicit memory.
(A) An example of an original scene in the relational manipulation experiment by Whitlow, Althoff, and Cohen (1995). Participants viewed the scene twice, then saw either
the original scene again or (B) a manipulated version in which relations among the objects in the scene were changed. Superimposed on the scenes in (A) and (B) are eye
movements made by one of the neurologically intact participants in the study (the circles represent the eye fixations). When the participant viewed the original version,
most eye movements were directed to the three objects in the center foreground: the
person, the wooden trash receptacle, and the sign. When viewing the manipulated
scene, the participant looked to the position where the person had been standing, even
though it was empty and the person was positioned elsewhere. Hence, eye movements
provide an implicit measure of the person's knowledge about the scene.

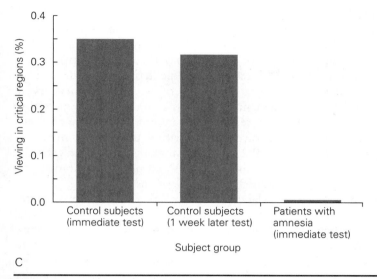

C

Figure 9.13 (Continued)
(C) A graph of data from this experiment. Control individuals tested either immediately after viewing the scenes or 1 week later (at which point they were at-chance in explicitly distinguishing between the manipulated and unmanipulated scenes) exhibited implicit memory for the relations among objects because they spent much time viewing the region of the scene in which the relations had been manipulated. In contrast, patients with amnesia did not spend time looking at that region, an indication that they lacked the ability to remember relational information even when it was assessed implicitly. (Courtesy of Neal J. Cohen; used by permission.)

ers have memory for the relations among the critical objects from their experience with the unmanipulated, original version of the scene, the manipulated scene will be deviant in the region(s) where items were manipulated. In fact, neurologically intact individuals spent the most time viewing the critical manipulated regions (Figure 9.13C). This effect could be detected in the eye-movement measures even when a 1-week delay occurred between the second presentation of the scenes and the final (test) presentation of the scenes. Moreover, at this point in time, participants' explicit knowledge of the scenes were at-chance and they could no longer correctly judge which scenes were presented in their original form as opposed to their manipulated form.

Thus, eye movements provided an indirect measure of memory for the relationships among objects in scenes and did not depend on explicit remembering of the previous presentation of the scenes. Yet, even with this implicit measure of memory, patients with amnesia were impaired in their memory for relations. As can be seen in Figure 9.13C, they directed eye movements to the critical regions no more often in the manipulated scenes than in the unmanipulated scenes, thereby failing to show the normal effect.

Declarative and Procedural Memory

Patients with amnesia are impaired on all tasks, or components of tasks, that depend on or benefit greatly from the ability to learn new relationships, particularly among arbitrarily associated items. These individuals have exceptional difficulty in learning the arbitrary relations among items that we explicitly learn in our everyday lives, such as the names connected with particular people's faces or the addresses and telephone numbers that we learn to associate with them. These relations are arbitrary in that rarely are people's names derived from their appearance; nor are telephone numbers and addresses in any way meaningfully related to people's names or appearance. They cannot be derived from other knowledge about the people but must be explicitly memorized. Similar arbitrary relationships can be assessed in the laboratory, such as by the paired-associate test that we learned about earlier in the chapter in which arbitrary pairs of words must be remembered.

This emphasis on memory for the arbitrary relationships among items is at the heart of a different theory of memory, one that distinguishes between declarative and procedural memory. As offered by Cohen and Eichenbaum (N. J. Cohen & Eichenbaum, 1993; Eichenbaum, Otto, & Cohen, 1994), reflecting an elaboration and expansion of the declarative-procedural theory offered initially by Cohen and Squire (N. J. Cohen, 1981, 1984; Squire & Cohen, 1984), this theory posits that the hippocampal system contributes to the mediation of and amnesia is a selective deficit of **declarative memory,** a fundamentally relational memory system. Other brain systems, which are not damaged in amnesia, are involved in mediating **procedural memory.** Table 9.2 lists the features and characteristics of these investigators' proposed declarative and procedural memory systems.

Declarative memory provides a way of representing experience that is fundamentally relational in nature, allowing not only the relationships among objects in a scene or in an event to be remembered, but also relationships to other memories to be remembered as well. This ability of new inputs to activate related already-stored memories produces the *flexibility* of declarative memory. Related declarative memories can be activated regardless of the current context, by all manner of external sensory or even purely internal inputs. They can be manipulated and flexibly expressed in any number of novel situations, independent of the circumstances in which the

Table 9.2 Features and Characteristics of Declarative and Procedural Memory

Type of memory	Features and characteristics
Declarative	Accumulates facts and events
	Represents the outcomes of processing operations
	Binds or chunks the inputs converging onto the hippocampal system
	Supports representations of experience that are fundamentally relational
	Is accessible to various processing systems
	Can be retrieved flexibly and used in novel contexts.
Procedural	Supports the acquisition and expression of skilled performance
	Involves tuning and modifying specific processing systems
	Supports representations that are dedicated to the modified processors (and thus unavailable to other processors)
	Supports representations of experience that are fundamentally individual (nonrelational)
	Can be expressed only inflexibly, only in a repetition of the original processing situation

Figure 9.14   A schematic depiction of the convergence of different streams of information onto the hippocampal system.
The following information converges onto the hippocampal system: temporal information from the frontal region (depicted by the clock); spatial information from the parietal region (depicted by a floor plan); information about specific people, places, and events (depicted by the young girl, the building, and the calendar, respectively); and even affective information from limbic regions evoked by particular situations such as a snow-covered field. (By permission of Neal J. Cohen and Larry Kanfer.)

information was initially acquired. For example, if all goes well, you should be able to bring to mind the information presented in this chapter when you reread it while studying for an examination, and also when you respond to questions on that examination. You will also be able to bring this information to mind when you read about related issues in a subsequent chapter of this book, when you watch a science-fiction movie in which a not-yet-discovered medical procedure for restoring memory is used, or when your grandmother tells you about her decreasing ability to remember recent events.

The central neural structure for declarative memory is the hippocampal system and related structures, which receive converging input from all the higher order neocortical (sensory, motor, and limbic) processors in the brain. These connections make the hippocampal system the recipient of information about the people and objects, the temporal and spatial contexts, and the affective and behavioral responses and actions that compose learning experiences. This convergence of information is represented pictorially in Figure 9.14. The hippocampal system then binds or chunks these converging inputs in a manner that is crucial in mediating the remembering of relationships among multiple distinct objects.

By contrast, procedural memory, supported by brain systems outside the hippocampal system and midline diencephalic regions, is *inflexible* and dedicated. Its representation of experience is inextricably tied to the processing operations that were engaged during initial learning. This type of memory therefore does not involve the storage of the outcomes of processing, in the way we described for declarative memory, but rather the tuning of and changes in the way these processing operations actually run—that is, modification of the processing elements themselves. Accordingly, procedural memory can be retrieved and expressed only when the original processing operations are again engaged. Procedural memories exert their influence only when the testing circumstances constitute a repetition of the original learning situation.

For example, the processing systems of the brain that are engaged in reading, having been organized by a lifetime of reading experience, continue to be shaped and molded, making and keeping them maximally tuned to the inputs they receive most frequently and recently. This tuning results in the widely observed frequency effects in word identification and reading speed, in which we have become, through experience, fastest at reading the words in the language that occur in text most often (similarly, we identify fastest the objects and the people that we encounter most frequently, and we type the letter combinations that we use most often the fastest). Procedural memory for a recent experience of reading can be expressed only when a person is again reading, without the requirement for any involvement of conscious recollection of any specific learning experiences. The subject need not be able to articulate verbally any of the information embodied in her or his ability to read skillfully. That is, we don't need to be able to report what the frequencies of various words in the language are in order for our reading speed to be influenced by those frequencies. Likewise, few people can actually report which letter combinations occur most frequently in typing despite the fact that everyone's typing shows some effect of those frequencies of occurrence. In a similar vein, Posner (1973) long ago observed that although highly skilled typists are poor at pointing out the locations of the letters on a schematic keyboard when not actually in the process of typing, their excellent knowledge of the spatial locations of the letters *a* to *z* is revealed whenever they type words.

This inflexibility of procedural memory allows it to be expressed only in limited contexts—those that permit the reengaging of the processors that participated in the original learning situation.

By focusing on amnesia as a deficit in declarative memory processing rather than focusing on the issue of conscious recollection, we can describe impaired versus spared memory abilities in both humans and animals with a single account of amnesia. Furthermore, this view can explain why patients with amnesia exhibit deficits on direct tests of memory but not on indirect tests. Direct tests of memory often require memory for the relationship between particular test items and a specific learning episode or study context. In contrast, indirect tests of memory require only memory for individual items, independent of their relationship to particular learning episodes, which is not disrupted by a deficit in relational memory processing.

The idea that declarative memory, critically dependent on the hippocampal system, is fundamentally relational and is selectively compromised in amnesia is supported by several converging lines of evidence, as summarized in Table 9.3. These lines of evidence include neuropsychological findings from humans and animals with amnesia, anatomical and physiological data, and results from functional neuroimaging studies.

The major line of evidence tying relational memory to hippocampal function comes from the neuropsychological findings from patients and animals with amnesia. As we have seen, the performance of patients and animals with amnesia is impaired whenever task performance depends on memory for the relations among items, whether for memory of public and personal events or recall and recognition memory of items in list context in humans, or for spatial learning in animals. This inability to appreciate the conjoining of information can cause patients with hippocampal damage to assume that new objects composed of conjunctions of elements of previously seen objects have been previously viewed (Kroll et al., 1995).

A different line of evidence for a role of the hippocampus in relational processing comes from functional brain imaging studies. Despite the over-

Table 9.3 Hippocampal System and Declarative Memory: Converging Evidence for a Role in Relational Memory Processing

Method or approach	Examples of evidence

Human neuropsychology	Deficit in memory for public and personal events
	Deficit in recall and recognition for items in (list) context
	Deficit in memory for arbitrary relationships:
	    Turns in a maze
	    Words and definitions
	    Spatial relations among objects (relational manipulation effect)

Animal neuropsychology	Deficit in spatial learning:
	    Radial arm maze
	    Water maze
	Deficit in contextual and conditional discrimination

Functional neuroimaging	Hippocampal activation when relational binding is required
Neuroanatomy	Converging inputs from all the higher order processing areas

Animal electrophysiology	"Relational cells" in the hippocampus:
	    Cells responding to spatial relations ("place cells")
	    Cells responding to second-order spatial relations
	    Cells responding to relations between places, higher order behaviors, and task relevance
	    Cells responding to temporal relations

Biophysical and molecular	Possession of a "learning" mechanism superb for detecting conjunctions of inputs in close temporal proximity

whelming neuropsychological evidence linking the hippocampal system to memory, most functional neuroimaging studies have been unsuccessful in finding reliable hippocampal activation during tasks involving explicit memory as compared with implicit memory (see Buckner et al., 1995). Recently, however, a functional magnetic resonance imaging (fMRI) study by N. J. Cohen et al. (1994) yielded hippocampal activation when participants performed a task that specifically required binding of multiple streams of information. Stimuli were color images of faces, each presented with a name and an occupation-related icon superimposed. When participants were required to bind in memory the faces, names, and icons to subsequently distinguish the studied face-name-icon triplets from other triplets not viewed, they showed increased activation of hippocampal system structures compared with activation in a condition in which they had to make only gender decisions about the faces.

Examination of the neuroanatomy and physiology of the hippocampal system suggests that it possesses the anatomical connections and the neural mechanisms required to support relational binding. It receives inputs from, and in return projects to, the neocortical brain regions that serve as the highest order processors of the various categories and modalities of information handled by the brain. Accordingly, it is in a position to receive, and bind, information about the objects and people present in the environment, the spatial relations among them, the events in which they play roles, and the temporal relations among those events. The hippocampal system also supports a mechanism for handling memory for conjunctions. It exhibits a particularly robust form of synaptic plasticity called *long-term potentiation* (LTP), in which brief patterned activation of particular pathways produces a stable increase in synaptic efficacy lasting for hours to weeks. This form of plasticity is mediated by a class of neurotransmitter receptors (*N*-methyl-D-aspartate [NMDA] receptors) that constitute superb con-

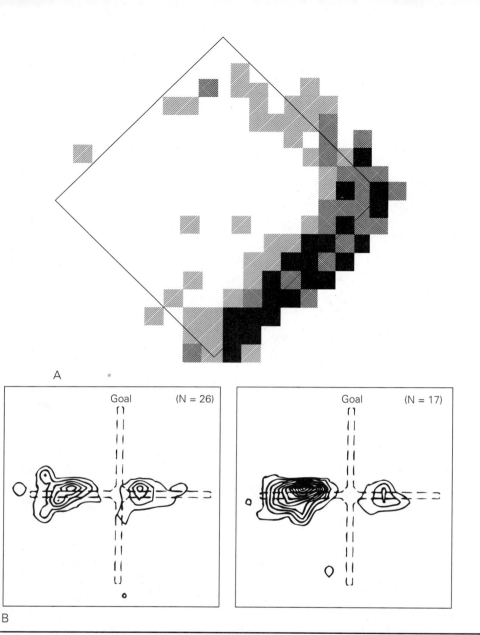

A

B

Figure 9.15 Examples of firing rates and patterns of hippocampal neurons with place fields in rats as they explore their environment.
(A) This display indicates the rate of neuronal firing as a function of the animal's location in the environment. The darker the box, the higher the firing rate. Note that the neuron fired preferentially and at the highest rate when the animal was in one specific place in the environment, namely along the lower right edge of the diamond-shaped environment. (B) Shown here is the firing pattern of a neuron whose place field (within the contour lines) caused it to fire preferentially when the rat was in two arms of the maze (dashed lines); the neuron fired more so in response to one arm than in response to the other. A similar pattern occurred both when the animal could see the surroundings (perceptual condition, left) and when those cues were taken away after the animal had been oriented within the environment (memory condition, right). (*Note.* A, Adapted from O'Keefe, 1976, p. 377; B, Adapted from O'Keefe & Speakman, 1987; C, Adapted from Muller et al., 1987.)

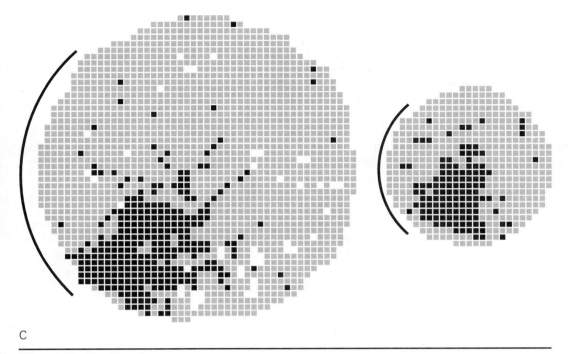

C

Figure 9.15 (Continued)
(C) These figures show the firing rate of a neuron (dark, high; light, low) when an animal was in a given location within an environment. When the animal was placed within a small circular environment (right), the cell fired preferentially to a location within that environment. When the animal explored the larger circular environment (left), the neuron's place field was "scaled up": The neuron still fired preferentially to the same quadrant of space even though that quadrant now encompassed more total area.

junction detectors, being activated specifically by converging inputs arriving in close temporal contiguity (Wigstrom & Gustafsson, 1985).

A final line of converging evidence comes from electrophysiological studies of the hippocampal system in which the activity of neurons has been shown to encode various relationships among significant cues or objects in the environment. For example, in rats who are actively exploring their environment, hippocampal neurons are found to have **place fields.** When the animal is in a particular "place" in the environment, the corresponding cell fires preferentially (Figure 9.15A). Such neuronal behavior is relational in that firing of these cells does not depend on any one of the many environmental stimuli, but rather on the relationships among them. For exam-

ple, as illustrated in Figure 9.15B, once place fields are established through the animal's exploration of its environment, they persist even when the experimenter removes a subset of the cues or even all of the specific sensory cues (O'Keefe & Speakman, 1987). Furthermore, they "scale up" in size, as shown in Figure 9.15C, when the environment that the animal is exploring is scaled up in size (Kubie & Ranck, 1984).

Moreover, the activity of hippocampal neurons is driven by a variety of higher order relationships between spatial location and the animal's behavioral activity. Neuronal activity while the animal is in the place field depends heavily on the speed with which the animal is moving and the direction in which it is heading and turning. Furthermore, the same neurons have different firing properties depending on which behaviors are task relevant at any given time. These neurons have a preference for one place in the behavioral apparatus when the animal is engaged in spatial navigation but a preference for a different place in the same apparatus when the animal is engaged in an olfactory discrimination task.

Given the evidence for different declarative and procedural systems, we now need to revisit a claim we made at the beginning of the chapter: Our memory in the real world reflects the contributions of multiple memory systems of the brain that under ordinary circumstances operate together seamlessly to support our memory. As with these other systems, declarative and procedural memory systems, too, ordinarily act in parallel, each contributing to behavioral performance to the extent that they are able. Thus, in the normal course of affairs, a given learning event leads both to storage of relational memory, through the hippocampal-dependent binding of the different elements of the event of the declarative system, and to the tuning of the processing operations engaged during the learning event, through the participation of the procedural system. As one example, the ardent student who picks up this textbook and reads the same chapters more than once should find that comprehending this text becomes progressively easier. This is because of both the increased fluency in the perceptual parsing of the words and illustrations in subsequent viewings—a purely procedural memory effect—and the accumulating knowledge of the substantive content of the text and figures that permits various sections to be related to one another and more easily understood—a declarative memory effect.

Other Multiple-System Viewpoints

Although we believe that the declarative-procedural memory theory is most capable of addressing the full range of neuropsychological, neuroanatomical, and neurophysiological evidence that has emerged in the literature on humans and animals (see Table 9.3), many memory dichotomies have been proposed concerning the nature of amnesia and the organization of normal memory, each of which emphasizes a different aspect of the distinctions between impaired and spared memory performances of patients with amnesia. A brief listing of most of these proposed dichotomies is provided in Table 9.4. Many of these have important commonalities with the ideas discussed previously, even if their range is somewhat more limited. We now turn our attention to some of the more prominent of the proposed multiple system viewpoints.

Episodic and Semantic Memory

Endel Tulving (1972) distinguished between **episodic memory,** containing autobiographical records of personally experienced events occurring in specifiable temporal and spatial contexts, and **semantic memory,** consisting of world knowledge stored in a context-free fashion. For example, your ability to remember the circumstances of buying this textbook involves episodic memory, whereas your ability to remember various facts about neuropsychology that were gleaned from this book and from class lectures and discussions involves semantic memory. This proposal about systems of normal human memory (and its continuing development over the years by Tulving [e.g., Tulving, 1994]) has been applied to the pattern of impairment and

Table 9.4 Some Proposals of Multiple Memory Systems

Declarative memory versus procedural memory

Explicit memory versus implicit memory

Episodic memory versus semantic memory

Knowing "that" versus knowing "how"

Memory with record versus memory without record

Memory with awareness versus memory without awareness

Memory versus habit

Locale (place) versus taxon

Representational memory versus dispositional memory

Working memory versus reference memory

sparing in patients with amnesia (e.g., Parkin, 1987). In this view, amnesia represents a selective impairment of episodic memory.

The commonality of this account with those discussed previously is that the difference between impaired and preserved memory performance revolves around whether memory for specific prior learning episodes is required. According to the episodic-semantic distinction, the performance of patients with amnesia during tasks involving skill learning and repetition priming is intact because these tasks do not require memory for particular episodes, whereas performance is impaired on tests that specifically probe (e.g., with recall or recognition) memory for the connection between items and a specified learning episode. This idea can be put into accord with the declarative-procedural distinction if memory for specific episodes is seen as one example of relational memory—that is, as memory for the relationship between certain items and their original context. In this view, episodic memory is seen as a subset of declarative memory.

However, the episodic-semantic distinction, as offered, does not address findings on amnesia in animals nor does it address the neuroanatomical and physiological facts about the hippocampal system. Moreover, it does not account for the full pattern of impairment and sparing in human amnesia. The phenomenology of anterograde and retrograde amnesia that we considered previously suggests impairment of both episodic and semantic memory, at least as those categories of memory are usually defined. Patients with amnesia show impairment in learning about and remembering not only the activities of daily life (that is, the episodes in which they participate), but also such prototypically semantic information as new vocabulary. They also show retrograde loss of memory for both personal (episodic) events and for world (semantic) knowledge, the latter in the form of memory for public events or the identity of famous persons (see Kopelman, 1989; Ostergaard, 1987; Zola-Morgan, Cohen, & Squire, 1983).

The impairment shown by these patients in learning such semantic information as public events and new vocabulary can also be subsumed within the declarative-procedural framework in that this knowledge, too, necessarily involves relational memory. Learning new vocabulary requires learning the relation between words and their meanings; learning about public events requires learning a set of facts about people, places, and objects, and about the actions and circumstances that describe the events in which they are involved. According to this view, semantic memory should also be seen as a subset of declarative memory (see N. J. Cohen, 1984; Schacter & Tulving, 1983; Squire, 1987).

When we turn to other neuropsychological deficits, however, we see an important place for a distinction between episodic and semantic memory—one that distinguishes between semantic knowledge overlearned early in life, which forms the foundation for object recognition, language, and the like, and the ability to learn and remember new facts and data. Amnesia, as we have seen, impairs the ability to learn and remember new facts and data while leaving intact the overlearned semantic knowledge supporting perceptual, motor, and linguistic competence. Various other neuropsychological disorders—such as the aphasias, agnosias, apraxias, and certain other selective neuropsychological deficits that we learned about elsewhere in this textbook (see chapters 8, 5, and 4, respectively) selectively impair semantic knowledge systems (see McCarthy & Warrington, 1990; Warrington, 1985) without causing amnesia. We have more to say about semantic knowledge impairments later in this chapter.

Memory for Context

A number of authors have emphasized memory for context as an important aspect of amnesia (Hirst & Volpe, 1984; Mayes, Meudell, & Pickering, 1985; Stern, 1981; Winocur, 1980), pointing to the fact that patients with amnesia have a well-documented deficit in learning and remembering contextual relationships. For example, the list-based tasks usually used in the laboratory require the subject to remember which items, all of which are familiar from many previous occurrences, appeared on a particular study list. Performance on such tasks is clearly impaired in cases of amnesia. Indeed, the failure of patients with amnesia to remember the context in which something was learned was an important part of the motivation for the episodic-semantic account of amnesia. However, by focusing on only contextual relationships, this proposal is unnecessarily limited in its scope. As we learned earlier, neurons in the hippocampus encode all sorts of relationships among multiple stimuli, and the impairment in amnesia affects learning and remembering all manner of relationships (names and faces, words and their meanings, and all types of arbitrary pairings of items). Indeed, the ability to remember the context in which something occurred—for example, the context in which you first learned of your admission to college, in which you first tasted chili peppers, or in which you discovered reggae music—requires the ability to learn (frequently arbitrary) relationships. Context, in this view, is seen as one subset of the relations that declarative memory can support.

Spatial Mapping

O'Keefe and Nadel (1978) proposed that amnesia, at least in rats, was characterized by an inability to construct, maintain, and/or make use of spatial maps. In support of this view are the many reports of profound impairment on various spatial learning tasks following hippocampal system damage in rats. It is also supported by the striking and well-documented findings of hippocampal neurons with place fields, which fire preferentially when the animal is in one or another specific location within its environment (see Figure 9.15).

However, although little doubt exists that the hippocampal system plays a critical role in much spatial learning, the focus of the proposal by O'Keefe and Nadel (1978) is unnecessarily limited in its scope. As we know, the impairment of learning and memory in animals with hippocampal amnesia extends well beyond spatial learning and is by no means the most striking aspect of memory impairment in human amnesia. Moreover, spatial relation-

ships are not the only type of relationships for which the hippocampal system plays a critical role. Rather, the hippocampal system and declarative memory are critical for memory for all types of relations, spatial and nonspatial.

WHERE LONG-TERM MEMORY IS STORED IN THE BRAIN

If the hippocampal system and related structures damaged in amnesia are not the site of permanent long-term storage, as we indicated previously, where in the brain is long-term memory stored? This question has long been at the heart of research on the neural bases of learning and memory. In this section, we attempt to offer some answers.

Historical Perspectives

Early efforts to understand where memory is stored in the brain were disappointingly unsuccessful. In his famous paper "In Search of the Engram," Karl Lashley (1950) summarized his many years of researching the effects of experimental lesions placed in different brain areas in various animals on this resigned note:

> I sometimes feel, in reviewing the evidence on the localization of the memory trace, that the necessary conclusion is that learning is just not possible. It is difficult to conceive of a mechanism which can satisfy the conditions set for it. (p. 501)

He argued against the idea of specific brain regions dedicated for memory storage and instead proposed the notions of *mass action* and *equipotentiality,* suggesting that there was equivalence of various regions of cortex for storing memories in a distributed fashion.

Later efforts, using various other methods to discover where memory is stored, had more optimistic outcomes. Contrary to Lashley's conclusion, learning is possible and we now have a reasonable understanding of how memory can be stored in the brain. One line of work of considerable historical interest is the classic set of studies by Penfield (e.g., Penfield & Perot, 1963). Using electrical stimulation of the exposed neocortex of patients with epilepsy, he attempted to map the functions of some of the subdivisions of the human brain. In the course of his work, Penfield reported a number of instances in which stimulation of particular regions in the temporal neocortex elicited what seemed to be memories, which unfolded in time as long as the stimulating current was on. The patient was aware of being on the operating table and speaking to the medical staff but reported the sense of seeing, hearing, and/or feeling some remembered event unfold with time. For example, the patient might report hearing the performance of a particular song or seeing and hearing children playing in a certain scene that seemed to be from the patient's childhood. Frequently, stimulation of the same region of the patient's temporal cortex repeatedly elicited the same memory, and the longer the stimulating current stayed on, the longer the memory played out.

This work seemed to suggest that the temporal cortex must be the repository of long-term memories, which were stored in a manner similar to audiovisual taping of events that transpire, such that electrical stimulation of the system caused the stored memories to be replayed. Some apparent support for this interpretation was provided by other electrical stimulation studies performed at about the same time by Bickford and colleagues (e.g., Bickford et al., 1958). These researchers implanted electrodes in the depths of the temporal lobe and reported a number of instances of retrograde and anterograde amnesia during delivery of current to the electrodes. While the stimulating current was on, patients were unable to remember memories from their past. The extent of this retrograde amnesia stretched further back in time the longer the electrical simulation proceeded. The patients were also unable to create new, enduring memories during electrical stimulation. After the period of stimulation ended, these individuals had an anterograde amnesia for what transpired during the session.

Current-day investigators believe that Penfield's conclusion that the temporal lobes are *the* storage site of memory was premature. Although the phenomena he reported are compelling, experts doubt whether these were true memories that were being elicited in the patients. No attempt was made to verify that the events the patients reported during stimulation had actually occurred as reported. More recent work has suggested that the reports of memories incorporate information actually present in the operating room (the faces and the conversations of the staff, or the music playing in the background) rather than events in the patient's life prior to the electrical stimulation, much as people tend to incorporate into their dreams information broadcast over their clock radios. More damaging to the claim that whole memory episodes are stored in the temporal lobes was the finding that even after the surgeon removed the temporal cortical sites that, when stimulated, caused the elicitation of "memories," those "memories" were not lost. Hence, the temporal lobes do not appear to store all the records of our experience. Indeed, Lashley was undoubtedly correct in rejecting the idea, which was prevalent in his time, of specific brain regions dedicated for memory storage. Temporal cortex does play a role in memory, but, like other cortical areas, it is involved both in the processing of certain domains of information (such as auditory information and specific visual form) and in the storage of the same domains of information.

Storage of Declarative Memory

Perhaps the best way to outline the current view of memory storage in the brain is to return to what we learned about amnesia and the hippocampal system. Because amnesia is global in the sense that the memory deficit is general across modalities (e.g., visual, auditory, olfactory) and categories of to-be-remembered materials (e.g., verbal, spatial), it is distinguishable from the agnosias, aphasias, and other disorders in which a loss of specific categories of knowledge is often tied to particular modalities. Such generality has been crucial in identifying that the role of the medial temporal lobe and midline diencephalic structures damaged in amnesia is specifically tied to *mnemonic* functions rather than to specific perceptual, linguistic, or other cognitive functions.

However, the retention of information from the remote past and information overlearned early in life by patients with amnesia indicates that the hippocampal system is not the site where memories are stored. Rather, this system receives converging input from each of the higher order processing areas of the cortex. The various elements of a given scene or event are processed by different cortical processors, differentially specialized for visual, auditory, linguistic, or spatial information. The connections between the hippocampal system and these various neocortical systems are all reciprocal, permitting the hippocampal system to communicate back with the same neocortical regions involved in processing the original event or scene. The distinct attributes or elements of the event can thus be stored in the different neocortical areas: Memory for visual aspects or elements of the experience is stored in visual-processing areas, memory for linguistic elements is stored in language areas, and so forth. Memory for the whole event would thereby be stored in a distributed fashion.

The evidence for this scheme is perhaps clearest for inferotemporal cortex (see Figure 5.1). Anatomical, neurophysiological, neuropsychological, and neuroimaging data all suggest that this region of the brain constitutes the site of long-term storage of memory for visual objects. Area TE is at the end of a line of increasingly sophisticated visual processors in the ventral ("what") visual pathway (see page 166, chapter 5, for discussion of the "what" visual pathways). It receives information from earlier visual processors that provide the information necessary to compute three-dimensional (3-D) form, then, in turn, projects to the hippocampal system

(see Mishkin, 1982). Its neurons are responsive to whole objects, positioned anywhere within large receptive fields, often invariant across changes in size, illumination, and viewing angle. As discussed in chapter 5, patients with damage to inferotemporal regions or to its input show a visual agnosia, a selective deficit in visual object recognition. The same area is activated in positron emission tomography (PET) or fMRI studies of neurologically intact control subjects during any task requiring visual object identification (e.g., Grady et al., 1992; Haxby et al., 1994; Sergent, 1994).

Recent neurophysiological studies of visual learning in monkeys also provide evidence that inferotemporal regions store visual information acquired during specific learning experiences. Consider the elegant experiment conducted by Sakai and Miyashita (1991) involving paired-associate learning of arbitrarily related visual shapes. After monkeys were trained to a criterion on arbitrary pairings of the visual shapes, they were tested with various correct and incorrect pairings. The first member of a given pair would be presented. Then, after a delay, the correct choice and an incorrect choice would be presented (Figure 9.16A). After training, neurons in inferotemporal cortex that were responsive to one or another of the visual shapes were found to have coded the newly learned associations (Figure 9.16B). Such neurons fired when presented with the first member of a given learned pair and then continued firing in anticipation of and during the presentation of the matching item of that pair. However, they ceased firing when presented with an item that was not the appropriate match for the first item. Such neural activity in the brain region provides a mechanism of memory for the co-occurrences of visual objects. On logical grounds it makes sense for memory about visual objects to be stored

Figure 9.16 Evidence that inferotemporal cortex is involved in the memory for visual objects.
(A) In the experiment of Sakai and Miyashita (1991), the monkey had to learn to associate specific pairs of these 24 visual shapes. (B) Neurons in temporal cortex that were responsive to a specific visual shape developed sensitivity to the visual shape that was arbitrarily paired with it during training. In this case, the cell was differentially sensitive to Item 12 and during the course of learning also became sensitive to Item 12'. (*Note.* Reprinted with permission from *Nature,* "Neural Organization for the Long-Term Memory of Paired Associates," by K. Sakai and Y. Miyashita, 1991, 354, pp. 152–155. Copyright 1991 Macmillan Magazines Limited.)

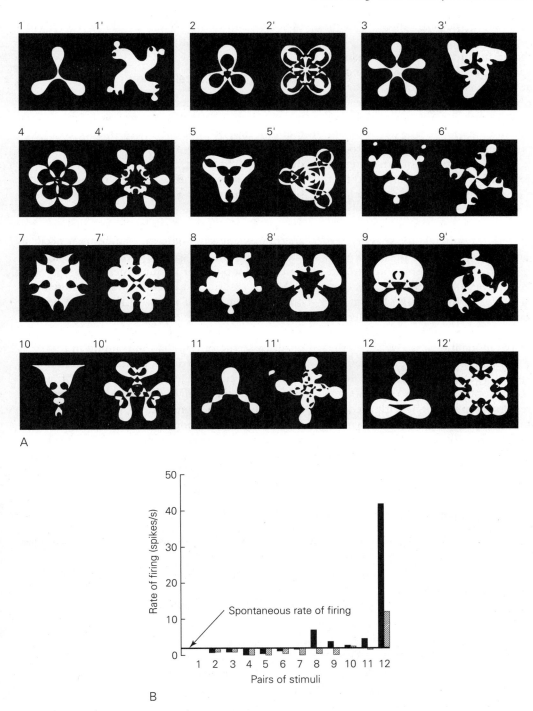

A

B

in the same system that provides the ability to identify and attach meaning to visual objects.

With this scheme in mind, we can understand some of the research done earlier in the 20th century. Consistent with Lashley's views, memory is stored in a distributed fashion. However, instead of resulting from equipotentiality and mass action, the distributed nature of memory storage derives from the localized storage within separate cortical processors of different, specific elements or attributes of events. The temporal lobes do play an important role in memory storage, although not the role that Penfield envisioned. Processes necessary for the identification of objects and for the identification of faces are supported by temporal lobe systems (see chapter 5), as are certain language processes (see chapter 8), which together support our stored knowledge of visual objects and their names (see A. R. Damasio, 1989). The functional role in memory performed by the temporal lobe is paralleled by the role of the highest order cortical processors in the other sensory modalities, as well as the multimodal and supramodal cortical areas that are involved in language, spatial processing, planning and organizing behavioral acts, and so forth. They have the same reciprocal interactions with the hippocampal system as temporal regions do, by virtue of which they serve as the storage site of long-term declarative memory about the elements or attributes of scenes and events that fall within each system's processing domain.

Storage of Procedural Memory

Unlike declarative memory, which requires hippocampal system participation, storage of procedural memory supporting skilled performance of a given task (e.g., typing, mirror-image reading) seems to depend only on cortical systems that are engaged in performance of the task. This form of memory seems to reflect tuning and modification of the cortical processing systems themselves. Table 9.5 summarizes several lines of evidence documenting the anatomical and physiological changes that occur in the brain, within the specific cortical processing systems, that support procedural memory.

Several studies have documented rearrangements of representations of the world in either primary somatosensory cortex or primary auditory cortex in response to behavioral learning. For example, as a result of tactile discrimination training in monkeys involving learning to detect punctate stimulation of small skin loci, neurons representing the "trained" areas of the skin's surface developed larger receptive fields (Merzenich, Rencanzone, Jenkins, & Grajski, 1990). Similarly, changes in the receptive field patterns of neurons in auditory cortex were seen in rats trained in tone discrimination (D. M. Diamond &

Table 9.5 Evidence for Changes in Cortical Processors Supporting Procedural Memory

Method or approach	Examples of evidence
Animal physiology	Rearrangements in primary somatosensory cortex following somatosensory discrimination training
	Rearrangements in primary auditory cortex following auditory discrimination training
Functional neuroimaging	Decrease in occipital cortex activation for primed visual stimuli
	Changes in distribution of activation in motor cortex and in cerebellum following learning of simple motor sequences
	Decrease in frontal cortex activation for primed semantic encodings
Human neuropsychology	Right occipital lobe damage producing selective deficit of visual-perceptual priming

Weinberger, 1986). Importantly, these changes in sensory representation occurred gradually along with increments in discriminative capacity, which suggests that they are part of the neural basis for the skilled performance supported by procedural memory.

The advent of functional imaging technologies, specifically PET and fMRI, enabled researchers to search for possible learning-induced changes within cortical processing areas in humans. In such studies, activity within specific processing areas is assessed during relevant processing tasks, with the goal of detecting changes in the extent or pattern of activity as procedural learning occurs. A series of PET studies (Buckner et al., 1995; Squire et al., 1992) have shown that repetitions of words in conditions that produce word priming result in changes (decreases in activation) in the occipital lobe visual-processing areas engaged by the reading task. Perceptual learning resulted in changes in fMRI activation seen in the visual cortical areas that were engaged in the original perceptual processing (Ungerleider, 1994). The learning of specific finger-movement sequences resulted in changes in the distribution of activation in motor cortex (Karni et al., 1995) and the cerebellum (Kim, Ugurbil, & Strick, 1994) from that seen during the initial performance of the sequences. Finally, regions in left prefrontal cortex that were activated during semantic encoding of words showed a decrease in activation for repeated (already-processed) words compared with that for new words (Demb et al., 1995). In each of these cases, priming effects or skill learning, which we consider procedural memory phenomena, were associated with modifications of the specific processors dedicated for the performance of that skill.

If the changes within cortical processors that were just discussed are actually responsible for some aspects of procedural memory, damage to these cortical systems would be expected to prevent similar procedural memory phenomena. In fact, neuropsychological confirmation of the link between procedural memory and specific cortical processing systems was recently obtained. In two single case studies, perceptual priming performance was evalu-

ated in patients with damage to right occipital lobe areas—the same areas that were shown to be activated in association with perceptual priming in the functional imaging studies noted previously. Patient L.H. (Keane, Clarke, & Corkin, 1992) and patient M.S. (J. D. E. Gabrieli et al., 1995) both show a selective deficit of visual word priming even though these patients do not have deficits of explicit remembering of words or, for that matter, of other items. These data further bolster the claim that procedural memory phenomena are supported by modifications of specific cortical processors.

OTHER MEMORY IMPAIRMENTS AND OTHER TYPES OF MEMORY

Most work on the neuropsychology of memory is devoted to the study of amnesia because the way in which memory breaks down in amnesia tells us much about the nature and organization of normal memory. However, other neuropsychological disorders reveal information about other aspects or other types of memory. Some of these disorders are discussed in other chapters of this textbook, in the context of deficits in specific domains of semantic knowledge, such as language (chapter 8) and visual object recognition (chapter 5). In the remaining pages of this chapter, we discuss the neurological bases for other aspects of memory deficits, such as working memory and strategic memory.

Working Memory

As discussed previously, amnesia impairs long-term memory but leaves working memory intact. The fact that working memory is intact permits patients with amnesia to comprehend scenes, events, and language normally and to engage in reasonable discourse, which provides us with some sense of what working memory is about. A more complete picture comes from the study of neuropsychological cases in which patients have selective working memory deficits, and from anatomical, physiological, and functional imaging studies of the dorsolateral prefrontal cortical areas critically involved in working memory functions. A full treatment of this topic is beyond the scope of this chapter, but a brief outline is offered.

A number of patients have now been studied who exhibit a selective impairment in working memory, demonstrating a deficit in temporarily maintaining in some active state, or in otherwise affording a special status to, whatever material they are currently working on (e.g., Shallice & Warrington, 1979; Vallar & Baddeley, 1984a,b). Two important observations about these impairments are that such patients are not impaired in their long-term memory abilities and that the deficit in working memory is narrowly defined, tied to specific processors. We discuss these two observations in turn.

In these cases, the dissociation between impaired working memory and intact long-term memory is the opposite of that seen in amnesia; this phenomenon constitutes a double dissociation of these memory systems. The fact that a deficit in working memory does not also cause a deficit in long-term memory is in some ways surprising and helps to clarify the nature of the relationship between these memory systems. Earlier theoretical work on memory had suggested that working memory and long-term memory handled information in a strictly serial manner. Information was first held in working memory and then, if it were to be remembered for any significant length of time, transitioned to a long-term memory store. Consolidation of memory was seen as the process of mediating the transition of memories from a labile short-term store to a more stable long-term store (see McGaugh & Herz, 1972)—the same process that Milner (B. Milner, 1962b; Scoville & Milner, 1957) saw as the likely locus of impairment in H.M. in her early discussions of medial temporal lobe amnesia.

However, current findings indicate that working memory can be so compromised as to prevent immediate verbatim recall of as few as two items (e.g., two digits), at the same time not interfering with long-term memory, including, for example, the ability to learn word lists or to succeed in paired-associate learning. Such a finding argues strongly against the early serial-processing notion of information be-ing transferred from working memory to long-term memory. Instead, working memory and long-term memory must be seen as systems working in parallel, one operating to maintain information in an active state to support on-line processing, and the other operating to create enduring records of experience for later use.

The other important observation about deficits of working memory is that they are tied closely to individual information-processing systems. Thus, the best known example of a working memory deficit involves impairment of **auditory-verbal working memory,** or what is currently known as the *phonological store.* This deficit consists of difficulty in repeating aloud and verbatim the contents of the immediately preceding verbal utterance, such as in the digit span test. However, patients with working memory deficits can retain and recover the informational content of the verbal input string and can even learn word lists. More to the current point, their working memory for other processing domains, such as spatial processing or arithmetic, is perfectly intact. Caramazza, Miceli, Silveri, and Laudanna (1985) have reported further specificity among working memory deficits, distinguishing between impairment in a system that holds auditory-verbal information received by the listener while language parsing occurs—the **input phonological buffer**—and impairment in a system that holds the phonological code being constructed by a speaker while he or she is preparing his or her own utterance—the **output phonological buffer.** Other patients have been reported with deficits of **visual-verbal working memory,** involving difficulty in the ability to hold visual-verbal information during reading while language processing occurs, and still others with deficits in what Baddeley (1986) refers to as the **visuospatial scratch pad,** which involves deficits in the ability to hold nonverbal visual information while performing perceptual analyses of the stimulus array. Thus, each of these deficits is tied to a very specific processing domain, leaving working memory for other processing domains intact, which suggests the existence of multiple working memory capacities, each intimately tied to the operation of specific information-processing modules of the brain.

Goldman-Rakic's work with the monkey (e.g., Goldman-Rakic, 1988; see also chapter 10) suggests that although these multiple working memory capacities are all distinct, they may all depend on the same brain region, the dorsolateral prefrontal cortex. The role of frontal cortex in memory has been known since 1935, when Fulton first used the spatial delayed-response task with dogs. In each trial of this task, the experimenter puts food in one of several food wells in view of the animal and covers them. After a delay interval, the animal is given the opportunity to choose one of the food wells. Only if the animal can remember which well was baited prior to the delay will it be able to consistently pick a well with food. Following frontal lobe damage, animals are unable to perform this task with delay intervals as short as 1 s. Subsequent work by various investigators also showed that the deficit in performing such tasks is caused by damage to the dorsolateral prefrontal cortex (see Goldman-Rakic, 1988).

The dorsolateral prefrontal area appears to have neurons that are particularly well suited to hold information on-line for brief periods. For example, in the spatial delayed-response task, they respond to particular spatial locations and fire preferentially during a delay interval, maintaining their firing throughout the delay (Funahashi, Bruce, & Goldman-Rakic, 1989, 1991; Fuster, 1989; Niki & Watanabe, 1976). Furthermore, when monkeys make errors on the spatial delayed-response task, these neurons fail to maintain their firing. Both findings suggest that the firing of prefrontal cortical neurons maintains the information during the delay interval (Funahashi, Bruce, & Goldman-Rakic, 1989, 1991).

The prefrontal cortex appears to have various subdivisions, all of which are involved in working memory, but each of which is dedicated to a certain type of working memory. Neurons in these various prefrontal subdivisions all fire preferentially during the delay interval, but some respond only to particular objects that must be remembered across the delay, whereas others respond to particular locations. Damage to the various prefrontal subdivisions causes deficits in different types of delayed-response performance, either for spatial locations, objects, or motor movements. Each area receives input from a distinct cortical processor in accordance with the type of information it holds on-line. For example, in the case of the spatial delayed-response task, a particular subdivision of the prefrontal cortex holds spatial information on-line that it received as input from the inferior parietal gyrus, which is the cortical processor capable of providing the spatial information that must be maintained across the delay. Other cortical processors, such as inferotemporal cortex (area TE) and motor systems, each send projections to just one distinct subdivision of prefrontal cortex. Moreover, PET and fMRI studies show activation of prefrontal cortex as well as specific cortical processors when humans perform working memory tasks (Jonides et al., 1993). For example, the PET study by Jonides et al. (1993) (which was discussed in chapter 6 with regard to spatial memory, see page 223) revealed activation in prefrontal cortex for both a spatial working memory task and for an object-recognition working memory task. However, activation was observed only in the temporal lobe for the object-recognition task and only in the parietal lobe for the spatial task.

These various lines of evidence suggest that the dorsolateral prefrontal cortex serves a general working memory function and that each of its various subdivisions maintain in an active state the information currently being processed within different dedicated cortical processors. This memory function supports the on-line processing ability of the brain's various processors, permitting them to comprehend and produce complicated utterances, motor acts, scenes, events, and so forth. As we learn in chapter 10, working memory also plays an important role in executive function.

Frontal Lobes and Strategic Memory

Working memory deficits are not the only memory deficits associated with damage to prefrontal cortex.

Damage to prefrontal cortex, due to traumatic lesions or to the effects of aging (which seem to target frontal lobe function disproportionately), produces impairment of **strategic (prospective) memory,** which is the ability to organize, search, and query declarative memory (Daigneault, Braun, & Whitaker, 1992; A. Shimamura, 1990). Although patients with such damage have no difficulty recognizing items that they recently studied, they are impaired in going beyond that to reconstruct the learning circumstances and/or to infer further information about the items.

These strategic memory deficits manifest in a number of ways. After frontal lobe lesions, poor performance is seen for tasks requiring **memory for temporal order** (e.g., judging which of two study items occurred more recently in a list: B. Milner, Corsi, & Leonard, 1991; A. P. Shimamura, Janowsky, & Squire, 1990), **source memory** (recollecting the source of a particular piece of information: Janowsky, Shimamura, & Squire, 1989), and **self-ordered pointing** (pointing to one item at a time from an array of items; the task is to select a different item in each trial while the locations of the items within the array are being manipulated: Petrides & Milner, 1982). Yet, in all these tasks, recognition memory for the items themselves is intact. Another way in which this deficit manifests is by impaired recall of items requiring recollection based only on context cues—(for example, "Report all the words that were on the previous study list") despite intact recognition (Jetter, Poser, Freeman, & Markowitsch, 1986).

Each of these deficits is also exhibited by neurologically intact older persons (Craik & McDowd, 1987; McIntyre & Craik, 1987; Naveh-Benjamin, 1990; A. Shimamura & Jurica, 1994). According to both behavioral and neuroradiologic assessments, the results of aging apparently have a disproportionate effect on the frontal lobes.

Each deficit in strategic memory is also a part of the behavioral impairment seen in patients with Korsakoff's disease, who have frontal lobe dysfunction superimposed upon their amnesia (Janowsky, Shimamura, & Squire, 1989; A. P. Shimamura, Jernigan, & Squire, 1988). Such deficits are not an obligatory part of the memory impairment in amnesia but instead occur only whenever frontal lobe dysfunction is part of the picture.

All these findings clearly illustrate the dissociation between the strategic aspects of memory processing and nonstrategic memory for items. The association between strategic aspects of memory and the frontal lobes makes sense, given the role of the frontal lobes in executive functioning, which involves planning, organizing, and monitoring behavior, an issue discussed in more detail in chapter 10.

Semantic Knowledge Systems

As we know, amnesia impairs the ability to learn and remember new facts and data, without impairing the semantic knowledge overlearned early in life that supports perceptual, motor, and linguistic competence. In contrast, various other neuropsychological disorders, such as agnosias, aphasias, and apraxias, impair particular **semantic knowledge systems** selectively, interfering with object recognition, aspects of language, or aspects of voluntary motor acts. Each semantic knowledge deficit seems to reflect damage to the cortical substrate for the relevant domain of semantic knowledge. In patients with stable but chronic impairment, the deficit manifests both in the apparent loss or inaccessibility of previously acquired semantic knowledge and in the ability to reacquire it. Thus, a patient with a profound deficit in face recognition is no longer able to recognize familiar people by their faces (see chapter 5) and is unable to relearn to do so. Semantic knowledge about faces, objects, or language is undoubtedly stored in the specific higher order cortical processors dedicated to face processing, to object processing, or to language processing (see chapter 8), respectively.

The fact that these deficits occur for narrow domains of semantic knowledge leads us to believe that various semantic knowledge systems operate separately from one another, and in parallel, to process information within their distinct domains. However, in the course of processing and storing information, they must interact with other brain systems. To process and maintain on-line the information critical for the task at hand, they must interact with dorsolateral prefrontal cortex. To store new semantic knowledge within their own domains and to store information about the relationships among the objects that have occurred in various scenes and events, they must interact with the hippocampal system.

SUMMARY

Selective impairments of various aspects of memory provide convincing evidence that memory is not a unitary process. Rather, memory should be thought of as a collection of memory systems that operate cooperatively to produce memory performance. The most extensively studied memory impairment is amnesia, which includes both an anterograde component, impairing the learning of new information after the onset of amnesia, and a retrograde component, impairing memory for information that was acquired prior to the onset of amnesia. Amnesia results from a number of causes, all of which damage various structures in medial temporal lobe (hippocampal system) or midline diencephalic structures of the brain. Although the amnesias observed after each of these various causes differ in some respects, such as severity and natural history of the impairment, they all impair processing for a particular domain of memory.

Anterograde amnesia selectively affects the ability to retain information in long-term memory, leaving intact working memory—the ability to hold information on-line temporarily while it is being processed. This deficit is global in the sense that it affects memory across all modalities of stimulus presentation, across numerous categories of materials, and across a variety of testing methods. However, amnesia is nonetheless a selective deficit, profoundly affecting memory for new facts and events but sparing the acquisition and expression of skilled performance. Such skilled performance can be expressed only in an inflexible manner, more specifically under

the same set of constrained circumstances under which it was originally acquired.

Although all amnesias include some amount of retrograde amnesia, the temporal extent of the retrograde impairment varies widely. Some retrograde amnesias are temporally limited, affecting only recent memories out to a few months or years and leaving more remote memories intact. Other amnesias affect a longer period, compromising memory for decades. Even such extensive retrograde amnesias often have a temporal gradient, leaving remote memories relatively more spared. Retrograde amnesia tends to spare information overlearned early in life, and, like anterograde amnesia, supports skilled performance. In part because of the variability in the extent of retrograde amnesia (as well as some differences among anterograde amnesias), some researchers have suggested that multiple forms of amnesia exist. Other researchers argue that evidence to support such a claim is insufficient and consider these forms to be variants of the same basic disorder.

Some debate has been generated as to where in the time line of memory processing amnesia exerts its effect. Amnesia does not seem to reflect a disorder in the encoding or laying down of memories because all amnesias include a retrograde deficit and yet these memories were laid down normally. Likewise, amnesia is probably not a disruption in the consolidation of memories because extensive retrograde amnesias imply that the consolidation process continues for decades, and the variable extent of retrograde amnesia among different individuals implies a large variability in consolidation rates among individuals. A failure to retrieve memories or the loss of memories in amnesia is supported by findings that retrograde amnesias can extend back many decades and that the performance of patients with amnesia can improve significantly when they are given cues for retrieval. However, retrieval cues might be useful regardless of whether the information was encoded poorly, consolidated poorly, stored poorly, maintained poorly, or retrieved poorly. Thus, which of these processes accounts for the memory loss in amnesia remains undetermined.

The phenomenology of amnesia provides us with

three basic lessons about the organization of memory. First, it indicates that long-term memory and working memory are distinct because anterograde amnesia selectively compromises certain aspects of long-term retention but leaves working memory intact. Second, it indicates that memory is dynamic and undergoes change with time because temporally limited and temporally graded retrograde amnesia clearly indicate a difference between recent memory and remote memory in terms of their susceptibility to amnesia. Third, we know that the hippocampal system and related structures cannot constitute the storage site of all long-term memories because memory for the remote past remains intact in all patients with temporally limited retrograde amnesia and because even patients with extensive retrograde amnesia retain information (over)learned early in life.

The fact that some memory capabilities are lost in amnesia while others are retained has led many researchers to conclude that multiple memory systems exist in the brain. How to best characterize the nature of information spared versus information impaired in amnesia, however, has been a matter of some debate. Some researchers have suggested that patients with amnesia lack the ability to recall material explicitly, or consciously, even though they can do so implicitly, or indirectly. Although accounting for a large amount of the data, this theory does not hold in some notable exceptions, and it does not provide a good explanation for animal models of amnesia. Other suggested deficits in patients with amnesia include difficulty in remembering episodic information, in remembering memory for context, and in remembering spatial maps. However, each of these explanations is limited in domain and/or can account for only a subset of the observed phenomena in amnesia. A more inclusive theory distinguishes between declarative and procedural memory systems. Declarative memory mediates the binding of multiple items, supporting memory for relations among the objects and the actions that constitute events. As a result of this relational memory processing, declarative memory enables the explicit remembering of facts and events and the ability to express this information flexibly in novel contexts. Procedural memory supports the acquisition and expression of skilled performance through online tuning and modification of cortical processing systems. This type of memory is inflexibly tied to the cortical processors engaged during the original learning experience and can be expressed only when the same processors are engaged. It is assessed in indirect, or implicit, tests of memory that do not require the subject to consciously recollect a prior learning experience. This memory system operates independently of the hippocampal system and thus remains preserved despite amnesia.

The question of where memory is stored in the brain has intrigued researchers since the beginning of the 20th century. The retention of information from the remote past and information overlearned early in life by patients with amnesia indicates that the hippocampal system and the midline diencephalic brain structures (damaged in amnesia) cannot be the repositories of all long-term memory. Instead, evidence suggests that memory is stored in the neocortex. Declarative memory is stored in various neocortical areas with the participation of the hippocampal system. The various elements or attributes of a given scene or event are stored by the relevant cortical processors (visual, auditory, language, spatial, planning, and so forth) by virtue of each of these cortical systems' reciprocal connections with the hippocampal system. Memory for the whole scene or whole event is thus stored in a distributed fashion, with the different attributes separated into separate cortical areas. Procedural memory, by contrast, is stored within individual cortical processing systems, as tunings and modifications of the processing operations themselves.

Other neuropsychological disorders reveal much about other aspects or other types of memory. Some patients exhibit a selective impairment in working memory, demonstrating a deficit in temporarily maintaining the information that they are currently processing in an active state, while having intact long-term memory. These deficits occur for a narrow domain of processing (e.g., limited to auditory-verbal working memory), which suggests that multiple working memory subsystems exist. All these working memory systems appear to rely on frontal regions. The frontal lobes are also important for the use of strategic, or prospective, memory, which is the ability to organize, search, and query declarative memory. Other neuropsychological disorders selectively impair particular semantic knowledge systems without causing amnesia. Such patients exhibit aphasias, agnosias, apraxias, and so forth. Each semantic knowledge deficit seems to reflect damage to the cortical substrate for the relevant domain of semantic knowledge; the deficit manifests both in the inaccessibility of previously acquired semantic knowledge and in the inability to reacquire it.

*E*xecutive
*F*unction

Dr. P. was a successful middle-aged surgeon who used the financial rewards of his practice to pursue his passion for traveling and playing sports. Tragically, while he was undergoing minor facial surgery, complications caused his brain to be deprived of oxygen for a short period. The ensuing brain damage had profound negative consequences on his mental functioning, compromising his ability to plan, to adapt to change, and to act independently.

After the surgery, standard IQ tests revealed Dr. P.'s intelligence to be, for the most part, in the superior range. Yet, he could not handle many simple day-to-day activities and was unable to appreciate the nature of his deficits. His dysfunction was so severe that not only was returning to work as a surgeon impossible for him, but in addition his brother had to be appointed his legal guardian. As a surgeon, Dr. P. had skillfully juggled many competing demands and had flexibly adjusted to changing situations and demands. Now, however, he was unable to carry out all but the most basic routines and then only in a rigid, routinized manner. Furthermore, he had lost his ability to initiate actions and to plan for the future. For example, his sister-in-law had to tell him to change his clothes, and the only way the family could get him to do so on his own was after years of rule setting. He managed to work as a delivery truck driver for his brother's business, but only because his brother could structure the deliveries so that they involved minimal planning. Dr. P. could not be provided with an itinerary for the deliveries of the day because he was incapable of advance planning. Rather, his brother would give him information about one delivery at a time. After each delivery, Dr. P. would call in for directions to the next stop.

Dr. P. also was totally unaware of his situation. He seemed unconcerned and uninterested in how he was provided with the basic necessities of life, such as clothes, food, and lodging, and was totally complacent about being a ward of his brother and sister-in-law. Formerly an outgoing man, he now spoke in a monotone and expressed little emotion. He did not initiate any activities or ask questions about his existence, being content to spend his free time watching television.[1]

The case of Dr. P. illustrates the deficits in **executive functions**—which include the ability to plan actions toward a goal, to use information flexibly, to realize the ramifications of behavior, and to make reasonable inferences based on limited information—that can occur after brain damage. As illustrated by the case, difficulties in executive function can arise despite normal functioning in other domains of intellectual processing, such as those generally measured by IQ tests (e.g., retention of knowledge, vocabulary, spatial-processing abilities, and so forth).

As we learn in this chapter, *executive function* is a term that covers many abilities and, as such, is a concept for which providing a precise definition is difficult. To better understand the types of abilities that we discuss throughout this chapter, let's consider, by analogy, the skills and attributes that are required of an executive of a company. First, an executive must have a master plan or a general conception of how the company should work. For example, the executive's goal may be to increase customer satisfaction, diversify markets, or raise production. He or she must be able to translate that general goal into specific actions, whether by increasing quality control, expanding the sales force, or automating factories. Second, the executive must be able to assimilate new information and use it to

[1]Adapted from *Neuropsychological Assessment* (2nd ed., pp. 39–40), by M. D. Lezak, 1983, New York: Oxford University Press.

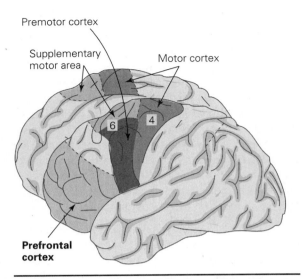

Figure 10.1 The divisions of the frontal lobes, including motor, premotor, supplementary motor, and prefrontal cortices.
Damage to prefrontal cortex is most likely to interfere with executive function. (*Note.* Adapted from Kandel et al., 1991, p. 495.)

modify plans as the need arises; that is, the executive must be flexible and responsive to change. For example, fluctuations in the stock market or political changes in foreign governments may necessitate a modification of plans or a new course of action. Such planning and flexibility are not usually demanded to as large a degree of assembly line workers, who in many cases are told what task to perform, how to do it, and when to do it. Third, an executive must keep track of multiple tasks simultaneously and understand the relationships among them, knowing which should come first and which should come second. As a result, the executive must often prioritize both decisions and actions. For example, if limited cash flow does not allow for an increase in the sales force *and* the automation of factories, priorities must be set. In a related vein, the executive must be able to assess the effect of each decision and to estimate its relative worth. Finally, an executive must be a person who projects the company image and serves as its spokesperson. As such, this job

requirement calls for a certain amount of social skill and political savvy and the ability to get along with other people.

These abilities—to create a plan and follow through with it, to adapt flexibly, to sequence and prioritize, to make cognitive estimations, and to interact in a socially astute manner—are multifaceted and share many characteristics. For example, the ability to prioritize often requires creating a plan and being flexible. When prioritizing, you must have an overall plan so that you can determine which actions will best help you reach your goal. Furthermore, you must be flexible because you need to consider a variety of paths toward your goal (rather than invoking a rigid rule). Because of the multifaceted nature of these executive functions, more than one function usually contributes to performance of many of the complex tasks we discuss in this chapter. Consequently, linking one particular type of function to a specific brain region, as we did in previous chapters (e.g., linking reading to the angular gyrus of the left hemisphere), is difficult for executive functions.

Even though the concept of executive function is used to describe a family of related abilities, it has been useful to neuropsychologists because it provides a way to conceptualize a constellation of deficits that are commonly observed in patients with frontal lobe damage. Although disruptions in executive function do not *prove* that the damaged region of brain tissue is anterior (because disruptions in executive function can occur after posterior damage as well; e.g., Anderson, Damasio, Jones, & Tranel, 1991; Grafman, Jones, & Salazar, 1990), deficits in executive function are much more common after anterior damage. They can also occur after closed head injury in which diffuse axonal damage is sustained (Stuss, 1987), especially when the injury has certain causes such as vehicular accidents, which are associated with a significant probability of localized frontal damage. As discussed in subsequent sections of this chapter, patients with frontal lobe damage, specifically damage to prefrontal areas, perform poorly on many of the executive functions that we discuss (Figure 10.1).

BREAKDOWN OF EXECUTIVE FUNCTION AND GOAL-DIRECTED BEHAVIOR

We now turn our attention to discussing how each set of abilities referred to as an executive function is compromised by brain damage. Although we save our discussion of the ability to interact in a socially astute manner for the next chapter, which discusses the neural basis of emotional processing, you should remember as you read that such abilities are not independent of other executive functions. For example, Dr. P.'s flat affect, apathy, and lack of concern about his condition surely interfere with his ability to plan, initiate, and sustain activity.

Deficits in Initiation, Cessation, and Control of Action

One difficulty often observed in individuals with executive dysfunction is what Luria (1966) and Lezak (1983) have referred to as **psychological inertia.** Inertia is the tendency of a body at rest to stay at rest or of a body in motion to stay in motion unless acted on by an outside force; it is resistance or a disinclination to motion, action, or change. Thus, these individuals are poor at starting an action or a behavior, but once engaged in it, they have great difficulty shifting or stopping it.

Such difficulties in overcoming psychological inertia can profoundly affect actions in everyday life. As illustrated by the vignette at the beginning of the chapter, psychological inertia can permeate much of a person's existence. Dr. P. took no initiative in terms of his personal hygiene or his day-to-day activities, did not inquire about either the state of events in his life or those in the world, and tended not to speak unless spoken to. In fact, patients with left frontal lobe damage often exhibit a marked reduction in spontaneous speech (B. Milner, 1971). Yet the difficulties go beyond that. A waitress explaining why she had lost her job after frontal lobe surgery said, "You have to have a 'push' to wait on several tables at once, and I just didn't have it any more" (Malmo, 1948, p. 542, cited in Duncan, 1986).

Once engaged in a course of action, individuals with executive dysfunction have difficulty deviating from that path. This tendency is easily observed in everyday behavior. Once engaged in an activity, the patient has trouble stopping, whether she or he is watching television or beating an egg. These individuals appear to get caught in a behavioral loop and have little internal control over behavior. This tendency to engage in repetitive behavior is often referred to as **perseveration.**

Difficulties in overcoming psychological inertia can be detected on various neuropsychological tests that are commonly used to assess executive function. One such class of tests are those designed to evaluate fluency, either verbal (Thurstone & Thurstone, 1943) or nonverbal (Jones-Gotman & Milner, 1977). These tests do not assess how coherently the individual can output information, as might be assessed in a patient with aphasia, but rather how easily, fluidly, and imaginatively a person can draw upon knowledge.

In these tests of fluency, an individual must, within a limited amount of time (e.g., 4 min), generate as many items as possible that meet certain constraints. For example, in the case of verbal fluency an individual might be asked to think of words beginning with the letter *s* or in the case of nonverbal fluency to create figures that can be constructed from four straight lines. When told to begin, neurologically intact individuals begin the task immediately and continue to produce items during the entire time period. In contrast, individuals with executive dysfunction typically appear to mull over the possibilities, seeming to deliberate as they slowly begin to start the task. Whereas a neurologically intact person might steadily reel off, "snail, snake, soil, shark, stem, stuck, stencil, storage, sullen," a person with executive dysfunction might get out only "snail" in an equivalent amount of time. Furthermore, few words are subsequently produced, and many are likely to be identical to or similar to those already mentioned. For example, after taking much time to generate just a few items such as "snake.....................stand.................stall," a person with frontal lobe damage might then continue with ".............snake.....................snow ....snaked." Relative to neurologically intact individuals and individuals with damage to other brain regions such as the temporal lobe, patients with left frontal lobe damage exhibit poor verbal fluency (B. Milner, 1964) and patients with right frontal lobe damage exhibit poor nonverbal fluency (Jones-Gotman & Milner, 1977).

Another test in which individuals exhibit difficulties in overcoming psychological inertia, and specifically exhibit perseveration, is the **Wisconsin Card Sorting Test (WCST).** In this test, four cards are lying on the table in front of the individual. Each card is distinct from all the others on the basis of three attributes: the number of items on the card (1, 2, 3, or 4), the shape of the items on the card (circle, triangle, cross, or star), and the color of the items on the card (red, green, yellow, or blue). For example, one card might have 3 green crosses; another 2 yellow stars; and still another 1 blue circle. The individual is given a stack of cards and is told to sort these cards into four piles below the four cards on the table. However, the individual is not explicitly told which criterion to use to sort the cards. Instead, as the individual places each card onto one of the four piles, the experimenter indicates only whether the response is correct or incorrect. So, for example, if color is the attribute by which the individual should be sorting, the examiner lets the individual know that the response is incorrect if the person places a card with 3 blue triangles on the pile below the card with 1 red triangle (Figure 10.2A). In contrast, if the same card is placed on the pile below the card with 4 blue circles, the examiner designates the response as correct (Figure 10.2B).

After the individual correctly sorts 10 cards on the basis of one particular attribute, such as color, the experimenter, without explicitly telling the individual, changes the criterion that must be used to sort the cards (e.g., to shape). Neurologically intact individuals quickly realize that the behavior that previously led to a correct response no longer does so and adjust their behavior accordingly. In contrast, individuals with executive dysfunction perseverate, continuing to sort the cards by color despite the negative feedback.

Because individuals who have difficulty overcoming psychological inertia do not seem to be able to regulate or control their actions, their behavior is often triggered by some object in the environment, a syndrome that has been referred to as an **environmental dependency syndrome** (e.g., R. Lhermitte, 1983; F. Lhermitte, Pillon, & Serdaru, 1986). Individuals with this syndrome take actions as if impelled or obligated to do so by their physical and social environment. For example, when told not to touch certain objects, such as a computer keyboard in a neuropsychologist's office, they type on it anyway. Other examples of this type of behavior are presented in Figure 10.3. As you can imagine, this sort of behavior makes the person appear as if he or she is acting impulsively. Such vulnerability is not limited to physical objects in the world but can extend into the social realm as well. For example, in one case a doctor suggested to a patient that if he was thirsty, he should go ahead and take a drink. After hearing this, the patient poured a glass of water and drank most of it, but left a little at the bottom because, he said, he was not thirsty. Interspersed throughout their ensuing conversation, the doctor mentioned to the patient that he should drink if thirsty. Each time upon hearing this suggestion, the patient poured himself a full glass of water and drank it. By the end of the conversation, the patient had consumed about a liter of water, even though when asked, he stated that he was not thirsty. Because of difficulties such as these, some researchers have wondered, philosophically, whether individuals with this type of executive dysfunction have lost their "free will."

The expression of this environmental dependency syndrome can often be influenced by an individual's personal history prior to injury. Illustrative examples are provided by the case of two patients with executive dysfunction, each of whom reacted differently to attending a buffet dinner (F. Lhermitte, 1986). One patient, a man from an upper-class background, behaved like a guest expecting to be served. In contrast, the other patient, a woman who had been a modest housekeeper for most of her life, immediately began serving the other guests.

Also noteworthy about the impulsivity and lack of control of action is that it can occur even when

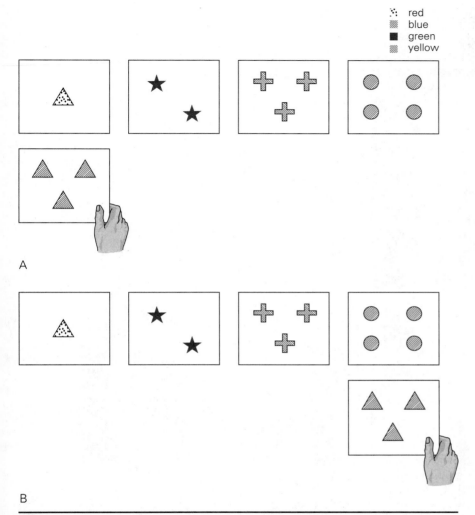

Figure 10.2 Two examples of sorting behavior on the Wisconsin Card Sorting Test (WCST).
In this particular series of trials, the subject must sort on the basis of color. (A) An example of an incorrect sort because the individual matched the card on the basis of shape instead of color. (B) An example of a correct sort because the individual matched the card on the basis of color rather than shape or number.

the person appears to "know" how to act, which suggests that the deficit may in part be characterized as a disconnection between thought and action. A classic example of this behavior is observed in patients performing the WCST. Many anecdotal reports exist of individuals who persist in sorting on the basis of a previously correct but now incorrect category even as they state that they *know* their action is wrong (e.g., B. Milner, 1964). Even when told explicitly which attribute to use to sort the

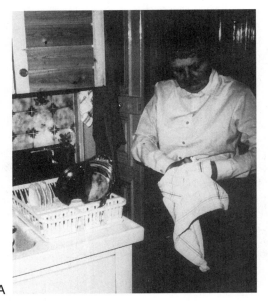

A

B

Figure 10.3 Two examples of the environmental dependency syndrome exhibited by patients with frontal lobe damage when they visited their physician's home.
(A) The woman, upon seeing dishes in the kitchen, began to wash them. (B) The man, upon seeing two pictures lying on the floor, picked up a hammer and nails and hung the pictures on the wall. (*Note.* From ''Human Autonomy and the Frontal Lobes: Part II. Patient Behavior in Complex and Social Situations. The 'Environmental Dependency Syndrome''' by F. Lhermitte, 1986, *Annals of Neurology*, 19(4), pp. 339, 340. Copyright © 1986 by the American Neurological Association. Used with permission of Lippincott-Raven Publishers, Philadelphia, PA.)

cards, in a modified version of the WCST, individuals with executive dysfunction may remain unable to translate these directions into action (Delis, Squire, Bihrle, & Massman, 1992). Another example of this disconnection between thought and action can be observed when such individuals are given a problem in which partial information toward a solution is given one step at a time. Although individuals with frontal lobe damage can provide a reasonable estimate of how many clues they will need to solve a sample problem successfully, they nonetheless attempt to solve the problem with fewer clues than they estimated they need (L. A. Miller, 1992).

Many of the findings we just discussed suggest that executive dysfunction disrupts the ability to control action or to translate intention into action. The deficit may lie in the ability to start, stop, or modulate an action, as can often be observed in tests of fluency or card sorting. In other cases, the problem may lie in using information to direct behavior, even when the individual appears to have knowledge of how behavior should be directed.

Impairments in Abstract and Conceptual Thinking

Individuals with executive dysfunction often have difficulty processing material in an abstract rather than a concrete manner. The WCST can reveal not only perseverative tendencies (as we just discussed), but also deficits in abstract and conceptual thinking. As we now know, in the WCST the individual must use feedback on each response to determine the criterion for sorting the cards (e.g., color). Making such a determination requires the use of logic and deduction as well as attention to the conceptual categories into which items fall, such as color. Individuals with problems in abstraction have difficulty even deducing the rule by which the cards should be sorted. In contrast, persons with only perseverative tendencies can deduce the rule but then are unable to switch their sorting criterion.

These difficulties in conceptualization (as compared with perseverative tendencies) have been examined by using a modification of the standard WCST (Delis, Squire, Bihrle, & Massman, 1992).

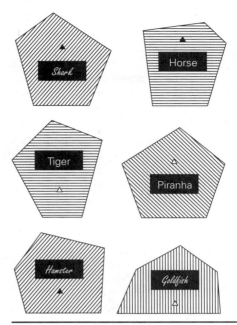

Figure 10.4 Examples of stimuli similar to those used to demonstrate abstraction difficulties in patients with frontal lobe damage.

These cards can be sorted into two equal groups on eight dimensions: (1) whether the animal lives on land or in the water, (2) whether the animal is domestic or dangerous, (3) whether the animal is large or small, (4) whether the triangle is above or below the word, (5) whether the triangle is black or white, (6) whether the lines are oblique or nonoblique, (7) whether the animal's name is five letters or longer, and (8) whether the animal's name is written in block letters or cursive letters. Patients with frontal lobe damage have difficulty sorting the cards into meaningful piles and sometimes cannot even do so when given concrete cues ("The animals are either man-eating or domestic"). (*Note.* Adapted from Delis et al., 1992, p. 688.)

In this test, an individual is given a set of six cards that must be sorted into two equal piles. Each card contains an animal's name and a triangle placed against a background of lines. The cards are constructed so that eight possible dimensions can be used to divide them into piles. For example, cards can be divided on the basis of whether the animal lives on land or in the water, whether the triangle is black or white, or whether the animal's name is above or below the triangle (Figure 10.4).

Individuals with frontal lobe damage exhibit deficits on this task in a variety of ways, all of which suggest that they have difficulty in abstract conceptualization. First, they have trouble determining how to sort the cards into meaningful groups. These difficulties don't always diminish when these persons are given abstract cues, such as "It has to do with how these animals behave around people," or even more concrete ones such as "These animals are man-eating or domestic" (the problem seen under these conditions may be due to either difficulty in abstraction or difficulty in translating thought to action, as we discussed previously). Second, the patients are often deficient at describing the rule by which they sort. For example, they are unable to state something to the effect of "The animals on the cards I am putting in this pile live in water, whereas the animals on the cards in this pile live on land." Even when the examiner sorts the cards into piles, the individuals cannot identify the rule used to sort the items. Furthermore, the difficulties in generating or recognizing categories cannot be accounted for by perseverative tendencies. All these findings point to the conclusion that individuals with frontal lobe damage may have difficulty with conceptualizing information in an abstract manner and using that information to guide behavior. These difficulties in abstraction may contribute, in part, to difficulties in strategy formation, which we discuss in more detail later.

Deficits in Cognitive Estimation

A third type of deficit often observed in individuals with executive dysfunction is an inability to use known information to make reasonable judgments or deductions about the world, a process often referred to as **cognitive estimation.** Remember that the knowledge base of individuals with executive dysfunction usually remains relatively unaffected; that is, individuals can retain knowledge about information such as the year of Canada's independence or the name of Henry VIII's second wife. Yet patients with executive dysfunction cannot make inferences based on this knowledge. For example,

patients with frontal lobe damage have difficulty estimating the length of the spine of an average woman. Such information is not usually stored in someone's memory or easily obtained from reference material, such as an encyclopedia. Instead, making a realistic estimate requires inference based on other knowledge. Estimating the length of a woman's spine requires using knowledge that the height of the average woman is about 5 ft 6 in. (168 cm) and considering that the spine runs about one third to one half the length of the body, which provides an estimate of 22 to 33 in. (56–84 cm). Patients with frontal lobe damage have difficulty making such estimates, often stating absurd or outrageous values (Shallice & Evans, 1978).

Poor cognitive estimation can be observed in other domains as well, such as estimating the price of items. For example, in one study, subjects were shown miniature replicas of real-life items, such as cars and washing machines, and were asked to estimate the cost of each. Once again, individuals with frontal lobe damage performed poorly, providing bizarre estimates on 25% of all responses (e.g., 10 cents for a washing machine) (Smith & Milner, 1984). Not only are their estimates of cognitive information incorrect, but so are their estimates of their own capabilities, such as their ability to direct activity in a goal-oriented manner or to control their emotions. For example, Prigatano, Altman, and O'Brien (1990) report that when patients with anterior lesions associated with diffuse axonal injury to other brain areas are asked how capable they are of performing tasks such as scheduling their daily activities, fending off depression, or preventing their emotions from affecting daily activities, they grossly overestimate their abilities in comparison with the ratings provided by relatives.

Estimation of information in the temporal domain is also affected, in particular estimating how frequently an event or item has occurred. In a paradigm used by Smith and Milner (1988), individuals are shown a series of nonsense items, some of which appear only once, whereas others appear 3, 5, 7, or 9 times nonconsecutively. After this initial series of items, individuals are given a series of test items.

For each test item, the person must decide whether it appeared in the initial sequence, then estimate how often it occurred. Although individuals with frontal lobe damage have no difficulty determining whether an item was in the inspection series (an ability that is compromised by temporal lobe damage, as discussed in chapters 5 and 9), they have difficulty estimating how frequently an item occurred, especially if it occurred often.

The difficulty in determining relative frequency of occurrence may not reflect difficulties in just cognitive estimation. It may also reflect a more general difficulty in memory tasks that place a premium on remembering temporal information, such as *how often* and *when* something occurred as opposed to remembering *whether* it occurred. As we learn later in the chapter, individuals with executive dysfunction and frontal lobe damage are impaired on a variety of sequencing tasks. Thus, both difficulty in cognitive estimation and difficulty in temporal sequencing may contribute to a reduced ability to estimate frequency of occurrence. Such impairments could interfere with planning and prioritizing behavior. If a person cannot estimate whether the likelihood of something is high or low, choosing a suitable plan of action becomes difficult.

Despite the impairments we just discussed, in some domains estimation abilities are preserved in patients with frontal lobe damage. For example, although such patients are poor at estimating how well they can prevent their emotions from affecting their daily activities, their estimates for more concrete tasks, such as preparing meals, dressing themselves, and personal hygiene, concur well with their relatives' estimates. Likewise, as we discussed earlier, these patients are as competent as patients with temporal lobe damage or neurologically intact individuals at judging how many clues they will need to solve a puzzle. However, when asked to solve the puzzle, patients with frontal lobe damage guess the answer before being given the requisite number of clues that they said they needed (L. A. Miller, 1992). Thus, the ability to estimate, evaluate, or make reasonable guesses is not entirely lost but is definitely compromised in a number of arenas.

Lack of Cognitive Flexibility and Deficits in the Response to Novelty

Individuals with executive dysfunction have an inability to be cognitively flexible—that is, to look at situations from a multiplicity of vantage points and to produce a variety of behaviors. The ability to be flexible is extremely important when a person is dealing with novel or new situations. Novelty, of course, is a relative concept, but we define it as an event, a situation, or an action that has a low probability of occurring given a particular context. Flexibility is also required when a new reaction must be made to an old stimulus. Some theorists suggest that the prefrontal areas play an especially important role in novel situations because damage to these brain areas results in difficulties in dealing with such situations (Fuster, 1985). Cognitive inflexibility can be considered distinct from, but related to, the perseverative tendencies and environmental dependencies we discussed previously. Having responses triggered by objects in the environment or being influenced by prior actions clearly adds to the challenge when a person is called upon to respond or act in an atypical manner.

A relatively simple model of novelty that is examined by using event-related potentials (ERPs) implicates the frontal regions in processing novel information. As we discussed in chapters 2 and 7, the P_{300} (a positive deflection in the amplitude of the brain's electrical response that generally occurs 300 ms after presentation of a stimulus) accompanies the on-line monitoring of attentional processing, a change in the information flow to the brain. For example, the P_{300} can be reliably evoked every time a person hears a low-probability item, such as a "boop," when it is embedded within a series of high-probability items, such as "beeps." This classic paradigm is known as the *oddball paradigm* because the low-probability item, the oddball, evokes a P_{300} response (sometimes called the P_{3b}), which is recorded most prominently over parietal regions of the brain. However, if a totally novel item, such as a dog bark, is inserted into the string of items, a prominent P_{300} is observed over frontal regions. This frontal P_{300} (often called the P_{3a} to differentiate it from the P_{3b}) suggests a role for the frontal lobes in processing novel information (R. T. Knight, 1991). Additional evidence is provided by findings that the amplitude of the P_{3a} is correlated with the volume of gray matter in the frontal lobes in neurologically intact men. In contrast, the amplitude of the P_{3b} is correlated with the volume of gray matter in parietal regions (Ford et al., 1994).

The ability to respond to novelty and be cognitively flexible can contribute to performance on some other tasks of executive function that we already discussed. For example, fluency tests can be considered, in part, to measure the response to novelty because individuals must apply knowledge in a fluid, novel, and flexible manner. However, as we discussed, these tasks also require a person to successfully initiate behavior. Therefore, we might be interested to learn the relative contribution of each function—cognitive flexibility and initiation of behavior—to fluency tasks. One way to do so is to compare two versions of the task that place different emphases on each of these components. When asked to name all the animals that they can think of in a limited amount of time, individuals with frontal lobe damage do not show extensive deficits (Newcombe, 1969). More severe deficits, however, are observed on fluency tasks in which individuals must generate all the words beginning with a certain letter (B. Milner, 1964). Both tasks obviously involve the initiation and cessation of behavior. However, the animal-naming task is not as novel as the word-naming task because we are often required to search our memory for items that are categorically related. In contrast, we rarely ever have to search our memory for words beginning with the same letter (unless you spend hours watching educational television programs for children, such as Sesame Street!). The larger deficit observed on the word-naming fluency task suggests that fluency tasks do not assess only the ability to initiate behavior; they also assess the ability to act in a novel manner.

Our discussion of how the brain allows us to respond in a novel and flexible manner now becomes more complicated because researchers have attempted to clarify the nature of flexibility by distinguishing among various types. From one perspective, flexibility allows an individual to make a variety of responses to the same stimulus. In some cases, an individual may need to learn to reverse a response made previously; this is known as **reversal learning.** For example, after learning to press the right-hand key when a blue light appears and the left-hand key when a yellow light appears, the individual must now press the right-hand key when the *yellow* light appears and the left-hand key when the *blue* light appears. Although patients with frontal lobe damage can exhibit normal reversal learning when the stimulus-response pairs are relatively arbitrary (e.g., blue light, right-hand key), difficulties are encountered when the task requires a typical stimulus-response association to be overridden. For example, individuals with frontal lobe damage exhibit difficulties when they must move a joystick to the left in response to a rightward-moving target and to the right in response to a leftward-moving target (Gauggel, 1996).

Another perspective on flexibility distinguishes between reactive flexibility and spontaneous flexibility (Eslinger & Grattan, 1993). Under this conception, **reactive flexibility** occurs when an individual reacts to information contained in the environment but in a different way than was done previously. One situation in which reactive flexibility must occur is during the WCST. In this situation, the cards contain information that guides the sorting behavior, and the person must switch from allowing one attribute of the items on the cards (e.g., color) to govern the response to allowing another criterion (e.g., shape) to dictate the response. In **spontaneous flexibility,** a diversity of ideas must be generated when environmental input provides relatively little structure to guide the response. An example of a task requiring spontaneous flexibility is the Alternative Uses Test, in which an individual must generate as many *atypical* uses for a common object as possible (e.g., using a newspaper to start a fire, swat a fly, wrap packages). Researchers have suggested that these two types of flexibility may rely on different neural substrates. Whereas individuals with frontal lobe damage perform poorly on both reactive and spontaneous flexibility tasks, as measured by the WCST and the Alternative Uses Test, respectively, patients with damage to the basal ganglia (which, as you may remember from chapter 4, is a structure with extensive connections to the frontal lobe) exhibit only impaired reactive flexibility. These findings suggest that reactive flexibility can be disrupted by damage to more than one brain region but that the frontal lobes play a special role in spontaneous flexibility.

Other researchers distinguish between different types of flexibility according to the amount of information available to guide novel responses and the degree to which old associations must be broken (R. W. Butler, Rorsman, Hill, & Tuma, 1993). For example, verbal fluency is considered not quite so taxing because the manner in which an individual must search through memory in verbal fluency is specified (i.e., by a designated letter) and old associations for the words need not be broken. Design fluency is more taxing because it requires the individual to use four straight lines to create a novel figure; however, the existence of various four-line figures (e.g., square and diamond) means that no one dominant association needs to be broken. However, in other tasks, such as the Alternative Uses Test, the individual must devise novel uses of an object (e.g., using a shoe as a bookend) and must inhibit a dominant old standard use (i.e., using a shoe as footwear). This latter type of fluency, in which old associations must be broken and novel ones formed (sometimes referred to as *ideational fluency*), appears to rely on a different neural substrate than that of the other types of fluency (i.e., verbal and design fluency). Deficits on verbal and design fluency tasks are observed only after substantial frontal lobe damage, which suggests that many subdivisions of the frontal region can support these functions and that deficits emerge only after a critical mass of tissue is lost. In contrast, even a small degree of frontal lobe damage disrupts ideational fluency tasks, which suggests that these tasks require the active integration of information across various subdivisions of the frontal lobe, so that the loss of any subdivision disrupts performance.

As we learned in this section, executive dysfunction is characterized by a lack of flexibility in perfor-

mance. This inflexibility can manifest as a person's inability to vary his or her response or as an inflexibility in the manner in which information is conceptualized or retrieved. Regardless of whether the problem occurs in terms of conceptualization or responding, executive dysfunction is usually characterized by an especially keen difficulty in being able to override well-learned associations. We revisit this issue later in the chapter when we discuss a theory of frontal lobe function that suggests the frontal lobes control behavior in nonroutine situations (Stuss & Benson, 1986).

Deficits in Goal-Directed Behaviors

The final executive ability that we discuss is the ability to organize behavior toward a goal. Such an ability is multifaceted, and as we learn shortly, the loss of any facet of goal-oriented behavior can cause the entire plan to be derailed.

Consider the multiple aspects of the simple task of making yourself a peanut butter and jelly sandwich. First, the ultimate goal must be kept in mind throughout the procedure, even though subgoals must be met along the way. For example, although locating the bread may be the first step in making the sandwich, after attaining that subgoal you must remember the ultimate goal and switch to finding the peanut butter or the jelly. Second, attaining the goal requires flexibility and adaptability. For example, if you remember that the jelly is on the top shelf of the refrigerator but do not find it there, you must devise an alternative strategy, such as searching the other shelves or looking among the racks in the door. Third, to reach the ultimate goal, the completed portions of the task must be distinguished from those yet to be attained. For example, after locating the jelly, you must remember not to turn your attention to finding some pieces of bread (because you already completed that part of the task). Fourth, you must evaluate the actions that will best help you to reach the goal. For example, you must realize that although a fork is in front of you, it is not the utensil best suited for making your sandwich. Instead, you must decide that the best course of action is to search through the silverware drawer for a knife. Finally, actions must be sequenced toward the goal. For example, once you find the ingredients—the bread, the peanut butter, and the jelly—as well as the necessary utensil, the knife, you must then proceed to make the sandwich.

In describing the construction of a peanut butter and jelly sandwich, we listed a number of skills: the ability to sequence or plan information, the ability to modify strategies, the ability to use knowledge in your plans, and the monitoring of your actions. We now examine each of these components of goal-oriented behavior and determine how it is affected by brain dysfunction.

Ability to Sequence

One of the basic processes involved in reaching a goal is determining what steps to take to attain the goal. Yet just knowing the steps is not enough because the ability to order or sequence the steps is also critical. Little in life can be accomplished in just one step, and even the most basic functions, such as feeding yourself, require multiple steps. In this section, we review evidence that such sequencing and planning abilities are important aspects of executive function and that they rely mainly on frontal regions. As we discussed in chapter 4, anterior regions of the brain are important for sequencing movements. These areas support not only motoric sequencing, but the sequencing of mental thoughts as well.

A basic ability required for sequencing behavior is to know what comes before and what comes after. Compared with individuals who have brain damage in other cortical regions, individuals with frontal lobe damage have difficulty in this arena, as exemplified by a poor ability in determining which of two items occurred more recently (B. Milner, 1982). One task that reveals these deficits requires an individual to look at an inspection series of items, such as line drawings. After the inspection series is a test phase involving multiple trials; in each trial, two items are shown on a choice card. In some trials, *recognition trials,* only one item on the choice card was viewed in the inspection series, and the participant must identify that item. In other trials, *recency*

trials, both items on the choice card were present in the inspection series, and the participant must decide which of the two appeared more recently. In this manner, the task can be used to assess both recognition memory ("Which one have you seen before?") and memory for item order ("Which one was seen more recently?") (Figure 10.5).

These two types of memory are dissociable and rely on different neural substrates. The ability to remember the sequence in which information was presented is disrupted by damage to frontal regions. In contrast, the ability to remember whether an item was presented in the inspection series is disrupted by damage to temporal regions (this dissociation was discussed briefly in chapter 9). Although individuals with frontal lobe damage have no difficulty distinguishing between an item that was previously presented and one that was not (an indication that their recognition memory is intact), they do have difficulty remembering the order in which material was viewed.

The degree to which patients with frontal lobe damage manifest such a deficit is not homogeneous but varies according to which hemisphere has sustained frontal lobe damage and the nature of the material whose order must be remembered. Patients with lesions to the frontal lobe of the left hemisphere exhibit moderate deficits with words but relatively little impairment with abstract designs or line drawings of common objects. In contrast, individuals with right frontal lobe lesions have difficulty with words and even greater problems with abstract designs and line drawings. These results suggest that frontal regions of the right hemisphere play a larger role in recency judgments than that of left frontal regions of the left hemisphere, which seem to be involved only when the material is verbal.

In the study just described, the individuals passively watched a sequence of events whose order was controlled by the experimenter. We might want to consider the possibility that these patients' performance might be better if *they* could control the order of events. However, this is not the case because other studies suggest that the ability to control the order of events also relies on frontal regions, although these areas are somewhat different than

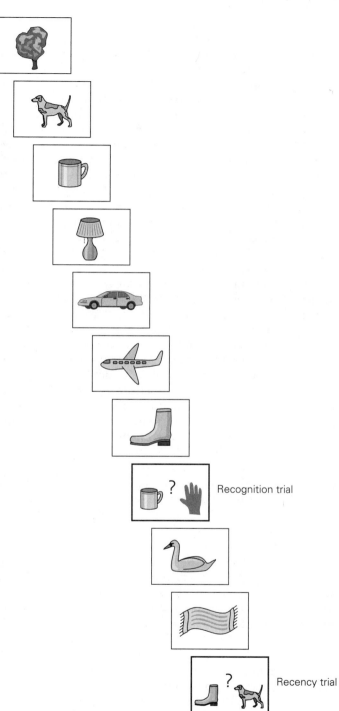

Figure 10.5   An example of the format of the recency judgment task.
First, the participant views an inspection series of line drawings. Then, in each trial, the individual must point either to the item that was previously viewed (recognition trial) or to the item viewed more recently (recency trial). Individuals with frontal lobe damage exhibit no difficulties on recognition trials but poor performance on recency trials.

those important for comprehending recency of occurrence. Because the procedure used to assess the ability of a person to sequence her or his behavior is complicated, we discuss it now in some detail.

In this procedure, individuals are shown an array of either 6, 8, 10, or 12 items. The items within each array are from the same category, either abstract designs, line drawings of objects, high-imagery words, or low-imagery words. Assume for the moment that we are using a 6-item array. On each trial, the participant is given six sheets of paper presented sequentially. Although each sheet contains all 6 items (arranged in a 2-by-3 matrix), the position of each item in the array varies from sheet to sheet. On each sheet, the participant must point to an item that was not previously chosen. Because a given item appears in a different location on each page, the individual must keep track of which items were previously selected (Figure 10.6). To prevent the person from using strategies that would make the task too easy, examiners do not allow participants to point to the same position on each page (e.g., point to the bottom left-hand item on each page) or in the case of words or items with names, to point to them in alphabetical order (Petrides & Milner, 1982).

Further implicating the frontal lobes in sequencing abilities is the fact that damage to frontal but not temporal regions disrupts performance on this task. However, the regions of the frontal lobe that are important for self-ordered sequencing are different than those needed for recency judgments. Frontal lobe lesions of the left hemisphere significantly impair performance on both the verbal and nonverbal tasks, whereas frontal lobe damage to the right hemisphere impairs performance on only the longest lists of nonverbal items. Thus, for the self-ordered pointing task, deficits are most profound after left frontal lobe damage, whereas for recency judgments, where order is determined by outside forces, deficits are most noticeable after right frontal lobe damage. Damage to left frontal regions may cause the most profound disruptions on both the verbal and nonverbal versions of the self-ordered pointing tasks because these tasks involve the sequencing of motor behavior, an ability for which the left hemisphere plays a predominant role.

The frontal lobes may contribute to the self-ordered pointing task and the recency judgment task not only because these tasks involve sequencing, but also because they require working memory. As we learned in chapter 9, working memory is used to keep information on-line to control behavior and as a sort of mental scratch pad during everyday actions. Working memory is important in the self-ordered pointing task because the person must keep track of which items have been pointed to and which remain to be selected. Likewise, the recency judgment task requires an individual to keep information on-line in working memory because the person must maintain the information about the order in which events occurred. As was mentioned in chapter 9 and is discussed later in this chapter in more detail, research on monkeys, involving a variety of behavioral and physiological techniques, has implicated frontal regions, specifically the dorsolateral prefrontal region, as extremely important for working memory (e.g., Goldman-Rakic, 1987). Providing some support for the idea that working memory plays a role in recency judgments, damage to lateral regions of the frontal lobe (approximately analogous to dorsolateral prefrontal regions in the monkey) disrupts recency judgments more than damage to other regions of the frontal cortex does (B. Milner, Corsi, & Leonard, 1991).

Thus far, we discussed sequencing abilities from two perspectives: being able to appreciate the sequence in which events occur and being able to generate sequential behavior. Another important aspect of sequencing behavior is the ability to choose which sequence or strategy best allows a goal to be attained. We now examine how this ability is compromised in individuals with executive dysfunction. To preview, compared with individuals with damage to other brain regions, patients with frontal lobe damage are less likely to report that they use strategies, and when a strategy is used, it tends to be ill defined or invoked inconsistently.

One task designed specifically to examine the ability to use strategies to sequence action is the Tower of London task designed by Shallice (1982) (which is distinct from the Tower of Hanoi puzzle discussed in chapter 9). This task is shown in Figure 10.7. The apparatus for the task consists of three

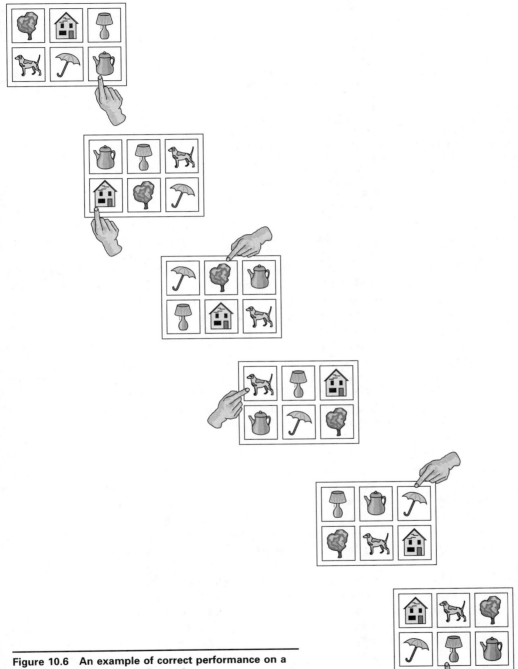

Figure 10.6   An example of correct performance on a six-item self-ordered pointing task.
The person must point to a different item on each page, and the position of each picture varies from page to page.

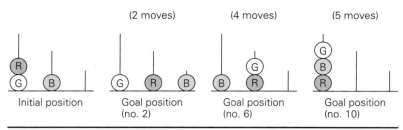

Figure 10.7   An example of three problems in the Tower of London task.
The same initial position is used in each problem. The balls must be moved to the goal position one at a time in as few moves as possible. The number of moves required to reach each goal is noted. R, red; G, green; B, blue. (*Note.* From "Specific Impairments of Planning," by T. Shallice, 1982, *Philosophical Transactions of the Royal Society of London, B298,* fig. 2, p. 204. Reprinted with permission from The Royal Society.)

prongs of varying height and three colored balls with holes that allow them to be placed on the prongs. The first prong can hold three balls, the second can hold two, and the last can hold only one. The individual is shown the balls in an initial position and must move the balls one at a time to reach a target configuration. The object is to get from the starting position to the goal configuration in as few moves as possible, keeping in mind the constraints imposed by the height of each prong and the restriction that only one ball can be moved at a time. Individuals with frontal lobe damage, most notably in the left hemisphere, are both inefficient and ineffective at performing this task (Shallice, 1982). They are inefficient because they take many moves to reach the end position and are ineffective because they engage in behaviors that don't lead toward the goal. Overall, their actions cause their behavior to appear aimless rather than directed.

Corroborative evidence for the role of frontal regions in the Tower of London task comes from experiments measuring regional blood flow, by means of single photon emission computed tomography (SPECT), in neurologically intact individuals performing a computerized touch-screen version of the task (R. G. Morris, Ahmed, Syed, & Toone, 1993). To explicitly examine the planning-sequencing aspect of the task, the researchers asked individuals to perform two versions of the task that were identical in their sensorimotor requirements but differed in the degree to which they required planning.

In the first, or control, version, the person was passively guided by the computer to solve the puzzle. The computer placed an *X* on the disk that should be moved, and the subject touched the disk. Next, the computer moved the disk to the correct position, at which point the individual had to touch that location. An *X* then appeared over the next disk that should be moved and so forth until the puzzle was solved. In the experimental condition, the individual saw the same displays and made the movements, except he or she had to plan the sequence of the moves (rather than being guided by the computer).

The results indicated that activation in the left prefrontal region and the left superior frontal region was greater when the participants had to actively plan the moves than when they were passively guided. Further indicating that these regions play a major role in sequencing and planning, the *degree* of activation of these regions in the experimental condition relative to the control condition predicted how well an individual performed the task. The individuals who solved the puzzle in fewer moves exhibited greater activation of left prefrontal areas than the subjects who took longer. Thus, this study provides converging evidence for the role of frontal regions in planning sequential behavior.

In this section, we review the many ways in which the conceptualization, understanding, and production of sequential behavior are disrupted by frontal lobe damage. Even though some aspects of sequencing depend more on frontal regions of the left hemisphere, whereas others depend more on frontal regions of the right hemisphere, for the most part, these skills appear to depend on overlapping neural structures in the frontal lobes.

Ability to Shift Set and Modify Strategies

So far we presumed that attaining a goal simply requires determining the series of steps to follow and then performing them. However, as we all know, reaching a goal may not always be a simple linear progression. Often we embark on what appears to be a clear path, only to encounter some unexpected twists and turns. Such a situation arose in the example of preparing a peanut butter and jelly sandwich, when the plan called for retrieving the jelly from the top shelf of the refrigerator, but, alas, the jelly was not there. At this point, continuing on the path toward the goal required the person to deviate from an expected or previously invoked plan, known as a shift in set, and to modify his or her strategy.

Individuals with executive dysfunction exhibit difficulties in switching set in many ways. We already mentioned some of these. For example, deficits emerge during sorting tasks when a switch must be made to a different conceptual set (e.g., switching a sorting strategy from one based on whether an animal lives on land or in water to one based on whether an animal is domestic or dangerous—Delis, Squire, Bihrle, & Massman, 1992) or to a different perceptual feature (e.g., switching from sorting on the basis of color to sorting on the basis of shape).

The degree of difficulty that individuals with frontal lobe damage have in making a shift depends, in part, on the nature of the shift. For example, look at the task illustrated in Figure 10.8. In this task, which was originally designed for use with animals, individuals are first taught to discriminate between two items (e.g., two black shapes) and to respond to only one of them (Figure 10.8A). Then, another dimension is added to the items (e.g., a simple white line pattern), which the individual must ignore (Figure 10.8B). At this point, new stimuli consisting of novel shapes and novel white line patterns are introduced. In one condition, the intradimensional shift condition, the participants

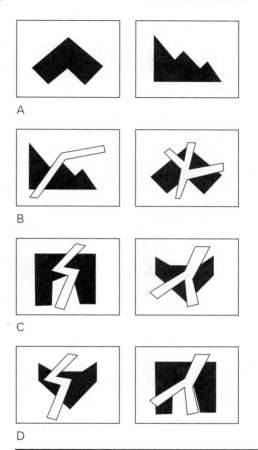

Figure 10.8 Examples of different types of conceptual shifts.
(A) In simple discrimination, an individual must simply learn to discriminate between two black shapes.
(B) Compound discrimination requires ignoring the white shapes and responding just on the basis of the black shapes. (C) In the intradimensional shift condition, the person must learn to discriminate between the two new black shapes while continuing to ignore the white shapes. (D) In the extradimensional shift condition, the person must discriminate between the two white shapes, which is a feature that was previously ignored. Individuals with frontal lobe damage have difficulty with this extradimensional shift. (*Note.* Adapted from Owen et al., 1991.)

must make their discrimination, as they did previously, solely on the basis of the same dimension used previously (e.g., on the basis of the black shapes while ignoring the white line pattern) (Figure 10.8C). In the other, the extradimensional shift condition, the participants must respond to the dimension that was previously ignored (e.g., the white line patterns) (Figure 10.8D).

Compared with patients who have temporal lobe lesions and with neurologically intact individuals, patients with frontal lobe damage are deficient at the extradimensional shift but not at the intradimensional shift (Owen et al., 1991). This difficulty may, in part, explain why individuals with executive dysfunction have difficulty on the WCST. They are unable to make the extradimensional shifts between color, form, and number. These difficulties in extradimensional shifting suggest that individuals with frontal lobe damage cannot generalize rules across boundaries that are dissimilar from the situation in which they were originally learned. Thus, if a new strategy is similar enough to the old one, performance is unimpaired; otherwise, patients with executive dysfunction are deficient in their ability to shift responses and strategies.

These difficulties in switching set may also occur because patients with executive dysfunction cannot generate alternative plans of action, or because they become "locked" onto one way of dealing with information, which precludes them from finding alternative responses. This problem is reminiscent of the perseveration problems discussed earlier. One task that has been used to demonstrate such a phenomenon is illustrated in Figure 10.9. Two items (stimuli) are shown on every trial, and the participant must choose one of the two. Each item can be characterized on four dimensions (whether the item is black or white, large or small, an *X* or a *T*, and to the left or to the right). In a pretest sequence of trials, the person attempts to discover the solution to the problem (e.g., always pointing to the black item) on the basis of the examiner's feedback as to whether each choice is correct or incorrect. This pretest ensures that the person has the conceptual skills to perform the task, because the actual test does not begin until the individual demonstrates the capacity to perform the task and can explicitly state the rule for choosing a stimulus. Then the test trials begin, which are used to examine the generation of strategies and the switching of hypotheses (Cicerone, Lazar, & Shapiro, 1983). Patients with frontal lobe damage have difficulty forming a strategy for performing the task because they

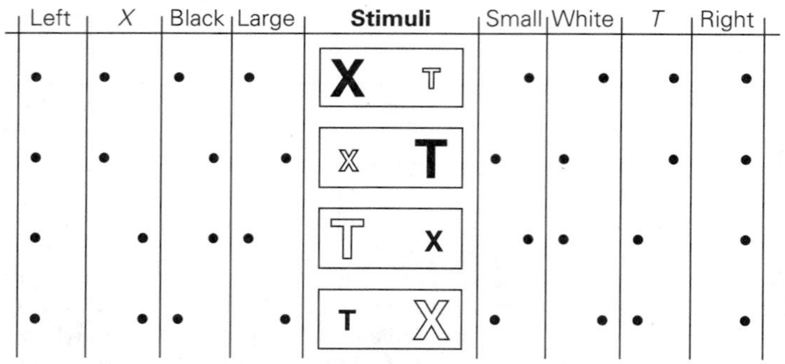

Figure 10.9 Examples of the stimuli used by Cicerone, Lazar, and Shapiro (1983).
Each item on a card (under the Stimuli column) can be classified according to four variables: its position (left, right), its identity (*X*, *T*), its color (black, white), and its size (large, small). Individuals must deduce, or hypothesize, which one of the variables is important (e.g., letter name but not color, size, or position) and then the item that they should choose (e.g., the *X*s but not the *T*s). The position of the circle (left, right) within each column indicates which of the two items would be chosen to be consistent with the hypothesized critical feature listed at the top of the column. (*Note.* Reprinted from *Neuropsychologia*, vol. 21, K. Cicerone, R. Lazar, and W. Shapiro, "Effects of Frontal Lobe Lesions on Hypothesis Sampling During Concept Formation," p. 515, Copyright 1983, with permission from Elsevier Science, Ltd., The Boulevard, Langford Lane, Kidlington OX5 1GB, UK.)

use fewer appropriate hypotheses than patients with damage to posterior brain regions do.

In other situations, patients with frontal lobe damage may appear to follow through on an appropriate hypothesis, only to abandon it later. For example, in a case described by Grafman, Sirigu, Spector, and Hendler (1993), a patient was asked to play the game Twenty Questions, in which a person can ask as many as 20 questions in attempting to determine the object about which another individual is thinking. In this case, the object was "tank." The patient had already determined that the object was inanimate and a vehicle. Yet after guessing a series of vehicle names, he suddenly stopped and asked if the object was an animal.

Individuals with frontal lobe damage also have trouble switching from one hypothesis to another, often continuing to focus on an incorrect hypothesis even though enough information has accrued to eliminate it as a possibility. This tendency was well illustrated with the task just described (see Figure 10.9). The patients' verbal output suggested to the researchers that the patients couldn't switch hypotheses because of a "tunnel vision" in which they zeroed in on one aspect of the stimulus and ignored others. Once they decided that a particular attribute was salient, they couldn't switch their focus to another attribute that might lead to the correct solution (Cicerone, Lazar, & Shapiro, 1983).

The tendency of individuals with frontal lobe damage to start down a particular path and not consider alternative solutions is demonstrated by another task in which a series of items, such as words or pictures, must be ordered (Della Malva, Stuss, D'Alton, & Willmer, 1993). In this task, two types of trials are used. In one type of trial, two items, which form a common association, are presented in succession. Yet they needn't be separated to form a valid sequence. An example is "sky/the/lit/*full*/*moon*/a," which should be ordered to read "A *full moon* lit the sky." In the other type of trial, the associated items must be separated, as in the set "of/full/the/was/*coffee*/*cup*," in which *coffee* and *cup* must be broken to correctly order the sentence to read "The *cup* was full of *coffee*." Although patients with frontal lobe damage can break the

association when making their responses, they cannot then go on to correctly order the words. In contrast, they have no trouble ordering the sentence when the associated words do not need to be broken. Thus, the association of two related words appears to preclude them from successfully generating a valid reordering of the words.

So far, we discussed mainly situations in which the individual must shift or redirect his or her response within the context of the same task (e.g., sorting cards). These situations can be considered a redirecting of a strategy or a response. We can also ask whether the actual *act of switching*, especially between different tasks, poses particular difficulty for patients with frontal lobe damage. Evidence from neurologically intact individuals suggests that task switching is directed by an executive control system that is independent of the systems that actually perform each task (e.g., Allport, Styles, & Hsieh, 1992; Rogers & Monsell, 1995). Patients with frontal lobe damage, specifically to the dorsolateral prefrontal cortex, are slower at switching between two tasks even when they perform each of the two tasks perfectly, which suggests that they have a specific deficit in task switching. This pattern of performance contrasts with that of individuals who have medial, frontal pole, or white-matter lesions, who are as slow at performing the tasks as they are at switching between them (J. S. Rubenstein, unpublished manuscript, 1993). Difficulties in switching between tasks can make goal-oriented behavior difficult when a series of distinct subtasks are required to reach the goal. For example, in the task of making a peanut butter and jelly sandwich, an individual must switch from the search subtask ("find the peanut butter and jelly") to the construct subtask ("make the sandwich"). Such a switch could be difficult for individuals with frontal lobe damage and executive dysfunction.

Ability to Use Information About Contingencies to Guide Behavior

The effective and efficient attainment of a goal often requires available information to be evaluated so that the appropriate strategy for a given situation can be selected. One set of conditions may favor one strategy, whereas a different set of conditions may favor an alternative strategy. At least in some cases, individuals with frontal lobe damage do not use information that would enable them to effectively guide subsequent action.

One example of the disregard for information that would help attain a goal comes from a study in which participants were asked to decide whether an upright letter or a rotated target letter (e.g., rotated 180 degrees clockwise) was in a normal or a mirror-image orientation. Cognitive psychologists have studied this task extensively and have found that most people perform the task by mentally rotating the letter to its upright position and then making the decision (e.g., R. N. Shepard & Cooper, 1982, see page 214, chapter 6). Not surprisingly, the more the letter is rotated from upright, the longer the person takes to reach a decision. This experiment, however, contained an additional condition to the traditional one just described. In this new condition, a precue, which was always presented in the normal orientation and rotated to the same degree as the subsequently appearing target, was presented 1,500 ms before the target. If the participant used information in the precue, the task could be performed simply, without any mental rotation. When the cue and the target had identical orientations, the target could be deduced to be in the normal orientation (because the cue was always in the normal orientation). In contrast, when they looked different, the person could deduce that the target must be in a mirror-image orientation (Figure 10.10). The experimenter could determine whether the participant was using the precue effectively because when a participant did so, the degree of rotation of the item no longer predicted the speed of a response.

Although patients with temporal lobe lesions and neurologically intact subjects used the cue to avoid having to rotate the letter mentally, individuals with frontal lobe damage still used the inefficient strategy of rotating the letters to their normal positions. Other possible explanations for their poor performance, such as difficulties in matching letters or retaining cues for 1,500 ms, were ruled out (Alivisatos, 1992). In a similar study, researchers found that individuals with frontal lobe damage do not use information provided by cues that indicate the position in space at which a target will subsequently appear (Alivisatos & Milner, 1989). Hence, individuals with frontal lobe damage frequently appear not to use extra information that is available in their environment that would allow them to effectively plan and guide their behavior.

Ability to Self-Criticize or Self-Monitor

The last skill we discuss that is important for attaining a goal is the ability to evaluate whether your performance is actually bringing you closer to your goal. Stated more simply, it is the ability to accurately answer the question "How am I doing?" Individuals with frontal lobe damage are notorious for not monitoring themselves or their performance, a tendency that manifests most noticeably as "wandering off task." For example, if asked to draw a square, persons with frontal lobe damage may start drawing a square but then begin to incorporate words from a nearby conversation into the drawing without seeming to realize or care that such actions are incompatible with what they set out to do (Luria, 1966). This behavior contrasts with that of individuals with nonfrontal lesions in similar situations. For example, a person whose visuospatial abilities have been compromised by a right posterior lesion will have difficulty drawing the square but will nonetheless continue in the attempt rather than engaging in some irrelevant activity.

In addition to having difficulties staying on task, individuals with executive dysfunction have difficulty determining whether an objective has been reached. For example, given cards that need to be rearranged in a sequence, individuals with executive dysfunction may simply move a card or two and then declare themselves done. Lack of motivation or concern about their performance level might account for some of these difficulties, especially considering the changes in emotional processing that accompany frontal lobe damage (which we discuss in chapter 11). Lack of motivation, however, is unlikely to be the sole explanation for these difficulties

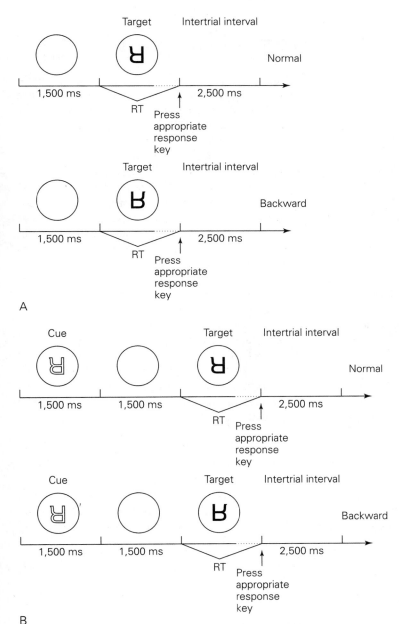

A

B

Figure 10.10 An example of an advance-information paradigm.

(A) In the standard (no-information) condition, the individual must decide whether the target item is in its normal orientation (top row) or is backward (bottom row). In general, the more the item is rotated from upright, the longer an individual takes to respond because he or she must rotate the letter mentally before answering. (B) In the advance-information condition, a cue that is always in the normal orientation is given, followed after by a brief delay by a target. This cue makes mental rotation unnecessary. If the cue and the target have identical orientations (top row), the individual should know immediately that the target is in the normal orientation, whereas if they have different orientations (bottom row), the individual should know that the target is in its mirror-image (backward) orientation. Individuals with frontal lobe damage do not use such information but instead continue to rotate the target letter mentally to reach their decision. RT, reaction time. (*Note.* Reprinted from *Neuropsychologia*, vol. 30, B. Alivisatos, ''The Role of Frontal Cortex in the Use of Advance Information in a Mental Rotation Paradigm,'' p. 151, Copyright 1992, with permission from Elsevier Science Ltd., The Boulevard, Langford Lane, Kidlington OX5 1GB, UK.)

Frontal Lobotomy as a "Cure" for Schizophrenia

In the 1930s, 1940s, and 1950s, frontal lobotomy was touted as a procedure to cure schizophrenia and other mental disorders. The history of the extensive use of this procedure is shameful but worth discussing because it provides useful lessons about the ethics of research with human participants and the methods used for evaluating the efficacy of new types of therapies.

Scientists often find that knowledge gained in animal studies is invaluable in their understanding of the human brain and in the design of new therapies. However, in the case of frontal lobotomy, this transfer of information from animals to humans ran amuck as a result of the ambitions of Egas Moniz, a Portuguese neurologist. Attending a conference in 1935, Moniz heard about a case study in which frontal lobectomy had made one of two chimpanzees tamer and less belligerent. Because psychiatrists were having minimal success in treating schizophrenia, Moniz was intrigued by this finding. Just 3 months later, Moniz, with little or no sound theoretical basis but this single case report, began performing bilateral frontal lobectomies on humans as a cure for schizophrenia. Compounding the problem was Moniz's seriously flawed method for evaluating the success of his operations. He examined his patients between 11 days and 2 months postoperatively—a time frame in which the generalized effects of brain trauma such as edema (swelling) are often still present. Thus, although Moniz observed reduced agitation in his patients, it probably reflected a groggy and stuporous state resulting from the brain surgery,

not a cure induced by the specific removal of frontal tissue. Moniz's grand claims about his informal and poorly controlled studies led him to win the Nobel Prize in 1949 for "his discovery of the therapeutic value of prefrontal leukotomy in certain psychoses." Awarding this prize to Moniz was probably one of the worst decisions that the Swedish Academy ever made.

The rationale provided for frontal lobectomies was that delusions (e.g., thinking that you are Napoleon reincarnated) and hallucinations (e.g., hearing voices telling you to burn down houses) were fueled by frontal lobe dysfunction, and that such behavior would cease if the frontal regions were disconnected from the rest of the brain. Today we know that disconnecting the frontal lobes is counterproductive because of their critical role in executive functions and because they are actually *underactive,* not overactive, in patients with schizophrenia (an issue we revisit in chapter 11). The difficulties in initiating behavior that are often observed after frontal lobe damage were interpreted by medical professionals earlier in the 20th century as a positive result because the patients acted out less. We now know that this lack of behavior doesn't represent a solution but is instead indicative of a problem.

Naturally, the question arises as to why the deleterious effects of frontal lobectomy weren't recognized earlier. The answers are many. First, psychiatry was groping for ways to deal with an illness for which it had no cure. Second, a neurologist in the United States, Walter Freeman, took it upon himself to proselytize the use of frontal lobotomy as he practiced it. The

---

because, as discussed earlier, in some situations patients verbally declare that they should do something but then fail to follow through. The verbal declarations provide some evidence that the individual is actually engaged by the task and has some interest in reaching the goal. However, the ability to monitor performance or to specifically translate that idea into action is disrupted.

THEORIES OF FRONTAL LOBE FUNCTION IN EXECUTIVE CONTROL

So far in this chapter, we reviewed the many types of difficulties in executive functions that can occur after frontal lobe damage. We now turn our attention to the issue of whether any general conceptual framework exists that can help us to understand this

technique was barbaric, so you might want to brace yourself for the description that follows. To avoid the use of anesthetics, Freeman administered electroshock to the patient, which would rack the person's body with convulsions until he or she lost consciousness. At this point, Freeman gained access to the brain through the eye socket, using a specifically designed tool that he slipped between the eyeball and the socket so as to avoid having to remove any skull. Then, using a blunt scalpel, which he moved back and forth, he destroyed frontal tissue. The entire procedure could be performed in 15 min.

The desperation of doctors searching for a cure, the ease of the procedure, the proselytizing by Freeman (who was thought to be knowledgeable because he was associated with the most famous U.S. military psychiatric hospital, St. Elizabeth's), and a state hospital system in which many of the patients were wards of the state (which meant that family members needn't be consulted prior to the procedure and often weren't around to provide impressions of their relative's postoperative state) all contributed to the acceptance of the technique in the United States. Because of these factors, many years passed before the uselessness of frontal lobotomy became apparent (a longer and very readable account of this and other misuses of psychosurgery is provided by Valenstein, 1986).

What did result, however, from this unfortunate period in the annals of psychiatry was a much greater sensitivity to the notion of the rights of humans who participate in experiments and an examination of how

experiments should be designed if the efficacy of an experimental treatment is to be evaluated. Today, in the United States and elsewhere, government-mandated and -regulated procedures must be used to obtain consent for participation in an experimental procedure of any sort, whether it is a simple study of behavior or trials for a new medical therapy. These rules state explicitly that a person cannot be coerced into participation and that individuals must be informed not only of a study's potential benefits, but of all its possible risks as well. In addition, researchers must follow special guidelines for including individuals who may not be completely capable of understanding what giving consent to participate means, such as individuals with a psychiatric illness. In terms of evaluating a new therapy, the status of individuals who receive treatment is compared with that of those who receive no treatment. To prevent any experimenter bias, a researcher who is "blind," not knowing whether the participant is in the treatment group or not, evaluates the participant's performance or responses. Furthermore, a therapy's efficacy must be proved on a small sample of individuals before trials with a larger population can begin. These rules regarding participation of individuals and the conduct of experiments are enforced by a Human Subjects Rights committee at the local level of the university or hospital where the experiment occurs. This committee reviews experiments to make certain that they meet the government guidelines, which were created with the goal of ensuring that situations such as those surrounding frontal lobectomy never occur again.

diversity. Although we do not resolve this issue with a simple solution, we discuss some major approaches to conceptualizing the role of frontal regions in executive function. The premise of the first approach, which has been explored extensively with animal models, is that the dorsolateral prefrontal cortex is critical for working memory. This conceptualization suggests that the lack of working mem-

ory precludes sequential analysis and the organization of behavior toward a goal. The underlying assumption of the second approach is that there are two ways to control behavior, one that is relatively automatic and one that is more controlled. Frontal lobe damage is believed to specifically disrupt the controlled processes. According to a third approach, the frontal lobes allow for complex behavior because they store memories for scripts that indicate the conditions under which actions should occur, the organization of those actions, and the end state that indicates those actions should cease. Damage to frontal areas leads to loss of these scripts and to executive dysfunction. A fourth approach derives from work on means-end analysis in artificial intelligence and machine learning, in which the difference between the current state of events and the goal state is computed so that actions can be chosen to minimize the difference. Proponents of this approach posit that frontal lobe damage prevents such analysis from occurring.

All these approaches need not be mutually exclusive, and each may shed light on how to conceptualize the role of the frontal lobes in executive functioning. As you read each theory, you may find it instructive to pause for a moment and evaluate it. You might, for example, want to consider how well each theory can explain Dr. P.'s problems.

Role of Working Memory

In the first approach that we discuss, a specific portion of the frontal lobe, the dorsolateral prefrontal area, is assumed to be critical for working memory. This theory, which is the most anatomically specific of those that we discuss, was not designed to account for the broad array of dysfunctions in executive control that can be observed. Nonetheless, we can examine the degree to which disruption of this underlying fundamental function of the prefrontal cortex might contribute to some of the deficits seen in executive function.

As discussed in chapter 9, working memory is the portion of memory that keeps information on-line for use in performing a task. It is to be distinguished from long-term memory, which is believed to be important for storing material for later retrieval. Much research performed on monkeys has documented the role of the dorsolateral prefrontal cortex in working memory (e.g., Goldman-Rakic, 1987). A classic example of such impairments is those exhibited on the delayed-response paradigm illustrated in Figure 10.11. In this paradigm, the monkey watches through a barred window as an experimenter places a morsel of food in one of two recessed bowls and then covers both bowls with identical pieces of cardboard (Figure 10.11A). Afterward, a screen drops, blocking the monkey's view of the cardboard covers for 1 to 10 s (Figure 10.11B). After the delay, the screen is lifted and the monkey is allowed to search for the food morsel in one of the two bowls (Figure 10.11C). If a monkey with dorsolateral prefrontal damage is allowed to choose between the two covered bowls immediately, no deficit in performance is observed. However, if the delay is longer than 1 s, which requires the information about the food's location to be sustained, the animal's performance plummets, presumably because a representation of the food's location cannot be kept in working memory. As mentioned in chapter 9, electrophysiologic evidence from neurologically intact animals also suggests that this region of the brain holds information in working memory. The firing rate of cells in prefrontal cortex increases at the time a target is shown and then is sustained through a waiting interval until the response display is shown, at which point cell activity decreases (Funahashi, Bruce, & Goldman-Rakic, 1989).

How might difficulties in working memory account for some of the deficits we observed? First, such difficulties may interfere with the ability to keep a goal in mind and thus may interfere with a person's ability to direct behavior toward a goal or to formulate a strategy that allows the goal to be attained. Second, difficulty in keeping information on-line may disrupt a person's understanding of temporal relations between items and events. If what has just happened cannot be kept on-line, its relation to subsequent happenings will be lost. In such cases, advance information that can aid in solving problems will be of little use, and deficits in self-ordering and making recency judgments will also occur. Third, because of a lack of working memory, behavior may be driven by the immediate stimuli in the environment or by recently rewarded behavior, which may explain some aspects of environmental dependency and perseveration observed in patients with frontal lobe damage. Thus, difficulties in working memory may account for a number of the diffi-

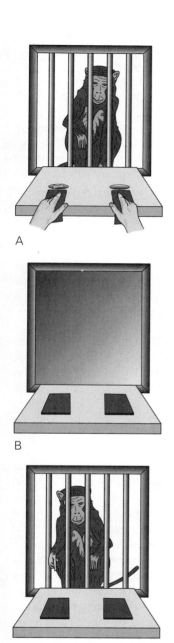

culties that are observed in cases of executive dysfunction (for a computational model demonstrating that a disruption in working memory can lead to deficits on four tasks on which patients with frontal lobe damage have difficulty, such as the WCST, see Kimberg & Farah, 1993).

Role of Controlled Versus Automatic Processes

Two theories emphasize the role of the frontal lobes in the controlled regulation of behavior, one put forth by Stuss and Benson (1986) and one by Shallice (1982). Stuss and Benson (1986) suggest that the frontal lobes are especially important in regulating behavior in nonroutine situations or in situations when behavior must be carefully constrained. These researchers suggest that control over behavior occurs in a hierarchical manner. At the lowest level, sensory information and basic knowledge are processed by posterior regions of the brain in a relatively automatic manner that varies little from day to day. Processing of this information is difficult to control consciously. The next level is associated with the executive, or supervisory, functions of the frontal lobe. At this level of control, the use of lower level sensory information is adjusted so that behavior can be guided toward a goal. Control of behavior is effortful and slow and requires conscious control. At the highest level are self-reflection, which allows the individual to have self-awareness and to realize the relationship of the self to the environment, and metacognition, which is the ability to reflect upon a process. Such a level allows for abstract mental

Figure 10.11   The delayed-response paradigm, used with monkeys, that illustrates the importance of dorsolateral prefrontal areas for working memory.
(A) In the cue period, the animal watches as the experimenter places a piece of food in one of two recessed food bowls, which are then concealed by identical cardboard covers. (B) Then a screen drops, precluding the monkey from viewing the bowls. (C) After a delay of 1 to 10 s, the screen is raised and the animal gets to choose one of the two covers, obtaining the food morsel if the correct choice is made (response phase). Monkeys with dorsolateral prefrontal damage cannot perform the task when the delay is longer than 1 s. (*Note.* From ''The neurobiology of cognitive development,'' by P. S. Goldman-Rakic, A. Isseroff, M. L. Schwartz, and N. M. Bugbee, in *Handbook of Child Psychology: Biology and Infancy Development* (pp. 281–344), edited by P. Mussen, 1983, New York: Wiley. Copyright © 1983 John Wiley & Sons, Inc. Reprinted by permission of John Wiley & Sons, Inc.)

representation of choices of actions and understanding of the world. This process is considered under control of the prefrontal cortex.

Like the working memory approach, this model is useful in explaining some of the deficits observed in patients with frontal lobe damage and executive dysfunction. Clearly, such a model can explain deficits in goal-oriented behavior, because it posits that organizing such behaviors is one of the main functions of frontal regions. It can also explain deficits in dealing with novelty and lack of cognitive flexibility because the frontal lobes are assumed to be important for nonautomatic behavior. Damage to frontal regions can also explain the environmental dependency syndrome, because, according to the model, responses to sensory stimuli would be automatic. The model could also explain the inability to consciously control action because these functions would be compromised by frontal lobe damage. Finally, the inability to self-criticize or self-monitor could be explained by this model as resulting from prefrontal region damage, which would leave patients devoid of any ability to reflect upon themselves or the processes in which they become engaged.

Another way in which the dichotomy between controlled and automatic behavior has been incorporated into a model of frontal lobe function is exemplified by the approach of Shallice (1982). He suggests that a two-pronged system influences the choice of behavior. One part, **contention scheduling,** is a cognitive system that allows for more automatic processing. This automaticity is engendered over time, because stimuli or situations become linked to actions, routines, or processing schemes, then groups of these become linked to one another. In this manner, a single stimulus may result in a relatively automatic string of actions (e.g., the way a red light can cause a relatively automatic string of actions when you are driving). Furthermore, this system is organized so that once any action is initiated it continues to be active until inhibited, and mutually incompatible processes inhibit one another. The other part, the **supervisory attentional system,** is the cognitive system required to effortfully direct attention and guide action through

decision processes. It is active only in certain situations: when no processing schemes are available, when the task is technically difficult, when problem solving is required, and when certain response tendencies must be overcome.

According to this theory, frontal lobe damage disables the supervisory attentional system and thus leaves actions to be governed totally by contention scheduling, a situation that has a number of implications. First, it means that individuals with frontal lobe damage will show few deficits, if any, in fairly routine situations in which the appropriate response is evoked by a stimulus in a simple and obvious way. So, for example, their behavior is intact on many tests assessed in a standard IQ battery because these tasks, such as providing a definition for a word, are often familiar and well practiced and because such tasks can be accomplished by contention scheduling. However, when a situation is novel or requires flexibility, these individuals will fail to respond appropriately. When given a novel task, such as the Tower of London task (see Figure 10.7), or a less practiced task, like the Block Design subtest of the Wechsler Adult Intelligence Scale—Revised (WAIS-R), these persons have difficulty because such a problem has not been encountered previously, hence no schemes in contention scheduling exists for dealing with it. Second, when these patients see a stimulus, it governs their behavior, so they appear to act impulsively. For example, they may pick up writing implements off a desk and begin to write even when they have been explicitly told not to touch them. Usually, when you sit at a desk with pens and pencils, you intend to write, so that with time the stimuli of the desk and the writing implements have been linked to certain actions— picking them up and writing. When neurologically intact individuals are told not to touch the objects on the desk, their supervisory attentional system overrides the typical response to the stimuli of the desk and writing implements. Without such a system, however, the typical schemes of contention scheduling are invoked. Third, this theory explains why individuals often perseverate. Once a strong trigger activates a scheme or an action, this process will continue to be invoked until some mutually incompatible process is activated. Without the supervisory attentional system, iterative actions triggered by contention scheduling are difficult to interrupt, thus perseveration results.

Use of Scripts

Another approach to understanding the role of the frontal lobes in executive function borrows from work examining how individuals represent stories or events in their lives. Such knowledge is thought to be organized into a set of events, actions, or ideas that are linked to form a unit of knowledge often referred to as a script (schema) (e.g., Schank, 1982). In this theory, managerial knowledge units (MKUs) are memories that are stored in prefrontal cortex and contain information on how to perform, use, or manage simple actions that have a single unifying theme (e.g., paying a bill). In general, a MKU specifies information about the setting in which such an event occurs, the set of events that must occur to achieve the goal, and the end event that terminates the action. Furthermore, these MKUs are organized hierarchically (Grafman, 1989). For example, at the top of the hierarchy may be an abstract MKU that represents any series of events that has a beginning, a goal, an action, and an ending. Next is a MKU that represents a general behavior such as eating a meal. At a still lower level is a representation of how a person eats a meal in a restaurant. Even further below are more specific rules, such as "Wait for the host or hostess to seat you." The linkage among these MKUs is believed to occur through learning and experience, and the more commonly a particular MKU is invoked, the more likely is that behavior.

This theory also can account for some of the deficits observed in patients with frontal lobe damage. First, because MKUs provide a means for conceptualizing actions needed for a goal and the MKUs are compromised by frontal lobe damage, the patient will have difficulty with goal-directed behavior. Second, because novel events occur less frequently, after frontal region damage a patient will have more difficulty retrieving a MKU for a relatively novel event, such as eating in an Afghani restaurant, than retrieving a MKU for something much more common, such as eating in an Italian restaurant. Third, because the MKU specifies the starting and stopping conditions for many behaviors, deficits in the initiation and cessation of action will also occur.

Role of a Goal List

Another approach to understanding deficits in frontal lobe functioning that shares some characteristics with the previous theory comes from the perspective of artificial intelligence and machine learning. The premise of this approach is that a person has a list of task requirements or goals that she or he wants to achieve—a *goal list*. Because typically a variety of behaviors or strategies can be used to reach a goal, a means-end analysis is performed in machine learning in which each of several possible actions is evaluated to determine how well it will enable the goal to be met. In practice, the system computes the difference between the current state of the machine (or organization) and the goal state, then selects the actions that will minimize the difference (i.e., that will change the current state of the system to one that will allow the goal to be reached most effectively).

According to this theory, frontal lobe damage disrupts the ability to form a goal list. Because this list is so fundamental to guiding behavior, the loss of this list should lead to difficulties across a large variety of domains. Indeed, individuals with frontal lobe damage have difficulty in many arenas, including abstract thinking, perceptual analysis, verbal output, and so forth. The loss of a goal list would also imply that an individual would have difficulty staying on task (because the goal that would guide behavior is missing), would be unduly influenced by environmental stimuli (because no internal goal would be guiding behavior), and would have difficulty organizing actions toward a goal, all symptoms exhibited by individuals with frontal lobe damage (Duncan, 1986).

All these theories can explain some of the problems that are seen in executive dysfunction, yet no one approach totally captures all the nuances that are observed in the clinic. Some of the theories we discussed are broad, which enables them to account in a general way for many of the difficulties that we observed, but such broadness impairs the usefulness of these theories for making more specific hypotheses about the nature of executive dysfunction. Other theories are more specific and can help to generate refined hypotheses, but they account for only a subset of the deficits in executive function that are typically observed. Perhaps better understanding of executive function will be gained only when these functions are conceptually divided into coherent subtypes or subclasses, much as researchers have differentiated between different memory processes (e.g., working memory vs. long-term memory). A more satisfactory understanding may also require us to acquire different conceptual frameworks that provide a means of thinking about neuropsychological dysfunction that cuts across many domains of behavior, as opposed to the more traditional approach, which seeks to identify the one neural structure critical for a specifically defined and discrete function (e.g., language output).

SUMMARY

Executive functions cover a variety of skills that are critical to everyday living but are often not assessed on standard IQ tests. These skills include the ability to initiate, control, or discontinue action; to use information flexibly; to make reasonable inferences; to think abstractly; to respond to novel information and situations; to sequence information; and to direct behavior in a goal-oriented manner. Although these abilities can be disrupted after damage to a variety of brain regions, they are most typically impaired after frontal lobe damage.

Individuals with such brain damage have difficulty in five main areas of executive function. The first difficulty they exhibit is psychological inertia, which is the disinclination to initiate, change, or end an action. Difficulties in the initiation of behavior manifest in reduced spontaneous speech and the lack of spontaneous actions. Difficulties in the cessation of behavior most often manifest as perseveration. Sometimes individuals with executive dysfunc-

tion can verbally describe the behavior that they should be performing but fail to engage in that behavior, which indicates a difficulty in translating intention into action. Because of the lack of internal control over behavior, individuals with executive dysfunction can be susceptible to having their actions driven by environmental stimuli (e.g., seeing a pen and picking it up); this phenomenon is known as the environmental dependency syndrome.

Abstract and conceptual thinking is a second class of abilities often compromised by executive dysfunction. For example, although individuals with such dysfunction may be able to sort cards on the basis of perceptual information, such as color, they have difficulty sorting according to an abstract category, such as whether the animal depicted on a card is domesticated or ferocious.

A third type of ability compromised by executive dysfunction is cognitive estimation. When a patient has a deficit in cognitive estimation, known information cannot be used to make reasonable inferences about the world. This problem occurs across many domains of information, ranging from the cost of household items to the self-evaluation of emotional control.

A fourth skill compromised by executive dysfunction is the ability to cope with novelty or to react flexibly. Such problems are particularly exacerbated when novel responses must be generated that require previously learned associations, either motoric or conceptual, to be overridden.

The final class of skills adversely affected in individuals with executive dysfunction is the ability to organize behavior toward a goal. This ability consists of a number of subskills, including the ability to sequence information, the ability to shift response set and modify strategies, the ability to use information about contingencies to guide behavior, and the ability to monitor self-performance. The sequential behaviors disrupted in executive dysfunction include the ability to remember the sequence in which an examiner presents information, the ability to perform a self-ordered sequencing task, and the ability to successfully sequence behavior to reach a goal. Individuals with executive dysfunction have difficulty switching their responses, becoming locked onto one particular method of solving a problem even though that method cannot bring them any closer to the solution. These persons also do not use the relationships among events to aid in preparing their responses. Finally, patients with executive dysfunction are notoriously poor at staying on task and don't seem to be disturbed when they fail to reach a goal.

A number of theories have been generated that may help us understand the role of frontal regions in executive functioning. According to one approach, derived from research with animals, damage to the dorsolateral prefrontal cortex disrupts working memory, which makes keeping information on-line difficult. Such a problem could help to explain why individuals with executive dysfunction have difficulty sequencing information and using contingencies among events to direct behavior, why they perseverate, and why their actions often appear to be driven by information immediately available in the environment. The underlying assumption of a second approach is that the frontal lobes are especially important for controlling behavior in nonroutine situations and for overriding typical stimulus-response associations, but contribute little to automatic and effortless behavior. This theory could explain why individuals with executive dysfunction have difficulty with novelty, exhibit an environmental dependency syndrome, and engage in perseverative behavior. Proponents of a third approach posit that scripts about actions and the context in which they occur are stored in memory in frontal regions. This theory could explain why goal-directed behavior, initiation and cessation of tasks, and the ability to respond in novel situations are disrupted after frontal lobe damage. A fourth approach, derived from theories in the field of artificial intelligence and machine learning, is based on the idea that executive dysfunction represents the inability to keep a goal list or list of task requirements in mind. This theory could explain why a person with frontal lobe damage is unable to stay on task, is unduly influenced by environmental stimuli, and cannot organize his or her actions to reach a goal.

*E*motion

Contributed by Wendy Heller

"While I paced softly on, the last sound I expected to hear in so still a region, struck my ear. It was a curious laugh; distinct, formal, mirthless. I stopped: the sound ceased only for an instant; it began again, louder: for at first, though distinct, it was very low. It passed off in a clamorous peal that seemed to wake an echo in every lonely chamber . . . the laugh was as tragic, as preternatural a laugh as any I have ever heard; and, but that it was high noon, and that no circumstance of ghostliness accompanied the curious cachinnation, but that neither scene nor season favored fear, I should have been superstitiously afraid."[1]

Many a reader has been enthralled by the story of Jane Eyre and Mr. Rochester, written by Charlotte Brontë in the first half of the 19th century. In it, a young governess, Jane Eyre, falls in love with Mr. Rochester, who, on the eve of marrying her, is revealed to have a wife concealed in the attic. By his description, "Bertha Mason is mad; and she came of a mad family; —idiots and maniacs through three generations!" (Brontë, 1962, p. 349). This revelation explains the "goblin" laugh occasionally echoing through the house, which Mr. Rochester had attributed to a servant and which Jane Eyre had thought represented the laugh of someone who might be possessed by a demon. At that time in history, attributing characteristics we now regard as symptoms of mental or neurological disorders to "possession" was common, and the family of a person with such a disorder usually sequestered and hid the unfortunate individual.

Although Brontë's description of the madwoman Bertha Mason could conceivably fit that of a number of mental illnesses, the focus on her disturbing laugh is intriguing. Note that Brontë described Bertha's laughter as "mirthless" and "preternatural." Perhaps intended merely as a literary device to build suspense and terror, the madwoman's laugh happens also to be a symptom of a certain type of epilepsy, in which seizures are accompanied by involuntary and uncontrollable outbursts of laughing (Figure 11.1). These strange laughing fits, termed **epileptic laughing,** are more often associated with an epileptic focus (an area of abnormal electrical discharge) in the left cerebral hemisphere, particu-larly in the temporal lobe region (Sackheim et al., 1982; see Heller, 1990, for a review). You may wonder why this phenomenon occurs; indeed, it provides a hint that something about the organization of the brain plays a role in the expression of emotions. Epileptic laughing can also be accompanied by involuntary turning movements toward the right side. The person might turn the head, an arm, or a shoulder; might deviate the eyes; or might do a complete turn (Myslobodsky, 1983). Small wonder that such odd, and indeed frightening, behaviors, arising seemingly out of the blue, were at one time attributed to madness or demon possession!

As in other areas of neuropsychology, much of what we know about the brain and emotion derives from or was stimulated by observations of individuals with neurological disorders. People with seizure disorders have provided intriguing data about the brain and different emotions; so have people who have sustained damage to different areas of the brain. In this chapter, we discuss the ways in which the brain is involved in emotion, and we review the evidence from studies of patients with neurological impairments, persons with clinical disorders such as depression and anxiety, and neurologically intact individuals. We also critically examine the theories that have been put forth to account for the findings. First, however, we must consider how to define *emotion* and some other terms.

---

[1]From *Jane Eyre* (p. 124), by C. Brontë, 1962, New York: Macmillan.

Figure 11.1 A woodcut depicting Bertha Mason, the madwoman in the attic, from Charlotte Brontë's book *Jane Eyre*.
As described by Brontë, Bertha's mirthless laugh sounds strikingly similar to changes in emotional expression that accompany epilepsy. (*Note.* Reprinted with the permission of Simon & Schuster Books for Young Readers, an imprint of Simon & Schuster Children's Publishing Division from *Jane Eyre* by Charlotte Brontë, illustrated by Ati Forberg. Copyright © 1962 Macmillan Publishing Company.)

DEFINITION OF EMOTION

The *American Heritage Dictionary of the American Language* defines *emotion* as "1. Agitation of the passions or sensibilities often involving physiological changes. 2. Any strong feeling, as of joy, sorrow, reverence, hate, or love, arising subjectively rather than through conscious mental effort." At first glance, this decription seems to capture our everyday sense of the word. However, when we examine this definition more closely, we begin to appreciate the complexity of trying to understand emotion. Embedded in this passage are some of the most fundamental debates about the nature of emotion. For instance, what does it mean for a feeling to arise "subjectively rather than through conscious mental effort"? This phrase raises the issue of whether cognition is a prerequisite for feelings to occur—a topic that has aroused heated debate in the literature. Most of us would recognize the role that conscious mental effort can play in generating or maintaining emotions. Imagine the jealous lover who dwells on thoughts of the beloved in someone else's arms, making him- or herself more and more miserable in the process. However, a number of neuroscientists who study emotion have suggested that relatively unconscious, but nevertheless cognitive, appraisals influence our emotional experiences, particularly our beliefs about the desirability of a situation or the extent to which a circumstance furthers our goals.

Another debate highlighted by this definition is the role of physiological changes in emotion. Historically, changes in heart rate, electrodermal response (the degree to which the skin conducts electricity depending on the amount of perspiration), blood pressure, and skin temperature have been viewed as generalized indicators of emotionality. As S. S. Tompkins (1984) described,

> It had been known for centuries that the face became red and engorged with blood in anger. . . that in terror the hair stood on end and the skin became white and cold with sweat . . . that the blood vessels dilated and the skin felt warm and relaxed in enjoyment. (p. 190)

In 1890, William James said that "bodily changes follow directly the perception of the exciting fact, and our feeling of the same changes as they occur is the emotion" (p. 449). A Danish physician, Carl G. Lange, proposed a similar idea in 1887. He said, "We owe all the emotional side of our mental life, our joys and sorrows, our happy and unhappy hours, to our vasomotor system" (Lange & James, 1967 p. 80). This notion came to be called the **James-**

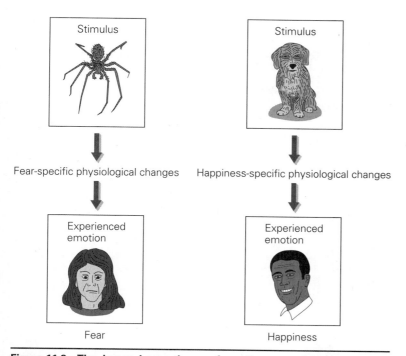

Figure 11.2 The James–Lange theory of emotion.
The underlying assumption of this theory is that the perception of an
event or an object causes a specific pattern of physiological changes that
evoke a specific emotional experience. For example, seeing a hairy spider
causes physiological reactions that are distinct from those that occur
when you see a puppy. The pattern of physiological change associated
with seeing the spider induces an experience of fear, whereas the change
associated with seeing the puppy induces the experience of happiness.

Lange theory, which states that each emotion is
caused by a specific physical response to a stimulus
(e.g., we feel afraid because we see a spider and
tremble). If this view were correct, it would imply
that before we could experience different emotions,
we would have to experience different "bodily
changes." This theory of emotion is graphically depicted in Figure 11.2.

These ideas led to a great deal of work in which
researchers tried to identify specific physiological
states that would uniquely characterize each emotion. These studies were relatively unsuccessful, and
an alternative view was eventually introduced. Phys-
iologists Walter Cannon (1927, 1931) and Philip
Bard believed that people could experience emotions even without the perception of bodily changes.

For instance, people who are completely paralyzed
from the neck down and who have little awareness
of sensory stimulation can still experience emotion.
Furthermore, research had revealed that the same
physiological states occur in many different emotions. The **Cannon–Bard theory** states that an
emotion is produced when an event or an object
is perceived by the thalamus, which conveys the
relevant information not only to the skeletal muscles
and autonomic nervous system, but simultaneously
to the cerebral cortex (Figure 11.3). Hence, according to this theory, the experience of emotion
is equally influenced by physiological changes in the
body and the processing of information by the brain.
This theory also asserts that similar physiological
changes can have different consequences for the

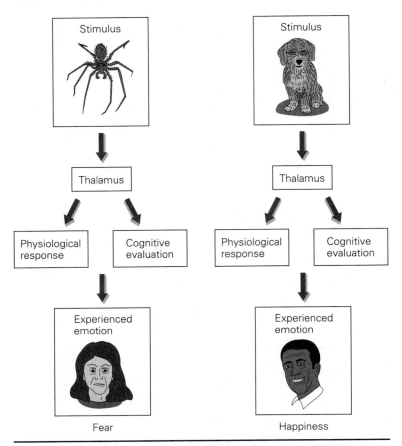

Figure 11.3 The Cannon–Bard theory of emotion.
According to this theory, an emotion is produced when an event or an object is perceived by the thalamus, which then conveys the relevant information simultaneously to the cerebral cortex and to the skeletal muscles and autonomic nervous system. The underlying assumption of this theory, unlike that of the James–Lange theory, is that the cerebral cortex plays an important role in evaluating the emotional significance of the stimulus.

experience of the emotion depending on the context of the changes. For example, although people shed tears when they are sad or when they are cutting onions, few people will claim that cutting onions is associated with an experience of sadness.

An extreme case of the latter view was put forth by Stanley Schachter in the **two-factor theory** of emotion, which suggests that emotional experience

is the outcome of physiological arousal and the attribution of a cause for that arousal (Figure 11.4). In a well-known study, Schachter and Singer (1962) used a chemical substance to induce a state of physiological arousal in their subjects. They then manipulated the situation, giving it a different emotional tone by changing the actions of the experimenters (e.g., in some cases the experimenter was rude and

annoying). As a result of their research, they claimed that "given a state of [physiological] activation . . . human subjects can be readily manipulated into states of euphoria, anger, and amusement" (p. 396).

More recent research, however, has shown that different emotions do have certain physiological signatures (e.g., Levenson, Eckman, & Friesen, 1990), although not to the dramatic extent that was once envisioned. More subtle, but nonetheless distinct, patterns of heart rate, electrodermal response, and physiological changes in the brain have been associated with specific emotions. Figure 11.5 shows different patterns of physiological responses as a function of different emotions.

Why are these issues important to our understanding of the neuropsychology of emotion? As we learned in previous chapters, different regions of the brain handle different kinds of tasks. If cognition plays only a minor role in emotion, perhaps the most important regions of the brain for emotion are subcortical structures, which are known to be associated with "emotional" behavior in animals. In contrast, if cognition plays a major role in the experience of emotion, perhaps the cerebral cortex plays a larger role, perhaps having a modulatory effect on the subcortex by facilitating or inhibiting emotional behavior. Indeed, research in neuropsychology has shown that both subcortical and cortical areas of the brain play an important role in emotional behavior and experience. These results are compatible with information-processing theories of emotion suggesting that not only are emotions part of a physiological system that readies the body for

Figure 11.4 The two-factor theory of emotion.
According to this theory, no unique physiological reaction is associated with each emotion. Instead, the physiological state can be interpreted in various ways. Thus, two factors, the physiological state and the causal attribution, dictate the emotional experience. Although the person in these pictures is having a similar physiological reaction, that of sweating and shaking, the context determines how the physiological reaction is interpreted.

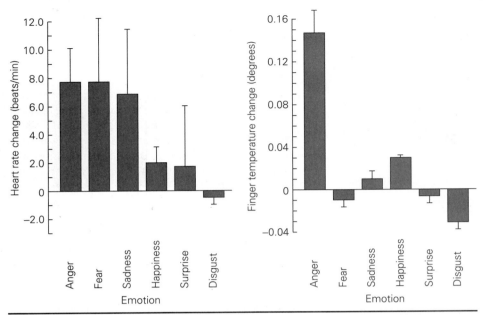

Figure 11.5 Examples of the unique physiological signatures of different emotions.
These graphs show that heart rate and finger temperature can vary with particular emotions. For example, anger is associated with marked increases in both heart rate and finger temperature, whereas fear is associated with a marked increase in heart rate but a slight decrease in finger temperature. (*Note.* Adapted with permission from "Autonomic Nervous System Activity Distinguishes Among Emotions," by P. Ekman, R. W. Levenson, and W. V. Friesen, 1983, *Science, 221,* p. 1209. Copyright 1983 American Association for the Advancement of Science.)

action, but they also provide important information that serves to guide behavior.

Normal emotional functioning most likely depends upon the interaction of a number of subsystems in the brain. The evidence suggests that these probably include the so-called limbic system (a primarily subcortical circuit, long thought to be important in emotion, containing among other structures the amygdala, hippocampus, hypothalamus, mammillary bodies, anterior thalamus, and cingulate cortex), the posterior parietal cortex of the right hemisphere, and the prefrontal cortex. These major regions of the brain that play an important role in emotion are depicted in Figure 11.6.

Subcortical structures, including the amygdala, anterior thalamus, and hypothalamus, are believed to play a role in attributing affective significance to different stimuli and in mediating the physiological responses associated with emotional reactions. The posterior region of the right hemisphere, in contrast, is important for the ability to interpret emotional information, which is more of a cognitive skill. This capacity has been shown to be relatively independent of the experience of emotion. For instance, you can know what an emotion is without feeling it; conversely, you can experience emotions but not understand what they mean. (Under normal circumstances, however, these events—experience and understanding—are likely intertwined and interdependent, informing each other both over time and within a particular situation.) Finally, the prefrontal cortex is involved in both the experience of emotion and, perhaps, the ability to express emotion by means of certain motor pathways. The ability to produce a grimace, for example, seems to be affected by frontal lobe damage.

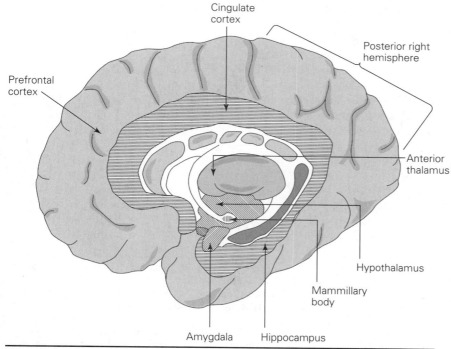

Figure 11.6 **The complex network of neural structures important for emotional functioning.**
Medial view of the right hemisphere showing the major regions involved. These regions include the prefrontal cortex, the posterior parietal cortex of the right hemisphere, and the limbic system (lined areas), a mainly subcortical circuit that includes the amygdala, hippocampus, mammillary bodies, hypothalamus, anterior thalamus, and cingulate cortex. (*Note.* Adapted from Kalat, 1992, p. 112.)

These brain regions are all interconnected, and the information processed in one region is combined with the information processed by another. Although various researchers place differential emphasis on which part of the brain is most important, or most involved, in affective computations, most agree that our "experience" of emotion is a product of the interaction of these regions. Thus, we typically experience an emotion as having a "feeling" component (often linked with a physiological experience—"rigid with fury" or "flushed with shame") accompanied by both sensory and cognitive processes that allow us to interpret and act upon the signals we perceive in the environment. We now examine in more detail the roles that these various brain regions play in emotion.

SUBCORTICAL NETWORKS FOR EMOTION

Many emotions are uncomfortable to experience. However, their survival value is obvious. When an animal is threatened, its body needs to mobilize its resources and take some kind of protective action: withdrawal (flight), perhaps, or aggression (fight). Furthermore, often these responses must be made quickly, before the animal has time to perform elaborate conscious cognitive computations and assessments of the situation. Therefore, we should not be surprised that emotional experience has been shown to be separable from conscious cognitive processing (e.g., LeDoux, 1989; Zajonc, 1980, 1984).

The results of research with animals have suggested that parts of the brain that are presumed to be older in evolutionary terms are particularly involved in emotion. When animals have lesions or are stimulated in certain parts of the subcortex, emotional responding is often affected. On the basis of these observations, James W. Papez (rhymes with "grapes") described in 1937 a particular brain circuit involved in emotion that included the hypothalamus, hippocampus, mammillary bodies, anterior thalamus, and cingulate cortex (see Figure 11.6).

Paul MacLean (1949, 1952) carried the idea further and proposed that these structures were part of what he termed the *limbic system*, one of three brain layers that developed during the course of evolution (what he called the *triune brain* or *visceral brain*). His conception of the structure of the brain is depicted in Figure 11.7.

More recent research has cast some doubt on the role of the structures that have been identified as part of the limbic system (see Brodal, 1981). Although investigators agree that emotions depend on this neural network, they now believe that the structures thought to be involved are not necessarily those that were perceived to be important in the past. For example, the hippocampus, once thought to be the hub of the limbic system, is actually relatively more important in memory functions than in emotional processing. In contrast, the amygdala, which in the past was not identified as a key component of the limbic system, has been receiving more attention from neuroscientists who study emotion (see LeDoux, 1989, 1993).

The role of the amygdala in emotion was highlighted when it was discovered to be responsible for the set of behavioral changes (known as *Klüver–Bucy syndrome*) that occurred in monkeys who sustained large temporal lobe lesions. These monkeys showed extremely abnormal reactions to the environment. They stopped being afraid of things they

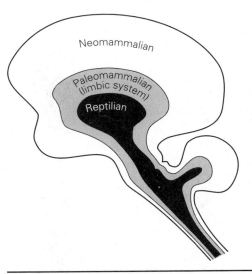

Figure 11.7 Paul MacLean's conception of the evolution of neural structures.
MacLean proposed that three main neural levels—the reptilian brain, the paleomammalian brain, and the neomammalian brain—reflected anatomical and biochemical commonalities with reptiles, early-evolving mammals, and late-evolving mammals, respectively. The paleomammalian brain includes the structures that compose the limbic system. (*Note.* Adapted from MacLean, 1967, p. 377.)

had feared in the past, attempted to engage in sexual behaviors with other species, and tried to ingest objects indiscriminately (including feces and rocks). Klüver and Bucy (1937) called the disconnection that they observed between the ability of the animals to process the sensory properties of objects and their understanding of the affective properties of these objects a *psychic blindness*.

Subsequent research demonstrated that lesions of the amygdala seem to cause a variety of vertebrates to lose the ability to respond to or make use of previous information about the affective significance of sensory stimuli. Consistent with these findings, the results of electrical stimulation studies have revealed that neurons in the amygdala respond more to the affective significance of stimuli than to their physical properties. LeDoux and colleagues have thus argued that the amygdala plays a critical role in ascribing affective meaning to stimulus configu-

rations (for an overview of this work and some recent interpretations, see LeDoux, 1993).

Thus, the subcortical structure at the hub of the
neural circuit involved in emotion may be the amygdala, instead of the hypothalamus or the hippocampus, although these structures are still viewed as
part of the network that mediates emotional response. The amygdala, hypothalamus, and hippocampus are interconnected with one another and
with various regions of the cortex, including those
that process sensory information, and the frontal
lobes.

The hippocampus, which (as we discussed in
chapter 9) is critical in allowing for long-term memory storage, is likely to be important in providing,
on the basis of previous experience, the contextual
information that frames a particular stimulus configuration. It may therefore play a modulatory role
in the affective response. An interesting illustration
of this possibility comes from animal studies in
which the development of gastric ulcers in response
to stress was examined. When lesions were made in
the amygdala, ulcers in response to stress were much
less likely to develop. In contrast, when lesions were
made in the hippocampus, ulcers were more likely
to develop (Henke, 1982). Thus, the hippocampus
appears to normally exert a mitigating, or calming,
effect on the output from the amygdala, perhaps
by providing an informational context that "puts
things in perspective."

LeDoux also argues that two important pathways
exist for communicating sensory information in a
neural network of emotion. One pathway seems
to be important for quick, instinctive, emotional
responses. For example, this pathway allows a jogger
to leap away from a shape on the road that looks
like a snake before the conscious mind has even had
the thought "That might be a snake." This pathway
projects straight from the anterior thalamus (an
early relay center for the sensory projections that
ultimately find their way to the cortex) to the amygdala. Another pathway connects the sensory areas of
the neocortex (regions that process visual, auditory,
somatosensory, gustatory, and olfactory information) to the amygdala—a corticoamygdala projection (in humans, the right hemisphere may be espe-

cially important in this regard, as is reviewed later
in this chapter). This pathway seems to provide a
more comprehensive context for processing the
emotional information. For example, after leaping
to safety, the jogger might study the shape more
carefully and realize that it is only a stick and therefore not something to be feared. Thus, the amygdala
appears to receive a progressively more complete
image of the same information, like the photograph
produced by a Polaroid camera in which the image
emerges in more and more detail while you watch.
Consequently, the thalamoamygdala pathway
would carry a crude, preliminary sketch of some
basic properties of the stimulus—not enough to
clearly identify the object, but enough, perhaps, to
ready a response. In contrast, the corticoamygdala
pathway, which is slower because it involves more
synapses, would deliver enough information to give
rise to an affective reaction that takes into account
the complexity of the eliciting stimulus configuration.

On the output side, interconnections between
the hypothalamus and the amygdala are likely to
mediate some of the autonomic and endocrine phenomena that we discussed earlier as typical manifestations of emotional states. The hypothalamus is
also involved in many of these regulatory physiological functions. Thus, the subcortical structures, by
virtue of their connections with one another and
with cortical regions, form a circuit, or network,
that is involved in emotional processing.

Although relatively little is known about the precise role of the frontal lobes in this complex emotional network, the richness of the interconnections
between subcortical regions and forebrain areas
leaves little doubt of a strong interdependency. In
fact, the neuroanatomist Walle Nauta once suggested that the frontal lobes are the neocortex of
the limbic system (Nauta, 1971). This conclusion
is consistent with evidence (to be reviewed later in
this chapter) that activity in the frontal lobes co-
varies with different emotional states. In an interesting speculation, LeDoux (1989) suggested that for
an emotion to be experienced, three types of representations must coincide in short-term memory.
These are event or stimulus representations,

affective representations that have been activated by the stimulus representations, and representations of the "self" as an "agent or experiencer." He suggested that the frontal lobes may play a critical role in providing representations of the self and hence may play a critical role in the conscious experience of an emotion. Proof of this possibility awaits further research.

ROLE OF THE CORTEX IN EMOTION

The cerebral cortex has been shown to play a role in several aspects of emotional function. These aspects are (a) the cognitive ability to interpret emotional information—to perceive, comprehend, and recall emotionally meaningful material; (b) the ability to express emotion, through tone of voice, gesture, or facial expression; and (c) the experience of emotion, or emotional state. We examine each of these emotional functions in turn and discuss which cortical regions play a role in each. In this discussion, we learn that the right hemisphere plays a special role in the ability to interpret and express emotional information. In contrast, the relative balance of activity between the frontal regions of the brain seems to be important for the experience of emotion.

Perception of Emotion

In this section of the chapter, we review evidence that the right hemisphere is important in understanding emotional information.

Interpretation of Emotional Signals

Most of us take for granted knowing that a frown means something different from a smile, say, or a wrinkled nose. Sometimes, a frown means puzzlement, suggesting a need for clarification or explanation. Often, a frown signals displeasure or disapproval. It might cue us that something we said or did annoyed or disturbed another person. That facial expression then becomes an important piece of information that we can take into account as we engage further in the interaction. We can decide to ignore the frown and continue on our path, know-

ing that we are in danger of a confrontation, or we can decide to avoid the confrontation and steer clear of the disturbing conversation or behavior. Human beings, who coexist with one another in highly complex social structures, depend on such nonverbal signals to communicate effectively.

Several channels are used to express nonverbal signals; these channels include facial expression, tone of voice (often referred to as *prosody*), and gestures. Whenever investigators compare the ability of patients with left-hemisphere brain damage and the ability of patients with right-hemisphere damage to make sense of emotional information conveyed through any of these channels, these researchers typically conclude that the right hemisphere is specialized for nonverbal skills. Compared to patients with left-hemisphere lesions, patients with right-hemisphere lesions in parietal and parietotemporal regions are significantly impaired in comprehending emotional tone of voice (e.g., K. M. Heilman, Scholes, & Watson, 1975; D. M. Tucker, Watson, & Heilman, 1977). Patients with right-hemisphere brain damage also perform more poorly than patients with left-hemisphere damage (a) when trying to discriminate between emotional faces and when attempting to name emotional scenes (e.g., DeKosky, Heilman, Bowers, & Valenstein, 1980), (b) when matching emotional expressions (e.g., Cicone, Wapner, & Gardner, 1980), and (c) when grouping both pictorially presented and written emotional scenes and faces (e.g., N. L. Etcoff, 1984; Kolb & Taylor, 1981). Patients with right-hemisphere damage are also impaired in the comprehension and appreciation of humorous or affective aspects of cartoons, films, and stories (H. Gardner, King, Flamm, & Silverman, 1975; Wapner, Hamby, & Gardner, 1981). Some of the facial expressions that individuals with right-hemisphere damage have difficulty distinguishing between are depicted in Figure 11.8.

The conclusion that the right hemisphere plays a special role in understanding emotional information is supported by many studies with neurologically intact participants as well. Left-ear advantages have been found for judging emotional tone of voice (e.g., Ley & Bryden, 1982) and for discriminating

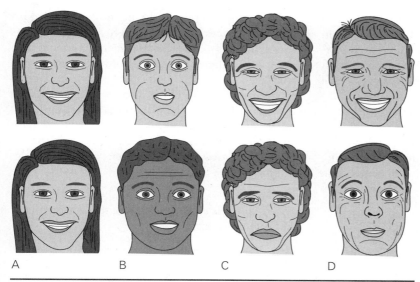

A   B   C   D

Figure 11.8 Examples of various facial expressions of emotion that individuals with right-hemisphere damage have difficulty distinguishing between.
Individuals with right-hemisphere damage are likely to have difficulty on a test such as the one shown here, in which they must decide whether the two faces in each column are expressing the same emotion. To ensure that the subject is not using other facial cues to perform the task, such as the poser's facial features, researchers use the following technique: In half of the trials the poser's identity remains constant, and in half it is changed. (A) Same face, same expression. (B) Different face, same expression. (C) Same face, different expression. (D) Different face, different expression. (*Note.* Adapted from Strauss & Moscovitch, 1981, p. 314.)

vocal nonspeech sounds such as shrieking, laughing, and crying (e.g., King & Kimura, 1972). Using divided visual field techniques, various researchers have found a left visual field (LVF), or right-hemisphere, advantage on tasks that require participants (a) to discriminate emotional expressions on faces (H. Buchtel, Campari, deRisio, & Rota, 1978; Ladavas, Umilta, & Ricci-Bitti, 1980; Pizzamiglio, Zoccolotti, Mammucari, & Cesaroni, 1983; Strauss & Moscovitch, 1981), (b) to remember emotionally expressive faces (Suberi & McKeever, 1977), and (c) to match an emotional face to a spoken word (Hansch & Pirozzolo, 1980) or to a cartoon drawing of a face (Landis, Assal, & Perret, 1979).

In other studies of neurologically intact adults, researchers have used a paradigm involving face chi-meras, each of which is composed of two half-faces spliced together to make a whole face (which you were introduced to in chapters 3 and 7; see pages 97 and 267 and Figure 7.15). In studies of emotion perception, half the face is expressing one emotion (e.g., smiling) and half the face is expressing another (e.g., sad or neutral). The faces can be presented either by using divided visual field techniques or in free vision. Typically, right-handed people judge a face as happier when the smile appears in their LVF or in their left hemifield, which suggests that the information is judged as more emotionally salient when it is received by the right hemisphere (Campbell, 1978; Heller & Levy, 1981; Levy, Heller, Banich, & Burton, 1983b). Again, these results have been interpreted to mean that the processing of emotional faces preferentially engages the right hemisphere. Thus, all the evidence reviewed from a variety of paradigms involving patients with brain damage and neurologically intact individuals suggests that the right hemisphere is better than the left at interpreting emotional information, regardless of how that information is expressed.

The left hemisphere, however, is not without a role in interpreting emotion. According to Dawn Bowers and her colleagues, who have studied many patients with right-hemisphere damage, the ability to understand emotional information depends upon a knowledge base that stores nonverbal information about the meaning of emotion (referred to as a **nonverbal affect lexicon;** Bowers, Bauer, & Heilman, 1993). These investigators contrast this ability with another type of emotional information processing, which is the ability to label emotions and to understand the link between certain situations and specific emotions (they call this **emotional semantics**). They distinguish, therefore, between the ability to comprehend the meaning of a facial expression, a gesture, or a tone of voice, which, as we just learned, relies on the right hemisphere, and the ability to know, for example, that fear is likely to be the response to a holdup, or sadness the response to a death. Whereas the nonverbal affect lexicon appears to be housed in the right hemisphere, the mechanisms that mediate emotional semantics seem to be distributed widely and are not right-hemisphere specific.

This idea is well illustrated in a study by Safer and Leventhal (1977), who asked participants to rate the emotionality of passages that varied in both emotional tone of voice and emotional content. Sometimes the emotional content was consistent with the emotional tone of voice (e.g., a story about something happy described in a happy tone of voice), and sometimes the emotional content was inconsistent with the emotional tone of voice (e.g., a story about something happy described in a sad tone of voice). The passages were presented to either the left ear or the right ear. These researchers found that participants who attended to the left ear based their ratings of emotionality on tone of voice, whereas participants who attended to the right ear based their ratings on the content of the passages.

In this study, therefore, the hemispheres relied on different sources of information to make judgments about the emotion presented in the passage: The right hemisphere used the nonverbal emotional content, and the left hemisphere used the verbal emotional content. These data are consistent with Bowers and colleagues' notion that the right hemisphere is important for nonverbal understanding of emotion but that the left hemisphere is able to process certain ideas about emotion.

Ramifications of Being Unable to Interpret Emotional Signals

How important is the ability to identify the kinds of emotional signals that pose a problem for individuals with right-hemisphere damage? The significance of these right-hemisphere skills is highlighted when we examine the effect of their loss on the quality of a person's life. Patients with right-hemisphere damage can be extremely difficult to deal with on a daily basis. They often seem to have lost the most basic social skills, such as knowing when to take turns in a conversation (typically cued by facial expression and voice intonation) or knowing how close to stand to someone while engaged in a conversation. They tend to be talkative, but listeners often describe the content of their conversation as shallow and inconsequential. These patients laugh during inappropriate moments, or they display other emotions that don't seem to fit the context. To the dismay of those around them, they seem to have difficulty putting themselves in someone else's shoes and often alienate their family members and friends. The ability to comprehend nonverbal signals is probably at the root of many of these problems. Thus, in trying to help these patients and their families adjust, one focus of rehabilitation is to modify these behaviors and to help the patient to become more sensitive to emotional and social cues.

Even more of a problem, these patients often seem to be unaware of their disabilities, a syndrome called *anosognosia,* in which persons with brain damage fail to appreciate the fact that they are disabled or that their behavior has changed (we discussed this syndrome in chapter 7 with regard to hemineglect, see page 256). Patients with anosognosia don't realize that they aren't thinking clearly or that they can't do all the things they used to do. For example, an airplane pilot with a right-hemisphere stroke and a left hemiparesis talked about going back to work the next day, ignoring even the fact that he was in the hospital. Clearly, such deficits in self-evaluation constitute a fundamental roadblock on the path to independent living and optimal rehabilitation. Thus, one of the main challenges facing rehabilitation professionals is to devise ways that enable such patients to become more aware of their disabilities.

The difficulty that patients with right-hemisphere brain damage have in understanding social situations seems to extend to a difficulty in contextualizing all sorts of information. In an interesting study, Howard Gardner and his colleagues asked patients with right-hemisphere damage and patients with left-hemisphere damage to listen to a series of narratives (H. Gardner, Brownell, Wapner, & Michelow, 1983). The narratives were designed so that each included something that didn't make sense in the context of the story. When asked to recall the story, the patients with left-hemisphere brain damage and the neurologically intact individuals either changed the nonsensical detail to fit the story or simply left it out. In contrast, the patients with right-hemisphere brain damage not only remembered the detail but tried to make the rest of the story fit around it. This process caused them to sacrifice the essence of the narrative and end up with a highly implausible construction. On the basis of these results, Gardner and his colleagues suggested that the right hemisphere houses a system that assesses the plausibility of events. This system, they suggest, is important for the ability to judge the likelihood or probability that an event could actually take place. This notion fits well with some other data showing that patients with right-hemisphere damage violate the contextual reality of objects (drawing things like a "potato bush," for example, even though potatoes grow underground). These results might also remind you of the situation we discussed previously in which the airplane pilot

with right-hemisphere damage seemed to be unaware of the magnitude of his deficits—an example of another way in which these patients seem out of touch with reality.

The idea that the right hemisphere is in a special position to judge the reality of something seems to be compatible with its other specializations, such as the ability to judge spatial relationships (as we discussed in chapter 6) and the ability to distribute attention across both sides of space (as we discussed in chapter 7). The fact that patients with right-hemisphere damage have difficulty understanding the gist of a narrative suggests that this hemisphere is also good at judging relationships among many kinds of concepts, a skill that would be needed to put things in an appropriate context (i.e., to assess how realistic they might be). These considerations deepen our understanding of the social and emotional difficulties of people with deficits in these right-hemisphere skills: Imagine trying to interact with other people when you cannot evaluate a situation realistically or judge which types of activities will be most appropriate to meet your goals.

Distinction Between Emotional Processing and Visuospatial Processing

Even after considering all the evidence implicating the involvement of the right hemisphere in the interpretation of emotion, we may want to contemplate whether comprehending emotional information is just one specific example of a complex perceptual task involving relational information, rather than a distinct process for which the right hemisphere is specialized (this issue is somewhat reminiscent of our discussion in chapter 5 as to whether the right hemisphere was specifically specialized for processing faces or for processing all complex mono-oriented visual stimuli with which we are experienced, see page 188). After all, face perception is fundamentally a visuospatial task that involves a configuration of features organized in a particular pattern relative to one another. Perhaps no unique right-hemisphere mechanism exists for processing emotional expression; maybe this hemisphere merely engages the same machinery that would be called upon to recognize a face or to organize a spatial pattern into a conceptual whole.

A common approach in neuropsychology, which you are familiar with by now, is to infer the presence of separate systems or modules by the demonstration of dissociations. If two tasks depend on a common region of the brain, damage to that region will presumably interfere with performance on both tasks. If, however, one task is spared and the other impaired (a dissociation), each may depend on a distinct brain mechanism. Even more convincing is the case in which the opposite dissociation is observed (a double dissociation). In this case, the possibility is reduced that one of the tasks is being performed by using some alternative pathway or strategy.

Many examples of dissociations between the ability to recognize a face, or perform a perceptual task, and the ability to interpret a facial emotion exist. These findings suggest that the right hemisphere has a separate specialization for processing emotional information above and beyond the stimuli, such as faces, upon which that emotional information is conveyed. Cases have been reported of patients with prosopagnosia (i.e., people who can't recognize the faces of specific individuals) who can identify facial emotions (Tranel, Damasio, & Damasio, 1988). Conversely, other patients can recognize faces but can't identify facial emotion. DeKosky, Heilman, Bowers, and Valenstein (1980) reported that a small subgroup of their sample of patients with right-hemisphere damage was not impaired on a nonemotional visuospatial task but was impaired on an emotional one. Likewise, Bowers, Bauer, Coslett, and Heilman (1985) reported that a group of patients with right-hemisphere damage remained impaired relative to neurologically intact individuals and patients with left-hemisphere damage on several emotional tasks, even when the patient groups were statistically equated on a measure of general visuospatial ability.

Nancy Etcoff (1989) used a clever paradigm to study the same issue. She based her study on a task that had been developed earlier to examine the independence or separateness of attentional or cognitive functions. In the original version of the task, subjects are asked to sort cards in which two dimensions are represented, say color (e.g., red vs. blue) and shape (e.g., square vs. circle). The task comprises three conditions: a "correlated" condition, in which the two dimensions co-vary (e.g., the deck might consist of only blue squares and red circles); a "constant" condition, in which one dimension stays the same while the other varies (e.g., the deck might have only red circles and red squares or only blue circles and red circles); and an "orthogonal" condition, in which both attributes vary randomly (e.g., the deck would have red circles, blue circles, red squares, and blue squares). Participants are told to sort the stimuli into two piles on the basis of one of the dimensions. If they do this equally quickly in all three conditions, the researcher concludes that the dimensions are "separable" (i.e., that each is processed independently of the other). If not, they are considered to be "integral" (i.e., that each is *not* processed independently of the other).

In a variation of this task, Etcoff used facial stimuli in which the two dimensions that were varied were physical identity and emotional expression. Neurologically intact individuals and patients with left-hemisphere damage were equally fast in all three conditions, which suggested that the two dimensions were separable. However, 4 of 12 patients with right-hemisphere damage showed a dissociation. Specifically, 2 patients were slowed when they had to sort by physical identity, but not when they had to sort by emotional identity, and 2 others showed the opposite pattern. Not surprisingly, these patients were distinguished by damage to different regions of the right hemisphere: The former 2 patients had damage to the posterior right temporal lobe, whereas the latter 2 had parietal region damage. This dissociation suggests that a different right-hemisphere region is specialized for processing facial identity than that which is specialized for processing facial affect.

Researchers examining face versus emotion perception in neurologically intact individuals have reached similar conclusions (e.g., Strauss & Moscovitch, 1981). In a number of studies, researchers have found that when emotional and nonemotional faces are projected by means of divided visual field techniques either to the LVF or to the right visual field (RVF), participants exhibit a greater LVF (right-hemisphere) advantage for the emotional faces than for the nonemotional faces (Suberi & McKeever, 1977). For example, in one divided visual field study (Ley & Bryden, 1979), the researchers used a large set of emotional faces that ranged from extremely positive to extremely negative, as shown in Figure 11.9A. They found that the largest LVF advantage occurred for the faces with the most extreme emotional expressions (Figure 11.9B). This larger LVF advantage seems to indicate that the emotional quality of the faces engages the right hemisphere above and beyond the recognition of faces in general.

However, the argument could be made that a greater right-hemisphere advantage in emotional face recognition results simply because recognition of emotion is somehow a more complex visuospatial task than face recognition is (hence it engages the right hemisphere to a greater degree). To address this issue, McKeever and Dixon (1981) used only neutral faces. They showed two sets of participants the exact same faces. This experimental design eliminated the argument that one condition involved more complex stimuli than the other. One group, however, was given a set of emotional instructions that they were told would aid them in remembering the faces. They were told, "I want you to imagine that something terribly sad has just happened to the two people whose faces you are studying. They have just suffered a terrible loss and now feel very saddened, frantically unhappy, and deeply depressed. As you continue to study the faces, imagine these sad feelings. Perhaps you can think of a situation in your own life in which you've experienced such sad emotions. Imagine that these same kinds of sad feelings are occurring in these individuals." The other group was given nonemotional instructions that were identical in length and wording, except the posers were described as "composed," "at ease," and "relaxed." The more the participants perceived the faces as emotional, the greater the LVF (right-hemisphere) advantage for remembering the faces they had seen. The results of this study suggest that the enhanced right-hemisphere advan-

tage for recognizing emotional faces is not just due to an increased visuospatial complexity in emotional faces—because the emotional and nonemotional faces were exactly the same. The right hemisphere seems to respond to the emotional meaning ascribed to the face, above and beyond its specialization for processing facial identity.

In summary, we can point to converging evidence from various experimental approaches suggesting that face recognition is separate from the identification of facial emotion and that the right hemisphere is critically involved in both tasks, although separate regions of the hemisphere appear to be involved in each.

Expression of Emotion

The expression of emotion is an extremely important component of social communication. In Western culture, when one person is speaking with another person, not looking at the other person's face is considered socially unacceptable and rude. Many of our opinions about people are based on aspects of facial expression, and we often hear statements such as "He has a shifty look on his face" or "She has kind eyes." On the basis of facial expressions, we make judgments about all sorts of personal traits and qualities, such as whether a person is honest or dishonest; whether the person is attracted to us or dislikes us; whether she or he is kind, compassionate, cold, or cruel; or whether the person is sensible or spacy. Both the phenomena of "love at first sight" and "I took an instant dislike to him" are frequently a function of the response to a person's face. Tone of voice carries a similar weight in affecting our emotional reactions to other people; a person who is soft-spoken is often believed to be gentle and nonjudgmental, whereas a person who is loud is perceived as arrogant and pushy.

Facial Expression

Researchers have taken a variety of approaches to studying the neuropsychology of facial expression, but two are the most common. In one approach, the faces of patients with left- or right-hemisphere

A

Figure 11.9 Evidence of enhanced right-hemisphere involvement in facial processing when emotional processing is required.
(A) The faces used by Ley and Bryden (1979) that varied in emotional intensity. Facial expressions are ordered from very positive (top row) to very negative (bottom row).
(B) The results of the Ley and Bryden study indicated that the right hemisphere's involvement in facial processing was greatest for extreme emotions. Although fewer errors were made on left visual field (LVF) trials for all expressions, this advantage was greatest when the expression was either extremely positive or extremely negative. (*Note.* From "Hemispheric Differences in Recognizing Faces and Emotions," by R. G. Ley and M. P. Bryden, 1979, *Brain and Language, 7,* p. 130. Copyright 1979 by Academic Press. Reprinted by permission.)

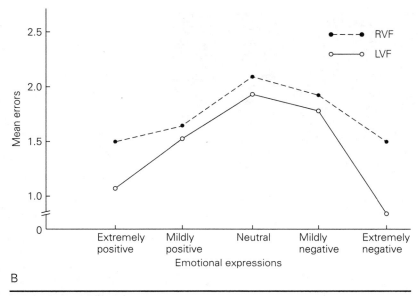

B

Figure 11.9 (Continued)

brain damage are photographed or videotaped while these individuals are talking, watching emotional films, or doing other tasks. The photographs or videotapes are then rated, either subjectively by judges or by using coding schemes to identify the muscle movements in the face (such as the Facial Action Coding System developed by Paul Ekman; Ekman, Hager, & Friesen, 1981). For example, if the corrugator muscles that control creasing of the eyebrows are judged to be active, the person can be inferred to be frowning, and if the zygomatic muscles that lift the edges of the mouth are judged to be active, the person can be scored as smiling (Figure 11.10). The emotion is then inferred from the facial expression.

In another approach, typically used with neurologically intact individuals, the emotional expression appearing on the left side of the face is compared with that appearing on the right side. Often, we can observe facial asymmetries merely by looking at a face, as shown in Figure 11.11. However, one way to quantitatively evaluate facial asymmetry is to cut a picture of a person's face in half and to splice each half-face together with its mirror image to create a composite. The result is two chimeras, each

consisting of two left half-faces or two right half-faces. When this is done, we can instantly see large differences in the appearance of the two sides of the face (Figure 11.12).

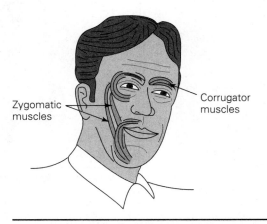

Figure 11.10 One method of studying facial expression.
This method involves using a coding scheme that catalogs movements of specific facial muscles. For example, contraction of the zygomatic muscles is important for smiling, whereas contraction of the corrugator muscles is important for frowning.

Figure 11.11 Striking asymmetries in the expression of emotion on the face.
Although we think of people's faces as symmetrical, asymmetries can be seen. Note the asymmetrical expressions on some well-known faces: (A) the Mona Lisa, (B) Marilyn Monroe, (C) Elvis Presley, and (D) John Wayne. (*Note.* A & B, Corbis-Bettmann; C & D, UPI/Corbis-Bettmann.)

Some of the earliest comments about these differences between the two sides of the face are interesting. Hallervorden (1902, 1929; cited in J. C. Borod, 1993), using the composite photograph technique, described the right side of the face as "apperceptive, thinking capably, lucid, and active" (p. 310). In contrast, the left side of the face was "perceptive, affective, having dark unformed content, and directionless" (p. 310). Somewhat later, Wolff (1933; cited in J. C. Borod, 1993) suggested that the right side of the face projects the social façade, whereas the left side reveals the passive unconscious self. Current descriptions based on these kinds of studies are less fanciful and poetic, although they sometimes

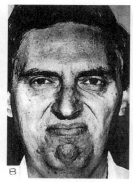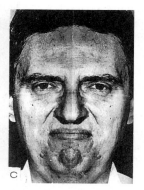

Figure 11.12 One method for demonstrating asymmetry of emotional expression on the face.
An original photograph of the face, shown here in (B), is bisected. Then, each half-face is spliced together with its mirror image to create a composite. Note the difference between the two composites depicted in (A) and (C). Which one looks more emotionally intense to you? Usually, individuals choose the composite composed of two left half-faces, depicted in (A), as more intense than the composite composed of two right half-faces, depicted in (C). This result suggests that the right hemisphere, which controls the lower left half of the face, has a larger role in producing facial emotional expression. (*Note.* Reprinted with permission from "Emotions Are Expressed More Intensely on the Left Side of the Face," by H. A. Sackeim, R. C. Gur, M. C. Saucy, 1978, *Science*, 202, p. 434. Copyright 1978 American Association for the Advancement of Science.)

parallel the previous descriptions. Generally, the left side of the face is found to be more expressive than the right side for both posed and spontaneous expressions, particularly for negative emotions (see J. C. Borod for an overview, 1993). These results are most consistently found in studies that examine neurologically intact adults. In contrast, the two sides of the face are more often judged to be symmetrical for positive emotions, such as smiles. Some researchers have even reported greater right-sided expressivity for positive emotions. Reminiscent of Wolff's suggestion, some people have argued that such expressivity may occur because positive emotional expressions are more related to the conventions of social communication (e.g., in a public setting a person is perceived as more polite if he or she looks pleasant and smiles) and hence are less likely to reflect sincere emotional experience.

However, findings vary across studies, especially among those examining facial asymmetry in individuals with brain damage. In a recent review of the literature on this topic, J. C. Borod (1993) argued that multiple factors besides which hemisphere is damaged may affect facial expression. These factors include the location of the lesion (anterior or posterior), the gender and age of an individual, and the cause of damage. If these factors all influence or moderate the degree to which the right hemisphere is involved in facial emotional expression, inconsistencies across studies would not be surprising.

In addition, the different methods used in the studies may have affected the results. In studies in which judges rate the faces, the right hemisphere is typically found to play a more important role, whereas in studies in which coding systems are used, usually no special role is reported. Although debate continues about the reasons for these differences, one possibility is that something about the configuration, or combinations, of movements (as opposed to the exact muscle movements) that signal emotion may be affected by right-hemisphere damage in a way that human perceivers can discern but that are not detected by coding schemes.

In summary, experts commonly believe that the right hemisphere plays a prominent role in facial expression in neurologically intact individuals.

However, in studies of persons with brain damage, some methods of inquiry reveal deficits after right-hemisphere injury, whereas others do not. To date, the reasons for this discrepancy are not fully apparent to researchers.

Tone of Voice

We just discussed the brain mechanisms important for controlling the expression of emotion through the face, but we have yet to consider whether the right hemisphere is also more important than the left in conveying emotion through tone of voice. Monrad-Krohn wrote several papers (e.g., 1947) in which he argued that language consists of more than finding the right word and putting it in the appropriate position with reference to other words. He coined the term *prosody* to refer to aspects of communication that had to do with tone of voice, including pitch, stress, and duration. Two types of prosody have been described. **Affective prosody** communicates the emotional context or tone of an utterance; for example, "My mother is coming to dinner" could be stated in a way that expresses elation or in a way that expresses dismay. **Propositional·prosody** communicates lexical or semantic information—for example, "What's that in the road ahead?" versus "What's that in the road, a head?" Studies of patients with brain damage have provided evidence that affective prosody seems to depend on the right hemisphere.

A common approach has been to present patients with brain damage with neutral sentences and to ask them to repeat the sentence in different tones of voice (e.g., happy, sad, angry, or indifferent). Typically, individuals with right-hemisphere damage speak in more of a monotone (e.g., D. M. Tucker, Watson, & Heilman, 1977). Furthermore, E. D. Ross and Mesulam (1979) provided data suggesting that difficulty with prosody (i.e., **aprosodia**) was not just a result of an overall impairment in emotional functioning associated with the right hemisphere. In one case, for example, a 39-year-old schoolteacher who had lost the capacity to convey emotion vocally and spoke in a monotone was still able to decode the emotions of other people and seemed to have a normal experience of emotion and an awareness of her own emotional state.

In summary, some evidence exists that the right hemisphere is differentially involved in the expression of emotion, regardless of whether it is expressed through tone of voice or through facial changes. In the case of facial expression, this finding appears to be true particularly when negative emotions are examined in neurologically intact adults.

Experience of Emotion

Thus far, we discussed how emotional information is perceived and expressed. In this section, we discuss the neural mechanisms that are important for the experience (feeling) of emotion and find that this experience depends on a delicate balance of activation between the two cerebral hemispheres, more specifically the frontal lobes.

Valence Theories

Previous decades have seen an evolution in our understanding of the neural mechanisms associated with the experience of emotion. The relatively clear evidence that the right hemisphere is superior at comprehending emotional information led researchers early on to claim that the right hemisphere is involved in all aspects of emotion (e.g., Levy, Heller, Banich, & Burton, 1983a). Various contradictory findings, however, soon led to another theory of the neuropsychology of emotion—that is, that the right hemisphere is specialized for negative affect (e.g., sadness), whereas the left hemisphere is specialized for positive affect (e.g., happiness) (e.g., Silberman & Weingartner, 1986). This type of theory has been called a **valence theory** because its main premise is that the emotional state of one hemisphere has a particular valence (e.g., positive), whereas the emotional state of the other hemisphere has the opposite valence (e.g., negative).

Valence theories were inspired by a set of observations, systematically described by Gainotti (1972), in which different emotional behaviors were

documented in people with right- versus left-hemisphere damage. Left-hemisphere damage was associated with the so-called **catastrophic reaction,** in which patients were described as emotionally volatile and especially prone to depression and crying. In contrast, right-hemisphere damage was observed to be frequently accompanied by a **euphoric-indifference reaction,** in which patients were inappropriately cheerful, were prone to laughter, and displayed a remarkable lack of awareness with regard to their disabilities and other consequences of changes wrought by brain damage. These observations led researchers to speculate that the left hemisphere is specialized for positive, or cheerful, affect and that the right hemisphere is specialized for negative, or depressed, affect. Note that one of the underlying assumptions of this hypothesis is that brain damage immobilizes or diminishes the functioning of the damaged hemisphere and that the behavior observed reflects the functioning of the intact hemisphere more or less on its own. A variant of this theory, although similar, reversed the attribution of emotion to each hemisphere (D. M. Tucker, 1981). According to this hypothesis, the observed behavior was not a function of the intact hemisphere but instead reflected the emotional tone of the subcortical areas on the damaged side that were released from cortical inhibition because of the lesion.

More recently, frontal lobe function, in particular, has been found to be associated with these differential emotional responses. In a series of studies of patients with unilateral brain damage, 60% of the patients with left frontal lobe lesions had the symptom cluster of major affective disorder described by *Diagnostic and Statistical Manual of Mental Disorders (DSM)* criteria, the standard diagnostic criteria used by psychiatrists and psychologists in the United States. Furthermore, the more anterior the lesion in the left hemisphere, the more severe the depressive symptoms (e.g., Lipsey et al., 1983). The differences between patients with left anterior lesions and patients with lesions located elsewhere can be seen in Figure 11.13A. In contrast, frontal lobe lesions in patients with right-hemisphere damage were associated with indifferent or euphoric behavior. Again, depression scores corre-

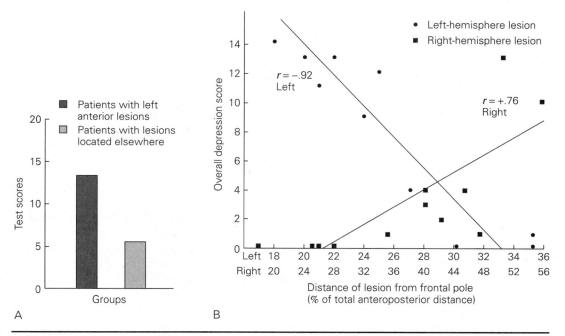

Figure 11.13 Relationship between the degree of depression exhibited after cerebral insult and the location of the lesion.
(A) Patients with damage to anterior regions of the left hemisphere often exhibit depressive symptomatology. Depicted here are scores on the Hamilton Depression Scale, which is a commonly used measure in clinical settings. A higher score indicates more severe depression. The average score for patients with left anterior lesions (dark bar) is higher than that for patients with lesions in other brain regions (light bar). (B) The relationship between lesion location and degree of depression differs between the hemispheres. The closer the lesion is to the most anterior portion of the left frontal lobe, the higher the overall depression score as indicated by a significant negative correlation ($r = -.92$) between depression score and distance of the lesion from the frontal pole. The opposite is true of the right hemisphere: The closer to the most anterior region, the lower the depression score as indicated by a significant positive correlation ($r = +.76$) between depression score and distance of the lesion from the frontal pole. (*Note.* A, Adapted from Lipsey et al., 1983, p. 266; B, Adapted from Robinson et al., 1984, p. 81.)

lated significantly with the distance of the lesion from the frontal lobes, but in the opposite direction than that observed in the patients with left-hemisphere damage (Figure 11.13B). In this case, the more anterior the lesion, the less the depression.

Similar emotional responses have been described in patients undergoing the sodium amobarbital test (which was discussed first in chapter 3 and then in chapter 8, see pages 99 and 293, respectively). When an injection of this barbiturate deactivates the left hemisphere, a catastrophic reaction is usually observed, whereas when an injection deactivates the

right hemisphere, a euphoric-indifference reaction is usually observed (e.g., Lee et al., 1988).

The notion that the left hemisphere is specialized for positive emotion and the right hemisphere for negative emotion seems further supported by findings from electroencephalographic (EEG) recordings taken during different emotional states. Mood changes in individuals with clinical depression were associated with variations in activation of the frontal lobes. During a resting, eyes-closed condition, individuals with depression showed more activity in right frontal regions than in the left

(Schaffer, Davidson, & Saron, 1983). Individuals who were not depressed showed the opposite pattern.

Integrative Theories

Is all emotion specialized to the right hemisphere, or is the left hemisphere specialized for positive emotion and the right hemisphere for negative emotion? How can these various findings be integrated? As long as emotional experience was considered indistinguishable from the ability to interpret emotional information, the findings remained contradictory. However, eventually investigators realized that just because a hemisphere is associated with a particular emotional state, that hemisphere is not necessarily specialized to process information corresponding to that emotion. Evidence from patients with brain damage and other clinical populations suggests that "feeling" an emotion can be distinguished from "knowing" about an emotion. Just as speech output seems to be localized to one region of the left hemisphere (Broca's area) and speech comprehension to another (Wernicke's area), a neuropsychological system involved in feeling could be independent of another system involved in the interpretation of that feeling. Therefore, the right hemisphere could be specialized for the interpretation of emotion without necessarily being specialized for the regulation of emotional experience.

Most researchers would currently agree that, although the evaluation of emotion and the experience of mood may not be entirely independent of each other, they do need to be distinguished (Davidson, 1993). Furthermore, they appear to depend primarily upon different regions of the brain. In particular, the evaluation of emotion is clearly specialized to the posterior regions of the right hemisphere, whereas the experience of emotion seems to be associated with the frontal regions. In particular, different emotions are accompanied by different patterns of activity between the left and right hemispheres.

Many of the earlier findings of asymmetrical frontal lobe activity during different emotional states have been extensively replicated and extended in more recent research (see Davidson, 1993; Davidson & Tomarken, 1989). Negative affect, including disgust, fear, and sadness, tends to be associated with relatively greater activation of the right frontal lobe than that of the left. Positive affect, in contrast, is associated with relatively greater activation of the left frontal lobe.

Davidson and his colleagues (see Davidson, 1993, for a review) have argued that the left frontal region houses a system involved in approach behaviors and that increased activity of the left frontal area is associated with emotions that tend to be accompanied by approach behaviors, including most positive emotions. In addition, some negative emotions, such as anger, that tend to be associated with approach behaviors might also be associated with increased activity of the left frontal region. In contrast, the right frontal region houses a system involved in withdrawal behaviors, and increased activity of the right frontal area is associated with emotions that are accompanied by withdrawal behaviors, such as fear, disgust, and depression. This theory is based on the notion that approach and withdrawal are the most basic and rudimentary actions that organisms take in responding adaptively to the environment. As emotions evolved, they became associated with already-established approach-and-withdrawal action systems. Davidson views the frontal region as a convergence zone where information from the posterior perceptual processing regions (the parietal cortex) is combined with information from the subcortical areas involved in attributing emotional significance to sensory input (the amygdala, as discussed previously). This notion is compatible with the views of LeDoux (1993), who also views emotional function as regulated by a system involving multiple regions of the brain. Both researchers would likely agree that the frontal region of the cortex is important for the most complex and coordinated decision making and action planning. As such, it would be crucial for it to have access to the various sources of emotional information processed or stored in other areas of the brain.

NEUROPSYCHOLOGICAL BASES OF MOOD AND EMOTION DISORDERS IN PSYCHOPATHOLOGY

So far, we discussed emotional processing in the brains of individuals who do not have psychiatric disorders or who had normal emotional functioning prior to the brain insult. In this section, we consider whether the same brain mechanisms that we already discussed also play a role in psychopathology.

Depression

Depression is considered to be a mood disorder characterized by chronic feelings of sadness and hopelessness, and loss of interest or pleasure. According to *DSM IV,* the current version of the standard diagnostic criteria, a number of syndromes have been identified in which depression is the predominant emotional state. In *bipolar disorder,* the person cycles through depressed and manic emotional periods. The manic state involves a distinct period of abnormally and persistently elevated, expansive, or irritable mood. The depressed state involves severe depression that exists most of the day nearly every day for at least 2 weeks. In *unipolar depression,* the person experiences only the depressed state, not the manic state. Depression can also be seasonal, defined by the existence of a regular temporal relationship between the onset of an episode of depression and a particular 60-day period of the year. A milder state of chronic depression that does not qualify as a major depressive episode has been termed *dysthymia* (or depressive neurosis) and is diagnosed if a person has experienced symptoms of depression for at least 2 years (1 year for children or adolescents). Typical symptoms of depression, in addition to sadness, hopelessness, and loss of interest or pleasure, include poor appetite or overeating, insomnia (difficulty falling asleep or early morning awakening) or hypersomnia (too much sleeping), low energy or fatigue, low self-esteem, and poor concentration or difficulty making decisions.

Quite a bit of evidence indicates that, in depression, right frontal activity is relatively higher than left frontal activity. The results of a number of studies suggest that this phenomenon might be due to a hypoarousal of the left frontal region in particular (e.g., Henriques & Davidson, 1991). Henriques and Davidson believe that such hypoarousal of the left frontal region reflects a vulnerability to a deficit in the approach system housed in this brain region. They argue that although not everyone with reduced activation of the left frontal region will become depressed, people who display such a pattern are more vulnerable to depression if other disturbing life events occur. This concept might explain why although many studies have revealed a higher proportion of patients with left frontal lobe lesions to be depressed (e.g., Robinson et al., 1984), some have not (e.g., Gainotti, 1989). If hypoarousal of the left frontal region (relative to the right) is a vulnerability factor, other factors (such as disturbing life events, degree of social support, financial worries, personality traits) would play an important role in whether a person becomes depressed after experiencing brain damage. This kind of conceptualization is called a **diathesis-stress model,** in which environmental factors (the stressors) interact with or exacerbate a biological predisposition (the diathesis).

Depression also seems to be accompanied, quite often, by a relative decrease in activation of posterior regions of the right hemisphere and decreases in performance on tasks dependent on this region (see Heller, 1993b). In studies in which regional electrical activity or regional blood flow of different areas of the brain has been measured in depressed individuals, activity has been found to be reduced in posterior regions of the right hemisphere (e.g., Davidson, Chapman, & Chapman, 1987). Depressed individuals also show relatively poor performance on various neuropsychological tasks that depend on the right hemisphere, such as judgment of line orientation, three-dimensional constructional skills, face recognition, spatial association learning, and performance with the nondominant hand on the Tactual Performance Test (as reviewed by Banich, Stolar, Heller, & Goldman, 1992). Depressed patients di-

Causes of Gender Differences in Depression: Biology, Environment, or Both?

The rates of depression in our society constitute a significant mental health problem, one that is receiving growing attention from governmental agencies, such as the National Institutes of Health in the United States. The problem is particularly acute for women: Many studies have revealed a female-to-male ratio of approximately two to one (Weissman et al., 1984).

Much literature has been generated on the causes of depression; researchers have examined factors inherent to the individual (e.g., genetic, neurochemical, and neuropsychological traits), as well as factors related to the environment, such as extreme loss (e.g., death of a parent), socialization processes that foster helplessness, and severe trauma (e.g., physical or sexual abuse). In general, it seems most likely that a complex interaction between biological vulnerability and environmental stress predisposes some people to depression.

In the attempt to explain gender differences in depression, many researchers have focused on the differing neurobiological tasks that must be carried out by the brain of a woman as compared to that of a man. Some researchers have argued that the neurochemical messenger systems in a woman's brain are more finely tuned and therefore more likely to be chronically disrupted when normal developmental processes are interrupted or modified. For example, a link has been found between various regions of the brain that regulate reproductive hormones (e.g., hypothalamus, pituitary gland) and the part of the body that produces adrenaline, a chemical that mediates a physical response to stress and threat. If the regulation of these hormones requires more intricate neural programming in women than in men, early experiences of threat or stress may cause a greater dysregulation of the whole system in women that contributes to a vulnerability toward depression in later years. Some authors have suggested, for example, that this system might become hyperresponsive in reaction to stress.

Another neurobiological phenomenon that has been identified in depression has to do with the relative activity of the two hemispheres of the brain. As described in the text, two patterns of relative activation in specific regions of the brain have been identified. In one, the left frontal region of the brain is relatively less active than the right frontal region in persons who are depressed than in those who are not. In the other, functions of the right posterior hemisphere are impaired in persons who are depressed, but not in individuals without depression.

Do these findings tell us anything about gender differences in depression? Unfortunately, few research-

agnosed with either bipolar illness or *melancholia* (i.e., sad mood along with possible disrupted sleep cycle, psychomotor slowing, excessive guilt, and weight loss) according to *DSM* criteria have also been found to show abnormal perceptual asymmetries on lateralized tasks as a result of impairments in right-hemisphere performance. Bruder et al. (1989) used a listening paradigm in which either consonant-vowel syllables or complex tones were presented to each ear; these researchers found that patients with melancholia showed poor left-ear (right-hemisphere) performance for all types of stimuli. Patients with bipolar disorder also failed to show the normal right-hemisphere advantage on a dot enumeration task.

Converging results have been obtained from studies on nondepressed subjects who undergo mood inductions. Ladavas, Nicoletti, Umilta, and Rizzolatti (1984) found that reaction time was selectively slowed for right-hemisphere responses when subjects were simply asked to feel sad. Banich, Stolar, Heller, and Goldman (1992) obtained similar results using a more complex conceptual task and a more elaborate mood-induction procedure.

ers have examined this issue. The possibility exists that females are born with relatively higher right frontal activity than left frontal activity and that they therefore are more likely to be vulnerable to depression. Conversely, the distribution of asymmetrical activity is just as likely to start out identical in males and females, but more environmental elicitors or stressors may exist for females than for males. For example, convincing evidence suggests that childhood sexual abuse is associated with depression later in life, and females are much more likely than males to be sexually abused. Similarly, women are socialized to feel helpless more often than men are. Thus, there may be just as many females as males with a neurological vulnerability (relatively reduced left frontal activity), but more of the females with this vulnerability would develop depression as a result of a disparity in the number and intensity of environmental elicitors. One important route for future research is to include equal groups of males and females in research studies. Infants must also be compared with adults. Only then will examining these alternative explanations for the observed gender differences in depression be feasible.

The possibilities we just described have interesting implications for certain psychological tendencies reported in the literature. More specifically, Nolen-Hoek-sema (1987) found that women are more likely to ruminate when depressed, whereas men are more likely to involve themselves in a distracting activity, such as a sport. Furthermore, physical activity has been found to enhance the self-concept of women who are depressed. These findings may be related to recent research that has shown exercise to produce a shift in cerebral activation such that the left frontal region becomes more active relative to the right (Petruzzello & Landers, 1992). Thus, perhaps the rate of depression in women versus men is affected by certain behavioral coping strategies (e.g., engaging in athletic activities) that influence the neurophysiological mechanisms underlying different emotional states.

To date, no definitive conclusions can be drawn about the reasons why more women than men are depressed. However, a number of promising pathways are open for investigation. Regardless of the methodology or aspect of brain function or psychology under investigation, researchers must consider the interplay of environmental and biological factors when attempting to construct hypotheses about brain-behavior relationships. This consideration is particularly important in light of the evidence for potentially large differences in the social and educational forces that are at play in the lives of women and men.

Heller (1993a,b) has argued that these findings suggest a role for the posterior right hemisphere in a dimension of emotion referred to in many theories as *arousal*. The results of studies in which the psychological factors that best characterize emotions were examined suggest two fundamental dimensions: valence (pleasant vs. unpleasant, or positive vs. negative) and arousal (high vs. low) (e.g., J. A. Russell, 1979). Heller (1993a,b) proposed a neuropsychological model of emotion suggesting that the frontal regions are involved in the valence aspect of emotion and that the posterior right hemisphere is involved in the arousal aspect (Figure 11.14). The arousal aspect of emotion is thought to relate to the physiological and autonomic functions described at the beginning of this chapter as critical components of emotion.

Consistent with Heller's proposal, evidence is accumulating to suggest that the right hemisphere plays a critical role in the regulation of autonomic and physiological responses. First, damage to the right hemisphere is associated with marked decreases in electrodermal responses (e.g., L. Morrow, Vrtunski, Kim, & Boller, 1981) and with slowing

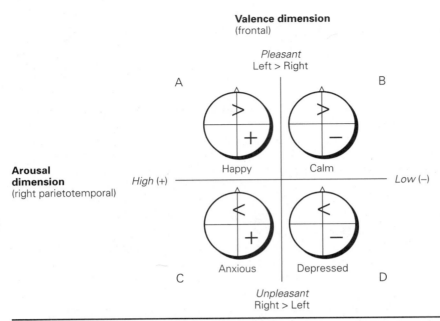

Figure 11.14 A model of regional brain activity and mood as proposed by Heller (1993a).
This model posits that the valence dimension of mood (positive, or pleasant, vs. negative, or
unpleasant; *y* axis) is mainly affected by activation of frontal regions of the brain, whereas
the arousal dimension (high vs. low; *x* axis) is mainly affected by activation of the right posterior region. Depicted here are the patterns of brain activation for four mood states. (Top left)
When activation of left frontal regions is greater than that of right frontal regions (which
leads to pleasant emotion) and the right posterior region is highly activated (which leads to
arousal), the individual is happy. (Top right) The pattern of activation is identical over frontal
regions for a calm state, but the activity over the right posterior region is reduced, which
leads to a lower level of arousal for a calm state than for happiness. (Bottom left) In anxiety,
higher right than left frontal activation leads to a negative valence, and high activity in the
right posterior region leads to increased arousal. (Bottom right) Finally, the brain activation in
depression is similar to that of anxiety in that higher right than left frontal activation leads to
a negative valence. However, the low activity in the right posterior region causes the decreased arousal that differentiates depression from anxiety. (*Note.* From "Neuropsychological
Mechanisms of Individual Differences in Emotion, Personality, and Arousal," by W. Heller,
1993, *Neuropsychology, 7,* p. 477. Copyright © 1993 by the American Psychological Association. Reprinted with permission.)

on certain reaction-time tasks above and beyond
that observed in patients with other types of brain
damage (e.g., A. Benton, 1986). Second, stimuli
presented to the right hemisphere but not the left
have been found to affect heart rate and blood pressure (Walker & Sandman, 1979; Wittling, 1990).
Finally, the right hemisphere seems to play a special
role in the secretion of cortisol, which is a physiolog-

ical response to certain stressful emotional events.
Wittling and Pflüger (1990) found significant
changes in salivary cortisol secretion when an emotionally aversive film was projected to the right
hemisphere but not when it was projected to the
left hemisphere. The data just described suggest
that the hypoarousal and decreased overall activity
level in at least some patients who are depressed

(e.g., Myslobodsky & Horesh, 1978), as well as the slowed reaction time and the decreased psychomotor speed (Knott & Lapierre, 1987), may be related to deficits in posterior right-hemisphere activation.

Anxiety

Patterns of hemispheric activity also seem to vary as a function of anxiety, although the findings have been more inconsistent than those for depression. In some studies, increased right-hemisphere activity has been observed, in others increased left hemisphere activity, and in still others no asymmetries in activity. In early work using behavioral measures, D. M. Tucker and colleagues (D. M. Tucker, Antes, Stenslie, & Barnhardt, 1978; D. M. Tucker, Roth, Arneson, & Buckingham, 1977; S. K. Tyler & Tucker, 1982) found that anxiety-producing experimental conditions were associated with a specific decrement in RVF (left-hemisphere) performance (D. M. Tucker, Antes, Stenslie, & Barnhardt, 1978). They also found that high trait-anxious subjects showed a significant tendency to report right-ear tones as louder and displayed a reduction in left lateral eye movements (an indication of reduced activity in the opposite hemisphere). Such findings led these researchers to hypothesize that anxiety is accompanied by increased left-hemisphere activation. According to their hypothesis, because the left hemisphere is trying to take on too many tasks, a processing overload is produced that leads to an overall decrement in performance. This conclusion is supported by the results of EEG studies, which have revealed increased left-hemisphere activity in people who are anxious (Carter, Johnson, & Borkovec, 1986).

However, in some studies in which a variety of imaging techniques were used, more activity was observed in right than in left parietotemporal regions during anxious states (e.g., Buchsbaum et al., 1987; Reiman et al., 1984), whereas in other studies no asymmetries were found (e.g., Fredrikson et al., 1993). The variability of findings has thus made it difficult to make generalizations about brain activity and anxiety.

In an attempt to account for the inconsistencies in these data, Heller (1993a,b) suggested that anxiety and depression may be associated with opposite patterns of activity in the cerebral hemispheres, particularly in right parietotemporal regions. Recall that depression is associated with reduced activity in this area. If anxiety is associated with increased activity in this area, these opposing tendencies might tend to suppress each other in populations where both anxiety and depression are present. For example, if the level of depression in a given population of anxious individuals is high, a tendency toward higher right parietotemporal activity associated with anxiety might be canceled out or diminished by the tendency toward lower right parietotemporal activity associated with depression. Furthermore, such opposing tendencies would cause the patterns that emerge in different studies to be highly variable, depending on the ratio of anxiety to depression in the particular population under investigation.

These considerations will be important to take into account in future studies of people who are depressed and anxious, because the frequency with which anxiety and depression co-occur is high. Among individuals who meet *DSM* criteria for major depression or panic disorder (a severe form of anxiety), 25% of all patients who are depressed have a history of panic disorder, and 40 to 80% of all patients with panic disorder have had an episode of major depression (see Katon & Roy-Byrne, 1991, for a review). Furthermore, as the severity of symptoms decreases, the overlap between symptoms of anxiety and depression becomes even larger; 50% or more of all people with subclinical symptoms of depression or anxiety (i.e., some symptoms of major depression or anxiety neurosis but not enough to meet *DSM-III-R* criteria) have mixed symptoms (Hiller, Zaudig, & Rose, 1989). Thus, the variability among the results of studies of regional brain activity in anxiety may indicate that varying degrees of comorbidity of depression and anxiety existed in the samples.

Another possibility is that different types of anxiety may be associated with disordered function in different regions of the brain (see Heller, 1993b).

Distinctions have been drawn between panic, typically defined as a state associated with many physiological symptoms (including changes in heart rate, frontal electromyograms [EMGs], and temperature; see D. H. Barlow, 1991), and worry, defined for example by Carter, Johnson, and Borkovec (1986) as an "uncontrollable verbally mediated cognitive activity, or thoughts, about self-relevant issues, such as interpersonal relations, finances, and work . . . concerned primarily with future events" (p. 193).

When the data on brain activity and anxiety are examined from this perspective, we can clearly see that a number of the studies pointing to higher right-hemisphere activity in anxious states have involved subjects diagnosed with panic disorder or have focused on states of panic (e.g., Reiman et al., 1984). In contrast, the results of studies that have been interpreted as reflecting either no asymmetry or higher left-hemisphere activity have tended to focus on anxious states that might be better characterized as worry (e.g., Carter, Johnson, & Borkovec, 1986; Reiman, Fusselman, Fox, & Raichle, 1989; D. M. Tucker, Antes, Stenslie, & Barnhardt, 1978; S. K. Tyler & Tucker, 1982). Therefore, posterior

right-hemisphere functions may be associated specifically with fear or panic responses, whereas left frontal functions may be involved in the experience of worry, as suggested by Tucker and colleagues, especially to the extent that it involves verbal rumination. Further research is needed to clarify this issue.

Schizophrenia

Schizophrenia is a serious mental disorder that is the primary diagnosis for approximately 50% of all people in mental institutions in the United States. Currently, schizophrenia is viewed as a brain disease, although a diathesis-stress model has been strongly supported in its etiology.

Schizophrenia is currently classified into five types: disorganized, catatonic, paranoid, undifferentiated, and residual. Each type presents a somewhat different clinical picture, and the symptoms vary considerably among the types. Typically, however, patients show a combination of symptoms from a set of eight categories (Table 11.1).

Given the background you now have in neuropsychology, you can see, by looking at these eight

Table 11.1 Symptom Categories in Schizophrenia

Category	Symptom(s)
Content of thought	A delusion or false belief.
Form of thought	A formal thought disorder involving abnormalities in the way a person's thought processes are organized. "Loose association," in which ideas shift from one unrelated topic to another, is a common example of this type of symptom.
Perception	Hallucinations or the reporting of experiences for which no observable eliciting stimuli appear to exist.
Affect	Disturbed emotions. Most common are emotions that are blunted, flat, or inappropriate to the situation.
Sense of self	Confusion about self-identity. The person may feel unreal or controlled by outside forces.
Volition	Reduced motivation and interest in pursuing almost any sort of goal. These symptoms interfere severely with a person's ability to work.
Relationship to the external world	Withdrawal from the external world and preoccupation with internal fantasies and odd ideas. These symptoms are sometimes called *autistic*.
Psychomotor behavior	Abnormalities of movement, including rocking, pacing, stereotyped actions, and bizarre behavioral rituals. Some patients diagnosed with schizophrenia become almost totally immobile; others take on a disheveled look or dress oddly, against social norms.

categories, that many regions of the brain might be involved in schizophrenia. Content and form of thought might be related to the left hemisphere; perception and affect, to the right hemisphere, to subcortical areas, or to both; and sense of self, volition, and psychomotor behavior, to the frontal areas, to subcortical regions, or to both. Indeed, researchers have examined many aspects of function in patients diagnosed with schizophrenia and have used many methodological approaches in the process. Buchsbaum (1990) reviewed evidence from neuroimaging studies suggesting that schizophrenia involved pathology of the temporal lobes, the frontal lobes, and the basal ganglia, and argued that these three areas might be part of a single neural system that is dysfunctional in schizophrenia. However, the findings across studies are varied, and although brain abnormalities are persistently found, an integrated model of neural pathology in schizophrenia remains elusive.

Early studies using divided visual field techniques argued for a pathology of the left hemisphere, which was accompanied by an overactivation (R. E. Gur, 1978). Subsequent examinations using brain imaging techniques and electrophysiological recording have upheld the notion that some type of problem exists in the left temporal lobe. An overall reduction in the normal amplitude of the P_{300} component of the event-related potential (ERP) has been replicated a number of times in patients diagnosed with schizophrenia (see McCarley et al., 1993). Furthermore, these abnormalities have been found to be correlated with reductions in the amount of brain tissue present in the left temporal regions as measured by magnetic resonance imaging (MRI) (McCarley et al., 1993). These findings are intuitively appealing given the often dramatic symptoms of thought disorder, including bizarre verbalizations and nonlinear thinking, that such patients demonstrate.

In other studies, researchers have found evidence for frontal lobe pathology on behavioral tests like the Wisconsin Card Sorting Test (WCST) (Weinberger, Berman, & Illowsky, 1988); abnormally low distributions of blood flow to the frontal regions have been found in some studies but not in others (see Rubin et al., 1991). Evidence has also been found for tissue loss in these areas (Raz, 1993) and in related subcortical areas. Again, these findings make sense, given the difficulty with volitional behavior often seen in patients with schizophrenia. Similarly, frontal lobe and basal ganglia pathology seem likely to be implicated in the abnormalities of motor behavior, such as rocking, pacing, and stereotyped motor movements, often exhibited by such patients.

Efforts have also been made to relate the different types of schizophrenia to different patterns of neuropsychological and neurophysiological functioning (e.g., Bernstein, Riedel, & Graae, 1988). Another approach is to examine the specific symptoms (e.g., flat affect) and attempt to link them to specific neuropsychological substrates (e.g., Stolar, Berenbaum, Banich, & Barch, 1994). Although these attempts have been promising, we await further research for definitive answers. In the meantime, we can be sure only that schizophrenia involves brain pathology in a number of regions.

SUMMARY

Defining emotion is an issue that has long vexed psychologists. One early theory of emotion, the James–Lange theory, suggested that emotion is our experience of the internal state of our bodies. For example, when our blood vessels are dilated and we feel warm, we automatically experience that as contentment or happiness. Such a view of emotion does not consider the brain to play a direct role. Later theorists, such as Cannon, said that the brain plays an important role in evaluating the nature of experience. For example, although a similar physiological reaction occurs anytime a person cries, regardless of whether the individual has been cutting onions or his or her feelings have been hurt, the brain interprets this same bodily reaction in two different ways. Later theorists, such as Singer and Schachter, took an even more extreme position, suggesting that depending on the setting, the same physiological reaction could be interpreted in vastly different ways. More recent research, however, has revealed that different emotions do have certain physiological signatures (e.g., Levenson, Eckman, & Friesen, 1990), although not to the dramatic extent that was once envisioned.

Research in neuropsychology has shown that both subcortical and cortical areas of the brain play an important role in emotional behavior and experience. Subcortical structures of primary importance include the amygdala, the hypothalamus, and the anterior thalamus. Certain subcortical pathways are thought to be important in emotional responses that are critical for adaptive responding, such as recoiling in fear. These types of responses are thought to happen quickly, sometimes even before conscious evaluation of a situation occurs.

Cortical regions of the brain are important for three major aspects of emotional processing: the ability to perceive and interpret emotionally meaningful information, the ability to communicate and express emotion, and the experience of emotion. The right hemisphere of the brain plays a critical role in the ability to interpret emotionally meaningful information, whether it is conveyed in tone of voice or in facial expression. Right-hemisphere damage that results in the loss of these skills can have a profound effect on an individual's quality of life as well as on the quality of life of her or his loved ones. For example, the individual may have difficulty knowing when someone is being kind or cruel, which may lead to inappropriate responses, such as lashing out when someone is trying to lend a hand. These problems are compounded when an individual has anosognosia, a lack of awareness of his or her deficits.

Emotions are often conveyed in a manner that requires the types of skills for which the right hemisphere is best suited. For example, understanding someone's intent can often rely on interpreting the emotional expression on the person's face, and face processing is a task at which the right hemisphere excels. This fact has led some researchers to examine whether the right-hemisphere contribution to processing emotional information is above and beyond any involvement it has in processing the material in which the emotional information is embedded. Evidence to date from patients with double dissocia-

tions suggests that the two contributions may be separable. For example, electrical stimulation of parieto-occipital regions of the right hemisphere disrupts the ability to recognize faces, whereas stimulation to the posterior middle temporal gyrus impairs the ability to interpret facial emotion while leaving recognition of faces intact.

The brain regions that are important for communicating emotion through facial expression or tone of voice remain controversial although evidence suggests that they may rely on the right hemisphere. Some of the contradictory findings that have been reported regarding individuals with brain damage may arise because of variability in lesion location and cause of damage. In addition, the way in which emotional expression is measured may lead to some of the contradictory findings. For example, the results of studies in which individuals are asked to rate emotional expression generally support the hypothesis that the right hemisphere plays a role in the expression of emotion. In contrast, when a coding system that rates movements of certain facial muscles is used, the contribution of the right hemisphere does not seem to be as great.

The frontal regions of the brain have been found to play a critical role in the experience of emotion or mood. On the basis of clinical reports that patients with left-hemisphere damage generally exhibit different emotional states than those with right-hemisphere damage, some investigators suggested that each hemisphere has a different emotional valence: The right hemisphere is specialized for negative affect and the left for positive affect. More recent research, however, revealed that changes in mood after brain damage are associated with frontal regions, so that lower activation of left than right frontal regions is associated with sad or negative moods and lower activation of right than left frontal regions is associated with happy or positive moods.

Particular types of emotional disorders and psychopathology have been linked to the dysfunction of specific brain regions. Not surprisingly, given the preponderance of evidence that differences in activation of frontal regions are associated with certain moods, individuals with mood disorders, such as depression, tend to exhibit relatively higher activity of the right frontal lobe than that of the left. Yet, other brain areas have been implicated in depression as well. For example, individuals with depression also appear to do poorly on neuropsychological tests that assess the functioning of right posterior regions, which suggests that these regions of the brain may be functioning atypically. Making generalizations about brain mechanisms underlying anxiety disorders is more difficult because different studies have implicated different regions (e.g., the right hemisphere vs. the left hemisphere). Part of the difficulty in determining the neural underpinnings of anxiety may occur because anxiety and depression often co-occur. Furthermore, different types of anxious states (e.g., panic vs. worry) may exist, each of which has a unique neural substrate. A tentative suggestion that must be examined more carefully in the future is that panic is associated with higher right-hemisphere activity, whereas worry is associated with higher left-hemisphere activity. Schizophrenia seems to involve dysfunction of a number of brain regions, including portions of the frontal and temporal lobes of each cerebral hemisphere, as well as subcortical regions, such as the basal ganglia. However, variability exists across studies, which may occur in part because of the variability with which schizophrenia manifests itself. Although we know that schizophrenia involves brain pathology in a number of regions, the exact nature of the neural circuit that is involved has yet to be adequately described.

*A*rtistry

430

Loring Hughes was a successful artist, who, after sustaining right-hemisphere brain damage, was told that she would probably never paint again. She was determined, however, to persevere in the pursuit that she loved, even though many obstacles blocked her path. At first she was unaware that her drawing had "problems," only realizing the flaws in her creations when other people pointed them out. However, with time, the consequences of the damage began to become apparent to her. She discovered that she had great difficulty appreciating spatial relations; hence the shapes and lines she drew were distorted. This problem was particularly devastating because her trademark had been a realistic painting style. Unfortunately, no matter how much effort she devoted to replicating her traditional style, she was unable to produce just the right perspective, just the right line. Only gradually, over a period of years, did she learn to accept that her style would never be the same. Thankful that she could at least still draw, she decided to be more open-minded about what appeared on her canvases, refraining from asking whether what she painted was "correct" or not.

The process of adjusting to her new painting style caused Loring to gain new insights into the nature of artistic expression. Because her difficulties with spatial relationships precluded her from providing a real-life representation of the world on her canvases, Loring was forced to turn to her inner vision—to her imagination and her feelings. Previously she had used the outside world as the gold standard by which she judged her work. Now, with that standard removed, she found that she had more freedom of expression. As she became more comfortable with her newfound style, producing satisfying works became progressively easier for her. However, she still had difficulty with the idea of showing her newer work in public, especially because it represented such a profound change in her artistic identity. Finally, though, she took the plunge and went public with her new style. To her delight, the new work was accepted with critical acclaim.[1]

As the case study in the opening vignette illustrates, there are many methods and means of artistic expression (Figure 12.1). However, regardless of the method used, the successful completion of a work of art, whether realized in visual form or in sound, is likely to require the integration of a variety of skills, and hence, as is demonstrated at various points in this chapter, is likely to depend on many regions of the brain. Also in this chapter, we debunk the popular myth that only certain portions of the brain are critical to creativity whereas others interfere with artistic expression. For example, proponents of one drawing technique purport that better artistic skills can be gained by unlocking the artistic and sensitive nature of the right hemisphere only when the busybody left hemisphere is distracted or tricked into lessening its control (Edwards, 1989). Although this particular technique may make a person a better artist, the explanation for such an effect is likely to be false because, as we mentioned, artistic expression rarely relies solely on one region of the brain.

You might think that compared with other cognitive skills, such as the ability to process language or the ability to orient in space, artistic skills would be the least consequential to lose, unless art was your profession. Yet, the role that artistic expression and appreciation can play in an individual's quality of life and in rehabilitation from brain damage may be extremely important. Many of us have diversions, from writing poetry to playing the piano, from listening to music to watching movies. These activities serve as a release from tension and are a source of solace and contentment away from tribulations in other arenas of our life. If such diversions are no longer possible, the world becomes a more difficult

[1]Adapted from "New Territory: Creativity and Brain Injury," by W. Heller, 1991, *The Creative Woman, 11*, pp. 16–18.

A   B

Figure 12.1   A change in artistic style as a result of brain damage.
(A) An example of a realistic portrait by Loring Hughes before her brain damage. (B) An example of her less literal and more interpretative style after she sustained right-hemisphere brain damage. (*Note.* Reprinted with permission from "Cognitive and Emotional Organization of the Brain: Influences on the Creation and Perception of Art," by W. Heller, in *Neuropsychology* (pp. 277, 278), edited by D. Zaidel, 1994, San Diego, Academic Press. Courtesy of Loring Hughes.)

place in which to live. Furthermore, at least some researchers consider certain artistic abilities to be one aspect of the multifaceted nature of human intelligence. In his book *Frames of Mind,* Howard Gardner (1983) argues that we possess not only linguistic, spatial, and interpersonal intelligence, but musical intelligence as well.

In this chapter, we examine the neuropsychological contributions to three types of artistic endeavors: the visual arts, the musical arts, and the language arts. In the first major section of the chapter, we begin by considering the basic spatial and motoric skills underlying the production of art and the emotional influences on picture production. Next, we gain insight into the neurological underpinnings of the visual arts by examining the work of skilled artists who have sustained brain trauma. Afterward,

we discuss how the brain influences both the way we perceive and the way we remember art. In the second major section of the chapter, we explore the neural structures involved in processing the basic components of music, including pitch, rhythm, and melody. This discussion is followed by a review of the neural bases for musical memory. We then examine what the performance of highly skilled and creative musicians can tell us about the neurological bases for musical processing. In the final section of the chapter, we examine the neurological bases for the literary skills that allow us to write an engaging and moving novel (as compared with a term paper!).

In our exploration of these issues, a few general themes continue to reemerge. One theme is that, regardless of the type of artistic endeavor, artistic expression is truly a product of integrative brain functioning. Another theme is that because artistic abilities are multifaceted, many highly skilled artists can adapt their style of performance after brain trauma. Although these individuals' abilities differ after brain damage, often enough skills remain intact to allow for continued artistic expression, albeit in a different way. To begin our discussion, let's turn our attention to the visual arts.

VISUAL ARTS

By their nature, the creation and the appreciation of visual art require multimodal integrative functions. Consider the multiple processes that contribute to the creation of a piece of visual artwork. A visual artist is not simply a draftsperson who "copies" either external objects or vistas nor internally generated ones. Instead, the artist must generate an abstract idea for a piece of art. Often, this idea is one in which the artist attempts to make us see something from an unusual vantage point, whether a different perspective from which to view a landscape, a different political perspective from which to view an event, or a different emotional perspective from which to understand our world. This abstract idea must then be translated into an explicit mental image, which in turn must be translated into a series of motor commands used to mold clay, to manipulate a blowtorch, or to place paint on the canvas. Visual perceptual mechanisms are also required to provide feedback to the artist as to whether her or his actions are producing the desired effect.

The appreciation of art also requires multiple processes. Because the tools available to the artist to communicate his or her vision are devices such as color, perspective, lighting, texture, form, and composition, the viewer must process these visual attributes of a sculpture or a painting before he or she can appreciate the artist's work. Yet, such processing alone is inadequate. The viewer must also appreciate the overall composition of a work of art and its unique perspective, and he or she must often interpret the emotional feeling or tenor transmitted through a piece of art.

At this point, we examine in more detail the specific abilities that are required to produce visual art. Our discussion centers mainly on painting and drawing, but much of what is discussed can be applied to sculpture and photography as well.

Production of Art

Artistic expression clearly requires the integrity of some basic sensory and motor regions of the brain. Primary and secondary visual cortices are needed to process visual information about form, color, and motion, whereas primary motor areas are needed to allow for the fine motor control necessary to create brushstrokes or to delicately mold material. Above and beyond these basic perceptual and motoric skills, however, three categories of abilities are of paramount importance for artistic expression in the visual modality: visuospatial processing, planning of motor movements, and emotional expression. We next discuss each of these abilities in more depth.

Visuospatial Processing

As you might imagine, the ability to perceive spatial relations is of profound importance for artistic production. As we discussed in chapter 6, many spatial abilities rely on the posterior sections of the right hemisphere. Thus, you should not be surprised to learn that drawing is severely compromised by damage to this region of the cortex. Individuals with such damage often lose the ability to correctly produce the overall form of an item and in severe cases cannot even depict the most basic spatial relationships, such as two parallel lines instead of two intersecting ones. In less severe cases, the ability to depict such basic relationships is intact, but the interrelationships among parts of an item cannot be correctly arranged to produce an entire figure (Kirk & Kertesz, 1989; McFie & Zangwill, 1960). At times, individuals with right-hemisphere damage focus on depicting the details of an object and may include extra details that are irrelevant or may create pictures that are repetitive in content (Lezak, 1983), fragmented (Belleza, Rappaport, Hopkins, & Hall,

1979), or overblown in size (Larrabee, Kane, Morrow, & Goldstein, 1982). The result is often a complex picture with details that seem to have been slapped down one on top of the other without any particular rhyme or reason.

The specific nature of the visuospatial deficit is generally influenced by which area of the posterior right hemisphere is damaged. For example, difficulty in using color, which provides visual information about form, is more often associated with damage to temporal regions, whereas difficulty in expressing the correct spatial relations among items or parts of an item is often exhibited after damage to parietal regions. Such relationships make sense, considering that in chapters 5 and 6 we learned that visual information about form is processed more ventrally in the brain, whereas visual information about spatial location and orientation is processed more dorsally.

Damage to anterior regions of the right hemisphere can also lead to problems with visuospatial processing, such as difficulty in correctly depicting the relative size of items (Grossman, 1988). Difficulties in processing spatial relations may also be observed after damage to subcortical regions in the right hemisphere, either because these regions contribute directly to these abilities or because they disrupt pathways to cortical regions (e.g., Kirk & Kertesz, 1993).

Although the role of the right hemisphere in producing visual art should be obvious, what may not be so obvious is that the left hemisphere can contribute as well. One way in which this contribution can be clearly demonstrated is by comparing the drawings produced by individuals with left-hemisphere damage with those produced by individuals who sustained right-hemisphere damage, as shown in Figure 12.2. When an individual with a damaged left hemisphere (but an intact right hemisphere) is asked to draw pictures, the overall form, or gestalt, is correctly depicted, but certain features or parts are missing. Furthermore, the drawings tend to contain fewer details, lines, and angles than would be expected. For example, in the drawing of the bicycle in Figure 12.2A, the overall form is scantly drawn at best, but it nevertheless depicts a correct configuration. The same can be said of the drawing of the house: The details are conspicuously absent, but the general shape is certainly recognizable. Hence, having a damaged left hemisphere clearly diminishes a person's drawing abilities.

Right-hemisphere damage has a different effect. In this case, the overall gestalt of the figure is usually missing or distorted, although the details in the picture are produced correctly. For example, in the drawing of the bicycle in Figure 12.2B, the individual clearly has the wrong overall configuration because a bar extends to the bottom of the rear wheel. Certainly a bicycle created like this one wouldn't get very far very fast! Nonetheless, the drawing contains many details, including a light, fenders, and spokes on the wheels. Likewise, in the picture of the house the overall form is distorted and the left side is missing, a testimony to neglect. However, details such as windowpanes and bricks in the chimney are included (e.g., N. Gardner, 1974; Lézak, 1983). These separable effects of right- and left-hemisphere damage on drawing are reminiscent of a distinction we discussed in chapter 5 on the hemispheric differences in global and local aspects of spatial processing with the right hemisphere being most adept at processing the global form of items and the left at processing local information.

Although not a disruption in visuospatial processing per se, disorders in directing attention to particular regions of space can disrupt the creation of visual art as well. As we learned in chapter 7, damage to posterior sections of the right hemisphere compromises the ability to distribute attention evenly and consistently across both sides of space. When damage occurs to this region, neglect is often manifest in drawings (as seen in the picture of the house in Figure 12.2B). Generally, the left side of the page is left blank entirely or features of objects on the left are blurred, distored, or missing (Kirk & Kertesz, 1989). Although this tendency is particularly obvious in freehand drawing, it can also occur when patients are asked to copy or reproduce a picture, even a simple one of a flower or a clock, for example (J. Borod, Goodglass, & Kaplan, 1980). In fact, so common is the manifestation of neglect in drawing that clinicians often ask individuals to copy a picture as a means of detecting neglect. Thus, right-hemisphere damage can disrupt the creation

A   B

Figure 12.2 A comparison of drawings by individuals with left-hemisphere damage and drawings by patients with right-hemisphere damage.
(A) After left-hemisphere damage, the overall gestalt of an item is correctly depicted, but details are scant or absent. (B) In contrast, after right-hemisphere damage the drawings lack an overall gestalt and show signs of hemineglect. However, detailed information, such as the bricks in the chimney and the fenders and light on the bicycle, is retained. (*Note.* From *The Shattered Mind* (pp. 306–307), by H. Gardner, 1974, New York: Vintage Books.)

of visual art forms not only because it affects basic visuospatial processing abilities, but because it can impair visuospatial attention as well.

Motor Sequencing

Producing visual art requires not only an ability to understand the spatial relationships among items, but also the ability to plan and control motor commands (Warrington, James, & Kinsbourne, 1966). In this capacity, the left hemisphere plays an especially important role for two reasons: It is the hemisphere that controls motor output for the dominant hand of most people, and it is specialized for the

control of skilled movements that require fine motor control. Hence, damage to motor regions of the left hemisphere may severely disrupt drawing and painting by causing weakness or paralysis of the dominant hand. Left-hemisphere damage can also result in apraxia, which, as we learned in chapter 4, disrupts the production of fine skilled motor movements and the sequencing of such actions. Not surprisingly, such disorders seriously disrupt drawing abilities and other modes of visual artistic abilities. For example, Kimura and Faust (1987) reported that compared with patients who had damage to other regions of the cortex, patients with apraxia produced the largest proportion of poor drawings and exhibited impairments in almost every aspect of drawing.

Emotional Influences on Production

So far, we discussed the neural bases for various perceptual and motor skills required for the production of a piece of art but did not consider the role that emotion might play. Although at present the evidence linking particular brain regions to emotional aspects of artistic expression is scant, some intriguing findings suggest that the emotional state of a neurologically intact individual can influence certain aspects of picture composition.

The asymmetries in frontal activation associated with particular mood states (which we discussed in chapter 11) may induce concomitant motoric and attentional biases, which in turn may influence the composition of drawings. As discussed in chapter 11, negative moods are accompanied by greater activation of right than left frontal regions, whereas positive moods are accompanied by greater activation of left than right frontal regions. Greater activation of one frontal region that accompanies a particular mood may also induce a motoric and attentional bias to the side of space contralateral to the more active hemisphere. For example, when persons who are not depressed must respond to emotionally negative questions (which would induce greater right frontal activity), they tend to direct more eye movements to the left. In contrast, when responding to emotionally positive questions (which would induce greater left frontal activity), they direct more eye movements to the right (Ahern & Schwartz, 1979). Similarly, when responding to neutral questions, individuals diagnosed with clinical depression, who by virtue of their depression are likely to have greater right frontal activation, exhibit more leftward eye movements (Myslobodsky & Horesh, 1978). Hence happy moods are associated with motoric and attentional biases to the right side of space, whereas sad moods are associated with a bias toward the left side of space.

Heller (1986, 1987) hypothesized that these distinct patterns of brain activity observed during different moods might influence the way people position objects in space when they are creating a picture or a drawing. She proposed that when individuals are sad, they displace emotionally salient information toward the left side of the page because of higher activation of the right frontal region. Likewise, when they are happy, emotionally salient information is displaced toward the right side of the page as a result of higher activation of the left frontal region. To test this possibility, she had grade-school children draw pictures while they were experiencing particular emotions (because mood, but not the perception of emotional cues, is associated with asymmetrical activation of frontal regions; see page 421, chapter 11). The children were asked to draw three pictures: one of something that made them feel happy, one of something that made them feel sad, and one of anything that they wanted to draw. Because previous studies of school children's drawings suggested that human figures tend to be the emotional focus of their composition, the placement of these figures was compared in the various drawings produced during different mood states.

As predicted, the human figures in the "sad" pictures were significantly displaced toward the left (Figure 12.3A) relative to the position of the figures in the "happy" pictures (Figure 12.3B). A follow-up study performed with adults who were being trained as art therapists, and who viewed artwork as a medium for emotional expression, yielded the same effect, but even to a larger degree than in the children's drawings (Heller, 1986, 1987). The results of these studies suggest that the artist's mood at the moment of creation may be related to specific patterns of brain activity, which in turn affects the organization of space during the composition of a work of art.

In summary, the foregoing discussion has elucidated some of the neuropsychological influences on the creation of art in the cognitive, motor, and emotional domains. To date, research has identified several distinct aspects of cortical organization that play a role in artistic creation. These include the specialization of the right hemisphere for spatial and attentional processing, and the specialization of the left hemisphere for fine motor coordination and planning. In addition, the activity of the frontal regions, which are involved in emotional experience, may influence the creation of art. These influences may include the emotional "spark," or feel-

A

B

Figure 12.3 Influence of the creator's mood on artistic composition.
Shown here are two drawings by children who were told to draw (A) something that made them feel sad and (B) something that made them feel happy. Note that in the "sad" picture the emotional object (the human figure) is positioned more to the left than the one in the "happy" picture. (*Note.* From "Cognitive and Emotional Organization of the Brain: Influences on the Creation and Perception of Art," by W. Heller, in *Neuropsychology* (pp. 281, 282), edited by D. Zaidel, 1994, San Diego, CA: Academic Press. Copyright 1994 by Academic Press. Reprinted by permission.)

ing, that motivates creation as well as attentional effects on composition.

Skilled Artistic Production

Although massive brain damage clearly interferes with the artistic abilities of anyone, regardless of their degree of training, the few case reports about professional artists who sustained brain damage suggest that the effects are not as devastating as might be imagined. In many of these cases, neither right-nor left-hemisphere damage precludes the artist's capacity to continue to produce works of merit (see Levy, 1988; Winner, 1982). Rather, as in the case of Loring Hughes, the most common sequela tends to be a change in artistic style. In fact, even in the face of some persistent deficits, such as those associated with hemineglect, artistic expression can continue. For example, Lovis Corinth, a German impressionist painter who experienced a massive stroke in the right hemisphere, continued his career with great success despite severe left-sided neglect. However, his style of painting changed; it became bolder, more expressive, and less representational. A similar, more recent example is that of Reynold Brown, an American artist known for his exquisitely detailed Hollywood movie posters in the 1950s and 1960s. He experienced a stroke in the right hemisphere, and like Corinth, exhibited severe hemineglect. As vividly illustrated by a series of his drawings that were included in a special show at the Art Institute of Chicago associated with a symposium called "Art and the Brain" (1989), his neglect was severe at first (Figure 12.4A) but diminished with time. As he adjusted to this deficit, his drawing style changed in a way that appeared to minimize the effect of his neglect (Figure 12.4B). Rather than drawing people straight on so that both sides of the face were equally prominent, he began to draw faces at a 45-degree angle, possibly so that the information on his left was not so prominent.

Furthermore, his subject matter and other aspects of his style changed as well. Prior to his stroke, his work was characterized by fine lines and intricate detail (Figure 12.5A), afterward his lines became bolder and more impressionistic (Figure 12.5B). In addition, whereas previously he would conjure elaborate pictures in his mind and then create them on paper, after his stroke he could no longer do so. Because of this newfound need to rely on external models, he switched to painting landscapes.

Similar effects can be seen for artists who work in three-dimensional media. Ginny Ruffner, a contemporary artist known for her glasswork, sustained a severe closed head injury in a 1991 car crash and

A   B

Figure 12.4   Changes in the severity of hemineglect and artistic expression after a stroke.
Shown here are two pictures by the American artist Reynold Brown. (A) Soon after his stroke, his neglect is so severe that no part of the face is depicted on the left side of the page. (B) Later, the neglect has dissipated somewhat, but not completely. Although the parts of the figure on the left are more elaborate than those in the previous picture, details, such as the collar, remain missing. Furthermore, the faces are drawn at such an angle that the portion on the left is minimized. (*Note.* A, Reprinted with permission from "Cognitive and Emotional Organization of the Brain: Influences on the Creation and Perception of Art," by W. Heller, in *Neuropsychology* (p. 273), edited by D. Zaidel, 1994, San Diego, Academic Press. B, From *Natuur en Techniek*, 1991, vol. 1, pp. 50–51. Reprinted with permission of Wendy Heller and the Reynold Brown estate.)

was comatose for 6 weeks. After a long recuperation in which she had to "relearn" about art, she found that her aesthetic sense was altered. "I have a much more tolerant definition of beauty now," she says. "I include things that earlier would have been 'gaudy'—lots of gold, swirly decoration." In addition, the nature of her work changed to accommodate the long-lasting deficits sustained as a result of the accident. Originally left-handed, she now must rely on her right hand. To accommodate this loss of dexterity, she sculpts items that are much sturdier and less delicate than before. Previously known for addressing intellectual themes associated with the history of art, she now addresses more emotional and personal (as well as intellectual) issues in her work, perhaps as a result of the damage to her frontal

lobes that has made her mood more labile (Pall, 1995). Two of her works, one created before the injury and the other afterward, are shown in Figure 12.6.

Because brain damage may not rob the trained artist of all his or her artistic skills, some scientists have suggested that the neural organization for art production may differ between artists and nonartists. For example, some researchers have suggested that the right hemisphere is more crucial than the left for artists, but not for nonartists (e.g., Winner, 1982). In contrast, other investigators argue that the cognitive functions necessary for artistic expression are more bilaterally represented in the artist than in the nonartist (Levy, 1988). The consequence of such an organization would be that after

A

B

Figure 12.5 Another example of a change in artistic style after brain damage.
Both of these works are by Reynold Brown. (A) A drawing completed prior to his stroke, which did not rely on an external model but instead was the result of his imagination. Note the highly detailed nature of this drawing, which was one signature of his style. (B) A painting completed after his stroke. The brushstrokes are much bolder and more impressionistic than those in his previous work, and his subject matter, a landscape, is drawn from an external model. (*Note.* Reprinted with permission from "Cognitive and Emotional Organization of the Brain: Influences on the Creation and Perception of Art," by W. Heller, in *Neuropsychology* (pp. 275, 276), edited by D. Zaidel, 1994, San Diego, Academic Press.)

brain damage each hemisphere of the artist would be capable of carrying out activities that in nonartists are normally restricted to one side of the brain.

An alternative hypothesis, however, is that artists and nonartists have a similar brain organization and do experience the same kinds of deficitis after brain damage (Heller, 1994). However, artists may exhibit less severe deficits because their training has provided them with a larger toolbox of skills to apply to artistic creation. After brain damage, they compensate for their disabilities by using the tools and abilities that can still be wielded with craft, forsaking those that have been rendered useless by brain damage. This adjustment in the prominence with which artists use various tools would explain why brain damage often necessitates a change in style. In contrast, an unskilled person who can create by using only one technique will be unable to produce art if brain damage interferes with that one ability. Considered in this light, what may be more important in the skilled artist is not so much the honed perceptual and motor skills that artistic training imparts, as much as the ability to flexibly turn a creative vision into reality. From this perspective, we might speculate that frontal regions of the brain, which as we learned in chapter 10 are important for novel solutions to problems and for goal-oriented behavior, play a more critical role in artistic expression, especially after brain damage. This speculation, however, must await confirmation.

In sum, although brain damage can clearly affect the artistic production of skilled artists, in some cases the individuals have continued to produce art even after sustaining a large neurological insult. The result observed most often after brain damage in the skilled artist is a change in style that circumvents the loss of specific abilities. Whether this ability of artists to continue to create art after neurological insult results because they have a different brain organization than that of nonartists or because they have greater flexibility in artistic expression due to years of experience remains to be determined (see Heller, 1994, for a discussion of many of the issues raised in the preceding section).

Perception of Art

Until this point, we discussed the neurological bases for the production of art rather than its perception. Generally, when we view a painting or a sculpture, we assume that whether we like it or not depends

A

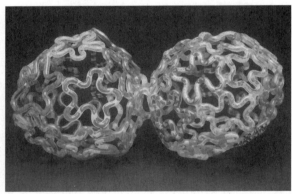

B

Figure 12.6   Two pieces of artwork created by a contemporary glass artist Ginny Ruffner.
(A) This piece, entitled "Beauty Deconstructing Portraiture," was produced in 1990, 1 year before her injury, and exhibits many of the characteristics of her art from that period. Note how delicate and fine the piece is. The subject of the piece concerns art history, in particular classic depictions of the female face in the canon of Western art. (B) This piece, entitled "The Hemispheres of the Brain Containing Pattern," was produced in 1993, 2 years after her injury. Note that the glasswork is much sturdier and that the subject of the piece is especially poignant and personally relevant given the artist's recent personal history. (*Note.* From "Starting from Scratch," by E. Pall, 1995, *The New York Times Magazine*, September 24, pp. 40, 43. Courtesy of Ginny Ruffner. Photos by Mike Seidl.)

on our individual artistic and aesthetic sensibilities. However, in certain circumstances the neurological organization of the brain may influence not only what we view as aesthetically pleasing or distasteful, but also what we remember about a piece of art. Such findings are another bit of evidence indicating that the organization of the nervous system influences the way in which we perceive the world. We now examine these findings in more detail.

Aesthetic Preference

One of the more intriguing findings regarding the neurological bases for artistry is that the organization of your brain may influence what you view as aesthetically pleasing. To investigate whether a person's brain organization influences his or her aesthetic preference, Levy (1976) asked right-handed individuals to view mirror-imaged pairs of vacation slides of scenic vistas photographed at various locations around the world. For each pair, the individuals decided which of the two mirror-image slides was more aesthetically pleasing. Because the visual content of the slides was identical regardless of its orientation (i.e., mirror-image or not), a preference among all individuals for the slide in one orientation over the other would indicate a communal aesthetic preference. Levy found that right-handed individuals clearly agreed that they preferred one orientation of the slide over the other for a small but significant proportion of her slides, about 10%. For the other slides, the individuals did not indicate a consistent preference; some liked one orientation, and others liked the opposite orientation.

Levy then wanted to know what factors made right-handers strongly prefer this small group of slides in one orientation rather than the other. To find the answer, she asked a new group of individuals to view these slides in their preferred orientation. When asked whether the most important content in these slides was situated to the left, to the right, or equally balanced on both sides, these individuals judged the slides to have their most interesting content on the right. In contrast, slides that were liked equally well in both orientations were not judged to have important content asymmetrically located to one side. These findings suggest that when a picture is considered more aesthetically pleasing in

PREFERRED PICTURES   NON-PREFERRED PICTURES

A   B

Figure 12.7   Brain organization and aesthetic preference.
Shown here are two slides that right-handers find more aesthetically pleasing in one orientation than in the mirror-image orientation. (A) The preferred orientation. The more interesting or more important content is asymmetrically represented on the right. (B) The nonpreferred orientation. (*Note.* Reprinted from *Neuropsychologia*, vol. 14, J. Levy, "Lateral Dominance and Aesthetic Preference," pp. 431–445, Copyright 1976, with kind permission from Elsevier Science, Ltd., The Boulevard, Langford Lane, Kidlington OX5 1GB, UK.)

one orientation than in its mirror image, the preferred orientation will have the more interesting or more prominent material situated to the right rather than to the left (Figure 12.7).

Levy went on to further demonstrate that the organization of the brain influences aesthetic preference because the same 10 slides that right-handers strongly preferred in one orientation were judged by left-handers to be equally pleasing in either orientation. This finding suggests that the organization of a right-hander's brain somehow induces the aesthetic bias, a bias that is not induced by the brain organization of left-handers (Levy, 1976). This basic phenomenon is well substantiated. It has been replicated by numerous other researchers, who used vacation slides (Banich, Heller, & Levy, 1989), simple compositions of drawings (Beaumont, 1985),

and in one experiment works of art (McLaughlin, Dean, & Stanley, 1983).

Although the influence of brain organization on aesthetic preference has been observed in numerous studies, researchers do not have a clear answer as to what mechanism induces the bias, although a number of possibilities exist. When she first observed this phenomenon, Levy (1976) suggested that the preference for slides with right-biased content occurred as a means of balancing an intrinsic bias of right-handers' brains to pay more attention to the left side of the slide. Her idea was that aesthetic judgments require complex visuospatial analysis, which would cause the right hemisphere of right-handers to become more active. This greater activity would induce an attentional bias to the left side of the picture, which would make it seem more

Preferred slide   **Nonpreferred slide**

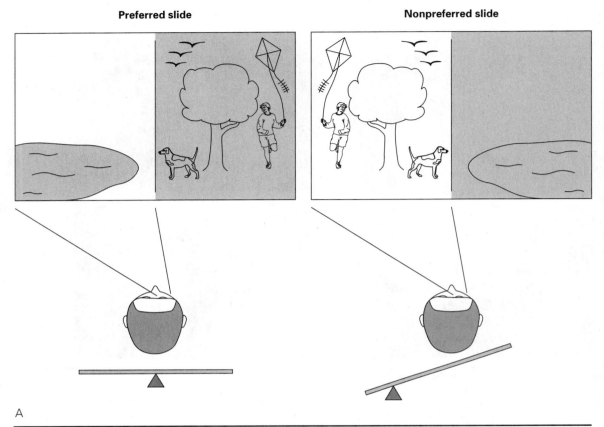

A

Figure 12.8   Possible explanations for right-handers' bias for pictures that have detailed content on the right.
(A) According to Levy, the complex visuospatial analysis engendered by a judgment of aesthetics induces greater right-hemisphere activation, which in turn causes an attentional bias toward the left side of space. In the pre-ferred slide, this attentional bias is counteracted by the busier content of the right side of the slide, which makes it appear more balanced and hence more aesthetically pleasing. In contrast, in the nonpreferred slide, the busier content on the left accentuates the leftward attentional bias, which makes the slide appear unbalanced and hence not aesthetically pleasing. (B) According to Beaumont, the location of busier content influences fixation. In the preferred slide, fixation is drawn to the more interesting right side, which means that most of the slide falls within the left visual field (LVF) and can be processed by the right hemisphere, which is specialized for complex visuospatial processing. In contrast, in the nonpreferred slide, fixation is drawn to the left side, which causes most of the slide to fall in the right visual field (RVF), where it must be processed by the left hemisphere, which is not adept at complex visuospatial processing. (C) According to Banich, the compatibility between the hemi-spheric mode of processing and slide content is important. In the preferred slide, detailed information in the RVF projects to the left hemisphere, which is specialized for local processing, and holistic aspects of the picture in the LVF project to the right hemisphere, which is specialized for global processing. In the nonpreferred slide, a mis-match occurs between the hemispheric mode of processing and the information being received: The right hemi-sphere receives local information and the left receives global information.

Preferred slide   **Nonpreferred slide**

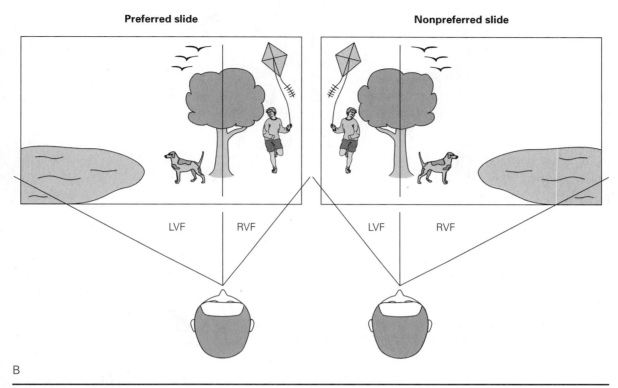

B

Figure 12.8   (Continued)

prominent. Hence, right-sided content would offset this left-sided bias, and make the picture appear more "balanced" and thus aesthetically pleasing. In contrast, left-handers, in whom visuospatial functions are more symmetrically organized, would not have a strong leftward attentional bias during visuospatial processing. Hence, they would find the pictures equally aesthetically pleasing regardless of orientation (Figure 12.8A).

Other researchers, however, provide different explanations for the effect. Beaumont (1985) has suggested that more important content on the right of the picture causes the eyes to fixate there, which means that most of the picture is situated in the left visual field (LVF). Hence, most of the picture projects directly to the right hemisphere, which is specialized for visuospatial processing in right-handers, and this leads the individual to judge the slide as more appealing (Figure 12.8B).

Another suggestion is that hemispheric differ-

ences in global and local aspects of a stimulus may affect aesthetic preference (see page 108–109, chapter 3) (M. T. Banich, unpublished manuscript, 1993). According to this explanation, slides are preferred when their orientation allows detailed information to be projected to the left hemisphere (which is superior at local processing) and holistic information to be projected to the right hemisphere (which is superior at global processing). When the mirror-image orientation is viewed, the person experiences a mismatch between the hemispheric mode of processing and the information being received (i.e., detailed information goes to the right hemisphere and holistic information projects to the left) (Figure 12.8C).

Still another possible mechanism for the phenomenon is based on hemispheric differences in emotional processing. According to this idea, the more interesting content on the right causes attention to be drawn to that side of space, which results

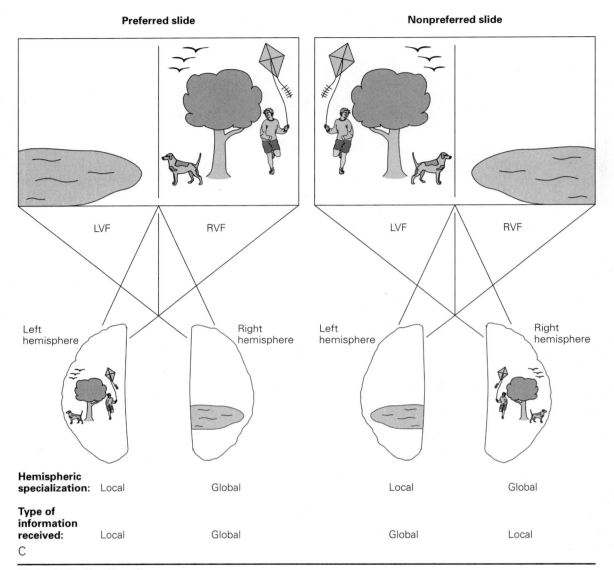

Figure 12.8 (Continued)

in activation of the contralateral hemisphere (the left). As discussed in chapter 11 and reviewed earlier in this chapter, greater activation of the left hemisphere, specifically the frontal regions, biases people toward a positive, cheerful, and optimistic view of the world, which would influence the viewer to see a picture as more aesthetically pleasing. This explanation is plausible because adults (Davidson, 1984) and children (Heller, 1988, 1990) will judge the identical picture as more negative when it is presented in the LVF than when it is presented in the right visual field (RVF), regardless of the emotion that the picture is expressing (see Heller, 1990).

At present, which of these four hypotheses best explains the preference for compositions with right-biased content is unclear. What is clear, however, is that although the effect has been observed numerous times for vacation slides and advertisements, it does not occur for recognized works of art, such as famous paintings (Freimuth & Wapner, 1979; McLaughlin, Dean, & Stanley, 1983), which in some cases may even be considered more pleasing when the most detail appears on the left (Mead & McLaughlin, 1992). Heller (1994) has argued that this dissociation favors the last of the four explanations. She notes that the first three explanations all assume that the effect is due to hemispheric differences in information processing—regardless of whether those differences affect the balance of a picture, affect which hemisphere does the majority of visuospatial processing, or affect which hemisphere receives local information and which receives global information. She argues that these three explanations suggest that similar preference should be observed regardless of whether the composition is a slide or a famous painting. However, if the effect is due to hemispheric differences in emotional processing, we may be able to explain the dissociation. Famous paintings differ from advertisements and vacation slides in that the artist's purpose may not be to create an enticing picture that will induce a positive emotional state in the viewer, unlike the advertiser, who wants to make the viewer like the product enough to buy it, or the individual who wants to have fond memories of a particular trip. An artist's skill may lie in her or his ability to arouse surprise, shock, wonder, or fear. In fact, an artist may have little desire to produce an optimistic, cheerful experience for the viewer. In such a case, the artist would not create a picture in which the more salient information is on the right because she or he is not interested in inducing a positive mood but is trying to evoke some other emotion.

Thus, although our sense of aesthetics and our appreciation of artistic creations appear to be influenced by the organization of the brain, researchers have not yet empirically determined whether this phenomenon is induced by hemispheric differences in information processing or hemispheric differences in emotional processing.

Memory for Artwork

In the previous section, we discussed factors that influence the way in which we perceive artwork while we view it. However, what if we are not judging a piece of art in front of us but instead are trying to remember a painting that we encountered previously? Although few researchers have investigated the neural bases for remembering artwork, the data that do exist suggest that the right hemisphere may play a more prominent role than the left, which is not surprising given the nonverbal nature of artwork. In a series of studies designed to examine another issue, namely the role of frontal and temporal regions in memory, B. Milner (1982) found that memory for abstract designs and drawings of common objects is disrupted by right temporal lobe lesions that include the hippocampus. Damage to right, but not left, frontal regions, will disrupt remembering which of two abstract paintings or line drawings was viewed most recently. These findings are consistent with what we learned in chapter 5 about the role of the right hemisphere in spatial memory and with what we learned in chapters 5 and 9 about the role of temporal and frontal regions in different types of memory.

Another approach to examining hemispheric differences in memory for artwork is to initially present pictures in central vision to neurologically intact individuals and then to assess the memory of each hemisphere for these pictures by presenting them again either in the RVF or in the LVF (e.g., D. W. Zaidel & Kasher, 1989). In one study, memory for two types of paintings was examined: realistic paintings, which conform with the characteristics of the world as we know it, and surrealistic paintings, which portray impossible representations of objects. Memory for the realistic paintings was identical regardless of the visual field in which the pictures were presented, whereas for surrealistic paintings, superior performance was observed in RVF trials. Furthermore, when the pictures were assigned metaphoric or literal titles, the surrealistic-metaphoric pairs were better remembered when they were presented to the RVF than when they were presented to the LVF. These findings have been interpreted to indicate that the left hemisphere is superior to the right in transcending the constraints of concrete reality and that this hemisphere demonstrates less rigid (i.e., more flexible) thought patterns (D. W. Zaidel & Kasher, 1989). However, another possibility is that the right hemisphere is more sensitive to the relations among items in the world, and violations of these relational categories may make remembering surreal items more difficult (Heller, 1994).

Now that we discussed the multifaceted nature of the skills involved in the production of visual art in general and in the production of visual art by artists who sustained brain trauma, as well as the hemispheric contributions to aesthetic preference and memory for artwork, we turn our attention to similar issues within the domain of music.

MUSICAL ARTS

In discussing music, we must differentiate between the ability to perceive music and the ability to perform it, much as we distinguished between the perception and the production of visual art. Thus, we begin by discussing the ways in which music is perceived by the brain. From there, we go on to discuss the brain regions that are involved in musical performance.

Basic Components of Music

In this section, we first consider the basic components of music and the neural mechanisms that underlie their perception.

Pitch

One of the most basic attributes of music is pitch, which is the listener's perception of the frequency of the sound waves comprising a musical sound. The frequency of a sound is measured in units of Hertz (Hz, or cycles per second). In music, each musical sound of a distinct frequency is known as a note. Thus, in more common parlance, pitch indicates how high or low a note is. Notes of different frequencies, and hence different pitches, sound distinct to us. For example, the frequency of the note A (which is the note that the modern orchestra tunes to before a performance) is 440 Hz, whereas the frequency of the note middle C is 262 Hz. Because the frequency of C is lower than that of A, C sounds lower in pitch (Askil, 1979).

The ability to distinguish between two pitches appears to be a rudimentary ability of the nervous system that can be performed by subcortical areas. Although the primary auditory cortex has a tonotopic map so that different regions of it are maximally sensitive to different frequencies (pitches) (as we discussed in chapter 1, see pages 36 and 37), the major disruption observed after damage to primary auditory cortex is in localizing auditory signals in space rather than in the ability to distinguish one pure pitch from another (e.g., Sidtis & Volpe, 1988). Thus, the computation of pure pitch appears not to require cortical areas but can be performed by subcortical auditory areas instead.

Music often consists of multiple tones, or notes, occurring simultaneously in time. When these tones temporally co-occur and their frequencies have a certain relationship to one another, they are called a **chord.** Chords fall into different classes depending on the relationship among the notes (usually three) that form the chord. For example, major chords are often perceived as sounding "happy," whereas minor chords are generally perceived as "sad." The only difference between a major chord and a minor chord is that the middle note of the minor chord is a little lower in pitch than that of the major chord.

When more than one tone is present, the brain receives a sound spectrum because there are different frequencies at which bands of energy are present in the sound (sound is energy in the form of pressure waves). For example, if the note middle C is played on a piano simultaneously with the note E, there are two bands of sound energy, one at 262 Hz (C) and another at 330 Hz (E). When a chord is played, a sound spectrum reveals the basic frequencies at which sound energy is produced and the degree of sound energy at each of those frequencies. Often, complex sounds consist of not only the basic components of the chord, but also harmonics of particular frequencies. A *harmonic* is a band of energy that is an integer multiple of the frequency of the basic tone, which is called the *fundamental*. For example, if the fundamental has a frequency of 262 Hz (middle C), its second harmonic will have a frequency of 524 Hz (in music, the second harmonic is called an *octave*). The third harmonic is the frequency of the fundamental multiplied by 3 (e.g., 786 Hz). Such spectral information provides important cues for distinguishing among different sounds.

Although subcortical areas can process a single tone, cortical regions, particularly those of the right hemisphere, appear to be important when the sound comprises a variety of pitches. For example, in one study, individuals with right- but not left-hemisphere damage had difficulty performing a dichotic listening task in which they were asked to discriminate complex tones (Sidtis & Volpe, 1988). Another study provided more precise localization for this ability, demonstrating that Heschl's gyrus of the right temporal lobe is critically important for complex pitch discrimination. In this study, such discrimination was tested in four groups of neurosurgical patients: those who underwent left temporal lobe removal that spared Heschl's gyrus, those who underwent right temporal lobe removal that spared Heschl's gyrus, those who underwent left temporal lobe removal including Heschl's gyrus, and those who underwent right temporal lobe removal including Heschl's gyrus. These patients' task was to decide whether the perceived pitch of two sets of tones went up or down. The tricky aspect of this task, however, was that the information needed to judge the perceived pitch of the two sets was missing from the actual stimuli. For example, tones at 600, 800, 1000, and 1200 Hz were presented simultaneously (Set 1), followed by the simultaneous presentation of tones at 600, 900, and 1200 Hz (Set 2). Notice that in both sets the individuals heard frequencies covering the same range—600 to 1200 Hz. However, each set had a different fundamental frequency. For the first set, the fundamental frequency was 200 Hz, and the tones that were presented represented the third, fourth, fifth, and sixth harmonics, respectively. In contrast, the fundamental frequency for the second set was 300 Hz because the tones that were presented represented the second, third, and fourth harmonics, respectively. Even though the fundamental was not present in the stimuli, a person who could discriminate complex pitches would hear a difference between the two sets of sounds because the fundamental could be inferred: The individual would perceive the second set as higher in pitch because its fundamental frequency, 300 Hz, was higher than that of the first set, 200 Hz (Figure 12.9A). In the control task, the same two sets of tones were presented, except the fundamental was now included in each set; consequently, the individual would not need to infer it on the basis of other information (Figure 12.9B).

All four patient groups could perform the task when the fundamental was present. However, when the fundamental frequency was missing, the group who underwent right temporal lobe removal including Heschl's gyrus was the only group that performed more poorly than neurologically intact individuals. These results implicate this brain region as critically important for the task (Zatorre, 1988). A corroborative piece of evidence implicating right temporal regions in extracting fundamental pitch information from complex sound spectra comes from the finding that individuals with right-hemisphere damage who have difficulty interpreting prosody tend to have specific difficulty processing it with regard to its fundamental frequency (Robin, Klouda, & Hug, 1991).

Evidence from positron emission tomography (PET) studies also indicates that the right hemisphere is involved in pitch perception of complex tones, even when that information is embedded within verbal information. Brain activation as measured by PET was compared in two conditions: one in which the individual heard two words and had to decide whether the second word had a higher pitch than the first, and one in which the same individuals just passively listened to speech. An increase in activation over the right prefrontal cortex was observed in the pitch condition relative to the passive listening condition. This increased activation is specific to pitch because it did not occur when individuals had to monitor for a phonologic attribute of speech (e.g., had to determine whether two words had the same final consonant) (Zatorre, Evans, Meyer, & Gjedde, 1992). Because prefrontal areas have been implicated in working memory in studies of both humans and animals (see page 361, chapter 9, and page 392, chapter 10), researchers have suggested that the right prefrontal area may be especially important for the on-line maintenance of pitch information.

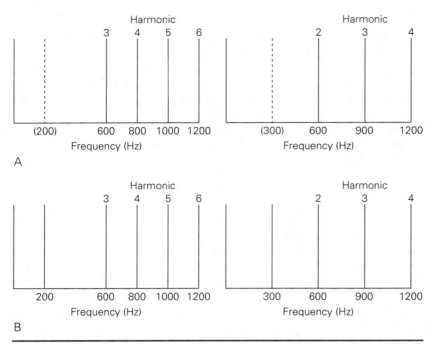

A

B

Figure 12.9 Musical stimuli used to examine the perception of complex pitch.
(A) Shown here are two musical stimuli in which the fundamental is absent. The missing fundamental is depicted by a dotted line and its frequency is noted in parentheses. The range of frequencies is similar for both stimuli (600–1200 Hz). To determine that the sound spectrum on the right is higher than that on the left, the fundamental must be deduced from the relationship of the component sounds. Patients with right temporal lobe damage that includes Heschl's gyrus cannot perform this task. (B) This depicts two musical stimuli in which the fundamental is present; hence no deduction is necessary to perform the task. Patients with right temporal lobe damage that includes Heschl's gyrus can perform this task. (*Note.* Adapted from Zatorre, 1988.)

Rhythm

Another important aspect of a musical composition is **rhythm,** which is the temporal relationship among sounds. Music consists not only of notes (having particular pitches) but also of each note having a specific duration of time. Because the left hemisphere is specialized for precise temporal processing, we might suspect that it plays an important role in rhythmic processing. However, in actuality, the results of empirical studies are equivocal.

The results of some studies indicate small or nonexistent hemispheric differences in processing rhythm. For example, B. Milner (1962a) found that the perception of rhythmic processing was not disrupted by either left or right temporal lobectomy, and other investigators found that damage to central regions of either hemisphere as well as right anterior damage can disrupt a sense of rhythm (e.g., Shapiro, Grossman, & Gardner, 1981). Other researchers, however, found a left-hemisphere superiority either for the detection of sounds with varying temporal parameters or for the production of rhythm. For example, Robin, Tranel, and Damasio (1990) asked small groups of patients with damage to one hemisphere or the other to perform numerous tasks requiring precise temporal processing of tones, such as determining which two tones in a series of six were offset by a smaller temporal gap than the others. The patients with left-hemisphere damage performed poorly on these temporal tasks, even though they had no difficulty with tasks requiring an analysis of pitch, such as adjusting an unmarked dial to change the pitch of one tone so that it matched a target tone. Wada studies (see chapter 3, pg. 99) also provide evidence for a greater degree of left-hemisphere participation in rhythm. An injection of sodium amobarbital that anesthetizes the left hemisphere has been found to disrupt a person's ability to produce the correct rhythm when he or she is singing (J. W. Gordon & Bogen, 1974), whereas right-hemisphere deactivation does not interfere with the production of musical rhythm (although under such circumstances tonal control is lost) (Borchgrevink, 1980). Thus, when hemispheric differences in rhythm are found, they tend to suggest a greater role for the left hemisphere.

Melody

In music, when pitches occur in a series and they have a certain rhythmic relationship to one another, the result is considered to be a **melody.** Melody, therefore, combines both temporal and pitch aspects of musical processing. Results from studies of individuals with brain damage suggest that processing melody relies on two separate brain regions and that each makes a unique contribution. The ability to distinguish between two melodies can be compromised by damage to either the anterior right temporal lobe or Heschl's gyrus (of either hemisphere). Nonetheless, these two areas appear to make separate contributions because lesions that impinge simultaneously on anterior temporal regions of the right hemisphere *and* Heschl's gyrus in the right hemisphere lead to poorer performance than if only one region is damaged. Although speculative, one idea is that damage to Heschl's gyrus interferes with a basic aspect of auditory memory that is required for comparing melodies, and that anterior regions of the right temporal lobe aid in more complex cognitive processing of melodic information. Thus, deficits are most severe when both mechanisms are simultaneously affected rather than when only one is compromised (Zatorre, 1985).

These findings hold not only for complicated melodies, but also for simple three-note melodies (Samson & Zatorre, 1988).

Musical Memory

So far we discussed the neural processing of abilities that are important for discriminating different aspects of music, such as pitch, rhythm, and melody, but we did not consider any situations in which these types of information must be retained in memory. The neural substrates that are important for discriminating pitch, rhythm, and melody overlap somewhat but are not entirely synonymous with those required to retain such information in memory.

As we learned previously, discrimination of complex spectral information relies on temporal and frontal regions of the right hemisphere. These same cortical regions are also important for short-term memory for pitch, but only when intervening or distracting material occurs between the two pitches. When individuals with cortical damage hear a target tone of a single frequency (e.g., the note C at 262 Hz) followed 1,650 ms later by a comparison tone, they have no difficulty determining whether the two tones are identical (which is consistent with findings that subcortical areas are sufficient for analysis of simple pitch). However, if any information intervenes between the presentation of the two tones, more specifically a set of six other tones, individuals with right temporal lobe and right frontal lobe damage perform poorly (Zatorre & Samson, 1991). Although the right anterior temporal region appears to be involved both in the discrimination of complex melodies and in short-term memory for pitch, it does not necessarily play the identical role in each task. Remember that the anterior temporal region and Heschl's gyrus appear to make identical contributions to short-term memory for pitch but distinct contributions to melody discrimination. Hence, this dissociation provides the possibility that anterior temporal regions perform different functions in each of these tasks.

The neural substrate for perceiving other musical or musically related information has also been found to differ from the substrate that is necessary for remembering such information. For example, although not specifically musical in nature, another situation in which the brain must process complex spectral information is when particular human voices must be recognized. Individuals with either right or left temporal lobe damage have an impaired ability to discriminate among the voices of people that the individuals do not know, although the ability to identify familiar voices is not disrupted. In contrast, the ability to recognize familiar voices is impaired after damage to right parietal regions (Van Lancker, Kreiman, & Cummings, 1989). In the case of melody, damage to right anterior regions or Heschl's gyrus of either hemisphere results in deficits in distinguishing between melodies, as we previously discussed. In contrast, temporal regions of both the right and left hemisphere are important for remembering a previously heard melody (Zatorre, 1985) or birdsong (B. Milner, cited in Zatorre, 1985).

Because both hemispheres have been implicated in memory for melody, researchers have attempted to examine whether each hemisphere plays a distinct role. After left-hemisphere damage, deficits in melody recognition are more likely to be observed when the task involves processing familiar melodies and when naming or identifying the melody is important. For example, in one study, patients heard a familiar melody unaccompanied by lyrics and had to identify a picture that went along with the melody. Patients with left-hemisphere damage did poorly when choosing the correct response depended on knowing the lyrics to the song (e.g., matching a picture of a boat to the song "Row, Row, Row Your Boat"). In contrast, patients with right-hemisphere damage did poorly when choosing the correct response required knowing the circumstances under which the melody is usually played (e.g., matching a picture of a person in a graduation gown to the graduation march) (J. Gardner et al., 1977).

Researchers have also examined the contribution of each hemisphere to memory for *songs*, which are melodies or tunes that are accompanied by words (Samson & Zatorre, 1991). In one experiment, individuals were taught obscure folk songs to ensure that they would have to learn both the melody and the words during the course of the experiment. After hearing the songs, the individuals were asked to listen to a series of items. Each item could be one of the following: one of the original songs, a new tune coupled with the same words as in an original song, the same tune as in an original song but with new words, or a new tune with new words. Individuals determined whether they had heard the song before, just the tune before, just the words before, or neither the words nor the tune before. As expected, left temporal lobe removal impaired the ability to recognize previously heard words. However, the researchers found to their surprise that patients who underwent right temporal lobe removal and patients who underwent left temporal lobe removal were both at-chance in recognizing the tune when an old tune was paired with new words.

Because these findings contradicted the expectation that the right hemisphere would be better at remembering the tune and the left hemisphere would be better at remembering the words, another study was performed. This time, rather than presenting words and tunes together as usually occurs in a song, the examiners presented a new set of individuals with *just* tunes or *just* words. Under these conditions, the distinct hemispheric contributions to musical memory were more apparent. Patients with left temporal lobe removal had poorer memory for lyrics than either patients with right temporal lobe damage or neurologically intact individuals did. In contrast, patients with right temporal lobe removal had poorer scores in tune recognition than those of either patients with left temporal lobe damage or neurologically intact individuals.

The authors interpreted their findings to suggest that the context in which a tune is heard influences the way it is stored in memory. Although the right hemisphere may be more sensitive to pitch and the left to words, when these features are combined in a song, they may not be stored in memory in a completely separable manner. For example, providing different words to accompany the same tune may alter the line of the melody (because different words have different phonetic properties) in such a way as to influence subsequent recognition (Crowder, Serafine, & Repp, 1990). You may have experienced this effect if you ever heard a song you know well in English sung in another language.

In such cases, you often don't recognize the song immediately because the words in the foreign language alter the tune enough to make it difficult to discern. The net result of all these studies is the suggestion that both hemispheres can contribute to memory for songs and that the more integrated the words and the tune, the more likely the contributions of the hemispheres overlap.

Skilled Musical Performance

In the previous sections, we discussed only the neural underpinnings of the regions of the brain that are important for the perception of music; we did not address how the brain influences musical production. This issue is much more difficult to examine because obtaining measures of brain activity during musical performance is nearly impossible, which may account for the scant amount of literature on the topic. Nonetheless, two points are clear from the fragments of information available. First, many component abilities underlie skilled musical performance, and these component abilities rely on diverse brain regions. Second, the brain modules used to read and write music are distinct from those used to read and write language.

Singing

One type of musical performance that has been examined from a neurological perspective is singing. In a handful of studies, researchers examined the effects of unilateral injection of sodium amobarbital on singing abilities and across these studies found that singing may be disrupted by either right- or left-hemisphere deactivation. However, the relative contributions of each hemisphere are difficult to determine because the patterns observed among individuals vary considerably (Zatorre, 1984). Nonetheless, one important point gleaned from such studies is that injections of sodium amobarbital (usually that which deactivates the right hemisphere) can disrupt singing but leave speech intact, which suggests that these two abilities are separate. This separability is noteworthy because it is consistent with evidence from other arenas (which is discussed subsequently) in suggesting that the ability

to process music and the ability to process language are distinct.

Instrumental Performance

Another means of investigating the neural bases for skilled musical performance is to use PET to measure regional brain activity during instrumental performance. In one such study, researchers examined the ability of musicians with 10 or more years of training to play a little-known partita by Bach (Sergent, Zuck, Terriah, & MacDonald, 1992). While in the PET machine, the musicians played the piece with the right hand and simultaneously listened to their performance. To determine the different component skills required for such a performance, researchers used a large number of control conditions and a subtractive methodology to isolate the brain regions responsible for each component. The control conditions and the skills that these conditions most likely assess are listed in Table 12.1.

By comparing performance under these different conditions, we can determine which brain regions contribute to the different aspects of musical performance. When the person was actually playing something (which he or she did with the right hand), activation occurred in motor areas including the left motor cortex, the left premotor area, and the right cerebellum. Given what you learned in chapter 4 about motor control, this finding should not surprise you: Left motor cortex is required to control finger movement, left premotor areas contribute to planning movement, and the cerebellum aids in skilled motor performance (remember that cerebellar control is ipsilateral, not contralateral, which explains why right but not left cerebellar regions were active during right hand movement). Listening to musical scales activated auditory regions, more specifically the secondary auditory cortex of both hemispheres and the superior temporal gyrus of the left hemisphere (which was active regardless of whether the subject played scales or passively listened). When the person listened to a piece of music, which is a more complex task than listening to scales, activation was observed over the right superior temporal gyrus. This finding is consistent with data indicating

Table 12.1 Conditions and the Skills Each Assessed in the Instrumental Performance Study by Sergent, Zuck, Terriah, and MacDonald (1992)

Condition	Skills assessed
Looking at visual-fixation cross	Basic visual processing
Listening to scales on a piano	Hearing musical stimuli
Playing scales and listening to them	Performing motor movements related to music; processing auditory feedback
Looking at dots and responding manually according to the quadrant in which the dot is located	Processing the spatial location of an item and translating it into a motor command
Sight-reading an unknown piece	Translating musical notation to motor commands; processing novel information
Reading a score and hearing its performance on a piano	Translating musical notation to an auditory image; processing auditory feedback; processing novel information

that individuals with damage to this region exhibit deficits in many aspects of musical processing (e.g., melody discrimination, complex pitch analysis).

When the person read a musical score, visual areas were activated; more specifically, bilateral activation of extrastriate visual areas occurred. What was noteworthy was that the activity was centered in the left occipitoparietal junction, in a region dorsal to that activated during the reading of language. This finding suggests that reading words and reading musical notation rely on separate neural substrates. More dorsal regions may be involved in reading musical notation because this task places larger demands on spatial-processing abilities. In musical notation, specific notes have particular spatial positions on the musical staff, and the position of the note on the staff indicates how high or low it is in pitch. Furthermore, the distance between two notes indicates their difference in pitch (Figure 12.10).

The areas of the brain that are activated while a person is listening to music and following its musical score, a task that requires the ability to translate the musical notation to an auditory image of the piece, were distinct from those activated when the person was required to just read a score or just listen to the music. Because listening to music and following its musical score is a multimodal task, you should not be surprised that the focus of activation was in the parietal lobe of both hemispheres, more specifically the superior and posterior parts of the supra-

marginal gyrus. Like reading, this task requires a translation between a visual notation system and sound. Yet, the area of activation was adjacent to, but not identical with, the area that when damaged typically causes alexia with agraphia. This finding provides yet another piece of evidence that reading music relies on a different neural substrate than that of reading language.

Finally, during performance of the partita, two regions of the brain were activated that were not activated in any of the other conditions. The first region was the superior parietal lobe of both hemispheres. This region of the brain is probably important for deriving spatial information from the musical staff and linking it to motor performance. As we learned in chapter 4, the parietal lobe is important for guiding movements in space, such as moving your fingers in a skilled manner to play certain keys on the piano. The second area that was active was also motoric in nature: the supplementary motor area and the adjacent portion of the left inferior frontal gyrus immediately above Broca's area. Also as we learned in chapter 4, this region of the brain is important for planning and sequencing motor acts and probably plays a prominent role in planning the pattern of motor control for the fingers that will create the tune on the keyboard (Sergent, Zuck, Terriah, & MacDonald, 1992).

This study reveals that many abilities are required for skilled musical performance and that a multiplicity of brain regions are required to carry out these

F   G   C

Figure 12.10 The spatial aspects of musical notation.
In musical notation, each note has a particular location on the musical staff (which comprises five lines): either between two lines (as in the case of the notes F and C) or intersecting a line (as in the case of the note G). The higher the location, the higher the pitch (e.g., F at 343 Hz is lower in pitch than G at 384 Hz, which in turn is lower than C at 512 Hz). The relationship between the pitch of two notes is depicted in musical notation by the spatial distance between the notes. Because G is only slightly higher in pitch than F, it is located just a little above F, whereas because C is significantly higher in pitch than G, it is located substantially above G.

skills. Note that musical performance relies heavily on multimodal association areas because such performance requires multiple translations: from a visuospatial representation to an auditory pattern (in the case of following a score), from a visuospatial representation to a motoric pattern (in the case of playing a score), and from a motoric pattern to an auditory pattern (in the case of monitoring what you are playing). As an example, Figure 12.11 shows the multiplicity of brain regions that are activated for the sight-reading condition of this study.

Differences Between Skilled and
Nonskilled Musicians

Another way to attempt to understand the neural substrates for musical skills is to examine the effects of brain damage on skilled musicians. As done by Sergent (1993), surveying knowledge about 20th-century composers who had cerebral dysfunction can be informative, even though the consequences of brain trauma on composers can vary widely. Vissarion I. Shebalin (1902–1963), a Russian composer, had two strokes in his left temporal lobe, one at the age of 51 years and the other at the age of 57 years. Despite these strokes, his colleagues claimed that he experienced no loss in musical ability. A French organist and composer, Jean Langlais

(1907–1991) had a cerebral hemorrhage in the left temporoparietal region, which left him aphasic, alexic, and agraphic. Nonetheless, he retained the ability to read musical notes and the ability to compose and improvise. Benjamin Britten (1913–1976), a British composer, had a cerebral embolism that did not influence his musical skills, and George Gershwin (1898–1937) had a right temporal lobe tumor that was "silent" and did not affect his mental abilities until shortly before his death.

These case studies, however, should not be over-interpreted to suggest that all musicians are totally unaffected by brain damage. One of the most detailed cases of a musician whose abilities were affected by cerebral dysfunction is that of Maurice Ravel (1875–1937), who was studied during a 2-year period by the neurologist Théophile Alajouanine. Although the source of Ravel's illness has never been definitively determined, his symptoms suggest that he experienced progressive degeneration in a relatively focal area of the left hemisphere. Ravel's problems first manifested in the linguistic domain: One of his pupils noticed spelling errors

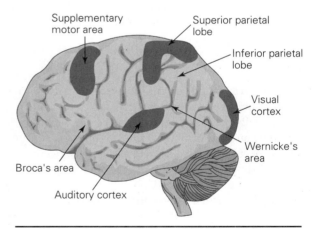

Figure 12.11 Regions of the brain active during the sight-reading, listening, and right-hand performance of a piano piece.
Shown here are the diverse brain regions activated as measured by positron emission tomography (PET). Notice that they include frontal, occipital, temporal, and parietal regions. Also notice that parts of the inferior parietal lobe that are important for reading words are not active. (*Note.* Adapted from Sergent, 1993, p. 169.)

Using Basic Aspects of Music as Therapy for Aphasia

As discussed in the text, music appears to rely on a different neural substrate than that used for language. One therapy for individuals with aphasia, Melodic Intonation Therapy (MIT), takes advantage of this dissociation to help these persons learn to speak more fluently. The basic idea behind this therapy is to aid the recovery from aphasia by engaging brain regions that are not traditionally involved in language (Helm-Estabrooks, 1983).

MIT highlights to patients the tonal and rhythmic qualities of verbal materials in a syllable-by-syllable manner. As the individual becomes more fluent in his or her production, the reliance on such cues is diminished. This therapy is hierarchically structured, consisting of three stages, and the ultimate goal is for the person to be able to produce language with normal prosody and cadence.

Stage 1 has five basic steps. During all of them, the clinician accentuates the rhythmic aspects of language by tapping the patient's left hand for every syllable that is said. In the first step, the clinician hums and then intones the target item, which generally is a multisyllabic word or a well-known phrase. For example, in the first step a person might say a sentence such as "Open the door" with the following tonal qualities:

High		O		door
Low			pen	the

In the second step, the patient and the clinician intone the items together. Once the patient can do this, the procedure is repeated, except the clinician fades out at the end of the phrase and lets the patient complete it without aid. Once the patient can master this step, the clinician intones the phrase and the patient repeats it immediately. In the last step, the clinician poses a question, and the patient must answer it with the target phrase. Thus, during these five steps, the clinician's role as a model increasingly diminishes.

Stages 2 and 3 increase the memory demands on the patient and reduce the reliance on tonal and rhyth-

on his scores and in his correspondence, even though he was still composing. With time, his language skills worsened so that he became alexic and agraphic and had a mild Wernicke's aphasia. About the same time, his musical abilities became more profoundly disturbed. He lost his ability to dictate music, to sight-read, to play from a score, and to play by heart. Most important, he lost his ability to compose. He claimed that although he could hear potential compositions in his head, such as an opera, he could not write them down. Despite these tragic losses in certain domains of his musical abilities, Ravel retained his ability to play scales, and his auditory abilities were intact. In addition, he could remember his compositions perfectly and had no difficulty determining whether a performer departed from what he had written.

Sergent (1993) has interpreted the pattern of Ravel's difficulties to suggest that his ability to translate musical representations across modalities was lost, even though his ability to process musical information in each modality was intact. For example, he lost his ability to sight-read, which requires the translation of a visual pattern into a pattern of motor movements. Furthermore, he was unable to compose because he could not translate the music in his head into notes. Nonetheless, his intact motor abilities enabled him to play scales, and his intact auditory functions allowed him to hear performances of his own pieces and know whether they were being played correctly.

The case studies of musicians who sustained brain damage allow two generalizations to be made about the neural organization of music. First, these stud-

mic qualities. In Stage 2, the corpus of phrases is expanded, as well as the length of the phrases. In addition, a delayed-recall condition is included so that the individual must wait at least 6 s before responding. In Stage 3, the subject must repeat phrases after a 6-s delay with a less exaggerated singsong manner until sentences can be produced in a normal manner.

Why does MIT seem to help patients with aphasia? As discussed in the text, musical and language abilities appear to dissociate, and the right hemisphere plays an important role in important aspects of musical processing. Thus, the creators of MIT suggest that this therapy allows intact right-hemisphere mechanisms to be invoked in the recovery process. More direct evidence for a role of the right hemisphere in MIT comes from a study examining the response of patients to this therapy. Individuals with lesions confined to the left hemisphere tended to respond well, whereas those whose lesions extend into the right hemisphere responded poorly. Hence, MIT was not effective when the right hemisphere was damaged, which suggests that this hemisphere plays an important role in the efficacy of MIT.

Notice that in MIT a linkage is made between language and music because music is used as a crutch on which the reacquisition of language processing rests. How are we to reconcile this type of therapeutic intervention with the idea that music and language are distinct? Although the brain's processing of language and music can be distinct, as we discussed, these processes can also be linked. In practice, language and music are often intertwined, such as when you sing a song. In fact, the study by Samson and Zatorre (1991), discussed in the text, suggests that although melody is predominantly processed by the right hemisphere, both the words and the melody of a song may become woven together in memory. Perhaps MIT is a useful therapy because although music has a somewhat distinct neural substrate for language, brain mechanisms that are damaged in aphasia do not impede the ability of music and language to interface in useful ways.

ies, especially that of Ravel, suggest that like other complicated cognitive functions, musical ability is not a unitary entity. Rather, it is composed of many subskills (sight-reading, composing, memorizing a piece, playing a piece), some of which can be lost after brain damage while others are retained. Currently, there are not enough case studies to provide clear evidence from double dissociations that different musical subskills are independent (e.g., sight-reading and composing). Nonetheless, the evidence to date suggests at least some separability of different musical functions in the brain. The second generalization that can be made is that the neural substrates underlying musical skills are distinct from those for other cognitive abilities. In numerous cases, musicians have sustained brain damage that interferes with other cognitive abilities but spares musical skill. This dissociation is particularly clear with regard to language because in a number of cases composers with severe language problems retained their musical ability. Moreover, the cases of Shebalin and Langlais corroborate the conclusion of PET studies that reading music and reading words are separate abilities.

Musical skills may be separable from other cognitive skills in musicians, in part, because of training that causes musicians to approach musical tasks differently than nonmusicians do. For example, in one study, when nonmusicians listened to dichotic melodies, they exhibited a left-ear advantage, whereas trained musicians who listened to the same melodies exhibited a right-ear advantage (Bever & Chiarello, 1974). In another study (Hirshkowitz, Earle, & Paley, 1978), the electroencephalographic (EEG) responses to musical chords differed between individuals with musical training and those without, whereas EEG responses to linguistic or atonal stimuli did not. Consistent with the Bever and Chiarello findings, greater left-hemisphere involvement was found on the part of trained musicians. However, differences between musicians and nonmusicians are not always observed (see Messerli, Pegna, & Sordet, 1995, for a discussion of this issue).

When differences *are* observed between musicians and nonmusicians, what might account for the disparity? Generally, musical tasks can be performed in multiple ways, and musical training is likely to influence the strategy that a person uses. For example, in the case of chords, a musically naive individual hears some notes played simultaneously and derives a general feeling about them, such as that they sound upbeat or sorrowful. In contrast, the musically trained individual knows that a chord is composed of three notes that have a particular relationship to one another. The trained musician also knows that chords that sound "happy" tend to be major chords whose middle note is slightly higher in frequency than the middle note of minor chords, which tend to sound "sad." Thus, the trained musician understands the relationship between the components of the sounds he or she is hearing, whereas the musically naive individual does not. Under such conditions, the left hemisphere, which is more detailed and piecemeal in its approach to analyzing information may play a greater role in processing music for the musician than for the nonmusician.

In addition, some recent findings suggest that the brains of certain musicians may have specific characteristics. For example, one group of researchers found that the brains of musicians with perfect pitch are distinguishable from those of individuals without perfect pitch, musicians and nonmusicians alike. *Perfect pitch* is a relatively rare ability that allows an individual to hear a tone and immediately know its pitch (e.g., middle C). It is a skill that a person is usually born with and is rarely acquired through practice. Compared with nonmusicians and musicians without perfect pitch, individuals with perfect pitch have been found to have a larger asymmetry of the planum temporale (Schlaug, Jancke,

Huang, & Steinmetz, 1995). As you may remember from chapter 3, the planum temporale is a region of the temporal lobe near Wernicke's area (see page 91) that typically is larger on the left than on the right in right-handers. At first this finding may seem at odds with the evidence discussed previously that suggests that the right hemisphere plays an important role in pitch. However, musicians with perfect pitch can correlate a tone with a particular *verbal* label in a way that other musicians cannot, which may explain the importance of the left hemisphere.

Another structural difference that has been noted between musicians and nonmusicians is the size of the anterior section of the corpus callosum. In particular, musicians (keyboard or string instrument players) who started their musical training before the age of 7 years were found to have a larger anterior section of the corpus callosum than that of nonmusicians and musicians who commenced training after this age. The increased size of these anterior regions may reflect a developmentally influenced phenomenon in which early musical training on an instrument requiring bimanual coordination influences the development of frontal areas and their interhemispheric connections (Schlaug et al., 1995). As you may remember from chapter 4, the supplementary motor area, which is connected by anterior regions of the callosum, has been suggested to play an important role in bimanual coordination.

LANGUAGE ARTS

As we learned in chapter 8, the left hemisphere plays a predominant role in reading and writing, which are disrupted by lesions to the angular gyrus, and knowledge of the grammatical structure and the meaning of language relies on Broca's and Wernicke's areas, respectively. Hence, we should not be surprised to learn that left-hemisphere damage severely disrupts the ability for artistic creation in the linguistic domain. Does this mean, however, that the work of either the professional writer or the amateur storyteller is solely a product of the left hemisphere? Most probably not. As we discussed in chapter 8 (see page 309), the right hemisphere plays an important role in certain language-related tasks, such as making inferences and constructing a narrative. These abilities are important skills for a large number of literary genres. How intriguing would a mystery novel be if the author couldn't construct a coherent narrative that led you to infer which character was likely to be the murderer? How comprehensible would a science writer's article be if she or he couldn't explain, in a narrative fashion, the series of experiments performed by scientists and the inferences drawn from each? The ability to create a narrative and to use language so that people come to a common inference are skills very much required in the creative use of language.

Evidence that the right hemisphere plays an important role in understanding and constructing a narrative comes from various studies showing that individuals with right-hemisphere damage have difficulty extracting the theme of a story (e.g., Moya, Benowitz, Levine, & Finklestein, 1986) or using information about a story's theme to help them in other tasks, such as arranging sentences into coherent paragraphs (e.g., Schneiderman, Murasugi, & Saddy, 1992). Studies also show that these individuals have difficulty judging the plausibility of story lines, often responding with embellishments or confabulations (e.g., Hough, 1990), and have difficulty determining whether an utterance is relevant to a conversation—that is, judging whether it builds upon previously presented material (e.g., Rehak, Kaplan, & Gardner, 1992).

Another type of language processing that is often invoked in creative writing is the use of atypical or figurative language, especially in the creation of a novel or a poem. Nonliteral uses of language, such as metaphor, in which the author attempts to use language in a poetic, an atypical, or a nonconcrete manner (Lakoff, 1987), appear to be a type of language processing at which the right hemisphere is particularly adept (Winner & Gardner, 1977). For example, the statement "My job is a jail" doesn't literally mean that the speaker's job is just like a jail. Rather, the meaning is influenced by the viewpoint of the speaker and the listener (Glucksberg & Keysar, 1990). When someone who must punch a time clock everyday exclaims, "My job is a jail!" it is likely to be a statement about the lack of autonomy. The same statement said by a workaholic, however, is more likely to be a statement about how work confines the person's interactions with the outside world and other people. Hence, this type of language must be interpreted with reference to outside context, or what Lakoff (1987) calls the "experiential Gestalt." As we discussed in chapter 3, the right hemisphere is particularly adept at gestalt processing; hence its role in this type of language processing is not surprising.

The difficulties experienced by patients with right-hemisphere damage in interpreting metaphor do not appear to derive from more basic differences in how the hemispheres process language, such as in the organization of the semantic lexicon (mental dictionary of word meaning). The right hemisphere's access to a broader range of words (e.g., *scalpel* and *bandage* in response to *doctor*) than that of the left (e.g., *nurse* and *surgeon* in response to *doctor*) (Beeman et al., 1994) might be posited as leading to deficits in the processing of metaphor after right-hemisphere damage. Although a reasonable hypothesis, it is unlikely to be true because at least some studies suggest that patients with right-hemisphere brain damage have a specific deficit in retrieving metaphorical meaning above and beyond any difficulty in activating multiple meanings of a word. In one study supporting this conclusion, researchers examined the processing of words that have two meanings (H. H. Brownell et al., 1990). Some of the words had both a metaphorical and a nonmetaphorical meaning, such as the word *warm*, whose nonmetaphorical meaning is related to temperature and whose metaphorical meaning relates to an emotional state. Other words had two meanings but neither was metaphorical, such as *cabinet*, which can mean either "a cupboard" or "a group of advisers." For each word, subjects decided which of two probe words was its synonym. For example, for a metaphorical word such as *warm*, subjects would need to choose between the correct answer "loving" and the incorrect answer "blanket." For a nonmetaphorical word such as *suit*, they would have to decide between the correct answer "trial" and the incorrect answer "tailor." Patients with right-hemisphere damage had more difficulty making the correct decision for the metaphorical words than for the nonmetaphorical words, which suggests a selective right-hemisphere deficit in processing metaphorical language, not an overall difficulty in retrieving multiple meanings of words.

The evidence reviewed in this section suggests that the right hemisphere can contribute to the creative use of language in a number of ways. It appears to be important in constructing narrative and making inference, which are critical to any coherent story line. It also contributes to the use of language in a nonconcrete or nonliteral manner that makes reading a novel or a poem so enjoyable. Clearly, these abilities are linked with left-hemisphere language-processing mechanisms, which indicates that the language arts, just like the visual and musical arts, require the integrative action of different brain regions.

SUMMARY

All creative endeavors, whether they be in the visuospatial, auditory, or linguistic domains, require the integration of a large variety of skills that rely on distinct brain regions. As such, these endeavors are often affected after brain damage, and their loss is detrimental to an individual's quality of life.

Visuospatial skills, one of the basic classes of skills required for creation in the visual arts, can be compromised after both right- and left-hemisphere damage, albeit in different manners. After right-hemisphere damage, individuals have difficulty correctly depicting spatial relationships, particularly the gestalt, or overall form, of items. In contrast, after left-hemisphere damage, constructions tend to be scant and devoid of detail, although the overall form is usually depicted correctly. In addition, right-hemisphere damage sometimes leads to hemineglect, which can cause the left side of a construction to be ill formed or missing entirely.

Another important ability for the creation of visual art is skilled motor sequencing. Because most people are right-handed, damage to central regions of the left hemisphere leads to weakness or paralysis of the dominant hand, which in turn results in poor motor control. Apraxia, typically associated with left-hemisphere damage, disrupts the purposeful fine motor movements and the sequencing of such movements required for visual creations.

A third important component for creation in the visual arts is emotion, which appears to influence how pieces of art are composed. Sad mood states, associated with higher activation of frontal regions of the right hemisphere than of the left, are accompanied by an attentional bias to the left side of space, which causes both children and adults to place the emotionally salient object in their drawings to the left of midline. In contrast, happy mood states, associated with higher activation of frontal regions of the left hemisphere than of the right, are accompanied by an attentional bias to the right side of space that causes the emotionally salient object to be placed to the left of midline.

Another manner in which to investigate the neurological contributions to the visual arts is to examine the consequences of brain damage in skilled artists, which surprisingly often may not be as devastating as expected. These findings have led some researchers to suggest that the brain of an artist is organized differently than that of a nonartist— either with greater right-hemisphere involvement for art or greater bilateral representation of artistic abilities than that in nonartists. However, other researchers have suggested that similar brain regions are involved in composing art in artists and nonartists, but extensive training allows skilled artists to create in a more flexible manner, allowing them to continue to create art after brain damage. Supporting this viewpoint is the fact that artists who sustain brain damage often have difficulty resuming painting in the style that they used prior to injury and must revert to a new style that circumvents their reduced capabilities.

The organization of the brain also influences the way in which art is perceived. Two populations known to differ in brain organization, right-handers and left-handers, perceive art differently. When right-handers prefer a picture in one orientation rather than in its mirror-image orientation, the preferred orientation contains the more interesting content on the right. Left-handers, in contrast, show no such preference, presumably because their brains are less lateralized than that of right-handers.

Although the exact mechanism that creates such an effect has not been elucidated, the phenomenon is well substantiated. This effect most likely results either from hemispheric differences in cognitive styles of processing information or from hemispheric differences in emotional processing.

Memory for artwork appears to rely on neural structures similar to those responsible for memory for other complex visuospatial material. In particular, memory for abstract designs and drawings of common objects is disrupted by lesions to right temporal regions including the hippocampus. Memory for recency of abstract painting relies on right frontal regions.

The basic components of music are pitch and rhythm. The perception of simple pitch relies on subcortical regions because this skill usually is not disrupted by cortical lesions. However, when complex pitch must be analyzed, such as discerning that multiple notes are being played simultaneously, right temporal regions, specifically Heschl's gyrus, play an important role. Right frontal regions also play a role in pitch discrimination, such as in determining whether a pitch is rising or falling. The neurological basis for rhythmic processing is more controversial because the findings are conflicting. Nonetheless, when differences between the hemispheres are noted, the left hemisphere appears to play a larger role than that of the right.

In melody, the elements of pitch and rhythm are combined. Damage to anterior temporal regions of the right hemisphere or to Heschl's gyrus in either the right or left hemisphere disrupts the ability to process melody, and each region appears to make separate contributions because damage to both results in more severe deficits than those observed after damage to either region alone.

The neural substrates for memory of musical information appear to be distinct from those required for musical perception. Although the perception of pitch is processed subcortically, memory for pitch depends on right temporal and frontal regions, at least when intervening material occurs between the two tones to be compared. Likewise, whereas the

perception of melody relies on Heschl's gyrus and right anterior temporal regions, memory for melody relies on temporal regions of either hemisphere. Although the left hemisphere may be more important for remembering the words to a tune and the right hemisphere for remembering the sequence of notes, these two attributes are often intertwined, so that damage to either hemisphere interferes with memory for a tune.

Many brain regions are involved in musical performance; right hemisphere regions play a predominant role in processing tonal information, and left hemisphere regions play a predominant role in the motoric aspects of performance. In addition, multimodal association areas play an especially important role—for example, in translating musical notation into an auditory image or into a motor sequence. Each hemisphere makes a different contribution to singing. The rhythmic aspects of singing are disrupted by an injection of sodium amobarbital that disables the left hemisphere, and the tonal aspects of singing are disrupted by an injection that deactivates the right hemisphere.

Furthermore, the sodium amobarbital studies indicate a separation of musical and language skills because injections can disrupt singing but not speech. In addition, the investigation of case studies of highly trained musicians who sustained brain damage confirms a separability of musical and language abilities. Research into how neurologically intact musicians process music suggests that they may process it in a more analytic, left-hemisphere manner than nonmusicians because they understand the structure underlying musical composition, whereas nonmusicians do not. Futhermore, certain types of musical abilities and training are associated with particular types of brain structures.

As with other artistic abilities, the language arts also appear to rely on both hemispheres. Although the left hemisphere's grammatical and semantic skills are clearly essential for creative writing, the right hemisphere contributes by aiding in the nonliteral use of language (such as metaphor), in the construction of a narrative, and in inference.

Chapter 13

Plasticity Across the Life Span

To all who knew him, Dan appeared to be a relatively intelligent 12-year-old with a friendly and cooperative manner. Yet, he was struggling in his schoolwork, especially in spelling and reading. These troubles were nothing new, for these subjects had always been difficult for him even though he had received considerable remedial training. When a school counselor suggested neuropsychological assessment, his parents agreed willingly, hoping that it might shed some light on his problems.

Neuropsychological testing revealed no evidence of gross brain damage because his sensory, perceptual, and motor abilities all appeared normal and his overall IQ was in the average range. A more detailed analysis of his abilities revealed that his visuospatial skills were quite good. His score on the Performance subscale of the Wechsler Intelligence Scale for Children—Revised (WISC-R), which emphasizes visuospatial abilities, was above average, and he performed well on a number of tests assessing nonverbal problem solving. In contrast, his performance on the Verbal subscale of the WISC-R was below average, and a number of additional verbal tests revealed that he had little appreciation for the phonemic structure of words. He read words by guessing what they were on the basis of their salient visual features, or configuration, rather than by trying to sound them out. For example, he read *form* as "farm," *theory* as "those," *grieve* as "great," and *tranquillity* as "train track." He exhibited similar problems in the spelling of orally presented words, spelling *square* as "scar," *cross* as "cors," and *triangle* as "trere."

Given that his difficulties were long-standing and had not been effectively overcome with remediation, the neuropsychologist diagnosed Dan as having a specific verbal learning disability that is commonly known as *dyslexia*. She suggested that further remediation in reading be geared to capitalize on Dan's good visuospatial abilities, such as teaching him to carefully distinguish words on the basis of their visual features and using flash cards to drill him on the form of words. This approach could be designed to incrementally increase his knowledge; he could first acquire knowledge about simple words then apply it toward reading more complicated material. For example, once Dan could learn to recognize *fly*, he could then use that knowledge to help read other words, such as *butterfly*. The neuropsychologist also explained to Dan's parents that even with such interventions, he would probably never become a fluent reader, which would likely continue to make some aspects of formal schooling difficult. However, she also emphasized that such difficulties did not necessarily preclude future occupational success for Dan, especially if his parents encouraged him to pursue areas of study and interests that would capitalize on his above-average visuospatial abilities.[1]

The case study in the opening vignette of this chapter illustrates some of the ways in which neuropsychological disorders observed developmentally can differ from those observed later in life. In adults, the inability to read is associated with insult to particular regions of the left hemisphere (see chapter 8, page 296). However, in Dan's case, no evidence of brain damage or a localized lesion was apparent. Whereas adults with alexia have acquired the ability to read and then lost it, Dan never acquired reading abilities to a reasonable degree of proficiency.

The case of Dan and children with other developmental disorders should help us to realize something that we may have inadvertently been lulled into forgetting, namely that the brain exhibits **plasticity,** meaning that it has the ability to change. Although this plasticity is most apparent during development, it is a process that occurs throughout

[1]Adapted from *Child Neuropsychology: An Introduction to Theory, Research, and Clinical Practice* (pp. 343–350), by B. P. Rourke, D. J. Bakker, J. L. Fisk, and J. D. Strang, 1983, New York: Guilford Press.

the course of an individual's life, providing the brain with a way of being continually responsive to environmental input. In this chapter, we examine plasticity from a life-span perspective, centering on changes early in development as well as changes that occur with old age. The developing brain and the aging brain are substantially different from the adult brain, so we examine the consequences of these differences for cognitive and emotional processes. We also consider how the brain can adapt in response to damage or insult.

DEVELOPMENTAL NEUROPSYCHOLOGY

In this section of the chapter, we examine developmental aspects of neuropsychological function. To provide some perspective on the differences between the immature brain and the mature brain, we begin by discussing brain changes during development and how these changes are influenced by the environment.

Changes in the Brain During Development

Early in fetal development, after the simple primordial fertilized egg differentiates into specific types of tissue (e.g., muscle, skeletal, cardiovascular, nerve), the spinal cord and brain are nothing more than a hollow tube. With time, the tube folds, twists, turns, and expands to become the fetal brain, whereas the hole becomes the ventricular system (Figure 13.1). Around the 6th week of gestation, the nerve cells (and glia) near the inside of the tube (what later becomes the ventricles) divide, proliferate, and then begin to migrate outward. In this process, the ventricles act much like a port around which the initial neural settlers will reside. As more neurons are generated (*neurogenesis*), the initial core or central areas are already settled and the new neurons, like new immigrants to a city, must traverse farther out to find a place to live. As the brain grows, new neurons, like new waves of immigrants, travel farther and farther out to the metaphorical suburbs of the brain. Thus, the six layers of cortex are built from the inside out; the first set of cells migrate to the deepest layer of the cortex (the sixth), the second to the

fifth, and so forth (e.g., Marin-Padilla, 1970). By 6 months' gestational age, most neurons have been produced.

Neurobiologists have long been puzzled by the nature of the mechanism that allows such an orderly migration of neurons. Currently, two major mechanisms are proposed to explain this migration. The first proposed mechanism involves a particular type of glia known as *radial glia,* which are organized so that they radiate away from the ventricles toward the outside surface of the developing brain. These cells are believed to act as highways or paths that guide neurons on their migration outward (Figure 13.2) (e.g., Rakic, 1981). Eventually, these radially oriented glia transform into astrocytes, a type of glia aptly named because they are star-shaped.

The second proposed mechanism is the **chemoaffinity (chemospecificity) hypothesis** put forth by Roger Sperry, who is also well known for his research on patients with the split-brain syndrome (see page 94 in chapter 3). He suggested that cells are genetically programmed to have a certain affinity for a particular chemical milieu. The cell then follows a chemical gradient to reach the site of this specific milieu in the brain, much the way a dog would follow the trail of a scent to reach the location of an animal it is tracking. Sperry's support for this hypothesis came from experiments with newts, whose optic fibers, if cut, regenerate and reestablish connections with the tectum (the portion of the newt brain that processes vision), which allows the animal to see again. After cutting the optic nerve, Sperry either reattached the eyeballs in their regular orientation or upside down (180-degree rotation). He reasoned that if these optic fibers reconnect in a random manner, the behavior of the two groups of animals, those with the reoriented eyeballs and those without, should be the same. However, if specific neural connections exist, the animals with the rotated eyes should see the world upside down (which would make catching a fly for dinner exceedingly difficult for these animals!). In fact, the movements of the animals with the rotated eyes were off by exactly 180 degrees, which showed that the neurons in the optic nerve had connected to the same region with which they had been linked before

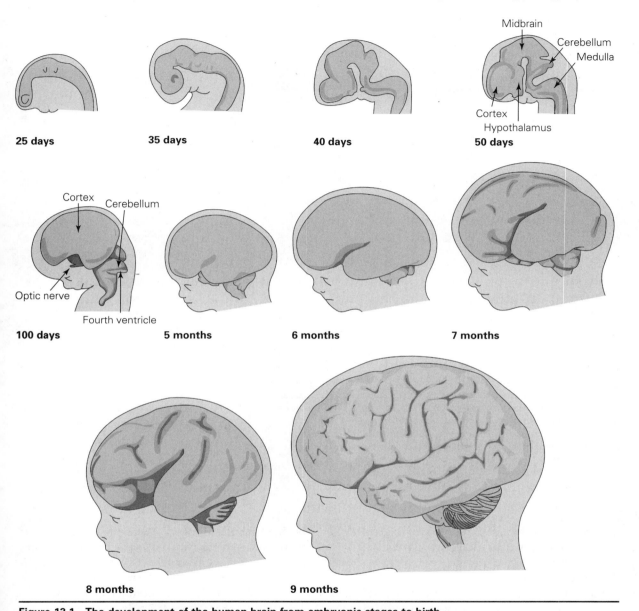

Figure 13.1 The development of the human brain from embryonic stages to birth.
During the first 2 months of development, the nervous system evolves from a hollow curved tube to a structure that is folding and starting to differentiate into discrete sections. By 100 days, the major divisions of the cortex have been formed. From then until birth, the brain continues to expand and to develop gyral patterns, all of which are present at birth. (*Note.* Adapted from Reynolds & Fletcher-Jansen, 1989, p. 19; Spreen et al., 1984, p. 25.)

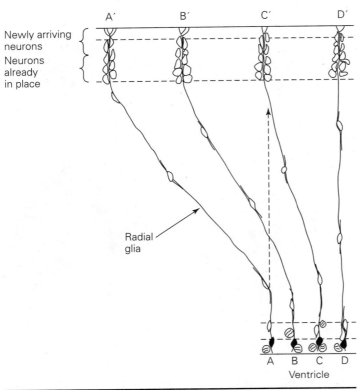

Figure 13.2 Neuronal migration, after proliferation, from the ventricles by means of radial glia to the layers of the cortex.
The development is from the inside out; later migrating neurons must pass through layers of neurons that are already in place. (*Note.* Adapted from Rakic, 1981.)

the transection (for a recent review of this work and the chemoaffinity hypothesis, see Gaze, 1982).

In humans, cell migration is complete by birth. Furthermore, neurons, unlike other cells in our body, do not regenerate after injury, which means that we can never acquire more brain cells. Hence the basic blueprint of the nervous system is set in place by birth. Nonetheless, the newborn's brain is different from that of an adult. The changes that occur are numerous, and we now discuss them, beginning with changes in the cells themselves: neurons and glia.

Although no new neurons are generated after birth, the number of connections (synapses) that these neurons make with other neurons continues to increase, a process known as **synaptogenesis.** In fact, this process occurs so rapidly within the first year of life that the total number of synapses increases more than 10-fold. The increase in the complexity of the neurons themselves and their connections with other neurons early in life can be seen in Figure 13.3.

Although neurons do not continue to proliferate during the course of development, glia do. Furthermore, their functions become more complicated with age. For example, early in life extra glia are

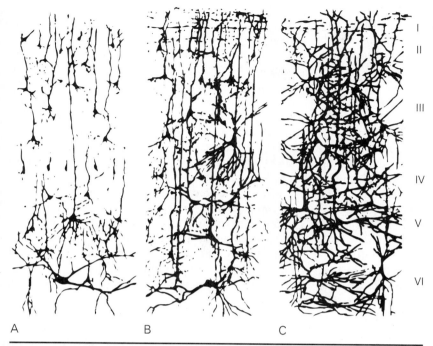

Figure 13.3   Increases in the dendrites of neurons and their interconnections during early development.
Shown here are representative sections of the brain of (A) a 3-month-old child, (B) a 15-month-old child, and (C) a 24-month-old child. The Roman numerals to the right of (C) indicate the six layers of cortex. (*Note.* Modified from the work of Conel, A, 1946; B, 1955; and C, 1959. With the permission of Dr. Karl H. Pribram.)

not produced in response to injury although later in life this is a common response. Furthermore, the growth of a specific type of glia, the oligodendrocyte, increases the myelin sheath around neurons, which as you may remember from chapter 1 increases nerve-conduction velocity. A baby's brain is relatively unmyelinated, which means that brain regions cannot interact quickly. It is as if the baby's brain is connected by a series of old country roads that meander from town to town. It doesn't make for fast travel. Myelin transforms those roads into faster roads, such as regional highways, and even more myelin transforms them into national superhighways, over which large volumes of traffic can travel quickly.

The process of myelination is drawn out, and for certain brain regions may continue even into the late teens and early 20s. Myelination first begins to appear between the fourth gestational month and the first year after birth. Not surprisingly, the brain regions that are most myelinated early in life, such as the spinal cord and the medulla, are those that support basic functions. During the first year after birth, basic sensory and motor systems become myelinated, after which myelination tends to involve connections between integrative systems, such as those connecting cortical and subcortical areas and those linking different cortical regions. For example, myelination of the corpus callosum continues through the late teens (e.g., Giedd et al., 1996;

Yakovlev & Lecours, 1967). Only then does the nerve-conduction velocity between the hemispheres reach the adult value of approximately 5 ms, which is four to five times as quick as that observed in children aged 4 years (Salamy, 1978).

Other generalized changes also occur in the brain, such as those relating to electrical and biochemical activity. Two main trends emerge with regard to electrophysiological activity: The dominant frequency of activity increases, and the pattern of electrical activity becomes more cyclic. During the first 2 years of life, electrophysiological activity tends to be low frequency (delta rhythm, <3.5 Hz). Such low-frequency activity is not typically observed in awake adults. Between the ages of 1 year and 5 years, the dominant frequency band is theta (4–7 Hz), which in awake adults is associated with relaxation with the eyes closed. After the age of 5 years, the alpha rhythm (8–13 Hz) becomes discernible, a frequency band associated with relaxation but alertness in adults. In adults, the specific suppression of this band of electrical activity as compared with other frequencies is thought to index higher brain activity (such as we discussed with regard to frontal lobe functioning and mood in chapter 11). By age 10 to 13 years, the alpha rhythm becomes similar to that of adults, and beta activity (>14 Hz) becomes discernible. As for the cyclicity of electrophysiological activity, no pattern is obvious in the infant, but as the child grows older, a clear sleep-wake cycle develops (Harmony, 1989).

Biochemical changes also occur in the brain during development. For example, evidence from monkeys suggests that neurotransmitter production increases during infancy (Kolb & Fantie, 1989), and aspects of brain metabolism, such as the rate of glucose consumption, change as well. As shown in Figure 13.4, during the first year after birth the metabolic rate of the entire cerebral cortex, as indexed by positron emission tomography (PET), is less than that for adults. After this point, the metabolic rate climbs steadily until it is double the adult value between the ages of 3 and 8 years. After this peak, it begins to decrease, but remains above adult levels during the early teen years. The changes in brain metabolism do not occur equally across the

brain, but, like myelination, they reflect changes in regional maturation across the brain. For example, during the first year of life, the highest metabolic rate occurs in subcortical structures. High metabolic rates for the cortex are observed only after that time (Chugani, Phelps, & Mazziotta, 1987). Glucose consumption may be high during childhood because fuel is needed to support structural changes in the brain. The oligodendroglia may need extra energy to generate myelin, and neurons may need energy to undergo both elaboration and pruning, a topic to which we turn next.

The development of the mammalian nervous system appears to be characterized by an initial proliferation of neurons and their connections, which is then followed by a process of pruning that occurs through one of two mechanisms: programmed cell death or elimination of synapses. In **programmed cell death,** vast numbers of neurons die at specific stages of development. It was believed that this mechanism seems to be most likely to occur when neural connections or systems are less complex. For example, whereas mice lose 30% of their cortical neurons during development (e.g., Heumann & Leuba, 1983) and visual areas of the monkey sustain a 15% loss (e.g., O'Kusky & Colonnier, 1982), it was believed not to occur in humans (e.g., Huttenlocher, 1990). However, recent studies suggest that programmed cell death may occur in humans late in gestation (Rabinowicz, Courten-Myers, Petetot, Xi, & Los Reyes, 1996).

Pruning during development in the human cortex also occurs by the **elimination of synapses,** in which the number of connections between neurons is reduced. The rate at which the pruning of neuronal connections can occur is staggering. For example, LaMantia and Rakic (1990) found that in the adult monkey, the number of axons in the corpus callosum (which allow for connections between cells in opposite hemispheres) is only one fourth that in the newborn monkey. On the basis of this study and others, these researchers estimate that as many as 60 axons per *second* are lost in the first few weeks of a monkey's life, and they speculate that in humans the loss may be even greater—as many as *200* axons per second (Rakic, 1991). The time course of synap-

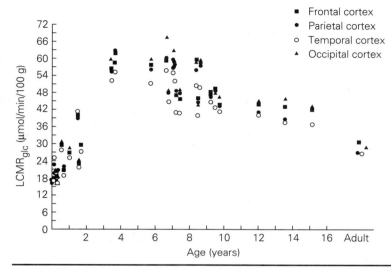

Figure 13.4 Changes in the metabolic rate of the brain's four major lobes during development.
During the first few years of life, metabolic rates are less than those of an adult (far right-hand side of the graph).
However, in preschool years the rate of brain metabolism begins to accelerate, reaching a peak value around the
age of 8 years, after which the metabolic rate slowly declines through the teenage years to adult values. LCMR$_{glc}$, lo-
cal cerebral metabolic rate for glucose. (*Note.* From "Positron Emission Tomography Study of Human Brain Func-
tional Development," by H. T. Chugani, M. E. Phelps, and J. C. Mazziotta, 1987, *Annals of Neurology*, 22(4), p. 492.
Copyright © 1987 by the American Neurological Association. Used with permission of Lippincott-Raven Publishers,
Philadelphia, PA.)

tic elimination can vary among cortical regions in
humans; for example, it is complete in the visual
cortex by age 10 years but continues until adolescence in frontal cortex (Figure 13.5) (Huttenlocher, 1979).

Programmed neuronal death and synaptic pruning are thought to be mechanisms by which the
nervous system can fine-tune itself. The brain over-
produces neurons or their processes, which allows
for a multiplicity of possible connections. Then,
during development, the neurons or connections
that don't receive much stimulation or are little used
wither away (Huttenlocher, 1990).

This neuronal or synaptic overproduction may
allow the brain to initially have maximal capacity to
respond to the environment, whereas the subsequent death and pruning may provide the capacity
for the brain to fine-tune and specialize itself for the
environment (Huttenlocher, 1994). For example,
although the structure of the human brain has

evolved in a way that allows almost all members of
the species to process language, the actual linguistic
environment into which an individual is born will
vary. A large set of synaptic connections may aid in
the capacity to learn any of the languages spoken
around the world, but the pruning may allow for a
fine-tuning for acquisition of a specific language
system.

You should not get the impression that once
synaptic pruning occurs, the connections in the cortex remain totally static. Some degree of plasticity
must be retained across the lifetime so that new
knowledge can be integrated and incorporated
while prior knowledge is reorganized. One proposed mechanism for such plasticity is a change in
the strength of a given synaptic connection. According to this viewpoint, often-used synaptic connections become stronger and more effective,
whereas those that are little used become weaker
(this idea is sometimes referred to as a *Hebbian*

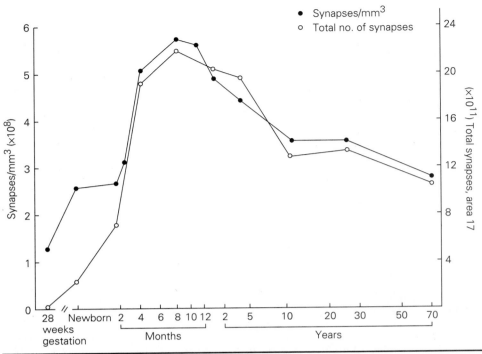

Figure 13.5 Proliferation and pruning of synaptic connections in the human visual cortex.
Within the first year of life, the total number of synapses (white) and the density of synapses (black) increase substantially. Pruning begins toward the end of the first year and continues until age 10 years. Thereafter, the number of synaptic connections remains static until the effects of aging begin to cause loss. (*Note.* Adapted from *Neuropsychologia*, vol. 28, P. R. Huttenlocher, "Morphometric Study of Human Cerebral Cortex Development," p. 519, Copyright 1990, with permission from Elsevier Science Ltd., The Boulevard, Langford Lane, Kidlington OX5 1GB, UK.)

synapse, after Donald Hebb, who suggested this type of processing). Another possible mechanism for plasticity is synaptogenesis, which, as we already discussed, is the creation of new synapses. Although the proliferation of synapses and their elimination occur at high rates early in development, the nervous system retains its ability to form new synapses throughout the lifetime. Early in development these connections are generated at random, but later in life the creation of new synapses has been proposed to become more specific and selective, guided strongly by the animal's experience (see Greenough, 1987, for a discussion of such a viewpoint).

All these changes in brain physiology, such as changes in metabolic rate, myelination, and synaptic density, are mirrored by changes in the behavioral repertoire of the child. In the motor domain, newborns exhibit a characteristic set of basic reflexes. Some of them are the rooting, grasping, and Babinski reflexes (Figure 13.6). These reflexes, which are relatively primitive reponses controlled by the brain stem, aid in the infant's survival (e.g., the rooting reflex, in which the infant turns toward the side of the face that is touched, helps the infant orient to the mother's breast). With age, these reflexes disappear because cortical areas inhibit their expression. Thus, when observed in an adult, they indicate cortical damage so severe as to release these primitive reflexes from inhibition. For this reason, checking for the Babinski reflex is a standard part of the neurological examination because this test provides a gross but quick method of ascertaining the extent of corti-

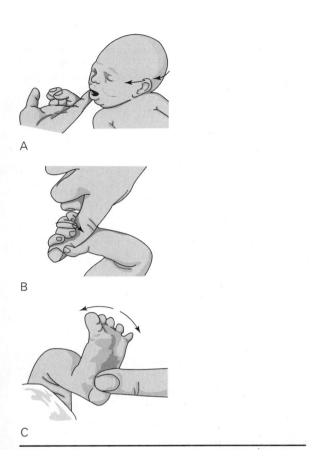

Figure 13.6 Three of the basic reflexes observed in infancy.
Shown here are the (A) rooting, (B) grasping, and (C) Babinski reflexes. As the child matures, these reflexes become inhibited by higher cortical control and disappear. After head trauma, neurologists often test for a Babinski reflex as a gross means of quickly determining the severity of brain damage. If the reflex is observed, cortical damage has occurred. (*Note.* Adapted from Kalat, 1992, p. 317; Kandel, 1991.)

cal damage after brain trauma. As the child ages, motor control moves out of the realm of reflexes into more controlled actions. At first the child's motor control is so poor that he or she cannot even turn over. With time, the child masters this skill, begins to crawl, and by age 18 months or so begins to walk.

Not only do the physical capacities of a child change with age, but so do higher order cognitive functions, such as language. The child progresses from cooing to babbling to speaking.

Children in all cultures tend to acquire both cognitive and motoric skills in an orderly fashion: Babbling precedes speaking, and crawling precedes walking. Furthermore, specific abilities are acquired within specific age ranges. Because these changes occur in an orderly fashion and at a particular age, they are known as **developmental milestones** (Spreen et al., 1984). The major physiological and behavioral changes during development are listed in Table 13.1. (Two good reviews of changes in the brain with development are Kolb & Fantie, 1989, and Majovski, 1989.)

Although development undoubtedly entails changes in brain functioning as well as changes in behavior, finding a direct one-to-one link between a change in a specific aspect of neural functioning and the emergence of a certain cognitive function has proven to be surprisingly difficult. Currently, there are relatively few cases in which we have a biological marker that predicts development of a specific cognitive process. Furthermore, even when we do find such a marker, the connection between the physiological process and the cognitive function is unclear. To illustrate this difficulty, we examine some research conducted by D. Molfese and Molfese (1994). They found that an infant's electrical response to auditory stimuli (i.e., AER–auditory evoked response) (in this case, the stimuli were speech sounds) recorded a week or so after birth can approximate how competent (good or poor) a child will be at processing language 3 years later. Although the AER appears to act as a biological marker for future language competence, we do not know what aspect of nervous system function is indexed by the AER. Furthermore, we do not know how variations in that function lead to varying competence in language. In response to this dilemma, D. Molfese has speculated that a larger AER may reflect a heightened capacity to discriminate among different speech sounds. Thus, children who can make fine discriminations sooner may have a head start in learning words early in life, which in turn helps them to have more developed language capacities at age 3 years.

Table 13.1 Developmental Changes During Early Childhood

Age	Visual and motor function	Social and intellectual function	EEG[a]	Average brain weight (g)
Birth	Exhibits sucking, rooting, swallowing, and Moro reflexes; engages in infantile grasping; blinks to light	—	Asynchronous; low voltage, 3–5 Hz; period of flattening; no clear distinction awake or asleep	350
6 weeks	Extends and turns neck when prone; regards mother's face; follows objects with eyes	Smiles when played with	Similar to birth records, with slightly higher voltages; rare 14-Hz parietal spindles in sleep	410
3 months	Exhibits infantile grasping and sucking modified by volition; keeps head above horizontal for long periods; turns to objects presented in visual field; may respond to sound	Watches own hands	When awake, asynchronous 3–4 Hz, some 5–6 Hz; low voltages continue; sleep better organized and more synchronous; more spindles but still often asynchronous	515
6 months	Grasps objects with both hands; will place weight on forearms or hands when prone; rolls supine to prone; supports almost all weight on legs for brief periods; sits briefly	Laughs aloud and shows pleasure; emits primitive articulated sounds, "ga-goo"; smiles at self in mirror	More synchronous; 5- to 7-Hz activity frequent; many lower voltages, slower frequencies; drowsy bursts can be seen; humps may first be seen in sleep	660
9 months	Sits well and pulls self to sitting position; uses thumb-forefinger grasp; crawls	Waves bye-bye; plays pat-a-cake; uses "dada," "baba"; imitates sounds	Mild asynchrony; predominant frequencies, 5–7 Hz and 2–6 Hz, especially anteriorly; drowsy bursts frequent; humps and spindles seen frequently in sleep	750
12 months	Is able to release objects; cruises and walks with one hand held; exhibits plantar reflex (50% of children)	Says two to four words with meaning; understands several proper nouns; may kiss on request	5–7 Hz in all areas; usually synchronous; some anterior 20–25 Hz; some 3–6 Hz; humps often seen in sleep and usually synchronous	925

Table 13.1 Developmental Changes During Early Childhood (*Continued*)

Age	Visual and motor function	Social and intellectual function	EEG[a]	Average brain weight (g)
24 months	Walks up and down stairs (using two feet a step); bends over and picks up objects without falling; turns knob; can partially dress self; exhibits plantar reflex (100% of children)	Uses two- to three-word sentences; uses "I," "me," and "you" correctly; plays simple games; points to four to five body parts; obeys simple commands	6- to 8-Hz activity predominates posteriorly, with some 4–6 Hz seen, especially anteriorly; humps in sleep always synchronous	1,065
36 months	Goes up stairs (using one foot a step); pedals tricycle; dresses and undresses fully except for shoelaces, belt, and buttons; visual acuity 20/20	Asks numerous questions; knows nursery rhymes; copies circle; plays with others	When awake, synchronous 6–9 Hz predominates posteriorly; less 4- to 6-Hz activity seen; in sleep, spindles usually synchronous	1,140

[a]EEG, electroencephalogram.
Note. Adapted from Spreen et al., 1984, pp. 32–33.

Another case in which speculative linkages can be made between brain development and behavior involves changes in visual cortex that appear to parallel changes in visual processing. At birth, few synaptic connections are present in visual cortex—about 20% of those at adulthood. This neural state is accompanied by low visual alertness and difficulties in tracking moving objects efficiently. At 4 months, a rapid burst in synaptogenesis is associated with a sudden increase in visual alertness. At this age, binocular perception, which depends on cortical rather than subcortical control, begins to emerge. Synaptic density remains high until 4 years of age, at which point it decreases. After this age, the ability to modify certain aspects of visual processing are lost. For example, strabismic amblyopia (i.e., crossing of the eyes), which is a relatively common condition of childhood, can be reversed if it is treated prior to this age (Huttenlocher, 1990). However after this point, the condition is irreversible. Researchers have suggested that the decrease in synaptic density after 4 years of age may be related to a decrease in plasticity.

Even if more specific linkages can be found between biological markers and developmental changes in mental ability, researchers will have difficulty determining whether the biological marker is indexing a neural process that is critical for a developmental change in behavior or whether the marker is just indexing a general level of brain maturity (which in turn predicts the onset of behavior). To make this distinction more concrete, think about the case of visual processing that we just discussed. Perhaps the biological process indexed by synaptic density specifically determines a child's competence in visual processing. Alternatively, synaptic density may not *directly* affect visual processing but may be only one measure of overall brain maturity, which is also reflected by increased myelination, changes in metabolic level, increased electroencephalographic

(EEG) coherence, and so forth. Although a deeper understanding of such linkages has evaded researchers, the general assumption is that a particular neurobiological substrate must be in place before specific motoric, cognitive, and emotional abilities can manifest themselves.

Influence of the Environment on the Developing Brain and Sensitive Periods

In discussing the biological timetable for development, we mentioned but did not elaborate upon the idea that environmental input has profound influences on the developing brain. We now review in more detail some of the evidence from research on animals that illustrates the substantial effects that environmental input can have on the structure and organization of the brain during development.

One well-known effect observed in animals is that an enriched or stimulating environment can affect the structure of neurons (e.g., Rosenzweig, Bennett, & Diamond, 1972) by causing the dendrites of the neurons to become bushier and the number of synapses per neuron to increase (e.g., Turner & Greenough, 1985). In the laboratory, an enriched environment for the rat consists of a complex spatial environment (e.g., with ramps and ladders) that contains many objects and toys for exploration (e.g., blocks, Ping-Pong balls), which are changed daily to provide variety. To furnish an enriched social environment as well, experimenters allow the animals to explore the environment along with other rats for a specified number of hours per day (Figure 13.7A). In contrast, the control environment consists of a small standard-issue clear plastic cage that the animal lives in alone (Figure 13.7B).

Dendritic elaboration and increasing synaptic connectivity as a result of an enriched environment occurs not only early during development but also in adulthood (e.g., Greenough & Chang, 1988). These neural changes may provide for more and varied connections, increasing the brain's computational power so that it can effectively deal with a more cognitively demanding and complicated environment. In fact, animals raised in complex environ-

ments are superior to control animals in solving various maze learning tasks (e.g., Juraska, Henderson, & Muller, 1984). Likewise, sparse dendritic elaboration may preclude certain mental processes. For example, in humans, the mental deterioration associated with Alzheimer's disease is also associated with a thinning of dendritic branches (Figure 13.8).

Although certain environmental effects can influence the organism across a lifetime, as in the case of dendritic elaboration, in other cases the organism is particularly sensitive to certain external stimuli only during a specific developmental period. This time is known as a **sensitive period** and generally has a specific onset and offset. Such time periods allow the brain to incorporate information from the environment and then to "lock" that information in. An example of a sensitive period that we already discussed is the limited time period during which intervention can correct walleye or crossed eyes. If the problem is not corrected during that time, irreversible difficulties in depth perception result.

The means by which the sensitive period for binocular disparity is thought to be reflected in changes in neuronal organization is as follows. Depth perception depends on binocular disparity (see page 209 in chapter 6), which is provided by the offset between the retinal image obtained by each eye. To compute depth, then, the brain must have a means for comparing information obtained by the left eye about a given point in space with that obtained by the right eye. This need is reflected in the organization of the visual cortex. Information about a given region of space is received by separate but adjacent regions of visual cortex, known as **binocular columns** (or ocular dominance columns), each of which is sensitive to input from only one eye. These columns, however, appear only after birth, when the infant has had some visual experience. Hence, the brain is plastic so that visual experience in a variety of settings and environments can influence connections in visual cortex that will aid in visual processing, including depth perception. However, this sensitive period then ends, most likely because the essential information needed to organize the cortex has been extracted from the environment and because maintaining unneeded connections is

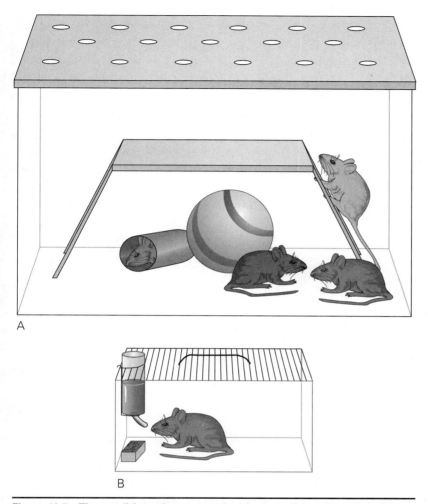

Figure 13.7   The conditions that are used with rats to investigate the effects of different environments on brain structure and behavior.
(A) In the complex environment condition, the animals are allowed to spend hours each day in an environment characterized by a large area in which the spatial arrangement of items and toys is changed daily (for variety) and in which the rats have the opportunity to interact with other rats. (B) In contrast, in the control condition the rat remains alone in a small plastic cage all day.

too costly. Hence, eye problems, like crossed eyes and walleye need to be corrected before the close of the sensitive period and the loss of sensitivity to such environmental inputs.

A more cognitive example of a function that has a sensitive period is language. When children are born, they are able to perceive almost all phonetic contrasts that occur in different language systems around the world. Such flexibility is important because the linguistic culture into which a child will be born is unpredictable. Within the first year of life, however, the child's ability to perceive particular

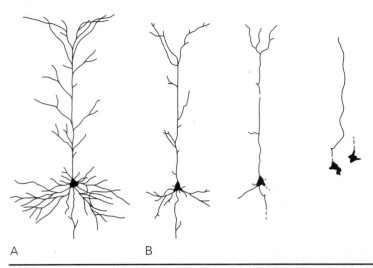

A   B

Figure 13.8 A loss of dendritic elaboration that accompanies mental deterioration.
(A) Shown here is a neuron from the brain of a normal adult human. Note the dark cell body in the lower part of the figure and the many dendrites feeding into it. Also note the axon emanating upward away from the cell body. (B) Neurons in individuals with increasing degrees of deterioration (left to right) as a result of Alzheimer's disease. Note the reduction in dendritic elaboration and other neuronal processes. (*Note.* From *Biological Psychology*, by J. W. Kalat. Copyright © 1992, 1988, 1984, 1981 Wadsworth, Inc. By permission of Brooks/Cole Publishing Company, Pacific Grove, CA 93950, a division of International Thomson Publishing Inc.)

contrasts is honed, becoming more sensitive to the contrasts relevant for the baby's linguistic environment and less sensitive to contrasts important in other languages (Kuhl et al., 1992).

The examples just provided illustrate a salient feature of sensitive periods: The neural organization that develops during the sensitive period is relatively irreversible. For example, if you cover one eye of a kitten during the sensitive period for the creation of binocular columns, the column of cortex for information from the patched eye will be smaller than normal, whereas the column for information from the unpatched eye will be larger than normal. If you remove the patch after the sensitive period is over, the brain does not revert to the standard configuration in which the columns for each eye are approximately equal in size. Rather, the ocular dominance column for the patched eye remains large and that of the unpatched eye remains small (e.g.,

Hubel & Wiesel, 1970; see LeVay, Wiesel, & Hubel, 1980, for a discussion of similar effects in the monkey).

Irreversible effects of sensitive periods have also been observed for more complicated cognitive skills. For example, the ability to acquire sophisticated grammatical competence in a second language appears to be limited by the age at which the second language is acquired. If acquisition occurs before the ages of 5–7 years or so, the person's competence will be equivalent to that of a native speaker (Figure 13.9A). For each year that passes after the age of 7 years without exposure to the second language, an incremental decline is seen in the ability to understand the particular grammatical constructions of that language (Figure 13.9B). Introduction to the second language after the age of 15 years is associated with poorest acquisition of these constructions, which suggests the end of the sensitive period. After

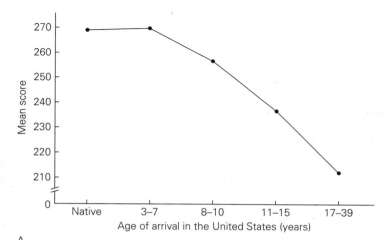

A

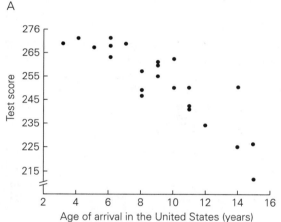

B

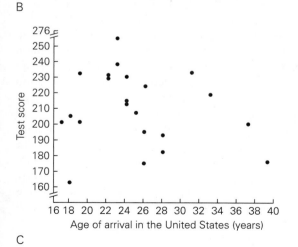

C

Figure 13.9 A sensitive period for the acquisition of grammatical competence in a second language.
(A) The relationship between age of acquisition of a second language (indicated here by age of arrival in the United States) and grammatical competence. The graph illustrates that individuals who arrive in the United States around the age at which formal schooling begins can acquire grammatical skills equivalent to those of a native speaker. However, the older the age of acquisition, the lower the level of competence. (B) The relationship between age of arrival in the United States and grammatical competence for individuals arriving between ages 3 and 15 years ($r = -.87$). With each year that passes after the age of 5 years, the ability to acquire grammatical competence decreases. (C) In contrast, after the age of 15 years, the age at which an individual arrives in the United States does not predict the person's grammatical competence ($r = -.16$). The relationships between competence and age of arrival shown in (B) and (C) suggest that the sensitive period for acquisition of sophisticated grammatical competence in a second language ends around the age of 15 years. (*Note.* Adapted from Johnson & Newport, 1989, pp. 79, 80.)

this age, even total immersion in a new linguistic environment cannot offset the lack of earlier exposure, an indication that the brain has organized in such a way as to preclude the possibility of processing such information. Thus, before age 15 years, age of acquisition of the second langage is a good predictor of adult level of sophisticated grammatical competence, even when other possible influences on competence are taken into account, such as how long the person has been in the environment in which the second language is spoken and the degree to which the second language is spoken at home and in the workplace. After this age, age of acquisition becomes unimportant (Figure 13.9C) and these other factors exert more influence. Such a pattern of results suggests that the ability to acquire a high degree of grammatical competence in a second language is limited by biological factors that signal the end of the sensitive period around the age of 15 years (Johnson & Newport, 1989). Although these biological factors remain to be identified, they may be associated with the onset of puberty because the sensitive period ends around that time.

DEVELOPMENTAL DISORDERS

Because the brain is developing in children, the nature of neuropsychological disorders observed in children is distinct from the nature of those occurring in adults. In this section of the chapter, we review some of the more common developmental disorders that appear to have neurological involvement. Some of these have identifiable causes, whereas the causes of others are unknown.

Learning Disabilities

Learning disabilities are syndromes in which a child has difficulty acquiring cognitive skills in only one particular domain or area. The two major subtypes of learning disabilities that we discuss are those that affect skills in the verbal domain and those that affect skills in the nonverbal domain.

Dyslexia and Other Verbal Learning Disabilities

Dyslexia is a specific inability to learn to read at an age-appropriate level, despite adequate opportunity, training, and intelligence (it is sometimes referred to as a *specific reading disability*). Usually, an individual is considered to have dyslexia when his or her general intelligence is adequate to support the cognitive demands imposed by reading, the individual's other cognitive functions seem to be age and grade appropriate, and exposure to written language and instruction in reading have been provided. For example, an 8-year-old child with a specific reading disability would be unable to read but could perform age-appropriate math problems, such as simple multiplication. As the child gets older, acquisition of knowledge in other subjects besides written language is likely to be compromised because of the heavy reliance in schools on reading materials for conveying such information.

Dyslexia is one of the more common developmental disorders, affecting approximately 5% of all children. In the United States alone, for example, more than 11 million persons have a severe reading disability (Hynd & Cohen, 1983). The number of individuals affected by dyslexia surpasses the combined total of those affected by cerebral palsy, epilepsy, and severe mental retardation.

Although all children with dyslexia are lumped together under the same diagnostic umbrella, behaviorally a fair amount of heterogeneity can be seen in the nature of the difficulties that these children exhibit. To make sense of this heterogeneity, researchers have provided various classification schemes for dividing dyslexia into subtypes (e.g., Boder, 1973; Denckla, 1979; Mattis, French, & Rapin, 1975). Examination of these various classification schemes reveals certain commonalities. The typical scheme involves two distinctly identified subgroups: one that has difficulty with the auditory-linguistic aspects of processing and one that has difficulty with the visuoperceptual aspects of reading. In some classifications, two other groups are identified: one that has difficulties in a mixture of auditory-linguistic and visuoperceptual processes and one that has difficulty in sequencing, especially in the articulatory and graphomotor domains.

Although most people assume that the cardinal sign of dyslexia is writing letters backward, children without reading disabilities commonly write letters backward, so this is not a specific sign of dyslexia. Instead, most persons with dyslexia (85%) appear to have difficulty not so much in the visuospatial aspects of reading as in linking a particular letter, which is a linguistic symbol, to a particular sound. These individuals have difficulty parsing words and assigning particular sound values to specific letters. This disorder is sometimes referred to as *dysphonetic dyslexia*. The remaining 15% of persons with dyslexia have specific difficulty with visuospatial aspects of language (Boder, 1973). These individuals are said to have *dyseidetic dyslexia*.

If you think back to the discussion on language in chapter 8, you may remember that we described two routes from print to meaning, the phonologic route and the direct route. Remember that learning new words usually requires the phonologic route—converting print to sound to meaning. Unfortunately, most children with dyslexia cannot use this route. You may be thinking, "Well why can't they learn to read using the direct route?" In fact, teachers often attempt to teach these children to read by using techniques that emphasize the direct route, such as the "look-see" (whole-word) method, in which an entire word is associated with a concept. However, this is a difficult means by which to acquire reading skills because each new word has a different form that must be memorized. Typically, the direct route is used only after an individual encounters a word frequently or becomes a fluent reader. To appreciate the difficulties of acquiring language by this route, consider that if your reading vocabulary consists of 20,000 words, you would have to memorize the association between the word, its meaning, and its pronunciation for each word—20,000 associations. Although making such associations is possible (e.g., the Chinese language requires the memorization of many ideograms), mastering a large reading vocabulary by using this

method would be difficult for any individual. Because of their reliance on visual form, readers with dyslexia often make errors not typically made by readers without the disorder—such as misreading *house* as "hose," a word that looks similar but sounds dissimilar.

Although on gross examination the brain of a person with dyslexia appears normal, researchers have postulated since the late 1920s, when Orton first introduced the idea, that dyslexia might result from some type of neural miswiring (e.g., Orton, 1937). At present, a few theories exist that might explain the neural basis for dyslexia. One prominent theory is that a developmental anomaly disrupts left-hemisphere function, specifically in the left parietal regions, which in adults are associated with processing written language (see page 296, chapter 8). Some support for this viewpoint has been provided by postmortem anatomical examination of the brains of patients with dyslexia. These findings must be viewed as tentative, however, because the sample size was small, consisting of the brains of four males (Galaburda et al., 1985) and three females (P. Humphreys, Kaufmann, & Galaburda, 1990).

The brains of the males were characterized by developmental anomalies in the organization of cellular layers, whereas those of the females exhibited anomalies in the process of myelination. All the brains of the males contained regions in which cells did not segregate into a typical laminar organization but instead aligned themselves more haphazardly. This misalignment, in which cells from a given cortical layer are situated in a different layer, is known as an *ectopia* and indicates a problem during neuronal migration. Such ectopias tended to appear most often in the inferior frontal and superior temporal regions, predominantly in the left hemisphere (Figure 13.10). Because neuronal migration occurs early in fetal development, the ectopias suggest a problem in early development whose functional significance manifests only much later in life, when a child begins to read. The brains of the females, rather than being characterized by ectopias, contained myelin scars, which indicate difficulties in development before myelination is complete. Because myelination oc-

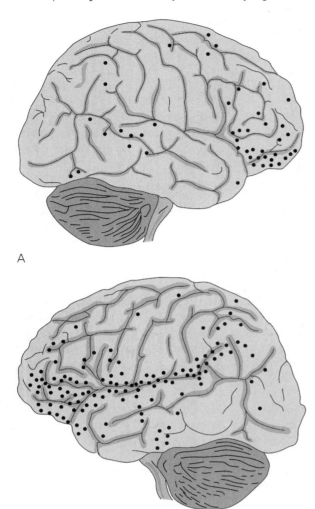

A

B

Figure 13.10 Locations of developmental anomalies in the brains of males diagnosed with dyslexia.
Shown here as black circles are sites that on postmortem examination were found to exhibit abnormalities in brain structure in (A) the right hemisphere and (B) the left hemisphere. Many more abnormalities can be seen in the left hemisphere than in the right. These abnormalities tend to occur in the peri-Sylvian area (in the vicinity of the Sylvian fissure) and in frontal regions. (*Note.* Adapted from Bigler, 1992, p. 489.)

curs after neural migration and females mature faster than males, the anomalies in the development of females and males with dyslexia may occur at approximately the same gestational age.

At present, the interpretation of these results is unclear. Although ectopias and myelin scars are rarely if ever observed in the brains of neurologically intact individuals, researchers do not know whether such anomalies are observed *only* in patients with dyslexia. To make that determination, investigators will have to examine the brains of children with other developmental disorders, such as autism, attention-deficit hyperactivity disorder, and mental retardation. If children in these populations are also found to have ectopias and myelin scars, such anomalies would then have to be considered a general indicator of a problem in brain development. However, if the ectopias and scars occur only in children with dyslexia, and not other groups of children with developmental disabilities, these anomalies would more likely represent the disordered physiological substrate for dyslexia (Hynd & Semrud-Clikeman, 1989).

Proponents of another theory suggest that dyslexia is caused by dysfunctional interaction between the cerebral hemispheres. Such a suggestion seems reasonable, considering that learning to read necessitates visual discrimination and recognition of letters, a purported right-hemisphere function (e.g., Hellige & Webster, 1979), which must be linked with their phonetic representations, a purported left-hemisphere function (e.g., Levy & Trevarthen, 1977). Thus, children with dyslexia might have difficulty reading because information processed by the right hemisphere cannot be translated to the left. However, to date, no one has explicitly determined whether such a translation process is critical for reading acquisition. Furthermore, all evidence of disrupted interhemispheric interaction in these individuals comes from studies examining other skills besides reading. For example, boys with dyslexia have been found to have difficulties on a bimanual coordination task that appears to rely critically on interhemispheric interaction through the corpus callosum (because the task cannot be performed after the callosum is severed) (Gladstone, Best, &

Davidson, 1989). They also exhibit deficits in the execution and timing of bimanual, but not unilateral, motor movements (e.g., Rousselle & Wolff, 1991; Wolff, Cohen, & Drake, 1984).

Accurate interpretation of these findings is difficult because dyslexia is a specific problem in reading, not motor control. Although difficulties in bimanual coordination might reflect a larger problem in all aspects of interhemispheric interaction, disruption in the transfer of motoric information might be totally unrelated to the transfer of graphemic or phonemic information. Such independence is possible because different sections of the corpus callosum transfer different types of information (e.g., semantic, visual, auditory, motoric). Hence, in dyslexia, the callosal region transferring motoric information might be dysfunctional but the regions transferring visual or phonetic information might be intact (for a more detailed discussion of how to determine the role of interhemispheric interaction in dyslexia and other neurological syndromes, see Banich & Shenker, 1994b).

Although a clear picture of the neurological contributions to dyslexia remains elusive, the disorder does appear to have a genetic component. Dyslexia tends to run in families, and monozygotic twins, who share all the same genes, have a higher concordance rate for dyslexia (i.e., both twins are dyslexic) than that for dizygotic twins, who share only half their genes (Vellutino, 1987). Although traditionally individuals with dyslexia have been considered more likely to be left-handed than right-handed (e.g., Critchley, 1970) and male than female (DeFries, 1985), more recent work examining twins and their family members suggests that this is not true. Rather, the genders differ in the severity of their deficits: As they reach adulthood, females are less likely than males to have severe problems (Gilger et al., 1992).

Before we leave the topic of dyslexia, we should note that although it is one of the most common developmental disorders, it is not the only developmental disorder involving language. Whereas dyslexia is a specific problem in reading, **developmental dysphasia** is a disorder of expressive language in which children have difficulty understanding and producing speech. These children may have a larger underlying problem in the ability to process temporal information of short duration or temporal information that follows quickly in time, which would result in pervasive and multimodal language difficulties (e.g., Tallal, Sainburg, & Jernigan, 1991). As we learned in chapters 3 and 8, many aspects of language processing rely on fine temporal resolution. In fact, some recent therapies, in which these children are trained with language-like information that is slowed, have been effective, presumably because they increase these children's sensitivity to particular perceptual contrasts, which can then be generalized to regular speech (Tallal et al., 1996).

As reviewed by Rapin, Allen, and Dunn (1992), many other aspects of developmental dysphasia remain a mystery. Information on its prevalence varies widely; lower estimates are 2% and upper estimates are 14%. Because most children who receive a brain insult usually retain the ability to acquire language, the cause of developmental dysphasia is unlikely to be a specific lesion but may involve dysfunction of various regions of both hemispheres. To date, however, a clear causative neurological factor has not been isolated. Furthermore, no direct link has been found to environmental toxins, intrauterine exposure to alcohol, drugs, or an impoverished linguistic environment. However, like dyslexia, developmental dysphasia appears to have a genetic component. Children with developmental language delays were more likely than matched control individuals to have a relative (parent, sibling, or more distant relative) who also had a developmental language disorder or learning disability.

Because language is the medium by which we most often communicate and the medium by which we are schooled, developmental disorders in language processing, regardless of the domain, visual or oral, can have profound implications for the subsequent level of achievement in school and work. Because formal schooling emphasizes language, individuals with developmental language disabilities must find alternative ways to acquire information, and persons with dyslexia need to choose careers that do not emphasize the written word. Although acquiring information through reading is not impossible for persons with dyslexia, it is indeed difficult.

Nonverbal Learning Disabilities

Although developmental disabilities in the language domain have received the most attention and study, learning disabilities are not limited to this arena. Another class of learning disabilities, **nonverbal learning disabilities,** is characterized by difficulty in acquiring spatial and nonverbal skills while verbal abilities remain unaffected. Whereas developmental language disabilities tend to affect processes performed by the left hemisphere, nonverbal learning disabilities tend to affect those performed by the right hemisphere.

Children with nonverbal learning disabilities are doubly at risk because their difficulties in the nonverbal domain affect not only cognitive functions but also emotional functions. Although any child with a learning disability must deal with its social implications (e.g., being called "stupid," being excluded from play by other children), the compromise of emotional processing in children with nonverbal learning disabilities compounds the problem. We first examine the cognitive aspects of nonverbal learning disabilities, then the emotional ones.

Children with nonverbal learning disabilities exhibit a broad range of cognitive difficulties making for some disagreement across researchers as to the essential set (e.g., Myklebust, 1975; Rourke & Finlayson, 1978). Overall, however, these children have difficulty appreciating the significance of nonverbal information despite having normal verbal intelligence. The tasks with which they may have difficulty include aspects of perception, imagery, learning to tell time, being able to get from place to place (geographical and spatial orientation), reading maps, appreciating visuospatial organization, understanding the significance of events, and performing arithmetic. (Although arithmetic is often considered a left-hemisphere task, these children encounter problems because their difficulties in spatial relations do not enable them to align numbers correctly.) Anecdotally, their parents report that these children rarely play with toys that require vi-

suoconstructive skills, such as puzzles and blocks. In addition, these children often have signs of neurological impairments, such as disorders in reflexes, impaired muscle tone, and tremors, that manifest only on the left side, indicative of right-hemisphere dysfunction (Semrud-Clikeman & Hynd, 1990). Despite these difficulties, nonverbal learning disabilities are considered to be underdiagnosed, in part because the intact verbal skills of these children do not alert teachers and parents to their problems.

In addition to the cognitive deficits, a concomitant constellation of social and emotional difficulties characterize nonverbal learning disabilities. As we learned in chapter 11, the right hemisphere is especially important for the interpretation and expression of emotion. In general, these children lack the ability to understand the social environment. Their difficulties may be exhibited in many domains. Perceptually, they may lack an ability to understand facial expression or gesture, to understand tone of voice, and to link those signals with verbal messages. In terms of production, their speech tends to be either flat and monotonous or hyperemotional and effusive. These difficulties are accompanied by difficulties in comprehending the social world, which is characterized by an avoidance of new situations, a lack of friends, and an inability to benefit from past experience in the social world. Their poor social competence is exhibited by their lack of empathy and their attempts to keep a listener's attention with a lot of verbal jargon that does little to foster communication or dialogue. All these difficulties manifest on personality testing, which, on average, shows elevated levels of anxiety, withdrawal, and depression (Strang & Rourke, 1985). Learning can be difficult for these children, not only because they have difficulty acquiring information in certain content areas, but also because they cannot process the social signals that are critical to the interactive nature of learning environments.

Autism and Pervasive Developmental Disorders

The **pervasive developmental disorders,** the most well-known of which is probably **autism,** have four basic characteristics: qualitative impairment in social interaction; delays and abnormalities in language as well as other aspects of communication; restricted, repetitive, and stereotyped patterns of behaviors, interests, or activities; and an onset of the problems in at least one of these three areas before the age of 3 years (American Psychiatric Association, *Diagnostic and Statistical Manual of Mental Disorders,* 4th ed., 1994). Most children with pervasive developmental disorders (75%) are also mentally retarded, meaning that their IQs are significantly below average. What is striking, however, about an autistic child, as compared with a child who is mentally retarded but not autistic, are the profound social deficits that the autistic child displays. Children with mental retardation seek interaction with adults, smile, and appreciate being held when hurt. Autistic children, on the other hand, are more likely to want to engage in routinized robotic behavior such as hand flapping, to scream if approached (as if being seriously intruded upon or violated), and to avoid the gaze of other people. They appear not to care whether people are present, and when others are around seem to act as if they were pieces of furniture or to "look through" them as if they didn't exist. When these children do become attached to something, it is usually an inanimate object, such as a piece of string or a rubber band (Fein et al., 1986).

Children with autism tend to do best on cognitive tasks that do not require human interaction or are not learned through human interaction. For example, their performance on certain mathematical or constructional puzzles (which require little human interaction) is much better than their performance on language tasks would predict. On recognition tests, they often can identify inanimate objects, such as a screwdriver, more readily than objects representing something human, such as a face. Their cognitive interests are usually narrow and unemotional, such as an obsession with baseball statistics, and they are often absorbed by mechanical movement (e.g., the spinning of an electric fan). They lack flexibility, becoming upset if any aspect of a routine is broken, and exhibit stereotypical and repetitive motor behaviors (e.g., hand flapping, head banging) (*DSM-IV,* 1994).

Throughout the history of thought on autism, which Kanner first described in 1943, people have debated whether it is primarily a cognitive disorder or an emotional disorder, a debate that continues today (e.g., Sigman, 1994). Early theories attributed autism to factors in the child's social environment, such as "cold mothering," which would leave the child socially isolated from the world and emotionally disturbed (Bettleheim, 1967). Such an emotional disconnection was hypothesized to preclude the types of interaction that would allow autistic children to acquire adequate cognitive skills. Although environmental models of autism have fallen by the wayside, many neurologically based models of autism view disturbances in emotional functioning as a primary component of the syndrome. This position is based on evidence that other developmental syndromes characterized by severe cognitive deficits are not accompanied by such profound defects in emotional functioning and that even when autistic individuals have adequate cognitive skills, they still manifest difficulty in the social realm (see Fein et al., 1986, for the details of this position).

Other theorists suggest that the basic problem in autism is not one of emotion but rather of cognition. They base their position on findings that wide and severe cognitive problems, especially in language, can linger, even if the child's social withdrawal improves with age. According to this viewpoint, the autistic child has a basic cognitive problem in understanding and modifying rules, using information symbolically, or using information in a sequential manner (e.g., Rutter, 1983). The central cognitive deficits would make the world, to an autistic child, a weird and incomprehensible place, a place to be avoided. Viewed from this perspective, the social and emotional deficits result from the lack of an adequate cognitive system to handle the demands of social interaction. Although the debate over the basic underlying problem in autism remains, most individuals will agree that autistic children seem to avoid interacting with the environment and people and act as if the world around them is intrusive, behavior that leads to both social isolation and cognitive deprivation.

At present, autism is assumed to be a heterogeneous disorder with many potential causes, including genetic disorders, infectious disease, birth injury, metabolic diseases, and structural disorders of brain development (e.g., Coleman, 1987). The constellation of brain structures involved in autism remains unclear, although a number of regions have been implicated. The potential contribution of each is beyond the scope of this chapter, so they are mentioned only briefly here. Some researchers have suggested that autism reflects an attentional disorder that is caused by abnormalities in the cerebellum, brain stem, thalamus, and striatum (i.e., the caudate, putamen, and globus pallidus) (Courchesne et al., 1988). Other investigators have emphasized the role of temporal lobe regions, specifically medial temporal areas (Bachevalier, 1994). Still other researchers have implicated a dysfunctional frontal-limbic system (A. R. Damasio & Maurer, 1978). Yet, at present, damage to none of these regions alone appears to account for all the behavioral symptoms observed in autistic children.

Notice that all the regions purported to be involved in autism share two main characteristics. First, a number of them, such as regions of the limbic system and temporal lobe, are typically associated with emotional functioning. Second, they tend to be part of a system that involves many different brain regions. The diffuse nature of brain structures affected in autism likely explains why this disorder affects so many aspects of intellectual and emotional functioning, in contrast to the specific verbal and nonverbal developmental disorders considered earlier, which affect a more circumscribed set of abilities.

Attention-Deficit Disorder

Attention-deficit disorder (ADD) is a developmental disorder in which the affected child is much more inattentive and distractible than is typical for the average child of the same age. Furthermore, individuals with ADD tend to be hyperactive and impulsive (*DSM-IV*, 1994) and are often guided by environmental dependencies similar to those discussed in chapter 10. These children *are* capable of paying attention and sitting still, because they may spend hours playing a video game, but overall their ability to do so is much less than is typical for their age. ADD often impedes a child's progress in learning, especially in a structured environment, because the child's impulsivity and distractibility do not allow him or her to sit still long enough to absorb material or to listen to instructions. Because of these tendencies, such children may find themselves cherished by neither teachers nor parents. If their behavior leads to difficulty with peers and authority figures, they can be at risk for engaging in antisocial behavior. Furthermore, although ADD is a distinct disorder, it can occur simultaneously with other learning disabilities such as dyslexia.

The primary means of treating children with ADD is with dextroamphetamine, which is related to amphetamine (Gadow, 1981), or methylphenidate (often known by its trade name, Ritalin). Amphetamine is known to increase concentration and the ability to focus (in fact, when taken in inappropriately large doses, amphetamine can cause overfocusing on a specific task or idea). Methylphenidate is known to affect the dopaminergic neurotransmitter system by slowing the rate of dopamine reuptake on postsynaptic sites. For children with ADD, these medications have been found to improve cognitive performance (e.g., Barkley, 1977), classroom behavior (e.g., Whalen, Henker, & Dotemoto, 1981), and interaction with parents (e.g., Barkley, Karlsson, Pollard, & Murphy, 1985). Because this medication is effective for most children with ADD, researchers assume that irregularities in the dopaminergic system cause the disorder.

A variety of other evidence also links ADD to the dopaminergic system. Anatomically, this system originates in the brain-stem regions and projects diffusely to many target areas, including frontal cortex. This system is thought to affect overall arousal and attention, as well as some aspects of motor functioning. The symptoms exhibited by children with ADD are sometimes reminiscent of those exhibited by individuals with damage to the frontal lobe (e.g., Barkley, Grodzinsky, & DuPaul, 1992), a region that receives many dopaminergic projections. PET studies comparing brain activation in children with ADD in medicated versus nonmedicated states also implicate the dopaminergic system.

Off methylphenidate, the children had hypoperfusion (less activity) in the caudate, putamen, and globus pallidus (i.e., the striatum), as well as in frontal regions. In addition, primary sensorimotor areas appeared to be overactivated. With methylphenidate, activation of striatal regions increased, whereas that of primary sensory regions decreased (Lou et al., 1989).

As we reviewed in the last three sections, development disorders can seriously hamper a child's ability to proceed along the normal developmental course with regard to the acquisition of cognitive and emotional skills. These disorders either affect specific areas of cognition, as in the case of dyslexia and nonverbal learning disabilities, or impair a broad array of cognitive functions, as in pervasive developmental disorders and ADD. These disorders may affect social functioning directly, as in pervasive developmental disorders, or indirectly, as in the case of dyslexia, because of their present and future effects on a child's social status. Because the problems rarely disappear with age (although they may dissipate), interventions that can mitigate the child's disabilities (e.g., tutoring, counseling) are often started as early as possible.

Mental Retardation

Many of the developmental disabilities that we discussed so far manifest in relatively specific ways, such as the inability to read or the inability to pay attention. When children do not acquire intellectual abilities across practically all cognitive domains in the rate and manner expected during the course of normal development, and when they have difficulties in adaptive functioning, such as self-care, the disorder is termed **mental retardation.** Mental retardation is generally divided into four categories based on severity. This classification system and the characteristics of individuals in each category are presented in Table 13.2.

Mental retardation can be caused by numerous

Table 13.2 The Four Classes of Mental Retardation Based on Severity

Degree of retardation	IQ level	Percentage[a]	Typical presentation
Mild	50–55 to 70	85	Previously known as "academically educable."
			Develop normally during preschool but don't acquire academic abilities above the 6th-grade level.
			As adults can usually be self-supportive although at times may need supervision and guidance.
Moderate	35–40 to 50–55	10	Previously known as "academically trainable."
			Can acquire communication skills during early childhood.
			As adults, need supervision for living and work.
Severe	20–25 to 35–40	3–4	Can learn some elementary self-care and language skills.
			As adults, can perform simple tasks in closely supervised settings.
Profound	<20–25	1–2	Usually have an identifiable neurologic disorder that accounts for the retardation.
			Have impairments during childhood in sensorimotor functioning.
			Need highly structured environment with constant supervision by an individual caregiver.

[a]Percentage of all mentally retarded children who fall into that category.
Note. Data from American Psychiatric Association, 1994.

Table 13.3 The Various Causes of Mental Retardation

Cause	Cases (%)	Example mechanisms	Example syndromes
Heredity	5	Error of metabolism	Phenylketonuria (PKU)
		Chromosomal aberrations	Fragile X syndrome
Early alteration of embryonic development	30	Prenatal exposure to a toxin	Fetal alcohol syndrome (FAS)
Problems in pregnancy and perinatally	10	Infection	Rubella
		Maternal malnutrition	Low birth weight
Medical conditions in child-hood and infancy	5	Poisoning	Ingestion of lead
		Malnutrition	Kwashiorkor
Environmental influences	15–20	Deprivation	No parental nurturance
No clear cause	30–40	?	?

Note. Data from American Psychiatric Association, 1994.

factors, including infections, genetic disorders, toxins, anoxia, and malnutrition. In the discussion that follows, we describe these as **risk factors,** which means that although they increase the likelihood of observing a general cognitive deficit, they do not ensure that one will be observed. These risk factors act much the way that a drunken driver, a slippery road, and bald tires act to increase the probability that the driver will be involved in a vehicular accident, although they don't ensure that an accident will ensue. The major predisposing factors for mental retardation are provided in Table 13.3

As we learned earlier in the chapter, the developing brain is plastic and can be affected by the environment to a greater degree than the adult brain can. Although the virtues of this plasticity are that the brain can fine-tune itself to the environment, it is also more vulnerable to influences that can affect it negatively, such as the risk factors for mental retardation. Risk factors for retardation can exert themselves either prenatally or postnatally. A growing public appreciation for the prenatal risk factors is reflected in public service announcements and packaging labels directed at pregnant women; such precautionary information advises pregnant women to limit their ingestion of certain substances (e.g.,

alcohol), emphasizes adequate nutrition, or warns the women to avoid individuals with certain infectious diseases, such as German measles (rubella). We now review the major risk factors for mental retardation and the means by which they have negative effects.

Infections

A variety of infections may damage the developing fetus by crossing the *placenta,* which is the membranous organ by which nutrients and blood are passed from the mother to the fetus. These infections, which are thought to occur in as many as 2% of all newborns, include toxoplasmosis, rubella, cytomegalovirus, and herpes simplex. One of the best known of these is rubella. If acquired by the mother before the 13th gestational week (even if during the last menstrual period before conception), rubella affects 50% of all infants and is associated with mental retardation and behavioral disorders (e.g., Chess, Fernandez, & Korn, 1979). The herpes virus is also a problem because it may exist undetected in many adults yet have devastating consequences for a developing organism. In addition to causing mental retardation, many viruses may cause anomalous development of the auditory tract, which leads to deafness and hampers the acquisition of speech and other aspects of language (e.g., Eichhorn, 1982).

Genetic Disorders

Many genetic disorders cause mental retardation. In this section, we briefly review only the major syndromes. Like the infections just described, genetic disorders affect not only the brain, but also other aspects of physical development.

One of the major genetic disorders leading to mental retardation is **Down syndrome,** which occurs in 1 in 100 cases. Then retardation is usually severe, and IQs are typically lower than those exhibited by less than 2% of the unimpaired population. This syndrome is caused by a defective egg or sperm or defects in early cell division, or more rarely because chromosomes translocate (move to other positions) during mitosis (the replication and subsequent division of DNA). It can also be caused by trisomy 21, which is a condition in which the 21st pair of chromosomes contains three chromosomes (hence *tri*somy) rather than the usual two. One well-known risk factor for Down syndrome is the mother's age. The probability of having a Down syndrome child increases significantly if the mother is older than 35 years (e.g., Lilienfeld, 1969). As they enter the fourth or fifth decade of life, many individuals with Down syndrome begin to exhibit symptoms similar to those of Alzheimer's disease (which we discuss in chapter 14), and postmortem examination of the brain reveals the tangles and plaques typical of Alzheimer's disease (e.g., Karlinsky, 1986; Oliver & Holland, 1986).

Another commonly inherited form of mental retardation is **fragile X syndrome** (sometimes referred to as *Martin–Bell syndrome*), which affects 1 in 1,500 boys and 1 in 2,500 girls (e.g., Webb, Bundey, Thake, & Todd, 1986). Because of this high incidence rate, some localities, such as Alberta, Canada, routinely screen newborns for this genetic disorder. In this syndrome, an individual inherits an X chromosome (from the mother in the case of boys or from either parent in the case of girls) with a fragile section at which a normally repeating sequence of genetic material occurs an unusually large number of times, much like a genetic stutter (see C. A. Ross, McInnis, Margolis, & Li, 1993, for a discussion of unusually large repeating sequences causing not only fragile X syndrome but other neuropsychiatric disorders as well). If a male receives this gene, he has an 80% chance of being mentally retarded, whereas for girls the chance is 30%. The degree of retardation varies, ranging from profound to borderline in boys and from mild to borderline in girls (see Table 13.2) (S. T. Warren & Nelson, 1994). Unlike Down syndrome, which is associated with a specific morphology of the body and face (Figure 13.11A), the changes in morphology are not as noticeable in individuals with fragile X syndrome, although an affected individual may have a long, narrow face; a long prominent chin, and large ears (Figure 13.11B) (Cianchetti et al., 1991). Because the physical characteristics of this syndrome are often subtle and screening for the disorder is not routine in many places, and because the manifestations of the disorder can vary, children with fragile X syndrome are often not diagnosed until later in childhood when they begin to fall behind their peers in development. Because children with this disorder can display autistic symptoms and approximately 12% of all males diagnosed as autistic have a fragile X chromosome, some researchers have suggested that these two disorders are related, although this viewpoint is by no means universally accepted (e.g., see W. T. Brown et al., 1986, and Fisch, 1992, for opposing viewpoints).

Another genetic disorder, which if untreated leads to severe mental retardation, is **phenylketonuria (PKU),** which occurs in 1 of every 18,000 births. In this disorder, individuals lack phenylalanine hydroxylase, an enzyme, that allows phenylalanine, a specific amino acid, to be converted to tyrosine. As a result, phenylalanine builds up in the blood, and there is a deficit in tyrosine and tryptophan, a metabolic precursor to the neurotransmitter dopamine. Hence, the brain is deprived of a critical neurotransmitter, and mental retardation results. Currently, newborns are screened for PKU; such screening allows dietary measures that restrict the intake of phenylalanine to be instituted immediately

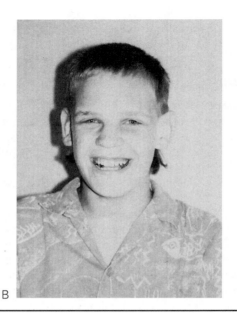

A   B

Figure 13.11   Physical features associated with genetic causes of mental retardation.
(A) Individuals who have Down syndrome typically have certain physical features that make this type of retardation relatively easy to detect in infancy. These features include an upper eyelid that, at the corner of the eye, folds over the bottom eyelid, and a face with a relatively flat profile. (B) In fragile X syndrome, the associated physical features are much less pronounced. As shown here in this adolescent male who has the syndrome, they include a long face, a prominent forehead, and large ears. However, as can be seen, these features are not so out of the ordinary as to make the diagnosis obvious. (*Note.* A, From *Child Psychology: A Contemporary Viewpoint* (4th ed., p. 72), by E. M. Hetherington and R. D. Parke, 1993, New York, McGraw-Hill. Reproduced with permission of The McGraw-Hill Companies. B, Reprinted with permission from "Advances in Molecular Analysis of Fragile X Syndrome," by S. T. Warren and D. L. Nelson, 1994, *Journal of the American Medical Association*, 271(7), p. 537. Copyright 1994, American Medical Association.)

after birth. (You may already be aware of PKU if you noticed labels on diet soda cans warning people with PKU, phenylketonurics, that the soda contains phenylalanine.) Although these procedures can ameliorate the negative mental consequences of this condition, problems can still arise because the children typically dislike this diet and want to "cheat." Furthermore, some evidence exists that even with early treatment, children with PKU can still exhibit intellectual deficits, especially in the realm of attention (e.g., Craft et al., 1992).

Other genetic disorders can affect specific aspects of intellectual functioning. One such disorder is **Turner's syndrome,** in which a female inherits just one X chromosome (XO) rather than two (XX)

(fetuses who inherit just a Y chromosome are not viable). Although these individuals' overall intelligence is normal and their verbal abilities tend to be above average, their spatial and perceptual skills are below average. At present, no specific brain abnormalities that would explain such a pattern of cognitive disabilities have been identified (e.g., Bender, Linden, & Robinson, 1994). In contrast, the inheritance of an additional X chromosome in both males (XXY) and females (XXX) is associated with poor verbal skills (e.g., Netley & Rovet, 1982; Pennington, Puck, & Robinson, 1980).

The exact mechanism whereby these genetic anomalies cause disruption in mental functioning is not yet clear. Because no cure exists for these disorders, the emphasis is on prevention or early intervention. Genetic counseling can help individuals decide whether they want to have a child, and amniocentesis can help women decide whether they want to carry an affected fetus, such as one with Down syndrome, to term. Screening for disorders at birth allows for intervention early in life (as in the case of PKU).

Toxins

Toxins are another cause of mental retardation. Recently, the public has been made more aware of this association because of discussion in the media and admonishments on cigarette packages and liquor bottles regarding the negative effects of tobacco and alcohol, respectively, on the developing fetus. The long-term effects of alcohol abuse by the mother during pregnancy are clear-cut and result in **fetal alcohol syndrome (FAS),** which is the leading cause of mental retardation (and is entirely preventable if the mother refrains from excessive drinking). FAS may also cause hyperactivity, poor attention span, social and emotional difficulties, retarded physical growth, and abnormalities of the face and cranium (see N. L. Day, 1992, and Streissguth, 1992, for a discussion of FAS and Goodlett & West, 1992, for an animal model of its effects on the brain). To provide some perspective, the amount of alcohol that these mothers typically consume is between 24 and 32 shots of hard liquor a week (or about 3.5 to 4.5 a day). Lower (but excessive) alcohol consumption during pregnancy, especially the early stages, can cause less severe effects, which are known as **fetal alcohol effects.**

Another drug whose negative effects on the developing fetus have received much attention is cocaine. However, some studies suggest that certain effects in crack babies (i.e., babies whose mothers are addicted to cocaine that is smoked) may be transient (e.g., L. F. Allen et al., 1991) and that with adequate support, children of crack-addicted mothers can make adequate academic progress. Nonetheless, difficulties in social interaction have been noted in children of substance abusers. For example, as infants they may not be responsive to

a mother's touch or attention (e.g., Beckwith et al., 1994). Whether these early difficulties have future negative implications for their ability to sustain relationships in academic, occupational, and personal arenas is one that will be answered only by longitudinal research on these children as they grow older. Ascertaining the specific effects of the mother's drug abuse on the subsequent mental status of the developing fetus is often difficult because other factors typically associated with the mother's cocaine use, such as poor nutrition, can also lead to mental retardation (a point often overlooked in the media's discussion of this issue) (e.g., N. L. Day & Richardson, 1993).

Anoxia

The brain is the most metabolically demanding of all organs, and because oxygen is critical for the conversion of glucose into energy, deprivation of oxygen (anoxia) for as few as 3 min is sufficient to cause brain death. Oxygen is even more critical for the developing nervous system because, as we learned previously, the metabolic needs of the developing nervous system can exceed those of the adult nervous system. Oxygen deprivation can occur during development in a variety of ways. Before birth, a child may experience reduced oxygen because the placenta (which allows blood to pass from the mother to the child) may be underdeveloped or damaged or because the mother doesn't have adequate oxygen herself (e.g., as a result of anemia). During birth, damage to the placenta or entanglement of the umbilical cord may reduce the oxygen supply to the infant. After birth, some populations of infants, such as those born very prematurely, are at risk for anoxia because their lungs are not developed enough for breathing (Spreen et al., 1984; for a review of the implications of oxygen deprivation at birth, see Blackman, 1989).

Children who have an anoxic episode early in life are at increased risk for later mental retardation (Lipper et al., 1986) and **cerebral palsy,** which is an umbrella term for many motor disorders resulting from nonprogressive damage to neural structures important for motor control (e.g., K. B.

Nelson & Ellenberg, 1986). However, mental retardation is not an inevitable consequence of anoxia early in life, and some children such as those with congenital heart problems, may exhibit substantial improvement if interventions are enacted to increase the oxygen supply to the brain (e.g., O'Dougherty, Wright, Loewenson, & Torres, 1985).

Malnutrition

Malnutrition either prenatally or postnatally can have serious consequences for later development because without enough nutrition, the child's organ systems, including the brain, will be underdeveloped (for a discussion of how undernutrition affects brain development, see Patel, 1983). In some situations, children receive adequate nutrition as long as they are breast-fed, but thereafter they may be in an environment in which their diet is deficient. Starvation due to a lack of protein in the diet, known as **kwashiorkor,** and starvation due to a deficiency in caloric intake, known as **marasmus,** are problems seen especially in developing countries (Spreen et al., 1984). Children with these disorders often have much edema, which accounts for the rounded faces and greatly bloated stomachs that we commonly see in journalists' pictures of children who live in famine-stricken regions of the world. Although inadequate nutrition often leads to mental retardation (e.g., Hoorweg & Stanfield, 1976), proper nutrition after early starvation (e.g., Bartel et al., 1977), as well as a stimulating environment, may diminish or overcome such effects. One difficulty in interpreting the results of studies of children who were malnourished during development is that the nutritional deficiency often coexists with other conditions, such as inadequate medical care and impoverished social and physical environments, that also have negative consequences for intellectual development (e.g., Ricciuti, 1993).

Adult Outcomes of Developmental Disorders

So far, we discussed the effects of developmental disorders on children but did not consider the level of functioning that these children show as adults.

For some of the disorders we discussed, the outcome is relatively straightforward. For instance, individuals who exhibit mental retardation or pervasive developmental disorders as children also exhibit intellectual impairment as adults. However, what about some of the more specific learning disabilities such as dyslexia and ADD? Do children outgrow these disorders, or do these syndromes hinder them for life?

One theory put forth to explain specific learning disabilities was the **maturational lag hypothesis,** which postulated that individuals with learning disabilities were slower to mature than their peers and that with time they would outgrow the problem much the way that children shed baby fat. Given our increasing knowledge regarding the neural bases for these disorders, however, the idea that these learning disabilities miraculously disappear at adulthood seems improbable. Nonetheless, some evidence exists that learning disabilities may become less severe with age in certain subpopulations of children. For example, some children with ADD have dramatic improvement in attentional skills around age 12 years, which is when children typically show an increase in attentional abilities. For the most part, however, learning disabilities in childhood also manifest in adulthood.

The fact that learning disabilities can endure across the life span is supported by both anatomical and behavioral evidence. Let's consider dyslexia as an example. As mentioned previously, atypical cell migration or atypical myelination occurs prenatally. These anatomical anomalies remain for the individual's entire life. The question then arises as to whether the brain can reorganize itself, despite this atypical substrate, to allow normal behavioral development. Such reorganization apparently isn't possible because compared with the performance of neurologically intact adults on neuropsychological test batteries, especially on tests that emphasize phonologic processing, the performance of adults with dyslexia is impaired. A difference is observed even if the individuals with dyslexia and the control individuals are matched for socioeconomic status (which is important because a poor reading ability may limit job opportunities for persons with dyslexia, and such limitations may lead to a lower-than-average socioeconomic status). Furthermore, neuropsychological test results for adults with dyslexia exhibit a profile that is suggestive of left posterior temporoparietal dysfunction and that is similar to profiles of individuals who acquire alexia as a result of brain injury (see chapter 8, page 296, for a discussion of alexia). Moreover, adults who had poor reading scores as children exhibit little focal activation (as measured by regional cerebral blood flow) of these left parietal regions during reading (Bigler, 1992). All these findings suggest that the brain of a person with dyslexia cannot compensate for certain aspects of the neural disorganization that occurred early in development.

Although we used dyslexia as an example, other childhood syndromes may extend into adulthood as well. For instance, because of their social inadequacy, childen with nonverbal learning disabilities may have mental health difficulties as adults. In one study, 7 of 8 adults who had been diagnosed with a nonverbal learning disability were prone to depression, 4 of them so severely as to require hospitalization. In addition, all were working at lower status jobs than would be anticipated on the basis of their schooling (Rourke, Young, Strang, & Russell, 1985). Likewise, as mentioned previously, children with ADD may have problems that evolve into antisocial behavior, especially in the later teen and adult years.

As we learn in the next section, the brain has a large potential for reorganizing itself in response to trauma and deprivation. This plasticity may account for some of the diminution in learning disabilities that can occur as a child ages. Yet it does not occur either in the manner or to the degree necessary to preclude learning disorders from manifesting themselves. We now turn our attention to an examination of the reorganization and plasticity of the brain.

RECOVERY OF FUNCTION

Our discussion so far centered on the development of the brain and the anomalies that may occur in the course of that development. We now need to examine how the brain reacts when it sustains a specific insult (e.g., a gunshot wound). First, we describe, in a general manner, the brain's responses to injury on a neurophysiological level. Then we discuss the possible mechanisms for recovery. Finally, we compare the differences in recovery of function between adults and children.

Neurophysiological Responses to Insult

Damage to the brain sets a number of physiological processes in motion, some of which occur directly at the site of the lesion and others of which occur at more distant points. At the site of the lesion, cells begin to die, a process called **necrosis.** (Remember that unlike other cells in the body, neurons do not regenerate but are lost forever.) Dead cells are engulfed and broken down (a process known as *phagocytosis*) by astrocytes and microglia. Other changes at the site of damage include the formation of new capillaries as well as the introduction of fluid to fill the spaces where cells once resided. The process of phagocytosis and capillary formation may continue for several months until only glial cells remain, a process known as **gliosis.** Astrocytes mark off the region, forming a scar.

The type of degeneration observed in nerve cells varies and depends in part on the component of the neuron that was damaged (Figure 13.12A) **Anterograde (wallerian) degeneration** occurs when the axon of a neuron in the central nervous system is severed from the cell body. Because the cell body is responsible for all synthesis of proteins and neurotransmitters, a severed axon is like a town whose critical supply route from the city has been washed out in a flood. The axon and the associated oligodendrocyte that forms its myelin sheath will die (Figure 13.12B). Another type of degeneration after injury is **retrograde degeneration,** in which not only does the portion of the cell distal to the site of injury die, but so does the rest of the axon and the cell body (Figure 13.12C). In some cases, cell loss may extend past the actual site of damage to more distal neurons, a process called **transneuronal degeneration** (Figure 13.12D). Such degeneration occurs because neurons require an optimal level of stimulation, certain chemical (probably nutritional)

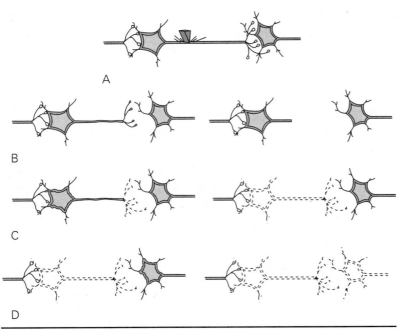

Figure 13.12   Different types of neuronal degeneration in response to injury.
(A) Site of injury. Here the axon is severed from the cell body. (B) In antero-grade degeneration, the cell body of the damaged neuron remains intact but portions of the axon distal to the site of injury die (left, early degeneration; right, late degeneration). (C) In retrograde degeneration, the entire neuron, in-cluding the cell body, dies (left, early degeneration; right, late degeneration). (D) In transneuronal degeneration, neurons that received inputs from the damaged neuron also die (left, early degeneration; right, late degeneration). (*Note.* Adapted from Kolb, 1985, p. 643; Rosenzweig & Leiman, 1989, p. 118.)

factors, or both from other nerve cells. Thus, if a substantial proportion of a neuron's inputs are damaged, that cell may die. Transneuronal degener-ation can occur across more than one synapse, hav-ing a domino-like effect. For example, if the optic nerve is cut, cells of the lateral geniculate body de-generate completely. Then, as the lateral geniculate begins to degenerate, cells in the visual cortex may degenerate as well. Often transneuronal degenera-tion is accompanied by accumulations of calcium, a process known as **calcification** which can easily be detected by brain imaging techniques, such as computerized axial tomography (CAT) scanning.

In addition to changes in the neurons themselves, other processes occur with damage. One of these, **edema,** is the swelling of tissue after trauma, which occurs in the brain just as it does in any other part of the body. However, swelling of the brain involves dangers not associated with bruising of other body parts. When other body parts are bruised, they just take up more space under your clothing. But the brain shares a confined space with cerebrospinal fluid within the skull, and when it is bruised, the situation is similar to one in which you have a badly bruised toe that must be shoved into your shoe. The edema associated with brain trauma leads to an increase in intracranial pressure because more fluid now occupies the same amount of space. This increased pressure can interfere with neuronal func-tion not only at the site of damage, but elsewhere as well. When the edema exerts pressure on brain-stem regions controlling vital functions, it can cause a person to become comatose, or, in more severe cases, even die. Hence, cortisone, a steroid, is often given after cerebral trauma to help reduce edema. Because edema may last for some time (e.g., weeks), the behavioral consequences of a lesion may not be apparent shortly after damage because such consequences are difficult to disentangle from the effects of generalized edema.

In addition to the changes just discussed, some of the basic aspects of brain functioning, such as its metabolic rate, neurotransmitter release, and oxygen consumption, may also be disrupted by a lesion. Generally after brain damage an immediate reduction in brain metabolism occurs both at the site of damage and in other brain regions, with subsequent reductions in blood flow that may linger for as long as 1 month. Brain trauma may also cause changes in neurotransmitter levels, with an initial decrease sometimes followed later by an increase over normal levels (which may be an attempt by remaining neurons to compensate for those that have been lost). The oxygen supply to the brain is also often decreased after damage, which not only damages neurons immediately, but also may cause more long-term effects. For example, oxygen deprivation allows a certain set of cells in the hippocampus (CA_1 cells) to release too much of a particular neurotransmitter, glutamate, which in turn overexcites the CA_1 cells; this overexcitation then leads to the death of these cells (Kolb & Whishaw, 1990).

Given these multiple changes in brain function in response to injury and the long time span during which they manifest themselves, you can begin to appreciate why the clinician often cannot immediately assess the degree of damage sustained from an injury. If swelling is extensive, the person may show severe impairments at first but significant improvement as the edema decreases. On the other hand, responses immediately after oxygen deprivation may overestimate later levels of functioning because the detrimental effects of the oxygen deprivation continue to accrue. Thus, measures based on the person's behavior immediately after injury can only crudely predict the prognosis for functioning a

month or even a year into the future (we discuss one of these measures, the Glasgow Coma Scale, in chapter 14).

Mechanisms for Recovery of Function

Once the brain sustains an insult, the central nervous system uses various processes to attempt to compensate for the loss. Some of these mechanisms occur at the cellular level, whereas others involve larger regions of brain tissue. These changes in which the brain tries to override and adapt its typical organization in the face of damage, trauma, or unusual circumstances (e.g., sensory deprivation) is known as **reorganization.** This process is observed both in developing organisms (i.e., children) and in adults. Reorganization can occur at a very gross level, such as the pattern of gyri and sulci of the brain (if the damage is inflicted in utero) (Goldman-Rakic & Rakic, 1984), or on a neuronal level. As we learn in the following sections, reorganization of the brain that occurs after damage early in life is usually more profound than that which can occur later in life. Although scientists originally believed that little if any reorganization was possible in the adult brain, that notion is slowly fading. With these general concepts in mind, we now examine in more detail the changes that occur in the nervous system in response to injury.

Cellular Processes

At the cellular level, a number of changes occur that may aid in recovery of function. Although **regeneration,** the reestablishment of a prior connection by a damaged nerve fiber, can occur in the peripheral nervous system, once a connection in the central nervous system is lost, it cannot be regenerated (in part because glial cells appear to inhibit neural growth; see Bahr & Bonhoeffer, 1994). Other processes that occur in response to damage in both the central and peripheral nervous systems involve neurochemical adaptations. One of these is **denervation supersensitivity,** in which intact cells become hypersensitive to stimulation. This process is thought to occur especially when reductions in the level of neurotransmitters, such as dopamine, occur. The number of receptors on the remaining cells increases so that the same amount of neurotransmitter can produce a much larger result. Such a mechanism may help to explain why deficits are not observed in Parkinson's disease until the vast majority of the dopamine-producing neurons are destroyed (see chapter 4, in which we discussed this disease). Responses to brain damage may also involve changes in the rate of synthesis or release of neurotransmitters or decreases in the rate at which transmitters are inactivated.

Two other cellular mechanisms for recovery are rerouting and sprouting. In **rerouting,** a neuron that has lost its target seeks a new target and connects with it instead. This process is distinct from **sprouting,** in which the nerve fiber grows, becomes bushier, and makes new connections. Thus, sprouting involves not only rerouting, but a proliferation of nerve growth as well. Sprouting may occur not only near an injury, but also at other sites far away (see Feinberg, Mazlin, & Waldman, 1989, for a discussion of the relevance of these mechanisms in humans).

One possible means by which regeneration, sprouting, and rerouting may occur is through a substance known as nerve growth factor (NGF), which is transported to nerve cells from glia. NGF was discovered in the 1940s by Rita Levi-Montalcini and colleagues, a discovery for which she received the Nobel Prize (for an interesting account of how doing experiments in a closet while hiding from the Nazis during World War II led her to this discovery, read her autobiography entitled *In Praise of Imperfection*). These researchers found that an antibody to NGF injected into newborn mice and rats reduced the number of neurons in the dorsal root ganglion of the spinal cord, which suggests that NGF is an important substance for sustaining neuronal growth. NGF has a large effect on three classes of neurons, only one of which is located within the central nervous system: cholinergic neurons of the basal forebrain and septum. Cutting the septal cholinergic neurons leading into the hippocampus (a region with one of the highest concentrations of NGF in the central nervous system) causes about

half the neurons to die. However, if NGF is injected into the ventricle immediately after the transection, neuronal death decreases. These findings suggest that NGF may be an important substance in sustaining neurons, especially after injury (Jessell, 1991). An interesting point to note is that neurons in the basal forebrain are markedly degenerated in Alzheimer's disease (see chapter 14 for more on Alzheimer's disease). Hence, a reduction in NGF may be one of the mechanisms whereby cell death occurs in this syndrome (e.g., Hefti & Weiner, 1986).

The efficacy of these various cellular mechanisms in promoting neuronal responses after injury is important because neuronal elaboration after injury appears to be linked to the degree to which behavior is restored. In a series of studies, Kolb and colleagues examined the effects of damage to various areas of a single hemisphere of rat cortex at different ages during development. Afterward, the rats were given the equivalent of a rodent neuropsychological test battery to determine their degree of impairment on species-specific behavioral tasks (such as grooming and exploring) and more cognitive and novel tasks, such as maze learning. These investigators found that when skills were recovered, the recovery was always accompanied by extensive dendritic arborization in the remaining intact cortex (Kolb, 1989).

Regional Processes

Not only can damage to the nervous system cause changes at the cellular level, but it can also cause regional changes in brain organization. Probably the best evidence that brain reorganization can occur in adult mammals comes from studies in which the brain loses specific types of sensory input or in which sensory regions are destroyed. Hence, we discuss these studies first and then examine whether similar effects can occur in humans after brain trauma.

Although at one time not a commonly held view, we now know that the adult brain is capable of reorganization. Probably some the most compelling research comes from a series of studies done by Merzenich and colleagues, who demonstrated

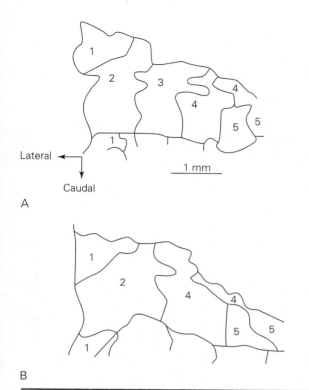

Lateral ←

Caudal

A

1 mm

B

Figure 13.13 Changes in the maps of the somatosensory cortex in the monkey in response to changes in the sensory information that it receives.
These maps indicate the areas of the brain that are sensitive to touch for the first (1) through fifth (5) digits (A) prior to amputation and (B) 62 days after amputation of the third digit. The region of brain tissue that previously was sensitive to touch from the third digit is now sensitive to tactile information from the second and fourth digits. The change between the map depicted in (A) and that depicted in (B) indicates the ability of the brain to reorganize even during adulthood. (*Note.* Adapted from Jenkins et al., 1990, p. 577.)

changes in the organization of somatosensory cortex in the adult monkey as a result of drastic changes in environmental input. In all their studies, they first determined the map of the somatosensory cortex, isolating the regions of brain that receive sensory input from each of the digits on the hand (Figure 13.13A). Such a map indicates clear borders between the regions responsible for sensory input from each finger. Then these researchers drastically changed the input into the brain's somatosensory region by means of a number of manipulations. In one study, they amputated the middle digit (such a manipulation is clearly not done lightly but provides information on brain reorganization that is difficult to obtain otherwise, and it can aid in providing information useful for the treatment of humans who have lost a limb). About 2 months later, they reexamined the somatosensory map and discovered that the brain region that had previously received information from the middle digit now responded to sensory input from the two adjacent digits (Figure 13.13B). In another study, these researchers "fused" two digits by sewing them together. They did so because they thought that the distinct boundaries in the somatosensory cortex result because separate digits usually have different functions and hence usually receive different somatosensory information. Fusing two digits should make their input more similar, and if reorganization occurs, should cause a blurring of the border between the regions in somatosensory areas that are sensitive to each digit. The results of this study confirmed these investigators' expectations: Before fusing, the brain region for a finger responded only to input from that finger, but after fusing it responded to adjacent regions on the two fused digits. Finally, Merzenich and colleagues altered the environmental input by training monkeys for a long period (i.e., months) on a task that caused only particular parts of the hand to receive tactile input, and found that the representation of the often-used digits was greatly increased. Moreover, after the monkey ceased performing the behavior frequently, the map reverted to its original state. In sum, these studies demonstrate that the organization of the brain in adulthood can flexibly adapt to environmental input (Jenkins, Merzenich, & Recanzone, 1990).

These researchers also demonstrated that reorganization can occur as a result of damage. They unilaterally lesioned specific portions of the somatosensory cortex that received information from particular regions of the hand. These lesions had immediate and important behavioral consequences. Animals would use the hand contralateral to the lesion only for gross grasping behaviors such as climbing bars, but not for more fine motor manipulation, such as grasping food, which relies on somatosensory feedback. With time, however, the animals' behavior became more and more normal. These behavioral changes were found to be accompanied by changes in the somatosensory map. When the brain tissue was first destroyed, certain portions of the contralateral hand were not represented anywhere in somatosensory cortex. With time, however, the skin surfaces that had been mapped to regions that were destroyed by the lesion were now represented in the cortex surrounding the lesion (Jenkins, Merzenich, & Recanzone, 1990). This study provides strong proof of reorganization of function after brain lesions, which appears to be linked to recovery of function.

Evidence from humans who have a limb amputated accidentally or for medical reasons (e.g., gangrene) suggests a similar capacity for the reorganization of brain maps. Individuals who undergo amputation of either the upper limb or a digit of the hand report feelings of the amputated limb when the face is stimulated (Ramachandran, Rogers-Ramachandran, & Steward, 1992). The regions of somatosensory cortex receiving information from the face and the hand are located next to each other and typically have a discrete boundary. After amputation, however, these regions reorganize so that the brain region previously sensitive solely to the hand has connections with neurons receiving information from the face. The result is that a touch to the face causes a sensation of touch from the amputated (phantom) limb.

Our discussion so far was limited to changes in brain organization that occur in sensory regions. Clearly a critical question for the rehabilitation of mental function after brain injury is the degree to which such mechanisms also work for cognitive functions, and the degree to which previously uninvolved brain regions can be recruited to aid in a task. A number of examples of such reorganization exist, and we discuss them next. For the most part, they fall within the domain of language functioning.

One example of seeming reorganization after brain injury comes from a case study of a French speaker with a left temporoparietal lesion who had the oral equivalent of deep dyslexia. The lesion disrupted his ability to repeat pronounceable nonwords and abstract words and caused him to make semantic substitutions when using concrete words (e.g., saying "cherry" for "raspberry" and "ballet" instead of "theater"). The researchers used SPECT to compare activation of his right hemisphere for two verbal tasks: pressing a button upon hearing the French noun for *bird* (a semantic task) and pressing a button every time he heard /e/ at the end of a word (a phonological task). He did reasonably well at detecting the word *bird* (77% accurate), and during this task a focal increase in activity in the right middle temporal region occurred. In contrast, he could never detect the phoneme, and no concomitant increase in activation in the right middle temporal region occurred during this task (Cardebat et al., 1994). These findings suggest that the right hemisphere may have reorganized to aid in semantic processing as a result of his damage. However, a definitive conclusion cannot be drawn because the individual was not tested prior to the insult. Thus, his right hemisphere might have been engaged in processing semantic information even *before* he sustained brain damage.

One way to avoid the difficulties of interpretation in the case study just described is to obtain a baseline estimate of right-hemisphere involvement in a linguistic task, such as can be provided by neurologically intact individuals, and to compare that with the degree of right-hemisphere involvement in individuals with left-hemisphere damage. Taking such an approach by using evoked potential (EP) and dichotic listening methods, researchers have found evidence for a right-hemisphere role in recovery of function. In this study, the experimenters used a paradigm in which they examined the amplitude of the EP in response to a sensory probe, such as a light flash or a tone. First, they obtained a base-line response of each hemisphere to the sensory probe. Then they gave their participants another task simultaneously with the sensory probe (to which they no longer had to respond). Typically, when the additional task is verbal, the EP to the sensory probe is attenuated over the left hemisphere relative to the base-line condition, which suggests that the left hemisphere is otherwise engaged in the verbal task and cannot respond to the sensory stimulus. Conversely, when the task is nonverbal, the EP is attenuated over the right hemisphere, which suggests that the right hemisphere is otherwise engaged in the nonverbal task.

To test the degree to which the right hemisphere can take over language capacities after left-hemisphere damage, the researchers tested a group of patients with aphasia who had unilateral left-hemisphere damage, a group of patients with right-hemisphere damage, and a group of neurologically intact individuals. These investigators reasoned that if the left hemisphere of persons with aphasia was still responsible for language processing, these individuals should exhibit the same pattern as neurologically intact individuals and individuals with right-hemisphere damage, namely greater attenuation of the response to the sensory stimulus over the left hemisphere when the person was engaged in a verbal task. On the other hand, if the right hemisphere had taken over some aspects of processing language in patients with aphasia, they should exhibit a different pattern from that of the other two groups, namely greater attenuation over the right hemisphere, which is in fact what was observed (Papanicolaou et al., 1988).

Although these studies provide evidence of possible brain reorganization after trauma, they leave many questions unanswered. First, researchers and clinicians do not know how to manipulate conditions so that such reorganization is likely to occur, and they do not know what parameters limit the extent of reorganization. Certainly, the potential for reorganization has limits because many individuals with brain damage do not exhibit substantial recovery of function. Second, researchers do not know whether brain regions truly reorganize to subsume a function previously performed by damaged tissue or whether the individual begins to use a new strategy that allows for good performance. In some cases, an individual can use a **compensatory strategy,** which is a strategy that generally would not be used to perform a task but is invoked to minimize the loss of a specific skill. Compensatory strategies usually do not represent reorganization because the

strategy is apt to rely on brain regions distinct from those used to perform the task prior to injury. For example, in chapter 9 we discussed the case of a woman who became amnesic after temporal lobe damage and carried a notebook with a description of her car because she could not remember where her car was parked or what it looked like. Such a strategy is compensatory because it is used specifically to compensate for her memory loss and because people do not normally take such an approach to remembering where they parked their car. Furthermore, this strategy is not likely to rely on the brain region that aided memory processing prior to damage, the temporal lobes, but instead probably depends on the angular gyrus of the left hemisphere (for reading) and posterior regions of the right and left hemispheres (for object recognition).

An **alternative strategy,** which is a strategy that falls within the realm of everyday behavior but is distinct from the way in which the individual typically performs the task, may also allow for good performance on a task without accompanying brain reorganization. As one example, a person may navigate while driving by creating a mental map of the current location, the desired destination, and the required direction of travel (e.g., northeast). However, damage to posterior regions of the right hemisphere may preclude this means of navigating, so the individual may switch to the alternative strategy of using a more verbally mediated and landmark-based method of navigation (e.g., "I go four blocks to the gas station and turn right, continuing until I reach the bakery"). Because a good proportion of neurologically intact individuals may use this verbally mediated strategy, it is an alternative strategy, distinct from a compensatory strategy, which tends to be outside the bounds of everyday behavior (e.g., carrying a notebook with a description of your car).

Such compensatory and alternative strategies are so effective that neuropsychologists often try to train individuals to use them to help cope with their disabilities. However, the potential use of these strategies can impede the ability of researchers and clinicians to determine the extent of brain reorganization after injury. For example, patients with aphasia who have left-hemisphere damage may begin to remember words not on the basis of their phonemic, or sound-based, codes, but by using imagery or other visual-based codes. If such an alternative strategy is used, greater right-hemisphere involvement can be observed after damage. However, in this situation such involvement does not indicate that the right hemisphere reorganized to perform the task in the same way that the left hemisphere performed it prior to injury, but only that an alternative strategy is being used. Teasing apart these possibilities requires a researcher not only to identify the brain regions involved in performing a task, but also to analyze how the task is being performed (i.e., the strategy used). At present, few studies have provided such an analysis, so this issue requires further exploration.

Recovery of Function in Children

The recovery of function in children is distinct from that in adults because of the greater plasticity of the developing nervous system. We now turn to some specific issues regarding this topic.

Kennard Principle

Probably the most dramatic difference between adults and children after brain insult is the seemingly miraculous recovery that children appear to make. For example, lesions that would leave adults with little or no capacity for language do not have such dire consequences for children. For decades, scientists have thought that the earlier in life damage is sustained, the better the recovery. This maxim became known as the **Kennard principle,** which was named after the individual who first proposed such an effect (Kennard, 1936, 1942). As we learn in this section, the Kennard principle is now known not to be entirely true: It holds in some cases but not in others.

When damage occurs early in life, the reorganizational capacity of the brain is large. One example of the huge potential for structural reorganization is provided by work with monkeys who received lesions in utero. In response to these lesions, drastic changes are noted in the gyral patterns of the brain, indicative of massive reorganization (Figure 13.14)

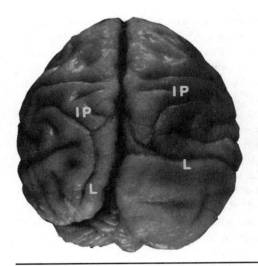

Figure 13.14 Massive reorganization in brain structure as the result of an insult that occurs very early in life. Shown here is reorganization of the left hemisphere of a rhesus monkey whose left occipital lobe was removed at gestational day 83 (note the lack of cortical mass at the back of the brain on the left-hand side). Changes in brain organization can be seen by comparing the size of the inferior parietal lobule in each hemisphere. The right hemisphere's inferior parietal lobule is the normal size and extends from the intraparietal (IP) sulcus to the lunate (L) sulcus. In the left hemisphere, the inferior parietal lobule extends from the intraparietal sulcus all the way to the back of the brain and is almost twice as large as normal. (*Note.* Reprinted with permission of the publisher from *Cerebral Dominance: The Biological Foundations,* edited by A. M. Galaburda and N. S. Geschwind, Cambridge, Mass.: Harvard University Press, Copyright © 1984 by the President and Fellows of Harvard College.)

(Goldman-Rakic & Rakic, 1984). Such drastic reorganization can have positive behavioral consequences. For example, damage early in life to the primary visual cortex in cats causes the enhancement of particular visual pathways and the retention of other pathways that usually disappear with age. In the intact cat, direct links from the lateral geniculate nucleus (LGN) to the extrastriate cortex occur for only a very brief time during development. These two areas are mainly linked indirectly through primary visual cortex. A lesion to primary visual cortex in infancy, however, will cause the normally ephem-

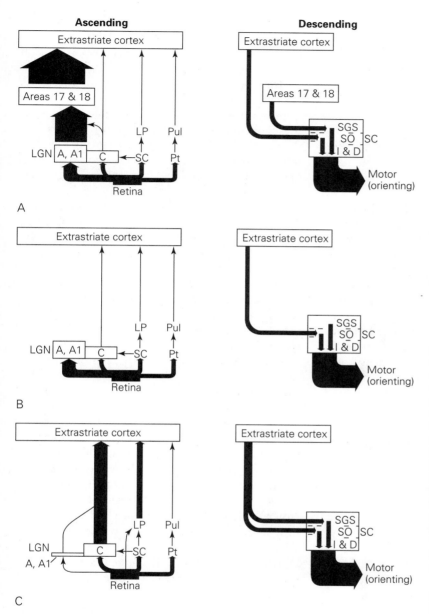

Ascending

Descending

A

B

C

Figure 13.15 A comparison of the degree of brain reorganization after damage in adulthood and after damage in infancy.

The ascending pathways from the retina to the extrastriate cortex and the descending pathways from extrastriate cortex to the superior colliculus (SC) in the cat are depicted for (A) intact adults, and those with ablation of the primary visual cortex during (B) adulthood and (C) infancy. In these diagrams, the width of the arrow indicates the size of the connection. After a lesion in infancy, the ascending pathway from the C layer of the lateral geniculate nucleus (LGN) to extrastriate cortex increases in size (large thick arrow), as does the pathway from the retina through the superior colliculus and the lateral posterior (LP) nucleus. Furthermore, two novel pathways not observed in intact animals are formed: an ascending pathway from the retina to the lateral posterior nucleus and a descending pathway from extrastriate cortex to the stratum griseum superficiale (SGS) of the superior colliculus. In contrast, none of these changes are seen after lesions in adult animals, a finding that demonstrates the greater plasticity of the immature nervous system. A and A1, layers A and A1; Pul, pulvinar nucleus; Pt, pretectum; SO, stratum opticum; I & D, intermediate and deep layers. (*Note.* From B. R. Payne and P. Cornwell, "System-wide Repercussions of Damage to the Immature Visual Cortex," *Trends in Neuroscience,* 17(3), p. 127, 1994. Reprinted with permission from Elsevier Science Ltd.)

eral links from certain layers of the LGN to extrastriate cortex to become established. In addition, pathways from extrastriate cortex to the superior colliculus are also increased. These changes are not observed in cats who sustain damage as adults (Figure 13.15).

Furthermore, these changes in neuronal wiring have important behavioral consequences. In adult cats, bilateral removal of visual cortex results in deficits in pattern discrimination, depth perception, and visual orienting, whereas removal of these same regions shortly after birth causes much less severe deficits. Similar trends are observed for visual function in both monkeys and humans, who have better abilities if a lesion to visual cortex occurs earlier rather than later in life (Payne & Cornwell, 1994). Thus, in these cases, the Kennard principle is correct: Early damage does lead to better reorganization and recovery. However, this is not the case for all functions. For example, recent studies attempting to replicate Kennard's findings that motor behaviors are less disrupted by early lesions have not been successful (e.g., Passingham, Perry, & Wilkinson, 1983).

The Kennard principle also may not hold in humans with regard to cognitive skills because damage at an early age does not always lead to better recovery (e.g., Woods, 1980). However, obtaining a clear picture of the effects of early damage in humans is complicated by a number of factors. First, findings from studies of monkeys and humans indicate that the consequences of early damage to the nervous system may not be revealed immediately but may become apparent only sometime later (Goldman, 1974). Hence, researchers must consider not only the age at which a child sustains a lesion, but also the age at which the child is being assessed and the amount of time that has passed since the injury. Second, the type of task used to assess cognitive ability is important, whether it measures general intellectual ability, as in the case of IQ tests, or a specific skill, such as language. To illustrate some of the complicated ways in which these factors interact, let's discuss one study in which I participated (Banich, Levine, Kim, & Huttenlocher, 1990; S. C. Levine, Huttenlocher, Banich, & Duda, 1987).

In this study, children who sustained unilateral brain damage were assessed, at some time after their brain injury, on a variety of neurological and intellectual tasks. The children were divided into two groups, those who had sustained damage either before or during birth, known as the *congenital group,* and those who had sustained damage between the ages of 1 month and 9½ years (average age at insult, 3¼ years), known as the *acquired group.* For the congenital group, the cause of damage was mostly unknown, whereas for the acquired group, the

causes varied from trauma to stroke to tumor. To understand what factors contributed to subsequent intellectual ability, a number of variables were examined, including the age at which the lesion occurred, the size of the lesion, the location of the lesion, the child's age at testing, and how much time had elapsed since the child sustained the damage (for the congenital group, these last two factors were the same, whereas for the acquired group they were not). My colleagues and I also assessed a wide range of cognitive abilities, including reading, mathematical skills, vocabulary, and general intelligence.

In one respect, we found evidence for the Kennard principle: Early damage led to maximal reorganization. Regardless of lesion location, all the children with congenital lesions acquired language and basic social skills. Thus, there seemed to be enough neural reorganization to support almost all cognitive functions, regardless of whether the initial damage was to the right hemisphere or the left. In another respect, however, we did not find evidence for the Kennard principle. Children with congenital lesions did not have maximal recovery. Instead, these children exhibited a substantial disruption in their overall intellectual abilities as measured by IQ tests.

We also found that the effect of the age at which the lesion occurred did not explain the whole story regarding subsequent intellectual ability and that the relationship was different for the two groups. For the acquired group, the best predictor of subsequent IQ was lesion size (Figure 13.16A): The larger the lesion, the poorer the child's IQ, regardless of the time elapsed since the lesion (Figure 13.16B) and the age at which the lesion was sustained. In contrast, for the congenital group, there was no good predictor of IQ for children younger than age 6 years. However, after that point a strong negative relationship was seen between the child's age and IQ: The older the child, the lower the IQ (Figure 13.16C), regardless of lesion size (Figure 13.16D).

How are we to interpret these results with regard to reorganization of function? When the damage occurs to the very young brain, the brain appears to be maximally flexible for reorganization and no

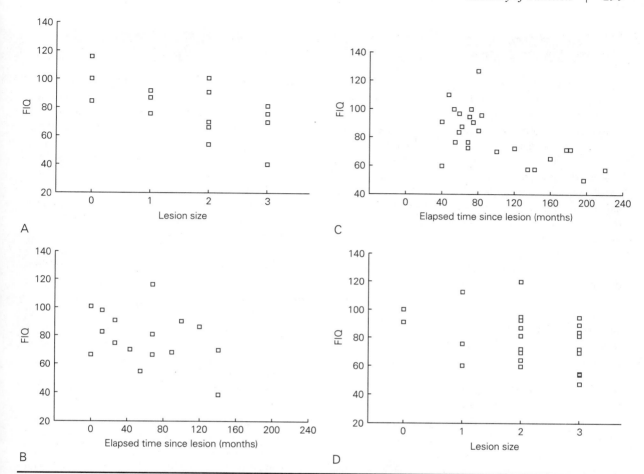

Figure 13.16 The relationship between neurologic factors and intellectual status (full-scale IQ [FIQ]) in children who sustain unilateral brain lesions.
(A) For children who sustain a lesion after birth (acquired group), lesion size (0 = small, 3 = extensive) predicts subsequent intellectual status: The larger the lesion, the lower the IQ ($r = -.669$). (B) In contrast, for the same children, a longer time elapsed since the lesion is only mildly associated with lower intellectual performance ($r = -.451$). (C) For children who sustain a lesion prior to or at birth (congenital group), a significant relationship exists between FIQ and the elapsed time since the lesion (which is equivalent to the child's age when tested), such that older age is associated with poorer intellectual performance ($r = -.648$). Note, however, that this relationship holds only for children older than approximately age 6 years. (D) In contrast, for the same children, lesion size as measured by brain scanning methods has no relationship to intellectual status ($r = -.283$). The factors predicting the intellectual performance of children who sustain lesions after birth differ substantially from those for children who sustain damage before or during birth. (*Note.* Adapted from *Neuropsychologia*, vol. 28, M. T. Banich, S. C. Levine, H. Kim, and P. Huttenlocher, "The Effects of Developmental Factors on IQ in Hemiplegic Children," pp. 40, 42, Copyright 1990, with permission from Elsevier Science Ltd., The Boulevard, Langford Lane, Kidlington OX5 1GB, UK.)

Can Deprivation Lead the Brain to Reorganize in a Way That Produces Extraordinary Abilities?

In the text, we discussed the ways in which the brain reorganizes in response to insult or atypical environments (e.g., sensory deprivation) so that it can attain or reacquire the normal complement of abilities. However, we did not discuss the possibility that reorganization might cause some abilities to be better than average or extraordinarily good. In at least one documented case, reorganization appears to actually boost some aspects of the brain's processing capacity: The brain reorganization that accompanies congenital deafness leads to enhanced processing of visual materials.

Researchers had determined that deprivation of a particular sensory input (e.g., auditory input) from birth did not enhance the basic processing in the remaining sensory modalities (e.g., the thresholds at which light or sound can be detected), which suggested that at least at the level of primary sensory cortex, little if any reorganization occurs. However, these findings did not preclude the possibility that higher level sensory processing areas or multimodal regions of the brain might reorganize in response to deprivation. To examine this issue, Helen Neville and colleagues examined individuals who are deaf from birth. The cochleae of these individuals' ears do not form correctly; hence, their nervous systems, including the auditory portions, are perfectly intact, but these people are unable to hear because they lack the peripheral receptor that is required to transduce sound waves into electrical signals.

In trying to address the question of whether higher level visual processing might be enhanced in individuals who experience auditory deprivation from birth, Neville and colleagues faced a difficult problem. Most, if not all, of these individuals learn American Sign Language (ASL). As we discussed in chapter 8 (see page 303), ASL is a visually based language that requires an individual to pay attention to a large expanse of visual space in front of him or her and to appreciate subtleties of movement within that space. The acquisition of such skills might make interpretation of experimental results difficult. If the researchers found that these persons had better visual abilities than those of hearing individuals, the researchers would have difficulty disentangling whether the brain of an individual who was deaf reorganized to handle visual information more efficiently than the brain of a hearing individual or whether the years of training and practice in ASL had caused the individual who was deaf to become an especially keen observer of the visual world.

To solve their dilemma, the researchers included a third group of individuals in their study: hearing individuals who also had learned to sign in ASL at a young age. Such individuals typically are the hearing children of parents who are deaf, and they learn ASL early so that they can communicate with their parents. If the brains of individuals who are deaf (and have learned ASL) reorganize because they lack auditory input, then the visual processing of these individuals should differ from

---

loss in cognitive ability is apparent at first. However, declines in mental function begin to be observed in children older than 6 years. It is not without precedent that damage sustained earlier in life does not manifest until later. Not only has this effect been observed in work with monkeys (i.e., Goldman, 1974), but such effects have also been observed in both human children and adults. For example, children with early damage have been found

not to exhibit deficits on an auditory localization task until age 11 years (Teuber & Rudel, 1962), and veterans who sustained penetrating head wounds in World War II began to show cognitive deficits relative to neurologically intact individuals of a similar age only decades later as both groups entered their 50s and 60s (Corkin, Rosen, Sullivan, & Clegg, 1989).

The deficits in children with congenital lesions

that of both hearing individuals who know ASL and hearing individuals who are not fluent in ASL. However, if learning ASL at an early age causes changes in visual processing, the pattern of processing by both groups of signers of ASL should differ from that observed in hearing individuals who never learned ASL.

These three groups of individuals were tested with both event-related potential (ERP) and behavioral methods. The researchers conducted a series of studies involving either tasks that required central vision, and hence were likely to rely on the ventral "what" system, or tasks involving the processing of spatial information, movement, and visuospatial attention, which were likely to rely on the dorsal "where" system (see chapters 5 and 6, respectively, for information on each of these systems).

Three important findings were gleaned from these studies. First, the processing of central stimuli did not differ for signers who were deaf, hearing signers, or hearing individuals, which suggests that little reorganization of the "what" system occurs in individuals who are deaf. Second, signers who were deaf were much faster to respond to peripheral stimuli than either hearing signers or hearing nonsigners were. Moreover, individuals who were deaf exhibited an attention-related N_{150} over occipital regions that was much larger than that observed in either group of hearing individuals. These findings suggest an enhancement of visuospa-

tial attentional processing in individuals who are deaf that is specifically related to the "where" system (because it occurred only for peripheral stimuli). Third, attention-related effects recorded over the temporal and parietal regions of the left hemisphere were much larger in signers who are deaf and in hearing signers than in nonsigners. These findings suggest that the exposure to ASL causes changes in the processing of motion detection by the left hemisphere. Such changes would arise because temporal sequencing of motion is a critical component of ASL and because the left hemisphere is specialized for language processing.

The results of these studies suggest two types of reorganization in individuals who are deaf. First, the greater responses observed over temporal regions in these individuals suggest that these regions may reorganize somewhat from processing auditory stimuli to processing visual stimuli. Second, increased attention-related ERP responses to peripheral stimuli over occipital regions in individuals who are deaf suggest a hypertrophy of the visual-processing areas. Such a hypertrophy would appear to instill individuals who are deaf with extraordinary abilities because these individuals are more than 100 ms faster at responding to the stimuli than hearing individuals are, even those who know ASL (see Neville, 1990, for a summary of this work, which was described in more detail in Neville & Lawson, 1987a–c).

that occur after the age of 6 years may be explained by the **crowding hypothesis** (e.g., Teuber & Rudel, 1962). According to this hypothesis, the young brain compensates for early damage by instituting a maximal rewiring of the available neural space. Although this reorganization works well initially, consequences develop later in life because the system cannot adapt to or acquire later developing mental skills. In the study in which I took part,

the age at which the developing brain seemed to become "overcrowded" was exactly the age when schooling begins and the brain must acquire a vast array of new cognitive skills. Thus, early reorganization appears to preclude the brain from meeting these higher cognitive demands and as such has a subsequent cost.

In contrast, the brains of the children with lesions acquired later in life had time to organize normally prior to the lesion. Thus, what predicts subsequent IQ is the size of the lesion: Larger cognitive deficits are associated with larger lesions because more regions of brain tissue are affected. Nonetheless, the pattern observed in these children is not identical to that observed in adults. Whereas left-hemisphere lesions in adults would have led to specific language deficits and posterior lesions would have led to more receptive deficits, no relationship was found between the lesion location and the profile of cognitive abilities as assessed by the WISC-R, reading, language, and visuospatial tests. Hence, the pattern of recovery in children with acquired lesions was different from that of adults, and this difference probably indicates greater plasticity in children.

The pattern of results that we just discussed should not be taken as the final word on recovery of function. One of the caveats regarding this study was that it was cross-sectional, meaning that it compared the performance of children at different ages. My colleagues and I *inferred* that the IQs of children with congenital lesions decreases with age from findings that the older children had lower IQs than those of the younger children. However, the only way to address this issue directly is to examine children longitudinally with time—that is, to chart the IQ of children with congenital lesions from age 6 years onward and to determine whether their IQs decrease year by year (a project that is ongoing; S. S. Levine, personal communication, 1994). This issue is important because some researchers have claimed that when such children are examined longitudinally, their verbal IQs may not show such declines (e.g., Aram & Eisele, 1994). Rather, we discussed the study in which I took part to provide but one example of the multiplicity of factors that can influence the subsequent level of functioning after early brain damage (see Vargha-Khadem, Isaacs, & Muter, 1994, for a review of studies examining the cognitive effects of early unilateral lesions). Future research will be required to disentangle the contribution of each factor more systematically.

Left-Hemisphere Sparing

When damage occurs early in life, certain functions may be spared at the expense of others. We already considered one variant of this idea, the crowding hypothesis, in which it was posited that earlier developing functions are spared relative to those acquired later. Another suggestion has been that left-hemisphere functions may be spared relative to those of the right hemisphere. Researchers have noted that when children sustain unilateral brain damage, their verbal IQs (VIQs) tend to be better than their performance IQs (PIQs) regardless of the hemisphere with the lesion (e.g., Nass, Peterson, & Koch, 1989; Riva & Cazzaniga, 1986). Some investigators have suggested that this pattern indicates a preeminence of language with regard to other cognitive functions, such that it is spared at all costs. However, other researchers have proposed that this pattern may be explained by the crowding hypothesis because many spatial abilities undergo large developmental changes later in life (e.g., changes in face-recognition abilities occur around age 10 years), whereas language abilities tend to develop earlier (e.g., the ability to speak emerges around age 2 years). Thus, by the age at which these spatial abilities should emerge, the developing nervous system may have little or no room left to reorganize, so they are crowded out.

Still other investigators suggest, on the basis of evidence from anatomical asymmetries, that there is a gradient of development across the hemispheres: that right motor and premotor areas develop more quickly than those on the left, followed by faster development of left posterior association regions (including Wernicke's area) than homologous areas on the right. It has been further hypothesized that later maturing areas would have greater plasticity, meaning that left-hemisphere frontal motor areas and right-hemisphere posterior association areas would be most able to reorganize (Best, 1988). Such a gradient might help to explain why right-hemisphere lesions early in life would have a more deleterious effect than left-hemisphere lesions on subsequent measures of IQ (e.g., Aram & Eisele, 1994; Woods, 1980). Because cognitive function as assessed by IQ tests generally relies on posterior brain regions, a person's IQ would decrease after a right-hemisphere lesion because posterior sections of the left hemisphere would have little room to reorganize. In contrast, after a left-hemisphere lesion, the more immature and hence more molten posterior regions of the right hemisphere could reorganize, which would allow for a better acquisition of mental functions.

However, we must consider another possible explanation for poorer performance after right-hemisphere damage. As discussed previously, difficulties in right-hemisphere function not only disrupt intellectual abilities, but also compromise the ability to interact socially. A lack of understanding of basic social concepts will impede learning not only in formal classroom settings, but in more informal settings, such as at home as well. For example, Heller, Hopkins, and Cox (1991) found that infants who sustained a right-hemisphere hemorrhage at birth had reduced eye contact and showed less reciprocal interaction with caretakers from a very early age than that exhibited by their counterparts with a left-hemisphere hemorrhage. Such poor social skills may hinder the ability of children with right-hemisphere damage to learn. These various explanations for poorer performance after early right-hemisphere damage should not be considered mutually exclusive. Right-hemisphere damage could lead to poorer intellectual recovery both because of effects to the neural substrate itself (i.e., slower right-hemisphere maturation) and because that neural substrate is particularly important for the skills that make learning possible.

Issues in Rehabilitation and Therapy

Inarguably, the single most important issue for anyone who has sustained brain damage is the degree to which rehabilitation and therapy can aid in recovery of function. Before anyone goes through the time, expense, and emotional hardships associated with rehabilitation, she or he would probably like to be reassured that a rehabilitation program will allow for a higher level of functioning than could be obtained without such an intervention. Fortunately, a strong scientific basis supports the assumption that rehabilitation programs can have a positive effect. Research with animals suggests that the environment into which they are placed after sustaining

damage can influence recovery. Moreover, research with humans suggests that a better quality of life and a higher level of cognitive performance can be attained when appropriate interventions are provided after brain damage (see Cope, 1995, for a recent review evaluating the effectiveness of rehabilitation after brain injury, and Rattok, et al., 1992, for an example of how the efficacy of a treatment program is evaluated).

Research on animals that examines how an environment can affect recovery of function after brain damage typically compares the anatomical, physiological, and behavioral responses of two groups of animals: those placed in an isolated environment after damage and those placed in an enriched environment. The enriched environments are just like those discussed earlier that lead to more extensive dendritic elaboration in neurologically intact rats (i.e., large complex environments with many toys and in which the rats can interact with other rats). Damage is generally induced either by surgery, by exposure to toxins (such as alcohol, lead, or radiation), by metabolic disruption, or by malnutrition.

Although some researchers find that the environment doesn't affect recovery, others find that the enriched environment has a positive effect. For example, some researchers, but not all, find that compared with rats living in an isolated environment, rats living in an enriched environment have increased cortical weight and higher DNA levels. The variability in results across studies probably can be attributed to differences in methods, the animals' ages, the causes of brain damage, and the nature of testing. However, as a whole, these studies suggest that under certain conditions the environment can attenuate the effects of damage, although the optimal conditions that yield such an attenuation are still unknown (Rose, 1988).

Concretely extrapolating from these studies of animals to humans is difficult. For instance, what would be an "enriched" environment for a human? Clearly, we couldn't simply place persons with lesions in an environment with complex objects and lots of people. In fact, too high a degree of complexity may be confusing to the patient with brain injury. Furthermore, the patient must negotiate not only a complex cognitive world, but a socially complex one as well. Let's now examine the factors that must be considered in designing rehabilitation programs for patients with brain injury.

Some experts have argued that an adequate rehabilitation program must have three components: one that addresses changes in cognitive capacity; one that addresses emotional changes, such as reactions to the trauma and any changes in personality resulting from brain damage; and one that addresses changes in behavior that will affect the person's lifestyle, such as pain and diminished energy (O'Hara, 1988). These three components must be considered simultaneously because they are interrelated. For example, the inability to cognitively evaluate a situation may interfere with emotional processing. We often use cognitive judgments about a situation to determine our emotional reaction, such as judging whether or not to feel hurt after hearing a comment that might be either sincere or sarcastic. Changes in emotional processing, especially personality, will in turn affect cognitive capacity. Damage to frontal areas, for example, leads to impulsivity and poor decision making. Likewise, an individual's physical condition will influence both cognition and emotion. For example, chronic pain is likely to affect a person's emotional state and to induce a negative bias that would pervade much of that person's thinking. Interpersonal interactions are especially vulnerable to disruption. For instance, reduced cognitive capacities may hamper the ability to communicate, whereas emotional dysfunction may cause an individual to retain an egocentric frame of reference (L. Miller, 1992).

Although various models of how to treat brain injury exist (see D. C. Burke, 1995, for a review), probably the most common one is an integrated multidisciplinary approach that is organized as a small "therapeutic community" in which the different domains affected by the injury (i.e., cognitive, emotional, family, social, behavioral, and vocational issues) are addressed simultaneously. For example, a treatment program might include training using hierarchically organized microcomputer tasks to alleviate attentional disorders, individualized remediation of cognitive skills (including eye-hand coordi-

nation, constructional praxis, visual information processing, and logical reasoning), small-group interpersonal communication exercises, therapeutic community activities, and personal counseling. If an individual makes sufficient progress, vocational counseling might be added (see, for example, Ben-Yishay & Diller, 1983; Ben-Yishay & Prigatano, 1990).

Rehabilitation with regard to emotional functioning is especially important. Although you may be tempted to think that cognitive and physical disabilities would be the most dire consequences of brain injury, a long-term study suggests that individuals who sustain head injury are most disabled by emotional and personality disturbances (Lezak, 1987). Unfortunately, rehabilitation of emotional functioning is also especially difficult. In typical psychotherapy, a person is encouraged to disucss the problems at hand. Such discussion requires a certain level of cognitive sophistication, good language and interpersonal conversational skills, and a capacity for self-evaluation. Clearly, these abilities are all taxed in individuals with brain injury.

Probably one of the most pervasive problems with these patients is their lack of self-awareness and lack of self-evaluatory capabilities (e.g., Prigatano, 1991). Furthermore, these individuals are likely to interpret information in the most concrete of manners and cannot generalize information learned in one setting to another. Hence, if they are in a situation even slightly different than the one they previously experienced (e.g., at home rather than in the hospital), they are likely to miss the similarity (e.g., Thomas & Trexler, 1982). Because their self-monitoring skills can be so poor and their thinking so concrete, individuals with brain damage must be given very specific feedback. For example, increased self-monitoring by these individuals can be accomplished by giving them formal checklists to use to evaluate their behavior; by making them view themselves on videotape; by having materials around the room, such as posters, that remind them of what they should be doing; and by having the staff be a "prosthetic conscience" telling the patient when he or she is behaving inappropriately. Eventually, the patient should learn to internalize this conscience, maybe at first by saying aloud things that the therapist would have said, then finally doing so silently.

A rehabilitation program also must address an individual's premorbid personality because this personality is likely to have a strong influence on emotional reactions after brain trauma. If someone was suspicious and withdrawn before brain trauma, that characteristic may be exaggerated and may cause the therapist to be viewed as an adversary rather than as an ally. In contrast, if the person was passive and dependent, he or she may use the brain trauma as an excuse for impulsive, inconsiderate, and egocentric behavior. Generally problem areas in personality (as well as family dynamics) are highlighted and enhanced by brain trauma (e.g., Lishman, 1973). Knowledge of a person's premorbid personality is also important because it can assist in designing more effective rehabilitation. For example, N. F. Cohen (1989) discussed a case in which rehabilitation of language difficulties, especially as related to conversation, was helped along by having a young man, who was a "Trekkie" premorbidly, watch and then verbally discuss Star Trek movies.

The rehabilitation program must also address the patient's physical status. If a person is in severe pain or has reduced energy, her or his ability to concentrate for long periods may be diminished, and adjustments will need to be made. For example, even if the person has the cognitive capacity to return to work full-time, physical ailments may require an adjustment to part-time work, or a staggered schedule may be required so that the person does not become too exhausted. Clearly, sensory and motor deficits, such as loss of vision and paralysis, are also likely to influence the nature and type of rehabilitation employed.

The final factor that must be considered in any rehabilitation plan is the nature of the support system available to the patient. If an individual has a caring family that is economically stable, a greater chance exists that a therapeutic intervention can continue at home and that additional problems imposed by the brain damage can be minimized. Nonetheless, the quality of life for family members is profoundly altered (e.g., Lezak, 1978) and by some estimates so negatively that 50% of all family

members resort to taking prescription drugs to reduce anxiety (Panting & Merry, 1972). Hence, when rehabilitation programs are being designed for individuals with brain damage, not only must the cognitive and emotional consequences of the damage be considered, but the effect on the individual's social system must be evaluated and addressed as well.

CHANGES IN THE BRAIN WITH AGING

Changes in brain functioning occur not only during childhood and as a result of brain damage, but also during the aging process. These changes begin to become more noticeable as a person approaches the later adult years. In this last section of the chapter, we consider some of the cognitive changes that accompany old age and the degree to which they may be neurologically based. Before we turn to this discussion, however, we should note that one of the most prominent neuropsychological issues with regard to aging and cognition is that of dementia, such as that which accompanies Parkinson's or Alzheimer's disease. In the present chapter, we discuss changes associated with normal aging and leave issues of dementia for the final chapter of the book.

Theories of Cognitive Changes With Aging

At present, there are two major theoretical camps with regard to how cognitive functions change with age. One camp argues that a general decline across all abilities occurs with age. This decline is believed to represent a general reduction in the mental resources that can be brought to bear on a problem or a general slowing in the speed of processing (e.g., Cerella, 1990; Salthouse, 1985). Evidence for this theory comes from comparing the performance of young adults and older adults (usually early retirement age or older) across a variety of tasks from different experiments. Generally, older individuals perform more poorly than younger persons, and this difference is accentuated for tasks that place more demands on central aspects of processing (e.g., memory search) than on peripheral aspects of processing in perceptual tasks (e.g., quickly identifying viewed items) (Cerella, 1985). The assumption derived from these types of data is that aging diminishes the ability to process tasks, especially those that are complex.

In contrast, the second camp argues that the deficits that emerge with age are not general, but rather more specific, such as a specific deficit in inhibitory processes (e.g., Hasher & Zacks, 1988). And still other researchers find a more variable picture of performance with age, in which some aspects of processing are compromised in older persons and other aspects are not (e.g., Kramer, Larish, & Strayer, 1995).

Given these two conflicting pictures of cognitive changes with aging, is there any way that neuropsychological evidence can help disentangle the two? As we review next, neuropsychological evidence is much more consistent with the hypothesis that aging is associated with specific cognitive deficits rather than general slowing. Tasks that show declines with age depend on particular brain regions, such as the frontal lobes and posterior association areas, whereas tasks relying on other areas tend not to be affected. Furthermore, the types of processes that are compromised, such as aspects of inhibitory control, tend to rely on the regions (e.g., frontal regions) that exhibit more severe changes during old age. We now turn our attention to the physiological and behavioral evidence that certain brain regions are more affected by aging than others are.

Brain Regions Most Susceptible to the Effects of Aging

The regions of the brain that appear to be most affected by aging are those that support higher order associative functions, namely frontal and parietal cortices, and to a lesser degree, medial temporal regions.

Frontal Regions

Both physiological and behavioral evidence exists for changes in frontal regions as a result of increasing age. From a physiological perspective, reductions in blood flow to the brain with age appear to be most pronounced for frontal regions (R. C. Gur et al., 1987; Shaw et al., 1984; L. R. Warren, Butler, Katholi, & Halsey, 1985). Furthermore, studies examining loss of neural tissue in various brain regions (e.g., Haug et al., 1983) suggest that changes are most prominent for the frontal lobes and the regions to which they connect, such as the basal ganglia and the thalamus.

These physiological changes in brain function appear to have behavioral consequences. Cognitive functions generally considered to be supported by frontal regions are particularly compromised with age. For example, older adults (aged 45–65 years) exhibit deficits on a battery of tests comprised of tasks described in prior chapters as dependent on frontal areas, such as the self-ordered pointing task, the Wisconsin Card Sorting Test, verbal fluency tasks, design fluency tasks, and the Stroop task (Daigneault, Braun, & Whitaker, 1992). More important, however, these deficits are selective and are not observed for tasks dependent on other brain regions. For example, in one study, subjects were given a battery of 12 neuropsychological tests to measure functioning of the frontal, parietal, and temporal regions of the left hemisphere, as well as functioning of the same areas of the right hemisphere (Mittenberg, Seidenberg, O'Leary, & DiGiulio, 1989). The performance of young adults (20-35 years old) was compared with that of older individuals (aged 55–75 years) who were matched for FIQ (i.e., matched for overall intelligence). Age was best predicted by scores on tests that measured frontal functioning, specifically design fluency, recency for words, and recency for pictures, rather than by tests thought to tap either parietal or temporal lobe function. Similar results have been obtained for samples of older individuals (aged 76–92 years) (Whelihan & Lesher, 1985). Age-related declines were found for all six frontal tasks in a test battery, but declines were observed for only two of nine nonfrontal tasks. Furthermore, with advancing age, decrements in verbal fluency (e.g., Obler & Albert, 1981; Villardita, Cultrera, Cupone, & Mejia, 1985) stand in stark contrast to the relative stability of other measures of verbal ability (e.g., Flicker et al., 1986).

Schacter (1987b) and Squire (1987) have suggested that frontal cortex might be involved in a "metamemory" function because frontal lobe damage has been found to affect recency judgments (e.g., Petrides & Milner, 1982) as well as judgments of the frequency of occurrence of an item (e.g., Smith & Milner, 1988). The ability to remember the temporal order of items is affected with age, but spatial memory is not. Moreover, these deficits in memory for temporal order are related to other measures of frontal lobe function such as flexibility (Parkin, Walter, & Hunkin, 1995).

Other evidence that older persons have frontal region dysfunction is the fact that they often have **source amnesia,** which is the inability to remember under what circumstances particular information was learned, despite the fact that the information itself can be remembered (e.g., an inability to remember *where* you learned that the earth orbits the sun, although you still remember that the earth does indeed orbit the sun) (McIntyre & Craik, 1987). Whereas some researchers have found these deficits to be related to deficits on other measures of frontal lobe functioning, such as verbal fluency tasks and certain aspects of performance on the Wisconsin Card Sorting Test (Craik, Morris, Morris, & Loewen, 1990), not all investigators have been able to confirm such a relationship (e.g., Spencer & Raz, 1994).

Parietal Regions

Some evidence suggests that tasks dependent on the parietal regions are also susceptible to aging effects, although these findings are not as strong as those for frontal regions. With age, decrements are found on certain tasks whose performance is disrupted by parietal lesions, most notably constructional and visuomotor tasks (e.g., Ardila & Rosseli, 1989; Farver & Farver, 1982). There are some hints (e.g., Farver & Farver, 1982) that the right parietal lobe may be more vulnerable to aging effects than the left is, and in fact some researchers have suggested that overall the right hemisphere is more susceptible to aging effects (e.g., Klisz, 1978). However, an important caveat is in order. Many of the tests on which older persons show right-hemisphere deficits are those on which speedy motor responses lead to high scores. To the degree that these more peripheral processes (e.g., motoric actions) are slowed with age, they will hinder the level of performance on such tasks. Furthermore, other studies have yielded no evidence of selective deficits on right-hemisphere tasks when the tasks do not emphasize motor skills but instead emphasize problem-solving skills (e.g., determining how to reassemble disassembled parts into a whole) (e.g., Libon et al., 1994).

Temporal Regions

As we learned in chapter 9, the temporal lobes are a region of the brain that is critically important for the ability to create new long-term memories of the declarative sort, which allows information to be used flexibly and in a variety of contexts. Whereas damage to temporal lobe structures does not affect the integrity of previously acquired memories, it severely compromises the ability to lay down new memories. By the sixth and seventh decades of life, healthy older adults begin to perform more poorly than younger individuals on direct tests of declarative memory. Older persons especially have problems with recall and on tasks that require an organized search through memory to retrieve the information rather than in structured situations in which a person must only recognize information (Craik, 1989). Relative to declarative memory, procedural memory tends to remain intact in healthy older individuals, although it too may show a decline with age (Davis et al., 1990).

SUMMARY

During gestation, nerve cells proliferate then migrate from the ventricles outward. By birth, all neurons that an individual will have for her or his entire lifetime are in place. After birth, glia proliferate; these cells play an important role in supporting neuronal function and in creating myelin. Other physiological changes during development include an increase in the brain's metabolic rate, a greater coherence in electrical activity, and an overproduction and then pruning of synaptic connections.

These developmental changes in brain structure and function are accompanied by changes in the cognitive capacities of the child. Children acquire cognitive skills in an orderly fashion, such as crawling before walking, and the unfolding of these specific skills, often referred to as developmental milestones, is presumed to represent a systematic increase in the maturation of the nervous system. Unfortunately, at present, we do not understand exactly which aspects of brain functioning cause which changes in cognitive functioning.

The environment has profound effects on the brain. Such effects are clearly seen during sensitive periods, which are time periods during development when an organism is particularly sensitive to certain external stimuli. One example in humans is that a person cannot acquire sophisticated grammatical competency in a second language if it is acquired after puberty.

Developmental disorders are syndromes in which the developing nervous system never acquires specific skills or acquires them in a less than optimal manner. One common developmental learning disability is dyslexia, which is an inability to read despite adequate intelligence in other domains and an adequate environment for reading acquisition (e.g., formal or informal schooling in the reading process). The cause of dyslexia remains unclear, although it may have a neurological basis, which many scientists assume is a dysfunction of the left hemisphere, impaired integration of information between the hemispheres, or both. Developmental dysphasia is a disorder in which children never learn to understand or produce adequate oral language. This syndrome is thought to arise from difficulties in sequencing temporal information. Nonverbal learning disabilities, which seem to result from right-hemisphere dysfunction, involve difficulty with spatial relations, geographic orientation, and puzzle construction. In addition, nonverbal learning disabilities affect social relations and peer interaction, probably as a result of deficient right-hemisphere processing of emotional information. Autism and pervasive developmental disorders are syndromes in which children show not only a profound lack of desire to interact emotionally or socially with other people, but also profound delays and disturbances in cognitive functioning, especially those that relate to communication (e.g., language). These disorders are thought to involve a large number of brain regions that may include the cerebellum, temporal lobes, frontal lobes, and other aspects of the limbic system. Children with attention-deficit disorder (ADD) have difficulty concentrating, are physically restless, cannot focus their attention on a task, and tend to be impulsive. This syndrome is believed to result from a dysregulation of the dopaminergic system. Children with learning disabilities rarely outgrow them. Rather, they seem to manifest them in adulthood as well, although the disabilities diminish in severity.

Mental retardation is characterized by a lack of intellectual ability across a wide range of cognitive skills. Many factors increase the risk of mental retardation, including infections, such as rubella (German measles); viruses, such as herpes simplex and cytomegalovirus; and genetic disorders, such as Down syndrome, fragile X syndrome, and phenylketonuria (PKU). Other environmental factors, such as toxins and malnutrition, can also lead to mental retardation.

A vast physiological response occurs to brain injury, including the degeneration and death of nerve cells, the cleaning up of debris by glia, swelling (known as edema), and eventually the formation of a scar. In addition, other aspects of brain functioning, such as metabolic rate, neurotransmitter release, and oxygen consumption, may be disrupted by a lesion. Compensatory mechanisms for neural injury include an increased sensitivity to neurotransmitters and the formation of new connections by rerouting and sprouting. These latter two processes appear to be important because research with rats suggests that the elaboration of the remaining neuronal processes can predict the degree of behavioral recovery.

Evidence from animals and humans also confirms that the brain has the capacity to reorganize its functional maps in response to extreme changes in environmental input and injury. The mapping of somatosensory regions has been shown to change in the monkey in response to brain lesions, limb amputation, and modified patterns of hand use, and in humans in response to amputation. Such reorganization can also occur with regard to cognitive functions. In addition, individuals can acquire compensatory strategies to overcome their deficits. Such strategies involve engaging in behaviors that they would not have engaged in before (e.g., carrying a notebook and writing down all important information to compensate for a memory problem). Individuals may choose instead an alternative strategy to perform a task (e.g., navigating by landmarks rather than by compass points).

The pattern of recovery observed in children is markedly different than that observed in adults. Decades ago, recovery of function in children was thought to always be superior to that in adults because children usually retain skills that adults often lose after sustaining similarly located lesions. However, children also experience the consequences of brain damage, even if it occurs early in life. Although the developing brain is capable of reorganization on a scale that does not occur in adults, the cost of such reorganization may be a decrease in the overall level of intellectual functioning. Some evidence suggests that after brain damage at a young age, language abilities are spared at the expense of other cognitive capabilities.

Rehabilitation after brain damage is complicated and requires taking many factors into account. Research with animals suggests that the environment in which an individual is placed may affect the degree of recovery. When designing rehabilitation programs for individuals with brain injury, the rehabilitation team must consider changes in cognitive capacity, in emotional functioning and personality, and in physical functioning (e.g., pain, paralysis). Many rehabilitation programs take a multifaceted approach in which cognitive, emotional, social, and vocational issues are dealt with simultaneously. Making the patient aware of his or her deficit is often a critical component of a successful rehabilitation program. In addition, the nature of the social environment can have profound effects on the degree of recovery.

Not only does the brain undergo change during the early years, but it changes with age. Although cognitive theories posit a general slowing or overall reduction in capacity with age, neuropsychological evidence suggests that the changes with age are more specific. In particular, changes in brain physiology are observed chiefly for association areas, mainly the frontal and parietal lobes. With age, deficits are seen in cognitive flexibility, fluency, and recency judgments. Deficits in cognitive functioning suggestive of parietal lobe dysfunction include difficulties with mazes and constructional tasks. Finally, when in their 60s and 70s, healthy individuals may also begin to exhibit some deficits in memory tasks that are suggestive of a decline in the functioning of medial temporal lobe structures.

*G*eneralized Cognitive *D*isorders

A strong and determined woman, L.F. immigrated to the United States from Italy in the early 1900s when she was in her 20s. She came alone, without family or friends—a journey that few women dared to make at that time under such circumstances. After arriving in the United States, she bucked tradition and didn't marry immediately, even though she was already considered an "old maid." Eventually she married a fellow Italian immigrant and they had four children, the last two of whom were born when L.F. was in her 40s.

Although life in her adopted country started out well because her husband had a successful carpentry business, the debt he incurred building multifamily dwellings caused him to lose everything when the financial markets collapsed at the beginning of the Depression. Determined that her four children would nonetheless get a college education (which they all eventually did), L.F. worked 10- to 14-hour days for years as a seamstress, doing intricate embroidery and beadwork for numerous garment makers in New York City. Despite the family's dire poverty, she instilled in her children a strong work ethic, a love of learning, and a sense of pride.

When she was in her early 80s, the apartment building in which L.F. and her husband had lived for 40 years was sold for conversion into a bank. As a result, she and her husband went to live with their second eldest daughter, who was married and had two children. L.F.'s memory had been deteriorating for some time, and moving into a new house was exceedingly difficult for her. Beset by forgetfulness and disorientation, this once-vibrant, resourceful, and proud woman, who had traveled the streets of New York City with ease, now had difficulty navigating from the room where she slept to the dining room, even though only one room intervened. L.F. was disoriented not only with regard to space, but also with regard to time, often confusing whether the time of day was morning or night. She would wander aimlessly around the house, especially at night, often searching for an item whose location she couldn't remember. On rare occasions she would even have a brief bout of paranoia. Once, for example, while her daughter was adjusting her seat belt for a trip to the grocery store, L.F. muttered in Italian that her ungrateful daughter was taking her to be killed.

The strain on the family of L.F.'s daughter was great. The house was small and didn't include a separate bedroom for L.F. and her husband, so they slept each night on a sofa bed in the family room. This meant that L.F.'s nightly wanderings disrupted everyone in the house. Moreover, during her nightly jaunts, she would disrupt the placement of various items all over the house and sometimes would even leave her dentures in bizarre locations. L.F.'s grandchildren had difficulty accommodating her need for the world to be orderly and set. They were also embarrassed on the occasions when friends came over to play and their grandmother became paranoid. She would determinedly follow their friends around the house to ensure that they weren't stealing anything.

About 9 months later, a tenant vacated the other half of the duplex in which L.F.'s eldest daughter and her family lived, and L.F. and her husband moved there. These new living arrangements were more suitable for the couple because L.F. could wander without disturbing others and the house could be organized specifically to accommodate her mental deterioration. Moreover, her eldest daughter's family was always next door and generously helped whenever L.F.'s husband, who was also in his 80s, had difficulty handling her or the daily chores. However, even with these new arrangements, L.F.'s ability to care for herself continued to deteriorate. Despite the strain of the constant care that she required, she was never institutionalized because of the love and patience of her husband of more than 50 years, who outlived her. He was able to provide such care because, unlike his wife, who had become incapacitated and dependent, he remained intellectually sharp and physically active until a few weeks before his death at the age of 90 years.

The case history described in the opening vignette is that of my maternal grandmother and describes, in part, the 9-month period when she lived with my family. Although never formally diagnosed, my grandmother surely had Alzheimer's, multi-infarct, or some similar dementia. In many ways, her case was typical, characterized by loss of memory, difficulties in spatial processing, disorientation, and changes in personality, especially paranoia. The course was unremittingly downward, although she died from heat stroke before becoming totally bedridden.

In this chapter, we discuss disorders, such as Alzheimer's disease, that are distinct from the neuropsychological syndromes that were the focus of most of this book. In our discussions so far, we emphasized the breakdown of specific cognitive functions, such as item recognition, and precisely described the circumscribed nature of the deficits. For example, in the case of visual object agnosia, we emphasized that the compromised function was a specific problem in visually identifying objects because of a disruption in the linkage of visual form to meaning. Yet in many syndromes that the neuropsychologist encounters, such as Alzheimer's disease, the breakdown of function is not restricted to one cognitive domain but affects multiple cognitive abilities simultaneously. We refer to these syndromes as **generalized (nonspecific) disorders.**

You should not be surprised to learn that the causes of generalized disorders vary significantly from that of the specific disorders that we discussed in chapters 4 through 12. Specific disorders usually result from causes that result in focal damage to the brain, such as bullet wounds and strokes (i.e., where damage is confined to the path of the projectile and to the brain regions deprived of oxygen, respectively). In contrast, the causes of generalized disorders tend to be different. They include closed head injury (which results from falls, vehicular accidents, assaults, and sports injuries), dementing disorders (which result from pathological changes in the brain), demyelinating diseases (which result from damage to the myelin sheath surrounding neurons), and exposure to toxins, all of which are likely to

have more distributed, rather than focal, effects on brain tissue. Even though all these causes of brain damage are likely to affect more than one cognitive system at the same time, their effects are not identical, so subtle but important differences in their neuropsychological manifestations can be seen. We now turn to a more detailed discussion of these various etiologies and the nature of the generalized cognitive disorders that they produce.

CLOSED HEAD INJURY

Closed head injury occurs when the brain sustains damage because the head forcefully comes into contact with another object (e.g., a car windshield, the ground, a blunt instrument such as a baseball bat), but no object penetrates the brain. This type of injury is a significant source of neuropsychological dysfunction; approximately 600,000 cases are seen each year. In two thirds of these cases, the patients require hospitalization. Closed head injury is most common in younger adults (<age 30 years), caused mainly by motor vehicle accidents, and in older individuals (>age 65 years) is predominantly attributed to falls (Kraus, 1987). The brain injury is typically diffuse, as is seen most commonly after motor vehicle accidents, but it may also have focal elements, as is usually the case with falls (Alberico et al., 1987). We now briefly discuss the mechanisms by which both diffuse and focal damage can occur in closed head injury and then discuss the neuropsychological consequences of such damage.

Etiology and Neuropsychological Consequences

The main mechanism of damage in closed head injury is a rapid acceleration of the head followed by a deceleration, hence it is sometimes referred to as **acceleration-deceleration injury.** The energy imparted to the brain causes it to move within the skull. This movement can lead to diffuse damage, as a result of the twisting and shearing of neurons, as well as focal damage, due to the impact of the brain with the hard inner surface of the skull. The neurons most vulnerable to this twisting are those that compose white-matter tracts, which have long axons and connect distant brain regions (e.g., Adams, Graham, Murray, & Scott, 1982). At the time of injury, such diffuse damage is not readily revealed by anatomical brain imaging studies because it does not result in a focal lesion. Instead, the major telltale sign of closed head injury that can be detected at the time of injury is edema (i.e., swelling). As time passes, a diffuse loss of neural tissue may be detected as an enlargement of the ventricles and a loss of volume in large myelinated tracts, such as the corpus callosum. Some of these anatomical changes, such as ventricular enlargement (e.g., Levin, Meyers, Grossman, & Sarwar, 1981) and the degree of damage to specific white-matter tracts (e.g., Gale, Johnson, Bigler, & Blatter, 1995), have been found to correlate with the degree of intellectual impairment observed (Figure 14.1).

The brain regions most likely to sustain focal injury are the orbitofrontal and temporal regions because the bones at these points in the skull are rough and protrude (e.g., Adams, Graham, Murray, & Scott, 1982). Focal damage at the site of impact is known as a **coup injury,** whereas focal damage opposite the site of impact is known as a **contrecoup injury.** For example, if the head strikes a windshield, not only might a coup injury in the frontal areas be sustained, but a contrecoup injury might occur at occipital sites as well. In sum, closed head injury involves diffuse damage to neurons throughout the brain, especially those with long axons, as well as possible localized damage, either at the site or opposite the site of impact (Grafman & Salazar, 1987).

One of the most prominent clinical signs of closed head injury is unconsciousness because it occurs even in cases of mild head injury (i.e., concussion) and doesn't usually accompany brain injury resulting from missile wounds. The level of consciousness provides a gross estimate of the damage sustained to the entire brain because the injury interferes with functioning of the brain stem (which controls wakefulness and consciousness) as much as it interferes with functioning of other brain regions. Hence, scales such as the **Glasgow Coma Scale (GCS)** (Teasdale & Jennett, 1974), which assess the level of consciousness, are widely used in emer-

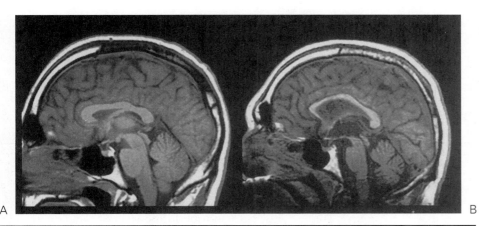

Figure 14.1 Effects of closed head injury on long myelinated nerve-fiber tracts in the brain.
Compared with an age- and gender-matched neurologically intact individual (A), an individual who sustains a closed head injury (B) exhibits a neuronal loss in white matter that is especially prominent in the corpus callosum as shown in these midsagittal MRI images. (*Note.* From "Nonspecific White Matter Degeneration Following Traumatic Brain Injury," by S. D. Gale, S. C. Johnson, E. D. Bigler, and D. D. Blatter, 1995, *Journal of the International Neuropsychological Society*, 1, p. 26. Copyright © 1995 Cambridge University Press. Reprinted with the permission of Cambridge University Press.)

Table 14.1 The Glasgow Coma Scale, Which Is Used to Predict the Severity of Brain Trauma

An individual's consciousness is assessed in three separate arenas: visual responsiveness, motor capabilities, and verbal responsiveness. The scores obtained in each of these three arenas are totaled to provide the overall score. Scores less than or equal to 8 indicate severe head injury, scores of 9 to 12 indicate moderate head injury, and scores greater than 13 indicate mild head injury.

Response	Points	Index of wakefulness
Eye opening		
None	1	Not attributable to ocular swelling
To pain	2	Pain stimulus is applied to chest or limbs
To speech	3	Nonspecific response to speech or shout, but does not imply the patient obeys command to open eyes
Spontaneous	4	Eyes are open, but this does not imply intact awareness
Motor response		
No response	1	Flaccid
Extension	2	"Decerebrate." Adduction, internal rotation of shoulder, and pronation of the forearm
Abnormal flexion	3	"Decorticate." Abnormal flexion, adduction of the shoulder
Withdrawal	4	Normal flexor response; withdraws from pain stimulus with abduction of the shoulder
Localizes pain	5	Pain stimulus applied to supraocular region or fingertip causes limb to move so as to attempt to remove it
Obeys command	6	Follows simple commands
Verbal response		
No response	1	(Self-explanatory)
Incomprehensible	2	Moaning and groaning, but no recognizable words
Inappropriate	3	Intelligible speech (e.g., shouting or swearing), but no sustained or coherent conversation
Confused	4	Patient responds to questions in a conversational manner, but the responses indicate varying degrees of disorientation and confusion
Oriented	5	Normal orientation to time, place, and person

Note. Adapted from Kolb & Whiteshaw, 1990, p. 820.

gency rooms around the world to provide a gross method for classifying the severity of damage in someone who just sustained a head injury. This scale, which is shown in Table 14.1, evaluates three realms of functioning: visual responsiveness, motor capabilities, and verbal responsiveness.

Scores on the GCS are divided into three general categories: severe injury (a score of 8 or less), moderate injury (a score of 9–12), and mild injury (a

score of 13–15). Medical personnel find the GCS score useful because it has prognostic value for survival rates and the future level of functioning. For example, 6 hours after injury, an individual whose GCS score is 8 or less (i.e., a severe head injury) has a 35 to 50% chance of dying within the next 6 months (although most of these individuals die within 3 days), a 1 to 5% chance of remaining in a persistent vegetative state, a 20 to 30% chance of being so disabled that he or she can manage only basic self-care or employment in a sheltered workshop, and only a 25% chance of independent functioning, although not at the same level as prior to the injury (e.g., working at a less demanding job). Furthermore, gradations of scores even within the three basic categories of head injury are important for predicting outcome. For example, individuals with a GCS score of 3 have a fourfold greater chance of dying than those with a GCS score of 7 (Eisenberg & Weiner, 1987).

The profile of neuropsychological deficits observed in individuals who have closed head injury varies because the nature of the damage can differ substantially compared with that in individuals with well-defined focal lesions (e.g., Thomas & Trexler, 1982). Nonetheless, certain common characteristics tend to be present at specific times postinjury. Generally when a person initially regains consciousness, she or he is likely to be disoriented, to have difficulty sustaining attention, and to have posttraumatic amnesia (which is the inability to acquire new information for events after the injury, see page 321, chapter 9). The individual may also be disinhibited, agitated, and emotionally labile, and may confabulate (i.e., invent stories) (e.g., Levin & Grossman, 1978). The initial presentation of these symptoms tends to be predictive of the severity of injury and the subsequent level of functioning. For example, posttraumatic amnesia extending past 3 weeks is associated with a poor level of subsequent cognitive functioning.

More long-term effects of closed head injury include difficulty in abstract thought and conceptualization. Individuals' thought processes are disordered, not to the point, and disconnected, and the degree of this impairment is linked to the severity of damage. These patients typically have difficulty in attentional functioning, particularly in dividing attention, inhibiting responses, and being cognitively flexible. Their behavioral control is often poor and they appear impulsive, impatient, and distractible. In addition, the ability to plan toward a goal, or the motivation to do so, is compromised. This latter difficulty can be related to emotional changes after injury such as depression or the person's lack of appreciation of his or her deficits, which are often prominent after closed head injury (e.g., Levin, High, et al., 1987). Because the frontal and temporal regions are often involved, deficits in attentional functions, executive function, and long-term memory, as well as personality changes, are common. In addition, deficits in cognitive functions performed by the brain region at the site of coup or contrecoup injuries are likely to be observed (Orsini, Van Gorp, & Boone, 1988).

Even **mild head injury,** which occurs when individuals have a change in consciousness for 2 to 30 min but do not have other gross signs of neurological damage, can have consequences for mental functioning. Complaints tend to fall into three major areas. First, difficulties in cognition are noted, especially with regard to concentration and memory. Second, the person experiences somatic symptoms, such as dizziness, blurred vision, sensitivity to noise, sleep disturbances, alterations in taste and smell, and changes in appetite. Third, the individual undergoes emotional changes, including depression, anxiety, loss of patience, and increased temper (Levin, Gary, et al., 1987). Despite apparent recovery as evidenced on neuropsychological tests, some of these symptoms, such as irritability, anxiety, depression, insomnia, and fatigue can remain (e.g., Binder, 1986).

Not only does closed head injury have consequences in and of itself, but it also may be a risk factor for various subsequent neuropsychological problems. Case studies suggest that an individual who sustains a closed head injury is at higher risk for sustaining another head injury than someone who never sustained a head injury is (see Salcido & Costich, 1992, for a discussion of this issue). The subsequent head injury may occur, in part, because these individuals have certain personality and social characteristics (e.g., risk taking, alcohol abuse) that predispose them to accidents (e.g., Tsuang, Boor, & Fleming, 1985). However, decrements in attention and poor judgment associated with the initial head injury may also predispose these individuals to another head injury (e.g., inattention might cause a person to fall, or misjudging the duration of a traffic light might lead to a motor vehicle accident). Closed head injury also appears to put an individual at higher risk for epilepsy. Posttraumatic epilepsy does not always manifest itself immediately but may begin more than 1 year after the head injury. (Later in the chapter, we discuss epilepsy in more detail.)

Researchers have also proposed that a closed head injury, even a mild one, may put an individual at higher risk for dementing disorders such as Alzheimer's disease. As many as one fourth of all individuals with Alzheimer's disease have been found to have a history of closed head injury, a significantly higher proportion than that found for individuals without dementia (e.g., Mortimer, French, Hutton, & Schuman, 1985; Mortimer et al., 1991). This relationship between head injury and Alzheimer's disease has been found in both Canadian (Canadian Study of Health and Aging, 1994) and Japanese (Kondo, Niino, & Shido, 1994) samples as well, although not to as strong a degree. In contrast, in other studies researchers examined the predisposing factors for Alzheimer's disease and found no relationship with head injury (e.g., Mendez et al., 1992). Thus, although head injury and Alzheimer's disease appear to be linked, the strength of this association remains to be clarified.

The mechanism whereby head injury leads to increased risk is unclear, but a number of hypotheses have been proposed. One possibility is that patients with Alzheimer's disease have a compromised blood-brain barrier that allows substances, such as proteins, viruses, toxins, and other agents, to gain access to the brain, which leads to deleterious neurologic effects (Mortimer & Pirozzolo, 1985). This hypothesis is based on postmortem findings that the brain of the typical patient with Alzheimer's disease has a higher-than-normal level of certain proteins, which usually are too large to pass through the blood-brain barrier. Another possibility is that the head injury itself triggers a physiological reaction that leads to the disease (Roberts et al., 1994). Studies have indicated that within days of a severe closed head injury there is a buildup of a certain protein (beta-amyloid protein), which has been proposed to be a causative agent in Alzheimer's disease

(we discuss this protein buildup in more detail later in this chapter). The formation of this protein is then thought to set off a cascade of events that lead to Alzheimer's disease.

Closed Head Injury and Sports

Closed head injury is a common occurrence in sports, as can be attested to by any fan of Canadian or U.S. football. Although a commentator may reassure the audience that a player who receives a hard hit was "Just shook up on the play and will soon be back in fine form," as a student of neuropsychology you should know that if the hit caused an alteration in consciousness, the story is more complicated. As we discussed, even minor head injury is associated with symptoms that last for a few weeks, including headaches, nausea, tiredness, dizziness, and difficulties in sleeping, all of which suggest that our player may not be up to par in next weekend's game. Furthermore, even if these injuries do appear to heal within a couple of weeks, questions remain as to whether they will have longer term effects, affecting the player's performance 2 years later or compromising his mental status after retirement. As we learned earlier in this chapter, the effects of such damage may not manifest until years later.

Probably the clearest case of sports-related head trauma occurs in boxing in the syndrome known as *dementia pugilistic,* or *chronic posttraumatic encephalopathy.* This syndrome, which begins to exhibit itself at the end of a boxing career or soon thereafter, initially manifests as tremors, difficulties in speaking, and abnormal reflexes (due to damage to the cerebellum and other motor areas). Insidiously, these difficulties become worse and disorders in thinking and emotion manifest, indicative of the extensive nature of damage to more wide-ranging regions of the brain. Regardless of whether a boxer is a professional or an amateur, heavyweight or lightweight, the probability of exhibiting such symptoms is related to the number of bouts in which the person fought (Mortimer & Pirozzolo, 1985). In fact, so clear is the association between head trauma sustained in the ring and subsequent neurological deficits, that sectors of the medical establishment in the United States have called for boxing to be discontinued as a sport in the Olympics and the military (Lundberg, 1994).

Football is another sport that is associated with closed head injury. In one study, college football players at 10 U.S. colleges were examined during a 4-year period, and researchers found that 1 in 10 players received a head injury within any given season and that more than 40% of the athletes sustained at least one head injury during their high school and college careers. These investigators also found that even when the injury led to a change or loss of consciousness for less than 2 min, acute effects that exhibited as difficulty in attentional processes and memory were observed within 24 hours postinjury. These symptoms tended to recede within 5 to 10 days but in some cases were long-term because neuropsychological performance didn't return to base line (Barth et al., 1989).

Evidence of these long-lasting effects of seemingly minor sports-related injuries is provided by a study of professional football players in Australia (Cremona-Meteyard & Geffen, 1994). In this study, the researchers assessed the consequences of a mild head injury (defined as any 2- to 20-min change in consciousness with no accompanying gross signs of neurological damage, and a posttraumatic amnesia that lasted less than 24 hours) both 2 weeks after injury and 1 year later. Two weeks postinjury, they found, not surprisingly, a slowing of overall reaction time (RT) and an inability to direct attention to a cued location. A year later, when the individuals claimed that all the behavioral signs of the concussion had disappeared, overall RT had returned to normal, but the deficit in directing visual attention remained. These findings suggest that even mild head injuries may be associated with long-term consequences, which may not be recognized by the people who sustain these injuries.

Other sporting activities are associated with significant rates of head trauma, such as equestrian sports, in which riders fall off or are thrown from horses, and skiing, in which individuals collide with trees, other skiers, boulders, ski-lift equipment, or ice. Other sports that have been associated with head injury include ice hockey, lacrosse, and even squash. One 42-year-old neurosurgeon fell while skiing, hit his head, and lost consciousness for no more than a few seconds. His self-evaluation of his abilities after this injury is as follows:

> Upon returning home, the neurosurgeon noted that he was a bit more distractible than was his norm and he had a great deal of difficulty remembering recent events, including particularly the location of objects necessary for work, such as a dictaphone, briefcase, and keys. List making in order to recall meetings scheduled and tasks to be performed became necessary, whereas they were not necessary before. Referencing articles from memory storage was difficult: authors were frequently transposed and dates incorrectly recalled. Information processing did not appear to be affected, but the ability to attend to a task required a higher level of energy expenditure than previously. These symptoms persisted, but improved gradually over a period of approximately 18 months. . . . Function as judged by others remains good, but is not optimal. (L. F. Marshall & Ruff, 1989.)

Given the deleterious effects of even mild closed head injury, what can be done to minimize its effect? In this case, an ounce of prevention is worth a ton of cure, because most closed head injuries are avoidable. One of the best preventive measures is to use seat belts and to have cars equipped with air bags. They do not allow the driver's or the passenger's head to come into contact with the windshield and help to prevent individuals from being thrown from a car, an event that greatly increases the chance of head injury. A second preventive measure is to emphasize the responsible consumption of alcoholic beverages because a clear association exists between alcohol intoxication and accidents. A third measure is to train individuals to carefully evaluate the risks of the activities or behavior in which they engage because a predisposing factor for head injury is risk-taking and reckless behavior. Another simple measure is to wear protective headgear whenever two-wheeled transportation is involved, regardless of whether it is a bicycle, a motor scooter, or a motorcycle. A similar approach can be taken to avoid closed head injury associated with sports. Protective gear is more or less the norm in some sports, such as lacrosse, hockey, and football, and its use is increasing in others. For example, headgear is worn by windsurfers sailing in stiff winds (because the mast or the wishbone holding the sail might hit forcefully enough to cause a loss of consciousness), by mountain-bike enthusiasts (in case they fly over the handlebars or otherwise awkwardly dismount from the bicycle), and by skiers, both children and adults (to minimize head injuries associated with collisions and falls). To provide perspective on how much these measures would help, consider that a recent epidemiological study revealed that of the individuals who sustained a brain injury in a motor vehicle accident, three quarters were not wearing seat belts; that 84% of the persons who sustained a brain injury in a bicycle or motorcycle accident were not wearing a helmet; and half of all individuals were intoxicated at the time of the accident (e.g., W. A. Gordon, Mann, & Willer, 1993).

DEMENTING DISEASES

Dementia is a debilitating syndrome involving a loss of cognitive functions, sometimes accompanied by personality changes, that interferes significantly with work or social activities. Although a person can become demented after an acute neurological incident (i.e., very severe head injury), dementias typically progress in stages, generally termed *mild, moderate,* and *severe,* and eventually lead to death. In mild dementia, the person retains judgment, can live alone, and can maintain adequate personal hygiene, although work or social activities are significantly impaired. As the disease progresses to the moderate stage, independent living becomes hazardous (e.g., the individual forgets to turn off the stove) and some degree of supervision becomes necessary. In severe dementia, the person's abilities are so impaired that he or she requires constant supervision (e.g., the person is mute, cannot maintain minimal personal hygiene). Dementia is a growing problem because the average life span of individuals continues to lengthen and the risk of dementia increases with age. Approximately 2 to 10% of all individuals older than age 65 years are affected, and for individuals older than 80 years, the prevalence

rate is between 12 and 25% (e.g., Kay et al., 1985; Schoenberg, Kokmen, & Okazaki, 1987).

Although all dementias lead to the same depressing end, different varieties manifest in somewhat distinct ways, both with regard to the specific constellation of cognitive functions affected and with regard to the course of their decline. To aid our understanding of dementing diseases, we divide them into three major varieties loosely based on the region of the brain most affected: those that mainly affect cortical regions, those that mainly affect subcortical regions, and those that affect both, which are referred to as *mixed-variety dementias.* Because the behavioral deficits that manifest in each of these three groups are distinguishable, such a division not only provides a useful heuristic for understanding brain-behavior relationships, but can also provide, to families and caregivers of persons with dementia, an overview of the difficulties that lie ahead. We should be aware that the labels given to these dementias describe the brain regions *most* affected and do not imply that these regions are affected exclusively. For example, even in subcortical dementias, some cortical damage is likely. The term *subcortical dementia* suggests only that the major symptoms of the disease arise from damage to subcortical structures. We now turn to an overview of the three major subcategories of dementia: cortical, subcortical, and mixed.

Cortical dementias will probably seem most familiar because they manifest as the co-occurrence of many deficits with which we are already familiar, such as aphasia, apraxia, agnosia, acalculia, spatial deficits, and memory problems. Dementias that are considered cortical are Alzheimer's disease, Pick's disease, and Creutzfeldt–Jakob disease. These three dementias generally have an insidious onset in which the first symptoms are difficulty remembering events, disorientation in familiar surroundings, problems finding the correct words to use or difficulty naming objects, and changes in personality and mood. The cognitive decline thereafter is steady, and except for Creutzfeldt–Jakob disease, is slow.

In contrast, subcortical dementias, which occur

in Huntington's disease and Parkinson's disease, do not result in specific and striking cognitive deficits, such as aphasia and apraxia. Instead, they are much more likely to manifest first as changes in personality, slowness in the speed of cognitive processing, lapses in attention, and difficulties in goal-directed tasks or tasks that require formation of a strategy (see Cummings & Benson, 1984, for a review). Whether cognitive changes in these individuals predate the onset of motor dysfunction remains controversial. Nonetheless, by the time individuals show signs of major cognitive deficits, the motor symptoms of the disease are already manifest, so making the diagnosis is relatively simple. Unlike patients with cortical dementias, who have pervasive memory difficulties, individuals with subcortical dementias exhibit a dissociation, having relatively few difficulties on recognition tasks while simultaneously being impaired on recall, which requires a strategic search through memory. Individuals with subcortical dementias also show a different temporal pattern of forgetting: Their deficits in memory are relatively even across time periods, whereas individuals with cortical dementias tend to exhibit more difficulty with recently acquired information (within the past 2 decades) than with more distant information (events that occurred 40 years ago). Table 14.2 lists the major features that distinguish cortical and subcortical dementias.

Mixed-variety dementias are disorders in which both cortical and subcortical involvement seems to occur, such as vascular dementia (previously referred to as *multi-infarct dementia*) and AIDS dementia. In these cases, evidence of damage to both cortical and subcortical regions is apparent, and, as you might imagine, these dementias manifest as patterns of cognitive performance that are midway between those observed in cortical and subcortical dementias. We now turn our attention to a more detailed discussion of each syndrome.

Cortical Dementias

For each of the major cortical dementias—Alzheimer's, Pick's, and Creutzfeldt–Jakob—we first discuss its neuropsychological profile, then its neurophysiological bases and putative causes.

Alzheimer's Disease

The average person probably associates Alzheimer's disease with memory loss, which is a reasonable assumption considering that the inability to remember a 10-item word list after a delay is the best measure for distinguishing between a mildly demented individual and a healthy older adult (e.g., Welsh et al., 1991). Yet the consequences of the disease reach far beyond memory. **Alzheimer's disease** (or, as it is often called, **dementia of the Alzheimer's type [DAT]**) results in a decline in many aspects of cognitive functioning. It is characterized by a prominent impairment in memory along with at least one of the following: aphasia, apraxia, agnosia, and disturbance in executive function. Personality changes, which at first are subtle but later become profound, are typically observed as well. As we learn later, the damage sustained to the brain is diffuse, which accounts for the broad nature of the cognitive deficits observed.

Because Alzheimer's disease has been estimated to account for more than half of all cases of dementia observed in older persons, researchers are intensely examining it in an attempt to understand both its neuropsychological consequences and its causes (R. B. Knight, 1992). Generally, Alzheimer's disease is considered to comprise two subsyndromes. One, known as *early onset Alzheimer's,* is characterized by onset of the disease before age 65 years. It progresses more rapidly and is more likely to have a genetic component. The other, known as *late-onset Alzheimer's,* is characterized by an onset after age 65 years and is usually associated with a slower decline (American Psychiatric Association, *Diagnostic and Statistical Manual of Mental Disorders,* 4th ed., 1994). At present, no specific physiological test exists that can reveal the presence of Alzheimer's disease in living individuals. Because the defining characteristics of the disease, specific neuroanatomical changes to the brain (which we discuss later), can be determined only by postmortem examination

Table 14.2   The Major Characteristics That Distinguish Cortical and Subcortical Dementias

Characteristic	Type of dementia	
	Subcortical	Cortical
Mental status		
Language	No aphasia	Aphasia
Memory	Forgetful (difficulty retrieving learned material)	Amnesia (difficulty learning new material)
Cognition	Impaired (poor problem solving produced by slowness, forgetfulness, and impaired strategy and planning)	Severely disturbed (based on agnosia, aphasia, acalculia, and amnesia)
	Slow processing time	Response time relatively normal
Personality	Apathetic	Unconcerned or euphoric
Mood	Affective disorder common (depression or mania)	Normal
Motor system		
Speech	Dysarthric	Normal[a]
Posture	Abnormal	Normal, upright[a]
Gait	Abnormal	Normal[a]
Motor speed	Slow	Normal[a]
Movement disorder	Common (chorea, tremor, rigidity, ataxia)	Absent
Anatomy		
Cortex	Largely spared	Involved
Basal ganglia, thalamus, mesencephalon	Involved	Largely spared
Metabolism		
Fluorodeoxyglucose scan	Subcortical hypometabolism (cortex largely normal)	Cortical hypometabolism (subcortical metabolism less involved)
Neurotransmitters preferentially involved	Huntington's disease: γ-aminobutyric acid	Alzheimer's disease: acetylcholine
	Parkinson's disease: dopamine	

[a]Motor system involvement occurs late in the course of Alzheimer's disease and Pick's disease.
Note. Adapted from Cummings & Benson, 1984, p. 875.

of brain tissue, a probable diagnosis is made on the basis of behavior. When other causes of dementia have been ruled out (e.g., dementia due to substance abuse) and the person's behavioral pattern is consistent with the disease, a diagnosis of Alzheimer's disease is given.

From its typically gradual onset, the course of the disease is progressively downward. Usually, the last abilities to be affected rely on well overlearned knowledge acquired early in life, such as that tested by the Vocabulary subtest of the Wechsler Adult Intelligence Scale—Revised (WAIS-R) (e.g., Logsdon et al., 1989). Because of the variability of impairment seen at different stages of the disease, two scales are widely used to quantify the degree to which the abilities of patients with Alzheimer's disease are compromised. One scale, the clinical dementia rating (Berg, 1988), uses a semistructured interview to provide a 4-point rating (0, no impairment, to 3, severe) on six dimensions: memory, orientation, judgment and problem solving, community affairs, hobbies and home, and personal care. The Global Deterioration Scale (e.g., Reisberg, Ferris, Deleon, & Crook, 1988; Reisberg et al., 1989) uses an interview to examine memory, orientation to the world, and self-care skills to provide a 7-stage rating (1, no decline, to 7, very severe decline). An overview of the characteristics of each stage and its typical duration is provided in Table 14.3.

Now let us examine some of the more specific deficits associated with Alzheimer's disease, starting with memory impairment, which is one of the most prominent aspects of the disease. Such impairment includes a severe anterograde amnesia that is global, some degree of retrograde amnesia, and, especially in later stages of the disease, difficulties in short-term memory. Thus, patients with Alzheimer's disease cannot acquire new information and, like patients with amnesia, have significant discrepancies between their IQ scores and their scores on tests such as the Wechsler Memory Scale (e.g., Weingartner et al., 1981). Patients with Alzheimer's disease also are worse than neurologically intact elderly individuals at recalling information across their lifetime, an indication of retrograde amnesia (e.g., Beatty et al., 1988), and they show a temporal gradient in such effects (e.g., Kopelman, 1989). Finally,

Table 14.3 One of the Typical Rating Scales for Alzheimer's Dementia (AD)

Stage	Diagnosis	Characteristics	Estimated duration[a]
1	Normal adult	No decrement noted	
2	Normal older adult	Subjective deficit in word finding noted	
3	Compatible with incipient AD	Deficits noted on demanding job-related tasks	7 years
4	Mild AD	Assistance required for complex tasks (e.g., handling finances, planning a dinner party)	2 years
5	Moderate AD	Assistance required for choosing attire	18 months
6	Moderately severe AD	a. Assistance required for dressing	5 months
		b. Assistance required for bathing properly	5 months
		c. Assistance required with mechanics of toileting (e.g., flushing, wiping)	5 months
		d. Urinary continence lost	4 months
		e. Fecal continence lost	10 months
7	Severe AD	a. Speech ability limited to about one-half dozen intelligible words	12 months
		b. Intelligible vocabulary limited to a single word	18 months
		c. Ambulatory ability lost	12 months
		d. Ability to sit up lost	12 months
		e. Ability to smile lost	18 months
		f. Ability to hold up head lost	Unknown

[a]In subjects who survive and progress to the next stage.
Note. Adapted from Reisberg, 1986, pp. 30–46.

difficulties in short-term memory on tests such as the Digit Span subtest of the WAIS-R may sometimes be observed, especially in later stages of the disease (e.g., R. S. Wilson, Bacon, Fox, & Kaszniak, 1983).

Because of damage to cortical areas, especially association areas, memory and knowledge systems are disrupted in these patients. The fact that they have relatively greater difficulty retrieving words on the basis of a semantic category than on the basis of a certain letter (e.g., *s*) suggests that the underlying structure of their semantic memory system is compromised by the disease (Monsch et al., 1994). This pattern is opposite that observed in individuals with frontal lobe damage, who have difficulty on letter fluency tasks but not on semantic fluency tasks, a pattern suggestive of intact semantic processing but poor executive control. Other evidence indicative of impairment in retrieving semantic information in Alzheimer's disease includes difficulties in providing definitions (e.g., Hodges, Salmon, & Butters, 1992) and difficulty recalling the form or function of objects (e.g., Flicker, Ferris, Crook, & Bartus, 1987).

We should mention that the memory disruption observed in patients with Alzheimer's disease is distinct from that observed in patients with amnesia (see page 318, chapter 9). First, although individuals with Alzheimer's disease and persons with amnesia both have difficulty creating new long-term memories (i.e., anterograde amnesia), patients in the later stages of Alzheimer's disease may have short-term memory problems as well, whereas short-term memory is intact in patients with amnesia. Second, patients with Alzheimer's disease exhibit an extensive retrograde amnesia, whereas most patients with non-Korsakoff's amnesia exhibit only a limited retrograde amnesia. Third, patients with Alzheimer's disease do not exhibit the sparing of procedural knowledge that is observed in individuals with amnesia. As we discussed in chapter 9, procedural memory has been hypothesized to depend on activating cortical processors in the same manner as when a skill is initially acquired and is thought to be independent of the hippocampal system. In Alzheimer's disease, many of the cortical processors in association areas are affected by the disease. Thus, unlike patients with amnesia, individuals with Alz-

heimer's disease for the most part do not exhibit priming effects. For example, whereas patients with Korsakoff's amnesia are biased to complete a stem (e.g., *mot___*) with a word that they recently read in a list of words (e.g., *motel*), patients with Alzheimer's dementia are not (e.g., A. P. Shimamura, Salmon, Squire, & Butters, 1987). Such a task requires knowledge about language and word meaning and presumably relies on parietotemporal regions that are often compromised in Alzheimer's disease. The only type of priming that occurs in Alzheimer's disease relies on the cortical regions that are least affected by the disease, such as sensory areas. For example, patients with this disease exhibit intact perceptual priming for visual form, which presumably relies on occipital regions that are relatively spared in the disease process (Keane et al., 1991).

Toward the later stages of the disease, language problems, such as aphasia, usually become prominent. At this time, the patient's speech becomes sparse and empty of meaning. For example, when asked to name an orange pictured in a photograph, a moderately demented patient replied, "Same thing, this is no, no, they may be this here and it didn't get here, but it got there, there, there" (Bayles, 1982, p. 276). Despite the lack of content, the syntactic structure of these individuals' language remains intact (e.g., Hier, Hagenlocker, & Shindler, 1985) and they show few phonemic disturbances or articulatory problems (e.g., Appell, Kertesz, & Fisman, 1982). This profile of language disturbance should remind you in part of some of the aphasic syndromes that we discussed in chapter 8, which are caused by posterior damage to the left hemisphere. In fact, some researchers have suggested that the language disorder seen in Alzheimer's disease is similar to that observed in Wernicke's aphasia or transcortical sensory aphasia, in which comprehension is disrupted but repetition and speech production are preserved (e.g., Cummings, Benson, Hill, & Read, 1985). However, the overall deterioration of the mental faculties, especially semantic knowledge, may preclude patients with Alzheimer's disease from producing meaningful speech and hence the language disturbances are unlike aphasias in the sense that they are not language specific.

In addition to memory and language problems, difficulty in other functions, such as visuospatial processing and apraxia, are common. Especially in the early phases of the disease, the observed neuropsychological impairments tend to be predicted by the specific pattern of decrease in regional brain metabolism as measured by positron emission tomography (PET) (e.g., Haxby et al., 1990). So, for example, patients with low metabolism in right parietal regions tend to have greater disturbances in spatial functions, whereas those with low metabolism in left parietal regions are more likely to have difficulties in reading and language functions or to be apraxic (see S. Hart & Semple, 1990, for a book-length discussion of profiles of neuropsychological impairment not only in Alzheimer's disease, but in other dementias as well).

In addition to compromising cognitive functioning, Alzheimer's disease causes personality changes. Caregivers rate patients with this disease, relative to their premorbid personality, as more neurotic, vulnerable, and anxious; less extroverted; more passive; less agreeable; less open to new ideas; and more depressed, although this depressed mood does not tend to be profound. Individuals with Alzheimer's disease do not exhibit odd or socially inappropriate behaviors, which are more common in subcortical dementias. For the most part, personality changes are not correlated with the duration of the illness and may begin to manifest relatively early in the disease. In some cases, the patients may exhibit psychiatric symptoms. For example, at later stages of the disease, delusions, especially of persecution, infidelity, and theft, may occur. However, these delusions do not tend to be elaborate and pass quickly. The more atypical an individual's personality before she or he is diagnosed with the disease, the more likely the person is to exhibit psychiatric symptoms such as depression and paranoid delusions (Chatterjee, Strauss, Smyth, & Whitehouse, 1992).

Now that we discussed the neuropsychological profile of impairment in Alzheimer's disease, we turn our attention to its neurophysiological bases and some of its possible causes. The defining symptoms of the disease are a brain riddled with large numbers of neurofibrillary tangles and amyloid plaques. **Neurofibrillary tangles,** twisted pairs of helical filaments found within the neurons, are similar to microtubules, normal cell structures that allow neurotransmitters and other proteins made within

the cell body to be transported to other regions of the cell. Because of their structure, it has been hypothesized that neurofibrillary tangles disrupt a neuron's structural matrix. Although these tangles can be found in the brain of the average healthy older individual, they are greatly increased in the cortex of an individual with Alzheimer's disease (e.g., Tomlinson, 1980, 1982) and their number predicts the severity of the dementia (e.g., Bierer et al., 1995; Nagy et al., 1995) (Figure 14.2). (Large numbers of neurofibrillary tangles are not unique to Alzheimer's disease but are also observed in other neurologic conditions such as Down syndrome, dementia from boxing, and Parkinson's disease resulting from encephalitis.) These tangles are not

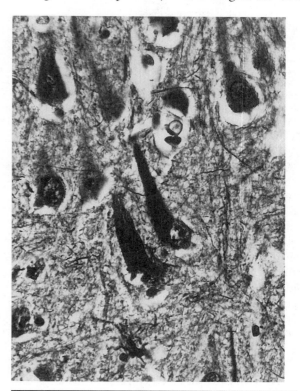

Figure 14.2 Neurofibrillay tangles that are typically observed in Alzheimer's disease.
Shown here is a section of hippocampus from a patient with Alzheimer's disease. The flame-shaped neurofibrillary tangles stain darkly because of their affinity for a silver stain. (*Note.* Reprinted with permission from *Principles of Neural Science* (3rd ed., p. 979), edited by E. R. Kandel, J. H. Schwartz, and T. M. Jessel, 1991, New York, Elsevier. Copyright held by Appleton & Lange.)

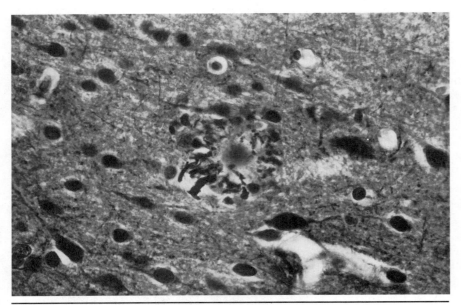

Figure 14.3 Amyloid plaques that are observed in Alzheimer's disease.
Shown here is an amyloid plaque (large round sphere), which is composed of proteins, in the cortex of a patient with Alzheimer's disease. (*Note.* From *Neuropsychology and the Dementias* (p. 32), by S. Hart and J. M. Semple, 1990, London, Erlbaum. Copyright © 1990. Reprinted by permission of Erlbaum (UK) Taylor & Francis.)

equally distributed throughout the brain but have an affinity for structures associated with the so-called limbic system, including medial temporal, inferior parietal, and frontal regions, whereas primary motor and sensory areas are relatively spared (e.g., Kemper, 1984). The presence of these tangles in medial temporal areas may functionally disconnect the hippocampus from the rest of the cortex. Tangles are also found in brain regions that contain the cell bodies for some of the major neurotransmitter systems (e.g., the basal forebrain nuclei and brainstem nuclei including the locus ceruleus and the raphe nucleus), which as we discuss later may play a role in causing memory impairments.

Amyloid plaques are deposits consisting of aluminum silicate and amyloid peptides, meaning that they are basically a buildup or a conglomeration of proteins (Figure 14.3). The plaques, typically surrounded by neurons containing neurofibrillary tangles, are believed to cause vascular damage and neuronal cell loss. As with neurofibrillary tangles, amyloid plaques can be observed in the brain of the average older individual without dementia. What distinguishes individuals with Alzheimer's disease from the neurologically intact older population is the number of plaques, which tend to concentrate in the cortex and the hippocampus, although they are sometimes seen in the basal ganglia, thalamus, and cerebellum. Large numbers of plaques are not unique to Alzheimer's disease; they are observed in patients with other brain diseases such as kuru, a disease caused by a virus, and amyotrophic lateral sclerosis (ALS), a demyelinating disease.

The net result of all these tangles and amyloid deposits is cell loss, which at later stages of the disease can be seen on anatomical brain images as cortical atrophy and ventricular expansion (Figure 14.4). As might be expected from the description of the location of tangles and plaques, cell loss in cortical regions is greatest in frontal, anterior temporal, and parietal regions, and the subcortical and midbrain structures most affected include the hippocampus, amygdala, and olfactory system.

The subcortical cell loss, specifically neuronal de-

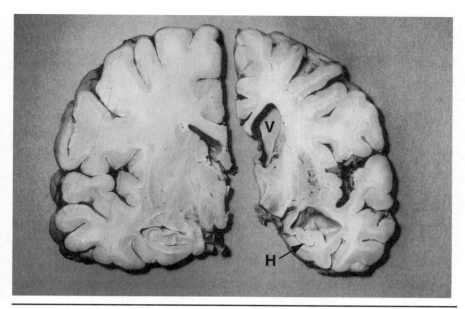

Figure 14.4 Cell loss due to Alzheimer's disease.
(Left) Coronal postmortem hemisection taken from the brain of a neurologically intact older person. (Right) Coronal postmortem hemisection taken from the brain of a 75-year-old patient with Alzheimer's disease who died approximately 5 years after the onset of the disease. Note the extensive atrophy of this patient's brain, especially that of the hippocampus (H). Also note that the ventricles (V) are extremely enlarged because as cortical cells die, cerebrospinal fluid fills the remaining space. (*Note.* From *Neuropsychology and the Dementias* (p. 30), by S. Hart and J. M. Semple, 1990, London, Erlbaum. Copyright © 1990. Reprinted by permission of Erlbaum (UK) Taylor & Francis.)

struction of the *nucleus basalis of Meynert* (e.g., Whitehouse et al., 1981, 1982), may explain some of the difficulties in Alzheimer's disease. Output from the nucleus basalis provides the main route for cholinergic input to the cortex and hippocampus. Because low levels of acetylcholine have been linked to memory performance, this cell loss may explain some of the memory deficits associated with the disease. For example, drugs that block acetylcholine, such as scopolamine, cause a memory impairment in neurologically intact young adults (e.g., Caine et al., 1981). In fact, this effect of scopolamine has been known for some time because this drug was used in ancient witchcraft rituals and in obstetrics to produce "twilight sleep" with amnesia for painful events (e.g., Drachmann, 1978; Warburton, 1979). Individuals with Alzheimer's disease reportedly have reductions (as much as 60–90%) in

the levels of enzymes that synthesize and break down acetylcholine (e.g., Davies & Maloney, 1976). Such reductions are correlated with the density of the plaques as well as declines in cognitive function (e.g., Perry, Tomlinson, & Blessed, 1978). Figure 14.5A shows the location of the nucleus basalis of Meynert in relation to midbrain structures, and Figure 14.5B depicts cholinergic projections to cortical areas.

These findings have led to the testing of potential drug therapies for Alzheimer's disease. Initial trials attempted to boost acetylcholine levels by providing more precursors to acetylcholine, such as lecithin and choline. This approach did not meet with much success, however, because the levels of the enzyme needed to create acetylcholine, choline acetyltransferase, are also reduced. Another strategy was to try to retain as much acetylcholine as possible in the

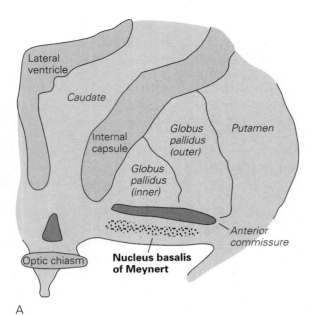

A

B

Figure 14.5 The nucleus basalis of Meynert and cholinergic projections, which are affected by Alzheimer's disease.

(A) A coronal section at the level of the optic chiasm illustrating the position of the nucleus basalis of Meynert relative to the striatum, and anterior commissure. (B) A midsagittal view of the brain showing the major cholinergic projections to the cortex, including those from the nucleus basalis of Meynert. 1, Nucleus basalis of Meynert; 2, nucleus of the diagonal band of Broca; 3, medial septal nucleus; 4, hippocampus; 5, olfactory bulb; 6, neocortex; 7, cingulate cortex. (*Note.* Adapted from Kandel et al., 1991, p. 980; B, Adapted from Hart & Semple, 1990, p. 48.)

patient's brain by giving the person physostigmine, a drug that inhibits the activity of acetylcholinesterase, the enzyme that breaks down acetylcholine. Administered orally, it had little effect, and when given intravenously, it provided only short-lived gains along with undesirable side effects (Koranyi, 1988). Because other neurotransmitters, such as dopamine, noradrenaline, and gamma-aminobutyric acid (GABA), are also depleted in Alzheimer's disease, drug therapies that simultaneously address multiple systems may prove to be the most effective. Hence, the search continues for a drug or a "cocktail" of drugs that will reduce memory loss in patients with this disease (for a review of the different neurotransmitter systems affected in dementia and potential drug treatments, see Whalley, 1989). Another approach is to give neurotrophic compounds, such as nerve growth factor (NGF), to prevent or retard the loss of cholinergic cells and thereby reduce the magnitude of acetylcholine depletion. Such an approach is being investigated because, as we learned in chapter 13 (see page 492), the *basal forebrain system* (of which the nucleus basalis is a part) is the main site in the cortex that has receptors for NGF (see Wilcock, 1994, for a discussion of this approach).

At present the etiology of Alzheimer's disease is unknown, although many theories about possible causes have been formulated (see Henderson, 1988, and Koranyi, 1988, for brief reviews). According to one set of theories, the disease results from an autoimmune disorder in which the body's immune system turns against itself and destroys brain tissue. The idea behind another class of theories is that a blood-brain barrier disruption lets toxins into the brain (e.g., aluminum, see Birchall & Chappel, 1988). Still another theory is that a DNA deficiency causes inadequate transcription of messenger RNA resulting in inadequate production of proteins necessary for neuronal function. Other researchers have argued that the amyloid plaques are a reaction to a virus that disrupts brain function many years after initial infection. Because amyloid proteins are seen not only in the brain (in the microtubules and plaques), but in other parts of the body as well, such as in the blood vessels, other investigators have posited that Alzheimer's disease may have a systemic nature. Finally, because the production of amyloids may occur in response to chronic inflammation, some researchers have suggested that the disease has a chronic inflammatory component.

Of all these theories, however, the most intense research has been directed at understanding the overproduction of amyloids. Amyloid buildup has been suggested as the causative agent in Alzheimer's disease, leading to the other aspects of Alzheimer's pathology such as neurofibrillary tangles, cell loss, and dementia (e.g., Hardy & Higgins, 1992). This suggestion is based on findings that a rare inherited form of the disease appears to be linked to three mutations of the gene responsible for a larger amyloid precursor protein that when broken down forms the amyloid beta protein found in the brain of the patient with Alzheimer's disease. Furthermore, this gene is contained in the same region of chromosome 21 that causes Down syndrome. As we discussed in chapter 13, individuals with Down syndrome have a higher-than-average probability of exhibiting signs of Alzheimer's disease in their 40s and 50s. According to the amyloid buildup hypothesis, one or more other agents (e.g., a head injury) would trigger the initial overproduction of amyloid beta protein, which would then have a cascade effect. However, such a viewpoint is not universally accepted because the amyloid buildup may be a byproduct of the "real" cause, much the way a fever doesn't cause the flu but always accompanies it.

Scientists will probably never find a single cause of Alzheimer's disease. Rather, a number of genetic and environmental factors likely combine to cause the disease. The genetic contribution may be a predisposition for biochemical aspects of neuronal function to go awry, which is then aggravated by the aging process, such as the increased accumulation of environmental toxins or the higher likelihood of compromised physiological functioning. A genetic predisposition may also be aggravated by late-emerging effects of specific medical events, such as a previous head injury or exposure to particular viruses. Thus, although none of these factors may be causative per se, they all may increase the risk.

One of the more intriguing risk factors for Alzheimer's disease appears to be minimal formal schooling, which increases a person's risk of developing the disease twofold relative to that of the person with elementary or middle school training. Moreover, there seems to be a "dose-related" function, in that the more schooling an individual has, the lower the person's chance of getting the disease. Such effects have been observed cross-culturally, even when the effects of age and gender are taken into account (e.g., when researchers consider that older individuals and females are likely to have had less formal schooling) (Katzman, 1993). The reason for a relationship between schooling and Alzheimer's disease remains a mystery. Perhaps minimal schooling is associated with other risk factors (e.g., living in an environment contaminated by toxins, or having a job in which head injuries are common). On the other hand, more education may increase the probability of living a life with high cognitive demands. If, as in animals, a complex environment leads to greater neuronal elaboration, individuals with more schooling and lifelong mental demands may have an extra reserve capacity to .offset the neuronal loss that accompanies old age.

Because Alzheimer's disease is so debilitating and so prevalent (the fourth leading cause of death among older individuals), scientists are working diligently to try to understand it. The greatest risk factor seems to be age, and the segment of the world's population that is older than age 65 years is increasing drastically; therefore, the care and management of individuals with the disease will be a significant problem in the years to come. In addition to its devastating effects on the individual, Alzheimer's disease, like other dementias, places a severe strain on the persons who must care for individuals with the disease.

Pick's Disease

Another cortical dementia, **Pick's disease,** has behavioral manifestations that are similar to those of Alzheimer's disease. However, it is about 10 to 20 times less common. Despite its similarities to Alzheimer's disease, some notable differences exist. Unlike the initial symptom in Alzheimer's disease, which

tends to be memory impairment, the first symptoms of Pick's disease usually occur in the realm of social-emotional functioning. The most marked symptoms are mood changes, notably biases toward euphoria, changes in personality, and a deterioration of social skills (Cummings & Benson, 1983). Although not as striking, problems with language, such as word-finding difficulty, naming difficulty, and empty speech, also are often observed initially (e.g., Holland, McBurney, Mossy, & Reinmuth, 1985). Only later, as the disease progresses, do other problems, such as difficulties in memory and apraxia, occur. Another feature that distinguishes Pick's disease from Alzheimer's disease is that the affected person may exhibit some aspects of Klüver–Bucy syndrome, which was first described in monkeys who had lesions of the temporal lobes, amygdala, and hippocampus (Klüver & Bucy, 1939). These animals were known for their inclination to place inappropriate objects in the mouth (e.g., fabric), to be hypersexual, to be placid, and to have object-recognition difficulties (recall from chapter 5 that this last difficulty is associated with damage to anterior temporal regions). Individuals with Pick's disease may exhibit gluttony, hyperorality, and affective disturbances (e.g., Cummings & Duchen, 1981).

In addition to having different behavioral manifestations than those of Alzheimer's disease, Pick's disease has different physiological characteristics. In typical cases, gross brain atrophy is noted only in temporal and frontal regions, which at later stages of the disease can be detected by structural brain imaging. This pattern differs from that in Alzheimer's disease, in which parietal areas are usually affected also. An example of the severe atrophy of the frontal regions in Pick's disease is shown in Figure 14.6. Cellular characteristics of the brain of an individual with Pick's disease, examined at autopsy, also distinguish it from that of an individual with Alzheimer's disease because of the noteworthy absence of neurofibrillary tangles and amyloid plaques. Instead, Pick's disease is characterized by two main features: pale neurons swollen as if they had "ballooned," and clumps of fibers in the cytoplasm that are stained by silver and are known as

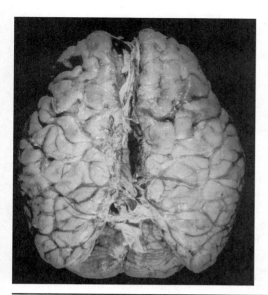

Figure 14.6   Brain atrophy in Pick's disease.
Shown here is the brain, as viewed from above, of an individual with Pick's disease. Note the amount of degeneration in the frontal regions relative to that in other areas of the cortex. (*Note.* From "Case Records of the Massachusetts General Hospital: Case 16-1986," by R. E. Scully, 1986, *New England Journal of Medicine*, 314, p. 1108. Copyright 1986, Massachusetts Medical Society. Reprinted by permission of *The New England Journal of Medicine*.)

Pick's bodies. These fibers are distinguishable from the neurofibrillary tangles seen in Alzheimer's disease because they are straight rather than paired and helical (see Scully, 1986, for a particularly vivid case report of Pick's disease).

Creutzfeldt–Jakob Disease

Creutzfeldt–Jakob disease, which is extremely rare, is unlike the two cortical dementias discussed so far because it has a known cause: a group of transmissible protein agents known as *prions* (*pro*teinaceous *in*fectious particles), or "slow viruses" (e.g., Gibbs et al., 1968), which are so-named because their symptoms manifest years to decades after the individual is infected (see Harrison & Roberts, 1991, for a discussion of how these agents cause various kinds of dementia). The prion responsible

for Creutzfeldt–Jakob disease is highly transmissible. For example, it can be transmitted between species. In bovines, it causes a neurological disorder known as *mad cow disease,* which humans can contract by eating tainted meat. (Because some individuals contracted the disease in this manner from infected cows in Great Britain, other European countries banned the importing of British meat during the spring of 1996.) This agent can also be transmitted from one person to the next during medical procedures, such as corneal implants, injections of human growth factor, and the implantation of intracranial electroencephalography (EEG) electrodes. It can even be contracted from contact with brain tissue during dissection if gloves are not worn. Although the actual virus causing the disease has not been isolated, it is known to be hardy (unlike the HIV virus) because it is resistant to boiling, formalin, alcohol, and ultraviolet radiation. Fortunately, the virus can be inactivated by autoclaving or by bleach.

Creutzfeldt–Jakob disease has characteristics that easily distinguish it from Alzheimer's and Pick's disease. This dementia is accompanied by involuntary movements and a characteristic EEG that has periodic sharp synchronous spikes at a rate of 0.5 to 2 Hz. In addition, it typically involves a course of decline that is much quicker than that observed in either of the other two cortical dementias we discussed. Although Creutzfeldt–Jakob disease may occur at any age, it manifests most frequently in the 50s or 60s. The initial complaints tend to be fatigue, anxiety, problems in concentration, difficulties with appetite or sleep, and occasionally an elated mood. Because of these symptoms, individuals are sometimes given a psychiatric diagnosis. Several weeks later, these symptoms are typically followed by motor symptoms, such as contractions of muscle groups, which then may be followed by a lack of coordination, involuntary movements, difficulty in gait, and altered vision. A swift and progressive neurological collapse, of which dementia is invariably a component, follows (e.g., P. Brown, Cathala, Sadowski, & Gajdusek, 1979; *DSM-IV,* 1994; Will & Matthews, 1984). The overall course of the disease, once manifest, is usually not longer than 1 year; the median duration is 4 months from the onset of the dementia. The decline is so rapid that it can be seen week by week or in some cases even day by day (e.g., R. Knight, 1989). Neuropathologically, the changes seen in the cortex are widespread neuronal loss and a proliferation of glial cells. In addition, the brain appears "spongy," which is why this disease is sometimes referred as to as *spongiform encephalopathy*.

Subcortical Dementias

Patients with subcortical dementias present with a pattern of cognitive disabilities that are distinct from those observed in patients with cortical dementias. Thought tends to be slowed and symptoms related to frontal lobe dysfunction are prominent. These latter difficulties probably result because the main subcortical regions affected in these dementias have intimate connections with frontal regions.

Huntington's Disease

As we discussed in chapter 4, Huntington's disease is an inherited progressive neurological disease that generally first manifests around age 40 years and inevitably leads to death about 15 years later. The incidence of this disease is about 5 cases per 100,000 people. As we discussed in some detail in chapter 4, the disease destroys cholinergic and GABA-ergic neurons in the striatum (caudate nucleus and putamen) and to some degree the globus pallidus (Figure 14.7), which leads to a movement disorder characterized by jerky, rapid, and uncontrollable movements (i.e., choreiform movements). In this section, we examine the intellectual impairments that accompany the disease.

The decline in cognitive functioning in individuals with Huntington's disease approximately parallels their decline in motor functioning, and, according to estimates, 90% of all patients with the disease eventually become demented (Lieberman et al., 1979). Individuals with Huntington's disease have difficulties in processing spatial information (e.g., Brouwers et al., 1984), retrieving information from memory (e.g., Butters et al., 1985), per-

forming executive functions, and paying attention (e.g., Josiassen, Curry, & Mancall, 1983). These symptoms are often accompanied by disorganized speech and changes in personality and emotional functioning. As with other subcortical dementias, profound aphasia and apraxia are rare, a factor that allows clinicians to easily differentiate between Alzheimer's disease (or other cortical dementias) and Huntington's disease (or other subcortical dementias). We now look at the constellation of cognitive and emotional deficits in Huntington's disease in more detail (for a good review, see Brandt, 1991).

Patients with this disease are likely to exhibit deficits on spatial tasks. We might speculate that these difficulties occur because many spatial tasks emphasize motor speed, which is compromised in Huntington's disease. Yet spatial deficits may be observed on tasks in which motor demands are not prominent, especially on tasks of spatial learning, which suggests that more cognitive aspects of spatial processing are also affected. Such findings are consistent with research performed on monkeys in which damage to the caudate nucleus has been found to cause difficulty on spatial learning tasks, such as spatial alternation (e.g., respond to the left stimulus on Trial 1, to the right stimulus on Trial 2, to the left stimulus on Trial 3, etc.).

The memory disorder in patients with Huntington's disease is characterized by two main features, each of which distinguishes it from the memory problems observed in patients with Alzheimer's disease. The first feature is the lack of a temporal gradient to the memory impairment. Typically, patients in the early stages of Alzheimer's disease have a temporal gradient to their retrograde amnesia, which is characterized by superior memory for historical events that occurred earlier in life (e.g., when they were 20 or 30 years old) than for events that occurred more recently (e.g., when they were 40, 50, or 60 years old). In contrast, patients with Huntington's disease tend to show more equal memory impairment across all time periods, without a selective sparing of older memories (e.g., Beatty et al., 1988) (Figure 14.8). The second main feature of memory processing in patients with Huntington's disease is that they exhibit a large dissociation be-

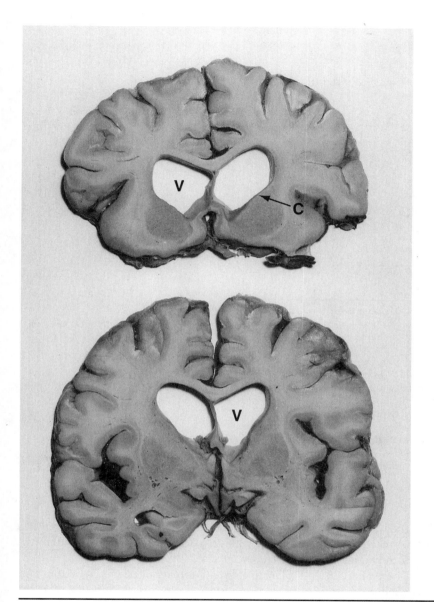

Figure 14.7   Neurological degeneration in Huntington's disease.
Coronal postmortem slices from a 65-year-old individual who had Huntington's dementia. The caudate (C) nucleus has shrunk to only a small thin strip below the ventricle
(top slice), and the ventricles (V) have become greatly enlarged (both slices). To compare how these structures look in a neurologically intact older person, refer to the left-
hand portion of Figure 14.4. Also note that the main area of neural degeneration in
Huntington's disease is distinct from that in Alzheimer's disease (see the right-hand portion of Figure
14.4). (*Note.* From *Neuropsychology and the Dementias* (p. 39), by S. Hart and J. M. Semple, 1990, London, Erlbaum. Copyright © 1990. Reprinted by permission of Erlbaum (UK) Taylor & Francis.)

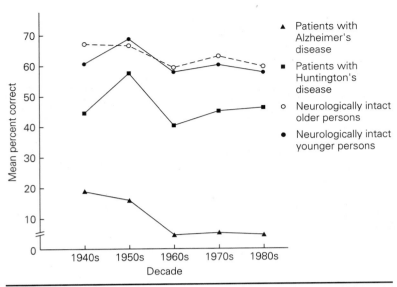

Figure 14.8 Memory across the life span in patients with Huntington's disease.
This graph depicts the performance of individuals with Huntington's disease (black squares), Alzheimer's disease (black triangles), young neurologically intact individuals (black circles), and older neurologically intact individuals (white circles) on tasks requiring the free recall of famous faces and public events pertaining to different decades of the 20th century. Two trends are noticeable. First, the memory deficit of patients with Huntington's disease is not as severe as that of patients with Alzheimer's disease. Second, the pattern of remembering in patients with Huntington's disease is similar to that of neurologically intact individuals and is distinct from that shown by patients with Alzheimer's disease, who have better memory for more remote events than for more recent events. (*Note.* Adapted from Beatty et al., 1988, p. 182.)

tween their ability to recognize and their ability to recall material: They are much better at recognition than at recall. In contrast, patients with Alzheimer's disease are equally impaired at both. These findings suggest that, unlike people with Alzheimer's disease, patients with Huntington's disease can store new information. However, their access to that information appears to be limited to situations in which aids for retrieval are provided, as in memory recognition tasks in which the person is given a choice of potential answers. In contrast, they have difficulty making a self-guided search through memory, which is required to recall (rather than recognize) information. In addition, the results of some

studies suggest that these patients may have less difficulty with verbal memory than with other forms of memory.

The final broad domain of cognitive dysfunction observed in Huntington's disease is in the realm of executive control and other tasks mediated by the frontal lobe. Patients with this disease have specific difficulties in initiating behavior, selecting a response, or selecting a stimulus on the basis of particular attributes. These deficits are not surprising if you consider that the head of the caudate nucleus, which is damaged by Huntington's disease, receives much input from the dorsolateral and orbital frontal cortex. The effects of the disintegration of the connections between the frontal lobe and the basal ganglia appear to manifest early, because one of the most common early complaints of individuals with Huntington's disease is that they have difficulty planning their activities and scheduling their lives. Other manifestations of decreased competency on tasks relying on frontal regions include reduced verbal fluency, perseverative tendencies, difficulty switching set, and loss of cognitive flexibility. Difficulties in response selection and abstract conceptualization become apparent from poor performance on tasks such as the Wisconsin Card Sorting Test (WCST) and the Stroop test.

Because Huntington's disease affects specific brain structures, researchers have investigated the degree to which behavioral deficits are correlated with brain atrophy as measured by anatomical brain imaging. Atrophy of the caudate nucleus, as measured by computerized axial tomography (CAT) or magnetic resonance imaging (MRI), is a good predictor of performance, especially with regard to tests such as the Stroop test, the Digit Symbol subtest of the WAIS-R, and the Trail Making Test. Although PET studies suggest that dopamine binding in both the caudate and the putamen is reduced, the degree of binding in the caudate predicts performance on cognitive tests, such as the Trail Making Test, the Digit Symbol subtest of the WAIS-R, verbal paired-associate learning, and the memory quotient of the Wechsler Memory Scale, to a much greater degree than binding in the putamen does. Because caudate binding does not correlate with the severity of motor functions such as chorea, these findings suggest that the caudate plays a larger role in cognitive functions, whereas the putamen plays more of a role in motor functions.

Besides being affected cognitively, individuals with Huntington's disease typically manifest changes in their emotional functioning (observed in 80% of all cases) (Lieberman et al., 1979). About half of all individuals with this disease have major depressive episodes or exhibit a depressed mood. You might think that such a reaction is a normal response to dealing with a fatal illness. However, the constellation of emotional symptoms is similar to that observed in individuals with Parkinson's dis-

ease, whose prognosis for subsequent functioning is not as bleak. The commonality of emotional symptoms in the two diseases suggests that they may be caused by damage to subcortical areas that occurs in both diseases. Patient's with Huntington's disease also tend to be irritable and apathetic and to have an increased prevalence of personality disorders (which are ingrained and maladaptive ways of interacting with the world—e.g., being paranoid). At times, these individuals even exhibit psychotic symptoms such as delusions (e.g., thinking you are being persecuted by the FBI or that you are Napolean reincarnated). Hallucinations (e.g., hearing voices), however, are rarer. In addition, these patients often act in socially inappropriate ways that are reminiscent of the behavior of individuals with frontal lobe damage (Cummings & Benson, 1988).

Parkinson's Disease

As we learned in chapter 4, patients with Parkinson's disease have a specific cell loss in the substantia nigra, the major source of dopaminergic neurons in the brain, and to a lesser degree in the locus ceruleus. Along with the motor symptoms that accompany the disease, dementia manifests in approximately 20 to 60% of these individuals. The cardinal neuropsychological symptoms of Parkinson's disease are a slowing in motor and thought processes, impairment in memory retrieval, and dysfunction of executive processes (see Dubois, Boller, Pillon, & Agid, 1991, for a good review). For the most part the cognitive decline is relatively slow in patients who are treated with L-dopa, a precursor to dopamine that can cross the blood-brain barrier. A somewhat faster cognitive decline is observed in individuals with an earlier rather than a later onset of the disease. In addition, greater cognitive impairments are observed in patients with rigidity and akinesia than in those with tremor.

The first aspect of cognitive compromise that we discuss with regard to Parkinson's disease is the slowing of motor and thought processes known as **bradyphrenia**. Although patients with Parkinson's disease can arrive at a correct answer, they do so slowly, seeming to need to overcome some type of mental inertia. Such slowing is more likely to occur on tasks requiring planning (e.g., Tower of London) than on simpler tasks. This slowness may influence a variety of mental functions, contributing to poor performance in other domains, such as language and visuospatial functioning. For example, motor and initiation-related problems that exhibit themselves within the domain of language include a reduction in the ability to name items, poor vocabulary, and disruptions in articulatory capacities. These difficulties, however, are unlike those observed in aphasic disorders and hence are not language specific. Some of the slowing of mental and motoric functions may also be exacerbated by the depression that often accompanies the disease.

A second area in which these patients manifest difficulty is in memory, specifically in retrieving information in nonstructured situations. Long-term memory for both verbal and visuospatial material appears to be intact when recognition procedures are used (e.g., "Have you seen this item before?"). Yet, deficits appear if they must recall information. As with Huntington's disease, the ability to plan a strategic search through memory is impaired. Thus, the pattern of memory functions observed in Parkinson's disease suggests that memory functions dependent on the temporal lobes are spared, whereas memory dependent on the integrity of the frontal lobes is more severely compromised (e.g., memory for recency). Finally, short-term memory is generally spared in Parkinson's disease, although performance deteriorates if a distracting stimulus intervenes. This probably relates to difficulties in attentional processes rather than difficulties in short-term memory (e.g., Pillon, Deweer, Agid, & Dubois, 1993).

The third domain in which patients with Parkinson's disease exhibit cognitive dysfunction is in the realm of executive function (e.g., Dalrymple, Kalders, Jones, & Watson, 1994). For example, these patients have difficulty with the WCST, not so much because they act in a perseveratory manner but because they do not seem to be able to think abstractly, being deficient at identifying the categories into which the cards should be sorted. They also exhibit deficits in switching between categories, such as on

Part B of the Trail Making Test, in which the individual must draw a line between letters and numbers in an alternating manner (e.g., A-1-B-2-C-3). Finally, these patients' ability to stay on task and not be driven to give standard responses to a stimulus is compromised. For example, patients with Parkinson's disease have difficulty on the Stroop task, in which the individual must name the color of ink in which the letters are printed (e.g., red) while simultaneously ignoring the competing color name spelled out by the letters (e.g., blue) (e.g., Henik, Singh, Beckley, & Rafal, 1993).

What neurobiological mechanisms account for the intellectual decline observed in patients with Parkinson's disease? A number of findings suggest that the loss of dopaminergic cells accounts for relatively little of the cognitive loss. First, at early stages of the disease, only dopaminergic neurons are affected, and at this point cognitive deficits are minimal. Second, patients with early onset Parkinson's disease (onset around age 40 years), who have a good long-term response to L-dopa treatment, have minimal intellectual impairment despite the long duration of the disease. Moreover, administration of L-dopa, which is used to decrease the motor symptoms, only moderately improves cognitive functions, and then only a subset of them. Third, the severity of the motor symptoms known to result from degeneration of the nigrostriatal dopaminergic system (e.g., akinesia) has only a modest correlation with intellectual performance, whereas other motor symptoms, such as gait disorder and dysarthria, which respond little if at all to L-dopa, are much more predictive of the cognitive decline. Fourth, patients who have Parkinson's disease as a result of MPTP (1-methyl-4-phenyl-1,2,3,6-tetrahydropyridine), a synthetic drug that specifically destroys dopaminergic neurons (see page 150, chapter 4), show little cognitive impairment. Fifth, postmortem studies reveal little relationship between degeneration of nigrostriatal neurons, as estimated from striatal concentrations of dopamine and loss of cells in the substantia nigra, and intellectual functioning (see Dubois, Boller, Pillon, & Agid, 1991, also for a review of these findings).

If damage to the dopaminergic system cannot

explain all the intellectual deficits, what can? One suggestion is that other regions of the brain, namely the deep gray-substance nuclei, which include the locus ceruleus, the raphe nuclei, and the substantia innominate, are also damaged. These nuclei are important because they are the sites of origin of other neurotransmitter systems: the long ascending noradrenergic, serotonergic, and cholinergic systems. Hence, damage to these systems may, in part, explain some of the cognitive deficits observed in patients with Parkinson's disease.

In sum, these patients do not exhibit global dysfunction but have difficulty in their speed of processing (which affects tasks such as word naming, word fluency, and certain visuospatial tasks), memory tasks that require frontal regions (e.g., estimates of recency and temporal ordering), and executive control. Although this profile, especially with regard to executive control, is consistent with that of a selective impairment in frontal functioning, these patients do not exhibit some of the signs of frontal lobe damage. They do not perseverate in sorting and fluency tasks, they are less disrupted in their ability to plan (e.g., on the Tower of London), and they do not seem to have the lack of insight or to be as inhibited as patients with frontal lobe damage usually are (Dubois, Boller, Pillon, & Agid, 1991).

Patients with Parkinson's disease also show changes in emotional functioning. Estimates of depression in these patients range from 12 to 90% with an average of 46%. This depression may have two major causes. On one hand, it may to be a reaction to the disabilities imposed by the illness. On the other hand, the neurobiological substrate of the disease may lead to depression. Suggesting the possibility of a neurobiological contribution is the fact that the levels of depression in patients with Parkinson's disease are higher than those observed in patients with other debilitating illnesses, especially those that involve motor impairments, such as paraplegia and hemiplegia. Compromise of the serotonergic system is associated with depression, and such a compromise is characteristic of Parkinson's disease. Low concentrations of serotonin have been found in the striatal-pallidal complex, hippocampus, frontal cortex, cingulate cortex, and entorhinal cortex of these patients. Furthermore, the main metabolite of serotonin is found in lower concentrations in the cerebrospinal fluid of patients with Parkinson's disease who are depressed than in patients with the disease who aren't depressed. In general, patients with Parkinson's disease who exhibit depression are more likely to be younger, to be less functionally impaired, and to have a family history of the disease.

In addition to mood changes, other aspects of emotional function are compromised. One prominent symptom of the disease is the **Parkinsonian mask,** which is an expressionless face. In part, this masklike facial appearance may reflect a dampening of motor movements because the patients can link the correct facial expression with an emotional situation and can produce a particular facial expression when asked (although rarely do they do so spontaneously). Nonetheless, the patients appear to have a dampening of emotional responsiveness. Their facial expressions and tone of voice lack emotional intensity, even in response to pictures with strong affective value.

Before we leave our discussion of Parkinson's disease, we need to mention another type of Parkinson's known as **hemi-Parkinsonism,** which results from *unilateral* disease of the basal ganglia and causes motor symptoms to be exhibited on only one side of the body. The manifestations of hemi-Parkinsonism—biochemical, motoric, and cognitive—vary depending on whether the destruction occurs to the right half of the basal ganglia or the left half. Biochemically, patients with left-sided symptoms (right-sided basal ganglia destruction) have less severe dopamine depletion than that of individuals with right-sided symptoms. This conclusion is based on studies such as those showing that individuals with left-sided symptoms, relative to those with right-sided symptoms, have higher levels of homovanillic acid (a product that results from the breakdown of dopamine), which implies that they have more dopamine to break down. Motorically, individuals with left-sided symptoms have deficits on tapping tasks only with the hand contralateral to the affected side, whereas those with right-sided symptoms have bilateral impairment. Finally, the laterality of hemi-Parkinsonism also predicts the nature of the cognitive disturbance observed. Individuals with left-sided symptoms generally have more difficulty processing visuospatial material, such as the WAIS-R Block Design and Object Assembly subtests and the Benton Facial Recognition Test, and memory for figures. In some cases, they may even exhibit hemineglect. In contrast, those with right-sided symptoms generally have more difficulty with verbal material, such as the verbal subtests of the WAIS-R, digit span, verbal fluency, and sentence repetition (Raskin, Borod, & Tweedy, 1990).

Mixed-Variety Dementias

Mixed-variety dementias are characterized by a substantial degree of both cortical and subcortical damage, which makes the clinical profile of these disorders an amalgam of the cortical and subcortical dementias we discussed. At present, our ability to characterize the constellation of the two main types of mixed-variety dementias, vascular dementia and AIDS dementia, is not as clear-cut for the other types of dementia we discussed. One reason for this murkiness is that the mixed-variety dementias affect the nervous system in a heterogeneous manner. In vascular dementia, the regions of the circulatory system that fail may vary from person to person. In the case of AIDS dementia, we are just beginning to get a clear picture of how this disorder affects the nervous system, and the profile of some aspects of neuropsychological functioning may vary between different groups of individuals (e.g., gay or bisexual men vs. intravenous drug users; e.g., E. M. Martin et al., 1995).

Vascular (Multi-infarct) Dementia

Vascular dementia, which until recently has been called **multi-infarct dementia,** is the second most common form of dementia. It results not from a single stroke, which tends to compromise a specific mental capacity (e.g., speech output), but from the cumulative effects of many strokes that tend to in-

volve both cortical and subcortical lesions, with a higher frequency of lesions in the frontal lobes than in other lobes of the cortex (e.g., Erkinjuntti, Haltia, Palo, & Paetau, 1988). In some cases, the vascular damage is mainly cortical. However, in other cases, especially with hypertension, lesions occur in the small blood vessels supplying subcortical areas, especially those that supply the basal ganglia, internal capsule, thalamus, and pons. When the damage is restricted to the subcortical white matter, the dementia is sometimes referred to as *Binswanger's disease* (e.g., Libon, Scanlon, Swenson, & Coslet, 1990).

The presentation of patients with vascular dementia is often similar to that of patients with Alzheimer's disease. However, there are a number of ways to distinguish between the two, including the patient's medical history, brain imaging, and neuropsychological testing. Patients with vascular dementia present with a medical history of cerebrovascular disease. Evidence for a vascular contribution to dementia comes from a long-standing history of arterial hypertension, focal neurological signs (such as weakness of an extremity) that are suggestive of a stroke, and MRI scans revealing specific and multiple infarcts of the cortex (which can be in either the white or gray matter). Typically, vascular dementia occurs with a relatively abrupt onset (although in some cases it can be insidious), is accompanied by a stepwise and fluctuating course, and is not restricted to an onset in the later years. This pattern contrasts with that observed in Alzheimer's disease, which has a slow progression, has an unremittingly downward course, and tends to occur later in life. Finally, treating hypertension and the associated vascular disease can aid in preventing further progression of the disease, which clearly is not the case in Alzheimer's disease (*DSM-IV,* 1994).

Exactly how vascular dementia can begin abruptly without a prior history of specific focal deficits is unclear. One possibility is that prior to the onset of the dementia the individual sustains one or more "silent" strokes that go undetected either because they have no severe behavioral manifestations, are limited in extent, or are quickly compensated for in behavior. Dementia would result when, after additional strokes, a critical volume of brain tissue has been damaged and compensatory mechanisms are no longer effective. Because newer areas of damage are generally indicated by edema or the presence of blood, whereas older "silent" strokes manifest as regions of brain atrophy, anatomical brain imaging can help determine whether the dementia results form the cumulative effects of compromised blood supply to the brain (Tatemichi, 1990).

In terms of their neuropsychological profile, individuals with vascular dementia usually present with the same type of pattern observed in patients with Alzheimer's disease, except they are more likely to exhibit deficits on tasks relying on frontal lobe function and to exhibit a pattern suggestive of subcortical involvement (e.g., Kertesz & Clydesdale, 1994). For example, patients with vascular dementia and Alzheimer's disease usually perform similarly on tests assessing visuospatial ability, language, and memory. However, patients with vascular dementia usually perform more poorly on tests measuring executive function, verbal fluency, and attention, all of which are believed to rely on the frontal lobes (see Almkvist, 1994, for a review). Consistent with the idea of greater subcortical involvement in vascular dementia than in Alzheimer's disease, patients with vascular dementia tend to exhibit slowing of performance on motor tasks and, to a lesser degree, on cognitive tasks (Almkvist, Backman, Basun, & Wahlund, 1993).

AIDS Dementia

AIDS is a viral disease that is passed through the exchange of blood or bodily fluids (mainly contracted during sexual relations between male-female, male-male, and possibly female-female partners), which acts to devastate the immune system and eventually leads to death. Because no cure exists for the disease, prevention is paramount and requires the one-time use or bleaching of hypodermic needles, the wearing of latex gloves to protect against contamination by infected blood, safe sex in which a barrier is used to prevent the exchange of bodily fluids, monogamy with a noninfected partner, or abstinence from sexual activity that involves the exchange of bodily fluid.

As AIDS ravages the systems of the body, it does so evenhandedly, not sparing the brain. Studies suggest that brain pathology exists in 75 to 90% of all individuals who have died of AIDS. Some of the effects are direct. As soon as a few weeks after infection, HIV can be found in cerebrospinal fluid; therefore, it crosses the blood-brain barrier (although the exact mechanism whereby it does so is not yet clear). Once in the brain, it appears to cause neuronal death, as evidenced by a reduction in the density of neurons, and to destroy oligodendrocytes, which leads to a loss of the brain's white matter. Brain imaging studies suggest that AIDS is associated with both cortical atrophy and subcortical damage, especially the white matter and subcortical nuclei, in particular the striatum and the thalamus (Navia, Cho, Petito, & Price, 1986). As we learn shortly, this pattern of regional brain atrophy significantly influences the nature of the neuropsychological disorders that accompany AIDS. Other effects on the brain occur indirectly. Because AIDS represents a breakdown in immunological competence, the brain becomes more susceptible to many factors that have negative consequences, such as opportunistic infections (both fungal and viral), infections by parasites, tumors, and cerebrovascular lesions (most common in patients who have hemophilia) (Everall & Lantos, 1991).

AIDS dementia, which affects between 6 and 30% of all adult AIDS patients, almost always occurs in the late stages of the disease when immunosuppression exists and other AIDS-defining illnesses manifest (e.g., Kaposi's sarcoma) (e.g., J. J. Day et al., 1992). As with any dementia, it causes serious declines in cognitive functioning. The most notable consequences are slowing of mental and motor functions, disruptions in concentration and attention, and memory disturbances. In contrast, naming and vocabulary are more likely to be spared. Often, AIDS dementia is also accompanied by changes in affect. Emotionally, individuals tend toward a flattened affect manifesting as apathy, reduced spontaneity, social withdrawal, increased irritability, and emotional lability. Furthermore, depression is often noted. Hence, the profile of neuropsychological dysfunction is more similar to that observed in a subcortical dementia than that associated with cortical dementia. In fact, atrophy of the basal ganglia, a subcortical structure, is a better predictor of the severity of AIDS dementia than measures of cortical atrophy are (e.g., Alyward et al., 1993). The progression of the dementia is variable, and at present no good predictors of its course are known, although individuals usually die within 6 months of its onset (e.g., Maj, 1990; Navia, Jordan, & Price, 1986).

However, the effects of AIDS on neuropsychological function may not be limited to cases in which it causes dementia. Because the AIDS virus affects the brain so early in the course of the disease, much recent research has focused on trying to determine whether asymptomatic individuals who are infected with HIV exhibit any neuropsychological impairment. In addition, investigators have attempted to determine whether increasing degrees of neuropsychological impairment are associated with increasing stages of immunological compromise (as defined by the U.S. Centers for Disease Control and Prevention, the CDC). The CDC criteria divide individuals who test positive for HIV into three groups: Class A, who are asymptomatic or have generalized lymphatic effects; Class B, who have minor opportunistic infections, constitutional symptoms, peripheral neuropathies, or any combination of the three; and Class C, who have had an AIDS-defining illness such as Kaposi's sarcoma or *Pneumocystis carinii.*

A recent review of 57 studies comparing neuropsychological functioning in asymptomatic individuals who were seropositive (i.e., infected) with functioning in individuals who were seronegative (i.e., uninfected) revealed inconsistencies across studies: In 32%, differences were observed, 21% yielded inconclusive results, and in 47% no differences were found. However, the studies in which a large neuropsychological battery was given (which provides a more sensitive measure of neuropsychological status) were more likely to detect differences. Furthermore, the *rates of impairment* for asymptomatic individuals who were seropositive were about three times higher than those for individuals who were seronegative (i.e., 35% vs. 12%) (White, Heaton, Monsch, & the HNRC Group, 1995). These findings suggest that HIV can have neuropsychological consequences even at asymptomatic stages of the disease. Tests on which asymptomatic individuals who are seropositive are likely to perform poorly include those requiring speeded psychomotor or mental functioning and those that require new learning (e.g., R. A. Bornstein et al., 1993; Heaton et al., 1995).

At the symptomatic stage, a 44% rate of impairment in mildly symptomatic individuals (Class B) and a 56% rate in the AIDS group (Class C) have been reported (Heaton et al., 1995). As the disease progresses, measures of frontal lobe function (e.g., perseverative errors on the WCST, verbal fluency) are more likely to be impaired (e.g., R. A. Bornstein et al., 1993; Heaton et al., 1995). The findings among asymptomatic and symptomatic individuals suggest that the early neuropsychological manifestations of HIV infection reflect compromise of subcortical structures and that the later stages of the disease affect frontal and frontal-striatal regions.

Given the devastating nature of the disease, you might wonder whether some aspects of the neuropsychological impairment observed in individuals infected with HIV reflect depression resulting either from their response to being diagnosed with a fatal illness or from accompanying organic changes in the brain (e.g., due to decreased activation of particular brain regions, due to compromise of particular neurotransmitter systems). However, this does not seem to be the case because the degree of depression cannot predict the severity and nature of neuropsychological impairments (e.g., Grant et al., 1993).

DEMYELINATING DISEASES

One of the most common neurological diseases of nontraumatic origin affecting the neuropsychological functioning of young and middle-age adults is multiple sclerosis, which occurs in approximately 60 of every 100,000 individuals. **Multiple sclerosis (MS)** is so named because it is characterized by multiple discrete areas, ranging in size from 1 mm to several centimeters, in which neurons have a complete absence of myelin. The neurons themselves remain relatively unaffected, although other pathological processes are associated with the disease (e.g., inflammation). The destruction of myelin in MS is thought to occur because of a disruption in immunological response in which the body incorrectly identifies part of its own system as a foreign agent or invader and attacks it (i.e., autoimmune disorder). Such demyelinated areas interfere or block neural transmission and cause symptoms specific to the location of these areas. Although the sites affected tend to be diffuse and multifocal, certain sites may be more affected than others. These tend to include the periventricular (*peri*, "near"; *ventricular*, "having to do with the ventricles") white matter and specific regions in one of the four major lobes of the cortex. The lobe most affected varies from individual to individual.

The etiology of MS is unknown, although evidence suggests both an environmental and a genetic contribution. In general, MS is linked to geographical locale; it is much less prevalent near the equator and more prevalent as you move geographically toward the Poles. Individuals who move after the age of 15 years retain the risk rate associated with their birthplace rather than that of the environment to which they move, which has led some researchers to suggest that the causative agent may be a slow virus that is more common in temperate and colder locales (Kurtzke, 1980). A genetic risk for the disease is suggested by findings that 1 in 5 patients with MS have a family member with the disease and that a higher concordance rate occurs in monozygotic twins (who share identical genetic material) than in dizygotic twins (who have only half their genetic endowment in common). Furthermore, researchers have found similarities among individuals with MS with regard to two of the genes that influence the immunologic response of the body: the human lymphocyte antigen (HLA) gene (on chromosome 6) and the T-cell receptor gene. The genetic risk factor appears to be independent of the environmental factor because, for example, the incidence rate among the Japanese is low regardless of whether they live in Japan, Hawaii, or the Pacific

Coast of the United States (R. Martin & McFarland, 1993).

Because of the diffuse nature of the lesions in MS and the variability of their location, MS has multiple manifestations. Initially, it tends to manifest as weakness in the extremities or as difficulty in some aspect of sensory processing, which is not surprising given that it selectively disrupts white-matter tracts (remember that sensory and motor tracts are often myelinated because information must travel long distances from the peripheral receptor to the brain or from the brain to the muscle). For the individual, the first manifestations of the disease can be extremely petrifying. A common initial symptom is a loss of vision in either one or both visual fields, or weakness or paralysis on one side of the body. Unlike many of the other syndromes we discussed in this chapter, the course of MS is highly variable. A person can have an acute flare-up that results in a hemianopsia, only to have that dissipate and remit, although a subsequent attack is more likely to leave the person with a permanent visual loss. Because MS usually affects individuals in the prime of their lives and its course is highly unpredictable, the disease is extremely stressful for those who have it, as well as their families. An individual never knows whether he or she will have the next attack 20 years later or a series of exacerbations will lead to permanent blindness or paralysis in the near future.

Some individuals with MS exhibit little if any cognitive disability, whereas others show clear cognitive declines. Researchers have estimated that cognitive deficits occur in 40 to 60% of all MS patients (e.g., S. M. Rao, Leo, Bernardin, & Unverzagt, 1991). When cognitive difficulties do occur, they tend to be variable and not affect as large a range of function as observed in dementia. If a typical pattern of cognitive disability exists in MS, it involves difficulty in memory and conceptual reasoning along with a general sparing of verbal and language skills. On memory tasks, individuals with MS have difficulty recalling information but display good recognition memory, which suggests an impairment of memory search patterns. In terms of conceptual skills, patients with MS have difficulty on the types of tasks that require abstraction and are thought to rely on the frontal lobes. These individuals may also exhibit deficits on visuospatial tasks, but because many of these tasks rely on either speeded performance or manual dexterity, the clinician may have difficulty disentangling the degree to which the deficit results from peripheral sensory and motoric consequences of MS and the degree to which it arises from more cognitively based difficulties. As such, the pattern of neuropsychological difficulties exhibited in MS is similar to that of disorders with subcortical as well as frontal involvement, which is consistent with the affinity of the disease for periventricular white matter. Given the distribution of demyelination MS likely disrupts the transmission of information between subcortical structures (such as the thalamus and the basal ganglia) and the cortex, mainly the frontal lobes (S. Rao, 1986). Finally, in reports of mood and personality changes with MS, depression is cited most commonly. These mood changes are difficult to interpret because they could be normal reactions to having a lifelong debilitating disease (patients with MS have a normal life expectancy) or they may in part reflect some of the organic changes that accompany the disease. At present, no clear connection has been found between depression and organic aspects of the disease as evaluated by brain imaging. However, some evidence exists that a mood disorder in MS characterized by inappropriate euphoria (rather than depression) is associated with cognitive impairments and diffuse brain abnormalities as detected by imaging (see S. M. Rao, Huber & Bornstein, 1992, for a review).

With the advent of functional magnetic resonance imaging (fMRI), which allows fine resolution between white and gray matter, research has been directed at attempting to determine whether the pattern and degree of white-matter destruction in MS can be linked to specific patterns of cognitive disabilities. If such correlations exist, brain scans could provide information about a patient's prognosis. Unfortunately, the relationships are not always clear-cut. For example, in a study comparing patients who had a relatively benign form of MS with those who had a more chronic and progressive variety, pathology was actually greater in 20% of the patients with a benign version and the overlap between the two groups in pathological manifestations was considerable (Koopmans et al., 1989). Furthermore, although lesions are observed four times more often in the parieto-occipital region than in frontal and temporal regions, the extent of frontal lesions has been found to predict impairment on nearly half the tests in a wide-ranging neuropsychological test battery (which confirms other findings that disruption of a subcortical-frontal axis plays an important role in the manifestation of the disorder) (Swirsky-Sacchetti et al., 1992). However, other indices of the scope and extent of the disease do predict the level of cognitive function. Not surprisingly, a relationship has been found between the total amount of brain tissue affected and the degree of cognitive decline, especially on memory tests and tasks of abstract or conceptual reasoning. A less expected result is that the size of the corpus callosum predicts declines on tasks that involve quick processing speed and attention (e.g., mental arithmetic). This finding may result either because rapid problem solving requires quick integration among brain regions, which is compromised by demyelination (S. M. Rao, et al., 1989), or because the corpus callosum plays an important role in attentional functioning (e.g., Banich, 1995a).

At present, no cure exists for MS. However, certain drugs can be given to reduce the severity of the disease, all of which act to suppress the immune system and reduce tissue inflammation. The drugs of choice vary depending on which of two varieties of MS the individual has: one whose course is relapsing and remitting or one whose course is more progressive and chronic (e.g., difficulty walking within 2 years and practically no motor function within 10 years of disease onset). For individuals with relapsing MS, ACTH (adrenocorticotropic hormone), which both modulates immunological function and has anti-inflammatory properties, improves the performance of individuals who have an acute relapse, reducing its severity and shortening its duration. An alternative therapy is intravenous methylprednisolone, which is often given when ACTH is ineffective or the person is experiencing a major motor disability (e.g., hemiparesis). However, neither drug changes the long-term course of the disease. In cases of progressive MS, more aggressive immunosuppressive therapy is usually used. However, some of the side effects of these therapies are life-threatening and increase the individual's risk of getting cancer and opportunistic infection. An experimental therapy that is currently being tested in large-scale clinical trials is interferon beta. Interferons are proteins produced by the body that have antiviral characteristics and modulate the immune response (they have also been explored with regard to their efficacy in treating cancers). Unlike other therapies, which just stay the course of the disease, interferon appears to actually reduce exacerbations of the disease (Jacobs, Munschauer, & Pullicino, 1993). This promising therapy is now being tested on a wide scale. Because of the potential usefulness of this treatment and the small supply of the drug, experimenters were faced with the ethical question of how to distribute the potential life-altering therapy fairly. They settled upon a lottery system in which individuals are randomly chosen for inclusion in the trials. As part of the clinical trials, the effect of interferon on neuropsychological function is being evaluated.

BRAIN SYNDROMES RESULTING FROM SUBSTANCE ABUSE AND EXPOSURE TO TOXINS

The diseases that we discussed in the preceding sections are not the only means by which generalized neuropsychological disorders can occur. Many substances to which we are exposed, either where we work or where we live, or that we ingest voluntarily can have deleterious effects on mental functions. We now discuss some of these agents and outline their neuropsychological effects.

Substance Abuse

A variety of substances that individuals abuse can have neuropsychological consequences. However, getting a clear picture of the deficits associated with a particular substance can be difficult for various reasons. First, these substances have both acute effects, which occur during or soon after exposure, and cumulative effects, which accrue with prolonged abuse. The contribution of each is difficult to tease apart. Typically, researchers try to determine a substance's long-term effects by testing abusers only after they go through a detoxification program for 2 to 3 weeks, which is a time period considered adequate to preclude acute effects. Second, individuals often abuse more than one substance, so obtaining a clear picture of the effect of a particular drug is difficult. Third, substance abuse may be associated with other variables that can adversely affect neuropsychological function and may either precede or exist concomitantly with the substance abuse, such as a history of childhood learning disabilities (e.g., Tarter & Alterman, 1984). Fourth, although researchers try to control for such variables, obtaining a sample of substance abusers and control individuals who are matched with regard to all the relevant factors is often impossible. All these difficulties are worth mentioning because as we learn in a moment, discrepancies in results can sometimes be found across studies. Nonetheless, clear evidence indicates that the abuse of certain substances can have deleterious effects on neuropsychological functioning.

One of the most widely abused substances in the world is alcohol. The number of cases of alcoholism in the United States alone is estimated at 9 million. The approximate cost of this alcohol abuse, including costs from hospitalization, institutionalization, motor vehicle crashes, and crime, is $85.8 billion (Rice, Kelman, & Miller, 1991). Generally, patients with chronic alcoholism exhibit a profile of cognitive deficits that includes poor visuospatial functioning, along with difficulties in learning, memory, and executive functioning. Other than having these specific difficulties, the patients appear relatively intact and exhibit little decrease, for example, in overall IQ. The difficulties in spatial processing tend to be the most pervasive deficits observed and can be detected by the Block Design subtest of the WAIS-R, the Rod and Frame Test (in which a person is placed in a darkened room with no spatial cues and must align a rod parallel to the floor when the frame in which it is viewed is tilted), and the Embedded

Figures **Designs** **Embedded items**

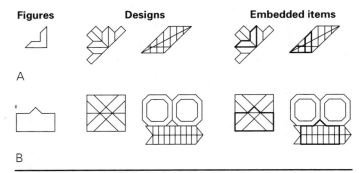

A

B

Figure 14.9 **An example of a visuospatial task that can be compromised by long-term alcohol abuse.**
Shown here are two sample items from the Embedded Figures Test. The object of the test is to find the small figure that is embedded within the larger one. (*Note.* Adapted from Talland, 1965.)

Figures Test, in which a specific pattern must be disembedded from the background in which it is presented (Figure 14.9). Patients with chronic alcoholism also exhibit deficits on tests that measure frontal region functioning, such as the WCST, and have difficulty switching between categories, such as on Part B of the Trail Making Test (responding by connecting A to 1 to B to 2, etc.). In addition, these individuals often have subtle memory deficits on tasks such as the serial list learning tasks, paired-associate learning tasks, and immediate and delayed recall tests (e.g., Errico, Parsons, & King, 1991; Parsons, Butters, & Nathan, 1987).

As discussed in chapter 9 (see Table 9.1, page 321), long-term binge drinking can induce a thiamin (vitamin B_1) deficiency that causes damage to midline diencephalic structures, including the mammillary bodies and regions of the thalamus, and results in Korsakoff's disease. Individuals with this syndrome have a dense anterograde amnesia in which the person can learn little if any new information, although short-term memory is intact. They also have a retrograde amnesia with a temporal gradient characterized by an ability to recall temporally more distant materials (events that occurred 4 or 5 decades ago) but not those that occurred more recently (within the last 2 decades). Patient's with

Korsakoff's disease are also likely to show symptoms associated with frontal lobe damage, and within the first year postonset of the disease, they may confabulate, creating elaborate stories to fill the gaps in their knowledge.

Although less research has been directed toward the neuropsychological deficits associated with the use of other drugs, certain agents have been found to have effects as well. For instance, marijuana has acute effects, 12 to 24 hours after use, that involve decrements in attention, short-term memory, and psychomotor skills. Although some researchers suggest attentional problems in long-term users of marijuana (e.g., Page, Fletcher, & True, 1988), debate continues as to whether long-term use is associated with neuropsychological deficits (for a review, see Pope, Gruber, & Yurgelun, 1995). Difficulties in temporal aspects of visual processing and increased visual sensitivity have been found to remain 2 to 3 years after the use of LSD (Abraham & Wolf, 1988), and individuals followed up 4 to 6 years after being treated for abuse of sedative or hypnotic agents, although improved, still exhibited neuropsychological deficits (Bergman, Borg, Engelbrekston, & Viker, 1989). Like chronic alcoholic abuse, chronic cocaine abuse has been associated with difficulties in attention and memory (e.g., O'Malley, Adamse,

Heaton, & Gawin, 1992), and conceptual flexibility, abstracting abilities, and visuospatial skills may also be affected.

Currently, much effort has been directed at trying to determine whether such effects can be reversed if the individual abstains from abuse of the substance. For example, neuropsychological performance can be within normal limits for alcoholics who refrain from drinking if they are relatively young (ages 18–35 years) and had a drinking problem of relatively short duration (e.g., 6 years as opposed to 30) (Eckardt et al., 1995). Such findings provide hope that early intervention and treatment that enable the individual to cease drinking can stave off long-lasting deleterious effects. Yet other studies do not provide evidence of such a recovery (e.g., Beatty, Katzung, Moreland, & Nixon, 1995). Similarly, researchers debate whether abstinence reduces deficits in memory and concentration in persons who abuse cocaine. Some findings indicate that deficits remain (e.g., Berry et al., 1993), whereas other findings provide some evidence of recovery of function (e.g., Azrin, Millsaps, Burton, & Mittenberg, 1992). The discrepancies among studies may arise because of differences in the premorbid status of particular samples (e.g., IQ and educational background, history of depression or attention-deficit disorder [ADD], family history of substance abuse) as well as their current status (e.g., age, amount of time abstinent), along with some of the factors discussed previously, all of which may contribute to the neuropsychological profile that is observed.

In conceptualizing the effects that chronic alcohol abuse has on the brain, some researchers have suggested that it ages the brain prematurely. This hypothesis is consistent not only with declines on visuospatial tasks that require speeded performance and impairment on tasks relying on frontal regions, but also with CAT scans indicating enlarged ventricles and atrophy that is most notable in frontal and parietal regions of the brain (Parsons & Farr, 1981). As for cocaine, some researchers suggest that, much like alcoholism, it leads to generalized brain dysfunction, whereas others suggest that it may have more specific effects on frontal-limbic areas because reductions in cerebral blood flow to these areas are observed for as long as 4 months after the cessation of drug use (e.g., Volkow et al., 1992).

Toxins

Toxins are substances that have the ability to destroy neural toxins and are another means by which the brain can incur nonspecific damage. Toxins take various forms, but in this section we focus our discussion on the neurotoxic effects and neuropsychological consequences of metals, organic solvents, and pesticides. Exposure to these materials can take place in a variety of settings but often occurs in the workplace. Consequently, exposure to toxins is an occupational hazard for 20 million workers in the United States alone and scores of individuals in other countries.

Metals

Many heavy metals (known as such because of their atomic weight) have been found to be toxic. Probably the best known of these is lead. The connection between lead and mental dysfunction has been known for some time and has historical significance. For instance, some scientists have suggested that drinking from lead vessels caused the deranged behavior of certain Roman emperors and the eventual downfall of that empire. Lead used in England in the 1700s and 1800s in the making of hats was thought to cause hat makers to go insane, an image immortalized by Lewis Carroll's Mad Hatter character in *Alice in Wonderland*. Our exposure to lead continues today with smelting and steel plants, battery reprocessing plants, and the use of leaded gasoline (although unleaded gas has become the mainstay in the United States and Canada, leaded gasoline is still common in other countries, so it is a health hazard in some European, Asian, Central American, and South American cities).

Lead has deleterious effects on both cognitive and emotional functioning that vary with the degree of exposure. These effects may be observed after

How to Detect Malingering

As we learned in the text, a number of nonspecific cognitive disorders, including mild head injury, exposure to organic solvents, and sports-related injury, can present signs that are vague and diffuse (e.g., amorphous difficulties in memory and concentration). Such symptoms can sometimes impede the clinical neuropsychologist's ability to determine the consequences of these injuries, especially when she or he must do so for legal purposes. For example, closed head injury may be a consequence of an automobile accident in which a driver is being sued for negligence, or exposure to toxic substances at work may lead a person to sue for disability insurance. How is a neuropsychologist to distinguish between the individual who has a legitimate disability and an individual who is faking it? This exaggeration or creation of symptoms for personal gain, either for money or to avoid responsibility for personal actions, is referred to as **malingering.** An important point about malingering is that the perpetrator's symptoms disappear when having them is no longer advantageous. You may have been a malingerer on occasion yourself. For example, to avoid going to elementary school one day you may have presented with all the symptoms of a severe stomachache only to have them miraculously disappear when the other children came home from school and it was time to go out and play.

Neuropsychologists generally have a number of ways to detect the presence of malingering, the most prominent of which is based on the analysis of the response pattern that an individual exhibits on standard tests of mental function. Malingerers act the way that they *think* they should act given their complaints. However, because they generally do not know much about neuropsychology, their common wisdom generates a profile of impairment that is at odds with that which is typically observed.

Some general telltale signs can alert the clinical neuropsychologist to the fact that he or she is dealing with a malingerer. Let's examine some examples from a case described by Orsini, Van Gorp, and Boone (1988). The most obvious sign of malingering is inconsistency in performance across tests. In true cases of brain injury, an individual generally has difficulties on a specific class of tests, such as memory tasks. Furthermore, the pattern across tasks is relatively stable, although, of course, some systematic differences may exist between different types of memory (short-term vs. long-term, verbal vs. spatial). For example, a suspicious profile of memory performance would be one in which a person denies being able to remember how old she or he is, where she or he was born, or how much schooling she or he has completed but has good memory for the accident for which she or he is attempting to receive compensation. Another example of such inconsistency is a sharp mismatch between the person's test performance and performance in everyday life. For example, a red flag should be raised if a person who can't remember when or where he or

only a few weeks or a few months of exposure. At low levels of exposure, emotional or nonspecific complaints are most common. These include fatigue, depression, and apathy. At higher levels, more specific neuropsychological complaints are manifest. These tend to center around difficulties in memory, visuospatial abilities, and visuomotor functions. In addition, reductions in psychomotor speed and manual dexterity are noted. Severe exposure is associated with greater memory deficits as well as deficits in attention, concentration, and abstract thought, along with complaints of depression, anger, and tension. In extremely severe cases, dementia can result (Hartman, 1987). Although removing an individual from an environment in which he or she is exposed to lead (such as a foundry) can reduce

she was born manages to take the bus to the hospital for neuropsychological testing without any problems.

Another tip-off that a person is faking a neuropsychological deficit is a pattern of performance that is highly atypical from a neuropsychological perspective. One such example would be poorer performance on tests of recognition memory than on tests of recall. As we know from our discussion of memory disorders and generalized cognitive disorders, recall is usually worse than recognition, or in the case of cortical dementia, is equally affected. Another example of an atypical pattern of performance would be an inability to count to 10 or to recite the days of the week while being able to follow directions or maintain even a minimally coherent conversation. Automatic tasks, such as recitation of the days of the week, can be preserved even in patients with severe dementia.

Yet another clue to malingering is a systematic pattern to incorrect responses. For example, if a person's answers to mental arithmetic problems are always off by a certain number (e.g., the answer is always one number greater than the true answer), the individual may be malingering. Further evidence that a person is systematically faking a deficit would be performance on a recognition memory task that is significantly below chance. Let's say that a person is given a test with three possible answers for each question. If the person has a serious memory impairment, he or she should perform at-chance (33%). However, if performance is significantly below chance (only 5–10% of the questions are answered correctly), it indicates a deliberate selection of the incorrect answer.

When faced with a potential malingerer, neuropsychologists administer particular tests designed to detect malingering. For example, forced-choice memory tasks may be used to determine whether the subject is responding below-chance. Other tests designed to highlight atypical performance may be administered as well. For example, in one such test, a person is given a series of 15 items and told to memorize them. The examiner emphasizes that 15 items far exceed the normal memory span. However, the items can be easily categorized into five conceptual groups of three (e.g., 1 2 3; a b c), which should make the list relatively easy to learn. Thus, if the individual being tested has an inability to recall at least three groups of items, she or he is likely to be malingering. Because malingering represents a particular level of cognitive sophistication, including strategy formation and goal-directed behavior, the individual's neuropsychological functioning cannot be very compromised. Nonetheless, the ability to malinger does not preclude the possibility that the individual does indeed have some disability. A useful strategy for a clinical neuropsychologist is to point out to the individual being tested that cooperation is likely to be a better approach than deception because neuropsychological testing can provide exactly the type of information that would bolster a legitimate claim.

the emotional symptoms for about one fifth to one third of the individuals, performance on memory and psychomotor tasks does not improve (E. L. Baker, White, & Murawski, 1985).

Lead poisoning in children has received much attention because it leads to mental retardation and can readily occur when children eat paint chips in older buildings because such paint typically contains as much as 50% lead. Even when the level of lead in a child's blood is below that considered toxic, she or he will show significant slowing in RT, and the higher the lead level, the more severe the dysfunction. Children with high levels of lead have been found to exhibit difficulties in a wide variety of domains, including problem solving, perceptual-motor tasks, visuomotor tasks, and visuospatial tasks. These children also exhibit depressed performance on subtests of the Wechsler Intelligence Scale for Children—Revised (WISC-R) that are highly correlated with overall IQ, such as the Information, Comprehension, and Vocabulary subtests, and may exhibit hyperactivity. Clearly, not every child will show all these symptoms, but the evidence suggests that lead toxicity can compromise intellectual functioning in many ways. Because lead exposure in children is associated with certain living conditions (e.g., living in an older building), which in turn may be associated with other factors that have deleterious effects on neuropsychological function (e.g., poor socioeconomic status, an impoverished environment), researchers have been careful to evaluate the effects of lead independent of these other factors. Even when such factors are considered, exposure to lead appears to be related to a cognitive decline (Hartman, 1987).

Organic Solvents

Organic solvents are toxic materials derived from naturally occurring substances. Individuals are exposed to them in the workplace (as in the case of carbon disulfide or carbon monoxide) or voluntarily abuse them, as in the case of toluene, which is the solvent found in glue and in cans of spray paint. Exposure to organic solvents tends to have large effects on the motor system, affecting the cerebellum, cranial nerves, and pyramidal motor system. Signs indicative of cerebellar compromise include gait ataxia, dysarthria, nystagmus, eye flutter, hearing loss, and poor arm coordination.

As with other toxic substances, deficits in processing appear to be related to the level of exposure. At low levels, individuals complain of fatigue, irritability, depression, and anxiety, as in the case of heavy metals. Few if any deficits are observed on standard neuropsychological tests. With higher levels of exposure, changes in mood, personality, and impulse control are found, along with intellectual deficits in memory, learning, concentration, and psychomotor functions. The most severe stage, more commonly reported with substance abuse rather than exposure

in the workplace, leads to pervasive neuropsychological dysfunction and dementia (Hartman, 1987).

What happens when individuals who are exposed to an organic solvent in the workplace no longer frequent that environment? This action has positive effects in about 50% of all individuals because they show improvements in neuropsychological performance. However, half remain at the same level of functioning or show deterioration. The distinguishing factor between these two groups is not their level of neuropsychological functioning prior to removal from the hazardous environment, but rather whether they had a peak exposure (brief but intense) to the solvent that required treatment or hospitalization. Poorer performance is associated with such a peak exposure (L. A. Morrow, Ryan, Hodgson, & Robin, 1991).

Pesticides

The use of pesticides is commonplace in farming and agriculture, and 2 to 5 million workers in the United States are exposed to pesticides each year. Of these individuals, about 1,200 experience acute pesticide poisoning annually. Yet the effects of pesticides are not limited to farmers or even home gardeners. Concern is growing that in many agricultural regions of the United States and elsewhere people are unknowingly being exposed to high levels of pesticides because these substances are seeping into the ground-water supply that is used to provide drinking water for rural communities. Exposure to these agents is also a concern in many developing countries because pesticides outlawed in the West are routinely sold there.

Because pesticides are clearly designed to be deadly to certain life forms, such as insects, the fact that they can have negative effects on humans is not surprising. One particularly large class of pesticides, organophosphates, are derived from the highly toxic nerve gases developed during World War II. Pesticides differ from these nerve gases mainly in potency and function. Many of the organophosphate pesticides are lipid soluble, meaning that, like alcohol, they can dissolve fats. This characteristic allows them to be easily absorbed through the skin, eyes, and respiratory tract. Generally, they have toxic effects by inhibiting acetylcholinesterase, which results in a buildup of acetylcholine in the synapse. With exposure to large amounts of these pesticides, a person can die. Other pesticides, such as fungicides, contain manganese, which is toxic because it interferes with catecholamine metabolism in the central nervous system.

Various cognitive dysfunctions are associated with pesticides, including reduced concentration, slowing of psychomotor function, memory problems, and language disturbances. Emotional changes, such as depression, anxiety, irritability, and personality changes have also been reported. Bodily symptoms include headaches, dizziness, stomach problems, cardiorespiratory problems, weakness, and weight loss. These symptoms may continue for as long as 11 years following pesticide exposure. Furthermore, they can be observed even when levels of acetylcholinesterase in the blood are within normal limits (Reidy, Bowler, Rauch, & Pedroza, 1992).

Other Substances

So far, we discussed metals, organic solvents, and pesticides, which are toxins that individuals either abuse or are exposed to during employment. However, sometimes people voluntarily take toxins for legitimate (rather than abusive) reasons. For example, lithium carbonate, a metal, is considered the drug of choice in treating manic-depression. Nonetheless, at high levels lithium is toxic and can lead to disintegration of neuropsychological function. Likewise, popular minor tranquilizers such as Valium, which comes from a family of medications known as benzodiazepines (named after their chemical structure); steroids; and drugs used to fight cancer have all been shown to have neuropsychological sequelae. For example, tranquilizers affect short-term memory and learning, and steroid use (popularized by athletes) leads to declines in cognitive performance. Thus, the neuropsychologist must know not only an individual's occupational history, but also his or her current medical status to determine whether declines in cognitive functioning can result from either toxins or drugs.

EPILEPSY

Throughout much of history, epilepsy has had a negative connotation; epileptic seizures have been referred to as "fits," and individuals with epilepsy have been stigmatized. We now know that such characterizations are unfair and that the disease is indicative of a neurological problem that does not reflect on the person's character. Epilepsy is a disease in which seizure activity is recurrent but intermittent. **Epileptic seizures** are episodes in which synchronous activity of nerve cells increases so that a gigantic hyperpolarization of neurons spreads over a large area in an atypical and abnormal manner. On the EEG record, these gigantic hyperpolarizations are seen as "spikes" (Figure 14.10). Seizures for which a cause is known are termed *symptomatic*. These causes include head trauma, metabolic disorders, infection, toxins, and tumors. For example, approximately 20% of all individuals who sustain a penetrating brain injury develop epilepsy (epilepsy is much less common after closed head injury) (see, for example, Dalmady-Israel & Zasler, 1993, for a review of issues related to posttraumatic seizures). Seizures that occur for no apparent reason are known as *idiopathic*.

Seizures come in many varieties, which are divided into two major classes. One major classification is *generalized seizures,* so-called because they involve the entire body. The second class is *focal seizures,* in which the activity starts in a particular region of the brain and then spreads, at times so much that it becomes generalized. During seizure activity, consciousness is disturbed. The major types of seizures, along with their motoric effects and usual changes in consciousness, are outlined in Table 14.4.

Epileptic seizures can be triggered by a variety of stimuli, and the evoking agent varies from individual to individual. Generally a person tries to avoid the situation or stimulus that leads to a seizure,

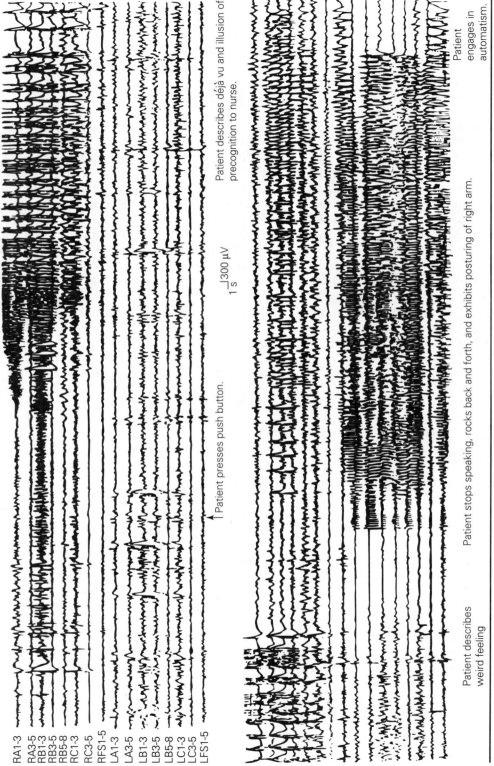

R.H. (age 32) 80–1989

RA1-3
RA3-5
RB1-3
RB3-5
RB5-8
RC1-3
RC3-5
RFS1-5
LA1-3
LA3-5
LB1-3
LB3-5
LB5-8
LC1-3
LC3-5
LFS1-5

300 μV
1 s

↑ Patient presses push button.

Patient describes déjà vu and illusion of precognition to nurse.

Patient describes weird feeling

Patient stops speaking, rocks back and forth, and exhibits posturing of right arm.

Patient engages in automatism.

Figure 14.10 The spiking of electrical brain activity that typically accompanies an epileptic seizure.
Reproduced here are recordings from eight electrodes over each hemisphere (R, right hemisphere; L, left hemisphere). The behavioral manifestations of the seizure are listed below the recordings. The spiking activity can be seen most prominently over the right hemisphere soon after the beginning of the seizure, but it manifests over the left hemisphere only when the patient stops speaking and begins to rock back and forth. (*Note.* Adapted with permission from "Neurobiological Substrates of Ictal Behavioral Changes," by P. Gloor, in *Advances in Neurology: Vol. 55, Neurobehavioral Problems in Epilepsy,* edited by D. B. Smith, D. M. Treiman, and M. R. Trimble, 1991, New York: Raven Press.)

Table 14.4 Classification of Epileptic Seizures and Their Manifestations

Type of seizure	Motor manifestations	Changes in consciousness
Generalized seizures		
Grand mal (tonic-clonic)	1. *Tonic phase*: The person shouts or makes a loud noise and falls. Then, the person exhibits upward or sideways turning of the eyes and tonic tension of the muscles in which the whole body stiffens and breathing stops. 2. *Clonic phase*: Rhythmic jerking of body parts begins and continues for minutes	1. *Tonic phase*: The person loses conscious control of movement and loses consciousness. 2. *Clonic phase*: Disorientation or comatose behavior is exhibited following clonic motor activity.
Clonic	Same as clonic phase of grand mal seizures described above	Same as clonic phase of grand mal seizures described above.
Tonic	Same as tonic phase of grand mal seizures described above.	Same as tonic phase of grand mal seizures described above.
Petite mal	A slight movement of the eyes or turning of the head can be observed.	A brief change in consciousness occurs, which is often overlooked by untrained individuals. The person seems to "space out" briefly (i.e., is unresponsive for about 10 s).
Focal seizures		
Jacksonian (originate in a specific region of the motor strip but sometimes in other regions such as the somatosensory strip)	The seizure starts as a clonic movement of one specific body part. The seizure spreads in an orderly progression down the motor strip to neighboring regions, involving more and more body parts; this progression is known as a Jacksonian march.	Little impairment of consciousness occurs.
Complex partial seizures (originate in the temporal or frontal lobe)	*During seizures*: The person engages in automatisms—repetitive motions including buttoning and unbuttoning the same button, lip smacking, swallowing, and chewing. This phase may then be followed by one in which the person seems catatonic or frozen.	*Preceding seizures*: The person experiences an aura, which is a feeling, sensation, smell, or taste that signals the onset of the seizure. In some cases, these auras can be elaborate and may involve mood changes, feelings of déjà vu, hallucinations, repetitive thoughts, or a warping of the sense of time and place. *During seizures*: A limited clouding of consciousness occurs.

although determining exactly what the exacerbating stimulus is may initially take a while. Stressful situations, especially those induced by sleep deprivation, can lead to seizure activity. In fact, so potent is sleep deprivation in bringing on seizure activity that neurologists often require a patient to go without sleep the night before they record the individual's EEG activity. Seizures may also be triggered by certain sensory stimuli, such as flashing lights; particular sounds; reading or laughing; certain classes of drugs, including alcohol; specific foods; and hormonal changes. For example, hormonal changes at puberty often cause a seizure (Kolb & Whishaw, 1990; Spreen et al., 1984).

Epilepsy can impair cognitive and psychosocial functioning. Clearly, consciousness is disrupted during the seizure and this disruption impairs cognition, but interictal (i.e., between-seizure) consequences occur as well. Neuropsychological deficits usually seem to reflect dysfunction of the area from where the seizure originated. The results of a recent study suggest that the cognitive consequences tend to be most related to the location of the seizure (frontal, temporal), the age of onset, and the individual's handedness; an earlier age of onset, left-handedness, and a frontal source of seizure activity are associated with poorer overall intellectual functioning (Strauss, Hunter, & Wada, 1995). However, sometimes the relationship between seizure activity and neuropsychological impairments is not always clear-cut (e.g., Williamson et al., 1993). Nonetheless, epileptiform EEG discharges that are not large enough to produce a seizure interfere with cognitive processing in about half of all cases (Binnie, 1994). Epilepsy is sometimes also associated with psychiatric disorders that occur postictally or chronically. The postictal disorders tend to be most common in individuals who have bihemispheric temporal lobe foci and clustering of seizures. A relatively young age at onset and low IQ are associated with more chronic psychotic symptoms (Umbricht et al., 1995) (for a review of the neuropsychological consequences of epilepsy, see Dodrill, 1992).

The two main forms of therapy for epilepsy are drug therapy and surgery. The first step in any treatment involves the administration of anticonvulsant medication, which reduces the likelihood of epileptic discharges. The two major types of drugs most commonly given are diphenylhydantoin (Dilantin) and phenobarbital. Exactly how these drugs work is not well understood, but they have proven effective in reducing seizures and hence are used. As with all other drugs, they have side effects and given in too large of doses can impair cognition (for a review of the side effects of anticonvulsant medication, see Nichols, Meador, & Loring, 1993). Therefore, the drug administration must be *titrated*, that is, adjusted bit by bit, so that the physician can find the dosage that has the greatest efficacy against seizures with the fewest side effects on cognition. In some cases, drugs may be ineffective in reducing seizures (Bannister, 1992).

If the focal origin for the seizure is clear, the physician and the patient may opt for surgery to remove the source of the seizure activity, especially if it seems to be recruiting previously healthy areas. As we discussed in the preceding section, focal seizures are most often localized to temporal and frontal areas. Especially when the focus is in the temporal areas, resection may be associated with memory loss.

SUMMARY

In this chapter, we discussed generalized cognitive disorders, which are neuropsychological disorders that affect multiple aspects of cognitive function simultaneously. The various etiologies of generalized cognitive disorders include closed head injury, dementing diseases, demyelinating diseases, exposure to toxins, and substance abuse. Closed head injury occurs when the head hits or is hit by a blunt object. Focal injury can occur at, or opposite, the site of impact, and diffuse damage occurs due to tearing and shearing of the neurons, which mainly affects long myelinated nerve-fiber tracts. Closed head injury is associated with loss of consciousness, even in cases of mild concussion. The degree of unresponsiveness of an individual, especially as measured by the Glasgow Coma Scale (GCS), provides a gross estimate of the prognosis for future functioning. The most common acute consequences of head injury are difficulties in concentration, attentional problems, and posttraumatic amnesia. More long-term effects include difficulties in abstract thought and conceptualization, flexibility, behavioral control, and planning, along with a lack of an appreciation of the deficits. Emotional changes such as anxiety, depression, and anger also occur frequently. Closed head injury has been suggested to put an individual at risk for other neurological disorders, such as another head injury or Alzheimer's disease. Activity in particular sports, such as boxing and football, can also predispose an individual to a closed head injury. Preventive measures to avoid head injury include wearing protective headgear during participation in sports that have a risk of head injury or during the use of two-wheeled transportation, using seat belts and equipping cars with air bags, responsibly consuming alcohol, and not engaging in risky or reckless behavior.

Generalized cognitive disorders are also observed in dementia, which is characterized by a progressive and steady decline in cognitive function. Dementias are usually divided into three classes: cortical, subcortical, and mixed. The cortical dementias, including Alzheimer's, Pick's, and Creutzfeldt–Jakob, are all typified by the simultaneous confluence of specific cognitive disorders such as aphasia, apraxia, agnosia, acalculia, spatial deficits, and memory problems. Alzheimer's disease is the most common cortical dementia. It's main feature is a prominent memory impairment, but other cognitive functions, such as language, object recognition, and spatial processing are also affected. Typically, personality changes are noted as well. Neurophysiologically, Alzheimer's disease is associated with specific neuroanatomical changes: the presence of neurofibrillary tangles and amyloid plaques in brain tissue. Although the mechanism by which these neuroanatomical structures interfere with neuronal function is not exactly known, they are linked to massive neuronal death in association cortex. The etiology of Alzheimer's disease is unknown, but the list of possible causes is long, including an autoimmune disorder, a breakdown in the blood-brain barrier, DNA deficiencies, a slow virus, and an inflammatory disease affecting multiple body systems.

Another disorder leading to a cortical dementia, Pick's disease, tends to affect mainly the frontal and temporal regions. Unlike Alzheimer's disease, in which memory impairment is usually the first symptom, difficulty in language and changes in personality are more likely to be the initial complaints. No tangles and plaques are seen in Pick's disease, but the neurons appear pale and swollen. Creutzfeldt–Jakob disease, which is caused by a communicable slow virus, leads to a much faster cognitive decline than that of either Alzheimer's or Pick's disease. The dementia is accompanied by involuntary movements, and the characteristic EEG pattern contains sharp spikes.

Subcortical dementias, such as those caused by Huntington's and Parkinson's disease, have a different profile of cognitive decline than that observed in patients with cortical dementias. Deficits are usually observed on tasks related to motor functioning, attention, and executive control. Memory impairments are exhibited on tests of recall but not recognition. Emotional changes, most notably depression, are often observed. In Huntington's disease, which is an inherited disorder, difficulties in spatial learning may also be present. In contrast, in Parkinson's disease, which results from cell loss in the substantia nigra, general slowing of both motor functioning and thinking occurs. In hemi-Parkinsonism, damage is sustained by only one half of the basal ganglia. In this situation, the cognitive deficits are linked to the side of the basal ganglia affected: Verbal disruptions are observed with left-sided damage, and visuospatial disruptions are observed after right-sided damage.

Mixed-variety dementias appear to have a cortical and a subcortical component and include vascular dementia and AIDS dementia. Vascular dementia results from the cumulative effect of many individual strokes. Because the brain damage may occur either cortically or subcortically and varies among individuals, the profile of neuropsychological dysfunction varies depending on the brain region involved. Typically, however, functions related to frontal regions and the frontal-striatal system are most often compromised. Individuals with AIDS dementia have difficulties in attention, problem solving, and memory and may exhibit psychiatric symptoms. Typically, the pattern of impairment is more like that associated with subcortical dementia than that observed in cortical dementia. At present, mild neuropsychological dysfunction appears to accompany HIV infection even when the individual is seropositive but asymptomatic.

The most common demyelinating disease is multiple sclerosis (MS), which seems to be caused by a genetic vulnerability combined with exposure to an environmental pathogen, which as yet is undefined. This disease attacks the myelin surrounding neurons while leaving the neurons themselves more or less intact. Because the regions of brain tissue that are affected vary among individuals, some variability in the cognitive dysfunction is observed, although sensory and motor deficits, along with difficulties in memory, conceptual reasoning, and attention, are common.

Cognitive functioning can also be disrupted in various ways in individuals who abuse substances or are exposed to toxins. Patients with alcoholism, even those who have abstained for some time, typically exhibit deficits on visuospatial functioning, learning, memory, and executive functioning. Similar effects are seen in the abuse of other substances. At present, debate continues as to whether abstinence from a substance after years of abuse leads to a recovery of neuropsychological functioning. Toxins, such as metals, organic solvents, and pesticides, lead to diffuse complaints, including problems in attention and memory, and slow psychomotor speed. Emotional complaints of increased depression and irritability are also common. When exposure to the toxin ceases, gains in neuropsychological function may be seen but are less common if an individual has had at least one intense exposure to the toxin that resulted in hospitalization.

Epilepsy, which is caused by synchronous and atypical firing of nerve cells, usually results from a factor that has a negative effect on brain functioning, such as toxins, head injury, and metabolic disturbances. The two main classes of seizures are generalized seizures and focal seizures. In generalized seizures, many regions of brain tissue misfire, whereas focal seizures affect only one region of the brain, usually the frontal or temporal lobes. Epilepsy may compromise both cognitive and emotional functioning. Cognitively, deficits are usually seen on tasks dependent on the region from which the seizures originate. In some cases, psychiatric symptoms may manifest as well. Drug therapy and surgery are the two main means of treating epilepsy, but drug therapy may have cognitive consequences, and surgery, most notably when it involves removal of temporal areas, is associated with memory loss.

Glossary

2½-D representation—A more elaborate representation of the visual world than the primal sketch. It contains information about the relative depth of surfaces.

3-D representation—A volumetric representation of an object that truly describes its 3-D characteristics so that the object can be identified regardless of the orientation from which it is viewed.

Acceleration-deceleration injury—See *Closed head injury*.

Action potential—The firing of a neuron in which the charge of the cell increases from the resting potential to +40 mV, then becomes more negative than the resting potential, and finally rebounds to the resting potential.

Action tremor (intention tremor)—A tremor causing movement to occur in a staggered manner during a motor act. It is typically associated with cerebellar damage and is distinct from the tremors usually observed in Parkinson's disease, which occur at rest.

Activating-orienting model—The idea that perceptual asymmetries arise from hemispheric differences in activation. The underlying assumption is that depending on the task demands (e.g., verbal vs. spatial), one hemisphere will become more activated than the other. This activation will cause an attentional bias to the side of space contralateral to the more activated hemisphere, which will lead to better processing of information on that side of space.

Affective prosody—The aspect of an utterance that communicates the emotional context or tone. For example, "My mother is coming to dinner" could be stated in a way that expresses elation or in a way that expresses dismay.

Agnosia—A modality-specific deficit occurring after brain damage that results in an inability to recognize objects even though basic sensory processing in that modality and memory are intact.

Agrammatical aphasia—An aphasia characterized by an inability to produce and comprehend the correct grammatical markers. The lesion causing it is generally located in left frontal regions.

Agraphia—The inability to write as a result of parietal lobe damage.

Akathisia—Compulsive, hyperactive, fidgety movements of the legs.

Akinesia—The lack of spontaneous movement. One of the main symptoms of Parkinson's disease.

Alertness and arousal—The basic aspects of attention that enable a person to extract information from the environment or to select a particular response.

Alexia—The inability to read as a result of parietal lobe damage.

Alien limb syndrome—A disorder in which a person feels unable to control the movements of a body part, believes the limb is alien, or believes that the body part has its own personality. It is typically associated with lesions in the supplementary motor area or those affecting blood flow to the anterior regions of the corpus callosum and the anterior cingulate cortex.

Alpha suppression—A decrease in the electroencephalographic (EEG) activity in the 9- to 12-Hz range (alpha activity) that generally accompanies mental activity.

Alternative strategy—An approach to a task that falls within the realm of everyday behavior but is distinct from the way in which the individual typically performs the task.

Altitudinal neglect—Disregard for one-half of vertical space (e.g., the upper half).

Alzheimer's disease—A cortical dementia that results in a decline in many aspects of cognitive functioning. It is characterized by a prominent impairment in memory along with at least one of the following: aphasia, apraxia, agnosia, and disturbance in executive functioning. It is sometimes called *dementia of the Alzheimer's type (DAT)*.

Amnesia—A memory deficit, including both anterograde and retrograde components, for facts and data (i.e., for declarative memory). It is caused by damage to the medial temporal lobes, midline diencephalic brain regions, or both.

Amyloid plaques—Deposits of aluminum silicate and amyloid peptides, which are basically a buildup or a conglomeration of proteins, that are not in the neurons themselves. They are believed to cause vascular damage and neuronal cell loss. Like neurofibrillary tangles, they are much more numerous in patients with Alzheimer's disease than in neurologically intact older individuals.

Anosognosia—A condition observed after hemiplegia in which a person denies, with both verbal and nonverbal behaviors, that his or her limb is paralyzed.

Anterior—Located toward the front of the brain (by the face).

Anterior cingulate cortex—A region of the brain located below the cingulate sulcus but above the corpus callosum that is important for motor control, especially when it involves novel responses to a stimulus (e.g., pressing the gas pedal when a red light appears).

Anterograde amnesia—The impairment of memory for information acquired after the onset of amnesia.

Anterograde (Wallerian) degeneration—The deterioration of an axon of a neuron in the central nervous system that has been severed from its cell body.

Aphasia—A class of syndromes, resulting from brain damage, that are characterized by a deficit in language processing.

Apperceptive agnosia—A type of visual agnosia in which a fundamental difficulty in forming a percept exists. Although basic visual information is processed (e.g., areas of light and dark), it cannot be bound together so that a meaningful whole is perceived.

Apraxia—An inability to perform skilled, purposeful movement even though the affected individual has intact motor innervation of the muscles, can spontaneously coordinate sensorimotor actions, and can comprehend what is being asked. It is generally observed bilaterally and is typically associated with lesions to the parietal region of the left hemisphere.

Aprosodia—Difficulty with prosody, usually as a result of brain damage.

Aprosodic—Lacking prosody.

Association Area—An area of the brain where information from multiple sensory modalities is processed.

Associative agnosia—A type of visual agnosia in which basic visual information can be integrated to form a meaningful perceptual whole but that particular perceptual whole cannot be linked to knowledge stored in memory.

Athetosis—Involuntary writhing contractions and twisting of the body into abnormal postures. It is a symptom of Huntington's disease.

Attention—A psychological process that allows us, because of the limited capacity of the human brain, to select only certain types of information and not others.

Attentional dyslexia—A syndrome in which an individual can recognize a single letter or a single word in isolation but cannot recognize the same letter or word if it is presented along with items of the same kind (i.e., other letters or other words).

Attention-deficit disorder (ADD)—A developmental disorder in which a child is extremely inattentive and distractible (much more so than is typical for the average child of the same age), and which may be accompanied by hyperactivity and impulsivity.

Auditory agnosia—A condition in which basic aspects of auditory stimuli can be processed but the person is unable to link that sensory information to meaning, despite the fact that memory, as assessed through other modalities, appears to be normal.

Auditory nerve—The conduit whereby information is carried from the ear to the brain.

Auditory-verbal working memory—Memory that allows us to hold and repeat verbatim the contents of the immediately preceding verbal utterance. It is sometimes called the *phonological store*.

Autism—A type of pervasive development disorder that is characterized by particularly profound social deficits as well as difficulties in learning.

Axon—The appendage of the cell along which a large electrical signal, the action potential, is propagated.

Axon hillock—The region of the cell near the cell body at which excitatory and inhibitory postsynaptic potentials summate to cause an action potential.

Balint's syndrome—A disorder in which individuals have difficulty localizing items in space, groping for objects as if blind. These individuals have optic ataxia, ocular apraxia, and simultanagnosia. The syndrome is sometimes referred to as *dorsal simultanagnosia* because it is generally seen after bilateral lesions to the dorsal occipitoparietal region and because the individual is unable to pay attention to two points in space simultaneously.

Ballistic movement—A movement that occurs so quickly that little or no time is available for it to be modified by feedback while it is being performed. The cerebellum controls this type of movement.

Basal ganglia—A group of subcortical structures, including the putamen and the caudate nucleus (known collectively as the *striatum*) and the globus pallidus (or *pal-*

lidum), located near the thalamus, that are responsible for motor control. The substantia nigra and the subthalamic nucleus are two other nuclei associated with the basal ganglia.

Bilateral—Pertaining to both sides of the brain (or space).

Bilateral presentation—A method in divided visual field studies in which two items are presented, one in each visual field.

Binocular columns—Separate but adjacent regions of visual cortex that receive information about a given region of space. Each column is specifically sensitive to input from only one eye. They are also known as *ocular dominance columns.*

Binocular disparity—The difference in the retinal images received by each eye that aids in determining the relative depth of items.

Blood-brain barrier—An impediment that prevents nutrients and other elements (including harmful substances such as toxins) that are in the bloodstream from entering neurons directly. It is created by a tight packing of glia between blood vessels and neurons.

Body schema—A conceptual spatial framework of the body that allows for an understanding of the spatial relationships among different body parts.

Bradykinesia—Slowness of movement. One of the main symptoms of Parkinson's disease.

Bradyphrenia—The slowing of motor and thought processes that typically accompanies Parkinson's disease.

Broca's Aphasia—A syndrome in which fluent speech is lost even though the person's speech comprehension is relatively spared. It is caused by a lesion to posterior regions of the left frontal lobe located directly in front of the face area of the motor strip.

Brodmann map—A neuroanatomical map of the cortex. It differentiates brain regions based on the nature of cells within a region and their laminar organization.

Calcification—Accumulations of calcium that are associated with transneuronal degeneration.

Callosal apraxia—An apraxia resulting from damage to the corpus callosum that prevents motor plans devised in the left hemisphere from reaching the right hemisphere. Skilled motor movements cannot be executed with the left hand because the right hemisphere cannot receive information about the motor program.

Callosal relay model—The idea that perceptual asymmetries arise because of degradation of information as it is transferred across the corpus callosum. The underlying assumption is that information received by a hemisphere less suited for a task is transferred to the opposite hemi-

sphere through the corpus callosum and that the fidelity of the information is reduced during that transfer.

Caloric stimulation—The introduction of 20 ml of water that is at least 7 °C warmer or colder than body temperature into the ear canal during the course of 15 s. It has been found to reduce neglect but cannot be used as a therapy because its effects dissipate with time and because of its side effects (e.g., nausea).

Cannon–Bard theory—The idea that an emotion is produced when an event or an object is perceived by the thalamus, which conveys this information simultaneously to the cerebral cortex and to the skeletal muscles and autonomic nervous system.

Catastrophic reaction—A condition in which patients are described to be emotionally volatile and especially prone to depression and crying. It occurs most frequently after left-hemisphere damage.

Categorical spatial relations—One position in relation to another (e.g., above vs. below, top vs. bottom, front vs. back, left vs. right). This type of spatial relation is believed to rely on left-hemisphere mechanisms and to be independent of a system in the right hemisphere that is believed to compute metric spatial relations.

Category-specific deficit—An inability to recognize a particular subclass of items, such as fruits and vegetables, while the ability to recognize other classes of items, such as human-made objects, remains relatively intact. This difficulty seems to reflect a disruption in the organization of semantic memory rather than a problem in linking specific perceptual forms to meaning.

Caudal—Located toward an animal's tail.

Caudate nucleus—A portion of the basal ganglia that, along with the putamen, receives all the input into the basal ganglia. It degenerates in Huntington's disease.

Cell body—The part of the neuron containing the nucleus and other cellular apparatus responsible not only for manufacturing proteins and enzymes that sustain cell functioning, but also for producing neurotransmitters.

Central fissure—The main fissure that divides anterior and posterior sections of the brain. It is sometimes called the *Rolandic fissure.*

Central nervous system—The portion of the nervous system that consists of the brain and the spinal cord.

Cerebellum—The brain region posterior to the medulla that is important for regulating muscle tone, guiding motor activity, and allowing motor skills to be learned.

Cerebral dominance—The idea that one hemisphere dominates or leads mental thought. In the late 19th and early 20th centuries, the left hemisphere was considered the dominant hemisphere because it is involved with language processing (and language was equated with thought).

Cerebral hemisphere—One half of the cortex. It is the region of the brain that plays a primary role in most of our mental skills, such as language, attention, and artistry.

Cerebral palsy—A disorder of motor functioning that occurs as a result of motor system damage during or preceding birth rather than from a progressive disease.

Cerebrospinal fluid (CSF)—The substance, similar in composition to blood plasma, in which the spinal cord and brain float. It cushions these structures from their bony encasements and transports nutrients to neurons.

Chemoaffinity (chemospecificity) hypothesis—The idea that during development the orderly migration of cells from a site near the ventricle to their final location within the brain occurs because a nerve cell travels until it finds a specific chemical milieu.

Chord—The co-occurrence of pitches whose frequencies have a certain relationship to one another.

Chorea—A variety of jerky movements that appear to be well-coordinated but are performed involuntarily, ceaselessly, and in an irregular manner. It is one of the main symptoms of Huntington's disease.

Chronic vegetative state—A state of consciousness that occurs after coma, in which the person regains a normal sleep-wake cycle, may follow people with his or her eyes, and responds with primitive reflexes but has no additional awareness of the external world or internal needs.

Cingulate cortex—The interface between subcortical and cortical brain regions that imparts emotional significance to information that has captured attention. It is involved when attention must be used to override automatic motor responses.

Closed head injury—Brain damage sustained when the head forcefully comes into contact with another object (e.g., a car windshield, the ground, a blunt instrument such as a baseball bat), but no object penetrates the brain. It is also called *acceleration-deceleration injury* because the damage usually occurs when a rapid acceleration of the head is followed by a rapid deceleration.

Coarticulation—Variations in the production of sounds by the vocal muscles depending on the preceding sounds.

Cognitive estimation—Using known information to make reasonable judgments or deductions about the world.

Cogwheel rigidity—The stiffness observed in Parkinson's disease due to increased muscle tone in extensor and flexor muscles. The increased tone causes the limbs to move in specific rigid steps, much as a cogwheel does.

Coma—An impaired state of consciousness in which individuals are seemingly unresponsive to most external stimuli, lying with their eyes closed. In severe cases, they may not even exhibit defensive movements to noxious or painful stimuli, although in less severe cases they will do so.

Compensatory strategy—An approach to a task that generally would not be used to perform the task but is invoked to minimize the loss of a specific skill.

Components—Characteristic portions of the event-related potential (ERP) waveform that have been linked to certain psychological processes, such as attention and memory.

Computational theory—A hypothesis that outlines the computations that must be performed by a system to solve a particular problem, such as recognizing an object.

Computerized axial tomography—A technique for imaging the brain with x-rays that provides information on the density of brain structures. It is also known as *CAT* or *CT*.

Conduction aphasia—A syndrome in which a person can comprehend and produce speech but cannot repeat what was just said. It is associated with damage to the region between Wernicke's and Broca's areas, damage that has been conceptualized as preventing information from Wernicke's area from being conducted forward to Broca's area for speech output.

Conjugate lateral eye movements—Rapid eye movements in a sideways direction that some researchers use to index hemispheric activation.

Constructional apraxia—Difficulty with spatial aspects of motor functioning. It may not be considered a true apraxia because the difficulty seems to arise not so much from motor problems as from spatial problems.

Constructional praxis—The ability to motorically produce or manipulate items so that they have a certain spatial relationship.

Contention scheduling—The cognitive system that allows for automatic processing. This automaticity is engendered over time, because stimuli or situations become linked to actions, routines, or schemata, and then groups of these become linked to one another.

Contingent negative variation (CNV)—An electroencephalographic (EEG) signal often recorded after the brain receives a warning signal that puts the brain in an alert state to receive information. This potential is thought to involve the reticular activating system, which then activates the rest of the cortex: first prefrontal areas, then more posterior regions.

Contralateral—On the opposite side from.

Contrecoup injury—Focal damage that occurs opposite the site of impact in closed head injury.

Coronal view—A plane that divides the front of the brain from the back.

Corpus callosum—The massive neural tract of more than 250 million nerve fibers that connects the cerebral hemispheres.

Corticobulbar pathway—The motor pathway that connects motor cortex to the face region and is important for motor control of the face.

Corticospinal pathway—The motor pathway that connects motor cortex to the spinal cord. Two major tracts within it are the lateral corticospinal tract and the ventral corticospinal tract.

Coup injury—Focal damage that occurs at the site of impact in closed head injury.

Cranial nerves—The nerves responsible for receipt of sensory information and motor control of the head as well as for neural control of internal organs.

Creutzfeldt–Jakob disease—A rare cortical dementia caused by an infectious agent, a prion. The initial symptoms, which are psychiatric, are followed by motor symptoms, then a swift mental decline and death.

Crossed aphasia—Aphasia in a right-handed individual that results from a right-hemisphere lesion. It occurs very rarely.

Crowding hypothesis—The theory that the young brain compensates for early damage by instituting a maximal rewiring of the available neural space. Although this reorganization works well initially, deleterious consequences are seen later in life because the system cannot adapt to or acquire later developing mental skills.

Cued recall—A direct (explicit) test of memory that samples the ability to recover items from memory in response to direct cues, such as the name of the actor who starred in the first Batman movie or the word from the study list that was an example of a vehicle.

Customized neuropsychological assessment—An approach in which a small set of standard tests is used to assess general intelligence, after which the administrator generates hypotheses about the nature of an individual's deficits and tests the hypotheses by using specialized tests to assess specific abilities.

Declarative memory—A memory system, which is dependent on the hippocampus and related structures, that supports a fundamentally relational form of memory that allows it to be retrieved and used flexibly in a number of contexts.

Decomposition of movement—The breakdown of complex, multijoint movement into single, serial movements. This phenomenon is often observed after cerebellar damage.

Deep alexia—A syndrome similar to phonologic alexia in that the phonologic route from print to meaning is disrupted. However, additional symptoms include misreading words as those with similar meaning (e.g., reading *ship* as "boat"), difficulty in reading words that serve as grammatical markers, and difficulty in reading abstract words (e.g., *faith*) although reading concrete words (e.g., *chair*) is preserved.

Deep cerebellar nuclei—Three nuclei (fastigial, interpositus, and dentate) embedded within the cerebellum, each of which connects to a different region of the cerebellum.

Delayed nonmatch-to-sample task—A task in which an animal must remember the identity of recently presented objects. Each trial of the task consists of a sample phase and a match phase.

Dementia—A debilitating syndrome involving a loss of cognitive funtions, sometimes accompanied by personality changes, that interferes significantly with work or social activities.

Dementia of the Alzheimer's type (DAT)—See *Alzheimer's disease.*

Dendritic tree—The part of the neuron that receives input from other cells.

Denervation supersensitivity—A process occurring after damage or cell loss by which the remaining intact cells become hypersensitive to stimulation.

Dentate nucleus—One of the deep cerebellar nuclei. It receives input from the lateral zone of the cerebellum.

Developmental dysphasia—A disorder of expressive language in which children have difficulty understanding and producing speech.

Developmental milestones—Specific changes in behavior and skills that manifest at certain ages during development.

Diathesis-stress model—A model of psychopathology in which environmental factors (the stressors) interact with or exacerbate a biological predisposition (the diathesis).

Dichaptic presentation—A method for testing lateralization of function in the tactile modality, in which an individual feels two items simultaneously, one in each hand, and then must identify these items in some manner. A superiority in processing by one hand is believed to indicate a superiority of the contralateral hemisphere.

Dichotic presentation—A method for examining hemispheric differences in the auditory modality in which *different* information is presented simultaneously to each ear. An advantage for information presented to one ear is believed to indicate a superiority of the contralateral hemisphere.

Diencephalon—The hypothalamus and the thalamus.

Digit span—The number of digits that can be held in working memory and repeated verbatim.

Dipole—A small region of electrical current with a relatively positive end and a relatively negative end produced by the common alignment and firing of dendritic fields in the brain.

Direct access theory—The idea that perceptual asymmetries arise because the hemispheres have differing competencies and any information received by a hemisphere is processed by that hemisphere. From this perspective, perceptual asymmetries arise because the hemisphere more suited for a task will exhibit superior processing of the information received than the hemisphere that is less suited for the task will.

Direct route to reading—The method of linking print to meaning without a phonologic intermediary.

Direct (explicit) tests of memory—Tests of memory that depend upon conscious recollection of the learning event and refer the subject to a particular study episode or learning event.

Disconnection syndrome—A disruption in cognitive function that occurs when a brain region is damaged, not because that region controls the function but because fibers connecting two brain regions critical to the function are destroyed.

Distal—Located toward the periphery or toward the end of a limb.

Divided visual field technique—A method whereby information is presented separately in each visual field. By comparing performance for information presented in the right visual field (received by the left hemisphere) and performance for that presented in the left visual field (received by the right hemisphere), researchers can determine hemispheric differences in processing.

L-Dopa—A precursor to dopamine that can cross the blood-brain barrier when given orally. It is used to treat Parkinson's disease.

Dorsal—Located toward an animal's back (in people sometimes toward the top as in the case of the brain).

Dorsal simultanagnosia—See *Balint's syndrome.*

Dorsomedial nucleus—The thalamic nucleus typically damaged in diencephalic amnesia.

Double dissociation—A method for determining that two cognitive functions are independent of each other. It occurs when lesions have converse effects on two distinct cognitive functions: One brain lesion causes a disruption in Cognitive Function A but not Cognitive Function B, whereas a different lesion causes a disruption in Cognitive Function B but not Cognitive Function A.

Double simultaneous stimulation technique—A method in which the patient is confronted with two similar items on each side of space simultaneously and is asked how many items have been presented. Under these conditions, a patient with neglect typically says that she or he sees, hears, or feels only a single item. However, if the same item is presented in isolation on the neglected side of space, it will be noticed.

Down syndrome—One of the leading genetic causes of mental retardation. It occurs because of a defective egg, a defective sperm, or defects in cell division; gene translocation; or trisomy 21, in which the 21st pair of chromosomes contains an extra (third) chromosome. This disorder is associated with maternal age older than 35 years.

Dressing apraxia—Difficulty performing the correct spatial manipulations and motor actions required to dress yourself. Like constructional apraxia, it may not be considered a true apraxia because the difficulty seems to arise not so much from difficulties in motor processing as from difficulties in spatial processing

Dual-task methodology—A method for investigating the existence of multiple resources in which the simultaneous performance of two tasks is examined. If the two tasks compete for resources, interference should occur when both tasks are performed simultaneously. If they do not compete for resources, no such decrement should be observed.

Dyslexia—The inability to learn to read at an age-appropriate level, despite adequate opportunity, training, and intelligence. It is sometimes called *a specific reading disability.*

Dysprosodic—Having disordered intonation.

Dystonia—Painful, continual muscle spasms.

Early selection viewpoint—The idea that selection occurs early in the stream of processing, soon after the receipt of sensory information and before an item is identified.

Echolalia—The compulsion to repeat what was just said. It is common in individuals with transcortical motor and transcortical sensory aphasia.

Edema—Tissue swelling after trauma.

Electrical potential—The summed or superimposed signal of the electrical activity of fields of neuronal dendrites that are all similarly aligned. It is typically recorded at the scalp.

Electroconvulsive therapy (ECT)—A series of treatments for the relief of severe depressive illness. When it is performed bilaterally, in which electrical current is applied across two electrodes placed on the surface of the head, it produces an amnesia that dissipates with time.

Electroencephalography (EEG)—A method of recording the electrical signals produced by the synchronous firing of neurons that provides information on the frequency at which neurons are firing.

Elimination of synapses—The process whereby numerous synaptic connections are lost during development. It allows pruning of neural connections after their proliferation early in life.

Emotional semantics—The ability to label emotions and to understand the link between certain situations and specific emotions. It is thought to depend partly on the left hemisphere.

Encoding of memories—The process whereby information is placed in memory storage so that it can be retrieved later.

Endogenous components—Event-related potential (ERP) components that are independent of stimulus characteristics, driven by internal cognitive states, and typically occur later in the waveform.

Environmental dependency syndrome—A disorder in which objects in the environment trigger individuals with executive dysfunction to act, even though the actions are inappropriate.

Epileptic laughing—Involuntary and uncontrollable outbursts of laughing, most often associated with an epileptic focus (an area of abnormal electrical discharge) in the left cerebral hemisphere, particularly in the temporal lobe region.

Epileptic seizure—A pathological neural phenomenon in which a vast number of neurons misfire in great bursts, or volleys, called *spikes.*

Episodic memory—Memory containing autobiographic records of personally experienced events occurring in specifiable temporal and spatial contexts.

Estimate of premorbid functioning—An approximation of the level at which a person was functioning before a brain injury.

Euphoric-indifference reaction—A condition in which patients are inappropriately cheerful, prone to laughter, and display a lack of awareness with regard to their disabilities and other consequences of changes wrought by brain

damage. It occurs most frequently after right-hemisphere damage.

Event-related potentials (ERPs)—Recordings of the brain's electrical activity that are linked to the occurrence of an event.

Excitatory postsynaptic potentials (EPSPs)—Small graded electrical potentials induced in a postsynaptic neuron after the binding of neurotransmitters to its membrane that serve to make the electrical charge of the postsynaptic cell more positive than the resting potential.

Executive functions—A family of functions that include the ability to plan actions toward a goal, to use information flexibly, to realize the ramifications of behavior, and to make reasonable inferences based on limited information. They can be compromised by damage to a variety of brain regions but most commonly occur after frontal lobe damage.

Exogenous components—Even-related potential (ERP) components linked to the physical characteristics of a stimulus. They usually occur early in the waveform.

Extended digit span—The number of digits that can be repeated verbatim if a person is given multiple repetitions of the same digit string with an additional digit added to extend the span. It provides an index of long-term memory.

Eye-movement monitoring techniques—Methods in which the eye movements of individuals are recorded.

Fastigial nucleus—One of the deep cerebellar nuclei. It receives input from the vermis.

Fetal alcohol effects—Negative consequences of alcohol intake by the mother during pregnancy that are not severe enough to be characterized as fetal alcohol syndrome.

Fetal alcohol syndrome (FAS)—A disorder characterized by mental retardation as well as stunted growth and congenital defects of the face and cranium. It is caused by excessive alcohol intake by the mother during pregnancy.

Fiber tract—A group of cells whose axons all project to the same region of the brain.

Figure-ground separation—The process of distinguishing a visual object from the background against which it is embedded. Color is an attribute that aids in such separation.

Finger agnosia—The bilateral inability of a person to recognize or localize his or her own fingers that is often associated with left-right confusion and is typically caused by a lesion to the left parietal cortex.

Fissure—A particularly deep sulcus.

Flicker fusion—The time delay between the presentation of two successive flashes of light, which is brief enough so that a person perceives the flashes as a steady stream of light.

Fragile X syndrome—A common form of mental retardation that is inherited. It is caused by a fragile section of the X chromosome; therefore, it has a much higher incidence rate in males than in females. It is sometimes called *Martin–Bell syndrome*.

Free recall—A direct (explicit) test of memory that samples the ability to recover items from memory in response to only a general cue about an event or a circumstance, such as the names of all the students in a particular class or the words on a given study list.

Frequency effects—The phenomenon in which words that are encountered most frequently in the language are read most quickly and objects that are encountered most frequently in the world are identified most quickly.

Frontal eye fields—A region of the brain located anterior to the supplementary motor area and dorsal to Broca's area. It is important for the control of voluntary eye movements.

Frontal lobe—The region of cortex in front of the central fissue.

Functional magnetic resonance imaging (fMRI)—A method, using magnetic resonance imaging (MRI) techniques, for assessing brain metabolism either through use of a magnetic contrast agent that enables blood flow to be determined or through measures of blood oxygenation.

Generalized (nonspecific) disorders—Syndromes in which the loss of function is not restricted to one cognitive domain but affects multiple cognitive abilities simultaneously.

Gerstmann syndrome—A disorder that was proposed to be caused by damage to the left parietal cortex and behaviorally characterized by four major attributes: right-left disturbances, finger agnosia, dysgraphia (an inability to write), and dyscalculia (the inability to perform arithmetic). Although these four symptoms can co-occur, they do not do so with such frequency that they represent a unique syndrome.

Glasgow Coma Scale (GCS)—A metric for assessing a person's level of consciousness that is widely used to provide a gross method for classifying the severity of damage in someone who just sustained a head injury.

Glia—The basic support cells of the central nervous system.

Gliosis—The filling in of a site of damage by glial cells.

Global aphasia—The inability to produce and comprehend language. It is usually associated with extensive left-hemisphere damage.

Global precedence—An idea advanced by the gestalt psychologists in the early 20th century, which says that the overall shape or relation among parts may be analyzed before the parts themselves.

Global processing—Analysis of the overall form, or gestalt, of objects. It is thought to rely on right-hemisphere mechanisms, most likely those in temporal regions.

Globus pallidus—The region of the basal ganglia from which almost all outputs emanate. It connects with the thalamus. It is sometimes called the *pallidum*.

Gradient field—A magnetic field that varies in intensity over the area being imaged and provides the ability to localize the points in space from which different portions of the signal are emanating.

Grandmother cell theory—The idea that a small set of particular cells would fire only in response to a highly specific object, such as your grandmother's face, and no other objects. These cells alone would be responsible for recognizing your grandmother. They would fire in response to her face because they received information from other cells that analyzed the parts of her face (e.g., cells that recognized her nose, her hair, her eyes, her chin line) and then conjoined the information.

Grapheme-to-phoneme correspondence rules—The guidelines that let us know how each grapheme should sound and how graphemes should be combined. Graphemes are the smallest units of written language that are combined to form words (e.g., "c").

Group studies—Neuropsychological investigations in which individuals with brain damage who have similar characteristics (e.g., lesions in similar areas) are studied as a group.

Gyrus—A ridge or mound of cortical tissue.

Hemi-inattention—See *Hemineglect*.

Hemineglect—The lack of attention to one side of space, usually the left, as a result of parietal lobe damage. It occurs despite intact sensory and motor functioning and is sometimes called *hemi-inattention*.

Hemi-Parkinsonism—A form of Parkinson's disease that results from unilateral disease of the basal ganglia and causes motor symptoms to be exhibited on only one side of the body. The cognitive deficits observed depend on whether damage occurs to the left or right half of the basal ganglia.

Hemiplegia—Paralysis on one entire side of the body. It typically results from damage to primary motor cortex and the basal ganglia.

Hemispherectomy—The surgical removal of an entire cerebral hemisphere.

Hemispheric specialization—The specialization of each cerebral hemisphere for different aspects of cognitive and emotional functioning. It is also referred to as *lateralization of function*.

Heschl's gyrus—The superior portion of the posterior temporal lobe in which primary auditory cortex is located.

Hippocampal system—The hippocampus, amygdala, and adjoining regions of cortex (parahippocampal and entorhinal gyri), whose damage results in amnesia.

Homonymous hemianopsia—The loss of vision in one entire visual field.

Homovanillic acid (HVA)—A by-product of dopamine synthesis.

Horizontal view—A plane in which the top of the brain is separated from the bottom.

Human neuropsychology—An area of study that is devoted to understanding how the neurological organization of the brain influences the way that people think, feel, and act.

Huntington's disease—A rare inherited neurologic disease caused by degeneration of the striatum that produces abnormal movements, cognitive deficits (eventually dementia), and psychiatric symptoms. It eventually leads to death.

Hyperkinesias—Involuntary undesired movements. They are observed in Huntington's disease.

Hypothalamus—The brain region that is responsible for regulatory behaviors, such as eating and drinking, that maintain the integrity of bodily systems.

Ideational apraxia—Difficulty performing a movement when the "idea" of the movement is lost. According to Liepmann, who proposed this concept, it occurs when individuals can perform simple one-step movements but not multistep movements.

Ideomotor apraxia—Difficulty performing a movement when a disconnection occurs between the idea of a movement and its execution. According to Liepmann, who proposed this concept, simple movements of an abstract nature are most affected.

Indirect (implicit) tests of memory—Tests of memory in which participants are referred to a previously experienced task but aren't required to consciously recall a specific learning experience. Changes in performance on the task as a consequence of prior experience are considered indices of memory.

Inference—The ability to "fill in the blanks" and make assumptions about material that is implied.

Inferior—Located toward the bottom of the brain.

Inferior colliculus—A structure in the midbrain that is important for integrating head and eye movements in response to sounds and for localizing sounds.

Inhibitory postsynaptic potentials (IPSPs)—Small graded electrical potentials induced in a postsynaptic neuron after the binding of neurotransmitters to its membrane that serve to make the electrical charge of the postsynaptic cell more negative than the resting potential.

Input phonologic buffer—The system that holds auditory-verbal information received by the listener while language parsing occurs.

Intermediate zone of the cerebellum—The region of the cerebellum that is located between the vermis and the lateral zone. It is important for smooth, nonrigid limb movements.

Interpositus nucleus—One of the deep cerebellar nuclei. It receives input from the intermediate zone of the cerebellum.

Inversion effect—Greater difficulty remembering inverted stimuli than upright stimuli. It is thought to assess the degree to which configural properties of an item are important for recognition and is greater for faces than for other mono-oriented stimuli.

Ipsilateral—On the same side as.

Irregular words—Words that do not follow the standard English grapheme-to-phoneme correspondence rules and thus require the direct route to reading.

James–Lange theory—The idea that each emotion is caused by a specific physical response to a stimulus (e.g., we feel afraid because we see a snake and tremble).

Kennard principle—The maxim suggesting that the earlier in life damage is sustained, the better the recovery. This generalization is now known not to be entirely true.

Korsakoff's amnesia—Amnesia related to chronic alcoholism. A gradual worsening of cognitive abilities is followed by acute hemorrhaging of midline diencephalic structures of the brain, which results in amnesia.

Kwashiorkor—Starvation due to a protein-deficient diet.

Lateral—Located toward the outside of the brain (away from the brain's midline).

Lateral corticospinal tract—The tract within the corticospinal pathway that is important for the control of distal muscles. When it is damaged, the ability to grasp and manipulate items with the far extremities is disrupted.

Lateral geniculate nucleus—The area of the thalamus onto which visual information from the optic tract synapses.

Lateralization of function—See *Hemispheric specialization*.

Lateral zone of the cerebellum—The most lateral region of the cerebellum. It is important for ballistic movements, multijoint movements, motor learning, and the timing of actions. It has been implicated in both motor and cognitive behaviors.

Late selection viewpoint—The idea that selection occurs later in processing, only after information is identified and categorized.

Learning disabilities—Syndromes in which a child has difficulty acquiring cognitive skills in only one particular domain or area.

Left visual field—The portion of space that falls to the left of the fixation point of gaze and projects to primary visual cortex of the right hemisphere.

Lesion method—The method of inferring that a mental function is supported by a particular region of brain tissue if that function is lost after damage to that region.

Letter-by-letter reading—A syndrome caused by damage to the left ventral occipital area, in which individual letters can be identified but they cannot be integrated to form a word. It is sometimes referred to as *spelling dyslexia* or *pure alexia*.

Lexical agraphia—A writing disorder in which the ability to use the direct route from meaning to writing is lost but the ability to use the phonologic route remains intact.

Limb apraxia—Difficulty performing voluntary movements with a limb, such as manipulating scissors, using a key to open a door, or waving good-bye.

Limbic system—A series of subcortical structures, including the amygdala, hypothalamus, cingulate cortex, anterior thalamus, mammillary bodies, hippocampus, and parahippocampal gyrus, that are thought to play a prominent role in emotional functions. However, they are also involved in many other diverse functions, including motor control, attention, memory.

Localization of function—The idea that particular mental functions are carried out by particular brain regions.

Local processing—Analysis of the features or details of objects. It is thought to rely on left-hemisphere mechanisms, most likely those in temporal regions.

Longitudinal fissure—The fissure that separates the right cerebral hemisphere from the left.

Macrosomatagnosia—A disturbance of body schema in which a person perceives a portion of his or her body as being too big. It is usually associated with the auras that precede epileptic seizures.

Magnetic resonance imaging (MRI)—A brain imaging technique that relies on electromagnetic radiation to provide highly precise anatomical images of the brain. The images can be tuned to different substances, such as water or fat, to emphasize different regions of brain tissue.

Malingering—The exaggeration or creation of symptoms for personal gain, either for money or to avoid responsibility for personal actions.

Mammillary bodies—The hypothalamic nuclei typically damaged in diencephalic amnesia.

Marasmus—Starvation due to a lack of adequate caloric intake.

Mass action—The idea that all regions of the brain contribute to almost all functions.

Material-specific memory disorders—Selective impairment of memory for a particular type of material. Impairment in remembering verbal material is observed after left-hemisphere damage, whereas impairments in remembering nonverbal material is observed after right-hemisphere damage.

Maturational lag hypothesis—The theory that individuals with learning disabilities are slower to mature than their peers and that with time they will outgrow the problem.

Medial—Located toward the middle of the brain.

Medial geniculate of the thalamus—The thalamic relay station for auditory information.

Medial temporal lobe region—The medial portion of the temporal lobes, including the hippocampal system.

Medulla—The section of the brain directly superior to the spinal cord that contains many of the cell bodies of the cranial nerves. It is also the region of the brain where motor information crosses from one side of the body to the other. It is important not only for the control of many essential functions, such as respiration and heart rate, but also for overall arousal and attention.

Melody—A series of pitches that have a certain rhythmic relationship to one another.

Memory consolidation—Processes that occur during the time after learning to increase resistance to disruption of surviving memories.

Memory for temporal order—Memory that, for example, allows us to judge which of two study items occurred more recently in a list. It depends on the integrity of frontal lobe systems.

Mental retardation—An inability to acquire intellectual abilities across practically all cognitive domains in the rate and manner expected during normal development. It is also characterized by difficulties in adaptive functioning, such as self-care.

Metacontrol—A type of interaction between the hemispheres in which one hemisphere dominates performance.

Metamemory—The abilities that allow for the strategic use, deployment, and retrieval of memories.

Method of converging operations—Examination of the same research question by using various methods and different subject populations to determine whether the results all converge on the same conclusion regarding a particular brain-behavior relationship.

Metric (coordinate) spatial relations—The distance between two locations. This type of spatial relation is thought to rely on right-hemisphere mechanisms and to be independent of a system in the left hemisphere that is thought to compute categorical spatial relations.

Microsomatagnosia—A disturbance of body schema in which a person perceives a portion of his or her body as being too small. It is usually associated with the auras that precede epileptic seizures.

Midbrain—A major section of the nervous system containing nuclei of the cells for some of the cranial nerves. It is the location of the inferior and superior colliculi, which are important for allowing a person to orient eye and head movements in response to auditory and visual stimuli, respectively.

Midline diencephalic region—Structures along the medial aspect of the thalamus and the hypothalamus. Damage to this region (particularly the dorsomedial nucleus of the thalamus and the mammillary bodies of the hypothalamus) results in amnesia.

Mild head injury—A head injury that results in a change in consciousness for 2 to 30 minutes but is unaccompanied by other gross signs of neurologic damage.

Mirror-image reading task—A task in which mirror-image text must be read aloud as quickly and accurately as possible. It is an example of a perceptual skill that can be learned normally despite amnesia.

Mirror tracing task—A task that requires the outline of a figure to be traced when visual information is conveyed only by means of a mirror. It is an example of a perceptual-motor skill that patients with amnesia can learn normally.

Mixed auditory agnosia—An auditory agnosia in which the ability to attach meaning to both verbal and nonverbal sounds is affected.

Modality specific—Manifesting in one sensory modality (e.g., vision) but not in others (e.g., hearing, touch).

Morris water maze—A test in which rats must learn and remember the spatial location of an escape platform submerged just below the surface of milky water in a circular tank or pool. Profound impairment on this task is seen following hippocampal system damage.

Motor program—An abstract representation of an intended movement that contains a plan for both general and specific aspects of an action. It is created before a complex motor act begins.

Multiple-case study approach—A neuropsychological investigation technique in which findings are obtained for a series or a group of patients, each of whom is also treated as a single-case study.

Multiple-resource theory—The viewpoint that attention consists of a limited set of attentional pools of resources. The capacity of the system to process information is greater when tasks draw from distinct resource pools rather than from the same one.

Multiple sclerosis (MS)—An autoimmune disorder that is characterized by multiple discrete areas, ranging in size from 1 mm to several centimeters, in which neurons have a complete absence of myelin. The cognitive concomitants include difficulty in memory and conceptual reasoning along with a general sparing of verbal and language skills.

Myelin—The fatty sheath around neurons formed by specific glial cells that causes increased conduction velocity of an action potential.

Narrative—The construction or understanding of a story line.

Necrosis—A process in which cells die at a site of damage.

Neglect dyslexia—A syndrome associated with parietal lobe damage, in which an individual consistently misreads a specific portion of words (e.g., just the beginning).

Neologisms—Sounds produced by persons with aphasia that follow the rules by which sounds are produced in a language but do not comprise a real word (e.g., "galump," "trebbin").

Neurofibrillary tangles—Twisted pairs of helical filaments found within neurons in neurologically intact older individuals and patients with Alzheimer's disease. These tangles tend to displace the cell body and are much more numerous in the cortex of a person with Alzheimer's disease than in a neurologically intact individual.

Neuromuscular junction—The place at which a neuron synapses on a muscle. When the neuron fires, the muscle contracts.

Neurons—The cells in the nervous system that are responsible for transmitting information by means of a combination of electrical and chemical signals.

Neuropsychological assessment—An evaluation of a person's cognitive, behavioral, and emotional functioning, which a neuropsychologist performs to determine the degree to which central nervous system damage may have compromised the person's abilities.

Neuropsychological test battery—A large number of neuropsychological tests that are designed to assess a range of sensory and cognitive abilities.

Neurotransmitters—The chemical substances that neurons use to communicate with one another.

Nigrostriatal bundle—The nerve-fiber tract that runs from the substantia nigra to the basal ganglia.

Nonverbal affect lexicon—A knowledge base that stores nonverbal information about the meaning of emotion. It is thought to reside in the right hemisphere.

Nonverbal auditory agnosia—An auditory agnosia in which the ability to attach meaning to words is intact, but the ability to do so for nonverbal sounds is disrupted.

Nonverbal learning disabilities—Specific learning disabilities in which a child has difficulty with nonverbal and spatial skills but not verbal skills. They have been linked to right-hemisphere dysfunction.

Nuclei—Distinct groups of neurons whose cell bodies are all situated in the same region of the nervous system.

Object-based viewpoint of attention—The idea that attention is directed toward particular objects.

Object-centered representation—A representation of an object that is based on a coordinate system with regard to the object's main attributes (center of mass, overall size, principle axis of elongation or principle axis of symmetry). This representation is invariant regardless of the direction from which the person views the object and hence allows the object to be recognized as equivalent across many orientations.

Occipital lobe—The region of cortex behind the endpoint of the Sylvian fissure and below the parietal lobe.

Ocular apraxia—The inability to voluntarily shift your gaze toward a new visual stimulus. It is one of the three main symptoms of Balint's syndrome.

Olfactory bulb—The region of the brain that is responsible for processing information about odors.

Oligodendrocytes—Glia in the central nervous system responsible for creating a myelin sheath around neurons.

Optic ataxia—The inability to point to a target under visual guidance. It is one of the three main symptoms of Balint's syndrome.

Optic chiasm—The point at which information from the nasal hemiretinae crosses the midline to the opposite side of the brain.

Optic nerve—The axons of retinal ganglion cells that serve as the conduit whereby information is carried from the eye to the brain.

Oral (buccofacial) apraxia—Difficulty performing voluntary movements with the tongue, lip, cheek, and muscles of the larynx, such as blowing a kiss or sucking on a straw.

Orientation invariant—The situation in which the relationships among an object's parts can be specified regardless of the angle from which the object is viewed.

Output phonological buffer—The system that holds the phonologic code being constructed by a speaker while he or she is preparing an utterance.

Paired-associate learning—The ability to learn word pairs or pairs of other objects that have no preexisting association. This type of learning is profoundly impaired in amnesia.

Paraphasias—Speech errors made by an individual with aphasia.

Parietal lobe—The region of cortex directly behind the central fissure but above the Sylvian fissure.

Parkinsonian mask—The expressionless face that typically accompanies Parkinson's disease.

Parkinson's disease—A syndrome associated with degeneration of the substantia nigra that leads to a slowness in movements, muscle rigidity, tremors, and cognitive dysfunction.

Perceptual asymmetries—Differences in the perception of sensory information that are interpreted as reflecting differences in hemispheric processing.

Perceptual categorization—The ability to classify an object as the same item despite variations in the information received by the sensory system, such as variations in size, color, and position.

Peripheral nervous system—All neural processes beyond the central nervous system, such as neurons that receive sensory information or synapse on muscle, and those that relay information to or from the spinal cord or the brain.

Perseverate—To engage in the same behavior or thought pattern repeatedly.

Perseveration—The tendency to engage in repetitive behavior.

Pervasive developmental disorders—Developmental disorders that have four basic characteristics: qualitative impairment in social interaction; delays and abnormalities in language as well as other aspects of communication; restricted, repetitive, and stereotyped patterns of behaviors, interests, or activities; and an onset of the problems in at least one of these three areas before the age of 3 years.

Phenylketonuria (PKU)—A genetic disorder that leads to mental retardation. It is caused by the lack of phenylalanine hydroxylase, an enzyme that breaks down the amino acid, phenylalanine. Its effects can be minimized by an appropriate diet beginning at birth.

Phonemic paraphasia—A paraphasia in which a similar-sounding word is substituted for another (e.g., "table" becomes "trable" or "fable").

Phonological agraphia—A writing disorder in which the ability to use the phonological route from meaning to writing is lost but the ability to use the direct route remains intact.

Phonological alexia—A reading disorder in which the ability to use the phonological route from print to meaning is lost but the ability to use the direct route remains intact.

Phonological route to reading—The method of linking the written word to meaning by using sound as the intermediary.

Phonology—The set of rules governing the sounds of language. It is one of the three fundamental components of language.

Pick's disease—A cortical dementia that mainly affects the temporal and frontal lobes. Its most notable effects are in the realm of social-emotional functioning and language.

Pitch—The perception of the frequency of a musical sound, or note. The higher the frequency of a sound, the higher its pitch is perceived.

Place of articulation—The location in the vocal tract where airflow is obstructed during the production of consonants.

Place fields—The regions of space that cause hippocampal cells to fire preferentially when they are traversed by an animal.

Planum temporale—The temporal plane; the region of the brain at the end of the Sylvian fissure that has been implicated in language processing. It is often larger in the left hemisphere than in the right.

Plasticity—The ability of the brain to change, especially in response to environmental input.

Pons—A major section of the nervous system located directly superior to the medulla and anterior to the cerebellum. It is involved in vestibular functions, auditory functions and in relaying information to the cerebellum.

Positron emission tomography (PET)—A method of investigating the metabolic activity of the brain by introducing a radioactive substance, which emits a positron that causes the substance to go from a radioactive state to a nonradioactive one. After being emitted, the positron is annihilated by an electron, and two photons of light, which travel in 180-degree opposite directions, are produced. Regions of high metabolic activity are determined by a series of light detectors placed around the head that detect the coincident arrival of photons.

Posterior—Located toward the back of the brain.

Posttraumatic amnesia—Amnesia for events following a brain injury.

Praxis—A system that is proposed to control all aspects of motor planning, including speech production, nonspeech oral movements, and limb movements. It is thought to be specialized to the left hemisphere.

Primal sketch—A "rough draft" of information in the visual world that is easily derived from the basic information that reaches the retina. This sketch contains information about things such as light-dark contrast, edges, and lines.

Primary motor cortex—A region of the cortex that is the final exit point for neurons controlling the fine motor control of the body's muscles.

Primary sensory cortex—The first region of cortex to receive information about a particular sensory modality (e.g., visual information).

Procedural memory—A memory system, operating independently of the hippocampal system, in which information is stored in an inflexible manner related to the context in which it was first acquired.

Programmed cell death—The process whereby numerous neurons die during a specific stage of development. It allows pruning of neurons after their proliferation early in life.

Propositional prosody—The aspect of an utterance that communicates lexical or semantic information—for example, "What's that in the road ahead?" versus "What's that in the road, a head?"

Proprioception—The perception of the position of body parts and their movements.

Prosody—The intonation pattern, or sound envelope, of an utterance.

Prosopagnosia—A selective inability to recognize or differentiate among faces, although other objects in the visual modality can be correctly identified.

Proximal—Located near the trunk or center.

Psychological inertia—The tendency if at rest, to stay at rest, or if in motion, to stay in motion, unless acted on by an outside force. It is the resistance or disinclination to motion, action, or change. Such inertia must be overcome to initiate action or to cease an ongoing course of action.

Pulse sequence—A magnetic field that is quickly applied and then stopped in a pulsing manner. These pulses perturb the static field, and are tuned to the energy of the atom under investigation. They cause these specific atoms, but not others, to flip 180 degrees.

Pulvinar—A nucleus of the thalamus that aids in attentional processing by filtering out specific information from the barrage of information that constantly impinges upon our sensory systems.

Pure tone audiometry—A method in which an individual is tested for the ability to perceive a tone that consists of only one frequency (e.g., 1000 Hz). In the test, numerous trials are given so that the ability to process pure tones is assessed over the range of frequencies that humans can detect (e.g., ~125–8000 Hz).

Pure word deafness—see *Verbal auditory agnosia*.

Putamen—A portion of the basal ganglia that, along with the caudate nucleus, receives all the input into the basal ganglia. It degenerates in Huntington's disease.

Quadranopsia—The loss of vision in one half of a visual field (a quadrant of visual space).

Reactive flexibility—The ability to react to information contained in the environment but in a different way than was done previously.

Receiver coil—The coil that picks up the signal from the atoms as they return to their static state after the pulse sequence.

Receptive field—The region of the sensory world to which a cell will respond if an appropriate stimulus appears within that region.

Receptor sites—Specific places on the postsynaptic dendritic tree that have a particular configuration allowing neurotransmitters to bind there, much as a key fits into a lock.

Recognition—A direct (explicit) test of memory that samples the ability to make judgments about a previous occurrence or to distinguish between items that were and items that were not previously encountered.

Regeneration—The reestablishment of a prior connection by a damaged nerve fiber. This mechanism of recovery of function is limited to the peripheral nervous system.

Relay center—A brain region in which the neurons from one area of the brain synapse onto other neurons that then go on to synapse somewhere else in the brain.

Reorganization—Changes in which the brain tries to override and adapt its typical organization in the face of damage, trauma, or unusual circumstances.

Repetition priming—An item-specific facilitation of performance based on previous experience. It is preserved in amnesia and is an indirect (implicit) test of memory.

Rerouting—A process by which a given neuron seeks and connects with a new target after losing an old one.

Resources—The components of attention, or the effort, that must be devoted to processing certain information.

Resting potential—The resting state of the cell in which the electrical charge inside the cell is −70 mV relative to the charge outside the cell.

Reticular activating system (RAS)—A brain system whose cell bodies are located in the medulla and other brain regions. It is responsible for alerting and arousal aspects of attention and for regulation of sleep-wake cycles. Damage to this system causes coma.

Retrieval of memories—The process whereby previously stored memories are recalled.

Retrograde amnesia—The impairment of memory for information that was acquired normally prior to the onset of amnesia.

Retrograde degeneration—Deterioration in which not only does the portion of the neuron distal to the site of injury die, but so does the rest of the axon and the cell body.

Reversal learning—A situation in which a previously learned set of responses must be reversed (e.g., learning to press the right-hand key when a yellow light appears and the left-hand key when a blue light appears after previously having learned to press the right-hand key when a blue light appeared and the left-hand key when a yellow light appeared).

Rhythm—The temporal relationship among sounds in music.

Ribot's Law—The law, posited by Theodule Ribot in the late 19th century, which states that the most recently acquired memories are most susceptible to disruption by brain damage.

Right visual field—The portion of space that falls to the right of the fixation point of gaze and projects to primary visual cortex of the left hemisphere.

Risk factors—Factors that, although they increase the likelihood that a syndrome will be observed, do not ensure that it will occur.

Rostral—Located toward an animal's head.

Rotary pursuit—A task requiring manual tracking of a circularly moving target. It is an example of a perceptual-motor skill that patients with amnesia can learn normally.

Rubrospinal pathway—The motor pathway that is important for control of forearm and hand movement independent from trunk movement. This pathway is less important in humans than in other species.

Saccade—An eye movement in which the eyes jump from one position to the next (rather than moving smoothly) with seemingly no processing of the intervening visual information.

Sagittal view—A plane that divides the brain along a left-right dimension.

Scotomas—Particular regions in the visual field in which light-dark contrast cannot be detected.

Selective attention—The aspect of attention that is used to select either specific incoming information or specific responses for priority in processing.

Self-ordered pointing—A test requiring the ability to keep track of which items in an array were already selected because the subject must point to a new item each time the array is viewed. It depends on the integrity of frontal lobe systems.

Semantic knowledge systems—The separate cortical systems that support knowledge of objects, language, motor abilities, and so forth.

Semantic memory—Memory of world knowledge that is stored in a context-free fashion.

Semantic paralexias—Reading errors in which a word is misread as a word with a related meaning.

Semantic paraphasia—A paraphasia in which a semantically related word is substituted for the desired word (e.g., "barn" for "house").

Semantics—The meaning of language. It is one of the three fundamental components of language.

Sensitive period—A developmental time period, which has a specific onset and offset, when the organism is especially sensitive to specific external stimuli. After this period ends, any organization that has occurred is generally irreversible.

Shrinking retrograde amnesia—The resolution of an extensive retrograde amnesia with time into a temporally limited retrograde amnesia.

Simultanagnosia—An inability to perceive different pieces of information in the visual field simultaneously because the person cannot direct attention to more than one small location in the visual world at a time. The person can recognize individual elements of a scene but not the scene as a whole. It is one of the three main symptoms of Balint's syndrome.

Single-case studies—Neuropsychological investigations in which researchers intensively study the performance of a single person with brain damage on a variety of neuropsychological tests.

Skill learning—The gradual acquisition of new skills such as motor, perceptual, and cognitive skills. These skills are generally preserved in amnesia.

Somatoparaphrenia—A relatively rare condition occurring in hemineglect in which the individual claims that a limb on the neglected side belongs to someone else.

Somatosensory agnosia—A condition in which a person is unable to recognize an item by touch but can recognize it in other modalities. As with other agnosias, memory is intact. It is also called *tactile agnosia* or *astereognosia*.

Source amnesia—The inability to remember under what circumstances particular information was learned, despite the fact that the information itself can be remembered (e.g., an inability to remember *where* you learned that the earth orbits the sun, although you still remember that the earth does orbit the sun).

Source memory—Recollecting the source of a particular piece of information. It depends on the integrity of frontal lobe systems.

Space-based viewpoint of attention—The idea that attention is directed toward a particular point in space and that the information at this location is processed more fully.

Spatial frequency hypothesis—The idea that hemispheres differ in their ability to process visual information, depending on spatial frequency. The left hemisphere is posited to excel at processing information of high spatial frequency and the right at processing information of low spatial frequency.

Spinal cord—The portion of the central nervous system where most (but not all) sensory neurons synapse on their way to the brain and whereby motor commands output from the brain are sent to the muscles.

Split-brain procedure—An operation in which the corpus callosum and other cortical commissures are severed precluding any communication between the cerebral hemispheres at the cortical level. Individuals who underwent this procedure are known as *patients with the split-brain syndrome*. It is sometimes referred to as *commissurotomy*.

Spontaneous flexibility—The ability to generate a diversity of ideas when environmental input provides relatively little structure to guide the response.

Sprouting—A process in which a nerve fiber grows, becomes bushier, and makes new connections. It involves not only rerouting, but also a proliferation of nerve growth.

Static field—A magnetic field of high field strength that causes all the atoms to spin and orient in the same direction. Magnets are classified according to the strength of this field, such as 1.5 tesla.

Stereopsis—Depth perception.

Storage, maintenance, or consolidation of memories—Processes operating during the time after learning that allow information to be retained in memory.

Strategic (prospective) memory—The ability to organize, search, and query declarative memory. It depends on the integrity of frontal lobe systems.

Stupor—A state of consciousness in which the individual can be aroused when shaken vigorously or called by name but cannot speak rationally and falls back into unconsciousness quickly.

Substantia nigra—A midbrain nucleus that is associated with the basal ganglia. The cell bodies of dopaminergic neurons are located there. This structure degenerates in Parkinson's disease.

Sulcus—A valley between gyri.

Superior—Located toward the top of the brain.

Superior colliculus—A structure in the midbrain that is important for allowing a person to orient her or his eyes to large moving objects in the periphery of the visual field. It allows a person to move his or her focus of attention.

Supervisory attentional system—The cognitive system required to effortfully direct attention.

Supplementary motor area (SMA)—A region of the frontal lobe located on the medial surface of each hemisphere (in the longitudinal fissure) anterior to the region of primary motor cortex and dorsal to the cingulate sulcus. It is important for planning, preparing, and initiating movements.

Surface alexia—A reading disorder in which the ability to use the direct route from print to meaning is lost but the ability to use the phonologic route remains intact.

Sylvian (lateral) fissure—The fissure that divides the temporal lobe from the rest of the brain.

Synapses—The points at which neurons connect with one another.

Synaptic vesicles—Little packages filled with neurotransmitters and located at the terminal, or buton, of the axon.

Synaptogenesis—The process whereby a neuron makes new connections (synapses) with other neurons.

Syntax—The grammar of language. It is one of the three fundamental components of language.

Tactile agnosia—See *Somatosensory agnosia*.

Tactile asymbolia—A form of tactile agnosia in which an individual can form a percept in the tactile modality but cannot link it to meaning (e.g., the 1.5-in.-long metal object that is big at the top and thin at the bottom with a jagged edge on one side cannot be linked to the concept of a key).

Tardive dyskinesia—A movement disorder that occurs in 20 to 40% of all individuals who are long-term users of antipsychotic drugs that block dopamine. It is characterized by increased motor movements, especially of the face and lips.

Telegraphic speech—Speech that contains content words, such as nouns and verbs, but is devoid of function words and word endings. It is characteristic of the speech output of patients with anterior lesions of the left hemisphere.

Temporal gradient—A gradient in memory loss in which recent memories are affected to a greater degree than more remote memories.

Temporal lobe—The region of cortex below the Sylvian fissure.

Temporally extensive retrograde amnesia—An amnesia that extends backward in time for decades from the onset of injury.

Temporally limited retrograde amnesia—An amnesia that extends backward in time from the onset of injury for a period of only several months or years.

Thalamus—A brain region that helps to regulate and organize information from the outer reaches of the nervous system as it ascends to the cortex. It also modifies information descending from the cortex.

Tics—Repetitive involuntary movements such as compulsive twitching of facial or limb muscles.

Tonotopic—A spatial organization of structures with regard to a tone's frequency.

Topographic disorientation—Difficulty remembering the way around the world after brain trauma. It may affect either the ability to learn routes in a new environment, such as a hospital, or the ability to remember routes through familiar places.

Tourette's syndrome—A relatively rare disorder that manifests as a variety of motor and vocal tics. It has its onset in childhood, usually before the age of 11 years.

Tower of Hanoi puzzle—A task involving rearranging a set of discs onto a set of pegs, requiring at least 31 moves. It is an example of a cognitive skill that can be learned normally despite amnesia.

Transcortical motor aphasia—A syndrome in which an individual loses the ability to produce spontaneous speech but retains the ability to repeat. It is associated with damage that is either anterior or superior to Broca's area.

Transcortical sensory aphasia—A syndrome in which an individual loses the ability to comprehend language but retains the ability to repeat. It is associated with damage to regions posterior to Wernicke's area.

Transneuronal degeneration—A process in which neuronal loss extends past the site of damage to more distal cells.

Tremors—Rhythmic, oscillating movements, usually of a limb or the head. One of the main symptoms of Parkinson's disease.

Turner's syndrome—A genetic disorder in which a female inherits just one X chromosome (XO) rather than two (XX). It is associated with especially poor spatial and perceptual skills.

Two-factor theory—The idea that emotional experience is the outcome of physiological arousal and the attribution of a cause for that arousal.

Unilateral—Pertaining to only one side of the brain (or space).

Unilateral presentation—A method in divided visual field studies in which a single item is presented in only one visual field.

Valence theory—The idea that the emotional state of one hemisphere has a particular valence (e.g., positive), whereas the emotional state of the other hemisphere has the opposite valence (e.g., negative).

Vascular dementia—A mixed-variety dementia that results from the cumulative effects of many individual strokes that tend to involve both cortical and subcortical lesions, with a higher frequency of lesions in the frontal lobes than in other cortical lobes. It was previously called *multi-infarct dementia*.

Ventral—Located toward an animal's stomach (in people sometimes toward the bottom as in the case of the brain).

Ventral corticospinal tract—The tract within the corticospinal pathway that is important for control of the trunk and upper legs. When it is damaged, locomotion and posture are disrupted.

Ventral visual system—Regions of the occipital and temporal lobes that respond only to visual stimuli and are important for object recognition. This system is often referred to as the *"what" visual system*.

Ventromedial pathway—The motor pathway that controls the trunk and proximal limb muscles. It is important for various functions including posture, coordination of eye movements with movements of the trunk and head, autonomic functions, and walking.

Verbal auditory agnosia—An auditory agnosia in which words cannot be understood but the ability to attach meaning to nonverbal sounds is intact. It is sometimes called *pure word deafness*.

Verbal paraphasia—A paraphasia in which one word is incorrectly substituted for another.

Vermis—The medial region of the cerebellum that is important for postural adjustments and walking.

Viewer-centered representation—A representation of an object that is based on the coordinate system of information falling on the retina. As the viewer's position changes relative to an object, so does the representation of the object.

Vigilance—The ability to maintain alertness continuously without "tuning in" and "tuning out." It is also called *sustained attention*.

Visual agnosia—An inability to recognize an object from information provided in the visual modality. It cannot be attributed either to a basic deficit in processing visual information or to a pervasive memory disorder. Furthermore, the deficit is modality specific because the item can be recognized through other sensory channels.

Visual-verbal working memory—Memory that allows us to hold visual-verbal information "on-line" during reading while language processing occurs.

Visuospatial scratch pad—Memory that allows us to hold nonverbal visual information while we perceptually analyze the stimulus array.

Voicing—The timing between the release of air for a stop consonant and the vibration of the vocal cords. When a sound is voiced, the release of air and vocal cord vibration coincide, whereas when a sound is unvoiced, the vocal cords don't begin to vibrate until after the release.

Volumetric representation—A true 3-D representation of an object that describes its volumetric properties, including its center of mass, its overall size (mean diameter or volume), and the principle axis of elongation or principle axis of symmetry.

Wada technique—A method used with patients about to undergo surgery for the removal of epileptic tissue to determine the hemisphere responsible for speech output. It involves injecting a barbiturate into the carotid artery to anesthetize one hemisphere.

Watershed lesion—A lesion caused by lack of oxygen to brain regions that are more susceptible to oxygen deprivation because they fall between the main "watershed" areas for the arterial blood supply. The cause of Balint's syndrome.

Wernicke's aphasia—A syndrome in which speech comprehension is disrupted but speech output is fluent although nonsensical. It is associated with a lesion to the temporal lobe typically near the junction with parietal and occipital regions.

Wisconsin Card Sorting Test (WCST)—A test often used to assess executive dysfunction. It requires individuals to discover which of three attributes (color, number, or shape) should be used to sort cards and to flexibly change the attribute used for sorting.

Word-stem completion—An indirect (implicit) test of memory in which the completion of three-letter word stems into whole words is influenced by recent study of words composed of the same stems.

Working memory—Short-term memory. The memory that we use to hold information for a brief amount of time or to hold information "on-line" as we perform a task.

References

Abraham, H. D., & Wolf, E. (1988). Visual function in past users of LSD: Psychophysical findings. *Journal of Abnormal Psychology, 97,* 443–447.

Adams, J. H., Graham, D. I., Murray, L. S., & Scott, G. (1982). Diffuse axonal injury due to nonmissile head injury in humans: An analysis of 45 cases. *Annals of Neurology, 12,* 557–563.

Adams, K. M. (1980). In search of Luria's battery: A false start. *Journal of Consulting and Clinical Psychology, 48,* 511–516.

Ahern, G. L., & Schwartz, G. E. (1979). Differential lateralization for positive versus negative emotion. *Neuropsychologia, 17,* 693–698.

Akshoomoff, N. A., & Courchesne, E. (1992). A new role for the cerebellum in cognitive operations. *Behavioral Neuroscience, 106*(5), 731–738.

Alberico, A. M., Ward, J. M., Choi, S. C., Marmarou, A., & Young, H. F. (1987). Outcome after severe head injury: Relationship to mass lesions, diffuse injury, and ICP course in pediatric and adult patients. *Journal of Neurosurgery, 67,* 648–656.

Albert, M. L. (1973). A simple test of visual neglect. *Neurology, 23,* 658–664.

Albert, M. L., & Bear, D. (1974). Time to understand: A case study of word deafness with reference to the role of time in auditory comprehension. *Brain, 97,* 373–384.

Albert, M. S., Butters, N., & Levin, J. (1979). Temporal gradients in the retrograde amnesia of patients with Korsakoff's disease. *Archives of Neurology, 36,* 211.

Albin, R. L., Young, A. B., & Penney, J. B. (1989). The functional anatomy of basal ganglia disorders. *Trends in Neurosciences, 12,* 366–375.

Alexander, G. E., & Crutcher, M. D. (1990). Functional architecture of basal ganglia circuits: Neural substrates of parallel processing. *Trends in Neurosciences, 13,* 266–271.

Alexander, G. E., DeLong, M. R., & Strick, P. L. (1986). Parallel organization of functionally segregated circuits linking basal ganglia and cortex. *Annual Review of Neuroscience, 9,* 357–381.

Alivisatos, B. (1992). The role of the frontal cortex in the use of advance information in a mental rotation paradigm. *Neuropsychologia, 30,* 145–159.

Alivisatos, B., & Milner, B. (1989). Effects of frontal or temporal lobectomy on the use of advance information in a choice reaction time task. *Neuropsychologia, 27,* 495–503.

Allen, L. F., Palomares, R. S., DeForest, P., Sprinkle, B., & Reynolds, C. R. (1991). The effects of intrauterine cocaine exposure: Transient or teratogenic? *Archives of Clinical Neuropsychology, 6*(3), 133–146.

Allen, L. S., Richey, M. F., Chai, Y. M., & Gorski, R. A. (1991). Sex differences in the corpus callosum of the living human being. *Journal of Neuroscience, 11,* 933–942.

Allison, T., McCarthy, G., Nobre, A., Puce, A., & Belger, A. (1994). Human extrastriate visual cortex and the perception of faces, words, numbers, and colors. *Cerebral Cortex, 5,* 544–554.

Allport, A., Styles, E., & Hsieh, S. (1994). Non-spatial orienting of attention: Exploring the dynamic control of tasks. In *Attention and performance XV.* Umilta, C. A., & Moscovitch, M. (Eds.). *Conscious and nonconscious information processing.* Cambridge, MA: The MIT Press.

Almkvist, O. (1994). Neuropsychological deficits in vascular dementia in relation to Alzheimer's disease: Reviewing evidence for functional similarity or divergence. *Dementia, 5,* 203–209.

Almkvist, O., Backman, L., Basun, H., & Wahlund, L. O. (1993). Patterns of neuropsychological performance in Alzheimer's disease and vascular dementia. *Cortex, 29,* 661–673.

Althoff, R. R., Maciukenas, M., & Cohen, N. J. (1993). Indirect assessment of memory using eye movement monitoring. *Society for Neuroscience Abstracts, 19,* 439.

Alyward, E. H., Henderer, J. D., McArthur, J. C., Brettschneider, P. D., Barta, P. E., & Pearlson, G. D. (1993). Reduced basal ganglia volume in HIV-1 associated dementia: Results from quantitative neuroimaging. *Neurology, 43,* 1099–2104.

American Psychiatric Association. (1994). *Diagnostic and statistical manual of mental disorders* (4th ed.). Washington, DC: Author.

Andersen, R. A. (1988). The neurobiological basis of spatial cognition: Role of the parietal lobe. In J. Stiles-Davis, M. Kritchevsky, & U. Bellugi (Eds.), *Spatial cognition: Brain bases and development* (pp. 57–80). Hillsdale, NJ: Erlbaum.

Andersen, R. A., & Mountcastle, V. B. (1983). The influence of the angle of gaze upon the excitability of the light-sensitive neurons of the posterior parietal cortex. *Journal of Neuroscience, 3,* 532–548.

Anderson, S. W., Damasio, H., Jones, R. D., & Tranel, D. (1991). Wisconsin Card Sorting Test performance as a measure of frontal lobe damage. *Journal of Clinical and Experimental Neuropsychology, 13,* 909–922.

Andreasen, N. (1989). Nuclear magnetic resonance imaging. In N. Andreasen (Ed.), *Brain imaging: Applications in psychiatry* (pp. 67–121). Washington, DC: American Psychiatric Press.

Andreassi, J. L. (1989). *Psychophysiology: Human behavior and physiological response* (2nd ed.). Hillsdale, NJ: Erlbaum.

Annett, M. (1985). *Left, right, hand and brain.* London: Erlbaum.

Appell, J., Kertesz, A., & Fisman, M. (1982). A study of language functioning in Alzheimer patients. *Brain and Language, 17,* 73–91.

Aram, D. M., & Eisele, J. A. (1994). Intellectual stability in children with unilateral brain lesions. *Neuropsychologia, 32,* 85–95.

Ardila, A., & Rosselli, M. (1989). Neuropsychological characteristics of normal aging. *Developmental Neuropsychology, 5,* 307–320.

Aretz, A. J. (1991). The design of electronic map displays. *Human Factors, 33,* 85–101.

Aretz, A. J., & Wickens, C. D. (1992). The mental rotation of map displays. *Human Performance, 5,* 303–328.

Askil, J. (1979). *Physics of musical sounds.* New York: Van Nostrand.

Atkinson, J., & Egeth, J. (1973). Right hemisphere superiority in visual orientation matching. *Canadian Journal of Psychology, 27,* 152–158.

Auerbach, S. H., Allard, T., Naeser, M., Alexander, M. P., & Albert, M. L. (1982). Pure word deafness: Analysis of a case with bilateral lesions and a defect at the prephonemic level. *Brain, 105,* 271–300.

Azrin, R. L., Millsaps, C. L., Burton, D. B., & Mittenberg, W. (1992). Recovery of memory and intelligence following chronic cocaine abuse. *Clinical Neuropsychologist, 6,* 344–345.

Bachevalier, J. (1994). Medial temporal lobe structures and autism: A review of clinical and experimental findings. *Neuropsychologia, 32,* 627–648.

Baddeley, A. D. (1986). *Working memory.* Oxford, England: Oxford University Press.

Bahr, M., & Bonhoeffer, F. (1994). Perspectives on axonal regeneration in the mammalian CNS. *Trends in Neurosciences, 17,* 473–478.

Baillargeon, R. (1994). How do infants learn about the physical world? *Current Directions in Psychological Science, 3,* 133–139.

Baker, E., Blumstein, S. E., & Goodglass, H. (1981). Interaction between phonological and semantic factors in auditory comprehension. *Neuropsychologia, 19,* 1–16.

Baker, E. L., White, R. F., & Murawski, B. J. (1985). Clinical evaluation of neurobehavioral effects of occupational exposure to organic solvents and lead. *British Journal of Mental Health, 14,* 135–158.

Banich, M. T. (1993). *Possible mechanisms underlying the linkage between aesthetic preference and cerebral lateralization.* Unpublished manuscript, University of Illinois at Urbana-Champaign.

Banich, M. T. (1995a). Interhemispheric interaction: Mechanisms of unified processing. In F. L. Kitterle (Ed.), *Hemispheric communication: Mechanisms and models* (pp. 271–300). Hillsdale, NJ: Erlbaum.

Banich, M. T. (1995b). Interhemispheric processing: Theoretical and empirical considerations. In R. Davidson & K. Hugdahl (Eds.), *Brain asymmetry* (pp. 427–450). Cambridge, MA: MIT Press.

Banich, M. T., & Belger, A. (1990). Interhemispheric interaction: How do the hemispheres divide and conquer a task? *Cortex, 26,* 77–94.

Banich, M. T., & Federmeier, K. D. (1995). Distinguishing categorical and metric spatial processes. In *Paper presented at the second annual meeting of the Cognitive Neuroscience Society,* San Francisco.

Banich, M. T., Heller, W., & Levy, J. (1989). Aesthetic preference and picture asymmetries. *Cortex, 25,* 187–196.

Banich, M. T., & Karol, D. L. (1992). The sum of the parts does not equal the whole: Evidence from bihemispheric processing. *Journal of Experimental Psychology: Human Perception and Performance, 18,* 763–784.

Banich, M. T., Levine, S. C., Kim, H., & Huttenlocher, P. (1990). The effects of developmental factors on IQ in hemiplegic children. *Neuropsychologia, 28,* 35–47.

Banich, M. T., Nicholas, C. D., & Karol, D. L. (1996). *Putting the pieces together: Integration of information between the cerebral hemispheres.* Manuscript submitted for publication.

Banich, M. T., & Shenker, J. I. (1994a). Dissociations in memory for item identity and item frequency: Evidence from hemispheric interactions. *Neuropsychologia, 32,* 1179–1194.

Banich, M. T., & Shenker, J. I. (1994b). Investigations of interhemispheric processing: Methodological considerations. *Neuropsychology, 8*(2), 263–277.

Banich, M. T., Stokes, A., & Elledge, V. C. (1989). Neuropsychological evaluation of aviators: A review. *Aviation Space and Environmental Medicine, 60,* 361–366.

Banich, M. T., Stolar, N., Heller, W., & Goldman, R. (1992). A deficit in right-hemisphere performance after induction of a depressed mood. *Neuropsychiatry, Neuropsychology and Behavioral Neurology, 5,* 20–27.

Banks, G., Short, P., Martinez, A. J., Latchaw, R., Ratcliff, G., & Boller, F. (1989). The alien hand syndrome: Clinical and postmortem findings. *Archives of Neurology, 46,* 456–459.

Bannister, R. (1992). *Brain and Bannister's clinical neurology* (7th ed.). Oxford, England: Oxford University Press.

Barbizet, J. (1970). *Human memory and its pathology.* San Francisco: Freeman.

Barkley, R. A. (1977). The effects of methylphenidate on various measures of activity level and attention in hyperkinetic children. *Journal of Abnormal Child Psychology, 5,* 351–369.

Barkley, R. A., Grodzinsky, G., & DuPaul, G. J. (1992). Frontal lobe functions in attention deficit disorder with and without hyperactivity: A review and research report. *Journal of Abnormal Child Psychology, 20,* 163–188.

Barkley, R. A., Karlsson, J., Pollard, S., & Murphy, J. V. (1985). Developmental changes in the mother–child interactions of hyperactive boys: Effects of two dose levels of Ritalin. *Journal of Child Psychology and Psychiatry and Allied Disciplines, 24,* 705–715.

Barlow, D. H. (1991). Disorders of emotion. *Psychological Inquiry, 2,* 58–71.

Barlow, H. B. (1985). The twelfth Bartlett Memorial Lecture: The role of single neurons in the psychology of perception. *Quarterly Journal of Experimental Psychology, 37A,* 121–145.

Bartel, P. R., Burnett, L. S., Griesel, R. D., Freiman, I., Rosen, E. G., & Grefhuysen, G. (1977). The effects of kwashiorkor on performance on tests of neuropsychological function. *Psychologia Africana, 17,* 153–160.

Barth, J. T., Alves, W. M., Ryan, T. V., Macchiocchi, S. N., Rimel, R. W., Jane, J. A., & Nelson, W. E. (1989). Mild head injury in sports: Neuropsychological sequelae and recovery of function. In H. S. Levin, H. M. Eisenberg, & A. L. Benton (Eds.), *Mild head injury.* New York: Oxford University Press.

Bates, E., Wulfeck, B., & MacWhinney, B. (1991). Cross-linguistic research in aphasia: An overview. *Brain and Language, 41,* 123–148.

Bayles, K. A. (1982). Language function in senile dementia. *Brain and Language, 16,* 265–280.

Beatty, J. (1995). *Principles of behavior neuroscience.* Madison, WI: Brown & Benchmark.

Beatty, W. W., Katzung, V. M., Moreland, V. J., & Nixon, S. J. (1995). Neuropsychological performance of recently abstinent alcoholics and cocaine abusers. *Drug and Alcohol Dependence, 37,* 247–253.

Beatty, W. W., Salmon, D. P., Butters, N., Heindel, W. C., & Granholm, E. L. (1988). Retrograde amnesia in patients with Alzheimer's disease or Huntington's disease. *Neurobiology of Aging, 9,* 181–186.

Beaumont, J. G. (1985). Lateral organization and aesthetic preference: The importance of peripheral visual asymmetries. *Neuropsychologia, 23,* 103–113.

Beauvois, M.-F., & Derouesne, J. (1981). Lexical or orthographic dysgraphia. *Brain, 104,* 21–50.

Beckwith, L., Rodning, C., Norris, D., Phillipsen, L., Khandabi, P., & Howard, J. (1994). Spontaneous play in two-year-olds born to substance-abusing mothers. *Infant Mental Health Journal, 15*(2), 189–201.

Beeman, M. (1993). Semantic processing in the right hemisphere may contribute to drawing inferences during comprehension. *Brain and Language, 44,* 80–120.

Beeman, M. (1997). Discourse comprehension and coarse semantic coding. In M. Beeman & C. Chiarello (Eds.), *Right hemisphere language comprehension: Perspectives from cognitive neuroscience.* Hillsdale, NJ: Erlbaum.

Beeman, M., & Chiarello, C. (Eds.). (1997). *Right hemisphere language comprehension: Perspectives from cognitive neuroscience.* Hillsdale, NJ: Erlbaum.

Beeman, M., Friedman, R. B., Grafman, J., Perez, E., Diamond, S., & Lindsay, M. B. (1994). Summation priming and coarse semantic coding in the right hemisphere. *Journal of Cognitive Neuroscience, 6,* 26–45.

Behrens, S. (1988). The role of the right hemisphere in the production of linguistic stress. *Brain and Language, 33,* 104–127.

Behrmann, M., & Moscovitch, M. (1994). Object-centered neglect in patients with unilateral neglect. *Journal of Cognitive Neuroscience, 6,* 1–16.

Belger, A., & Banich, M. T. (1992). Interhemispheric interaction affected by computational complexity. *Neuropsychologia, 30,* 923–931.

Belleza, T., Rappaport, M., Hopkins, H. K., & Hall, K. (1979). Visual scanning and matching dysfunction in brain-damaged patients with drawing impairment. *Cortex, 15,* 19–36.

Belliveau, J. W., Kennedy, D. N., McKinstry, R. C., Buchbinder, B. R., Weisskoff, R. M., Cohen, M. S., Vevea, J. M., Brady, T. J., & Rosen, B. R. (1991). Functional mapping of the human visual cortex by magnetic resonance imaging. *Science, 254,* 716–718.

Belmont, L., & Birch, H. G. (1963). Lateral dominance and right-left awareness in normal children. *Child Development, 34,* 257–270.

Bender, B. G., Linden, M. G., & Robinson, A. (1994). Neurocognitive and psychosocial phenotypes associated with Turner syndrome. In S. H. Broman & J. Grafman (Eds.), *Atypical cognitive deficits in developmental disorders* (pp. 197–216). Hillsdale, NJ: Erlbaum.

Benowitz, L. I., Bear, D. M., Rosenthal, R., Mesulam, M.-M., Zaidel, E., & Sperry, R. W. (1983). Hemispheric specialization in nonverbal communication. *Cortex, 19,* 5–12.

Benson, D. F. (1985). Aphasia. In K. M. Heilman & E. Valenstein (Eds.), *Clinical neuropsychology* (2nd ed.). New York: Oxford University Press.

Benson, D. F., & Geschwind, N. (1972). Aphasia and related disturbances. In A. B. Baker (Ed.), *Clinical neurology.* New York: Harper and Row.

Benson, D. F., & Greenberg, J. P. (1969). Visual form agnosia. *Archives of Neurology, 20,* 82–89.

Benton, A. (1986). Reaction time in brain disease: Some reflections. *Cortex, 22,* 129–140.

Benton, A. L. (1961). The fiction of the Gerstmann syndrome. *Journal of Neurology, Neurosurgery and Psychiatry, 24,* 176–181.

Benton, A. L. (1967). Constructional apraxia and the minor hemisphere. *Confinia Neurologica, 29,* 1–16.

Benton, A. L. (1969). Disorders of spatial orientation. In P. J. Vinken & G. W. Bruyn (Eds.), *Handbook of clinical neurology.* Amsterdam: North Holland.

Benton, A. L. (1985). Body schema disturbances: Finger agnosia and right-left disorientation. In K. M. Heilman & E. Valenstein (Eds.), *Clinical neuropsychology* (2nd ed.). New York: Oxford University Press.

Benton, A. L., Hannay, H. J., & Varney, N. R. (1975). Visual perception of line direction in patients with unilateral brain disease. *Neurology, 25,* 907–910.

Benton, A. L., & Hécaen, H. (1970). Stereoscopic vision in patients with unilateral cerebral disease. *Neurology, 20,* 1084–1088.

Benton, A. L., Levin, H. S., & Van Allen, M. W. (1974). Geographic orientation in patients with unilateral cerebral disease. *Neuropsychologia, 12,* 183–191.

Ben-Yishay, Y., & Diller, L. (1983). Cognitive remediation. In E. A. Griffith, M. Bond, & J. Miller (Eds.), *Rehabilitation of the head injured adult* (pp. 367–380). Philadelphia: F A Davis.

Ben-Yishay, Y., & Prigatano, G. (1990). Cognitive remediation. In M. Rosenthal, E. R. Griffith, M. R. Bond, & J. D. Miller (Eds.), *Rehabilitation of the adult and child with traumatic brain injury* (pp. 393–409). Philadelphia: F A Davis.

Berg, L. (1988). Clinical Dementia Rating (CDR). *Psychopharmacology Bulletin, 24,* 637–639.

Bergman, J., Borg, S., Engelbrekston, K., & Viker, B. (1989). Dependence on sedative-hypnotics: Neuropsychological impairment, field dependence and clinical course in a 5-year follow-up study. *British Journal of Addiction, 84,* 547–553.

Bernheimer, H., Birkmayer, W., Hornykiewicz, O., Jellinger, K., & Seitelberg, F. (1973). Brain dopamine and the syndromes of Parkinson and Huntington: Clinical, morphological and neurochemical correlations. *Journal of Neuroscience, 20,* 415–455.

Bernstein, A. S., Riedel, J. A., & Graae, F. (1988). Schizophrenia is associated with altered orienting activity. *Journal of Abnormal Psychology, 97,* 3–12.

Berquier, A., & Ashton, R. (1992). Language lateralization in bilinguals: More not less is needed. A reply to Paradis (1990). *Brain and Language, 43,* 528–533.

Berry, J., Van Gorp, W. G., Herzberg, D. S., Hinkin, C., Boone, K., Steinman, L., & Wilkins, J. N. (1993). Neuropsychological deficits in abstinent cocaine abusers: Preliminary findings after two weeks of abstinence. *Drug and Alcohol Dependence, 32,* 231–237.

Berti, A., & Rizzolatti, G. (1992). Visual processing without awareness: Evidence from unilateral neglect. *Journal of Cognitive Neuroscience, 4,* 345–351.

Bertoncini, J., Morais, J., Bijeljac-Babic, R., McAdams, S., Peretz, I., & Mehler, J. (1989). Dichotic perception and laterality in neonates. *Brain and Language, 37,* 591–605.

Best, C. T. (1988). The emergence of cerebral asymmetries in early human development: A literature review and a neuroembryological model. In D. L. Molfese & S. J. Segalowitz (Eds.), *Brain lateralization in children: Developmental implications* (pp. 5–34). New York: Guilford Press.

Best, C. T., Hoffman, H., & Glanville, B. B. (1982). Development of infant ear asymmetries for speech and music. *Perception and Psychophysics, 31*(1), 75–85.

Bettleheim, B. (1967). *The empty fortress.* New York: Free Press.

Bever, T., & Chiarello, R. (1974). Cerebral dominance in musicians and nonmusicians. *Science, 185,* 137–139.

Bickford, R. G., Mulder, D. W., Dodge, H. W., Svien, H. J., & Rome, H. P. (1958). Changes in memory function produced by electrical stimulation of the temporal lobe in man. *Research Publications—Association for Research in Nervous and Mental Disease, 36,* 227–243.

Bierer, L. M., Hof, P. R., Purohit, D. P., Carlin, L., Schmeidler, J., Davis, K. L., & Perl, D. P. (1995). Neocortical neurofibrillary tangles correlate with dementia severity in Alzheimer's disease. *Archives of Neurology. 52,* 81–88.

Bigler, E. D. (1992). The neurobiology and neuropsychology of adult learning disorders. *Journal of Learning Disabilities, 25,* 488–506.

Binder, L. M. (1986). Persisting symptoms after mild head injury: A review of the post-concussive syndrome. *Journal of Clinical and Experimental Neuropsychology, 8,* 323–346.

Binnie, C. D. (1994). Cognitive impairment: Is it inevitable? *Seizure, 3*(Suppl. A), 17–22.

Birchall, J. D., & Chappel, J. S. (1988). Aluminum, chemical physiology, and Alzheimer's disease. *Lancet, 2,* 1008–1010.

Bisiach, E., Capitani, E., & Porta, E. (1985). Two basic properties of space representation in the brain. *Journal of Neurology, Neurosurgery and Psychiatry, 48,* 141–144.

Bisiach, E., Geminiani, G., Berti, A., & Rusconi, M. L. (1990). Perceptual and premotor factors of unilateral neglect. *Neurology, 40,* 1278–1281.

Bisiach, E., & Luzzatti, C. (1978). Unilateral neglect of representational space. *Cortex, 14,* 129–133.

Bisiach, E., & Rusconi, M. L. (1990). Break-down of perceptual awareness in unilateral neglect. *Cortex, 24,* 643–649.

Bisiach, E., Rusconi, M. L., & Vallar, G. (1991). Remission of somatoparaphrenic delusion through vestibular stimulation. *Neuropsychologia, 29,* 1029–1031.

Black, F. W., & Strub, R. L. (1976). Constructional apraxia in patients with discrete missile wounds of the brain. *Cortex, 12,* 212–220.

Blackman, J. A. (1989). The relationship between inadequate oxygenation of the brain at birth and developmental outcome. *Topics in Early Childhood Special Education, 9,* 1–13.

Bleier, R. (1984). *Science and gender.* New York: Pergamon Press.

Blumstein, S. (1991). Phonological aspects of aphasia. In M. Sarno (Ed.), *Acquired aphasia* (pp. 129–155). New York: Academic Press.

Blumstein, S. E., Baker, E., & Goodglass, H. (1977). Phonological factors in auditory comprehension in aphasia. *Neuropsychologia, 15,* 19–30.

Blumstein, S. E., Cooper, W. E., Zurif, E., & Caramazza, A. (1977). The perception and production of voice-onset time in aphasia. *Neuropsychologia, 15,* 371–383.

Blumstein, S. E., Tarter, V. C., Nigro, G., & Statlender, S. (1984). Acoustic cues for perception of place of articulation in aphasia. *Brain and Language, 22,* 128–149.

Boder, E. (1973). Developmental dyslexia: A diagnostic approach based on three reading-spelling patterns. *Developmental Medicine and Child Neurology*, *15*, 663.

Bogen, J. (1979). The callosal syndrome. In K. E. Heilman & E. Valenstein (Eds.), *Clinical neuropsychology*. New York: Oxford University Press.

Boll, T. J. (1981). The Halstead-Reitan Neuropsychological Battery. In S. B. Filskov & T. J. Boll (Eds.), *Handbook of clinical neuropsychology*. New York: Wiley Interscience.

Borchgrevink, H. M. (1980). Cerebral lateralization of speech and singing after intracarotid amytal injection. In M. T. Sarno & O. Hook (Eds.), *Aphasia: Assessment and treatment*. Stockholm: Almqvist and Wiksell.

Bornstein, B. (1963). Prosopagnosia. In L. Hapern (Ed.), *Problems of dynamic neurology* (pp. 283–318). Jerusalem: Hadassah Medical School.

Bornstein, B., Sroka, M., & Munitz, H. (1969). Propsoagnosia with animal face agnosia. *Cortex*, *5*, 164–169.

Bornstein, R. A., Nasrallah, H. A., Para, M. F., Whitacre, C. C., Rosenberger, P., & Fass, R. J. (1993). Neuropsychological performance in symptomatic and asymptomatic HIV infection. *AIDS*, *7*, 519–524.

Borod, J., Goodglass, H., & Kaplan, E. (1980). Normative data on the Boston Diagnostic Aphasia Examination Parietal Lobe Battery, and the Boston Naming Test. *Journal of Clinical Neuropsychology*, *2*, 209–216.

Borod, J. C. (1993). Cerebral mechanisms underlying facial, prosodic, and lexical emotional expression: A review of neuropsychological studies and methodological issues. *Neuropsychology*, *7*, 445–463.

Borod, J. C., Carper, M., Naeser, M., & Goodglass, H. (1985). Left-handed and right-handed aphasics with left hemisphere lesions compared on nonverbal performance measures. *Cortex*, *21*, 81–90.

Bowers, D., Bauer, R. M., Coslett, H. B., & Heilman, K. M. (1985). Processing of faces by patients with unilateral hemispheric lesions. I. Dissociations between judgements of facial affect and facial identity. *Brain and Cognition*, *4*, 258–272.

Bowers, D., Bauer, R. M., & Heilman, K. M. (1993). The nonverbal affect lexicon: Theoretical perspectives from neuropsychological studies of affect perception. *Neuropsychology*, *7*, 433–444.

Bradshaw, J. L., Phillips, J. G., Dennis, C., Mattingley, J. B., Andrewes, D., Chiu, E., Pierson, J. M., & Bradshaw, J. A. (1992). Initiation and execution of movement sequences in those suffering from and at-risk of developing Huntington's disease. *Journal of Clinical and Experimental Neuropsychology*, *14*, 179–192.

Brandt, J. (1991). Cognitive impairments in Huntington's disease: Insights into the neuropsychology of the striatum. In F. Boller & J. Grafman (Eds.), *Handbook of neuropsychology* (Vol. 5, pp. 241–264). New York: Elsevier.

Brandt, J., & Butters, N. (1986). The neuropsychology of Huntington's disease. *Trends in Neurosciences*, *9*, 118–120.

Breedlove, S. M. (1992). Sexual differentiation of the brain and behavior. In J. B. Becker, S. M. Breedlove, & D. Crews (Eds.), *Behavioral endocrinology* (pp. 39–68). Cambridge, MA: MIT Press.

Breggin, P. R. (1993). Parallels between neuroleptic effects and lethargic encephalitis: The production of dyskinesias and cognitive disorders. *Brain and Cognition*, *23*, 8–27.

Brinkman, C. (1984). Supplementary motor area of the monkey's cerebral cortex: Short- and long-term deficits after unilateral ablation and the effects of subsequent callosal section. *Journal of Neuroscience*, *4*, 918–929.

Brodal, A. (1981). *Neurological anatomy in relation to clinical medicine* (3rd ed.). New York: Oxford University Press.

Brontë, C. (1962). *Jane Eyre*. New York: Macmillan.

Brooks, D. N., & Baddeley, A. (1976). What can amnesic patients learn? *Neuropsychologia*, *14*, 111–122.

Brouwers, P., Cox, C., Martin, A., Chase, T. N., & Fedio, P. (1984). Differential perceptual-spatial impairment in Huntington's and Alzheimer's dementias. *Archives of Neurology*, *41*, 1073–1076.

Brown, J. (1977). *Mind, brain and consciousness*. New York: Academic Press.

Brown, P., Cathala, F., Sadowski, D., & Gajdusek, D. (1979). Creutzfeldt–Jakob disease in France: II. Clinical characteristics of 124 consecutively verified cases during the decade 1968–1977. *Annals of Neurology*, *6*, 430–437.

Brown, W. T., Jenkins, E., Cohen, I. L., Fisch, G. S., Wolf-Schein, E. G., Gross, A., Waterhouse, L., Fein, D., Mason-Brothers, A., Ritvo, E., Ruttenberg, B., Bentley, W., & Castells, S. (1986). Fragile X and autism: A multi-center survey. *American Journal of Medical Genetics*, *23*, 341–352.

Brownell, H. (1988). Appreciation of metaphoric and connotative word meaning by brain-damaged patients. In C. Chiarello (Ed.), *Right hemisphere contributions to lexical semantics* (pp. 19–31). New York: Springer-Verlag.

Brownell, H. H., Michel, D., Powelson, J. A., & Gardner, H. (1983). Surprise but not coherence: Sensitivity to verbal humor in right hemisphere patients. *Brain and Language*, *18*, 20–27.

Brownell, H. H., Simpson, T. L., Bihrle, A. M., Potter, H. H., & Gardner, H. (1990). Appreciation of metaphorical alternative word meanings by left and right brain-damaged patients. *Neuropsychologia*, *28*, 375–383.

Bruder, G. E., Quitkin, F. M., Stewart, J. W., Martin, C., Voglmaier, M. M., & Harrison, W. M. (1989). Cerebral laterality and depression: Differences in perceptual asymmetry among diagnostic subtypes. *Journal of Abnormal Psychology*, *98*, 177–186.

Bruyer, R., Laterre, C., Seron, X., Feyereisen, P., Strypstein, E., Pierrard, E., & Rectem, D. (1983). A case of prosopagnosia with some preserved covert remembrance of familiar faces. *Brain and Cognition*, *2*, 257–284.

Bryden, M. P. (1965). Tachistoscopic recognition, handedness, and cerebral dominance. *Neuropsychologia*, *3*, 1–8.

Bryden, M. P. (1976). Response bias and hemispheric differences in dot localization. *Perception and Psychophysics*, *19*, 23–28.

Bryden, M. P., & Allard, F. (1976). Visual hemifield differences depend on typeface. *Brain and Language*, *3*, 191–200.

Bryden, M. P., McManus, I. C., & Bulman-Fleming, M. B. (1995). GBG, hormones, genes, and anomalous dominance: A reply to commentaries. *Brain and Cognition, 27,* 94–97.

Buchsbaum, M. S. (1990). Frontal lobes, basal ganglia, temporal lobes—Three sites for schizophrenia? *Schizophrenia Bulletin, 16,* 379–390.

Buchsbaum, M. S., Wu, J., Haier, R., Hazlett, E., Ball, R., Katz, M., Sokolski, K., Lagunas-Solar, M., & Langer, D. (1987). Positron emission tomography assessment of effects of benzo-diazepines on regional glucose metabolic rate in patients with anxiety disorder. *Life Sciences, 40,* 2393–2400.

Buchtel, H., Campari, F., De Risio, C., & Rota, R. (1978). Hemispheric differences in discriminative reaction time to facial expressions. *Italian Journal of Psychology, 5,* 159–169.

Buchtel, H. A., & Stewart, J. D. (1989). Auditory agnosia: Apperceptive or associative disorder? *Brain and Language, 37,* 12–25.

Buckner, R., Petersen, S. E., Ojemann, J. G., Miezin, F. M., Squire, L. R., & Raichle, M. E. (1995). Functional anatomical studies of explicit and implicit memory retrieval tasks. *Journal of Neuroscience, 15,* 19–29.

Burgess, C., & Simpson, G. B. (1988). Cerebral hemispheric mechanisms in the retrieval of ambiguous word meanings. *Brain and Language, 33,* 86–103.

Burke, D. C. (1995). Models of brain injury rehabilitation. *Brain Injury, 9,* 735–743.

Burke, K. A., Letsos, A., & Butler, R. A. (1994). Asymmetric performances in biaural localization of sound in space. *Neuropsychologia, 32,* 1409–1417.

Burton, L. A., Wagner, N., Lim, C., & Levy, J. (1992). Visual field differences for clockwise and counterclockwise mental rotation. *Brain and Cognition, 18,* 192–207.

Butler, R. A. (1994). Asymmetric performances in monaural localization of sound in space. *Neuropsychologia, 32,* 221–229.

Butler, R. W., Rorsman, I., Hill, J. M., & Tuma, R. (1993). The effects of frontal brain impairment on fluency: Simple and complex paradigms. *Neuropsychology, 7,* 519–529.

Butters, N., & Cermak, L. S. (1986). A case study of the forgetting of autobiographical knowledge: Implications for the study of retrograde amnesia. In D. C. Rubin (Ed.), *Autobiographical memory* (pp. 253–272). Cambridge, England: Cambridge University Press.

Butters, N., Soeldner, C., & Fedio, P. (1972). Comparison of parietal and frontal lobe spatial deficits in man: Extrapersonal vs. personal (egocentric) space. *Perceptual and Motor Skills, 34,* 27–34.

Butters, N., Wolfe, J., Martone, M., Granholm, E., & Cermak, L. S. (1985). Memory disorders associated with Huntington's disease: Verbal recall, verbal recognition, and procedural memory. *Neuropsychologia, 23,* 729–743.

Byne, W., Bleier, R., & Houston, L. (1988). Variations in human corpus callosum do not predict gender: A study using magnetic resonance imaging. *Behavioral Neuroscience, 102,* 222–227.

Caine, E. D., Weingartner, H., Ludlow, C. L., Cudahy, E. A., & Wehry, S. (1981). Qualitative analysis of scopolamine-induced amnesia. *Psychopharmacology, 74,* 74–80.

Calvanio, R., Petrone, P. N., & Levine, D. M. (1987). Left visual spatial neglect is both environment-centered and body-centered. *Neurology, 37,* 1179–1183.

Campbell, R. (1978). Asymmetries in interpreting and expressing a posed facial expression. *Cortex, 19,* 327–342.

Canadian Study of Health and Aging. (1994). The Canadian Study of Health and Aging: Risk factors for Alzheimer's disease in Canada. *Neurology, 44,* 2073–2080.

Cancelliere, A., & Kertesz, A. (1990). Lesion localization in acquired deficits of emotional expression and comprehension. *Brain and Cognition, 13,* 133–147.

Cannon, W. B. (1927). The James–Lange theory of emotions: A critical examination and an alternative theory. *American Journal of Psychology, 39,* 106–124.

Cannon, W. B. (1931). Again the James–Lange and the thalamic theories of emotion. *Psychological Review, 38,* 281–295.

Caplan, D. (1987). *Neurolinguistics and linguistic aphasiology.* Cambridge, England: Cambridge University Press.

Cappa, S., Sterzi, R., Vallar, G., & Bisiach, E. (1987). Remission of hemineglect and anosognosia during vestibular stimulation. *Neuropsychologia, 25,* 775–782.

Caramazza, A., & Badecker, W. (1989). Patient classification in neuropsychological research. *Brain and Cognition, 10,* 256–295.

Caramazza, A., & Hillis, A. (1990). Spatial representation of words in the brain implied by studies of a unilateral neglect patient. *Nature, 346,* 267–269.

Caramazza, A., Hillis, A. E., Rapp, B. C., & Romani, C. (1990). The multiple semantics hypothesis: Multiple confusions? *Cognitive Neuropsychology, 7,* 161–189.

Caramazza, A., Miceli, G., Silveri, M. C., & Laudanna, A. (1985). Reading mechanisms and the organization of the lexicon: Evidence from acquired dyslexia. *Cognitive Neuropsychology, 2,* 81–114.

Cardebat, D., Demonet, J.-F., Celsis, P., Puel, M., Viallard, G., & Marc-Vergnes, J.-P. (1994). Right temporal compensatory mechanisms in a deep dysphasic patient: A case report with activation study by SPECT. *Neuropsychologia, 32,* 97–103.

Carey, S., & Diamond, R. (1977). From piecemeal to configurational representation of faces. *Science, 195,* 312–314.

Carlson, N. (1986). *Physiology of behavior* (3rd ed.). Boston: Allyn & Bacon.

Carlson, N. (1994). *Physiology of behavior.* (5th ed.). Boston: Allyn & Bacon.

Carmon, A., & Bechtoldt, H. P. (1969). Dominance of the right cerebral hemisphere for stereopsis. *Neuropsychologia, 7,* 29–39.

Carpenter, M. B. (1976). *Human neuroanatomy* (7th ed.). Baltimore: Williams & Wilkins.

Carter, W. R., Johnson, M. C., & Borkovec, T. D. (1986). Worry: An electrocortical analysis. *Advances in Behavioral Research and Therapy, 8,* 193–204.

Caselli, R. J. (1993). Ventrolateral and dorsomedial somatosensory association cortex damage produces distinct somesthetic syndromes in humans. *Neurology, 43,* 762–771.

Cavalli, M., DeRenzi, E., Faglioni, P., & Vitale, A. (1981).

Impairment of right brain-damaged patients on a linguistic cognitive task. *Cortex, 17*, 545–556.

Cerella, J. (1985). Information processing rates in the elderly. *Psychological Bulletin, 98*, 67–83.

Cerella, J. (1990). Aging and information processing rate. In J. Birren & K. Schaie (Eds.), *Handbook of psychology and aging* (pp. 201–221). New York: Academic Press.

Cermak, L. S., Lewis, R., Butters, N., & Goodglass, H. (1973). Role of verbal mediation in performance of motor tasks by Korsakoff patients. *Perceptual and Motor Skills, 37*, 259–262.

Cermak, L. S., & O'Connor, M. (1983). The anterograde and retrograde retrieval ability of a patient with amnesia due to encephalitis. *Neuropsychologia, 21*, 213–234.

Chastain, G. (1987). Visually presented letter strings are encoded phonologically: Some converging evidence. *Journal of Experimental Psychology: General, 114*, 147–156.

Chatterjee, A., Strauss, M. E., Smyth, K. A., & Whitehouse, P. J. (1992). Personality changes in Alzheimer's disease. *Archives of Neurology, 49*, 486–491.

Chess, S., Fernandez, P., & Korn, S. (1979). Behavioral consequences of congenital rubella. *Annual Progress in Child Psychiatry and Child Development*, 467–475.

Chiarello, C. (1991). Interpretation of word meanings by the cerebral hemispheres: One is not enough. In P. J. Schwanenflugel (Ed.), *The psychology of word meanings* (pp. 251–278). Hillsdale, NJ: Earlbaum.

Christman, S. (1989). Perceptual characteristics in visual field research. *Brain and Language, 11*, 238–257.

Christman, S., Kitterle, F. L., & Hellige, J. B. (1991). Hemispheric asymmetry in the processing of absolute versus relative spatial frequency. *Brain and Cognition, 16*, 62–73.

Chugani, H. T., Phelps, M. E., & Mazziotta, J. C. (1987). Positron emission tomography study of human brain functional development. *Annals of Neurology, 22*(4), 487–497.

Cianchetti, C., Sannio-Fancello, G., Fratta, A. L., Manconi, F., Orano, A., Pischedda, M. P., Pruna, D., Spinicci, G., Archidiacono, N., & Filippi, G. (1991). Neuropsychological, psychiatric, and physical manifestations in 140 members from 18 fragile X families. *American Journal of Medical Genetics, 40*, 234–243.

Cicerone, K., Lazar, R., & Shapiro, W. (1983). Effects of frontal lobe lesions on hypothesis sampling during concept formation. *Neuropsychologia, 21*, 513–524.

Cicone, M., Wapner, W., & Gardner, H. (1980). Sensitivity to emotional expressions and situations in organic patients. *Cortex, 16*, 145–158.

Clarke, S., Assal, G., & deTribolet, N. (1993). Left hemisphere strategies in visual recognition, topographical orientation and time planning. *Neuropsychologia, 31*, 99–113.

Cohen, N. F. (1989). Staying in the community after a head injury. In E. Perecman (Ed.), *Integrating theory and practice in clinical neuropsychology*. Hillsdale, NJ: Erlbaum.

Cohen, N. J. (1981). *Neuropsychological evidence for a distinction between procedural and declarative knowledge in human memory and amnesia*. Unpublished doctoral dissertation, University of California, San Diego.

Cohen, N. J. (1984). Preserved learning capacity in amnesia: Evidence for multiple memory systems. In L. R. Squire & N. Butters (Eds.), *Neuropsychology of memory* (pp. 83–103). New York: Guilford Press.

Cohen, N. J., Althoff, R. R., Webb, J. M., McConkie, G. W., Holden, J. A., & Noll, E. L. (1995). *Eye movement monitoring as an indirect measure of memory*. Manuscript submitted for publication.

Cohen, N. J., Banich, M. T., Kramer, A. F., Morris, H. D., Lauterbur, P. C., Potter, C. S., Cao, Y., & Levin, D. N. (1993). Assessing test-retest reliability of functional MRI data. *Society for Neuroscience Abstracts, 23*, 1494.

Cohen, N. J., & Eichenbaum, H. E. (1993). *Memory, amnesia, and the hippocampal system*. Cambridge, MA: MIT Press.

Cohen, N. J., Eichenbaum, H. E., Deacedo, B. S., & Corkin, S. (1985). Different memory systems underlying acquisition of procedural and declarative knowledge. *Annals of the New York Academy of Sciences, 444*, 54–71.

Cohen, N. J., Ramzy, C., Hu, Z., Tomaso, H., Strupp, J., Erhard, P., Anderson, P., & Ugurbil, K. (1994). Hippocampal activation in fMRI evoked by demand for declarative memory-based binding of multiple streams of information. *Society for Neuroscience Abstracts, 20*, 1290.

Cohen, N. J., & Squire, L. R. (1980). Preserved learning and retention of pattern-analyzing skill in amnesia: Dissociation of knowing how and knowing that. *Science, 210*, 207–210.

Cohen, N. J., & Squire, L. R. (1981). Retrograde amnesia and remote memory impairment. *Neuropsychologia, 19*(3), 337–356.

Cohen, R. M., Semple, W. E., Gross, M., Holcomb, H. J., Dowling, S. M., & Nordahl, T. E. (1988). Functional localization of sustained attention. *Neuropsychiatry, Neuropsychology and Behavioral Neurology, 1*, 3–20.

Colby, C. L., & Zeffiro, T. (1990). Cortical activation in humans during visual and oculomotor processing measured by positron emission tomography (PET). *Society for Neuroscience Abstracts, 16*, 621.

Cole, M., Schutta, H. S., & Warrington, E. K. (1962). Visual disorientation in homonymous half fields. *Neurology, 12*, 257–263.

Coleman, M. (1987). The search for neurological subgroups in autism. In E. Schopler & G. Mesibov (Eds.), *Neurobiological issues in autism* (pp. 163–178). New York: Plenum Press.

Coltheart, M. (1980). Reading, phonological recoding and deep dyslexia. In M. Coltheart, K. E. Patterson, & J. C. Marshall (Eds.), *Deep dyslexia* (pp. 197–226). London: Routledge.

Coltheart, M. (1982). The psycholinguistic analysis of acquired dyslexias: Some illustrations. *Philosophical Transactions of the Royal Society of London, B298*, 151–164.

Cope, D. N. (1995). The effectiveness of traumatic brain injury rehabilitation: A review. *Brain Injury, 9*, 649–670.

Corballis, M., & McLaren, R. (1984). Winding one's *p*'s and *q*'s: Mental rotation and mirror image discrimination. *Journal of Experimental Psychology: Human Perception and Performance, 10*, 318–327.

Corballis, M., & Sergent, J. (1989). Hemispheric specialization for mental rotation. *Cortex, 25,* 15–25.

Corbetta, M., Miezin, F. M., Dobmeyer, S., Shulman, G. L., & Petersen, S. E. (1991). Selective and divided attention during visual discriminations of shape, color, and speed: Functional anatomy by positron emission tomography. *Journal of Neuroscience, 11,* 2383–2402.

Corbetta, M., Miezin, F. M., Shulman, G. L., & Petersen, S. E. (1993). A PET study of visuospatial attention. *Journal of Neuroscience, 13,* 1202–1226.

Coren, S., & Halpern, D. F. (1991). Left-handedness: A marker for decreased survival fitness. *Psychological Bulletin, 109,* 90–106.

Coren, S., & Halpern, D. F. (1993). A replay of the baseball data. *Perceptual and Motor Skills, 76,* 403–406.

Corina, D. P., Poizner, H., Bellugi, U., Feinberg, T., Dowd, D., & O'Grady-Batch, L. (1992). Dissociations between linguistic and nonlinguistic gestural systems: A case for compositionality. *Brain and Language, 43,* 414–447.

Corina, D. P., Vaid, J., & Bellugi, U. (1992). The linguistic basis of left hemisphere specialization. *Science, 255,* 1258–1260.

Corkin, S. (1968). Acquisition of motor skill after bilateral medial temporal-lobe excision. *Neuropsychologia, 6,* 255–265.

Corkin, S. (1982). Some relationships between global amnesias and the memory impairments in Alzheimer's disease. In S. Corkin, K. L. Davis, J. H. Growdon, & E. Usdin (Eds.), *Alzheimer's disease: A report of progress in research* (pp. 149–164). New York: Raven Press.

Corkin, S. (1984). Lasting consequences of bilateral medial temporal lobectomy: Clinical course and experimental findings in H.M. *Seminars in Neurology, 4,* 249–259.

Corkin, S., Milner, B., & Rasmussen, T. (1970). Somatosensory thresholds: Contrasting effects of postcentral-gyrus and posterior parietal-lobe excisions. *Archives of Neurology, 23,* 41–58.

Corkin, S., Rosen, T. J., Sullivan, E. V., & Clegg, R. A. (1989). Penetrating head injury in young adulthood exacerbates cognitive decline in later years. *Journal of Neuroscience, 9,* 3876–3883.

Coslett, H. B., Bowers, D., & Heilman, K. M. (1987). Reduction in cerebral activation after right hemisphere stroke. *Neurology, 37,* 957–962.

Courchesne, E., Yeung-Courchesne, R., Press, G. A., Hesselink, J. R., & Jernigan, T. L. (1988). Hypoplasia of cerebellar vermal lobules VI and VII in autism. *New England Journal of Medicine, 318,* 1349–1354.

Craft, S., Gourovitch, M. L., Dowton, S. B., Swanson, J., & Bonforte, S. (1992). Lateralized deficits in visual attention in early treated PKU. *Neuropsychologia, 30,* 341–351.

Craik, F. I. M. (1989). In R. Wurtman (Ed.), *Alzheimer's disease: Advances in basic research and therapy.* Cambridge, MA: Center for Brain Sciences.

Craik, F. I. M. & McDowd, J. M. (1987). Age differences in recall and recognition. *Journal of Experimental Psychology: Learning, Memory, and Cognition, 13,* 474–479.

Craik, F. I. M., Morris, L. W., Morris, R. G., & Loewen, E. R. (1990). Relations between source amnesia and frontal lobe functioning in older adults. *Psychology and Aging, 5,* 148–151.

Crawford, J. R. (1992). Current and premorbid intelligence measures in neuropsychological assessment. In J. R. Crawford, D. M. Parker, & W. W. McKinlay (Eds.), *A handbook of neuropsychological assessment.* Hillsdale, NJ: Erlbaum.

Cremona-Meteyard, S. L., & Geffen, G. M. (1994). Persistent visuospatial attention deficits following mild head injury in Australian Rules football players. *Neuropsychologia, 32,* 649–662.

Critchley, M. (1970). *Developmental dyslexia.* Springfield, IL: Charles C Thomas.

Crowder, R. G., Serafine, M. L., & Repp, B. (1990). Physical interaction and association by contiguity in memory for the words and melodies of songs. *Memory and Cognition, 18,* 469–476.

Cumming, W. J. K. (1988). The neurobiology of body schema. *British Journal of Psychiatry, 153*(Suppl. 2), 7–11.

Cummings, J. L. (1991). Behavioral complications of drug treatment in Parkinson's disease. *Journal of the American Geriatrics Society, 39,* 708–716.

Cummings, J. L., & Benson, D. F. (1983). *Dementia: A clinical approach.* Boston: Butterworth.

Cummings, J. L., & Benson, D. F. (1984). Subcortical dementia: Review of an emerging concept. *Archives of Neurology, 41,* 874–879.

Cummings, J. L., & Benson, D. F. (1988). Psychological dysfunction accompanying subcortical dementias. *Annual Review of Medicine, 39,* 53–61.

Cummings, J. L., Benson, D. F., Hill, M. A., & Read, S. (1985). Aphasia in dementia of the Alzheimer type. *Neurology, 35,* 394–397.

Cummings, J. L., & Duchen, L. W. (1981). Kluver–Bucy syndrome in Pick's disease: Clinical and pathologic correlations. *Neurology, 31,* 1415–1422.

Daigneault, S., Braun, C. M. J., & Whitaker, H. A. (1992). Early effects of normal aging on perseverative and non-perseverative prefrontal measures. *Developmental Neuropsychology, 8,* 99–114.

Dalmady-Israel, C., & Zasler, N. D. (1993). Post-traumatic seizures: A critical review. *Brain Injury, 7,* 263–273.

Dalrymple, A. J. C., Kalders, A. S., Jones, R. D., & Watson, R. W. (1994). A central executive deficit in patients with Parkinson's disease. *Journal of Neurology, Neurosurgery and Psychiatry, 57,* 360–367.

Damasio, A. R. (1985). Disorders of complex visual processing: Agnosia, achromatopsia, Balint's syndrome, and related difficulties of orientation and construction. In M.-M. Mesulam (Ed.), *Principles of behavioral neurology* (pp. 259–288). Philadelphia: F A Davis.

Damasio, A. R. (1989). The brain binds entities and events by multiregional activation from convergence zones. *Neural Computation, 1,* 123–132.

Damasio, A. R., Damasio, H., & Chui, H. C. (1980). Neglect following damage to frontal lobe or basal ganglia. *Neuropsychologia*, *18*, 123–132.

Damasio, A. R., Damasio, H., & Van Hoesen, G. W. (1982). Prosopagnosia: Anatomical basis and behavioral mechanisms. *Neurology*, *32*, 331–341.

Damasio, A. R., & Maurer, R. G. (1978). A neurological model for childhood autism. *Archives of Neurology*, *35*, 777–786.

Damasio, H., & Damasio, A. R. (1989). *Lesion analysis in neuropsychology*. New York: Oxford University Press.

Damasio, H. C. (1991a). Neuroanatomical correlates of the aphasias. In M. T. Sarno (Ed.), *Acquired aphasia* (2nd ed., pp. 45–70). New York: Academic Press.

Damasio, H. C. (1991b). Neuroanatomy of frontal lobe in vivo: A comment on methodology. In J. S. Levin, H. M. Eisenberg, & A. L. Benton (Eds.), *Frontal lobe function and dysfunction*. New York: Oxford University Press.

Daniel, W. F., & Yeo, R. A. (1994). Accident proneness and handedness. *Biological Psychiatry*, *35*, 499.

Danly, M., & Shapiro, B. (1982). Speech prosody in Broca's aphasia. *Brain and Language*, *16*, 171–190.

Danta, G., Hilton, R. C., & O'Boyle, D. J. (1978). Hemisphere function and binocular depth perception. *Brain*, *101*, 569–590.

Davidson, R. J. (1984). Affect, cognition, and hemispheric specialization. In C. E. Izard, J. Kagan, & R. Zajonc (Eds.), *Emotion, cognition, and behavior* (pp. 320–365). New York: Cambridge University Press.

Davidson, R. J. (1992). Emotion and affective style: Hemispheric substrates. *Psychological Science*, *3*, 39–43.

Davidson, R. J. (1993). Parsing affective space: Perspectives from neuropsychology and psychophysiology. *Neuropsychology*, *7*, 464–475.

Davidson, R. J., Chapman, J. P., & Chapman, L. J. (1987). Task-dependent EEG asymmetry discriminates between depressed and non-depressed subjects. *Psychophysiology*, *24*, 585.

Davidson, R. J., & Tomarken, A. J. (1989). Laterality and emotion: An electrophysiological approach. In F. Boller & J. Grafman (Eds.), *Handbook of neuropsychology* (pp. 419–441). Amsterdam: Elsevier.

Davies, P., & Maloney, A. J. F. (1976). Selective loss of central cholinergic neurons in Alzheimer's disease. *Lancet*, *2*, 1403.

Davis, H., Cohen, A., Gandy, M., Colombo, P., Van Dusseldorp, G., Simolke, N., & Romano, J. (1990). Lexical priming deficits as a function of age. *Behavioral Neuroscience*, *104*, 288–297.

Day, J. J., Grant, I., Atkinson, J. H., Brysk, L. T., McCutchan, J. A., Hesselink, J. R., Heaton, R. K., Weinrich, J. D., Spector, S. A., & Richman, D. D. (1992). Incidence of dementia in a two year follow-up of AIDS and ARC patients on an initial Phase II AZT placebo-controlled study: San Diego Cohort. *Journal of Neuropsychiatry*, *4*, 15–20.

Day, N. L. (1992). Effects of prenatal alcohol exposure. In I. S. Zagon & T. A. Slotkin (Eds.), *Maternal substance abuse and the developing nervous system* (pp. 27–44). New York: Academic Press.

Day, N. L., & Richardson, G. A. (1993). Cocaine use and crack babies: Science, the media, and miscommunication. *Neurotoxicology and Teratology*, *15*(5), 293–294.

Dee, H. L., Benton, A. L., & Van Allen, M. W. (1970). Apraxia in relation to hemisphere locus of lesion and aphasia. *Transactions of the American Neurological Association*, *95*, 147–148.

DeFries, J. C. (1985). Colorado reading project. In D. B. Gray & J. F. Kavanaugh (Eds.), *Biobehavioral measures of dyslexia*. Parkton, MD: York Press.

De Haan, E. H., Young, A., & Newcombe, F. (1987). Faces interfere with name classification in a prosopagnosic patient. *Cortex*, *23*, 309–316.

DeKosky, S. T., Heilman, G. E., Bowers, D., & Valenstein, I. (1980). Recognition and discrimination of emotional faces and pictures. *Brain and Language*, *9*, 206–214.

deLacoste, C., Kirkpatrick, J. B., & Ross, E. D. (1985). Topography of the human corpus callosum. *Journal of Neuropathology and Experimental Neurology*, *44*, 578–591.

deLacoste-Utamsing, C., & Holloway, R. L. (1982). Sexual dimorphism in the human corpus callosum. *Science*, *216*, 1431–1432.

Delis, D. C., Robertson, L. C., & Efron, R. (1986). Hemispheric specialization of memory for visual hierarchical stimuli. *Neuropsychologia*, *24*, 205–214.

Delis, D. C., Squire, L. R., Bihrle, A., & Massman, P. (1992). Componential analysis of problem-solving ability: Performance of patients with frontal lobe damage and amnesic patients on a new sorting test. *Neuropsychologia*, *30*, 683–697.

Delis, D. C., Wapner, W., Gardner, H., & Moses, J. A. (1983). The contribution of the right hemisphere to the organization of paragraphs. *Cortex*, *19*, 43–50.

Della Malva, C. L., Stuss, D. T., D'Alton, J., & Willmer, J. (1993). Capture errors and sequencing after frontal brain lesions. *Neuropsychologia*, *31*, 363–372.

Demb, J. B., Desmond, J. E., Wagner, A. D., Stone, M., Lee, A. T., Glover, G. H., & Gabrieli, J. D. E. (1994). A functional MRI (fMRI) student of semantic encoding and memory in the left inferior frontal gyrus. *Society for Neuroscience Abstracts*, *20*, 1290.

Denckla, M. B. (1979). Childhood learning disabilities. In K. M. Heilman & E. Valenstein (Eds.), *Clinical neuropsychology*. New York: Oxford University Press.

Dennett, D. C., & Kinsbourne, M. (1992). Time and the observer: The where and when of consciousness in the brain. *Behavioral and Brain Sciences*, *17*, 175–180.

Dennis, M., & Kohn, B. (1975). Comprehension of syntax in infantile hemiplegics after cerebral hemidecortication: Left-hemisphere superiority. *Brain and Language*, *2*, 472–482.

Dennis, M., & Whitaker, W. (1976). Language acquisition following hemidecortication: Linguistic superiority of left over right hemisphere. *Brain and Language*, *3*, 404–433.

DeRenzi, E. (1980). The Token Test and the Reporter's Test: A measure of verbal input and a measure of verbal output. In M. T. Sarno & O. Hook (Eds.), *Aphasia: Assessment and treatment*. New York: Masson.

DeRenzi, E. (1986). Current issues in prosopagnosia. In H. D. Ellis, M. A. Jeeves, F. Newcombe, & Y. A. (Eds.), *Aspects of face processing*. Dordrecht, The Netherlands: Martinus Nijhoff.

DeRenzi, E., Faglioni, P., & Previdi, P. (1977). Spatial memory and hemispheric locus of lesion. *Cortex, 13*, 424–433.

DeRenzi, E., & Lucchelli, F. (1988). Ideational apraxia. *Brain, 111*, 1173–1188.

DeRenzi, E., Motti, F., & Nichelli, P. (1980). Imitating gestures: A quantitative approach. *Archives of Neurology, 37*, 6–10.

DeRenzi, E., & Nichelli, P. (1975). Verbal and non-verbal short-term memory impairment following hemispheric damage. *Cortex, 11*, 341–354.

DeRenzi, E., Perani, D., Carlesimo, G. A., Silveri, M. C., & Fazio, F. (1994). Prosopagnosia can be associated with damage confined to the right hemisphere—An MRI and PET study and review of the literature. *Neuropsychologia, 32*, 893–902.

DeRenzi, E., Pieczuro, A., & Vignolo, L. A. (1968). Ideational apraxia: A quantitative study. *Neuropsychologia, 6*, 41–52.

DeRenzi, E., & Spinnler, H. (1966). Visual recognition in patients with unilateral cerebral disease. *Journal of Nervous and Mental Disease, 142*, 513–525.

Desimone, R., Albright, T. D., Gross, C. G., & Bruce, C. (1984). Stimulus selective properties of inferior temporal neurons in the macaque. *Journal of Neuroscience, 4*, 2051–2062.

Desimone, R., & Gross, C. G. (1979). Visual areas in the temporal cortex of the macaque. *Brain Research, 178*, 363–380.

Desmedt, J. E., & Robertson, D. (1977). Differential enhancement of early and late components of the cerebral somatosensory evoked potentials during forced-paced cognitive tasks in man. *Journal of Physiology (London), 271*, 761–782.

Deutsch, G., Bourbon, W., Papanicolaou, A., & Eisenberg, H. (1988). Visuospatial tasks compared during activation of regional cerebral blood flow. *Neuropsychologia, 26*, 445–452.

Deutsch, J. A., & Deutsch, D. (1963). Attention: Some theoretical considerations. *Psychological Review, 70*, 80–90.

Diamond, A. (1990). Developmental time course in human infants and infant monkeys, and the neural bases of inhibitory control in reading. *Annals of the New York Academy of Sciences, 608*, 637–676.

Diamond, D. M., & Weinberger, N. M. (1986). Classical conditioning rapidly induces specific changes in frequency receptive fields of single neurons in secondary and ventral ectosylvian cortical fields. *Brain Research, 372*, 357–360.

Diamond, R., & Carey, S. (1986). Why faces are and are not special: An effect of expertise. *Journal of Experimental Psychology: General, 115*, 107–117.

Dimond, S. J., & Beaumont, J. G. (1973). Difference in the vigilance performance of the right and left hemisphere. *Cortex, 9*, 259–265.

Ditunno, P., & Mann, V. (1990). Right hemisphere specialization for mental rotation in normals and brain damaged subjects. *Cortex, 26*, 177–188.

Dodrill, C. B. (1992). Neuropsychological aspects of epilepsy. *Psychiatric Clinics of North America, 15*, 383–394.

Donchin, E. (1984). Report of Panel III: Preparatory processes. In E. Donchin (Ed.), *Cognitive psychophysiology* (pp. 179–219). Hillsdale, NJ: Erlbaum.

Donchin, E., & Coles, M. (1988). Is the P_{300} component a manifestation of context updating? *Behavioral and Brain Sciences, 11*, 406–417.

Doody, R. S., & Jankovic, J. (1992). The alien hand and related signs. *Journal of Neurology, Neurosurgery and Psychiatry, 55*, 806–810.

Doyon, J., & Milner, B. (1991). Right temporal-lobe contribution to global visual processing. *Neuropsychologia, 29*, 343–360.

Drachman, D. A. (1978). Memory, dementia, and the cholinergic system. In R. Katzman, R. D. Terry, & K. L. Bick (Eds.), *Alzheimer's disease: Senile dementia and related disorders* (pp. 141–148). New York: Raven Press.

Drachman, D. A., & Arbit, J. (1966). Memory and hippocampal complex. II. Is memory a multiple process? *Archives of Neurology, 15*, 52–61.

Driver, J., Baylis, G., Goodrich, S. J., & Rafal, R. D. (1994). Axis-based neglect of visual shapes. *Neuropsychologia, 32*, 1353–1365.

Dror, I. E., Kosslyn, S. M., & Waag, W. L. (1993). Visual-spatial abilities of pilots. *Journal of Applied Psychology, 78*, 763–773.

Dubner, R., & Zeki, S. M. (1971). Response properties and receptive fields of cells in an anatomically defined region of the superior temporal sulcus in the monkey. *Brain Research, 35*, 528–532.

Dubois, B., Boller, F., Pillon, B., & Agid, Y. (1991). Cognitive deficits in Parkinson's disease. In F. Boller & J. Grafman (Eds.), *Handbook of neuropsychology* (Vol. 5, pp. 195–240). New York: Elsevier.

Duncan, J. (1986). Disorganisation of behaviour after frontal lobe damage. *Cognitive Neuropsychology, 3*, 271–290.

Eckardt, M. J., Stapleton, J. M., Rawlings, R. R., Davis, E. Z., & Grodin, D. M. (1995). Neuropsychological functioning in detoxified alcoholics between 18 and 35 years of age. *American Journal of Psychiatry, 152*(1), 45–52.

Edwards, B. (1989). *Drawing on the right side of the brain: A course in creativity and artistic confidence*. Los Angeles: Jeremy P Tarcher.

Ehrlichman, H., & Weinberger, A. (1978). Lateral eye movements and hemispheric asymmetry: A critical review. *Psychological Bulletin, 85*, 1080–1101.

Eichenbaum, H. (1994). The hippocampal system and declarative memory in humans and animals: Experimental analysis and historical origins. In D. L. Schacter & E. Tulving (Eds.), *Memory systems 1994*. Cambridge, MA: MIT Press.

Eichenbaum, H., Otto, T., & Cohen, N. J. (1994). Two component functions of the hippocampal memory system. *Behavioral and Brain Sciences, 17*, 449–517.

Eichenbaum, H., Stewart, C., & Morris, R. G. M. (1990). Hippocampal representation in spatial learning. *Journal of Neuroscience, 10*, 331–339.

Eichhorn, S. K. (1982). Congenital cytomegalovirus infection: A significant cause of deafness and mental deficiency. *American Annals of the Deaf, 127*(7), 838–843.

Eidelberg, D., & Galaburda, A. M. (1984). Inferior parietal lobule: Divergent architectonic asymmetries in the human brain. *Archives of Neurology, 41*, 843–852.

Eisenberg, H. M., & Weiner, R. L. (1987). Input variables: How information from the acute injury can be used to characterize groups of patients for studies of outcome. In H. S. Levin, J. Grafman, & H. M. Eisenberg (Eds.), *Neurobehavioral recovery from head injury.* New York: Oxford University Press.

Ekman, P., Hager, J. C., & Friesen, W. V. (1981). The symmetry of emotional and deliberate facial actions. *Psychophysiology, 18*, 101–106.

Ellis, A. W., Flude, B. M., & Young, A. W. (1987). "Neglect dyslexia" and the early visual processing of letters in words. *Cognitive Neuropsychology, 4*, 439–464.

Entus, A. K. (1977). Hemispheric asymmetry in processing of dichotically presented speech and nonspeech stimuli by infants. In S. J. Segalowitz & F. A. Gruber (Eds.), *Language development and neurological theory* (pp. 64–73). New York: Academic Press.

Erkinjuntti, T., Haltia, M., Palo, J., & Paetau, A. (1988). Accuracy of the clinical diagnosis of vascular dementia: A prospective clinical and post-mortem neuropathological study. *Journal of Neurology, Neurosurgery and Psychiatry, 51*, 1037–1044.

Errico, A. L., Parsons, O. A., & King, A. C. (1991). Assessment of verbosequential and visuospatial cognitive abilities in chronic alcoholics. *Psychological Assessment, 3*, 693–696.

Eslinger, P. J., & Grattan, L. M. (1993). Frontal lobe and frontal-striatal substrates for different forms of human cognitive flexibility. *Neuropsychologia, 31*, 17–28.

Etcoff, N. (1989). Asymmetries in recognition of emotion. In F. Boller & J. Grafman (Eds.), *Handbook of neuropsychology: Vol. 3. Emotional behavior and its disorders* (pp. 363–382). New York: Elsevier.

Etcoff, N. L. (1984). Selective attention to facial identity and facial emotion. *Neuropsychologia, 22*, 281–295.

Everall, I. P., & Lantos, P. L. (1991). The neuropathology of HIV: A review of the first 10 years. *International Review of Psychiatry, 3*, 307–320.

Falzi, G., Perrone, P., & Vignolo, L. (1982). Right-left asymmetry in anterior speech region. *Archives of Neurology, 39*, 239–240.

Farah, M. J. (1984). The neurological basis of mental imagery: A componential analysis. *Cognition, 18*, 245–272.

Farah, M. J. (1988). Is visual imagery really visual? Overlooked evidence from neuropsychology. *Psychological Review, 95*, 307–317.

Farah, M. J. (1990). *Visual agnosia: Disorders of object recognition and what they tell us about normal vision.* Cambridge, MA: MIT Press.

Farah, M. J., Gazzaniga, M. S., Holtzman, J. D., & Kosslyn, S. M. (1985). A left hemisphere basis for visual imagery? *Neuropsychologia, 23*, 115–118.

Farah, M. J., Hammond, K. M., Mehta, Z., & Ratcliff, G. (1989). Category-specificity and modality-specificity in semantic memory. *Neuropsychologia, 27*, 193–200.

Farah, M. J., & McClelland, J. L. (1991). A computational model of semantic memory impairment: Modality-specificity and emergent category-specificity. *Journal of Experimental Psychology: General, 120*, 339–357.

Farah, M. J., Soso, M. J., & Dasheiff, R. M. (1992). Visual angle of the mind's eye before and after unilateral occipital lobectomy. *Journal of Experimental Psychology: Human Perception and Performance, 18*, 241–246.

Farver, P. F., & Farver, T. B. (1982). Performance of normal older adults on tests designed to measure parietal lobe functioning. *American Journal of Occupational Therapy, 36*, 444–449.

Fein, D., Pennington, B., Markowitz, P., Braverman, M., & Waterhouse, L. (1986). Towards a neuropsychological model of infantile autism: Are the social deficits primary? *Journal of the American Academy of Child Psychiatry, 25*(2), 198–212.

Feinberg, T. E., Mazlin, S. E., & Waldman, G. E. (1989). Recovery from brain damage: Neurologic considerations. In E. Perecman (Ed.), *Integrating theory and practice in clinical neuropsychology* (pp. 49–73). Hillsdale, NJ: Erlbaum.

Fiez, J., Petersen, S. E., Cheney, M. K., & Raichle, M. E. (1992). Impaired non-motor learning and error detection associated with cerebellar damage: A single case study. *Brain, 115*, 155–178.

Fiez, J. A., & Petersen, S. E. (1993). PET as part of an interdisciplinary approach to understanding processes involved in reading. *Psychological Science, 4*, 287–293.

Fisch, G. S. (1992). Is autism associated with the fragile X syndrome? *American Journal of Medical Genetics, 43*, 47–55.

Flicker, C., Ferris, S. H., Crook, T., & Bartus, R. T. (1987). Implications of memory and language dysfunction in the naming deficit of senile dementia. *Brain and Language, 31*, 187–200.

Flicker, C., Ferris, S. H., Crook, T., Bartus, R. T., & Reisberg, B. (1986). Cognitive decline in advanced age: The psychometric differentiation of normal and pathological age changes in cognitive function. *Developmental Neuropsychology, 2*, 309–322.

Fodor, J. (1985). The modularity of mind. *Behavioral and Brain Sciences, 8*, 1–42.

Foldi, N. S. (1987). Appreciation of pragmatic interpretation of indirect commands: Comparison of right and left brain-damaged patients. *Brain and Language, 31*, 88–108.

Fontenot, D. J. (1973). Visual field differences in the recognition of verbal and nonverbal stimuli in man. *Journal of Comparative and Physiological Psychology, 85*, 564–569.

Ford, J. M., Sullivan, E. V., Marsh, L., White, P. M., et al. (1994). The relationship between P$_{300}$ amplitude and regional gray matter volumes depends upon the attentional system engaged. *Electroencephalography and Clinical Neurophysiology*, *90*, 214–228.

Foundas, A. L., Leonard, D. M., Gilmore, R., Fennell, E., & Heilman, K. M. (1994). Planum temporale asymmetry and language dominance. *Neuropsychologia*, *10*, 1225–1231.

Fox, P. T., Raichle, M. E., Mintun, M. A., & Dence, C. (1988). Nonoxidative glucose consumption during focal physiologic neural activity. *Science*, *241*, 462–464.

Franco, L., & Sperry, R. W. (1977). Hemisphere lateralization for cognitive processing of geometry. *Neuropsychologia*, *15*, 107–114.

Fredrikson, M., Gustav, W., Greitz, T., Eriksson, L., Stone-Elander, S., Ericson, K., & Sedvall, G. (1993). Regional cerebral blood flow during experimental phobic fear. *Psychophysiology*, *30*, 126–130.

Freeman, E. A. (1991). Coma arousal therapy. *Clinical Rehabilitation*, *5*, 241–249.

Freiberg, L., Olsen, T. S., Roland, P. E., Paulson, O. B., & Lassen, N. A. (1985). Focal increase of blood flow in the cerebral cortex of man during vestibular stimulation. *Brain*, *108*, 609–623.

Freimuth, M., & Wapner, S. (1979). The influence of lateral organization on the evaluation of paintings. *British Journal of Psychology*, *70*, 211–218.

Fried, I., Mateer, C., Ojemann, G., Wohns, R., & Fedio, P. (1982). Organization of visuospatial functions in human cortex. *Brain*, *105*, 349–371.

Friedman, A., & Polson, M. C. (1981). The hemispheres as independent resource systems: Limited capacity processing and cerebral specialization. *Journal of Experimental Psychology: Human Perception and Performance*, *7*, 1031–1058.

Friedman, A., Polson, M. C., Dafoe, C. G., & Gaskill, S. J. (1982). Dividing attention within and between hemispheres: Testing a multiple resources approach to limited-capacity information processing. *Journal of Experimental Psychology: Human Perception and Performance*, *8*, 625–650.

Frisk, V., & Milner, B. (1990). The role of the left hippocampal region in the acquisition and retention of story content. *Neuropsychologia*, *28*(4), 349–359.

Frith, C. D., Friston, K. J., Liddle, P. F., & Frackowiak, R. S. J. (1991). A PET study of word finding. *Neuropsychologia*, *29*, 1137–1148.

Fudin, R., Renninger, L., Lembessis, E., & Hirshon, J. (1993). Sinistrality and reduced longevity: Reichler's 1979 data on baseball players do not indicate a relationship. *Perceptual and Motor Skills*, *76*, 171–182.

Fulton, J. F. (1935). A note on the definition of the "motor" and "premotor" areas. *Brain*, *58*, 311–316.

Funahashi, S., Bruce, C. J., & Goldman-Rakic, P. S. (1989). Mnemonic coding of visual space in the monkey's dorsolateral prefrontal cortex. *Journal of Neurophysiology*, *61*(2), 331–349.

Funahashi, S., Bruce, C. J., & Goldman-Rakic, P. S. (1991). Neuronal activity related to saccadic eye movements in the monkey's dorsolateral prefrontal cortex. *Journal of Neurophysiology*, *65*(6), 1464–1483.

Fuster, J. M. (1985). The prefrontal cortex, mediator of cross-temporal contingencies. *Human Neurobiology*, *4*, 169–179.

Fuster, J. M. (1989). *The prefrontal cortex* (2nd ed.). New York: Raven Press.

Gabrieli, J. D., Cohen, N. J., & Corkin, S. (1988). The impaired learning of semantic knowledge following bilateral medial temporal-lobe resection. *Brain and Cognition*, *7*(2), 157–177.

Gabrieli, J. D. E., Fleischman, D. A., Keane, M. M., Reminger, S. L., & Morrell, F. (1995). Double dissociation between memory systems underlying explicit and implicit memory in the human brain. *Psychological Science*, *6*(2), 76–82.

Gadow, K. D. (1981). Drug therapy for hyperactivity: Treatment procedures in natural settings. In K. D. Gadow & J. Loney (Eds.), *Psychosocial aspects of drug treatment for hyperactivity* (pp. 325–378). Boulder, CO: Westview Press.

Gaffan, D. (1974). Recognition impaired and association intact in the memory of monkeys after transection of the fornix. *Journal of Comparative and Physiological Psychology*, *86*, 1100–1109.

Gaffan, D. (1977). Monkey's recognition memory for complex pictures and the effects of fornix transection. *Quarterly Journal of Experimental Psychology*, *29*, 505–514.

Gainotti, G. (1972). Emotional behavior and hemisphere side of lesion. *Cortex*, *8*, 41–55.

Gainotti, G. (1989). Disorders of emotions and affect in patients with unilateral brain damage. In F. Boller & J. Grafman (Eds.), *Handbook of neuropsychology* (pp. 345–361). Amsterdam: Elsevier.

Gainotti, G., Cianchetti, C., & Tiacci, C. (1972). The influence of hemispheric side of lesions on non-verbal tasks of finger localization. *Cortex*, *8*, 364–381.

Galaburda, A. M., LeMay, M., Kemper, T. L., & Geschwind, N. (1978). Right-left asymmetries in the brain. *Science*, *199*, 852–856.

Galaburda, A. M., Sherman, G. F., Rosen, G. D., Aboitiz, F., & Geschwind, N. (1985). Developmental dyslexia: Four consecutive patients with cortical anomalies. *Annals of Neurology*, *18*, 222–233.

Gale, S. D., Johnson, S. C., Bigler, E. D., & Blatter, D. D. (1995). Nonspecific white matter degeneration following traumatic brain injury. *Journal of the International Neuropsychological Society*, *1*, 17–28.

Gardner, H. (1974). *The shattered mind*. New York: Vintage Books.

Gardner, H. (1983). *Frames of mind*. New York: Basic Books.

Gardner, H., Brownell, H. H., Wapner, W., & Michelow, D. (1983). Missing the point: The role of the right hemisphere in the processing of complex linguistic materials. In E. Perecman (Ed.), *Cognitive processing in the right hemisphere* (pp. 169–191). New York: Academic Press.

Gardner, H., King, P. K., Flamm, L., & Silverman, J. (1975). Comprehension and appreciation of humorous material following brain damage. *Brain*, *98*, 399–412.

Gardner, H., Silverman, J., Denes, G., Semenza, C., & Rosenstiel, A. K. (1977). Sensitivity to musical denotation and connotation in organic patients. *Cortex*, *13*, 242–256.

Garrett, M. F. (1975). The analysis of sentence production. In G. H. Bower (Ed.), *The psychology of learning and motivation* (pp. 133–177). New York: Academic Press.

Gasquoine, P. G. (1993). Alien hand sign. *Journal of Clinical and Experimental Neuropsychology, 15,* 653–667.

Gauggel, S. (1996). *Control of action after frontal lobe damage.* Manuscript submitted for publication.

Gaze, R. M. (1982). R. W. Sperry and the neuronal specificity hypothesis. *Trends in Neurosciences, 5*(10), 330–332.

Gazzaniga, M. S. (1970). *The bisected brain.* New York: Appleton-Century-Crofts.

Gazzaniga, M. S. (1983a). Reply to Levy and Zaidel. *American Psychologist, 38,* 547–549.

Gazzaniga, M. S. (1983b). Right hemisphere language following brain bisection: A 20-year perspective. *American Psychologist, 38,* 525–537.

Gazzaniga, M. S., Bogen, J. E., & Sperry, R. W. (1962). Some functional effects of sectioning the cerebral commissures in man. *Proceedings of the National Academy of Science, USA, 48,* 1765–1769.

Gazzaniga, M. S., & LeDoux, J. E. (1978). *The integrated mind.* New York: Plenum Press.

Geffen, G., Bradshaw, J. L., & Wallace, G. (1971). Interhemispheric effects on reaction time to verbal and nonverbal visual stimuli. *Journal of Experimental Psychology, 87,* 415–422.

Georgopoulos, A. P., Schwartz, A. B., & Kettner, R. E. (1986). Neuronal population coding of movement direction. *Science, 233,* 1416–1419.

Gerstmann, J. (1957). Some notes on the Gerstmann syndrome. *Neurology, 7,* 866–869.

Geschwind, N., & Galaburda, A. M. (1985a). Cerebral lateralization: Biological mechanisms, associations, and pathology: I. A hypothesis and a program for research. *Archives of Neurology, 42,* 428–459.

Geschwind, N., & Galaburda, A. M. (1985b). Cerebral lateralization: Biological mechanisms, associations, and pathology: II. A hypothesis and a program for research. *Archives of Neurology, 42,* 521–552.

Geschwind, N., & Galaburda, A. M. (1985c). Cerebral lateralization: Biological mechanisms, associations, and pathology: III. A hypothesis and a program for research. *Archives of Neurology, 42,* 634–654.

Geschwind, N., & Levitsky, W. (1968). Human brain: Left-right asymmetries in temporal speech region. *Science, 161,* 186–187.

Gibbs, C. J., Gajdusek, D. C., Asher, D. M., Alpers, M. P., Beck, E., Daniel, P. M., & Matthews, W. B. (1968). Creutzfeldt–Jakob disease (spongiform encephalopathy): Transmission to the chimpanzee. *Science, 161,* 388–389.

Gibson, C., & Bryden, M. P. (1983). Dichaptic recognition of shapes and letters in children. *Canadian Journal of Psychology, 37,* 132–143.

Giedd, J. N., Rumsey, J. M., Castellanor, F. X., Rajapakse, J. C., Kaysen, D., Vaituzis, A. C., Vauss, Y. C., Hamburger, S. D., & Rapoport, J. L. (1996). A quantitative MRI study of the corpus callosum in children and adolescents. *Developmental Brain Research, 91,* 274–280.

Gilger, J. W., Pennington, B. F., Green, P., Smith, S. M., & Smith, S. D. (1992). Reading disability, immune disorders and non-right-handedness: Twin and family studies of their relations. *Neuropsychologia, 30,* 209–227.

Gladstone, M., Best, C. T., & Davidson, R. J. (1989). Anomalous bimanual coordination among dyslexic boys. *Developmental Psychology, 25,* 236–246.

Glick, S. D., Ross, A. D., & Hough, L. B. (1982). Lateral asymmetry of neurotransmitters in human brain. *Brain Research, 234,* 53–63.

Glisky, E. L., & Schacter, D. L. (1987). Acquisition of domain-specific knowledge in organic amnesia: Training for computer-related work. *Neuropsychologia, 25*(6), 893–906.

Glisky, E. L., Schacter, D. L., & Tulving, E. (1986). Computer learning by memory-impaired patients: Acquisition and retention of complex knowledge. *Neuropsychologia, 24*(3), 313–328.

Glosser, G., & Friedman, R. B. (1990). The continuum of deep/phonological alexia. *Cortex, 26,* 343–359.

Glucksberg, S., & Keysar, B. (1990). Understanding metaphorical comparisons: Beyond similarity. *Psychological Review, 97,* 3–18.

Godwin-Austen, R. B. (1965). A case of visual disorientation. *Journal of Neurology, Neurosurgery and Psychiatry, 28,* 453–458.

Goetz, C. G., Tanner, C. M., Stebbins, G. T., Leipzig, G., & Carr, W. C. (1992). Adult tics in Gilles de la Tourette's syndrome: Description and risk factors. *Neurology, 42,* 784–788.

Goldberg, G. (1985). Supplementary motor area structure and function: Review and hypotheses. *Behavioral and Brain Sciences, 8,* 567–616.

Golden, C. J. (1981). A standardized version of Luria's neuropsychological tests. In S. Filskov & T. J. Boll (Eds.), *Handbook of clinical neuropsychology.* New York: Wiley Interscience.

Golden, C. J., Hammeke, T. A., & Purisch, A. D. (1978). Diagnostic validity of a standardized neuropsychological test battery derived from Luria's neuropsychological tests. *Journal of Consulting and Clinical Psychology, 46,* 1258–1265.

Golden, G. S. (1990). Tourette syndrome: Recent advances. *Pediatric Neurology, 8,* 705–714.

Goldman, P. (1974). An alternative to developmental plasticity: Heterology of CNS structures in infants and adults. In D. G. Stein, J. J. Rosen, & N. Butters (Eds.), *Plasticity and recovery from brain damage* (pp. 149–174). New York: Academic Press.

Goldman-Rakic, P. S. (1987). Circuitry of the prefrontal cortex and the regulation of behavior by representational knowledge. In F. Plum & V. Mountcastle (Eds.), *Handbook of physiology, Vol. 5.* Bethesda, MD: American Physiological Society.

Goldman-Rakic, P. S. (1988). Topography of cognition: Parallel distributed networks in primate association cortex. *Annual Review of Neuroscience, 11,* 137–156.

Goldman-Rakic, P. S. (1990). Cellular and circuit basis of working memory in prefrontal cortex of nonhuman primates. *Progress in Brain Research, 85,* 325–336.

Goldman-Rakic, P. S., & Rakic, P. (1984). Experimental modification of gyral patterns. In N. S. Geschwind & A. M. Galaburda (Eds.), *Cerebral dominance: The biological foundations.* Cambridge, MA: Harvard University Press.

Goodale, M. A., & Milner, A. D. (1992). Separate visual pathways for perception and action. *Trends in Neurosciences, 15,* 20–25.

Goodglass, H. (1976). Agrammatism. In H. Whitaker & H. A. Whitaker (Eds.), *Studies in neurolinguistics* (pp. 237–260). New York: Academic Press.

Goodlett, C. R., & West, J. R. (1992). Fetal alcohol effects: Rat model of alcohol exposure during the brain growth spurt. In I. S. Zagon & T. A. Slotkin (Eds.), *Maternal substance abuse and the developing nervous system* (pp. 45–76). New York: Academic Press.

Gordon, H. W. (1980). Degree of ear asymmetries for perception of dichotic chords and for illusory chord localization in musicians of different levels of competence. *Journal of Experimental Psychology: Human Perception and Performance, 6,* 516–527.

Gordon, J. W., & Bogen, J. E. (1974). Hemispheric lateralization of singing after intracarotid sodium amylobarbitone. *Journal of Neurology, Neurosurgery and Psychiatry, 37,* 727–738.

Gordon, W. A., Mann, N., & Willer, B. (1993). Demographic and social characteristics of the traumatic brain injury model system database. *Journal of Head Trauma Rehabilitation, 8,* 26–33.

Grady, C. L., Haxby, J. V., Horwitz, B., Schapiro, M. B., Rapoport, S. I., Ungerleider, L. G., Mishkin, M., Carson, R. E., & Herscovitch, P. (1992). Dissociation of object and spatial vision in human extrastriate cortex: Age-related changes in activation of regional cerebral blood flow measured with (-sup-1-sup-5O)water and positron emission tomography. *Journal of Cognitive Neuroscience, 4*(1), 23–34.

Graf, P., & Schacter, D. L. (1985). Implicit and explicit memory for new associations in normal and amnesic subjects. *Journal of Experimental Psychology: Learning, Memory, and Cognition, 11*(3), 501–518.

Graf, P., Squire, L. R., & Mandler, G. (1984). The information that amnesic patients do not forget. *Journal of Experimental Psychology: Learning, Memory, and Cognition, 10*(1), 164–178.

Grafman, J. (1989). Plans, actions, and mental sets: managerial knowledge units in the frontal lobes. In E. Perecman (Ed.), *Integrating theory and practice in clinical neuropsychology* (pp. 93–138). Hillsdale, NJ: Erlbaum.

Grafman, J., Jones, B., & Salazar, A. (1990). Wisconsin Card Sorting Test performance based on location and size of neuroanatomical lesion in Vietnam veterans with penetrating head injury. *Perceptual and Motor Skills, 71,* 1120–1122.

Grafman, J., & Salazar, A. (1987). Methodological considerations relevant to the comparison of recovery from penetrating and closed head injury. In H. S. Levin, J. Grafman, & H. M.

Eisenberg (Eds.), *Neurobehavioral recovery from head injury* (pp. 43–54). New York: Oxford University Press.

Grafman, J., Sirigu, A., Spector, L., & Hendler, J. (1993). Damage to the prefrontal cortex leads to decomposition of structured event complexes. *Journal of Head Rehabilitation, 8,* 73–87.

Grant, I., Olshen, R. A., Atkinson, J. H., Heaton, R. K., Nelson, J., McCutchan, J. A., & Weinrich, J. D. (1993). Depressed mood does not explain neuropsychological deficits in HIV-infected persons. *Neuropsychology, 7,* 53–61.

Gray, J. A. (in press). The contents of consciousness: A neuropsychological conjecture. *Behavioral and Brain Sciences.*

Graybiel, A. M. (1990). Neurotransmitters and neuromodulators in the basal ganglia. *Trends in Neurosciences, 13,* 246.

Graybiel, A. M., Aosaki, T., Flaherty, A. W., & Kimura, M. (1994). The basal ganglia and adaptive motor control. *Science, 265,* 1826–1831.

Greenblatt, S. H. (1973). Alexia without agraphia or hemianopia. Anatomical analysis of an autopsied case. *Brain, 96,* 307–316.

Greenough, W. T. (1975). Experiential modification of the developing brain. *American Scientist, 63,* 37–46.

Greenough, W. T. (1987). Experience effects on the developing and the mature brain: Dendritic branching and synaptogenesis. In N. A. Krasnegor, E. Blass, M. Hofer, & W. P. Smotherman (Eds.), *Perinatal development: A psychobiological perspective* (pp. 195–221). New York: Academic Press.

Greenough, W. T., & Chang, F.-L. F. (1988). Plasticity of synaptic structure in the cerebral cortex. In A. Peters & E. G. Jones (Eds.), *Cerebral cortex* (pp. 391–439). New York: Plenum Publishing.

Gross, C. G. (1992). Visual stimuli and the inferior temporal cortex. *Philosophical Transactions of the Royal Society of London, B335,* 3–10.

Gross, C. G., Bender, D. B., & Rocha-Miranda, C. E. (1969). Visual receptive fields of neurons in inferotemporal cortex of the monkey. *Science, 166,* 1303–1306.

Gross, C. G., & Mishkin, M. (1977). The neural basis of stimulus equivalence across retinal translation. In S. Harnad, R. Doty, J. Jaynes, L. Goldstein, & G. Krauthamer (Eds.), *Lateralization in the nervous system* (pp. 109–122). New York: Academic Press.

Gross, C. G., Rocha-Miranda, C. E., & Bender, D. B. (1972). Visual properties of neurons in inferotemporal cortex of the macaque. *Journal of Neurophysiology, 35,* 96–111.

Grossman, M. (1988). Drawing deficits in brain-damaged patients' freehand pictures. *Brain and Cognition, 8,* 192–213.

Groves, P. M., & Rebec, G. V. (1988). *Introduction to biological psychology* (3rd ed.). Dubuque, IA: William C. Brown.

Guariglia, C., & Antonucci, G. (1992). Personal and extrapersonal space: A case of neglect dissociation. *Neuropsychologia, 30,* 1001–1009.

Guitton, D., Buchtel, H. A., & Douglas, R. M. (1985). Frontal lobe lesions in man cause difficulties in suppressing reflexive glances and in generating goal-directed saccades. *Experimental Brain Research, 58,* 455–472.

Gunderson, C. H. (1990). *Essentials of clinical neurology.* New York: Raven Press.

Gur, R. C., Gur, R. E., Obrist, W. D., Skolnick, B. E., & Reivitch, M. (1987). Age and regional cerebral blood flow at rest and during cognitive activity. *Archives of General Psychiatry, 44,* 617–621.

Gur, R. C., Mozley, L. H., Mozley, P. D., Resnick, S. M., Karp, J. S., Alvai, B., Arnold, S. E., & Gur, R. E. (1995). Sex differences in regional cerebral glucose metabolism during a resting state. *Science, 267,* 528–531.

Gur, R. E. (1978). Left hemisphere dysfunction and left hemisphere overactivation in schizophrenia. *Journal of Abnormal Psychology, 87,* 226–238.

Gusella, J. G., Wexler, N. S., Conneally, P. A., Naylor, S. L., Anderson, M. A., Tanzi, R. E., Watkins, P. C., Ottina, K., Wallace, M. R., Sakaguchi, A. Y., Young, A. B., Shoulson, I., Bonillo, E., & Martin, J. B. (1983). A polymorphic DNA marker genetically linked to Huntington's disease. *Nature, 306,* 234–238.

Habib, M., Gayraud, D., Oliva, A., Regis, J., Salamon, G., & Khalil, R. (1991). Effects of handedness and sex on the morphology of the corpus callosum: A study with brain magnetic resonance imaging. *Brain and Cognition, 16,* 41–61.

Habib, M., & Sirigu, A. (1987). Pure topographical disorientation: A definition and anatomical basis. *Cortex, 23,* 73–85.

Haist, F., Shimamura, A. P., & Squire, L. R. (1992). On the relationship between recall and recognition memory. *Journal of Experimental Psychology: Learning, Memory, and Cognition, 18*(4), 691–702.

Halpern, D. F., & Coren, S. (1993). Left-handedness and life span: A reply to Harris. *Psychological Bulletin, 114,* 235–241.

Hannay, H. J., Rogers, J. P., & Durant, R. F. (1976). Complexity as a determinant of visual field effects for random forms. *Acta Psychologica (Amsterdam), 40,* 29–34.

Hannay, H. J., Varney, N., & Benton, A. L. (1976). Visual localization in patients with unilateral cerebral brain disease. *Journal of Neurology, Neurosurgery and Psychiatry, 39,* 307–313.

Hansch, E. C., & Pirozzolo, F. J. (1980). Task relevant effects on the assessment of cerebral specialization for facial emotion. *Brain and Language, 10,* 51–59.

Hardy, J. A., & Higgins, G. A. (1992). Alzheimer's disease: The amyloid cascade hypothesis. *Science, 25,* 184–185.

Harmony, T. (1989). Psychophysiological evaluation of children's neuropsychological disorders. In C. R. Reynolds & E. Fletcher-Janzen (Eds.), *Handbook of clinical child neuropsychology* (pp. 265–270). New York: Plenum Press.

Harris, L. J. (1993a). Do left-handers die sooner than right-handers? Commentary on Coren and Halpern's (1991) "Left-handedness: A marker for decreased survival fitness." *Psychological Bulletin, 114,* 203–234.

Harris, L. J. (1993b). "Left-handedness and life span": Reply to Halpern and Coren. *Psychological Bulletin, 114,* 242–247.

Harrison, P. J., & Roberts, G. W. (1991). "Life, Jim, but not as we know it?" Transmissible dementias and the prion protein. *British Journal of Psychiatry, 158,* 457–470.

Hart, J., Berndt, R. S., & Caramazza, A. (1985). Category-specific naming deficit following cerebral infarction. *Nature, 316,* 439–440.

Hart, S., & Semple, J. M. (1990). *Neuropsychology and the dementias.* London: Ehrlbaum.

Hartman, D. E. (1987). Neuropsychological toxicology: Identification and assessment of neurotoxic syndromes. *Archives of Clinical Neuropsychology, 2,* 45–65.

Harwood, K., & Wickens, C. D. (1991). Frames of reference for helicopter electronic maps: The relevance of spatial cognition and componential analysis. *International Journal of Aviation Psychology, 1,* 5–23.

Hasher, L., & Zacks, R. (1988). Working memory, comprehension, and aging: A review and a new view. In G. Bower (Ed.), *The psychology of learning and motivation* (pp. 193–225). New York: Academic Press.

Hatta, T. (1977). Functional hemisphere asymmetries in an inferential thought task. *Psychologia, 20,* 145–150.

Haug, H., Barmwater, U., Eggers, R., Fischer, D., Kuhl, S., & Sass, N. L. (1983). Anatomical changes in aging brain: Morphometric analysis of the human prosencephalon. In J. Cerbos-Navarro & H. I. Sarkander (Eds.), *Neuropharmacology: Vol. 21. Aging* (pp. 1–12). New York: Raven Press.

Hauser, T. (1991). *Muhammad Ali: His life and times.* New York: Simon & Schuster.

Hawrylak, N., & Greenough, W. T. (1995). Plasticity of astrocytes: A review and hypothesis.

Haxby, J. V., Grady, C. L., Koss, E., Horwitz, B., Heston, L., Scapiro, M., Friedland, R. P., & Rapoport, S. I. (1990). Longitudinal study of cerebral metabolic asymmetries and associated neuropsychological patterns in early dementia of the Alzheimer type. *Archives of Neurology, 47,* 753–760.

Haxby, J. V., Horwitz, B., Ungerleider, L. G., Maisog, J. M., Pietrini, P., & Grady, C. L. (1994). The functional organization of human extrastriate cortex: A PET-rCBF study of selective attention to faces and locations. *Journal of Neuroscience, 14*(11), 6336–6353.

Heaton, R. K., Grant, I., Butters, N., White, D. A., Kirson, D., Atkinson, J. H., McCutchan, J. A., Taylor, M. J., Kelly, M. D., Ellis, R. J., Wolfson, T., Velin, R., Marcotte, T. D., Hesselink, J. R., Jernigan, T. L., Chandler, J., Wallace, M., Abramson, I., & Group, T. H. (1995). The HNRC 500—Neuropsychology of HIV infection at different disease stages. *Journal of the International Neuropsychological Society, 1,* 231–251.

Hécaen, H. (1962). Clinical symptomology in right and left hemisphere lesions. In V. B. Mountcastle (Ed.), *Interhemispheric relations and cerebral dominance* (pp. 215–243). Baltimore: Johns Hopkins University Press.

Hécaen, H., & Kremin, H. (1976). Neurolinguistic research on reading disorder from left hemisphere lesions: Aphasic and "pure" alexias. In H. A. Whitaker & H. Whitaker (Eds.),

Studies in neurolinguistics II (pp. 269–329). New York: Academic Press.

Hécaen, H., & Rondot, P. (1985). Apraxia as a disorder of signs. In E. Roy (Ed.), *Neuropsychological studies of apraxia and related disorders*. Amsterdam: Elsevier-North Holland.

Hefti, E., & Weiner, W. J. (1986). Nerve growth factor and Alzheimer's disease. *Annals of Neurology, 20,* 275–281.

Heilman, K., Bowers, D., Speedie, L., & Coslett, H. B. (1984). Comprehension of affective and nonaffective prosody. *Neurology, 34,* 917–921.

Heilman, K. M., Bowers, D., Coslett, H. B., Whelan, H., & Watson, R. T. (1985). Directional hypokinesia: Prolonged reaction times for leftward movements in patients with right hemisphere lesions and neglect. *Neurology, 35,* 855–859.

Heilman, K. M., Rothi, L. J., & Valenstein, E. (1982). Two forms of ideomotor apraxia. *Neurology, 32,* 342–346.

Heilman, K. M., & Rothi, L. J. G. (1985). Apraxia. In K. M. Heilman & E. Valenstein (Eds.), *Clinical neuropsychology* (2nd ed., pp. 131–150). New York: Oxford University Press.

Heilman, K. M., Scholes, R., & Watson, R. T. (1975). Auditory affective agnosia: Disturbed comprehension of affective speech. *Journal of Neurology, Neurosurgery and Psychiatry, 38,* 69–72.

Heilman, K. M., & Valenstein, E. (1972). Frontal lobe neglect in man. *Neurology, 22,* 660–664.

Heilman, K. M., Watson, R. T., & Valenstein, E. (1985). Neglect and related disorders. In K. M. Heilman & E. Valenstein (Eds.), *Clinical neuropsychology* (2nd ed.). New York: Oxford University Press.

Heller, W. (1986). *Cerebral organization of emotional function in children*. Unpublished doctoral dissertation, University of Chicago.

Heller, W. (1987). Lateralization of emotional content in children's drawings. *Scientific proceedings of the annual meeting of the American Academy of Child and Adolescent Psychiatry, 3,* 63.

Heller, W. (1988). Asymmetry of emotional judgements in children. *Journal of Clinical and Experimental Neuropsychology, 10,* 36.

Heller, W. (1990). The neuropsychology of emotion: Developmental patterns and implications for psychopathology. In N. Stein, B. L. Leventhal, & T. Trabasso (Eds.), *Psychological and biological approaches to emotion* (pp. 167–211). Hillsdale, NJ: Erlbaum.

Heller, W. (1991). New territory: Creativity and brain injury. *Creative Woman, 11,* 16–18.

Heller, W. (1993a). Gender differences in depression: Perspectives from neuropsychology. *Journal of Affective Disorders, 29,* 129–143.

Heller, W. (1993b). Neuropsychological mechanisms of individual differences in emotion, personality, and arousal. *Neuropsychology, 7,* 476–489.

Heller, W. (1994). Cognitive and emotional organization of the brain: Influences on the creation and perception of art. In D. Zaidel (Ed.), *Neuropsychology* (pp. 271–292). San Diego: Academic Press.

Heller, W., Hopkins, J., & Cox, S. (1991). Effects of lateralized brain damage on infant socioemotional development. *Journal of Clinical and Experimental Neuropsychology, 13,* 64.

Heller, W., & Levy, J. (1981). Perception and expression of emotion in right-handers and left-handers. *Neuropsychologia, 19,* 263–272.

Hellige, J. B. (1993a). *Hemispheric asymmetry: What's right and what's left*. Cambridge, MA: Harvard University Press.

Hellige, J. B. (1993b). Unity of thought and action: Varieties of interaction between the left and right cerebral hemispheres. *Current Directions in Psychological Science, 2,* 21–25.

Hellige, J. B., & Cox, P. J. (1976). Effects of concurrent verbal memory on recognition of stimuli from the left and right visual fields. *Journal of Experimental Psychology: Human Perception and Performance, 2,* 210–221.

Hellige, J. B., & Michimata, C. (1989). Categorization versus distance: Hemispheric differences for processing spatial information. *Memory and Cognition, 17,* 770–776.

Hellige, J. B., Taylor, A. K., & Eng, T. L. (1989). Interhemispheric interaction when both hemispheres have access to the same stimulus information. *Journal of Experimental Psychology: Human Perception and Performance, 15,* 711–722.

Hellige, J. B., & Webster, R. (1979). Right hemisphere superiority for initial stages of letter processing. *Neuropsychologia, 17,* 653–660.

Helm-Estabrooks, N. (1983). Exploiting the right hemisphere for language rehabilitation: Melodic intonation therapy. In E. Perecman (Ed.), *Cognitive processing in the right hemisphere*. New York: Academic Press.

Henderson, A. S. (1988). The risk factors for Alzheimer's disease: A review and hypothesis. *Acta Psychiatrica Scandinavica, 78,* 257–275.

Henik, A., Singh, J., Beckley, R. J., & Rafal, R. D. (1993). Disinhibition of automatic word reading in Parkinson's disease. *Cortex, 29,* 589–599.

Henke, P. G. (1982). Telencephalic limbic system and experimental gastric pathology: A review. *Neuroscience and Biobehavioral Reviews, 6,* 381–390.

Henriques, J. B., & Davidson, R. J. (1991). Left frontal hypoactivation in depression. *Journal of Abnormal Psychology, 100,* 535–545.

Hess, R. F., Baker, C. L., & Zihl, J. (1989). The motion-blind patient: Low-level spatial and temporal filters. *Journal of Neuroscience, 9,* 1628–1640.

Heumann, D., & Leuba, G. (1983). Neuronal death in the development and aging of the cerebral cortex of the mouse. *Neuropathology and Applied Neurobiology, 9,* 297–311.

Hicks, R. A., Johnson, C., Cuevas, T., Deharo, D., & Bautista, J. (1994). Do right-handers live longer? An updated assessment of baseball player data. *Perceptual and Motor Skills, 78*(3, Pt. 2), 1243–1247.

Hicks, R. A., Pass, K., Freeman, H., Bautista, J., et al. (1993).

Handedness and accidents with injury. *Perceptual and Motor Skills, 77*(3, Pt. 2), 1119–1122.

Hier, D. B., Hagenlocker, K., & Shindler, A. G. (1985). Language disintegration in dementia: Effects of etiology and severity. *Brain and Language, 25*, 117–133.

Hiller, W., Zaudig, M., & Rose, M. (1989). The overlap between depression and anxiety on different levels of psychopathology. *Journal of Affective Disorders, 16*, 223–231.

Hilliger, L. A., & Koenig, O. (1991). Separable mechanisms in face processing: Evidence from hemispheric specialization. *Journal of Cognitive Neuroscience, 3*, 42–58.

Hillis, A. E., & Caramazza, A. (1991). Deficit to stimulus-centered, letter shape representations in a case of "unilateral neglect." *Neuropsychologia, 29*(12), 1223–1240.

Hillyard, S. A., Hink, R. F., Schwent, V. L., & Picton, T. W. (1973). Electrical signs of selective attention in the human brain. *Science, 182*, 177–180.

Hillyard, S. A., & Kutas, M. (1983). *Annual Review of Psychology, 34*, 33–61.

Hirshkowitz, M., Earle, J., & Paley, B. (1978). EEG alpha asymmetry in musicians and non-musicians: A study of hemispheric specialization. *Neuropsychologia, 16*, 125–128.

Hirst, W., Johnson, M. K., Kim, J. K., Phelps, E. A., Risse, G., & Volpe, B. T. (1986). Recognition and recall in amnesics. *Journal of Experimental Psychology: Learning, Memory, and Cognition, 12*, 445–451.

Hirst, W., & Volpe, B. T. (1984). Automatic and effortful encoding in amnesia. In M. S. Gazzaniga (Ed.), *Handbook of cognitive neuroscience.* New York: Plenum Press.

Hiscock, M., Inch, R., Jacek, C., Hiscock-Kalil, C., & Kalil, K. M. (1994). Is there a sex difference in human laterality? I. An exhaustive survey of auditory laterality studies from six neuropsychology journals. *Journal of Clinical and Experimental Neuropsychology, 16*, 423–435.

Hiscock, M., Israelian, M., Inch, R., Jacek, C., Hiscock-Kalil, C. (1995). Is there a sex difference in human laterality? II. An exhaustive survey of visual laterality studies from six neuropsychology journals. *Journal of Clinical and Experimental Neuropsychology, 17*, 590–610.

Hochberg, F., & LeMay, M. (1975). Arteriographic correlates of handedness. *Neurology, 25*(3), 218–222.

Hodges, J. R., Salmon, D. P., & Butters, N. (1992). Semantic memory impairment in Alzheimer's disease: Failure of access or degraded knowledge? *Neuropsychologia, 30*, 301–314.

Hoffman, J. E. (1990). Event-related potentials and automatic and controlled processes. In J. W. Rohrbaugh, R. Parasuraman, & R. Johnson (Eds.), *Event-related brain potentials: Basic issues and applications* (pp. 145–157). New York: Oxford University Press.

Holland, A. L., McBurney, D. H., Mossy, J., & Reinmuth, O. M. (1985). The dissolution of language in Pick's disease with neurofibrillary tangles: A case study. *Brain and Language, 24*, 36–58.

Holloway, R. L. (1980). Indonesian "solo" (Ngandong) endocranial reconstructions: Some preliminary observations and comparisons with Neanderthal and Homo erectus groups. *American Journal of Physical Anthropology, 53*, 285–295.

Holmes, G. (1919). Disturbances of visual orientation. *British Journal of Ophthalmology, 2*, 449–468, 506–518.

Holtzman, J. D., & Gazzaniga, M. S. (1982). Dual task interactions due exclusively to limits in processing resources. *Science, 218*, 1325–1327.

Hoorweg, J., & Stanfield, J. P. (1976). The effects of protein energy malnutrition in early childhood on intellectual and motor abilities in later childhood and adolescence. *Developmental Medicine and Child Neurology, 18*, 330–350.

Hornak, J. (1992). Ocular exploration in the dark by patients with visual neglect. *Neuropsychologia, 30*, 547–552.

Hough, M. S. (1990). Narrative comprehension in adults with right and left hemisphere brain-damage: Theme organization. *Brain and Language, 38*, 253–277.

Hubel, D. H., & Wiesel, T. N. (1970). The period of susceptibility to the physiological effects of unilateral eye closure in kittens. *Journal of Physiology, 206*, 419–436.

Huber, S. J., Christy, J. A., & Paulson, G. W. (1991). Cognitive heterogeneity associated with clinical subtypes of Parkinson's disease. *Neuropsychiatry, Neuropsychology and Behavioral Neurology, 4*, 147–157.

Hughes, H. C., Fendrich, R., & Reuter-Lorenz, P. A. (1990). Global versus local processing in the absence of low spatial frequencies. *Journal of Cognitive Neuroscience, 2*, 272–282.

Humphreys, G. W., & Riddoch, M. J. (1984). Routes to object constancy: Implications from neurological impairments of object constancy. *Quarterly Journal of Experimental Psychology: Human Experimental Psychology, 36A*(3), *36A*, 385–415.

Humphreys, P., Kaufmann, W. E., & Galaburda, A. M. (1990). Developmental dyslexia in women: Neuropathological findings in three patients. *Annals of Neurology, 28*, 727–738.

Huttenlocher, P. R. (1979). Synaptic density in human frontal cortex: Developmental changes and effects of aging. *Brain Research, 163*, 195–205.

Huttenlocher, P. R. (1990). Morphometric study of human cerebral cortex development. *Neuropsychologia, 28*, 517–527.

Huttenlocher, P. R. (1994). Synaptogenesis in human cerebral cortex. In G. Dawson & K. W. Fischer (Eds.), *Human behavior and the developing brain* (pp. 137–152). New York: Guilford Press.

Hynd, G. W., & Cohen, M. (1983). *Dyslexia: Neuropsychological theory, research, and clinical differentiation.* New York: Grune & Stratton.

Hynd, G. W., & Semrud-Clikeman, M. (1989). Dyslexia and brain morphology. *Psychological Bulletin, 106*, 447–482.

Ivry, R. B., & Keele, S. W. (1989). Timing functions of the cerebellum. *Journal of Cognitive Neuroscience, 1*, 136–152.

Ivry, R. B., & Lebby, P. C. (1993). Hemispheric differences in auditory perception are similar to those found in visual perception. *Psychological Science, 4*(1), 41–45.

Jacobs, L., Munschauer, F. E., & Pullicino, P. (1993). Current treatment strategies and perspectives of multiple sclerosis. In

U. Halbreich (Ed.), *Multiple sclerosis: A neuropsychiatric disorder*. Washington, DC: American Psychiatric Press.

Jacoby, L. L. (1984). Incidental versus intentional retrieval: Remembering and awareness as separate issues. In L. R. Squire & N. Butters (Eds.), *Neuropsychology of memory* (pp. 145–156). New York: Guilford Press.

Jakobson, L. S., Archibald, Y. M., Carey, D. P., & Goodale, M. A. (1991). A kinematic analysis of reaching and grasping movements in a patient recovering from optic ataxia. *Neuropsychologia, 29*, 803–809.

James, W. (1890). *The principles of psychology*. New York: Holt.

Janowsky, J. S., Shimamura, A. P., & Squire, L. R. (1989). Source memory impairment in patients with frontal lobe lesions. *Neuropsychologia, 27*(8), 1043–1056.

Jenkins, W. M., Merzenich, M. M., & Recanzone, G. (1990). Neocortical representational dynamics in adult primates: Implications for neuropsychology. *Neuropsychologia, 28*, 573–584.

Jernigan, T. L., & Ostergaard, A. L. (1993). Word priming and recognition memory are both affected by mesial temporal lobe damage. *Neuropsychology, 7*, 14–26.

Jessell, T. M. (1991). Reactions of neurons to injury. In E. R. Kandel, J. H. Schwartz, & T. M. Jessell (Eds.), *Principles of neural science* (3rd ed., pp. 258–282). New York: Elsevier.

Jetter, W., Poser, U., Freeman, R. B. J., & Markowitsch, H. J. (1986). A verbal long term memory deficit in frontal lobe damaged patients. *Cortex, 22*, 229–242.

Johnson, J. S., & Newport, E. L. (1989). Critical period effects in second language learning: The influence of maturational state on the acquisition of English as a second language. *Cognitive Psychology, 21*(1), 60–99.

Jones-Gotman, M. (1986a). Memory for designs: The hippocampal contribution. *Neuropsychologia, 24*, 193–203.

Jones-Gotman, M. (1986b). Right hippocampal excision impairs learning and recall of a list of abstract designs. *Neuropsychologia, 24*, 659–670.

Jones-Gotman, M., & Milner, B. (1977). Design fluency: The invention of nonsense drawings after focal cortical lesions. *Neuropsychologia, 15*, 653–674.

Jonides, J., Smith, E. E., Koeppe, R. A., Awh, E., Minoshima, S., & Mintun, M. A. (1993). Spatial working memory in humans as revealed by PET. *Nature, 363*, 623–625.

Josiassen, R. C., Curry, L. M., & Mancall, E. L. (1982). Patterns of intellectual deficit in Huntington's disease. *Journal of Clinical Neuropsychology, 4*, 173–183.

Julesz, B. (1964). Binocular depth perception without familiarity cues. *Science, 145*, 356.

Juraska, J. (1991). Sex difference in "cognitive" regions of the rat brain. *Psychoneuroendocrinology, 16*, 105–119.

Juraska, J. M., Henderson, C., & Muller, J. (1984). Differential rearing experience, gender, and radial maze performance. *Developmental Psychobiology, 17*, 209–215.

Kahle, Leonhardt, & Platzer. *Color atlas and textbook of human anatomy: Vol. 3. Nervous system and sensory organs*. Chicago: Year Book Medical.

Kahneman, D. (1973). *Attention and effort*. Englewood Cliffs, NJ: Prentice Hall.

Kalat, J. W. (1992). *Biological psychology* (4th ed.). Belmont, CA: Wadsworth.

Kandel, E. R., Schwartz, J. H., & Jessell, T. M. (Eds.). (1991). *Principles of neural science* (3rd ed.). New York: Elsevier.

Kandel, E. R., Schwartz, J. H., & Jessell, T. M. (1995). *Essentials of neural science and behavior*. Norwalk, CT: Appleton & Lange.

Kaplan, E., Fein, D., Morris, R., & Delis, D. C. (1991). *Manual for the WAIS-R as a neuropsychological instrument*. San Antonio, TX: Psychological Corporation.

Kaplan, J. A., Brownell, H. H., Jacobs, J. R., & Gardner, H. (1990). The effects of right hemisphere damage on the pragmatic interpretation of conversational remarks. *Brain and Language, 38*, 315–333.

Kapur, N. (1993). Focal retrograde amnesia in neurological disease: A critical review. *Cortex, 29*(2), 217–234.

Karlinsky, H. (1986). Alzheimer's disease and Down's syndrome: A review. *Journal of the American Geriatrics Society, 34*, 728–734.

Karni, A., Meyer, G., Jezzard, P., Adams, M., Turner, R., & Ungerleider, L. G. (1995). Functional MRI evidence for adult motor cortex plasticity during motor skill learning. *Nature, 377*, 155–158.

Katon, W., & Roy-Byrne, P. P. (1991). Mixed anxiety and depression. *Journal of Abnormal Psychology, 100*, 337–345.

Katzman, R. (1993). Education and the prevalence of Alzheimer's disease. *Neurology, 43*, 13–20.

Kay, D. W. K., Henderson, A. S., Scott, R., Wilson, J., Rickwood, D., & Grayson, D. A. (1985). Dementia and depression among the elderly living in the Hobart community: The effect of the diagnostic criteria on the prevalence rates. *Psychological Medicine, 15*, 771–788.

Keane, M. M., Clarke, H., & Corkin, S. (1992). Impaired perceptual priming and intact conceptual priming in a patient with bilateral posterior cerebral lesions. *Society for Neuroscience Abstracts, 18*, 386.

Keane, M. M., Gabrieli, J. D., Fennema, A. C., Growdon, J. H., & Corkin, S. (1991). Evidence for a dissociation between perceptual and conceptual priming in Alzheimer's disease. *Behavioral Neuroscience, 105*(2), 326–342.

Keele, S. (1968). Movement control in skilled motor performance. *Psychological Bulletin, 70*, 387–403.

Kemper, T. (1984). Neuroanatomical and neuropathological changes in normal aging and dementia. In M. A. Albert (Ed.), *Clinical neurology of aging*. New York: Oxford University Press.

Kendrick, K. M., & Baldwin, B. A. (1987). Cells in temporal cortex of conscious sheep can respond preferentially to the sight of faces. *Science, 236*, 448–450.

Kennard, M. A. (1936). Age and other factors in motor recovery from precentral lesions in monkeys. *Journal of Neurophysiology, 1*, 477–496.

Kennard, M. A. (1942). Cortical reorganization of motor function. *Archives of Neurological Psychiatry, 48*, 227–240.

Kent, R. D., & Rosenbek, J. (1982). Prosodic disturbance and neurologic lesion. *Brain and Language, 15,* 259–291.

Kertesz, A., & Clydesdale, S. (1994). Neuropsychological deficits in vascular dementia vs. Alzheimer's disease: Frontal lobe deficits prominent in vascular dementia. *Archives of Neurology, 51,* 1226–1231.

Kertesz, A., Ferro, J. U., & Shewan, C. M. (1984). Apraxia and aphasia: The functional anatomical basis for their dissociation. *Neurology, 34,* 40–47.

Kim, S. G., Ugurbil, K., & Strick, P. L. (1994). Activation of a cerebellar output nucleus during cognitive processing. *Science, 265,* 949–951.

Kimberg, D. Y., & Farah, M. J. (1993) A unified account of cognitive impairments following frontal lobe damage: The role of working memory in complex, organized behavior. *Journal of Experimental Psychology: General, 122,* 411–428.

Kimble, D. P. (1990). Functional effects of neural grafting in the mammalian central nervous system. *Psychological Bulletin, 108,* 462–479.

Kimura, D. (1967). Functional asymmetry of the brain in dichotic listening. *Cortex, 3,* 164–178.

Kimura, D. (1969). Spatial localization in left and right visual fields. *Canadian Journal of Psychology, 23,* 445–458.

Kimura, D. (1977). Acquisition of a motor skill after left hemisphere damage. *Brain, 100,* 337–350.

Kimura, D. (1980). Neuromotor mechanisms in the evolution of human communication. In H. D. Steklis & M. J. Raleigh (Eds.), *Neurobiology of social communication in primates: An evolutionary perspective.* New York: Academic Press.

Kimura, D. (1982). Left-hemisphere control of oral and brachial movements and their relation to communication. *Philosophical Transactions of the Royal Society of London, B298,* 135–149.

Kimura, D., & Faust, R. (1987). Spontaneous drawing in an unselected sample of patients with unilateral brain damage. In D. Ottoson (Ed.), *Duality and unity of the brain: Unified functioning and specialisation of the hemispheres* (pp. 114–146). New York: Plenum Press.

Kimura, D., & Hampson, E. (1994). Cognitive pattern in men and women is influenced by fluctuations in sex hormones. *Current Directions in Psychological Science, 3,* 57–61.

Kimura, D., & Watson, N. (1989). The relation between oral movement control and speech. *Brain and Language, 37,* 565–590.

King, F. L., & Kimura, D. (1972). Left-ear superiority in dichotic perception of vocal nonverbal sounds. *Canadian Journal of Psychology, 26,* 111–116.

Kinsbourne, M. (1974). Lateral interaction in the brain. In M. Kinsbourne & W. L. Smith (Eds.), *Hemispheric disconnections and cerebral function* (pp. 239–259). Springfield, IL: Charles C Thomas.

Kinsbourne, M. (1975). The mechanisms of hemispheric control of the lateral gradient of attention. In P. M. A. Rabbitt & S. Dornic (Eds.), *Attention and performance.* New York: Academic Press.

Kinsbourne, M., & Warrington, E. K. (1962). A study of finger agnosia. *Brain, 85,* 47–66.

Kirk, A., & Kertesz, A. (1989). Hemispheric contributions to drawing. *Neuropsychologia, 27,* 881–886.

Kirk, A., & Kertesz, A. (1993). Subcortical contributions to drawing. *Brain and Cognition, 21,* 57–70.

Kitterle, F. L., Hellige, J. B., & Christman, S. (1992). Visual hemispheric asymmetries depend on which spatial frequencies are task relevant. *Brain and Cognition, 20,* 308–314.

Klein, D., Moscovitch, M., & Vigna, C. (1976). Attentional mechanisms and perceptual asymmetries in tachistoscopic recognition of words and faces. *Neuropsychologia, 14,* 335–338.

Klisz, D. (1978). Neuropsychological evaluation of older persons. In M. Storandt (Ed.), *The clinical psychology of aging* (pp. 71–95). New York: Plenum Press.

Klüver, H., & Bucy, P. C. (1937). "Psychic blindness" and other symptoms following bilateral temporal lobectomy in rhesus monkeys. *American Journal of Physiology, 119,* 352–353.

Klüver, H., & Bucy, P. C. (1939). Preliminary analysis of the functions of the temporal lobes in monkeys. *Archives of Neurology and Psychiatry, 42,* 979–1000.

Knight, R. (1989). Creutzfeldt–Jakob disease. *British Journal of Hospital Medicine, 41,* 165–171.

Knight, R. B. (1992). *The neuropsychology of degenerative brain diseases.* Hillsdale, NJ: Erlbaum.

Knight, R. T. (1991). Evoked potential studies of attention capacity in human frontal lobe lesions. In H. S. Levin, H. M. Eisenberg, & A. L. Benton (Eds.), *Frontal lobe function and dysfunction* (pp. 139–153). New York: Oxford University Press.

Knight, R. T., Scabini, D., Woods, D. L., & Clayworth, C. C. (1989). Contribution of temporal-parietal junction to the human auditory P_3. *Brain Research, 502,* 109–116.

Knott, V. J., & Lapierre, Y. D. (1987). Electrophysiological and behavioral correlates of psychomotor responsivity in depression. *Biological Psychiatry, 22,* 313–324.

Knowlton, B. J., Ramus, S. J., & Squire, L. R. (1992). Intact artificial grammar learning in amnesia: Dissociation of classification learning and explicit memory for specific instances. *Psychological Science, 3,* 172–179.

Knowlton, B. J., & Squire, L. R. (1994). The information acquired during artificial grammar learning: Item similarity vs. grammaticality. *Journal of Experimental Psychology: Learning, Memory, and Cognition, 20,* 79–91.

Kohn, B., & Dennis, M. (1974). Selective impairments of visuospatial abilities in infantile hemiplegics after right cerebral hemidecortication. *Neuropsychologia, 12,* 505–512.

Kolb, B. (1989). Brain development, plasticity, and behavior. *American Psychologist, 44,* 1203–1212.

Kolb, B., & Fantie, B. (1989). Development of the child's brain and behavior. In C. R. Reynolds & E. Fletcher-Janzen (Eds.), *Handbook of clinical child neuropsychology* (pp. 17–39). New York: Plenum Press.

Kolb, B., & Milner, B. (1981). Performance of complex arm and facial movements after focal brain lesions. *Neuropsychologia, 19,* 291–308.

Kolb, B., & Taylor, L. (1981). Affective behavior in patients with localized cortical excisions: Role of lesion site and side. *Science, 214,* 89–91.

Kolb, B., & Whishaw, I. Q. (1985). *Fundamentals of human neuropsychology* (2nd ed.). New York: Freeman.

Kolb, B., & Whishaw, I. Q. (1990). *Fundamentals of human neuropsychology* (3rd ed.). New York: Freeman.

Komatsu, H., & Wurtz, R. H. (1988). Relation of cortical areas MT and MST to pursuit eye movements. I. Localization and visual properties of neurons. *Journal of Neurophysiology, 60,* 580–603.

Kondo, K., Niino, M., & Shido, K. (1994). A case-control study of Alzheimer's disease in Japan: Significance of life-styles. *Dementia, 5,* 314–326.

Koopmans, R. A., Li, D. K., Grochowski, E., Cutler, P. J., & Paty, D. W. (1989). Benign versus chronic progressive multiple sclerosis: Magnetic resonance imaging features. *Annals of Neurology, 25,* 74–81.

Kopelman, M. D. (1989). Remote and autobiographical memory, temporal context memory and frontal atrophy in Korsakoff and Alzheimer patients. *Neuropsychologia, 27,* 437–460.

Koranyi, E. K. (1988). The cortical dementias. *Canadian Journal of Psychiatry, 33,* 838–845.

Kosslyn, S. M. (1973). Scanning visual images. Some structural implications. *Perception and Psychophysics, 14,* 90–94.

Kosslyn, S. M. (1987). Seeing and imagining in the cerebral hemispheres: A computational approach. *Psychological Review, 94,* 148–175.

Kosslyn, S. M. (1990). Mental imagery. In D. N. Osherson, S. M. Kosslyn, & J. M. Hollerbach (Eds.), *Visual cognition and action* (pp. 73–97). Cambridge, MA: MIT Press.

Kosslyn, S. M., Alpert, N. M., Thompson, W. L., Maljkovic, V., Weise, S. B., Chabris, C. F., Hamilton, S. E., Rauch, S. L., & Buonanno, F. S. (1993). Visual mental imagery activates topographically organized visual cortex: PET investigations. *Journal of Cognitive Neuroscience, 5,* 263–287.

Kosslyn, S. M., Chabris, C. F., Marsolek, C. J., & Koenig, O. (1992). Categorical versus coordinate spatial relations: Computational analyses and computer simulations. *Journal of Experimental Psychology: Human Perception and Performance, 18,* 562–577.

Kosslyn, S. M., Holtzman, J. D., Farah, M. J., & Gazzaniga, M. S. (1985). A computational analysis of mental image generation: Evidence from functional dissociations in split-brain patients. *Journal of Experimental Psychology: General, 114,* 311–341.

Kosslyn, S. M., Koenig, O., Barrett, A., Cave, C., Tang, J., & Gabrieli, J. D. E. (1989). Evidence for two types of spatial representations: Hemispheric specialization for categorical and coordinate relations. *Journal of Experimental Psychology: Human Perception and Performance, 15,* 723–735.

Kosslyn, S. M., & Ochsner, K. N. (1994). In search of occipital activation during visual mental imagery. *Trends in Neurosciences, 17,* 290–292.

Kramer, A., Larish, J., & Strayer, D. (1995). Training strategies for attentional control in dual-task settings: A comparison of young and old adults. *Journal of Experimental Psychology: Applied, 1,* 50–76.

Kramer, A. F., Wickens, C. D., & Donchin, E. (1985). Processing of stimulus properties: Evidence for dual-task integrity. *Journal of Experimental Psychology: Human Perception and Performance, 11,* 393–408.

Kraus, J. (1987). Epidemiology of head injury. In P. R. Cooper (Ed.), *Head injury.* Baltimore: Williams & Wilkins.

Kroll, N. E. A., Knight, R. T., Metcalfe, J., Wolf, E. S., & Tulving, E. (1995). *Cohesion failure as a source of memory illusions.* Manuscript submitted for publication.

Kubie, J. L., & Ranck, J. B., Jr. (1984). Hippocampal neuronal firing, context, and learning. In L. R. Squire & N. Butters (Eds.), *Neuropsychology of memory* (pp. 417–423). New York: Guilford Press.

Kuhl, P. K., Williams, K. A., Lacerda, F., Stevens, K. N., & Lindblom, B. (1992). Linguistic experience alters phonetic perception in infants by 6 months of age. *Science, 255,* 606–608.

Kurtzke, J. F. (1980). Epidemiologic contributions to multiple sclerosis: An overview. *Neurology, 30,* 61–79.

Kutas, M., & Hillyard, S. A. (1980). Reading senseless sentences: Brain potentials reflect semantic incongruity. *Science, 207,* 203–205.

Kwong, K. K., Belliveau, J. W., Chesler, D. A., Goldberg, I. E., Weisskoff, R. M., Poncelet, B. P., Kennedy, P. N., Hoppel, B. E., Cohen, M. S., Turner, R., Cheng, H.-M., Brady, T. J., & Rosen, B. R. (1992). Dynamic magnetic resonance imaging of human brain activity during primary sensory stimulation. *Proceedings of the National Academy of Sciences, USA, 89,* 5675–5679.

LaBerge, D., & Buchsbaum, M. S. (1990). Positron emission tomographic measurements of pulvinar activity during an attention task. *Journal of Neuroscience, 10,* 613–619.

LaBerge, D. L. (1990). Attention. *Psychological Science, 1,* 156–162.

Ladavas, E. (1987). Is the hemispatial deficit produced by right parietal lobe damage associated with retinal or gravitational coordinates? *Brain, 110,* 167–180.

Ladavas, E., Nicoletti, R., Umilta, C., & Rizzolatti, G. (1984). Right hemisphere interference during negative affect: A reaction time study. *Neuropsychologia, 22,* 479–485.

Ladavas, E., Umilta, C., & Ricci-Bitti, P. E. (1980). Evidence for sex differences in right hemisphere dominance for emotions. *Neuropsychologia, 18,* 361–367.

Lakoff, G. (1987). *Women, fire, and dangerous things: What categories reveal about the mind.* Chicago: University of Chicago Press.

LaMantia, A. S., & Rakic, P. (1990). Axon overproduction and elimination in the corpus callosum of the developing rhesus monkey. *Journal of Neuroscience, 10,* 2156–2175.

Landis, T., Assal, G., & Perret, E. (1979). Opposite cerebral hemispheric superiorities for visual associative processing of emotional facial expressions and objects. *Nature, 278,* 739–740.

Landis, T., Cummings, J. L., Benson, D. F., & Palmer, E. P. (1986). Loss of topographic familiarity: An environmental agnosia. *Archives of Neurology, 43,* 132–136.

Lange, C. C., & James, W. (1967). *The emotions.* New York: Hafner.

Lange, C. S. (1887). The emotions. W. James & C. G. Lange (Trans.). Baltimore: Williams & Wilkins. (Original work published 1887)

Larrabee, G. J., Kane, R. L., Morrow, L., & Goldstein, G. (1982). Differential drawing size associated with unilateral brain damage. In *Paper presented at the tenth annual meeting of the International Neuropsychological Society,* Pittsburgh, PA.

Lashley, K. (1950). In search of the engram. *Symposia of the Society of Experimental Biology, 4,* 454–482.

Lashley, K. S. (1929). *Brain mechanisms and intelligence.* Chicago: University of Chicago Press.

Lavergne, J., & Kimura, D. (1987). Hand movement asymmetry during speech: No effect of speaking topic. *Neuropsychologia, 25,* 689–693.

Lawrence, D. G., & Kuypers, G. J. M. (1968). The functional organization of the motor system in the monkey. II. The effects of lesions of the descending brain-stem pathways. *Brain, 91,* 15–36.

Lechevalier, B., Petit, M. C., Eustache, F., Lambert, J., Chapon, F., & Vaider, F. (1989). Regional cerebral blood flow during comprehension and speech (in cerebrally healthy subjects). *Brain and Language, 37,* 1–11.

LeDoux, J. E. (1989). Cognitive-emotional interactions in the brain. *Cognition and Emotion, 3,* 267–289.

LeDoux, J. E. (1993). Emotional networks in the brain. In M. Lewis & J. M. Haviland (Eds.), *Handbook of emotions* (pp. 109–118). New York: Guilford Press.

Lee, G. P., Loring, D. W., Meador, K. J., Flanigin, H. F., & Brooks, B. S. (1988). Severe behavioral complications following intracarotid sodium amobarbital injection: Implications for hemispheric asymmetry of emotion. *Neurology, 38,* 1233–1236.

Leehey, S. C., Carey, S., Diamond, R., & Cahn, A. (1978). Upright and inverted faces: The right hemisphere knows the difference. *Cortex, 14,* 411–419.

Lees, A. (1990). Tics. *Behavioural Neurology, 3,* 99–108.

Lehmkuhl, G., & Poeck, K. (1981). A disturbance in the conceptual organization of actions in patients with ideational apraxia. *Cortex, 17,* 153–158.

LeMay, M. (1976). Morphological cerebral asymmetries of modern man, fossil man, and nonhuman primate. *Annals of the New York Academy of Sciences, 280,* 349–366.

Lembessis, E., & Rudin, R. (1994). Sinistrality and reduced longevity: Reply to Coren and Halpern's replay. *Perceptual and Motor Skills, 78,* 579–582.

Lenneberg, E. H. (1967). *Biological foundations of language.* New York: Wiley.

Leung, C. M., Chan, Y. W., Chang, C. M., Yu, Y. L., & Chen, C. N. (1992). Huntington's disease in Chinese: A hypothesis of its origin. *Journal of Neurology, Neurosurgery and Psychiatry, 55,* 681–684.

LeVay, S., Wiesel, T. N., & Hubel, D. H. (1980). The development of ocular dominance columns in normal and visually deprived monkeys. *Journal of Comparative Neurology, 191,* 1–51.

Levenson, R. W., Eckman, P., & Friesen, W. V. (1990). Voluntary facial action generates emotion-specific autonomic nervous system activity. *Psychophysiology, 27,* 363–383.

Levin, H. S., Gary, H. E., High, W. M., Mattis, S., Ruff, R. M., Eisenberg, H. M., Marshall, L. F., & Tabaddor, K. (1987). Minor head injury and the postconcussional syndrome: Methodological issues in outcomes studies. In H. S. Levin, J. Grafman, & H. M. Eisenberg (Eds.), *Neurobehavioral recovery from head injury* (pp. 262–275). New York: Oxford University Press.

Levin, H. S., Goldstein, F. C., Williams, D. H., & Eisenberg, H. M. (1991). The contribution of frontal lobe lesions to the neurobehavioral outcome of closed head injury. In H. S. Levin, H. M. Eisenberg, & A. L. Benton (Eds.), *Frontal lobe function and dysfunction* (pp. 318–338). New York: Oxford University Press.

Levin, H. S., & Grossman, R. G. (1978). Behavioral sequelae of closed head injury. *Archives of Neurology, 35,* 720–727.

Levin, H. S., High, W. M., Goethe, K. E., Sisson, R. A., Overall, J. E., Rhoades, H. M., Eisenberg, H. M., Kalisky, Z., & Gary, J. (1987). The Neurobehavioural Rating Scale: Assessment of the behavioural sequelae of head injury by the clinician. *Journal of Neurology, Neurosurgery and Psychiatry, 50,* 183–193.

Levin, H. S., Meyers, C. A., Grossman, R. G., & Sarwar, M. (1981). Ventricular enlargement after closed head injury. *Archives of Neurology, 38,* 623–629.

Levine, D. N., Kaufman, K. J., & Mohr, J. P. (1978). Inaccurate reaching associated with a superior parietal lobe tumor. *Neurology, 28,* 556–561.

Levine, S. C. (1984). Developmental changes in right-hemisphere involvement in face recognition. In C. Best (Ed.), *Hemispheric function and collaboration in the child* (pp. 157–191). New York: Academic Press.

Levine, S. C., & Banich, M. T. (1982). Lateral asymmetries in the naming of words and corresponding line drawings. *Brain and Language, 17,* 34–45.

Levine, S. C., Banich, M. T., & Koch-Weser, M. (1988). Face recognition: A general or specific right hemisphere capacity? *Brain and Cognition, 8,* 303–325.

Levine, S. C., Huttenlocher, P., Banich, M. T., & Duda, E. (1987). Factors affecting cognitive functioning of hemiplegic children. *Developmental Medicine and Child Neurology, 29,* 27–35.

Levy, J. (1976). Lateral dominance and aesthetic preference. *Neuropsychologia, 14,* 431–445.

Levy, J. (1983). Language, cognition, and the right hemisphere: A response to Gazzaniga. *American Psychologist, 38,* 538–541.

Levy, J. (1988). Cerebral asymmetry and aesthetic experience. In I. Rentschler, B. Herzberger, & D. Epstein (Eds.), *Beauty and the brain* (pp. 219–242). Basel, Switzerland: Birkhäuser Verlag.

Levy, J., Heller, W., Banich, M. T., & Burton, L. A. (1983a). Are variations among right-handed individuals in perceptual asymmetries caused by characteristic arousal differences between hemispheres? *Journal of Experimental Psychology: Human Perception and Performance, 9,* 329–359.

Levy, J., Heller, W., Banich, M. T., & Burton, L. A. (1983b). Asymmetry of perception in free viewing of chimeric faces. *Brain and Cognition, 2,* 404–419.

Levy, J., & Kueck, L. (1986). A right hemispatial field advantage on a verbal free-vision task. *Brain and Language, 27,* 24–37.

Levy, J., & Trevarthen, C. W. (1976). Metacontrol of hemispheric function in human split-brain patients. *Journal of Experimental Psychology: Human Perception and Performance, 2,* 299–312.

Levy, J., & Trevarthen, C. W. (1977). Perceptual, semantic and phonetic aspects of elementary language processes in split-brain patients. *Brain, 100,* 105–118.

Levy, J., Trevarthen, C. W., & Sperry, R. W. (1972). Perception of bilateral chimeric figures following "hemispheric deconnexion." *Brain, 95,* 61–78.

Ley, R. G., & Bryden, M. P. (1979). Hemispheric differences in processing emotions and faces. *Brain and Language, 7,* 127–138.

Ley, R. G., & Bryden, M. P. (1982). A dissociation of right and left hemispheric effects for recognizing emotional tone and verbal content. *Brain and Cognition, 1,* 3–9.

Lezak, M. D. (1978). Living with the characterologically altered brain injured patient. *Journal of Clinical Psychiatry, 39,* 63–72.

Lezak, M. D. (1983). *Neuropsychological assessment* (2nd ed.). New York: Oxford University Press.

Lezak, M. D. (1987). Relationships between personality disorders, social disturbances, and physical disability following traumatic brain injury. *Journal of Head Trauma Rehabilitation, 2,* 57–69.

Lezak, M. D. (1995). *Neuropsychological assessment* (3rd ed.). New York: Oxford University Press.

Lhermitte, F. (1986). Human autonomy and the frontal lobes: Part II. Patient behavior in complex and social situations: The "Environmental Dependency Syndrome." *Annals of Neurology, 19*(4), 335–343.

Lhermitte, F., Pillon, B., & Serdaru, M. (1986). Human autonomy and the frontal lobes: Part I. Imitation and utilization behavior: A neuropsychological study of 75 patients. *Annals of Neurology, 19,* 326–334.

Lhermitte, F., & Signoret, J.-L. (1976). The amnesic syndromes and the hippocampal-mammillary system. In M. Rosenzweig & E. L. Bennett (Eds.), *Neural mechanisms of learning and memory* (pp. 49–56). Cambridge, MA: MIT Press.

Lhermitte, R. (1983). "Utilization behavior" and its relation to lesions of the frontal lobes. *Brain, 106,* 237–255.

Libon, D. J., Glosser, G., Malamut, B. L., Kaplan, E., Goldberg, E., Swenson, R., & Sand, L. P. (1994). Age, executive functions, and visuospatial functioning in healthy older adults. *Neuropsychology, 8,* 38–43.

Libon, D. J., Scanlon, M., Swenson, R., & Coslet, H. B. (1990). Binswanger's disease: Some neuropsychological considerations. *Journal of Geriatric Psychiatry and Neurology, 3,* 31–40.

Lieberman, A., Dziatolowski, M., Neophytides, A., Kupersmith, M., Aleksic, S., Serby, M., Koerin, J., & Goldstein, H. (1979). Dementias of Huntington's and Parkinson's disease. In T. N. Chase, N. Wexler, & A. Barbeau (Eds.), *Advances in neurology* (pp. 273–289). New York: Raven Press.

Lilienfeld, A. M. (1969). *Epidemiology of mongolism.* Baltimore: Johns Hopkins University Press.

Lipper, E. G., Voorhies, T. M., Ross, G., Vannucci, R. C., & Auld, P. A. M. (1986). Early predictors of one-year outcome for infants asphyxiated at birth. *Developmental Medicine and Child Neurology, 28,* 303–309.

Lipsey, J. R., Robinson, R. G., Pearlson, G. D., Rao, K., & Price, T. R. (1983). Mood change following bilateral hemisphere brain injury. *British Journal of Psychiatry, 143,* 266–273.

Lishman, W. A. (1973). The psychiatric sequelae of head injury: A review. *Psychological Medicine, 3,* 304–318.

Logsdon, R. G., Teri, L., Williams, D. E., Vitiello, M. V., & Prinz, P. N. (1989). The WAIS-R profile: A diagnostic tool for Alzheimer's disease? *Journal of Clinical and Experimental Neuropsychology, 11,* 892–898.

Longden, K., Ellis, C., & Iversen, S. D. (1976). Hemispheric differences in the discrimination of curvature. *Neuropsychologia, 14,* 195–202.

Lou, H. D., Henriksen, L., Bruhn, P., Borner, H., & Nielsen, J. G. (1989). Striatal dysfunction in attention deficit and hyperkinetic disorder. *Archives of Neurology, 46,* 48–52.

Luh, K., & Levy, J. (1995). Interhemispheric cooperation: Left is left and right is right, but sometimes the twain shall meet. *Journal of Experimental Psychology: Human Perception and Performance, 21,* 1243–1258.

Lundberg, G. D. (1994). Let's stop boxing in the Olympics and the United States Military. *Journal of the American Medical Association, 271,* 1790.

Luria, A. R. (1966). *Higher cortical functions in man.* New York: Basic Books.

Lynch, J. C. (1980). The functional organization of posterior parietal association cortex. *Behavioral and Brain Sciences, 3,* 485–534.

Lynch, J. C., Mountcastle, V. B., Talbot, W. H., & Yin, T. C. (1977). Parietal lobe mechanisms for directed visual attention. *Journal of Neurophysiology, 40,* 362–389.

MacLean, P. D. (1949). Psychosomatic disease and the "visceral brain": Recent developments' bearing on the Papez theory of emotion. *Psychosomatic Medicine, 11,* 338–353.

MacLean, P. D. (1952). Some psychiatric implications of physiological studies on frontotemporal portion of limbic system (visceral brain). *Electroencephalography and Clinical Neurophysiology, 4,* 407–418.

MacLean, P. D. (1967). The brain in relation to empathy and medical education. *Journal of Nervous and Mental Disease, 144,* 374–382.

MacNiven, E. (1994). Increased prevalence of left-handedness in victims of head trauma. *Brain Injury, 8,* 457–462.

Maj, M. (1990). Psychiatric aspects of HIV-1 infection and AIDS. *Psychological Medicine, 20,* 547–563.

Majovski, L. V. (1989). Higher cortical functions in children: A developmental perspective. In C. R. Reynolds & E. Fletcher-Janzen (Eds.), *Handbook of clinical child neuropsychology* (pp. 41–67). New York: Plenum Press.

Malloy, P. (1987). Frontal lobe dysfunction in obsessive-compulsive disorder. In E. Perecman (Ed.), *The frontal lobes revisited* (pp. 207–224). New York: IRBN Press.

Mangun, G. R., & Hillyard, S. A. (1988). Spatial gradients of visual attention: Behavioral and electrophysiological evidence. *Electroencephalography and Clinical Neurophysiology, 70,* 417–428.

Mangun, G. R., & Hillyard, S. A. (1990). Electrophysiological studies of visual selective attention in humans. In A. R. Scheibel & A. F. Wechsler (Eds.), *Neurobiology of higher cognitive function* (pp. 271–295). New York: Guilford Press.

Marin-Padilla, M. (1970). Prenatal and early postnatal ontogenesis of the motor cortex: A Golgi study. 1. The sequential development of cortical layers. *Brain Research, 23,* 167–183.

Mark, V. W., Kooistra, C. A., & Heilman, K. M. (1988). Hemispatial neglect affected by non-neglected stimuli. *Neurology, 38,* 1207–1211.

Marr, D. (1982). *Vision.* San Francisco: Freeman.

Marr, D., & Nishihara, H. K. (1978). Visual information processing: Artificial intelligence and the sensorium of sight. *Technology Review, 81,* 2–23.

Marsden, C., Merton, P., Morton, H., Hallett, M., Adam, J., & Rushton, D. (1977). Disorders of movement in cerebellar disease in man. In F. Rose (Ed.), *Physiological aspects of clinical neurology* (pp. 179–199). Oxford, England: Blackwell.

Marsden, C. D. (1986). Movement disorders and the basal ganglia. *Trends in Neurosciences, 9,* 512–515.

Marshall, J. C., & Halligan, P. W. (1988). Blindsight and insight in visuospatial neglect. *Nature, 336,* 766–767.

Marshall, L. F., & Ruff, R. M. (1989). Neurosurgeon as victim. In H. S. Levin, H. M. Eisenberg, & A. L. Benton (Eds.), *Mild head injury.* New York: Oxford University Press.

Marsolek, C. J., Kosslyn, S. M., & Squire, L. R. (1992). Form-specific visual priming in the right cerebral hemisphere. *Journal of Experimental Psychology: Learning, Memory and Cognition, 18*(3), 492–508.

Martin, E. M., Pitrak, D. L., Pursell, K. J., Mullane, K. M., & Novak, R. M. (1995). Delayed recognition memory span in HIV-1 infection. *Journal of the International Neuropsychological Society, 1,* 575–580.

Martin, M. (1979). Hemispheric specialization for local and global processing. *Neuropsychologia, 17,* 33–40.

Martin, R., & McFarland, H. F. (1993). Role of genetic factors for the autoimmune pathogenesis of multiple sclerosis. In U. Halbreich (Ed.), *Multiple sclerosis: A neuropsychiatric disorder* (pp. 73–96). Washington, DC: American Psychiatric Press.

Martone, M., Butters, N., Payne, M., Becker, J. T., & Sax, D. (1984). Dissociations between skill learning and verbal recognition in amnesia and dementia. *Archives of Neurology, 41*(9), 965–970.

Masterton, R. B. (1992). Role of the central auditory system in hearing: The new direction. *Trends in Neurosciences, 15*(8), 280–285.

Mattis, S., French, J. H., & Rapin, I. (1975). Dyslexia in children and young adults: Three independent neuropsychological syndromes. *Developmental Medicine and Child Neurology, 17,* 150.

Maunsell, J. H. R., & Newsome, W. T. (1987). Visual processing in monkey extrastriate cortex. *Annual Review of Neuroscience, 10,* 365, 367.

Mayes, A. R., Meudell, P. R., & Pickering, A. (1985). Is organic amnesia caused by a selective deficit in remembering contextual information? *Cortex, 21,* 167–202.

Mazzoni, M., Pardossi, L., Cantini, R., Giorgetti, V., & Arena, R. (1990). Gerstmann syndrome: A case report. *Cortex, 26,* 459–467.

McCarley, R. W., Shenton, M. E., O'Donnell, B. F., Faux, S. F., Kikinis, R., Nestor, P. G., & Jolesz, F. A. (1993). Auditory P_{300} abnormalities and left posterior superior temporal gyrus volume reduction in schizophrenia. *Archives of General Psychiatry, 50,* 190–197.

McCarthy, R. A., & Warrington, E. K. (1990). *Cognitive neuropsychology: A clinical introduction.* New York: Academic Press.

McClelland, J. L., McNaughton, B. L., & O'Reilly, R. C. (1995). Why there are complementary learning systems in the hippocampus and neocortex: Insights from the successes and failures of connectionist models of learning and memory. *Psychological Review, 102*(3), 419–457.

McFie, J., Piercy, M. F., & Zangwill, O. L. (1950). Visual spatial agnosia associated with lesions of the right cerebral hemisphere. *Brain, 73,* 167–190.

McFie, J., & Zangwill, O. L. (1960). Visual-constructive disabilities associated with lesions of the left cerebral hemisphere. *Brain, 83,* 242–260.

McGaugh, J. L., & Herz, M. J. (1972). *Memory consolidation.* San Francisco: Albion.

McGlinchey-Berroth, R., Milberg, W. P., Verfaellie, M., Alexander, M., & Kilduff, P. T. (1993). Semantic processing in the neglected visual field: Evidence from a lexical decision task. *Cognitive Neuropsychology, 10,* 79–108.

McGlone, J. (1980). Sex differences in human brain asymmetry: A critical survey. *Behavioral and Brain Sciences, 3*(2), 215–263.

McIntyre, J. S., & Craik, F. I. M. (1987). Age differences in memory for item and source information. *Canadian Journal of Psychology, 41,* 175–192.

McKeever, W. F., & Dixon, M. S. (1981). Right-hemisphere superiority for discriminating memorized from nonmemorized faces: Affective imagery, sex, and perceived emotionality effects. *Brain and Language, 12,* 246–260.

McLaughlin, J. P., Dean, P., & Stanley, P. (1983). Aesthetic preference in dextrals and sinistrals. *Neuropsychologia, 21,* 147–153.

McManus, I. C., & Bryden, M. P. (1991). Geschwind's theory of cerebral lateralization: Developing a formal, causal model. *Psychological Bulletin, 110,* 237–253.

McNeil, J. E., & Warrington, E. K. (1993). Prosopagnosia: A face-specific disorder. *Quarterly Journal of Experimental Psychology, 46A,* 1–10.

Mead, A. M., & McLaughlin, J. P. (1992). The roles of handedness and stimulus asymmetry in aesthetic preference. *Brain and Cognition, 20,* 300–307.

Meerwaldt, J. D., & Van Harskamp, F. (1982). Spatial disorientation in right-hemisphere infarction. *Journal of Neurology, Neurosurgery and Psychiatry, 45,* 586–590.

Mehta, Z., & Newcombe, F. (1991). A role for the left hemisphere in spatial processing. *Cortex, 27,* 153–167.

Mendez, M. F., & Geehan, G. R. (1988). Cortical auditory disorders: Clinical and acoustic features. *Journal of Neurology, Neurosurgery and Psychiatry, 51,* 1–9.

Mendez, M. F., Underwood, K. L., Zander, B. A., Mastri, A. R., et al. (1992). Risk factors in Alzheimer's disease: A clinicopathologic study. *Neurology, 42,* 770–775.

Mennemeier, M., Wertman, E., & Heilman, K. M. (1992). Neglect of near peripersonal space. *Brain, 115,* 37–50.

Merckelbach, H., Muris, P., & Kop, W. J. (1994). Handedness, symptom reporting, and accident susceptibility. *Journal of Clinical Psychology, 50,* 389–392.

Mertens, I., Siegmund, H., & Gruesser, O. J. (1993). Gaze motor asymmetries in the perception of faces during a memory task. *Neuropsychologia, 31(9),* 989–998.

Merzenich, M. M., Recanzone, G. H., Jenkins, W. M., & Grajski, K. A. (1990). Adaptive mechanisms in cortical networks underlying cortical contributions to learning and nondeclarative memory. In *Cold Spring Harbor Symposia on Quantitative Biology: Vol. 55: The brain.* New York: Cold Spring Harbor Laboratory.

Messerli, P., Pegna, A., & Sordet, N. (1995). Hemispheric dominance for melody recognition in musicians and non-musicians. *Neuropsychologia, 33,* 395–405.

Mesulam, M.-M. (1981). A cortical network for directed attention and unilateral neglect. *Annals of Neurology, 10,* 309–325.

Mesulam, M.-M. (Ed.). (1985). *Principles of behavioral neurology.* Philadelphia: F A Davis.

Meyer, D., Schvaneveldt, R., & Ruddy, M. G. (1974). Functions of graphemic and phonemic codes in visual word recognition. *Memory and Cognition, 2,* 309–321.

Miceli, G. (1982). The processing of speech sounds in a patient with cortical auditory disorder. *Neuropsychologia, 20,* 5–20.

Miceli, G., Gainotti, G., Caltagirone, C., & Masullo, C. (1980).

Some aspects of phonological impairment in aphasia. *Brain and Language, 11,* 159–169.

Miller, L. (1992). Cognitive rehabilitation, cognitive therapy, and cognitive style: Toward an integrative model of personality and psychotherapy. *Journal of Cognitive Rehabilitation, 10,* 18–29.

Miller, L. A. (1992). Impulsivity, risk-taking, and the ability to synthesize fragmented information after frontal lobectomy. *Neuropsychologia, 31,* 69–79.

Milner, A. D., Perrett, D. I., Jonston, R. S., Benson, P. J., Jordan, T. R., Heeley, D. W., Bettucci, D., Mortara, F., Mutani, R., & Terazzi, E. (1991). Perception and action in "visual form agnosia." *Brain, 114,* 405–428.

Milner, B. (1962a). Laterality effects in audition. In V. B. Mountcastle (Ed.), *Interhemispheric relations and cerebral dominance* (pp. 177–195). Baltimore: Johns Hopkins Press.

Milner, B. (1962b). Les Troubles de la mémoire accompagnat des lésions hippocampiques bilatérales. In P. Passouant (Ed.), *Physiologie de l'hippocampe* (pp. 257–272). Paris: Centre National de la Recherche Scientifique.

Milner, B. (1964). Some effects of frontal lobectomy in man. In J. M. Warren & K. Akert (Eds.), *Frontal granular cortex and behavior* (pp. 313–331). New York: McGraw-Hill.

Milner, B. (1965). Visually-guided maze learning in man: effects of bilateral hippocampal, bilateral frontal and unilateral cerebral lesions. *Neuropsychologia, 3,* 317–338.

Milner, B. (1966). Amnesia following operation on the temporal lobes. In C. W. M. Whitty & O. L. Zangwill (Eds.), *Amnesia* (pp. 109–133). London: Butterworth.

Milner, B. (1968). Visual recognition and recall after temporal lobe excisions in man. *Neuropsychologia, 6,* 191–209.

Milner, B. (1971). Interhemispheric differences in the localization of psychological processes in man. *British Medical Bulletin, 27,* 272–277.

Milner, B. (1978). Clues to the cerebral organization of memory. In P. Buser & A. Rougeul-Buser (Eds.), *Cerebral correlates of conscious experience.* Amsterdam: Elsevier.

Milner, B. (1982). Some cognitive effects of frontal-lobe lesions in man. *Philosophical Transactions of the Royal Society of London, B298,* 211–226.

Milner, B., Corkin, S., & Teuber, H. L. (1968). Further analysis of the hippocampal amnesia syndrome. *Neuropsychologia, 6,* 215–234.

Milner, B., Corsi, P., & Leonard, G. (1991). Frontal-lobe contribution to recency judgements. *Neuropsychologia, 29,* 601–618.

Milner, B., & Petrides, M. (1984). Behavioural effects of frontal-lobe lesions in man. *Trends in Neurosciences, 7,* 403–407.

Milner, B., Taylor, L., & Sperry, R. W. (1968). Lateralized suppression of dichotically presented digits after commissural section in man. *Science, 161,* 184–185.

Mink, J. W., & Thach, W. T. (1993). Basal ganglia intrinsic circuits and their role in behavior. *Current Opinion in Neurobiology, 3,* 952.

Mishkin, M. (1978). Memory in monkeys severely impaired by combined but not separate removal of the amygdala and hippocampus. *Nature, 273,* 297–298.

Mishkin, M. (1982). A memory system in the monkey. *Philosophical Transactions of the Royal Society of London, B298,* 85–95.

Mishkin, M., & Delacour, J. (1975). An analysis of short-term visual memory in the monkey. *Journal of Experimental Psychology: Animal Behavior Processes, 104,* 326–334.

Mishkin, M., Ungerleider, G., & Macko, K. A. (1983). Object vision and spatial vision: Two cortical pathways. *Trends in Neurosciences, 6,* 414–417.

Mittenberg, W., Seidenberg, M., O'Leary, D. S., & DiGiulio, D. V. (1989). Changes in cerebral functioning associated with normal aging. *Journal of Clinical and Experimental Neuropsychology, 11,* 918–932.

Mize, K. (1980). Visual hallucinations following viral encephalitis: A self report. *Neuropsychologia, 18,* 193–202.

Molfese, D., & Molfese, V. J. (1994). Short-term and long-term developmental outcomes: The use of behavioral and electrophysiological measures in early infancy as predictors. In G. Dawson & K. W. Fischer (Eds.), *Human behavior and the developing brain* (pp. 493–517). New York: Guilford Press.

Molfese, D. L., Freeman, R. B., & Palermo, D. S. (1975). The ontogeny of brain lateralization for speech and nonspeech stimuli. *Brain and Language, 2,* 356–368.

Money, J. A. (1976). *A standardized road map test of directional sense. Manual.* San Rafael, CA: Academic Therapy Publications.

Monrad-Krohn, G. H. (1947). Dysprosody of altered "melody of language." *Brain, 70,* 405–415.

Monsch, A. U., Bondi, M. W., Butters, N., Paulsen, J. S., Salmon, D. P., Brugger, P., & Swenson, M. R. (1994). A comparison of category and letter fluency in Alzheimer's disease and Huntington's disease. *Neuropsychology, 8,* 25–30.

Moran, J., & Desimone, R. (1985). Selective attention gates visual processing in the extrastriate cortex. *Science, 229,* 782–784.

Moray, N. (1959). Attention in dichotic listening: Affective cues and the influence of instruction. *Quarterly Journal of Experimental Psychology, 11,* 56–60.

Morgenstern, H., Glazer, W. M., Niedzwiecki, D., & Nourjah, P. (1987). The impact of neuroleptic medication on tardive dyskinesia: A meta-analysis of published studies. *American Journal of Public Health, 77,* 717–724.

Morris, R. G., Ahmed, S., Syed, G. M., & Toone, B. K. (1993). Neural correlates of planning ability: Frontal lobe activation during the Tower of London test. *Neuropsychologia, 31,* 1367–1378.

Morris, R. G. M. (1981). Spatial localization does not require the presence of local cues. *Learning and Motivation, 12,* 239–260.

Morrow, L., Ratcliff, G., & Johnston, C. S. (1985). Externalising spatial knowledge in patients with right hemisphere lesions. *Cognitive Neuropsychology, 2,* 265–273.

Morrow, L., Vrtunski, P. B., Kim, Y., & Boller, F. (1981).

Arousal responses to emotional stimuli and laterality of lesions. *Neuropsychologia, 19,* 65–71.

Morrow, L. A., Ryan, C. M., Hodgson, M. J., & Robin, N. (1991). Risk factors associated with persistence of neuropsychological deficits in persons with organic solvent exposure. *Journal of Nervous and Mental Disease, 9,* 540–545.

Morselli, P. L., & Lloyd, K. G. (1985). Mechanisms of action of antiepileptic drugs. In R. J. Porter & P. L. Morselli (Eds.), *The epilepsies* (pp. 40–81). Boston: Butterworth.

Mortimer, J. A., French, L. M., Hutton, D. J., & Schuman, L. M. (1985). Head trauma as a risk factor for Alzheimer's disease. *Neurology, 35,* 264–267.

Mortimer, J. A., & Pirozzolo, F. J. (1985). Remote effects of head trauma. *Developmental Neuropsychology, 1,* 215–229.

Mortimer, J. A., van Duijn, C. M., Chandra, V., Fratiglioni, L., Graves, A. B., Heyman, A., Jorm, A. F., Kokmen, E., Konda, K., Rocca, W. A., Shalat, S. L., Soininen, H., & Hofman, A. (1991). Head trauma as a risk factor for Alzheimer's disease: A collaborative re-analysis of case-control studies. *International Journal of Epidemiology, 20*(Suppl. 2), S28—S35.

Moscovitch, M. (1979). Information processing and the cerebral hemispheres. In M. S. Gazzaniga (Ed.), *Handbook of behavioral neurobiology: Neuropsychology.* New York: Plenum Press.

Moscovitch, M. (1994). Memory and working-with-memory: A component process model based on modules and central systems. In D. L. Schacter & E. Tulving (Eds.), *Memory systems 1994.* Cambridge, MA: MIT Press.

Moscovitch, M., Behrmann, M., & Winocur, G. (1994). Do PETS have long or short ears? Mental imagery and neuroimaging. *Trends in Neurosciences, 17,* 292–294.

Moscovitch, M., & Radzins, M. (1987). Backward masking of lateralized faces by noise, pattern, and spatial frequency. *Brain and Cognition, 6,* 72–90.

Moscovitch, M., Winocur, G., & McLachlan, D. (1986). Memory as assessed by recognition and reading time in normal and memory-impaired people with Alzheimer's disease and other neurological disorders. *Journal of Experimental Psychology: General, 115*(4), 331–347.

Motter, B. C., & Mountcastle, V. B. (1981). The functional properties of light-sensitive neurons of the posterior parietal cortex studies in waking monkeys: Foveal sparing and opponent vector organization. *Journal of Neuroscience, 1,* 3–26.

Mountcastle, V. B., Lynch, J. C., Georgopoulos, A., Sakata, H., & Acuna, C. (1975). Posterior parietal association cortex of the monkey: Command functions for operations within extrapersonal space. *Journal of Neurophysiology, 38,* 871–908.

Moya, K. L., Benowitz, L. I., Levine, D. N., & Finklestein, S. (1986). Covariant defects in visuospatial abilities and recall of verbal narrative after right hemisphere stroke. *Cortex, 22,* 381–397.

Mozaz, M. J. (1992). Ideational and ideomotor apraxia: A qualitative analysis. *Behavioural Neurology, 5,* 11–17.

Muller, R. U., Kubie, J. L., & Ranck, J. B., Jr. (1987). Spatial firing patterns of hippocampal complex spike cells in a fixed environment. *Journal of Neuroscience, 7.*

Murray, M. (1994, February 13). Nancy Wexler's test. *The New York Times Magazine*, p. 28.

Myklebust, H. R. (1975). Nonverbal learning disabilities: Assessment and intervention. In H. R. Myklebust (Ed.), *Progress in learning disabilities: Vol. 3* (pp. 85–121). New York: Grune & Stratton.

Myles-Worsley, M., Johnston, W. A., & Simons, M. A. (1988). The influence of expertise on x-ray image processing. *Journal of Experimental Psychology: Learning, Memory, and Cognition, 14*, 553–557.

Myslobodsky, M. S. (1983). Epileptic laughter. In M. S. Myslobodsky (Ed.), *Hemisyndromes: Psychobiology, neurology, psychiatry.* New York: Academic Press.

Myslobodsky, M. S., & Horesh, N. (1978). Bilateral electrodermal activity in depressive patients. *Biological Psychiatry, 6*, 111–120.

Naatanen, R., Gaillard, A. W. K., & Mantysalo, S. (1978). The N_1 effect of selective attention reinterpreted. *Acta Psychologica (Amsterdam), 42*, 313–329.

Naeser, M. A., & Borod, J. C. (1986). Aphasia in left-handers: Lesion site, lesion side and hemispheric asymmetries on CT. *Neurology, 36*, 471–488.

Nagy, Z., Esiri, M. M., Jobst, K. A., Morris, J. H., King, E. M. F., McDonald, B., Litchfield, S., Smith, A., Barnetson, L., & Smith, A. D. (1995). Relative roles of plaques and tangles in the dementia of Alzheimer's disease: Correlations using three sets of neuropathological criteria. *Dementia, 6*, 21–31.

Nakanishi, A. (1980). *Writing systems of the world.* Tokyo: Charles E. Tuttle.

Nass, R., Peterson, H., & Koch, D. (1989). Differential effects of congenital left and right brain injury on intelligence. *Brain and Cognition, 9*, 258–266.

Nauta, W. (1971). The problem of the frontal lobe: A reinterpretation. *Journal of Psychiatric Research, 8*, 167–187.

Naveh-Benjamin, M. (1990). Coding of temporal order information: An automatic process? *Journal of Experimental Psychology: Learning, Memory, and Cognition, 16*, 117–126.

Navia, B. A., Cho, E., Petito, C. K., & Price, R. W. (1986). The AIDS dementia complex: II. Neuropathology. *Annals of Neurology, 19*, 525–535.

Navia, B. A., Jordan, B. D., & Price, R. W. (1986). The AIDS dementia complex: I. Clinical features. *Annals of Neurology, 19*, 517–524.

Navon, D. (1977). Forest before trees: The precedence of global features in visual perception. *Cognitive Psychology, 9*, 353–383.

Nebes, R. D. (1978). Direct examination of cognitive function in the right and left hemispheres. In M. Kinsbourne (Ed.), *Asymmetrical function of the brain* (pp. 99–137). Cambridge, England: Cambridge University Press.

Neill, W. T. (1977). Inhibition and facilitation processes in selective attention. *Journal of Experimental Psychology: Human Perception and Performance, 3*, 444–450.

Nelson, H. E. (1982). *National Adult Reading Test: Test manual.* Windsor, England: NFER-Nelson.

Nelson, K. B., & Ellenberg, J. H. (1986). Antecedents of cerebral palsy: Multivariate analysis of risk. *New England Journal of Medicine, 315*, 81–86.

Nespoulous, J. L., Joanette, Y., Béland, R., Caplan, D., & Lecours, A. R. (1984). Phonological disturbances in aphasia: Is there a "markedness" effect in aphasic phonemic errors? In F. C. Rose (Ed.), *Progress in aphasiology: Advances in neurology, Vol. 42.* New York: Raven Press.

Netley, C., & Rovet, J. (1982). Verbal deficits in children with 47,XXY and 47,XXX karyotypes: A descriptive and experimental study. *Brain and Language, 17*, 58–72.

Neville, H. J. (1990). Intermodal competition and compensation in development: Evidence from studies of the visual system in congenitally deaf adults. *Annals of the New York Academy of Sciences, 608*, 71–91.

Neville, H. J., & Lawson, D. (1987a). Attention to central and peripheral visual space in movement detection task: An event-related potential and behavioral study. I. Normal hearing adults. *Brain Research, 405*, 253–267.

Neville, H. J., & Lawson, D. (1987b). Attention to central and peripheral visual space in movement detection task: An event-related potential and behavioral study. II. Congenitally deaf adults. *Brain Research, 405*, 268–283.

Neville, H. J., & Lawson, D. (1987c). Attention to central and peripheral visual space in movement detection task: An event-related potential and behavioral study. III. Separate effects of auditory deprivation and acquisition of a visual language. *Brain Research, 405*, 284–294.

Newcombe, F. (1969). *Missile wounds of the brain: A study of psychological deficits.* Oxford, England: Oxford University Press.

Newcombe, F. (1985). Neuropsychology of consciousness: A review of human clinical evidence. In D. A. Oakley (Ed.), *Brain and mind* (pp. 152–196). New York: Methuen.

Newcombe, F., & Russell, W. R. (1969). Dissociated visual perceptual and spatial deficits in focal lesions of the right hemisphere. *Journal of Neurology, Neurosurgery and Psychiatry, 32*, 73–81.

Nichols, M. E., Meador, K. J., & Loring, D. W. (1993). Neuropsychological effects of antiepileptic drugs: A current perspective. *Clinical Neuropharmacology, 16*, 471–484.

Niki, H., & Watanabe, M. (1976). Prefrontal unit activity and delayed response: Relation to cue location versus direction of response. *Brain Research, 105*, 79–88.

Nolen-Hoeksema, S. (1987). Sex differences in unipolar depression: Evidence and theory. *Psychological Bulletin, 101*, 259–282.

Novelly, R. A. (1992). The debt of neuropsychology to the epilepsies. *American Psychologist, 47*, 1126–1129.

Obler, L. K., & Albert, M. (1981). Language and aging: A neurobiological analysis. In D. S. Beasley & G. A. Davis (Eds.), *Aging: Communication processes and disorders* (pp. 107–121). New York: Grune & Stratton.

O'Boyle, M. W., Van Wyhe-Layler, F., & Miller, D. A. (1987). Recognition of letters traced in the right and left palms: Evidence for a process-oriented tactile asymmetry. *Brain and Cognition, 6*, 474–494.

O'Dougherty, M., Wright, F. S., Loewenson, R. B., & Torres, F. (1985). Cerebral dysfunction after chronic hypoxia in children. *Neurology, 35*, 42–46.

Ogden, J. A. (1985). Antero-posterior interhemispheric differences in the loci of lesions producing visual hemineglect. *Brain and Cognition, 4*, 59–75.

O'Hara, C. (1988). Emotional adjustment following minor head injury. *Cognitive Rehabilitation, 6*, 26–33.

Ojemann, G. A. (1983). Brain organization for language from the perspective of electrical stimulation mapping. *Behavioral and Brain Sciences, 6*, 189–230.

Ojemann, G. A. (1991). Cortical organization for language. *Journal of Neuroscience, 11*, 2281–2287.

Ojemann, G. A., Ojemann, J., Lettich, E., & Berger, M. (1989). Cortical language localization in left, dominant hemisphere. *Journal of Neurosurgery, 71*, 316–326.

Oke, A., Keller, R., Mefford, I., & Adams, R. (1978). Lateralization of norepinephrine in human thalamus. *Science, 200*, 1411–1413.

O'Keefe, J. A. (1976). Spatial memory within and without the hippocampal system. In W. Seifert (Ed.), *Neurobiology of the hippocampus*. New York: Academic Press.

O'Keefe, J. A., & Nadel, L. (1978). *The hippocampus as a cognitive map*. London: Oxford University Press.

O'Keefe, J. A., & Speakman, A. (1987). Single unit activity in the rat hippocampus during a spatial memory task. *Experimental Brain Research, 68*, 1–27.

O'Kusky, J., & Colonnier, M. (1982). Postnatal changes in the number of neurons and synapses in the visual cortex (A17) of the macaque monkey. *Journal of Comparative Neurology, 210*, 291–296.

Oliver, C., & Holland, A. J. (1986). Down's syndrome and Alzheimer's disease: A review. *Psychological Medicine, 16*, 307–322.

O'Malley, S., Adamse, M., Heaton, R. K., & Gawin, F. H. (1992). Neuropsychological impairment in chronic cocaine abusers. *American Journal of Drug and Alcohol Abuse, 18*, 131–144.

Orsini, D. L., Van Gorp, W. G., & Boone, K. B. (1988). *The neuropsychology casebook*. New York: Springer-Verlag.

Orton, S. T. (1937). *Reading, writing and speech problems in children*. New York: Norton.

Ostergaard, A. L. (1987). Episodic, semantic, and procedural memory in a case of amnesia at an early age. *Neuropsychologia, 25*(2), 341–357.

Owen, A. M., Roberts, A. C., Polkey, C. E., Sahakian, B. J., & Robbins, T. W. (1991). Extra-dimensional versus intra-dimensional set shifting performance following frontal lobe excisions, temporal lobe excisions or amygdalo-hippocampectomy in man. *Neuropsychologia, 29*, 993–1006.

Page, J. B., Fletcher, J., & True, W. R. (1988). Psychosocial perspectives on chronic cannabis use: The Costa Rican follow-up. *Journal of Psychoactive Drugs, 20*, 57–65.

Pall, E. (1995, September 24). Starting from scratch. *The New York Times Magazine*, pp. 39–43.

Panting, A., & Merry, P. (1972). The long term rehabilitation of severe head injuries with particular reference to the need for social and medical support for the patient's family. *Rehabilitation, 38*, 33–37.

Papagno, C., della Sala, S. D., & Basso, A. (1993). Ideomotor apraxia without aphasia and aphasia without apraxia: The anatomical support for a double dissociation. *Journal of Neurology, Neurosurgery and Psychiatry, 56*, 286–289.

Papanicolaou, A. C., Moore, B. D., Deutsch, G., Levin, H. S., & Eisenberg, H. M. (1988). Evidence for right-hemisphere involvement in recovery from aphasia. *Archives of Neurology, 45*, 1025–1029.

Papez, J. W. (1937). A proposed mechanism of emotion. *Archives of Neurological Psychiatry, 38*, 725–743.

Paradis, M. (1977). Bilingualism and aphasia. In H. Whitaker & H. A. Whitaker (Eds.), *Studies in neurolinguistics* (pp. 65–122). New York: Academic Press.

Paradis, M. (1990). Language lateralization in bilinguals: Enough already! *Brain and Language, 39*, 576–586.

Paradis, M. (1992). The Loch Ness Monster approach to bilingual language lateralization: A response to Berquier and Ashton. *Brain and Language, 43*, 534–537.

Paradis, M., Goldblum, M. C., & Abidi, R. (1982). Alternate antagonism with paradoxical translation behavior in two bilingual aphasic patients. *Brain and Language, 15*, 55–69.

Paradis, M., Hagiwara, H., & Hildebrandt, N. (1985). *Neurolinguistic aspects of the Japanese writing system*. New York: Academic Press.

Pardo, J. V., Pardo, P. J., Janer, K. W., & Raichle, M. E. (1990). The anterior cingulate cortex mediates processing selection in the Stroop attentional conflict paradigm. *Proceedings of the National Academy of Science, USA, 87*, 256–259.

Parkin, A. J. (1987). *Memory and amnesia*. Oxford, England: Basil Blackwell.

Parkin, A. J., Walter, B. M., & Hunkin, N. M. (1995). Relationships between normal aging, frontal lobe function, and memory for temporal and spatial information. *Neuropsychology, 9*, 304–312.

Parsons, O. A., Butters, N., & Nathan, P. (Eds.). (1987). *Neuropsychology of alcoholism: Implications for diagnosis and treatment*. New York: Guilford Press.

Parsons, O. A., & Farr, S. P. (1981). The neuropsychology of alcohol and drug use. In S. B. Filskov & T. J. Boll (Eds.), *Handbook of clinical neuropsychology* (pp. 320–365). New York: Wiley.

Passingham, R. E., Perry, V. H., & Wilkinson, F. (1983). The long-term effects of removal of sensorimotor cortex in infant and adult rhesus monkeys. *Brain, 106*, 675–705.

Patel, A. J. (1983). Undernutrition and brain development. *Trends in Neurosciences, 6*(4), 151–154.

Patterson, K. (1982). Reading and phonological coding. In A. W. Ellis (Ed.), *Normality and pathology in cognitive functions* (pp. 77–112). New York: Academic Press.

Patterson, K. E., & Kay, J. (1982). Letter-by-letter reading: Psychological descriptions of a neurological syndrome. *Quarterly Journal of Experimental Psychology, 34A*, 411–441.

Patterson, K. E., Seidenberg, M. S., & McClelland, J. L. (1989). Connections and disconnections: Acquired dyslexia in a computational model of reading processes. In R. G. M. Morris (Ed.), *Parallel distributed processing: Implications for psychology and neurobiology* (pp. 131–181). Oxford, England: Oxford University Press.

Paus, T., Kalina, M., Patockova, L., Angerova, Y., Cerny, R., Mecir, P., Bauer, J., & Krabec, P. (1991). Medial versus lateral frontal lobe lesions and differential impairment of central-gaze fixation maintenance in man. *Brain, 114,* 2051–2067.

Paus, T., Petrides, M., Evans, A. C., & Meyer, E. (1993). Role of the human anterior cingulate cortex in the control of oculomotor, manual, and speech responses: A positron emission tomography study. *Journal of Neurophysiology, 70,* 1–18.

Payne, B. R., & Cornwell, P. (1994). System-wide repercussions of damage to the immature visual cortex. *Trends in Neurosciences, 17*(3), 126–130.

Penfield, W., & Perot, P. (1963). The brain's record of auditory and visual experience. *Brain, 86,* 595–696.

Penfield, W., & Rasmussen, T. (1950). *The cerebral cortex of man: A clinical study of localization of function.* New York: Macmillan.

Pennington, B., Puck, M., & Robinson, A. (1980). Language and cognitive development in 47,XXX females followed since birth. *Behavior Genetics, 10,* 31–41.

Perrett, D. I., Mistlin, A. J., & Chitty, A. J. (1987). Visual neurones responsive to faces. *Trends in Neurosciences, 10,* 358–364.

Perry, E. K., Tomlinson, B. E., & Blessed, G. (1978). Correlation of cholinergic abnormalities with senile plaques and mental test scores in senile dementia. *British Medical Journal, 2,* 1457–1459.

Petersen, S. E., Fox, P. T., Posner, M. I., Mintun, M., & Raichle, M. E. (1988). Positron emission tomographic studies of the cortical anatomy of single-word processing. *Nature, 331,* 585–589.

Petersen, S. E., Fox, P. T., Snyder, A. Z., & Raichle, M. E. (1990). Activation of extrastriate and frontal cortical areas by visual words and word-like stimuli. *Science, 249,* 1041–1044.

Petrides, M., & Milner, B. (1982). Deficits on subject-ordered tasks after frontal- and temporal-lobe lesions in man. *Neuropsychologia, 20,* 249–262.

Petruzzello, S. J., & Landers, D. M. (1994). State anxiety reduction and exercise: Does hemispheric activation reflect such changes? *Medicine and Science in Sports and Exercise, 26,* 1028–1035.

Pettinati, H. M. (1988). *Hypnosis and memory.* New York: Guilford Press.

Peyser, J. M., & Poser, C. M. (1986). Neuropsychological correlates of multiple sclerosis. In S. B. Filskov & T. J. Boll (Eds.), *Handbook of clinical neuropsychology* (pp. 364–398). New York: Wiley.

Pigott, S., & Milner, B. (1993). Memory for different aspects of complex visual scenes after unilateral temporal- or frontal-lobe resection. *Neuropsychologia, 31,* 1–15.

Pigott, S., & Milner, B. (1994). Capacity of visual short-term memory after unilateral frontal or anterior temporal-lobe resection. *Neuropsychologia, 32,* 969–981.

Pillon, B., Deweer, B., Agid, Y., & Dubois, B. (1993). Explicit memory in Alzheimer's, Huntington's, and Parkinson's diseases. *Archives of Neurology, 50,* 374–379.

Pinek, B., Duhamel, J.-R., Cave, C., & Brouchon, M. (1989). Audio-spatial deficits in humans: Differential effects associated with left versus right hemisphere parietal damage. *Cortex, 25,* 175–186.

Pizzamiglio, L., Zoccolotti, P., Mammucari, A., & Cesaroni, R. (1983). The independence of face identity and facial expression recognition mechanisms: Relation to sex and cognitive style. *Brain and Cognition, 2,* 176–188.

Plaut, D. C., & Farah, M. J. (1990). Visual object representation: Interpreting neurophysiological data within a computational framework. *Journal of Cognitive Neuroscience, 2,* 320–343.

Plum, F., & Posner, J. B. (1980). *The diagnosis of stupor and coma* (3rd ed.). Philadelphia: F A Davis.

Poeck, K. (1986). The clinical examination for motor apraxia. *Neuropsychologia, 24,* 129–134.

Poeck, K., & Lehmkuhl, G. (1980). Das Syndrom der ideatorischen Apraxie und seine Localisation. *Nervenarzt, 51,* 217–225.

Pohl, W. (1973). Dissociation of spatial discrimination deficits following frontal and parietal lesions in monkeys. *Journal of Comparative and Physiological Psychology, 82,* 227–239.

Poirier, P., Lassonde, M., Villemure, J.-G., Geoffroy, G., & Lepore, F. (1994). Sound localization in hemispherectomized patients. *Neuropsychologia, 32,* 541–553.

Poizner, H., Klima, E. S., & Bellugi, U. (1987). *What the hands reveal about the brain.* Cambridge, MA: MIT Press.

Polson, M. C., & Friedman, A. (1988). Task-sharing within and between hemispheres: A multiple-resources approach. *Human Factors, 30,* 633–643.

Pope, H. G., Gruber, A. J., & Yurgelun, T. D. (1995). The residual neuropsychological effects of cannabis: The current status of research. *Drug and Alcohol Dependence, 38,* 25–34.

Posner, M. I. (1973). *Cognition: An introduction.* Glenview, IL: Scott, Foresman.

Posner, M. I. (1980). Orienting of attention. *Quarterly Journal of Experimental Psychology, 32,* 3–25.

Posner, M. I. (1992). Attention as a cognitive and neural system. *Current Directions in Psychological Science, 1,* 11–14.

Posner, M. I., Inhoff, A. W., Friedrich, F. J., & Cohen, A. (1987). Isolating attentional systems: A cognitive-anatomical analysis. *Psychobiology, 15,* 107–121.

Posner, M. I., & McCandliss, B. D. (1993). Converging methods for investigating lexical access. *Psychological Science, 4,* 305–309.

Posner, M. I., & Petersen, S. E. (1990). The attention system of the human brain. *Annual Review of Neuroscience, 13,* 25–42.

Posner, M. I., Petersen, S. E., Fox, P. T., & Raichle, M. E. (1988). Localization of cognitive operations in the human brain. *Science, 240,* 1627–1631.

Posner, M. I., & Raichle, M. E. (1994). *Images of mind*. New York: Freeman.

Posner, M. I., Sandson, J., Dhawan, M., & Shulman, G. L. (1989). Is word recognition automatic? *Journal of Cognitive Neuroscience, 1*, 50–60.

Posner, M. I., Walker, J. A., Friedrich, F. J., & Rafal, R. D. (1984). Effects of parietal injury on covert orienting of attention. *The Journal of Neuroscience, 4*, 1863–1874.

Prigatano, G. P. (1991). Disturbances of self-awareness of deficit after traumatic brain injury. In G. P. Prigatano & D. L. Schacter (Eds.), *Awareness of deficit after brain injury* (pp. 111–126). Oxford, England: Oxford University Press.

Prigatano, G. P., Altman, I. M., & O'Brien, K. P. (1990). Behavioral limitations that traumatic-brain-injured patients tend to underestimate. *Clinical Neuropsychologist, 4*, 163–176.

Prigatano, G. P., & Schacter, D. L. (1991) *Awareness of deficit after brain injury*. Oxford, England: Oxford University Press.

Pylyshyn, Z. W. (1973). What the mind's eye tells the mind's brain: A critique of mental imagery. *Psychological Bulletin, 80*, 1–24.

Pylyshyn, Z. W. (1981). The imagery debate: Analogue media versus tacit knowledge. *Psychological Review, 87*, 16–45.

Rabinowicz, T., Courten-Myers, G., Petetot, J., Xi, G., & Los Reyes, E. (1996). Human cortex development: Estimates of neuronal numbers indicate major loss during gestation. *Journal of Neuropathology and Experimental Neurology, 55*, 320–328.

Rafal, R., & Posner, M. I. (1987). Deficits in human visual spatial attention following thalamic lesions. *Proceedings of the National Academy of Sciences, USA, 84*, 7349–7353.

Rafal, R. D., Posner, M. I., Friedman, J. H., Inhoff, A. W., & Bernstein, E. (1988). Orienting of visual attention in progressive supranuclear palsy. *Brain, 111*, 267–280.

Raichle, M., Fiez, J., Videen, T. O., MacLeod, A. M. K., Pardo, J. V., Fox, P. T., & Petersen, S. E. (1994). Practice-related changes in human brain functional anatomy during nonmotor learning. *Cerebral Cortex, 4*, 8–26.

Raichle, M. E. (1994). Images of the mind: Studies with modern imaging techniques. *Annual Review of Psychology, 45*, 333–356.

Rakic, P. (1981). Developmental events leading to laminar and areal organization of the neocortex. In F. O. Schmitt, F. G. Worden, G. Adelman, & S. G. Dennis (Eds.), *The organization of the cerebral cortex* (pp. 7–28). Cambridge, MA: MIT Press.

Rakic, P. (1991). Plasticity of cortical development. In S. E. Brauth, W. S. Hall, & R. J. Dooling (Eds.), *Plasticity of development* (pp. 127–161). Cambridge, MA: MIT Press.

Ramachandran, V. S., Rogers-Ramachandran, D., & Steward, M. (1992). Perceptual correlates of massive cortical reorganization. *Science, 258*, 1159–1160.

Rao, S. (1986). Neuropsychology of multiple sclerosis: A critical review. *Journal of Clinical and Experimental Neuropsychology, 8*, 503–542.

Rao, S. M., Huber, S. J., & Bornstein, R. A. (1992). Emotional changes with multiple sclerosis and Parkinson's disease. *Journal of Consulting and Clinical Psychology, 60*, 369–378.

Rao, S. M., Leo, G. J., Bernardin, L., & Unverzagt, F. (1991). Cognitive dysfunction in multiple sclerosis: 1. Frequency, patterns, and prediction. *Neurology, 41*, 685–691.

Rao, S. M., Leo, G. J., Haughton, V. M., St. Aubin-Faubert, P., & Bernardin, L. (1989). Correlation of magnetic resonance imaging with neuropsychological testing in multiple sclerosis. *Neurology, 39*, 161–166.

Rapcsak, S. Z., Cimino, C. R., & Heilman, K. M. (1988). Altitudinal neglect. *Neurology, 38*, 277–281.

Rapin, I., Allen, D. A., & Dunn, M. A. (1992). Developmental language disorders. In S. J. Segalowitz & I. Rapin (Eds.), *Handbook of neuropsychology: Vol. 7. Child Neuropsychology* (pp. 111–137). New York: Elsevier.

Rapoport, J. L. (1990). Obsessive compulsive disorder and basal ganglia dysfunction. *Psychological Medicine, 20*, 465–469.

Raskin, S. A., Borod, J. C., & Tweedy, J. (1990). Neuropsychological aspects of Parkinson's disease. *Neuropsychology Review, 1*, 185–221.

Rasmussen, T., & Milner, B. (1977a). The role of early left-brain injury in determining lateralization of cerebral speech function. *Annals of the New York Academy of Sciences, 299*, 355–369.

Rasmussen, T., & Milner, B. (1977b). The role of early left-brain injury in determining lateralization of cerebral speech functions. In S. Dimond & D. Blizzard (Eds.), *Evolution and lateralization of function in the brain*. New York: New York Academy of Sciences.

Ratcliff, G. (1979). Spatial thought, mental rotation and the right cerebral hemisphere. *Neuropsychologia, 17*, 49–54.

Ratcliff, G., & Davies-Jones, G. A. B. (1972). Defective visual localization in focal brain wounds. *Brain, 95*, 49–60.

Ratcliff, G., Dila, C., Taylor, L., & Milner, B. (1980). The morphological asymmetry of the hemispheres and cerebral dominance for speech: A possible relationship. *Brain and Language, 11*, 87–98.

Ratcliff, G., & Newcombe, F. (1973). Spatial orientation in man: Effects of left, right, and bilateral cerebral lesions. *Journal of Neurology, Neurosurgery and Psychiatry, 36*, 448–454.

Ratcliff, G., & Newcombe, F. (1982). Object recognition: Some deductions from the clinical evidence. In A. W. Ellis (Ed.), *Normality and pathology in cognitive functions* (pp. 147–171). London: Academic Press.

Rattok, J., Ben-Yishay, Y., Ezrachi, O., Lakin, P., Piasetsky, E., Ross, B., Silver, S., Vakil, E., Zide, E., & Diller, L. (1992). Outcome of different treatment mixes in a multidimensional neuropsychological rehabilitation program. *Neuropsychology, 6*, 395–415.

Rayman, J., & Zaidel, E. (1991). Rhyming and the right hemisphere. *Brain and Language, 40*, 89–105.

Raz, S. (1993). Structural cerebral pathology in schizophrenia: Regional or diffuse? *Journal of Abnormal Psychology, 102*, 445–452.

Reed, C. L., & Caselli, R. J. (1994). The nature of tactile agnosia: A case study. *Neuropsychologia, 32*, 527–539.

Rehak, A., Kaplan, J. A., & Gardner, H. (1992). Sensitivity to conversational deviance in right-hemisphere-damaged patients. *Brain and Language, 42*, 203–217.

Reidy, T. J., Bowler, R. M., Rauch, S. S., & Pedroza, G. I. (1992). Pesticide exposure and neuropsychological impairment in migrant farm workers. *Archives of Clinical Neuropsychology, 7*, 85–95.

Reiman, E. M., Fusselman, M. J., Fox, P. T., & Raichle, M. E. (1989). Neuroanatomical correlates of anticipatory anxiety. *Science, 243*, 1071–1074.

Reiman, E. M., Raichle, M. E., Butler, F. K., Herscovitch, P., & Robins, E. (1984). A focal brain abnormality in panic disorder, a severe form of anxiety. *Nature, 310*, 683–685.

Reisberg, B. (1986). Dementia: A systematic approach to identifying reversible causes. *Geriatrics, 41*, 30–46.

Reisberg, B., Ferris, S. H., deLeon, M. J., & Crook, T. (1988). Global Deterioration Scale (GDS). *Psychopharmacology Bulletin, 24*, 661–663.

Reisberg, B., Ferris, S. H., deLeon, M. J., Kluger, A., Franssen, E., Borenstein, J., & Alba, R. C. (1989). The stage-specific temporal course of Alzheimer's disease: Functional and behavioral concomitants based upon cross-sectional and longitudinal observation. *Progress in Clinical and Biological Research, 317*, 23–41.

Reuter-Lorenz, P. A., & Brunn, J. L. (1990). A pre-lexical basis for letter-by-letter reading: A case study. *Journal of Cognitive Neuropsychology, 7*, 1–20.

Reuter-Lorenz, P. A., Kinsbourne, M., & Moscovitch, M. (1990). Hemispheric control of spatial attention. *Brain and Cognition, 12*, 240–266.

Reuter-Lorenz, P. A., & Posner, M. I. (1990). Components of neglect from right-hemisphere damage: An analysis of line bisection. *Neuropsychologia, 28*, 327–333.

Reynolds, C. R., & Fletcher-Jansen, E. (1989). *Handbook of clinical child neuropsychology*. New York: Plenum Press.

Rhodes, G., Tan, S., Brake, S., & Taylor, K. (1989). Expertise and configural coding in face recognition. *British Journal of Psychology, 80*, 313–331.

Ribot, T. (1881/1882). *Diseases of memory*. New York: Appleton.

Ricciuti, H. N. (1993). Nutrition and mental development. *Current Directions in Psychological Science, 2*, 43–46.

Rice, D. P., Kelman, S., & Miller, L. S. (1991). The economic cost of alcohol abuse. *Alcohol Health and Research World, 15*(4), 307–316.

Richardson-Klaven, A., & Bjork, R. A. (1988). Measures of memory. *Annual Review of Psychology, 39*, 475–543.

Riddoch, M. J., & Humphreys, G. W. (1983). The effect of cueing on unilateral neglect. *Neuropsychologia, 21*, 589–599.

Riva, D., & Cazzaniga, L. (1986). Late effect of unilateral brain lesions sustained before and after age one. *Neuropsychologia, 24*, 423–428.

Roberts, G. W., Gentleman, S. M., Lynch, A., Murray, L., et al. (1994). β Amyloid protein deposition in the brain after severe head injury: Implications for the pathogenesis of Alzheimer's disease. *Journal of Neurology, Neurosurgery and Psychiatry, 57*, 419–425.

Robertson, L. C., & Lamb, M. R. (1991). Neuropsychological contributions to part-whole organization. *Cognitive Psychology, 23*, 299–332.

Robertson, L. C., Lamb, M. R., & Knight, R. T. (1988). Effects of lesions of temporal-parietal junction on perceptual and attentional processing in humans. *Journal of Neuroscience, 8*, 3757–3769.

Robin, D. A., Klouda, G., & Hug, L. N. (1991). Neurogenic disorder of prosody. In M. Cannito & D. Vogel (Eds.), *Treating disordered speech motor control: For clinicians by clinicians* (pp. 241–271). Austin, TX: PRO-ED.

Robin, D. A., Tranel, D., & Damasio, H. (1990). Auditory perception of temporal and spectral events in patients with focal left and right cerebral lesions. *Brain and Language, 39*, 539–555.

Robinson, R. G., Kubos, K. L., Starr, L. B., Rao, K., & Price, T. R. (1984). Mood disorders in stroke patients. Importance of location of lesion. *Brain, 107*, 81–93.

Rode, G., Charles, N., Perenin, M. T., Vighetoo, A., Trillet, M., & Aimard, G. (1992). Partial remission of hemiplegia and somatoparaphrenia through vestibular stimulation in a case of unilateral neglect. *Cortex, 28*(2), 203–208.

Rodel, M., Cook, N. D., Regard, M., & Landis, T. (1992). Hemispheric dissociation in judging semantic relations: Complementarity for close and distant associates. *Brain and Language, 43*, 448–459.

Roeltgen, D. P., & Heilman, K. M. (1984). Lexical agraphia: Further support for the two strategy hypothesis of linguistic agraphia. *Brain, 107*, 811–827.

Rogers, R. D., & Monsell, S. (1995). Costs of a predictable switch between simple cognitive tasks. *Journal of Experimental Psychology: General, 124*, 207–231.

Roland, P. E., Larsen, B., Lassen, N. A., & Skinhøj, E. (1980). Supplementary motor area and other cortical areas in organization of voluntary movements in man. *Journal of Neurophysiology, 43*, 118–136.

Romani, G. L., Williamson, S. J., & Kaufman, L. (1982). Tonotopic organization of the human auditory cortex. *Science, 216*, 1339–1340.

Rose, F. D. (1988). Environmental enrichment and recovery of function following brain damage in the rat. *Medical Science Research, 16*, 257–263.

Rosenzweig, M. R., Bennett, E. L., & Diamond, M. C. (1972). Brain changes in response to experience. *Scientific American, 226*, 22–29.

Rosenzweig, M. R., & Leiman, A. L. (1989). *Physiological psychology* (2nd ed.). New York: Random House.

Ross, C. A., McInnis, M. G., Margolis, R. L., & Li, S. (1993). Genes with triplet repeats: Candidate mediators of neuropsychiatric disorders. *Trends in Neurosciences, 16*(7), 254–260.

Ross, E. D. (1981). The aprosodias: Functional-anatomic organization of the affective components of language in the right hemisphere. *Archives of Neurology, 38,* 561–569.

Ross, E. D., & Mesulam, M.-M. (1979). Dominant language functions of the right hemisphere? Prosody and emotional gesturing. *Archives of Neurology, 36,* 144–148.

Rourke, B. P., Bakker, D. J., Fisk, J. L., & Strang, J. D. (1983). *Child neuropsychology: An introduction to theory, research, and clinical practice.* New York: Guilford Press.

Rourke, B. P., & Finlayson, M. A. J. (1978). Neuropsychological significance of variations in patterns of academic performance: Verbal and visual-spatial abilities. *Journal of Clinical Neuropsychology, 6,* 121–133.

Rourke, B. P., Young, G. C., Strang, J. D., & Russell, D. L. (1985). Adult outcomes of central processing deficiencies in childhood. In I. Grant & K. M. Adams (Eds.), *Neuropsychological assessment in neuropsychiatric disorders: Clinical methods and empirical findings* (pp. 244–257). New York: Oxford University Press.

Rousselle, C., & Wolff, P. H. (1991). The dynamics of bimanual coordination in developmental dyslexia. *Neuropsychologia, 29,* 907–924.

Rubens, A. B. (1985). Caloric stimulation and unilateral visual neglect. *Neurology, 35,* 1019–1024.

Rubens, A. B., Geschwind, N., Mahowald, M. W., & Mastri, A. (1977). Posttraumatic cerebral hemispheric disconnection syndrome. *Archives of Neurology, 34,* 750–755.

Rubens, A. B., Mahowald, M. W., & Hutton, J. T. (1976). Asymmetry of lateral (Sylvian) fissure in man. *Neurology, 26,* 620–624.

Rubenstein, J. S. (1993). *Executive control of cognitive processes in task switching.* Unpublished manuscript.

Rubin, P., Holm, S., Friberg, L., Videbech, P., Andersen, H. S., Bendsen, B. B., Stromso, N., Larsen, J. K., Lassen, N. A., & Hemmingsen, R. (1991). Altered modulation of prefrontal and subcortical brain activity in newly diagnosed schizophrenia and schizophreniform disorder. *Archives of General Psychiatry, 48,* 987–995.

Ruff, R. M., Hersh, N. A., & Pribram, K. H. (1981). Auditory spatial deficits in the personal and extrapersonal frames of reference due to cortical lesions. *Neuropsychologia, 19,* 435–443.

Rugg, M. D., & Coles, M. G. H. (Eds.). (1995). *Electrophysiology of mind: Event-related brain potential and cognition.* New York: Oxford University Press.

Russell, J. A. (1979). Affective space is bipolar. *Journal of Personality and Social Psychology, 37,* 345–356.

Russell, W. R., & Nathan, P. W. (1946). Traumatic amnesia. *Brain, 68,* 280–300.

Rutter, M. (1983). Cognitive deficits in the pathogenesis of autism. *Journal of Child Psychology and Psychiatry, 24,* 513–531.

Rybash, J. M., & Hoyer, W. J. (1992). Hemispheric specialization for categorical and coordinate spatial representation: A reappraisal. *Memory and Cognition, 20,* 271–276.

Sackeim, H. A., Greenberg, M. S., Weiman, A. L., Gur, R. C.,

Hungerbuhler, J. P., & Geschwind, N. (1982). Hemispheric asymmetry in the expression of positive and negative emotions: Neurological evidence. *Archives of Neurology, 39,* 210–218.

Sackheim, H. A., Gur, R. C., & Saucy, M. C. (1978). Emotions are expressed more intensely on the left side of the face. *Science, 202,* 434.

Sacks, O. (1985). *The man who mistook his wife for a hat.* New York: Summit Books.

Safer, M. A., & Leventhal, H. (1977). Ear differences in evaluating emotional tones of voice and verbal content. *Journal of Experimental Psychology: Human Perception and Performance, 3,* 75–82.

Sagar, H. J., Cohen, N. J., Corkin, S., & Growdon, J. H. (1985). Dissociations among processes in remote memory. *Annals of the New York Academy of Sciences, 444,* 533–535.

Sagar, H. J., Cohen, N. J., Sullivan, E. V., Corkin, S., & Growdon, J. H. (1988). Remote memory function in Alzheimer's disease and Parkinson's disease. *Brain, 111,* 185–206.

Saito, H. A., Yukic, M., Tanaka, K., Hikosaka, K., Fukada, Y., & Iwai, E. (1986). Integration of direction signals of image motion in the superior temporal sulcus of the macaque monkey macaca-fuscafa. *Journal of Neuroscience, 6,* 147–157.

Sakai, K., & Miyashita, Y. (1991). Neural organization for the long-term memory of paired associates. *Nature, 354,* 152–155.

Sakata, H., Shibutani, H., & Kawano, K. (1983). Functional properties of visual tracking neurons in posterior parietal association cortex of the monkey. *Journal of Neurophysiology, 49,* 1364–1380.

Sakata, H., Shibutani, H., Kawano, K., & Harrington, T. L. (1985). Neural mechanism of space vision in the parietal association cortex of the monkey. *Vision Research, 25,* 453–463.

Salamy, A. (1978). Commissural transmission: Maturational changes in humans. *Science, 200,* 1409–1411.

Salcido, R., & Costich, J. F. (1992). Recurrent traumatic brain injury. *Brain Injury, 6,* 293–298.

Salthouse, T. (1985). Speed of behavior and its implications for cognition. In J. Birren & K. Schaie (Eds.), *Handbook of the psychology of aging* (pp. 400–426). New York: Van Nostrand Reinhold.

Sampson, G. W. (1985). *Writing systems.* Stanford, CA: Stanford University Press.

Samson, S., & Zatorre, R. J. (1988). Melodic and harmonic discrimination following unilateral cerebral excision. *Brain and Cognition, 7,* 348–360.

Samson, S., & Zatorre, R. J. (1991). Recognition memory for text and melody of songs after unilateral temporal lobe lesion: Evidence for dual encoding. *Journal of Experimental Psychology: Learning, Memory, and Cognition, 17,* 793–804.

Sandman, C. A., O'Halloran, J. P., & Isenhart, R. (1984). Is there an evoked vascular response? *Science, 224,* 1355–1367.

Saron, C. D., & Davidson, R. J. (1989). Visual evoked potential measures of interhemispheric transfer time in humans. *Behavioral Neuroscience, 103,* 1115–1138.

Sasanuma, S. (1980). Acquired dyslexia in Japanese: Clinical features and underlying mechanisms. In M. Coltheart, K. E. Patterson, & J. C. Marshall (Eds.), *Deep dyslexia* (pp. 91–118). London: Routledge & Kegan Paul.

Schacter, D. L. (1987a). Implicit memory: History and current status. *Journal of Experimental Psychology: Learning, Memory, and Cognition, 13,* 501–518.

Schacter, D. L. (1987b). Memory, amnesia, and frontal lobe dysfunction. *Psychobiology, 15,* 21–36.

Schacter, D. L., & Tulving, E. (1983). Memory, amnesia, and the episodic/semantic distinction. In R. L. Isaacson & N. E. Spear (Eds.), *Expressions of knowledge.* New York: Plenum Press.

Schachter, S., & Singer, J. E. (1962). Cognitive, social, and physiological determinants of emotional state. *Psychological Review, 69,* 379–399.

Schaffer, C. E., Davidson, R. J., & Saron, C. (1983). Frontal and parietal electroencephalogram asymmetry in depressed and nondepressed subjects. *Biological Psychiatry, 18,* 753–762.

Schank, R. (1982). *Dynamic memory: A theory of reminding and learning in computers and people.* Cambridge, England: Cambridge University Press.

Scheibel, A. B. (1984). A dendritic correlate of human speech. In N. Geschwind & A. M. Galaburda (Eds.), *Cerebral dominance: The biological foundations* (pp. 43–52). Cambridge, MA: Harvard University Press.

Schenck, F., & Morris, R. G. M. (1985). Dissociation between components of spatial memory in rats after recovery from the effects of retrohippocampal lesions. *Experimental Brain Research, 58,* 11–28.

Schiller, P. H., Sandell, J. H., & Maunsell, J. H. R. (1987). The effect of frontal eye field and superior colliculus lesions on saccadic latencies in the rhesus monkey. *Journal of Neurophysiology, 57,* 1033–1049.

Schiller, P. H., True, S. D., & Conway, J. L. (1980). Deficits in eye movements following frontal eye field and superior colliculus ablations. *Journal of Neurophysiology, 44,* 1175–1189.

Schlag-Rey, M., Schlag, J., & Dassonville, P. (1992). How the frontal eye field can impose a saccade goal on superior colliculus neurons. *Journal of Neurophysiology, 67,* 1003–1005.

Schlaug, G., Jancke, L., Huang, Y., Staiger, J. F., & Steinmetz, J. (1995). Increased corpus callosum size in musicians. *Neuropsychologia, 33,* 1047–1055.

Schlaug, G., Jancke, L., Huang, Y., & Steinmetz, H. (1995). In vivo evidence of structural brain asymmetry in musicians. *Science, 267,* 699–701.

Schneiderman, E. I., Murasugi, K. G., & Saddy, J. D. (1992). Story arrangement ability in right-brain damaged patients. *Brain and Language, 43,* 107–120.

Schoenberg, B. S., Kokmen, E., & Okazaki, H. (1987). Alzheimer's disease and other dementing illnesses in a defined United States population: Incidence rates and clinical features. *Annals of Neurology, 22,* 724–729.

Schroder, J., Buchsbaum, M. S., Siegel, B. V., Geider, F. J., & Niethammer, R. (1995). Structural and functional correlates of subsyndromes in chronic schizophrenia. *Psychopathology, 28,* 38–45.

Schwartz, M. F., Mayer, N. H., FitzpatrickDeSalme, E. J., & Montgomery, M. W. (1993). Cognitive theory and the study of everyday action disorders after brain damage. *Journal of Head Trauma and Rehabilitation, 8,* 59–72.

Scoville, W. B., & Milner, B. (1957). Loss of recent memory after bilateral hippocampal lesions. *Journal of Neurology, Neurosurgery and Psychiatry, 20,* 11–12.

Scully, R. E. (1986). Case records of the Massachusetts General Hospital. Case 16-1986. *New England Journal of Medicine, 314,* 1101–1111.

Segalowitz, S., & Gruber, F. (Eds.). (1977). *Language development and neurological theory.* New York: Academic Press.

Seidenberg, M. S., & McClelland, J. L. (1989). A distributed, developmental model of visual word recognition and naming. *Psychological Review, 96,* 523–568.

Semmes, J. (1965). A non-tactual factor in astereognosis. *Neuropsychologia, 3,* 295–315.

Semmes, J. (1968). Hemispheric specialization: A possible clue to mechanism. *Neuropsychologia, 6,* 11–26.

Semmes, J., Weinstein, S., Ghent, L., & Teuber, H.-L. (1955). Spatial orientation: 1. Analysis of locus of lesion. *Journal of Psychology, 39,* 227–244.

Semmes, J., Weinstein, S., Ghent, L., & Teuber, H.-L. (1963). Impaired orientation in personal and extrapersonal space. *Brain, 86,* 747–772.

Semrud-Clikeman, M., & Hynd, G. W. (1990). Right hemisphere dysfunction in nonverbal learning disabilities: Social, academic and adaptive functioning in adults and children. *Psychological Bulletin, 107*(2), 196–209.

Sergent, J. (1982a). About face: Left-hemisphere involvement in processing physiognomies. *Journal of Experimental Psychology: Human Perception and Performance, 8,* 1–14.

Sergent, J. (1982b). The cerebral balance of power: Confrontation or cooperation. *Journal of Experimental Psychology: Human Perception and Performance, 8,* 253–272.

Sergent, J. (1983). The role of the input in visual hemispheric asymmetries. *Psychological Bulletin, 93,* 481–514.

Sergent, J. (1985). Influence of task and input factors on hemispheric involvement in face processing. *Journal of Experimental Psychology: Human Perception and Performance, 11,* 846–861.

Sergent, J. (1990). Furtive incursions into bicameral minds. *Brain, 113,* 537–568.

Sergent, J. (1991). Judgments of relative position and distance on representations of spatial relations. *Journal of Experimental Psychology: Human Perception and Performance, 91,* 762–780.

Sergent, J. (1993). Music, the brain and Ravel. *Trends in Neurosciences, 16,* 168–172.

Sergent, J. (1994). Brain-imaging studies of cognitive functions. *Trends in Neurosciences, 17*(6), 221–227.

Sergent, J., Ohta, S., & MacDonald, B. (1992). Functional neuroanatomy of face and object processing. *Brain, 115,* 15–36.

Sergent, J., & Signoret, J.-L. (1992a). Functional and anatomical decomposition of face processing: Evidence from prosopagnosia and PET study of normal subjects. *Philosophical Transactions of the Royal Society of London, B335,* 55–62.

Sergent, J., & Signoret, J.-L. (1992b). Varieties of functional deficits in prosopagnosia. *Cerebral Cortex, 2,* 375–388.

Sergent, J., Zuck, E., Terriah, S., & MacDonald, B. (1992). Distributed neural network underlying musical sight-reading and keyboard performance. *Science, 257,* 106–109.

Shallice, T. (1981). Phonological agraphia and the lexical route in writing. *Brain, 104,* 413–429.

Shallice, T. (1982). Specific impairments of planning. *Philosophical Transactions of the Royal Society of London, B298,* 199–209.

Shallice, T. (1988). *From neuropsychology to mental structure.* Cambridge, England: Cambridge University Press.

Shallice, T., & Evans, M. E. (1978). The involvement of frontal lobes in cognitive estimation. *Cortex, 13,* 294–303.

Shallice, T., & Warrington, E. K. (1977). The possible role of selective attention in acquired dyslexia. *Neuropsychologia, 15,* 31–41.

Shallice, T., & Warrington, E. K. (1979). Auditory-verbal short-term memory impairment and conduction aphasia. *Brain and Language, 4,* 479–491.

Shallice, T., Warrington, E. K., & McCarthy, R. (1983). Reading without semantics. *Quarterly Journal of Experimental Psychology, 35,* 111–138.

Shapiro, B. E., Grossman, M., & Gardner, H. (1981). Selective processing deficits in brain damaged populations. *Neuropsychologia, 19,* 161–169.

Shaw, T. G., Mortel, K. F., Meyer, J. S., Rogers, R. L., Hardenberg, J., & Cutaia, M. M. (1984). Cerebral blood flow changes in benign and cerebrovascular disease. *Neurology, 34,* 855–862.

Shaywitz, B. A., Shaywitz, S. E., Pugh, K. R., Constable, R. T., Skudlarski, P., Fulbright, R. K., Bronen, R. A., Fletcher, J. M., Shankweiler, D. P., Katz, L., & Gore, J. C. (1995). Sex differences in the functional organization of the brain for language. *Nature, 373,* 607–609.

Shelton, P. A., Bowers, D., & Heilman, K. M. (1990). Peripersonal and vertical neglect. *Brain, 113,* 191–205.

Shenter, J. I., Banich, M. T., & Klipstein, S. (1993). Unpublished observations.

Shepard, R. (1988). The role of transformations in spatial cognition. In J. Stiles-Davis, M. Kritchevsky, & U. Bellugi (Eds.), *Spatial cognition: Brain bases and development* (pp. 81–110). Hillsdale, NJ: Erlbaum.

Shepard, R. N., & Cooper, L. A. (1982). *Mental images and their transformations.* Cambridge, MA: MIT Press.

Shimamura, A. (1990). Aging and memory disorders: A neuropsychological analysis. In M. L. Howe, M. J. Stones, & C. J. Brainerd (Eds.), *Cognitive and behavioral performance factors in atypical aging.* New York: Springer-Verlag.

Shimamura, A., & Jurica, P. J. (1994). Memory interference effects and aging: Findings from a test of frontal lobe function. *Neuropsychology, 8,* 408–412.

Shimamura, A. P., Janowsky, J. S., & Squire, L. R. (1990). Memory for the temporal order of events in patients with frontal lobe lesions and amnesic patients. *Neuropsychologia, 28*(8), 803–813.

Shimamura, A. P., Jernigan, T. L., & Squire, L. R. (1988). Korsakoff's syndrome: Radiological (CT) findings and neuropsychological correlates. *Journal of Neuroscience, 8,* 4400–4410.

Shimamura, A. P., Salmon, D. P., Squire, L. R., & Butters, N. (1987). Memory dysfunction and word priming in dementia and amnesia. *Behavioral Neuroscience, 101,* 347–351.

Sidtis, J. J., & Volpe, B. T. (1988). Selective loss of complex-pitch or speech discrimination after unilateral lesion. *Brain and Language, 34,* 235–245.

Sidtis, J. J., Volpe, B. T., Watson, D. H., Rayport, M., & Gazzaniga, M. S. (1981). Variability in right hemisphere language after callosal section: Evidence for a continuum of generative capacity. *Journal of Neuroscience, 1,* 323–331.

Sigman, M. (1994). What are the core deficits in autism? In S. H. Broman & J. Grafman (Eds.), *Atypical cognitive deficits in developmental disorders* (pp. 139–157). Hillsdale, NJ: Erlbaum.

Silberman, E. K., & Weingartner, H. (1986). Hemispheric lateralization of functions related to emotion. *Brain and Cognition, 5,* 322–353.

Simion, F., Bagnaro, S., Bisiachi, P., Roncata, S., & Umilta, C. (1980). Laterality effect, levels of processing and stimulus properties. *Journal of Experimental Psychology: Human Perception and Performance, 6,* 184–195.

Smith, M. L., & Milner, B. (1981). The role of the right hippocampus in the recall of spatial location. *Neuropsychologia, 19*(6), 781–793.

Smith, M. L., & Milner, B. (1984). Differential effects of frontal-lobe lesions on cognitive estimation and spatial memory. *Neuropsychologia, 22,* 697–705.

Smith, M. L., & Milner, B. (1988). Estimation of frequency of occurrence of abstract designs after frontal or temporal lobectomy. *Neuropsychologia, 26*(2), 297–306.

Spencer, W. D., & Raz, N. (1994). Memory for facts, source, and context: Can frontal lobe dysfunction explain age-related differences? *Psychology and Aging, 9,* 149–159.

Sperry, R. W. (1964). The great cerebral commissure. *Scientific American.*

Sperry, R. W. (1974). Lateral specialization in the surgically separated hemispheres. In F. Schmitt & F. Worden (Eds.), *The neurosciences: Third study program.* Cambridge, MA: MIT Press.

Sperry, R. W., Zaidel, E., & Zaidel, D. (1979). Self recognition and social awareness in the deconnected minor hemisphere. *Neuropsychologia, 17,* 153–166.

Spreen, O., Tupper, D., Risser, A., Tuokko, H., & Edgell, D. (1984). *Human developmental neuropsychology*. New York: Oxford University Press.

Springer, S. P., & Deutsch, G. (1993). *Left brain, right brain*. New York: Freeman.

Squire, L. R. (1982). Comparisons between forms of amnesia: Some deficits are unique to Korsakoff's syndrome. *Journal of Experimental Psychology: Learning, Memory, and Cognition, 8*(6), 560–571.

Squire, L. R. (1984). The neuropsychology of memory. In P. Marler & H. Terrace (Eds.), *The biology of learning (Dahlem-Konferenzen)*. Berlin: Springer-Verlag.

Squire, L. R. (1987). *Memory and brain*. New York: Oxford University Press.

Squire, L. R., & Cohen, N. J. (1979). Memory and amnesia: Resistance to disruption develops for years after learning. *Behavioral and Neural Biology, 25*, 115–125.

Squire, L. R., & Cohen, N. J. (1982). Remote memory, retrograde amnesia, and the neuropsychology of memory. In L. S. Cermak (Ed.), *Human memory and amnesia*. Hillsdale, NJ: Erlbaum.

Squire, L. R., & Cohen, N. J. (1984). Human memory and amnesia. In G. Lynch, J. L. McGaugh, & N. M. Weinberger (Eds.), *Neurobiology of learning and memory* (pp. 3–64). New York: Guilford Press.

Squire, L. R., Cohen, N. J., & Nadel, L. (1984). The medial temporal region and memory consolidation: A new hypothesis. In H. Weingartner & E. Parker (Eds.), *Memory consolidation* (pp. 185–210). Hillsdale, NJ: Erlbaum.

Squire, L. R., Cohen, N. J., & Zouzounis, J. A. (1984). Preserved memory in retrograde amnesia: Sparing of a recently acquired skill. *Neuropsychologia, 22*(2), 145–152.

Squire, L. R., Ojemann, J. G., Miezin, F. M., Petersen, S. E., Videen, T. O., & Raichle, M. E. (1992). Activation of the hippocampus in normal humans: A functional anatomical study of memory. *Proceedings of the National Academy of Sciences, USA, 89*, 1837–1841.

Starkstein, S. E., Brandt, J., Folstein, S., Strauss, M., Berthier, M. L., Pearlson, G. D., Wong, D., McDonnell, A., & Folstein, M. (1988). Neuropsychological and neuroradiological correlates in Huntington's disease. *Journal of Neurology, Neurosurgery and Psychiatry, 51*, 1259–1263.

Starkstein, S. E., & Robinson, R. G. (1988). Lateralized emotional response following stroke. In M. Kinsbourne (Ed.), *Cerebral hemisphere function in depression* (pp. 23–48). Washington, DC: American Psychiatric Press.

Steinmetz, H., Volkmann, J., Jancke, L., & Freund, H. J. (1991). Anatomical left-right asymmetry of language-related temporal cortex is different in left- and right-handers. *Annals of Neurology, 29*, 315–319.

Stern, L. D. (1981). A review of theories of amnesia. *Memory and Cognition, 9*, 247–262.

Sternberg, S. S., Monsell, S., Knoll, R. L., & Wright, C. E. (1978). The latency and duration of rapid movement sequences: Comparisons of speech and type-writing. In G. E. Stelmach (Ed.), *Information processing in motor control and learning* (pp. 118–152). New York: Academic Press.

Stokes, A., Banich, M. T., & Elledge, V. C. (1991). Testing the tests—An empirical evaluation of screening tests for the detection of cognitive impairment in aviators. *Aviation Space and Environmental Medicine, 62*, 783–788.

Stolar, N., Berenbaum, H., Banich, M. T., and Barch, D. (1994). Neuropsychological correlates of alogia and affective flattening in schizophrenia. *Biological Psychiatry, 35*, 164–172.

Strang, J. D., & Rourke, B. P. (1985). Arithmetic disability subtypes: The neuropsychological significance of specific arithmetic impairment in childhood. In B. P. Rourke (Ed.), *Neuropsychology of learning disabilities* (pp. 302–330). New York: Guilford Press.

Strauss, E., Hunter, M., & Wada, J. (1995). Risk factors for cognitive impairment in epilepsy. *Neuropsychology, 9*, 457–463.

Strauss, E., LaPointe, J. S., Wada, J. A., Gaddes, W., & Kosaka, B. (1985). Language dominance: Correlation of radiological and functional data. *Neuropsychologia, 23*, 415–420.

Strauss, E., & Moscovitch, M. (1981). Perception of facial expressions. *Brain and Language, 13*, 308–332.

Streissguth, A. P. (1992). Fetal alcohol syndrome and fetal alcohol effects: A clinical perspective of later developmental consequences. In I. S. Zagon & T. A. Slotkin (Eds.), *Maternal substance abuse and the developing nervous system* (pp. 5–26). New York: Academic Press.

Studdert-Kennedy, M., & Shankweiler, D. (1970). Hemispheric specialization for speech perception. *Journal of the Acoustical Society of America, 48*, 579–594.

Stuss, D. T. (1987). Contribution of frontal lobe injury to cognitive impairment after closed head injury: Methods of assessment and recent findings. In H. S. Levin, J. Grafman, & H. M. Eisenberg (Eds.), *Neurobehavioral recovery from head injury* (pp. 166–177). New York: Oxford University Press.

Stuss, D. T., & Benson, D. F. (1986). *The frontal lobes*. New York: Raven Press.

Suberi, M., & McKeever, W. F. (1977). Differential right hemispheric memory storage of emotional and non-emotional faces. *Neuropsychologia, 15*, 757–768.

Sutherland, R. J., Whishaw, I. Q., & Kolb, B. (1983). A behavioral analysis of spatial localization following electrolytic, kainate- or colchicine-induced damage to the hippocampal formation in the rat. *Behavioural Brain Research, 7*, 133–153.

Swirsky-Sacchetti, T., Mitchell, D. R., Seward, J., Gonzales, C., Lublin, F., Knobler, R., & Field, H. L. (1992). Neuropsychological and structural brain lesions in multiple sclerosis: A regional analysis. *Neurology, 42*, 1291–1295.

Taft, M. (1982). An alternative to grapheme-phoneme conversion rules? *Memory and Cognition, 10*, 465–474.

Taira, M., Mine, S., Georgopoulos, A. P., Murata, A., & Sakata, H. (1990). Parietal cortex neurons of the monkey related to the visual guidance of hand movement. *Experimental Brain Research, 83*, 29–36.

Tallal, P., Miller, S. L., Redi, G., Byma, G., Wang, X. Q., Nagarajan, S. S., Schneiner, C., Jenkins, W. M., & Merzenich, M. M. (1996). Language comprehension in language-learning impaired children with acoustically modified speech. *Science, 271*, 81–84.

Tallal, P., Sainburg, R. L., & Jernigan, T. (1991). The neuropathology of developmental dysphasia: Behavioral, morphological, and physiological evidence for a pervasive temporal processing disorder. *Reading and Writing, 3*, 363–377.

Talland, G. A. (1965). *Deranged memory.* New York: Academic Press.

Tanji, J., Taniguchi, K., & Saga, T. (1980). Supplementary motor area: neuronal response to motor instructions. *Journal of Neurophysiology, 43*, 60–68.

Tarter, R. E., & Alterman, A. I. (1984). Neuropsychological deficits in alcoholics: Etiological considerations. *Journal of Studies on Alcohol, 45*, 1–9.

Tatemichi, T. K. (1990). How acute brain failure becomes chronic: A view of the mechanisms of dementia related to stroke. *Neurology, 40*, 1652–1659.

Teasdale, G., & Jennett, B. (1974). Assessment of coma and impaired consciousness: A practical scale. *Lancet, 2*, 81–84.

Tecce, J. J., & Cole, J. O. (1974). Amphetamine effects in man: Paradoxical drowsiness and lowered electrical brain activity (CNV). *Science, 185*, 451–453.

Tecce, J. J., Cole, J. O., Mayer, J., & Lewis, D. C. (1977). Barbiturate effects on brain functioning (CNV) and attention performance in normal men. *Psychopharmacology Bulletin, 13*, 64–66.

Teuber, H. L. (1955). Physiological psychology. *Annual Review of Psychology, 6*, 267–296.

Teuber, H. L., & Rudel, R. G. (1962). Behavior after cerebral lesions in children and adults. *Developmental Medicine and Child Neurology, 3*, 3–20.

Thach, W. T., Goodkin, H. G., & Keating, J. G. (1992). Cerebellum and the adaptive coordination of movement. *Annual Review of Neuroscience, 15*, 403–442.

Thach, W. T., Jr. (1992). The cerebellum: Coordination and adaptation of movement. In K. W. Brocklehurst (Ed.), *Neuropsychology: The neuronal basis of cognitive function* (pp. 113–130). New York: Thieme.

Thomas, J. D., & Trexler, L. E. (1982). Behavioral and cognitive deficits in cerebrovascular accident and closed head injury: Implications for cognitive rehabilitation. In L. E. Trexler (Ed.), *Cognitive rehabilitation: Conceptualization and intervention* (pp. 27–62). New York: Plenum Press.

Thompson, P. (1980). Margaret Thatcher: A new illusion. *Perception, 9*, 483–484.

Thurstone, L., & Thurstone, T. (1943). *The Chicago Tests of Primary Mental Abilities.* Chicago: Science Research Associates.

Tian, J. R., Zee, D. S., Lasker, A. G., & Folstein, S. E. (1991). Saccades in Huntington's disease: Predictive tracking and interaction between release of fixation and initiation of saccades. *Neurology, 41*, 875–881.

Tipper, S. P. (1985). The negative priming effect: Inhibitory effects of ignored primes. *Quarterly Journal of Experimental Psychology, 37A*, 571–590.

Tognola, G., & Vignolo, L. A. (1980). Brain lesions associated with oral apraxia in stroke patients: A cliniconeuroradiological investigation with CT scan. *Neuropsychologia, 18*, 257–272.

Tomlinson, B. E. (1980). The structural and quantitative aspects of the dementias. In P. Roberts (Ed.), *Biochemistry of dementia* (pp. 15–52). London: Wiley.

Tomlinson, B. E. (1982). Plaques, tangles and Alzheimer's disease. *Psychological Medicine, 12*, 449–459.

Tompkins, C., & Flowers, C. R. (1985). Perception of emotional intonation by brain-damaged adults: The influence of task processing levels. *Journal of Speech and Hearing Research, 28*, 527–538.

Tompkins, S. S. (1984). Affect theory. In K. R. Scherer & P. Ekman (Eds.), *Approaches to emotion* (pp. 163–195). Hillsdale, NJ: Erlbaum.

Tranel, D., Damasio, A., & Damasio, H. (1988). Intact recognition of facial expression, gender, and age in patients with impaired recognition of face identity. *Neurology, 38*, 690–696.

Tranel, D., & Damasio, A. R. (1988). Non-conscious face recognition in patients with face agnosia. *Behavioural Brain Research, 30*, 235–249.

Treisman, A., & Gelade, G. (1980). A feature integration theory of attention. *Cognitive Psychology, 12*, 97–136.

Treisman, A. M., & Schmidt, H. (1982). Illusory conjunctions in the perception of objects. *Cognitive Psychology, 14*, 107–141.

Trimble, M. R. (1988). Body image and the temporal lobes. *British Journal of Psychiatry, 153*(Suppl. 2), 12–14.

Trimble, M. R., & Rogers, D. (1987). The neurobiology of schizophrenia. In L. DeLisi & F. Henn (Eds.), *Handbook of schizophrenia* (pp. 439–466). Amsterdam: Elsevier.

Tsuang, M. T., Boor, M., & Fleming, J. A. (1985). Psychiatric aspects of traffic accidents. *American Journal of Psychiatry, 142*, 538–546.

Tucker, D., & Williamson, P. (1984). Asymmetric neural control systems in human self-regulation. *Psychological Review, 91*(2), 185–215.

Tucker, D. M. (1981). Lateral brain function, emotion, and conceptualization. *Psychological Bulletin, 89*, 19–46.

Tucker, D. M., Antes, J. R., Stenslie, C. E., & Barnhardt, T. M. (1978). Anxiety and lateral cerebral function. *Journal of Abnormal Psychology, 87*, 380–383.

Tucker, D. M., Roth, R. S., Arneson, B. A., & Buckingham, V. (1977). Right hemisphere activation during stress. *Neuropsychologia, 15*, 697–700.

Tucker, D. M., Watson, R. T., & Heilman, K. M. (1977). Discrimination and evocation of affectively intoned speech in patients with right parietal disease. *Neurology, 27*, 947–958.

Tulving, E. (1972). Episodic and semantic memory. In E. Tulving & W. Donaldson (Eds.), *Organization of memory* (pp. 382–403). New York: Academic Press.

Tulving, E. (1994). Organization of memory: *Quo vadis?* In M. S. Gazzaniga (Ed.), *The cognitive neurosciences* (pp. 839–853). Cambridge, MA: MIT Press.

Turner, A. M., & Greenough, W. T. (1985). Differential rearing effects on rat visual cortex synapses: I. Synaptic and neuronal density and synapses per neuron. *Brain Research, 329,* 195–203.

Tyler, A., Morris, M., Lazarou, L., Meredith, L., Myring, J., & Harper, P. (1992). Presymptomatic testing for Huntington's disease in Wales: 1987–90. *British Journal of Psychiatry, 161,* 481–488.

Tyler, S. K., & Tucker, D. M. (1982). Anxiety and perceptual structure: Individual differences in neuropsychological function. *Journal of Abnormal Psychology, 91,* 210–220.

Umbricht, D., Degreef, G., Barr, W. B., Lieberman, J. A., Pollack, S., & Schaul, N. (1995). Postictal and chronic psychoses in patients with temporal lobe epilepsy. *American Journal of Psychiatry, 152,* 224–231.

Umilta, C., Bagnara, S., & Simion, F. (1978). Laterality effects for simple and complex geometrical figures and nonsense patterns. *Neuropsychologia, 16,* 43–49.

Umilta, C., Rizzolatti, G., Marzi, C. A., Zamboni, G., Franzini, C., Camarda, R., & Berlucchi, G. (1974). Hemispheric differences in the discrimination of line orientation. *Neuropsychologia, 12,* 165–174.

Ungerleider, L. G. (1994). Transient and enduring effects of experience: Functional studies of visual and motor cortex. *Society for Neuroscience Abstracts, 20,* 124.

Ungerleider, L. G., & Mishkin, M. (1982). Two cortical visual systems. In D. J. Ingle, M. A. Goodale, & R. J. W. Mansfield (Eds.), *Analysis of visual behavior* (pp. 549–586). Cambridge, MA: MIT Press.

Vaina, L. M., LeMay, M., Bienfang, D. C., Choi, A. Y., & Nakayama, K. (1990). Intact "biological motion" and "structure from motion" perception in a patient with impaired motion mechanisms: A case study. *Visual Neuroscience, 5,* 353–369.

Valenstein, E. S. (1986). *Great and desperate cures: The rise and decline of psychosurgery and other radical treatments for mental illness.* New York: Basic Books.

Vallar, G., & Baddeley, A. (1984a). Fractionation of working memory: Neuropsychological evidence for a phonological short-term store. *Journal of Verbal Learning and Verbal Behavior, 23,* 151–162.

Vallar, G., & Baddeley, A. (1984b). Phonological short-term store, phonological processing, and sentence comprehension: A neuropsychological case study. *Cognitive Neuropsychology, 1,* 121–141.

Vallar, G., & Perani, D. (1986). The anatomy of unilateral neglect after right-hemisphere stroke lesions. A clinical CT/scan study in man. *Neuropsychologia, 24,* 609–622.

Vallar, G., Sterzi, R., Bottini, G., Cappa, S., & Rusconi, M. L. (1990). Temporary remission of left hemi-anesthesia after vestibular stimulation. A sensory neglect phenomenon. *Cortex, 26,* 121–131.

van Haaren, F., van Hest, A., & Heinsbroek, R. P. (1990). Behavioral differences between male and female rats: Effects of gonadal hormones on learning and memory. *Neuroscience and Biobehavioral Reviews, 14,* 23–33.

Vanier, M., & Caplan, D. (1985). CT scan correlates of surface dyslexia. In K. E. Patterson, J. C. Marshall, & M. Coltheart (Eds.), *Surface dyslexia: Neuropsychological and cognitive studies of phonological reading* (pp. 511–525). Hove, London: Erlbaum.

Van Kleeck, M. H. (1989). Hemispheric differences in global versus local processing of hierarchical visual stimuli by normal subjects: New data and a meta-analysis of previous studies. *Neuropsychologia, 27,* 1165–1178.

Van Lancker, D. R., Kreiman, J., & Cummings, J. (1989). Voice perception deficits: Neuroanatomical correlates of phonagnosia. *Journal of Clinical and Experimental Neuropsychology, 11,* 665–674.

Van Voorhis, S., & Hillyard, S. A. (1977). Visual evoked potentials and selective attention to points in space. *Perception and Psychophysics, 22,* 54–62.

Vargha-Khadem, F., Isaacs, E., & Muter, V. (1994). A review of cognitive outcome after unilateral lesions sustained during childhood. *Journal of Child Neurology, 9,* 2S67–2S73.

Vega, A., Jr., & Parsons, O. A. (1967). Cross-validation of the Halstead-Reitan tests for brain damage. *Journal of Consulting Psychology, 31,* 619–623.

Vellutino, F. R. (1987). Dyslexia. *Scientific American, 256,* 34–41.

Villardita, C., Cultrera, S., Cupone, V., & Mejia, R. (1985). Neuropsychological test performances and normal aging. *Archives of Gerontology and Geriatrics, 4,* 311–319.

Vogt, B. A., Finch, D. M., & Olson, C. R. (1992). Functional heterogeneity in cingulate cortex: The anterior executive and posterior evaluative regions. *Cerebral Cortex, 2,* 435–443.

Volkow, N. D., Hitzemann, R., Wang, G. J., Fowler, J. S., Wolf, A. P., Dewey, S. L., & Handlesman, L. (1992). Long-term frontal brain metabolic changes in cocaine abusers. *Synapse, 11,* 183–190.

von Stockert, T. R., & Bader, A. L. (1976). Some relations of grammar and lexicon in aphasia. *Cortex, 12,* 49–60.

Wachsmuth, E., Oram, M. W., & Perrett, D. I. (1994). Recognition of objects and their component parts: Responses of single units in the temporal cortex of the macaque. *Cerebral Cortex, 5,* 509–522.

Wada, J. A., Clarke, R., & Hamm, A. (1975). Cerebral hemispheric asymmetry in humans. *Archives of Neurology, 32,* 239–246.

Wagner, H. N., Burns, D. H., Dannals, R. F., Wong, D. F., Langstrom, B., Duefler, T., Frost, J. J., Ravert, H. T., Links, J. M., Rosenbloom, S. B., Lucas, S. E., Kramer, A. V., & Kuhlar, M. J. (1983). Imaging dopamine receptors in the human brain by positron tomography. *Science, 221,* 1264–1266.

Walker, B. B., & Sandman, C. A. (1979). Human visual evoked responses are related to heart rate. *Journal of Comparative and Physiological Psychology, 93,* 717–729.

Wallesch, C. W., Henriksen, L., Kornhuber, H. H., & Paulson, O. B. (1985). Observations on regional cerebral blood flow in cortical and subcortical structures during language production in normal man. *Brain and Language, 25,* 224–233.

Wapner, W., Hamby, S., & Gardner, H. (1981). The role of the right hemisphere in the apprehension of complex linguistic materials. *Brain and Language, 14,* 15–33.

Warburton, D. M. (1979). Neurochemical basis of consciousness. In K. Brown & S. J. Cooper (Eds.), *Chemical influences on behavior* (pp. 421–462). New York: Academic Press.

Warren, L. R., Butler, R. W., Katholi, C. R., & Halsey, J. H. (1985). Age differences in cerebral blood flow during rest and during mental activation measurements with and without monetary incentive. *Journal of Gerontology, 40,* 53–59.

Warren, S. T., & Nelson, D. L. (1994). Advances in molecular analysis of fragile X syndrome. *Journal of the American Medical Association, 271*(7), 536–542.

Warrington, E. K. (1975). The selective impairment of semantic memory. *Quarterly Journal of Experimental Psychology, 27,* 187–199.

Warrington, E. K. (1982). Neuropsychological studies of object recognition. *Philosophical Transactions of the Royal Society of London, B298,* 15–33.

Warrington, E. K. (1985). A disconnection analysis of amnesia. *Annals of the New York Academy of Sciences, 444,* 72–77.

Warrington, E. K., & James, M. (1986). Visual object recognition in patients with right-hemisphere lesions: Axes or features? *Perception, 15,* 355–366.

Warrington, E. K., & James, M. (1988). Visual apperceptive agnosia: A clinico-anatomical study of three cases. *Cortex, 24,* 13–32.

Warrington, E. K., James, M., & Kinsbourne, M. (1966). Drawing disability in relation to laterality of cerebral lesion. *Brain, 89,* 53–82.

Warrington, E. K., & McCarthy, R. A. (1987). Categories of knowledge: Further fractionations and an attempted integration. *Brain, 110,* 1273–1296.

Warrington, E. K., & McCarthy, R. A. (1994). Multiple meaning systems in the brain: A case for visual semantics. *Neuropsychologia, 32,* 1465–1473.

Warrington, E. K., & Rabin, P. (1970). Perceptual matching in patients with cerebral lesions. *Neuropsychologia, 8,* 475–487.

Warrington, E. K., & Shallice, T. (1980). Word-form dyslexia. *Brain, 103,* 99–112.

Warrington, E. K., & Shallice, T. (1984). Category specific semantic impairments. *Brain, 107,* 829–854.

Warrington, E. K., & Taylor, A. M. (1973). The contribution of the right parietal lobe to object recognition. *Cortex, 9,* 152–164.

Warrington, E. K., & Taylor, A. M. (1978). Two categorical stages of object recognition. *Perception, 7,* 695–705.

Warrington, E. K., & Weiskrantz, L. (1968). A new method of testing long-term retention with special reference to amnesic patients. *Nature, 217,* 972–974.

Warrington, E. K., & Weiskrantz, L. (1970). The amnesic syndrome: Consolidation or retrieval? *Nature, 228,* 628–630.

Watson, R. T., Heilman, K. M., Cauthen, J. C., & King, F. A. (1973). Neglect after cingulectomy. *Neurology, 23,* 1003–1007.

Watson, R. T., Miller, B. D., & Heilman, K. M. (1978). Nonsensory neglect. *Annals of Neurology, 3,* 505–508.

Watson, R. T., Valenstein, E., & Heilman, K. M. (1981). Thalamic neglect. *Archives of Neurology, 38,* 501–506.

Webb, T. P., Bundey, S. E., Thake, A. I., & Todd, J. (1986). Population incidence and segregation ratios in the Martin–Bell syndrome. *American Journal of Medical Genetics, 23,* 573–580.

Wechsler, D. (1981). *Manual for the Wechsler Adult Intelligence Scale—Revised.* San Antonio, TX: Psychological Corporation.

Wechsler, D. (1989). *Manual for the Wechsler Preschool and Primary Scale of Intelligence—Revised.* San Antonio, TX: Psychological Corporation.

Wechsler, D. (1991). *Manual for the Wechsler Intelligence Scale for Children—Third Edition.* San Antonio, TX: Psychological Corporation.

Weinberger, D. R., Berman, K. F., & Illowsky, B. P. (1988). Physiological dysfunction of dorsolateral prefrontal cortex in schizophrenia: III. A new cohort and evidence for a monoaminergic mechanism. *Archives of General Psychiatry, 45,* 609–615.

Weiner, W. J., & Goetz, C. G. (Eds.). (1989). *Neurology for the non-neurologist* (2nd ed.). Philadelphia: Lippincott.

Weingartner, H., Kaye, W., Smallberg, S. A., Ebert, M. H., Gillin, J. C., & Sitaram, N. (1981). Memory failures in progressive idiopathic dementia. *Journal of Abnormal Psychology, 90,* 187–196.

Weingartner, H., Grafman, J., Boutelle, W., & Martin, P. (1983). Forms of cognitive failures. *Science, 221,* 380–382.

Weintraub, S., & Mesulam, M. (1987). Right cerebral dominance in spatial attention. *Archives of Neurology, 44,* 621–625.

Weintraub, S., Mesulam, M.-M., & Kramer, L. (1981). Disturbances in prosody: A right hemisphere contribution to language. *Archives of Neurology, 38,* 742–744.

Weiskrantz, L. (1985). On issues and theories of the human amnesic syndrome. In N. Weinberger, J. L. McGaugh, & G. Lynch (Eds.), *Memory systems of the brain* (pp. 380–418). New York: Guilford Press.

Weissman, M. M., Leaf, P. J., Holzer, C. E. I., Myers, J. K., & Tischler, G. L. (1984). The epidemiology of depression: An update on sex differences in rates. *Journal of Affective Disorders, 7,* 179–188.

Welsh, K. A., Butters, N., Hughes, J., Mohs, R., & Heyman, A. (1991). Detection of abnormal memory decline in mild cases of Alzheimer's disease using CERAD neuropsychological measures. *Archives of Neurology, 48,* 278–281.

Whalen, C. K., Henker, B., & Dotemoto, S. (1981). Teacher response to methylphenidate (Ritalin) versus placebo status of hyperactive boys in the classroom. *Child Development, 52,* 1005–1014.

Whalley, L. J. (1989). Drug treatment of dementia. *British Journal of Psychiatry, 155*, 595–611.

Whelihan, W. M., & Lesher, E. (1985). Neuropsychological changes in frontal functions with aging. *Developmental Neuropsychology, 1*, 371–380.

White, D., Heaton, R. K., Monsch, A. U., & the HNRC Group (1995). Neuropsychological studies of asymptomatic human immunodeficiency virus-type-1 infected individuals. *Journal of the International Neuropsychological Society, 1*, 304–315.

Whitehouse, P. J., Price, D. L., Clark, A. W., Coyle, J. T., & DeLong, M. R. (1981). Alzheimer disease: Evidence for selective loss of cholinergic neurons in the nucleus basalis. *Annals of Neurology, 10*, 122–126.

Whitehouse, P. J., Price, D. L., Stubble, R. G., Clark, A. W., Coyle, J. T., & DeLong, M. R. (1982). Alzheimer's disease and senile dementia: Loss of neurons in the basal forebrain. *Science, 215*, 1237–1239.

Whitlow, S. D., Althoff, R. R., & Cohen, N. J. (1995). Deficit in relational (declarative) memory in amnesia. *Society for Neuroscience Abstracts, 21*, 754.

Wickens, C., Kramer, A., Vanasse, L., & Donchin, E. (1983). Performance of concurrent tasks: A psychophysiological analysis of the reciprocity of information-processing resources. *Science, 221*, 1080–1082.

Wickens, C. D. (1980). The structure of attentional resources. In R. Nickerson & R. Pew (Eds.), *Attention and performance VIII*. Hillsdale, NJ: Erlbaum.

Wiggins, S., Whyte, P., Higgins, M., Adam, S., Theilmann, J., Bloch, M., Sheps, S. B., Schechter, M. T., & Hayden, M. R. (1992). The psychological consequences of predictive testing for Huntington's disease. *New England Journal of Medicine, 327*, 1401–1405.

Wigstrom, H., & Gustafsson, B. (1985). On long-lasting potentiation in the hippocampus: A proposed mechanism for its dependence on pre- and postsynaptic activity. *Acta Psychologia Scandinavica, 123*, 519–522.

Wilcock, G. K. (1994). The role of growth factors and neuropeptides in Alzheimer's disease. *Human Psychopharmacology Clinical and Experimental, 9*, 353–356.

Will, R. G., & Matthews, W. B. (1984). A retrospective study of Creutzfeld–Jakob disease in England and Wales, 1970–1979. I. Clinical features. *Journal of Neurology, Neurosurgery and Psychiatry, 47*, 134–140.

Williamson, P. D., French, J. A., Thadani, V. M., Kim, J. H., Novelly, R. A., Spencer, S. S., & Mattson, R. H. (1993). Characteristics of medial temporal lobe epilepsy: II. Interictal and ictal scalp electroencephalography, neuropsychological testing, neuroimaging, surgical results, and pathology. *Annals of Neurology, 34*, 781–787.

Wilson, B., Kaszniak, A. W., & Fox, J. H. (1981). Remote memory in senile dementia. *Cortex, 17*, 41–48.

Wilson, R. S., Bacon, L. D., Fox, J. H., & Kaszniak, A. W. (1983). Primary memory and secondary memory in dementia of the Alzheimer type. *Journal of Clinical Neuropsychology, 5*, 337–344.

Winner, E. (1982). *Invented worlds: The psychology of the arts.* Cambridge, MA: Harvard University Press.

Winner, E., & Gardner, H. (1977). The comprehension of metaphor in brain-damaged patients. *Brain, 100*, 719–727.

Winocur, G. (1980). The hippocampus and cue utilization. *Physiological Psychology, 8*(2), 280–288.

Wirshing, W. C., & Cummings, J. (1990). Tardive movement disorders. *Neuropsychiatry, Neuropsychology and Behavioral Neurology, 3*, 23–35.

Witelson, S. F. (1974). Hemisphere specialization for linguistic and nonlinguistic tactual perception using a dichotomous stimulation technique. *Cortex, 10*, 3–17.

Witelson, S. F. (1977). Early hemisphere specialization and interhemispheric plasticity: An empirical and theoretical review. In S. J. Segalowitz & F. A. Gruber (Eds.), *Language development and neurological theory* (pp. 213–289). New York: Academic Press.

Witelson, S. F., & Goldsmith, C. H. (1991). The relationship of hand preference to anatomy of the corpus callosum in men. *Brain Research, 545*, 175–182.

Witelson, S. F., & Nowakowski, R. S. (1991). Left out axons make men right: A hypothesis for the origin of handedness and functional asymmetry. *Neuropsychologia, 29*, 327–333.

Witelson, S. F., & Pallie, W. (1973). Left hemisphere specialization in the newborn: Anatomical evidence of asymmetry. *Brain, 96*, 641–646.

Wittling, W. (1990). Psychophysiological correlates of human brain asymmetry: Blood pressure changes during lateralized presentation of an emotionally laden film. *Neuropsychologia, 28*, 457–470.

Wittling, W., & Pflüger, M. (1990). Neuroendocrine hemisphere asymmetries: Salivary cortisol secretion during lateralized viewing of emotion-related and neutral films. *Brain and Cognition, 14*, 243–265.

Wolff, P. H., Cohen, C., & Drake, C. (1984). Impaired motor timing control in specific reading retardation. *Neuropsychologia, 22*, 587–600.

Wong, D. F., Wagner, H. N., Tune, L. E., Dannals, R. F., et al. (1986). Positron emission tomography revealed elevated D2 receptors in drug-naive schizophrenics. *Science, 234*, 1558–1563.

Woods, B. T. (1980). The restricted effects of right-hemisphere lesions after age one: Wechsler test data. *Neuropsychologia, 18*, 65–70.

Wright, C. E. (1990). Controlling sequential motor activity. In D. N. Osherson, S. M. Kosslyn, & J. M. Hollerbach (Eds.), *Visual cognition and action* (pp. 285–316). Cambridge, MA: MIT Press.

Wurtz, R. H., & Goldberg, M. E. (1972). Activity of superior colliculus in behaving monkey: III. Cells discharging before eye movements. *Journal of Neurophysiology, 35*, 575–586.

Wurtz, R. H., & Goldberg, M. E. (Eds.). (1988). *The neurobiology of saccadic eye movements*. Amsterdam: Elsevier.

Yakovlev, P. I., & Lecours, A. R. (1967). The myelogenetic cycles of regional maturation of the brain. In A. Minkowski (Ed.), *Regional development of the brain in early life* (pp. 3–65). Oxford, England: Blackwell.

Yamaguchi, S., & Knight, R. T. (1991). Anterior and posterior association cortex contributions to the somatosensory P_{300}. *Journal of Neuroscience, 11,* 2039–2054.

Yin, R. K. (1970). Face recognition by brain-injured patients: A dissociable ability? *Neuropsychologia, 8,* 395–402.

Yokoyama, K., Jennings, R., Ackles, P., Hood, P., & Boller, F. (1987). Lack of heart rate changes during an attention-demanding task after right hemisphere lesions. *Neurology, 37,* 624–630.

Young, A. W., DeHaan, E. H. F., Newcombe, F., & Hay, D. C. (1990). Facial neglect. *Neuropsychologia, 28,* 391–415.

Young, A. W., Hellawell, D. J., & Welch, J. (1992). Neglect and visual recognition. *Brain, 115,* 51–71.

Zaidel, D. W., & Kasher, A. (1989). Hemispheric memory for surrealistic versus realistic paintings. *Cortex, 25,* 617–641.

Zaidel, E. (1978). Auditory language comprehension in the right hemisphere following cerebral commissurotomy and hemispherectomy: A comparison with child language and aphasia. In A. Caramazza & E. B. Zurif (Eds.), *Language acquisition and language breakdown: Parallels and divergencies* (pp. 229–275). Baltimore: Johns Hopkins University Press.

Zaidel, E. (1983a). Disconnection syndrome as a model for laterality effects in the normal brain. In J. B. Hellige (Ed.), *Cerebral hemisphere asymmetry: Method, theory and application* (pp. 95–151). New York: Praeger.

Zaidel, E. (1983b). A response to Gazzaniga: Language in the right hemisphere, convergent perspectives. *American Psychologist, 38,* 542–546.

Zaidel, E. (1990). The saga of right-hemisphere reading. In C. Trevarthen (Ed.), *Brain circuits and functions of the mind: Essays in honor of Roger W. Sperry* (pp. 304–319). Cambridge, England: Cambridge University Press.

Zajonc, R. B. (1980). Feeling and thinking: Preferences need no inferences. *American Psychologist, 35,* 151–175.

Zajonc, R. B. (1984). On the primacy of affect. *American Psychologist, 39,* 117–123.

Zangwill, O. L. (1960). La problème de l'apraxie idéatoire. *Revue Neurologique (Paris), 102,* 595–603.

Zatorre, R. J. (1984). Musical perception and cerebral function: A critical review. *Music Perception, 2,* 196–221.

Zatorre, R. J. (1985). Discrimination and recognition of tonal melodies after unilateral cerebral excisions. *Neuropsychologia, 23,* 31–41.

Zatorre, R. J. (1988). Pitch perception of complex tones and human temporal-lobe function. *Journal of the Acoustical Society of America, 84,* 566–572.

Zatorre, R. J., Evans, A. C., Meyer, E., & Gjedde, A. (1992). Lateralization of phonetic and pitch discrimination in speech processing. *Science, 256,* 846–849.

Zatorre, R. J., & Samson, S. (1991). Role of the right temporal neocortex in retention of pitch in auditory short-term memory. *Brain, 114,* 2403–2417.

Zeki, S. (1980). The representation of colours in the cerebral cortex. *Nature, 284,* 412–418.

Zeki, S., & Shipp, S. (1988). The functional logic of cortical connections. *Nature, 335,* 311–317.

Zeki, S., Watson, J. D. G., Lueck, C. J., Friston, K. J., Kennard, C., & Frackowiak, R. S. J. (1991). A direct demonstration of functional specialization in human visual cortex. *Journal of Neuroscience, 11,* 641–649.

Zigmond, M. J., Abercrombie, E. D., Berger, T. W., Grace, A. A., et al. (1990). Compensations after lesions of central dopaminergic neurons: Some clinical and basic implications. *Trends in Neurosciences, 13,* 290–296.

Zihl, J., Von Cramon, D., & Mai, N. (1983). Selective disturbance of movement vision after bilateral brain damage. *Brain, 106,* 313–340.

Zola-Morgan, S., Cohen, N. J., & Squire, L. R. (1983). Recall of remote episodic memory in amnesia. *Neuropsychologia, 21(5),* 487–500.

Zola-Morgan, S., & Squire, L. R. (1985). Medial temporal lesions in monkeys impair memory on a variety of tasks sensitive to human amnesia. *Behavioral Neuroscience, 99,* 22–34.

Zurif, E. B., Gardner, J., & Brownell, H. H. (1989). The case against the case against group studies. *Brain and Cognition, 10,* 237–255.

Name Index

Note: (cap.) in citation refers to figure caption.

611

Subject Index

Abstract conceptualization, 158, 311, 375–376, 393–394, 515, 534, 539–540
Acceleration-deceleration injury, 512–513
Accurate fasciculus, 281
Acetylcholine, 127(cap.), 141, 525–527, 547
Acetylcholinesterase, 527, 547
Acquired immune deficiency syndrome (AIDS), 537
ACTH. *See* Adrenocorticotropic hormone
Action potential, 5, 6, 127(cap.)
Action tremor, 134
Activating-orienting model, 103
ADD. *See* Attention deficit disorder
Adrenaline, 422
Adrenocorticotropic hormone (ACTH), 540
AER. *See* Auditory evoked response
Aesthetic preference, 440–445
Affect, negative vs. positive, 418
Affective prosody, 417
Aging
    brain regions most susceptible to, 506–507
    cell loss and, 149
    cognitive changes with, 505–506
    frontal lobe function and, 364
    See also Development, human
Agnosia(s), 191, 321, 324, 355, 357, 364
    Alzheimer's disease and, 519
    auditory, 44, 197–198
    finger, 221
    somatosensory (tactile), 44, 198–200

visual, 43, 165–166, 170–175, 177–179, 181, 193, 358
Agrammatic aphasia, 291
Agraphia(s), 44, 296, 299, 452, 454
AIDS. *See* Acquired immune deficiency syndrome
AIDS dementia, 536, 537–538
Akathisia, 154
Akinesia, 139, 149, 151, 533, 534
Alcohol(ism), 321, 487, 541–542, 543
Alertness, attention and, 236, 268
Alexia(s), 44, 296, 297–299, 300, 452, 454
Alien limb syndrome, 155–156
Allophones, 287
Alpha activity, 75, 466
Alpha suppression, 77
ALS. *See* Amyotrophic lateral sclerosis
Alternative strategies, after brain damage, 495–496
Alternative Uses Test, 378, 379
Altitudinal neglect, 265
Alveolar stops, 289
Alzheimer's disease, 6, 88, 321, 335, 338, 339, 485, 492, 505, 512, 516, 518, 519–528, **525**, 530, 532, 536, 537
American Sign Language (ASL), 276, 303–305, 311, 500–501
Amnesia, 225, 271, 315, 316, 318–343
    anterograde. *See* Anterograde amnesia
    causes of, 318–319, 320
    cognitive deficits and, 321
    declarative memory and, 350
    episodic memory and, 355

global nature of, 357
Korsakoff's, 321
long-term memory and, 361, 362
multiple forms of, 339–341
natural history of, 321
organization of memory and, 343
posttraumatic, 321, 337, 515
retrieval deficit explanation of, 341–343
retrograde. *See* Retrograde amnesia
severity of memory impairment and, 319–321
source, 507
working memory and, 361
Amniocentesis, 487
Amphetamine, 482
Amputation, reorganization after, 494
Amygdala, 21, **21**, 318, **319**
    Alzheimer's disease and, 524
    damage to, 336, 528
    emotion and, 404, **405**, 406–407, 420
Amyloid plaques, 524, **524**, 527, 528
Amyotrophic lateral sclerosis (ALS), 524
Anemia, 72
Angular gyrus, 296, 370
Animals, nonhuman, 60–61
    development process and, 472
    emotion and, 406, 407
    enriched environments and, 503
    face recognition by, 182–184
    memory and, 325, 327, **328**, 334–335, 345
Anomia, selective, 193
Anosognosia, 221, 263, 410–411
Anoxia, 335, 336, 339, 484
Anterior aphasia, 291–292, 293, 304

Note: Page numbers set in boldfaced type refer to illustrations; (cap.) in citation refers to figure captions.

Free recall, 323, 339, 342
Frontal cortex, 307, 363
Frontal eye fields, 141, 142, **144**, 145–146, 151, 245
Frontal lobe(s), **23**, 24, **25**, 39–43
aging and, 506–507
AIDS dementia and, 538
alcoholism and, 542, 543
artistry and, 436, 438
attention and, 243, 250–252, **251**, 256, 268
damage to, 40–43, 54, 156, 159, 218, 219, 223, 256, 304, 308, 363, 370, 371–372, 376, 377, 378, 379, 380, 382, 384, 385, 386–387, 388, 392, 393, 394, 395, 421, 438, 482, 504, 522, 528, **529**, 535, 542
decision making and, 504
depression and, 41, 77, 418–420, 421
development process and, 467, **467**
divisions of, **40**
emotion and, 404, 407–408, 436, 438, 466
executive function(s) and, 370, 371–372, 376, 377, 378, 379, 380, 382, 384–385, 386–387, 388, 390–396
epilepsy and, 550
Huntington's disease and, 533
impulsivity and, 504
language processing and, 304, 308, 371, 522
memory and, 42–43, 74, 159, 222, 223, 363–364
motor planning and, 142
multiple sclerosis and, 540
Pick's disease and, 528
Parkinson's disease and, 534, 535
schizophrenia and, 390–391, 427
spatial processing and, 218, 219, 223
vascular (multi-infarct) dementia and, 536, 537
Frontal lobotomy, 390–391
Frontal opercular region, 25
Frontotemporal region, damage to, 157
Frown, 415
Functional magnetic resonance imaging (fMRI), 69, 71–74, 81, 351, 361, 363, 540
Function words, 277

Fundamental, in music, 446, 447, **448**
Fungicides, 547
Fusiform gyrus, 186–187, **186, 187**, 188

GABA. *See* Gamma-aminobutyric acid
Gait disorder, 534
Gamma-aminobutyric acid (GABA), 141, 527
Ganglion cells, 31
GCS. *See* Glasgow Coma Scale
Gender
brain organization and, 119–121
depression and, 422–423
dyslexia and, 477–478, 479
fragile X syndrome and, 485
Gender categorization, 186, **187**
Generalized (nonspecific) disorders, defined, 512
Generalized seizures, 547, 549
Genetics
Alzheimer's disease and, 519, 527
developmental dysphasia and, 479
Down syndrome, 485, 527
Huntington's disease and, 151, 152–153
mental retardation and, 484, 485–487
multiple sclerosis and, 539
Tourette's syndrome and, 153–154
Geographical knowledge, spatial processing and, 219–220
Geometric relations, spatial processing and, 211, 230
Gerstmann syndrome, 221
Gestalt psychology, 176, 179, 457
Glasgow Coma Scale (GCS), 513–515
Glia, 3, 7, 462, 464–465, 489, 491, 492
Gliosis, 489
Global aphasia, 282, 284
Global Deterioration Scale, 521
Global precedence, 179
Global processing
aesthetic preference and, 442(cap.)
hemispheric specialization and, 109, **109**
object recognition and, 179–181
Global stereopsis, 210
Globus pallidus, 20, 135, 137–138, 139, **139, 140**, 141, 150, 482, 530
Gluttony, 528

Goal-directed behavior, 379–390, 394, 395, 439
Goal list, 395
Gradient field, 65
Grammar, 284, 290–292, 474–476
Grandmother cell theory, 183–184
Grapheme(s), defined, 296
Grapheme-to-phoneme correspondence rules, 296–297
Grasping reflex, 468, **469**, 470
Gray matter, 7, **14**
Group studies, 57–58
Gyri, 22, **22**, 23

Hair cells, in cochlea, 25, 36
Half-life, 70, 71
Hallucinations, visual, 270
Haloperidol, 154
Halstead-Reitan test battery, 83, 84
Handedness, 57, 60
aesthetic preference and, 440–441, **442**
corpus callosum and, 120
hemispheric specialization and, 117–119
lateralization of language processing and, 293–294, 295
planum temporale and, 456
Hand movements, 144
Happiness, 418, 436, 437(cap.)
Harmonic(s), in music, 446–447
Head injury, closed. *See* Closed head injury
Hearing. *See* Auditory processing
Hebbian synapse, 467–468
Hematoma, 64(cap.)
Hemianopsia, 34, 257–258, 270, 539
Hemi-inattention, 44–45, 235, 255
Hemineglect, 44, 54, 160, 240, 241, 248, 249, 250, 252, 254, 255–270, 271, 300
artistry and, 434, **435**, 437
as attentional syndrome, 256–259
brain-behavior relationships and, 263–270
clinical features of, 255–262
conceptual representations and, 259–262
spatial processing and, 221, 226–227
treatment of, 262–263
Hemiparesis, 540
Hemi-Parkinsonism, 149, 535–536
Hemiplegia, 28, 221